Environmental Law, Policy,

Praise for *Environmental Law, Policy, and Economics*

"The inclusion of environmental science in the context of a treatise on environmental law, policy, and economics makes this book one of the most comprehensive, useful, and timeless treatments on the subject to date."
—Jennifer Sass, Senior Scientist, Natural Resources Defense Council

"This book is a timely and important contribution, written by authors who combine decades of academic excellence with significant real life experiences. It demonstrates the cutting edge potential for law to become a policy tool that can drive sustainable innovation when applied by knowledgeable and capable practitioners. The vast and comprehensive scope is both broad and deep; the synthesis of complex interconnections is a welcome tour de force."
—Ted Smith, Founder and former Executive Director, Silicon Valley Toxics Coalition and Coordinator, International Campaign for Responsible Technology

"This book explores not only the basic environmental pollution control laws but also, and of fundamental importance, the ways in which these laws do or do not lead to cleaner production. Its explanations of various concepts and legal tools will be useful to both students and practitioners."
—John C. Dernbach, Professor of Law, Widener University Law School

"A comprehensive and invaluable compendium of two decades of scholarship and jurisprudence on the legal, social, and economic dimensions of pollution regulation, control, and prevention. Written largely from an American perspective, the volume draws important lessons from the comparative, European experience, as well."
—David A. Sonnenfeld, Professor and Chair, Department of Environmental Studies, SUNY College of Environmental Science and Forestry

"Highly recommended for use both in the classroom and the law office. It is not only a highly useful treatise on the field, but a convincing affirmation of the central role law plays in environmental protection."
—William Futrell, President, Sustainable Development Law Associates

Environmental Law, Policy, and Economics

Reclaiming the Environmental Agenda

Nicholas A. Ashford
Charles C. Caldart

The MIT Press
Cambridge, Massachusetts
London, England

For information about special quantity discounts, please email special_sales@mitpress.mit.edu

This book was set in Times New Roman on 3B2 by Asco Typesetters, Hong Kong.
Printed on recycled paper and bound in the United States of America.

Library of Congress Cataloging-in-Publication Data

Ashford, Nicholas Askounes.
Environmental law, policy, and economics : reclaiming the environmental agenda / Nicholas A. Ashford, Charles C. Caldart.
    p.   cm.
Includes bibliographical references and index.
ISBN 978-0-262-01238-6 (hardcover : alk. paper)—978-0-262-53399-7(pb.)
  1. Environmental law—United States. 2. Environmental policy—United States. I. Caldart, Charles C. II. Title.

KF3775.A967   2007
344.7304′6—dc22

2007001995

Dedicated to the committed government employees, activists, scholars, and far-sighted firms who have helped protect the environment and public health.

Contents in Brief

Contents in Detail

Foreword

As a country, we have made substantial progress in cleaning up the environment, thanks to an ambitious statutory framework, impressive contributions by states, municipalities, and the private sector, and most importantly by the American public's unwavering support for clean air and water. And yet, we face a daunting array of challenges. The environment continues to be degraded by toxic chemicals such as pesticides, heavy metals, and synthetic organic compounds. We continue to lose wetlands, wildlife habitat, and other productive natural resources to development. Demand has exploded for clean water for all its many purposes, in some places out-stripping available supplies, as population and economic activity increase. We are notoriously inefficient in the way we use both water and energy. Numerous fisheries are excessively harvested or depleted, and coastal estuaries and waterways are degraded by runoff from sources of pollution dispersed across the landscape. Most obvious today is the threat of global climate change; as more greenhouse gases are pumped into the atmosphere, leading scientists report we may have reached, or be close to reaching, a "tipping point" that requires urgent action.

What is clear from this sampling of environmental concerns is that, notwithstanding the progress we have made, we have not yet fulfilled the promise of a clean, healthy environment for all Americans envisioned when President Nixon created the Environmental Protection Agency in 1970.

Is it time to rethink the roles and strategies of government and the private sector in safeguarding public health and the environment? Taking the twin pillars of regulation and enforcement as a foundation, tackling the challenges of global climate change and toxic pollution requires more of us to fashion nonpartisan solutions that enlist the creativity and entrepreneurial spirit of Americans. Technology, which has contributed to past problems, must be employed to reverse current energy and pollution trends, as they pose a clear risk to all of us. This requires the intelligent use of legal and economic tools to create appropriate incentives for those engaged in industry, agriculture, transportation, and business—as well as for consumers, and citizens generally—for we have learned over more than 30 years in this endeavor that environmental protection is by no means the exclusive province of EPA. Rather, we have to build the concern into all aspects of our economic and community life if we are to achieve a safe, healthy environment.

We need far more attention devoted to the means by which we can stimulate and deploy new, more environmentally sustainable technologies. We need to harness market forces on behalf of the environment. More and more companies are learning that improving efficiency and cutting waste pays off—in their bottom line. Ultimately, we need to reconcile consumer demand with the growing awareness of its impacts on a finite and, it seems, increasingly vulnerable planet.

Environmental Law, Policy, and Economics provides a valuable foundation for constructing multifaceted approaches to nonpartisan environmentalism. It offers, in one place, grounding in environmental science, economics, law, and policy. The authors examine the relative effectiveness of law and economics, including the emergence of information, or right-to-know, tools for addressing environmental challenges and spurring technological advancement. The book's subtitle, *Reclaiming the Environmental Agenda*, could well be its title. My hope is that this work will help provide the basis for renewing our commitment to environmental health in step with a modern industrial society. Our future may well depend on our ability to embrace a paradigm shift to sustainable development, in other words, to a model of economic prosperity that respects the essential contribution of the natural systems on which all human activities depend.

William K. Reilly
Administrator,
Environmental Protection Agency, 1989–1993

Acknowledgments

The authors are grateful to the Department of Civil and Environmental Engineering and the School of Engineering at MIT, both of which supported the teaching of the course upon which this text is based. We are also thankful for financial support from the Bernard Gordon Curriculum Development Fund and from the Bauman Foundation. We thank Robert F. Stone for his contributions to the writing of chapters 3 and 12, Simon Mui for his contributions to the writing of chapter 7, and Dale B. Hattis and Claire Franklin for their insightful comments and feedback on chapter 2. We also wish to thank Chris Mascara and Rita Adom for their assistance in the preparation of the manuscript, and Elizabeth Milnes for assistance in obtaining copyright clearance. We are especially grateful to Androniki A. Ashford for a creative cover design. Finally, we extend a special thanks to the hundreds of exceptional students it has been our privilege to teach in law and policy courses at MIT; their inspiration and feedback have been invaluable.

Introduction

This text on environmental law, policy, and economics grows out of courses taught by the authors at the Massachusetts Institute of Technology over the past 25 years. During that period, there has been a significant evolution in environmental policy. New environmental legislation has been added at the federal level, and older environmental legislation has been substantially reshaped by congressional amendments. There has also been a significant evolution in environmental science, and in the treatment of science (and scientific uncertainty) by the courts.

The concept of the cost-benefit analysis as an overriding normative principle has gained a firm foothold in both congressional and judicial thought, and it does periodic battle with the equally powerful notion that "technology forcing" is a legitimate function of environmental law. Increased citizen participation—in both legal and political processes—has been a focus of federal environmental legislation, and this has borne considerable fruit at the federal, state, and local levels. Yet, despite increased public involvement in environmental policy (or perhaps because of it), environmental law is under attack in several quarters.

Traditional (so-called command-and-control) legislative approaches are alleged to be increasingly ineffective and fragmented, and many argue that mandatory styles of governance should give way to—or at least be heavily influenced by—negotiated stakeholder processes. So-called end-of-pipe approaches for pollution control are now less favored than preventing pollution at the source, but analysts disagree as to whether regulations or economic incentives provide a more effective pathway to this end. Some argue that the polluting industry itself is in the best position to come up with the appropriate solutions, and that incentives should be structured accordingly, while others argue that many incumbent industries and products ought to be replaced with more sustainable ones. Finally, there appears to be an increased willingness in the federal courts to second guess (albeit often implicitly) the policy choices made by Congress, which makes environmental law more unpredictable than it would otherwise be.

One of the authors (NAA) brings to this treatise both a knowledge of, and involvement in, European approaches to environmental challenges and a long history of inter-country comparative research on the effects of regulation on technological change. The other author (CCC) brings years of experience in litigating violations of environmental statutes and regulations, and in the creative use of the law to protect citizens, workers, and consumers.

This work includes what might be found in a traditional course in environmental law and policy: common law and administrative law concepts; the standard air, water, and waste statutes; the Pollution Prevention Act; the National Environmental Policy Act; and the Endangered Species Act. We also include a chapter on enforcement. Beyond these more traditional topics, we also address the information-based obligations of industry (such as "right-to-know" laws), and the problems presented by sudden and accidental chemical releases of chemicals (which require different approaches from those focused on the gradual release of pollution). In addition, we include chapters on environmental economics and market-based and voluntary alternatives to traditional regulation. Finally, because we believe that an appreciation of the basics of environmental science and risk assessment, and a familiarity with the processes of technological innovation and diffusion, are essential complements to the understanding of legal concepts, we explore these topics as well.

The text focuses on pollution rather than energy, and addresses both pollution control and pollution prevention (what the Europeans call cleaner and inherently safer production). Perhaps the most distinguishing characteristic of the volume is its emphasis on the evaluation, design, and use of the law to stimulate technological change and industrial transformation, rather than to merely control pollution. We argue that the law can be used to implement an "industrial policy for the environment" and that beyond changes in industrial inputs, products, and processes, there is a need to address broader issues of sustainable development, which will involve the shift from products to product services, and further to larger system changes.

As the subtitle of the text—Reclaiming the Environmental Agenda—implies, we depart from those environmental law, environmental policy, and environmental economics texts that argue for a reduced role for government. The environmental record of the past 35 years suggests there is much to be gained when government provides clear, stringent legal requirements for environmental improvements and for technological transformations, although these requirements must be coupled both with flexible means to achieve environmental targets and with meaningful stakeholder participation.

The text is meant to provide a broad and detailed discussion of the most current pressing issues in environmental law, policy, and economics for the general reader, and to provide in one volume material for undergraduate and graduate-level courses taught in law, business, and public policy schools; schools of public health; and in departments of urban studies, civil and environmental engineering, environmental sciences, chemical engineering, chemistry, and economics. There is more material in this text than would ordinarily be taught in one semester. The material could easily span a two-semester—or two- or three-quarter—sequence of courses. Because of the broad expanse of the materials and their stand-alone nature, the instructor teaching a one-semester or one-quarter course could easily select only some of the regulatory systems—for example air and water pollution or waste—coupled with the tutorials on right to know and/or pollution prevention and/or tort and/or science and/or economics.

Because of the lengthy nature of this treatise, we have included very little statutory material in the text itself. The reader is encouraged to read selected statutory language provided at the website: http://mitpress.mit.edu/ashford_environmental_law. That website will also contain updated material considered essential for keeping abreast of the developing environmental law and policy, such as new cases and commentary.

1 The Nature and Origins of Environmental Contamination

A. The Nature of the Problem: Pollution and the Accidental Release of Chemicals into the Environment
B. The Causes of Pollution and Accidental Releases
    1. Increases in the Production and Use of Chemicals, and Changes in the Nature of Chemical Contamination
    2. Public Goods, the Tragedy of the Commons, and Free-Rider Problems: The Destructiveness of Pursuing Narrow Self-interest
        a. Pursuing Self-interest as a Pathway to an Improved Environment
        b. Moral Appeal
    3. Pollution as an Economic Problem
    4. Limits to Growth
C. Pollution and Accident Control, Mitigation, and Prevention
D. The Focus of Traditional Environmental Law
E. Beyond Pollution and Accident Control and Prevention: Sustainable Production and Products

---

In this introductory chapter, we address the origin and causes of pollution and accidental releases of chemicals into the environment. We distinguish the *expected* by-products of industrial production, transportation, and consumption—sometimes called *gradual pollution*—from the *unintentional or unexpected* (and sometimes sudden) accidental release of chemicals and energy associated with industrial spills, explosions, and fires. Of course, sudden and/or accidental releases may take time to permeate soil and water (or air), but the *initial loss of control* of toxic materials is the characterizing element that society seeks to eliminate or minimize. Environmental law addresses both types of pollution, traditionally focusing on the control of pollution and accidental releases, on mitigation (environmental cleanup and injury prevention), and to a lesser extent on *primary* prevention that eliminates or dramatically reduces, at the source, the probability of releases that could cause harm to human health and the environment.

A. THE NATURE OF THE PROBLEM: POLLUTION AND THE ACCIDENTAL RELEASE OF CHEMICALS INTO THE ENVIRONMENT

Figure 1.1 is a pictorial representation of the stages (life cycle) of a polluting industry, indicating sources of air, water, and waste associated with related production processes and products. Pollution control is traditionally focused on the waste streams emanating from the facility or from product use and disposal, while pollution prevention is centered within the production or manufacturing facility. All stages, from production to disposal, can contribute directly or indirectly to pollution and contamination.

The chemicals released into the environment during this industrial life cycle come in a variety of forms, and cause or contribute to a variety of known and potential harms. The following three excerpts discuss some of the more important human health problems emanating from pollution of the air, of drinking water, and of the food supply, and some of the more important chemicals associated with such pollution.

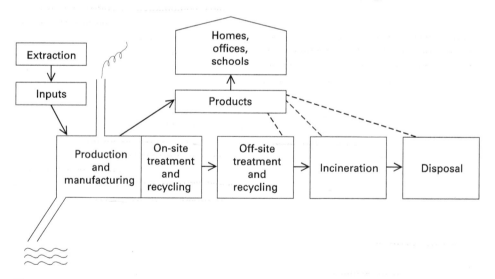

Figure 1.1
Stages of production leading to chemical exposure.

Specific Air Pollutants Associated with Adverse Respiratory Effects
David C. Christiani and Mark A. Woodin

Source: "Urban and Transboundary Air Pollution," in Michael McCally (ed.), *Life Support: The Environment and Human Health*. MIT Press, Cambridge, Mass., 2002, pp. 15–37, excerpted with permission.

Several major types of air pollution are currently recognized to cause adverse respiratory health effects: sulfur oxides and acidic particulate complexes, photochemical oxidants, and a miscellaneous category of pollutants arising from industrial sources....

SULFUR DIOXIDE AND ACIDIC AEROSOLS

Sulfur dioxide (SO_2) is produced by the combustion of sulfur contained in fossil fuels, such as coal and crude oil. Therefore, the major sources of environmental pollution with sulfur dioxide are electric power generating plants, oil refineries, and smelters. Some fuels, such as "soft" coal, are particularly sulfur-rich. This has profound implications for nations such as China, which possesses 12 percent of the world's bituminous coal reserves and depends mainly on coal for electric power generation, steam, heating, and (in many regions) household cooking fuel.

Sulfur dioxide is a clear, highly water-soluble gas, so it is effectively absorbed by the mucous membranes of the upper airways, with a much smaller proportion reaching the distal regions of the lung. The sulfur dioxide released into the atmosphere does not remain gaseous. It undergoes chemical reaction with water, metals, and other pollutants to form aerosols. Statutory regulations promulgated in the early 1970s by the U.S. Environmental Protection Agency (EPA) under the Clean Air Act resulted in significant reductions in levels of SO_2 and particulates. However, local reductions in pollution were often achieved by the use of tall stacks, particularly for power plants. This resulted in the pollutants being emitted high into the atmosphere, where pro-longed residence time allowed their transformation into acid aerosols. These particulate aerosols vary in composition from area to area, but the most common pollutants resulting from this atmospheric reaction are sulfuric acid, metallic acids, and ammonium sulfates. Sulfur dioxide, therefore, together with other products of fossil-fuel combustion (e.g., soot, fly ash, silicates, metallic oxides) forms the heavy urban pollution that typified old London, many cities in developing nations today that mainly burn coal, and basin regions in the United States, such as in areas of Utah where there are coal-burning plants.

In addition to this smog—a descriptive term generically referring to the visibly cloudy combination of smoke and fog—an acidic aerosol is formed that has been shown to induce asthmatic responses in both adults and children.... [B]oth epidemiological and controlled human studies have demonstrated remarkable sensitivity of persons with asthma while exercising to the bronchoconstrictive effects of acidic aerosols. Several studies have also linked exposure to acidic aerosols and mortality, documenting an increase in deaths of persons with underlying chronic heart and lung disease who had been exposed. Finally, acidic aerosols result in "acid rain," which may threaten aquatic life....

PARTICULATES

Particulate air pollution is closely related to SO_2 and aerosols. The term usually refers to particles suspended in the air after various forms of combustion or other industrial activity. In the epidemics noted earlier, the air pollution was characterized by high levels of particulates, sulfur dioxide, and moisture.

Recent studies have shown that particulate air pollution per se was associated with increases in daily mortality in London in both the heavy smog episodes of the 1950s and the lower pollution levels of the late 1960s and early 1970s....

Recent interest in particulate air pollution has focused on particle size. Specifically, particles < 2.5 microns in diameter ($PM_{2.5}$, also called "fine" particles), produced almost exclusively from combustion sources, have been closely studied under the hypothesis that such small particles can penetrate deeply into the lung, while larger particles would be trapped in the upper airway....

PHOTOCHEMICAL OXIDANTS

The other two most commonly generated industrial and urban pollutants are ozone and oxides of nitrogen. In contrast to sulfur dioxide, these two substances are produced not so much by heavy industry as by the action of sunlight on the waste products of the internal combustion engine. The most important of these products are unburned hydrocarbons and nitrogen dioxide (NO_2), a product of the interaction of atmospheric nitrogen with oxygen during high-temperature combustion. Ultraviolet irradiation by sunlight of this mixture in the lower atmosphere results in a series of chemical reactions that produce ozone, nitrates, alcohols, ethers, acids, and other compounds that appear in both gaseous and particulate aerosols. This mixture of pollutants constitutes the smog that has become associated with cities with ample sunlight (Los Angeles, Mexico City, Taipei, Bangkok) and with most other urban areas in moderate climates.

Ozone and nitrogen dioxide have been studied extensively in both animals and humans. Both gases are relatively water insoluble and reach lower into the respiratory tract. Therefore, these gases can cause damage at any site from the upper airways to the alveoli.

EXPOSURE TO OZONE AND NITROGEN DIOXIDE

Clinical research on the acute effects of exposure to ozone reveals symptoms and changes in respiratory mechanics at rest or during light exercise after exposure to 0.3–0.35 ppm. In exercising subjects, similar effects will occur with exposure to 150 ppb, a level currently found in urban air. There is also recent evidence that the upper-airway (nose) inflammation induced by ozone correlates with the lower-airway response, as demonstrated by simultaneous nasal and bronchoalveolar lavage.

Animal studies have clearly documented severe damage to the lower respiratory tract after high exposure, even briefly, to ozone. The pulmonary edema noted is similar to that noted in humans accidentally exposed to lethal levels. Animals exposed to sublethal doses develop damage to the trachea, the bronchi, and the acinar region of the lung.

...High concentrations of O_3 are most often observed in the summertime, when sunlight is most intense and temperatures are highest—conditions that increase the rate of photochemical formation. Strong diurnal variations also occur, with O_3 levels generally lowest in the morning hours, accumulating through midday, and decreasing rapidly after sunset....

While O_3 concentrations may be elevated in outdoor air, they are substantially lower indoors. The lower indoor concentrations are attributed to the reaction of O_3 with various surfaces, such as walls and furniture. Mechanical ventilation systems also remove O_3 during air-conditioning. For these reasons, staying indoors or closing car windows and using air-conditioning are generally recommended as protecting against exposure to ambient O_3.

Studies of the effect of nitrogen dioxide on healthy human subjects have demonstrated results similar to those found with ozone, with the exception that the concentration of nitrogen dioxide shown to produce mechanical dysfunction is above the concentrations noted in pollution episodes (i.e., 2.5 ppm). In animal studies, similar damage to alveolar cells is noted after exposure to relatively high concentrations of nitrogen dioxide.

In any case, current epidemiologic data show that exposure to photochemical oxidants, particularly ozone, can cause broncho-constriction in both normal and asthmatic people.

CARBON MONOXIDE (CO)

The health effects of carbon monoxide have been documented in clinical observations of patients with CO intoxication and in experimental and epidemiologic studies of persons exposed to low-level CO. Carbon monoxide is an odorless, colorless gas produced by incomplete combustion of carbonaceous fuels such as wood, gasoline, and natural gas. Because of its marked affinity for hemoglobin, CO impairs oxygen transport, and poisoning often manifests as adverse effects in the cardiovascular and central nervous systems, with the severity of the poisoning directly proportional to the level and duration of the exposure. Thousands of people die annually (at work and at home) from CO poisoning, and an even larger number suffer permanent damage to the central nervous system. Sizable

portions of the workers in any country have significant CO exposure, as do a larger proportion of persons living in poorly ventilated homes where biofuels are burned....

In addition to containing sulfur dioxide, particulates, and photochemical pollutants, urban air contains a number of known carcinogens, including polycyclic aromatic hydrocarbons (PAHs), n-nitroso compounds, and, in many regions, arsenic and asbestos. Exposure to these compounds is associated with increased risk of lung cancer in various occupationally exposed groups (e.g., coke-oven workers exposed to PAHs and insulators exposed to asbestos). Therefore, populations living near coke ovens or exposed to asbestos insulation at home and in public buildings also may be at increased risk of lung cancer.

In addition to these agents, airborne exposure to the products of waste incineration, such as dioxins and furans, may be on the increase in some communities. Though usually present in communities in concentrations much lower than those found in workplaces, airborne dioxins, furans, and other incineration products may still lead to increased lung cancer risks, particularly in neighborhoods or villages near point sources where their levels may be substantial. The degree of cancer risk for ambient exposures to these compounds has not been calculated to date.

Drinking-Water Pollution and Human Health
Howard Hu and Nancy K. Kim

Source: E. Chivian, M. McCally, H. Hu, and A. Haines (eds.), *Critical Condition: Human Health and the Environment*. MIT Press, Cambridge, Mass., 1993, pp. 31–48, excerpted with permission.

...Of the four (physical, chemical, biologic, and radioactive) general characteristics of water quality, we shall concentrate on chemical...pollutants....

SOURCES OF CONTAMINATION AND ROUTES OF EXPOSURE

Surface water can be contaminated by point or non-point sources. A runoff pipe from an industrial plant or a sewage-treatment plant discharging chemicals into a river is a point source; the carrying of pesticides by rainwater from a field into a lake is a non-point discharge. Fresh surface water can also be affected by groundwater quality; for example, approximately 30% of the stream flow of the United States is supplied by groundwater emerging as natural springs or other seepage.

Groundwater is contained in a geological layer termed an *aquifer*. Aquifers are composed of permeable or porous geological material, and may either be unconfined (and thereby most susceptible to contamination) or confined by relatively impermeable material called *aquitards*. Though they are located at greater depths and are protected to a degree, confined aquifers can nevertheless be contaminated when they are tapped for use or are in proximity for a prolonged period of time to a source of heavy contamination.

Contamination of aquifers can occur via the leaching of chemicals from the soil, from industrial discharges, from septic tanks, or from underground storage tanks. Fertilizers applied to agricultural lands contain nitrates which dissolve easily in water. Rainwater percolating through the soil can carry the dissolved nitrates with it into aquifers. Industry or homes can discharge wastewater directly into groundwater from septic tanks or waste holding tanks. Buried underground tanks used to store chemicals, such as gasoline or fuel oil, can leak, allowing their contents to seep into groundwater.

The chemical characteristics of a contaminant may change as it percolates through the soil zone to the aquifer. Attenuation may occur through a number of processes, such as dilution, volatilization, mechanical filtration, precipitation, buffering, neutralization, microbial metabolism, and plant uptake. These generally reduce the toxicity of the contaminant. Once a contaminant gains entry into an aquifer, transport usually results in an elliptical plume of contamination, the shape, flow rate, and dispersion of which depend on aquifer permeability, hydraulic gradients, contaminant chemistry, and many other factors.

People can be exposed to polluted groundwater or surface water through a number of routes. Most commonly, contaminated water can be collected or pumped and used directly for drinking or cooking. Significant exposure to chemicals in surface water can also occur when swimming in a lake or river. Some chemicals accumulate in fish that are subsequently caught and eaten. A chemical that volatilizes easily can escape from groundwater and rise through soil, and in gaseous form the chemical can then be released into surroundings or can enter homes through cracks in basements, exposing residents through inhalation. If water used for bathing is contaminated, some chemicals can also be absorbed through skin or inhaled in the fine spray of a shower. Of these routes of exposure, use of contaminated water for drinking and cooking is clearly the most dominant threat, followed by ingestion of contaminated fish (especially in areas where high fish consumption and pollution coexist).

Most of the contaminants in surface water and groundwater that are due to human activity derive from agricultural and industrial sources. The spectrum of contaminants is enormous. The most important ones are toxic heavy metals (such as lead, arsenic, cadmium, and mercury), pesticides and other agricultural chemicals (such as nitrates, chlorinated organic chemicals (DDT), organophosphate or carbamate (aldicarb) insecticides, and herbicides (2,4-D), and volatile organic chemicals (such as gasoline products and the halogenated solvents trichloroethene and tetrachloroethene). There are also some natural sources of hazardous chemical exposure; for example, deep wells are often contaminated with naturally occurring arsenic.

SPECIFIC HAZARDS

Nitrates and Nitrites

From a global perspective, biological processes such as nitrogen fixation and the conversion of organic nitrogen to ammonia (NH_3), or nitrate (NO_3^-) are the major sources of inorganic nitrogen compounds in the environment. However, on a local scale, municipal and industrial wastewaters (particularly sewage treatment plants, fertilizers, refuse dumps, septic tanks, and other sources of organic waste) are major nitrogen sources. Waste sources are significant, can greatly exceed natural sources, and are increasingly found in groundwater primarily because of a marked rise in the use of nitrogenous fertilizers around the world. . . .

The total nitrogen content of water is usually measured for both nitrates and nitrites. Nitrate or nitrite is more likely to be found in higher concentrations in groundwater than in surface water, and shallow wells (especially dug wells) are more likely to be contaminated than deep or drilled wells. . . .

Two potential health effects of concern from nitrate or nitrite in drinking water are the induction of methemoglobinemia and the formation of nitrosamines. Nitrate itself is relatively non-toxic to humans; however, when converted in the body to nitrite (primarily by bacteria in the colon) and absorbed, this nitrogen compound is capable of oxidizing hemoglobin (the principal oxygen-transport molecule of the body), with the consequent induction of methemoglobinemia and oxygen starvation. The symptoms of methemoglobinemia include bluish skin and lips, weakness, rapid pulse, and tachypnea. Infants are particularly at risk, because the higher pH of an infant's stomach contents provides a more favorable environment for the bacteria that convert nitrate to nitrite. Babies less than 1 year of age and babies with respiratory illnesses or diarrhea may be at greater risk from nitrite-induced methemoglobinemia.

The risk for methemoglobinemia drinking water containing less than 10 nitrate (as nitrogen) per liter is relatively With drinking water contaminated by nit at levels above 10 mg/l, however, the risk is significant; around 17–20% of infants develop methemoglobinemia when exposed to these higher levels.

It has been postulated that nitrates can also form nitrosating agents, which can react with secondary organic amines to form nitrosamines. Nitroso compounds are carcinogenic at high doses in animal studies. . . .

Heavy Metals

The heavy metals of greatest concern for health with regard to environmental exposure through drinking water are lead and arsenic. Cadmium, mercury, and other metals are also of concern, although exposure to them tends to be more sporadic. Significant levels of these metals may arise in drinking water, directly or indirectly, from human activity. Of most importance is seepage into groundwater of the run-offs from mining, milling, and smelting operations, which concentrate metals in ores from the earth's crust, and effluents and hazardous wastes from industries that use metals. Lead contamination in drinking water is of particular concern, as lead was used in household plumbing and in the solder used to connect it. Seepage of heavy metals (especially arsenic) from the earth's crust can be a natural source of contamination in some areas where deep wells are used for drinking water. Quantitative modeling of the movement of heavy metals in the environment suggests that accumulation of metals in water, in soil, and in the food chain is accelerating around the world. . . .

Lead

The sources of lead in drinking water that are of greatest concern are lead pipes, the use of which was highly prevalent until the 1940s, and lead solder, which was used (and is still being used in some countries) to connect plumbing. Also of concern is the seepage of lead from soil contaminated with the fallout from combusted leaded gasoline and the potential seepage of lead in hazardous-waste sites. In the United States, lead is prevalent in over 43% of hazardous-waste sites, and migration and groundwater contamination have been documented in almost half of these lead-containing sites.

Lead contamination of drinking water from lead pipes and solder is more likely to be found in water samples taken at the tap than at the treatment plant. Soft water leaches more lead than does hard water, and the greatest exposure is likely to occur when a tap is first turned on after not being used for six or more hours. (The water drawn in such a case is called *first-draw water*.)

Lake and river water, worldwide, contains about 1–10 micrograms of lead per liter. Because of lead in plumbing systems, lead levels in drinking water at the tap as high as 1,500 g/l have been found. Drinking water is only one of many potential sources of lead exposure; lead paint, dust, food, and air pollution are other important sources, particularly in old urban areas.

The current U.S. Centers for Disease Control level of concern for blood lead in children in 10 μg per deciliter. This level was set because of recent evidence linking low-level lead exposure to adverse effects on neurobehavioral development and school performance in children. That concentration can generally be reached when a child ingests 8 ounces of contaminated water per day (defined as tap water with "first-draw water" containing more than 100 μg of lead per liter). In order to create a margin of safety, the Environmental Protection Agency recently lowered the amount of lead that is acceptable in drinking water from 50 to 15 μg/l. The importance of reducing children's exposure to lead is underscored by new evidence that suggests that cogni-

tive deficits caused by lead are at least partly reversible.

Arsenic

Drinking water is at risk for contamination by arsenic from a number of human activities, including the leaching of inorganic arsenic compounds used in pesticide sprays, the contamination of surface water by fallout from the combustion of arsenic-containing fossil fuel, and the leaching of mine tailings and smelter runoff. For example, in Perham, Minnesota, groundwater contamination by an arsenic-containing grasshopper bait led to wellwater arsenic concentrations of 11–21 mg/l and to documented illness.

With chronic exposure at high levels, children are particularly at risk; the primary symptoms are abnormal skin pigmentation, hyperkeratosis, chronic nasal congestion, abdominal pain, and various cardiovascular manifestations. Some of these same problems were noticed in Taiwan by W. P. Tseng, who also documented "black foot" disease (a vasospastic condition thought to be caused by chronic arsenic exposure leading to gangrene of the extremities) and high rates of skin cancer.

At lower levels of exposure, cancer is the outcome of primary concern. Occupational and population studies have linked chronic high-dose arsenic exposure to cancer of the skin, the lungs, the lymph glands, the bone marrow, the bladder, the kidneys, the prostate, and the liver. Using a linear dose-response model to extrapolate risk, and imposing that risk on a large population, one would predict that significant numbers of people with chronic low-dose arsenic exposure would develop cancer. Understanding the true risk from low-level arsenic exposure is an area of active epidemiological research.

Other Heavy Metals

Contamination of water with other heavy metals has caused problems in isolated instances. In 1977, the National Academy of Sciences ranked the relative contributions of these metals in water supplies as a function of man's activities as follows.

very great	cadmium, chromium, copper, mercury, lead, zinc
high	silver, barium, tin
moderate	beryllium, cobalt, manganese, nickel, vanadium
low	magnesium.

Of these metals, mercury and cadmium are probably the most toxic at the levels found in water.

High levels of environmental exposure to mercury occur primarily through the consumption of food tainted by organic (and sometimes inorganic) mercury (see next excerpt). However, the uses of mercury compounds that give rise to these exposures, such as the treatment of seeds with phenyl mercury acetate (used for its antifungal properties), can also lead, through runoff, to the contamination of surface water and groundwater. Similarly, short-chain alkyl mercury compounds are lipid-soluble and volatile; therefore they pose a risk of skin absorption and inhalation from bathing in contaminated waters. The most common symptoms of high-level organic mercury poisoning are mental disturbances, ataxia (loss of balance), gait impairment, disturbances of speech, constriction of visual fields, and disturbances of chewing and swallowing. The toxicological implications of low-level mercury exposure are poorly understood.

Environmental exposure to cadmium has been increasing as a result of mining, refining, smelting, and the use of cadmium in industries such as battery manufacturing. Environmental exposure to cadmium has been responsible for significant episodes of poisoning through incorporation into foodstuffs; however, the same sources of cadmium for these overt episodes of poisoning, such as the use of cadmium-contaminated sewage sludge as fertilizer, can potentially cause contamination of ground and surface water used for drinking and bathing. High cadmium consumption causes nausea, vomiting, abdominal cramping, diarrhea, kidney disease, and increased calcium excretion (which leads to skeletal weakening). As in the case of mercury, the toxic effects of chronic exposure to low levels of cadmium are poorly understood. Recent studies have demonstrated an increased rate of mortality from cerebrovascular disease (e.g., stroke) in populations from cadmium-polluted areas. One study has also indicated an association between cadmium levels in drinking water and prostatic cancer.

Pesticides

In today's world, especially in developing countries, the use of pesticides has become inextricably linked with agricultural production. Included under the rubric of "pesticides" are insecticides, herbicides, nematicides, fungicides, and other chemicals used to attract, repel, or control pest growth. Insecticides and nematicides, including the bicyclophosphates, cyclodienes, and the pyrethroids, generally work by inhibiting neurotransmitter function in the peripheral and central nervous systems. Herbicides and fungicides interfere with specific metabolic pathways in plants, such as photosynthesis and hormone function.

Pesticides pose a major threat of contamination to both surface water and ground water. In the United States, approximately 1 billion pounds of pesticides are applied annually to crops. Persistent and broad-spectrum agents such as DDT were once favored. DDT was shown to accumulate in the food chain and in living systems, with profound effects, and was prohibited in the United States in 1972; however, it and related chlorinated compounds continue to be used widely outside North America. Moreover, the nonresidual and more specifically targeted chemicals and agents that are now in wide use in North

America still generate concern because of their long-term effects on ground and surface water.

Highly water-soluble pesticides and herbicides can leach into groundwater; the less soluble, more persistent chemicals can be carried in surface-water runoff to lakes and streams. More than 70 pesticides have been detected in groundwater. Specific chemicals, such as atrazine, are still routinely detected in aquifers and wells.

The most recognized hazard of pesticide exposure is the development of acute toxic effects at high levels of exposure, such as might be sustained by an agricultural worker. The health effects of low-level or prolonged pesticide exposures via drinking water are much less clear. Extrapolation of results from *in vitro* studies to humans suggests the possibility of incrementally increased risk of cancer for many of the pesticides in use. Epidemiological correlations have been found between elevated serum DDT plus DDE, its major metabolite, and subjects who reported hypertension, arteriosclerosis, and diabetes in subsequent years. Of particular concern are recent findings that demonstrate a strong association between breast cancer in women and elevated serum levels of DDE. The overall database of human epidemiological data is sparse, however. In addition, in view of the slower elimination of pesticides in humans and their greater life span, extrapolating toxicity data from experiments on animals to humans may underestimate risks.

The case of aldicarb, a pesticide that has been used widely in recent times in the United States, is illustrative of contemporary issues related to pesticides and groundwater. A carbamate insecticide, aldicarb has been used on a number of crops, including potatoes, which are grown in sandy soil. The combination of the chemical's being applied to soil rather than to plant leaves and the permeability of sandy soil has led to widespread groundwater contamination. Aldicarb has been detected in groundwater in Maine, Massachusetts, New

York, Rhode Island, Wisconsin, and other states. . . .

Volatile Organic Compounds

Other very common groundwater contaminants include halogenated solvents and petroleum products, collectively referred to as *volatile organic compounds* (VOCs). Both groups of chemical compounds are used in large quantities in a variety of industries. Among the most common uses of the halogenated solvents are as ingredients in degreasing compounds, dry-cleaning fluids, and paint thinners. Military dumps have recently been recognized for their widespread environmental contamination with solvents.

Historically, once used, these chemicals were discharged directly to land, given shallow burial in drums, pooled in lagoons, or stored in septic tanks. Sometimes the sites were landfills situated over relatively impermeable soils or impoundments lined with impenetrable material; often, however, the sites were in permeable soils, over shallow water tables, or near drinking-water wells. Petroleum products frequently were stored in underground tanks that would erode, or were spilled onto soil surfaces.

These compounds are major contaminants in recognized hazardous-waste sites. For instance, of the 20 chemicals most commonly detected at sites listed on the EPA's National Priority List, 11 were VOCs: trichloroethylene, toluene, benzene, chloroform, tetrachloroethylene, 1,1,l,-trichloroethane, ethylbenzene, trans-1,2-dichloroethane, xylene, dichloromethane, and vinyl chloride.

Unfortunately, the chemical and physical properties of VOCs allow them to move rapidly into groundwater. Almost all of the above chemicals have been detected in groundwater near their original sites, some reaching maximum concentrations in the hundreds to thousands of parts per million. Once in groundwater, their dispersion is dependent on a number of factors, such as aquifer permeability, local and regional groundwater flow patterns, chemical properties, and withdrawal rates from surrounding groundwater wells.

At high levels of exposure, VOCs can cause headache, impaired cognition, hepatitis, and kidney failure; at the levels of exposure most commonly associated with water contamination, however, cancer and reproductive effects are of paramount concern. Many of these compounds have been found to cause cancer in laboratory animals....

Animal Studies

HAZARDOUS-WASTE SITES AND GROUNDWATER CONTAMINATION

Many of the specific hazards discussed above threaten water supplies because of their presence at hazardous-waste sites. Epidemiological studies of communities near hazardous-waste sites are plagued by a number of methodological obstacles.... Even if studies are performed flawlessly, and an association is discovered, causality is far from proven; moreover, the complex mixtures of chemicals found at most hazardous-waste sites make it exceedingly difficult to pinpoint the culprit substance(s).

Nevertheless, such studies are vitally important. They provide information on the scope of the problem, and they serve to educate communities about the hazards and the possible (if not exact) risks. Moreover, methods of exposure assessment and outcome ascertainment are constantly improving, as is demonstrated by a recent study in which slight but significant increases in malformation rates were associated with residential proximity to hazardous-waste sites in New York State.

ISSUES RELATED TO WATER TREATMENT AND USE

Remedial action for a contaminated aquifer is complicated, time-consuming, expensive, and often not feasible. If a contamination plume is shallow and in unconsolidated material, excavation and removal is a possible solution; other strategies include *in situ* detoxification, stabilization, immobilization, and barrier formation. Similarly, decontamination of a surface water supply is often complicated by the multiplicity of contaminants involved. Methods of water treatment that might be employed include reverse osmosis, ultrafiltration, use of ion-exchange resins, and filtration through activated charcoal. Clearly, the best solution to the contamination of groundwater or surface water is prevention.

Methods used for disinfecting drinking water can have toxic effects, due to the disinfectants or by their by-products. In the United States chlorine is routinely used, because of its powerful and long-lasting antimicrobial effect and its low cost; however, as a by-product of chlorination, chlorine reacts with substances commonly found in water to generate trihalomethanes (THM), such as chloroform, which increase the risk of cancer. As a volatile organic compound, chloroform can be significantly absorbed through skin contact and inhalation during a shower. Treatment with chloramine or ozone instead of chlorine eliminates THM formation but is more expensive. Chlorination has also been recently implicated in the formation of nonvolatile polar furanone compounds that are powerfully mutagenic.

Chlorine

Contamination, water treatment, and expense must be considered in the context of usage patterns. In developed countries, high-quality water is used in huge quantities. In the United States, 50 gallons of high-quality water are consumed per capita per day for domestic uses alone (1165 gallons, if one counts commercial uses as well). Less than 1 gallon is actually consumed; the rest is utilized in a myriad of activities, most of which do not require high quality. Approaches to decreasing the use of high-quality water include increased attention to methods of conservation and the institution of dual water systems in which separate plumbing systems deliver high-quality water for culinary use and less pure water for other uses.

SUMMARY

The number of different industrial and agricultural chemicals that threaten public and private water supplies is enormous. Nitrates, heavy metals, pesticides, and volatile organic compounds are of most concern in terms of human health. The exact nature of the health risks from many of these exposures is not known; this is particularly true with respect to the relationship of low-level chronic exposures to cancer and other long-term effects. Additional epidemiological and toxicological research is important, as are improving risk-assessment methods and defining societal notions of "acceptable" risk. Of equal importance, however, is using existing research to target the prevention of additional contamination of this resource that is so critical to health and survival.

Food Contamination Due to Environmental Pollution
E. Bowen and H. Hu
Source: E. Chivian, M. McCally, H. Hu, and A. Haines (eds.), *Critical Condition: Human Health and the Environment*. MIT Press, Cambridge, Mass., 1993, pp. 49–69, excerpted with permission.

Human life is sustained by an environment that provides adequate food derived from plants, minerals, and animals. Whereas the spoilage of food and its contamination by infectious agents and their toxins have long been of concern in the field of public health, contamination by environmental pollution has been less well recognized. We will concentrate on the latter, and we will not discuss hazards related to food processing (such as food irradiation, food additives, cooking, and preservation techniques) or to natural food toxins.

Environmental contamination of food can occur through multiple pathways on land, by air, and in fresh and salt water. The polluting agents of most significance include pesticides, radionuclides, halogenated cyclic compounds, and heavy metals.

A great deal of overlap exists between contamination of food and contamination of drinking water (see the preceding [excerpt]) with respect to the toxins involved and the sources of pollution. In particular, aquatic animals serve as important contributors to the nutritional protein, lipid, and vitamin requirements of humans, and serve to cycle waterborne anthropogenic toxic chemicals back to human consumers in the form of food.

In general, one of the main differences between water contamination and food contamination is the tendency of plants and animals in the food chain to concentrate certain toxins, thereby increasing the exposure of unwary consumers. For instance, radioactive strontium concentrates in milk, and mercury (as the organic compound methyl mercury) concentrates in the tissues of fish.

The toxicity of contaminants in food can be compounded by malnutrition. For example, children who are deficient in iron, calcium, phosphorus, protein, or zinc absorb more lead than do well-nourished children with identical environmental lead exposures. And malnutrition weakens the immune system, thus making an affected person more vulnerable to infectious pathogens and possibly to chemical agents.

Exposure to environmental food contamination may not be borne equally. In the United States, approximately three-fourths of the toxic waste disposal sites that failed to comply with the regulations of the U.S. Environmental Protection Agency were located in impoverished communities of people of color, placing them at greater risk of food and water contamination. These are also the individuals who are at greatest risk for malnutrition and occupational exposures to pesticides, toxic metals, and other hazardous substances.

Responsibility for monitoring and control of contaminants in food is shared by a number of agencies. In the United States, the Food and Drug Administration (FDA) monitors dietary intake of selected contaminants; the Food Safety Inspection Service of the Department of Agriculture monitors residues in meat and poultry; and the Environmental Protection Agency's National Human Monitoring Program estimates total body exposure to toxic substances, including pesticides. Elsewhere, a growing number of countries are participating in the Global Environment Monitoring System, a program of food monitoring supported by the World Health Organization and the United Nations. By 1988, 35 countries participated, representing countries in every continent.

PESTICIDES

Pesticides are used in agriculture in all parts of the world. While most cases of acute, high-exposure pesticide poisoning are related to occupational exposure to the applicators themselves (there are more than 200,000 deaths worldwide each year, mainly in this population, from acute pesticide poisoning), significant exposure can occur through ingestion of treated food. At least 37 epidemics directly due to pesticide contamination of food have been reported.

The term *pesticides* includes insecticides, herbicides, rodenticides, food preservatives, and plant growth regulators. We will concentrate on chemical insecticides. Chemical insecticides include synthetic organic insecticides and inorganic chemicals (mostly metals, such as arsenic). Other insecticides, such as those from biological sources—nicotine, pyrethrin, pheromones, and insect-specific bacteria and viruses—will not be considered in this chapter. Synthetic organic insecticides can be further broken down into the chlorobenzene derivatives (e.g., dichlorodiphenyltrichloroethane (DDT)), cyclodienes (chlordane, aldrin, dieldrin), benzenehexachlorides (lindane), carbamates, and organophosphates (malathion).

While the mechanism of action differs among different classes of agents, most chemical pesticides are designed to be acutely toxic to their target organism. At high levels of exposure, they are also acutely toxic to humans, usually causing general symptoms of poisoning (nausea, vomiting, malaise, headache) as well as neurological symptoms (excitability, tremors, convulsions). Pesticide applicators are most at risk for high levels of exposure.

Pesticide contamination of food is mostly of concern because, while exposures are at lower levels, they involve much larger segments of the population (all consumers). In addition, many pesticides concentrate in the food chain and can accumulate in human tissue, where their slow metabolism and solubility in adipose (fat) tissue can lead to lifelong storage. Organochlorine pesticides have been found throughout the food chain, even in zooplankton and fish in the Arctic Ocean. One recent study in Asia found these same pesticides at particularly high levels in preserved fruits, eggs, and fish. Another study in Africa found the presence of chlorinated pesticides in over 80% of samples of eggs, poultry liver, and bovine liver and kidney; 7.5% of samples had levels higher than international tolerance levels. In the United States, the commercial milk supply in Hawaii was contaminated by heptachlor epoxide during 1981 and 1982. Isomers of dioxin have been found in crustaceans and finfish off the east coast, probably as the result of a combination of municipal and industrial combustion processes....

HEAVY METALS

Lead

The contamination of food with lead is of major concern because of the high levels of exposure experienced around the world and because of recent studies linking neurobehavioral toxicity to relatively minute quantities of lead in human tissues....

OTHER HEAVY METALS

Lead is not the only metal to contaminate food. Several highly toxic metals that are often used in agricultural and industrial applications may enter the food supply intentionally or inadvertently. Common domestic sources of exposure to arsenic, cadmium, copper, and mercury are pottery, metal pans, teapots, cooking utensils, and packaging materials. Arsenic, copper, and mercury are also used in herbicides, fungicides, and insecticides. Any and all of these routes of exposure can cause food contamination and can produce acute or chronic illnesses.

Cadmium

Cadmium can contaminate food by its presence in pesticides, pigments, paints, plastics, and cigarettes. In the United States, 500,000 individuals have occupational exposures to cadmium in mining, welding, galvanizing, battery production, and many other industries. Families who live near the sites of such industries or who are engaged in cottage industries involving cadmium-containing pigments or batteries may also develop cadmium toxicity through exposure to cadmium in food, air, soil, and water. Substantial cadmium pollution can occur in areas where arsenic, zinc, copper, lead, and cadmium are mined from iron ore. In Japan, cadmium runoff from mines has polluted rivers that were used to irrigate rice paddies. Individuals who consumed cadmium-contaminated rice developed chronic cadmium poisoning and had shortened life spans.

Cadmium accumulates throughout life. High exposure has been linked to osteomalacia, a softening of the bones. Cadmium damages renal tubules, causing proteinuria, a condition in which serum proteins are excreted in excess in the urine. A dose-response relationship has been shown between the prevalence of proteinuria and the cadmium content of rice in contaminated regions. Finally, substantial concern exists over the possibility, suggested by animal research and epidemiological studies, that chronic lower-dose cadmium exposure can cause cancer, particularly of the lung and of the prostate.

Mercury

Mercury contamination of food has been well documented in locations as diverse as Michigan, Iraq, and Japan. A classic episode occurred in the 1950s in Minamata Bay, Japan. A chemical factory that made vinyl chloride dumped mercury into the bay. Individuals who ate contaminated fish developed mercury toxicity accompanied by neurological disorders, including progressive peripheral paresthesias with numbness and tingling sensations in the extremities, loss of muscle coordination with unsteadiness of gait and limbs, slurred speech, irritability, memory loss, insomnia, and depression. Forty deaths and at least 30 cases of cerebral palsy with permanent disability were reported.

A much larger epidemic of similar neurological disorders occurred in Iraq when seed grain treated with mercury fungicide, instead of being planted, was mistakenly incorporated into wheat flour and baked into bread. More than 450 persons died, and more than 6,000 were hospitalized.

In the United States, an estimated 68,000 workers are exposed to mercury in the workplace. The major agricultural and industrial sources of mercury are fungicides, pesticides, paints, pharmaceuticals, batteries, electrical equipment, thermometers, and the industrial production of chlorine and vinyl chloride.

Ingestion of contaminated fish and fish products is a major source of environmental exposure to mercury. In the United States, mercury contamination of freshwater fish is prevalent in the Great Lakes region. Excessive levels of methylmercury have been reported in fish in scores of Michigan lakes. Public health authorities in 20 states have issued advisories that children, women of child-bearing age, and pregnant and lactating women should avoid eating certain fishes from contaminated lakes. However, an estimated 20% of the fish and shellfish consumed in the United States comes from subsistence fishing or recreational fishing and is not subject to adequate monitoring from an environmental health standpoint.

Mercury compounds from agricultural and industrial sources are converted by bacteria into methylmercury, which is soluble, mobile, and rapidly incorporated into aquatic food chains. Mercury concentrates as it moves up the food chain, accumulating in carnivorous fishes (such as the northern pike) to levels 10,000–100,000 times the concentrations in the surrounding water. Marine fishes, especially carnivorous ones such as the swordfish, have been found to contain high levels of mercury, exceeding 1 μg per gram. Between 70% and 90% of the mercury detected in fish muscle is in the bioavailable form of methylmercury and hence is readily absorbed.

Environmental agencies in New York, Wisconsin, and Minnesota have reported an association between lake acidification from acid rain and increasing levels of mercury in fish. Tropospheric ozone pollution and global warming may also lead to increased levels of mercury in freshwater fish, the former by increasing the rate of conversion of elemental mercury to methylmercury and the latter through increased atmospheric mercury deposition. . . .

Arsenic

Arsenic is used widely in insecticides, fungicides, and herbicides, and may contaminate food by all these routes. Diet represents the largest source of arsenic exposure for the general population, followed by groundwater contamination. In addition, an estimated 55,000 U.S. workers have had occupational exposures to arsenic.

Arsenic is found in 28% of U.S. "Superfund" hazardous-waste sites, and migration from those sites, with subsequent contamination of food and water, has been documented. And young children living near pesticide factories or copper smelters may ingest arsenic-contaminated soil on playgrounds, adding to the possibility of their developing arsenic toxicity.

Symptoms of acute arsenic toxicity are nausea, vomiting, diarrhea, abdominal pain, and metallic taste. Severe toxicity may cause circulatory collapse, seizures, and kidney failure due to acute tubular necrosis. Chronic exposure to moderately high levels of arsenic is associated with fatigue, weakness, gastroenteritis, dermatitis, and peripheral neuropathies that begin with painful feet and progress to a loss of normal sensation in the hands and feet in a "stocking and glove" pattern. . . .

The potential for carcinogenicity remains a primary concern for exposure to arsenic at low levels. As with many topics related to food toxicology, little epidemiological research exists which can address this issue; extrapolation from high-exposure studies using conventional methods suggests that significant risks may exist.

Copper

Copper is used widely in many industries, including agriculture; it is used in plumbing and in cookware; and has been identified in 18% of U.S. hazardous-waste sites. Acidic drinking water mobilizes copper from plumbing. In many countries, including the United States, copper sulfate is added directly to reservoirs to control algae. This sharply raises the level of copper in drinking water for several days.

With very high levels of exposure, acute copper poisoning results in nausea, vomiting, diarrhea, and metallic taste. Chronic copper toxicity has been studied in the context of Wilson's disease, a rare inherited metabolic disease in which copper accumulation leading to central-nervous-system degeneration, liver disease, and anemia. *In vitro* studies and mammalian *in vivo* studies suggest that copper may also be a human mutagen. Relatively little is known about the potential toxicity of copper at the levels of exposure most commonly encountered. There is reason for concern, however, because of the very broad human exposure to copper compounds.

MISCELLANEOUS CONTAMINATION

Food can be inadvertently contaminated by industrial chemicals mistakenly introduced during processing and distribution. For instance, the ingestion of refined aniline-adulterated rapeseed oil in Spain in 1981 was associated with the development of a toxic syndrome with autoimmunological features.

The recent introduction of food irradiation has generated some concerns regarding the potential induction of harmful radioactivity, radiolytic products (such as superoxide radicals), and mutant strains of microorganisms.

Little hard evidence exists that supports these concerns. Nevertheless, additional research seems prudent in view of the widespread potential application of this method of preserving food.

CONCLUSION

The integrity of food is threatened by a number of man-made pollutants that can be introduced at any step in the food chain and in the food-processing industry. There have been a number of instances in which high-level poisoning has occurred through human error and negligence. The potential toxicity of exposures to pesticides, metals, radionuclides, and other contaminants that have slowly accumulated in soils and the food chain is of growing concern.

Most of these toxins are invisible and are not easily detected by consumers. Moreover, the processing or cooking of food is generally not effective in neutralizing their impact. For instance, broiling fish contaminated with polychlorinated biphenyls and pesticides has not been found to significantly alter their levels.

Painfully slow research has begun to clarify the risks associated with food contamination. New tools are being developed to better define accumulated exposure and early health effects in humans; in the meantime, it would seem prudent to pursue primary prevention and to vigilantly guard against the contamination of the food supply by environmental pollutants.

The avowed focus of environmental law, of course, is the reduction of such pollution over time. The following article discusses one attempt to trace the prevailing trends in environmental quality over the period 1970–1995, which represents the first 20 to 25 years of the modern era of federal environmental legislation.

Environmental Trends

Peter Montague

Source: *Rachel's Environment and Health Weekly*, no. 613, August 27, 1998, excerpted with permission.

...Now, after 20 years of intense efforts to reverse the trends of environmental destruction, the question is, are we succeeding?

So far as we know, only one study has tried to answer this question in a rigorous way. The study, called INDEX OF ENVIRONMENTAL TRENDS, was published in April 1995 by the National Center for Economic and Security Alternatives in Washington, D.C. [1]. In it, the authors measured trends in a wide range of serious environmental problems facing industrial societies. The study relied on the best available data, most of it gathered and maintained by national governments.

The study examined 21 indicators of environmental quality, summarizing the data into a single numerical "environmental index." The index shows that, despite 20 years of substantial effort, each of the nine countries has failed to reverse the trends of environmental destruction. See table [1.1].

Here is a brief discussion of the 21 categories of data from which the summary index was calculated:

AIR QUALITY

The study used six measures of air quality: sulfur oxides, nitrogen oxides, volatile organic compounds, carbon monoxide, particulate matter (essentially, soot), and carbon dioxide. The first five are called "criteria pollutants" in the U.S. The sixth, carbon dioxide, is a greenhouse gas, now thought to be contributing to global warming.

The study found successful reductions of sulfur oxides in all nine countries, but also found that acid rain—caused by sulfur oxides—continues to damage forests in Denmark, Britain and Germany. The same is true in the U.S. and Canada, so additional reductions will be needed.

Table 1.1
Ranking from Least to Most Environmental Deterioration 1970–1995

Country	Environmental Quality
Denmark	−10.6%
Netherlands	−11.4%
Britain	−14.3%
Sweden	−15.5%
West Germany	−16.5%
Japan	−19.4%
United States	−22.1%
Canada	−38.1%
France	−41.2%

Source: Alpalovitz, Gar et al. (1995) "Index of Environmental Trends," National Center for Economic and Security Alternative, WDC, page 2.

The study did not include "the vast range of hazardous air pollutants, called 'air toxics' in the United States," because "regulatory bodies in the nine countries have failed to comprehensively monitor or regulate most hazardous air pollutants." The study says, "There are roughly 48,000 industrial chemicals in the air in the United States, only a quarter of which are documented with toxicity data" [1, p. 11].

The study also did not include indoor air pollution which is "virtually unmonitored and...probably on the rise in many of the countries surveyed."

The study notes that, "The necessary reductions in NOx [nitrogen oxides] and CO2 [carbon dioxide], it seems, may require far more change than seems politically possible—major reductions in the use of private automobiles, for example" [1. p. 11].

WATER QUALITY

Water quality in the index is represented by pollution trends of major rivers within countries. Specific measures include dissolved oxygen, nitrates, phosphorus, ammonium, and metals. Unfortunately, national trend data on water quality is generally poor, compared to data on air quality. For example, in the U.S., only 29% of the nation's river miles have been monitored.

The study did not include trends in groundwater quality "because most countries do not produce national trend data on groundwater pollution. Yet groundwater in all index countries is contaminated, and by most measures, the problem has worsened since 1970" the study says [1, p. 13]. The study did measure groundwater withdrawals, compared to the natural rate of replenishment of groundwater.

CHEMICALS

The study measured production of fertilizers, pesticides, and industrial chemicals. The chemical industry continues to grow at a rate

of 3.5% each year, thus doubling in size every 20 years.... Of the 70,000 chemicals in commercial use in 1995, only 2% had been fully tested for human health effects, and 70% had not been tested for any health effects of any kind. At least 1000 new chemicals are introduced into commercial use each year, largely untested. If all the laboratory capacity currently available in the U.S. were devoted to testing new chemicals, only 500 could be tested each year, the study notes [1, p. 14]. Therefore, even if the necessary funding were made available, there would be no way of ever testing all the chemicals that are currently in use, or all of the new ones being introduced each year.

WASTES

The study examined trends in municipal wastes and nuclear wastes in the nine countries. Both kinds of waste are increasing steadily. Trend data for industrial wastes and hazardous wastes are not available. The study concludes that, "The United States is arguably the most wasteful—that is, waste-generating—society in human history" [1, p. 8].

LAND

The study examined the area of wetlands, and the amount of land devoted to woods in each of the nine countries.

STRUCTURAL BAROMETERS OF SUSTAINABILITY

Two additional measures were used in developing the index of environmental trends: the amount of energy used by each country, and the total number of automobile miles traveled.

SUMMARY

In sum, this study of environmental quality in nine nations reveals that environmental destruction is continuing, and in some cases accelerating, despite 20 years of substantial effort to reverse these trends. The study concludes, "The index data suggest that achieving across-the-board environmental protection and restoration will require deeper, more fundamental change than has

yet been attempted in the countries surveyed" [1, p. 5].

REFERENCE

1. Gar Alparovitz, *et al.*, *Index of Environmental Trends*, Washington, D.C.: National Center for Economic and Security Alternatives, 1995.

■ **NOTES**

1. The information in the excerpt above is outdated, but the current state of air and water still leaves much about which to be concerned. Although air quality improved in 2006 and total air pollution declined by more than half since 1970, approximately 103 million people nationwide lived in counties with pollution levels above EPA's national air quality standards in 2006, most seriously for ozone and fine particulates [*Environment Reporter* 38(18): 1005–1006 (2007)]. More information on air quality trends is available at http://www.epa.gov/airtrends/econ-emissions.html. Information on the State of the Air report is available from the American Lung Association at http://www.lungusa.org.

2. Improvements in water quality are leveling off 35 years after the Clean Water Act was enacted. EPA reports that 9 percent of assessed river miles, 45 percent of assessed lake acres, and 51 percent of assessed square miles of estuaries are "impaired" because of unregulated agricultural and/or stormwater runoff. [*Environment Reporter* 38(9): 493 (2007)].

3. The reporting of chemical emissions to air and water by larger facilities, as compiled in the Toxics Release Inventory (discussed in chapter 12), indicates shifts to, and increases in, the production of toxic waste.   ■

What we don't know about the chemicals in our environment probably surpasses what we do know. We often lack adequate knowledge about the toxicity of even high-volume chemicals. Without the necessary scientific data, regulatory initiatives may be misdirected or absent entirely.

Executive Summary
David Roe, et al., Environmental Defense Fund
Source: *Toxic Ignorance: The Continuing Absence of Basic Health Testing for Top-Selling Chemicals in the United States*, 1997, excerpted with permission.

After DDT, after lead, after PCBs [polychlorinated biphenyls] and other unintended

chemical catastrophes, our knowledge about the chemicals we allow in commerce must have gotten much better. So Congress wrote into law, and so the public has a right to assume.

Yet for most of the important chemicals in American commerce, the simplest safety facts still cannot be found. Environmental Defense Fund research indicates that, today, even the most basic toxicity testing results cannot be found in the public record for nearly 75% of the top-volume chemicals in commercial use.

In other words, the public cannot tell whether a large majority of the highest-use chemicals in the United States pose health hazards or not—much less how serious the risks might be, or whether those chemicals are actually under control. These include chemicals that we are likely to breathe or drink, that build up in our bodies, that are in consumer products, and that are being released from industrial facilities into our backyards and streets and forests and streams.

In the early 1980s, the National Academy of Sciences' National Research Council completed a four-year study and found 78% of the chemicals in highest-volume commercial use had not had even "minimal" toxicity testing. Thirteen years later, there has been no significant improvement.

What we don't know may not be hurting us—or it may. But guinea pig status is not what Congress promised the public more than twenty years ago. Instead, it established a national policy that the risks of toxic chemicals in our environment would be identified and controlled. Ignorance, pervasive and persistent over the course of twenty years, has made that promise meaningless.

Chemical safety can't be based on faith. It requires facts. Government policy and government regulation have been so ineffective in making progress against the chemical ignorance problem, for so long, that the chemical manufacturing industry itself must now take direct responsibility for solving it. It is high time for the facts to be delivered.

Step one toward a solution lies in simple screening tests, which manufacturers of chemicals can easily do. All chemicals in high-volume use in the United States should long since have been subjected to at least preliminary health-effects screening, with the results publicly available for verification. There is already international consensus on just what needs to be done as a first step. A model definition of what should be included in preliminary screening tests or high-volume chemicals was developed and agreed on in 1990 by the U.S. and the other member nations of the Organisation for Economic Cooperation and Development, with extensive participation from the U.S. chemical manufacturing industry. All that is missing is the industry's commitment to act, without waiting any longer.

The possibility of sudden and accidental releases of chemicals during spills, explosions, and fires at plants that produce or use chemicals presents risks to worker and public safety, as well as to the environment. This risk was brought to the world's attention in 1984, when an explosion at a Union Carbide pesticide plant in Bhopal, India, released the chemical methyl isocyanate from a storage tank, killing more than 2,000 people. This dramatized an underappreciated source of risk, and ultimately helped lead to revisions of environmental and occupational safety and health legislation that placed an increased emphasis on accidental releases of chemicals. (See chapter 10 for a discussion of the chemical safety and reporting requirements created by the 1986 Superfund Amendment and Reauthorization Act, and see chapters 6 and 13 for a discussion of the chemical safety provisions of the 1990 Clean Air Act Amendments.)

Certain chemicals, and certain industrial sectors, are responsible for the majority of the risks from explosions and fires. Transportation accidents involving the movement of bulk chemicals are an additional concern. A report issued by EPA in 2000 discussed the risks and accident profile of chemical producing and using industries. Facilities required to submit risk management plans (RMPs) under the 1990 Clean Air Act number some 15,000, and together they utilize approximately 20,000 chemical processes. Of these processes, about 17,500 contain at least one toxic chemical, and about 8,000 contain at least one flammable chemical. Four chemical types—anhydrous ammonia, chlorine, propane, and flammable mixtures—are present in nearly 70% of all RMP processes. Fortunately, accidents are infrequent—fewer than 8% of facilities reported any accidents in the period 1990–1999—but when they occur, they can be dramatic and life threatening, both because of extreme toxicity and because of flammability. See James C. Belke (2000) *Chemical Accident Risks in U.S. Industry: A Preliminary Analysis of Accident Risk Data from U.S. Hazardous Chemical Facilities*. EPA, Washington, D.C. accidents scarce but devastating

B. THE CAUSES OF POLLUTION AND ACCIDENTAL RELEASES

One might well ask, what are the systemic causes of continuing pollution in a nation with a relatively high standard of living? One might also ask why concern for chemical pollution has steadily increased since the 1970s, in spite of the rather considerable governmental and private-sector attention given to the reduction of such pollution. Why do we continue to have chemical spills and disasters? The answers lie in a number of explanations, including increases in absolute and per capita levels of production of chemicals and the use and consumption of chemically based products, changes in the nature of pollution, the increasing tendency of people and firms to "free ride" on others, limits in the assimilative capacity of ecosystems to absorb the pollution, advances in scientific understanding of the toxic effects of chemicals, and increases in public awareness. Different commentators focus on different parts of the problem.

1. Increases in the Production and Use of Chemicals, and Changes in the Nature of Chemical Contamination

Barry Commoner, while acknowledging the large increases in the volume of chemicals produced and used, argues that it is the shift in the nature or kinds of chemicals that are entering the environment that should concern us most. In a 1987 essay in the

New Yorker, he also provides a political history of what he perceives as a retreat from environmentalism.

A Reporter at Large: The Environment
M. Barry Commoner
Source: *The New Yorker*, **June 15, 1987, pp. 46–71.**

. . . The total toxic-chemical problem is huge. The American petrochemical industry produces about two hundred and sixty-five million metric tons of hazardous waste annually; toxic chemicals generally make up about one per cent of this material, and the rest is made up of water and other non-toxic carriers. About a third of this waste is emitted, uncontrolled, into the environment. Moreover, most of the controlled, or "managed," waste . . . [ultimately] . . . becomes a long-term threat to the environment. Only about one per cent of the industry's toxic waste is actually destroyed. The chemical industry has, largely unrestrained, become the major threat to environmental quality.

. . . [T]here is a consistent explanation for the few instances of environmental success: they occur only when the relevant technologies of production are changed to eliminate the pollutant. If no such change is made, pollution continues unabated or, at best— if a control device is used—is only slightly reduced. . . . In essence, the effort to deal with environmental pollution has been trivialized. A great deal of attention has been paid to designing—and enforcing the use of—control devices that can reduce hazardous emissions only moderately. Much less attention has been given to the more difficult but rewarding task of changing the basic technologies that produce the pollutants. . . .

Unlike the steel, auto, and electric-power industries, the petrochemical industry—on its present scale, at least—is not essential. Nearly all its products are substitutes for perfectly serviceable preexisting ones: plastics for paper, wood, and metals; detergents for soap; nitrogen fertilizer for soil, organic matter, and nitrogen-fixing crops (the natural sources of nitrogen); pesticides for the insects' natural predators. . . . The petrochemical industry is inherently inimical to environmental quality. The only effective way to limit its dangerous impact on the environment is to limit the industry itself. . . .

There have been lively debates over whether environmental degradation can be reversed by controlling the growth of the world population. A decade ago, many if not most environmentalists were convinced that population pressure and "affluence," rather than inherent faults in the technology of production, were the chief reasons for environmental degradation. Since then, the hazards dramatized by Chernobyl, Three Mile Island, Seveso, Bhopal, Love Canal, and Agent Orange have convinced many people that what needs to be controlled is not the birth rate but the production technologies that have engendered these calamities. . . . The reason for malnutrition, starvation, and famine, then, is poverty, not overpopulation. Excess population is a symptom of poverty, not the other way around.

The three most important books of the past 50 years to warn of the great future damage chemical pollution may cause to humans and ecosystems—Rachel Carson's

Silent Spring (1962), Barry Commoner's *The Closing Circle* (1963), and Theo Colborn, Dianne Dumanoski, and John Peterson Myers's *Our Stolen Future* (1996)—all focused on synthetic organic compounds, especially those that are halogenated. The first two of these books make their case based on observations and intuition about biological systems, and the lack of consonance of synthetic halogenated hydrocarbons with our "evolutionary soup." The third book synthesizes the evidence from disparate observations tending to indicate that something has in fact gone terribly wrong with reproductive processes, and that this has affected all living species. This issue is discussed further in chapter 2. In addition, the seminal work *Limits to Growth* (1972) warned of the possible environmental collapse of industrial systems that do not take into account ecological, energy, and physical limits.

2. Public Goods, the Tragedy of the Commons, and Free-Rider Problems: The Destructiveness of Pursuing Narrow Self-Interest

In the following classic essay, Garrett Hardin interprets pollution in the context of the economic issue of "public goods."

The Tragedy of the Commons
Garrett Hardin

Source: Excerpted with permission from 162 *Science* 1243, 1244–1245 (1968). Copyright 1968 AAAS.

The tragedy of the commons develops in this way. Picture a pasture open to all. It is to be expected that each herdsman will try to keep as many cattle as possible on the commons. Such an arrangement may work reasonably satisfactorily for centuries because tribal wars, poaching, and disease keep the numbers of both man and beast well below the carrying capacity. Finally, however, comes the day of reckoning, that is, the day when the long-desired goal of social stability becomes a reality. At this point, the inherent logic of the commons remorselessly generates tragedy.

As a rational being, each herdsman seeks to maximize his gain. Explicitly or implicitly, more or less consciously, he asks, "What is the utility to me of adding one more animal to my herd?" This utility has one negative and one positive component.

1. The positive component is a function of the increment of one animal. Since the herdsman receives all the proceeds from the sale of the additional animal, the positive utility is nearly +1.

2. The negative component is a function of the additional overgrazing created by one more animal. Since, however, the effects of overgrazing are shared by all the herdsmen, the negative utility for any particular decision-making herdsman is only a fraction of −1.

Adding together the component partial utilities, the rational herdsman concludes that the only sensible course for him to pursue is to add another animal to his herd. And another; and another.... But this is the conclusion reached by each and every rational herdsman sharing a commons. Therein is the tragedy. Each man is locked into a system that compels him to increase his herd without limit—in a world that is limited. Ruin is the destination toward which all men rush, each pursuing his own best interest in a society that believes in the freedom of the commons. Freedom in a commons brings ruin to all. . . .

POLLUTION

In a reverse way, the tragedy of the commons reappears in problems of pollution. Here it is not a question of taking something out of the commons, but of putting something in—sewage, or chemical, radioactive, and heat wastes into water; noxious and dangerous fumes into the air; and distracting and unpleasant advertising signs into the line of sight. The calculations of utility are much the same as before. The rational man finds that his share of the cost of the wastes he discharges into the commons is less than the cost of purifying his wastes before releasing them. Since this is true for everyone, we are locked into a system of "fouling our own nest," so long as we behave only as independent, rational, free-enterprisers.

The tragedy of the commons as a food basket is averted by private property, or something formally like it. But the air and waters surrounding us cannot readily be fenced, and so the tragedy of the commons as a cesspool must be prevented by different means, by coercive laws or taxing devices that make it cheaper for the polluter to treat his pollutants than to discharge them untreated. We have not progressed as far with the solution of this problem as we have with the first. Indeed, our particular concept of private property, which deters us from exhausting the positive resources of the earth, favors pollution. The owner of a factory on the bank of a stream—whose property extends to the middle of the stream—often has difficulty seeing why it is not his natural right to muddy the waters flowing past his door. The law, always behind the times, requires elaborate stitching and fitting to adapt it to this newly perceived aspect of the commons. . . .

The pollution problem is a consequence of population. It did not much matter how lonely American frontiersman disposed of his waste. "Flowing water purifies itself every 10 miles," my grandfather used to say, and the myth was near enough to the truth when he was a boy, for there were not too many people. But as population became denser, the natural chemical and biological recycling processes became overloaded.

■ NOTES

1. Hardin traces the destruction of the public commons from the overgrazing of cattle to the fact that not all the damage produced by one cattle owner accrues to him or her. In addition, even if some cattle owners would be willing to spend their resources to mitigate all the damage, others would raise their cattle without doing so, and thus would "free ride" on their socially conscious neighbors, rather than join in the improvement of the commons. If there are enough cattle owners seeking to similarly raise more cattle without mitigating the damage, this results in the destruction of the commons for all. Pollution is produced in excess by the same mechanism, and Hardin argues that without coercive interventions by government, this is inevitable. Hardin also suggests that the pollution problem "is a consequence of pop-

ulation." Reduce population and the problem goes away. Alternatively, privatize parcels of the commons, or have government step in to coerce socially responsible behavior.

2. Note that Hardin and Commoner do not agree on the importance of population as a major factor in environmental degradation. See also Paul R. Ehrlich (1968) *The Population Bomb*, whose doomsday scenario of massive starvation failed to materialize. But also see Paul R. Ehrlich, Gretchen C. Daily, Scott C. Daily, Norman Myers, and James Salzman (1997) "No Middle Way on the Environment," *Atlantic Monthly*, December, pp. 98–104, which addresses overconsumption as a prime cause of environmental degradation.   ■

a.   Pursuing Self-Interest as a Pathway to an Improved Environment

In contrast to Garret Hardin, Matt Ridley and Bobbi S. Low argue that appealing to humankind's tendency toward selfishness can actually *save* the proverbial commons.

Can Selfishness Save the Environment?
M. Ridley and B. S. Low
Source: *The Atlantic Monthly*, September 1993, pp. 76–86, excerpted with permission.

FOR THE GOOD OF THE WORLD?

...At the center of all environmentalism lies a problem: whether to appeal to the heart or to the head—whether to urge people to make sacrifices in behalf of the planet or to accept that they will not, and instead rig the economic choices so that they find it rational to be environmentalist....

[Biologists and economists]...[b]oth think that people are generally not willing to pay for the long-term good of society or the planet. To save the environment, therefore, we will have to find a way to reward individuals for good behavior and punish them for bad. Exhorting them to self-sacrifice for the sake of "humanity" or "the earth" will not be enough.

This is utterly at odds with conventional wisdom "Building an environmentally sustainable future depends on restructuring the global economy, major shifts in human reproductive behavior, and dramatic changes in values and lifestyles," wrote Lester Brown, of the Worldwatch Institute, in his State of the World for 1992, typifying the way environmentalists see economics. If people are shortsighted, an alien value system, not human nature, is to blame.

...We are going to argue that the environmental movement has set itself an unnecessary obstacle by largely ignoring the fact that human beings are motivated by self-interest rather than collective interests. But that does not mean that the collective interest is unobtainable: examples from biology and economics show that there are all sorts of ways to make the individual interest concordant with the collective—so long as we recognize the need to.

THE TRAGEDY OF THE COMMONS

...In 1968 the ecologist Garrett Hardin wrote an article in *Science* magazine that explained "the tragedy of the commons"—

*Benifits to one
damage dispose
to all*

why common land tended to suffer from overgrazing, and why every sea fishery suffers from overfishing. It is because the benefits that each extra cow (or netful of fish) brings are reaped by its owner, but the costs of the extra strain it puts on the grass (or on fish stocks) are shared among all the users of what is held in common. In economic jargon, the costs are externalized. Individually rational behavior deteriorates into collective ruin.

The ozone hole and the greenhouse effect are classic tragedies of the commons in the making: each time you burn a gallon of gas to drive into town, you reap the benefit of it, but the environmental cost is shared with all five billion other members of the human race. You are a "free-rider." Being rational, you drive, and the atmosphere's capacity to absorb carbon dioxide is "overgrazed," and the globe warms. Even if individuals will benefit in the long run from the prevention of global warming, in the short run such prevention will cost them dear. As Michael McGinnis and Elinor Ostrom, of Indiana University at Bloomington, put it in a recent paper, "global warming is a classic dilemma of collective action: a large group of potential beneficiaries facing diffuse and uncertain gains is much harder to organize for collective action than clearly defined groups who are being asked to suffer easily understandable costs."

Hardin recognized two ways to avoid overexploiting commons. One is to privatize them, so that the owner has both costs and benefits. Now he has every incentive not to overgraze. The other is to regulate them by having an outside agency with the force of law behind it—a government, in short—restrict the number of cattle.

...The whole structure of pollution regulation in the United States represents a centralized solution to a commons problem. Bureaucrats decide, in response to pressure from lobbyists, exactly what levels of pollution to allow, usually give no credit for any reductions below the threshold, and even specify the technologies to be used (the so-

called "best available technology" policy). This creates perverse incentives for polluters, because it makes pollution free up to the threshold, and so there is no encouragement to reduce pollution further.

...A more general way, favored by free-market economists, of putting the same point is that regulatory regimes set the value of cleanliness at zero: if a company wishes to produce any pollutant, at present it can do so free, as long as it produces less than the legal limit. If, instead, it had to buy a quota from the government, it would have an incentive to drive emissions as low as possible to keep costs down, and the government would have a source of revenue to spend on environmental protection. The 1990 Clean Air Act set up a market in tradable pollution permits for sulfur-dioxide emissions, which is a form of privatization.

THE PITFALLS OF PRIVATIZATION

Because privatizing a common resource can internalize the costs of damaging it, economists increasingly call for privatization as the solution to commons problems....

It would be [im]possible to define private property rights in clean air. Paul Romer, of Berkeley, points out that the atmosphere is not like the light from a lighthouse, freely shared by all users. One person cannot use a given chunk of air for seeing through—or comfortably breathing—after another person has filled it with pollution any more than two people in succession can kill the same whale. What stands in the way of privatizing whales or the atmosphere is that enforcement of a market would require as large a bureaucracy as if the whole thing had been centralized in the first place.

...Moreover, there is no guarantee that rationality would call for a private owner of an environmental public good to preserve it or use it sustainably. Twenty years ago Colin Clark, a mathematician at the University of British Columbia, wrote an article in *Science* pointing out that under certain circumstances it might make economic sense to exterminate whales. What he meant was that because interest rates could allow money to grow faster than whales reproduce, even somebody who had a certain monopoly over the world's whales and could therefore forget about free-riders should not, for reasons of economic self-interest, take a sustainable yield of the animals. It would be more profitable to kill them all, bank the proceeds, sell the equipment, and live off the interest....

THE MIDDLE WAY

...[L]ocal people can and do get together to solve their difficulties, as long as the community is small, stable, and communicating, and has strong concern for the future...[C]ooperation is more likely in small groups that have common interests and the autonomy to create and enforce their own rules....

WHAT CHANGED DU PONT'S MIND?

...[W]hy [would] a corporation willingly abandon a profitable business by agreeing to phase out the chemicals that seem to damage the ozone layer[?] Du Pont's decision stands out as an unusually altruistic gesture amid the selfish strivings of big business. Without it the Montreal protocol on ozone-destroying chemicals, a prototype for international agreements on the environment, might not have come about. Why had Du Pont made that decision? Conventional wisdom, and Du Pont's own assertions, credit improved scientific understanding and environmental pressure groups. Lobbyists had raised public consciousness about the ozone layer so high that Du Pont's executives quickly realized that the loss of public good will could cost them more than the products were worth....It suggests that appeals to the wider good can be effective where appeals to self-interest cannot....

CAUSE FOR HOPE

...Let the United States drag its feet over the Rio conventions if it wants, but let it feel the sting of some sanction for doing so. Let people drive gas-guzzlers if they wish, but tax them until it hurts. Let companies lobby against anti-pollution laws, but pass laws that make obeying them worthwhile. Make it rational for individuals to act "green."

...We are merely asking governments to be more cynical about human nature. Instead of being shocked that people take such a narrow view of their interests, use the fact. Instead of trying to change human nature, go with the grain of it. For in refusing to put group good ahead of individual advantage, people are being both rational and consistent with their evolutionary past.

■ **NOTES**

Human nature Self interested
Use this to our advantage

1. DuPont's actions vis-á-vis chlorofluorocarbons (CFCs) were also motivated by the company's self-interest in preserving its markets; coming out quickly with its own substitutes before anyone else had time to develop them put the company in an advantageous financial position. In fact, DuPont was the driver behind the Montreal Protocol's relatively aggressive phaseout of CFCs. Is this example characteristic of industry's response to environmental regulation in general? Consider Michael Porter's argument, discussed in chapters 3, 12, and 13, that "first movers" can benefit by being ahead of the curve in environmental compliance.

2. Note the authors' focus on the success of voluntary initiatives in small communities with interests in common. Is the social cohesion necessary to encourage efforts toward the greater good likely to be similarly strong in large, anonymous urban areas?

3. Mandatory disclosure laws (discussed in chapter 10) may be one means to bring private behavior more in line with the public interest. See Mary Graham, "Regulation by Shaming," *The Atlantic* 285(4): 36 (April 2000).   ∎

b.   Moral Appeal

Can moral rectitude save the environment? The following conservative believes so.

A Conservative Speaks
G. K. Durnil

What about enforcement?

Source: *Rachel's Environment and Health Weekly*, no. 424, January 12, 1995, excerpted with permission.

[Ex]cerpts from a previously-unreported speech by Gordon K. Durnil, former U.S. Chairman of the International Joint Commission (IJC)....

... Let's wrap up this discussion with some practical reasons why conservatives should be interested in and leaders for environmental protection: interested in what we are doing to ourselves and to our children with some of the chemicals we use and the processes we employ. I start with the presumption that all reasonable people prefer clean air and clean water; that such people are opposed to unknowing exposures to various poisons to our children, our families and our friends. So where do we start? The best way, the least expensive way, the conservative way and the least painful way to accomplish the goal of protection from the most onerous pollutants is prevention. Just don't do it in the first place. Governments, jointly or singularly, will never have sufficient funds to continue cleaning up all those onerous substances lying on the bottom of lakes or working their way through the ground. So for economic reasons and for health reasons, prevention is a conservative solution. Let's not continue to put in what we now are paying to clean up.

never will have enough $ to clean & stop

Conservatives want lower taxes. Conservatives want smaller government, with less regulations and fewer regulators. Pollution prevention, instead of all the high-cost bureaucratic mandates and regulatory harassment at the tail end of the pollution trail, can achieve those conservative purposes. If you don't make an onerous substance in the first place, you won't later need to regulate it; you won't need regulators or the increased taxes and fees to pay their expenses. If you don't discharge it, you don't need to buy a government permit with all the attendant red tape and bureaucratic nonsense to which businesses are now subjected. Pollution prevention corrects not just the physical health of our society, it promotes economic health.

Conservatives believe in individual rights. We believe in the right to own private property, and to use it as we see fit. Private dry lands should not be deemed to be wet by a remote government. Such actions violate our basic constitutional rights. But is not the insidious invasion of our bodies by harmful unsolicited chemicals the most flagrant violation of our individual rights?

We conservatives bemoan the decline in values that has besieged our present day society. We abhor government and media assaults on our constitutional right to freely practice our religion in today's value neutral, politically correct society. Why then should we not abhor the lack of morality involved in discharging untested chemicals into the air, ground and water to alter and harm, to whatever degree, human life and wildlife?

We conservatives preach out against the decline in learning in our schools; the increased incidence of juvenile crime; we worry about abnormal sexual practices and preferences. Should there be evidence (as there is) that some of those things are being caused by chemicals tested and untested flowing into our environment, should we not add them to our litany of concerns?

We preach self-reliance, but can we be that if unbeknown to us mysterious chemicals are affecting our ability to be reliant upon ourselves?

We conservatives believe it unconscionable that government programs such as welfare are tearing at the fabric of the family. We are upset with the growing incidence of birth out of wedlock, of single parent families; with children bearing children. Why then are we not so concerned with the causes, and the increased incidence, of childhood cancers? Why not visit the local children's hospital

and visit with those brave youngsters with ineffective immune systems trying to fight off the devastating evils of cancer? Observe the parental pain. See how that circumstance tears at the family. Why not add childhood cancer to our concerns about the family; asking why the emphasis is still on how to cure it, instead of on how to prevent it?

...The symmetry of nature is loaned to us for human use over relatively short periods of time; seventy or eighty years, if we are fortunate. Each of us has a moral duty to not disrupt that balance. For centuries humans met that moral duty, but over the past one half century we have become just too urbane to worry about such mundane things. We have unknowingly done with chemicals what we would never have intentionally done had we pursued the moral basis of the conservative philosophy I described earlier.

Daily we are being exposed to more and more information about the need for environmental stewardship; about the need to exercise precaution before putting harmful chemicals into the environment....[W]e are unintentionally putting our children and our grandchildren in harms way. And I have concluded that we need a basic change of direction.

▪ NOTE

1. Note the author's endorsement of the "Precautionary Principle" (prevention). Conservationists seek to "preserve"—to "conserve"—nature and the environment. What are *political* conservatives trying to preserve or conserve? Is pollution a "conservative," "liberal," or "progressive" political issue, or does it transcend such ideologies (and labels)?   ▪

3.   Pollution as an Economic Problem

Garrett Hardin suggests that the failure to hold polluters liable for the damage they cause is an underlying reason for the failure of economic actors to police themselves.

Classical economists would agree. They tend to interpret pollution as an economic problem, as articulated in the following article by Larry Ruff, which has become something of a paradigm for the way in which modern economists approach the issue.

The Economic Common Sense of Pollution
Larry Ruff

Source: Robert Dorfman and Nancy S. Dorfman, *Economics of the Environment*. V. W. Norton, New York, 1972, pp. 3–19, excerpted with permission.

We are going to make very little real progress in solving the problem of pollution until we recognize it for what, primarily, it is: an economic problem, which must be understood in economic terms.... Engineers ... are certain that pollution will vanish once they find the magic gadget or power source. Politicians keep trying to find the right kind of bureaucracy; and bureaucrats maintain an unending search for the correct set of rules and regulations. Those who are above such vulgar pursuits pin their hopes on a moral regeneration or social revolution, apparently in the belief that saints and socialists have no garbage to dispose of. But as important as technology, politics, law, and ethics are to the pollution question, all such approaches are bound to have disappointing results, for they ignore the primary fact that pollution is an economic problem.

Before developing an economic analysis of pollution, however, it is necessary to dispose of some popular myths. First, pollution is not new.... Second, most pollution is not due to affluence, despite the current popularity of this notion.... Nor can pollution be blamed on the self-seeking activities of greedy capitalists.... What *is* new about pollution is what might be called the *problem* of pollution. Many unpleasant phenomena—poverty, genetic defects, hurricanes—have existed forever without being considered problems; they are, or were, considered to be facts of life, like gravity and death, and a mature person

simply adjusted to them. Such phenomena become problems only when it begins to appear that something can and should be done about them. It is evident that pollution had advanced to the problem stage. Now the question is what can and should be done?

... Pure self-interest, guided only by the famous "invisible hand" of competition, organizes the economy efficiently.

The logical basis of this rather startling result is that, under certain conditions, competitive prices convey all the information necessary for making the optimal decision....

Th[e] divergence between private and social costs is the fundamental cause of pollution of all types, and it arises in any society where decisions are at all decentralized—which is to say, in any economy of any size which hopes to function at all.... Without prices to convey the needed information, [the socialist or capitalist manager] ... does not know what action is in the public interest, and certainly would have no incentive to act correctly even if he did know.

Although markets fail to perform efficiently when private and social costs diverge, this does not imply that there is some inherent flaw in the idea of acting on self-interest in response to market prices. Decisions based on private cost calculations are typically correctly from a social point of view; and even when they are not quite correct, it often is better to accept this inefficiency than to turn to some alternative decision mechanism, which may be worse.... There is no point in trying to find something—some omniscient and omnipotent *deus ex machina*—to replace markets and self-interest. Usually it is preferable to modify existing institutions, where necessary, to make private and social interest coincide.

And there is a third relevant economic concept: the fundamental distinction between questions of efficiency and questions of equity or fairness. A situation is said to be efficient if it is not possible to rearrange things so as to benefit one person without harming any others. That is the *economic* equation for efficiency. *Politically*, this equation can be solved in various ways; though most reasonable men will agree that efficiency is a good thing, they will rarely agree about which of the many possible efficient states, each with a different distribution of "welfare" among individuals, is the best one. Economics itself has nothing to say about which efficient state is the best. That decision is a matter of personal and philosophical values, and ultimately must be decided by some political process. Economics can suggest ways of achieving efficient states, and can try to describe the equity considerations involved in any suggested social policy; but the final decisions about matters of "fairness" or "justice" cannot be decided on economic grounds....

But if we cannot directly observe market prices for many of the costs of pollution, we must find another way to proceed. One possibility is to infer the costs from other prices, just as we infer the value of an ocean view from real estate prices. In principle, one could estimate the value people put on clean air and beaches by observing how much more they are willing to pay for property in nonpolluted areas. Such information could be obtained; but there is little of it available at present.

Another possible way of estimating the costs of pollution is to ask people how much they would be willing to pay to have pollution reduced....

Once cost and benefit functions are known, the [government] should choose a level of abatement that maximizes net gain. This occurs where the marginal cost of further abatement just equals the marginal benefit... [T]here is a very simple way to accomplish all this. *Put a price on pollution....*

Once the prices are set, polluters can adjust to them any way they choose. Because they act on self-interest they will reduce their pollution by every means possible up to the point where further reduction would cost more than the price....

In general, the price system allocates costs in a manner which is at least superficially fair: those who produce and consume goods which cause pollution, pay the costs. But the superior efficiency in control and apparent fairness are not the only advantages of the price mechanism. Equally important is the case with which it can be put into operation. It is not necessary to have detailed information about all the techniques of pollution reduction, or estimates of all costs and benefits. Nor is it necessary to determine whom to blame or who should pay. All that is needed is a mechanism for estimating, if only roughly at first, the pollution output of all polluters, together with a means of collecting fees. Then we can simply pick a price—any price—for each category of pollution, and we are in business. The initial price should be chosen on the basis of some estimate of its effects but need not be the optimal one. If the resulting reduction in pollution is not "enough," the price can be raised until there is sufficient reduction. A change in technology, number of plants, or whatever, can be accommodated by a change in the price, even without detailed knowledge of all the technological and economic data. Further, once the idea is explained, the price system is much more likely to be politically acceptable than some method of direct control. Paying for a service, such as garbage disposal, is a well-established tradition, and is much less objectionable than having a bureaucrat nosing around and giving arbitrary orders. When businessmen, consumers, and politicians understand the alternatives, the price system will seem very attractive indeed. . . .

There are some objections that can be raised against the price system as a tool of pollution policy. Most are either illogical or apply with much greater force to any other method of control. . . . First, it is probably easier to get agreement on a simple schedule of pollution prices than on a complex set of detailed regulations. Second, a uniform price schedule would make it more difficult for any member of the "cooperative" group to attract

industry from the other areas by promising a more lenient attitude toward pollution. Third, and most important, a price system generates revenues for the [government], which can be distributed to the various political entities. While the allocation of these revenues would involve some vigorous discussion, any alternative methods of control would require the various governments to raise taxes to pay the costs, a much less appealing prospect; in fact, there would be a danger that the pollution prices might be considered a device to generate revenue rather than to reduce pollution, which could lead to an overly-clean, inefficient situation.

■ **NOTES**

1. Is Ruff's assertion that pollution is not new a convincing one? Have the nature, pervasiveness, and consequences of pollution changed?

2. Are prices associated with the public's "willingness to pay" for clean air, clean water, and other environmental amenities satisfying metrics? See the discussion in chapter 3.

3. Although Ruff acknowledges that economics cannot assist us in deciding questions of equity, does he appear to accept any justification for reducing pollution below the levels where marginal costs and benefits are equal; i.e., forcing industry to spend more on reducing pollution than the public demands?

4. Note that while Ruff also acknowledges that "[e]conomics itself has nothing to say about which efficient state is the best," he assumes that any efficient state is better than any inefficient state.

5. The following article addresses the justification for government intervention in the market on both efficiency and equity grounds, stressing the need to confront the efficiency-equity tradeoffs.   ■

Environmental and Safety Regulation: Reasons for their Adoption and Possible Effects on Technological Innovation

N. Ashford and G. Heaton

Source: *Environmental Policy and Law*, vol. 1, pp. 171–172 (1975/76), excerpted with permission.

THE JUSTIFICATION FOR GOVERNMENT INTERVENTION IN ENVIRONMENTAL/SAFETY MATTERS

In the United States, the rationale for government intervention in the marketplace through regulation is usually expressed in terms of two purposes: either (1) to improve the working of the market for goods and services by encouraging competition, economic efficiency and the diversity of available goods and services, or (2) to ameliorate the adverse consequences of market activities and technology in general by reducing the attendant social costs.

The underlying reason for pursuing these goals is not to improve the efficiency of the market for its own sake, but to "optimize" social welfare. *Economic* regulation generally addresses itself to the first purpose by attempting to insure that the "price mechanism" operates efficiently to allocate goods and services properly among economic sectors and between producers and consumers, but also to allocate resources properly between generations. Economic regulation, properly carried out, thereby is generally expected to reduce the price of the goods and services it seeks to regulate.

Environmental/safety regulation, on the other hand, attempts to internalize the social costs attending market activities—especially those associated with technology—and it does this by making sure that the prices of goods and services paid by the consumer reflect the true costs to society. Thus, it might be expected that prices increase in some cases. Including the costs of minimizing adverse health or safety consequences from

technology in the price of goods and services represents a shift in the way that costs are accounted for and not necessarily a true increase in the cost to society. Furthermore, ... environmental or safety regulation may not only decrease the total cost to the society but may reduce prices as well.

Thus, we can see that two kinds of regulation—economic and environmental/safety—are expected to operate differently because they address different aspects of market activity. There is, however, one further critical distinction: Environmental/safety regulation also may have as a fundamental purpose the protection of certain groups of people—for example, children, workers in an asbestos plant, or the less educated. This is justified under the principle of equity or fairness whereby some economic efficiency may be sacrificed for the health or safety of those special groups. Price increases which result from internalizing health or safety costs—for example in making products safe—do not necessarily result in a reduction of real economic efficiency, but protecting a group of workers may.

"Optimizing" the social welfare should not be confused with "maximizing" social welfare. To the extent that a regulatory decision seeks to protect a select group of people, additional costs (and benefits) arise above what might be expected if the only concern were to protect as many lives as possible, regardless of their distribution. For example, it is conceivable that asbestos might be banned for use as a brake lining with the result that more lives are lost on the highway (due to less efficient brakes) than are saved in asbestos manufacturing operations. These additional costs might be justified or even demanded by considerations of equity.

The fact that economic efficiency is sometimes traded for equity consideration should not be disturbing unless it is either unnecessary for the result or one forgets that economic efficiency is a measure of *maximizing* rather than *optimizing* social welfare. In the United States, for instance, we pay special attention to small business in formulating our economic regulatory strategies—and we do this as a conscious tradeoff between economic efficiency and equity considerations in order to maintain the viability of the small firm. Regulatory policies aimed at fairness to the consumer or worker are no less justified.

Lest one is left with the impression that environmental/safety regulations either contribute to economic inefficiency or at most do not improve economic efficiency, a further observation is helpful. The price mechanism is theoretically supposed to allocate resources properly between this generation and the next. If the price today does not reflect all the real *economic* costs, the commodity may be underpriced and too much consumed. This has been made fairly clear to us in the case of natural gas. Difficulties arise both from the fact that the economy is operating some distance from efficiency and because a rapid attempt to bring the market into equilibrium may cause immense adjustment and transient costs. If, in fact, the prices of goods and services today similarly do not reflect attendant *social* costs, and especially if these costs are increasing rapidly (like pollution) or will be included in the price at an increasing rate, we are also using material resources too rapidly because they are underpriced. In the language of the economist, we are made economically inefficient by not internalizing the externalities. . . .

Granger Morgan also confronts the tension between equity and efficiency, but in a different way.

Risk Management Should Be About Efficiency and Equity
Granger Morgan

Source: Reprinted in part with permission from *Environmental Science & Technology*, **January 1, 2000, pp. 32A–34A. Copyright 2000, American Chemical Society.**

[There have] been persistent calls for legislation to mandate cost-benefit analysis as the basis for managing risks to health, safety, and the environment. Listening to the proponents of these bills, one gets the idea that efficiency should be the sole objective of government. But efficiency is only one objective. And, most of the time, efficiency is not the *primary* objective of most government policy. Government is mainly preoccupied with distributional issues, that is, with equity.

This concern with equity is even reflected in some enabling risk management legislation. The Clean Air Act does not talk about cleaning up the nation's air to the point where a marginal improvement in air quality is just equal to the marginal social losses from pollution. It calls upon EPA to keep the nation's air clean enough to protect "the most sensitive [population]". . . .

. . . We need to acknowledge that both economic efficiency *and* social equity are legitimate goals in risk management, and we need to find regulatory strategies that allow us to explicitly combine the two. What might such a strategy look like? Here is a simple example:

No individual shall be exposed to a lifetime excess probability of death from this hazard of greater than X. Whether additional resources should be spent to reduce the risks from this hazard to people whose lifetime probability of death falls below X should be determined by a careful benefit-cost calculation.

Choosing the value of the equity threshold X is the first important social value judgment required in this method.... The key point is that in this formulation one says there is a level of risk above which we will not allow *anybody* in our society to be exposed. As it has in the past, that level may change over time.

Some might argue that X should only be specified for "uncompensated involuntary risks." However, for many health, safety, and environmental risks, I think that most people now believe that there is a level of risk above which compensation, even for risks "freely accepted" becomes a socially unacceptable solution.

This formulation does not stop at limiting individual lifetime risks to X. It also says that if there are cost-effective ways that people at or below a risk of X can be further protected (i.e., with $B - C > 0$, where B represents benefit and C represents cost), we should adopt them....

Why not just use benefit-cost alone without an equity threshold? Because, in some cases, a straight benefit-cost formulation could leave a few individuals exposed to levels of risk that are significantly greater than X....A traditional benefit-cost formulation would control those risks only to the extent that such control is economically justifiable. The hybrid approach at least reduces every person's risk down to the equity threshold, on the grounds that, independent of the costs of control, it is socially unacceptable to expose anyone to a higher risk.

---

4. Limits to Growth

A challenging complication, beyond what could be called "the pricing problem" discussed by Ruff, arises when the effects of current production and consumption are not apparent or recognized until some time considerably later; and by the time they are recognized, it may be impossible or prohibitively expensive to reverse or minimize these effects. This leads to what has been described as "overshoot and collapse" as a consequence of exceeding ecological limits.

Using system dynamics techniques developed by Jay Forrester at MIT,[1] the legendary 1972 *Limits to Growth* report discussed the results of a computer model

---

1. In 1971, the book *World Dynamics* presented the results of a computer model developed by Professor Forrester and his colleagues at MIT, called "World 2." Forrester describes how the model was created to support a two-week workshop at MIT (in 1970) during which the Executive Committee from the Club of Rome were invited to *learn* the process of model formulation and computer simulation. The "World 2" model was designed to analyze the problems facing the "world system," which was defined as incorporating mankind, his social systems, his technology, and the natural environment. Using five key variables—population, capital investment, natural resources, the fraction of capital devoted to agriculture, and pollution—the model provided evidence that within the next 100 years "man may face choices from a four-pronged dilemma—suppression of modern industrial society by a natural-resource shortage; decline of world population from changes wrought by pollution; population limitation by food shortage; or pollution

(called "World 3") designed to predict the future if current trends of increasing population, industrialization, pollution, food production, and resource depletion continued unabated. The report reached three salient conclusions:

1. "If the present growth trends in world population, industrialization, pollution, food production, and resource depletion continue unchanged, the limits to growth on this planet will be reached sometime within the next one hundred years. The most probable result will be a rather sudden and uncontrollable decline in both population and industrial capacity."

2. "It is possible to alter these growth trends and to establish a condition of ecological and economic stability that is sustainable far into the future. The state of global equilibrium could be designed so that the basic material needs of each person on earth are satisfied and each person has an equal opportunity to realize his individual human potential."

3. "If the world's people decide to strive for this second outcome rather than the first, the sooner they begin working to attain it, the greater will be their chances of success." (D. H. Meadows, D. L. Meadows, J. Randers, and W. Behrens (1972) *Limits to Growth.* Potomac Associates, New York, pp. 23–24.)

An important concept raised in *Limits to Growth* is "overshoot and collapse," the idea that once one inadvertently goes beyond the system's limits, it will be nearly impossible to reverse course (see id., p. 144). Overshoot can occur, the study's authors opined, because (1) growth leads to rapid change within the system; (2) there is a limit to the system beyond which it becomes unstable; and (3) delays in feedback mechanisms will mean that the system's limits will be exceeded before the problems are identified. For example, "[p]ollution generated in exponentially increasing amounts can rise past the danger point, because the danger point is first perceived years after the offending pollution was released. A rapidly growing industrial system

---

collapse from war, disease, and social stresses caused by physical and psychological crowding" [J. W. Forrester (1971) *World Dynamics.* Wright-Allen Press, Cambridge, Mass., p. 11].

In addition, the simulations indicated that the high standard of living in developed countries is likely to fall as industrialization reaches a "*natural-resource limit,*" and that developing countries might have "*no realistic hope*" of reaching the standard of living experienced in developed nations (Forrestr, infra, p. 12), predictions which fueled the developed-developing country debate about the sovereign right to, and best process of, development. Following the workshop at MIT, The Club of Rome, convinced that Forrester's model had identified many of the factors behind the "world problematique," decided to launch Phase One of their study into the predicament of mankind. This phase, headed by Dennis Meadows, led to the creation of a "World 3" model, upon which the *Limits to Growth* report was based. The "World 3" model contained about three times as many mathematical equations as its predecessor and used empirical data for many of its numerical relationships [H. S. D. Cole, C. Freeman, M. Jahoda, and K. L. R. Pavitt (eds.) (1973) *Thinking About the Future: A Critique of The Limits to Growth.* Sussex University Press, London]. Note: the phrase "world problematique," was created by The Club of Rome to describe the set of crucial problems—political, social, economic, technological, environmental, psychological, and cultural— facing humanity.

can build up a capital base dependent on a given resource and then discover that the exponentially shrinking resources reserves cannot support it" (id., p. 145).

In 1992, the authors of the *Limits to Growth* study published *Beyond the Limits*, which argued that the conclusions they reached in 1972 were still valid, but that the underlying logic needed to be strengthened.[2] This newer work argues that the limits to growth are not physical limits such as limits to population growth or to the number of automobiles on the road. Rather, they are limits to *throughput*, i.e., limits to the flows of energy and materials required to keep people alive, to build more automobiles, and the like. And by this they mean that the limits to growth are not only the limits to the earth's ability to provide the *resource streams* of energy and materials necessary to meet predicted consumption levels, but also limits to its ability to absorb the *pollution and waste streams* in natural "sinks" such as forests and oceans. One common criticism of the first "World 3" model was that it underestimated the influence of technological advance and did not adequately represent the adaptive nature of the market. *Beyond the Limits* utilized a new version of the model that did not rely solely on technology or the market, but instead on a smooth interaction between the two. The results of the new model indicated that in many cases resource and pollution flows had already surpassed levels that are physically sustainable.

The implications of these conclusions are far reaching. In essence, the *Limits to Growth* reports state that nothing short of a radical restructuring of the prevailing trends of industrialization and economic growth will suffice to prevent a sudden decline in both population and industrial capacity. In addition, if they are correct, a condition of ecological and economic stability will only be achieved if the limited natural resources are shared prudently and equally among the world population,

---

2. The revised conclusions are (1) "Human use of many essential resources and generation of many kinds of pollutants have already surpassed rates that are physically sustainable. Without significant reductions in material and energy flows, there will be in the coming decades an uncontrolled decline in per capita food output, energy use, and industrial production." (2) "This decline is not inevitable. To avoid it two changes are necessary. The first is a comprehensive revision of policies and practices that perpetuate growth in material consumption and in population. The second is a rapid, drastic increase in the efficiency with which materials and energy are used." and (3) "A sustainable society is still technically and economically possible. It could be much more desirable than a society that tries to solve its problems by constant expansion. The transition to a sustainable society requires a careful balance between long-term and short-term goals and an emphasis on sufficiency, equity, and quality of life rather than on quantity of output. It requires more than productivity and more than technology; it also requires maturity, compassion, and wisdom" [Meadows *et al.* (1992) *Beyond the Limits: Confronting Global Collapse, Envisioning a Sustainable Future*, Chelsea Green Publishing, White River Junction, Vermont, pp. xv–xvi].

In 2004, the 30-year update of *Limits to Growth* was published. "Now, three decades later, we are into the 21st century within 20 years of the time when our scenarios suggest that growth will near its end. The basic conclusions are still the same. . . . The world's use of materials and energy has grown past the levels that can be supported indefinitely. Pressures are mounting from the environment that will force a reduction. Rising oil prices, climate change, declining forests, falling ground water levels—all of these are simply symptoms of the overshoot" [Donella H. Meadows, Jorgen Randers, and Dennis Meadows (2004) *Facing the Limits to Growth*, AlterNet, http://www.alternet.org/story/18978/ (accessed on 06/25/04).]

and if the economic system provides the opportunity for each individual to achieve his or her full potential though employment. Finally, the sooner such changes begin the better. Such stark predictions[3] and conclusions[4] have obvious negative connotations for both developed and developing nations, and have not been received warmly. For developed nations, the idea of using substantially fewer resources (to allow developing nations to use their fair share of the terrestrial stock) raises the specter of lowered standards of living. Developing nations are equally distressed by the suggestion that they will never be able to achieve the standard of living experienced by developed nations.

An interesting response to *Limits to Growth* came from Sir Solly Zuckerman:

The only kind of exponential growth with which the book...does not deal, and which I for one believe is a fact, is the growth of human knowledge and of the increase in the kind of understanding with which we can imbue our efforts as we see to it that our increasing numbers do not become incompatible with a better life....[T]he alarm which we now experience in fact comes from our increased knowledge of what we are doing. (W. Rowland (1973) The Plot to Save the World. Clarke, Irwin, Toronto/Vancouver, p. 18.)

Similarly, Marie Jahoda argued that the introduction of an extra variable—the human—into the World 3 computer model used by the *Limits* authors might change the structure of the debate:

It is in the nature of purposeful adaptation that the course of events can be changed dramatically if social constraints are experienced as intolerable, if aspirations remain unfulfilled and if confidence in the ruling political powers disintegrates. It makes no sense in this context to talk of exponential growth in a finite world. Man's inventiveness in changing social arrangements is without limits, even if not without hazards. (M. Jahoda (1973) "Postscript on Social Change," in *Thinking About the Future: A Critique of The Limits to Growth*, H. S. D. Cole, C. Freeman, M. Jahoda, and K. L. R. Pavitt (eds.) Sussex University Press, London, pp. 209–215, at p. 215.)

---

3. Forrester and the *Limits* authors note they did not develop their models to accurately predict the future; instead their models were designed to indicate the behavior of the world system if certain changes were made to the system's structure and policies. *Limits to Growth* (pp. 185–186) notes that it "was intended to be, and is, an analysis of current trends, of their influence on each other, and of their possible outcomes. [Its]...goal was to provide warnings of potential world crisis if these trends are allowed to continue, and thus offer an opportunity to make changes in our political, economic, and social systems to ensure that these crises do not take place."

4. *Limits to Growth* does not make any explicit recommendations regarding how a "state of equilibrium" could be achieved. In the words of that study, "It presents a bold step toward a comprehensive and integrated analysis of the world situation, an approach that will now require years to refine, deepen, and extend" (id., p. 186). Regarding its pessimistic conclusions, the report offers the following comments. "Many will believe that, in population growth, for instance, nature will take remedial action, and birth rates will decline before catastrophe threatens. Others may simply feel that the trends identified in the study are beyond human control; these people will wait for "something to turn up." Still others will hope that minor corrections in present policies will lead to a gradual and satisfactory readjustment and possibly to equilibrium. And a great many others are apt to put their trust in technology, with its supposed cornucopia of cure-all solutions....We welcome and encourage this debate" (id., p. 189).

If we consider the events in the United States that led to the formation of a national environmental agenda in the 1960s and 1970s, Jahoda's insights are not without historical support. A real question exists, however, as to whether the international community, with its competing sovereign interests, can reach a consensus on how to adequately respond to these "intolerable" events. In addition, we need to ask the question of whether humankind can risk the formation of global hazards of this nature in the first instance, which brings us back to the original purpose of *Limits to Growth*.

Most assuredly, the *Limits* reports have not been without their detractors. Three particularly influential critiques of the initial *Limits to Growth* report were *The Doomsday Syndrome—An Attack on Pessimism*, written in 1972 by John Maddox, the editor of the British magazine *Nature*; *Thinking About the Future—A Critique of the Limits to Growth*, written in 1973 by a group of authors at the Science Policy Research Unit at the University of Sussex; and *The Computer that Printed Out W*O*L*F**, 50 *Foreign Affairs* 660–668, written in 1972 by MIT economist Carl Kaysen. *The Doomsday Syndrome* presents a contrasting (i.e., optimistic) view, in which resources are more abundant and human ingenuity leads to an increase in human well-being. In addition, Maddox argued that nations then facing food shortages were likely to have a food surplus by the 1980s, a prediction that sadly did not materialize for countries such as Somalia and Ethiopia. *Thinking About the Future* is an academic critique of *Limits to Growth*.[5] It also expressed the concern that what ultimately must be a somewhat subjective undertaking was clothed with the scientific respectability that came with having been generated by a computer by a research group based at MIT. As a result, they said, *Limits to Growth* was often cited in doomsday literature as an "authoritative source for views which otherwise might be rather difficult to justify" [C. Freeman (1973) "Malthus with a Computer," in *Thinking About the Future: A Critique of The Limits to Growth*. H. S. D. Cole, C. Freeman, M. Jahoda, and K. L. R. Pavitt (eds.) Sussex University Press, London, pp. 14–22, at p. 9]. The World 3 computer model, they noted, was a model of a social system, which necessarily involved critical assumptions about the workings of that system— assumptions that were in turn influenced by the attitudes and values of the researchers. Hence the output of the model was only as good as the "mental models"

---

5. The authors argue that the World 3 model failed to adequately consider the effects of politics, economics, and sociology, and did not, on the whole, provide an accurate representation of real world phenomenon and behavior. They also argue that the aggregation of inadequate data presented a gross oversimplification of the real world situation, and that the model's use of deterministic—as opposed to probabilistic—projections meant that it was impossible to determine how probable the output was. Finally, they believe that the model underestimated the impact of technological innovation. However, the authors also praise the MIT work, characterizing it as a "courageous and pioneering attempt to make a computer model of the future of the world" [H. S. D. Cole, C. Freeman, M. Jahoda, and K. L. R. Pavitt (eds.) (1973) *Thinking About the Future: A Critique of The Limits to Growth*. Sussex University Press, London, p. 6].

used to develop it, which also encapsulated the modelers' ideological positions.[6] *The Computer that Printed Out W*O*L*F** is a technologically optimistic critique of *Limits to Growth*. Kaysen, like Maddox, argues that the limits defined in the World 3 model are not fixed and can be extended by investment into new land and into exploration and discovery. He argues that once the problem is recognized as one of "cost limits," as opposed to "physical limits," the forces of increasing extraction costs and advancing technology will combine to identify new resources that were previously out of reach. Such action extends the physical limits, or supplies of fixed resources, which Kaysen argues has been occurring throughout human history.[7]

In a more recent reassessment, Reid argues that while *Limits to Growth* can be criticized on points of detail, the basic assumption that increasing rates of resource consumption could not continue in a finite world had to be right. He also notes that critics were not receptive to the idea that pollution—as opposed to energy shortages or scarcity of resources—would be a key factor in the eventual collapse of the world system, and that time has tended to prove this criticism wrong [D. Reid (1995) *Sustainable Development, An Introductory Guide*. Earthscan, London].

Regardless of the ultimate strength of the positions taken by advocates and opponents of *Limits to Growth*, the work has undeniably stimulated important national and international debates on the prospects for the human environment. These debates include but go well beyond the issue of pollution, and include resource scarcity, ecosystem stability, and global climate disruption, all part of the concerns voiced for sustainable development. We return to these broader concerns in the last chapter of this volume.

■ NOTES

1. Oddly enough, even though there is now evidence that limits are in fact being surpassed—as shown by global warming, the destruction of the ozone layer, widespread contamination of drinking water systems, and the possibility of widespread

---

6. In a lecture on "System Dynamics and Sustainability" given at MIT on January 18, 2002, Professor Jay Forrester explained that he never strayed from the capabilities and limitations of the "World 3" model when answering the criticism unleashed upon the Club of Rome once the report was published. While the "World 3" model had limitations, which were clearly articulated in the report, the model's output could easily be defended, but only by clearly articulating the foundations upon which the output was based.

7. Kaysen also highlights two other apparent flaws in the World 3 model. First, the price of resources is not adequately represented. Sharp adjustments to the price of a resource can lead to large shifts in the location and type of resources used, in population, and in the patterns of consumption. Hence, prices can make smooth transitions occur as limits begin to emerge. Second, the researchers did not always use available knowledge effectively. Specific attention is drawn to the manner in which population growth is formulated and to the fact that birth to death rates in the Western world have adjusted with rising income, a trend overlooked by the model. However, Kaysen does acknowledge the magnitude of the population problem.

species harm through endocrine disruption—*Beyond the Limits* has not received the serious attention it deserves.

2. In *Beyond the Limits*, which makes the case for limits in even stronger fashion than the prior work, the authors argue in a closing chapter that an environmental ethic backed by "love" is required to prevent system collapse. Do the authors strengthen their case by this appeal? Is it related to the hope that moral rectitude will save the environment?   ∎

C. POLLUTION AND ACCIDENT CONTROL, MITIGATION, AND PREVENTION

As noted at the outset of this chapter, the control of gradual pollution usually focuses on end-of-pipe approaches that leave the production system essentially unchanged. Bag houses to convert gaseous SO_2 into sulfates, and traps or filters or ion exchange columns to remove mercury and other heavy metals from water effluents, are examples of end-of-pipe responses to pollution. These activities are termed pollution *control*. A related type of "control" approach is commonly taken to chemical accidents. Accidents are typically controlled through such measures as strengthening vessel walls, venting high pressures built up in a runaway reaction, or using sudden thermal cooling to quench runaway chemical systems. A distinguishing feature of both pollution and accident control is that the fundamental industrial processes remain essentially unchanged.

If pollution does occur, cleanup activities (such as the removal of contaminated soil) can be used to minimize or ameliorate the extent of the harm. This is termed pollution *mitigation*. Similarly, after chemical accidents occur, measures can be taken to mitigate human injury and property damage, such as fire-fighting, evacuation, and emergency first aid.

Pollution and accident control and mitigation are increasingly regarded as having limited long-range effectiveness. Control is (at best) secondary prevention, and mitigation is tertiary prevention. *Primary* prevention—what characterizes *pollution prevention* and *inherent safety*—requires a redesign of production processes, their inputs, or their final products.

Pollution prevention, which the Europeans call *cleaner production*, attempts to prevent the possibility of harm, rather than reduce the probability of harm, by eliminating the problem at its source. Inherent safety, or inherently safer production, is a concept similar to or a natural extension of pollution prevention or cleaner production.[8] Both typically involve fundamental changes in production technology:

---

8. See N. A. Ashford (1997) "Industrial Safety: The Neglected Issue in Industrial Ecology," in Special Issue on Industrial Ecology, N. A. Ashford and R. P. Côté (eds.) *Journal of Cleaner Production* 5(1/2), pp. 115–121.

substitution of inputs, process redesign and reengineering, and/or final product reformulation. They may require organizational and institutional changes as well.[9] Inherently safer production is the analogous concept for the prevention of sudden and
accidental releases.

Throughout this book we examine the extent to which current environmental laws,
and alternatives to them, could stimulate the increased use of these primary prevention approaches. Toward the end of the book, in chapter 13, we examine pollution
prevention and inherent safety in more detail.

D. THE FOCUS OF TRADITIONAL ENVIRONMENTAL LAW

To a large extent, implementation of the current system of media-based environmental laws has focused on pollution and accident control, and has been slow to embrace
prevention as a superior approach to reducing pollution and chemical accidents. Although the drafters of the Clean Air Act, the Clean Water Act, the Safe Drinking
Water Act, and the legislation intending to control and mitigate the effects of hazardous waste all envisioned that these laws would bring about a fundamental transformation of industry, the implementation and enforcement of these laws often leave
highly polluting production processes unchanged. The Pollution Prevention Act of
1990, which states that reduction of pollution *at the source* is the preferred method
of reducing pollution, was designed to rectify this, and we evaluate its progress in
the later chapters of this book. Beyond the more traditional media-based statutes,
there are other environmental and public health laws under which questions of
changing industrial processes and products are more frequently addressed. These include the regulatory systems governing pesticides, pharmaceuticals, food safety, and
occupational health and safety.[10] Questions of this nature are addressed in these systems because changing the industrial process, or industrial or consumer products,
often is the only (or the only efficient) way to adequately protect the public health
and safety. Applying the lessons of these laws to the broader field of environmental
regulation is what we endeavor to do here.

---

9. See *Government Strategies and Policies for Cleaner Production* (1994) United Nations Environmental
Program, Paris, ISBN 92-807-1442-2, 32 pp. See also "Encouraging Inherently Safer Production in Euro-
pean Firms: A Report from the Field," N. A. Ashford and G. Zwetsloot (1999) Special Issue on Risk
Assessment and Environmental Decision Making, A. Amendola and D. Wilkinson (eds.) *Journal of
Hazardous Materials*, pp. 123–144.

10. The regulatory regimes for occupational health and safety are discussed in detail in N. A. Ashford and
C. C. Caldart (1996) *Technology, Law and the Working Environment.* 2nd. ed. Island Press, Washington,
D.C.

E. BEYOND POLLUTION AND ACCIDENT CONTROL AND PREVENTION: SUSTAINABLE PRODUCTION AND PRODUCTS

Finally, we are increasingly convinced that forging a more sustainable economy—in which there are shifts away from production and products[11] that can potentially result in pollution to the providing of services that satisfy human needs in entirely different ways—is a crucial and necessary long-range approach, given the present increased rates of both individual and industrial consumption.[12] At this point in time, sustainable development has not been sufficiently incorporated into either law or industrial practices. It is the focus of the closing chapter of this text.

---

11. See Kenneth Geiser (2001) *Materials Matter: Toward a Sustainable Materials Policy.* MIT Press, Cambridge, Mass., 479 pages.

12. See N. A. Ashford (2002) "Government and Innovation in Environmental Transformations in Europe and North America," in Special Issue on Ecological Modernization, David Sonnenfeld and Arthur Mol (eds.) *American Behavioral Scientist* vol. 45.

2 Nature and Assessment of the Harm

A. Life Cycle Analysis and the Biological Impact Pathway
B. Environmental and Ecosystem Degradation
C. Human Health Risks
   1. Classical Categorization: The Dose Makes the Poison
      a. Exposure and Dose
      b. Dose-Effect and Dose-Response Relationships
      c. Categorization of Health Effects Resulting from Exposures to Chemicals
      d. In vitro Studies
      e. Structure-Activity Relationships
   2. Multistage Disease Processes: The Dose Plus the Host Makes the Harm
      a. Endocrine Disruption
      b. Low-Level Chemical Sensitivity
      c. Toxicant-Induced Loss of Tolerance: A New Theory of Disease?
      d. Cancer, Repair Mechanisms, and Hormesis
D. The Basics (and Limitations) of Risk Assessment
   1. Risk Assessment Methodology
   2. The Limitations of Risk Assessment
   3. Epidemiology
E. Scientific Uncertainty, Values, and Implications for Policy: Can a "Safe" Level of Exposure be Unequivocally Determined?

A. LIFE CYCLE ANALYSIS AND THE BIOLOGICAL IMPACT PATHWAY

Figure 1.1 of the previous chapter is a representation of material and product flows stemming from industrial activity. A more generalized life cycle model developed at MIT in the 1970s is shown in figure 2.1. Life cycle analysis (LCA) is the name of the methodology used to track material and chemical flows from extraction to disposal

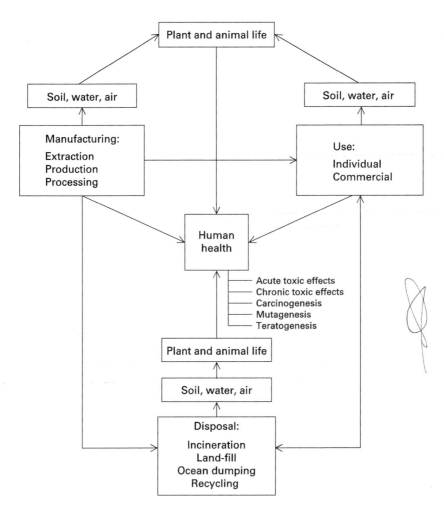

Figure 2.1
A simple general life cycle model. (Source: N. A. Ashford, D. B. Hattis, G. R. Heaton, J. I. Katz, W. C. Priest, and E. M. Zolt, "Life Cycle Models for the Production, Use, and Disposal of Chemicals," in *Evaluating Chemical Regulations: Trade-off Analysis and Impact Assessment for Environmental Decision-Making*. Final Report to the Council on Environmental Quality under Contract No. EQ4ACA35. CPA-80-13, 1980. NTIS PB81-195067.)

("cradle to grave"). The model facilitates a consideration of the options for intervention to reduce pollution and/or to reduce chemical exposures at various stages.

Life Cycle Models for the Production, Use, and Disposal of Chemicals
N. A. Ashford, D. B. Hattis, G. R. Heaton, J. I. Katz, W. C. Priest, and E. M. Zolt
Source: *Evaluating Chemical Regulations: Trade-off Analysis and Impact Assessment for Environmental Decision-Making.* **Final Report to the Council on Environmental Quality under Contract No. EQ4ACA35. CPA-80-13. NTIS PB81-195067, 1980, pp. 19–25.**

In order to analyze the costs and benefits associated with governmental restrictions placed on the production, use, and disposal of a given chemical, one first needs to know the material flows of the chemical through the economy. A schematic "life cycle model" can form a basic framework for economic analysis. Life cycle models depict the major steps in the production, processing, distribution, intermediate use, end use, and disposal of a chemical, and point out the routes of human exposure and possible environmental contamination. Such models must assure a proper accounting for all material flows. Mass has to be conserved throughout the models, and discrepancies between material flows and storages in various parts of the life cycle models have to be reconciled. This is often a way to discover that a significant pathway [for the loss of material]—e.g., to the environment—has been overlooked.

The life cycle models have three important uses in the assessment of regulatory systems:

1. The feasibility, effectiveness, and direct economic and environmental consequences of various control strategies can be evaluated in the context of examining how [changes] in material flows propagate through the model.
2. Areas of data deficiency in the models can suggest what additional information should be sought by the regulator.
3. An application of the model to the current regulatory framework for any particular class of chemicals can illuminate control deficiencies and suggest alternative regulatory strategies.

It is convenient to present the description of such material flows diagrammatically. Figure [2.1] illustrates a simple life cycle model. More detailed models can illustrate unique characteristics found in the production, distribution, use, or disposal of any individual chemical.

■ NOTE

1. As with other frameworks for analysis, life cycle analysis often suffers from an inappropriate truncation or simplification in its execution. Four areas typically underemphasized or ignored are (1) environmental contamination from the extraction and refinement of the basic starting materials before manufacturing begins; (2) worker exposures in the associated extraction, production, and transportation activities; (3) disposal of finished products, such as computers and electronic equipment; and (4) worker exposures associated with manufacturing, use, disposal, and waste management. The legendary quandary of whether to use paper or plastic shopping bags, for

example, depends on whether the analysis begins with forests and oil reserves, or with paper and plastic stock.

What is subsequently of interest for our purposes are the effects of resulting chemical exposures on human health and the environment. The *biological impact pathway* (also developed at MIT) is an aid to understanding the connection between loss of control of a chemical and eventual health and environmental effects. The biological impact pathway further facilitates the consideration of options for intervention.

The Biological Impact Pathway
N. A. Ashford, D. B. Hattis, G. R. Heaton, J. I. Katz, W. C. Priest, and E. M. Zolt

Source: *Evaluating Chemical Regulations: Trade-off Analysis and Impact Assessment for Environmental Decision-Making.* **Final Report to the Council on Environmental Quality under Contract No. EQ4ACA35. CPA-80-13, NTIS PB81-195067, 1980, pp. 20, 22–25.**

The production and use of chemicals generate a wide spectrum of material and energy flows. To the degree that a particular material/ energy flow is controlled and directed without loss within industrial processes, it will not affect biological systems and can properly be considered solely within a commercial life cycle model. However, whenever there is a flow of material or energy to some medium where effective control is lost, we can classify that flow as a *discharge* which may lead to a biological impact or response.

This definition of "discharge" is very broad. It includes a diverse spectrum of material/ energy flows from the conventional air and water pollution discharges to trapping of free vinyl chloride monomer in plastic (where it might later migrate to food or air). A discharge might also take the form of a child removing aspirin tablets from a bottle without a safety cap. The distinguishing feature of a discharge, however, is that after the discharge, further transfers of the material are usually beyond the direct control of the commercial producer or consumer. Even where

the release is intentional and the resulting biological response is desired (as in a pesticide sprayed onto a field or a drug injected into [or ingested by] a patient), the loss of control signals the end of the substance's commercial life cycle and the beginning of a pathway to potential biological impact.

To simplify discussion, all environmental impacts are treated here as if they were changes in the health of people or other organisms which are produced or influenced by some set of discharges. With small modifications, however, the form of analysis is also applicable when (1) the environmental disturbance does not originate from a discharge (e.g., from construction of an open pit mine), or (2) the eventual receptor of physical damage is not a living organism (e.g., materials which corrode more quickly in the presence of sulfur oxides). A general causal pathway relating discharge to ultimate biological impact[1] is shown in figure [2.2]. All of the steps in this pathway are not always present or important in the analysis of the effects of particular discharges, but the intermediate stages

---

1. Some environmental pollutants (e.g., sulfur dioxide) may also cause property damage. Although in these cases, the ultimate receptor of damage is not a biological organism, it is still possible to draw and analyze similar types of causal pathways, substituting the words "impact on property" for "biological impact."

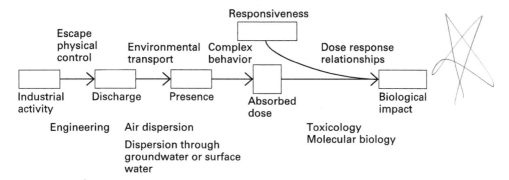

Figure 2.2
The biological impact pathway. (Source: N. A. Ashford, D. B. Hattis, G. R. Heaton, J. I. Katz, W. C. Priest, and E. M. Zolt, "The Biological Impact Pathway," in *Evaluating Chemical Regulations: Trade-off Analysis and Impact Assessment for Environmental Decision-Making*. Final Report to the Council on Environmental Quality under Contract No. EQ4ACA35. CPA-80-13, 1980. NTIS PB81-195067.)

shown are sometimes useful for purposes of analysis.

In the most general case, the discharge first comes under the influence of a transport mechanism such as diffusion in air, flow in a river, or migration from the plastic of a food container to the food. During transport, the substance in question may undergo physical and/or chemical transformation to materials with different properties. As a result, some potentially bioactive substance is *present* at definable concentrations in locations where it may contact living organisms. For example, locations where it may be useful to characterize the concentration of bioactive material may be the air in a workplace which is potentially breathed by a worker, fish muscle which may be eaten by a human consumer, or the lather of a soap which may be absorbed through the skin—anywhere, in short, where there is direct *opportunity* for entry of the chemical into the organism which will ultimately manifest the biological response.

The actual process of entry of the chemicals into the population of living organisms which ultimately responds is termed by us [as] *exposure*. In the entry process, the individuals may be actively involved to differing degrees. Such involvement can range from exposure through inadvertent skin absorption of a chemical to an exposure dependent upon some complex behavior pattern, such as workers performing a particular job and breathing air at a given rate, or fishermen with their own idiosyncratic habits of places to fish, types of fish to bring home, and quantities of fish eaten. In general, a description of exposure sufficient to allow further analysis must include the *distribution* of doses to the population of individuals at risk. That is, it must be determined how many individuals take in how much of the chemical over an appropriate time period for analysis.[2]

It is also sometimes necessary to note systematic differences in the *responsiveness* of particular subgroups within the exposed population. For example, a toxicant which is well tolerated at a given dosage by the majority of a population may be lethal to a subpopulation with unusual liver function. Similarly,

---

2. The appropriate time period for analysis depends upon how much time must elapse between

two exposure episodes before the biological effects of the two episodes are completely independent.

teratogenic effects (birth defects) can result only to the degree that the subpopulation of pregnant women is exposed to an active substance.

If it is possible to define the applicable relationships between dosage and response, the ultimate *biological impact or response* can finally be analyzed. Dose-response relationships occasionally may be inferred from toxicological or epidemiological research, or, more frequently, hypothesized from limited data and general models. The goal is to characterize overall biological impact in terms of:

• types of impact (cancer, kidney damage, enhancement of crop growth, etc.)

• severity and timing of impact (for each type of impact, the distribution of intensity of the impact over time among the affected population)

• number of individuals affected (for each category of type and severity)

Several biological impact pathways may occur in a complex production-use-disposal cycle. Regulatory activities may address some damage pathways and neglect others, but all must be considered in assessing health or environmental effects since they are connected through the life cycle of the chemical (or its substitutes). For example, regulation of workplace exposure may change external discharges.

■ **NOTES**

1. The last paragraph here deserves emphasis. Associated with *each* of the activities in figures 1.1 (from chapter 1) and 2.1 is a potential biological impact or response, reflecting the consequences of exposure to workers, consumers, the general public, and the environment.

2. Note that scientific activity and specialization contribute to knowledge at various places in the biological impact pathway. Scientists studying transport theory focus on the relationship between *discharge* and *presence*. Exposure modelers focus on the relationship between *presence* and *exposure*. Toxicologists (and epidemiologists) study the (dose-response) relationship between *exposure* and *biological impact and response*, as well as *differences in responsiveness*.   ■

B. ENVIRONMENTAL AND ECOSYSTEM DEGRADATION

In one sense, concern for the environment and ecosystem stems from its effects on human beings, which is an essentially anthropocentric view of nature. This includes the need to prevent eutrophication of water systems, to maintain air quality that permits good visibility, and to preserve species that might be the sources of medicinal benefits to humankind. Even the maintenance of ecosystems so that humans might enjoy nature is mainly anthropocentric. At one time, nature and wilderness preservation for its own sake was quite a separate issue, one that has strong cultural overtones for certain groups, such as Native American communities. With the

realization that humans are a part of the ecosystem, that they take food and suste-
nance from it, that threats such as endocrine disruption can affect *all* species, and
that human activity can seriously and perhaps permanently alter the earth's ecosystem, the environment-human health distinction becomes less meaningful. However,
to some extent, four distinct foci of environmental concern and activity remain:
human health, biological (animal and plant) systems and ecosystems, disruption of
global climate, and conservation of materials and resources (including preservation
of energy sources). Different legislation addresses these concerns, and interest groups
tend to distinguish themselves based on these allegedly separate issues. One aspect of
the increased interest in sustainable development has been for certain groups—
environmental, labor, religious, etc.—to not only see the interconnections among
these separate environmental issues, but also to see the connections of these issues
to employment and wages, occupational safety and health, indoor air pollution, and
the global economic order. (See the discussion of sustainable development in chapter
14.) The protests that began in Seattle, Washington, at the 1999 meeting of the
World Trade Organization, followed by protests in Washington, D.C., Stockholm,
Ottawa, and Genoa, represent a new political awareness on this score.

C. HUMAN HEALTH RISKS

The nature of the risk to human health from various exposures commonly is inferred
from a variety of sources: from the study of exposed cohorts of people, often workers
(epidemiology), from animal experiments (in vivo toxicology), from bacterial or other
assay systems (in vitro toxicology), and from the chemical structure-activity relationships of putative harmful substances. The available scientific information is used to
estimate human risks through *risk assessment*. Risk assessment is also used to estimate harm to the environment and ecosystems, although the specific models that
are used may sometimes be very different from those used in assessing risks to human
health. See Joanna Burger (1999) "Ecological Risk Assessment at the Department of
Energy: An Evolving Process," *International Journal of Toxicology* 18(2): 149–155.

1. Classical Categorization: The Dose Makes the Poison

a. Exposure and Dose
The concept of exposure is more complicated than depicted in figure 2.2. Conceptually, exposure can have at least five different meanings: *initial or ambient exposure*
(external dose in a medium, in food, or in a product), *contact exposure* (external
dose in contact with the respiratory tract, the gastrointestinal tract, and the skin), *uptake or absorption* (internal dose, i.e., in the body), *biologically effective dose* (dose at
the site of toxic action, e.g., organ or system), and *molecular dose* (the dose delivered

to target macromolecules). The latter two are most useful for understanding the mechanisms of disease, but they are the most difficult (and require the greatest invasiveness) to determine. See the discussion of biological markers in N. A. Ashford, C. J. Spadafor, D. B. Hattis, and C. C. Caldart (1990) *Monitoring the Worker for Exposure and Disease: Scientific, Legal, and Ethical Considerations in the Use of Biomarkers*. Johns Hopkins University Press, Baltimore.

Exposures can be *one-time*, *intermittent* (with no regularity), *periodic*, or *continuous*. The duration of the intermittent or periodic exposure may range from a day to many days, but is not continuous over a lifetime. While there is a tendency to define dose simply as the total amount of exposure integrated over time, from the perspective of biological impact, it matters a great deal how the dose is actually distributed.

b. Dose-Effect and Dose-Response Relationships

Exposure to Toxic Materials and Carcinogens
N. A. Ashford
Source: Reprinted in part with permission from *Crisis in the Workplace*. MIT Press, Cambridge, Mass., 1976, pp. 115–124 (references omitted). Copyright 1976, MIT Press.

The extent to which a particular health hazard should be controlled depends [among other things upon] both on [the] severity [and nature of its biological effect] and the dose-response relationship. [The effect on an organism is dose-dependent, e.g., the extent to which a rodent's liver is destroyed by a lifetime daily ingestion of alcohol—expressed as the percentage of the liver that becomes cirrhotic—depends on the magnitude (and duration) of the daily dose.] In simple terms, the *dose-effect relationship* indicates how a biological organism's response to a toxic substance changes as its exposure to the substance increases. [As another] example, a small dose of carbon monoxide [might cause a headache or] drowsiness, but a larger dose can cause death. [*Dose-effect* relationships should not be confused with the more familiar *dose-response* relationship, i.e., the incidence of effects of a given degree of severity in an exposed population as a function of dose and duration of exposure and other individual factors such as age at exposure.]

[Once the minimum effect of concern from a hazard is determined for regulatory purposes—for example the additional hearing loss over background for workers from exposure to noise—one needs to know what percentage of test animals (or humans observed in epidemiological studies) exhibit that effect or worse at a variety of doses. These data constitute a dose-response relationship.] This relationship is shown graphically in curve A of figure [2.3]. [Note that the curve is an *iso-effect* curve; i.e., it is a curve for a specific level of damage of concern, for example an extra 10dB hearing loss. If the level of damage of concern were chosen to be greater—such as a 25dB shift in hearing ability—the dose-response curve would be shifted to the right.]

In the determination of a dose-response relationship, it is often assumed that a threshold exposure exists below which no harmful effect occurs. However, there is considerable doubt that the threshold concept holds for radiation damage and carcinogenesis. To put it

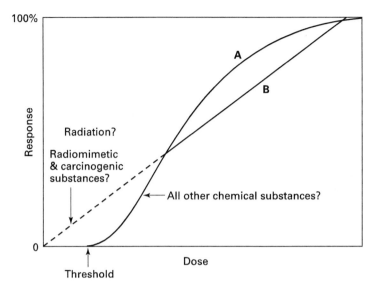

Figure 2.3
Dose-response relationship for a noncarcinogen (A) and a carcinogen (B) that acts by primary genetic mechanisms. (Source: N. A. Ashford, *Crisis in the Workplace*. MIT Press, Cambridge, Mass., 1976.)

another way, radiation damage and the initiation of cancer may exhibit a zero threshold, as indicated in curve B of figure [2.3], which means there is no dose that can be considered [to have zero chance of inducing an additional cancer].

[Classical] toxicity [can be described as]...the net result of two competing reactions, as shown in figure [2.4]. One reaction (shown on the left) represents the effects of the toxic agent on the body. The other reaction (shown on the right) is the body's adaptive or *homeostatic* reaction which [in the classical toxicological paradigm] counteracts the toxin's effect and attempts to return the body to equilibrium. The body's natural cleansing actions and the production of antibodies are good examples. Not until a certain level of toxin is present do the body's adaptive mechanisms fail to counteract the toxin; hence, a threshold is said to exist. It should be recognized that the threshold will usually be higher for acute effects than for slower act-

ing and longer-term chronic effects; i.e., the amount of toxin [intake per time period] needed to produce chronic effects is likely to be...less than the minimum amount required to demonstrate an immediate, acute toxic effect. (This may hold for the total amount over time as well as the unit dosage at a given time.) The mechanisms for the acute and chronic damage may be very different and may manifest themselves in different parts of the body....

The task of setting standards for safe levels of exposure is likewise difficult. It is not possible to determine all the points on a dose-response curve: the lower the dose, the lower the [incidence of] response—and we are limited by inherent difficulties in measuring both near zero. Thus, even for acute effects, we must [often] extrapolate [really interpolate] the curve to find the threshold [if it exists]; and this threshold for acute effects may bear no relation to the threshold for chronic effects.... Furthermore, if we were to test a

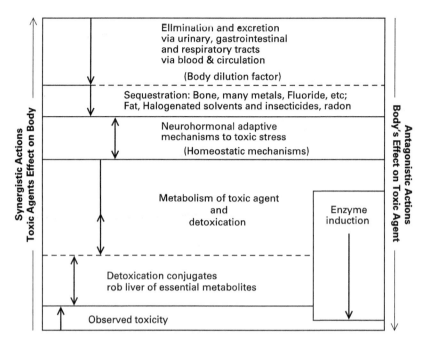

Figure 2.4
Analysis of the effects of a toxic substance. (Source: N. A. Ashford, *Crisis in the Workplace*. MIT Press, Cambridge, Mass., 1976. Adapted from Herbert E. Stokinger, "Concepts of Thresholds in Standards Setting," *Archives of Environmental Health* vol. 25, p. 155 September 1972.)

large number of people on any particular day, we might find a distribution of thresholds among them (see figure [2.5]).

The distribution can be caused by many factors: (1) natural variance, (2) genetic differences, and (3) other interacting toxins and stressors. The distribution is conveniently viewed as being made up of three parts: the average, the sensitive, and the resilient populations. The concept behind this distribution needs to be stressed because it is often misunderstood and abused in attempts to explain why some people get disease and why some do not.

Because of natural variations in a person's physiology from day to day, he may be [more susceptible to damage] one day, but resilient the next. Repeated measurements could determine the extent of this natural variance

for acute effects, but the effect of natural variance in the distribution for chronic effects is impossible to determine since an organism only lives once....

There is strong evidence that the mechanisms for radiation damage and carcinogenesis are quite different than those for ordinary toxic effects. The effects of exposure to harmful radiation are cumulative and irreversible. Each exposure causes permanent damage which adds to the damage caused by previous radiation exposures. Because every exposure, however small, can do permanent damage, the threshold below which no damage occurs is said to be zero.

[Chemically induced carcinogenesis] is [generally] thought to proceed through a two-step mechanism: initiation and promotion. The irreversible initiation process may result

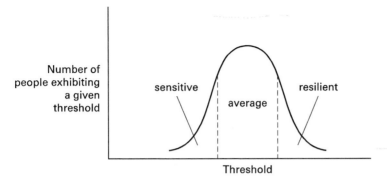

Figure 2.5
Normal bell-shaped distribution of thresholds for toxic effects. (Source: N. A. Ashford, *Crisis in the Workplace*. MIT Press, Cambridge, Mass., 1976.)

from the insult of a single molecule of a carcinogen on a single susceptible cell. Because exposure to a carcinogen, however small, can initiate a cancer, the threshold below which no "damage" occurs is said to be zero. Even if initiation were the rate-determining step in the cause of cancer, every exposure to a carcinogen would not result in cancer. The carcinogen–cell interaction would have to occur "correctly"—just as a full score in a bowling game requires a "correct hit." Thus, [stochastic] probability considerations can partly explain why all people exposed to carcinogens do not have cancer.

Promotion of the cancer to the status of a tumor (or detectable change in the blood or lymphatic system) may follow at different speeds in different species. The body's adaptive or immunological mechanisms may delay or avoid the manifestation of the cancer into recognizable form, but the potential for promotion to occur is there if initiation has occurred. The observation that skin cancer can be speeded up by the addition of a promoter (e.g., croton oil) after exposure and removal of the cancer initiator indicates that a

nonzero threshold may exist for the promotion step, but much controversy exists as to the general correctness of this statement for all cancers.

Decisions about what standards to adopt for carcinogens have to be made with the recognition of the good possibility that a zero threshold exists for these substances. This may or may not require the adoption of a zero standard (i.e., zero within the limitations of measurement). For example, if the standard for radiation is set at one-hundredth of the level to which human beings are exposed from naturally occurring uranium in the general environment, a nonzero (but small) standard may be justifiable. On the other hand, since no safe level has been determined for the liver carcinogen vinyl chloride, and humans are not exposed to vinyl chloride from natural sources, the recommendation for reducing workplace exposure "below measurable limits" seems sensible.[3]

For chronic effects, the extrapolation from animals to humans is difficult, partly because of biological differences and partly because of differences in life span. Whatever problems

[3. Since this writing first appeared, there has been considerable debate about whether finite thresholds exist for some mechanisms of cancer causation, suggesting that nonzero exposures could be justified.]

exist for predicting safe levels for ordinary toxic materials from animal studies, the problems are further complicated in the case of cancer. Many carcinogenic materials are also toxic [in other ways as well] (e.g., arsenic and vinyl chloride). The fact that a particular cancer is easily produced by certain agents in test animals is useful in identifying potentially powerful human carcinogens. The usefulness of animal data in the prediction of human cancer is diminished when (1) the cancer is a rare occurrence, (2) a long latency period is required (possibly longer than the animal's life span) or (3) different test species react differently to a carcinogen. Furthermore, the relative effects of a chemical's carcinogenic and toxic potential differ among species. . . . Where animal data indicates cancer, materials should be treated as suspect. However, where no indication of cancer is found, the suspect agent cannot be assumed safe [unless reinforced by gene toxicity studies, mechanistic studies, oncogenicity studies, and tests for other types of toxicity].

[In 1971 t]he Food and Drug Administration Advisory Committee on Protocols for Safety Evaluation addressed itself to the problems of using test animals for the prediction of human cancer:

Although a positive answer to the question as posed can be given in some particular instances, no unqualified negative answer is ever possible. Thus, if none out of n test animals exposed to the agent develop cancer, and n is a large number, the elevation, if any, is certainly small, but no matter how large the value of n, it is not logically possible to conclude on the basis of such evidence that no elevation has occurred. The agent might in fact induce one cancer in every 2n animals, and the experiment, being too small to detect it, would be incapable of providing cogent evidence for the absence of any elevation whatsoever. This is true no matter how large is the value of n.

Even with as many as 1000 test animals and using only 90% confidence limits, the upper limit yielded by a negative experiment is 2.3 cancers per 1000 test animals. No one would wish to introduce an agent into a human population for which no more could be said than that it would probably produce no more than 2 tumors per 1000 [persons exposed]. To reduce the upper limit of risk to 2 tumors per one million with a confidence coefficient of 0.999 would require a negative result in somewhat more than three million test animals.

The impracticably large numbers required to detect carcinogenic effects of possible public health importance, together with the uncertainties of downward extrapolation, set limits to the amount of protection that can be achieved [solely from direct projections (without high to low dose interpolation of risks) from] a routine [animal] testing program. [*Toxicology and Applied Pharmacology* (1971), 20: 419–438]

. . . Putting aside for the moment the issue of a threshold for carcinogens, it is not clear that an organism's adaptive mechanisms can be relied upon to combat continuous exposures. Although exercising a muscle creates a stressful condition, that exercise (when not continuous) is viewed as desirable. However, hanging a hundred pound weight from one's arm continuously cannot be said to be healthful. Toxic materials also initiate stresses which are measurable by physiological changes in the blood and in the nervous system. The whole body chemistry is affected by both the toxic material and the body's reactions as it tries to return to equilibrium. A common example of short-term adaptation is the body's development of a fever to counteract an infection. However, calling on the body's adjustment mechanisms continuously cannot be said to be harmless. Constant exposure of the body to toxic materials demands a continuous adjustment of the body chemistry which does not represent the normal state of body equilibrium even though the body system may be stable. On a cellular level, the body is asked to adjust to a stress not unlike hanging a weight from a muscle continuously. . . .

The discussion of exposure to toxic materials thus far has focused on the establishment of a safe level for an isolated substance. This make-believe world of isolated hazards does not exist in either the workplace or in the general environment. Most potential human exposure to chemicals is exposure to mixtures. Toxic materials exist in combination with one another, and their effects may be further complicated by stress caused by noise, abnormal temperatures, ergonomic factors, and psychosocial factors. Two toxic substances in combination can have effects on the body which are either (1) additive in an expected way, (2) synergistic (i.e., combining in such a way that the resultant effect is greater than the sum of the individual effects), or (3) antagonistic (i.e., combining in such a way that the resultant effect is less than the sum of the individual effects).... The question remaining is how commonplace and how predictable synergistic [or antagonistic] effects are.

Research on joint (acute) toxic action indicates that about 5% of the combinations investigated in one study exhibited synergistic (or antagonistic) behavior [Smyth et al., *Toxicology and Applied Pharmacology* 1969, vol. 14, p. 340]. The remaining 95% combined in a predictable way, i.e., additively. It has been pointed out, however, that the research data indicated that in many cases the substances tested were not the most highly toxic of industrial substances, and it is possible that the 5% figure for other-than-additive effects would have been enhanced had pairs of highly toxic substances been used in the investigations. It is not possible to "predict" which 5% of the combinations of all substances will behave synergistically.

Most current evidence of toxic interactions is based on acute responses, and there have been relatively few studies to evaluate possible interactions of chronic exposures to mixtures of chemicals....

A closer look at what the 5% figure means should convince the reader that the problems of synergism are very great indeed. [Suppose there] are 12,000 toxic materials in [significant] commercial use today. For n substances, the number of possible pairs is $n(n-1)/2$. Of the $12,000 \times 11,999/2$ pairs, 5% or 3.6 million pairs may behave synergistically (or antagonistically).[4] To this number are being added...new chemicals annually, which increases the number of possible combinations further.... The problems are even worse than indicated above. Some stressors, such as heat and noise, may enhance the toxicity of many toxic materials....

Toxic materials as stressors may promote cancer. The extent to which the synergistic effects of stressors may be important in both toxicity and in the promotion of cancer has not been determined. Research is seriously deficient in these areas.

Thus, serious consideration should be given to the question of whether we shall ever be able to generate the data base necessary to set safe levels for toxic materials and carcinogens. An alternative and more sensible approach may be to redesign our industrial processes, to automate where necessary, and to reduce unnecessary proliferation of new chemicals.

■ **NOTES**

1. Animal experiments employ exposed and unexposed control (comparison) groups and are used to detect *excess* disease or effects due to exposure. They are relatively insensitive (i.e., they tend to miss less frequent, but potentially important, effects of chemical exposures, especially at lower exposure levels). Following the usual practice of employing 100 test animals at each dose examined, a risk is not statistically

---

[4. Whether synergism presents a problem depends on the doses of interacting chemicals. At very low doses, synergistic interactions differ little from additive effects.]

significant if it is less than 5% in excess over the control group. Even where 24,000 animals are used, animal experiments are not sufficiently sensitive to measure less than a 1% increase in tumor incidence. (See the discussion by G. M. Masters in section D of this chapter, which addresses risk assessment in greater detail.)

2. Observations of disease or health effects in human cohorts (which is the province of epidemiology) may likewise be insensitive. Except where dose and response are deliberately measured a priori, as with clinical trials for pharmaceuticals, the potential for error in an epidemiologic study may be high. The reconstruction of past doses in an affected population often requires considerable assumptions (or even guesswork); there may be many confounding (or background) exposures that obscure the true relationship between the exposure and disease or health effect being studied, and assembling an appropriate reference or control group may be problematic. (See the discussion in section D.)

3. In the discussion excerpted in section D of this chapter, G. M. Masters argues that some models of cancer causation most likely overestimate the incidence in human populations. This observation needs to be put into context. While some of these mathematical models may overestimate cancer causation based solely on the inputs considered, these models also tend to ignore *synergism*, multiplicative interactions between chemical exposures that produce more profound human health effects than would occur simply with the additive effects of the two exposures individually. The synergistic effects of chemical carcinogens can be substantial in actual exposed populations, such as those exposed to both asbestos and cigarette smoke. Furthermore, the commonly used cancer causation models tend to ignore the effects of cancer *promoters*, chemicals that potentiate, rather than initiate, the growth of cancerous cells.

4. For a discussion of the difficulties of correctly assessing the risks posed by chemical mixtures, including the challenges posed by possible synergistic effects, see David O. Carpenter, Kathleen Arcaro, and David C. Spink (2002) "Understanding the Human Health Effects of Chemical Mixtures," *Environmental Health Perspectives* vol. 110, suppl. 1, pp. 25–42.   ∎

Relating Exposure to Damage
N. A. Ashford, D. B. Hattis, G. R. Heaton, J. I. Katz, W. C. Priest, and E. M. Zolt
Source: *Evaluating Chemical Regulations: Trade-off Analysis and Impact Assessment for Environmental Decision-Making.* **Final Report to the Council on Environmental Quality under Contract No. EQ4ACA35. CPA-80-13, NTIS PB81-195067, 1980, pp. 5-25 to 5-27.**

The subject of dose-response relationships for hazardous substances has been an area of great controversy over many decades. One common cause of these disputes is that experts trained in the perspectives of different disciplines examine incomplete available data and are led to radically different expectations about the likely behavior of relevant biological systems in regions of dosage where information cannot be obtained from direct observations. The clash of expectations has been especially acute between people trained in traditional toxicology and people trained in the newer molecular biological disciplines. . . .

A major theme, if not the central organizing principle of traditional physiology and toxicology, is the concept of the homeostatic system. Biological processes are seen as part of a complex interacting web, exquisitely designed so that modest perturbations in any parameter automatically give rise to adaptive negative feedback processes to restore optimal functioning. In this view, so long as an external stimulus does not push one or more parameters beyond a specified limit ("threshold"), adaptive processes can repair any damage which may have been temporarily produced and completely restore the system to the functional state prior to the stimulus. This paradigm has enjoyed great success in guiding the design and interpretation of a wide range of experimental findings on acute responses to toxic chemicals, heat, cold, and other agents where the mechanism of damage does, in fact, consist of grossly overwhelming a particular set of bodily defenses.[5]

Another type of damage mechanism dominates thinking in molecular biology and genetics. At the molecular level, some fundamental life processes are basically fragile—in particular, the integrity of the mechanism of inheritance depends on detailed fidelity in copying the massive amount of information coded within the DNA of each cell. An unrepaired error ("mutation") in copying will usually be passed on to all of the progeny of the mutated cell. Even if the mistake is confined to a single DNA base, massive adverse consequences may result if important genetic information has been altered in a functionally-significant way.

For the molecular biologist it is intuitively obvious that even a single molecule of a substance that reacts with DNA has some chance of producing a biologically significant result if it happens to interact with just the right DNA site.[6] For the traditional toxicologist, intuition leads to just the opposite expectation; that for any substance there is some level of exposure that will not significantly affect a biological system. Clearly, application of either intuition to a particular biological response is appropriate only to the degree that the causal mechanism for that response resembles the paradigmatic damage-producing process which is the basis for the intuition.

This, of course, begs the question "What are the rules for deciding whether the causal mechanism for a particular response 'resembles' homeostatic-system-overwhelming, mutation, or some other type of damage process?" [The next reading] suggests a classification system for health effects with four broad categories defined by different properties of the fundamental damage-producing processes. We believe that a useful first step in considering dose-response information for any health effect is to classify it into one of these broad groups. Then the analyst can use sets of a priori assumptions/presumptions appropriate for the group in assessing the likely shape of the dose-response curve for the effect in question. . . .

[5. See figure 2.4.]
[6. Errors can also randomly occur from incorrect transcription of DNA and, theoretically, these can be problematic. The capacity for the cell to repair the DNA may be important. In practical terms, when looking at potentially harmful substances, it may be difficult or impossible to determine whether the incidence of chemically induced changes is greater than that which occurs naturally; and while intellectually challenging, public policy decisions may not support efforts to delve deeply into these questions.]

■ **NOTES**

1. In figure 2.3, if actual data points were to be placed on the A and B curves, one could place "error bars" around those points signifying the 90 or 95% confidence levels reflecting the significance or "power" of the experimental data. As one places those confidence levels on points signifying lower and lower exposures, the confidence levels increase in size, reflecting greater uncertainty. This is a statistical artifact arising from the relatively small number of animals or people who are affected at low doses. Referring to the earlier discussion of the relative insensitivity of animal experiments, if curve A, for example, were to represent a classical toxicity study exposing 100 animals at each dose examined (usually three), an excess of disease or effect of 5% would be indistinguishable from 0% within the limits of statistical significance; i.e., the lower limit of the error bar would go through zero.

2. The threshold of curve A in figure 2.3 is an interpolation of higher-dose data points to their intersection with the horizontal axis. Would industry be justified in arguing that the threshold should be placed at the dose whose lower confidence level includes zero, rather than interpolation of the expected value of response at each dose? Is this good public policy? Why or why not?

3. Returning again to figure 2.3, if the two diseases were irreversible—or equally reversible—and involved equivalent degrees and duration of pain and suffering, would you prefer to subject yourself (or others) to an exposure to a substance with or without a no-effect threshold; e.g., would you rather increase your (or others') risk of emphysema or of lung cancer? The answer should depend both on what level of exposure is involved and on the shape and slope of the dose-response curve. If the exposure is below threshold, exposure to the threshold pollutant obviously is preferable, because no risk at all is involved. If you are above threshold, the choice depends both on the specific doses and on the relative slopes of the two dose-response curves. What is important is *the expected risks at the anticipated doses.*

4. The practice of rotating workers in and out of a particular workplace is sometimes used to ensure that no worker spends enough time exposed to a particular contaminant to be above the threshold for a health effect caused by that contaminant. This has been done, for example, with workplace exposures to lead and radiation. If such a worker rotation strategy does not guarantee a subthreshold dose (in the case of a classical toxicant), or if it is employed with nonthreshold toxicants (e.g., some carcinogens, mutagens, or other extremely low-level acting developmental toxicants), the strategy can actually create a higher total disease risk across the population of rotated workers. The determining factors are the shape of the dose-response curve and the location of the threshold. In figure 2.3, curve A is depicted as curvilinear up-

ward at low doses. For both threshold pollutants (curve A) and nonthreshold carcinogens (curve B), the dose-response curve could be curvilinear upward, linear, or curvilinear downward. In the latter case rotation could actually increase total disease. The possibility of rotation causing more disease is easily seen through an example. If, rather than exposing N workers for 8 hours to dose D, we expose 2N workers for 4 hours to a smaller dose, the risk could be greater or lesser than that formerly faced by the original N workers. For a dose-response curve that is curvilinear downward, the 4-hour risk will be greater than half the 8-hour risk and the total disease will be greater than if no rotation occurred because twice as many workers are exposed. The environmental analogy would be to dilute the pollution so that any particular individual in the general population receives a smaller dose, but more people are exposed. ∎

c. Categorization of Health Effects Resulting from Exposures to Chemicals

Health effects can be categorized in many ways, according to the purpose underlying the categorization. From the medical practices that focus on diagnosing and treating diseases of organs and systems of the body, we find, among others, the following descriptors of toxic chemical effects: *pulmonary* (lung), *cardiopulmonary* (heart-lung), *hepatotoxic* (liver), *nephrotoxic* (kidney), *dermatologic* (skin), *neurotoxic* (nervous system), and *immunotoxic* (immune system). Other descriptors of diseases by mechanism

Table 2.1
Types of Health Effects Requiring Fundamentally Different Risk Assessment and Risk Management Approaches

---

"Traditional" toxicity   Proceeds by overwhelming body compensatory processes; below some threshold, in individuals who are not already beyond the limits of normal function without exposure, response is reversible

   Traditional *acute* toxicity   Toxic action is completely reversible *or* proceeds to long term damage within about three days of exposure—lung damage from inhalation of chlorine; pesticide poisoning from unusually high exposures of farmworkers; probably many teratogenic effects.

   Traditional *chronic* toxicity   Toxic process typically proceeds to clinically noticeable damage or abnormal function over a time period from several days to several months, due to either (A) reversible accumulation of a toxic agent (e.g., methyl mercury or lead) or (B) accumulation of a slowly-reversible toxic response (e.g. cholinesterase inhibition).

Effects resulting from insidious processes that are irreversible or poorly reversible at low doses or early stages of causation

   Molecular biological effects (stochastic process)   Occur as a result of one or a small number of irreversible changes in information coded in DNA—Mutagenesis, much carcinogenesis (from exposure to vinyl chloride, benzene, radiation) and some teratogenesis.

   Chronic cumulative effects   Occur as a result of a chronic accumulation of many small-scale damage event—emphysema, asbestosis, silicosis, noise-induced hearing loss, atherosclerosis, and probably hypertension; possibly depletion of mature oocytes.

Source: *Evaluating Chemical Regulations: Trade-Off Analysis and Impact Assessment for Environmental Decision-Making*, N. A. Ashford, D. B. Hattis, G. R. Heaton, J. I. Katz, W. C. Priest, E. M. Zolt, Final Report to the Council on Environmental Quality under Contract No. EQ4ACA35. CPA-80-13, 1980. NTIS #PB81-195067, pp. 5-27 to 5-31.

are *carcinogenesis* (cancer), *teratogenesis* (birth defects), *genotoxic* (toxic to basic genetic material), *mutagenic* (causing mutations in either somatic or germ cells), and *endocrine disrupting*.

While these categorizations are useful for some purposes, we believe that another taxonomy, which classifies toxic effects according to the biological mechanism through which they act upon the human body, is more useful for establishing safe levels and for assessing various intervention strategies for reducing risk. This fourfold classification of toxic effects is summarized in table 2.1 and discussed in the reading that follows.

A Taxonomy of Biological Effects with Different Dose-Response Implications
N. A. Ashford, D. B. Hattis, G. R. Heaton, J. I. Katz, W. C. Priest, and E. M. Zolt
Source: *Evaluating Chemical Regulations: Trade-off Analysis and Impact Assessment for Environmental Decision-Making.* **Final Report to the Council on Environmental Quality under Contract No. EQ4ACA35. CPA-80-13, NTIS PB81-195067, 1980, pp. 5-27 to 5-31.**

In classifying particular toxic effects the analyst needs to focus on the kinds of events that are known or are likely to be occurring at subclinical dosage levels or at pre-clinical stages in the pathological process. The analyst should first ask,

"Are the events that are occurring ordinarily completely reversible, given a prolonged period with no further exposure to the hazard?"

If the answer to this question is yes, then it will generally be appropriate to treat the condition within the framework of traditional toxicology. Examples of such reversible changes . . . that require the use of time-weighting functions for accurately summarizing fluctuating exposures include:

• buildup of a contaminant in blood or other tissues,
• most enzyme inhibition, and
• induction of short-term biological responses which act to maintain homeostasis (e.g.,

sweating in response to heat, tearing in response to irritations).

After assigning a particular effect to the province of traditional toxicology, it is then usually helpful to characterize the time-course over which the sub-clinical or pre-clinical events are likely to be reversed. If reversal is likely to be essentially complete within a few hours or days, it should be considered under the heading of *acute toxicity*.[7] If reversal is likely to take longer than a few days before it can be considered substantially complete (and longer-term modeling of toxicant buildup or of other effects is therefore required for accurate prediction of the response), the condition should be considered under the heading of *classic chronic toxicity*.

If the answer to the question above is "No" and events are likely to be occurring at subclinical exposure levels or preclinical stages that are not ordinarily completely re-

---

[7. In the usual parlance of toxicology, the terms "acute," "subacute/subchronic," and "chronic" refer to the *duration of dosing*, and not the time frame for reversibility. Here, in making distinctions based

on pathological mechanism properties, we are laying the groundwork for more predictive quantitative risk assessment, rather than the usual toxicological "safety" evaluations.]

versible,[8] modeling of biological risks will generally need to be based on fundamentally different concepts from the homeostatic system/threshold paradigm of traditional toxicology.... [S]ome traditional toxicological elements such as pharmacodynamic modeling are still helpful in the supporting role of determining the effective delivery of hazardous substances to the sites where irreversible or poorly reversible damage events can occur. However, appropriate modeling for conditions that are the result of irreversible or poorly reversible processes must fundamentally be based on the likely dose-response characteristics of the events which cause the basic irreversible changes.

Once the primacy of such irreversible changes is established for a particular event, one should ask whether clinical manifestations are likely to be the direct result of only a few, or of very many individual irreversible damage events. If it is thought that only a few events directly contribute to a particular clinical manifestation (e.g., [where] a small number of heritable changes within a singe cell line lead ... to cancer) the effect can be considered to be a *molecular biological disease*. If thousands, millions, or billions of individual irreversible events directly contribute to a particular condition (e.g., very large numbers of individual alveolar septa must break in order to produce serious impairment from emphysema), we think it should be dealt with under the category of *chronic cumulative effects*.[9]

The aim of creating these four broad categories (acute toxicity, classic chronic toxicity, molecular biological, and chronic cumulative) is to help distinguish among types of risk analysis problems which must be approached from first principles in basically different ways.

■ NOTES

1. Not all carcinogens are thought to act primarily through DNA mutations. For example, PCBs and dioxins are thought to act through other mechanisms. This has

---

8. Examples of such irreversible or poorly reversible events include:

• changes in genetic information or in the heritable pattern of gene expression after these are effectively "fixed" into a cell's genome by replication,
• death of non-replicating types of cells (e.g., neurons),—destruction of non-regenerating structures (e.g., alveolar septa),
• generation and buildup of incompletely repaired lesions (e.g., atherosclerotic plaques), and
• apparently irreversible physiological changes produced by multiple, diverse fundamental mechanisms (e.g., long term increases in blood pressure from "essential" causes).

9. An important distinguishing feature of *chronic cumulative effects* is that because damage takes the form of many small irreversible steps, there is always a broad continuous distribution in the population of the number of steps (and resulting functional impairment) which have occurred in individuals. For example, hearing impairment and lung function can and do take on a whole range of intermediate values from excellent function, through mediocre function, to function which imposes a serious handicap. Because of this, for environmental agents which tend to move most members of an exposed population some distance in the direction of worse function, it will usually be inadequate to describe effects in terms of the number of "cases" of overt illness, defined as passage beyond some single critical value of function. Rather the effect must be described in terms of a shift of portions of the population from excellent to good function, from good to mediocre function, etc. The shift in the entire population distribution of function must be conveyed to the user of the results of the risk analysis.

caused some to argue for the use of the traditional toxicological paradigm, with thresholds and the use of safety factors, for these substances. Traditionally, U.S. regulatory agencies have not made distinctions among carcinogens in this manner, and have used linear, nonthreshold models in their risk assessments for all carcinogens. EPA's 2005 revised cancer guidelines, however, do provide for the use of threshold models for carcinogens classified as having nongenetic modes of action. See *Guidelines for Carcinogen Risk Assessment. U.S. Environmental Protection Agency, National Center for Environmental Assessment, Washington, D.C. Available at* http://cfpub.epa.gov/ncea/cfm/recordisplay.cfm?deid=116283

2. These revised EPA guidelines are controversial. Not only do they depart from the linear dose-response assumption for some carcinogens, they also depart from the traditional practice of inferring human carcinogenicity from animal data alone. The guidelines also encourage the calculation of central or "best estimates" of risk, rather than only "upper-bound estimates," and these could be used in the cost-benefit analyses performed by the Office of Management and Budget in evaluating regulations (discussed in chapters 3 and 5). The guidelines also call for the use of "expert elicitation" (formal probability judgments by scientists outside of the agency) to estimate risks where the data are weak. See *Environment Reporter* 36(13): 646 (2005).

3. Whatever the mechanism posited for the initiation of cancer, the promotion of carcinogenic cells to manifest tumors and disease is thought to proceed via a subsequent step, often with substances different from those that initiated the cancer acting as promoters. In some cases, however, initiators are also promoters. This is usually posited whenever there appears to be synergism or multiplicative effects between two carcinogens, such as occurs between tobacco smoke and asbestos.

4. There is no reason why a disease may not involve more than one process, or more than one type of process. See the discussion in section C2.

5. Toxicity to both the immune system (immunotoxicity) and the nervous system (neurotoxicity) is receiving increased attention in the assessment of risk. See Angela Veraldi, Adele Seniori Constantini, Vanessa Bolejack, Lucia Miligi, Paolo Vineis, and Henk van Loveren (2006) "Immonotoxic Effects of Chemicals: A Matrix for Occupational and Environmental Studies," *American Journal of Industrial Medicine* 49: 1046–1055, and L. Claudio, W. C. Kwa, A. L. Russell, and D. Wallinga (2000) "Testing Methods for Developmental Neurotoxicity of Environmental Chemicals," *Toxicology and Applied Pharmacology* 164(1): 1–14.   ∎

d.   In vitro Studies

Bruce Ames pioneered bacterial assay tests to detect the mutagenic (and hence presumably the carcinogenic) potential of organic chemicals. These tests are performed in vitro (in glass test tubes or other vessels) by adding a suspected mutagen to live bacteria. Not all classes of carcinogens can be tested by these assays, in particular heavy-metal compounds, because these substances test negative in these assays but turn out to be carcinogenic in living species. Many additional tests have been developed since the original assay, and the tests can be used seriatim (sequentially). Some tests involve the addition of enzymes thought to be necessary to metabolize or transform compounds into their ultimate mutagenic forms.

■ **NOTES**

1. Suppose 5% of chemicals are in fact carcinogenic. Further assume that an Ames-type bioassay yields 10% false negatives and 13% false positives for a given class of chemical compounds containing N compounds. What are the chances that a randomly chosen chemical is in fact carcinogenic if it tests positive?

Solution

The number of chemicals that are in fact positive divided by *the number expected to test positive* is:

$$\frac{\text{no. testing positive that are positive}}{\text{no. testing positive that are positive} + \text{no. testing positive that are in fact negative}}$$

$$= \frac{(0.05N)(0.9)}{(0.05N)(0.9) + (0.95N)(0.13)} = \frac{0.045}{0.045 + 0.124} = 0.27$$

Thus, the chances of the test indicating a true positive result are about one in four.

2. Note that in order to get this answer, the underlying a priori prevalence of carcinogens must be known. Satisfy yourself that if the facts of the problem were changed such that the a priori expectation was that only 1% of the chemicals in this class were carcinogenic, the chances of the test turning up a real positive would only be seven out of one hundred. What if the a priori expectation were that 10% of the chemicals in this class are carcinogenic? Note that the greater the a priori expectation, the more likely it is that the substance that tests positive is in fact positive.

3. Where two or more independent tests (tests using different methods) are used, the chances of being wrong are greatly diminished. This is why a battery of tests commonly is used. Even though the reliability of the Ames test alone is acknowledged not to be strong, many companies that use Ames at very early screening in their search for chemicals to be commercialized generally abandon Ames-positive chemicals even though they may not ultimately be shown to be genotoxic when a full battery of tests is applied. ■

traditional toxicology - ~~sts~~ organisms can receive dosage up to a limit where it will completely expunge it
modern biological - opposite

e. Structure-Activity Relationships

Chemical structure can often tell us a great deal about toxicity. For example, a chlorine group or a nitrogen-oxide group on the aromatic ring (found in benzene, naphthalene, etc.) can render a compound more toxic. Alkylating agents are putative mutagens or carcinogens. Halogenated organic compounds (containing chlorine or bromine, and sometimes iodine) behave somewhat similarly. For example, vinyl chloride is a well-known carcinogen, and it should not have been a surprise that vinyl bromide is even more potent. Sometimes the "shape" of a molecule—its stereochemistry—rather than its molecular constitution, determines toxicological behavior, as, for example, in the case of estrogenic activity. [See Weida Tong, Roger Perkins, Richard Strelitz, Elizabeth R. Collantes, Susan Keenan, William J. Welsh, William S. Branham, and Daniel M. Sheehan (1997) "Quantitative Structure-Activity Relationships (QSARs) for Estrogen Binding to the Estrogen Receptor: Predictions across Species," *Environmental Health Perspectives* 105(10): 1116–1124.] Much has been learned in the past few decades from studying chemical structure and its relationship to toxicity, and while toxic behavior is not perfectly predictable, predictions drawn from such analyses often are not far off the mark.[10] Sometimes they are the only available source of information for developing the appropriate initial approach to new and novel chemicals.

2. Multistage Disease Processes: The Dose Plus the Host Makes the Harm

Paracelsus' classical adage—"the dose makes the poison"—turns out to be too simplistic for multistage disease processes, especially those that change the host and render it more susceptible to toxic substances. Among the health problems that involve

---

10. See, for example, Organization for Economic Cooperation and Development (1993) *Application of Structure-Activity Relationships to the Estimation of Properties Important in Exposure Assessment.* OECD Environmental Monograph 67, OECD, Paris. In the 1970s, as U.S. regulation under the Clean Air Act and the Occupational Safety and Health Act was just beginning, knowledge about structure-activity relationships was limited. Replacing a known toxic material with a substitute chemical for which little actual toxicity or epidemiological data existed was then very risky. Thirty-five years later, we have accumulated a great deal of experience, and confidence that clearly safer substitutes can be identified is much more soundly based. In general, the chances of unfortunate surprises in this regard have been greatly diminished. A recent U.S. Government Accountability Office report stresses the increasing importance of structure-activity relationships. See U.S. GAO (June 2005) *Chemical Regulation: Options Exist to Improve EPA's Ability to Assess Health Risks and Manage Its Chemical Review Program.* GAO-05-458, GAO, Washington, D.C. The report observes: "EPA predicts potential exposure levels and toxicity of new chemicals by using scientific models and by comparing them with chemicals with similar molecular structures (analogues) for which toxicity information is available.... EPA believes that the models are generally useful as screening tools for identifying potentially harmful chemicals.... EPA believes that, based on limited validation studies, its models are more likely to identify a false positive...than a false negative" (pp. 3–4). OECD member countries are currently leading collaborative efforts to develop and harmonize structure-activity relationship methods for assessing chemical hazards. See also Thomas Hoefer et al. (2004) "Animal Testing and Alternative Approaches for the Human Health Risk Assessment under the Proposed New European Chemicals Regulation," *Archives of Toxicology* 78: 549–564.

multistage processes are endocrine disruption, low-level chemical sensitivity, and autoimmune diseases.

a. Endocrine Disruption

Endocrine disruption resulting from in utero exposure to toxic substances is of increasing concern.

Overview of the Endocrine Disruptor Issue
Environmental Protection Agency
Source: Endocrine Disruptor Screening Program: Report to Congress, EPA, Washington, D.C., August 2000.

There is concern that certain pesticide chemicals and other chemical substances, as well as certain naturally-occurring substances such as phytoestrogens in foods, may modify the normal functioning of human and wildlife endocrine, or hormone, systems. Endocrine disruptors (also referred to as hormonally active agents) may cause a variety of problems with, for example, development, behavior, and reproduction. They have the potential to impact both human and wildlife populations (US EPA, 1997; NAS, 1999).

Although many pesticides, and some industrial chemicals, may have already undergone extensive toxicological testing, conventional toxicity tests may be inadequate to determine whether these substances interact with specific components of the endocrine system and whether additional testing is needed for the EPA to assess and characterize more fully their impact on both human and ecological health. Scientific knowledge related to endocrine disruptors is still evolving; however, there is widespread scientific agreement that a screening and testing program would be useful in elucidating the scope of the problem (EDSTAC, 1998; EPA, 1999; NAS, 1999).

An endocrine system is found in nearly all animals, including mammals, non-mammalian vertebrates (e.g., fish, amphibians, reptiles, and birds), and invertebrates (e.g., snails, lobsters, insects, and other spe-

cies). The endocrine system consists of glands and the hormones they produce that guide the development, growth, reproduction, and behavior of human beings and animals. Some of the endocrine glands are the pituitary, thyroid, and adrenal glands, the female ovaries and male testes. Hormones are biochemicals, produced by endocrine glands, that travel through the bloodstream and cause responses in other parts of the body.

Disruption of this complex system can occur in various ways. For example, some chemicals may mimic a natural hormone, "fooling" the body into over-responding to the stimulus or responding at inappropriate times. Other chemicals may block the effects of a hormone in parts of the body normally sensitive to it. Still others may directly stimulate or inhibit the endocrine system, causing overproduction or underproduction of hormones. Certain drugs, such as birth control pills, are used to cause some of these effects intentionally.

A variety of effects on humans and wildlife have been attributed to endocrine disruptors (US EPA, 1997; NAS, 1999). Although there is controversy on the subject, EPA (US EPA, 1997) and the National Academy of Sciences (NAS, 1999) published recent reports based on reviews of the scientific literature on studies of declining human sperm counts over the last fifty years. Wildlife has been reported with malformed genitalia, aberrant mating behavior, sterility, and other physical and behavioral anomalies (US EPA, 1997; NAS 1999). A difficulty in attributing specific health effects to specific chemicals is that we do not currently know which chemicals may interfere with endocrine system function, the extent to which problems exist, or how widespread they may be in the environment. Nonetheless, in view of existing data, endocrine disruptors warrant further study (US EPA, 1997; NAS, 1999). The agency has, therefore, initiated a two-phased implementation strategy for its Endocrine Disruptor Screening Program: Standardization and validation of screens and tests in accordance with statutory mandates of the FFDCA; and a research program directed toward reducing uncertainty in this complex and scientifically controversial area....

REFERENCES

EDSTAC (Endocrine Disrupter Screening and Testing Advisory Committee), (1998) *Final Report* EPA/743/R-98/003, Washington, DC.

US EPA (1997) *Special Report on Environmental Endocrine Disruption: An Effects Assessment and Analysis* EPA/630/R-96/012, Washington, DC.

US EPA (1999) *Review of the EPA's Proposed Environmental Endocrine Disruption Screening Program by a Joint Subcommittee of the Science Advisory Panel* EPA-SAB-EC-99-013, Washington, DC.

NAS (1999) *Hormonally Active Agents in the Environment* National Academy Press, Washington, DC.

■ **NOTES**

1. In part because hormones themselves provide very potent chemical signals (at very low concentrations in the body), endocrine disruption challenges the sufficiency of regulatory approaches that control exposures to toxic substances at the parts per million (ppm) level. See Peter Waldman (2005) "Common Industrial Chemicals in Tiny Doses Raise Health Issue," *Wall Street Journal*, July 25, p. A1. Exposures of a fetus to an endocrine disrupter at a much lower parts per billion (ppb) level can be sufficient to cause damage to its development and later reproductive health, depending on the affinity of the "disruptor" chemical for the hormonal receptor compared to that of the real hormone. This has important implications for controlling toxic substances in the general environment, because bioaccumulation and biomagnification allow fat-soluble substances to accumulate and concentrate up the food chain. Endocrine disruption is still observed in lakes in the Florida Everglades, even though the concentration of PCBs in the water of the lakes themselves is below the limits of detection, because PCBs are already in the fatty tissues of fish and other species inhabiting the lakes. Some persistent organic pollutants can reach high concentrations in humans and other air-breathing animals, even though they don't bioaccumulate in fish, suggesting that EPA screening mechanisms may need revision. See Celia Arnaud, "Persistent Organic Pollutants," http://www.cen-online.org, July 16, 2007.

2. Estrogenic activity associated with cosmetics has been implicated in increased risk of breast cancer. See Maryann Donovan, Chandra M. Tiwary, Deborah Axelrod,

Annie J. Sasco, Lowell Jones, Richard Hajek, Erin Sauber, Jean Kuo, and Devra L. Davis, "Personal Care Products That Contain Estrogens or Xenoestrogens May Increase Breast Cancer Risk," *Medical Hypotheses* (2007) 68(4): 756–766.

3. There is now a report on what is believed to be the first demonstration and explanation of how a toxin-induced disorder in a pregnant female can be passed on to children and succeeding generations without changes in her genetic code or in gene sequences in the DNA. See M. D. Anway, A. S. Cupp, M. Uzumcu, and M. K. Skinner (2005) "Epigenetic Transgenerational Actions of Endocrine Disruptors and Male Fertility," *Science* 308: 1466–1469. The standard view of heritable disease is that for any disorder or disease to be inherited, a gene must mutate, and must then be passed on to the offspring. Skinner and his colleagues showed that exposing a pregnant rat to high doses of a class of pesticides that are endocrine disruptors causes an inherited reproductive disorder in male rats that is passed on without any genetic mutation. These changes are called "epigenetic" changes. Epigenetics refers to modifying DNA without mutations in the sequences of the genes, e.g., by the addition of a methyl group (methylation). The common wisdom has been that any artificially induced epigenetic modifications will remain as an isolated change in an individual. Because no genes are altered, the changes presumably could not be passed on. In the reported work, the male in the breeding pair was born with a low sperm count and other disorders because of the mother's exposure to toxins. Further, the male *offspring* of the pair also had these problems, as did the next two generations of male rats. See also Bob Weinhold (2006) "Epigenetics: The Science of Change," *Environmental Health Perspectives* 114(3): A160–A167.   ■

b. Low-Level Chemical Sensitivity

Persons experiencing more or less immediate adverse reactions from low-level exposures include persons suffering from "sick-building syndrome" and "multiple chemical sensitivity." These are controversial diagnoses.

Low-Level Chemical Sensitivity: Implications for Research and Social Policy
Nicholas A. Ashford

Source: Amy Brown and Myron Mehlman (eds.), *Toxicology and Industrial Health: Special Issues on Multiple Chemical Sensitivity,* **April–June 1999, 15(3–4), pp. 421–427, excerpted with permission.**

INTRODUCTION

While sensitivity to low levels of chemical exposures is not a new problem, it has been approached with renewed interest, and controversy, in the last decade, first in North America and more recently in Europe.... Chemical hyper-reactivity continues to engender scientific debate and controversy around issues relating to etiology, diagnosis, and treatment. While an increasing number of patients voice their concern and dissatisfaction with the response of the medical community and government to their illnesses which they believe are caused by exposure to low levels of chemicals in their environments, the scientific debate rages on; and the medical community continues to engage in sometimes acrimonious discussions about the nature of the problem.

As a result of an overview of the problem in North America [7], it is increasingly clear that low-level chemical sensitivity, rather than a clearly-defined disease entity, might be more correctly described as a class of disorders—like infectious disease—the members of which may present with similar symptoms, but which have a myriad of precipitating agents and pathophysiological pathways. Chemical sensitivity may be viewed as the *consequence* of a variety of disease processes resulting from "Toxicant-Induced Loss of Tolerance" (TILT). TILT is a new theory of disease providing a phenomenological description of those disease processes [7, 18].

DISTINGUISHING DIFFERENT TYPES OF SENSITIVITY

The different meanings of the term *sensitivity* are at least partially responsible for the confusion surrounding chemical sensitivity. Chemical sensitivity encompasses three relatively distinct categories [6]:

1. The response of *normal* subjects to known exposures in a traditional dose-response fashion. This category includes responses of persons at the lower end of a population distribution of classical responses to toxic substances [such as CO or lead], as well as classical allergy [for example to pollen or dust mites] or other immunologically-mediated sensitivity.

2. The response of *normal* subjects to known or unknown exposures, unexplained by clas-

sical or known mechanisms. This category includes:

a. Sick building syndrome (SBS) in which individuals respond to known or unknown exposures, but whose symptoms resolve when they [leave] . . . the building, and

b. Sensitivity, such as that induced by toluene di-isocyanate (TDI), which begins as specific hypersensitivity to a single agent (or class of substances) but which may evolve into non-specific hyper-responsiveness described in category 3) below.

3. The heightened, extraordinary, or unusual response of individuals to known or unknown exposures whose symptoms do not completely resolve upon removal from the exposures and/or whose "sensitivities" seem to spread to other agents. These individuals may experience:

a. a heightened response to agents at the same exposure levels as other individuals;

b. a response at lower levels than those that affect other individuals; and/or

c. a response at an earlier time than that experienced by other individuals.

Patients suffering from . . . multiple chemical sensitivity (MCS) [12] exhibit the third type of sensitivity. Their health problems often (but not always) appear to involve a two-step process. The first step originates with some acute or traumatic exposure [very often reported to be some types of pesticides, organic solvents, and anesthesia], after which the triggering of symptoms and observed sensitivities occur at very low levels of chemical exposure (the second step). The inducing chemical or substance may or may not be the same as the substances that thereafter provoke or "trigger" responses. (Sometimes the inducing substance is described as "sensitizing" the individual, and the affected person is termed a "sensitized" person.) Acute or traumatic exposures are not always necessary. Repeated or continuous lower-level exposures may also lead to sensitization.

These "sensitized individuals" are not those on the tails of a *normal* distribution. They are thought to make up a distinct subset of the population. The fact that normal persons do not experience even at higher levels of exposure those symptoms that chemically-sensitive patients describe at much lower levels of exposure probably helps explain the reluctance of some physicians to believe that the problems are physical in nature. To compound the problem of physician acceptance of this illness, multiple organ systems may be affected, and multiple substances may trigger the effects. Over time, sensitivities seem to spread, in terms of both the types of triggering substances and the systems affected [7].

Avoidance of the offending substances is reported to be effective but much more difficult to achieve for these patients than for classically sensitive patients because symptoms may occur at extremely low levels and the exposures are ubiquitous....

REFERENCES

6. Ashford, N., B. Heinzow, K. Lütjen, C. Marouli, L. Mølhave, B. Mönce, S. Papadopoulos, K. Rest, D. Rosdahl, P. Siskos and E. Velonakis (1995). *Chemical Sensitivity in Selected European Countries: An Exploratory Study: A Report to the European Commission*, Ergonomia, Athens, Greece.

7. Ashford, N. A. and Miller, C. S. (1998). *Chemical Exposures: Low Levels and High Stakes*, John Wiley Press, New York, 440 pp.

12. Cullen, M. (1987). "The worker with multiple chemical sensitivities: An overview." In: Workers with Multiple Chemical Sensitivities, *Occupational Medicine: State of the Art Reviews*, M. Cullen, ed., Hanley & Belfus, Philadelphia, 2(4): 655.

18. Miller, C. S. (1997). "Toxicant-induced Loss of Tolerance: An Emerging Theory of Disease." *Environmental Health Perspectives*, 105 (Suppl 2): 445–453.

■ NOTES

1. Because persons with chemical sensitivity often report symptomatic responses to exposures to many common chemicals at levels that are in the ppb range, regulatory approaches focused on technologies controlling exposures at the ppm range in the ambient air and water may be insufficient to protect them. However, control at the ppb range, or outright bans of these common chemicals, often will not be technologically or economically feasible. Accordingly, the regulatory focus should instead be on preventing people from becoming extraordinarily sensitive in the first place, by eliminating exposures to those substances thought or reported to *initiate* the condition. These are predominantly classical neurotoxins such as some pesticides, some anesthetics, and some organic solvents.

2. In indoor environments, both workplaces and residences, "safe" spaces can be created for the chemically sensitive. Arguably, the Americans with Disabilities Act (ADA) requirement for "reasonable accommodation" demands this of employers and landlords. As interpreted by the United States Supreme Court, a person is not considered "disabled" by a particular physical or mental condition unless one or more of the person's "ordinary activities of life" are compromised by the condition. If the disability only affects a person's ability to do a specific task at work, the person

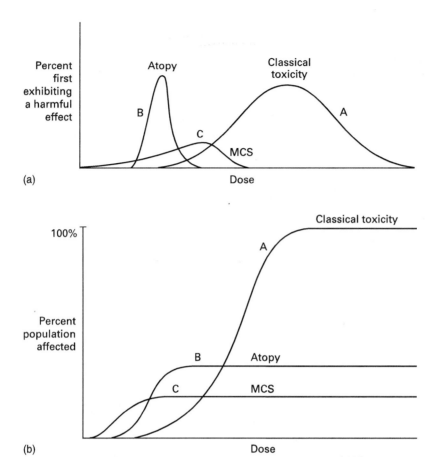

Figure 2.6
Distinctions between different types of chemical sensitivity. (a) Hypothetical distribution of different types of sensitivities as a function of dose. Curve A is a sensitivity distribution for classical toxicity, e.g., to lead or a solvent. Sensitive individuals are found in the left-hand tail of the distribution. Curve B is a sensitivity distribution of atopic or allergic individuals in the population who are sensitive to an allergen, e.g., rag-weed or bee venom. Curve C is a sensitivity distribution for individuals with multiple chemical sensitivities who, because they are already sensitized, subsequently respond to particular incitants, e.g., formaldehyde or phenol. (b) Hypothetical population dose-response curves for different effects. Curve A is a cumulative dose-response curve for classical toxicity, e.g., to lead or a solvent. Curve B is a cumulative dose-response curve for atopic or allergic individuals in the population who are sensitive to an allergen, e.g., ragweed or bee venom. Curve C is a cumulative dose-response curve for individuals with multiple chemical sensitivities who, because they are already sensitized, subsequently respond to particular incitants, e.g., formaldehyde or phenol. (Source: N. A. Ashford and C. S. Miller, 1998. Taken from *Chemical Exposures: Low Levels and High Stakes*. Wiley, New York, 1998.)

is not "disabled" under the ADA. *See Toyota Motor Mfg. Kentucky, Inc. v. Williams*, 534 U.S. 184 (2002). Since the "ordinary activities" of chemically sensitive persons are considered compromised in any environment that contains small amounts of offending chemicals, this decision should not affect the chemically sensitive.

3. Figures 2.6a and b provide a pictorial representation of differences among different kinds of chemical sensitivity. Note that the first panel (the sensitivity distributions) shows three different groups. The chemically sensitive subgroup is *not* on the tail of a normal distribution that constitutes the *classically* more-sensitive people in a so-called normal population. The chemically sensitive comprise a separate group, reacting at much lower doses than those on the tail of a normal distribution. Note also in the second panel (depicting population dose-response curves) that while at some dose 100% of the population exhibits the monitored (classically toxic) effect, this is not true for the atopic (classically allergic) or chemically sensitive populations. Not everyone is allergic within normal exposure parameters. And the kinds of multi-symptomatic reactions characteristic of the chemically sensitive are not exhibited by most of the normal population, even at high levels of exposure.   ▪

c. Toxicant-Induced Loss of Tolerance: A New Theory of Disease?

The following article discusses the differences between classical disease processes and multistage disease processes, as well as possible connections among the emerging public health concerns.

Low-Level Exposures to Chemicals Challenge Both Science and Regulatory Policy

N. A. Ashford and C. S. Miller

Source: Adapted from *Environmental Science and Technology*, November 1998, pp. 508A–509A, excerpted with permission.

THE PROBLEM

There is mounting evidence that human exposure to chemicals at levels once thought to be safe (or presenting insignificant risk) could be harmful. So-called low-level exposures have been linked with adverse biological effects including endocrine disruption *(1)*, chemical sensitivity *(2)*, and cancer *(3)*. In the 16th century, Paracelsus observed that *the dose makes the poison*. A more apt and modern revision might be that *the host plus the dose makes the poison*. Prior susceptibility of the host, whether inborn or environmentally induced, followed by other lifetime exposures, can cause irreversible injury. Humans in their most vulnerable developmental state, whether in the womb or during infancy, warrant special consideration, both in their own right and as sentinel indicators. The emerging science associated with low-level chemical exposures requires that we change both (1) the way we think about chemicals and health, including the adequacy of quantitative risk assessment, and (2) the solutions we devise to prevent and address chemically-caused injury.

CHEMICALS AND HEALTH

In his seminal work, *The Structure of Scientific Revolutions*, Thomas Kuhn described the process by which scientific knowledge evolves *(4)*.... New theories emerge only after much difficulty. At this point in time, we are just beginning to recognize the link between chemicals and a host of new public health problems that challenge the tenets of traditional toxicology and medicine. These include birth defects (and other damage) due to developmental toxicants; autoimmune diseases, including lupus, scleroderma, and Sjøgren's Syndrome; certain chronic conditions in children such as attention deficit hyperactivity disorder, depression, and asthma that have become more prevalent in the past few decades; chemical sensitivity including its overlaps with sick building syndrome, the unexplained illnesses of Gulf War veterans, chronic fatigue syndrome, fibromyalgia, and toxic encephalopathy; and, finally, new links to cancer, including childhood cancers.

These emerging public health problems are characterized by six common threads which provide a new perspective on disease: (1) They represent a departure from many classic diseases such as tuberculosis and heart disease in that *communication systems or networks*, rather than specific organs of the body appear to be the target. These include the *endocrine* system, the *immune* system, and the *neurological* system; (2) No *single* cause has been identified for each of these conditions. Further, there are often no clear biomarkers for either exposure or disease. Because of the current lack of clear biomarkers, classical epidemiology is less able to identify susceptible or sensitive subgroups; (3) Disease becomes manifest after two or more stages or events occur. For example, some cancer (and

of course cancer is not a single disease) may proceed first by *initiation*—a mutation that alters the genetic material of the cell—followed by the *promotion* of cancer cells to a recognizable tumor. These two stages can involve different chemicals, radiation, or viruses. It has been hypothesized that Toxicant-induced Loss of Tolerance (TILT) leading to chemical sensitivity also proceeds via a two-stage process: (a) an initial exposure to high levels of certain chemicals (or repeated exposures at lower levels), followed by (b) triggering of symptoms by everyday chemical exposures at levels that do not appear to affect most people *(2)*; (4) The time between the first and subsequent stages of disease can be long enough to obscure the connection between exposures and ultimate disease.... Furthermore, the *timing* of the initial exposure can be crucial because there are crucial periods in the developmental process that are especially susceptible to damage. Chemical sensitivity reportedly can develop months after the initial exposure and remain manifest for years. Furthermore, the timing of the initiating doses appears important. Loss of tolerance does not always require a high initial dose; smaller doses, strategically timed, might also cause pathological loss of tolerance; (5) The classical approaches and models used in both toxicology and epidemiology, premised on single agents disrupting individual organs, do not explain these diseases. Moreover, the relationship between the initiating exposure and ultimate health effects/disease (the dose-effect/response curve) is not monotonic—i.e., the extent of disease does not increase in a regular way as a function of dose. We have seen this vividly in the recent work of Fred vom Saal on the endocrine-disrupting effects of bis-phenol A *(5)*; and (6) Endocrine disruption (ED), TILT, and some cancers [especially those related to *in utero* exposure leading to increased numbers of certain receptors rendering the person more susceptible to cancer, or related to chemical brain injury causing immune system dysfunction in the individual] appear to represent a failure in functional and/or adaptive processes in important systems or networks as a result of chemical exposures at concentrations three to six orders of magnitude lower than those associated with classical toxic effects in normal individuals. Today, individuals may be exposed to multiple xenobiotics simultaneously, as in a sick building in which hundreds of volatile organic compounds might be present in the air.

ED, TILT, and some cancers may be interrelated. ED disrupts normal development, and possibly the immune system, resulting in increased susceptibility to certain cancers. ED might also affect the neurological system, leading to increased susceptibility to sensitization by chemicals. TILT manifests as a loss of tolerance to everyday chemical, food, and drug exposures in affected persons, possibly leaving these individuals more susceptible to other disease. TILT may, in fact, represent a new theory of disease *(2)*. Just as the general category of "infectious diseases" encompasses a diverse spectrum of diseases involving different organisms (which affect different organs via different *specific* disease mechanisms), TILT may arise from different chemical exposures (which, like the infectious diseases, could affect different organ systems via different *specific* disease mechanisms).

With Toxicant-Induced Loss of Tolerance, key systems of the body appear to lose their ability to adapt to low-level chemical exposures. Finally, it is possible that [some cancers proceed when the immune system no longer functions as it should because of chemical brain injury]. The cause of the loss of protective function is not well understood....

REFERENCES

1. Colborn, T.; Dumanowski, D.; Myers, J. P. *Our Stolen Future*; Dutton Press, New York, 1996, 306 pages.

2. Ashford, N. A.; Miller, C. S. *Chemical Exposures: Low Levels and High Stakes*; John Wiley Press, New York, 1998, 440 pages.

3. Davis, D. L.; Telang, N. T.; Osborne, M. P.; Bradlow, H. L. "Medical Hypothesis: Bifunctional Genetic-Hormonal Pathways to Breast Cancer," *Environmental Health Perspectives*, 1997, 101 (3), 571–576, April 1997. See also National Toxicology Program, "Seventh Annual Report on Carcinogens"; National Institute of Environmental Health Sciences, Research Triangle Park, North Carolina 1996.

4. Kuhn, T. *The Structure of Scientific Revolutions*; University of Chicago Press, Chicago, IL, Third Edition 1996.

5. Hileman, B. "Bisphenol A: Regulatory, Scientific Puzzle"; 1997, *Chemical and Engineering News*, 37, March 24, 1997. See also vom Saal, F. *Proceedings of the National Academy of Sciences*, 1997, 94, 2056.

d. Cancer, Repair Mechanisms, and Hormesis

The discussion above focuses on multistage disease processes in which both steps or stages contribute to the development of the disease. We have already discussed the fact that in classical toxicological disease, *homeostatic* processes may act to bring the body back into equilibrium by some compensatory action, such as excretion, sweating, and the like. In the case of molecular biological disease, DNA or other genetic repair mechanisms may act to some extent to correct the "mistakes" of mutation and other damage. Although these are not compensatory mechanisms per se, they are beneficial and can reduce the risk of cancer at low levels of chemical exposure.

Some researchers have even argued that low levels of carcinogens are actually good for you. See, e.g., Edward J. Calabrese and Linda A. Baldwin (1998) "Can the Concept of Hormesis Be Generalized to Carcinogenesis? *Regulatory Toxicology and Pharmacology* 28: 230–241. See also Edward Calabrese (2004) "Hormesis: Basic, Generalizable, Central to Toxicology and a Method to Improve the Risk-assessment Process," *International Journal of Occupational and Environmental Health* 10(4): 446–447. The concept of "hormesis" posits that at low levels, the dose-response curve can be "U" shaped, rather than linear. While this may be an interesting scientific issue, it is unlikely to be particularly relevant to regulatory policy, both because the science supporting this position is highly controversial and because, on a molecular basis, exposures are still very large indeed.

For a vigorous discussion of the relevance of hormesis to environmental regulation, see BELLE (Biological Effects of Low Level Exposures) NEWSLETTER, 9(2) 1–47, ISBN 1092-4736, Northeast Regional Environmental Public Health Center, University of Massachusetts, School of Public Health, Amherst, Massachusetts. For a critical view of hormesis in the context of the law, see John Appelgate (2001) "Getting Ahead of Ourselves: Legal Implications of Hormesis," Belle On-Line http:// www.belleonline.com/n3v92.html. For a scientific critique, see Deborah Axelrod, Kathy Burns, Devra Davis, and Nicolas von Larebeke (2004) "Hormesis: An Inappropriate Extrapolation from the Specific to the Universal," *International Journal of Occupational and Environmental Health* 10: 335–339, and Stephen M. Roberts (2001) "Another View of the Scientific Foundations of Hormesis," *Critical Reviews in Toxicology* 31(4&5): 631–635.

▪ NOTES

1. Note that for endocrine disruption from bis-phenol A, the dose-response curve has actually been empirically determined to be an *inverted* "U". This means that at the lowest of exposures the response (in rodents) increases regularly with dose as expected, then tapers off, but finally actually decreases as the dose increases further. There are good mechanistic reasons for this, but they challenge conventional notions of toxicology. See F. vom Saal, cited in reference 5 of the previous article.

2. Some carcinogens, such as selenium, are essential for life. However, the biological processes underlying that essentiality may still be totally independent of carcinogenesis processes. Caution should be exercised in arguing that because some substances (which also happen to be carcinogens) are good for you, all carcinogens are good for you at some level. ▪

D. THE BASICS (AND LIMITATIONS) OF RISK ASSESSMENT

1. Risk Assessment Methodology

What Is Risk Assessment?
Veerle Heyvaert
Source: "Reconceptualizing Risk Assessment," *Reciel* 8(2): 135–143, 1999, excerpted with permission.

Before evaluating its pros and cons, it is obviously necessary to have a common understanding of what risk assessment signifies in the context of environmental regulation. In its broadest possible meaning, risk assessment is a methodology for making predictions about the risks attached to the introduction, maintenance or abandonment of certain activities (for example, the introduction of new technology in the workplace) based on available information relating to the activity under examination [3]. In other words, risk assessment is a way of ordering, structuring and interpreting existing information with the aim of creating a qualitatively new type of information, namely estimations on the likelihood (or probability) of the occurrence of adverse effects [4].

Applied to the study of chemical safety, risk assessment combines data on adverse environmental or health effects (such as toxicity and ecotoxicity) with information on foreseeable exposure. The procedure most frequently used to make this assessment, which is also the one prevailing in European Community legislation, consists of a four-step analysis [5]. The first level of analysis is called *hazard identification*, and aims to determine the intrinsically hazardous physico-chemical and (eco)toxicological properties of a substance. During the hazard identification stage, chemical substances are subjected to a series of tests to establish their intrinsic characteristics, including their boiling point, density and corrosivity, but also qualities which are far

more difficult to examine, such as carcinogenicity and effects on reproduction. When this "chemical identity card" is mapped out, risk assessors move on to the second stage: *dose-response assessment*. This assessment seeks to clarify the relation between the required quantity or concentration of a dangerous substance, and the occurrence of adverse effects. To this end, risk assessors determine significant levels of concentration, such as the "lowest observable adverse effect level" (LOAEL) and the "no observable adverse effect level" (NOAEL) for health risk assessment, and the "predicted no-effect concentration" (PNEC) for environmental assessments. The objective of the third step, *exposure assessment*, is to make a quantitative or qualitative estimate of the dose or concentration of the substance to which a population is or may be exposed, and of the size of the population exposed. In the case of environmental risks, exposure assessment aims to predict the concentration of the substance that will eventually be found in the environment. This concentration is tagged by the term "predicted environmental concentration" (PEC). Finally, the fourth stage is dedicated to the process of *risk characterization*. Here, risk assessors combine the test results, data and estimates generated during the identification, dose-response measurement and exposure assessment stages, and on this basis try to determine, or even calculate, the likelihood that the examined substance will adversely [a]ffect human health or the environment, and the severity of the anticipated negative effects. It is this final determination that should be used as a basis for legal and policy decision-making. [emphasis added]

REFERENCES

3. David A. Wirth and Ellen K. Silbergeld (1995) "Risky Reform" 95 *Col L Rev* 1857 (at 1866).

4. Joseph V. Rodricks (1992) *Understanding the Toxicity and Human Health Risks of Chemicals in our Environment*, Cambridge University Press (at 185).

5. ...See...John S. Applegate (1991) "The Perils of Unreasonable Risk: Information, Regulatory Policy and Toxic Substances Control" 95 *Col L Rev* 261 (at 278).

■ **NOTE**

1. The four steps of risk assessment highlighted in the preceding article were actually developed in a study by the U.S. National Academy of Sciences. See *Risk Assessment in the Federal Government: Managing the Process.* National Academy Press, Washington, D.C., 1983.   ■

The following reading provides a deeper tutorial in risk assessment methodology.

Risk Assessment
G. M. Masters

Source: *Introduction to Environmental Engineering and Science*, 2nd ed. Prentice Hall, Englewood Cliffs, N.J., 1998, p. 117 et seq. (references omitted). Adapted by permission of Pearson Education, Inc., Upper Saddle River, NJ.

4.1 INTRODUCTION

One of the most important changes in environmental policy in the 1980s was the acceptance of the role of risk assessment and risk management in environmental decision making. In early environmental legislation, such as the Clean Air and Clean Water Acts, the concept of risk is hardly mentioned; instead, these acts required that pollution standards be set that would allow adequate margins of safety to protect public health. Intrinsic to these standards was the assumption that pollutants have thresholds, and that exposure to concentrations below these thresholds would produce no harm. All of that changed when the problems of toxic waste were finally recognized and addressed. Many toxic substances are suspected carcinogens; that is they may cause cancer, and for carcinogens the usual assumption is that even the smallest exposure creates some risk.

If any exposure to a substance causes risk, how can air quality and water quality standards be set? When cleaning up a hazardous waste site, at what point is the project completed; that is, how clean is clean? At some point in the cleanup, the remaining health and environmental risks may not justify the continued costs and, from a risk perspective, society might be better off spending the money elsewhere...so policy makers have had to grapple with the tradeoff between acceptable risk and acceptable cost. Complicating those decisions is our very limited understanding of diseases such as cancer coupled with a paucity on the tens of thousands of synthetic chemicals that are in widespread use today. Unfortunately, those who have responsibility for creating and administering environmental regulations have to take action even if definitive answers from the scientific community on the relationship between exposure and risk are not available.

The result has been the emergence of the controversial field of environmental risk assessment. Hardly anyone is comfortable with it. Scientists often deplore the notion of condensing masses of frequently conflicting, highly uncertain, often ambiguous data, which has been extrapolated well beyond anything actually measured, down to a single number or two. Regulatory officials are battered by the public when they propose a level of risk that they think a community living next to a toxic waste site should tolerate. Critics of government spending think risks are being systematically overestimated, resulting in too much money being spent for too little real improvement in public health. Others think risks are underestimated since risk assessments are based on data obtained for exposure to individual chemicals, ignoring the synergistic effects that are likely to occur when we are exposed to thousands of them in our daily lives.

Some of the aforementioned conflicts can best be dealt with if we make the distinction between risk assessment and risk management. *Risk assessment* is the scientific side of the story. It is the gathering of data that are used to relate response to dose. Such dose-response data can then be combined with estimates of likely human exposure to produce overall assessments of risk. *Risk management,* on the other hand, is the process of deciding what to do. It is decision making, under extreme uncertainty, about how to allocate national resources to protect public health and the environment. Enormous political and social judgment is required to make those decisions. Is a one-in-a-million lifetime risk of getting cancer acceptable and, if it is, how do we go about trying to achieve it? . . .

4.4   RISK ASSESSMENT

Our concern is with the probability that exposure of some number of people to some combination of chemicals will cause some amount of response, such as cancer, reproductive failure, neurological damage, developmental problems, or birth defects. That is, we want to begin to develop the notions of risk assessment. The National Academy of Sciences (1983) suggests that risk assessment be divided into the following four steps: Hazard identification, dose-response assessment, exposure assessment, and risk characterization. After a risk assessment has been completed, the important stage of risk management follows, as shown in figure [2.7].

• *Hazard identification* is the process of determining whether or not a particular chemical is causally linked to particular health effects such as cancer or birth defects. Since human data are so often difficult to obtain, this step usually focuses on whether a chemical is toxic in animals or other test organisms.

• *Dose-response assessment* is the process of characterizing the relation between the dose of an agent administered or received and the incidence of an adverse health effect. Many different dose-response relationships are possible for any given agent depending on such conditions as whether the response is carcinogenic (cancer causing) or noncarcinogenic and whether the experiment is a one-time acute test or a long-term chronic test. Since most tests are performed with high doses, the dose-response assessment must include a consideration for the proper method of extrapolating data to low exposure rates that humans are likely to experience. Part of the assessment must also include a method of extrapolating animal data to humans.

• *Exposure assessment* involves determining the size and nature of the population that has been exposed to the toxicant under consideration, and the length of time and toxicant concentration to which they have been

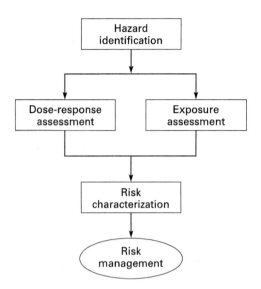

Figure 2.7
Risk assessment is usually considered to be a four-step process, followed by risk management. (Source: G. M. Masters, "Risk Assessment," in *Introduction to Environmental Engineering and Science*, 2nd ed. Prentice Hall, Englewood Cliffs, N.J., 1998.)

exposed. Consideration must be given to such factors as the age and health of the exposed population, smoking history, the likelihood that members of the population might be pregnant, and whether or not synergistic effects might occur due to exposure to multiple toxicants.

• *Risk characterization* is the integration of the above three steps that results in an estimate of the magnitude of the public-health problem.

4.5   HAZARD IDENTIFICATION

The first step in a risk analysis is to determine whether the chemicals that a population has been exposed to are likely to have any adverse health effects. This is the work of toxicologists, who study both the nature of the adverse effects caused by toxic agents as well as the probability of their occurrence. We shall start our description of this hazard identification process by summarizing the path-

ways that a chemical may take as it passes through a human body and the kinds of damage that may result. . . .

A toxicant can enter the body using any of three pathways: by ingestion with food or drink, through inhalation, or by contact with the skin (dermal) or other exterior surfaces, such as the eyes. Once in the body it can be absorbed by the blood and distributed to various organs and systems. The toxicant may then be stored (for example in fat as in the case of DDT), or it may be eliminated from the body by excretion or by transformation into something else. The biotransformation process usually yields metabolites that can be more readily eliminated from the body than the original chemicals; however, metabolism can also convert chemicals to more toxic forms. . . .

There are several organs that are especially vulnerable to toxicants. The liver, for example, which filters the blood before it is pumped through the lungs, is often the target.

Since toxics are transported by the bloodstream, and since the liver is exposed to so much of the blood supply, it can be directly damaged by toxics. Moreover, since a major function of the liver is to metabolize substances, converting them into forms that can more easily be excreted from the body, it is also susceptible to chemical attack by toxic chemicals formed during the biotransformation process itself. Chemicals that can cause liver damage are called *hepatotoxins*. Examples of hepatoxic agents include a number of synthetic organic compounds, such as carbon tetrachloride (CCl_4), chloroform ($CHCl_3$), and trichloroethylene (C_2HCl_3); pesticides such as DDT and paraquat; heavy metals such as arsenic, iron, and manganese; and drugs, such as acetaminophen and anabolic steroids. The kidneys are also responsible for filtering the blood, and they too are frequently susceptible to damage.

Toxic chemicals often injure other organs and organ systems as well. The function of the kidneys is to filter blood to remove wastes that will be excreted in the form of urine. Toxicants that damage the kidneys, called *nephrotoxics*, include metals such as cadmium, mercury, and lead, as well as a number of chlorinated hydrocarbons. Excessive kidney damage can decrease or stop the flow of urine, causing death by poisoning from the body's own waste products. *Hematotoxicity* is the term used to describe the toxic effects of substances on the blood. Some hematotoxins, such as carbon monoxide in polluted air, and nitrates in groundwater, affect the ability of blood to transport oxygen to the tissues. Other toxicants, such as benzene, affect the formation of platelets which are necessary for blood clotting. The lungs and skin, due to their proximity to pollutants, are also often affected by chemical toxicants. Lung function can be impaired by such substances as cigarette smoke, ozone, asbestos, and quartz rock dust. The skin reacts in a variety of ways to chemical toxicants but the most common,

and serious, environmentally related skin problem is cancer induced by excessive ultraviolet radiation....

Mutagenesis

...Deoxyribonucleic acid (DNA) is an essential component of all living things and a basic material in the chromosomes of the cell nucleus. It contains the genetic code that determines the overall character and appearance of every organism. Each molecule of DNA has the ability to replicate itself exactly, transmitting that genetic information to new cells. Our interest here in DNA results from the fact that certain chemical agents, as well as ionizing radiation, are *genotoxic*; that is, they are capable of altering DNA. Such changes, or *mutations*, in the genetic material of an organism can cause cells to malfunction, leading in some cases to cell death, cancer, reproductive failure, or abnormal offspring. Chemicals that are capable of causing cancer are called *carcinogens*; chemicals that can cause birth defects are *teratogens*.

Mutations may affect somatic cells, which are the cells that make up the tissues and organs of the body itself, or they may cause changes in germ cells (sperm or ovum) that may be transmitted to future offspring. As is suggested in figure [2.8], one possible outcome of a mutagenic event in a somatic cell is the death of the cell itself. If the mutation is in a somatic cell and it survives, the change may be such that the cell no longer responds to signals that normally control cell reproduction. If that occurs, the cell may undergo rapid and uncontrolled cellular division, forming a tumor. Mutations in somatic cells may damage or kill the affected individual, and if the individual is a pregnant female, the embryo may be damaged, leading to a birth defect. Germ cell mutations, on the other hand, have the potential to become established in the gene pool and be transmitted to future generations.

Many organs
& functions
affected

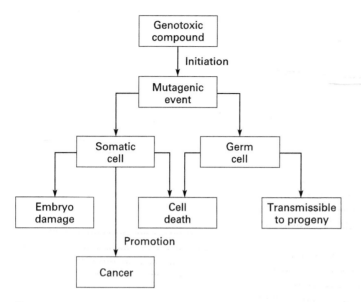

Figure 2.8
Possible consequences of a mutagenic event in somatic and germinal cells. (Source: G. M. Masters, "Risk Assessment," in *Introduction to Environmental Engineering and Science*, 2nd ed. Prentice Hall, Englewood Cliffs, N.J., 1998.)

Carcinogenesis

Cancer is second only to heart disease in terms of the number of Americans killed every year. Every year close to 1 million people are diagnosed with cancer, and over one-half million die each year. Cancer is truly one of the most dreaded diseases.

Chemically induced carcinogenesis is thought to involve two distinct stages, referred to as *initiation* and *promotion*. In the initiation stage, a mutation alters a cell's genetic material in a way that may or may not result in the uncontrolled growth of cells that characterizes cancer. In the second, or promotion, stage of development, affected cells no longer recognize growth constraints that normally apply and a tumor develops. Promoters can increase the incidence rate of tumors among cells that have already undergone initiation, or they can shorten the latency period between initiation and the full

carcinogenic response. The model of initiation followed by promotion suggests that some carcinogens may be initiators, others may be promoters, and some may be complete carcinogens capable of causing both stages to occur. Current regulations do not make this distinction, however, and any substance capable of increasing the incidence of tumors is considered a carcinogen, subject to the same risk assessment techniques. Tumors, in turn, may be *benign* or *malignant* depending on whether or not the tumor is contained within its own boundaries. If a tumor undergoes *metastasis*—that is, it breaks apart and portions of it enter other areas of the body—it is said to be malignant. Once a tumor has metastasized it is obviously much harder to treat or remove.

The theoretical possibility that a single genotoxic event can lead to a tumor is referred to as the *one-hit hypothesis*. Based on this hypothesis, exposure to even the smallest

No threshold for carcinogens (conservative)

amount of a carcinogen leads to some non-zero probability that a malignancy will result. That is, in a conservative, worst-case risk assessment for carcinogens, it is assumed that there is no threshold dose below which the risk is zero....

Toxicity Testing in Animals

With several thousand new chemicals coming onto the market each year, and a backlog of tens of thousands of relatively untested chemicals already in commerce, and a limited number of facilities capable of providing the complex testing that might be desired, it is not possible to fully test each and every chemical for its toxicity. As a result, a hierarchy of testing procedures has been developed that can be used to help select those chemicals that are most likely to pose serious risks....

The prevailing carcinogenesis theory, that human cancers are initiated by gene mutations, has led to the development of short-term, *in vitro* (in glassware) screening procedures, which are one of the first steps taken to determine whether a chemical is carcinogenic. It is thought that if a chemical can be shown to be mutagenic, then it *may* be carcinogenic, and further testing may be called for. The most widely used short-term test, called the *Ames mutagenicity assay*, subjects special tester strains of bacteria to the chemical in question. These tester strains have previously been rendered incapable of normal bacterial division [in the absence of specific nutrients], so unless they mutate back to a form that is capable of growth and division, they will die [if grown in medium that lacks the nutrients they require]. Bacteria that survive and form colonies do so through mutation [which restores their ability to grow in deficient media]; therefore, the greater the survival rate of these special bacteria, the more mutagenic is the chemical.

Intermediate testing procedures involve relatively short-term (several months' duration)

carcinogenesis bioassays in which specific organs in mice and rats are subjected to known mutagens to determine whether tumors develop.

Finally, the most costly, complex, and long-lasting test, called a *chronic carcinogenesis bioassay*, involves hundreds...of animals over a time period of several years. To assure comparable test results and verifiable data, the National Toxicology Program in the United States has established minimum test requirements for an acceptable chronic bioassay which include:

• *Two species of rodents must be tested.* Mice and rats, using specially inbred strains for consistency, are most often used. They have relatively short lifetimes and their small size makes them easier to test in large numbers.

• *At least 50 males and 50 females of each species for each dose must be tested.* Many more animals are required if the test is to be sensitive enough to detect risks of less than a few percent.

• *At least two doses must be administered (plus a no-dose control).* One dose is traditionally set at the maximum tolerated dose (MTD), a level that can be administered for a major portion of an animal's lifetime without significantly impairing growth or shortening the lifetime. The second dose is usually one-half or one-fourth the MTD.

Exposure begins at 6 weeks of age, and ends when the animal reaches 24 months of age. At the end of the test, all animals are killed and their remains are subjected to detailed pathological examinations. These tests are expensive as well as time consuming. Testing a typical new chemical costs between $500,000 and $1.5 million, takes up to two or three years, and may entail the sacrifice of [a great number] of animals....

Notice that, following the aforementioned protocol, the minimum number of animals required for a bioassay is 600 (2 species × 100 animals × 3 doses), and at that number it is

in vitro nage for carcin...

still only relatively high risks that can be detected. With this number of animals, for the test to show a statistically significant effect, the exposed animals must have at least 5 or 10 percent more tumors than the controls in order to conclude that the extra tumors were caused by the chemical being tested. That is, the risk associated with this chemical can be measured only down to roughly 0.05 or 0.10 unless we test a lot more animals.

A simple example may help clarify this statistical phenomenon. Suppose we test 100 rats at a particular dose and find one tumor. To keep it easy, let's say the control group never gets tumors. Can the actual probability (risk) of tumors caused by this chemical at this dose be 1 percent? Yes, definitely. If the risk is 1 percent we would expect to get one tumor, and that is what we got. Could the actual probability be 2 percent? Well, if the actual risk is 2 percent, and *if we were able to run the test over and over again* on sets of 100 rats each, some of those groups would have no tumors, some would certainly have one tumor and some would have more. So our actual test of only one group of 100, which found one tumor, is not at all inconsistent with an actual risk of 2 percent. Could the actual risk be 3 percent? Running many sets of 100 rats through the test would likely result in at least one of those groups having only one tumor. So it would not be out of the question to find one tumor in a single group of 100 rats even if the actual risk is 3 percent. Getting back to the original test of 100 rats and finding one tumor, we have just argued that the actual risk could be anything from 0 percent to 2 or 3 percent, maybe even more, and still be consistent with finding just one tumor. We certainly cannot conclude that the risk is only 1 percent. In other words, with 100 animals we cannot perform a statistically significant test and be justified in concluding that the risk is anything less than a few percent. Bioassays designed to detect lower risks require many thousands of animals. In fact, the largest experiment ever performed involved over 24,000 mice and yet was still insufficiently sensitive to measure a risk of less than 1 percent (Environ, 1988).

The inability of a bioassay to detect small risks presents one of the greatest difficulties in applying the data so obtained to human risk assessment. Regulators try to restrict human risks due to exposure to carcinogens to levels of about 10^{-6} (one in a million), yet animal studies are only capable of detecting risks of down to 0.01 to 0.1. It is necessary, therefore, to find some way to extrapolate the data taken for animals exposed to high doses to humans who will be exposed to doses that are at least several orders of magnitude lower.

Human Studies

Another shortcoming in the animal testing methods just described, besides the necessity to extrapolate the data toward zero risk, is the obvious difficulty in interpreting the data for humans. [*Some prefer to refer to this as an interpolation rather than an extrapolation, because the point of zero excess risk for zero excess exposure is required. One is therefore interpolating between the high dose data points and the required zero zero point.*] How does the fact that some substance causes tumors in mice relate to the likelihood that it will cause cancer in humans as well? Animal testing can always be criticized in this way, but since we are not inclined to perform the same sorts of tests directly on humans, other methods must be used to gather evidence of human toxicity. [*Such tests can include measurements of genetic toxicity in humans (e.g., chromosome breakage and somatic mutation assays) or human cells cultured in vitro.*]

Sometimes human data can be obtained by studying victims of tragedies, such as the chemical plant explosion that killed and injured thousands in Bhopal, India, and the atomic bombing of Hiroshima and Nagasaki, Japan. The most important source of human risk information, however, comes from epidemiological studies. Epidemiology is the study of the incidence rate of diseases in real populations. By attempting to find correlations between disease rates and various environmental factors, an epidemiologist attempts to show in a quantitative way the relationship between exposure and risk. Such data can be used to complement animal data, clinical data, and scientific analyses of the characteristics of the substances in question. . . .

Caution must be exercised in interpreting every epidemiologic study, since any number of confounding variables may lead to invalid conclusions [as well as chance statistical fluctuations in the occurrence of particular cancers in particular groups of people]. For example, the study may be biased because workers are compared with nonworkers (workers are generally healthier) [and have lower incidences of mortality and morbidity], or because relative rates of smoking have not been accounted for, or there may be other variables that are not even hypothesized in the study that may be the actual causal agent. As an example of the latter, consider an attempt to compare lung cancer rates in a city having high ambient air pollution levels with rates in a city having less pollution. Suppose the rates are higher in the more polluted city, even after accounting for smoking history, age distribution, and working background. To conclude that ambient air pollution is causing those differences may be totally invalid. Instead, it might well be different levels of radon in homes, or differences in other indoor air pollutants associated with the type of fuel used for cooking and heating, that are causing the cancer variations.

Weight-of-Evidence Categories for Potential Carcinogens

Based on the accumulated evidence from case studies, epidemiologic studies, and animal data, the EPA uses [five] categories to describe the likelihood that a chemical substance is carcinogenic (USEPA, 1986a).

[The categories and criteria for classifying substances as carcinogens were revised in 2005. See http://cfpub.epa.gov/ncea/raf/ recordisplay.cfm?deid=116283. Based on human and animal data, structure activity relationships, and short-term in vitro testing, the five revised categories are:

- carcinogenic to humans
- likely to be carcinogenic to humans
- suggestive evidence of carcinogenic potential
- inadequate information to assess carcinogenic potential
- not likely to be carcinogenic to humans. The full characterization is reproduced in the notes following this reading.]

4.6 DOSE-RESPONSE ASSESSMENT

As the name suggests, the fundamental goal of a dose-response assessment is to obtain a mathematical relationship between the amount of a toxicant to which a human is exposed and the risk that there will be an unhealthy response to that dose. We have seen dose-response curves for acute toxicity, in which the dose is measured in milligrams per kilogram of body weight. The dose-response curves that we are interested in here are the result of chronic toxicity; that is, the organism is subjected to a prolonged exposure over a considerable fraction of its life. For these curves the abscissa is dose, which is usually expressed as the average milligrams of substance per kilogram of body weight per day (mg/kg/day). The dose is an exposure averaged over an entire lifetime (for humans, assumed to be 70 years). The ordinate is the response, which is the risk that there will be some adverse health effect. As usual, response (risk) has no units; it is a probability that there will be some adverse health effect. For example, if prolonged exposure to some chemical would be expected to produce 700 cancers in a population of 1 million, the

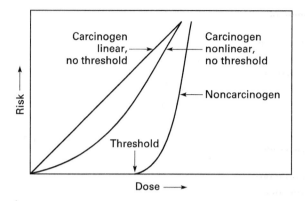

Figure 2.9

Dose-response curves for carcinogens are assumed to have no threshold; that is, any exposure produces some chance of causing cancer. (Source: G. M. Masters, "Risk Assessment," in *Introduction to Environmental Engineering and Science*, 2nd ed. Prentice Hall, Englewood Cliffs, N.J., 1998.)

response could be expressed as 0.0007×10^{-4}, or 0.07 percent. The annual risk would be obtained by spreading that risk over an assumed 70-year lifetime, giving a risk of 0.00001 or 1×10^{-5} per year.

For substances that induce a carcinogenic response [by a putative mutagenic mode of action], it is always conventional practice to assume that exposure to any amount of the carcinogen will create some likelihood of cancer. That is, a plot of response versus dose is required to go through the origin. For noncarcinogenic responses, it is usually assumed that there is some *threshold dose*, below which there will be no response. As a result of these two assumptions, the dose-response curves and the methods used to apply them [can be] quite different for carcinogenic and noncarcinogenic effects, as suggested in figure [2.9]. The same chemical, by the way, may be capable of causing both kinds of response.

To apply dose-response data obtained from animal bioassays to humans, a *scaling factor* must be introduced. Sometimes the scaling factor is based on the assumption that doses are equivalent if the dose per unit of body weight in the animal and human is the same.

Sometimes, if the exposure is dermal, equivalent doses are normalized to body surface area rather than body weight when scaling up from animal to human. [*EPA's 2005 guidance calls for equating doses across species on a mg/kg body weight basis. This is the scaling factor for metabolism and is the base case for scaling of drug and chemical clearance processes.*] In either case, the resulting human dose-response curve is specified with the standard mg/kg/day units for dose. Adjustments between animal response and human response may also have to be made to account for differences in the rates of chemical absorption. If enough is known about the differences between the absorption rates in test animals and in humans for the particular substance in question, it is possible to account for those differences later in the risk assessment. Usually though, there [are] insufficient data and it is simply assumed that the absorption rates are the same.

Extrapolations from High Doses to Low Doses

The most controversial aspect of dose-response curves for carcinogens is the method

[Handwritten margin note at top: "For #Q no agreed upon method to extrapolate high dose animal studies to low dose chronic exposure. No way to know which is most accurate"]

chosen to extrapolate from the high doses actually administered to test animals to the low doses to which humans are likely to be exposed. Recall that even with extremely large numbers of animals in a bioassay, the lowest risks that can be measured are usually a few percent. Since regulators attempt to control human risk to several orders of magnitude less than that, there will be no actual animal data anywhere near the range of most interest.

Many mathematical models have been proposed for the extrapolation to low doses. Unfortunately, no model can be proved or disproved from the data, so there is no way to know which model is the most accurate. That means the choice of models is strictly a policy decision. . . .

To protect public health, [in the past] the EPA [chose] to err on the side of safety and overemphasize risk, [using] a modified multistage model, called the *linear multistage model* [Crump, 1984]. It is linear at low doses with the constant of proportionality picked in a way that statistically will produce less than a 5% chance of underestimating risk. [Crump's linearized multistage model, which was the default under the 1986 guidance, has been replaced in the 2005 guidance by a procedure under which models of different forms are used to estimate the lower confidence limit on a dose that causes a 10% excess risk, followed by a linear interpolation of risk between that dose and a zero dose.]

Potency Factor for Carcinogens

For chronic toxicity studies, a low dose is administered over a significant portion of the animal's lifetime. The resulting dose-response curve has the incremental risk of cancer (above the background rate) on the y-axis, and the lifetime average daily dose of toxicant along the x-axis. At low doses, where the dose-response curve is assumed to be linear, the slope of the dose-response curve is called the *potency factor* (PF), or *slope factor*.

$$\text{Potency factor} = \text{Incremental lifetime cancer risk} / \text{Chronic daily intake (mg/kg-day)} \quad (4.11)$$

The denominator in (4.11) is the dose averaged over an entire lifetime; it has units of average milligrams of toxicant absorbed per kilogram of body weight per day, which is usually written as (mg/kg-day) or (mg/kg/day). Since risk has no units, the units for potency factor are therefore (mg/kg-day)$^{-1}$.

If we have a dose-response curve, we can find the potency factor from the slope. In fact, one interpretation of the potency factor is that it is the risk produced by a chronic daily intake of 1 mg/kg-day, as shown in figure [2.10].

Rearranging (4.11) shows us where we are headed. If we know the chronic daily intake CDI (based on exposure data) and the potency factor (from EPA), we can find the lifetime, incremental risk from

$$\text{Incremental lifetime cancer risk} = \text{CDI} \times \text{Potency factor} \quad (4.12)$$

The linearized multistage risk-response model assumptions built into (4.12) should make this value an upper-bound estimate of the actual risk. Moreover, (4.12) estimates the risk of getting cancer, which is not necessarily the same as the risk of dying of cancer, so it should be even more conservative as an upper-bound estimate of cancer death rates. . . .

The other factor we need to develop more fully in order to use the basic risk equation (4.12) is the concept of chronic daily intake. The CDI is, by definition,

$$\text{CDI (mg/kg-day)} = \text{Average daily dose (mg/day)} / \text{Body weight (kg)} \quad (4.13)$$

The numerator in (4.13) is the total lifetime dose average over an assumed 70-year lifetime. . . .

[It should be understood that the upper confidence limit takes into account only some usually minor statistical sampling error

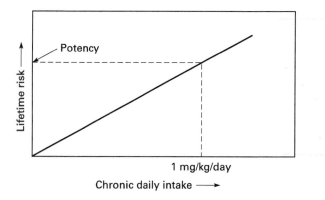

Figure 2.10
The potency factor is the slope of the dose-response curve. It can also be thought of as the risk that corresponds to a chronic daily intake of 1 mg/kg-day. (Source: G. M. Masters, "Risk Assessment," in *Introduction to Environmental Engineering and Science*, 2nd ed. Prentice Hall, Englewood Cliffs, N.J., 1998.)

sources of uncertainty in fitting the animal cancer bioassay data—not the larger uncertainties involved in the shape of the basic dose-response relationship, interspecies projection, and other considerations such as the extent of human interindividual variability.]

The Reference Dose for Noncarcinogenic Effects

The key assumption for noncarcinogens is that there is an exposure threshold: that is, any exposure less than the threshold would be expected to show no increase in adverse effects above natural background rates. One of the principal goals of toxicant testing is therefore to identify and quantify such thresholds. Unfortunately, for the usual case, inadequate data are available to establish such thresholds with any degree of certainty and, as a result, it has been necessary to introduce a number of special assumptions and definitions.

Suppose there exists a precise threshold for some particular toxicant for some particular animal species. To determine the threshold experimentally, one might imagine a testing program in which animals would be exposed to a range of doses. Doses below the threshold would elicit no response: doses above

the threshold would produce responses. The lowest dose administered that results in a response is given a special name: *the lowest-observed-effect level* (LOEL). Conversely, the highest dose administered that does not create a response is called the *no-observed-effect level* (NOEL). NOELs and LOELs are often further refined by noting a distinction between effects that are [considered] *adverse* to health and effects that are not. Thus, there are also *no-observed-adverse-effect levels* (NOAELs) and *lowest-observed-adverse-effect levels* (LOAELs).

Figure [2.11] illustrates these levels and introduces another exposure called the *reference dose*, or RfD. The RfD [is sometimes] called the *acceptable daily intake* (ADI) and, as that name implies, it is intended to give an indication of a level of human exposure that is likely to be without appreciable risk. The units of RfD are mg/kg-day averaged over a lifetime [just as they were for the CDI]. The RfD is obtained by dividing the NOAEL by an appropriate *uncertainty factor* (sometimes called a safety factor). A 10-fold uncertainty factor is used to account for differences in sensitivity between the most sensitive individuals in an exposed human population, such as pregnant women, babies, and the elderly,

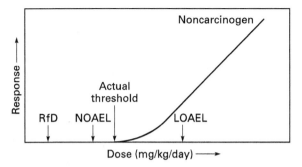

Figure 2.11
The reference dose (RfD) is the no-observed-adverse-effects-level (NOAEL) divided by an uncertainty factor typically between 10 and 1000. (Source: G. M. Masters, "Risk Assessment," in *Introduction to Environmental Engineering and Science*, 2nd ed. Prentice Hall, Englewood Cliffs, N.J., 1998.)

and "normal, healthy" people. Another factor of 10 is introduced when the NOAEL is based on animal data that are to be extrapolated to humans. And finally, other factors of 10 [or 3, up to a maximum overall factor of 3000, are sometimes introduced] when there are no good human data and the animal data bases available are limited [e.g., of less duration than a full lifetime exposure-effect study; missing studies of reproductive or developmental endpoints; or the study did not establish a NOAEL, that is, the lowest dose tested still induced effects considered "adverse"]. Thus, depending on the strength of the available data, human RfD levels are established at doses that are anywhere from one-tenth to one [three-]thousandth of the [NOAEL], which itself is [intended to be] somewhat below the actual threshold [for inducing a statistically significant excess of observed adverse effects in the limited groups of animals tested]. Table [2.2] gives a short list of some commonly encountered toxicants and their RfDs.

The Hazard Index for Noncarcinogenic Effects

Since the reference dose RfD is established at what is intended to be a safe level, well below the level at which any adverse health effects have been observed, it makes sense to compare the actual exposure to the RfD to see whether the actual dose is supposedly safe. The hazard quotient is based on that concept:

$$\text{Hazard quotient} = \text{Average daily dose during exposure period (mg/kg-day)} / \text{RfD} \quad (4.16)$$

Notice that the daily dose is averaged only over the period of exposure, which is different from the average daily dose used in risk calculations for carcinogens. For noncarcinogens, the toxicity is important only during the time of exposure. Recall that for a cancer risk calculation (e.g., Eq. 4.13) the dose is averaged over an assumed 70-year lifetime.

The hazard quotient has been defined so that if it is less than 1.0, there should be no significant risk of systemic toxicity. Ratios above 1.0 could represent a potential risk, but there is no way to establish that risk with any certainty.

When exposure involves more than one chemical, the sum of the individual hazard quotients for each chemical is used as a measure of the potential for harm. This sum is called the *hazard index*:

$$\text{Hazard index} = \text{Sum of the hazard quotients} \quad (4.17)$$

Table 2.2
Oral RfDs for Chronic Noncarcinogenic Effects of Selected Chemicals

Chemical	RfD (mg/kg/day)
Acetone	0.100
Arsenic	0.0003
Cadmium	0.0005
Chloroform	0.010
1,1-Dichloroethylene	0.009
cis-1,2-Dichloroethylene	0.010
Fluoride	0.120
Mercury (inorganic)	0.0003
Methylene chloride	0.060
Phenol	0.600
Tetrachloroethylene	0.010
Toluene	0.200
1,1,1-Trichloroethane	0.035
Xylene	2.000

Source: U.S. EPA. http://www.epa.gov/iris.

4.7 HUMAN EXPOSURE ASSESSMENT

One of the most elementary concepts of risk assessment is one that is all too often overlooked in public discussions: that risk has two components—the toxicity of the substance involved, and the amount of exposure to that substance. Unless individuals are exposed to the toxicants, there is no human risk.

A human exposure assessment is itself a two-part process. First, pathways that allow toxic agents to be transported from the source to the point of contact with people must be evaluated. Second, an estimate must be made of the amount of contact that is likely to occur between people and those contaminants.... Substances that are exposed to the atmosphere may volatilize and be transported with the prevailing winds.... Substances in contact with soil may leach into groundwater and eventually be transported to local drinking water wells.... As pollutants are transported from one place to another, they may undergo various transformations that can change their toxicity and/or concentration.... A useful summary of exposure pathway models that the EPA uses is given in the Superfund Exposure Assessment Manual (USEPA, 1988).

Once the exposure pathways have been analyzed, an estimate of the concentrations of toxicants in the air, water, soil, and food at a particular exposure point can be made. With the concentrations of various toxic agents established, the second half of an exposure assessment begins. Human contact with those contaminants must be estimated. Necessary information includes numbers of people exposed, duration of exposure, and amounts of contaminated air, water, food, and soil that find their way into each exposed person's body. Often, the human intake estimates are based on a lifetime of exposure, assuming standard, recommended daily values of amounts of air breathed, water consumed, and body weight.... In some circumstances, the exposure may be intermittent and adjustments might need to be made for various body weights, rates of absorption, and exposure periods....

4.8   RISK CHARACTERIZATION

The final step in a risk assessment is to bring the various studies together into an overall risk characterization. In its most primitive sense, this step could be interpreted to mean simply multiplying the exposure (dose) by the potency to get individual risk, and then multiplying that by the number of people exposed to get an estimate of overall risk to some specific population.

While there are obvious advantages to presenting a simple, single number for extra cancers, or some other risk measure, a proper characterization of risk should be much more comprehensive. The final expressions of risk derived in this step will be used by regulatory decision makers in the process of weighing health risks against other societal costs and benefits, and the public will use them to help them decide on the adequacy of proposed measures to manage the risks. Both groups need to appreciate the extraordinary "leaps of faith" that, by necessity, have had to be used to determine these simple quantitative estimates. It must always be emphasized that these estimates are preliminary, subject to change, and extremely uncertain.

The National Academy of Sciences (1983) suggests a number of questions that should be addressed in a final characterization of risk, including the following:

• What are the statistical uncertainties in estimating the extent of health effects? How are these uncertainties to be computed and presented?
• What are the biological uncertainties? What are their origins? How will they be estimated? What effect do they have on quantitative estimates? How will the uncertainties be described to agency decision-makers?
• Which dose-response assessments and exposure assessments should be used?
• Which population groups should be the primary targets for protection, and which provide the most meaningful expression of the health risk? . . .

4.9   COMPARATIVE RISK ANALYSIS

In 1987, the EPA released a report entitled *Unfinished Business: A Comparative Assessment of Environmental Problems* (USEPA, 1987), in which the concepts of risk assessment were applied to a variety of pressing environmental problems. The goal of the study was to attempt to use risk as a policy tool for ranking major environmental problems in order to help the agency establish broad, long-term priorities.

At the outset it was realized that direct comparisons of different environmental problems would be next to impossible. Not only are the data usually insufficient to quantify risks, but the kinds of risk associated with some problems, such as global warming, are virtually incomparable with risks of others, such as hazardous waste. In most cases, considerable professional judgment rather than hard data was required to finalize the EPA's rankings. In spite of difficulties such as these, the report is noteworthy in terms of both its methodology and its conclusions.

The study was organized around a list of 31 environmental problems, including topics as diverse as conventional (criteria) air pollutants, indoor radon, stratospheric ozone depletion, global warming, active hazardous waste sites regulated by the Resource Conservation and Recovery Act (RCRA), and inactive (Superfund) hazardous waste sites, damage to wetlands, mining wastes, and pesticide residues on foods. Each of these 31 problems was analyzed in terms of four different types of risk: cancer risks, noncancer health risks, ecological effects, and welfare effects (visibility impairment, materials damage, etc.). In each assessment, it was assumed that existing environmental control programs continue so that the results represent risks as they exist now, rather than what they would have been had abatement programs not already been in place.

The ranking of cancer risks was perhaps the most straightforward part of the study since the EPA already has established risk assessment procedures and there are considerable data already available from which to work. Rankings were based primarily on overall cancer risk to the entire U.S. population, though high risks to specific groups of individuals, such as farm workers, were noted. A number of caveats were emphasized in the final rankings on such issues as lack of complete data, uneven quality of data, and the usual uncertainties in any risk assessment that arise from such factors as interspecies comparisons, adequacy of the low-dose extrapolation model, and estimations of exposures. Ordinal rankings were given, but it was emphasized that these should not be interpreted as being precise, especially when similarly ranked problems are being compared.

Given all of the uncertainties, in the cancer working group's final judgment two problems were tied at the top of the list: (1) worker exposure to chemicals which does not involve a large number of individuals, but does result in high individual risks to those exposed; and (2) indoor radon exposure, which is causing considerable risk to a large number of people. Inactive (Superfund) hazardous waste sites ranked eighth and active (RCRA) hazardous waste sites were thirteenth. Interestingly, it was noted that with the exception of pesticide residues on food, the major route of exposure for carcinogens is inhalation. Their ranking of carcinogenic risks is reproduced in table [2.3].

The other working groups had considerably greater difficulty ranking the 31 environmental problem areas since there are no accepted guidelines for quantitatively assessing relative risks. As noted in *Unfinished Business*, a perusal of the rankings of the 31 problem areas for each of the four types of risk (cancer and noncancer health effects, ecological, and welfare effects) produced the following general results:

• No problems rank relatively high in all four types of risk, or relatively low in all four.

• Problems that rank relatively high in three of the four risk types, or at least medium in all four, include criteria air pollutants; stratospheric ozone depletion; pesticide residues on food; and other pesticide risks (runoff and air deposition of pesticides).
• Problems that rank relatively high in cancer and noncancer health risks but low in ecological and welfare risks include hazardous air pollutants; indoor radon; indoor air pollution other than radon; pesticide application; exposure to consumer products; and worker exposures to chemicals.
• Problems that rank relatively high in ecological and welfare risks, but low in both health risks, include global warming; point and nonpoint sources of surface water pollution; physical alteration of aquatic habitats (including estuaries and wetlands), and mining wastes.
• Areas related to groundwater consistently rank medium or low.

In spite of the great uncertainties involved in making their assessments, the divergence between EPA effort in the 1980s and relative risks is noteworthy. As concluded in the study, areas of relatively high risk but low EPA effort include indoor radon; indoor air pollution; stratospheric ozone depletion; global warming; nonpoint sources; discharges to estuaries, coastal waters, and oceans; other pesticide risks; accidental releases of toxics; consumer products; and worker exposures. Areas of high EPA effort but relatively medium or low risks include RCRA sites, Superfund sites, underground storage tanks, and municipal nonhazardous waste sites.

The *Unfinished Business* report was the first major example of what has come to be known as *comparative risk analysis*. Comparative risk analysis differs from conventional risk assessment since its purpose is not to establish absolute values of risk, but rather to provide a process for ranking environmental problems by their seriousness. A subsequent 1990 report, *Reducing Risks*, by EPA's Science Advisory Board, recommended that

Table 2.3
Consensus Ranking of Environmental Problem Areas on Basis of Population Cancer Risk

Rank	Problem area*	Selected Comments
1 (tied)	Worker exposure to chemicals	About 250 cancer cases per year estimated based on exposure to 4 chemicals; but workers face potential exposures to over 20,000 substances. Very high individual risk possible.
1 (tied)	Indoor radon	Estimated 5,000–20,000 lung cancers annually from exposure in homes.
3	Pesticide residues on foods	Estimated 6,000 cancers annually, based on exposure to 200 potential oncogenes.
4 (tied)	Indoor air pollutants (nonradon)	Estimated 3,500–6,500 cancers annually, mostly due to tobacco smoke.
4 (tied)	Consumer exposure to chemicals	Risk from 4 chemicals investigated is about 100–135 cancers annually: an estimated 10,000 chemicals in consumer products. Cleaning fluids, pesticides, particleboard, and asbestos-containing products especially noted.
6	Hazardous/toxic air pollutants	Estimated 2,000 cancers annually based on an assessment of 20 substances.
7	Depletion of stratospheric ozone	Ozone depletion projected to result in 10,000 additional annual deaths in the year 2100. Not ranked higher because of the uncertainties in the future risk.
8	Hazardous waste sites, inactive	Cancer incidence of 1,000 annually from 6 chemicals assessed. Considerable uncertainty since risk based on extrapolation from 35 sites to about 25,000 sites.
9	Drinking water	Estimated 400–1,000 annual cancers, mostly from radon and trihalomethanes.
10	Application of pesticides	Approximately 100 cancers annually; small population exposed but high individual risks.
11	Radiation other than radon	Estimated 360 cancers per year. Mostly from building materials. Medical exposure and natural background levels not included.
12	Other pesticide risks	Consumer and professional exterminator uses estimated cancers of 150 annually. Poor data.
13	Hazardous waste sites, active	Probably fewer than 100 cancers annually: estimates sensitive to assumptions regarding proximity of future wells to waste sites.
14	Nonhazardous waste sites, industrial	No real analysis done, ranking based on consensus of professional opinion.
15	New toxic chemicals	Difficult to assess: done by consensus.
16	Nonhazardous waste sites, municipal	Estimated 40 cancers annually, not including municipal surface impoundments.
17	Contaminated sludge	Preliminary results estimate 40 cancers annually, mostly from incineration and landfilling.
18	Mining waste	Estimated 10–20 cancers annually, largely due to arsenic. Remote locations and small population exposure reduce overall risk though individual risk may be high.
19	Releases from storage tanks	Preliminary analysis, based on benzene, indicates lower cancer incidence (<1)

Table 2.3
(continued)

Rank	Problem area*	Selected Comments
20	Nonpoint source discharges to surface water	No quantitative analysis available: judgment.
21	Other groundwater contamination	Lack of information: individual risks considered less than 10^{-6}, with rough estimate of total population risk at <1.
22	Criteria air pollutants	Excluding carcinogenic particles and VOCs (included under hazardous/toxic air pollutants): ranked low because remaining criteria pollutants have not been shown to be carcinogens.
23	Direct point-source discharges to surface water	No quantitative assessment available. Only ingestion of contaminated seafood was considered.
24	Indirect point-source discharges to surface water	Same as above.
25	Accidental releases, toxics	Short-duration exposure yields low cancer risk: noncancer health effects of much greater concern.
26	Accidental releases, oil spills	See above. Greater concern for welfare and ecological effects.

*Not ranked: Biotechnology: global warming; other air pollutants; discharges to estuaries, coastal waters and oceans; discharges to wetlands.
Source: Based on data from *Unfinished Business: A Comparative Assessment of Environmental Problems*, 1987b, Office of Policy, Planning and Evaluation, EPA/230/2-87/025 WDC.

the EPA reorder its priorities on the basis of reducing the most serious risks. The combination of these two reports has had considerable influence on the way that the EPA perceives its role in environmental protection. EPA's Office of Research and Development (U.S. EPA, 1996) has incorporated these recommendations in setting forth its strategic principles, which include the following:

• Focus research and development on the greatest risks to people and the environment, taking into account their potential severity, magnitude and uncertainty.
• Focus research on reducing uncertainty in risk assessment and on cost-effective approaches for preventing and managing risks.
• Balance human health and ecological research.

Based on those strategic principles, the EPA [in 1996] defined its six highest-priority research topics for the next few years (U.S. EPA, 1996):

• *Drinking water disinfection* Some microorganisms, especially the protozoan *Cryptosporidium*, are able to survive conventional disinfection processes, and some carcinogens, such as chloroform, are created during chlorination of drinking water. Questions to be addressed include the comparative risk between waterborne microbial disease and the disinfection byproducts formed during drinking water disinfection.
• *Particulate matter* Inhalation of particulate matter in the atmosphere poses a high potential human health risk. The relationship between morbidity/mortality and low ambient levels of particulate matter, and cost-effective methods to reduce particulate matter emissions, are principal areas of interest.
• *Endocrine disruptors* Declines in the quality and quantity of human sperm production and increased incidence of certain cancers that may have an endocrine-related basis form the basis of concern for this high-priority research topic.

• *Improved ecosystem risk assessment* Understanding the impacts of human activities on ecosystems has not developed as rapidly as human health impacts. Topics such as forest decline, toxic microorganisms in estuaries, reproductive failure of wildlife, and the reappearance of vectorborne epidemic diseases need to be addressed.

• *Improved health risk assessment* Continued focus on reducing the uncertainty in the source-exposure-dose relationship, including the impacts of mixtures of chemical insults, is needed.

• *Pollution prevention and new technologies* Avoiding the creation of environmental problems is the most cost-effective risk-management strategy, but it is not clear how best to integrate pollution prevention into government and private-sector decision making.

REFERENCES

Crump, K. S., 1984, An improved procedure for low-dose carcinogenic risk assessment from animal data. *Journal of Environmental Pathology. Toxicology, and Oncology* 5(4/5): 339–349.

Environ, 1988, *Elements of Toxicology and Chemical Risk Assessment*, Environ Corporation, Washington, DC.

National Academy of Sciences, 1983, *Risk Assessment in the Federal Government: Managing the Process*, National Academy Press, Washington, DC.

USEPA, 1986a, *Guidelines for Carcinogen Risk Assessment*, Federal Register, Vol. 51, No. 185, pp. 33 992–34 003, September 24, 1986.

USEPA, 1987, *Unfinished Business: A Comparative Assessment of Environmental Problems*, Office of Policy, Planning and Evaluation, EPA/230/2-87/025, Washington, DC.

USEPA, 1988, *Superfund Exposure Assessment Manual*, Environmental Protection Agency, Office of Remedial Response, EPA/540/1-88/001, Washington, DC.

USEPA, 1996, *Strategic Plan for the Office of Research and Development*, United States Environmental Protection Agency Research and Development (8101) EPA/600/R-96/059 Office of Research and Development http://www.epa.gov/OSP/strtplan/documents/ord96strplan.pdf

■ NOTES

1. The preceding discussion of dose assumes a more-or-less *continuous* dose over a lifetime (in the case of animals or citizens) or a working lifetime (40 hours per week in the case of exposed workers). The reference dose (RfD), determined in figure 2.11, represents a safe level of continuous exposure. As previously noted, exposures can be one-time, intermittent (with no regularity), periodic, or continuous. Especially in the case of workers (or even consumers) subject to a short period of very high exposure—which could come, for example, from a chemical spill, from cleaning a chemical reactor vessel or handling hazardous waste, or from the use of a toxic product for a short task—safe levels (reference doses) are also often determined for short exposure times. These are expressed as short-term exposure limits (STELs). The dose-response curve for a high short-term exposure may have a different slope and threshold than the dose-response curve for a continuous exposure (such as the ones depicted in figure 2.3). Thus, exposure of a group of animals to 25 ppm of vinyl chloride for 15 minutes will cause more cancer among those animals than will the same dose spread

out over an 8-hour period. Similarly, the practice of rotating workers in and out of a particular workplace to limit their time of exposure may also lead to a higher incidence of disease among those workers if the effect of the rotation is to expose the workers to higher doses over shorter periods of time. (See the previous discussion of worker rotation in note 4 on page 60.)

2. Note the following cautionary statement from the risk assessment discussion excerpted earlier: "Many mathematical models have been proposed for the extrapolation to low doses. Unfortunately, no model can be proved or disproved from the data, so there is no way to know which model is the most accurate. That means the choice of models is strictly a policy decision." While it is true that scientific uncertainty can mean that policy considerations must necessarily enter into the choice of the model, this is not always the case. When there is evidence supporting one theory of the underlying *mechanism* of biological damage over another theory, the simple mathematical "best fit" of the data to alternative models should not dominate the risk assessment exercise. For a detailed discussion of this point, see D. Hattis and A. Smith (1986) "What's Wrong with Quantitative Risk Assessment?" in *Biomedical Ethics Reviews*, R. Almeder and J. Humber (eds.), Humana Press, Totowa, N.J., pp. 57–105 (ISBN 0742-1796).

3. There has been a great effort in recent years to "harmonize" methods for cancer and noncancer effects. Unfortunately, the thrust of such efforts has often been to make the cancer analysis look more like the noncancer analysis, where it can then be argued that there is likely to be a nonmutagenic mode of action.[11] An alternative approach is to "harmonize" methods by making the noncancer risk analysis more quantitative, albeit by utilizing a basic probit (lognormal tolerance distribution) assumption for the population dose-response relationship. For details, see D. Hattis (2001) "We Can Move Beyond the Rigidity of Single-Point 'Uncertainty' Factors," *Risk Policy Report* pp. 31–33, September 18; and D. Hattis, S. Baird, and R. Goble (2002) "A Straw Man Proposal for a Quantitative Definition of the RfD," in *Human Variability in Parameters Potentially Related to Susceptibility for Noncancer Risks*. Final Technical Report, U.S. Environmental Protection Agency STAR grant R825360. US.EPA, Washington, D.C. Full version available on the web at http://www2.clarku.edu/faculty/dhattis; a shortened version is in *Drug and Chemical Toxicology* vol. 25, pp. 403–436.

---

11. A nongenotoxic carcinogen acts through a metabolic pathway and only when that pathway is saturated is a second pathway started. It is this second pathway that produces the putative carcinogen. It is through mechanistic studies that this is determined. The "threshold" would be taken as the level of the chemical that is metabolized through the first (nongenotoxic) pathway. Not many chemicals have been investigated to the extent necessary to make these determinations, but for those that have been, the data support a nongenotoxic mechanism below the threshold level.

4. EPA's 2005 guidance for determining when a substance will be considered a carcinogen (http://cfpub.epa.gov/ncea/cfm/recordisplay.cfm?deid=116283) is reproduced here:

"Carcinogenic to Humans"
This descriptor indicates strong evidence of human carcinogenicity. It covers different combinations of evidence.

• This descriptor is appropriate when there is convincing epidemiologic evidence of a causal association between human exposure and cancer.
• Exceptionally, this descriptor may be equally appropriate with a lesser weight of epidemiologic evidence that is strengthened by other lines of evidence. It can be used when all of the following conditions are met: (a) there is strong evidence of an association between human exposure and either cancer or the key precursor events of the agent's mode of action but not enough for a causal association, and (b) there is extensive evidence of carcinogenicity in animals, and (c) the mode(s) of carcinogenic action and associated key precursor events have been identified in animals, and (d) there is strong evidence that the key precursor events that precede the cancer response in animals are anticipated to occur in humans and progress to tumors, based on available biological information. In this case, the narrative includes a summary of both the experimental and epidemiologic information on mode of action and also an indication of the relative weight that each source of information carries, e.g., based on human information, based on limited human and extensive animal experiments.

"Likely to Be Carcinogenic to Humans"
This descriptor is appropriate when the weight of the evidence is adequate to demonstrate carcinogenic potential to humans but does not reach the weight of evidence for the descriptor "Carcinogenic to Humans." Adequate evidence consistent with this descriptor covers a broad spectrum. As stated previously, the use of the term "likely" as a weight of evidence descriptor does not correspond to a quantifiable probability. The examples below are meant to represent the broad range of data combinations that are covered by this descriptor; they are illustrative and provide neither a checklist nor a limitation for the data that might support use of this descriptor. Moreover, additional information, e.g., on mode of action, might change the choice of descriptor for the illustrated examples. Supporting data for this descriptor may include:

• an agent demonstrating a plausible (but not definitively causal) association between human exposure and cancer, in most cases with some supporting biological, experimental evidence, though not necessarily carcinogenicity data from animal experiments;
• an agent that has tested positive in animal experiments in more than one species, sex, strain, site, or exposure route, with or without evidence of carcinogenicity in humans;
• a positive tumor study that raises additional biological concerns beyond that of a statistically significant result, for example, a high degree of malignancy, or an early age at onset;
• a rare animal tumor response in a single experiment that is assumed to be relevant to humans; or
• a positive tumor study that is strengthened by other lines of evidence, for example, either plausible (but not definitively causal) association between human exposure and cancer or evidence that the agent or an important metabolite causes events generally known to be

associated with tumor formation (such as DNA reactivity or effects on cell growth control) likely to be related to the tumor response in this case.

"Suggestive Evidence of Carcinogenic Potential"
This descriptor of the database is appropriate when the weight of evidence is suggestive of carcinogenicity; a concern for potential carcinogenic effects in humans is raised, but the data are judged not sufficient for a stronger conclusion. This descriptor covers a spectrum of evidence associated with varying levels of concern for carcinogenicity, ranging from a positive cancer result in the only study on an agent to a single positive cancer result in an extensive database that includes negative studies in other species. Depending on the extent of the database, additional studies may or may not provide further insights. Some examples include:

• a small, and possibly not statistically significant, increase in tumor incidence observed in a single animal or human study that does not reach the weight of evidence for the descriptor "Likely to Be Carcinogenic to Humans." The study generally would not be contradicted by other studies of equal quality in the same population group or experimental system (see discussions of *conflicting evidence* and *differing results*, below);
• a small increase in a tumor with a high background rate in that sex and strain, when there is some but insufficient evidence that the observed tumors may be due to intrinsic factors that cause background tumors and not due to the agent being assessed. (When there is a high background rate of a specific tumor in animals of a particular sex and strain, then there may be biological factors operating independently of the agent being assessed that could be responsible for the development of the observed tumors.) In this case, the reasons for determining that the tumors are not due to the agent are explained;
• evidence of a positive response in a study whose power, design, or conduct limits the ability to draw a confident conclusion (but does not make the study fatally flawed), but where the carcinogenic potential is strengthened by other lines of evidence (such as structure-activity relationships); or
• a statistically significant increase at one dose only, but no significant response at the other doses and no overall trend.

"Inadequate Information to Assess Carcinogenic Potential"
This descriptor of the database is appropriate when available data are judged inadequate for applying one of the other descriptors. Additional studies generally would be expected to provide further insights. Some examples include:

• little or no pertinent information;
• conflicting evidence, that is, some studies provide evidence of carcinogenicity but other studies of equal quality in the same sex and strain are negative. *Differing results*, that is, positive results in some studies and negative results in one or more different experimental systems, do not constitute *conflicting evidence*, as the term is used here. Depending on the overall weight of evidence, differing results can be considered either suggestive evidence or likely evidence; or
• negative results that are not sufficiently robust for the descriptor, "Not Likely to Be Carcinogenic to Humans."

"Not Likely to Be Carcinogenic to Humans"
This descriptor is appropriate when the available data are considered robust for deciding that there is no basis for human hazard concern. In some instances, there can be positive results in

experimental animals when there is strong, consistent evidence that each mode of action in experimental animals does not operate in humans. In other cases, there can be convincing evidence in both humans and animals that the agent is not carcinogenic. The judgment may be based on data such as:

• animal evidence that demonstrates lack of carcinogenic effect in both sexes in well-designed and well-conducted studies in at least two appropriate animal species (in the absence of other animal or human data suggesting a potential for cancer effects),
• convincing and extensive experimental evidence showing that the only carcinogenic effects observed in animals are not relevant to humans,
• convincing evidence that carcinogenic effects are not likely by a particular exposure route . . . or
• convincing evidence that carcinogenic effects are not likely below a defined dose range.

A descriptor of "not likely" applies only to the circumstances supported by the data. For example, an agent may be "Not Likely to Be Carcinogenic" by one route but not necessarily by another. In those cases that have positive animal experiment(s) but the results are judged to be not relevant to humans, the narrative discusses why the results are not relevant.

Multiple Descriptors
More than one descriptor can be used when an agent's effects differ by dose or exposure route. For example, an agent may be "Carcinogenic to Humans" by one exposure route but "Not Likely to Be Carcinogenic" by a route by which it is not absorbed. Also, an agent could be "Likely to Be Carcinogenic" above a specified dose but "Not Likely to Be Carcinogenic" below that dose because a key event in tumor formation does not occur below that dose.

5. As discussed in chapters 3 and 5, the White House Office of Management and Budget (OMB) has long pressed regulatory agencies to use cost-benefit analysis to determine whether, and to what extent, to regulate chemical and other hazards. The benefit side of cost-benefit analysis is informed by quantitative risk assessment. In January 2006, OMB issued controversial and detailed draft guidelines on how agencies should conduct and harmonize their risk assessments to make them "objective, reproducible, and transparent" (http://www.whitehouse.gov/omb/inforeg/proposed_risk_assessment_bulletin_010906.pdf). Environmental groups and state regulators were extremely critical of this attempt to regularize the conduct of risk analysis, and charged that OMB was seeking to impose conventions on methodologies that favored industry positions, such as the use of "central tendencies" or "best estimates" of risk rather than estimates based on 95% confidence levels. The National Research Council of the National Academy of Sciences issued a scathing report (http://www.nap.edu/catalog/11811.html) that recommended OMB withdraw the entire proposal, and OMB subsequently did so. See Cornelia Dean (2007) "Risk Assessment Plan is Withdrawn," *New York Times*, January 12, p. 19. ■

2.   The Limitations of Risk Assessment

[handwritten: ef. item enormously time & cost consuming]

[The] ... Trouble with Risk Assessment
Veerle Heyvaert

Source: "Reconceptualizing Risk Assessment," *Reciel* 8(2): 135–143, 1999 (references omitted), excerpted with permission.

... [R]isk assessment has to contend with a number of challenges that call into question the adequacy of the technique on a more general, fundamental, or even conceptual, level. A detailed discussion of these critiques would exceed the scope of this article. The sections below briefly outline the basic tenets of the prevalent lines of attack against risk assessment for regulation.

RISK ASSESSMENT IS UNRELIABLE

A first major challenge to risk assessment focuses on the reliability of test results. Many commentators have argued that, even when a great deal of time, money and expertise is spent, risk assessments produce results that are, at best, plausible. Uncertainties complicate each of the four assessment stages. For instance, to determine the toxicity of a substance, risk assessors traditionally rely either on animal tests, or epidemiological studies. Both pose difficulties. In the case of animal tests, the problem is obvious: the applicability of animal test data to humans is by no means a given, and even though some rules of thumb exist, there are no general, universally valid rules of extrapolation. In the case of ecotoxicity testing, studies are usually conducted on a limited group of test organisms (such as fish and earthworms), which represent entire ecological systems. Needless to add, the risks of oversimplification are enormous.

To their advantage, epidemiological studies are conducted outside the artificial confines of testing laboratories, and focus on real people or ecosystems rather than test organisms. On the other hand, such studies are enormously time-consuming and costly. Furthermore, their unavoidably limited scope may prevent the discovery of certain adverse exposure effects, particularly those that have a relatively low occurrence rate, but nevertheless pose a significant risk. Finally, ruling out alternative causes for observed health or ecological effects is an extremely difficult, precarious exercise that leaves significant room for error. Hence, the statistical power of epidemiological studies—which are generally considered the most reliable and conclusive kind of data available for risk assessment—is debatable.

Matters get worse when the stages of dose-response assessment and exposure assessment are taken into account. Neither of these stages produces incontestable data; both rely on models, predictions and, at times, informed guesses. The fourth stage, risk characterization, draws together the information produced during the three preceding stages, and thus compounds all the uncertainties inherent in the process. In light of all these limitations, the exclamations of a number of critics, denouncing risk assessment as "mythological", "a charade", or even "an exercise in clairvoyance," begin to appear less far-fetched.

SCIENCE, RISK AND REGULATION: A PRECARIOUS PARTNERSHIP

I suggested previously that the scientific outlook of risk assessment may serve to legitimize risk assessment as a basis for decision-making, particularly for decisions that transcend the national level. Yet the close links between science and risk assessment are as much a source of contention as they are one of legitimacy. It is possible to identify three sets of controversies relating to the scientific status of risk assessment.

The "Bad Science" Problem

However sophisticated the information at their disposal, risk assessors must deploy certain heuristic tools and assumptions to arrive at risk characterizations. They rely on extrapolation models to infer human health effects from animal testing data, on assessment factors to go from "lowest observable adverse effect levels" to "no observable adverse effect levels" and on estimates to determine exposure. These tools and assumptions are as much part and parcel of risk assessment, as the "hard data" of test results. They are, however, not value-free. For instance, an assessment factor of 1,000 clearly incorporates a broader margin of safety than a factor of 10. The latter assessment factor reflects the following reasoning: if "less than 10" have no observable effect, then "1" is certainly safe. The assessment factor of 1,000, however, reasons: if "less than 10" have no observable effect, then "0.01" is certainly safe, and is therefore the most conservative, or cautious, of the two.

One might argue that the presence of these normative assumptions disqualifies risk assessment as a scientific discipline. More frequently, however, commentators implicitly accept that science works with assumptions, but disagree with the level of caution incorporated in the assumptions that underscore risk assessment. In particular, many have taken issue with risk assessment's tendency to "err on the safe side." Excessively conservative assumptions produce "bad science," and lead to systematic overestimations of risks. The result is that regulatory bodies spend too much attention and resources over-regulating too few chemicals.

The "Inappropriate Science" Problem

A second strand of criticism questions whether the use of scientific methodologies, to the exclusion of other modes of reasoning, is appropriate within a regulatory context. This issue is raised, first, in the context of evidentiary standards. The works of the US author Carl Cranor make a compelling case that scientific standards of proof to establish causation between a substance and an effect are too stringent to suit regulatory goals. This is because, for scientists, it is a far graver mistake erroneously to attribute an effect to an identified cause (this is a false positive), than to overlook one (a false negative). Hence, scientific proof rules are designed to minimize the chance of false positives occurring, and are less concerned about the occasional false negative. For the purposes of environmental regulation, on the other hand, mistakenly overlooking the connection between a chemical and adverse effects (false negative) is, or should be, more serious than wrongly accepting a causal link. Consequently, evidentiary standards for regulation should differ from evidentiary standards for science. To the extent that risk assessment incorporates scientific proof rules, Cranor concludes, the technique is insufficiently attuned to its regulatory objectives.

A second issue pertaining to the appropriateness of science, is whether scientific data and methodologies should be the sole basis of risk assessment. Risk, it is argued, is not only a function of dangerous properties and probabilities, but is co-determined by sets of social values, which affect the acceptability of risk and, hence, the relative importance the public attaches to the availability of regulatory protection against particular risks. Public appreciation of risks may be influenced by a number of non-scientific factors, such as the origin of the risk (natural or man-made), whether the risk is assumed voluntarily or involuntarily (smoking v inhaling exhaust fumes), the degree of familiarity (sun tanning or indoor radiation), the distribution of the risk over people (localized or diffuse) and time (affecting present or future generations), etc. A responsive risk assessment should incorporate and reflect these social values. Currently established assessment methodologies, however, leave hardly any scope for the integration of nonscientific factors.

The "Undemocratic Science" Problem

EC [European Community] authorities did not intend for risk assessment to be a deliberative, democratic process. Making assessments is the prerogative of risk assessors, typically experts trained in toxicology, biochemistry, or one of the other scientific disciplines that are relevant to risk assessment. The reasoning behind this arrangement is clear: since risk assessment is a technical, analytical and objective exercise, it does not require any public involvement. However, the preceding discussion illustrates that the qualification of risk assessment as "purely technical" is, mildly put, debatable. If we accept

that some of the assumptions deployed in risk assessment are normative, it becomes questionable whether independent scientific experts should be solely responsible for them. If we furthermore adhere to the view that risk is determined by social values as well as facts, the assertion that risk assessment is strictly a matter for scientists to decide becomes untenable.

The "democratic deficit" of risk assessment may well acquire particular urgency within the EC framework. Following EC legislation, risk assessors are not only responsible for drawing up risk characterizations, but furthermore make risk recommendations, which may include recommendations to adopt risk reduction measures. Even though European, or national, decision-makers are not bound by these recommendations, their authoritative force is considerable. And, it is particularly unlikely that, if risk assessors conclude that a substance should not be subjected to risk reduction measures, public authorities would undertake regulatory action in spite of their advice....

---

3. Epidemiology

Epidemiology and Risk
Richard Monson

Source: D. C. Christiani and K. T. Kelsey (eds.), *Chemical Risk Assessment and Occupational Health.* **Auburn House, Westport, Com., 1994, pp. 39–41, excerpted with permission.**

Epidemiology is a descriptive discipline. Epidemiologists collect data on exposure and on disease from human populations. The association between exposure and disease is termed *risk*. It is desirable that the data collected on exposure and disease and the measure of risk assessed bear some relationship to the true association in the underlying population from which the data derive.

At one level, therefore, *risk assessment* is a synonym for epidemiology. The usual caveats that are attached to the interpretation of epidemiological data should also be attached to any risk assessment. These include issues of selection bias, information bias, confounding, stability of data, and generalizability. At this level, risk assessment can be viewed as a scientific exercise devoid of policy implications.

One makes a judgment about the meaning of data in one study or in a set of studies. That judgment is a scientific opinion as to the likelihood of a relationship between some exposure and some disease.

However, science in the abstract is useful primarily for one's pleasure. Since few scientists are self-supporting, it follows that there must be some utility to the results of scientific inquiry. A second level in which risk assessment has a utilitarian function is policy. The results of scientific inquiry become part of the information available for the development of political decisions, for example, the setting of permissible levels of exposure to chemicals in the workplace. Epidemiological data have utility not only in the assessment as to whether some exposure and some disease are associated, possibly causally, but also in evaluating the level of exposure at which there is no apparent increase in risk.

However, even this second level is not an accurate description of the current use of the term *risk assessment*. My perception is that risk assessment today is an all-encompassing term used to describe the process through which society sets priorities for action. Although I have not heard the term used in the context of deciding which candidate to vote for in a presidential election, each voter's choice ultimately is an assessment of the risks and benefits (negative risks?) attached to each candidate. There is an implicit weighing of these risks and benefits; for example, a candidate's position on abortion may receive a 100 percent weight.

While this example on voting is not an attempt to trivialize the use of the term *risk assessment*, it does illustrate the difficulty of attempting to engage in a focused discussion on risk assessment. One participant may be thinking of how to measure the level of exposure to benzene in the workplace; a second may be pondering the problems related to assessing whether the existence of a cluster of workers with benzene exposure and leukemia can add to the scientific information on this

chemical; a third may be questioning the utility of epidemiological information in protecting service station employees from the hazards of pumping gasoline; and a fourth may be trying to figure out how to enact a law on benzene in drinking water without having to suffer the indignity of dealing with scientists who are unable to reach a consensus.

For most information currently available on human populations, a qualitative assessment of risk is all that is indicated. However, such epidemiological data do allow for rough quantitative estimates of risk to be determined, and methods to improve such analysis are under development. . . . In addition to epidemiological data, much information is also available from experiments on animal populations, where quantification of the observed relationship between exposure and disease is relatively straightforward. Having done a quantitative risk assessment in animals, there is the tendency to transfer that assessment to humans. The major problem, of course, is that there is a large qualitative step that must be made in using data on animals to assess risk in humans. We do not know now, and it is unlikely that we will ever know in a quantitative manner, how animal data relate to human risk. This observation reinforces the potential utility of epidemiological data in risk assessment.

Because of the fundamental uncertainties in both epidemiological and animal data, the term *quantitative risk assessment* must be used with extreme caution. In fact, quantitative risk assessment almost always requires qualitative judgments about the underlying science. While quantification of the association between exposure and disease is the ultimate goal of any risk assessment, be it an individual epidemiological study or the national policy on benzene in drinking water, it must be recognized that assessment of risk is ultimately a matter of judgment rather than of data.

Epidemiology in Occupational Health Risk Assessment

M. Jane Teta

Source: D. C. Christiani and K. T. Kelsey (eds.), *Chemical Risk Assessment and Occupational Health.* Auburn House, Westport, Com., 1994, pp. 57–66, excerpted with permission.

During the last 10 years, I have spent a great deal of my time as an occupational epidemiologist working with toxicologists and struggling with risk assessment issues, particularly those relating to the optimal uses of both animal and human data. I've made some observations with which you may or may not agree. What is the difference between a toxicologist and an epidemiologist? The epidemiologist is always apologizing. We routinely make excuses and focus on the limitations of our work. Our sample sizes are too small, especially for rare diseases; we don't have adequate information on potential confounders; our exposure information is not quantitative and precise; and on and on. The curricula at our schools of public health teach us to be experts in critiquing the work of ourselves and others. The toxicologists seem to have been spared from this perpetual skepticism, perhaps because laboratory data have traditionally been viewed as free from the sources of error inherent in human observational data. Concerns, however, have recently been raised about mechanistic differences in toxic responses between animals and humans and even over the fundamental design of the chronic animal carcinogenicity bioassay itself. These unsettling questions have led to a renewed interest in using epidemiological data in risk assessment.

I would like to discuss the contribution epidemiological data can make to the risk assessment process. I, for one, feel that epidemiological data should play a very important role in this area, not because it has all the answers but because the uncertainties in using epidemiology may not be any greater than the uncertainties in the risk assessment process as it has traditionally been practiced. There are, however, numerous unanswered questions about how epidemiological data should be applied in risk assessment. We don't currently have appropriate guidelines for this endeavor, in part because epidemiology lacks the history and tradition that lies behind the use of toxicological data in risk assessment. Thus, we have the challenge of building consensus on how to make the best use of the human data that are available to us now and how to collect the kind of data that might be more useful in the future.

What has occurred in the epidemiological discipline itself that we are so much more interested in human data? Before about 1950, there were very few completed epidemiology studies, particularly chemical-specific ones, upon which to draw inferences related to human health risks. This has changed radically, and an example illustrating some of these changes will be given later. Yes, epidemiology continues to have problems associated with statistical power: Such studies can't prove the negative and can't detect risks at very low levels of exposure or potency. Classical toxicology shares many of these problems as well. Epidemiology has also had study quality issues, but overall the field is improving in this regard, with efforts being made to codify appropriate practices. Examples of this can be found in the "Guidelines for Good Epidemiology Practices" developed by the Epidemiology Task Group of the Chemical Manufacturers Association [reference omitted]. Epidemiologists, as a group, want to continue to improve the quality of their work and make it more useful in efforts to assess workplace risks. An example of this is the ongoing efforts being made by many research groups to improve exposure assessments, an area that has been a very definite limitation in epidemiological research. The

National Institute for Occupational Safety and Health (NIOSH), the National Cancer Institute (NCI), industry, and university exposure assessors and statisticians have been developing new methodologies of estimating occupational exposures retrospectively [i.e., exposure reconstruction] [references omitted], and these promise to enhance the usefulness of such human studies. Thus, although epidemiologists will be quick to agree that issues of validity and reliability certainly remain in the field, we question whether these limitations result in any greater uncertainty than those associated with extrapolations from high-dose animal toxicity tests to humans.

META-ANALYSIS

One approach to reducing the power limitations associated with using epidemiological data is the application of meta-analysis to observational data. This involves a qualitative review of the available, relevant studies and a quantitative summarization of the evidence from multiple studies into a single, more precise, risk estimate. Meta-analysis provides an approach to *moving in the bounds of uncertainty* about risks. It also attempts to take advantage of all the relevant studies of suitable quality, irrespective of study size or outcome, to make a judgment about hazard in the initial phase of risk assessment.

While meta-analysis holds promise to enhance the value of human data in the risk assessment process, there are some caveats related to its use that merit consideration I believe that careful attention to the following recommendations is essential to the appropriate use of these techniques:

1. Meta-analysis should not be reduced to a statistical exercise devoid of expert judgment in the design, analysis, and interpretation of results.
2. It should be preceded by the development of a protocol that describes the outcomes of a priori interest, criteria for study inclusion and

exclusion, the analytic tests to be employed, the weighting system to be used, how heterogeneity will be handled, and how study quality will be assessed and incorporated into the process.
3. A thorough, qualitative assessment of the characteristics, strengths, and limitations of all the available studies should also precede any quantitative treatment of the data.

USE OF EPIDEMIOLOGICAL DATA IN THE HAZARD IDENTIFICATION STEP OF RISK ASSESSMENT

I would propose that when good epidemiology studies are available that they be given greater weight in the hazard identification phase of risk assessment than has previously been the case; that a weight of evidence, not a strength of evidence, approach be taken; and that expert judgment be applied. It is not scientifically justifiable to conclude that an agent is a carcinogen because one epidemiology study reports an excess risk, in the presence of numerous others that do not provide such evidence. It is important to examine all the evidence simultaneously. Is there consistency in study results? Are the outcomes biologically plausible? In the selection of a target organ, patterns across the spectrum of studies, not the end point in the single study that provides the highest risk estimate, should be used. These would seem to constitute basic principles in the application of good science to risk assessments using epidemiological data.

For example, let's examine the process of incorporating human and animal data into the hazard identification process as it exists today (figure [2.12]). Assume that there are health concerns about a particular chemical. The risk assessor queries, "What evidence do we have from experimental data?" If there is evidence of carcinogenicity, then the human evidence is examined. There are four outcomes related to the human evidence; yes, no, inadequate, or there are no human data.

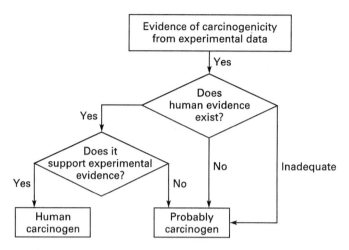

Figure 2.12
Carcinogenicity hazard identification paradigm: "as is." (Source: M. Jane Teta, "Epidemiology in Occupational Risk Assessment," in D. C. Christiani and K. T. Kelsey (eds.), *Chemical Risk Assessment and Occupational Health*. Auburn House, Westport, Conn., 1994.)

There is no dispute on an overall conclusion related to carcinogenicity if the human evidence is also positive. But what happens when the human evidence is nonpositive or inadequate or doesn't exist? The chemical typically lands in the same box, with a classification of probable carcinogen. What this communicates to the epidemiologist is that, for purposes of risk assessment, it does not really matter whether your data are inadequate, whether they are nonpositive or whether studies were conducted at all. It doesn't really impact the classification unless it is positive. I would suggest that risk assessors put more weight on solid human evidence when it exists and start the process by examining the human data first. An alternative hazard identification paradigm making fuller use of epidemiological results is presented in figure [2.13]. If the data are nonpositive from both animal and epidemiological sources, while you can't conclude with absolute certainty that the agent is not a carcinogen, it should not be suspected of being one based on the evidence that is currently avail-

able. The challenge occurs when there is conflicting information. What happens when animal and human data don't agree? Currently, the animal evidence takes precedence, irrespective of the statistical power and quality of the epidemiological evidence. Positive animal data drive the classification.

I would suggest that there is a range of outcomes that should be considered when the animal and human data are not consistent. First, an attempt should be made to assess the possible reasons for the inconsistency. These may be related to mechanistic differences between the species, power limitations in the human data, or issues related to study design or conduct, in either the animal or human studies, that may have impacted their overall quality or conclusions. In such cases, additional information may be needed to reach a defensible conclusion. In the absence of such information, there are currently no guidelines on an approach to addressing inconsistencies, short of completely ignoring the result of human studies. This should be rectified.

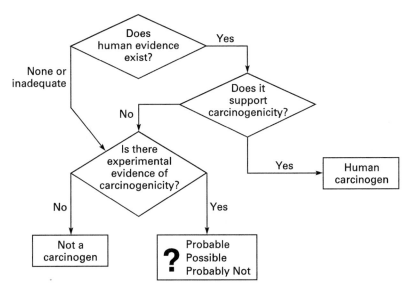

Figure 2.13
Carcinogenicity hazard identification paradigm: "should be?" (Source: M. Jane Teta, "Epidemiology in Occupational Risk Assessment," in D. C. Christiani and K. T. Kelsey (eds.), *Chemical Risk Assessment and Occupational Health.* Auburn House, Westport, Conn., 1994.)

USE OF EPIDEMIOLOGICAL DATA IN POTENCY AND EXPOSURE PHASES OF RISK ASSESSMENT

Methods for dose response assessment will not be discussed here in any detail because this topic has been covered elsewhere. I would like to propose, however, criteria for the use of human data in quantitative dose response assessment when data exist from both chronic animal bioassays and epidemiological studies. The question to be answered is, When [are] the human data good enough to use? I think we need at least general guidelines to follow in addressing this question and I would like to suggest the following to promote discussion.

First of all, there should be reasonable evidence of carcinogenicity in the body of human data related to a specific type of cancer or cancers. This would preclude using for risk assessment purposes the upper bound of the 95 percent confidence interval from an epidemiological study for a target organ that

is of concern based solely on animal data but not of concern based on the totality of the human evidence. For example, the upper bound of the human data for brain cancer (an EtO [ethylene oxide] target organ in female rats) should not be used in a mathematical model to estimate EtO potency when the body of human data does not support that the agent actually causes human brain cancer.

Other possible criteria to evaluating the appropriateness of using epidemiological data in risk assessment include the availability of quality studies with reasonable estimates of exposure covering the likely range of human experience, a sufficient observation period, and a reasonable sample size. These are not hard and fast rules because expert judgment is needed to evaluate the suitability of the human data on a case-by-case basis. For example, the latency and rarity of the cancer of interest might impact the decision of whether the observation period is sufficient or the sample size is reasonable.

The issue of reasonable estimates of exposure warrants some discussion, since it is often the reason epidemiological studies are discounted in setting exposure limits. Human studies will never achieve the accuracy and precision of controlled laboratory studies. However, reasonable estimates of exposures are often achievable, which together with a sensitivity analysis can yield less uncertainty than the results of animal to human extrapolation. Sensitivity analyses can also be applied to characterize the impact of different choices of statistical models. These approaches result in a distribution of potential exposures and, ultimately, in cancer potency estimates as well. This is consistent with the recommendation made previously that we move away from bright-line estimates and present plausible ranges or risk estimates that provide more scientific information about the likelihood of risk and the uncertainties surrounding these estimates.

EPIDEMIOLOGY AND RISK CHARACTERIZATION

I also envision epidemiology being used more effectively in the risk characterization phase of risk assessment, even when the studies are not suitable for dose response assessment. Animal-based potency estimates can be modified either up or down, by reflecting on whether the observable human data are consistent with the predictions based on animal data. This goes beyond the conservative, but often stated, notion that epidemiology can at least be used to provide an upper bound on risk.

The first challenge to such efforts is proper identification of inconsistent results between animal assays and human epidemiology. This is not a straightforward process. There are numerous examples in the literature of attempts to test the consistency of human and animal data in which one group of investigators will say that they are consistent, while another will contend they are not [references omitted]. How do we define consistency or inconsistency? There may be inconsistency in terms of gender sensitivity. For example, the female rat was used to estimate the carcinogenic potency of EtO because this species and sex yielded the largest potency estimate. However, when the human data, which included women, are examined, there is no evidence that females are more sensitive. In fact, quite the opposite was seen in the NIOSH EtO study. This is just one aspect of consistency. Another is cancer site concordance. There is general agreement that this provides strong support of carcinogenicity, but its absence does not preclude such a conclusion. There is one aspect of consistency that I strongly urge risk assessors to reconsider. I call it the *95 percent UCL rule*. This technique assumes consistency if the animal-based estimate applied to humans results in an excess risk that is less than the 95 percent upper confidence limit produced by the epidemiology data. While this purely statistical approach provides some perspective on consistency, it forces the risk assessor into relying on a single number to make a scientific judgment and places an unreasonable burden on the epidemiology data to rule out the animal-based prediction. A more useful approach might be one that answers the question, If the animal-based predictions are truly reflective of human risk, how likely would it be to observe the results seen in the totality of investigated human experience? The response to this question could be a combination of a probability estimate and expert judgment. Common sense dictates that a likelihood of only 8 to 10 percent should not be ignored because it is not 5 percent, which provides the requisite 95 percent certainty.

For example, in the Teta study (table [2.4]), we can rule out a risk greater than 2.7 with 95 percent certainty. We cannot rule out with 95 percent confidence anything less than 2.7, and an excess risk this high may be similar to or greater than what would be predicted based on the animal-based potency estimate. An animal-based prediction for humans of 2.0, for example, would be highly unlikely

Table 2.4
Mortality Study of 1,896 Ethylene Oxide Workers in Chemical Manufacturing

Follow-Up: 1940–1988/ave. = 27 yrs.
Assignment: 1925–1978/ave. = 5 yrs.

	Obs.	Exp.	SMR.
All Cancer	110	128.1	0.86
Lymphopoietic Cancer	7	11.8	0.59
Leukemia	5	4.7	1.06

*95% upper confidence limit = 2.7.
Source: Teta, M. J., L. Benson and J. N. Vitale (1993) "Mortality Study of Ethylene Oxide Workers in Chemical Manufacturing," *British Journal of Industrial Medicine* 50(8): 704–709.

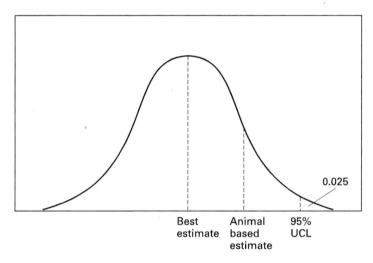

Figure 2.14
How likely is it that the animal-based predictive risk ratio is true, given the probability distribution of risks from epidemiologic data? (Source: M. Jane Teta, "Epidemiology in Occupational Risk Assessment," in D. C. Christiani and K. T. Kelsey (eds.), *Chemical Risk Assessment and Occupational Health*. Auburn House, Westport, Conn., 1994.)

but supposedly consistent with the human evidence using the 95 percent UCL rule (figure [2.14]). In such a scenario, 49 years of human observation with leukemia rates similar to those expected for control populations would be dismissed in favor of an observed increase in brain gliomas and leukemia in the female rat.

Finally, epidemiology data may also be useful in the identification of susceptible populations. The NCI is doing some cutting-edge work in molecular epidemiology, which in the future will identify genetic markers of susceptible populations. . . .

CONCLUSION

By way of summary, I urge my colleagues in risk assessment, epidemiology, and toxicology to collaborate in consensus building on the critical issues related to the use of epidemiology in the risk assessment process. These include:

• Guidelines for using epidemiological data for dose-response assessment;

• A methodology for testing the consistency of human and animal data; and

• Approaches to conducting hazard identification when the animal and human data conflict. . . .

■ **NOTES**

1. Teta suggests that "[i]t is not scientifically justifiable to conclude that an agent is a carcinogen because one epidemiology study reports an excess risk, in the presence of numerous others that do not provide such evidence." Given that there may be many confounders in real-life exposure situations that would render many epidemiological studies inconclusive, is the author's position a prudent (or precautionary) one?

2. While Teta is correct that "epidemiology data may be useful in the identification of susceptible populations," epidemiologic data can serve this purpose only if the prevalence of identifiable subcohorts is high enough to be statistically significant, which is often not the case. See N. A. Ashford, C. J. Spadafor, D. B. Hattis, and C. C. Caldart (1990) *Monitoring the Worker for Exposure and Disease: Scientific, Legal, and Ethical Considerations in the Use of Biomarkers.* Johns Hopkins University Press, Baltimore.

3. A recent paper argues that exposure misclassification is a more serious problem than confounding in epidemiological studies of occupational exposures. See Aaron Blair, Patricia Stewart, Jay H. Lubin, and Francesco Forastiere (2007) "Methodical Issues Regarding Confounding and Exposure Misclassification in Epidemiological Studies of Occupational Exposures," *American Journal of Industrial Medicine* 50: 199–207.   ■

Applied Epidemiology and Environmental Health: Emerging Controversies
Carolyn Needleman
Source: *American Journal of Infection Control* 25(3): 262–274, 1997 (references omitted), excerpted with permission.

This review article assesses the state of the science in environmental epidemiology, not by summarizing current scientific findings but rather by examining conceptual controversies in the study of how environmental factors influence human health. This approach seems necessary because environmental epidemiology presently stands at a crossroads—in fact, at a number of overlapping crossroads. The field teems with epistemologic debates concerning appropriate paradigms for framing research questions, interpreting data, and applying research findings to policy. The present review focuses on emerging controversies related to three questions: What is considered "environmental"? What counts as credible research in environmental epidemiology? And what does "applied epidemiology" mean in the context of environmental health? The goal is to organize the presently fragmented critical literature on these issues and to promote productive dialogue by identifying central themes in current conceptual debates.

In recent years the field of environmental epidemiology has flourished, producing a voluminous scientific literature on the human health effects of environmental hazards. However, signs of strain abound...A growing number of scientists argue that the field's traditional epistemologic assumptions provide a conceptual framework too limited for detecting, analyzing, and controlling environmental causes of disease....

WHAT IS "ENVIRONMENTAL"?

In 1991, in an effort to consolidate the burgeoning findings of environmental epidemiology, the National Research Council issued the first of a planned series of reports on this relatively new field. Noting how widely used the term "environmental epidemiology" has become, the report's authors offer the following general definition: "Environmental epidemiology is the study of the effect on human health of *physical, biologic, and chemical factors in the external environment,* broadly conceived" (emphasis added).

...Current definitions of "environment" reflect three distinctly different conceptions of how environmental epidemiology should be oriented.

The first conception centers on health impact. In this view, every external factor affecting human health in any way, singly or in combination, holds interest for the environmental epidemiologist. From a health perspective, it would be pointless to study chemical exposures in the community without also considering the population's work-related chemical exposures. It would be illogical to study "environmental" injuries at home or at work while excluding injuries caused by car accidents, criminal assaults, or suicide attempts. In this framework, cumulative hazardous exposures in multiple settings are relevant; cultural values and social behavior are relevant; malnutrition, inadequate shelter, and unsafe consumer products are relevant; and disregarding nicotine and alcohol as environmental toxins makes no sense at all.

The second conception aims to advance health knowledge. Here the main point is to understand, through rigorous scientific research, the human health effects of specific toxic substances and harmful conditions. In this framework, however compassionate the investigator, the exposed human populations essentially serve as scientific study subjects. Because the inclusion of vaguely defined and hard-to-measure social and cultural variables might complicate the research, it makes sense to narrow the boundaries of the variables considered and to examine health effects of toxic substances one by one.

A third conception is based on health turfs. Here the guiding logic is jurisdictional and pragmatic. Deliberately or unconsciously, researchers adapt their work to fit the boundaries of existing regulatory mandates, professional domains, legal precedents, and competing interest groups....Occupational and nonoccupational health hazards are separated conceptually even when they involve identical toxic exposures because this division holds significance for regulatory and professional concerns. Injuries can be studied as environmental health problems, but only if they do not involve intentional interpersonal violence, which belongs in the realm of social science, social work, and criminal justice. Although such arbitrary distinctions may seem indefensible from a health standpoint, they reflect compelling political and administrative interests within professions, government, academia, and the larger society.

All three perspectives value scientific evidence. All three claim public health as their ultimate goal. Often mixed in practice, they do not form clear opposing camps. However, as discussed in the next section, differing conceptions of the field's boundaries imply divergent research directions for environmental epidemiology.

WHAT COUNTS AS CREDIBLE RESEARCH?

As a general type of research, epidemiology faces a number of unavoidable practical difficulties. These limitations loom particularly large in environmental epidemiology, where liability concerns and inadequate record-keeping so often cloud the picture. Good information on exposures is often lacking; key epidemiologic studies often get buried in the unpublished "gray literature" of state health departments or sealed by court order as part of legal settlements. Physicians, lacking incentives and appropriate training, substantially underreport environmental health problems. Registries and programs of biological monitoring to measure human exposure are still few and far between and fraught with ethical dilemmas. With statistical power limited by the small numbers involved, even very dramatic disease clusters in local communities prove hard to link conclusively with environmental factors. Overall, as the National Research Council has observed, "the conditions for development of environmental epidemiology and programs and methods are so adverse as to impede useful scientific investigations of many important questions."

However, as much as these practical and technical concerns need attention, equally important debates about environmental epidemiology's research utility take place on a conceptual level. What kind of research does it take to build a credible case that environmental factors cause or contribute to specific diseases in human populations?

The National Research Council's 1991 report on environmental epidemiology explains the research goal this way "By examining specific populations or communities exposed to different ambient environments, [environmental epidemiology] seeks to clarify the relationship between physical, biologic or chemical factors and human health."

This broad statement leaves much room for disagreement about what "clarification" means in practice. When the Occupational Safety and Health Administration (OSHA) proposed in the mid-1990s to regulate ergonomic hazards, many scientists—including those in OSHA—believed that the available literature on musculoskeletal disorders provided "solid evidence" of environmental causation. Others considered the same scientific literature inadequate as scientific proof, allowing the standard's opponents to charge "no consensus in the scientific community" and defeat the proposed regulation. The controversy over "Gulf War Syndrome" provides another case in point. Assessing the evidence on possible environmental factors in Gulf War veterans' health problems, government scientific advisory panels have reached sharply divergent conclusions. Are these illnesses related to stress, to chemical exposures, to multiple factors operating in combination? What would constitute convincing evidence for the various explanations? Granted, access to relevant Defense Department information has been problematic, but scientific interpretation of the data presently available is perplexing in itself. A recent editorial by Landrigan [Landrigan, P. J. (1997) "Illness in Gulf War Veterans; Causes and Consequences" *Journal of the American Medical Association* 277: 259–261] observes that the nation may need to give these veterans the support they merit, without ever achieving full scientific understanding of their illness and its etiology.

Although such debates may well involve interest group politics, they also touch on at least five areas of assumption-related scientific controversy: (1) the nature of valid causal inference in science; (2) differential susceptibility within exposed populations; (3) the appropriate unit of analysis; (4) appropriate indicators of health effects; and (5) ways of dealing with residual uncertainty.

Issue 1: The Nature of Valid Causal Inference

Modern epidemiology relies on a causal model rooted in the philosophical tradition of positivism. In this model, the goal of scientific study is to isolate single independent variables and relate them to single dependent variables, controlling for confounders, for the purpose of developing universal principles with predictive value. The causal connection is assumed to be linear, even if complex; effective control of confounding variables is assumed to be possible, even if hard to implement. This causal model has proved a powerful engine for research. However, it has also stimulated much debate, particularly in relation to environmental health problems.

For one thing, environmental exposures do not occur one by one in the real world. People encounter multiple health hazards simultaneously, possibly with synergistic as well as additive effects; the results are hard to disentangle, especially at low dose levels. A simple model based on isolating single cause-and-effect relationships sheds little light on cumulative multiple exposures with a common health outcome, such as asthma. Although the problem of multifactorial causation is well acknowledged, satisfactory research solutions have so far proved elusive.

Moreover, some health effects of great interest to environmentalists turn out to be exceedingly slippery as dependent variables: multiple chemical sensitivity, chronic fatigue, vague symptoms apparently related to indoor air pollution and electromagnetic fields, and some forms of cancer. They seem to involve complex nonlinear mechanisms that are quite different from the clear-cut dose-response relationships usually investigated in epidemiology. For example, toxic chemicals may function as "initiators," "promoters," and/or "progressors" in the multistage development of cancer. They may "kindle" reactions at previously tolerated low dose levels, spread sensitivity to other chemically unrelated substances, and change the body's natural systems in ways that produce disease and affective disorders with no obvious link to the original exposure. Initial symptoms of sensitization may seem to disappear, masked through a process of "adaptation" in which the body builds up tolerance to a toxic substance [see the discussion of TILT in section C2c].

Considerable effort has gone into developing better clinical definitions of vaguely defined illnesses with possible links to environmental exposures; for example, Cullen has developed criteria for diagnosing multiple chemical sensitivity. However, Ashford and Miller suggest that when dealing with "a diversity of agents causing equally diverse effects at extraordinarily low levels with no true unexposed control group," even the most detailed *clinical* definitions of health effects will fail to yield meaningful epidemiologic insight. They recommend instead an *operational* definition, assessing patients' reactions to a period of fasting and isolation in a toxin-free "environmental unit" followed by re-entry into the everyday environment.

Complex diseases of this sort pose conceptual problems for epidemiology's traditional reliance on the "black box" approach, in which statistical associations are sought between exposures and health effects in a population, without much concern for mechanisms to explain the apparent connection. Nonlinear processes of disease causation fit awkwardly with this model. In recent years, with fuller insight into the complexities of disease development, environmental epidemiologists increasingly feel impelled to frame their research in more sophisticated terms. Susser, a leading voice for paradigm change, calls for replacing the "black box" metaphor entirely with a new one based on "Chinese boxes," where causal processes occur nested inside one another. By contrast, Schulte argues that although disease mechanisms need to be better explicated, a different causal paradigm is probably unnecessary given the "new resolving power in the assessment of exposure-disease relationships" promised by biomarker research. He anticipates that the rapidly developing field of molecular epidemiology will eventually be able to show, in previously unobtainable detail, exactly what goes on inside the "black box."

Either way, with or without a change of underlying paradigm, environmental epidemiology faces enormous methodologic challenges in dealing with nonlinear models of causation. It may be many years before scientific understanding catches up with the possibilities suggested by recent research....

Issue 2: Differential Susceptibility

The field of epidemiology has traditionally worked in terms of average responses to exposure. Although variations in individual physiology are, of course, recognized, the emphasis has been on finding probabilities of disease for the at-risk population as a whole. However, in relation to environmental hazards, some definable subpopulations seem to have distinct and unique susceptibilities.

One such subpopulation is children. This point was made powerfully in a recent investigation of children's dietary risks from pesticides, carried out by a National Research Council committee chaired by Landrigan. The committee found that children differ greatly from adults in terms of exposure to pesticides and also (to a lesser degree) in physiologic response. Their bodies are rapidly growing and developing; compared with adults, they eat and drink more per pound of

weight and have different dietary preferences; they ingest more contaminants because of normal childhood hand-to-mouth behavior; and they have a longer lifetime ahead in which to develop long-latency diseases. For these reasons, when a population is exposed to an environmental hazard such as pesticides, the resulting disease burden falls disproportionately on the children in the population. The authors of the report note that children who are poor or ill may be even more vulnerable to environmental hazards because of malnutrition, interacting medications, and already damaged organ systems. They recommend that *"risk distributions* rather than a point estimate such as a mean, median, or outer bound should be used where possible to provide a more complete characterization of risk" (emphasis added).

The special susceptibility of children, particularly children in poverty, is beginning to receive more attention in environmental health research and policy. But the broader conceptual implications for epidemiologic methodology have not yet been faced. Children are only one of a variety of subpopulations plausibly at special risk for environmental hazards. Exposures safely tolerated by an average healthy adult might cause health harm in adults who are malnourished, in those whose immune systems are compromised because they have AIDS, or in those with genetically based susceptibilities. Other subgroups may be especially vulnerable because their exposure is atypically high for special reasons not usually assessed. For example, many low-income adults eat fish caught in the wild, which may expose them disproportionately to chemical hazards that bioaccumulate in aquatic life. An expanding literature raises the possibility that dietary differences may play an even more fundamental role in environmental disease because some foods and methods of food preparation expose people to naturally occurring toxic substances; certain foods also provide protective micronutrients whose presence or absence can influence the severity of DNA damage from environmental exposures.

For these reasons, distributional risk analysis may be appropriate not only for children but also for a number of other subpopulations whose greater susceptibility and/or exposure is currently masked by epidemiologic analysis that blends them in with larger populations. Such analysis would require primary data collection (for example, on personal behavior and health history) to supplement the sketchy information offered by the usual preexisting information sources. . . .

Issue 4: Appropriate Indicators of Health Outcomes

A more muted controversy, but one with important policy implications, centers on reification—treating a measure as identical to the thing being measured. In environmental epidemiology, hospital admission records are commonly used as indicators of disease in populations. However, some health effects of great interest for environmental studies do not typically result in hospitalization and thus do not "count" in research. Moreover, using hospital admissions as an indicator of illness almost certainly introduces biases related to health care access. Recent investigations of health problems among Gulf War veterans have highlighted this problem dramatically, with various federally sponsored studies reaching entirely different conclusions. One large-scale study by the Navy and Department of Defense examined admissions to military hospitals among Gulf War veterans and reported no excess risk of disease in this population. By contrast, a study by the Centers for Disease Control and Prevention measured health effects through surveys rather than hospital admissions; preliminary findings show substantially increased rates of disease among troops deployed to the Persian Gulf.

As critics sometimes note in passing, many additional simplifying assumptions are built into the field's usual approach to measuring health effects. Chronic illnesses tend to be treated as permanent states rather than as fluctuating and intermittent; but, in reality, many chronic health problems wax and wane or go into remission, making them hard to describe within a conceptual framework that assumes a steady or worsening condition. Contrary to everyday experience, disease is often dichotomized in epidemiologic research as present or absent with no degrees in between. The emphasis on manifest disease makes it hard to capture more subtle health effects such as long-term developmental deficits in children of parents exposed to environmental toxins. The strong medical orientation of the field can cloud the interpretation of mental health issues in individuals claiming environmental health damage, converting all their emotional problems (including legitimate anger) into "stress reactions" that suggest a psychosomatic base to the illness. And, although research often concentrates on mortality as the health outcome of interest, both science and disease prevention might be better served by using morbidity or even subclinical health effects.

The standard quantitative criteria used to interpret findings in environmental epidemiology have also been attacked. Critics ask, What is so sacrosanct about 10 to the sixth power as an estimate of acceptable risk? Why should the 0.05 level of probability hold any special magic for separating epidemiologic findings into "positive" and "negative" categories, especially in small populations? Instead of arbitrary standards, shouldn't we be using interpretative criteria that are health-based, plausible in light of other available evidence, and matched to the specific context?

Even commonly understood categories of race and ethnicity become suspect when used acritically for epidemiologic purposes. These categories represent social constructs, not genetically accurate descriptors. Biologically, it makes little sense to lump those who are Jewish by conversion in with the rest of the Jewish population, or to treat individuals with widely varying levels of African ancestry as a genetically similar pool of "African-Americans."

These various forms of simplification may be useful as pragmatic adaptations to the limitations of available data. But when mistakenly equated with reality, they become conceptual traps that obscure actual environmental health effects and distort the base of scientific evidence needed for public health intervention.

Issue 5: Dealing with Residual Uncertainty

A fifth methodologic debate revolves around concepts of uncertainty and risk. In the prevailing epidemiologic paradigm, uncertainty represents a void that must be filled. The mission of science is to reduce the level of uncertainty one way or another, either directly through research or indirectly through developing estimates that are based on extrapolation where appropriate research is still lacking. This conceptual orientation has led a number of federal regulatory and environmental health science agencies to place great emphasis on precise quantitative risk assessments.

In principle, human epidemiologic research offers the most logical grounding for environmental risk assessments, especially for low-dose exposures. But, in practice, epidemiologic studies have historically been considered a weak research base because of their practical and methodologic limitations. Various approaches have been suggested to improve the utility of human epidemiology for risk assessment, including statistical combination ("convolution") of data on multiple factors that affect exposure dose, refining exposure assumptions through mapping and computer modeling, and using biologic markers as indicators of exposure. However, these approaches as yet remain fairly undeveloped. Environmental risk assessors customarily construct their estimates by analogy, extrapolating from experimental studies done on animals.

Although a valuable and well-established tool, the reliance on animal studies for human risk assessment has raised concern. The practice involves numerous assumptions about interspecies comparability, raises methodologic questions concerning dose equivalency, and cannot address the complexity of environmental exposures for human populations in their natural social settings. Providing more controlled research conditions but no guarantee of relevance, animal toxicology creates the appearance of reducing uncertainty about human health risks without necessarily doing so in fact.

With animal-based risk assessment being an imperfect guide and human epidemiology hampered by practical obstacles, some environmental scientists suggest shifting to a different way of dealing with uncertainty: weight of the evidence (WOE). In the WOE approach, if existing research strongly suggests a causal link between an environmental exposure and a health effect, health risk should be presumed even though considerable uncertainty remains. WOE encourages combination of relevant findings from all available sources—human epidemiology, animal toxicology, and biomolecular research. The process yields conclusions about human risk without attempting to generate precise quantitative risk estimates.

More radical approaches to dealing with uncertainty appear in the field of ecology, where "chaotic" global processes of weather, climate change, and population growth routinely thwart the deterministic assumptions of traditional scientific research. A provocative article by Dovers and Handmer [Dovers S. R. and Handmer J. W. (1995) "Ignorance, the Precautionary Principle, and Sustainability" *Ambio* 24: 92–97] presents the idea that, for environmental health problems, a certain level of uncertainty may be irreducible. These health problems not only involve the differential susceptibilities and complex disease mechanisms already discussed, but they also occur in dynamic ecologic systems where toxic substances move around, bioaccumulate, and combine in unanticipated ways to form "daughter" by-products. Some part of the resulting contingent interactions will be inherently unpredictable; some level of uncertainty will always remain. In this paradigm, the challenge is not to eliminate uncertainty (because that is impossible), but rather to define it more creatively as a phenomenon to be analyzed and managed. Uncertainty is usually thought of as a problem and dichotomized as completely present or completely absent. Instead, it could be considered a variable interesting in its own right, with degrees and sub-types worthy of analysis. Dover and Handmer go on to present an analytic framework for "ignorance auditing" when action must be based on incomplete knowledge.

The notion of inherently irreducible uncertainty is as yet foreign to environmental epidemiology; some have argued that public health researchers will never be able to accept it. Yet this idea holds promise for breaking through some of the current conceptual deadlocks in applying research to environmental health policy, to which we now turn.

WHAT DOES "APPLIED" MEAN?

. . . Some innovative strategies have been suggested as ways around the various impasses over application. One idea is to reorient environmental epidemiology and its policy applications around "sentinel" categories or events representing the high susceptibility subgroups or individuals within a population exposed to environmental hazards. Exposure levels determined safe for the sentinels could then be used as the upper limit of safe exposure for the general population. This approach follows a logic different from current practice, which emphasizes probabilities for the whole population and measures health effects among maximally exposed individuals. Depending on the hazard, some promising

sentinels might be children, occupational groups such as farmers with relatively high exposure to general environmental hazards, and individuals manifesting diseases unusual for their age and gender.

Another approach, suggested by Silbergeld [Silbergeld E. K. (1994) "Evaluating the success of environmental health programs in protecting the public's health." In: Andrews J. S., Frumkin H., Johnson B. L., Mehlman M. A., Xintaras C., Bucsela J. A., editors. Hazardous waste and public health: international congress on the health effects of hazardous waste. Princeton (NJ): Princeton Scientific; pp. 43–44], is to monitor closely a few selected health problems with potential links to many different environmental hazards—for example, low birth weight, neurodegenerative diseases of aging, and asthma. High rates of these targeted health problems in a population would signal a need to investigate intensively for possible environmental causes, building a WOE explanation that accommodates the possibility of multiple, cumulative, and interactive hazards.

These alternative approaches start with human beings instead of chemicals, consistent with a "health impact" orientation in epidemiology rather than a hazard-centered "health knowledge" orientation. Clearly both perspectives contribute to the welfare of society. They are not mutually exclusive in any sense. However, within the realm of applications, health impact logically should take primacy. In *applied* epidemiology, advancement of scientific knowledge is a means toward the end of improving public health, not an end in itself. For this reason, the health impact orientation seems a more appropriate guide for environmental health programs and policy. . . .

CONCLUSIONS

Given the immense social and economic interests involved, value choices inevitably arise at the boundary line between science and public policy in environmental epidemiology. As this discussion shows, such choices also lie embedded in the methods, goals, and assumptions of the research itself. The challenge for environmental epidemiology as a field is to appreciate the deeper significance of its recurrent controversies and to make the underlying nonempirical assumptions of research more transparent, not necessarily reaching consensus but opening the widest possible range of legitimate tools for dealing with the diverse research problems and social pressures now confronting the field.

■ NOTES

1. Many prospective epidemiological studies (those that follow a particular population for several years and record exposure levels and disease outcomes) are done with workers. Such studies are also sometimes done with persons who volunteer as subjects (e.g., from the military). Retrospective studies (which attempt to determine past exposures in diseased populations) may be done on workers, or on any group thought to have been exposed to harmful substances and whose disease prevalence suggests a possible problem. The health of workers and volunteer populations is— at least in some important ways—better than that of a more representative part of the general population containing more susceptible subgroups. The result is that when the prevalence of a particular disease in chemically exposed workers or volunteers is compared with the prevalence of that disease in the general population, there may not appear to be an increased risk attributable to the exposure. Because these study groups tend to be healthier than the general population, their likelihood of developing a disease is, in general, lower than that of the general population *by a factor of 0.6 to 0.8*, depending on the disease. See T. J. Sterling and J. J. Weinkam (1986) "Extent, Persistence, and Constancy of the Healthy Worker or Healthy Person Effect by All and Selected Causes of Death," *Journal of Occupational Medicine* 28(5): 348–353; and T. J. Sterling and J. J. Weinkam (1985) "The 'Healthy Worker Effect' on Morbidity Rates," *J. Occup. Med.* 27(7): 477–482. See also J. Baillargeon, G. Wilkinson, L. Rudkin, G. Baillargeon, and L. Ray, Laura (1998) "Characteristics of the Healthy Worker Effect: A Comparison of Male and Female Occupational Cohorts," *J. Occup. Med.* 40(4): 368–373.

2. Thus, when one of these subject groups has an "odds ratio" of, for example, 1.05 for the prevalence of disease (the odds ratio is the ratio of disease prevalence in the subject population compared with that in the general population), this may be interpreted as "normal," but it may actually be 25–45% higher than would ordinarily be expected for this population. This is called "the healthy worker effect" or the "healthy volunteer effect." It is unfortunate that so many epidemiological studies ignore this effect in reporting their results, thus potentially hiding real risks to health.

3. Death (mortality) from a particular disease or condition, rather than disease or illness itself (morbidity), is often the focus of epidemiologic investigations. In part, this is because death records (from public health, insurance, or other sources) are often more readily accessible. The odds ratio for mortality is abbreviated SMR (standard *mortality* ratio), while SmR represents the standard *morbidity* ratio in a studied population.

4. Note the subtle distinction between the concept of disease "prevalence" and disease "incidence." The former measures the disease at a particular moment in time, no matter when the disease was contracted. The latter is the rate of disease creation within a specific time period, usually a year, e.g., new cases of lung cancer diagnosed in 2002. Of course, the proper measurement of incidence depends on timely diagnosis. When new attention is placed on diseases of possible chemical causation, e.g., lupus or reproductive diseases, the resulting incidence figures may suffer from a reporting bias. It is possible for the incidence to be affected in opposite ways, by increased correct reporting on the one hand, and by decreased causative exposures, or interventions intended to arrest or reverse the disease, on the other.

5. Epidemiological studies look for excess disease or health effects in a target population. When excess disease or effects are not statistically significant, they are often ignored or not reported. Because of the long latency of some diseases, such as lung cancer in asbestos workers, the statistics don't "ripen" for many years. However, looking at regular increases in prevalence over time can give an early signal that a health problem exists in the target population long before the excess disease becomes statistically significant.

6. Statistically significant associations between dose and disease prevalence—leading to a dose-response relationship—are customarily constructed by fitting data over the entire set of available empirical data, from low exposures to medium exposures to high exposures. But when there are confounding factors (i.e., where there are other causes of the disease or a high background incidence of the disease in some of the population), the association (and the dose-response relationship) may not be statistically significant. This is especially true at medium exposure levels. In such cases, however, the excess disease in the 90th percentile of exposure (the highest 10%) relative to the 10th percentile (the lowest 10%) may be statistically significant and could be used to guide public policy.

7. Professor Kristin Shrader-Frechette of Notre Dame University describes the "methodological disagreements over the causal inferences used to interpret epidemiological statistics and risk data" as "the epidemiology wars." Three putative decisional "rules" over which the wars are being waged are "the *epidemiological-evidence rule* (EER), according to which causal inferences about harm require

(human) epidemiological data, not merely animal or laboratory data; the *statistical-significance rule* (SSR), according to which the null or no-effect hypothesis ought to be rejected only if there is statistically significant evidence of harm (p ≤ 0.05); and the *relative-risk rule* (RRR), according to which hazard identification (alleging that some agent has caused a given harm) requires evidence of a relative risk of at least two" (Kristin Shrader-Frechette, personal communication 1 April 2007).   ∎

In a recent study, the European Environmental Agency reviewed the 2002 history of suspect environmental and occupational hazards and concluded that many of the hazards recognized as confirmed and serious today first came to our attention as the result of evidence of disease and health effects that was not statistically significant at the time. Virtually none of the early suggestions turned out to be "false positives." Some have argued that random disease causation would result in one out of 20 disease cluster studies (5%) being a "false positive" at the $p = 0.05$ level (almost by definition). However, because there may be a lack of a clear relationship between a causative exposure and an observable health effect given the variety of confounding factors in the real world, in practice only the most robust effects show through the "noise." Therefore, simple reliance on the possibility of a disease cluster being random will not usually constitute an informed public policy. See European Environmental Agency (2002) *Late Lessons from Early Warning: The Precautionary Principle 1896–2000*. Environmental Issue Report No. 22, ISBN 92-9167-323-4, Copenhagen, Denmark.

8. Over the past decade, as information on the human genome has been gathered, there has been an increased focus on genetic factors in disease causation. One outgrowth of this has been the emergence of what many now call genetic epidemiology—the use of epidemiology to investigate the inherited causes of disease in given populations. For any given disease, the primary goal of genetic epidemiology is to determine whether the disease has a genetic component and, if so, to estimate the relative contribution of one's genetic makeup in comparison to other factors (such as environmental exposures) in disease causation. See Jaakko Kaprio (2000) "Genetic Epidemiology," *BMJ* 320: 1257–1259. However, a workshop convened by the National Academy of Sciences in 2002 concluded that "only a small percentage of cancer is attributed to the powerful dominant single genes or the strongest toxicants." See "Cancer and the Environment: Gene-Environment Interactions" (Free Executive Summary) http://www.nap.edu/catalog/10464.html from Samuel Wilson, Lovell Jones, Christine Couseens, and Kathi Hanna, Editors, Roundtable on Environment Health Sciences, Research, and Medicine, in *Cancer and the Environment: Gene-Environment Interactions*, ISBN 978-0-309-08475-8, National Academy Press, Washington, D.C.

E. SCIENTIFIC UNCERTAINTY, VALUES, AND IMPLICATIONS FOR POLICY: CAN A "SAFE" LEVEL OF EXPOSURE BE UNEQUIVOCALLY DETERMINED?

Several types of uncertainty plague the determination of dose-response relationships and safe (or acceptably low) exposure levels. Uncertainty can be associated with an accurate point estimate of risk, risk profiles, indeterminacy, and ignorance. A point estimate of annual risk, e.g., a 0.1% chance of being killed if you ride a motorcycle, may be determined from data on motorcycle deaths in large urban populations and describes a well-defined probability, but the certainty of a particular individual being killed is not known. Second, it should be recognized that point estimates of expected risk from pollution or health hazards are extremely rare. Although a few risks, such as the risk of hearing loss in a population with continuous noise exposure, are unusually well defined, most risks are expressed as a range bounded by defined levels of uncertainty. Here, risk is itself a *probability distribution* (of the probability of harm versus the degree of harm), and the tails of the distribution are usually not well defined. As a result, a data point on a dose-response curve usually has a fairly large range of uncertainty associated with it, often expressed as a 95 percent confidence level. The lower the dose, the greater the degree of uncertainty. This is a direct consequence of the limitations of animal data or epidemiological evidence, as discussed earlier. This is the most commonly understood concept of uncertainty, but there are additional uncertainties.

Indeterminacy compounds the problem. This is where one knows what one does not know, but more experimentation and observation will not yield useful results in a timely fashion. We know that cancers that begin by mutagenesis are promoted by other chemicals, for example, but it would be nearly impossible to identify which of the many chemicals to which people are exposed are the promoters.

Moreover, there is abject *ignorance*, where we don't even know what we don't know. For example, endocrine disruption was not a known effect of chemical exposure until relatively recently, and thus it was not a focus of toxicological or epidemiological research. The fact that our risk assessments can be compromised by these various types of uncertainty, many believe, argues for precaution, especially with exposure to persistent, bioaccumulative, and/or halogenated compounds or alkylating agents.

Public Policy Response
N. A. Ashford and C. S. Miller

Source: "Low-Level Exposures to Chemicals Challenge Both Science and Regulatory Policy," *Environmental Science and Technology* 508A–509A, November 1998.

We propose that a systems-focused approach to disease best fits the pattern of the emerging illnesses of the 21st Century. It is our view that a systems approach likewise is needed as we fashion our public policy responses. The lack of clear biomarkers and the time lag between initiating exposures and ultimate disease make it technically, and increasingly politically, difficult to develop the extensive body of evidence needed to *regulate* many chemicals and industrial processes or to *compensate* the chemically injured. For this reason, we must seriously consider adoption of the *Precautionary Principle*, a concept endorsed at the UN Conference on Environment and Sustainable Development in Rio de Janeiro and already implemented in some European and U.S. regulatory systems. That is, we must act preventively in the face of uncertainty, erring on the side of caution. This requires education of the public, government, and industry, as well as political courage and conviction.

Over the past 25 years, scientific concern over emerging environmental or public health problems generally has begun with a suggestion—sometimes a mere whisper—that trouble was brewing. Those suggestions and whispers ultimately ripened into full-fledged confirmations that our worst fears were true. Examples include asbestos-related cancer, and the toxic effects of benzene, lead, and persistent pesticides. The frightening but enlightening reality is that with few excep-

tions the early warnings warranted heeding and the bulk of predictions were certainly in the right direction, if not understated. In retrospect, not only were our precautionary actions justified, but we waited far too long to take those actions. Endocrine disrupting chemicals [and neurotoxic chemicals] present an opportunity to act more quickly than we have in the past, although some damage has already been done. Intervening now to prevent the next generation of developmentally or immunologically compromised or chemically intolerant persons, many of them children, is both possible and necessary.

Admittedly, there is considerable uncertainty about some aspects of endocrine disruption and other systemic damage or injury. We are told that this uncertainty places environmental legislators and regulators on the horns of a dilemma. They must risk making one of two types of mistakes: a Type I error is committed if they regulate a chemical, imposing large costs on industry and the consumer, and the chemical later turns out to be safe; a Type II error is committed if they fail to regulate a chemical which turns out later to be harmful. The Precautionary Principle argues for regulation when the scientific evidence is sufficiently compelling—but not perfect. It states a preference for avoiding a Type II error. As long as there is some scientific uncertainty, even if it is small, a potentially regulated industry is understandably more interested in avoiding a Type I error.

- ■ NOTES

1. Some have argued that a "Type III" error can occur when we are working on the wrong problem. Here the existence of indeterminacy and ignorance are especially relevant.

2. While she critiques risk assessment as it is currently practiced, Ellen Silbergeld also advocates a move to outright bans or technology-based approaches for controlling risk rather than try to improve imperfect risk assessment methodologies. Later in this book, we (like Barry Commoner in chapter 1) argue that even much more of a shift is needed, one that focuses on changing the technology of production as a strategic approach. See Ellen K. Silbergeld (1993) "Risk Assessment: The Perspective and Experience of U.S. Environmentalists," *Environmental Health* Perspectives 101(2): 100–104, June.   ■

The following article discusses the relative contributions of science and values to the regulatory process, and challenges the notion that risk assessment and risk management decisions can be neatly separated.

Science and Values: Can They Be Separated?
Nicholas A. Ashford

Source: "Science and Values in the Regulatory Process," *Statistical Science* 3(3): 377–383 (August 1988) (references omitted), excerpted with permission.

Although scientific inquiry often claims to be value-neutral (i.e., non-normative), the same cannot be said for the uses of scientific information in decisions concerning the control of science and technology. It is therefore important to ask whether the conduct of policy-relevant scientific inquiry, such as risk assessment, can ever really be value neutral. The practice of science has been described as reductionist, that is, science teases out the most likely correct truth in an uncertain world by using simplifying assumptions and theories. The traditions and conventions adopted by science in order to establish "truth" are traditions and conventions to deal with uncertainties in both scientific theory and data. In the evolution of a scientific paradigm or methodology, for example, science often establishes clearly visible standards which must be achieved for something to be considered true. The things that are considered true according to these standards are called facts. When we are certain about scientific explanations, we call these explanations laws. When we are less certain, we call them theories. To change a scientific theory into a scientific law, we need both confirmation of the theory by existing data and acceptable explanations of data that appear to deviate from the predictions of the theory. Science recognizes that such confirmation or explanations cannot be 100% certain. Scientific tradition and conventions establish the minimum scientifically acceptable probability of being correct and the maximum scientifically acceptable probability of being wrong in reaching a conclusion.

Legal actions seek to be fair and to encourage the correct outcome in societal activities, including the applications of science and technology. In prescribing or prohibiting a given activity, the law, like science, is sensitive to the probability that a certain view of the world might be right or might be wrong. What the law calls a fact—sometimes called a legal fact—is based on a set of data that is certain enough to justify a given directive or conclusion. But the law also seeks to encourage the correct result in the normative sense, that is, what John Rawls would call the just thing. The law and the policy process recognize that something must be true enough to justify an action, but the same basis for truth is not required as a prerequisite to arriving at a just outcome in different situations. Law thus seemingly creates a paradox whereby things can be regarded as true for some purposes but not for others. Science, on the other hand, insists that things are either true or untrue, and by marshalling established scientific conventions as the tests, encourages us to believe that no value judgment ever attends the establishment of truth.

It is, however, clear that those who undertake scientific inquiry today, in fact, hold values concerning the use of their science. Within a given framework of scientific traditions and conventions, there are many ways to analyze and present data. There are also many ways to frame the scientific question and choose which data to collect. A scientist's choice among these possibilities is shaped by values. By either speaking out about those values or by remaining silent, scientists exercise a value judgment about the way science is used in regulation. Accordingly, as Professor Mark Rushefsky has observed, "Ostensible disputes over the science are, in reality, over the values inherent in the assumptions."

If science is not value-free, then how can it best inform the public policy debate? Many would address that question by requiring agencies to establish a two-step process for dealing with risk: risk assessment and risk management. The former is expected to be a non-normative scientific determination, and the latter a value-laden political decision to control a given hazard. However, the key question for policy makers is this: at what level of proof does a showing of risk or danger trigger a requirement for regulatory action? What is considered sufficient proof is a social policy determination, requiring a judgment about the consequences of both regulating and not regulating a possibly hazardous activity. Science can inform, but should not necessarily dictate, the results of that analysis.

Such judgments can be in error because of uncertainties with regard to the nature and extent of the risk or the economic and technologic feasibility of regulatory controls. Type I errors are committed when society regulates an activity which turns out not to be harmful and resources are needlessly expended. Type II errors are committed when, because of insufficient evidence, society fails to regulate an activity which turns out to be harmful. Aversion to making Type I and Type II errors reflects differing value decisions about (1) the nature of the mistakes made and (2) the extent, prevalence or magnitude of the mistakes. An aversion to Type I errors underlies the often expressed pleas that we "move the regulatory process toward better science." In some cases this may simply be a request to be more permissive in controlling technologic activities.

The interplay of facts, or science, and values can be illuminated by three general scenarios concerning carcinogen regulation:

1. If a causal relationship is shown which satisfies the accepted scientific conventions for establishing that a chemical causes cancer, then a scientific determination has been made which can inform the public policy process. (An example is the overwhelming evidence that asbestos exposure causes mesothelioma.) Then, the decision to notify, regulate, or compensate is essentially a social or public policy decision.

2. If a sizable majority of the relevant and respected scientific community believes that a

substance is probably carcinogenic (perhaps more likely than not), although causality has not been proven at the conventional (high) level of statistical significance or with sufficient strength of association, then a science policy determination has been made that justifies treating the substance as if it were carcinogenic. The scientists who reach such a consensus have similar values regarding the use to which the scientific data will be put. Specifically, the decision to view the substance as a probable carcinogen in this scenario reflects an aversion to Type II errors, that is, erring on the side of caution. Their science policy decision can then inform the social policy decision taken by the regulatory agency.

3. If the scientific community reaches no consensus about labeling a substance as carcinogenic (for regulatory purposes), then there is no scientific or science policy determination to inform regulatory decision making. However, it may still be sound social policy to control that substance. A decision to regulate under these circumstances would merely mean that the regulator's preference for making Type I versus Type II errors is different from that of the scientists who reviewed the evidence.

These three scenarios, of course, represent points on what is really a continuum of scientific uncertainty. They merely illustrate the varying relationship of science and values encountered in the regulatory process. Under conditions of uncertainty, the nature of the scientific consensus or science policy determination, may depend on the use to which data and information will be put. Consensus on the minimum evidence required for action will, and probably should, differ according to whether the purpose is notification, regulation or compensation.

Thus, while a uniform intellectual approach to the question of risk assessment and risk management is theoretically desirable, uniform conventions, such as statistical

significance or the rejection or acceptance of negative studies, are not advisable in deciding what level of proof is acceptable for policy purposes. Value judgments clearly attend decisions whether to lean in favor of Type I or Type II errors in specific cases. This is because the cost of being wrong in one instance may be vastly different from the cost of being wrong in another. For example, banning a chemical which is essential to a beneficial societal activity (such as the use of radionuclides in medicine) has potentially more drastic consequences than banning a nonessential chemical for which there is a close, cost-comparable substitute. It may be perfectly appropriate to rely on most likely estimates of risk in the first case and on worst case analysis in the second. This approach illustrates not only a preference for making Type I rather than Type II errors, but also illustrates the dependence of that preference on the size of the Type I error.

In each of the three scenarios described above, both a fair process and a fair outcome are desirable. A fair process has its origins in the legal tradition of due process, but more generally means that a procedure for the determinations of both science and policy has provided adequate opportunity for presentation and discussion of the data, their relevance for society and the underlying values and preferences of the participants regarding the use of the data or findings. Whether a process is fair or not can usually be determined objectively by any observer without deciding questions of fact or policy one way or another. In contrast, a fair outcome has as its reference or basis a particular observer's view of the same issues. People who would make different decisions concerning a fact or policy might not call the outcome fair, although they might agree that the process leading to it was fair.

In Scenario 1, scientists can contribute their work product (or publish their findings) and hope that the facts will speak for themselves when considered by the decision makers. Of course, there may be vigorous dissent about the scientific studies themselves, and this may require open discussion of the science. But this process can usually be handled with fairness by the scientists themselves in an informal way through peer review and other avenues for open exchange and criticism. A more formal process targeted toward elucidating facts and values will then be required for the subsequent policy decision to ensure that the data are put to an appropriate use for regulatory purposes. It is within this scenario that a cost-benefit analysis, in which either net benefits of a proposed action, or a benefit-to-cost ratio, is sometimes the basis for a decision. Type I and Type II errors are small and hence play no part in the decision process. Instead, the decision maker's values regarding net benefits or a benefit-to-cost ratio is the basis.

In Scenario 2, a fair process is needed not only for the risk management decision, but also during risk assessment in order that the science policy determinations are properly arrived at. Such a process is required to illuminate the values that may be hidden behind science policy conclusions. In this scenario, uncertainty (and error avoidance) plays a larger role, and values enter in arriving at science policy conclusions. A cost-benefit basis for a decision appears to be, but is not the sole basis for the decision.

In Scenario 3 we are unsure about the correctness of the outcome, that is, Type I and/or Type II errors are large. The best we can do is to provide a fair process for the resolution of competing values, because the final social policy decision turns largely on value choices concerning Type I and Type II errors.

■ **NOTES**

1. For an insightful treatment of the problems with risk analysis within the context of environmental law, see D. Hornstein (1992) "Reclaiming Environmental Law: A Normative Critique of Comparative Risk Analysis," *Columbia Law Review* vol. 92, pp. 562–633.

2. For a laudatory treatment of risk assessment in environmental law, see Mathew D. Adler (2004) "Against 'Individual Risk': A Sympathetic Critique of Risk Assessment," University of Pennsylvania, Institute for Law & Economics Research Paper 04-01; and University of Pennsylvania Law School, Public Law Working Paper 49. Access at http://papers.ssrn.com/sol3/papers.cfm?abstract_id=487123   ■

3 Economics and the Environment

A.   INTRODUCTION

The relevance of economics for the evaluation and design of environmental policy has numerous dimensions. Some relate to the basis for environmental decision making, e.g., the use of cost-benefit analysis to determine whether and to what extent to regulate, while others are instrumental, e.g., the use of market-based instruments to achieve environmental goals. First, environmental resources, amenities, and quality have *economic value*. Second, while markets are useful in providing society with goods and services in general, there are serious *market imperfections* (what some describe as market failures) that justify government intervention to protect the environment. Third, in the proper context, economics can contribute to *evaluating and prioritizing alternative policies* for improving the environment, both within a given area of concern (such as the reduction of air pollution from a variety of sources) and among different areas of concern (such as air pollution, water pollution, and hazardous wastes). Fourth, economics, through the application of *cost-benefit* analysis, offers an alternative policy rationale for determining whether, and to what extent, a particular environmental problem should be controlled or addressed. Finally, as discussed in chapter 12, *market-based instruments* are increasingly promoted as complements to, and sometimes as substitutes for, traditional regulatory approaches.

In general, the trend toward market-based decision making and control represents a shift away from some of the values underlying the congressional mandates embodied in many of the nation's bedrock environmental statutes. This is illustrative of the fact that economics and law compete politically for dominance in environmental policy formulation. Further, within the discipline of economics there are radically different schools of thought. In the United States, neoclassical environmental economics predominates over both ecological economics[1] and socioeconomics.[2] A central tenet of neoclassical environmental economics is that the goal of environmental policy should be to achieve economic efficiency. As we will see, this "economic efficiency" is commonly defined with reference to production and pollution control technology currently in existence, and thus generally fails to incorporate the dynamics of technological change. One goal of this text is to shift the discussion away from the preoccupation of neoclassical economics and traditional decision making with *static* efficiency, and to enlarge the discussion to include the *dynamic* efficiency that can be achieved through technological change.

We also offer a word or two about underlying biases. Often, what are presented as academic or intellectual arguments about issues such as the value of human life,

---

1. See Daly (1991) and Costanza and Daly (1991).
2. See R. H. Ashford (2004).

the importance of achieving efficiency in fashioning solutions, or the effects of a particular strategy on technological innovation are in reality attempts to cloak political and disciplinary ideology in non-normative frameworks. One of the goals of this chapter is to identify the *normative* implications of the various ways in which economics influences environmental policy and to explore the associated underlying values.

B. THE ECONOMIC VALUE OF ENVIRONMENTAL AMENITIES, RESOURCES, AND QUALITY

Our economy and our natural environment are inextricably linked, both because the environment contributes to our economic welfare and because the economic decisions we make affect the quality of our environment. From an economic perspective, the environment performs four valuable functions. First, the environment supplies natural resources—including minerals, timber, and oil and other energy resources—that are used as inputs in the production of economic goods and services.[3] Second, in some cases, the environment serves as a potential receptor of wastes generated by production and consumption activities to the extent that waste products can be biologically or chemically processed by the environment; for example, wetlands can provide a natural cleansing mechanism for water systems. However, the environment has a limited *assimilative* capacity for these wastes.[4] Third, the environment contributes fresh water and food necessary to sustain life and provides other life-support functions as well, such as maintaining temperature, climate, and an atmospheric composition suitable for life. Fourth, the environment provides direct amenities that

---

3. A distinction is sometimes made between natural resources that are *renewable* and those that are *nonrenewable* (or *depletable*). Trees are a frequently used example of a renewable resource, since timber can be generated indefinitely as long as the stock of trees is maintained through replanting and forestry management. (Note that trees are not a *fully* renewable resource, however, because many people place a higher value on old-growth forests.) In contrast, coal is a nonrenewable resource whose stock inevitably decreases as the resource is used in production.

4. The notion of the environment's assimilative capacity—usually with reference to a medium's capacity to maintain itself, such as in the case of a lake—has been criticized insofar as it implies that there is no associated environmental damage below some threshold level of assimilative capacity. In most cases, there is some increased level of environmental damage even before these threshold levels are reached. In addition, even if the waste levels do not exceed the assimilative capacity of the environment, humans and other animal life exposed to the waste may suffer serious, and sometimes fatal, health effects. As discussed in chapter 1, for example, endocrine-disrupting chemicals can cause damage to all species at remarkably low levels. Some types of pollutants are incapable of being transformed into harmless or less harmful substances by natural processes. These persistent pollutants—which include metals such as mercury and lead, and manmade substances such as PCBs (polychlorinated biphenyls) and DDT (dichlorodiphenyltrichloroethane)—build up (bioaccumulate) in the environment or in animal life. See, for example, Nisbet (1991).

enhance human enjoyment, education, and spiritual well-being.[5] Examples of what many, or most, individuals consider environmental amenities include beautiful landscapes, recreational sites, and the existence of diverse life forms on the earth. These four functions can be viewed as economic services in the sense that they all have a positive economic value: if these services could be purchased and sold in the marketplace, people would willingly pay to receive more of them, or to avoid receiving less of them. It is sometimes assumed that economic and commercial activity leads inevitably to environmental degradation, but that is not necessarily so. Many economic activities have only an incidental effect on the environment, and some economic activities may specifically, and by intention, reduce environmental damage in the first place. Typically, however, it is economic activity that causes environmental damage.[6] Aside from diminishing the positive aspects of environmental resources, amenities, and systems, the production, use, and disposal of toxic substances directly damages human and wildlife health and indirectly damages them through stratospheric ozone depletion and climate disruption.

In this textbook, our investigation of economic aspects of the environment is focused on environmental pollution and excludes what has come to be known as "natural resource economics," an important field that concerns the management and use, over time, of renewable and nonrenewable resources such as fisheries, forests, minerals, and energy sources.[7]

In this chapter and later in chapter 12 (which focuses on alternative forms of government intervention to promote pollution reduction) we examine three major issues associated with the economics of environmental protection: (1) imperfections in the workings of private markets that result in excessive levels of pollution and environmental damage relative to what individuals or society may desire, (2) various types of government policies that can be introduced in an effort to remedy these market imperfections and thus increase environmental protection through improved economic performance, and (3) methods for evaluating and choosing among candidate government programs to remedy environmental problems.[8]

---

5. See Kellert and Wilson (1993).

6. For a perspective of the world in which economic activity takes place within ecological limits, see the work on "ecological economics" pioneered by Herman Daly (1991). See also Constanza and Daly (1991).

7. For an introduction to the field of natural resource economics, see Harris (2005). Also see relevant sections of Fisher (1981), Tietenberg (2003), and Hanley, Shogren, and White (1997).

8. The literature on environmental economics is vast, and we can only hope here to provide an overview of the major issues. For a more comprehensive and more technical discussion, see Baumol and Oates (1988), Tietenberg (2003), United States Environmental Protection Agency (2000), and Hanley, Shogren, and White (1997). For a dated, but useful, survey of the literature, see Cropper and Oates (1992).

C. MARKET IMPERFECTIONS[9] AS THE BASIS FOR GOVERNMENT INTERVENTION

In our society it is often argued that the preferred mechanism for conducting economic and social activities, and for making economic and social decisions, is the private market—a decentralized network of private transactions through which information about individual preferences is imparted. The theoretical well-functioning ("perfect") market system possesses two important properties. First, the perfect market is *economically* (allocatively) *efficient*. This means that resources are allocated to those who value them most highly (an alternative formulation is that resources are put to their most valued use); the appropriate mix of goods and services, embodying the desired grouping of characteristics (for example, size, color, and style for clothing) is produced; and all possible mutually beneficial exchanges take place, so that further improvements in the welfare of any member of society cannot be attained without making at least one other member worse off. Second, consistent with libertarian values, transactions in the perfect market are entirely *voluntary*; only if the interested parties are able to negotiate to mutual advantage will a market exchange occur.

For private markets to function as postulated by economic theory, however, four conditions must be satisfied. First, those parties engaging in marketplace transactions must bear all of the costs and derive all of the benefits of their actions; that is, the market must not generate *externalities*. Second, market participants must have *perfect information*; they must be fully informed about their market options and about the consequences of exercising those options. Third, markets must be *perfectly competitive*, so that individual economic agents (sellers or buyers) do not have undue influence over the price of goods sold (e.g., through monopoly pricing). Fourth, since market outcomes will vary according to the preexisting distribution of wealth and other social parameters that underlie and reflect issues of equity and justice, the legitimacy and desirability of market outcomes require that the *ethical and distributional* setting in which private markets function be socially acceptable.

In practice, of course, these conditions are violated in important ways. In the following paragraphs we discuss these market imperfections and their effects on the level of environmental pollution. Much of the focus will be on issues of *static efficiency*, by which we mean the allocation of resources using current technology. However, consistent with a main theme of this work—that environmental regulation

---

9. We prefer the term "market imperfections" to the term "market failure," for two reasons. First, as discussed later in this chapter, perfectly working markets may only achieve static, rather than dynamic, efficiency. Second, economic efficiency—whether static or dynamic—may result in outcomes that are nonetheless socially undesirable (e.g., because of equity considerations).

can (and should) serve as a mechanism to promote technological changes that reduce environmental and human risk—we will also be examining the effect of market imperfections on *dynamic efficiency*, particularly as it concerns the development of technological innovations that create new opportunities for reducing pollution.

1. Externalities

Externalities arise when the actions of one party impose costs or bestow benefits on other parties that are direct (as opposed to those caused indirectly by price adjustments), but that are not recognized in market transactions. The classic example of an externality is, in fact, environmental pollution. Where, for instance, a factory's pollution of a river diminishes the welfare of individuals downstream, but the downstream residents receive no compensation for this from the firm that owns the factory, a *negative externality* (what is sometimes called a "public bad," in contrast to a "public good") has been created. The presence of externalities undermines the efficiency of the market because, given the resulting divergence between social and private costs, the market imparts inaccurate signals.[10] In the water pollution example, the (unregulated) firm is able to regard water as a costless resource, even though the firm's production decisions impose social costs on the individuals downstream. As a consequence, the firm will find it profitable to pollute the water resource beyond the socially optimal level.

This is illustrated in figure 3.1. The horizontal axis depicts the amount of pollution discharged by the firm. A movement from right to left indicates that less pollution is being discharged. Curve A represents the marginal cost *to the firm* of reducing pollution. As the firm reduces its emissions from E' to 0, it becomes increasingly costly for the firm to make additional discharge reductions. Curve B is the marginal *social* cost (what might be called "disbenefits") of pollution damage—not to the firm, but to the individuals downstream. This curve is sometimes referred to as the marginal "willingness to pay" to avoid pollution, or the marginal value of clean air or water. Thus, this curve also represents the marginal *benefits* to those individuals of pollution reduction.

The marginal social cost increases as the firm increases its discharge from 0 to E'. According to classical economic theory, the *socially optimal* amount of pollution discharge is E^*, the point at which the damage caused by an additional unit of pollution

---

10. While externalities cause markets to function inefficiently—and result in excessive amounts of environmental pollution—these problems are hardly unique to market economies. Evidence from centrally planned economies, such as those of the former Soviet Union, indicates that pollution problems there are every bit as large as, if not larger, than they are in the United States and other market-based economies. See, for example, Goldman (1985).

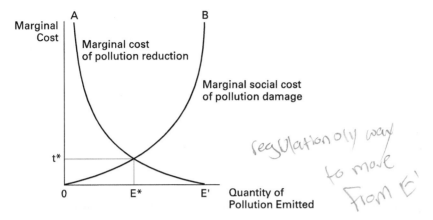

Figure 3.1
The socially optimal level of pollution derived from the marginal costs and benefits of pollution control.

is just equal to the marginal cost t^* of avoiding it.[11] Operating in an unregulated market, however, the firm would instead choose to discharge pollution at point E', in excess of the socially optimal amount. The reason is that, since the marginal cost of pollution damage *to the firm* is zero, the firm will not find it profitable to incur any costs to reduce its discharge of pollutants.

■ NOTES

1. Note that the points on the cost curve A are derived from the costs of alternative (technological) means to control or reduce pollution. These include, e.g., end-of-pipe air and water pollution control, waste management, substitution of feedstocks or starting materials, process redesign, and product reformulation. The latter three are known as "pollution prevention" or "cleaner production approaches." Combinations of pollution reduction technologies may be used. Sometimes industrial systems can be continuously tuned to reduce pollution to any desired level (for example, by systematically choosing fuels with different sulfur content). In other, and perhaps most cases, technologies are discrete and the corresponding cost curves are not smooth; instead different combinations of technologies are used to achieve stepwise progressions from one level of risk reduction to another.

11. The socially optimal level of pollution is that which minimizes the sum of (1) the costs of pollution control and (2) the costs of pollution damage. At pollution levels in excess of E^* in figure 3.1, total social costs are higher since the increase in pollution damage exceeds the reduction in the costs of pollution reduction. At pollution levels below E^*, total social costs are also higher since the increase in pollution reduction costs exceeds the amount by which pollution damage is lessened.

2. The points on the social cost (societal demand) curve B are determined either from revealed willingness-to-pay preferences (discussed later) for pollution reduction or a calculus attached to valuing lives saved or illness and injury prevented, and are derived from risk assessments and the observed willingness of persons to work in more dangerous occupations in return for higher wages (where the increase in wages is known as the "wage differential" or "wage premium for risk").   ▪

What causes externalities to exist? Economists have identified several overlapping factors, including the following: (1) an absence of property rights, (2) nonrival consumption and nonexcludability, (3) free-rider problems, and (4) high transaction costs.

• *Property rights* refer to a set of entitlements defining the owner's privileges and limitations for the use of a resource. These encompass the right to exclude others from using, encroaching upon, damaging, or seizing the resource. Because many environmental resources are not privately owned and their property rights are not well defined, it is difficult for private markets to allocate them efficiently.

• *Nonrival consumption* is a characteristic of goods that can be "consumed" by one person without reducing the ability of others to consume them as well. For example, within limits (that is, until congestion sets in), one person's enjoyment of a beautiful landscape does not prevent others from deriving equal pleasure from it.

• *Nonexcludability* refers to a situation in which it is technically impossible or excessively expensive to prevent others from consuming an existing resource. For example, it is virtually impossible to exclude a resident from enjoying the benefits of improved air quality in the area.

• *Free-rider problems*—which are closely connected with the characteristics of nonrival consumption and nonexcludability—arise when individuals can enjoy the use of a resource without having to compensate the owner for it. Hence, the individuals have no incentive to pay for the resource or to reveal the value of the resource to them.

• *High transaction costs* apply when the negotiations needed to successfully accomplish a market transaction are complicated and time-consuming, and consequently expensive.[12] Where property rights are absent and a large number of individuals are able to enjoy the use of a resource—again because of nonrival consumption and nonexcludability—then transaction costs will typically be enormous.[13]

---

12. High transaction costs may also apply because of the difficulty and expense of enforcing property rights arising from a market transaction.

13. This suggests that the law ought to be used to minimize transaction costs, but Driesen and Ghosh (2005) argue that finite transaction costs may serve positive purposes such as in expending effort, time, or costs to avoid bad transactions or to acquire needed valuable information. See the discussion on imperfect information in the following section.

In general, environmental resources, such as ambient air and natural waterways, are characterized by an absence of well-defined property rights, by nonrival consumption and nonexcludability, by free-rider problems, and by prohibitively high costs of putting together and enforcing transactions to protect their quality.[14] It is these features of environmental resources that cause externalities to exist.

The effects of externalities on the level of environmental pollution are normally portrayed in terms of *static* efficiency; that is, at a point in time when technological opportunities are fixed. This was the approach taken, for instance, in figure 3.1. The effects of externalities on *dynamic* efficiency—over time, as technological opportunities are allowed to vary—generally are even more pronounced. The reason is not difficult to understand. It can be a costly and risky endeavor for firms to attempt to develop new production processes or new products that reduce the amount of environmental pollution. Firms will undertake such projects only with the expectation of recovering those costs and earning economic profits when the new pollution-reducing technologies are brought to market. Because of externalities, however, a firm operating in a free market generally does not bear the costs of the pollution it creates. The firm thus would have no incentive either to develop pollution-reducing technologies itself or to purchase pollution-reducing processes or products from other firms. Consequently, in the absence of potential demand for pollution-reducing innovations, no firm would invest in the development of such technologies unless they offered other economic advantages as well.[15]

2. Imperfect Information

The economist's model of an idealized market system assumes that the participants are fully informed of their options. Applied to environmental pollution, this

---

14. The famous Coase Theorem holds that in a competitive market, *if* affected parties are able to negotiate freely with each other and transaction costs are small, assigning unilateral property rights to environmental resources, regardless of which party is assigned those rights, is sufficient to lead to an efficient market outcome without any (other) government intervention (Coase, 1960). (According to this theorem, applying the so-called *Polluter Pays Principle*—discussed at the end of this chapter—does not change the ultimate use of resources or extent of damage, although it does impose costs preferentially on the polluting party.) The Coase Theorem is more of a theoretical curiosity than a practical solution to environmental problems because the conditions necessary for it to apply—ease of negotiation and negligible transaction costs to strike a bargain—are quite often absent. This certainly is the case where pollution has an adverse effect on numerous parties, all of whom have an incentive to strategically misrepresent their willingness-to-pay to eliminate the pollution, or to take a "free ride" on others' willingness-to-pay.

15. See, however, the later discussion of "first-mover" advantages of firms who respond first to new environmental requirements, articulated independently by Ashford et al. (1979, 1983; Ashford, Ayers, and Stone, 1985) and Porter and van der Linde (1995a, 1995b) who argued, respectively, that there are "ancillary benefits" or "innovation offsets" to compliance costs for the firm in terms of the benefits of correcting production inefficiencies resulting from pollution. These may be of great economic benefit to innovating firms.

assumption requires that all interested parties know: (1) the magnitude and composition of environmental pollution, as well as its sources—the firms and consumers responsible for emitting the pollutants; (2) the effects of pollutants on human health and the environment; and (3) the availability, cost, and effectiveness of pollution-reducing processes, equipment, and products. These informational assumptions are rarely realized in practice. Moreover, placing an economic value on human health and environmental amenities is fraught with difficulty.[16]

In general, the types and concentrations of air and water pollution are site-specific and are likely to vary significantly over time. An interested party may be able to sense the presence of pollutants by their accompanying odors or irritating effects, but typically is not able to discern their magnitude or composition. Furthermore, because pollutants migrate in air and water and soil, and because the same pollutant typically is emitted by many firms, it is usually difficult to identify the original source of pollution at a specific site and time. (Polluters might be aware of their own hazardous emissions, but it certainly is not in their interest to share that information with others.) Of course, interested parties could monitor pollution sites and the emissions of suspected polluters. Monitoring, however, is a costly activity and because externalities deaden incentives to reduce pollution, monitoring is unlikely to be pursued in an unfettered market system.

In the vast majority of cases, it is also difficult to determine the effects of specific environmental pollutants on human health. Many human diseases associated with environmental exposure have multiple potential causes, and may be the result of synergistic effects. This often makes it virtually impossible to ascertain whether an individual's disease was caused or exacerbated by environmental exposure rather than by nonenvironmental factors such as diet, genetic predisposition, or physiological or psychological stress.[17] This problem is compounded by the fact that there frequently is a long latency period—sometimes 20 years or more—between exposure to the environmental health hazard and the manifestation of the consequent disease. Similarly, in many cases the environmental damage—such as deforestation, soil erosion, acid rain, depletion of stratospheric ozone, reduction of dissolved oxygen in water, and animal poisonings—caused by specific amounts and types of pollutants have not yet been quantitatively established.

---

16. For an examination of the theoretical and empirical problems associated with imputing a monetary value for human health and environmental amenities, see, for example, Ortolano (1997, pp. 117–143), and section E.1 in this chapter.

17. It is true that on rare occasions the cause of a disease is unique, or nearly so. Examples of such "signature" diseases are angiosarcoma, which is caused by exposure to vinyl chloride, and mesothelioma, which is caused by exposure to asbestos. Even in the case of signature diseases, however, individuals may not know whether their exposure to the hazardous substance in question was occupationally or environmentally related.

Finally, many polluting firms are unaware of the existence of pollution-reducing technologies and, again because externalities deaden incentives to reduce pollution in an unfettered market system, they lack an economic motive to incur the costs of searching for such technologies.

3. Imperfect Competition

The economist's idealized competitive market system is also predicated on a model of perfect competition. That is, the market for each commodity is assumed to contain such a large number of buyers and such a large number of sellers that no individuals are able, through their actions, to influence the price of the commodity. Each buyer and seller therefore treats prices as given and makes profit-maximizing decisions by comparing marginal gains or losses against the corresponding market price.

In actuality, firms in some industries possess an appreciable degree of market power and are therefore able to influence or even control the price at which their products are sold. This is especially the case with specialty chemicals that have unique properties and uses and thus have no real competitors offering close substitutes either as inputs to a production process or as final products. Thus, the idealized concept of substitution operating to replace "bad" chemicals with "better" ones often does not reflect reality unless markets are competitive.[18] Even large-volume chemicals tend to be produced by a small number of firms, often operating more or less as an oligopoly.

When it comes to the amount, as opposed to the nature of, environmental pollution, the static effects of imperfect competition appear to be of secondary importance, certainly relative to externalities and imperfect information. In fact, because industries in which firms possess significant market power tend to restrict output, they will also tend to generate less pollution (assuming the level of pollution per unit of output is constant) than if those industries were perfectly competitive.[19] In terms of the dynamic effects on environmental pollution, however, the presence of significant market power may play a more crucial and less desirable role. Recall that it is the spur of competition and the lure of profitable opportunities that induce firms to undertake innovative activity. Firms that possess significant market power— and thus are already earning excess profits and are at least somewhat insulated from

---

18. For a discussion from the perspective that substitution can be used to offset concerns about sustainable development, see Solow (1991).

19. Although it is beyond the scope of our discussion here, it is for this reason that measures to reduce the excessive amount of pollution caused by externalities theoretically need not be as stringent when they are applied to monopolistic industries as when they are applied to competitive industries. See, for example, Baumol and Oates (1988, pp. 79–85).

competitive pressures—should be far less likely to expose themselves to the techno-logical and financial risks associated with attempts to develop less costly and more effective methods of limiting environmental pollution.

4. Market-Related Inequities and Injustices

The economist's idealized market system allocates resources efficiently, but not nec-essarily optimally in a social sense. In the economist's "efficient" market, it is impos-sible to *reallocate* resources in a way that makes someone better off without making someone else worse off. Economists refer to such an allocation of resources as the "Pareto optimal" (or, more accurately, "Pareto efficient") outcome.[20] A market that has attained this state of Pareto efficiency is known as an economically efficient market. However, market transactions do not take place in a vacuum. They occur in a social setting with a preexisting distribution of wealth and a specified set of individ-ual rights and obligations. Market outcomes will vary according to these prevailing social conditions.

If the initial endowment of wealth were distributed in an unjust or socially undesir-able manner, the resulting market outcome would in all likelihood not be *socially* op-timal, partly because winners do not generally compensate losers in the real world and partly because some suffer more than others. For example, the poor, or certain racial and ethnic groups, might bear a disproportionate share of risks from expo-sure to hazardous pollutants.[21] A socially preferred outcome could in principle be achieved by some more equitable, nonmarket reallocation of resources, even though there would be associated losses in efficiency from an *economic* standpoint.[22]

In addition, some individual actions are circumscribed by rights and duties, which take precedence over market opportunities. Market transactions in such circum-stances may be socially unacceptable on ethical grounds, even if they are voluntarily made. For example, we do not permit individuals to sell themselves into slavery or to bring their children into factories to assist them in earning wages for the family. Sim-ilarly, the right to vote and criminal penalties are privileges and sanctions, respec-tively, that cannot be transferred to others, through the market or otherwise.

Several types of ethical considerations arise in the case of environmental protec-tion. First, regardless of what the market-determined outcome might be, we as a so-

---

20. Pareto optimality is named after the Italian economist and sociologist, Vilfredo Pareto, who first proposed it as a criterion for measuring improvements in social welfare.

21. The concept of "environmental justice" has arisen to reflect this concern. See Ashford and Rest (2001).

22. In economic terms, unless a market outcome is socially optimal as well as Pareto optimal, then non-Pareto optimal allocations exist that are "socially preferred." See Mishan (1981, pp. 345–353).

ciety tend to want to place a limit on the environmental risks to which any person is exposed.[23]

Second, many communities affected by contamination have experienced significant economic, social, and health impacts. Some of these communities were socially disadvantaged prior to the discovery of the contamination and have suffered disproportionate environmental burdens. They have voiced considerable objection to the "environmental injustice" and disparate impacts they have suffered in connection with the contamination in their communities. This injustice is seen to result from the (1) prejudicial location of hazardous and polluting facilities in low-income or minority communities and/or (2) the absence of or inadequate attention to remediation or cleanup in these communities. In the latter case, the communities may decry government attention as "too little, too late" (Foreman, 1998; Bryant, 1995; GAO, 1983, 1995; Hofrichter, 1993; United Church of Christ, 1987).[24]

Furthermore, where government has responded, it has been accused of operating more or less in a vacuum, and the communities have reacted negatively, expressing dissatisfaction with both the outcomes and the process of cleanup activities. It is fair to say that the different governmental agencies operating at the federal, state, and local level have not always had a clear vision of their respective roles, nor have they always spoken consistently or "with one voice" to the community. When independent contractors also are active at the site—especially when they change over time—there is often community dissatisfaction with "the whole lot." Government involvement in contaminated communities continues to be a challenge and an ongoing learning experience for both the agencies and the community.

Finally, there is the crucial matter of *intergenerational equity*. Many of our environmental assets are nonrenewable, and once they are depleted or destroyed, the multifunctional services they provide—environmental amenities, life support, assimilative capacity, and productive resources—could be irreversibly lost to all future generations.[25] Furthermore, a large proportion of these environmental services are

---

23. It is sometimes argued that this is particularly so for environmental hazards because for the individuals at risk, the exposure to hazardous pollutants is generally neither voluntary nor compensated. It is true, however, that individuals may in some cases take actions that increase their exposure to environmental hazards. For instance, some individuals, typically because of financial hardship, choose to live near industrial sites where pollution levels are high or risk exposure to agricultural pesticides by accepting a job as a farm worker. Nevertheless, we as a society consider it unconscionable to allow individuals to be exposed to avoidable, life-threatening environmental risks, even if those risks arise as part of market decisions to which the individuals were deemed to have consented (in the same sense that we outlaw "voluntary" blackmail transactions because they are morally unacceptable).

24. The commentary on these assertions goes both ways and has now surfaced as contentious debate. In order to fully appreciate the social and political dynamics of contaminated communities of color or low economic status, it is important to realize that they believe both to be true.

25. Another intergenerational equity concern is that certain environmental pollutants—such as endocrine-disrupting chemicals—may affect yet-to-be-born individuals while they are still in the womb. See the discussion in chapter 2 and Colborn, Dumanoski, and Myers (1996).

unique, or at least without effective substitutes, so that the goods and services resulting from the depletion of our environmental assets cannot, in any meaningful sense, be said to compensate for them or to replace them. Many in our society share the view that this generation has an ethical responsibility to maintain its global inheritance for future generations.[26] While the terms of this responsibility are subject to debate and interpretation, it suggests, at a minimum, an obligation to ensure both that the environment will remain habitable (by preserving some sensible standard of environmental quality) and that some reasonable stock of environmental assets will be sustained for the next and future generations.[27]

D.   ECONOMIC EFFICIENCY AND THE TECHNOLOGICAL DYNAMIC

The preceding discussion of market imperfections indicates why the operation of an unfettered market economy most likely would result in levels of pollution and environmental damage that society would find excessive. Indeed, the existence of these imperfections is the classical market-based argument in favor of government intervention on behalf of public health and the environment. A certain amount of government intervention is necessary, the economist will say, to compensate for the imperfections of the market. But, in any given case, *how much* intervention is necessary? From an economics perspective, the "right" amount of intervention would be the amount necessary to bring the market into a condition of economic efficiency. This, however, leads to an important second question: What *type* of economic efficiency do we want?

As suggested earlier, the concept of economic efficiency can take either a static or a dynamic view of technology. In a state of *static efficiency*, all variables (including technological capability) are fixed. One thus calculates the "efficient" use of resources with reference to *existing* technology. Traditionally, it has been this notion of economic efficiency that economists have used in analyzing the need for, and predicting the effects of, environmental regulation. Referring again to figure 3.1, application of this traditional efficiency approach would dictate that the firm be required to reduce its pollution from E' to E^*, because E^* is the amount of pollution dictated by the intersection of curve A (the marginal cost to the firm of reducing pollution) with curve B (the marginal cost of the firm's pollution to society or the societal demand for pollution reduction). According to this viewpoint, requiring any *greater* pollution reduction from the firm would be counterproductive because it would lead

---

26. United Nations (1992).

27. For a more detailed examination of the issues surrounding intergenerational equity, see, for example, Pearce and Turner (1990, pp. 211–238) and Ortolano (1997, pp. 20–40).

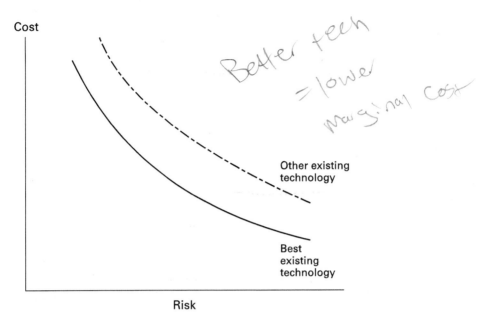

Figure 3.2
The efficiency frontier for risk reduction compliance.

to an economically "inefficient" result.[28] A lower reduction in pollution would likewise be socially suboptimal. E^* is the point of *static* economic efficiency. Again, it is termed "static" because the shape and location of curve A are determined by the cost to the firm of reducing pollution through the use of *existing* technology. Typically, this cost is calculated with reference to off-the-shelf pollution control technology—or pollution prevention technology—already in use within the industry or easily available from others.

The existing technology options are represented in figure 3.2. The solid curve in this figure differs from the marginal cost curve A in figure 3.1 in that the *total* cost of pollution (i.e., risk) reduction is depicted. For comparison, less effective technological choices are represented by the dashed curve.

The curve labeled "best existing technology" in figure 3.2 depicts the risk reduction costs a polluter faces by utilizing a variety of different technological approaches as a function of different levels of risk. At any given risk level, the curve represents the lowest-cost approach using the best existing technology, and is known as the

28. See, for example, the following description from a popular economics textbook: "The efficient level of emissions is at a point where the marginal social cost of emissions is equal to the marginal cost of abating emissions.... Note that if emissions are lower, the marginal cost of abating emissions is greater than the marginal social cost, so emissions are *too low*" (Pindyck and Rubinfeld, 1999, emphasis added).

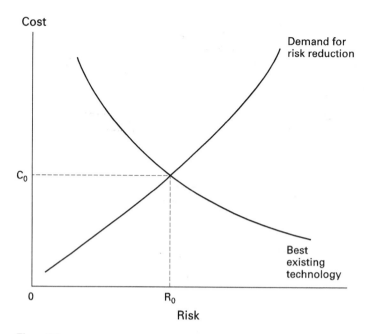

Cost

Demand for
risk reduction

Best
existing
technology

C_0

0 R_0

Risk

Figure 3.3
Optimal level of environmental risk as determined by costs of existing technology controls and perceived benefits.

efficiency frontier for compliance with a risk reduction goal. As more and more risk reduction is required (proceeding to the left along the risk axis), the cost per unit of additional risk reduction increases to what economic analysts call the point of diminishing returns, where enormous costs are incurred for small reductions in risk.

The efficiency frontier is also depicted in figure 3.3 along with a curve representing societal demand for risk reduction as a function of risk. Where the two curves cross is the point where the benefits of risk reduction equal the costs. This is the "optimal" level of risk R_0 at a cost C_0 using quasi-economic efficiency criteria.[29] Of course,

29. Strictly speaking, economically "efficient" solutions require that society reduce risk as long as the *marginal*, i.e., incremental, benefits of further risk reduction exceed the *marginal* costs. Protection beyond this point would impose marginal costs that would exceed the marginal benefit realized and thus would be rejected if efficiency is to be achieved. In order to be able to undertake a marginal cost and marginal benefit analysis, the policy designer would have to know the shapes of both the cost and the benefit curves, an essentially impractical, if not unachievable, goal. Reflecting this reality and the essentially political demand that the benefits of a policy equal (or exceed) its costs—often cited by the courts in pursuit of "reasonable regulation"—those advocating market-based solutions are usually content if the benefits of environmental policies equal their costs. Indeed, the Office of Management and Budget (OMB), overseeing executive orders relating to regulatory impact analysis (required of federal agencies in promulgating "major" rules having an economic impact of at least $100 million annually) regards this as a fundamental goal. (See chapter 5 for a discussion of OMB's role in reviewing proposed rulemaking.)

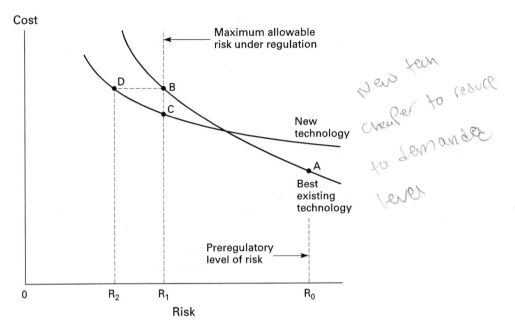

Cost

Maximum allowable
risk under regulation

D   B

C

New
technology

A

Best
existing
technology

Preregulatory
level of risk

0   R₂   R₁   R₀

Risk

*New tech
cheaper to reduce
to demanded
level*

Figure 3.4
Comparison of costs of new and existing technologies for reducing environmental risks.

societal demand must be expressed in monetary terms to determine the efficient or optimal level of risk.

While employing a new technology may be a more costly method of attaining *current* environmental standards[30] (assuming existing technologies are optimal at the current risk level required), it may allow the achievement of *stricter* standards at a lower cost than would the adoption of existing technology. Figure 3.4 illustrates the difference, as explained in the following paragraphs.

Suppose that as a result of either market demand or regulatory fiat, a reduction in risk from R_0 to R_1 is desirable. Use of the most efficient existing technology would impose a cost represented by point B. (Again, the "existing technology" curve represents the supply of lowest-cost technologies from among existing technological options for achieving various levels of environmental risk.) However, if it were possible to stimulate technological innovation, a new, more efficient technology "supply curve" could arise, allowing the same degree of risk reduction at a lower cost represented by point C. Alternatively, a greater degree of health protection (R_2) could be

30. Thus, the cost of new technology at current levels of tolerated risk is shown in figure 3.4 to be initially higher than the cost of existing technology currently in use.

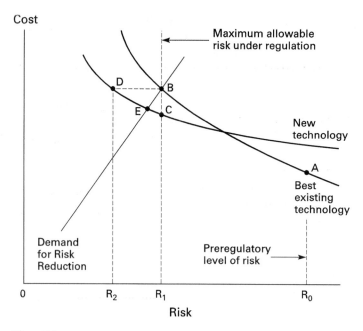

Figure 3.5
Comparison of optimal levels of risks as determined by new and existing technologies.

offered if expenditures equal to costs at point B using existing technology were applied instead to new technological solutions (point D). Note that co-optimization (the proverbial ability to have your cake and eat it too) can occur when a new *dynamic* efficiency is achieved; the triangular area BCD represents a "win-win" situation. Referring to figure 3.5, which adds the societal demand curve for risk reduction, the equilibrium point E would occur at both lower cost and lower risk than that represented by the static equilibrium point B.[31]

In a particular instance, if end-of-pipe approaches have been used for a long time and improvements in pollution control have probably reached a plateau, the new

---

31. The "Porter Hypothesis" has been proposed to explain why firms would find it in their economic advantage to invest in compliance technology ahead of others in an industry (Porter and van der Linde, 1995a, 1995b). Beginning in 1979 a number of MIT studies found that regulation could stimulate significant *fundamental changes in product and process technology* that benefited the industrial innovator, provided the regulations were stringent and focused. This empirical work supports a much stronger link between government regulation and technological change that emerged some 15 years later as the Porter Hypothesis, which argued that firms on the cutting edge of developing and implementing pollution reduction technology would benefit economically through "innovation offsets" by being first-movers to comply with regulation. In Europe, where regulation was arguably less stringent and formulated with industry consensus, regulation was not found to stimulate much significant innovation (Kemp, 1997). Analysis of the U.S. situation since the earlier MIT studies reinforces the strategic usefulness of properly designed and implemented regulation complemented by economic incentives (Strasser, 1997). See also Reinhardt (1999).

technology curve or frontier will arguably be occupied predominantly by pollution prevention technologies (i.e., new products, inputs, or production processes) rather than pollution control technologies. We refer to programs to bring firms into environmental compliance using new technologies as innovation-driven pollution prevention initiatives.[32]

The U.S.-based empirical studies of innovative responses to stringent regulation confirm that these win-win situations do in fact exist (Ashford et al., 1985; Strasser, 1997). The next logical step is to design environmental, health, and safety regulations to achieve an innovative response. One can immediately see from this discussion that if the new regulated level of allowable risk R_l is not stringent enough (i.e., not far enough to the left), the firm may simply elect to adopt off-the-shelf existing technology, rather than embark on a technically risky, innovation-generating strategy. Paradoxically, less stringent regulation may be more expensive for the firm because it encourages the diffusion of existing technology rather than innovation.

Information-based policies can also be used to encourage innovation (see Koch and Ashford, 2006). Instead of technology assessment, two alternative informational activities could be employed: (1) a technology improvement opportunity analysis (TIOA) and (2) a technology options analysis (TOA). The first encourages the firm to ask *where* in the production process is *what* needed for an environmentally sounder approach? Input substitution? Process change? Final product reformulation? Having thus determined *where* and *what kind* of improvements are desirable, the firm then engages in a technology options analysis, which focuses on whether and what kind of specific changes are possible. Analysis of the reporting of toxic emissions in the United States confirms that merely asking these questions leads to significant pollution prevention activity (see the discussion in chapter 13). A study undertaken for the European Commission in the allied area of inherently safer technologies indicates the value and success of this approach (see Ashford and Zwetsloot, 1999). Persuading firms to engage in a meaningful process of identifying opportunities and areas for technology development, however, is likely to require a legal mandate. Otherwise, they are unlikely to do it.

Summary

The concept of *dynamic efficiency* allows us to take the potential for technological advance into account. In contrast to static efficiency, dynamic economic efficiency

---

32. A given firm could improve its efficiency in risk management by using better end-of-pipe control technology or by engaging in pollution prevention, which could be accomplished if the firm changed its inputs, reformulated its final products, or altered its process technology by adopting technology new to the firm but not new to the market. This latter approach would be characterized as diffusion-driven pollution prevention, and the changes, while beneficial, would probably be suboptimal because the firm would achieve static, but not dynamic, efficiency.

assumes a constantly shifting set of alternatives, particularly in the technological realm.[33]

The difference between static and dynamic efficiency has significant implications for the design of regulation. A key feature of environmental regulation is that under the right conditions it can create a meaningful incentive for technological advance. If we design environmental regulation with only *static* efficiency in mind, however, we very likely will not take advantage of this potential. If we have reason to believe that there is a meaningful potential for the use of "cleaner" or more environmentally sound technology within a polluting industry, our regulatory goal should be to stimulate the development of new technology that is sufficient to produce a downward *shift* in the technology cost curve. Conversely, if we set the lawful emission level at the modest point dictated by traditional static economic efficiency, the firm likely can comply by moving a short way up the existing technology cost curve. Unless the increased cost associated with this move is significant enough to capture the firm's attention, or unless the firm has some other reason (unrelated to regulation) to invest in relevant technological change, the firm is likely to comply with the regulation through the application of existing technology.

If we set a *stringent* new risk reduction level, the firm may still be able to meet this new regulatory requirement with the application of existing technology, but the cost of doing so will be higher. The relevant cost differential is more likely to be significant enough to persuade at least one firm in the industry to devote some of its energies toward the design of a *more efficient* technological solution.[34] If no firm in the industry could meet the new emission requirement with existing technology and none succeeded in developing new technology, new entrants may arise to displace the incumbent firms and industry.[35] An emission limit that is more stringent than that suggested by notions of static economic efficiency might be fashioned to cause the incumbent firms to be more innovative, or alternatively, it could be set deliberately to

---

33. The differences between dynamic and static efficiency are well described in the work of Burton Klein (1977). In the context of environmental law, see Driesen (2003) and Ashford (1999).

34. In a much-quoted econometric study challenging the Porter Hypothesis, Jaffe et al. (1995) find little *statistical* evidence that stringent regulation leads firms to innovate. These authors are missing the point, however. It could be argued that, in general, regulation does not stimulate innovation in *most* firms. The point is that it can stimulate innovation in *some* firms—those who turn out to become the technological leaders and gain considerable advantage over the others. The evidence here is necessarily anecdotal. Much regulation is "captured" or heavily influenced by the dominant firms, who persuade government to set standards that they themselves can already meet. Why, then, should it be a surprise that not much innovation occurs in the majority of firms subject to regulation and that no "statistical correlation" can be found between regulation and widespread innovation in those firms? See Ashford (1999).

35. In chapter 12, we argue that a "fail-soft" strategy should be followed by regulatory agencies, whereby firms who make good-faith efforts at developing new technologies, but who fall short of new stringent regulatory requirements, are treated leniently so as not to discourage others from taking technological risks.

encourage new entrants.[36] This approach enables the regulator to create a direct incentive for the kind of technological advance that results in lower emissions at a lower cost, and thus achieves dynamic efficiency. Note that unlike static efficiency, there is no *unique* dynamic efficiency point. The extent of significant changes in the cost-reduction and risk-reduction potential depends on the particular new technological response that arises from the regulatory signal.

■ **NOTE**

1. Chapter 12 of this text is devoted to an investigation of the various types of governmental policies potentially capable of remedying market imperfections, and of improving economic and environmental performance by encouraging dynamic efficiency. There we explore some of the circumstances under which government intervention is likely to be more, or less, effective in promoting technological advance. In the next section of this chapter we examine cost-benefit analysis, a policy-analytic tool (grounded in economics) that has, over the past two-and-a-half decades, become the dominant method used by policymakers to evaluate government health, safety, and environmental policies. ■

E. THE USE OF COST-BENEFIT ANALYSIS AS A MEANS OF EVALUATING AND DESIGNING OPTIONS FOR ENVIRONMENTAL REGULATION

The need for a formal methodology for choosing from among alternative environmental policies is obvious. The candidate government programs to improve the environment will normally impose social costs as well as benefits. Thus there is a natural tendency to want to have a mechanism for identifying which environmental policies will, on balance, make society "better off" in some meaningful sense, and for selecting from among these the policy or mix of policies that will provide the largest social improvement. This is the promise of cost-benefit analysis.

As conceived in theory, cost-benefit analysis: (1) enumerates *all* possible consequences, both positive and negative, that might arise in response to the implementation of a candidate government policy; (2) estimates the probability of each consequence occurring; (3) estimates the benefit or loss to society should each occur, *expressed in monetary terms*; (4) computes the *expected* social benefit or loss from each possible consequence by multiplying the amount of the associated benefit or loss by its probability of occurrence; and (5) computes the net *expected* social benefit

---

36. See Jänicke and Jacob (2004) for an excellent discussion of the importance of creating lead markets for environmentally friendly technologies in the context of ecological modernization. Unlike many others, these authors stress the need for radical innovations and the limitations of relying on existing firms to achieve them.

Table 3.1
Matrix of Policy Consequences for Different Actors

Group	Effects		
	Economic	Health/Safety	Environmental
Producers	$C_\text{\$}$, $B_\text{\$}$	$C_{H/S}$, $B_{H/S}$	$C_{Env't}$, $B_{Env't}$
Workers	$C_\text{\$}$, $B_\text{\$}$	$C_{H/S}$, $B_{H/S}$	$C_{Env't}$, $B_{Env't}$
Consumers	$C_\text{\$}$, $B_\text{\$}$	$C_{H/S}$, $B_{H/S}$	$C_{Env't}$, $B_{Env't}$
Others	$C_\text{\$}$, $B_\text{\$}$	$C_{H/S}$, $B_{H/S}$	$C_{Env't}$, $B_{Env't}$

Notes: $C_\text{\$}$ refers to the economic costs of reducing environmental risks; $B_\text{\$}$ refers to the economic benefits of reducing environmental risks; $C_{H/S}$ refers to the health and safety costs of reducing environmental risks; $B_{H/S}$ refers to the health and safety benefits of reducing environmental risks; $C_{Env't}$ refers to the environmental costs of reducing environmental risks; $B_{Env't}$ refers to the environmental benefits of reducing environmental risks.

or loss associated with the government policy by summing over the various possible consequences. The reference point for these calculations (commonly termed the "baseline") is the state of the world in the absence of the candidate government policy.

A cost-benefit analysis usually begins with the accumulation of a set of data such as that shown in table 3.1. This table presents a relatively disaggregated matrix of the various positive and negative consequences of a government policy for a variety of actors. Here the consequences are separated into economic, health and safety, environmental, and other effects, and the parties affected are organized into policy-relevant groups of actors: firms, workers, consumers, and "others." Initially, the consequences are represented in their natural units. Economic effects are expressed in monetary units, health and safety effects are expressed in mortality and morbidity terms, environmental effects are expressed in damage to ecosystems, and so on. In addition, the consequences are described solely in terms of the time period during which they occur. What cost-benefit analysis does is translate all of these consequences into "equivalent" monetary units, discount each to its present value (that is, reduce the value assigned to future effects to reflect the fact that they will not be experienced until later),[37] and aggregate them into a single dollar value intended to express the net social effect of the government policy.

The cost-benefit calculation can be expressed in simple mathematical terms by the following equation:

---

37. Even after adjusting for inflationary effects, the timing of costs and benefits still matters. As explained later in this chapter, the real value of a dollar of costs or benefits in a future period is worth less than such a dollar today. In order to make the costs and benefits from different periods commensurate, as required by cost-benefit analysis, future costs and benefits are adjusted downward, using a specified discount rate, to derive their present value.

$$V = \sum_{i=1}^{n} \sum_{j=1}^{m} \frac{(B_{ij} - C_{ij})}{(1 + r)^{i}}$$

where B_{ij} and C_{ij} are the jth type of policy benefit and cost, respectively, in the ith year after the policy is introduced, and B and C are expressed in monetary units; r is the appropriate discount rate; and V is the (discounted) present value of the policy. Note that this cost-benefit procedure, in effect, collapses the matrix in table 3.1 into a single monetary value.

This value can then be used to evaluate (present or proposed) government policies. When there is only one policy option under consideration, the cost-benefit criterion dictates that the option should be implemented only if its anticipated net social effect, when compared with the baseline, is positive. When there are several policy alternatives under consideration, the cost-benefit criterion dictates that the policy that promises the largest positive net social benefit, when compared with the baseline, should be implemented.

As a decision-making tool, cost-benefit analysis has several positive features. First, it can clarify choices among alternatives by evaluating consequences in a consistent and systematic manner. Second, it has the potential to foster an open and fair policy-making process by making explicit the estimates of costs and benefits and the assumptions on which those estimates are based. Third, by expressing all of the gains and losses in monetary terms, discounted to their present value, cost-benefit analysis permits the total impact of a policy to be summarized using a common metric, and to be represented by a single dollar amount. (In contrast, *cost-effectiveness* analysis—which attempts to find the minimum cost of achieving a target level of environmental protection—expresses the benefits and costs of a policy as a *ratio* of (fixed) benefits to costs and does not attempt to monetize the environmental benefits. The environmental target may be chosen based on public health or environmental considerations, or by political processes alone, and may be socially endorsed through legislation.)[38]

As a practical matter, however, cost-benefit analysis possesses several serious limitations, and we will explore some of these here. Our examination of the shortcomings of cost-benefit analysis will frequently parallel our previous discussion of market defects. This should hardly come as a surprise, since market imperfections affect the market-derived estimates of costs and benefits on which cost-benefit analysis relies.

---

38. Costs and benefits can also be expressed as a benefit-to-cost ratio, B/C, where the benefits need not be monetized. The dimensions of the benefit/cost ratio are, for example, reductions in environmental pollution (of, say, a given toxicity or concentration) per dollar expended. A related approach is *health-effectiveness* analysis, which evaluates different prospective targets and looks for the largest health benefit for a given (fixed) expenditure level. This allows a comparison of benefit/cost ratios, although a straightforward comparison among different public health goals (e.g., morbidity reduction vs. mortality reduction) may be difficult. Such comparisons become even more difficult if one expands the analysis to a similar evaluation of different environmental targets. For example, how does a policymaker trade off environmental improvements that provide recreational benefits against those that prevent the extinction of an endangered species?

Moreover, it is important to keep in mind that cost-benefit analysis utilizes economic methods and economic terminology, and that these tend to be inappropriate or inaccurate measures of those policy effects whose importance transcends considerations of economic efficiency. Nevertheless, this dissection of cost-benefit analysis is not intended to suggest a wholesale rejection of the technique, but rather to caution against both the uncritical application of this imperfect methodology and the unqualified acceptance of its results.[39]

▪ NOTES

1. The home page of EPA's Center for Environmental Economics is found at http://www.epa.gov/economics. The EPA Guidelines for Preparing Economic Analysis are listed under "reports." They address major analytical issues on key topics, including:

· Treatment of uncertainty and nonmonetary information
· Estimating the value of reducing fatal risks
· Defining baseline conditions (i.e., contrasting the state of the economy and environment with and without a proposed regulatory policy)
· Discounting and comparing differences in the timing of benefits and costs
· Examining environmental justice concerns in economic analyses
· Assessing who pays the costs and receives the benefits of regulation
· Locating available data sources for conducting economic analyses

Publications and journal articles authored by EPA staff are also found on the home page.

2. Recognizing some of the limitations of traditional cost-benefit analysis, the OMB Office of Information and Regulatory Affairs now requires cost-effectiveness analysis for economically significant environmental, health, and safety rules (*Environmental Reporter* 34: 1962, 2003). Cost-effectiveness analysis avoids the problematic monetization of environmental, health, and safety benefits, but still invites comparisons of these benefits against monetary costs. In 2006, the National Academies' Institute of Medicine issued a report generally supporting cost-effectiveness analysis, but cautioning that it also poses significant challenges for regulatory agencies, including the "time and cost" of doing such analyses and limitations of available data. See "Valuing Health for Regulatory Cost-Effectiveness Analysis" at http://www.nap.edu/catalog/11534.html?send.

3. See note 3 in section E-5 of this chapter.   ▪

---

39. An alternative approach to cost-benefit analysis is trade-off analysis, discussed later in section E-7 of this chapter.

1. Problems in Estimating Environmental Policy Benefits

Government programs that reduce environmental pollution can yield several different types of benefits. These include reduction in human illness, reduction in damage to environmental resources used in production (and, in some cases, to finished products), and increases in environmental amenities.

There are several formidable tasks associated with estimating the magnitude of these policy benefits. First, the "baseline" level of environmental pollution must be established for each site or region to be affected by the policy. Second, the regulated industry's response to the policy—expressed in terms of pollution reduction—must be predicted. Third, the effect of this expected pollution reduction on human health and environmental resources must be estimated. This last task depends on the application of risk assessment and epidemiology and can be an especially difficult exercise because the relationship between exposure to pollutants and human disease and/or environmental degradation often is not understood in sufficient detail (see chapter 2).

In addition, many of the benefits of environmental policy are not bought and sold in the market and thus have no clearly defined economic value. In the next sections, we examine some of the techniques that have been employed to assign a monetary value to (a) health-related benefits and (b) environmental resources and amenities.

a. Valuing Health-Related Benefits

One of the main benefits of environmental policies often is a reduction in the number (or severity) of the cases of human illness resulting from exposure to pollutants. Prominent examples of such health-related benefits include decreases in medical expenses; decreases in physical disability, pain and suffering, and death; and concomitant increases in productivity. Some of these health benefits, such as reductions in the need for medical services or reductions in wages from workdays lost to disease or disability, have an economic value that has been accurately determined by market prices. However, many other health benefits—such as reductions in physical disability, pain and suffering, and death—do not.

The traditional methods of monetizing these latter benefits—surveys and market studies—have, to a large extent, proven unsuccessful. Interviews and questionnaires asking individuals what they would be willing to pay for a stated reduction in risk have inherent limitations since answers to hypothetical questions have been shown to be poor indicators of a person's actual behavior.[40]

---

40. This is particularly so for decisions involving health hazards, when the mood and motive of actual choice are difficult to simulate. In drawing the subject's attention to a particular risk, a willingness-to-pay question may elicit a response that measures the immediate anxiety accompanying any contemplation of mortality or bodily harm rather than a representative value. The likelihood of an unrealistic answer is increased because the respondent has little incentive to determine or to reveal his true preferences. See Ashford and Stone (1988, p. 18).

Imputing the value of risk reduction from an individual's behavior as a consumer is also a seriously flawed approach (Fischer, 1979). Individual purchases are normally undertaken for a variety of reasons, and it is difficult to isolate what portion is motivated by, say, a desire to reduce the risk of bodily impairment, pain and suffering, or premature death versus other product attributes. Furthermore, consumers are rarely well informed about the risks confronting them and have a well-documented history of being unable to process the risk information at their disposal in an expected manner.[41] As a result, the assumption of economic efficiency underlying attempts to value risks from consumer market decisions is untenable in practice.

Policy analysts seeking to derive the value of a reduction in health or safety risks frequently turn to the job market. According to economic theory, a worker's valuation of job risk will be represented by a *risk-compensating wage premium*—the extra amount of salary the worker requires in order to take a risky job (see Viscusi, 1992). But the job market is subject to several significant market imperfections that undermine the usefulness of the risk premium as a measure of the worker's risk valuation (see Graham and Shakow, 1990 and Dorman, 1996). For example, job-related diseases that are not known to the worker will not be reflected in the wage premium for risk. Moreover, workers may not understand or appreciate the long-term consequences of on-the-job risks. In theory, workers are just as likely to overreact as underreact to information regarding workplace hazards. In practice, however, worker risk perception appears to be dominated by an "it-can't-happen-to-me" attitude. This results in known risks being understated, and thus undervalued.[42] Another job market defect, externalities, causes the observed wage premium for risk to measure only the *worker's* valuation of an incremental risk, but not the value family members, friends, and other interested parties attach to the worker's exposure to that risk.

Furthermore, models of the risk premium assume a perfectly competitive job market. Violation of this assumption means that the resulting estimates will "misinterpret" the true wage premium for risk. This is a particularly serious problem, both because many job markets fall far short of the competitive ideal, and because there may be no way to adjust the estimates to correct for the misspecification. Finally, comparisons of risk premiums among different workplaces indicate that there is a meaningful *wealth* differential: richer workers tend to place a higher value on risk than do poorer workers for the same risky job.[43] Use of the wage premium as

---

41. The literature documenting risk perception problems is large. See, for example, Tversky and Kahneman (1974, pp. 1124–1131), Machina (1987, pp. 141–147), and Fischhoff (1977, pp. 187–189).

42. See Ashford (1976, p. 357), which also explores other attitudinal factors that cause workers to understate the risks to which they are exposed.

43. Graham and Shakow (1990); Dorman (1996).

a means of valuing risk reduction, then, may be undesirable from a social equity perspective.

b. Valuing Environmental Resources and Amenities

The other major potential benefit of environmental policies is a reduction in damage to the environment itself, and a corresponding increase in environmental resources and amenities. The total economic value of these environmental benefits consists of several conceptually distinct elements. One is what is termed the *active use value*—which, as the name implies, derives from the actual utilization of environmental resources. The active use of a lake, for example, would include its use for fishing, sailing, and wastewater discharge, and its use as a water supply. A second source of economic value is called the *option value*—the value of preserving an environmental asset so that people will have the option of enjoying it at a later date. The option value exists, in this case, because of uncertainty about the future availability of the environmental asset, and because individuals are risk averse. An option value might also exist where: (1) there is uncertainty about whether specific pollutants will damage the environment; (2) the damage to the environment, if it occurs, will be irreversible; and (3) over time, new information is expected to emerge about the effects of the pollutant on the environment. In this case, preserving the environment *to take advantage of the new information* is what creates the option value (Fisher, 1981, pp. 137–139). A third type of economic value is the *existence value* of environmental assets. This value is distinct from actual use and arises because people derive satisfaction simply from the knowledge that an environmental asset—for instance, a particular animal species—continues to exist.

A few of these environmental benefits are directly traded in private markets, and their market price accurately reflects their value. For instance, the per unit economic value of improved crop yield due to a reduction in environmental pollution can be approximated by the price per unit of the crop in the agricultural market.[44] In most cases, however, some valuation technique must be employed to develop a surrogate market measure of the environmental benefit. Popular valuation methods include the weak complementary approach, the defensive expenditure approach, the hedonic valuation method, and the contingent valuation method. Each has its own set of problems and limitations (see United States Environmental Protection Agency, 2000, chapter 7).

The *weak complementary* approach is based on the proposition that the value of an environmental amenity is reflected by the (complementary) expenses individuals incur to use the environmental amenity. Examples of such expenses include the costs

---

44. Even in this relatively simple case, however, the economic value may be complicated by price shifts in response to the increase in crop yield. See, for example, Cropper and Oates (1992, p. 721).

of traveling to and from the environmental amenity, the value of the time spent in traveling to and from and using the amenity, and any entrance or rental fees associated with its use. The weak complementary approach is flawed in that it ignores both the option value and the existence value of the environmental asset and because the willingness-to-pay to use an environmental amenity may far exceed the expenses associated with its use. On the other hand, the weak complementary approach could also overstate the value of the environmental amenity because of the availability of nearby, similar environmental amenities (i.e., the availability of close substitutes is typically ignored using this approach).[45]

The *defensive expenditure* approach relies on the fact that the deleterious effects of pollution on environmental resources can often be offset by the purchase and use of other resources. For instance, households may respond to the diminished quality of their tap water by purchasing water filters or bottled water. These defensive expenditures reflect, to some extent, how much individuals value the environmental resource. One problem with this approach is that the substitute may only partially compensate for the effects of pollution; another is that the substitute may yield unrelated benefits as well.

Hedonic procedures attempt to impute the economic value of environmental amenities by decomposing the price of a good traded in the market into the price of the various attributes that make up the good.[46] For instance, the price of a house depends on a variety of characteristics, such as lot size, the number of bedrooms, the number of bathrooms, and the quality of the school system, as well as on environmental attributes related to air quality, water quality, and noise. By performing a statistical analysis of housing prices as a function of these various housing characteristics, one can attempt to isolate the effect of specific environmental attributes on the price of housing. The price thus imputed can be said to reflect the economic value of the particular attribute.[47] There are several reasons why hedonic estimates of this nature may not produce an accurate valuation of environmental amenities. First, it may be difficult to isolate the effect of environmental attributes that are closely associated with each other (for example, air pollution that is due to proximity to an air-

---

45. For attempts to deal with these problems, see, for example, Hanley, Shogren, and White (1997, pp. 404–411).

46. Estimates of the value of health and safety benefits derived from workers' imputed valuation of job risks—previously discussed—are, in fact, based on hedonic estimation techniques to isolate the risk-compensating wage premium. For a discussion of the use of hedonic methods to value environmental benefits, see Palmquist (1991) and Freeman (1993).

47. The imputed value of environmental attributes, using hedonic techniques, typically results from the intersection of demand and supply functions. For some purposes, this intersection yields the desired value. However, where the desired value is the willingness-to-pay for a marginal increase in the environmental attribute, additional statistical techniques must be deployed to identify the demand function for the environmental attribute. See, for example, Rosen (1974) and Palmquist (1991).

port is closely correlated with airplane noise). Second, market imperfections (e.g., home buyers not being fully informed about air pollution levels in the area or their adverse health consequences) also can affect the validity of imputed estimates. Third, important variables—particularly qualitative attributes (e.g., the level and quality of local public services, such as public schools; housing rentals versus housing ownership), but also sometimes quantitative attributes (such as the level of property taxes)—are often omitted.

The fourth method—*contingent* valuation—is probably the most widely used and most controversial of all the environmental valuation techniques. One reason for its popularity is that it is frequently the only technique available for estimating the option value and existence value of environmental benefits. The contingent valuation method essentially asks individuals—either by questionnaire or survey, or by "laboratory" experiment—what they would be willing to pay to receive an environmental benefit or, conversely, what they would have to be paid to willingly accept the loss of an environmental benefit.[48] While numerous procedures have been developed to enhance the reliability of these estimates (Hanemann, 1994; National Oceanic and Atmospheric Administration, 1993), the contingent valuation method is still potentially vulnerable to many of the limitations traditionally associated with valuations based on hypothetical rather than real market responses. In contrast to real market transactions, for example, there are no meaningful "budget" constraints for these hypothetical expenditures. In addition, many individuals are not able to process risk information and may not be sufficiently familiar with the environmental amenity at issue to have a well-considered value for it.

■ NOTE

1. For an early review of benefit estimation methodologies and an investigation of the benefits of health, safety, and environmental regulations, see Ashford et al. (1980). ■

---

48. Standard welfare theory predicts that the willingness-to-pay (WTP) and the willingness-to-accept payment (WTA) for an economic good should be equivalent, or close in value given small income effects. One of the early criticisms of the contingent valuation method was that WTP estimates of the value of an improvement in environment quality were significantly smaller than the WTA estimates. Since then, however, an increasing body of evidence from the field of experimental economics has confirmed that the divergence between WTP and WTA estimates of environmental assets is a real phenomenon rather than an artifact of the contingent valuation method. The theoretical underpinnings of the WTP-WTA divergence have not fully been resolved but, in general, the lower the degree of substitution between the good being valued and other market or nonmarket goods, the greater the divergence. The fact that environmental resources and amenities often have few, if any, substitutes therefore helps explain the large WTP-WTA divergence when estimating their value. See Hanemann (1991) and Hanley, Shogren, and White (1997, pp. 362–364, 395–396).

n Estimating Environmental Policy Costs: Static versus Dynamic
bout Technological Responses

:osts imposed by a government policy would seem at first glance to
    to identify and to express in economic terms, estimates of costs are
usually no more certain or reliable than are estimates of benefits. One reason is
that policy analysts rarely have access to detailed, independent information about
actual—and potential—production relationships and associated costs in an industry.
Instead, they must depend to a large extent on industry-provided data to develop
estimates of the costs to industry of complying with the public policy. Since higher
compliance costs make a policy less attractive, industries that would be subject to
the candidate policy may choose to inflate their reported compliance costs.

  In addition, compliance cost estimates often fail to take three significant factors
into account: (1) economies of scale, which reflect the fact that an increase in the production of compliance technology often reduces unit costs; (2) the ability of industry
to learn over time to comply more cost-effectively—to move upward on what the
management scientists refer to as the learning curve;[49] and (3) the crucial role that
can be played by technological innovation in reducing compliance costs (Ashford,
1998).

  To see the estimation bias caused by failing to accurately predict an innovative
technological response, consider figure 3.4, introduced earlier. Assume a firm's activities create a level of risk at point A prior to the introduction of a government policy,
in this case a performance standard specifying the maximum allowable emissions
level (represented by the dotted line). The cheapest way for the firm to comply with
the new standard, using existing technology, is to move to point B. Suppose, however, that in response to the regulation the firm develops a process innovation that
permits it to comply by moving to point C. Ignoring the firm's innovative activity
therefore results, in this example, in an overestimation of compliance costs by the
amount BC.[50]

  Other errors of omission and faulty attribution plague attempts to estimate policy
costs. A typical problem is the inclusion of the cost of activities that, although causally related to compliance efforts, are not necessary for compliance. The classic reason for this phenomenon is indivisibilities in investment decisions; it is usually less
costly to make multiple changes in production simultaneously rather than individu-

---

49. For a review of the evidence documenting productivity gains associated with organizational learning
curves, see Argote and Epple (1990).

50. A retrospective analysis of eight OSHA regulations issued between 1974 and 1989 concluded that the
agency's estimates of economic impacts systematically and significantly overestimated compliance costs by
ignoring the innovative response of industry to the enacted standards (United States Office of Technology
Assessment, 1995).

ally. Environmental regulation can provide the stimulus to make production-related improvements that, while viewed as too costly in isolation, become economically viable if done in conjunction with the changes needed to comply with the regulation. However, if the cost of these production modifications is assigned to the projected cost of the regulation, the cost of the regulation will be overstated. Conversely, costs ascribed to pollution reduction are frequently offset by concomitant productivity improvements. For example, sealing reactor vessels during manufacture to limit toxic air emissions offers the simultaneous advantages of reducing worker exposure to toxic substances and increasing production yield, since less material is now lost during processing. Furthermore, government intervention sometimes provides "leveraged" benefits by inducing firms to deal preventively with other (possibly unregulated) environmental and workplace hazards (Ashford, 1981, pp. 131–132). Such concomitant but indirect benefits of public policy are often omitted in cost-benefit calculations.

Finally, there is the possibility that government intervention will have derivative "competitiveness" effects, typically due to *differentially large* compliance costs borne by some or all regulated firms. If they attempt to pass on such costs to their customers by raising prices, firms burdened with differentially large compliance costs may lose substantial business to their lower-cost, and lower-priced, competitors. Alternatively, if these firms choose to absorb significant compliance costs, they may no longer remain profitable and could be forced out of business. In general, compliance costs may fall disproportionately on a specific industry segment (because, for example, the in-place production technology that characterizes that segment makes compliance particularly difficult and costly to achieve) or on specific firms within an industrial sector (because, for example, of the size or age of their plants).

In the case of environmental policies, however, the most frequently expressed concern is that compliance costs may affect the competitiveness of domestic producers relative to rival firms in foreign countries that are not subject to—or burdened by— U.S. environmental regulations. Although an examination of the contentious issue of international competitiveness is beyond the scope of our discussion here, we note that there is little evidence to suggest that environmental regulations have had a significant impact on the competitiveness of U.S. manufacturers.[51] Furthermore, researchers have reported numerous instances in which environmental regulations have spurred the development by domestic firms of lower-cost and more effective compliance technologies, which subsequently increased the competitiveness of the innovative firms in international markets.[52]

---

51. For a survey of the evidence, as well as a reasoned investigation of how to define and measure international competitiveness, see Jaffe, Peterson, Portnoy, and Stavins (1995).

52. See United States Office of Technology Assessment (1995). See also Stone (1994).

Table 3.2
Present Value of $1 at the End of Year *t* using Discount Rate *i*

Year *t*	Discount Rate *i*				
	2%	4%	6%	8%	10%
10	0.82	0.68	0.56	0.46	0.39
20	0.67	0.46	0.31	0.21	0.15
30	0.55	0.31	0.17	0.10	0.06
40	0.45	0.21	0.10	0.05	0.02
50	0.37	0.14	0.05	0.02	0.01
100	0.14	0.02	0.00	0.00	0.00

3. Problems in Selecting the Discount Rate

As previously noted, the process of *discounting* aims to put costs and benefits that occur during different time periods on a comparable basis. The rate at which future costs and benefits are discounted is termed the *discount rate*.[53]

The choice of discount rate can have a dramatic effect on the cost-benefit estimates used to evaluate the desirability of a government policy. Since most government programs involve an investment of resources in early periods that generate benefits in later periods, the major effect of discounting is to reduce the magnitude of the benefits—the larger the discount rate, the greater the reduction—and thereby to make government policies in general, and particularly those whose benefits are not realized until many periods later, less attractive.

Table 3.2 illustrates how the present value of a dollar of benefits decreases as the discount rate increases and as the benefits are delayed farther and farther into the future. For example, the present value of a dollar received 10 years from now will decline from $.82 to $.39 as the discount rate is increased from 2 to 10%. Even relatively low discount rates can significantly affect the present value as the time horizon is extended. Even at a 2% discount rate, for example, a dollar of benefits retains only 14% of its value when it is delayed 100 years into the future. At higher discount rates, benefits lose virtually all of their present value over time. For example, at a 10% discount rate, a dollar received 50 years into the future retains a mere 1% of its original value.

There are two fundamental reasons why the discount rate is positive (that is, why a dollar of costs or benefits in a later period is worth less, not more, than a dollar to-

---

53. The discount rate, net of inflationary effects, is sometimes referred to as the *real* discount rate. Throughout this chapter, for convenience we will use the term "discount rate" rather than "real discount rate" to denote the discount rate net of inflationary effects. Similarly, we assume that all costs and benefits are given in real rather than *nominal* terms (that is, *not* adjusted for inflation).

day). One reason is the productivity of capital. A dollar today can be invested to earn interest over time, where the interest earned reflects the productivity of capital. A dollar in a later period thus is worth less than a dollar today, since the future dollar will not have accrued interest from earlier periods. The second reason is time preference: people simply prefer to receive a dollar now rather than later. Individual time preference is sometimes characterized as human impatience, but it also reflects, at least in part, real uncertainty about the availability of the benefit at a future date and about whether the individual will be alive to enjoy it.

The reasons are similar when we consider the discount rate at the societal, rather than the individual, level. First, owing to the productivity of capital, any social investment under consideration involves a social opportunity cost equal to the social rate of return that could have been earned had the resources used for the social investment been productively invested elsewhere. Second, there is a social time preference that favors present benefits over future benefits. Social time preference presumably reflects some underlying degree of impatience—just as individual time preference does—but not uncertainty about individual longevity. An additional argument that is sometimes offered in support of social time preference is based on the following three propositions: (1) future societies are likely to be richer than current ones; (2) the marginal utility of consumption declines as consumption increases; and therefore (3) an additional dollar of benefits will be worth less—will have less utility—to future societies than a dollar of benefits will be worth to the current society.[54]

What remains to be answered is at what level to set the discount rate. This question has been a source of scholarly debate for several decades.[55] Nevertheless, there appears to be a reasonable consensus about several points concerning the choice of discount rate. First, there is no single "best" discount rate to apply to all government programs. The appropriate discount rate depends on a variety of factors, including how the investment is being financed, the degree of risk involved in the investment, and the nature and duration of the costs and benefits. Second, a major source of difficulty in setting the discount rate is how to adjust for market distortions caused by taxes on income from capital investment. It is, after all, the tax system that causes the opportunity cost of capital to exceed the rate of time preference (Lind, 1982, pp. 24–32). Third, for environmental policies, which typically require the private sector to

---

54. As we argue later in this section, these propositions in support of social time preference may be more than offset in the case of human health and environmental benefits because of the relative scarcity of these "commodities," because human health and environmental benefits are without close substitutes, or simply because of a shift in tastes and values over time. Whatever the reason, we observe that our society has over time spent an increasingly larger percentage of its income on human health and environmental benefits.

55. For a more detailed examination of the issues under debate, see, for example, Lind (1982), Pearce and Turner (1990, pp. 211–225), Farber and Hemmersbaugh (1993), and United States Environmental Protection Agency (2000, chapter 6).

undertake investments, the annualized investment costs must reflect the private cost of borrowing money (for the period of time until the amortized capital costs are recovered); however, the annualized costs and benefits should then be discounted at the social discount rate (Lind, 1990, p. S-24). Finally, for environmental programs with long-term effects, a reasonable measure of the social discount rate is the long-term real rate of return on riskless investments (Farber and Hemmersbaugh, 1993, pp. 280–287).

The real rate of return on government securities, such as Treasury notes and bonds, provides a good approximation of the real rate of return on riskless investments. Estimates of the long-run rate of return on government securities are relatively low, ranging from approximately 0.5 to 3.0%.[56]

For the benefits of environmental policy, the "effective" social discount rate should probably be even lower. The reason is that changes in individual incomes and tastes over time can influence the value of future policy benefits and costs. Environmental amenities and health benefits, in particular, have become more valuable relative to other goods over time in response to an increase in the standard of living, both because health and environmental amenities are without close substitutes and because environmental amenities are in relatively fixed or declining supply.[57] The "effective" social discount rate properly captures the temporal appreciation in the value of environmental and health amenities (assuming, as has traditionally been the case, that policy benefits have not been directly adjusted to reflect their temporal appreciation in real value).

---

56. See Farber and Hemmersbaugh (1993, pp. 280–282), as well as the references cited there.

57. Recall that the present value of a benefit B_i in year i can be expressed as:

$$\frac{B_i}{(1+r)^i}$$

However, if the benefit is an environmental or health amenity that increases in value relative to other goods at an annual rate of (ε), then the proper mathematical expression for the benefit's present value is:

$$\frac{B_i(1+\varepsilon)^i}{(1+r)^i}$$

For small values of (r) and (ε), that expression is approximately equivalent to:

$$\frac{B_i}{(1+r-\varepsilon)^i}$$

Thus the "effective" discount rate—or time rate of preference—is approximately $(r-\varepsilon)$. In principle, the effective discount rate for benefits could even be negative if the rate at which the value of environmental and health amenities increases over time exceeds the social discount rate; that is, if (ε) is larger than (r). A recent paper by Costa and Kahn (2003) confirms the existence of a sizable ε. For the period 1900–2000, the imputed value of ε was 3.4%; for the period 1980–2000, the imputed value of ε was 2.5%. This compares to the real discount rate, r, of about 1 to 3% for environmental programs with long-term effects.

Although the preceding discussion indicates that a relatively low social discount rate, probably no larger than 1 to 2%,[58] should be used to evaluate environmental policies, from 1972 to 1992, the federal Office of Management and Budget, with few exceptions, directed federal agencies, including the Environmental Protection Agency, to apply a 10% real discount rate when calculating the present value of the costs and benefits of federal programs (United States Office of Management and Budget, 1972). In 1992, after several years of review, OMB lowered its real discount rate requirement from 10 to 7% (United States Office of Management and Budget, 1992).[59] As suggested by table 3.2, OMB's past discount rate policy has profound implications for environmental policy, dramatically understating future policy benefits and therefore potentially leading to the rejection of many socially desirable environmental programs.

▪ NOTES

1. For an interesting collection of articles by German, American, and United Kingdom scholars on discounting, see Hampicke and Ott (2003).

2. EPA's policies for "discounting and comparing differences in the timing of benefits and costs" can be found in chapter 6, Analysis of Social Discounting, pp. 52–55 in EPA's *Guidelines for Preparing Economic Analysis* located in the "Select EPA Reports" on the home page for EPA's Center for Environmental Economics: http://www.epa.gov/economics.

3. Economists favor both monetizing benefits and discounting future benefits and costs. Sunstein and Rowell (2005a, 2005b), recognizing the equity implications for subsequent generations experiencing harm as a result of discounting the future, suggest that "a morally adequate response" is to compensate those suffering from "risks imposed on them by their predecessors." This of course does nothing to correct the cost-benefit bias against preventing long-term harms, although it may force an internalization of discounted future costs.   ▪

4. Problems of Equity and Ethics

Social policy determinations as to the "appropriate" level of environmental risk often turn on considerations of equity and on conceptions of individual and social

---

58. As noted earlier, the "effective" discount rate to be applied to environmental benefits should probably be even lower, and might even be negative.

59. OMB has more recently permitted the use of other discount rates if they can be justified. For example, OMB has noted that the social rate of time preference is often used to reflect the discount rate and that the government borrowing rate, roughly 3% in recent years, is, according to the economics literature, a good measure of the social rate of time preference. See United States Office of Management and Budget (2000).

justice. Yet, traditional cost-benefit analysis is unable to address these issues and thus often cannot assess whether implementation of a government policy truly constitutes an improvement in social welfare.

As discussed earlier, the economist's normative standard is Pareto optimality: achieving a situation in which it is impossible to make someone better off without making someone else worse off (because all mutually beneficial exchanges will already have occurred). The cost-benefit criterion closely resembles the test of Pareto optimality. If the net effects of a government policy are positive, then those who gain as a result of the policy *could, in theory,* pay off those who lose and still have some benefits left over for themselves. *Potentially,* no one loses and at least some gain. But a *potential* Pareto improvement (referred to by economists as the *Kaldor-Hicks criterion*) is not the same as an actual Pareto improvement *unless* the redistribution of benefits to the losers actually takes place. The fact that such redistribution normally does not occur in response to an environmental policy tends to undercut the value of cost-benefit analysis as a means of measuring the policy's effects on social welfare.

For some types of government policy, of course, the distributional consequences are negligible; in such instances, the cost-benefit criterion may serve as a reasonable indicator of real Pareto improvements. However, many individuals are involuntarily exposed to hazardous pollutants that pose serious health risks. Furthermore, the individuals at risk are not a random cross section of the general population; they frequently represent a disproportionate share of the poor, or racial and ethnic populations,[60] as well as geographically distinct populations (e.g., those working at or living near an industrial plant that emits toxic pollutants). Thus, for government policies involving environmental hazards, the distributional effects are likely to be substantial, in which case cost-benefit analysis will be an unsatisfactory measure of Pareto improvements. In addition, certain policy effects are not intrinsically economic; they touch on more fundamental social attributes, such as individual rights and justice.[61] Attempting to quantify and monetize these attributes as part of a cost-benefit analysis is more likely to obfuscate and misconstrue their essential qualities than to clarify their values.

In the case of environmental policies, particularly those with significant long-term health and environmental benefits, an important ethical issue surrounding the use of

---

60. In a 1992 study, EPA concluded that racial minorities and low-income populations experience higher than average exposure to selected air pollutants and hazardous wastes. Moreover, these populations live in areas that are likely to receive inadequate remediation efforts. See United States Environmental Protection Agency (1992) and the earlier discussion of environmental justice in section C.4 of this chapter.

61. Law, in particular, is concerned with the safeguarding of those rights. In a sense, then, law and economics represent different paradigmatic approaches to environmental protection.

cost-benefit analysis is intergenerational equity.[62] As previously explained, the process of discounting benefits as part of the cost-benefit procedure has the effect of making the weight we attach to future benefits smaller and smaller the farther we go into the future.[63] After 150–250 years or so, the benefits conferred on all future generations are effectively ignored because as a result of discounting they become microscopically small.[64] Benefits enjoyed 200 years from now that have been discounted by 7% annually—a rate that is consistent with OMB's current policy recommendations—would, for purposes of cost-benefit analysis, retain only one one-millionth of their original value. Even at a more plausible discount rate of 2%, benefits enjoyed 200 years into the future would be valued at less than 2% of their original amount. Because of discounting, traditional cost-benefit analysis tends to overlook any sense of ethical responsibility to future generations to maintain a habitable environment and preserve environmental assets.[65]

5. Misuses and Abuses of Cost-Benefit Analysis

Beyond the inherent limitations of cost-benefit analysis, the use of cost-benefit analysis, in practice, has been plagued by a host of other interrelated problems, such as suboptimization, quantification bias, "bottom-line" myopia, and politicization.

Suboptimization has been defined as discovering the best way to do things that might better be left undone (Boulding, 1974, p. 136). Cost-benefit analysis is an "instrumental technique" (Tribe, 1973, p. 635), concerned, not with selecting ultimate societal ends, but merely with helping to choose the best means to achieve those ends. A policy satisfying the cost-benefit criterion might still be socially undesirable because the policy objective itself is suboptimal. For instance, policies whose objective is to control the release of hazardous wastes into the environment might ignore the possibility of redesigning the production process to eliminate the use of the hazardous material in the first place.

---

62. See, for example, Portney and Weyant (1999).

63. Note that cost-benefit analysis does not incorporate the preferences of future generations. The discounted benefits of environmental policy enjoyed by future generations merely represent the way we—the current generation—have chosen to represent our concern for them.

64. For example, in estimating the effects of proposed regulations to protect stratospheric ozone, EPA formally truncated the stream of regulatory benefits and costs after the year 2165 for ease of calculation. Presumably, after discounting, the magnitude of effects on all subsequent generations was considered too minute to possibly influence the cost-benefit results from earlier years. See United States Environmental Protection Agency (1987, chapter 10). For a critique of the methodology EPA used to conduct its regulatory impact analysis, see Ashford and Stone (1988, pp. 50–51).

65. One possible remedy would be to impose ethical constraints on cost-benefit analysis. Violation of any of the ethical conditions would cause the policy in question to be rejected, even if the results of the cost-benefit calculations were otherwise favorable. For a discussion of such an approach applied to environmental policies, see Pearce and Turner (1990, pp. 224–225).

Quantification bias refers to the tendency of many policy analysts to identify policy effects that are difficult to quantify or to express in monetary terms—such as environmental benefits or distributional impacts—but to omit these effects entirely in the ensuing cost-benefit calculations. What this does, in essence, is to impose a value of zero on those policy effects for which no objective economic value is available, even though those effects may be of larger social significance than all of the monetized consequences combined. An illustration of quantification bias is the practice, popularized in recent years by some economists, of evaluating regulations based solely on their cost per life saved. The problem with this evaluation procedure is that it ignores all other benefits of regulations, including reductions in the number of injuries and chronic diseases and increases in environmental amenities. Use of this defective procedure will undervalue many regulations, particularly those whose benefits are primarily in the form of environmental improvements and reduced illnesses and injuries (Stone, 1997). Another manifestation of quantification bias is the valuation of certain policy effects on the basis of their readily available but inappropriate economic dimensions. The most obvious example is the long-time use of the sum of a person's discounted future earnings (the so-called "human capital" approach)—now discredited—to value lives saved as a result of to government policy. Despite its superficial appeal, the human capital approach bears no relation to the social valuation of a reduction in life-threatening risks and in fact is consistent with the morally offensive proposition that the death of a no-longer-productive retired or handicapped person confers a net benefit to society (Ashford and Stone, 1988, pp. 2–4; Ortolano, 1997, p. 132).

"Bottom-line" myopia flows from the ability of cost-benefit analysis to express the total (expected) effect of a policy in a single dollar amount. The summary cost-benefit value facilitates comparison of alternative government policies according to a common metric, but it does so at a price. Collapsing the various consequences of a policy into a single, bottom-line value does not reveal the myriad assumptions and data on which that value is based; it compresses them and removes them from view. As a practical matter, policymakers and the public are apt to accept the summary value of cost-benefit analysis as gospel without considering the plausibility of the underlying assumptions and the accuracy of the supporting data, particularly when such information is not readily available. Similarly, the uncertainty surrounding the estimates of the costs and the benefits, the sensitivity of the expected policy impacts to specific assumptions and data, and the confidence interval that represents the range within which the true effect of the policy will probably fall are all matters to be considered in making policy decisions, but which are suppressed by the reduction of the cost-benefit assessment to a single bottom-line value. For example, as previously noted, even a modest change in the discount rate may have a profound effect on the estimated impact of a policy. But unless this information accompanies the bottom-line value, the results of the cost-benefit analysis, for policy-making pur-

poses, are liable to be misleading and misunderstood. In that case, rather than promoting rational, candid policy making, cost-benefit analysis exposes the policy-making process to potential abuse.

The politicization of cost-benefit analysis is another way in which the policy-making process can be abused. Political groups, in the hope of furthering ideological or special interests, may endeavor to influence either the cost-benefit estimates themselves or the manner in which those estimates are used in policy making (McGarity, Shapiro, and Bollier, 2004). In the former case, policy analysts with a vested interest in the outcome might attempt to "construct" the cost-benefit analysis so as to arrive at a predetermined result.[66] Unless the underlying assumptions and data are revealed and subject to public scrutiny, such manipulation of the estimation procedure is likely to go unnoticed. In the latter case, the abuse of the policy-making process might typically be accomplished by improperly imposing cost-benefit decision rules on the policymaker (e.g., by circumvention of government checks and balances). Using the cost-benefit criterion as a *decision rule* for policies whose estimated impacts have been influenced by politically motivated "guidance" subverts rather than promotes the democratic process. The policymaker's ability to make decisions is compromised and his or her accountability eroded. When this happens, cost-benefit analysis no longer clarifies and facilitates the democratic process, but becomes a substitute for it.

■ **NOTES**

1. For an analysis of inappropriate use and oversight of regulatory cost-benefit analysis, see Heinzerling (1998). For a brief summary of both methodological and political shortcomings, see Heinzerling and Ackerman (2002) and Ackerman and Heinzerling (2004). For a retrospective analysis of whether the application of cost-benefit analysis would have justified important environmental regulations, see Ackerman, Heinzerling, and Massey (2005). Analyzing 25 government environmental, health, and safety rules that U.S. General Accounting Office (now the Government Accountability Office) identified as having been significantly affected by OMB, Driesen (2006) found that "OMB never supported changes that would make environmental, health, and safety regulations more stringent" and that "[i]n twenty-four of the twenty-five cases, all of the changes that OMB (GAO 2003) suggested would weaken environmental, health, or safety protections" (p. 365). Driesen (2003) concludes: "CBA [cost-benefit analysis] is not neutral in practice, and is, in many ways, anti-environmental in theory" (p. 402).

---

66. One striking example, previously described, is the discount rate policy previously used by OMB, which directed federal agencies to apply an exaggerated real discount rate when calculating the present value of the costs and benefits of federal regulations.

2. As discussed in chapter 5, executive orders directing regulatory impact (cost-benefit) assessments of major proposed federal regulations have been in place since the administration of Richard Nixon. OMB's role in reviewing these regulatory impact assessments came into prominence during the administration of Ronald Reagan. While the executive orders signed by President Reagan required that benefits *outweigh* costs, the orders signed by President Clinton required only that benefits *justify* costs. The Clinton executive orders acknowledged that not all benefits and costs can be monetized, and that nonmonetary consequences should be influential in regulatory analysis. See Hahn, Olmstead, and Stavins (2003).

3. In 2007, the administration of President George W. Bush issued two documents affecting the way agencies must conduct regulatory impact analysis in the future. President Bush amended President Clinton's executive order on cost-benefit review to add the requirement that the agency justify each proposed major regulation by demonstrating the existence of a specific market failure, or a specific failure of public institutions, that warrants the new action. See Executive Order 13422, January 18, 2007 (http://www.sba.gov/advo/laws/eo12866.pdf). The 2007 order also creates the position of "Regulatory Policy Officer" within federal agencies, as presidential appointees, and specifies OMB authority over the regulatory "guidance documents" required by an OMB bulletin issued a few days later. See Final Bulletin for Agency Good Guidance Practices, 72 *Fed. Reg.* 3432 (Jan. 25, 2007) (http://www.whitehouse.gov/omb/fedreg/2007/012507_good_guidance.pdf). The bulletin requires federal agencies to submit guidance documents for OMB review that detail the agency's regulatory philosophy. These guidance documents are ultimately to be submitted to the public for comment, but only after they have been reviewed and (presumably) shaped and edited by OMB. Although the bulletin stops short of requiring a formal regulatory impact analysis of the economic effects of an agency's guidance documents, it invites executive branch influence earlier in the regulatory policy process. The bulletin recognizes that agency guidance documents, though not legal requirements per se, could lead parties to alter their conduct in a manner that would have an economically significant impact, and the bulletin signals OMB intent to flag (and discourage) such potential effects prior to the issuance of any actual rules or regulations. For a critical commentary on these changes by OMB Watch, a non-profit group that monitors the activities of OMB and other federal government actors, see Madia and Melbirth (2007). ∎

6. The Value of Transparency

Although we have described a variety of theoretical and practical shortcomings of cost-benefit analysis, we acknowledge that its basic objective—to help evaluate government policy by enumerating all of its consequences—arguably is a desirable one.

Many of the limitations of cost-benefit analysis are in fact unavoidable by-products of any such systematic approach to decision making. For example, the imprecision of the cost-benefit estimates of the impacts of environmental protection simply mirrors the technical uncertainties and the social complexities surrounding the problem. Obviously, more accurate estimates of impacts could be achieved by improved scientific methods and knowledge, but the same could be said for any policy evaluation technique, not just cost-benefit analysis.

The fact that an objective, unambiguously correct assessment of policy impacts cannot be guaranteed reinforces the importance of the process by which a particular assessment is performed. It is in this area—the evaluative process—that cost-benefit analysis is most vulnerable. The process of conducting a cost-benefit analysis forces the policy analyst to make explicit assumptions and data choices. In practice, however, the typical reduction of the various policy impacts to a single, bottom-line (usually monetary) value has tended to conceal the underlying assumptions and data from public examination. Cost-effectiveness or health-effectiveness analysis avoids monetizing environmental, health, and safety benefits, but comparing the value of avoiding different kinds of impacts remains problematic.

One way to remedy this problem is for policy analysts to acknowledge the limitations of their craft and to provide policymakers and the public, in addition to the bottom-line expected value, a meaningful critique of the policy evaluation exercise through which that value was generated, including uncertainties, confidence intervals, and the sensitivity of the results to specific assumptions and data choices. Even if this were to be done, however, the specter of political misuse and abuse of cost-benefit analysis would remain a viable drawback to its use. In the next section, an alternative to cost-benefit analysis is explored.

▪ NOTES

1. For criticisms of using cost-benefit analysis to determine regulatory targets, see Thomas O. McGarity (2004). See also Driesen (2001).

2. For a general discussion of the use of feasibility, rather than cost-benefit analysis, as a central criterion, see Driesen (2005).

3. Note that to the extent environmental policy costs are *overestimated*, apparent cost curves will be shifted upward from and to the right of the true cost curves, leading to a (static) efficiency point with higher overall risk. Similarly, to the extent the risks are *underestimated*, the evaluation of reducing true risks—i.e., the true benefits or demand curves—will also be shifted upward from and to the left of the apparent benefits curve, leading to a lower demand for risk reduction. As a result, even from a static efficiency perspective, the "optimal" level of risk reduction dictated by these

curves will be artificially low. Two common features of the practices used to determine optimal levels of risk reduction will lead to this result: (1) the failure to take
into account alternative technologies that lower the cost of control and (2) the failure
to consider synergistic effects, unforeseen or a priori unquantifiable chemical releases,
or emerging theories of chemically caused disease and injury that would argue for
greater degrees of protection.   ■

7.   Trade-off Analysis as an Alternative to Cost-Benefit Analysis

One way to transcend many of the problems with using cost-benefit analysis to guide
environmental decision making is to have the policy analyst calculate the various
policy consequences, as was done in table 3.1, without translating the various economic, health, environmental, and other effects into a single dollar metric; without
discounting them to present value; and without summing the benefits and costs ac-
cruing to actors in order to come up with a net benefit or a benefit-to-cost ratio.
The consequences, when presented in disaggregated form, permit decisionmakers to
examine the real policy trade-offs, guided by the social expression of preferences provided in the law. For example, the Clean Air Act intends that certain sensitive subgroups are to be specially protected, such as protecting children from exposure to
lead. In these instances, Congress has already performed the social balancing of costs
and benefits, and collapsing the impacts of the regulation by cost-benefit analysis is
not permissible.[67] Of course, in some cases, a particular legislative mandate may be
consistent with collapsing the various consequences into a single value, as is done in
cost-benefit analysis; but in these cases, at least the application of the cost-benefit
procedure has not been prematurely imposed. Note that the level of disaggregation
in a "trade-off" matrix is not uniquely defined for all problems; it depends on the
particular social problem in question and the associated policy-relevant variables.
Trade-off analysis provides transparency as to what is traded for what, and who benefits and who loses.

   Trade-off analysis avoids unnecessarily obscuring the differences between non-
commensurables such as economic commodities, risks to life, and individual rights,
or between those who benefit and those who suffer from the public policy. This type
of analysis not only exposes to public scrutiny the policy analyst's disaggregated
estimates and the assumptions and data on which they are based, it also *forces policymakers to comply with legislative mandates* and to make explicit their value judg-

---

67. In the area of occupational health, the Supreme Court has held that OSHA may not use cost-benefit
considerations in formulating standards to protect worker health because "Congress itself defined the basic
relationship between costs and benefits [in the Occupational Safety and Health Act], by placing the 'benefit' of worker health above all other considerations save those making attainment of this 'benefit' unachievable." See *American Textile Manufacturers Institute v. Donovan*, 452 U.S. 490 (1981).

ments and trade-offs, thereby preventing them from abdicating responsit
their decisions. Thus, accountability, rather than accounting, is fostered.
way, instead of compromising congressional intent, economic analysis can co
to furthering legislative goals in environmental protection, occupational hea,ாா añū
safety, economic growth, and technological advance.

- **NOTE**

1. During the 1970s Ashford (1978, 2001a) and Söderbaum (1973, 2000) independently offered trade-off analysis (what Söderbaum calls *positional analysis*)[68] as an
alternative to cost-benefit analysis. One distinction between these two formulations
of trade-off analysis is that the former not only talks about the disaggregation of concerns but also includes the importance of technological innovation. Both formulations focus on "accountability" and the importance of allowing decisionmakers to
make transparent decisions; i.e., decisions made with the knowledge of who is most
likely to gain and lose under a new social arrangement or form of technology. While
environmental economics as currently practiced searches for optimal outcomes using
static efficiency, the use of trade-off analysis leads to a form of dynamic environmental economics that includes the consideration of technological change over time
(Ashford, 2001b; Driesen, 2003, 2004).   ■

F. PRIORITIZING ENVIRONMENTAL PROBLEMS WITHIN AND AMONG DIFFERENT PROBLEM AREAS

As discussed in chapter 2, risk assessment was described in 1983 in a now near-
legendary report by the National Academy of Sciences (NAS, 1983) as consisting of
four steps: (1) hazard identification, (2) dose-response assessment, (3) exposure assessment, and (4) risk characterization. Risk assessment, of course, has been and continues to be an activity fraught with methodological difficulties and challenges. It is
an activity where both values and science necessarily play a part, and its results will
vary with choices of data, models, and assumptions. This is especially the case where

---

68. Söderbaum (2000) argues that cost-benefit analysis makes the unrealistic assumption that all politicians and citizens adopt the market ideology built into the analysis framework. He suggests that positional
analysis (PA) is a more democratic process that incorporates the ideological orientation among politicians
and citizens. Instead of identifying the economically efficient outcome, PA is a many-sided analysis that
aims to articulate the options or alternatives of choice, the impacts associated with these, the interests and
stakeholders that are affected and whether there are conflicts among them, and whether the ideological ori-
entations can provide a new lens for valuation and decision making (ibid., p. 87). The basic idea of PA is
to reach "conditional conclusions," that is, "conclusions that are conditional in relation to each ideological
orientation articulated and considered. The idea is to facilitate learning processes and decision-making and
not to dictate the "correct" way of arriving at the best and optimal decision" (ibid., p. 66).

there is considerable uncertainty, notwithstanding assertions that risk assessment can be clearly separated from risk management. See Ashford (1988) and Hornstein (1992).

1. Perceptual and Political Influences on Risk-Based Priority Setting

Different environmental and health and safety statutes incorporate concerns for risk, costs, technology, and equity in different ways. While it might be said that there are inconsistencies among regulatory areas or regimes because the cost per fatality avoided differs markedly (Sunstein, 1990; Travis et al., 1987), those differences could well be explained by differences in the risk posture (i.e., risk neutrality or risk aversion) of various regulatory authorities, the nature of the risk addressed (e.g., voluntary versus involuntary, chronic versus acute, mortality versus morbidity), the characteristics of the risk bearers (such as sensitive populations, children, workers), and differing mandates in the statutes themselves regarding the appropriate balance between the costs and benefits of regulations. The regulatory systems are risk driven; action is triggered by the discovery or assessment of risk. However, the differences among regulatory agencies are not in fact necessarily "irrational," unless rationality is tautologically defined as minimizing cost per unit of population risk as quantified via a "best estimate" (Shrader-Frechette, 1991).

The exercise of priority setting becomes incredibly complicated, depending on the context. It is one thing to prioritize options for controlling occupational carcinogens, it is another to prioritize efforts to reduce hazards with such diverse consequences as cancer, emphysema, acute poisoning, and traumatic accidents, even within the same industry or context of exposure. Simply counting fatalities from each hazard does not fully capture the human impact of these hazards. While considerable energy has been devoted to developing a means of evaluating a lost life in economic terms, we scarcely know where to begin with the far more prevalent effects of morbidity attended by great differences in pain and suffering, or with ecological effects resulting in the loss of a species. Even when we are comparing like hazards, such as fatal accidents, it is not clear that we should place equal emphasis on valuing opportunities for, say, reducing occupational risk versus highway deaths.

Even if we were to make no distinctions among the types of injury sustained, society has seen fit through legislation to regard, for example, exposure to carcinogens (and more recently to endocrine disrupters) through additives to the food supply as different from other consumer exposures. If the priority-setting discussion intends to revisit the wisdom of existing legislative directives, it will need to decide on the weighting criteria and the principles to be applied to: issues of risk profiles, risk types, and distribution of risks among risk bearers and costs among cost bearers; the nature of the assumption of risk; and a host of other factors. While the political agenda can be altered, it is not clear that a rational, inherently correct system based on risk can be identified.

The problems are not simply political. Since regulation focuses on controlling or reducing particularized or specific hazards, political demands are translated into contests between affected publics and affected industries over a specific hazard and often within such specific regulatory regimes as food additives, occupational exposure, community contamination, or consumer products. The legislative structure and risk assessments on a specific hazard define the debate.

One cannot prioritize particularized political demands. Crisis-driven demands (such as those arising from Love Canal or from Alar on apples) divert resources from a general plan in order to address perceived emergencies in a timely fashion. More general political demands (such as for worker safety and environmental protection) are juggled in the annual budgeting process. On the other hand, even where political demands do not drive or bombard an agency, attempts to act ahead of political demand—for instance, by prioritizing chemicals to be tested, ranking chemicals according to risk, and finally regulating in accordance with these rankings— leads to difficulties. During the first years of its implementation of the 1976 Toxic Substances Control Act, EPA became hopelessly bogged down in its efforts to build a rational system, even though the administration of then President Jimmy Carter was supportive of the effort. Prioritization of even the 100 chemicals in most common use had hardly been started after 4 years of effort. In order to understand this lack of success, it is necessary to examine priority setting in greater detail.

2. The Inherent Nonuniformity in Priority Setting

Priority setting for addressing and remedying environmental problems involves the articulation of an organizing principle for setting priorities and the establishment of a social, political, and legal process for implementing the system. Even left to its own devices and free from political pressures, responsible government faces challenges at several levels.

Given that different environmental problems are managed by different regulatory agencies or offices, and fall under different legislative mandates, the first question of priority setting concerns the relative allocation of resources to different regulatory regimes. How, for example, do we value controlling air emissions compared with ensuring that new pesticides are relatively safe? In practice, this is influenced largely by the political process and is not based on some rational analytical scheme. However, even if this initial allocation does not seem to be rational, greater or fewer environmental benefits can be realized, depending upon the extent to which each regulatory regime coordinates its activities with the others. For example, simultaneous though separate requirements for controlling cadmium in occupational environments, water effluents, and consumer products can be more cost-effective than uncoordinated efforts spread out in time. Part of this cost-effectiveness stems from the fact that those firms responsible for cadmium use and production have an opportunity to adopt a multimedia focus, where changes in the technology of production can have multiple payoffs for reducing risks. The opportunity to achieve multiple environmental payoffs through coordination of various regulatory efforts could alter an agency's internal priority scheme (discussed later) by placing a particular substance or problem higher on a list than it would have been using a single regulatory focus.

Even in the most supportive of political times, such as when the U.S. Interagency Regulatory Liaison Group was formed in the late 1970s, the attempt to coordinate regulatory efforts was not entirely successful. Within EPA, the establishment of "multioffice clusters" to promote integrated cross-media problem solving on specific pollutants (such as lead), on specific industries (such as petrochemicals), or on specific issue areas (such as indoor air pollution) may eventually be more successful, but fundamental problems are likely to remain. An alternative approach worth considering is one in which the coordination of agency efforts focuses, not on regulation of a single substance or class of substances, but on establishing a concerted effort to change an industrial process or production technology. Such an approach is explored in chapter 13.

Given the influence of politics on the allocation of resources to different regulatory regimes, it is understandable that government would turn its attention to establishing priorities *within* each regime, rather than among them. The internal ranking system for taking action could take on any of three forms:

• ranking problems by the number of persons at risk;
• ranking problems by expected (maximum individual) risk (in such a scheme, a lifetime risk of cancer of one in 1,000 would rank higher than a risk of one in 10,000); or
• ranking regulatory interventions by their health-effectiveness, i.e., the amount of risk reduced per compliance dollar expended.

Generating these priority schemes would, of course, rely on risk assessments (and as mentioned earlier, a way of weighing different kinds of risks). The third option would need, in addition, estimates of compliance cost. All three options would also require a determination of how much residual risk would be "acceptable" or permissible under various legislative mandates, as well as an assessment of the means by which compliance would be achieved. Economically efficient means presumably would be preferred, except where unjustifiable inequities exist as to either the beneficiaries of protection (citizens, workers, consumers) or those who bear the costs (small versus large firms, different industrial sectors, and so forth). For example, it has been suggested that the Occupational Safety and Health Administration abandon efforts to protect all workers from asbestos or noise exposure when it becomes too expensive, but the inequity of protecting some workers more than others argues against this approach. On the other hand, the Clean Air and Clean Water acts require that new plants be regulated more stringently than old ones, but this, too, is based on equity concerns.

All the complexities involved in priority setting within regulatory regimes reveal priority-setting schemes that take many factors into account: risk, efficiency of reducing risk, equity, technological and economic feasibility, and responsiveness to public demands and private concerns. Many extant schemes are used to rank hazards, not industrial processes or industrial sectors, although there are striking examples of the use of regulation to promote technological change when the latter approach has been taken. See Ashford and Heaton (1983) for examples, such as PVC (polyvinyl chloride) polymerization, and substitutes for PCBs. For additional examples, see OTA (1995).

While there have been repeated calls for uniform approaches to risk assessment and uniform balancing of regulatory costs and benefits, the legal mandates and individual cultures of different regulatory regimes prevent the achievement of uniformity. And while uniformity might be a preferred goal of some analysts, differences between agency approaches should not be too quickly labeled as inconsistencies. The differences may be defensible. Demands for consistency that move all systems to a lower common denominator of environmental protection may be motivated by antiregulatory interests. Demands for *tighter* levels of protection to achieve consistency are not made by the same players who demand a relaxation of "overly restrictive" regulatory systems.

Given that priority setting for regulation involves an integration of benefits, cost, and equity concerns, determining the appropriate level of control or regulation for a particular risk is a necessary first step in creating a priority-setting scheme for many risks. Since priority setting depends on ranking the opportunities for risk reduction, a decision first has to be made as to how much of each risk type we would want to reduce. To facilitate this determination, an impact analysis of different amounts of regulation would need to be undertaken.

▪ NOTES

1. For an in-depth discussion of how the proponents of cost-benefit analysis view priority setting based on the ranking of hazards and programs by their cost-benefit ratios, and the confusion and difficulties inherent in such ranking systems, see Driesen (2001).

2. In a 1991 case overturning EPA's attempt to ban most uses of asbestos under the Toxic Substances Control Act (TSCA), the Fifth Circuit Court of Appeals held that the agency was required to examine the costs and benefits of all of the various

options for reducing asbestos exposure, including the relative risks and benefits of substitutes for asbestos, before it could determine whether its proposed regulation of that substance was "reasonable" within the meaning of TSCA (which authorizes the regulation of "unreasonable" chemical risks). See *Corrosion Proof Fittings v. EPA*, 947 F.2d 1201 (5th Cir. 1991). Because EPA views this as a daunting task, this decision has largely rendered TSCA a dead letter for the comprehensive regulation of industrial chemicals.

3. See the proposals for the use of risk-risk analysis by Keeney (1990 and Keeney and Winkler, 1985), which are based on the premise that the economic costs of environmental regulation tend to make the intended beneficiaries of that regulation poorer and thus subject them to greater environmental, health, and safety risks generally. Also see the resulting criticism of that approach by the U.S. Government Accountability Office (GAO, 1992). Rascoff and Revesz (2002) offer a more complete and balanced analysis of the consequences of regulating a single risk by arguing for not only the inclusion of the risks of substitutes, but also "ancillary benefits" in terms of positive spillovers in associated but indirect protections against risks not the intended target of the regulation, and other general environmentally positive behavioral changes that come from compliance with the regulation. On the subject of "ancillary benefits" associated by induced innovation, see the studies by Ashford and colleagues at MIT (1983 and 1985) and by Porter and van der Linde (1995a, 1995b) on the related concept of "innovation offsets." For an important treatise on comparative risk assessment, see Hornstein (1992).   ▪

G. LAW AND ECONOMICS AS COMPETING FRAMEWORKS FOR ENVIRONMENTAL DECISION MAKING: THE POLLUTER PAYS PRINCIPLE AND THE PRECAUTIONARY PRINCIPLE

The *Polluter Pays Principle* holds that polluting enterprises should bear the costs of controlling their polluting activities and should assume liability for the consequences of these polluting activities. This principle stands in contrast to an alternative perspective, often advanced by neoclassical economists, which is known as the Coasean view (after economist Ronald Coase). The difference between these two perspectives is illustrated by the following example. Imagine that the industrial producer of a certain product freely uses the air or water to dispose of a noxious waste, taking no steps to control or treat the waste prior to discharge. The adverse effects of this pollution are largely borne by individuals who live downstream or downwind of the site. The lower cost of this method of disposal may benefit consumers of the product (through lower prices), the producer of the product (through higher profits), or both. In either case, neither the producer nor the consumer has an incentive to account for the externality costs that the production of the product imposes on persons living downstream or downwind of the site.

In his famous article, *The Theory of Social Cost* (1960), Nobel Prize-winning economist Ronald Coase suggests that externality problems of this nature can be solved by marketlike transactions involving a negotiation between polluters and affected citizens. Coase characterizes the issue as being one in which there is a "reciprocal nature of the harm." Were it not for the polluter, there would be no problem. Conversely, were there no citizens living downstream or downwind (or if those living there were willing to move), there would likewise be no problem. Coase argues that in the absence of transaction costs, it makes no sense for the government to impose a solution. Through negotiation, no matter which group initially has property rights in the air or water, the same outcome would result. The resource (air or water) would be put to its most valued use. Coase argues that what is important is the value of the polluting activity (in excess of its options for alternative activities) compared with the value placed on a clean environment by humans by remaining in that environment (over the cost of moving). In this view, it makes no difference to the final outcome which party has "property rights" in the ecosystem. Either way, the market will give the same result, and the ecosystem will be put to its most valued use. Either the polluter will desist or move, or the humans will move. For a deeper discussion of the Coase Theorem and its detractors, see Simpson (1996).

In contrast, the Polluter Pays Principle calls attention to the fact that these results are not identical from an equity perspective; what *does* differ here is who bears the economic costs. The Polluter Pays Principle incorporates a moral judgment by placing responsibility for cessation of pollution (and for any necessary clean-up) directly on the polluter, even in situations in which it would be cheaper to have the humans move. When the law incorporates the Polluter Pays Principle, it reflects the symbolic value of a clean environment. Coasean economists reject the application of law in this context because it is said to be economically inefficient. Indeed, much of the environmental debate between law and economics reflects this tension, since the law here is primarily concerned with fairness and ethical principles, while economics is concerned with economic efficiency.

The *Precautionary Principle* is more subtle, less clearly defined, and often more controversial than the Polluter Pays Principle. It arose as a means of addressing the uncertainties often associated with even the best of environmental risk assessments. In many cases, the time scales and consequences of environmental changes are unknown and/or difficult to define in scientific terms. Moreover, environmental impacts from activities carried out today may not be seen for many generations, and may have implications well beyond current political terms and agendas. In a broad sense, there are two basic policy approaches that can be taken in the face of such uncertainties. The first cautions that regulatory action not be pursued until the uncertainties are sufficiently resolved, lest the regulated industry be made to incur needless costs. The second cautions that harm to the environment and public health can be far-reaching, and calls for regulatory action when the available (yet imperfect) data are sufficiently suggestive of harm. It is this second approach that forms the basis for the Precautionary Principle. The principle was independently developed in the United States and Germany and has now become recognized in international environmental law. Principle 15 of the Declaration of the 1992 United Nations Conference on Environment and Development (known as the Rio Declaration) states as follows: "In order to protect the environment, the precautionary approach shall be widely used by States according to their capabilities. Where there are threats of serious and irreversible damage, lack of full scientific certainty shall not be used as a reason for postponing cost-effective measures to prevent environmental degradation."

The Precautionary Principle not only appears in European Union environmental directives, it is also articulated as a fundamental legal principle in the treaties that bind the member countries. In 1992, the Maastricht treaty provided that European Community action on the environment "shall be based on the precautionary principle." The use of the Precautionary Principle was further extended to Community policy on the environment in the 1997 Treaty of Amsterdam.

In the United States, a precautionary approach has been applied in various ways in decisions about health, safety, and the environment for about 30 years, which is much longer than recent commentaries would have us believe, and earlier than the appearance of a formal Precautionary Principle in European law. See Ashford (2006) and de Sadeleer (2000, 2002). This is not to say, however, that the Precautionary Principle is currently enjoying a robust existence within the U.S. regulatory system. In general, the strength of the Precautionary Principle depends on (1) the extent to which the operative legislation (environmental, occupational, and consumer protection) can be read as requiring or permitting the use of a precautionary approach, (2) the extent to which administrative agencies are willing to take such an approach, and (3) the extent to which the courts are willing to read the operative legislation as requiring or permitting such an approach. Many health and environmental statutes employ strong precautionary language. A few mandate a strict precautionary approach. The Food, Drug, and Cosmetic Act, for example, forbids the Food and Drug Administration from approving any food or color additive that has been found to cause cancer in humans or animals, and the courts have given effect to this edict even when they questioned its wisdom. See, e.g., *Public Citizen v. Young*, 831 F. 2d 1108 (D.C. Cir. 1987). More often, however, the operative legislation contains general language that stops short of a direct mandate, but which strongly suggests a precautionary approach. It is in the implementation of these statutes that one can trace the waxing and waning of the Precautionary Principle.

In the 1970s, the first 10 years of the modern environmental era, the Precautionary Principle could generally be said to be on the rise in this country. As amended in

1970, for example, the Clean Air Act specifies that ambient air quality standards be set at the level that will ensure an "adequate margin of safety," and that emission standards for hazardous air pollutants ensure an "ample margin of safety." Similarly, the Occupational Safety and Health Act of 1970 (OSHAct) states that its "purpose and policy" is to "assure as far as possible every working man and woman in the Nation safe and healthful working conditions." Thus, in *Lead Industries Association, Inc. v. Environmental Protection Agency*, 647 F.2d 1130 (D.C. Cir. 1980), the District of Columbia (D.C.) Circuit Court of Appeals upheld EPA's ambient air standard for lead in the face of a vigorous industry challenge, noting that "Congress directed the Administrator to *err on the side of caution* in making the necessary decisions" (emphasis added). And in *The Society of Plastics Industry, Inc. v. Occupational Safety and Health Administration*, 509 F2d 1301 (2d Cir. 1975), the Second Circuit Court of Appeals upheld a very stringent workplace standard governing exposure to the carcinogen vinyl chloride, in the face of uncertain scientific and technological data, noting that it is OSHA's duty "to act where existing methodology or research is deficient." These and other endorsements by the courts of a precautionary approach were the origin of the Precautionary Principle in U.S. environmental law. See Ashford (2006).

Beginning in the 1980s, the political appointees in leadership positions in U.S. regulatory agencies became less willing to regulate without strong evidence of harm. This was a response both to the political predilections of the presidents who had appointed them and to the fact that the courts had made it increasingly difficult for aggressive health, safety, and environmental standards to survive judicial review. In 1980, for example, the Supreme Court held that OSHA's workplace standard for benzene exceeded the agency's authority under the OSHAct, and a plurality of the Court issued an opinion expressing the view that the agency may regulate a workplace toxicant only when it can show that exposure to that chemical places workers at a "significant risk" of harm. See *Industrial Union Department v. American Petroleum Institute*, 448 U.S. 607 (1980). The plurality also offered guidance as to what might be considered "significant," noting that it should lie somewhere between a lifetime risk of 10^{-3} (1 in 1,000, which the plurality cited as a clearly significant risk) and 10^{-9} (1 in 1,000,000,000, a clearly insignificant risk). Under President Reagan (and subsequent administrations), OSHA largely chose to use the least permissibly protective level (10^{-3}) as its cutoff point for regulation, and the number of new occupational exposure regulations dropped dramatically. This heralded the wane of the Precautionary Principle in toxic substance regulation.

Drawing on the plurality opinion in the benzene case, the D.C. Circuit Court of Appeals held in 1987 that the concept of significant risk was an (implicit) component of the Clean Air Act's directive that emission standards for hazardous air pollutants be set at the level that ensures an "ample margin of safety." Safe, reasoned the court, does not mean risk free, and only significant risks need be regulated. The court did, however, affirm the precautionary aim of the Clean Air Act: "Congress authorized and, indeed, required EPA to protect against dangers before their extent is conclusively ascertained. Under the 'ample margin of safety' directive, EPA's standards must protect against incompletely understood dangers to public health and the environment." See *Natural Resources Defense Council, Inc. v. Environmental Protection Agency*, 824 F.2d 1146 (D.C. Cir. 1987). Twenty years later, the Supreme Court affirmed the precautionary intent of another portion of the Clean Air Act, and directed EPA to reconsider its decision not to take action to curb global warming. See *Massachusetts v. Environmental Protection Agency*, 127 S. Ct. 1438 (2007).

Nonetheless, in today's political climate, the burden of scientific proof has posed a difficult barrier to overcome in any effort to protect health, safety, and the environment in the United States. Actions to prevent harm are usually taken only after significant proof of harm is established, at which point it may be too late to prevent significant damage. Typically, hazards are addressed by industry and government agencies one at a time, in terms of a single pesticide or chemical, rather than as broader initiatives such as the promotion of organic agriculture and nontoxic products, or the phaseout of particular classes of dangerous chemicals.

The Precautionary Principle has been criticized as being both too vague and too arbitrary to form a basis for rational decision making. The assumption underlying this criticism is that any scheme not based on cost-benefit analysis and risk assessment is both irrational and without secure foundation in either science or economics. See Ashford (2005, 2006) for a criticism of that view and an argument that the tenets of the Precautionary Principle are rational within an analytical framework as rigorous as uncertainties permit, and one that mirrors democratic values embodied in regulatory, compensatory, and common law. Furthermore, while risk assessment certainly has a place in a regulatory system based on a precautionary approach, cost-benefit analysis *as a decision-making criterion* will often be at odds with the Precautionary Principle. In a very real sense, this was the effect of the *Corrosion Proof Fittings* case, discussed in note 2 at the end of section F, in which the court's elevation of the cost-benefit principle above all other regulatory concerns appears to have substantially blunted the precautionary aspects of the Toxic Substances Control Act. Trade-off analysis, on the other hand, can help facilitate the application of the Precautionary Principle.

In general, policymakers must address uncertainty both about (1) the nature and extent of the health, safety, or environmental risks in question and about (2) the performance of an alternative technology said to be able to reduce that risk. First, they must choose whether to err on the side of caution or on the side of risk. With regard to the first type of uncertainty—scientific uncertainty—two mistakes can be made. A *Type I* error is committed if society regulates an activity that appears to be hazardous, but turns out later to be harmless (a "false positive" in the parlance of experimental analysis) and resources are needlessly expended. Another error, a *Type II* error, is committed if society fails to regulate an activity because the evidence is not initially thought to be strong enough, but the activity ultimately proves to be harmful (a "false negative") See Ashford (1988). Finally, a *Type III* error is said to occur when one provides an accurate (or precise) answer to the wrong problem. See Schwartz and Carpenter (1999). Not taking into account opportunities to change technology restricts the decision-maker to static solutions and thus gives rise to the further error of considering options within "bounded rationality."

Where uncertainty exists on the technology side, Type I errors can be said to be committed when society mandates the development or adoption of a technology that turns out to be much more expensive or less effective in reducing risk than anticipated, and resources thus are needlessly or foolishly expended. Type II errors might be said to be committed when, because of insufficient commitment of resources or political will, society fails to force or stimulate significant risk-reducing technology.[69] An important distinction between a cost-benefit approach and one based on precaution is that the former is risk neutral in the balancing of costs and benefits with their attendant uncertainties, and the latter is risk averse to Type II errors.

Value judgments clearly attend decisions whether to lean toward tolerating Type I or Type II errors with regard to *either* risk or technology choices. This is because the cost of being wrong in one instance may be vastly different from the cost of being wrong in another. For example, banning a chemical essential to a beneficial activity such as the use of radionuclides in medicine has potentially more drastic consequences than banning a nonessential chemical for which there is a close, cost-comparable substitute. It may be perfectly appropriate to rely on "most likely" estimates of risk in the first case and on "worst-case" estimates in the second. A Type II error regarding technology choice arguably was committed in the manner in which the Montreal Protocol banned CFCs. DuPont and ICI, the producers of CFCs, were allowed to promote the use of their own substitute, HCFCs; a more stringent protocol could have stimulated the development of still better substitutes.

Evaluating potential errors and deciding which way to lean is not a precise science. However, making those evaluations and valuations explicit within a trade-off analysis that acknowledges distributional effects, accounts for uncertainties in risk assessments, and considers opportunities for technological change will reveal the preferences upon which policies are based and may suggest priorities. That is one of

---

69. This may happen when, under pressure from cost constraints, standards are not as stringent as health or environmental concerns might justify. "Lax" standards may not stimulate serious changes in technology, while stringent standards would. Stringent standards may actually be more economically beneficial for society than lax standards, although there may be winners and losers within the industrial or product sectors. See the discussion of stimulating technological change through regulation in chapter 12. Also see Ashford (2002).

the reasons why trade-off analysis may often be more useful than cost-benefit analysis as a decision-making tool.

- ■ **NOTE**

1. Taking a strong stand against the Precautionary Principle, Richard Stewart (2002) argues that uncertain risks should be regulated under the same decisional framework as risks that are well characterized, and that "uncertainty as such does not justify regulatory precaution" (p. 71). He suggests that, "while preventive regulation of uncertain risks is often appropriate and should incorporate precautionary elements where warranted by risk aversion or information acquisition, strong versions of the [principle] do not provide a conceptually sound or socially desirable prescription for regulation" (p. 72). In other words, precaution is endorsed when the victims (the intended beneficiaries of the regulation) are themselves risk averse, but not when the government acts as trustee for the victims in the absence of expressed risk aversion. Is this always (or often) a sensible distinction? Are ordinary citizens experienced at relating to small-probability, high catastrophic risks of unknown magnitude or consequences?   ■

H. SCHOOLS OF ECONOMIC DISCOURSE AND POLICY FORMULATION

There are different schools of economic discourse, each with a different perspective concerning the appropriate role of economics in environmental policy making. *Environmental economics* represents the application of neoclassical economics to environmental problems, with an underlying concern for correctly pricing the uninternalized externalities. As we have seen, the focus is on achieving static economic efficiency. This is in sharp contrast to *ecological economics*, which argues that economic activities must take place within the ecological limits of the biosphere, and that advances in pollution prevention technology focusing on pollution prevention must be implemented before any growth is to occur. See Söderbaum (2000). In this view, the use of resources and the extent of permissible pollution are determined, not by prices, but by biophysical limits. Nonetheless, externalities are still priced, and the correct treatment of, and accounting for, "natural capital" are cornerstones of this approach. See Lewin (1995). Ecological economics and its reliance on the idea of limits to growth are often eclipsed in the environmental debate by a form of technological optimism that holds that more benign—or even environmentally sound—substitutes for products, materials, and processes will eventually be developed because of the inherent ingenuity of humankind.

Neoclassical economics may have found a more formidable competitor in technologically focused policy development. In a broad sense, two different approaches are vying for dominance in current environmental policy debates. The first, which might be termed the *co-evolutionary approach*, asks the following question: How can we best encourage the different sectors of society to work together to make the necessary changes to improve the environment and public health? This approach relies on measures designed to enhance efficiency and cooperation, such as the involvement of stakeholders, continuous learning, innovative governance, and regulatory streamlining, and it tends to focus on stepwise, incremental improvements, often relying on best existing technology. In contrast, a *technology-focused regulatory approach* asks a different question: How do we identify and exploit the opportunities for changing—through innovation where necessary—the basic technologies of extraction, production, agriculture, and transportation that cause damage to the environment and public health? In any given situation, this will involve a policy choice—based on considerations of risks, costs, equity, and timing—as to whether the goal is to effectuate a transformation of the existing polluting or problem industrial sectors or to stimulate more radical and disrupting innovation that might result in the replacement of one or more of these sectors with firms that employ a new technology.

Currently, EPA, like most economists, scientists, and risk analysts, is focused on the first approach. On the other hand, activists and others interested in significant industrial transformations have focused on the second approach and have argued for the application of political will and creative energy toward changing the ways that industrial systems are constructed. The first effort promotes rationalism within a more or less static world; the second promotes dynamic transformation of the industrial state.

If what is desired is a tenfold (or greater) reduction in pollution (or in material or energy use), a result that would be in line with the tenets of ecological economics, limiting policy options to those involving cooperation with existing firms undertaking incremental changes may well guarantee failure. As discussed in chapter 12, this is especially likely to be true if the regulatory targets, as well as the means and schedule for reaching those targets, are negotiated between government and the incumbent industry. Economically dynamic, innovation-focused environmental policy is far more likely to achieve a significant transformation.

■ NOTES

1. Further readings on these topics can be found in two journals that focus on ecological economics: the *Journal of Ecological Economics* and the *International Journal of Green Economics*.

2. For a textbook that compares traditional environmental economics with ecological economics, see Jonathan M. Harris (2005) *Environmental and Resource Economics: A Contemporary Approach*. 2nd ed. Houghton Mifflin, Boston. ■

ACKNOWLEDGMENT

The authors are indebted to Robert F. Stone for his contributions to the writing of this chapter.

REFERENCES

Ackerman, Frank, and Lisa Heinzerling. 2004. *Priceless: On Knowing the Price of Everything and the Value of Nothing.* New York: New Press.

Ackerman, Frank, Lisa Heinzerling, and Rachel Massey. 2005. "Applying Cost-Benefit Analysis to Past Decisions: Was Environmental Protection Ever a Good Idea?" 57 *Administrative Law Review* 155.

Argote, L., and D. Epple. 1990. "Learning Curves in Manufacturing," *Science* 247: 920–924.

Ashford, N. A. 1976. *Crisis in the Workplace: Occupational Disease and Injury.* Cambridge, Mass.: MIT Press.

Ashford, N. A. 1978. "The Role of Risk Assessment and Cost-Benefit Analysis in Decisions Concerning Safety and the Environment." *FDA Symposium on Risk/Benefit Decisions and the Public Health, February 17, 1978*, Colorado Springs, pp. 159–168.

Ashford, N. A. 1981. "Alternatives to Cost-Benefit Analysis in Regulatory Decisions," *Annals New York Academy of Science*, 129–137.

Ashford, N. A. 1988. "Science and Values in the Regulatory Process," *Statistical Science* 3(3): 377–383.

Ashford, N. A. 1998. "The Importance of Taking Technological Innovation into Account in Estimating the Costs and Benefits of Worker Health and Safety Regulation," in *Costs and Benefits of Occupational Safety and Health: Proceedings of the European Conference on Costs and Benefits of Occupational Health and Safety 1997*, The Hague, Holland, *May 28–30, 1997*, J. Mossink and F. Licher (eds.), pp. 69–78. Available at http://hdl.handle.net/1721.1/1585.

Ashford, N. A. 1999. "Porter Debate Stuck in 1970s," in *The Environmental Forum* (September/October) Washington, D.C.: Environmental Law Institute, p. 3.

Ashford, N. A. 2001a. "Implementing a Precautionary Approach in Decisions Affecting Health, Safety, and the Environment: Risk, Technology Alternatives, and Tradeoff Analysis," in The Role of Precaution in Chemicals Policy, *Favorita Papers* 01/2002, Elisabeth Freytag, Thomas Jakl, Gerhard Loibl, and Michael Wittmann (eds.) Vienna: Diplomatic Academy, pp. 128–140. Available at http://hdl.handle.net/1721.1/1587.

Ashford, N. A. 2001b. "Innovation—The Pathway to Threefold Sustainability," in *The Steilmann Report: The Wealth of People: An Intelligent Economy for the 21st Century*, F. C. Lehner, A. Charles, S. Bieri, and Y. Paleocrassas (eds.) Bochum, Germany: Brainduct ® Edition, pp. 233–274.

Ashford, Nicholas 2002. "Government and Innovation in Europe and North America," Special Issue on Ecological Modernization, David Sonnenfeld and Arthur Mol (eds.) *American Behavioral Scientist* 45(9): 1417–1434.

Ashford, Nicholas A. 2006. "The Legacy of the Precautionary Principle in U.S. Law: The Rise of Cost-Benefit Analysis and Risk Assessment as Undermining Factors in Health, Safety and Environmental Protection," in *Implementing Precaution: Approaches from Nordic Countries and the EU*, Nicolas de Sadeleer (ed.) London: Earthscan.

Ashford, N. A., and C. Ayers. 1985. "Policy Issues for Consideration in Transferring Technology to Developing Countries," *Ecology Law Quarterly*, 12(4): 871–906.

Ashford, N. A., C. Ayers, and R. F. Stone. 1985. "Using Regulation to Change the Market for Innovation," *Harvard Environmental Law Review* 9(2): 419–466.

Ashford, N. A., and C. C. Caldart. 1996. *Technology, Law and the Working Environment* rev. ed. Washington, D.C.: Island Press.

Ashford, N. A., G. R. Heaton, and W. C. Priest, W. C. 1979. "Environmental, Health and Safety Regulations and Technological Innovation," in *Technological Innovation for a Dynamic Economy*, C. T. Hill and J. M. Utterback (eds.). New York: Pergamon Press, pp. 161–221.

Ashford, N. A., and G. R. Heaton, Jr. 1983. "Regulation and Technological Innovation in the Chemical Industry," *Law and Contemporary Problems* vol. 46, no. 3, pp. 109–157, Duke University School of Law. Available at http://hdl.handle.net/1721.1/1556.

Ashford, N. A., and K. Rest. 2001. *Public Participation in Contaminated Communities*. Available at http://web.mit.edu/ctpid/www/tl/.

Ashford, N. A., and R. F. Stone. 1988. Cost-Benefit Analysis in Environmental Decision-Making: Theoretical Considerations and Applications to Protection of Stratospheric Ozone. Research supported by the Office of Policy Analysis and Review in the Office of Air and Radiation, U.S. Environmental Protection Agency.

Ashford, N. A., and G. Zwetsloot. 1999. "Encouraging Inherently Safer Production in European Firms: A Report from the Field," Special Issue on Risk Assessment and Environmental Decision Making, A. Amendola and D. Wilkinson (eds.) *Journal of Hazardous Materials* pp. 123–144.

Ashford, N. A. et al. 1980. *Analyzing the Benefits of Health, Safety, and Environmental Regulations*. Cambridge, Mass.: Center for Policy Alternatives at MIT, CPA-82-16.

Ashford, R. H. 2004. "What is Socio-Economics?" 41 *San Diego Law Review* 5.

Baumol, W. J., and W. E. Oates. 1988. *The Theory of Environmental Policy* 2nd ed. Cambridge: Cambridge University Press.

Boulding, K. E. 1974. "Fun and Games with the Gross National Product: The Role of Misleading Indicators in Social Policy," in *Environment and Society*, R. T. Roelofs, J. N. Crowley, and D. L. Hardesty (eds.) Englewood Cliffs, N.J.: Prentice-Hall.

Bryant B. (ed.) 1995. *Environmental Justice: Issues, Policies, and Solutions*. Washington, D.C.: Island Press.

Coase, R. H. 1960. "The Problem of Social Cost," *Journal of Law and Economics* 3: 1–44.

Colborn, T., D. Dumanoski, and J. P. Myers. 1996. *Our Stolen Future*. New York: Dutton.

Costa, D. L., and M. E. Kahn. 2003. "The Rising Price of Nonmarket Goods," *American Economic Review* 93(2): 227–232 (May).

Costanza, R., and H. Daly. 1991. "Goals, Agenda and Policy Recommendations for Ecological Economics," in *Ecological Economics*, Robert Costanza (ed.) New York: Columbia University Press.

Cropper, M. L., and W. E. Oates. 1992. "Environmental Economics: A Survey," *Journal of Economic Literature* 30(2): 675–740.

Daly, H. 1991. *Steady-State Economics*. Washington, D.C.: Island Press.

de Sadeleer, Nicolas. 2000. *Two Approaches of Precaution: A Comparative Review of EU and US Theory and Practice of the Precautionary Principle*. Brussels: Centre d'Étude du Droit de l'Environment.

de Sadeleer, Nicolas. 2002. *Environmental Principles: From Political Slogans to Legal Rules*. Oxford: Oxford University Press.

Dorman, P. 1996. *Markets and Mortality: Economics, Dangerous Work, and the Value of Human Life*. Cambridge: Cambridge University Press.

Driesen, David M. 2001. "Getting Our Priorities Straight: One Strand of the Regulatory Reform Debate," ELA 31: 10003–10020.

Driesen, D. M. 2003. *The Economic Dynamics of Environmental Law*. Cambridge, Mass.: MIT Press.

Driesen, D. M. 2004. "The Economic Dynamics of Environmental Law: Cost-Benefit Analysis, Emissions Trading, and Priority-Setting," *Boston College Environmental Affairs Law Review* 31(3), 501–528.

Driesen, David M. 2005. "Distributing the Costs of Environmental, Health and Safety Protection: The Feasibility Principle, Cost-Benefit Analysis, and Regulatory Reform," *Boston College Environmental Affairs Law Review* 32(1): 1–95.

Driesen, David M., and Shubha Ghosh. 2005. "The Functions of Transaction Costs: Rethinking Transaction Cost Minimization in a World of Friction," *Arizona Law Review* 47(1): 61–111.

Driesen, David M. 2006. "Is Cost-Benefit Analysis Neutral?" *University of Colorado Law Review* 77(2): 335–404.

Farber, D. A., and P. A. Hemmersbaugh. 1993. "The Shadow of the Future: Discount Rates, Later Generations, and the Environment," *Vanderbilt Law Review* 46(2): 267–304 (March).

Fischer, G. W. 1979. "Willingness to Pay for Probabilistic Improvements in Functional Health Status: A Psychological Perspective," in *Health: What Is It Worth? Measures of Health Benefits*, S. J. Mushkin and D. W. Dunlop (eds.) New York: Pergamon Press.

Fischhoff, B. 1977. "Cost Benefit Analysis and the Art of Motorcycle Maintenance," *Policy Sciences* 8: 177–202.

Fisher, A. C. 1981. *Resource and Environmental Economics*. Cambridge: Cambridge University Press.

Foreman, C. 1998. *The Promise and Peril of Environmental Justice*. Washington, D.C.: Brookings Institution.

Freeman, A. M. III. 1993. *The Measurement of Environmental and Resource Values: Theory and Methods*. Washington, D.C.: Resources for the Future.

GAO (U.S. Government Accountability Office). 1983. *Siting of Hazardous Waste Landfills and their Correlation with Racial and Economic Status of Surrounding Communities*. GAO/RCED-83-168 (June 1, 1983). Washington, D.C.: Government Printing Office.

GAO (U.S. Government Accountability Office). 1992. *Risk-Risk Analysis: OMB's Review of a Proposed OSHA Rule*. GAO/PEMD-92-33. Washington, D.C.: U.S. GAO.

GAO (U.S. Government Accountability Office). 1995. *Demographics of People Living Near Waste Facilities*. GAO/RCED-95-84 (June 1995). Washington, D.C.: Government Printing Office.

GAO (U.S. Government Accountability Office) 2003. *Rulemaking: OMB's Role in Reviews of Agencies' Draft Rules and the Transparency of Those Reviews* GAO-03-929 (September 22, 2003) 3, 17–21. Washington, D.C.: Government Printing Office.

Goldman, M. I. 1985. "Economics of Environmental and Renewable Resources in Socialist Systems," in *Handbook of Natural Resource and Energy Economics: Volume II*, A. V. Kneese and J. L. Sweeney (eds.) Amsterdam: North-Holland.

Graham, Julie, and Don Shakow. 1990. "Labor Market Segmentation and Job-Related Risk: Differences in Risk and Compensation Between Primary and Secondary Labor Markets," *American Journal of Economics and Sociology* 49(3): 307–323.

Hahn, Robert, Sheila M. Olmstead, and Robert N. Stavins. 2003. "Environmental Regulation in the 1990s: A Retrospective Analysis," 27 *Harvard Environmental Law Review* 377.

Hanemann, W. M. 1994. "Valuing the Environment Through Contingent Valuation," *Journal of Economic Perspectives* 8(4): 19–43 (Fall).

Hanley, N., J. F. Shogren, and B. White. 1997. *Environmental Economics: Theory and Practice*. New York: Oxford University Press.

Hampicke, Ulrich, and Konrad Ott (eds.) 2003. "Reflections on Discounting," Special issue of the *International Journal of Sustainable Development* 6(1): 7–149.

Hanemann, W. Michael. 1991. "Willingness to Pay and Willingness to Accept," *The American Economic Review* 81(3): 635–647.

Harris, Jonathan M. 2005. *Environmental and Resource Economics: A Contemporary Approach* 2nd ed. Boston: Houghton Mifflin.

Heinzerling, L. 1998. "Regulatory Costs of Mythical Proportions," *Yale Law Journal* 107: 1981–2070.

Heinzerling, L., and F. Ackerman. 2002. *Pricing the Priceless: Cost-Benefit Analysis of Environmental Protection*. Georgetown Environmental Law and Policy Institute, Georgetown Law Center, Georgetown University, Washington, D.C. 35 pp.

Hofrichter Richard (ed.) 1993. *Toxic Struggles: The Theory and Practice of Environmental Justice*. Philadelphia, Pa: New Society Publishers.

Hornstein, D.T. 1992. "Reclaiming Environmental Law: A Normative Critique of Comparative Analysis," *Columbia Law Review* 92(3): 562–633.

Jaffe, A. B., S. R. Peterson, P. R. Portney, and R. N. Stavins. 1995. "Environmental Regulation and the Competitiveness of U.S. Manufacturing: What Does the Evidence Tell Us?" *Journal of Economic Literature* 33(1): 132–163 (March).

Jänicke, M., and K. Jacob. 2004. "Ecological Modernisation and the Creation of Lead Markets," in *Towards Environmental Innovation Systems*, K. M. Weber and J. Hemmelskamp (eds.) Heidelberg: Springer.

Keeney, R. L. 1990. "Mortality Risks Induced by Economic Expenditures," *Risk Analysis* 10(1): 147–158.

Keeney, R. L., and R. L. Winkler. 1985. "Evaluating Decision Strategies for Equity of Public Risks," *Operations Research* (33): 955.

Kellert, S. R., and E. O. Wilson. 1993. *The Biophilia Hypothesis*. Washington, D.C.: Island Press.

Kemp, R. 1997. *Environmental Policy and Technical Change: A Comparison of the Technological Impact of Policy Instruments*. Cheltenham, UK: Edward Elgar.

Klein, B. 1977. *Dynamic Economics*. Cambridge, Mass.: Harvard University Press.

Koch, L., and N. A. Ashford. 2006. "Rethinking the Role of Information in Chemicals Policy: Implications for TSCA and REACH," *Journal of Cleaner Production* 14(1): 31–46.

Lewin, Jeff. 1995. Chapter 8: Towards a New Ecological Law and Economics," in *Law and Economics: New and Critical Perspectives*, Robin Paul Malloy and Christopher K. Braun (eds.) New York: Peter Lang.

Lind, R. C. 1982. "A Primer on the Major Issues Relating to the Discount Rate for Evaluating National Energy Options," in *Discounting for Time and Risk in Energy Policy*, R. C. Lind (ed.) Baltimore: Johns Hopkins University Press.

Lind, R. C. 1990. "Reassessing the Government's Discount Rate Policy in Light of New Theory and Data in a World Economy with a High Degree of Capital Mobility," *Journal of Environmental Economics and Management* 18: S8–S28.

Machina, M. J. 1987. "Choice Under Uncertainty: Problems Solved and Unsolved," *Economic Perspectives* 1(1): 121–154.

Madia, Matt and Rick Melbirth. 2007. "A Failure to Govern: Bush's Attack on the Regulatory Process," OMB Watch, Washington, D.C., available at: http://www.ombwatch.org/regs/PDFs/FailuretoGovern .pdf.

McGarity, Thomas O. 2004. "The Goals of Environmental Legislation," 31 *Boston College Environmental Affairs Law Review* 529–554.

McGarity, T. O., S. Shapiro, and D. Bollier. 2004. *Sophisticated Sabotage: The Intellectual Games Used to Subvert Responsible Regulation*. Washington, D.C.: Environmental Law Institute.

Mishan, E. J. 1981. *Introduction to Normative Economics*. New York: Oxford University Press.

NAS (National Academy of Sciences). 1983. *Risk Assessment in the Federal Government: Managing the Process*. Washington, D.C.: National Academy Press.

National Oceanic and Atmospheric Administration (NOAA). 1993. Appendix I—Report of the NOAA Panel on Contingent Valuation. *Federal Register* 58(10): 4602–4614.

Nisbet, E. G. 1991. *Leaving Eden—To Protect and Manage the Earth*. Cambridge: Cambridge University Press.

Ortolano, L. 1997. *Environmental Regulation and Impact Assessment*. New York: John Wiley & Sons.

OTA: see United States Office of Technology Assessment.

Palmquist, R. B. 1991. "Hedonic Methods," in *Measuring the Demand for Environmental Quality*, J. Braden and C. Kolstad (eds.) Amsterdam: Elsevier Science Publishers.

Pearce, D. W., and R. K. Turner. 1990. *Economics of Natural Resources and the Environment*. London: Harvester Wheatsheaf.

Pindyck, Robert S., and D. L. Rubinfeld 1999. *Microeconomics* 4th ed. Upper Saddle River, N.J.: Prentice Hall.

Porter, M. E., and C. van der Linde. 1995a. "Green and Competitive: Ending the Stalemate," *Harvard Business Review* 73: 120–134 (September/October).

Porter, M. E., and C. van der Linde. 1995b. "Toward a New Conception of the Environmental-Competitiveness Relationship," *Journal of Economic Perspectives* 9(4): 97–118.

Portney, P. R., and J. P. Weyant (eds.) 1999. *Discounting and Intergenerational Equity*. Washington, D.C.: Resources for the Future.

Rascoff, S. J., and R. L. Revesz. 2002. "The Bias of Risk Tradeoff Analysis: Towards Parity in Environmental and Health-and-Safety Regulation," *University of Chicago Law Review* 16: 1763–1836.

Reinhardt, F. 1999. "Market Failure and the Environmental Policies of Firms," *Journal of Industrial Ecology* (3)1: 9–21.

Rosen, S. 1974. "Hedonic Prices and Implicit Markets: Product Differentiation in Pure Competition," *Journal of Political Economy* 82(1): 34–55 (January/February).

Schwartz, S., and K. Carpenter. 1999. "The Right Answer for the Wrong Question: Consequences of Type III Error for Public Health Research," *American Journal of Public Health* 89: 1175–1180.

Shrader-Frechette, K. S. 1991. *Risk and Rationality*. Berkeley and Los Angeles: University of California Press.

Simpson, A. W. Brian. 1996. "Coase v. Pigou Reexamined," *Journal of Legal Studies* 25: 53–97.

Söderbaum, P. 1973. "Positionsanalys vid beslutsfattande of planering. Ekonomisk analys pa tvarvetenskaplig grund (Positional Analysis for Decision Making and Planning. Economic analysis on an interdisciplinary Decision basis)," Stockholm: Esselte Stadium.

Söderbaum, P. 2000. *Ecological Economics: A Political Economics Approach to Environment and Development*. London: Earthscan.

Solow, R. M. 1991. "Sustainability: An Economist's Perspective," in *Economics of the Environment: Selected Readings*, R. Dorfman and N. Dorfman (eds.) New York: W.W. Norton, pp. 179–187.

Stewart, Richard. 2002. "Environmental Regulatory Decision Making Under Uncertainty," *Research in Law and Economics* 20: 71–126.

Stone, R. F. 1994. A Retrospective Analysis of the Economic Impact on Foundries of OSHA's 1987 Formaldehyde Standard. Working paper, U.S. Congress, Office of Technology Assessment, NTIS PB96108626.

Stone, R. F. 1997. Correspondence: Benefit-Cost Analysis. *Journal of Economic Perspectives* 11(2): 187–188 (Spring).

Strasser, K. 1997. "Cleaner Technology, Pollution Prevention, and Environmental Regulation," *Fordham Environmental Law Journal* 9(1): 1–106.

Sunstein, C. 1990. *After the Rights Revolution: Reconceiving the Regulatory State*. Cambridge, Mass.: Harvard University Press.

Sunstein, Cass, and Arden Rowell. 2005a. "On Discounting Regulatory Benefits: Risk, Money, and Intergenerational Equity," Working Paper 05-08, American Enterprise Institute–Brookings Joint Center for Regulatory Studies.

Sunstein, Cass, and Arden Rowell. 2005b. "On Discounting Regulatory Benefits: Risk, Money, and Intergenerational Equity," John M. Olin Law and Economics Working Paper No. 252, the University of Chicago. Accessible at http://www.law.uchicago.edu/Lawecon/index.html.

Tietenberg, T. 2003. *Environmental and Natural Resource Economics* 6th ed. Boston: Addison-Wesley.

Travis, C., S. Richter, E. Crouch, R. Wilson, and E. Klema. 1987. "Cancer Risk Management," *Environmental Science and Technology* 21(5): 415–420.

Tribe, L. H. 1973. "Technology Assessment and the Fourth Discontinuity," *Southern California Law Review* 46(3): 617–660 (June).

Tversky, A., and D. Kahneman. 1974. "Judgment Under Uncertainty: Heuristics and Biases," *Science* 185: 458–468 (September).

United Church of Christ Commission for Racial Justice. 1987. *Toxic Waste and Race in the United States: A National Report on the Racial and Socioeconomic Characteristics of Communities Surrounding Hazardous Waste Sites*. New York, New York Commission for Racial Justice. Also see Robert Bullard, Paul Mohai, Robin Saha, and Beverley Wright. 2007. *Toxic Wastes and Race at Twenty: 1987–2007: Grassroots*

Struggles to Dismantle Environmental Racism in the United States, Report prepared for the United Church of Christ Justice and Witness Ministries.

United Nations. 1992. "The Rio Declaration on Environment and Development," *The Global Partnership for Environment and Development: A Guide to Agenda 21 (Post-Rio edition)*. New York: United Nations, pp. 3–9 and 13–17.

United States Environmental Protection Agency. 1987. *Regulatory Impact Analysis: Protection of Stratospheric Ozone*. Stratospheric Protection Program, Office of Program Development, Office of Air and Radiation, U.S. EPA (December).

United States Environmental Protection Agency. 1992. *Environmental Equity, Reducing Risk for All Communities*. vol. 1, EPA Report 230-R-92-008. Washington, D.C.: Environmental Protection Agency.

United States Environmental Protection Agency. 2000. *Guidelines for Preparing Economic Analyses*. EPA Report 240-R-00-003 (September). Washington, D.C.: Environmental Protection Agency Accessible under "reports" at http://www.epa.gov/economics.

United States Office of Management and Budget. 1972. Circular A-94 Revised (March 27).

United States Office of Management and Budget. 1992. Circular A-94 Revised (Transmittal Memo 64) (October 29).

United States Office of Management and Budget. 2000. Memorandum for the Heads of Departments and Agencies: Guidelines to Standardize Measures of Costs and Benefits and the Format of Accounting Statements (March 22).

United States Office of Technology Assessment. 1995. *Gauging Control Technology and Regulatory Impacts in Occupational Safety and Health—An Appraisal of OSHA's Analytic Approach*. OTA-ENV-635 (September). Washington, D.C.: U.S. Congress.

Viscusi, W. Kip. 1992. *Fatal Tradeoffs: Public and Private Responsibilities for Risk*. New York: Oxford University Press.

4 Addressing Pollution Through the Tort System

A. INTRODUCTION

Put simply, *common law* is judge-made law, and *tort* law is a branch of the common law that provides redress for certain types of wrongs committed by one party against another. Since modern environmental law is, in this country at least, largely a creature of federal and state legislation, one might well ask why we begin our study of environmental law with a look at the common law tort system, which is focused neither on legislation nor on the environment. Indeed, one might well ask why we look at the tort system at all. There are four primary reasons.

First, it was the weakness of the common law as a means of addressing environmental issues that led to the complex network of environmental statutes we have today. If we are to understand (and perhaps argue about) the continued need for environmental legislation, we must have an appreciation for the strengths and weaknesses of the legal system that would take its place were that legislation to be repealed.

Second, tort law is far from moribund when it comes to environmental issues. Although tort law takes a decided back seat to environmental statutes and regulation as a means of protecting the environment, tort lawsuits can still be an effective mechanism for abating pollution in appropriate cases.

Third, tort law remains an important—indeed, is often the only—legal mechanism for securing individual (as opposed to societal) relief for environmental harm, especially for those who seek compensation for personal injury or property damage allegedly caused by pollution.

Finally, many of the concepts and policy mechanisms that are now embedded in federal environmental statutes—such as the use of cost-benefit balancing to set regulatory standards, the imposition of strict liability for violating a standard, the use of court injunctions to stop pollution, the imposition of financial penalties for wrongdoing, and the use of the law to "force" the development of less-polluting technologies—have their origins in the common law.

1. The Common Law: Court-Made Law (and Policy)

The common law has its origins in the unwritten rules of conduct developed over time by the Anglo-Saxon peoples of ancient England. This body of law was brought to this country by the British colonists and was retained when those colonists declared their independence from England and formed the United States. As noted by the United States Supreme Court, "The common law includes those principles, usages, and rules of action applicable to the government and security of person and property, which do not rest for their authority upon any express and positive declaration of the will of the legislature" [*Western Union Telegraph Co. v. Call Pub. Co.*,

181 U.S. 92, 102 (1901)]. In other words, the common law is distinct from statutory law. It derives "from usages and customs of immemorial antiquity" (id.), as interpreted and applied by the courts. Moreover, the common law is a creature of state law, not federal law. Again, in the words of the Supreme Court, "There is no common law of the United States in the sense of a national customary law distinct from the common law of England *as adopted by the several states, each for itself,* applied as its local law, and subject to such alteration as may be provided by its own statutes" (id., emphasis added). Each state, then, is free to develop its own common law through its own courts, and (as is discussed more fully below) to override this court-made law through its own legislative process.

Three important principles emerge from this. The first is that the common law may vary from state to state. Indeed, in theory, the fifty different states could take fifty different common-law approaches to the same issue. Although this is rarely (if ever) the case, there often are important differences in the common law among various states. Furthermore, one state may have decided a particular issue where another state has not yet addressed it. The courts of New Jersey, for example, may have decided to impose strict liability on the operators of hazardous waste landfills, while the courts of Idaho may not have considered the question.

Second, the highest state court within a state (typically called the state supreme court) is the ultimate arbiter of the common law of that state. Thus, if a federal court (even the United States Supreme Court) is hearing a case that involves the common law of a particular state, the federal court is not free to impose its own version of the common law, but rather must apply the law in accordance with the rulings of the courts of that state.

Third, while the common law is applied with reference to relevant precedent (it is said to be derived, after all, from usages and customs of immemorial antiquity), the common law is nonetheless an evolving thing. When a state court is applying the common law, it is free to change that law to adapt to its own view of current social needs. The court is free to either expand or contract the law, even if doing so results in the reversal of one of its own long-standing precedents. This is not to suggest that the state courts make significant changes in the common law lightly, or that they do so often. Many principles of the common law, including some of those we will review in this chapter, have been in place for a century or more. However, significant changes in the common law of various states have occurred over this same century, and another such change could always be just one court opinion away.

In short, the common law is court-made policy. In contrast to the appropriate role of a court when it is interpreting state or federal statutes—when, as we discuss in the following chapter, the court is duty-bound to give effect to the will of the legislative body that wrote the law—the common law court is acting perfectly appropriately when it weighs social costs, benefits, and equities to determine its own view of desirable public policy. Unlike statutory law, the common law is created (and not just interpreted) through lawsuits. One party sues another, seeking particular relief, and the court applies the common law in resolving the issues raised in that lawsuit. In a very real sense, then, the common law is policy making through dispute resolution.

Generally speaking, the common law can be divided into three branches, each defined by a particular subject matter. *Contract* law is that portion of the common law that establishes the rules governing the formation, execution, and enforcement of contracts between two or more parties. *Property* law is that portion of the common law dealing with how interests in real property (land) are acquired and conveyed. And *tort* law, as noted, deals generally with wrongs committed by one party against another. The *Oxford English Dictionary* traces the origins of "tort" to the Middle English term for "wrong, injury," and to the Medieval Latin term *tortum*, meaning "wrong, injustice." It defines a modern-day tort as "a wrongful act or an infringement of a right (other than under contract) leading to legal liability." To this must be added the qualification that in the United States and other Anglo-Saxon judicial systems, a tort is a *civil*—as distinguished from a criminal—wrong. That is, the legal liability that attaches upon a court finding that a tort has been committed is not liability to the state for having committed a crime, and the remedy imposed by the court is not a jail sentence or a criminal fine. Rather, tort liability, when it is established, runs from the defendant to the plaintiff, and the remedy imposed by the court (generally speaking) is an order requiring the defendant to pay a sum of money to the plaintiff, to cease the activity found to be wrongful, or both.

It is through this concept of the common law tort—the social "wrong" to which civil liability attaches—that the common law most often addresses pollution (and concomitant issues of environmental and occupational health). In general, the plaintiff who seeks to use the tort system to halt ongoing pollution, or to obtain compensation for injury allegedly caused by past pollution, will endeavor to convince the court (judge and/or jury) that the creation of the pollution constitutes a tort under applicable state law.

■ **NOTES**

1. Other parts of the common law may also be relevant to a particular environmental issue. Contract law, for example, will govern the interpretation of so-called pollution insurance policies, whereby one party (usually an insurance company) agrees to indemnify another party for monetary liability resulting from certain types of polluting activities or events. Such a policy might, for example, pledge to defend a chemi-

cal company against lawsuits for damages stemming from off-site contamination by hazardous substances alleged to have been caused by the company's operations, and to pay any judgments awarded in these suits (up to a maximum amount specified in the policy). In general, however, the success or failure of any such lawsuits against the company would be determined under the tort system.

2. If you are unfamiliar with the United States court system, you may want to read section B.3, "Direction from the Judicial Branch," in chapter 5, which provides an overview of the (federal) judicial system and the nature of court decisions.   ∎

2. The Relationship Between the Common Law and Statutory Law

In a very real sense, the common law tort system creates standards of conduct for society. Thus, for example, a company that might feel tempted to simply (and cheaply) bury its hazardous waste in its back lot is likely to think twice about doing so, even in the absence of federal or state hazardous waste statutes, because of the tort lawsuits it might face if the waste contaminated an underlying aquifer. Given that such "backyard dumping" of hazardous waste would almost assuredly be deemed negligence (or worse), the tort system effectively imposes a legal standard prohibiting the company from taking this action. This does not guarantee that the company will not take the prohibited action, of course, but it does raise the specter of serious financial sanctions (monetary damages, attorneys fees, and court costs) if it does. The potential that an adverse court judgment would harm the firm's reputation (and bring with it the imprimatur of antisocial behavior) can provide an additional deterrent.

Obviously, however, modern common law exists within a society whose activities are governed by considerable legislation at both the state and federal level. The common law interacts with this body of statutory law in a number of ways. First, it is important to keep in mind that statutory law typically can *preempt* the common law. That is, unless doing so would conflict with the state constitution, the legislature of a state is free to override the policy choices made by the courts of that state. Similarly, unless something in the federal constitution prevents it from doing so, Congress may also step in and assert federal legislative control over a particular policy realm, and may preempt state law in doing so. Thus, one of the first steps to be taken in assessing whether a particular environmental issue could be appropriately addressed through the common law is to determine if there are any applicable federal or state laws and, if so, whether those laws leave any room for the application of the common law to this issue.

In the field of environmental torts, there are two categories of statutory law that may preempt the common law, in whole or in part. First, there may be statutes (usually at the state level) designed to channel or limit tort law. These *statutory tort laws* generally replace the operation of the state common law in the particular situations to which they apply. The common law tort of nuisance, for example, has been defined in whole or in part by statute in several states. In many instances these state nuisance statutes simply codify common law principles; in others, the statutes redefine nuisance law in certain ways. In either instance, when a court is hearing a case brought under a state nuisance statute, it is not applying common law. That is, the role of the court is to give effect to the policies of the legislature as expressed in the statute, rather than to formulate its own sense of appropriate policy under the (potentially evolving) common law. Thus, while it may be appropriate under the language and history of the statute to apply common law principles in applying the statute to particular situations, it is ultimately the will of the legislature that controls.

Also potentially relevant to environmental tort cases are state and federal statutes designed to protect the environment or public health. These statutes can, either explicitly or implicitly, preempt tort law remedies. Moreover, to the extent that a *federal* environmental statute preempts state tort law remedies, it will do so regardless of whether those remedies stem from state common law or from state statutory law. The existence of an applicable environmental statute, however, does not necessarily mean that state tort law is preempted. The key is whether Congress or the state legislature, as the case may be, intended to preclude the operation of tort law in the situations covered by the statute. Quite often tort law and environmental law are allowed to operate as independent mechanisms for "regulating" behavior. Where this is true, an applicable environmental statute or regulation may well still be deemed relevant to a court's determination as to what the appropriate tort law standard should be in a particular situation, but the court will be free to impose a tort law standard that is different from the applicable environmental law standard. If the court determines that the tort law standard is less stringent, however, the defendant will remain obligated to comply with the (more stringent) environmental law standard.

■ **NOTES**

1. If you were to create a "hierarchy" of laws by source for any state—including federal and state statutory law, federal and state administrative regulations, state common law, and the federal and state constitutions—where would you place the common law?

2. Some state constitutions contain provisions that can be read to place limitations on the authority of the state legislature to eliminate or truncate common law rem-

edies. See, e.g., *Johnson v. BP Chemicals, Inc.*, 707 N.E.2d 1107 (Ohio, 1999) (the Ohio statute limiting workers' right to sue an employer for intentional tort violates Ohio constitution). At the federal level, an attempt by Congress to limit state tort law remedies might, in some circumstances, be construed as being beyond its commerce clause authority (see chapter 5). In addition, the Fifth and Fourteenth amendment proscriptions against the "taking" of private property for anything other than a public purpose, and their concomitant requirement that just compensation be paid when private property is taken for an appropriate public purpose, may act as a restriction on the authority of Congress or the states to do away with nuisance law, which is designed to protect private parties against damage caused by the maintenance of "nuisances" that interfere with their enjoyment of their land. See, e.g., *Urie v. Franconia*, 218 A.2d 360, 362 (N.H. 1966) ("It seems doubtful [that] the Legislature has constitutional power to permit the defendant to continue to commit private nuisances . . . since such legislation would constitute taking private property for a non-public purpose.")

3. A classic example of state statutory law that has preempted the common law is the workers' compensation system that exists, by state statute, in every state. Although the statutes vary from state to state, a feature shared by all is a classic trade-off: workers lose their right to sue their employer (at least in a negligence suit) for injury and disease originating in the workplace, and gain in return the right to receive compensation for such harm (up to statutorily limited amounts) without having to prove that the harm was caused by the employer's negligence. As demonstrated by the decision of the Ohio Supreme Court cited in the previous note, however, courts in some states have held that the workers' compensation bar against tort suits does not extend to workers' claims against the employer for *intentional* tort. Some courts have applied this principle to suits alleging that the employer knowingly exposed the employee to hazardous chemicals in the workplace. See, generally, Nicholas A. Ashford and Charles C. Caldart (1996) *Technology, Law, and the Working Environment*. Island Press, Washington, D.C., pp. 447–495.

4. Some federal environmental statutes explicitly preserve the right of the states to impose more stringent standards, and this extends to the de facto standards imposed by the common law tort system. Section 510 of the Clean Water Act, for example, affirms the right of any state to "adopt or enforce . . . any standard or limitation respecting discharges of pollutants, or . . . any requirement respecting control or abatement of pollution," so long as it is not "less stringent" than the applicable federal standard. See 33 U.S.C. §1370. As this book goes to press, however, there are bills pending in Congress that would explicitly *prohibit* stricter state environmental, public health, and consumer safety standards ■

B. THE TORT SYSTEM

As the foregoing discussion suggests, the modern United States tort system is governed by state common law, state statutes, and, to a lesser extent, federal statutes.
Before looking at the particular type of statutory and common law tort claims that
tend to be relevant to the environmental field, we look first at a few general concepts
that apply to all of them. We begin with the underlying purposes of tort law.

1.   The Basic Functions of Tort Law

When contemplating the place of tort law in modern society, it is important to keep
in mind that tort law plays more than one legitimate social function. The most obvious function of the tort system, of course, is to provide a means through which individuals may obtain relief from, or monetary compensation for, a particular alleged
wrong. When a person is injured while using a consumer product, for example, the
tort system affords the injured party an opportunity to establish that *liability* should
attach to the manufacturer of the product, and that the manufacturer thus
should compensate the injured party in an amount commensurate with the extent of
the injury. Conversely, the tort system provides the manufacturer with an opportunity (though most likely an unwelcome one) to establish that liability should not
attach. In this way the tort system serves an important *dispute resolution* function.

It would be a mistake, however, to limit one's view of the tort system to this perspective, because tort law also serves important *social policy* functions. Part of the
value of the tort system to society is its deterrent effect. As discussed earlier, tort
law endeavors to channel human activity toward more desirable behavior by creating
a financial disincentive for undesirable behavior. Quite simply, the prospect of tort
suits for monetary damages will often be one deterrent against starting or continuing
an activity that poses a risk of harm to others.

Suppose, for example, that a company is considering an activity (such as continuing to operate a highly polluting factory, or manufacturing a toxic chemical product)
that poses a risk to human health. In all likelihood, company officials are aware that
pursuing this activity may expose the company to lawsuits in the future. If they cared
only about maximizing the company's profit, they likely would estimate the cost of
reducing the human health risk *now* (by installing pollution control equipment, for
example, or by reformulating the product to eliminate the use of the toxic chemical),
and compare it with the estimated *future* cost of litigation. To calculate this second
half of the equation, company officials would estimate the probable number of lawsuits the company would lose, the probable amount the company would be ordered
to pay to injured plaintiffs in those suits, and the probable amount the company
would have to pay, win or lose, for its own litigation costs (attorneys' fees, expert

witness fees, and the like). Once this number is calculated, it must be discounted to present value to reflect the fact that it would not be paid now, but rather would be paid some years from now. If the present value of the estimated cost of future lawsuits is larger than the present cost of reducing the human health risk, the company has a financial incentive to spend the money on risk reduction now, so that it can avoid the cost of litigation later.

This is a simplified example, of course, and probably a cynical one. For one thing, it ignores the fact that there may be a moral dimension to company decision making; company officials may want to reduce the risk to human health because they believe it to be the right thing to do. This example also ignores the potential role that aversion to adverse publicity (and to the attendant financial consequences that such publicity can bring) may play in a company's decision to attempt to avoid future lawsuits. Nonetheless, it does capture the financial dynamic that tort law can create. And while it would be unrealistic to assume that companies engage in this kind of cost comparison each time they decide to employ a process or product that creates a risk to public health or the environment, considerations of this nature do often factor into company decision making. Consider, for example, one manufacturer's decision to continue the manufacture of 1,2-dibromo-3-chloropropane (DBCP), a pesticide associated both with cancer and with male sterility.

In 1977, a group of workers learned that they had become sterile while manufacturing the chemical DBCP for Occidental Petroleum Co. in Central California. A lawsuit filed by those workers... unearthed a 1978 internal company memo which describes how [Occidental] calculate[s] costs and benefits. The document, written by the Director of Health, Safety and the Environment suggested that Occidental calculate how many people would become exposed to its DBCP, assume that a normal proportion of them would become sterile or get cancer and that half of those would sue, and then figure how much the company would have to pay in judgments, settlements and legal fees. "Should the product still show an adequate profit meeting corporate investment criteria, the project should be considered further," the memo said. (*San Jose Mercury*, November 20, 1985, as quoted in *Silicon Valley Toxics News*, vol. 3, no. 3, Winter 1985)

Another way of looking at tort law is as an embodiment of important social norms. In this view, tort law decisions serve as symbolic examples that underscore the importance of certain moral and cultural values, such as the notion that one should be responsible for the harm that one creates. (This is sometimes characterized in the environmental field as the Polluter Pays Principle, which is discussed in chapter 3). For a discussion of the symbolic significance of the tort system in lawsuits over exposure to toxic substances, see J. L. Mashaw (1985) "A Comment on Causation, Law Reform, and Guerrilla Warfare," 73 *Georgetown Law Journal* 1393, 1395–1396; and E. D. Elliot (1988) "The Future of Toxic Torts: Of Chemophobia, Risk as a Compensable Injury and Hybrid Compensation Systems," 25 *Houston Law Review* 781, 781–785.

■ **NOTES**

1. When reading a tort law decision, it is important to keep in mind both the dispute resolution function and the social policy functions that the court is endeavoring to fulfill. Quite often these will complement one another. In other situations, however, some observers will perceive a conflict between the two functions. A court may come to a decision, for example, because it believes that the result will serve a useful social policy outcome (generally because it will set an important precedent for future behavior), even though the result may not appear wholly just as applied to the particular facts of the case. This sometimes occurs when a court imposes tort liability for conduct to which tort liability had not previously been thought to attach.

2. It is also important to keep in mind that the tort system is an imperfect social policy mechanism and that its workings often spark spirited debate. Reasonable people may hold widely divergent views, both about the appropriateness of various decisions made by courts within the tort system, and about the appropriateness of allowing the tort system to serve this social policy function in the first place. At their core, these are social policy debates. How one resolves these issues depends on how one views a broad set of fundamental subissues. To what extent, for example, does one tend to emphasize notions of individual or personal responsibility over notions of corporate or collective responsibility? Does one favor "market-driven" innovation or "safety-driven" innovation? (That is, does one tend to err on the side of allowing new technology to develop, or on the side of protecting people from the potential dangers of new technology?) Does one tend to emphasize profits (and the economic growth that flows from them), or compensating injured parties (and the economic growth that flows from doing so)?

3. Since at least the mid-1970s, various groups (such as manufacturing associations, chambers of commerce, and insurance companies) have championed various forms of "tort reform" legislation. See, e.g., "The Devils in the Product Liability Laws," *Business Week*, February 12, 1979, p. 72 (characterizing products liability suits as "a horrendous problem"). The goal of this effort has been to "rein in" the tort system, through legislated limits on both liability and monetary damages. This approach has found a receptive audience in some state legislatures, and among many at the federal level (President Reagan, particularly, was a champion of the "tort reform" concept, and President George W. Bush has been a strong supporter). Thus far, a few states have enacted sweeping structural changes to their tort systems, and others have enacted more modest legislation affecting certain aspects of certain types of cases (usually medical malpractice and/or products liability suits). No similar federal legislation has been enacted, although President Clinton did veto a bill that would have placed certain limitations on products liability suits. Here again,

these are public policy decisions; "reform" is very much in the eye of the beholder. The effect of tort reform legislation of this nature is to limit the financial impact of the tort system and make it more predictable. This in turn reduces the deterrent effect of tort law. ∎

2. The Available Remedies

In general, the tort system provides two potential remedies for successful plaintiffs: monetary awards (damages) for harm caused by tortious behavior; and court orders (injunctive relief) to restrain future tortious behavior. Depending on the facts of the case and the nature of the claim, one or both of these forms of relief may be available.

a. Monetary Damages

i. Compensatory Damages In all states, the successful tort plaintiff is entitled to have the *trier of fact* (the jury, or if it is not a jury trial, the judge) determine an appropriate amount to be paid by the defendant to the plaintiff to compensate the plaintiff for the harm proven to have been caused by the defendant's tortious behavior. Straightforwardly enough, the sums so awarded are known as *compensatory damages*; in theory, they are to be no greater, and no less, than the amount deemed necessary to "make the plaintiff whole." Unless there is a statute detailing the factors to be considered in assessing compensatory damages (and such statutes are rare), the determination of the relevant factors and their appropriate value will be up to the trier of fact. This is not to suggest that there is no method to the process, however.

Assume, for example, that a jury must determine the amount of compensatory damages to award to a plaintiff who suffered permanent facial scarring and lung damage as a result of the defendant's negligent handling of a toxic chemical. To make a case for compensatory damages, the plaintiff's lawyer likely will present evidence of (1) the medical expenses already incurred by the plaintiff (or the plaintiff's insurance company) as a result of the injury, (2) any medical expenses likely to be incurred in the future as a result of the injury, (3) any wages already lost as a result of the injury, (4) if the plaintiff is disabled as a result of the injury, any lost future earnings likely to result from this disability, and (5) any psychological or emotional conditions said to be caused by the injury (or the ensuing disability). In addition, the plaintiff's lawyer will suggest that an amount be awarded for the plaintiff's "pain and suffering", that is, for the day-to-day discomfort and anxiety caused by the injury. The defendant's lawyer will have an opportunity to present evidence and arguments to counter some or all of this presentation. Quite likely, both sides will offer testimony from expert witnesses (medical professionals to speak to the degree of harm and the likelihood of future treatment, for example, and economists or accountants, and occupational or rehabilitation therapists, to speak to the loss of future earning capacity). The job of the jury will be to take in all of this information, decide whose presentation on each point was the more credible, and make its award accordingly.

ii.   Punitive Damages   In addition to compensatory damages, most states provide by statute for an award of *punitive damages* in certain situations. Punitive damages are designed to punish a defendant for particularly egregious behavior, and to act as a financial deterrent against repetition of the behavior (by the defendant or others) in the future. The criteria for an award of punitive damages will depend on the particular provisions of the relevant state statute. In general, the plaintiff must prove that the defendant's behavior went beyond mere negligence and rose to the level of egregiousness specified in the statute. Some states require a showing of malice, some require a showing of gross negligence, and most require a showing of conduct (such as recklessness) that is more egregious than gross negligence, but do not require proof of malice. Over half of the states with punitive damages statutes require proof of the specified level of egregiousness by clear and convincing evidence (that is, by more than just a preponderance of the evidence). *See* Richard L. Blatt, Robert W. Hammesfahr, and Lori S. Nugent (2002) *Punitive Damages: A State-By-State Guide to Law and Practice* §8.2, West, Eagan, Minn.

Although they receive considerable attention in the media, punitive damages are awarded only infrequently. A 1995 Department of Justice study of 762,000 tort cases, for example, found that only 12,000 of these went to trial, and that only 364 of those (3%) resulted in an award of punitive damages. See "Justice Department Study Finds Few Awards of Exemplary Damages in State Liability Claims," 10 *Toxics Law Reporter* 200 (July 26, 1995). Nonetheless, punitive damages have long been the target of legal challenges by business groups. Two primary constitutional arguments have been raised against punitive damages: that they violate the Eighth Amendment's prohibition against cruel, unusual, and excessive punishment, and that they violate the due process principles embodied in the Fifth and Fourteenth amendments. Although this first argument has found little favor with the United States Supreme Court, the Court has held that the due process clause of the Fourteenth Amendment places certain limitations on the right of the states to impose punitive damages.

In *BMW of North America v. Gore*, 517 U.S. 559 (1996), the Court held for the first time that a state punitive damage award was unconstitutionally excessive. In that case, an Alabama jury had awarded $4,000 in compensatory damages (to the purchaser of a "new" automobile that had been repainted by the manufacturer without his knowledge to disguise acid-rain damage) and $4,000,000 in punitive damages (because the manufacturer had engaged in this same practice with hundreds of other automobiles sold as "new" nationwide). On appeal, the Alabama Supreme Court had reduced the punitive damages verdict to $2,000,000. The United States Supreme Court, in a five to four opinion, held that imposition of the $2,000,000 award was a violation of the manufacturer's right to due process, both because the amount of the award was excessive, and because it was based, in part, on the defendant's out-of-state conduct. The Court's decision articulated three touchstones to be used by trial and appellate courts in reviewing punitive damage awards: the egregiousness (or reprehensibility) of the defendant's conduct; the ratio between the punitive and compensatory awards; and the size of the punitive award compared with criminal fines or statutory civil penalties available for similar conduct. This three-part inquiry is consistent with previous decisions, which have held that a punitive damage award is not unconstitutionally excessive merely because it is much larger than the compensatory damage award. See *TXO Production Corp. v. Alliance Resources Corp.* 509 U.S. 443 (1993) (upholding a punitive damage award that was 526 times greater than the compensatory damage award, where the defendant's conduct was found to be malicious).

In *State Farm Mutual Auto. Ins. Co. v. Campbell*, 538 U.S. 408 (2003), the Court placed three additional limitations on the states' authority to impose punitive damages. First, the Court held that a defendant's conduct directed at other persons may not be considered in assessing punitive damages unless that conduct also bears directly on the harm suffered by the plaintiff. Otherwise, noted the Court, a defendant could be too readily subject to multiple punitive damage claims (in multiple states) for the same conduct. Moreover, suggested the Court, if the conduct did not bear a reasonable relationship to the conduct that caused harm to the plaintiff, the state court would effectively be asserting jurisdiction over a dispute that was not before it. Second, the Court held that a judge or jury may not use evidence of *out-of-state* conduct to punish a defendant for action that was not considered wrongful in the jurisdiction where it occurred. Third, the Court held that the relative *wealth* of a defendant may not be used to justify an award of punitive damages that is "otherwise unconstitutional." To pass constitutional muster under the Court's reading of the due process clause, then, the focus of the punitive damages inquiry must be on the nature of the tortious conduct by which the defendant caused harm to the plaintiff, but this may be buttressed by a consideration of other tortious acts of the defendant as long as they bear a reasonable relationship to that conduct.

If assessed, punitive damages usually are awarded to the plaintiff. Since the plaintiff presumably has already been fully compensated (via the compensatory damage award) for the injuries suffered as a result of the defendant's actions, is there a justification for awarding the plaintiff additional money in the form of punitive damages? Could the public policy goals of punitive damages be fulfilled (or even enhanced) if punitive damages were instead paid into a public fund (such as, for example, one established to aid uncompensated accident victims)? What would this do to the plaintiff's incentive to invest the additional time and money necessary to pursue the claim for punitive damages? As of 2004, only nine states had statutes directing a portion of punitive damage awards to a public fund. See, e.g., Adam Liptak (2004) "Schwarzenegger Sees Money for State in Punitive Damages," *New York Times*, May 30.

■ NOTES

1. In the parlance of tort lawyers, compensatory damages that can be readily verified and quantified (such as medical expenses, the amount paid to repair a damaged vehicle, and other out-of-pocket costs) are commonly called "special damages," while damages whose value is more indeterminate (such as lost future earning capacity and pain and suffering) are commonly termed "general damages."

2. The plaintiff in a tort case has a duty to *mitigate* damages. That is, if there are reasonable steps that the plaintiff could take to reduce the severity or impact of the harm suffered (such as physical or occupational therapy), the plaintiff is generally said to have a duty to take them, and the award of compensatory damages is reduced by the amount attributable to a plaintiff's failure to mitigate damages.

3. Where an insurance company (or a state workers' compensation fund) provides benefits for an injury or disease for which the insured is later awarded damages in a tort action, there may be a right of subrogation, whereby the insurer is entitled to whole or partial reimbursement from the insured for the benefits paid.

4. Placing a "cap" (a specified upper limit) on pain and suffering awards has been the most common focus of "tort reform" legislation. Some states have, for example, placed such caps on awards to plaintiffs in medical malpractice cases. See, e.g., *Fein v. Permanente Medical Group*, 695 P.2d 665 (Cal. 1985) (the California statute limiting noneconomic damages in medical malpractice actions to $250,000 is not unconstitutional). Some state courts, however, have held that such limits violate guarantees in the state constitution. See, e.g., *Carson v. Maurer*, 424 A.2d 825 (N.H. 1980) (the New Hampshire statute limiting noneconomic damages in medical malpractice actions to $250,000 violates the equal protection clause of the New Hampshire constitution). See also *State ex rel. Ohio Academy of Trial Lawyers v. Sheward*, 715 N.E.2d 1062 (Ohio 1999) (a comprehensive Ohio "tort reform" statute imposing limits on punitive and noneconomic damages violates the Ohio constitution). A *federal* damage limitation, on the other hand, could not be invalidated under the constitution of a particular state. In the mid-1980s, the Reagan administration proposed limiting awards for pain and suffering and punitive damages to a combined total of $100,000 in all cases, although Congress never acted on this suggestion. *See* Bob

Hunter (1986) "The Insurance Industry is to Blame," *Washington Post*, April 13, p. C7. More recently, the George W. Bush administration proposed a federal limit on pain and suffering awards in medical malpractice cases. See, e.g., Sheryl Stolberg (2003) "Transplant Mix-Up Enters Debate on Malpractice," *New York Times*, Feb. 26, p. 1 (discussing a proposed federal law that would have placed a $250,000 limit on noneconomic damages in medical malpractice cases).

5. Many states do not allow an award of compensatory damages for negligently inflicted emotional harm unless the plaintiff has also suffered concomitant physical harm. In *Payton v. Abbott Labs*, 437 N.E.2d 171 (Mass. 1982), for example, the Supreme Judicial Court of Massachusetts held that women who are at increased risk of cancer because their mothers took the drug diethylstilbestrol (DES) during pregnancy may not sue the manufacturer for emotional harm without establishing that the drug had also caused them physical harm. The California Supreme Court has authorized negligence actions for fear of cancer in the absence of present physical harm, but "only if the plaintiff pleads and proves that the fear stems from a knowledge, corroborated by reliable medical and scientific opinion, that it is more likely than not that the feared cancer will develop in the future due to the toxic exposure." *Potter v. Firestone Tire & Rubber Co.*, 863 P.2d 795, 800 (Cal. 1993). However, if the defendant intentionally or recklessly exposed the plaintiff to carcinogens, under circumstances that would warrant an application of California's punitive damages statute, California courts will permit recovery for fear of cancer without requiring proof that it is more likely than not that the plaintiff will actually contract the cancer (id). This is consistent with the rule in many states that proof of concomitant physical injury is not required in cases alleging intentional or reckless infliction of emotional harm. See, e.g., *Payton v. Abbott Labs*, 437 N.E.2d at 176 ("this court has allowed recovery for emotional distress absent physical harm... where the defendant's conduct was extreme and outrageous, and was either intentional or reckless").

6. In interpreting the Federal Employee Liability Act (FELA), a federal statute that creates a compensation scheme for railroad employees, the Supreme Court has held that damages for mental anguish can be recovered only where the employee sustains a physical impact as a result of the defendant's negligence, or where that negligence places the employee within the zone of danger of manifesting an injury at some later date. See *Consolidated Rail v. Gottshall*, 512 U.S. 532 (1994). The Court has since held that FELA does not permit recovery for mental anguish stemming from mere exposure to asbestos [*Metro-North Commuter R.R. v. Buckley*, 521 U.S. 424 (1997)], but that it does permit recovery for mental anguish resulting from a "genuine and serious" fear of developing cancer, even if the risk of actually developing cancer is remote, where the employee has already contracted another asbestos-related disease, such as asbestosis [*Norfolk & Western Railway v. Ayers*, 538 U.S. 135 (2003)].

7. A related issue is whether property owners may recover damages for the devaluation of their property due to *public fear* of hazardous substances or other pollution risks on or near the property. The majority view is that they can, regardless of whether the public fear is reasonable. See, e.g., *San Diego Gas & Electric Co. v. Daley*, 253 Cal. Rptr. 144 (Cal. Ct. App. 1988). A minority of states allows recovery of such damages only if the public fear is reasonable, e.g. *Dunlap v. Loup River Public Power Districts*, 284 N.W. 742 (Neb. 1939), and a few disallow such recovery altogether, e.g., *Central Illinois Light Co. v. Nierstheimer*, 185 N.E.2d 841 (Ill. 1962).

8. Two of the justices who dissented from the Supreme Court's punitive damage decision in *BMW v. Gore*, Antonin Scalia and Clarence Thomas, take the position that since punitive damages are traditionally a matter of state law subject to state sovereignty, they should not be subjected to federal constitutional analysis. *See* 517 U.S. at 598–599.

9. All states have provisions (in statute and/or court rules) that authorize the judge hearing a case to reduce the size of a jury award (of compensatory and/or punitive damages) in certain limited circumstances (such as if the judge finds that the amount awarded is manifestly out of proportion to the evidence presented at trial). Such trial court rulings may in turn be appealed to the state appellate courts. This state statutory authority is in addition to the authority of the courts to review punitive damage awards on federal constitutional grounds. In *Cooper Industries, Inc. v. Leatherman Tool Group, Inc.*, 532 U.S. 424 (2001), the Supreme Court held that in reviewing lower court rulings on the constitutionality of punitive damage awards, appellate courts must apply a de novo standard of review. That is, rather than simply reviewing the lower court's decision to see if it represented an abuse of the court's discretion, the appellate court must conduct its own independent assessment of whether the punitive damage award comports with due process requirements.

10. In the closely watched environmental tort case involving the 1989 *Exxon Valdez* oil spill in Prince William Sound, Alaska, the Ninth Circuit Court of Appeals held that a $5 billion punitive damage award against ExxonMobil violated the Fourteenth Amendment's due process clause [*In re Exxon Valdez*, 270 F.3d 1215 (9th Cir. 2001)]. The court concluded that there was a 17 to 1 ratio between punitive and compensatory damages, and held that this was, under the circumstances of the case, excessive. On remand, the district court reexamined the ratio between punitive damages and compensatory damages, and concluded that it was only 9.5 to 1. This, and other factors, led the district court to conclude that the $5 billion punitive damage award was not unconstitutionally excessive. However, believing that the Ninth Circuit's decision required him to reduce the amount of the award, the district judge cut $1 billion from the punitive damage assessment, leaving an award of $4 billion [*In re Exxon Valdez*, 236 F.Supp.2d 1043 (D. Alaska 2002)]. Exxon and the plaintiffs

both appealed, and the decision was again vacated and remanded by the Ninth Circuit (Docket No. 03-35166, Aug. 18, 2003), which directed the district court to reconsider its opinion in light of the Supreme Court's decision in *State Farm Mutual Auto. Ins. Co. v. Campbell*, discussed earlier. After a detailed consideration of the factors set forth in *State Farm*, the district judge determined that the $5 billion punitive damages award was not unreasonable in light of those factors. Nonetheless, because the district judge still believed himself bound by the Ninth Circuit's earlier opinion to reduce the size of the award, he ultimately reduced it to $4.5 billion [*In re Exxon Valdez*, 296 F.Supp.2d 1071 (D. Alaska 2004)]. Both sides appealed once again, and the Ninth Circuit again addressed the issue. Noting that "Exxon's reckless misconduct in placing a known relapsed alcoholic in command of a supertanker, loaded with millions of barrels of oil, to navigate the pristine and resource abundant waters of Prince William Sound was reckless and warrants severe sanctions," the court concluded that, because the company had taken steps to remediate the damage, Exxon's conduct did not "warrant sanctions at the highest range allowable under the due process analysis." Noting further that "[i]t is time for this protracted litigation to end," the Ninth Circuit directed the district court to assess punitive damages in the amount of $2.5 billion [*In re Exxon Valdez*, 472 F.3d 600, 624–25 (9th Cir. 2006)].

11. The Federal Tort Claims Act precludes awards of punitive damages in tort suits against the federal government. See 28 U.S.C. §2674.   ∎

b. Injunctive Relief

An injunction is, by its nature, a prospective remedy; it is designed to prevent or reduce future harm. It takes the form of a court order directing the defendant to take, or to refrain from taking, certain action. In an environmental tort case, an injunction might order a factory owner to install certain pollution reduction technology, or to reduce pollution to a particular level by a specified date. Injunctions are never issued by juries, only by judges. In general, injunctions are not issued lightly, and the decision whether to grant an injunction is said to rest with the sound discretion of the judge. Moreover, if a judge does decide to grant an injunction, he or she has considerable discretion in framing the elements of that injunction.

When a court is ruling on a request for injunctive relief, it is said to be sitting as a *court of equity*. That is, one of its functions will be to perform a balancing of the equities, to determine whether they favor the issuance of the requested injunction. The nature of the relevant equities, of course, will vary with the particular facts of the case. As articulated by the Restatement of Torts, however, three considerations are likely to predominate: (1) "the relative hardship likely to result to defendant if an injunction is granted and to plaintiff if it is denied"; (2) "the interests of third persons and of the public"; and (3) "the practicability of framing and enforcing the order or judgment." See American Law Institute (1977) *Restatement (Second) of the Law of*

Torts §936. A key factor, then, will be the court's sense of the relative balancing of the social costs and benefits of the requested injunction.

■ **NOTE**

1. Throughout the rest of this chapter, we will be making reference (as in the preceding section) to the Restatement of Torts. A "restatement" of a particular area of the common law is an attempt by a group of legal scholars to convey the current state of the law in that area, to articulate the underlying conceptual framework, and to suggest—especially for those topics where a consensus approach has not emerged from the state courts—what the law *should* be. Although restatements of the law are not binding authority, they are often influential, and the courts often cite them. As one might expect, as the law grows and changes, the restatements are modified and expanded. The original Restatement of Torts was begun in 1923 and completed in 1939. This work was considerably revised in a Second Restatement published in the 1960s and 1970s, and portions of a Third Restatement—in draft and final form— have been published more recently.   ■

3.   The Central Elements of a Tort Claim

a.   In General
The common law tort system uses a deceptively simple framework to address the exceptionally complex issues of assigning responsibility for human injury and determining the level at which such injury should be compensated. In general, the injured party seeking monetary damages (the plaintiff) must prove three basic things in order to prevail: (1) that the defendant's actions were of a type that renders the defendant legally *liable* to the plaintiff (in the environmental context, this will generally be either because the defendant has committed negligence, nuisance, or trespass, or because strict liability applies); (2) that these actions *proximately caused* injury to the plaintiff (that is, that the defendant's actions actually caused or contributed to the injury); and (3) that the plaintiff suffered *actual harm* (economic, physical, psychological, or, in some states, emotional) as a result of the injury. The burden is on the plaintiff to prove all three of these, and the plaintiff must carry this burden by "a preponderance of the evidence." In general, this means that the plaintiff must show that it is more likely than not that the various factual assertions necessary to establish the case are in fact true. If the plaintiff is successful, it is then up to the trier of fact (the jury, or if it is not a jury trial, the judge) to place a monetary value on the plaintiff's injury.

If the plaintiff is seeking an injunction in addition to, or instead of, monetary damages, the plaintiff must prove (again, by a preponderance of the evidence): (1) that *neec all 3 & 4*

f wishing for injunction must prove that

the defendant will take (or threatens to take) actions of a type that would render the defendant legally liable to the plaintiff (again, either because the defendant has committed negligence, nuisance, or trespass, or because strict liability applies); (2) that this activity would proximately cause harm to the plaintiff; (3) that the harm caused would be *irreparable*; and (4) that the plaintiff has no other adequate remedies at law to address this harm. If all four of these elements are established, it will then be up to the judge, as discussed earlier, to determine after balancing the relevant equities whether an injunction should be issued restraining the offending activity and, if so, what shape that injunction should take. Beyond these basic touchstones, the nature of tort remedies tends to vary from state to state, and close attention to the specific laws of the particular state is essential.

■ **NOTES**

1. The "proximate causation" requirement—which we revisit toward the end of this chapter—is also sometimes expressed as the requirement of "legal causation." In general, there must be a sufficiently close causal connection between the defendant's actions and the plaintiff's injury. While this does not require the plaintiff to establish that the defendant was the *sole* cause of the injury, the plaintiff does have to show that the defendant's actions were a *cause in fact* of the injury. Thus, the existence of other causes—even intervening causes—of the plaintiff's injury is not fatal to a claim of proximate causation as long as the defendant's actions actually contributed to the causal chain giving rise to the injury.

2. Another principle that is often said to be embodied in the proximate causation requirement, especially in negligence cases, is that the plaintiff's injury must be of a type that was reasonably foreseeable at the time of the defendant's actions. If the defendant could not reasonably have foreseen that an injury of the type suffered by the plaintiff would be incurred, the argument runs, it would be unjust to hold the defendant liable for the plaintiff's injury. Sometimes this concept is instead treated as part of the determination as to whether the defendant's actions were negligent; if the injury to the plaintiff was not reasonably foreseeable, the argument runs, the defendant had no duty to the plaintiff not to engage in the activity that caused the injury. See, e.g., *Palsgraf v. Long Island Railroad Co.*, 248 N.Y. 339, 162 N.E. 99 (1928). The Second Restatement of Torts took a somewhat different approach, stating that the defendant will not be held liable for an injury which, *looking backward after the injury has been sustained*, with full knowledge of all that occurred, would appear to be "highly extraordinary." *See* American Law Institute (1977) *Restatement (Second) of the Law of Torts* §435(2). Regardless of how it is formulated, this general foreseeability principle, although it is neither often invoked nor clearly defined by the courts, does operate as a limitation on the reach of tort law.

3. As the foregoing discussion suggests, the foreseeability requirement really incorporates two different concerns. The first is a concern with particularly lengthy or convoluted chains of causation. At some point, the thought is, notions of justice and common sense should keep us from holding a defendant liable for the far-flung, incidental consequences of his actions. This would appear to fit nicely within the concept of proximate (or "legal") causation. The second is a concern that defendants not be held liable for behavior that cannot truly be labeled as unreasonable. This fits nicely within traditional concepts of negligence: If the defendant could not reasonably have anticipated that his actions would harm someone in the plaintiff's position, it is difficult to say that the defendant had a duty to the plaintiff to avoid taking those actions. As discussed later, however, not all tort liability is based on a finding that the defendant's conduct was unreasonable. For those tort claims that are not grounded in the unreasonableness of the defendant's conduct, this second concern would appear to have far less relevance.

4. Suppose the defendant's factory wrongfully exposes the plaintiff to airborne emissions of a particular chemical. Should the plaintiff be able to recover damages form the defendant even if it was not known at the time that the chemical emitted by the defendant could cause the type of injury suffered by the plaintiff? What if it was known that the chemical was a carcinogen, but that the injury claimed by the plaintiff is endocrine disruption that leads to birth defects? Keep in mind that, ultimately, whether to apply the foreseeability requirement to bar recovery in a particular case is a social policy judgment.

5. Although the third and fourth of the requisite elements for an injunction (irreparable harm and the inadequacy of other remedies) are conceptually distinct, it is often difficult to distinguish between them in practice. In theory, "the irreparable injury rubric is intended to describe the quality or severity of the harm necessary to trigger equitable intervention. In contrast, the inadequate remedy test looks to the possibilities of alternative modes of relief, however serious the initial injury" [*Lewis v. S.S. Baune*, 534 F.2d 1115, 1124 (5th Cir. 1976)]. However, courts often cite the irreparability of the harm as the basis for concluding that other legal remedies (such as a claim for monetary damages) are not adequate (see id.). Conversely, other courts measure the irreparability of the harm by the extent to which it could be satisfactorily redressed by other legal remedies. See, e.g., *Tropic Film Corporation v. Paramount Pictures Corp.*, 319 F. Supp 1247, 1255 (S.D.N.Y. 1970) (irreparable harm is harm that "cannot be fully and promptly remedied by the granting of a money judgment").

6. The existence of an applicable environmental statute may make it more difficult to obtain injunctive relief in an environmental tort case. If the court determines that the activity giving rise to the plaintiff's harm is or will be the subject of regulatory

action, the court may determine that this is an adequate alternative avenue of legal relief for the plaintiff, and may decline to issue an injunction (or delay a decision on an injunction pending the outcome of the regulatory process). ■

b. Tort Suits Against the Government

If the tort claim is against a governmental entity (federal or state), there is an additional requirement that the plaintiff must satisfy in order to prevail. Another concept that the courts of the United States imported from England was the principle of *sovereign immunity*. Based loosely on the notion that "the king (or queen) can do no wrong," this principle holds that the government cannot be sued for monetary damages unless it has consented to such suits. As a practical matter, then, a plaintiff with a claim against the government must demonstrate that the claim in question is one that the government has agreed (generally through legislation waiving its sovereign immunity) may be brought against it. The Federal Tort Claims Act governs most tort claims against agencies and instrumentalities of the federal government. That statute provides that the United States "shall be liable . . . in the same manner and to the same extent as a private individual under like circumstances" (28 U.S.C. §2674), but not where the alleged wrong constitutes "the failure to exercise or perform a discretionary function or duty on the part of a federal agency or an employee of the Government, whether or not the discretion involved be abused" (28 U.S.C. §2680).

This "discretionary function" exception acts as a substantial limitation on the types of tort claims that may be brought against the federal government. Clearly, one may not bring suit against the government when it is acting in its standard-setting role. The neighbors of a chemical factory, for example, could not seek money damages from the EPA for its alleged failure to set adequate air emission standards for the chemical industry. The courts have also held that the discretionary function exception precludes suits against federal agencies in their enforcement role. See, for example, *Irving v. U.S.*, 162 F.3d 154 (1st Cir. 1998), and *Cunningham v. U.S.*, 786 F.2d 1445 (9th. Cir. 1986), both of which hold that injured workers have no tort claim against the Occupational Safety and Health Administration for injuries arising from the agency's failure to uncover hazards during inspections of their workplace. However, where the government is conducting activities of a type that are usually conducted by private parties, such as operating a factory or supplying a product, courts have been more willing to allow suits under the Federal Tort Claims Act to go forward. See, e.g., *Dube v. Pittsburgh Corning*, 870 F.2d 790 (1st Cir. 1989), where the daughter of a worker at the Portsmouth Naval Shipyard who brought asbestos home on his clothes was allowed to sue the Navy for asbestos-related disease.

A key factor in such cases may be whether the governmental conduct at issue was governed by a specific statute, regulation, or articulated governmental policy. If it was, and the conduct giving rise to the plaintiff's tort claim was taken pursuant to

Federal Tort Claims act is what seps immunity

that statute, regulation, or policy, the courts are less likely to apply the discretionary function exception. This is so because a governmental representative who is simply carrying out a prescribed (and therefore mandatory) governmental policy cannot be said to be exercising any discretionary authority. Similarly, a governmental representative who *departs* from prescribed governmental policy may also be said to fall outside the discretionary function exemption, for the reason that he or she lacks the discretionary authority to change articulated governmental policy. The applicability of this line of reasoning may in turn depend on whether the governmental policy in question is sufficiently specific. For example, in *OSI, Inc. v. U.S.*, 285 F.3d 947 (11th Cir. 2002), hazardous waste disposal decisions made at Maxwell Air Force Base near Montgomery, Alabama, were deemed to be within the discretionary function exemption, even though the plaintiff argued that these decisions departed from Air Force instruction manuals addressing the procedures to be followed in the handling and disposal of hazardous wastes. Noting that "the manuals state only general principles and objectives and do not constitute specific, mandatory directives" (id. at 952 n.2), the Eleventh Circuit Court of Appeals held that the existence of the manuals did not overcome the applicability of the discretionary function exemption to the Federal Tort Claims Act.

C. THE FOUR CLASSIC ENVIRONMENTAL TORT CLAIMS

Keeping in mind the caveat that tort law doctrines can vary considerably from state to state, let us now turn to the four types of tort claims that are most commonly used to address past or prospective injuries alleged to stem from environmental pollution: negligence, nuisance, trespass, and strict liability for harm from an abnormally dangerous ("ultrahazardous") activity.

1. Negligence

The classic fault-oriented tort claim is one that alleges that the defendant has engaged in negligent behavior. The claim is "fault-oriented" in the sense that to prevail, the plaintiff must show that the defendant's conduct has fallen below a standard of care required by law. The central liability debate in a negligence case will focus on two questions: (1) What is the standard of behavior that the law requires in this circumstance? and (2) Did the defendant's conduct fall below ("breach") that standard? This second question is a factual one and it flows from the first, which is an issue of law. How, then, does tort law determine the standard of conduct required by law?

As discussed earlier, the state legislature (or Congress) may have defined the tort law standard applicable to circumstances such as those before the court. If so, unless the underlying legislation is constitutionally infirm, the court is bound to apply that standard. Where no legislative determination has been made, however, it is up to the courts to determine the appropriate standard of care. In general, the conceptual starting point for making this determination is the "reasonably prudent person." The conduct of this hypothetical person—who is, after all, reasonably prudent—is said to determine the standard to which negligence law will hold society. At least theoretically, then, what goes into a determination of the negligence standard are the various considerations that would logically go into a determination of what "reasonably prudent" behavior would be under the circumstances of the particular case. Some of these considerations could be expected to be the common behavior of persons facing circumstances similar to those faced by the defendant, the relationship (if any) between the plaintiff and the defendant, the ease with which the defendant could have avoided the conduct giving rise to the injury to the plaintiff, the standards imposed by applicable or relevant statutes or regulations (if any), and the way in which similar circumstances have been treated under the tort law of this and other states.

Thus, in tort cases seeking to restrain or seek compensation for industrial pollution under a negligence theory, the common practice of the industry, though relevant, is not determinative. Myriad considerations can affect a court's willingness to move beyond industry practice in setting the negligence standard, but chief among these are likely to be the economic and technological feasibility of reducing the pollution to below harmful levels, and the extent of the injury that will (or may) occur if the pollution is not so reduced. One famous tort scholar, Judge Learned Hand of the federal Court of Appeals for the Second Circuit, posited an "algebraic" formulation of the test for whether a court should require a more stringent standard of care than that which is dictated by industry practice. If we apply his formulation to the pollution context, the duty required by the law would be a function of three variables: (1) the probability that harm will occur if the industry does not change its behavior by polluting less, (2) the severity of that harm if it does occur, and (3) the burden to the industry of effecting a sufficient reduction in pollution. Thus, in Judge Hand's words, "if the probability be called P; the injury L; and the burden B; liability depends on whether B is less than L multiplied by P; i.e., whether $B < PL$" [*United States v. Carroll Towing Co.*, 159 F.2d 169, 173 (2d Cir. 1947)].

This is not to say, of course, that the courts will (or should) routinely base their decisions squarely on the results of a cost-benefit analysis of this nature. One court may look no further than the relevant precedent of past decisions, deciding the time is not right for "advancing" the law. Another court may be driven by its sense of the untapped technological potential of the industry, and may decide to set a more stringent standard to encourage the adoption of cleaner technology. Still another may eschew the cost-benefit approach in favor of notions of fundamental justice and fairness, or notions of individual human rights. Nonetheless, the twin notions of risk and

feasibility will often come to the fore, either explicitly or implicitly. While no court can be expected to perform the kind of formal cost-benefit analysis done by some regulatory agencies, some courts will base their decision, at least in part, on their general policy sense of whether the risks to be avoided by holding industry to a higher standard justify the costs to the industry of implementing that standard.

■ **NOTES**

1. As suggested by our earlier discussion of foreseeability, another issue that sometimes arises in negligence cases is whether the defendant had a duty *to this plaintiff* to adhere to the articulated standard of care. This question must be answered in the affirmative for the plaintiff to prevail.

2. In a negligence claim for environmental pollution, the activity giving rise to the pollution may already be the subject of a regulatory standard established under state or federal environmental law. As the foregoing discussion suggests, this may affect the negligence case in a number of ways. First, environmental statutes may wholly preempt the operation of tort law in a particular subject matter area. Where they do not, regulatory standards established under those statutes may well have a bearing on the standard of care established under negligence law. Sometimes the statute will provide explicit direction, specifying that it does, or does not, establish the tort law standard, or specifying whether it should or should not be considered in establishing the tort law standard. If the statute is silent on the point, the court must decide whether the regulatory standard is legally relevant to the tort law standard (that is, whether the trier of fact should be allowed to consider evidence of compliance or noncompliance with the regulatory standard). If the court finds that it is relevant (which is likely), the court may determine that violation of the regulatory standard is *negligence per se* (that is, that it irrefutably establishes negligence). Conversely, a court may conclude that compliance with the regulatory standard irrefutably establishes the lack of negligence. Whether either approach is taken likely depends on the court's view of the purpose of the regulatory standard in question. If the court determines that the government standard was meant to define minimally acceptable performance, it is unlikely to find that compliance with that standard shields the defendant from a negligence claim. Quite often, the court will determine that compliance or noncompliance with the regulatory standard is relevant to, but not conclusive of, the determination of the tort standard. Some states have enacted legislation addressing this issue, at least for certain types of cases. A Colorado products liability statute, for example, creates a (refutable) presumption against negligence in products liability cases where the product complies with applicable regulatory standards, and creates a similar presumption in favor of negligence for products that fail to comply with an applicable regulatory standard. See Colo. Rev. Stat. §13-21-403.

3. At the trial court level, it is the job of the judge to define the appropriate standard of care, and it is the job of the jury (if there is one) to determine whether that standard has been breached. ∎

2. Nuisance

Perhaps the most widely used tort claim in environmental cases is the nuisance claim. There are two forms of nuisance—private and public—and both have been used to address harm allegedly caused by polluting activities.

a. Private Nuisance

A *private nuisance* is the wrongful interference with another's use and enjoyment of his or her land. To be entitled to bring the claim, the plaintiff must have a lawful possessary interest in some parcel of real property, and the nuisance must interfere with his or her use or enjoyment of that property. In general, then, the plaintiff in a private nuisance suit will be one who owns or rents the property in question. Assuming that the plaintiff has the requisite interest in the property, the key determination in a private nuisance case will be whether the defendant's interference with the plaintiff's use and enjoyment of that property is sufficient to constitute a nuisance under the law of the particular state. To demonstrate that it is, the plaintiff generally must prove that the interference is both intentional and unreasonable.

The notion of "intentional" conduct in this context is rather broadly construed. As noted by one well-known treatise:

Occasionally, the defendant may act from a malicious desire to [do] harm for its own sake, but more often the situation involving the private nuisance is one where the invasion is intentional merely in the sense that the defendant has created or continued the condition causing the interference with full knowledge that the harm to the plaintiff's interests are occurring or are substantially certain to follow. (W. Page Keeton, Dan B. Dobbs, Robert E. Keeton, and David G. Owen, 1984, *Prosser and Keeton on Torts*, 5th edition, 624–625. St. Paul, Minn: West Publishing)

Thus, if a seafood processing plant discharges fish remains into a nearby river, causing the river to emit a foul stench as it passes by neighboring properties, the operator of the seafood plant most likely would be said to have intentionally interfered with the owners' use and enjoyment of those properties.

Often the more difficult element to prove is the requirement that the interference be "substantial and unreasonable." These are distinct but related concepts. The requirement that the interference be substantial embodies the general principle that the law of nuisance addresses significant harm rather than trifles. That is, the interference must be substantial enough to warrant the attention of the law. However, what may seem insignificant in one context may seem significant in another; this goes to the heart of the situational weighing of consequences and equities embodied in the requirement that the interference be unreasonable. Note that the test for "reasonableness" here is conceptually different from the one applied to a negligence claim. In negligence, the focus is on the reasonableness of the defendant's conduct; in nuisance, it is on the reasonableness of the defendant's interference with the plaintiff's use and enjoyment of property. Although this distinction can be fairly subtle in its practical application, it is an important one. For example, a company that exercises due care in operating its factory, both following accepted industry practices and employing the latest available technology, may nonetheless be said to be creating a nuisance if it is releasing toxic fumes that create a health risk for the surrounding neighbors.

In nuisance law, the definition of unreasonable interference is largely situational. Although a general statement of principle might be that unreasonable interference is interference that is greater than that which the plaintiff could reasonably have expected, this will not suffice in all situations. The unreasonableness determination usually involves a weighing of several factors. Among the key factors are likely to be the nature of the surrounding area, the respective natures of the plaintiff's and defendant's uses of their properties, the extent of the harm caused to the plaintiff, and the cost to the defendant of abating that harm. If the gravity of the harm to the plaintiff is found to outweigh the utility of the activity of the defendant that is causing that harm, the interference is likely to be deemed unreasonable. The converse, however, is not necessarily true. If the utility of the activity is found to outweigh the gravity of the harm, the activity may still be found to be unreasonable if the harm could be mitigated or avoided without materially diminishing the utility of the activity. Thus, if the interference is caused by pollution from a manufacturing plant, and if there is economically feasible technology that would reduce or eliminate the pollution without compromising the plant's capability to make its product, continuation of the interference might very well be deemed unreasonable.

Another factor that may be considered is the relative capacity of the parties to shift the cost of avoiding the loss to the general public. If both parties are businesses in an industrialized area, for example, and the plaintiff is able to pass along to its customers the costs of protecting against the interference, the court may determine that this is a reasonable result. It may also be important to know which party came to the area first. If a polluting factory decides to locate in a neighborhood that has long been exclusively residential, the residential neighbors are likely to have a stronger case for nuisance than is the plaintiff who decided to build her home next to an industrial park.

In some states, the law of private nuisance has been, in whole or in part, codified in state statute. Although state nuisance statutes often incorporate the general principles discussed here, the elements of a particular statutory nuisance claim may be more (or less) expansive.

■ NOTES

1. In discussing the elements of private nuisance, many courts cite the Restatement of Torts, which states that the defendant's interference with the plaintiff's use and enjoyment of his property must be either "intentional and unreasonable" *or* "unintentional and otherwise actionable under the rules governing negligent, reckless or ultrahazardous conduct." See American Law Institute (1977) *Restatement (Second) of the Law of Torts* §822. This alternative second criterion would appear to be unnecessary. If the defendant's conduct is negligent or reckless, and is causing harm to the plaintiff, the plaintiff presumably will have a cause of action for negligence. Similarly, if the harm stems from the defendant's pursuit of an ultrahazardous activity, the defendant presumably will be *strictly* liable for that harm under the principles discussed later in this chapter. There thus would appear to be no need to resort to nuisance law.

2. In some states, a guest may be said to have a sufficient property interest to bring a private nuisance claim.

3. Since environmental pollution is by its very nature the creation of an externality, it is often well suited to a nuisance law analysis. Keep in mind, however, that the twin requisites of substantial interference and unreasonable interference must be satisfied. If the state of the relevant science is not sufficiently developed to permit a determination of whether, or to what extent, the externality is causing actual harm to the plaintiff, a nuisance claim is unlikely to be successful. See, e.g., *Westchester Assoc., Inc. v. Boston Edison Co.*, 47 Mass. App. Ct. 133, 712 N.E.2d 1145 (1999) (electromagnetic fields generated by power lines do not constitute a nuisance, although "increasing knowledge or changing uses" may require a change in this rule "as a matter of public policy").

4. An alternative view of the law of private nuisance is that it is not really grounded in tort law principles, but rather involves conflicting property rights that a court attempts to resolve through judicial zoning. See, e.g., E. Rabin (1977) "Nuisance Law: Rethinking Fundamental Assumptions," 63 *Virginia Law Review* 1299; J. H. Beuscher and J. W. Morrison (1955) "Judicial Zoning Through Recent Nuisance Cases," 1955 *Wisconsin Law Review* 440. This view is consistent with the fact that the determination as to whether a particular interference is unreasonable involves a weighing of the parties' respective interests in the use of their property.   ■

b. Public Nuisance

As distinguished from a private nuisance, a *public nuisance* is one that affects the public generally, rather than simply affecting one or a few people in the use and enjoyment of their property. When a factory's air emissions substantially and unreasonably interfere with its neighbors' use and enjoyment of their property, this, as we have seen, is a private nuisance. But if the air emissions also kill birds and other wildlife (which are, in a broad sense, "owned" by all), it may well also be a public nuisance. Public nuisance law is usually defined by state statute, and the statutes of most states not only contain a general description of nuisance, but also identify particular activities (such as the harboring of diseased animals) as public nuisances. In many cases, the right to bring suit to abate a public nuisance belongs exclusively to the government, and some public nuisances are punishable as criminal behavior. To this extent, public nuisance laws that are used to address environmental pollution are simply one form of environmental statute. However, some public nuisance laws also provide for a right of enforcement and recovery of monetary damages by parties who are specifically affected by the public nuisance.

■ NOTES

1. Violation of an environmental statute or regulation is sometimes considered evidence tending to show the existence of a nuisance. When a nuisance is established in this fashion, nuisance law has the effect of helping to enforce environmental law. See, e.g., *Miotke v. City of Spokane*, 101 Wn.2d 307, 678 P.2d 803 (1984) (a determination that discharge of raw sewage into a lake constituted both a public and private nuisance was upheld because, inter alia, the discharge was a violation of the state water pollution control statute). Indeed, courts may give consideration to the public policies underlying a particular environmental law even if the defendant's conduct is not technically a violation of that law. See, e.g., *Village of Wilsonville v. SCA Services, Inc.*, 86 Ill.2d 1, 426 N.E.2d 824 (1981) (which upheld a determination that a chemical waste landfill, lawfully permitted when it was initially created, posed a public nuisance, in part because it could not have been permitted under a more recent state statute governing new landfills).

2. An innovative use of the public nuisance doctrine has come in lawsuits against paint manufacturers on behalf of children who suffered lead poisoning as a result of the lead-based paint found in older housing stock. As the paint decays and flakes with wear and age, it leaves dust and paint chips that are readily ingested by toddlers, often causing serious and sometimes permanent injury. The lawsuits target the companies who manufactured lead paint over the relevant time period, alleging that they created a public nuisance by selling for residential application a product containing a known toxicant. Not all such lawsuits have been successful, but a jury in Rhode Island found three paint manufacturers liable in a highly publicized 2006 verdict. For a series of articles offering a detailed—and highly critical—analysis of this type of litigation, see Richard O. Faulk and John S. Gray, "Getting the Lead Out?

The Misuse of Public Nuisance Litigation by Public Authorities and private Counsel," 21 *Toxics Law Reporter* 1071 (Nov. 30, 2006), 1124 (Dec. 7, 2006), and 1172 (Dec. 14, 2006).

3. Before the advent of the present era of federal environmental statutes, the federal courts sometimes recognized a *federal* common law of public nuisance governing interstate pollution. More recently, several states and environmental groups joined forces to bring suit against a number of power companies under this theory, alleging that the companies contributed to global warming by collectively emitting 650 million tons of carbon dioxide to the atmosphere annually. See *State of Connecticut v. American Electric Power Company*, 406 F. Supp. 2d 265 (S.D. N.Y. 2005). The states, "claiming to represent the interests of more than 77 million people and their related environments," sought to use the federal common law of public nuisance to compel the companies to substantially reduce their emissions. The United States District Court hearing the case did not reach the question of whether a federal common law of nuisance can still be said to exist. Instead, citing the national debate that raged over whether and how to address global warming, the court dismissed the case on the ground that it presented a "political question" that the federal courts had no authority to resolve. In the words of the court, "The Framers based our Constitution on the idea that a separation of powers enables a system of checks and balances, allowing our Nation to thrive under a Legislature and Executive that are accountable to the People, subject to judicial review by an independent Judiciary. While, at times, some judges have become involved with the most critical issues affecting America, political questions are not the proper domain of judges.... [C]ases presenting political questions are consigned to the political branches that are accountable to the People..."

4. Is there likely to be a clear distinction between "political" questions and those that are justiciable (i.e., appropriate for judicial resolution) in the federal courts? Note that this concept of a nonjusticiable political question arises only in situations (such as cases invoking a federal common law) in which the federal courts are being asked to make and carry out public policy. It does not arise, for example, when the courts are asked to resolve a dispute as to the meaning of a federal statute, because there the courts are (at least in theory) simply interpreting and giving effect to the policy choices made by Congress. This role of the federal courts is discussed in chapter 5. ∎

3. Trespass

Trespass is one of the oldest torts. Simply put, trespass is the intentional physical invasion of another's land. ("Intentional" in this context has the same meaning as in nuisance law, discussed above.) The law of trespass has been applied to pollution cases because some courts have been willing to characterize the emission of pollution onto another's land as an "invasion" sufficient to constitute trespass. The case most often cited for this principle is *Martin v. Reynolds Metals Co.*, 221 Or. 86, 342 P.2d 790 (1959), in which the Supreme Court of Oregon upheld a determination that the defendant's aluminum reduction plant had committed trespass because it "caused certain fluoride compounds in the form of gases and particulates to become airborne and settle upon the plaintiff's land rendering it unfit for raising livestock." See also, e.g., *Sheppard Envelope Co. v. Arcade Malleable Iron Co.*, 355 Mass. 180, 138 N.E.2d 777 (1956) (a foundry's emission of cinders and "other gritty substances" that fall on an adjacent envelope company constitutes a trespass). Where a trespass is found, the defendant is liable for the harm proximately caused without additional proof of wrongful conduct.

Some see trespass cases of this type as being "in reality, examples of either the tort of private nuisance or liability for harm resulting from negligence," especially because they appear to impose liability only if harm results (W. Page Keeton, Dan B. Dobbs, Robert E. Keeton, and David G. Owen, *Prosser and Keeton on Torts*, pp. 71–72). This may be true, but the availability of a separate cause of action for trespass may be of practical significance in a state that provides a longer statute of limitations for trespass than for nuisance or negligence. This was the situation in *Martin v. Reynolds Metals*. Oregon's statute of limitations provided that claims for "nontrespassory injuries to land" had to be brought within 2 years of the date of the injury, but allowed up to 6 years to bring an action for trespass. Since the plaintiffs filed their suit for damages more than 2 years after Reynolds ceased its operations, the characterization of the conduct as a trespass was essential to their recovery.

4. Strict Liability for Abnormally Dangerous Activity

A fourth type of tort claim that is sometimes asserted in environmental cases is strict liability for the conduct of an "abnormally dangerous" or "ultrahazardous" activity. Although there are some subtle differences between these two characterizations, they share the basic principle that society considers some activities to be so dangerous that it holds those who conduct these activities liable for the harm they cause *even though the utmost care was taken to conduct the activities safely*. That is, those who conduct such activities are *strictly liable*—liable without "fault"—for the harm proximately caused. Unlike negligence, then, the determining factor for liability is not whether the defendant's conduct fell below an applicable standard of care, but whether the activity giving rise to the harm is one that the law will label as one to which this type of liability applies.

The concept is generally attributed to the English case of *Rylands v. Fletcher*, L.R. 3 H.L. 330 (1868), in which the owners of a reservoir were held liable for harm caused when water from the reservoir broke through a shaft beneath the reservoir that led to an abandoned coal mine, and from there flooded through underground passageways into the plaintiff's mine. Although the owners were found to be neither negligent nor liable for trespass, the British House of Lords nonetheless upheld a judgment that they were strictly liable for the damage caused to plaintiff's property. The determinative factor, said the British tribunal, was that locating a reservoir (which poses an obvious risk of escaping water) in an area rife with coal mining activity (and thus with abandoned mines) was an abnormal and unnatural use of the property.

The cases in the United States recognizing this form of liability, while not uniform, have generally relied on the two general principles underlying *Rylands v. Fletcher* to hold that the activity in question must be both unduly dangerous and inappropriate to the area in which it is conducted. This second principle, which is sometimes characterized as the requirement that the abnormally dangerous activity be "a thing out of place," is what is said to keep such obviously dangerous activities as driving an automobile on a highway from being classified as "abnormally" dangerous. The Second Restatement of Torts offers a somewhat broader definition, detailing six factors to be considered in determining whether a particular activity is abnormally dangerous: (1) whether the activity poses a high risk of harm to person or property; (2) whether that harm, if it occurs, will be great; (3) whether the risk can be eliminated by the exercise of reasonable care; (4) whether, and to what extent, the activity is not a matter of common usage; (5) whether, and to what extent, the activity is inappropriate to the place in which it is being conducted; and (6) whether, and to what extent, the social value of the activity outweighs its dangerousness. See American Law Institute, *Restatement (Second) of the Law of Torts* §520 (1977).

As one might expect, very few activities have been classified as abnormally dangerous or ultrahazardous. The most oft-cited example of an activity to which this form of liability applies is blasting—the use of in-ground or underground explosives in mining, road building, and other extraction and construction endeavors. Here, because the activity poses a clear risk of substantial harm to surrounding properties, because even the exercise of the utmost care cannot wholly eliminate that risk, and because the use of explosives generally is not considered a "common" activity, courts have been willing to impose strict liability for damage caused by resultant shock waves. Courts have also dealt with blasting under negligence and trespass theories, however, and the success of a claim for strict liability may depend on the nature of the area in which the blasting is conducted. Blasting in an urban area, for example, likely will give rise to strict liability more easily than will blasting in a remote mountainous area.

To date, the importance of this theory of liability to the field of environmental torts has been largely conceptual rather than practical because it has rarely been applied in this context. The operation of a nuclear power plant, which poses clear environmental risks, is often cited as an example of an abnormally dangerous activity to which strict liability should attach. The significance of this view is lessened, however, by the fact that liability for damage caused by the operation of a nuclear plant will, in many instances, be prescribed by the provisions of the federal Price-Anderson Act. See 42 U.S.C. §2210.

There was considerable support in the 1980s for the proposition that the owner or operator of a hazardous waste landfill should be strictly liable for damage caused by wastes that migrated off-site, and in 1983 the Supreme Court of New Jersey held that the disposal of untreated hazardous wastes is an abnormally dangerous activity to which strict liability will attach. See *New Jersey Dept. of Environmental Protection v. Ventron Corp.*, 468 A.2d 150 (N.J., 1983). See, also, *T & E Industries, Inc. v. Safety Light Corp.*, 587 A.2d 1249 (N.J., 1991) (the processing, handling, and disposal of radium was held to be an abnormally dangerous activity). This approach to hazardous waste and hazardous materials has not been widely adopted in the tort law of other states. However, strict liability for certain remediation costs and damage to natural resources *has* been imposed on the operators of hazardous waste facilities, and on the generators of those wastes, under the federal Comprehensive Environmental Response, Compensation, and Liability Act (CERCLA, the "Superfund" statute), which is discussed in chapter 9.

▪ NOTES

1. The federal government cannot be held strictly liable under the Federal Tort Claims Act. See *Laird v. Nelms*, 406 U.S. 797 (1972).

2. The draft Third Restatement of Torts takes a more definitive approach to characterizing abnormally dangerous activity than its predecessor, and adds an explicit requirement of foreseeability. According to the first "tentative draft" of this section of the Third Restatement, an activity is abnormally dangerous if it both "creates a foreseeable and highly significant risk of physical harm even when reasonable care is exercised by all actors" and "is not a matter of common usage" [American Law Institute, *Restatement (Third) of the Law of Torts: Liab. Physical Harm* §20 (T.D. No. 1, 2001)]. If this became the accepted definition of abnormally dangerous activity, would it be likely to expand or to contract the universe of activities that could be declared abnormally dangerous? Does the disposal of hazardous waste, or the processing, handling, and disposal of hazardous materials generally, pose a "highly significant risk" of harm "even when reasonable care is exercised" by all concerned?   ▪

D. PRODUCTS LIABILITY CLAIMS

Another form of tort claim that is sometimes used to address environmental pollution, and is commonly used to address human exposure to toxic chemicals, is the products liability lawsuit. Here, the product either is itself a pollutant or gives rise to pollution; some familiar examples are cigarettes, toxic chemical products (such as asbestos), and sprays or air conditioners that release chlorofluorocarbons into the atmosphere. Products liability lawsuits may be brought by the purchaser or user of the product, which commonly means that these suits may be used to redress both consumer and worker exposure to toxic substances. (State workers' compensation statutes do not bar worker suits against third-party manufacturers of products used in the workplace.) Products liability suits can always be grounded in negligence; that is, they can be based on allegations that the manufacturer did not use reasonable care in the design or manufacture of the product, but the major development in products liability law over the past 50 years has been a move toward strict liability. Indeed, there is a popular perception today that all manufacturers are strictly liable for harm caused by their products. This, however, is not the case.

Perhaps the best current summary of the common law of the United States on products liability can be found in the Third Restatement of Torts. This formulation begins with the proposition that a manufacturer is liable for the harm (proximately) caused by its product if the product is "defective." A product is said to be defective if it "contains a manufacturing defect, is defective in design, or is defective because of inadequate instructions or warnings." *See* American Law Institute, *Restatement (Third) of the Law of Torts: Prod. Liab.* §2 (1998). These three types of defect are then defined as follows (emphasis added):

(a) a product contains a *manufacturing defect* when the product departs from its intended design even though all possible care was exercised in the preparation and marketing of the product;
(b) a product is *defective in design* when the foreseeable risks of harm posed by the product could have been remedied or avoided by the adoption of a reasonable alternative design by the seller or other distributor, or a predecessor in the commercial chain of distribution, and the omission of the alternative design renders the product not reasonably safe;
(c) a product is *defective because of inadequate instructions or warnings* when the foreseeable risks of harm posed by the product could have been reduced or avoided by the provision of reasonable instructions or warnings by the seller or other distributor, or a predecessor in the commercial chain of distribution, and the omission of the instructions or warnings renders the product not reasonably safe.

The standard by which the manufacturer's liability will be judged, then, depends on the type of product defect asserted. If it is a manufacturing defect—if it is the one item, out of the many produced by the factory, whose chemical formulation, say, differed from the manufacturer's design—strict liability will be applied. The courts have made a determination that from a social policy perspective it is appropriate to place the cost of the harm caused by such defects on the manufacturer, rather than on the injured consumer or user. This is said to be so both because the manufacturer is in the best position to keep the defect from occurring and because the manufacturer can spread the cost of the harm across all consumers of the product in the form of higher prices.

When the injured plaintiff alleges that the product was defective in design—that it performed precisely as designed, but that it was nonetheless defective—the situation becomes more complicated and pure strict liability does not apply. It is often said, however, that a showing of negligence is not required. Indeed, the Second Restatement of Torts, in an oft-cited formulation, states that liability should be imposed on the manufacturer if the product was both defective and unreasonably dangerous. See American Law Institute, *Restatement (Second) of the Law of Torts* §402A (1965). Thus, it was said, since the focus of the inquiry is on the reasonable safety of the product, rather than on the reasonableness of the manufacturer's design, this was a form of enhanced liability that differed from negligence. In practice, this often has been a distinction without a difference. To determine whether the product was reasonably safe, the courts generally employ a risk-utility analysis: Does the utility of the product outweigh its risk? The answer to that question, however, generally turns on whether there was an alternative design that would have made the product safer without unduly diminishing its utility. If so, the key question generally becomes whether the manufacturer knew, or reasonably should have known, about this alternative design. This is, generally speaking, a negligence question. Accordingly, the articulation of the standard of liability for design defects in the Third Restatement of Torts (quoted above) is phrased in negligence terms. See, e.g., David G. Owen (1996). "Defectiveness Redefined: Exploding the Myth of 'Strict' Products Liability," 1996 *University of Illinois Law Review* 743.

The third type of products liability case is the action based on the manufacturer's *failure to warn* consumers and users about the dangers of the product. Many toxic substance exposure cases—with the asbestos cases being the prime example—have been brought under this theory. By and large, these are handled by the courts as straightforward negligence cases. The key questions, then, generally are whether the manufacturer knew or reasonably should have known about the dangers of the product, and whether any warnings that were given were adequate to communicate those dangers to the consumer or user of the product.

The question of whether a manufacturer reasonably should have known about a particular alternative design (in design defect cases) or a particular product danger (in failure to warn cases) generally turns on the *state of the art* at the time the product was manufactured. That is, was the state of knowledge within the relevant scientific or engineering disciplines such that a reasonable person would have discovered the alternative design—or the product's danger—if he or she had surveyed the available journals, studies, and the like? A manufacturer asserting that the relevant knowledge base was not sufficiently developed at the time of manufacture and sale is often said to be raising the state-of-the-art defense. To the extent that this defense is not allowed, design defect and failure-to-warn cases move much closer to the strict liability paradigm. Indeed, a notable exception to the line of cases holding that failure-to-warn cases are to be governed by principles of negligence is *Beshada v. Johns-Manville Products Corp.*, 447 A.2d 539 (N.J. 1982), in which the New Jersey Supreme Court held that the state-of-the-art defense was not available to asbestos manufacturers being sued for failing to warn about the dangers of their product. The sole test, said the court, is whether the product was reasonably safe; if a warning can make the product safer without unduly diminishing its utility, the product will not be reasonably safe if it is sold without a warning.

Beshada v. Johns-Manville Products Corp.
447 A.2d 539 (N.J. 1982)
(New Jersey Supreme Court)

...As it relates to warning cases, the state-of-the-art defense asserts that distributors of products can be held liable only for injuries resulting from dangers that were scientifically discoverable at the time the product was distributed. Defendants argue that the question of whether the product can be made safer must be limited to consideration of the available technology at the time the product was distributed. Liability would be absolute, defendants argue, if it could be imposed on the basis of a subsequently discovered means to make the product safer since technology will always be developing new ways to make products safer. Such a rule, they assert, would make manufacturers liable whenever their products cause harm, whether or not they are reasonably fit for their foreseeable purposes....

The most important inquiry... is whether imposition of liability for failure to warn of dangers which were undiscoverable at the time of manufacture will advance the goals and policies sought to be achieved by our strict liability rules. We believe that it will.

RISK SPREADING

One of the most important arguments generally advanced for imposing strict liability is that the manufacturers and distributors of defective products can best allocate the costs of the injuries resulting from it. The premise is that the price of a product should reflect all of its costs, including the cost of injuries caused by the product. This can best be accomplished by imposing liability on the manufacturer and distributors. Those persons can insure against liability and incorporate the cost of the insurance in the price of the product. In this way, the costs of the product will be borne by those who profit from it: the manufacturers and distributors who profit from its sale and the buyers who profit from its use. "It should be a cost of doing business that in the course of doing that business an unreasonable risk was created." Keeton [Products Liability—Inadequacy of Information"], 48 *Tex. L. Rev.* [398] at 408 [1970]. *See* Prosser, *The Law of Torts*, §75, p. 495 (4th Ed. 1971).

Defendants argue that this policy is not forwarded by imposition of liability for unknowable hazards. Since such hazards by definition are not predicted, the price of the hazardous product will not be adjusted to reflect the costs of the injuries it will produce. Rather, defendants state, the cost "will be borne by the public at large and reflected in a general, across the board increase in premiums to compensate for unanticipated risks." There is some truth in this assertion, but it is not a bad result.

First, the same argument can be made as to hazards which are deemed scientifically knowable but of which the manufacturers are unaware. Yet it is well established under our tort law that strict liability is imposed even for defects which were unknown to the manufacturer. It is precisely the imputation of knowledge to the defendant that distinguishes strict liability from negligence. Defendants advance no argument as to why risk spreading works better for unknown risks than for unknowable risks.

Second, spreading the costs of injuries among all those who produce, distribute and purchase manufactured products is far preferable to imposing it on the innocent victims who suffer illnesses and disability from defective products. This basic normative premise is at the center of our strict liability rules. It is unchanged by the state of scientific knowledge at the time of manufacture.

Finally, contrary to defendants' assertion, this rule will not cause the price and production level of manufactured products to diverge from the so-called economically efficient level. Rather, the rule will force the price of any particular product to reflect the cost of insuring against the possibility that the product will turn out to be defective.

ACCIDENT AVOIDANCE

In *Suter v. San Angelo Foundry & Machine Co., 406 A.2d 140 (N.J. 1979)*, we stated:

"Strict liability in a sense is but an attempt to minimize the costs of accidents and to consider who should bear those costs. *See* the discussion in Calabresi & Hirschoff, 'Toward a Test for Strict Liability in Torts,' 81 *Yale L.J.* 1055 (1972), in which the authors suggest that the strict liability issue is to decide which party is the 'cheapest cost avoider' or who is in the best position to make the cost-benefit analysis between accident costs and accident avoidance costs and to act on that decision once it is made. *Id.* at 1060.

Using this approach, it is obvious that the manufacturer rather than the factory employee is 'in the better position both to judge whether avoidance costs would exceed foreseeable accident costs and to act on that judgment.' *Id.*"

Defendants urge that this argument has no force as to hazards which by definition were undiscoverable. Defendants have treated the level of technological knowledge at a given time as an independent variable not affected by defendants' conduct. But this view ignores the important role of industry in product safety research. The "state-of-the-art" at a given time is partly determined by how much industry invests in safety research. By imposing on manufacturers the costs of failure to discover hazards, we create an incentive for them to invest more actively in safety research.

FACT FINDING PROCESS

The analysis thus far has assumed that it is possible to define what constitutes "undiscoverable" knowledge and that it will be reasonably possible to determine what knowledge was technologically discoverable at a given time. In fact, both assumptions are highly questionable. The vast confusion that is virtually certain to arise from any attempt to deal in a trial setting with the concept of scientific knowability constitutes a strong reason for avoiding the concept altogether by striking the state-of-the-art defense.

Scientific knowability, as we understand it, refers not to what in fact was known at the time, but to what *could have been* known at the time. In other words, even if no scientist had actually formed the belief that asbestos was dangerous, the hazards would be deemed "knowable" if a scientist could have formed that belief by applying research or performing tests that were available at the time. Proof of what could have been known will inevitably be complicated, costly, confusing and time-consuming. Each side will have to produce experts in the history of science and technology to speculate as to what knowledge was feasible in a given year. We doubt that juries will be capable of even understanding the concept of scientific knowability, much less be able to resolve such a complex issue. Moreover, we should resist legal rules that will so greatly add to the costs both sides incur in trying a case.

The concept of knowability is complicated further by the fact, noted above, that the level of investment in safety research by manufacturers is one determinant of the state-of-the-art at any given time. Fairness suggests that manufacturers not be excused from liability because their prior inadequate investment in safety rendered the hazards of their product unknowable. Thus, a judgment will have to be made as to whether defendants' investment in safety research in the years preceding distribution of the product was adequate. If not, the experts in the history of technology will have to testify as to what would have been knowable at the time of distribution if manufacturers had spent the proper amount on safety in prior years. To state the issue is to fully understand the great difficulties it would engender in a courtroom.

In addition, discussion of state-of-the-art could easily confuse juries into believing that blameworthiness is at issue. Juries might mistakenly translate the confused concept of state-of-the-art into the simple question of whether it was defendants' fault that they did not know of the hazards of asbestos. But that would be negligence, not strict liability. . . .

■ **NOTES**

1. The *Beshada* case has not been widely followed. Indeed, even in New Jersey, most failure-to-warn cases outside of the asbestos context are handled as negligence cases, and the state-of-the-art defense is available. Are there valid policy reasons for treating failure-to-warn cases within the negligence paradigm? Assume that the *Beshada* approach had become the general rule in failure-to-warn cases. Could a product without a warning ever satisfy a risk-utility test? That is, would there ever be a situation in which the addition of a warning would *not* make a product safer without unduly diminishing its utility? Does the technology-forcing rationale articulated by the New Jersey Supreme Court in *Beshada* nonetheless justify the application of a strict liability paradigm?

2. Despite its limited applicability to other failure-to-warn cases, *Beshada* remains an articulate statement of the general policy rationale for the use of the strict liability paradigm in product liability cases.

3. For years, Johns-Manville was a major employer in New Jersey, with a large asbestos manufacturing operation in Manville, New Jersey. In the early 1980s, however, faced with mounting product liability suits from asbestos victims, the company filed for reorganization under Chapter 11 of the federal bankruptcy code and moved its corporate headquarters from New Jersey to Denver, Colorado. As the following excerpt indicates, it is likely that a certain bitterness toward the company remained in New Jersey.

The people of Manville, New Jersey have paid a high price for their piece of the American dream. The hard-working immigrants who settled this town struggled, and often succeeded, in earning the rewards our society promises. They bought houses, raised children and sent them to college. For many, their dream has ended with the cruel reality of oxygen tanks, and slow descents into weakness and incurable cancers. And they never made that choice for themselves. "The people I know, they feel bitter," [one asbestos worker] says. "When we were hired, they should have said, 'Hey, there's a risk involved. Do you want to take it with that risk?' And you'd have had the option to say no." (Jim Jubak, "They are the First," *Environmental Action*, February 1983, p. 9) ∎

A BRIEF COMMENTARY ON DEFENSES

There are defenses to each of the tort claims discussed here. To a certain extent, these will vary with the nature of the claim. However, there are three defenses that are somewhat more broadly applicable. The first of these is *comparative negligence*. If the plaintiff's own negligence is responsible (along with the defendant's actions) for his or her injury, the courts generally will reduce the award of monetary damages to the plaintiff in proportion to that portion of the injury caused by the plaintiff's own negligence. A related, but conceptually distinct, principle is *assumption of the risk*. If the plaintiff has put himself into a particular situation knowing full well the risk posed by the defendant's activity, he may be said to have "assumed the risk" that he would be harmed. If so, the plaintiff will not have a claim against the defendant for the damage caused. As one might expect, this defense is not recognized in all situations, for to do so would essentially be to allow activities that pose *obvious* risks to go undeterred. Nonetheless, this defense is often said to be available in negligence cases. Finally, it is a defense to a products liability claim that the plaintiff was injured because he or she put the product to a use that was not *reasonably foreseeable* by the manufacturer or seller.

E. THE TECHNOLOGY-FORCING POTENTIAL OF TORT LAW

Because it has the potential to require a standard of behavior that is more protective of health, safety, or the environment than that practiced by industry, tort law has an obvious potential to "force" the use (or development) of cleaner or safer technology. The classic example of this technology-forcing potential is another decision by aforementioned Judge Learned Hand of the Second Circuit Court of Appeals

---

The T. J. Hooper
L. HAND, Circuit Judge
60 F.2d 737 (2d Cir. 1932)

The barges No. 17 and No. 30, belonging to the Northern Barge Company, had lifted cargoes of coal at Norfolk, Virginia, for New York in March, 1928. They were towed by two tugs of the petitioner, the 'Montrose' and the 'Hooper,' and were lost off the Jersey Coast on March tenth, in an easterly gale. The cargo owners sued the barges under the contracts of carriage; the owner of the barges sued the tugs.... All the suits were joined and heard together, and the judge found that all the vessels were unseaworthy; the tugs, because they did not carry radio receiving sets by which they could have seasonably got warnings of a change in the weather which should have caused them to seek shelter in the Delaware Breakwater en route....

It is not fair to say that there was a general custom among coastwise carriers so to equip their tugs. One line alone did it; as for the rest, they relied upon their crews, so far as they can be said to have relied at all. An adequate receiving set suitable for a coastwise tug can now be got at small cost and is reasonably reliable if kept up; obviously it is a source of great protection to their tows. Twice every day they can receive these predictions, based upon the widest possible information, available to every vessel within two or three hundred miles and more. Such a set is the ears of the tug to catch the spoken word, just as the master's binoculars are her

eyes to see a storm signal ashore. Whatever may be said as to other vessels, tugs towing heavy coal laden barges, strung out for half a mile, have little power to manoeuvre, and do not, as this case proves, expose themselves to weather which would not turn back stauncher craft. They can have at hand protection against dangers of which they can learn in no other way.

Is it then a final answer that the business had not yet generally adopted receiving sets? There are, no doubt, cases where courts seem to make the general practice of the calling the standard of proper diligence; we have indeed given some currency to the notion ourselves. Indeed in most cases reasonable prudence is in fact common prudence; but strictly it is never its measure; a whole calling may have unduly lagged in the adoption of new and available devices. It never may set its own tests, however persuasive be its usages. Courts must in the end say what is required; there are precautions so imperative that even their universal disregard will not excuse their omission. But here there was no custom at all as to receiving sets; some had them, some did not; the most that can be urged is that they had not yet become general. Certainly in such a case we need not pause; when some have thought a device necessary, at least we may say that they were right, and the others too slack. The statute (section 484, title 46,

U.S. Code [46 USCA §484]) does not bear on this situation at all. It prescribes not a receiving, but a transmitting set, and for a very different purpose; to call for help, not to get news. We hold the tugs [liable] therefore because had they been properly equipped, they would have got the Arlington reports. The injury was a direct consequence of this unseaworthiness.

As one might expect, following this case radio receivers became common equipment on commercial vessels sailing in and around the United States. Similarly, years later, products liability suits against asbestos manufacturers helped spur the development of substitutes for this chemical in commercial and consumer products.

F. DRAWBACKS TO USING THE TORT SYSTEM AS A POLLUTION REDUCTION TOOL

One obvious disadvantage to using the tort system as a regulatory tool for environmental pollution is that it is a piecemeal way of making policy. Standards of conduct are established irregularly, in response to the particular lawsuits that parties choose to file, and then only on a state-by-state basis. This latter point can be particularly limiting when dealing with transboundary problems, such as certain types of air pollution, where we might prefer a regional or national approach. Even within a particular state, it may be difficult to use the tort system to address diverse harms because meaningful abatement may require the filing of a number of different suits by different people. Moreover, even when these issues are not significant, there are other limitations that often prevent the tort system from being an effective pollution reduction tool. Some of the more important of these are discussed here. For a more in-depth evaluation of the deterrent effect of tort law, and of liability systems generally, see chapter 12.

1. The Financial Investment Necessary to Mount a Credible Case

Cost barrier

Many plaintiffs simply will not be able to bring their case to court. Lawsuits cost money, and complex environmental tort cases often cost a substantial amount of money. The combination of plaintiff's attorneys' fees, expert witness fees, investigation costs, and other preparation and trial costs in a toxic chemical exposure case, for example, can easily run from several hundred thousand to a few million dollars. Most plaintiffs do not have the resources necessary to finance such suits. Thus, most of these claims are financed by lawyers who take the case on a *contingent fee* basis. That is, the lawyer agrees not to charge for his or her time in bringing the case unless the plaintiff wins, at which point the lawyer will be entitled to a specified percentage of the proceeds, in addition to reimbursement for all out-of-pocket costs (such as expert witness fees) advanced. As a practical matter, then, the plaintiff's ability to sue often depends on whether a lawyer can be found who will take the case for a contingent fee. Given the uncertainty of the outcome of many of these cases, however, finding such a lawyer may be a difficult proposition. Moreover, where the harm is a generalized one, the potential recovery available to each plaintiff may not be sufficient to warrant the investment of the lawyer's time and money. In certain cases, this problem may be surmounted through some kind of collective tort action, but this is not always practicable.

According to a 2001 report by LRP Publications that analyzed 2,751 product liability verdicts in several states, the median jury award in such suits rose from $500,300 in 1993 to over $1.8 million in 1999. *See* Greg Winter (2001) "Jury Awards in Product-Liability Suits Are Rising," *New York Times*, January 30, p. 1. At the same time, however, the number of product liability cases filed in federal court dropped from 32,856 in 1997 to 14,428 in 2000, according to the Administrative Office of the United States Courts (id.). When asked about these results, some plaintiffs' lawyers noted that the costs of bringing such suits have risen, leading to the rejection of many potentially meritorious suits whose potential recovery was deemed insufficient to justify a lawyer's investment of time and money:

'I've had plenty of defective product [cases], clearly defective, where I won't even talk to the people because their injuries aren't severe enough,' said Craig E. Hillborn, president of Hillborn & Hillborn, a small law firm in Birmingham, Mich. 'If they're not a quadriplegic, a paraplegic or losing some part of their body, there's no way I'm going to take that case.' ...

'I can't take cases on any more unless I am absolutely positive that I have one worth at least $2 million,' said James L. Gilbert, president of Attorney Information Exchange Group, an organization of about 500 plaintiffs' lawyers nationwide. 'I can no longer afford to spend $300,000 trying a case that is only worth $500,000, and that's ridiculous.' (Id.)

2.   The Difficulty in Moving Beyond Current Industry Practice

As discussed, to prevail in a tort case the plaintiff often has to demonstrate that the defendant "breached" an applicable legal standard. To the extent that *industry practice* is the reference point on which this legal standard is based, it may be difficult for the plaintiff to carry this burden. Often, it is industry practice itself that is the source of the pollution about which the plaintiff complains. To the extent that the court engages in a *cost-benefit* balancing to determine the appropriate standard, the court may conclude that the cost to industry (and to society in general) of imposing a stricter standard on industry outweighs the benefit to the plaintiff (and to society in general) of doing so.

3. The Difficulty in Proving Proximate Causation

Especially in cases alleging actual or potential damage to human health, it may be difficult or impossible for a plaintiff to prove *proximate causation* (that is, that the defendant's activities caused, or will cause, the harm of which the plaintiff complains). As discussed earlier, this proposition, like all elements of a tort case, must be proven by a preponderance of the evidence, which generally means that it must be shown to be more likely than not to be true. At least three types of questions may prove difficult to answer in this regard.

First: Does the kind of pollution emitted by the defendant cause the kind of harm alleged by the plaintiff? For example, do PCBs cause human cancer?

Second: Which defendant (among many potential defendants) caused (or will cause) the harm in question? If a plaintiff in New England alleges property or health damage from acid rain, for example, can the plaintiff identify those sources of sulfur and nitrogen oxides (some of which may be as far away as the Midwest) that cause acid rain to form in this particular locale? In a case involving alleged harm from a pharmaceutical, where scores of manufacturers had manufactured the identical drug according to a common formula, the California Supreme Court imposed liability according to a *market share* approach when the plaintiff could not identify the company that had made the particular quantities of this drug that allegedly caused her injury. Under this approach, the plaintiff was allowed to hold the defendant manufacturers liable for her injury in proportion to the percentage which the amount of the drug sold by each of them bore to the entire production of the drug (subject to the right of any of the manufacturers to avoid liability if it could affirmatively prove that it had not made the particular quantity of the drug that had harmed the plaintiff). As noted by the California court (over a spirited dissent):

In our contemporary complex industrialized society, advances in science and technology create fungible goods which may harm consumers and which cannot be traced to any specific producer. The response of the courts can be either to adhere rigidly to prior doctrine, denying recovery to those injured by such products, or to fashion remedies to meet these changing needs. [*Sindell v. Abbott Laboratories*, 26 Cal. 3d 588, 610, 607 P.2d 924, 936, (1980)]

Although an approach of this nature could also be extended to environmental harms caused by the collective actions of a number of defendants, fashioning a fair and equitable remedy in such situations is likely to be more difficult than it was in *Sindell*, where the potential harm from the allegedly wrongful actions of the defendants (making and marketing the defective drug) was known to be identical.

Finally, there is a third causation issue that plagues many environmental tort claims: Was the harm to the plaintiff caused by the activities of the defendant or by some other factor? For example, where the plaintiff alleges that his or her cancer was caused by exposure to chemical pollution generated by the defendant, the type of cancer in question will often be associated with other potential causes as well (diet, other environmental exposures, etc.). This type of issue may be the most difficult of all to overcome. If there is nothing, other than statistics, to tie the plaintiff's particular case of cancer to the defendant's pollution, the plaintiff may well be required to prove that exposure to the defendant's pollution more than doubled his or her risk of cancer over the background rate because this would establish, on a statistical basis, that it was more than 50% likely to be true. (In the parlance of epidemiology, this condition would be met where the *attributable risk* is greater than 50%.) The long latency period of many cancers can exacerbate the difficulty of making this showing.

A substantial part of the problem in this area is that the relevant science has not developed to the degree of certainty presently required by the tort system. This disjuncture between science and the law has led many commentators to call for systemic changes in tort law. Consider, for example, the following statement from Carl Cranor and David Eastmond, a philosopher and environmental toxicologist, respectively:

[S]cientific evidence about the universe of substances may be so great that current tort law rules of liability are inadequate to address properly the problems they pose. Current tort law liability rules, combined with evidentiary burdens and standards of proof, function well when both sides have plausible fact scenarios about the *likelihood* of what happened. When there is considerable *ignorance* on one side, however, as is the case in many tort suits, the party with the burden of proof will lose. To address widespread ignorance about substances, courts may need to consider different legal doctrines. To protect the public better and ensure the possibility of justice between parties, courts may need to tailor new standards of liability, or shift burdens of proof once a plaintiff has presented a prima facie case to induce better testing and safety investigations by firms that create and use potentially toxic substances. (Carl F. Cranor and David A. Eastmond, "Scientific Ignorance and Reliable Patterns of Evidence in Toxic Tort Causation: Is There a Need for Liability Reform?" 64 *Law and Contemporary Problems* 1, 2002)

Although the call for reform is a strong one, the remedy may not be easy to design (much less to convince a court or legislative body to adopt). For example, the statistical evidence may show that one of every ten persons exposed to a particular chemical who now has a particular disease actually contracted the disease as a result of the exposure. If the plaintiff both has the disease and was exposed to the chemical, how can he establish that he is the one person out of ten who actually has a valid claim against the party responsible for the exposure? If he does not have additional evidence—beyond the bare statistics—tying his particular case of the disease to the defendant's chemical, is shifting the burden of proof likely to help him? In one sense, the problem facing the plaintiff (and the tort system) is that we tend to rely on population-based evidence (statistical studies conducted across a human or animal population) to determine whether *individual* causation has been proven. One potential solution would be to devise some kind of *population-based* approach to causation, such as awarding partial damages to all exposed persons with the disease, with the damages calculated in proportion to the attributable risk. Although this approach has considerable conceptual appeal, a host of practical considerations (such as individual variability among the plaintiffs) would make it challenging (but certainly not impossible) to implement. Short of a systemic change of this nature, advances in the science, such as the recognition of "biomarkers" that serve to link a particular medical condition with a particular exposure, may hold the most promise.

4.   The Difficulty in Presenting "Novel" Scientific or Engineering Testimony

If the expert opinion on which the plaintiff must rely to prove his or her case is based on scientific principles or data that are relatively new and/or not yet widely accepted by the relevant scientific community, the plaintiff may have difficulty convincing the court to admit the opinion into evidence (that is, the court may refuse to allow the expert to testify). This issue has become particularly acute in the federal courts as a result of a series of decisions by the United States Supreme Court stressing the need for federal trial judges to act as "gatekeepers" of scientific, engineering, and other technical evidence. Before allowing scientists, engineers, or other technical experts to offer opinion testimony to the jury on these matters, the Court has held, the judge must ensure that the methodology used to arrive at the opinion is "reliable." See *Daubert v. Merrell Dow Pharmaceuticals, Inc.*, 509 U.S. 880 (1993) (addressing expert opinions regarding "scientific" knowledge); *General Electric Company v. Joiner*, 522 U.S. 136 (1997) (holding that the trial court's decision to admit or exclude such expert opinion testimony may be reversed by the court of appeals only if the decision constitutes an abuse of discretion); and *Kumho Tire Company, Ltd. v. Carmichael*, 526 U.S. 137 (1999) (extending these rules to expert opinions on engineering and other "technical" knowledge). At least initially, this requirement appears to have resulted in an increased level of exclusion of scientific and engineering opinion testimony offered by plaintiffs. See, e.g., "Admissibility of Expert Proof Subject to Closer Judicial Scrutiny Since *Daubert*," 15 *Toxics Law Reporter* 1117 (Nov. 2, 2000). Although the Supreme Court based these decisions on the Federal Rules of Evidence, which are not applicable to the courts of the states, many state courts have adopted similar requirements. See "States Move to *Daubert*, Even When They Say They're Stuck on *Frye*," 17 *Toxics Law Reporter* 376 (April 18, 2002).

■ NOTE

1. In *General Electric Company v. Joiner*, 522 U.S. 136 (1997), the Court upheld the ruling of a federal district court judge excluding the opinion of an expert who would

have testified that he believes that PCBs cause cancer in humans because they have been shown to cause cancer in animal tests. The exclusion of the evidence was proper, the Court concluded, because the expert had not explained in sufficient detail why it was reasonable to extrapolate from animal evidence to humans.   ∎

5. The Lengthy Delay Between Causation and Remedy

In suits for compensation for damage to human health, the long latency period for many pollution-induced diseases means that the suit is not likely to be brought until years after the harm was caused. This tends to blunt the deterrent effect (of the potential financial cost to the polluter from the lawsuit) on current behavior. That is, even if the defendant believes that some plaintiffs will eventually sue and recover monetary damages, the costs of future lawsuits, when discounted to present value, may not be sufficient to provide a financial incentive to the defendant to invest *now* in the pollution reduction that would be necessary to avoid the lawsuits.

∎ **NOTE**

1. As discussed in chapter 9, the Comprehensive Environmental Response, Compensation, and Liability Act specifies that the statute of limitations for claims alleging harm from environmental exposure to hazardous substances shall not begin to run until the plaintiff discovered, or reasonably should have discovered, that he or she was suffering harm related to such exposure. This provision appears not to apply to claims arising out of workplace exposure to hazardous substances, however.   ∎

6. The Difficulty in Securing an Injunction Against Ongoing Industrial Activity

Finally, in suits seeking to abate ongoing pollution, it may be hard to convince the court to issue an injunction ordering the defendant to cease (or sufficiently reduce) the pollution in question. In deciding whether to issue an injunction (and in deciding what the terms of any such an injunction should be), the court most likely will balance the costs of an injunction against the benefits. In doing so, a state court may well be inclined to sacrifice a societal interest in pollution reduction in favor of a local interest in economic security. Moreover, the court may be loath to question the representations of the polluting industry regarding its own technological capability. The following case, decided at the dawn of the modern era of federal environmental legislation, is perhaps the classic example of these considerations in operation.

Boomer et al. v. Atlantic Cement Company, Inc.
BERGAN, J.
26 N.Y.2d 219, 257 N.E.2d 870 (1970)
(New York Court of Appeals)

Defendant operates a large cement plant near Albany. These are actions for injunction and damages by neighboring land owners alleging injury to property from dirt, smoke and vibration emanating from the plant. A nuisance has been found after trial, temporary damages have been allowed; but an injunction has been denied.

The public concern with air pollution arising from many sources in industry and in transportation is currently accorded ever wider recognition accompanied by a growing sense of responsibility in State and Federal Governments to control it. Cement plants are obvious sources of air pollution in the neighborhoods where they operate. But there is now before the court private litigation in which individual property owners have sought specific relief from a single plant operation. The threshold question raised by the division of view on this appeal is whether the court should resolve the litigation between the parties now before it as equitably as seems possible; or whether, seeking promotion of the general public welfare, it should channel private litigation into broad public objectives.

A court performs its essential function when it decides the rights of parties before it. Its decision of private controversies may sometimes greatly affect public issues. Large questions of law are often resolved by the manner in which private litigation is decided. But this is normally an incident to the court's main function to settle controversy. It is a rare exercise of judicial power to use a decision in private litigation as a purposeful mechanism to achieve direct public objectives greatly beyond the rights and interests before the court.

Effective control of air pollution is a problem presently far from solution even with the full public and financial powers of government. In large measure adequate technical procedures are yet to be developed and some that appear possible may be economically impracticable.

It seems apparent that the amelioration of air pollution will depend on technical research in great depth; on a carefully balanced consideration of the economic impact of close regulation; and of the actual effect on public health. It is likely to require massive public expenditure and to demand more than any local community can accomplish and to depend on regional and interstate controls.

A court should not try to do this on its own as a by-product of private litigation and it seems manifest that the judicial establishment is neither equipped in the limited nature of any judgment it can pronounce nor prepared to lay down and implement an effective policy for the elimination of air pollution. This is an area beyond the circumference of one private lawsuit. It is a direct responsibility for government and should not thus be undertaken as an incident to solving a dispute between property owners and a single cement plant—one of many—in the Hudson River valley.

The cement making operations of defendant have been found by the court at Special Term to have damaged the nearby properties of plaintiffs in these two actions. That court, as it has been noted, accordingly found defendant maintained a nuisance and this has been affirmed at the Appellate Division. The total damage to plaintiffs' properties is, however, relatively small in comparison with the value of defendant's operation and with the consequences of the injunction which plaintiffs seek.

The ground for the denial of injunction, notwithstanding the finding both that there is a nuisance and that plaintiffs have been damaged substantially, is the large disparity in economic consequences of the nuisance and of the injunction. This theory cannot, however, be sustained without overruling a doctrine which has been consistently reaffirmed in several leading cases in this court and which has never been disavowed here, namely that where a nuisance has been found and where there has been any substantial damage shown by the party complaining an injunction will be granted. The rule in New York has been that such a nuisance will be enjoined although marked disparity be shown in economic consequence between the effect of the injunction and the effect of the nuisance. . . .

Although the court at Special Term and the Appellate Division held that injunction should be denied, it was found that plaintiffs had been damaged in various specific amounts up to the time of the trial and damages to the respective plaintiffs were awarded for those amounts. The effect of this was, injunction having been denied, plaintiffs could maintain successive actions at law for damages thereafter as further damage was incurred.

The court at Special Term also found the amount of permanent damage attributable to each plaintiff, for the guidance of the parties in the event both sides stipulated to the payment and acceptance of such permanent damage as a settlement of all the controversies among the parties. The total of permanent damages to all plaintiffs thus found was $185,000. This basis of adjustment has not resulted in any stipulation by the parties.

This result at Special Term and at the Appellate Division is a departure from a rule that has become settled; but to follow the rule literally in these cases would be to close down the plant at once. This court is fully agreed to avoid that immediately drastic

remedy; the difference in view is how best to avoid it.*

One alternative is to grant the injunction but postpone its effect to a specified future date to give opportunity for technical advances to permit defendant to eliminate the nuisance; another is to grant the injunction conditioned on the payment of permanent damages to plaintiffs which would compensate them for the total economic loss to their property present and future caused by defendant's operations. For reasons which will be developed the court chooses the latter alternative.

If the injunction were to be granted unless within a short period—e.g., 18 months—the nuisance be abated by improved methods, there would be no assurance that any significant technical improvement would occur.

The parties could settle this private litigation at any time if defendant paid enough money and the imminent threat of closing the plant would build up the pressure on defendant. If there were no improved techniques found, there would inevitably be applications to the court at Special Term for extensions of time to perform on showing of good faith efforts to find such techniques.

Moreover, techniques to eliminate dust and other annoying by-products of cement making are unlikely to be developed by any research the defendant can undertake within any short period, but will depend on the total resources of the cement industry Nationwide and throughout the world. The problem is universal wherever cement is made.

For obvious reasons the rate of the research is beyond control of defendant. If at the end of 18 months the whole industry has not found a technical solution a court would be hard put to close down this one cement plant if due regard be given to equitable

---

* Respondent's investment in the plant is in excess of $45,000,000. There are over 300 people employed there.

principles. On the other hand, to grant the injunction unless defendant pays plaintiffs such permanent damages as may be fixed by the court seems to do justice between the contending parties.

All of the attributions of economic loss to the properties on which plaintiffs' complaints are based will have been redressed. The nuisance complained of by these plaintiffs may have other public or private consequences, but these particular parties are the only ones who have sought remedies and the judgment proposed will fully redress them. The limitation of relief granted is a limitation only within the four corners of these actions and does not foreclose public health or other public agencies from seeking proper relief in a proper court. It seems reasonable to think that the risk of being required to pay permanent damages to injured property owners by cement plant owners would itself be a reasonable effective spur to research for improved techniques to minimize nuisance. The power of the court to condition on equitable grounds the continuance of an injunction on the payment of permanent damages seems undoubted.

The damage base here suggested is consistent with the general rule in those nuisance cases where damages are allowed. "Where a nuisance is of such a permanent and unabatable character that a single recovery can be had, including the whole damage past and future resulting therefrom, there can be but one recovery" (66 C. J. S., Nuisances, §140, p. 947). It has been said that permanent damages are allowed where the loss recoverable would obviously be small as compared with the cost of removal of the nuisance (*Kentucky-Ohio Gas Co. v. Bowling*, 264 Ky. 470, 477).

The present cases and the remedy here proposed are in a number of other respects rather similar to *Northern Indiana Public Serv. Co. v. Vesey* (210 Ind. 338) decided by the Supreme Court of Indiana. The gases,

odors, ammonia and smoke from the Northern Indiana company's gas plant damaged the nearby Vesey greenhouse operation. An injunction and damages were sought, but an injunction was denied and the relief granted was limited to permanent damages "present, past, and future" (p. 371). Denial of injunction was grounded on a public interest in the operation of the gas plant and on the court's conclusion "that less injury would be occasioned by requiring the appellant [Public Service] to pay the appellee [Vesey] all damages suffered by it.... than by enjoining the operation of the gas plant; and that the maintenance and operation of the gas plant should not be enjoined" (p. 349).

The Indiana Supreme Court opinion continued: "When the trial court refused injunctive relief to the appellee upon the ground of public interest in the continuance of the gas plant, it properly retained jurisdiction of the case and awarded full compensation to the appellee. This is upon the general equitable principle that equity will give full relief in one action and prevent a multiplicity of suits" (pp. 353–354).

It was held that in this type of continuing and recurrent nuisance permanent damages were appropriate. See, also, *City of Amarillo v. Ware* (120 Tex. 456) where recurring overflows from a system of storm sewers were treated as the kind of nuisance for which permanent depreciation of value of affected property would be recoverable....

Thus it seems fair to both sides to grant permanent damages to plaintiffs which will terminate this private litigation. The theory of damage is the "servitude on land" of plaintiffs imposed by defendant's nuisance. (See *United States v. Causby*, 328 U.S. 256, 261, 262, 267, where the term "servitude" addressed to the land was used by Justice Douglas relating to the effect of airplane noise on property near an airport.)

The judgment, by allowance of permanent damages imposing a servitude on land, which is the basis of the actions, would preclude future recovery by plaintiffs or their grantees (see *Northern Indiana Public Serv. Co. v. Vesey*, supra., p. 351).

This should be placed beyond debate by a provision of the judgment that the payment by defendant and the acceptance by plaintiffs of permanent damages found by the court shall be in compensation for a servitude on the land.

Although the Trial Term has found permanent damages as a possible basis of settlement of the litigation, on remission the court should be entirely free to re-examine this subject. It may again find the permanent damage already found; or make new findings. The orders should be reversed, without costs, and the cases remitted to Supreme Court, Albany County to grant an injunction which shall be vacated upon payment by defendant of such amounts of permanent damage to the respective plaintiffs as shall for this purpose be determined by the court.

DISSENTING OPINION BY JASEN, J.

I agree with the majority that a reversal is required here, but I do not subscribe to the newly enunciated doctrine of assessment of permanent damages, in lieu of an injunction, where substantial property rights have been impaired by the creation of a nuisance. It has long been the rule in this State, as the majority acknowledges, that a nuisance which results in substantial continuing damage to neighbors must be enjoined. To now change the rule to permit the cement company to continue polluting the air indefinitely upon the payment of permanent damages is, in my opinion, compounding the magnitude of a very serious problem in our State and Nation today.

In recognition of this problem, the Legislature of this State has enacted the Air Pollution Control Act (Public Health Law, §§1264–1299-m) declaring that it is the State policy to require the use of all available and reasonable methods to prevent and control air pollution (Public Health Law, §1265).[1]

The harmful nature and widespread occurrence of air pollution have been extensively documented. Congressional hearings have revealed that air pollution causes substantial property damage, as well as being a contributing factor to a rising incidence of lung cancer, emphysema, bronchitis and asthma.[2]

The specific problem faced here is known as particulate contamination because of the fine dust particles emanating from defendant's cement plant. The particular type of nuisance is not new, having appeared in many cases for at least the past 60 years. (See *Hulbert v. California Portland Cement Co.*, 161 Cal. 239 [1911].) It is interesting to note that cement production has recently been identified as a significant source of particulate contamination in the Hudson Valley. This type of pollution, wherein very small particles escape and stay in the atmosphere, has been denominated as the type of air pollution which produces the greatest hazard to human health.[4] We have thus a nuisance which not only is damaging to the plaintiffs,[5] but also is decidedly harmful to the general public.

1. See, also, Air Quality Act of 1967, 81 U.S. Stat. 485 (1967).
2. See U.S. Cong., Senate Comm. on Public Works, Special Subcomm. on Air and Water Pollution, Air Pollution 1966, 89th Cong., 2d Sess., 1966, at pp. 22–24; U.S. Cong., Senate Comm. on Public Works, Special Subcomm. on Air and Water Pollution, Air Pollution 1968, 90th Cong., 2d Sess., 1968, at pp. 850, 1084.

4. J. Ludwig, "Air Pollution Control Technology: Research and Development on New and Improved Systems," 33 *Law and Contemp. Prob.* 217, 219 (1968).
5. There are seven plaintiffs here who have been substantially damaged by the maintenance of this nuisance. The trial court found their total permanent damages to equal $185,000.

I see grave dangers in overruling our long-established rule of granting an injunction where a nuisance results in substantial continuing damage. In permitting the injunction to become inoperative upon the payment of permanent damages, the majority is, in effect, licensing a continuing wrong. It is the same as saying to the cement company, you may continue to do harm to your neighbors so long as you pay a fee for it. Furthermore, once such permanent damages are assessed and paid, the incentive to alleviate the wrong would be eliminated, thereby continuing air pollution of an area without abatement.

It is true that some courts have sanctioned the remedy here proposed by the majority in a number of cases,[6] but none of the authorities relied upon by the majority are analogous to the situation before us. In those cases, the courts, in denying an injunction and awarding money damages, grounded their decision on a showing that the use to which the property was intended to be put was primarily for the public benefit. Here, on the other hand, it is clearly established that the cement company is creating a continuing air pollution nuisance primarily for its own private interest with no public benefit.

This kind of inverse condemnation (*Ferguson v. Village of Hamburg*, 272 N.Y. 234) may not be invoked by a private person or corporation for private gain or advantage. Inverse condemnation should only be permitted when the public is primarily served in the taking or impairment of property. (*Matter of New York City Housing Auth. v. Muller*, 270 N.Y. 333, 343; *Pocantico Water Works Co. v. Bird*, 130 N.Y. 249, 258.) The promotion of the interests of the polluting cement company has, in my opinion, no public use or benefit.

Nor is it constitutionally permissible to impose servitude on land, without consent of the owner, by payment of permanent damages where the continuing impairment of the land is for a private use. (See *Fifth Ave. Coach Lines v. City of New York*, 11 N.Y. 2d 342, 347; *Walker v. City of Hutchinson*, 352 U.S. 112.) This is made clear by the State Constitution (art. I, §7, subd. [a]) which provides that "[p]rivate property shall not be taken for *public use* without just compensation" (emphasis added). It is, of course, significant that the section makes no mention of taking for a *private* use.

In sum, then, by constitutional mandate as well as by judicial pronouncement, the permanent impairment of private property for private purposes is not authorized in the absence of clearly demonstrated public benefit and use.

I would enjoin the defendant cement company from continuing the discharge of dust particles upon its neighbors' properties unless, within 18 months, the cement company abated this nuisance.[7]

It is not my intention to cause the removal of the cement plant from the Albany area, but to recognize the urgency of the problem stemming from this stationary source of air pollution, and to allow the company a specified period of time to develop a means to alleviate this nuisance.

I am aware that the trial court found that the most modern dust control devices available have been installed in defendant's plant, but, I submit, this does not mean that *better* and more effective dust control devices could

---

6. See *United States v. Causby* (328 U.S. 256); *Kentucky-Ohio Gas Co. v. Bowling* (284 Ky. 470, 477); *Northern Indiana Public Serv. Co. v. Vesey* (210 Ind. 338); *City of Amarillo v. Ware* (120 Tex. 456); *Pappenheim v. Metropolitan El. Ry. Co.* (128 N.Y. 436); *Ferguson v. Village of Hamburg* (272 N.Y. 234).

7. The issuance of an injunction to become effective in the future is not an entirely new concept. For instance, in *Schwarzenbach v. Oneonta Light & Power Co.* (207 N.Y. 671), an injunction against the maintenance of a dam spilling water on plaintiff's property was issued to become effective one year hence.

not be developed within the time allowed to abate the pollution.

Moreover, I believe it is incumbent upon the defendant to develop such devices, since the cement company, at the time the plant commenced production (1962), was well aware of the plaintiffs' presence in the area, as well as the probable consequences of its contemplated operation. Yet, it still chose to build and operate the plant at this site.

In a day when there is a growing concern for clean air, highly developed industry should not expect acquiescence by the courts, but should, instead, plan its operations to eliminate contamination of our air and damage to its neighbors. . . .

CHIEF JUDGE FULD and JUDGES BURKE and SCILEPPI concur with Judge BERGAN; JUDGE JASEN dissents in part and votes to reverse in a separate opinion.

Order reversed, without costs, and the case remitted to Supreme Court, Albany County, for further proceedings in accordance with the opinion herein.

■ NOTES

1. This case is interesting for the differing views on technological innovation taken by the majority and the dissent. Which view shows more faith in the technological capability of industry? Which view is likely to pose the bigger risk of harm if it proves incorrect?

2. The remedy endorsed by the majority—permanent monetary damages paid by the defendant to the plaintiffs as a condition for the authority to continue the polluting activity—obviously has some potential to "force" technological advance as well. If the monetary award were high enough, the firm would have an incentive to find a less polluting alternative so it could avoid paying the award. (As noted by the dissent, however, once the damages have been assessed and paid, that financial incentive disappears.) In a situation such as this, what factors are likely to determine the size of the award?

3. The *Boomer* decision was written by the New York Court of Appeals, which is the highest state court in the state of New York. Note that the Court of Appeals remanded the case back to the Supreme Court, which is the name that New York gives to its trial-level courts. As in other states, New York has a separate trial court for each county (the trial court that originally heard the *Boomer* case was in Albany County). In most other states, however, the county trial court is known as the "Superior" or "District" court, and the state's highest court is known as the Supreme Court. ■

5 Administrative Law: The Roles of Congress, the President, the Agencies, and the Courts in Shaping Environmental Policy

F. Two General Environmental Mandates to Agencies: The National Environmen-
    tal Policy Act and the Endangered Species Act
    1. The National Environmental Policy Act
        a. The Environmental Impact Statement
        b. The Council on Environmental Quality
    2. The Endangered Species Act

Most of the "law" referred to in the title of this text stems from federal regulatory
statutes that govern various aspects of U.S. industry and its technology. Administrative law is the key to understanding how these regulatory systems function.

In essence, administrative law is the body of law that governs the way in which administrative agencies make and implement decisions. Federal administrative law is
grounded in the U.S. Constitution and in various federal statutes. Although administrative law can appear to be little more than a series of seemingly arcane structural
and procedural rules, a basic understanding of administrative law is essential to an
understanding of how the regulatory system works. It is administrative law that
allows us to "push" the regulatory system in one direction or another—to propose
a regulation that we feel is needed, to challenge a regulation that we feel is too stringent (or not stringent enough), to obtain information from the records of an administrative agency, to provide input to the standard-setting process, and to do a host of
other things that give us some measure of control over the direction of environmental
policy. In this light, administrative law can be seen as the useful tool it often is.

This chapter provides an overview of the administrative system—highlighting the
relationships between Congress, the president, the agencies, and the courts—and
then explores some of the issues that are of particular importance to the regulation
of environmental and workplace pollutants. In addition, it provides a brief introduction to the legal system for those unfamiliar with its workings. Finally, it gives a brief
analysis of the National Environmental Policy Act and the Endangered Species Act,
two environmental statutes that broadly affect decision making by federal agencies.

A. QUESTIONS TO CONSIDER WHEN ANALYZING A REGULATORY FRAMEWORK

Before delving into the theories and practice of administrative law, it is useful to reflect for a moment on the broader picture. What is it that can be gained from a study
of administrative law and the administrative system? Certainly it should provide
some familiarity with the details of administrative procedure. Beyond the technical
details, however, administrative law gives us a conceptual basis from which we can

analyze, and actually come to understand, a particular regulatory system. The following questions provide a logical focus for conducting such an analysis in the area of health, safety, and environmental regulation. In each instance, an understanding of administrative law will help ferret out the appropriate answer.

1. How is the regulatory "problem" defined? What is being regulated, and how is it delineated?

2. What "risk reduction mandate" is embodied in the statutory standard? That is, how aggressive should the agency be in addressing the problem at hand? To what extent is the agency required to reduce the risks at which the regulations are directed? For example, what level of disease prevention or pollution abatement must the implementing agency attain and/or maintain?

• Is the standard health-based (i.e., designed to achieve the level of risk reduction deemed necessary to meet a particular public health or environmental endpoint)? Or is it technology-based (i.e., set at the level of performance deemed attainable by the use of a particular technology)?

• To what extent—if at all—is economics to be taken into consideration?

• Is the standard tied to economic feasibility?

• If so, does the standard look to the economics of the firm or to the economics of the entire industry?

• Is some form of social cost-benefit analysis required (or permitted)?

3. How has the agency interpreted and carried out its statutory mandate?

4. Through what procedures are the agency's regulations promulgated? To what extent are those outside the agency able to place issues onto—or remove issues from—the agency's regulatory agenda, and to participate in the agency's rulemaking procedures?

5. Who has the statutory burden of proof with regard to the various issues of importance? In a broad sense, is the burden on industry to prove that its product or process is "acceptable," or is the burden on the regulatory agency to prove that it is not?

6. What health or safety testing requirements, if any, does the statute impose (or allow)?

7. What avenues are available for appealing the agency's decision to take (or not to take) a particular regulatory action? Is there an express "citizen suit" provision that allows affected citizens to sue the agency and/or individual violators of the statute?

8. What enforcement options are available to the agency?

9. What role is left for state statutes or common law in this area? To what extent, if at all, does the federal regulatory system preempt state action?

With these general inquiries in mind, we now turn to the administrative system itself. The conceptual basis for administrative law may be somewhat familiar to any student who has taken a high school course on the U.S. government. Indeed, it is often so familiar that it is taken for granted or even overlooked completely. Almost all questions of administrative law in the United States are grounded in the tripartite model of government embodied in the Constitution: the separation of powers among the legislative, executive, and judicial branches of government. In general, it is this model that judges have in their mind's eye, either explicitly or implicitly, when they approach issues of administrative law.

This chapter is designed to guide the reader through this tripartite system. Although the chapter emphasizes the federal system, the broad concepts are largely applicable to the various state administrative and legal systems as well. There are, however, important differences between the federal system and many state systems. Any attempt to understand or use a particular state's administrative process should be preceded by careful attention to the specific features of that state's system.

B. THE CONSTITUTIONAL BASIS FOR HEALTH, SAFETY, AND ENVIRONMENTAL REGULATION

Typically, administrative agencies are created by the legislative branch, are run on a day-to-day basis by the executive branch, and are subjected to periodic review by the judicial branch. Thus, a functional analysis of agency behavior—one that asks both what it is that agencies do and how their activities can be influenced—must examine the manner in which each of the branches directs and controls agency behavior.

1. Direction from the Legislative Branch

The legislative branch can direct and influence agency behavior through a series of formal and informal controls.

a. The Substantive Statutory Mandate

The administrative process begins with an act of Congress that either creates a new agency to deal with a particular area of concern or grants new powers and responsibilities to an existing agency to deal with that area of concern. We will refer in this text to a statute that gives such authority to a new or existing agency as the agency's *originating* statute (also known as the *enabling* legislation) in that area. It is the originating statute that gives the agency its statutory mandate—its formal directive from Congress with regard to the subject matter at hand. Obviously, an agency often administers more than one originating statute, and the demarcation between subject areas is not always clear. For example, the Environmental Protection Agency has been given the directive to deal with toxic air pollutants under the Clean Air Act, toxic water pollutants under the Clean Water Act, toxic wastes deposited into the ground under the Resource Conservation and Recovery Act, and toxic chemicals generally under the Toxic Substances Control Act. See 42 U.S.C. §7412, 33 U.S.C. §1317, 42 U.S.C. §6901, *et seq.*, and 15 U.S.C. §2601, *et seq.* A close examination of each of these statutes reveals not only that EPA has a variety of statutory directives from Congress, but also that it could use any one of these statutes, especially the latter, in such a way as to limit the discharge of toxic substances into all environmental media. Furthermore, there are situations in which two or more agencies have overlapping statutory mandates. For example, both the Occupational Health and Safety Administration (OSHA) and EPA have the authority to regulate workers' exposure to harmful chemicals.

■ NOTES

1. Inconveniently enough, the sections of many federal statutes are known by two different numbers. When an act is passed by Congress, its sections are numbered sequentially, beginning with 1. Thus, the Occupational Safety and Health Act (OSH-Act) is numbered from Section 1 through Section 34. Longer statutes, such as the Clean Air Act or Clean Water Act, commonly are divided into "subchapters" or "titles." Within each subchapter or title, the various sections are numbered in sequential fashion: 101, 102, 201, 202, etc. It is by these original section numbers that the various sections of a statute usually become known to those who work with them on a regular basis. However, all federal statutes are grouped by subject matter area and placed into the United States Code (U.S.C.). The Clean Water Act, for example, is found in Title 33 of the Code, the area of the Code dealing generally with navigation and navigable waters, while the Clean Air Act is found in Title 42, the area of the Code dealing generally with public health and welfare. Federal statutes are cited by their title and section numbers. Thus, Section 101 of the Clean Water Act becomes 33 U.S.C. §1251. This is the "official" citation.

2. EPA is an exception to the general way administrative agencies are created. It was not created by an act of Congress, but by a presidential order in 1970.   ■

b.   The Commerce Clause

Congressional power to grant authority to administrative agencies flows from the U.S. Constitution. By now it is well settled that Congress has broad powers under the commerce clause of the Constitution to regulate in the general areas of health, safety, and the environment.

The Constitution grants Congress the power "to regulate commerce...among the States" (Article 1, Section 8). This commerce power allows Congress to regulate activities that substantially affect interstate commerce, a power that has broadened considerably over the years through judicial interpretation. For example, in uphold-ing the Civil Rights Act of 1964, the Supreme Court accepted as valid an asserted relationship between interstate commerce and racial discrimination in restaurants. It reasoned that restaurants that refused to serve African-Americans sold fewer inter-state goods, obstructed interstate travel by African-Americans, and generally affected the free flow of commerce across state lines. If the commerce clause could be used to sustain such social regulation, it is not difficult to see how it was extended to the environmental and occupational arenas as well, especially since the regulation of health, safety, and the environment involves the products and processes of industrial, agricultural, and energy production and their use.

To discourage any challenge to a statute enacted under its commerce powers on the grounds that it is not sufficiently connected to interstate commerce, Congress generally includes explicit findings as to the effect on commerce in the language of the statute itself. The Supreme Court emphasized the importance of such findings in *United States v. Lopez*, 514 U.S. 549 (1995), when it held unconstitutional a federal law prohibiting the possession of firearms within 1,000 feet of a school. The Court concluded that Congress had not demonstrated an adequate connection between the regulated activity and interstate commerce, and thus held that Congress had over-stepped its commerce clause authority. This was the first time in six decades that the Court had struck down a federal law for exceeding the power granted to Congress under the commerce clause.

Five years later, in *United States v. Morrison*, 529 U.S. 598 (2000), the Court indi-cated that there are some regulatory topics whose connection with interstate com-merce is so tenuous that even specific congressional findings cannot justify the use of the commerce clause to address them. At issue in *Morrison* was a federal statute giving the victims of certain *intrastate* acts of gender-motivated violence the right to pursue a claim for money damages against their assailants in federal court. Congress had supported this legislation with "numerous" findings as to the serious effects of such violence on victims and their families, and with a finding that such violence affects interstate commerce in several specific ways. See 529 U.S. at 614–615. None-theless, the Court held that Congress lacks authority under the commerce clause to promulgate such a law.

The Court noted that since the regulated activity (intrastate acts of gender-motivated violence) was neither interstate nor economic in nature, the burden on Congress to establish the requisite impact on interstate commerce was a heavy one. The congressional findings on this score, noted the Court, were based on the premise that such violence, in the aggregate, could logically be said to set in motion a chain of events that eventually leads to certain effects on interstate commerce. This premise, reasoned the Court, "would allow Congress to regulate any crime so long as the na-tionwide, aggregated impact of that crime has substantial effects on employment, production, transit, or consumption," and could "be applied equally as well to family law and other areas of traditional state regulation, since the aggregate impact of marriage, divorce, and childrearing on the national economy is undoubtedly significant" (id. at 615). Thus, although the Court declined to "adopt a categorical rule against aggregating the effects of... noneconomic activity" in commerce clause analyses (id. at 613), it held that Congress may not invoke the commerce clause to "regulate noneconomic, violent criminal conduct based solely on that conduct's aggregate effect on interstate commerce" (id. at 617). For the five justices in the majority, the key constitutional principle at stake was the distinction "between what is truly national and what is truly local" (id. at 617–618). "The regulation and punishment of intrastate violence that is not directed at the instrumentalities, channels, or goods involved in interstate commerce," they noted, "has always been the province of the states" (id. at 618).

This case does not appear to represent a departure from the principles that have supported the use of the commerce clause to enact health, safety, and environmental legislation. Indeed, the *Morrison* Court was careful to reaffirm its allegiance to the "modern, expansive interpretation of the Commerce Clause" (529 U.S. at 608). Moreover, since environmental legislation is almost always directed at activities (such as the operation of manufacturing facilities) that are economic in nature, and is often directed at effects (such as the pollution of interstate waters) that are interstate in nature, its grounding in the commerce clause would appear solid even under a broad interpretation of *Morrison*. Nonetheless, it would be prudent to expect that the case will embolden the regulated community to mount an increased number of commerce clause challenges to such legislation.

c. The "Regulatory Takings" Issue

Beyond the limitations imposed by the commerce clause itself, the Constitution places other potential restrictions on congressional policy making, depending on the specific nature of the legislation in question. One of these is the takings clause of the Fifth Amendment, which provides that private property shall not be "taken for public use, without just compensation." This is the portion of the Constitution that prevents the federal government from, say, demolishing someone's home to put in a freeway without first initiating a formal condemnation process and paying the homeowner the fair value of the property. Some regulatory statutes may also raise "takings" issues. From a policy perspective, the pivotal question is whether a particular statute regulating private sector behavior will be considered simply regulation, or whether it will be considered a regulatory taking of private property. If the latter, the law will be invalid unless (1) the taking is for a legitimate public purpose, and (2) there is a mechanism for fairly compensating the private parties whose property is so taken. Under current Supreme Court jurisprudence, very few, if any, provisions of federal environmental law would qualify as a taking. However, for several years there has been a strong push in some quarters to greatly expand the scope of the takings clause to the point where several current federal laws, such as those regulating the filling of wetlands, would come within its ambit. This push, which is both political and philosophical in nature, has been championed both by business groups and those with an antiregulatory or limited-government outlook.

The Supreme Court has often stated that the party seeking to establish that a regulation constitutes a taking faces a "heavy burden" of persuasion, and that the key inquiry will be "[t]he economic impact of the regulation on the claimant and...the extent to which the regulation has interfered with distinct investment-backed expectations" [*Penn Central Transportation Co. v. New York City*, 438 U.S. 104, 124 (1978)]. Thus in *Lucas v. South Carolina Coastal Council*, 505 U.S. 1003 (1992), the Court held that a law "that deprives land of all economically beneficial use" will be considered a taking, so long as the use to which the owner wishes to put the land "was previously permissible under relevant property and nuisance principles" (505 U.S. at 1027, 1030). Because the landowner had a reasonable expectation at the time he invested in the property that he would be allowed to put it to productive use, the subsequent regulation wholly prohibiting any such use was a taking. In the modern regulatory world, then, the question becomes the *reasonableness* of a party's expectation that an activity (development of land, operation of a business, etc.) may be conducted free of future regulation.

A case very much in point on this issue is *Ruckelshaus v. Monsanto*, 467 U.S. 986 (1984), in which a pesticide manufacturer sought to invalidate a provision in the 1978 amendments to the Federal Insecticide, Fungicide, and Rodenticide Act giving the public access to pesticide health and safety data submitted by the manufacturer to EPA as part of the pesticide registration process. These data, argued Monsanto, contain trade secrets, and by forcing the corporation to effectively disclose these secrets to the public, the government was taking private property without compensation. The Court agreed that trade secrets are "property" within the Fifth Amendment, but—except for a 6-year period from 1972 to 1978 during which the statute had explicitly promised that such data would be kept confidential—the Court disagreed that the forced disclosure of these data constitutes a taking. The Court reached this conclusion because it found that, outside of this 6-year period, Monsanto had not had a "reasonable investment-backed expectation" that the material it submitted to EPA would be put to further regulatory use. "In an industry that long has been the focus of great public concern and significant government regulation, the possibility was substantial that the Federal Government, which had thus far taken no position on disclosure of health, safety, and environmental data concerning pesticides, upon focusing on the issue, would find disclosure to be in the public interest" (467 U.S. at 1009). Under this rationale, regulations directed at reducing pollution—a matter "that long has been the focus of great public concern and significant government regulation"—generally would not appear to be amenable to a successful takings claim.

■ **NOTES**

1. The takings concept is applied to *state* government actions under the Fourteenth Amendment and under similar provisions in state constitutions.

2. In addition to constitutional protections against takings, some states have enacted laws requiring their own regulatory bodies to provide compensation to landowners whose property values are reduced as the result of new state regulations. In Oregon, this was enacted by the voters via the citizen initiative process, although the same approach was rejected by Washington State voters in 2006. There have been periodic moves in Congress over the past 15 years to enact similar legislation on the federal level. Obviously, depending on the scope of such legislation, it could have a chilling effect on regulation. Indeed, taken to its extremes, such legislation could effectively dismantle the current regulatory system.

3. In *Eastern Enterprises v. Apfel*, 524 U.S. 498 (1998), a four-justice plurality of the Supreme Court concluded that a federal statute that required a former coal company to fund health benefits for previously retired miners violated the takings provision of the Fifth Amendment because its retroactive application "substantially interferes with [the company's] reasonable investment-backed expectations" (id. at 532). This decision has led some to argue that retroactive liability statutes, such as the hazardous waste Superfund statute, similarly constitute a regulatory taking. As discussed in chapter 9, this argument has not been well received in the federal courts.   ■

d.   The Delegation Doctrine

Many statutory mandates to agencies—especially in the areas of health, safety, and the environment—are strikingly broad and nonspecific. For example, Section 6 of the Toxic Substances Control Act (15 U.S.C. §2605) directs EPA to regulate chemicals that pose "an unreasonable risk of injury to health or the environment." The statute does not, however, define the term "unreasonable risk." Beyond a general directive to EPA to "consider the environmental, social, and economic impact" of actions taken under the statute [see 15 U.S.C. §2501(c)], TSCA leaves the agency considerable discretion to determine which risks will be deemed unreasonable and which will not.

Earlier in this century such a broad grant of authority to an administrative agency might well have been considered unconstitutional. The relevant constitutional principle is known as the "delegation doctrine" (also sometimes known as the "nondelegation doctrine"). This doctrine stems from the classic understanding that Congress—as the duly elected representative of the American public—is the repository of all federal legislative power. According to the delegation doctrine, Congress cannot delegate this legislative power to another party, such as an administrative agency, because the agency has not been elected by the people. Under a strict application of the doctrine, Congress is required to provide reasonably clear and specific statutory standards to guide agency decision making.

The delegation doctrine reached its apex in 1935 when the U.S. Supreme Court struck down two separate statutes on the grounds that they granted improperly broad decision-making authority to administrative agencies. See *Panama Refining Co. v. Ryan*, 293 U.S. 388 (1935); *Schechter Poultry Corp. v. United States*, 295 U.S. 495 (1935). Since that time, however, the number of administrative agencies has increased dramatically, and agency decision making has become the principal means of federal regulation. Administrative agencies have even been said to comprise the "fourth branch" of government. In an apparent acquiescence to political reality, the courts have also relaxed the delegation doctrine considerably. Broad delegations of substantive authority to administrative agencies have become very much the rule rather than the exception. When an especially expansive statutory mandate is challenged, the courts have responded, not by invoking the delegation doctrine to strike down the statute, but by either (1) giving a narrower interpretation to the statutory language, or (2) ordering the agency to develop its own standards for interpreting the statutory language. Indeed, the Supreme Court has not invoked the delegation doctrine to invalidate a statute since 1935.

Nonetheless, on two occasions prior to his appointment as chief justice, Justice William Rehnquist authored a separate opinion in which he took the position that Section 6(b)(5) of the OSHAct—a provision directing OSHA to set standards for workplace exposures to toxic substances—violates the delegation doctrine. That section requires OSHA to "set the standard which most adequately assures, to the extent feasible...that no employee will suffer material impairment of health or functional capacity" [28 U.S.C. §655(b)(5)]. In failing to be more specific, Justice Rehnquist concluded, Congress had unconstitutionally delegated to an agency the responsibility for making the "fundamental policy decisions" that must properly be made by Congress itself [*Industrial Union Dept., AFL-CIO v. American Petroleum Institute*, 448 U.S. 607, 671 (1980) (Rehnquist, J., concurring)]. See also *American Textile Manufacturers Institute v. Donovan*, 452 U.S. 490, 543–45 (1981) (Rehnquist, J., dissenting). Were this position to be adopted by a majority of the Court, other broad statutory mandates in the area of health, safety, and the environment could also be called into question.

In 2001, however, Chief Justice Rehnquist joined a unanimous Court in rejecting a delegation doctrine challenge to Section 109(b)(1) of the Clean Air Act [42 U.S.C.

§7409(b)(1)], which directs EPA to set "ambient air quality standards the attainment and maintenance of which in the judgment of the Administrator [of EPA], based on [scientific criteria documents developed by EPA] and allowing an adequate margin of safety, are requisite to protect the public health." The scope of discretion given to the EPA by this provision, noted the Court, is "well within the outer limits of our non-delegation precedents" [*Whitman v. American Trucking Associations, Inc.*, 531 U.S. 457, 474 (2001)]. Significantly, the Court held that even though the air quality standards set by EPA have broad national applicability, Congress was not required to provide specific criteria to be used by EPA in determining when the specified "margin of safety" is "adequate," or in determining what level of protection is "requisite to protect public health."

It is true enough that the degree of agency discretion that is acceptable varies according to the scope of the power congressionally conferred. . . . But even in sweeping regulatory schemes we have never demanded . . . that statutes provide a "determinate criterion" for saying "how much [of the regulated harm] is too much." (id. at 475, citation omitted)

Thus, while there may be some federal health, safety, or environmental provisions that are so broadly drawn that they would be held in violation of the delegation doctrine, this case would appear to indicate that any such examples will be few and infrequent.

▪ NOTES

1. The *American Trucking* case was an appeal of a decision of the Court of Appeals for the District of Columbia holding, among other things, that EPA had violated the delegation doctrine by failing to articulate a set of specific criteria outlining how it would exercise its discretion under Section 109(b)(1). See *American Trucking Associations, Inc. v. EPA*, 175 F.3d 1027, 1034 (D.C. Cir. 1999), which is excerpted in chapter 6. In reversing this determination, the Supreme Court effectively rejected the notion that an agency, as opposed to Congress, could be said to violate the delegation doctrine. "We have never suggested," noted the Court, "that an agency can cure an unlawful delegation of legislative power by adopting in its discretion a limiting construction of the statute" (531 U.S. at 472). (As discussed in chapter 6, the Court also held in *American Trucking* that Section 109(b)(2) of the Clean Air Act does not permit EPA to consider the economic costs of implementation when setting primary ambient air quality standards.)

2. Although all nine members of the Supreme Court agreed on the delegation doctrine result in *American Trucking*, they did not all do so for the same reasons. Justice Antonin Scalia authored the majority opinion, which Chief Justice Rehnquist joined. This opinion distinguished the earlier opinions written by Justice Rehnquist in the

OSHAct cases by noting that "even then-Justice Rehnquist...would have upheld [Section 6(b)(5) of the OSHAct] if, like the statute here, it did not permit economic costs to be considered" (531 U.S. at 473–474). This is not an accurate characterization of those earlier OSHAct opinions. The primary view expressed by Justice Rehnquist in the OSHAct cases was that the use in Section 6(b)(5) of the phrase "to the extent feasible"—without further definition by Congress of what is meant by "feasible"—is unconstitutionally broad. The fact that OSHA has interpreted this language to mean *technological and economic* feasibility, he wrote then, represents policy making by the agency that, under the Constitution, should have been done by Congress.

3. Two justices, John Paul Stevens and David Souter, concurred in the Court's delegation doctrine result in *American Trucking*, but not in the Court's opinion on the issue. In a separate opinion, they noted that they would prefer the Court to acknowledge that the Clean Air Act *does* delegate legislative power to EPA, but to hold that such a delegation does not violate the Constitution. See 531 U.S. at 487–490. Justice Clarence Thomas, on the other hand, joined the Court's opinion, but wrote separately to note that, had the nondelegation argument been framed differently, he would have looked at the question more closely. "On a future day," he wrote, "I would be willing to address the question whether our delegation jurisprudence has strayed too far from our Founders' understanding of separation of powers" (id. at 487).   ■

e. The Procedural Mandate

In addition to being required to follow the substantive mandates of originating statutes, federal agencies are also required to adhere to the more general procedural directives of several other statutes. While the substantive mandate provides guidance to an agency on which decisions it should make, the procedural mandate provides guidance on how those decisions should be made. The most important procedural statute for federal agencies is the Administrative Procedure Act (APA), 5 U.S.C. §551, *et seq.* Passed in 1946, this statute remains the chief means through which Congress controls the procedures of the various federal agencies. The APA proscribes procedures for agency rulemaking and adjudication, for judicial review of administrative decision making, and for citizen access to these administrative and judicial processes.

Congress significantly expanded citizen access to the administrative process in the 1970s with the passage of the Freedom of Information Act, which requires agencies to make most of their internal documents available to the public; the Government in the Sunshine Act, which requires agencies to make many of their proceedings open to the public; and the Privacy Act, which gives private citizens access to agency documents and information concerning them. All three of these acts were incorporated as provisions of the APA. In addition, in 1972 Congress passed the Federal Advisory Committee Act, which specifies procedures for an agency's use of outside advisors. Each of these general procedural statutes is discussed in more detail in section D of this chapter.

In the 1990s, Congress turned its attention to the impacts of agency rulemaking on the regulated community and enacted a series of laws designed to reduce those impacts. The genesis of these laws was the election of 1994, when the Republican Party regained control of both houses of Congress for the first time in several years. Led by then-Speaker of the House Newt Gingrich, the Republicans brought with them an aggressive legislative agenda that they termed their "Contract with America." A chief plank in this agenda was "regulatory reform," which, broadly speaking, meant minimizing the costs and other burdens imposed by federal regulation on businesses and state and local governments. A key goal of this reform movement was that all, or virtually all, federal regulation be required to meet a cost-benefit criterion, which would have required a reduction in the stringency of those regulations whose costs were deemed not to be justified by the associated benefits. Although Congress came close to passing such sweeping legislation, it did not do so. However, Congress did enact two laws during this period that have had an impact on agency rulemaking, especially in the areas of health, safety, and the environment.

The first of these was the Unfunded Mandates Reform Act (2 U.S.C. §§551–559, 701–706), passed in 1995. This act requires agencies to prepare "a qualitative and quantitative assessment of the anticipated costs and benefits" of any proposed "major" rule (defined as a regulation whose aggregate impact is anticipated to be $100 million or more in any given year), unless the preparation of such an assessment "is otherwise prohibited by law" (2 U.S.C. §1532). The statute also specifies in some detail the contents of the required cost-benefit assessment. Since many federal rules will exceed the $100 million threshold, this law effectively imposes a cost-benefit "overlay" on major federal regulation. It is important to note, however, that this law does not require an agency to abandon its particular statutory mandate in favor of balancing costs and benefits. That is, it does not impose cost-benefit as a *substantive* decision-making criterion. Nonetheless, by requiring the agency to calculate the costs and benefits of major regulations, and to place this information in the administrative record, Congress clearly has elevated the importance of the cost-benefit criterion.

A year later, in 1996, Congress called for further review of agency decision making with the passage of the Small Business Regulatory Enforcement Fairness Act (Pub. L. 104–121, March 26, 1996). A key aspect of this law was a series of amendments strengthening a 1980 statute known as the Regulatory Flexibility Act (RFA), 5 U.S.C. §§601–612. As amended, the RFA requires agencies to publish a "regulatory flexibility analysis" with any proposed or final rule likely to have a significant economic impact on a substantial number of small entities. The analysis published with a proposed rule is to include, among other things, "a description of any significant alternatives to the proposed rule ... which minimize any significant impact of the proposed rule on small entities" [5 U.S.C. §603(c)]. The analysis published with a final rule in turn is to include "a description of the steps the agency has taken to minimize the significant economic impact on small entities," and a statement of the "factual, policy, and legal reasons" why the approach taken in the final rule was selected instead of the other regulatory alternatives considered [5 U.S.C. §603(a)(5)].

A second key aspect of the 1996 law was the creation of the Congressional Review Act (CRA), 5 U.S.C. §§801–808. As its name suggests, the CRA was designed to facilitate congressional review of agency rulemaking. It requires that before a final rule takes effect the promulgating agency provide a report to Congress that includes, among other things, "a complete copy of the cost-benefit analysis of the rule, if any," and the regulatory flexibility analyses prepared under the Regulatory Flexibility Act. If the regulation is a "major" rule under the Unfunded Mandates Reform Act, it does not take effect until 60 days after this report has been submitted, unless the president determines that the rule should take effect immediately because one of four designated criteria have been satisfied. See 5 U.S.C. §§801(a)(3) and 801(c). This is intended to give members of Congress time to review the regulation and, if they choose to do so, debate its merits. Moreover, Congress may (subject to a potential presidential veto) nullify any rule submitted under the CRA and prevent it from taking effect by passing a "joint resolution of disapproval" (5 U.S.C. §802).

A variety of other statutes also provide general procedural directives to federal agencies. Two of these are of particular importance to the field of environmental policy: the National Environmental Policy Act, which requires federal agencies to prepare and consider an environmental impact statement before approving a major action that significantly affects the environment; and the Endangered Species Act, which requires federal agencies to consult with the Department of Interior before approving major federal actions that may have an effect on species that have been listed under the act. These laws are discussed in more detail at the end of this chapter.

The originating statute may specify its own procedural requirements as well, and conflicts may arise between the procedural directives of the originating statute and the directives of one or more of the general procedural statutes mentioned here. The resolution of any such conflict depends on the intent of Congress. In general, the more recent statute addressing the point in question will control. For example, the OSHAct, passed in 1970, contains specifications for rulemaking that differ from those found in the Administrative Procedure Act, and the agency is required to follow the OSHAct procedures to the extent that they differ from the APA. Where an originating statute does not specify a different procedure, however, the agency will be required to follow the "generic" requirements set forth in the APA.

■ **NOTES**

1. The Unfunded Mandates Reform Act also imposes a substantive directive, albeit a "soft" one, on major federal regulations. For any proposed regulation meeting the monetary threshold identified earlier, the agency must "identify and consider a reasonable number of alternatives, and from those alternatives select the least costly, most cost-effective, and least burdensome alternative that achieves the objectives of the rule" [2 U.S.C. §1535(a)]. The agency can avoid this requirement, however, if it publishes "an explanation of why the least costly, most cost-effective, or least burdensome method of achieving the objectives of the rule was not adopted," or if the requirement is "inconsistent with law" [2 U.S.C. §1535(b)]. The focus of this latter exception would seem to be situations in which the agency's substantive mandate requires it to prefer a certain regulatory result even if it is not the cheapest effective alternative. In general, however, the directive to select the most cost-effective of those alternatives that will fulfill an agency's mandate should not in itself require the agency to compromise its substantive mandate.

2. For a discussion of the use of cost-benefit analysis in the design of regulations, see chapter 3. For an identification and discussion of some of the cost-benefit bills that Congress considered in the mid-1990s but did not pass, see the sources cited in David Driesen (2001) "Getting Our Priorities Straight: One Strand of the Regulatory Reform Debate," 31 *Environmental Law Reporter* 10003, 10004, n.8.

3. During the mid-1990s Congress also considered, but did not pass, legislation that would have required agencies to perform a detailed risk assessment, according to specified criteria, before promulgating health, safety, and environmental regulation. While it did not pass broad legislation of this nature, however, Congress did include risk assessment provisions in its 1996 amendments to the Safe Drinking Water Act, the statute under which EPA establishes health criteria for public drinking water supplies. Under these new provisions, risk assessments conducted under the act must be based on "the best available, peer-reviewed science and supporting studies conducted in accordance with sound and objective scientific practices," and on "data collected by accepted methods or best available methods (if the reliability of the method and the nature of the decision justifies the use of the data)" [42 U.S.C. §300g-1(b)(3)(A)]. Generally speaking, would such a requirement be expected to have an impact on the substance of environmental regulation (for example, a rule establishing a maximum exposure level for a toxic substance)? Would it be expected to provide increased opportunity for judicial review of the regulation?

4. Note that unless there is a concomitant increase in agency resources, legislation that expands the responsibilities that an agency must fulfill before issuing its regulations—such as by requiring a cost-benefit analysis or a complicated risk assessment—will tend to reduce the number of regulations that the agency can promulgate.

5. The D.C. Circuit Court of Appeals has held that the requirements of the Regulatory Flexibility Act are not triggered by the indirect effects of a regulation on small entities, but only by the effects on small entities that are directly regulated by the rule in question. See *Motor & Equp. Mrfrs. Ass'n. v. Nichols*, 142 F.3d 449, 467 and n.18 (D.C. Cir. 1998).

6. In 2000, in the waning days of the Clinton administration, Congress enacted the Information (Data) Quality Act, which was added as a short rider to an appropriations bill. The law, which was supported and largely written by business groups, directs the Office of Management and Budget to "issue guidelines ... that provide policy and procedural guidance to Federal agencies for ensuring and maximizing the quality, objectivity, utility, and integrity of information (including statistical information) disseminated by Federal agencies" (Section 515 of the Treasury, Postal Service, and General Government Appropriations Act for Fiscal Year 2001, enacted on December 21, 2000 as part of an omnibus spending bill). See Consolidated Appropriations FY 2001 of 2000, Pub. L. No. 106-554, 114 Stat. 2763A-153 to 2763A-154. Because it establishes guidelines for the "quality, objectivity, utility, and integrity" of scientific data used by federal agencies, and because also it affords interested parties the right to challenge an agency's adherence to those guidelines, the law could have a significant effect on agency rulemaking if it is vigorously enforced. See, generally, Andrew L. Revkin (2002) "Law Revises Standards for Scientific Study: Agencies Face Challenges on Health and Environment Research," *New York Times*, March 21, p. A24; Daniel M. Steinway, "The Data Quality Act: An Emerging Approach for Reviewing EPA and Other Regulatory Decisionmaking," 20 *Toxics Law Reporter* 700 (July 28, 2005).

7. Acting under the Data Quality Act, the White House Office of Management and Budget (OMB) issued a set of detailed draft guidelines in 2006 purporting to standardize the performance of risk assessments by federal agencies. As discussed in chapter 2, these guidelines were roundly criticized by environmental and public health groups as being heavily biased toward long-expressed industry views on risk assessment, and as being designed so as to weaken federal regulation of environmental and public health hazards. After a panel of the National Academy of Sciences concluded that the draft guidelines were "fundamentally flawed," and that OMB's definition of risk assessment itself "conflicts with long-established concepts and practices," OMB withdrew the guidelines. See Cornelia Dean (2007) "Risk Assessment

Plan is Withdrawn," *New York Times*, January 12, p. 19. The role of OMB in influencing agency rulemaking is explored in greater detail later in this chapter.   ■

f. Interpreting the Statutory Mandate

A central task for the agency—and for the courts in reviewing the agency's decisions—is interpreting the statutory mandate. Often this is far from easy. The broader and less specific the substantive mandate, the more difficult it is to divine the intent of Congress. To determine legislative intent, the agency and the courts start logically with the statutory language itself. This basic principle has been well stated by the Supreme Court. "First, always, is the question whether Congress has directly spoken to the precise question at issue. If the intent of Congress is clear, that is the end of the matter, for the court, as well as the agency, must give effect to the unambiguously expressed intent of Congress" [*Chevron U.S A. v. NRDC*, 467 U.S. 837, 842–843 (1984)]. Thus, where the language of the statute is sufficiently clear and unambiguous, the agency need not, and may not, look any further. It must carry out the intent of Congress as expressed in the language of the statute.

In many cases, however, the intent of Congress is not clear from the bare language of the statute. Here one must look behind the language to the statute's legislative history. There are three basic sources of this history. Prior drafts of the statute—the early House and Senate bills—can help reveal what Congress chose not to include in the final statute. This allows one to draw logical inferences about the language that did become law. Reports of the congressional committees that helped draft the language can also be helpful. These reports—the House report, the Senate report, and the Conference report (which is written by representatives of both committees when they meet to work out the compromise language for the final statute)—contain explanatory comments on the final statutory language. Because the Conference report represents something of a consensus document, the courts generally consider it to be the most instructive and influential. The third and generally least influential source of legislative history is the record of the congressional floor debates on the various versions of the statute. Such commentary is most useful when it elucidates positions on both sides of a particular issue and in doing so sheds light on why a particular provision was rejected in favor of another. Quite often, however, senators or representatives have a particular ax to grind and offer comments on a bill with the obvious intent of influencing court interpretations at a later time. Unless such commentary provides evidence of widespread congressional support for the proffered interpretation (or perhaps is given by the chief sponsor of the bill), it is given little weight by the courts.

Finally, courts look to how the agency has interpreted the statute. If the agency's interpretation does not conflict with the language, structure, or legislative history of the statute, the courts generally defer to the agency's interpretation, as long as it is reasonable. In the *Chevron* case cited here, the Supreme Court deferred to EPA's interpretation of an ambiguous phrase in the Clean Water Act. This form of deference to agency reasoning is commonly referred to as "*Chevron* deference."

g. Statutory Amendment and Informal Controls

If Congress believes that an agency is pursuing regulatory policies that run counter to legislative intent or directives (or if it believes that reviewing courts have taken the implementation of a statute in a direction not in concert with Congress' current desires), it has several ways to remedy the problem. The most direct course of action would be for Congress to formally amend the statute to clarify its mandate to the agency. This may not be accomplished easily, however. Congress does not often speak with a unified voice. The passage of a major piece of legislation usually requires considerable time and political compromise. Indeed, certain language may be intentionally left vague to permit such a compromise to be struck. Any attempt to inject further specificity into a piece of legislation by amending it may well face a long and difficult battle. This is not to say that statutes are never changed in response to congressional dissatisfaction with an agency's behavior. The Solid Waste Disposal Act (also known as the Resource Conservation and Recovery Act), for example, was substantially modified in 1984 in response to a widespread perception in Congress that EPA was not moving swiftly enough to regulate the disposal of hazardous waste. To prompt the agency to act, the amendments gave it an explicit timetable for regulating a wide array of specifically enumerated categories of hazardous waste. Congress took a similar approach when it amended the Safe Drinking Water Act in 1986, and when it amended the Clean Air Act provisions for hazardous air pollutants in 1990.

Congress also has a number of informal, more broadly "political" controls at its disposal. For example, members of Congress are free to make statements—on the floor of Congress and in other public fora—that criticize how an agency handles a particular matter. Especially if they receive media attention, such comments can effectively spur the agency to consider a change in direction. Congress also can use committee hearings to question and verbally admonish recalcitrant agency officials. These include oversight hearings held by congressional committees responsible for a particular subject area (such as air pollution), which permit close and often harsh questioning of agency officials, and budget hearings.

During the annual budget period, top agency officials come before Congress to explain and defend the administration's funding proposal for their agency. This gives members of Congress an opportunity to influence behavior by suggesting an increase or threatening a decrease in the agency's overall funding. In the early years of the Reagan administration, for example, both EPA and OSHA were called to task for requesting a budget that many members of Congress believed was too small to fulfill their statutory mandates. In addition, Congress can designate specific line items in an agency's authority for special funding.

h. Federal Regulatory Authority and the States

Federal health, safety, and environmental legislation often gives administrative agencies specific regulatory duties with regard to state governments. As we will see, state agencies play an important role in implementing congressional policy under several federal environmental statutes, subject to the overriding authority of the responsible federal agency. Moreover, some state government facilities can be a significant source of pollution, and they are subject to regulation under federal environmental statutes. The limits of congressional—and thus federal agency—power in this area are defined by the Constitution.

Once the federal government has chosen to take regulatory action in a particular area, what role is left for state and local governments? By and large, the answer is that they may play whatever role the federal government allows them to play, and they may choose to play no role at all. The supremacy clause of Article VI of the U.S. Constitution characterizes the acts of Congress as the "supreme Law of the Land," and the Supreme Court has long interpreted this provision as empowering Congress to preempt state and local laws. In some cases a federal statute or regulation will explicitly specify that state laws governing the same subject matter are prohibited. The National Labor Relations Act, the nation's primary labor law, has such a provision. Other statutes, such as the Clean Air Act and Clean Water Act, explicitly disavow any intent to preempt more stringent state laws. Where a federal statute is silent on the subject of preemption, it is up to the courts—as usual—to divine the intent of Congress. In general, courts will not find an intent to preempt unless (1) the federal law and the state law are so much in conflict that it is impossible to comply with both; (2) the federal government has so pervasively regulated the subject matter area that it can be said to have "preempted the field"; or (3) the state statute or provision can rightly be said to be "an obstacle to the accomplishment of the purposes of Congress." See *Silkwood v. Kerr-McGee Corporation*, 464 U.S. 238, 248 (1984).

May state laws ever preempt federal laws? That is, may a state impose a less stringent regulatory standard in place of a federal standard? This is really the flip side of the federal preemption question, and again the answer flows from the supremacy clause of the Constitution. So long as Congress is acting within its constitutional authority in enacting a regulatory statute, a state may not preempt the operation of that statute within its borders unless Congress has authorized it to do so. Although there are important exceptions, the approach typically taken by Congress in the environmental field has been to use federal legislation to establish minimum standards, and to allow the states to enforce more stringent, but not less stringent, standards of their own. As noted in chapter 4, however, there has been a more recent push in Congress to pass "omnibus" legislation that would explicitly prohibit the states from imposing more stringent environmental standards.

In many circumstances Congress would prefer to do more than simply leave the states free to promulgate their own regulations if they choose to do so. Often Congress deems it preferable to have the states play a key role in implementing and enforcing federal environmental policy. Such was the case with the Low Level Radioactive Waste Policy Act, which was designed to encourage the states to enter into interstate compacts governing the disposal of low-level nuclear waste. Several states challenged the law's basic structure under the Tenth Amendment to the Constitution, which provides that "[t]he powers not delegated to the United States by the Constitution, nor prohibited by it to the States, are reserved to the States." The cases were consolidated on appeal, and the Supreme Court's resolution of this controversy constitutes a primer on the relevant issues of federalism in this area.

New York v. United States
Justice O'CONNOR delivered the opinion of the Court
505 U.S. 144 (1992)
(United States Supreme Court)

These cases implicate one of our Nation's newest problems of public policy and perhaps our oldest question of constitutional law. The public policy issue involves the disposal of radioactive waste.... The constitutional question is as old as the Constitution: It consists of discerning the proper division of authority between the Federal Government and the States. We conclude that while Congress has substantial power under the Constitution to encourage the States to provide for the disposal of the radioactive waste generated within their borders, the Constitution does not confer upon Congress the ability simply to compel the States to do so....

II.   A

In 1788, in the course of explaining to the citizens of New York why the recently drafted Constitution provided for federal courts, Alexander Hamilton observed: "The

erection of a new government, whatever care or wisdom may distinguish the work, cannot fail to originate questions of intricacy and nicety; and these may, in a particular manner, be expected to flow from the establishment of a constitution founded upon the total or partial incorporation of a number of distinct sovereignties." The Federalist No. 82, p. 491 (C. Rossiter ed. 1961). Hamilton's prediction has proved quite accurate.... [T]he Court has resolved questions "of great importance and delicacy" in determining whether particular sovereign powers have been granted by the Constitution to the Federal Government or have been retained by the States.

These questions can be viewed in either of two ways. In some cases the Court has inquired whether an Act of Congress is authorized by one of the powers delegated to Congress in Article I of the Constitution. In other cases the Court has sought to determine whether an Act of Congress invades the province of state sovereignty reserved by the Tenth Amendment. In a case like these, involving the division of authority between federal and state governments, the two inquiries are mirror images of each other. If a power is delegated to Congress in the Constitution, the Tenth Amendment expressly disclaims any reservation of that power to the States; if a power is an attribute of state sovereignty reserved by the Tenth Amendment, it is necessarily a power the Constitution has not conferred on Congress.

It is in this sense that the Tenth Amendment "states but a truism that all is retained which has not been surrendered." United States v. Darby, *312 U.S. 100, 124, 85 L. Ed. 609, 61 S. Ct. 451 (1941).* As Justice Story put it, "this amendment is a mere affirmation of what, upon any just reasoning, is a necessary rule of interpreting the constitution. Being an instrument of limited and enumerated powers, it follows irresistibly, that what is not conferred, is withheld, and belongs to the state authorities." 3 J. Story, Commentaries on the Constitution of the United States 752 (1833). This has been the Court's consistent understanding: "The States unquestionably do retain a significant measure of sovereign authority...to the extent that the Constitution has not divested them of their original powers and transferred those powers to the Federal Government." *Garcia v. San Antonio Metropolitan Transit Authority,* 469 U.S. 528, 549 (1985) (internal quotation marks omitted).

Congress exercises its conferred powers subject to the limitations contained in the Constitution. Thus, for example, under the Commerce Clause Congress may regulate publishers engaged in interstate commerce, but Congress is constrained in the exercise of that power by the First Amendment. The Tenth Amendment likewise restrains the power of Congress, but this limit is not derived from the text of the Tenth Amendment itself, which, as we have discussed, is essentially a tautology. Instead, the Tenth Amendment confirms that the power of the Federal Government is subject to limits that may, in a given instance, reserve power to the States. The Tenth Amendment thus directs us to determine, as in this case, whether an incident of state sovereignty is protected by a limitation on an Article I power....

B

Petitioners [the State of New York and two New York counties] do not contend that Congress lacks the power to regulate the disposal of low level radioactive waste. Space in radioactive waste disposal sites is frequently sold by residents of one State to residents of another. Regulation of the resulting interstate market in waste disposal is therefore well within Congress' authority under the Commerce Clause. Petitioners likewise do not dispute that under the Supremacy Clause Congress could, if it wished, preempt state radioactive waste regulation. Petitioners contend only that the Tenth Amendment limits the power of Congress to regulate in the way it has chosen. Rather than addressing the problem of waste disposal by directly regulating the generators and disposers of waste, petitioners argue, Congress has impermissibly directed the States to regulate in this field....

This litigation [thus] concerns the circumstances under which Congress may use the States as implements of regulation; that is, whether Congress may direct or otherwise motivate the States to regulate in a particular field or a particular way. Our cases have established a few principles that guide our resolution of the issue.

1. As an initial matter, Congress may not simply "commandeer the legislative processes of the States by directly compelling them to enact and enforce a federal regulatory program." *Hodel v. Virginia Surface Mining & Reclamation Assn., Inc.,* 452 U.S. 264, 288, 69 L. Ed. 2d 1, 101 S. Ct. 2352 (1981). In *Hodel,* the Court upheld the Surface Mining

Control and Reclamation Act of 1977 precisely because it did *not* "commandeer" the States into regulating mining. The Court found that "the States are not compelled to enforce the steep-slope standards, to expend any state funds, or to participate in the federal regulatory program in any manner whatsoever. If a State does not wish to submit a proposed permanent program that complies with the Act and implementing regulations, the full regulatory burden will be borne by the Federal Government."...

2. This is not to say that Congress lacks the ability to encourage a State to regulate in a particular way, or that Congress may not hold out incentives to the States as a method of influencing a State's policy choices. Our cases have identified a variety of methods, short of outright coercion, by which Congress may urge a State to adopt a legislative program consistent with federal interests. Two of these methods are of particular relevance here.

First, under Congress' spending power, "Congress may attach conditions on the receipt of federal funds." *South* Dakota v. Dole, *483 U.S. 203, 206 (1987)*. Such conditions must (among other requirements) bear some relationship to the purpose of the federal spending....

Second, where Congress has the authority to regulate private activity under the Commerce Clause, we have recognized Congress' power to offer States the choice of regulating that activity according to federal standards or having state law preempted by federal regulation....

With these principles in mind, we turn to the three challenged provisions of the Low Level Radioactive Waste Policy Amendments Act of 1985.

III

...Construed as a whole, the Act comprises three sets of "incentives" for the States to provide for the disposal of low level radioactive waste generated within their borders. We consider each in turn.

A

...The Act's first set of incentives, in which Congress has conditioned grants to the States upon the States' attainment of a series of milestones, is...well within the authority of Congress under the Commerce and Spending Clauses. Because the first set of incentives is supported by affirmative constitutional grants of power to Congress, it is not inconsistent with the Tenth Amendment.

B

...In the second set of incentives, Congress has authorized States and regional compacts with disposal sites gradually to increase the cost of access to the sites, and then to deny access altogether, to radioactive waste generated in States that do not meet federal deadlines. As a simple regulation, this provision would be within the power of Congress to authorize the States to discriminate against interstate commerce....

The Act's second set of incentives thus represents a conditional exercise of Congress' commerce power, along the lines of those we have held to be within Congress' authority. As a result, the second set of incentives does not intrude on the sovereignty reserved to the States by the Tenth Amendment.

C

The take title provision is of a different character. This third so-called "incentive" offers States, as an alternative to regulating pursuant to Congress' direction, the option of taking title to and possession of the low level radioactive waste generated within their borders and becoming liable for all damages waste generators suffer as a result of the States' failure to do so promptly. In this provision, Congress has crossed the line distinguishing encouragement from coercion....

The take title provision offers state governments a "choice" of either accepting ownership of waste or regulating according to the instructions of Congress. Respondents [the United States and certain individual states supporting the law who had intervened in the case as defendants] do not claim that the Constitution would authorize Congress to impose either option as a freestanding requirement. On one hand, the Constitution would not permit Congress simply to transfer radioactive waste from generators to state governments. Such a forced transfer, standing alone, would in principle be no different [from] a congressionally compelled subsidy from state governments to radioactive waste producers. The same is true of the provision requiring the States to become liable for the generators' damages. Standing alone, this provision would be indistinguishable from an Act of Congress directing the States to assume the liabilities of certain state residents. Either type of federal action would "commandeer" state governments into the service of federal regulatory purposes, and would for this reason be inconsistent with the Constitution's division of authority between federal and state governments. On the other hand, the second alternative held out to state governments—regulating pursuant to Congress' direction—would, standing alone, present a simple command to state governments to implement legislation enacted by Congress. As we have seen, the Constitution does not empower Congress to subject state governments to this type of instruction.

Because an instruction to state governments to take title to waste, standing alone, would be beyond the authority of Congress, and because a direct order to regulate, standing alone, would also be beyond the authority of Congress, it follows that Congress lacks the power to offer the States a choice between the two. Unlike the first two sets of incentives, the take title incentive does not represent the conditional exercise of any congressional power enumerated in the Constitution. In this provision, Congress has not held out the threat of exercising its spending power or its commerce power; it has instead held out the threat, should the States not regulate according to one federal instruction, of simply forcing the States to submit to another federal instruction. A choice between two unconstitutionally coercive regulatory techniques is no choice at all. Either way, "the Act commandeers the legislative processes of the States by directly compelling them to enact and enforce a federal regulatory program," Hodel v. Virginia Surface Mining & Reclamation Assn., Inc., *452 U.S. at 288*, an outcome that has never been understood to lie within the authority conferred upon Congress by the Constitution.

Respondents emphasize the latitude given to the States to implement Congress' plan. The Act enables the States to regulate pursuant to Congress' instructions in any number of different ways. States may avoid taking title by contracting with sited regional compacts, by building a disposal site alone or as part of a compact, or by permitting private parties to build a disposal site. States that host sites may employ a wide range of designs and disposal methods, subject only to broad federal regulatory limits. This line of reasoning, however, only underscores the critical alternative a State lacks: A State may not decline to administer the federal program. No matter which path the State chooses, it must follow the direction of Congress.

The take title provision appears to be unique. No other federal statute has been cited which offers a state government no option other than that of implementing legislation enacted by Congress. Whether one views the take title provision as lying outside Congress' enumerated powers, or as infringing upon the core of state sovereignty reserved by the Tenth Amendment, the provision is inconsistent with the federal structure of our Government established by the Constitution....

VII

Some truths are so basic that, like the air around us, they are easily overlooked. Much of the Constitution is concerned with setting forth the form of our government, and the courts have traditionally invalidated measures deviating from that form. The result may appear "formalistic" in a given case to partisans of the measure at issue, because such measures are typically the product of the era's perceived necessity. But the Constitution protects us from our own best intentions: It divides power among sovereigns and among branches of government precisely so that we may resist the temptation to concentrate power in one location as an expedient solution to the crisis of the day. The shortage of disposal sites for radioactive waste is a pressing national problem, but a judiciary that licensed extraconstitutional government with each issue of comparable gravity would, in the long run, be far worse.

States are not mere political subdivisions of the United States. State governments are neither regional offices nor administrative agencies of the Federal Government. The positions occupied by state officials appear nowhere on the Federal Government's most detailed organizational chart. The Constitution instead "leaves to the several States a residuary and inviolable sovereignty," The Federalist No. 39, p. 245 (C. Rossiter ed. 1961), reserved explicitly to the States by the Tenth Amendment.

Whatever the outer limits of that sovereignty may be, one thing is clear: The Federal Government may not compel the States to enact or administer a federal regulatory program. The Constitution permits both the Federal Government and the States to enact legislation regarding the disposal of low level radioactive waste. The Constitution enables the Federal Government to preempt state regulation contrary to federal interests, and it permits the Federal Government to hold out incentives to the States as a means of encouraging them to adopt suggested regulatory schemes. It does not, however, authorize Congress simply to direct the States to provide for the disposal of the radioactive waste generated within their borders. While there may be many constitutional methods of achieving regional self-sufficiency in radioactive waste disposal, the method Congress has chosen is not one of them.

■ NOTES

1. Justice Byron White, joined by Justices John Paul Stevens and Harry Blackmun, dissented from that portion of the decision invalidating the act's "take title" provisions. The dissent did not dispute the basic Tenth Amendment principles enunciated by the majority, but rather argued that the majority had failed to appreciate the importance of the fact that Congress had enacted the low-level waste act at the urging of several states. The federal statute, noted Justice White, "resulted from the efforts of state leaders to achieve a state-based set of remedies to the waste problem. They sought not federal pre-emption or intervention, but rather congressional sanction of interstate compromises they had reached" (505 U.S. at 189–190). As Justice White read the case record, New York itself had agreed to the general structure of the law,

including the take-title provision, and had benefitted from the fact that the law had encouraged other states to enter into interstate compacts governing low-level nuclear waste. "The State should be stopped from asserting the unconstitutionality of a provision that seeks merely to ensure that, after deriving substantial advantages from the 1985 Act, New York in fact must live up to its bargain by establishing an in-state low-level radioactive waste facility or assuming liability for its failure to act" (id. at 198–199).

2. In a portion of the majority opinion not reprinted here, the Court was careful to note that the federal-state framework embedded in the Constitution had not prevented Congress from expanding the role played by the federal government in shaping public policy:

> This framework has been sufficiently flexible over the past two centuries to allow for enormous changes in the nature of government. The Federal Government undertakes activities today that would have been unimaginable to the Framers in two senses; first, because the Framers would not have conceived that *any* government would conduct such activities; and second, because the Framers would not have believed that the *Federal* Government, rather than the States, would assume such responsibilities. Yet the powers conferred upon the Federal Government by the Constitution were phrased in language broad enough to allow for the expansion of the Federal Government's role. (id. at 157)

3. Why might Congress choose to have the states, rather than EPA, do much of the day-to-day permitting and enforcement under federal statutes such as the Clean Air Act and the Clean Water Act?   ■

Beyond their role as regulators of pollution, state governments can also be sources of pollution themselves. A state prison discharging sewage into a river, for example, is a source of water pollution. Although the issue is perhaps not fully resolved, it appears fairly clear that Congress may subject the states to federal environmental laws and thus may regulate pollution emanating from state facilities. While it may empower federal agencies to enforce federal environmental regulations against the states, however, it appears that Congress may not authorize private citizens to bring enforcement suits against the states. The Eleventh Amendment to the Constitution, which deals with the "sovereign immunity" of the federal government (the right of the government, as a "sovereign," to choose the conditions under which it will be subject to a lawsuit), also provides that the federal courts may not be given jurisdiction over suits "against one of the United States by Citizens of another State." Although the Eleventh Amendment thus does not extend to suits brought against a state by its own citizens, the Supreme Court has long held that this language merely confirms the broader principle, deemed by the Court to be inherent in the structure of the Constitution, that states enjoy sovereign immunity from any suit brought against them in federal court.

Until recently, however, it had been thought that Congress could abrogate this immunity as part of a federal regulatory statute, thus subjecting the states to suits brought under that statute, and a plurality of the Supreme Court had affirmed this principle in *Pennsylvania v. Union Gas Co.*, 491 U.S. 1 (1989). In a subsequent 5 to 4 opinion, however, a majority of the Court rebuked this approach and held that Congress has no power under the commerce clause to abrogate the inherent sovereign immunity enjoyed by the states. See *Seminole Tribe of Florida v. Florida*, 517 U.S. 44 (1996). Accordingly, Congress would appear to lack the power to authorize private citizens to bring suit against a state under a federal environmental statute without the state's consent. This would apply both to suits to bring a state facility into compliance with the law and to suits to compel a state to carry out a regulatory duty it had agreed to perform under the law.

■ **NOTES**

1. In the *Seminole Tribe* case, the Court distinguished the power of Congress under the commerce clause from its power under the Fourteenth Amendment (which, among other things, prohibits the states from engaging in certain types of discrimination). The Fourteenth Amendment, noted the Court, expressly provides that "Congress shall have the power to enforce, by appropriate legislation, this article." This, said the Court, gives Congress the power to abrogate state sovereign immunity with regard to legislation enacted under the Fourteenth Amendment.

2. Sovereign immunity does not apply where the "sovereign" has consented to be sued. Is there a way that Congress could, consistent with the principles of federalism laid out in *New York v. U.S.*, implement a federal environmental program under which private citizens were authorized to enforce the federal requirements against noncompliant states in federal court? (Note that Congress has no power to affect the jurisdiction of state courts and thus could not create such a right in state court.)

3. In general, state sovereign immunity from federal court suit applies only to the state government itself, and not to separate governmental entities within the state, such as cities, counties, regional authorities, and the like. See, e.g., *Mancuso v. New York Thruway Auth.*, 86 F.3d 289 (2nd Cir. 1996) (the Thruway Authority is not a state agency for the purposes of Eleventh Amendment immunity). Furthermore, federal suits brought by citizens against state officials who fail to comply with federal law may be viable under the doctrine of *Ex Parte Young* 209 U.S. 123 (1908). See, e.g., *Strahan v. Coxe*, 127 F.3d 155 (1st Cir. 1997); *Natural Resources Defense Council v. California Dep't. of Transp.*, 96 F.3d 420 (9th Cir. 1996).

4. The issue of whether Congress has the power under the commerce clause to subject the states to federal environmental laws is likely to be addressed by the courts in the early part of this century. Recently, the State of Nebraska brought suit against the Environmental Protection Agency, seeking to bar enforcement against instrumentalities of the state of certain standards promulgated under the federal Safe Drinking Water Act. Nebraska argued that to the extent that the statute purports to apply to state facilities, it both exceeded the power granted to Congress under the commerce clause and violated the reservation of powers to the states set forth in the Tenth Amendment. Because the case was dismissed on procedural grounds (the state had not challenged the regulations within the time allowed by the statute), the court did not address these constitutional issues. See *Nebraska v. United States*, 238 F.3d 946 (8th Cir. 2001).

2. Direction from the Executive Branch

Although they are usually created by the legislative branch (as noted, EPA is an exception), administrative agencies sit within the executive branch. Accordingly, the executive also exercises considerable control over agency decision making. Much of the executive's influence over the direction of an agency stems from the president's control of the appointment process. Most statutes that create an administrative agency also permit the president to appoint the agency's top decisionmakers (the so-called political appointments), subject to the approval of the Senate. The power to appoint includes the power to remove from office, along with all the more subtle means of persuasion that lie between the two. The underlying theory, presumably, is that each new administration should be free, within the bounds of the applicable statutory mandates, to chart the direction of the agencies that operate within its purview. However, this approach often entails an inherent conflict because the direction favored by the administration frequently differs from that favored by Congress. This appears to be an accepted part of the political process.

The executive branch also wields considerable influence over the agencies through the budget process. Although final approval of the national budget rests with Congress, the budget is shaped in large part by the proposed budget submitted to Congress by the president. Even more directly than Congress, then, the executive branch can use its grip on the national purse strings to expand the size of those regulatory programs it favors and to reduce the size of those it does not. Furthermore, since 1980 the president has used the Office of Management and Budget to oversee an economic analysis of all proposed major regulations. This has had a significant effect on the regulatory initiatives proposed by OSHA and EPA, and, as the following commentary from the Reagan era indicates, has generated substantial controversy.

An Obstacle to Public Safety
William B. Schultz and David C. Vladeck
Source: *The Washington Post*, May 10, 1988, p. 20, reprinted with permission.

Before President Ronald Reagan was elected, the principal function of the Office of Management and Budget was to manage the federal budget. But [since 1980], OMB has taken on a new role that has had a chilling effect on regulations designed to protect consumers and workers.

OMB's authority comes from an executive order issued less than a month after Reagan took office. It requires that OMB review all major federal regulatory decisions and do an economic analysis of the costs of implementing each proposal. This little-noticed order from the White House has accomplished perhaps the most significant change in administrative law in the past 50 years.

Take the case of asbestos. In the early 1960s, asbestos was identified as a hazard that killed thousands of people annually, and in 1984 the Environmental Protection Agency proposed to phase out this substance over five to 15 years. But the proposal, like every important regulation issued by federal health and safety agencies during the Reagan administration, had a major hurdle to overcome: the Office of Management and Budget.

OMB performed a cost-benefit analysis, balancing the lives that would be lost if asbestos were permitted to be used in products such as insulation against the cost to industry of a ban. Its officials decided that a life is worth $1 million but then used an economist's tool called "discounting" to adjust for their expectation that most people would not die from asbestos-induced cancer until many years after their initial exposure. Using discounting, OMB's economists calculated the adjusted value of a human life at $208,000. OMB found that the regulation was not justified because its costs exceeded the value of

human lives saved, and sent it back to EPA for revision. . . .

The pace of standard-setting at the Occupational Safety and Health Administration (OSHA), which was always slow, is now glacial. Created in 1970, OSHA's mandate is to foster a safe environment for American workers. One of its principal tools is the strict limitations that it places on toxic substances in the workplace.

Although OSHA had been averaging two to three health regulations per year, the agency did not issue a single standard during the first 2 1/2 years of the Reagan administration, and it has issued only six standards during the past seven years [1981 through 1987]. Four of these—ethylene oxide, benzene, formaldehyde and field sanitation—were issued only after a court order setting a specific deadline for agency action.

In the process, OMB succeeded in delaying standards for several years or more. A good example is ethylene oxide (EtO), a highly toxic and carcinogenic gas widely used in hospitals to sterilize medical equipment. In 1981, OSHA estimated that at exposure levels then permitted in the workplace, from 6 to 10 percent of 75,000 exposed hospital workers would get cancer over the course of their lives.

In 1983, a federal appeals court found that OSHA had illegally delayed the stronger EtO standard and ordered the agency to act. OSHA drafted a standard that was generally acceptable to labor and consumer groups, but the hospital industry objected to the part of the regulation that limited the amount of EtO a worker could receive in a single burst.

Having lost at OSHA, the industry took its case to OMB, which adopted the industry's view and overruled OSHA. That decision

[handwritten margin notes at top: "estimated 1500 excess lung cancer cases b/c of OMB delay"; "OSHA deals with worker safety"]

was also reversed by the court of appeals, and, nearly two years later, the new regulation was issued in March [1988].

OSHA's benzene regulation suffered a similar fate; it was delayed three years before being issued in 1987.

One of the most troubling instances of current OMB interference involves cadmium, a metal used in electroplating and extensively in industrial processing. OSHA estimates that more than 213,000 workers are exposed to very high levels of cadmium. As a result, health officials estimate, there may be 1,106 excess cancer deaths per 10,000 workers, affecting 11 percent of the work force. Even greater numbers could suffer kidney damage, according to OSHA.

In the past, OSHA acted very quickly to curb exposures. Today, after factoring in OMB review, OSHA estimates that it will take three years to issue a cadmium standard. The agency projects that for each year it delays, nearly 500 workers could contract cadmium-induced lung cancer.

[handwritten margin note: "FDA"]

The Food and Drug Administration, one of the oldest federal regulatory agencies, is charged with regulating foods, drugs, and cosmetics. It has always been seen as relatively non-political. Yet today, every important FDA decision must survive a political review at OMB.

Unlike OSHA standards, most of the regulations that the FDA ultimately issues have not been significantly changed by OMB. But when important public health issues are at stake, OMB has delayed and indirectly blocked FDA regulations.

Take the case of aspirin and Reye's syndrome. Reye's syndrome is a rare but sometimes fatal disease that in the late 1970s was killing several hundred children a year. In the fall of 1981, the federal Centers for Disease Control, supported by four separate studies, identified a link between Reye's syndrome and the use of aspirin by children with flu and chicken pox.

No one suggested that aspirin be taken off the market, but the FDA drafted a proposed regulation that would have required a warning label.

[handwritten margin note: "Reyes Syndrom"]

The aspirin industry immediately began lobbying OMB. The president of its trade association, the Aspirin Foundation, met with a high-level OMB official, who, as he later recounted in a sworn deposition, reviewed the FDA's scientific data concerning the link between aspirin and Reye's syndrome. Within a few days, he rejected the work that it had taken scientists at the FDA more than six months to complete. Shortly thereafter, the FDA decided to kill the proposed regulation until an additional study was completed.

In February 1986, almost four years later, the FDA at last issued a final regulation requiring the warning label on aspirin products, and the incidence of Reye's syndrome, which also had received considerable publicity, has since declined significantly.

[handwritten margin note: "What does this have to do w/ costs?"]

OMB's impact on health and safety regulation is not limited to highly publicized cases such as aspirin. Often, FDA officials choose not to issue important regulations because they know that OMB will not give its approval. Usually, the public never learns about these efforts that are not pursued, but one extraordinary example, urethane in alcohol, has recently come to light.

Urethane is a carcinogen found in many alcoholic beverages. Canada, at the end of 1985, set limits in wine and liquor. While there are many uncertainties in applying data from animal research to humans, one study concluded that daily consumption of the amount of urethane in two shots of many brands of bourbon sold in the U.S. might cause cancer in one in 200 people. Gary Flamm, director of FDA's Office of Toxicological Sciences, ranks urethane among the top three carcinogens that should be feared. Concerned about these risks, the FDA and the industry have tested about 1,000 products to determine their urethane levels, and about

[handwritten margin note: "Possible correlation w/ cancer animal research"]

[handwritten note at bottom: "OMB Sucks"]

100 have been found to have levels that exceed the Canadian limits. The Center for Science in the Public Interest has petitioned the FDA to follow Canada's lead and regulate this carcinogen.

The agency seriously considered issuing a regulation, but, instead, entered into voluntary agreements with the wine and liquor industry under which the manufacturers would not meet the Canadian limits until 1995. The agreements, moreover, are not enforceable by the FDA.

The problem with OMB review is that it allows economists who have little contact with the regulatory agency and virtually no technical expertise to evaluate essentially scientific decisions. OMB compounds the damage by leaving no paper trail, so the public often blames other agencies for delays or inadequate regulations that were the fault of OMB.

Until now, most of the criticism of OMB has come from the public interest community. Industry lobbyists have kept quiet as they successfully use OMB to overrule agency decisions that displease their clients. But these same lobbyists privately have expressed concerns about OMB review. They realize that their success will come back to haunt them if there is a shift in the political winds.

President Reagan's 1981 Executive Order 12291 (the core substance of which remains in effect under a 1993 executive order issued by President Clinton) required OMB to review significant new regulatory actions to ensure that the potential benefits to society outweigh the potential costs, with such benefits and costs to be quantified in monetary terms. In essence, this order imposed the cost-benefit criterion as a prerequisite to promulgation of federal regulations. As noted in the Schultz and Vladeck article, OMB has used the review authority granted by this order to delay the promulgation of several regulations. A precursor to this executive order was President Ford's 1974 Executive Order 11821, which required that all regulations issued by executive branch agencies be accompanied by an inflationary impact statement, where "inflationary" was defined by the Council on Wage and Price Stability as a situation in which the costs of the regulation exceeded the benefits. However, it did not require that the regulation not be inflationary, only that the inflationary impacts be evaluated.

Similarly, President Carter's Executive Order 12044 required federal agencies to analyze the economic consequences of significant regulations and their alternatives, but it imposed no cost-benefit requirement. Although President Clinton's 1993 executive order expressly revoked President Reagan's order, it repromulgated many of the basic concepts and retained the cost-benefit review as a key part of OMB's role.

The Clinton order is Executive Order 12866, 58 *Fed. Reg.* 51735 (Sept. 30, 1993). This order requires agencies to submit detailed information on anticipated costs and benefits for OMB review before they take any "significant regulatory action," which is defined as an action that is likely to result in a rule that may have "an annual effect on the economy of $100 million or more," that may "adversely affect in a material way the economy, a sector of the economy, productivity, competition, jobs, the environment, public health or safety, or State, local, or tribal governments or communities," or that may meet another of the criteria enumerated therein. The cost and benefit information submitted is to be quantified "to the extent feasible." See Executive Order 12866, Sections 3(f) and 6(a)(3)(B). OMB in turn is directed to "provide meaningful guidance and oversight so that each agency's regulatory actions are consistent with applicable law, the President's priorities, and the principles set forth in the Executive Order" [id. Section 6(b)]. The cost-benefit criterion is incorporated in the following "Principle of Regulation" stated in the order:

Each agency shall assess both the costs and benefits of the intended regulation and, recognizing that some costs and benefits are difficult to quantify, propose or adopt a regulation only upon a reasoned determination that the benefits of the intended regulation justify its costs. (id., Section 1(b)(6))

In 2007, President George W. Bush amended the Clinton order to add to the cost-benefit review the requirement that the agency justify each proposed major regulation by demonstrating the existence of a specific market failure, or a specific failure of public institutions, that warrants the new action. See Executive Order 13422, 72 *Fed. Reg.* 2763 (Jan. 18, 2007) (http://www.sba.gov/advo/laws/eo12866.pdf). The 2007 order also creates the position of "Regulatory Policy Officer" within federal agencies, as presidential appointees, and specifies OMB authority over the regulatory "guidance documents" required by an OMB bulletin issued a few days later. See Final Bulletin for Agency Good Guidance Practices, 72 *Fed. Reg.* 3432 (Jan. 25, 2007) (http://www.whitehouse.gov/omb/fedreg/2007/012507_good_guidance.pdf). The bulletin requires federal agencies to submit for OMB review "guidance documents" that detail the agency's regulatory philosophy. These guidance documents are ultimately to be submitted to the public for comment, but only after they have been reviewed and (presumably) shaped and edited by OMB. For a critical commentary on these requirements, and of this expansion of OMB's behind-the-scenes role in agency decision making, see Matt Madia and Rick Melbirth. 2007. A Failure to Govern: Bush's Attack on the Regulatory Process, OMB Watch, Washington, D.C. (http://www.ombwatch.org/regs/PDFs/FailuretoGovern.pdf)

▪ NOTES

1. For a more detailed, scholarly review that comes to the same general conclusions about OMB's role as the Schultz and Vladek article, see E. D. Olson (1984) "The Quiet Shift of Power: Office of Management and Budget Supervision of Environmental Protection Agency Rulemaking Under Executive Order 12291," 4 *Virginia Journal of Natural Resources Law* 1. For two such articles coming to a contrary

conclusion, see Bernstein (1982) "The Presidential Role in Administrative Rulemaking: Improving Policy Directives: One Vote for Not Tying the President's Hands," 56 *Tulane Law Review* 818; and Comment, "Capitalizing on a Congressional Void: Executive Order 12291," 31 *American Unversity Law Review* 613 (1981). For a more detailed exploration of cost-benefit analysis as a guide for decision making, see chapter 3.

2. OMB has sought to impose the cost-benefit criterion on agency decision making even when the underlying statute has required that the regulation be promulgated according to criteria other than cost-benefit balancing. It uses this criterion in its review of workplace health regulations proposed by OSHA, for example, even though the Supreme Court has held that such regulations are to be set according to technological and economic feasibility, and not according to a weighing of costs and benefits. See *American Textile Manufacturers Institute v. Donovan*, 452 U.S. 490 (1981). Is this approach consonant with the executive order's directive that OMB endeavor to ensure that agency regulation is "consistent with applicable law?" Moreover, what issue of constitutional law does it raise? On the other hand, what arguments might OMB make to support its role in the face of a conflicting congressional mandate? And note that, even where OMB's legal authority to impose the cost-benefit criterion may be weak, its practical, political authority may be strong, especially when it is backed by a strong president.

3. The philosophical tension between Congress and the president on the cost-benefit issue would appear to have been lessened by the former's embrace of the cost-benefit criterion in the Unfunded Mandates Reform Act of 1995. As discussed earlier in this chapter, however, that law applies to a more limited class of "major" regulations, and it does not require that the benefits of a regulation outweigh its costs.

4. OMB has a limited, *congressionally delegated* authority to influence the content of agency regulations under the Paperwork Reduction Act (PRA), 44 U.S.C. §3501, *et seq*. The general purpose of the PRA is to reduce the public and private burdens incident to government data-gathering activities, and the act directs OMB to oversee the work of other agencies in furtherance of this purpose. One of OMB's responsibilities in this regard is to "maximize the practical utility of and public benefit from information collected by or for the Federal Government" [44 U.S.C. §3504(c)(4)]. OMB has used this authority to raise questions about the contents of various agency information requests, such as workplace health surveys conducted by the National Institute for Occupational Safety and Health. However, the Supreme Court held that the PRA did not authorize OMB to review OSHA's Hazard Communication Standard, which requires employers to generate and disclose to their workers certain information about chemicals used in the workplace, because the PRA pertains only to

the collection of information by, or for the use of, the federal government. See *Dole v. United Steelworkers of America*, 494 U.S. 26 (1990).   ■

3. Direction from the Judicial Branch

Absent a statutory or constitutional amendment, the ultimate arbiters of the meaning of a particular statute or constitutional provision are the courts. This principle flows from the venerable case of *Marbury v. Madison*, 1 Cranch 137, 2 L. Ed.60 (1803), in which the Supreme Court held that a court could invalidate an act of Congress if it found the statutory language to be in violation of the Constitution. In a very real sense, what an agency can or must do is what the courts—in interpreting the relevant statutory or constitutional provisions—say it can or must do. Congress can amend a statute to circumvent a judicial interpretation that it does not like, but even the new statutory language will face potential scrutiny by a reviewing court.

As powerful as the judicial branch is, however, it has at least one major Achilles heel. Unless someone brings a lawsuit, even the nine justices of the nation's most powerful judicial body—the United States Supreme Court—can do absolutely nothing to correct an agency action or decision that they believe to be unconstitutional or in violation of the agency's statutory mandate. Even if a lawsuit is filed, the Supreme Court cannot act on the matter until the case winds its way up from the lower courts, a process that can take years. (There are special circumstances in which a case can originate in the Supreme Court, but these are quite limited.)

Familiarity and comfort with the court system take time and cannot be gained through a few readings in a textbook. The following piece describes briefly what courts do and how the federal judicial system is organized.

Constitutional Courts
J. H. Ferguson and D. E. McHenry

Source: *The American System of Government*. McGraw-Hill, New York, 1981, pp. 441–453. Reprinted with permission of the McGraw-Hill Companies.

The judicial article of the Constitution, Article III, is amazingly brief. It consists of but six paragraphs, the reading of which provides little understanding of our judicial system. The key to understanding is the opening sentence: "The judicial power of the United States, shall be vested in one supreme Court, and in such inferior Courts as the Congress may from time to time ordain and establish." ...

FEDERAL JUDGES

The Omnibus Judgeship Act of 1978 provided additional judgeships, creating positions in 117 district courts and 35 courts of appeals [figure 5.1]—the largest single increase in Federal judgeships in American history... The filling of those 152 positions [brought] the total number of sitting judges

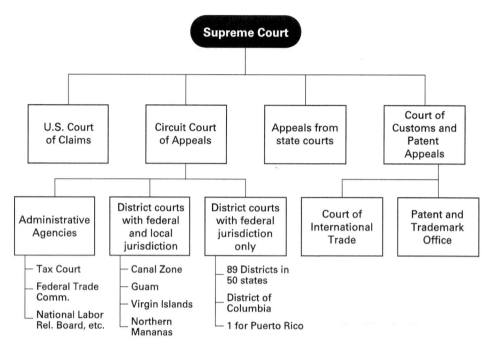

Figure 5.1
The federal judicial system, like that in each of the states, consists of trial and appellate courts. (Source: J. H. Ferguson and D. E. McHenry, *The American System of Government*. McGraw-Hill, New York, 1981.)

to about 650, more than three-fourths of whom preside at the district-court level. The new legislation also authorized the President to promulgate "standards and guidelines" for the selection of new judges on the basis of merit. Moreover, it stipulated that in making nominations the President should "give due consideration to qualified women, blacks, Hispanics and other minority individuals."

Selection and Appointment

All Federal judges are appointed by the President with the advice and consent of the Senate for terms of "good behavior." No qualifications are stated in the Constitution; hence the President is free to appoint anyone whom the Senate agrees to confirm. Although the President appoints judges, the rule of sen-

atorial courtesy has traditionally required that a name submitted be acceptable to one or both senators, when of the President's party, in whose state the vacancy exists. Critics have for years claimed that the system unduly politicizes judicial selection; slows down the appointing process; fosters discrimination for reasons of race, national origin, creed, partisanship, and sex; and reduces the likelihood of having a judiciary worthy of commanding the confidence and respect required during the uncertain times ahead. . . .

Judicial salaries are fixed by Congress; they can be raised at any time, but they cannot be lowered during the incumbency of any particular judge. At the age of seventy, or at sixty-five with fifteen years on the bench, judges may retire or resign at full pay. If they retire, they are eligible for special assignments of a

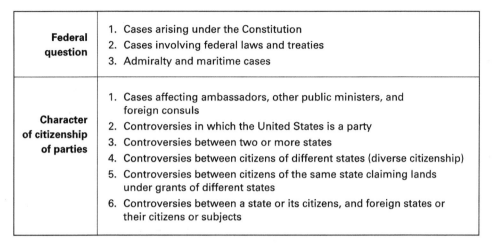

Federal question	1. Cases arising under the Constitution 2. Cases involving federal laws and treaties 3. Admiralty and maritime cases
Character of citizenship of parties	1. Cases affecting ambassadors, other public ministers, and foreign consuls 2. Controversies in which the United States is a party 3. Controversies between two or more states 4. Controversies between citizens of different states (diverse citizenship) 5. Controversies between citizens of the same state claiming lands under grants of different states 6. Controversies between a state or its citizens, and foreign states or their citizens or subjects

Figure 5.2
Types of cases and controversies. (Source: J. H. Ferguson and D. E. McHenry, *The American System of Government.* McGraw-Hill, New York, 1981.)

judicial character. Unlike most pension plans, the Federal one for judges requires no financial contributions from their own earnings during the course of employment.

After assuming office, judges are required by . . . canons of judicial ethics to refrain from such political activity as holding office in a political organization; making speeches for, or publicly endorsing, a political organization or candidate; soliciting funds, paying an assessment, or making a contribution to a political organization or candidate; attending political gatherings or purchasing tickets for political party dinners or other functions; and running for office without first resigning.

Removal from Office

The fact that no definite time limit is placed on judicial tenure has been understood to mean that terms run for life or until a judge chooses to resign or retire. It has also been understood that forcible removal was possible only by the impeachment process, although the Constitution does not explicitly state this to be the case. . . .

Jurisdiction

The term "jurisdiction" refers to the types of disputes and issues which may be taken to Federal courts for decision.

Constitutional courts may deal only with "cases" and "controversies." This explains why they will not give "advisory opinions" when asked by the President or Congress to clarify legal issues. Cases and controversies arise from contests between litigants who have rights and interests at stake and standing to sue in Federal courts. The rights and interests must be real and substantial, not hypothetical or trivial. . . .

The classes of cases and controversies which may come before Federal courts are shown [in figure 5.2]. Some of these raise Federal questions, i.e., they involve the Constitution, acts of Congress, treaties, or vessels on navigable waters. Others reach Federal courts because of the character or citizenship of the parties involved.

Item 4, diversity of citizenship, presents difficulties. After much confusion, two rules now govern: (1) United States courts decide

Exclusively federal	Civil actions in which states are parties (subject to exceptions noted)
	All suits and proceedings brought against (but not necessarily those initiated by) ambassadors, others possessing diplomatic immunity, and foreign consuls
	All cases involving federal criminal laws
	All admiralty, maritime patent-right, copyright, and bankruptcy cases
	All civil cases against the federal government where consent to sue has been granted
Denied federal	Civil suits involving citizens of different states where the amount at issue is less than [$75,000]
Concurrent with states	Civil suits involving citizens of different states where the amount at issue is [$75,000] or more

Figure 5.3
Jurisdiction of federal courts. (Source: J. H. Ferguson and D. E. McHenry, *The American System of Government*. McGraw-Hill, New York, 1981.)

cases involving citizens of different states according to the same rules of law as would govern the case in a State court. (2) In such cases, Federal procedures are followed.

Item 6 has been qualified by the Eleventh Amendment, Congress, and the courts, in keeping with the precept that a sovereign cannot be sued unless consent is given. States may now be sued in Federal courts without their consent only by another state or by the Federal government. If an alien, citizen of another state, or citizen of the same state wishes to sue a state, this can be done only with the consent of the state involved.... States may, however, initiate suits in Federal courts against aliens, citizens of other states, and foreign governments; although disputes with foreign governments are often settled by diplomatic negotiation.

Federal jurisdiction over the types of cases and controversies mentioned is not exclusive, however. Rather, Congress is free to distrib-

ute jurisdiction over most of them as it sees fit. Indeed, Congress may completely divest Federal courts of jurisdiction in certain instances. As matters stand, Federal courts have exclusive jurisdiction over some of them, have concurrent jurisdiction over others, and are totally denied consideration of still others. The division of responsibility is given in [figure 5.3]....

SUPREME COURT

Standing at the pinnacle of the Federal court system is the United States Supreme Court. Launched by the Judiciary Act of 1789, the Court held its first two terms on Wall Street in New York City, but in neither term were there any cases. Its next two terms were held in Philadelphia; thereafter it met in Washington. As first constituted it consisted of a Chief Justice and five associates. Congress by statute reduced the membership to five in 1801;

> *Warrant*—commands appearance, arrest, search, or seizure.
>
> *Summons*—directs defendant in civil suit to appear and answer complaint.
>
> *Writ of execution*—directs defendant to satisfy judgment awarded in civil suit.
>
> *Writ of ejectment*—ejects defendant from property held which court has found belongs to plaintiff.
>
> *Injunction*—directs person to do, or more commonly, not to do, damaging act.
>
> *Mandamus*—orders public official to perform act required by law.
>
> *Certiorari*—orders public official, especially inferior judicial tribunal, to send up record for review.

Figure 5.4
Common judicial writs. (Source: J. H. Ferguson and D. E. McHenry, *The American System of Government*. McGraw-Hill, New York, 1981.)

increased it to seven in 1807; increased it to nine in 1827 and ten in 1863; reduced it to seven in 1866; and fixed it at nine in 1869.…

Cases that do not originate in the Supreme Court come to it by what is technically known as an appeal or by writ of certiorari [see figure 5.4]. Appeals are allowed as a matter of right in cases involving Federal and state powers which obviously require a ruling by the highest Court. On petitions for certiorari the Court has the option of granting or denying review. If granted, as comparatively few are, lower Federal or state courts are directed to send up the entire record and proceeding for review or retrial. Typically, over three-fourths of the Supreme Court's business arises from petitions for certiorari.…

Decisions and Opinions

Several hundred cases and controversies reach the Supreme Court each year. A large number of appeals and petitions for writs of certiorari are disposed of without serious consideration for want of jurisdiction or merit. Many petitions for certiorari are merely granted or denied upon comparatively short briefs without oral argument. Others involving rather well-settled points of law about which the Court can come to a decision without oral hearings are disposed of as brief per curiam decisions. The remainder are decided after oral argument and in comparatively long written opinions setting forth reasons and justifications.

A decision may be unanimous or divided. If divided, both majority and dissenting opinions are usually written. Often one justice or more than one agrees with the conclusion reached in the majority or the dissenting opinion but for different reasons, in which case concurring opinions may be written. Thus, in a case involving complicated and controversial issues, there may be a majority opinion, a dissenting opinion, and concurring opinions. Six justices constitute a quorum, and at least a majority must concur before a decision is reached. *Obiter dicta* appear from time to time. Those are passing remarks, or observations, which are not binding on the case at hand but may have a bearing upon how opinions are interpreted, enforced, or decided at some time in the future. Published opinions once bore such titles as Dallas,

Cranch, Wheaton, Wallace, and Otto, reflecting the names of Court reporters; since 1882 they have appeared as United States Reports.

COURTS OF APPEALS

Immediately below the Supreme Court stand the courts of appeals, created in 1891. There is one for the District of Columbia and eleven others. The eleventh, including Alabama, Georgia, and Florida, was added in 1980, by splitting the fifth. . . .

Each court has four to twenty-six permanent judges and usually hears cases in divisions consisting of three judges, but all judges may sit. The justices of the Supreme Court may also sit within circuits to which each has been assigned, but time prevents them from "riding circuit," as they did in the early days of the Republic. District judges may also be assigned to serve in the appeals courts, although they may not judge cases which were before them on the lower bench. In some circuits, court is always held in the same city; in others, it may be held in two or more designated cities. The courts sit at irregular intervals in buildings owned or leased by the Federal government. Appeals judges are appointed by the President with the advice and consent of the Senate for terms of good behavior.

The appeals courts have slight original jurisdiction; they are primarily appellate courts. With few exceptions, cases decided in the district courts, special constitutional courts, legislative courts, and quasi-judicial boards and commissions go next to the appeals courts. Only the Supreme Court reviews the decisions of the appeals courts. . . .

DISTRICT COURTS

Eighty-nine district courts are located in the states. An additional one serves the District of Columbia. Districts have from one to twenty-seven judges; in a few instances, one judge serves two or more districts. The judges are appointed by the President with Senate approval for terms of good behavior.

A small state may itself constitute a district; otherwise, districts are arranged with regard for population, distance, and volume of business. Congress establishes district configuration.

Except for those assigned to the District of Columbia, district judges must reside in the district, or one of the districts, for which they are appointed. A permanent office must be maintained at a principal city, but court is usually held at regular intervals in various cities within each district.

Most cases and controversies [within the federal judicial system] start in district courts . . . [C]ases begun in state courts are occasionally transferred to them. . . . Ordinarily, cases are tried with only one judge presiding, but three judges must sit in certain types of cases.

Traditionally, the many bankruptcy cases arising under Federal law originated in the district courts, where they were handled by court-appointed "referees." In 1978, Congress changed that system when it approved the first major revision of the nation's bankruptcy laws in nearly forty years. After debating whether primary responsibility should be retained by the district courts or shifted to the circuit courts, Congress decided in favor of the former and elevated the rank and status of referees to bankruptcy judges.

Under the new system, bankruptcy judgeships were placed on a permanent basis rather than at the discretion of the United States Judicial Conference. The number of judgeships was increased substantially; they were made appointive by the President with Senate approval for fourteen-year terms; salaries and benefits were raised; and jurisdiction was broadened. Provision for merit selection was made by authorizing circuit-court counsels to recommend candidates, although, as in other instances when merit lists are supplied, the President is not required to nominate any of the candidates named.

Although bankruptcy judges remain adjuncts of the district courts, they have both constitutional and legislative status. They now have all the jurisdictional authority over bankruptcy proceedings that a district judge has in civil cases, but their terms are limited to a stated number of years... Most appeals are taken to district courts, although appeals may be heard by circuit courts with the consent of all parties, or to panels of three bankruptcy judges designated by the circuit courts....

FEDERAL MAGISTRATES

Until recent times, minor judicial functions were performed by commissioners appointed by district courts for terms of four years and paid from fees. Legal training was not a prerequisite, and partisan considerations usually determined who would be appointed. Legislation enacted in 1968 provided the first reform in more than a hundred years. The name "magistrate" was substituted for "commissioner"; legal training was required; and appointments were made by district courts for terms of eight years; salaries were substituted for fees; and trial jurisdiction was broadened.

Further upgrading resulted from legislation passed in 1979. That legislation allowed magistrates to preside, provided [litigants] consent in writing, at jury and nonjury civil trials; criminal misdemeanor trials; and juvenile trials which do not permit incarceration. Magistrates continue to [receive] eight-year appointments, although merit selection procedures promulgated by the United States Judicial Conference must now be used. Direct appeals [from a magistrate's opinion] can be taken to United States Circuit Courts of Appeals unless litigants consent before trial to appeal to United States District Courts. As presently constituted, magistrate courts play about the same role in the Federal system of justice as do the lowest state trial courts presided over by officers bearing such titles as magistrates, justices of the peace, or community court judges.

COURT OFFICERS

Attached to each Federal court are the usual clerks, reporters, stenographers, bailiffs, and other aides. Appointments are usually made by the courts themselves using merit standards set by the Administrative Office of the United States Courts.

■ NOTES

1. In addition to the sources of exclusive federal jurisdiction mentioned here, certain federal statutes require that cases involving those statutes be brought in federal court. The Clean Water Act, for example, specifies that a "citizen suit" against an alleged violator of the act must be brought in the federal district court in which the alleged violation occurred. See 33 U.S.C. §1365(c).

2. In addition to the twelve Courts of Appeals mentioned here, there is a Court of Appeals for the Federal Circuit, which hears appeals from such specialized tribunals as the Court of Claims, the Patent and Trademark Office, and the Court of International Trade. For the past several years, there has been interest in Congress in splitting the Ninth Circuit Court of Appeals, which currently covers nine western states and Guam.

3. There is also a United States Tax Court, a trial-level court that presides over certain disputes arising under the Internal Revenue Code.   ■

The following excerpt is from a lecture given by Professor Karl Llewellyn to incoming law students at Columbia University. First published in 1930, Professor Llewellyn's observations remain perhaps the classic statement on the difficulty, and importance, of that arcane branch of literature known as the "judicial opinion."

This Case System: What to Do with the Cases
K. N. Llewellyn
Source: *The Bramble Bush*. Oceana, Dobbs Ferry, N.Y., 1981, pp. 41–45.

[C]ases in casebooks have been assigned to you; what, then, are you to do with them? Now the first thing you are to do with an opinion is to read it. Does this sound commonplace? Does this amuse you? There is no reason why it should amuse you. You have already read past seventeen expressions of whose meaning you have no conception. So hopeless is your ignorance of their meaning that you have no hard-edged memory of having seen unmeaning symbols on the page. You have applied to the court's opinion the reading technique that you use upon the Satevepost. Is a word unfamiliar? Read on that much more quickly! Onward and upward— we must not hold up the story.

That will not do. It is a pity, but you must learn to read. To read each word. To understand each word. You are outlanders in this country of the law. You do not know the speech. It must be learned. Like any other foreign tongue, it must be learned: by seeing words, by using them until they are familiar; meantime, by constant reference to the dictionary. What, dictionary? Tort, trespass, trover, plea, assumpsit, nisi prius, venire de novo, demurrer, joinder, traverse, abatement, general issue, tender, mandamus, certiorari, adverse possession, dependent relative revocation, and the rest. Law Latin, law French, aye, or law English—what do these strange terms mean to you? Can you rely upon the crumbs

of language that remain from school? Does cattle levant and couchant mean cows getting up and lying down? Does nisi prius mean unless before? Or traverse mean an upper gallery in a church? I fear a dictionary is your only hope—a law dictionary—the one volume kind you can keep ready on your desk. Can you trust the dictionary, is it accurate, does it give you what you want? Of course not. No dictionary does. The life of words is in the using of them, in the wide network of their long associations, in the intangible something we denominate their feel. But the bare bones to work with, the dictionary offers; and without those bare bones you may be sure the feel will never come.

The first thing to do with an opinion, then, is read it. The next thing is to get clear the actual decision, the judgment rendered. Who won, the plaintiff or defendant? And watch your step here. You are after in first instance the plaintiff and defendant below, in the trial court. In order to follow through what happened you must therefore first know the outcome below; else you do not see what was appealed from, nor by whom. You now follow through in order to see exactly what further judgment has been rendered on appeal. The stage is then cleared of form—although of course you do not yet know all that these forms mean, that they imply. You can turn now to what you want peculiarly to know.

Given the actual judgments below and above as your indispensable framework—what has the case decided, and what can you derive from it as to what will be decided later?

You will be looking, in the opinion, or in the preliminary matter plus the opinion, for the following: a statement of the facts the court assumes; a statement of the precise way the question has come before the court—which includes what the plaintiff wanted below, and what the defendant did about it, the judgment below, and what the trial court did that is complained of; then the outcome on appeal, the judgment; and finally the reasons this court gives for doing what it did. This does not look so bad. But it is much worse than it looks.

For all our cases are decided, all our opinions are written, all our predictions, all our arguments are made, on certain four assumptions. They are the first presuppositions of our study. They must be rutted into you till you can juggle with them standing on your head and in your sleep.

1. The court must decide the dispute that is before it. It cannot refuse because the job is hard, or dubious, or dangerous.

2. The court can decide only the particular dispute which is before it. When it speaks to that question it speaks ex cathedra, with authority, with finality, with an almost magic power. When it speaks to the question before it, it announces Law, and if what it announces is new, it legislates, it makes the law. But when it speaks to any other question at all, it says mere words, which no man needs to follow. Are such words worthless? They are not. We know them as judicial dicta; when they are wholly off the point at issue we call them obiter dicta—words dropped along the road, wayside remarks. Yet even wayside remarks shed light on the remarker. They may be very useful in the future to him, or to us. But he will not feel bound to them, as to his ex cathedra utter-ance. They came not hallowed by a Delphic frenzy. He may be slow to change them; but not so slow as in the other case.

3. The Court can decide the particular dispute only, according to a general rule which covers a whole class of like disputes. Our legal theory does not admit of single decisions standing on their own. If judges are free, are indeed forced, to decide new cases for which there is no rule, they must at least make a new rule as they decide. So far, good. But how wide, or how narrow, is the general rule in this particular case? That is a troublesome matter. The practice of our case-law, however, is I think fairly stated thus: it pays to be suspicious of general rules which look too wide; it pays to go slow in feeling certain that a wide rule has been laid down at all, or that, if seemingly laid down, it will be followed. For there is a fourth accepted canon.

4. Everything, everything, big or small, a judge may say in an opinion, is to be read with primary reference to the particular dispute, the particular question before him. You are not to think that the words mean what they might if they stood alone. You are to have your eye on the case in hand, and to learn how to interpret all that has been said merely as a reason for deciding that case that way.

Now why these canons? The first, I take it, goes back to the primary purpose of law. If the job is in first instance to settle disputes which do not otherwise get settled, then the only way to do it is to do it. And it will not matter so much how it is done, in a baffling instance, so long as it is done at all.

The third, that cases must be decided according to a general rule, goes back in origin less to purpose than to superstition. As long as law was felt as something ordained of God, or even as something inherently right in the order of nature, the judge was to be regarded as a mouthpiece, not as a creator; and a mouthpiece of the general, who but made clear an application to the particular.

Else he broke faith, else he was arbitrary, and either biased or corrupt. Moreover, justice demands, wherever that concept is found, that like men be treated alike in like conditions.... That calls for general rules, and for their even application....

Back, if I may now, to the why of the two canons I have left: that the court can decide only the particular dispute before it; that all that is said is to be read with eyes on that dispute. Why these? I do believe...that here we have as fine a deposit of slow-growing wisdom as ever has been laid down through the centuries by the unthinking social sea. Here, hardened into institutions, carved out and given line by rationale. What is this wisdom? Look to your own discussion, look to any argument. You know where you would go. You reach, at random if hurried, more carefully if not, for a foundation, for a major premise. But never for itself. Its interest lies in leading to the conclusion you are headed for. You shape its words, its content, to an end decreed. More, with your mind upon your object you use words, you bring in illustrations, you deploy and advance and concentrate again. When you have done, you have said much you did not mean. You did not mean, that is, except in reference to your point. You have brought generalization after generalization up, and discharged it at your goal; all, in the heat of argument, were overstated. None would you stand to, if your opponent should urge them to another issue.

So with the judge. Nay, more so with the judge. He is not merely human, as are you. He is, as well, a lawyer; which you, yet, are not. A lawyer, and as such skilled in manipulating the resources of persuasion at his hand. A lawyer, and as such prone without thought to twist analogies, and rules, and instances, to his conclusion. A lawyer, and as such peculiarly prone to disregard the implications which do not bear directly on his case.

More, as a practiced campaigner in the art of exposition, he has learned that one must prepare the way for argument. You set the mood, the tone, you lay the intellectual foundation—all with the case in mind, with the conclusion—all, because those who hear you also have the case in mind, without the niggling criticism which may later follow. You wind up, as a pitcher will wind up— and as in the pitcher's case, the wind-up often is superfluous. As in the pitcher's case, it has been known to be intentionally misleading.

With this it should be clear, then, why our canons thunder. Why we create a class of dicta, of unnecessary words, which later readers, their minds now on quite other cases, can mark off as not quite essential to the argument. Why we create a class of obiter dicta, the wilder flailings of the pitcher's arms, the wilder motions of his gum-ruminant jaws. Why we set about, as our job, to crack the kernel from the nut, to find the true rule the case in fact decides: the rule of the case.

The professional charged with the responsibility of navigating the legal system, of course, is the lawyer. In litigation, and in administrative proceedings, the lawyer's role is to represent one of the interested parties and, under the rules of the adversary system, to advance that party's interest to the fullest extent allowed by the law. As is illustrated by the following tongue-in-cheek variation on Jonathan Swift's "A Modest Proposal," this role is not always seen as a productive one.

Lawyers for Cars

Russell Baker

Source: *The New York Times*, June 8, 1983, reprinted with permission.

While Japan was producing automobiles the United States was producing lawyers. American lawyer production has more than doubled since 1960, with the result that there are now 612,000 on the market, or one lawyer for every 390 Americans.

On a per capita basis, this is 20 times the number of lawyers available in Japan. These figures are the basis of my "lawyer-for-cars" proposal for solving our trade problem with the Japanese.

As first proposed to the White House, my plan called for exporting one lawyer to Japan for every car Japan exports to the United States. The Japanese objected to this. They argued that we would need to keep at least 200,000 lawyers for ourselves, leaving only 412,000 for export.

On a one-for-one basis, they noted, Japan would be permitted to ship us only 412,000 cars, which is far below their present export level.

As I explained to the White House, the Japanese estimate was far off base. Since the United States could function very happily with no more than three dozen lawyers, we should be able to send Japan 611,964 lawyers by the end of the year.

Under State Department pressure, however, we sought to please the Japanese by changing the car-to-lawyer ratio to a three-for-one swap. We would ship 611,964 lawyers, they would ship 1,835,892 cars in the present year.

Moreover, we would change the ratio in future years, in view of the fact that after the initial shipment our exports would decline.

At present we produce only 35,000 new lawyers each year. We proposed annual shipments from these inventories of 34,998 new lawyers at an exchange rate of between 50 and 75 cars per lawyer.

At this stage the Japanese revealed that they had been toying with us. A letter from the Japanese Lawyer Import Commission said, "We are dismayed to find that the 611,964 lawyers you propose to ship us are almost totally ignorant of the engineering and production skills necessary for the making of superior automobiles and highly sophisticated electronic machinery."

If we would agree to put the lawyers through a 10-year retraining program Japan would be prepared to consider a deal. "We do not believe this is an unreasonably long retraining period," they said, "since our studies show that to an American lawyer 10 years is virtually no time at all."

Simultaneously, lawyers began to raise obstacles. I was swamped with legal paper. Writs, injunctions, orders to show cause, requests for postponement, suits for damages on grounds of invasion-of-lawyers.

Among the most annoying were the 376,000 writs of habeas Japanus ordering me to produce the Japanese Government for the taking of depositions in suits to be prosecuted against me for "slanderously and maliciously asserting" that a lawyer was worth no more than 50 to 75 cars.

Not surprisingly, all my other activities have been brought to a halt. Though I expect to prevail eventually when my cases are finally decided by the Supreme Court in the second quarter of the next century, this is no comfort to one whose only dream is to see the day when Japan will be as blessed with lawyers as the United States.

For this reason it pains me to be attacked as I was last week by the Japanese Minister of Motion. "There are certain Western schemers, envious of Japan's ability to keep moving ahead," he said.

"These schemers have plans for infesting our society with hundreds of thousands of men cunningly trained in the arts of stopping all constructive activity, of bringing entire societies to a dead standstill. Yes, I speak of lawyers."

"There are plans afoot for shipping us enough lawyers to stop all forward motion in Japan, as they have stopped it in a certain country I need not identify. They call this trading lawyers for cars. To understand its true nature, however, I suggest that you try to imagine what kind of car Japan might produce if beset by 611,964 lawyers."

Well. I've been trying to imagine it, and I don't think it would be that terrible. The tires might have each other tied up in court when you wanted to drive to the seashore; the engine might sue every time you forgot to change the oil on time, and the gear shift on the showroom model might charge you with discrimination if you tried to buy an automatic transmission, but at least it would be a car that knew its rights and was willing to pay for their defense.

This, and not the insensate march of economic success, is the essence of civilization. I hope Japan will try it. Maybe, to show our friendship, we could give them 100,000 lawyers outright, just to get them started.

■ **NOTES**

1. One of the central themes sounded here by Russell Baker—that "to an American lawyer, 10 years is virtually no time at all"—echoes a complaint that has resonated throughout modern history. (The premise of Charles Dickens' *Bleak House* for example, was that litigation over the probate of a particular will was both interminable and intractable.) Baker's juxtaposition of the (presumably inefficient) American lawyer with the (presumably efficient) Japanese car manufacturer also echoes the oft-stated complaint that the legal system retards technological productivity and innovation. While there certainly are situations where this is true, keep in mind that productivity and innovation can be directed toward a variety of alternative goals, and that one legitimate function that the legal and regulatory systems can be asked to serve is to *redirect* productivity and innovation toward particular goals. As discussed in chapter 4, this is one of the functions of the tort system. If it works as intended, the production of safer technologies is promoted, while the production of more dangerous ones is discouraged. Similarly, as we will see in greater detail in the ensuing chapters, one of the key goals of environmental legislation is to promote cleaner technologies at the expense of more polluting ones. In doing so, the system will, by design, retard the development of certain kinds of technology.

2. There is no question, though, that Baker's description of a system prone to argumentation and delay strikes a responsive chord with most of us. Are there, nonetheless, legitimate values that are served by ensuring that the system allows ample time for investigation, argument, and analysis? Is there a value to the process, even if the process often is more lengthy or cumbersome than we might prefer? To what extent does the Constitution *require* such a process?   ■

C. ADMINISTRATIVE RULEMAKING

In the broad sense, an agency carries out its statutory mandate by promulgating administrative regulations. These regulations are first published in the *Federal Register* (*Fed. Reg.*), and are later codified in the Code of Federal Regulations (C.F.R.). Unless they are challenged successfully in court or in Congress, they have the force of law. This section explores the process by which agency rulemaking is effectuated.

1. The Distinction between Rulemaking, Adjudication, and Enforcement

Agencies perform legislative, judicial, and enforcement functions. When an agency engages in rulemaking, it is doing many of the things we normally associate with the legislative process, and it is making policy. Within the confines of its statutory mandate, the agency is laying out a policy that all who fall within its ambit will have to follow. When EPA sets an air emissions standard for a specific industry, for example, it is engaging in rulemaking and is establishing a requirement to which all facilities within that industry will be required to adhere.

However, agencies can be authorized to do more than develop and promulgate administrative rules; they are also often directed to enforce them as well. EPA, for example, is authorized to enforce the emission standards it sets under the Clean Air Act. In doing so, the agency performs a function that looks more like police work than legislation. This is the agency's enforcement function.

Finally, many regulatory statutes create some kind of administrative tribunal to adjudicate disputes that arise when the agency uses its enforcement power. The OSH-Act, for example, created the Occupational Safety and Health Review Commission. Employers cited for violating the act or some regulation promulgated under the act can appeal the citation to the review commission. The commission hears the facts and determines whether a violation of the act has occurred. It does not issue broad policy declarations, but rather issues an interpretation of the law as applied to the facts at hand. In doing so, the review commission is engaging in adjudication, not rulemaking. EPA plays a similarly adjudicative role when it hears appeals of water pollution discharge permits issued by the agency under the Clean Water Act, and it has created a separate adjudicatory tribunal for such purposes.

2. A General Look at Rulemaking under the Administrative Procedure Act

When an agency engages in rulemaking under the provisions of the Administrative Procedure Act, it must publish a "general notice of proposed rulemaking" in the *Federal Register*, setting forth (1) a statement of the time, place, and nature of the public

proceedings; (2) reference to the legal authority under which the rule is
and (3) either the terms or substance of the proposed rule or a description
ects and issues involved. See Section 4 of the APA (5 U.S.C. §553). Beyond
....., ...PA specifies two different general procedures that can be used by agencies
promulgating administrative regulations: formal rulemaking and informal (or notice
and comment) rulemaking.

Formal rulemaking, defined in Sections 7 and 8 of the APA (5 U.S.C. §§556 and
557), is to be performed only if Congress specifically requires it in the originating
statute. Since formal rulemaking can be a lengthy and cumbersome process, it has
been required in only a few modern regulatory statutes. The requisites of the formal
rulemaking process include a trial-type hearing before an impartial presiding officer;
an opportunity to present evidence and to cross examine witnesses; a decision made
on the record; an opportunity to submit proposed findings, exceptions, and supporting reasons; and a statement of findings and conclusions and the reasons for them.
As with a court trial, a verbatim record of the entire proceeding must be maintained.
If an agency engages in formal rulemaking, Section 10 of the APA directs the reviewing court to set aside the agency's action if the action is "found to be . . . unsupported
by substantial evidence [on the record as a whole]" [5 U.S.C. §706(2)(E)].

Unless the originating statute specifies otherwise, informal rulemaking is to be
used. This form of rulemaking, defined in Section 4 of the APA, is often called notice
and comment rulemaking. It requires that after giving the required notice in the *Federal Register*, the agency give "interested parties an opportunity to participate in the
rulemaking through submission of written data, views, or arguments with or without
opportunity for oral presentation." It does not require a hearing and allows the
agency to consider materials other than those brought forward at any hearing
the agency chooses to conduct. Unlike formal rulemaking, informal rulemaking
allows the agency to look beyond the hearing record in making rules. Agencies
engaging in informal rulemaking under the APA are not held to the "substantial evidence" standard of judicial review, but rather to the arguably less stringent requirement that their determinations not be "arbitrary" or "capricious." The nature and
scope of the courts' review of agency decision making are discussed in more detail
later in this chapter.

On occasion, an agency will utilize a group of advisors from outside the agency to
assist in its deliberations on one or more issues relevant to a proposed or ongoing
rulemaking. These advisory bodies may be specifically assembled to assist in a particular agency deliberation, or they may be of long-standing nature. They may be
specifically authorized by statute, or they may be assembled by the agency on an
informal basis. In general, these advisory committees do not supplant the agency's
regulatory power or responsibilities, but they do provide input to the agency on

selected technical and policy issues that arise in the course of the agency's delibera-tions. Accordingly, they can have a marked impact on the content and timing of agency rulemaking. Unless exempted by statute, all such advisory bodies are subject to the requirements of the Federal Advisory Committee Act, which is discussed in more detail later in this chapter.

in which cases would an agency be exempt?

■ **NOTES**

1. Under the APA, notice and comment is not required for "interpretative rules" (that is, rules that merely interpret, rather than substantively implement, statutory language), "general statements of policy," or "rules of agency organization, proce-dure, or practice" [5 U.S.C. §553(b)(A)]. As one might expect, the demarcation line between such rules—especially "interpretative" rules—and substantive regulation is not always clear. An agency's designation of a rule as one that does not require notice and comment is subject to judicial review, and agency rules of this nature have been struck down because of the agency's failure to provide the opportunity for notice and comment.

2. As part of the Environmental Research, Development, and Demonstration Authorization Act of 1978, Pub. L. 95-155, §8, Nov. 8, 1977, Congress created a Science Advisory Board (SAB) "to provide such scientific advice as may be requested" by EPA or certain designated congressional committees. The SAB is to be "composed of at least nine members," each of whom "shall be qualified by educa-tion, training, and experience to evaluate scientific and technical information on mat-ters referred to the Board." This provision was codified as 42 U.S.C. §4365, and added to the National Environmental Policy Act. Over the years, the SAB member-ship has grown much larger than nine.

3. Congress has also created advisory boards with functions associated with specific environmental legislation, such as the Clean Air Scientific Advisory Committee. ■

3. Negotiated Rulemaking

An agency may choose to augment the notice and comment process by convening a group of interested persons to negotiate some or all of the components—or even the precise language—of a proposed rule. The following articles present many of the arguments for and against the use of negotiation as a means of formulating regulations.

The Theory and Practice of Negotiated Rulemaking
Lawrence Susskind and Gerard McMahon

Source: 3 *Yale Journal on Regulation* 133 (1985), excerpted with permission.

Scholars, government officials, and practitioners have expressed concern over the weaknesses of the federal rulemaking process and the time it often takes to promulgate rules. Given the many instances in which rules have been challenged in court, both the process of rulemaking and the regulations produced seem to have lost legitimacy in the eyes of many regulatees.

Since the late 1970's, advocates of negotiated approaches to rulemaking have argued that the legitimacy of proposed rules could be restored—and time-consuming court challenges avoided—if informal, face-to-face negotiations were used to supplement the traditional review and comment process. Critics, however, have responded quite negatively to what they perceived as the dangers of "dealmaking behind closed doors." Nevertheless, proponents of the innovation have persisted, and during the last few years several federal agencies have experimented with negotiated approaches to rulemaking.

The Environmental Protection Agency (EPA) has undertaken the most elaborate tests of the concept. EPA's experiences shed new light on the advantages of negotiated rulemaking and suggest that some of the concerns of the critics have been misplaced. This article examines the results of the EPA demonstrations in order to test the models of

negotiated rulemaking advanced by advocates, to respond to the concerns of critics, and to inform and improve the provisional theory. With the refinements suggested in this article, EPA's approach to negotiated rulemaking appears to hold great promise for remedying the crisis of regulatory legitimacy.

I. NEGOTIATED RULEMAKING AS A REGULATORY REFORM

Almost all the parties involved in federal rulemaking—business associations, public interest groups, and many government officials—complain about the time and expense involved in developing and implementing regulations.[1] Businesses assert that delays are costly and increase the uncertainty surrounding investment decisions.[2] Advocacy groups complain that litigation delays implementation of important rules.[3] Each party tends to think that the agency favors the others.[4] Agency officials, on the other hand, feel that their autonomy has been unreasonably limited by procedural requirements mandated by Congress and the courts.[5] Courts, however, are inappropriate as final arbitrators of technically complex regulatory disputes. Many judges fear "government by the judiciary" and admit their inability to cope with complex technical issues.[6]

---

1. Morgan, Toward a Revised Strategy for Ratemaking, 1978 U. ILL. L.F. 21, 21–22 (1978); Note, Rethinking Regulation: Negotiation as an Alternative to Traditional Rulemaking, 94 HARV. L. REV. 1871 (1981).
2. W. Ruckelshaus, Environmental Negotiation: A New Way of Winning, Address to the Conservation Foundation's Second National Conference on Environmental Dispute Resolution 3 (Oct. 1, 1984) (on file with the Yale Journal on Regulation).

3. Id. at 14.
4. Harter, Dispute Resolution and Administrative Law: The History, Needs, and Future of a Complex Relationship, 29 VILL. L. REV. 1393, 1404 (1984).
5. W. Ruckelshaus, supra note 2, at 2.
6. See, e.g., Bazelon, Risk and Responsibility, 205 SCIENCE 277, 278 (1979); Leventhal, Environmental Decisionmaking and the Role of the Courts, 122 U. PA. L. REV. 509, 541–42 (1974).

These groups would certainly be less troubled if they believed that the conventional rulemaking process generated rules responsive to their interests, but few are satisfied with the time it takes to enact rules, the cost involved, or the quality of the rules produced.[7] In a speech delivered shortly before he left EPA, former Administrator William Ruckelshaus estimated that more than 80% of EPA's rules are challenged in court and that approximately 30% of the Agency's rules are significantly changed as a result of litigation.[8]

How did this situation develop? The roots of the problem can be found in the evolution of the regulatory process and in the changing nature of the issues that the process has been forced to address during the past several decades. Agency rulemaking from the New Deal to the early 1960's was characterized by broad deference to agency expertise and discretion. By the late 1960's, however, the groups being regulated, the newly emergent environmental advocacy organizations, and the courts had become unwilling to let such discretion go unchallenged.

Federal regulations typically are developed under procedures defined by the Administrative Procedure Act of 1946. Using in-house expertise and informal individual meetings with stakeholders (parties who are interested in or will be affected by the rule), an agency such as EPA first develops a Notice of Proposed Rulemaking, which is published in the Federal Register. Non-agency stakeholders, such as businesses or environmental organizations, are then able to respond by adding to a rulemaking record through a formal public comment process. Oral hearings are permissible but not required. The agency must base the final rulemaking on a consideration of the record, although in addressing ambiguities and uncertainties in the record it may make policy choices where necessary.

Many of the regulations promulgated over the past two decades have involved the resolution of complex factual questions.[9] More importantly, they have required difficult policy decisions that, at times, have lacked an operable political consensus. If all regulations had a clearly determinable factual basis, arguments about the exercise of agency discretion would be moot. Agencies, however, must also make policy choices in situations where either the desired facts are not available or the available "facts" are contested. In such situations, the agency exercises considerable discretion as it interprets inconsistent facts, balances various and often competing interests, and ultimately makes subjective policy choices with very real economic and political ramifications. In this context, an agency can expect opposition to almost every rule it develops.

Congress, the White House, and the courts have explored a variety of strategies to forestall concerns about the exercise of agency discretion and to increase agency accountability. However, the government's efforts to limit discretion have increased the time and

7. Harter, Negotiating Regulations: A Cure for Malaise, 71 GEO. L. J. 1, 6 (1981) [hereinafter cited as Cure for Malaise]; S. BREYER & R. STEWART, ADMINISTRATIVE LAW AND REGULATORY POLICY 592 (2nd ed. 1985).
8. W. Ruckelshaus, supra note 2, at 2. Ruckelshaus also noted the tremendous amount of time consumed by litigation over agency rules. He estimated that, each year, handling litigation from rulemaking challenges requires approximately 50 person-years from EPA's Office of General Counsel, 75 person-years from the EPA program offices, 25 person-years from the Department of Justice, and 175 person-years on the part of the plaintiffs' counsel. Id.
9. Harter, The Political Legitimacy and Judicial Review of Consensual Rules, 32 AM. U.L. REV. 471, 473 (1983) [hereinafter cited as Consensual Rules]; Susskind & Ozawa, Mediating Public Disputes: Obstacles and Possibilities, 41 J. SOCIAL ISSUES 151 (1985).

cost involved in rulemaking. Congress has enacted the Federal Advisory Committee Act (FACA), the Sunshine Act, the ex parte prohibitions of the Administrative Procedure Act, and the Freedom of Information Act. In issuing Executive Orders 12,291 and 12,498, the White House has given the Office of Management and Budget (OMB) greatly expanded responsibility for reviewing the probable cost-effectiveness of proposed regulations. Since 1970, the courts have expanded judicial supervision of agencies by broadening the rules of standing, issuing more specific criteria regarding the development and use of a factual record, expanding notice and comment requirements, and expressing a willingness to take a "hard look" at the reasonableness of proposed regulations. These changes have produced "hybrid rulemaking," so-called because it is intermediate between the informal notice and comment rulemaking and formal procedures which include evidentiary hearings.

While these developments have increased agency accountability, they have not fully responded to concerns about the legitimacy of regulatory actions. Limiting the role of non-agency participants to adversarial challenges to the rulemaking record has been an ineffective means of building support for the policy choices that agencies have had to make. The current rulemaking process is bound to generate dissatisfaction as long as regulatory agencies retain the exclusive responsibility for making the technical judgments and political compromises needed to develop a rule. By encouraging and empowering regulatees to challenge agency decision-

making in an effort to enhance the political legitimacy of the rulemaking process, Congress and the courts have simply increased the complexity, cost, and time it takes to generate rules that can be implemented.

A number of scholars have suggested negotiated rulemaking as a response to these problems of delay, increased cost, and loss of political legitimacy. In negotiated rulemaking, an agency and other parties with a significant stake in a rule participate in facilitated face-to-face interactions designed to produce a consensus. Together the parties explore their shared interests as well as differences of opinion, collaborate in gathering and analyzing technical information, generate options, and bargain and trade across these options according to their differing priorities. If a consensus is reached,[10] it is published in the Federal Register as the agency's notice of proposed rulemaking, and then the conventional review and comment process takes over. Because most of the parties likely to comment have already agreed on the notice of proposed rulemaking, the review period should be uneventful. The prospects of subsequent litigation should be all but eliminated....

II. THE PREVAILING THEORY

In order to evaluate EPA's negotiated rulemaking demonstrations systematically, a theoretical framework is required. There are two strands of theory that can presently be used to construct such a framework. The first addresses the hypothetical preconditions necessary for the success of a negotiated rule-

---

10. In practice, consensus is achieved when all the participants remain silent in response to the mediator's inquiry, "Is there anyone who cannot live with this latest restatement?" That moment is usually preceded by an elaborate effort to ensure that every participant's primary concerns have been satisfied. Such a consensus may be elusive, with the group

perhaps only able to agree on a range of acceptable alternatives. This at least narrows the scope of possibilities, and the agency can use this product to draft a rule that falls within the acceptable boundaries. See Harter, Regulatory Negotiation: The Experience So Far, RESOLVE, Winter 1984, at 9 [hereinafter cited as Harter, Experience So Far].

making, and the second sets forth criteria for evaluating rules produced through negotiation. The two strands are interrelated, and both draw on existing theories of negotiation and doctrines of administrative process.

A. The Hypothetical Preconditions for Success

In his seminal study of negotiated rulemaking, Philip Harter proposed a set of hypotheses about the conditions under which regulatory negotiation would be likely to succeed. In developing these criteria for success, Harter drew upon analogous situations in the broad area of dispute resolution, in which negotiation is used to resolve complex policy problems.[31] The Administrative Conference of the United States endorsed his model and adopted a set of recommendations encouraging agencies to experiment with negotiated rulemaking.[32] Eight of the criteria proposed by Harter and noted by the Administrative Conference seem especially relevant and worth testing here.

First, people will come to the bargaining table only as long as they believe negotiations will produce an outcome for them that is as good as or better than the outcomes that would result from other available methods of pursuing their interests. The concept that parties will pursue their own best interest in this way is a key assumption in negotiation theory, popularized by Fisher and Ury under

the heading of BATNA (Best Alternative to a Negotiated Agreement).[34]

Second, the acceptability of negotiation as a dispute resolution process is determined by relative power,[35] another common strand in negotiation theory. Negotiations will only proceed if the parties are interdependent, that is, if they are constrained from acting unilaterally. Furthermore, if the imbalance of power is too great, the less powerful party is sure to seek an alternative context in which to press its claims, away from the negotiation table.[36]

Third, with regard to the issue of scale, fifteen parties is considered the "rough practical limit" on the number of participants that can work effectively in a negotiated rulemaking.

Fourth, the issues must be readily apparent and the parties must be ready to address them.[38] Negotiation theorists, drawing in large part on the history of labor relations in the United States, have consistently identified "ripeness" as a criterion.[39] In the environmental mediation field, however, there is substantial disagreement about the relevance of the ripeness argument.[40]

Fifth, consensus building will be impeded if deeply held beliefs or values are in conflict.[41] If values are incontrovertible, there is no room for compromise or collaborative problem solving. This is linked to a sixth precondition that Raiffa and others have pointed out—namely, that there must be two or more issues "on the table" so that parties can

---

31. Harter, Cure for Malaise, supra note 7, at 42–51.

32. 1 C.F.R. §305.82–4 (1985).

34. R. FISHER & W. URY, GETTING TO YES 104 (1981).

35. Harter, Cure for Malaise, supra note 7, at 43; Cormick, Intervention and Self-Determination in Environmental Disputes: A Mediator's Perspective, RESOLVE 23 (Winter 1982).

36. Harter, Cure for Malaise, supra note 7, at 45; Fisher, Negotiating Power, 27 BEHAVIORAL SCIENCE 149–66 (1983).

38. Cormick, supra note 35, at 4, 6. See also Popper, An Administrative Law Perspective on Consensual Decision Making, 35 AD. L. REV. 255 (1983).

39. SIMPKIN, MEDIATION AND THE DYNAMICS OF COLLECTIVE BARGAINING 42 (1971).

40. Susskind, Environmental Mediation and the Accountability Problem, 6 VT. L. REV. 17–18 (1981).

41. This refers to deeply held, almost theological values, as opposed to how two parties might value the impact of an emission standard differently.

maximize their overall interests by trading or bundling issues.[42] This precondition for success can best be understood as a restatement of the basic distinction between "distributive" and "integrative" bargaining.[43] In distributive bargaining situations, one side can only win if another side loses—the classic "zero-sum" situation. In integrative bargaining situations, all sides can come out ahead by trading across issues or items that they value differently—the classic "win-win" situation.

Seventh, the pressure of a deadline is necessary for successful negotiation.[44] Without a deadline, parties may purposefully delay or fail to focus on reaching a settlement.

Finally, some method of implementing the final agreements must be available and acceptable to the parties.[45] Parties must believe that their agreement will be implemented and that their participation will be worthwhile. The importance of perceptions and commitments in negotiation cannot be emphasized strongly enough.

While Harter framed his discussion in terms of presumed preconditions for success, some of these same criteria can be recast in terms of a framework for evaluating the agreements reached through a negotiation process.

B. A Framework for Evaluating Negotiated Rules

Negotiated rulemaking will only be utilized more broadly if it achieves better results than the traditional rulemaking process.[46] The framework for evaluating negotiated rulemaking is premised on the baseline criteria that fairer and wiser rules will be produced at a lower cost. Following from Harter's discussion of preconditions for success, this framework should include the following specific criteria.

Each party must feel that the negotiated rule serves its interests at least as well as the version of the rule most likely to be developed through the conventional process.[47] The only way of testing this latter criterion is to compare the attitudes of the participants at the end of the process with their initial statements of expectations.

A negotiation should yield realistic commitments from all of those involved. A rule that satisfies everyone in principle but cannot be implemented is of little use. Not only is the support of the participants important, but so too is the support of any interested party. The measure of success on this score is whether the proposed rule, drafted through the informal process, can weather the close scrutiny of those who did not participate in the nego-

---

42. H. RAIFFA, THE ART AND SCIENCE OF NEGOTIATION, 164–165 (1982). However, as Harter points out, very few regulations involve single issues. Most proposals can be broken down into analyzing the scope of the remedy and the substantive and procedural elements of the regulation.
43. LEWICKI & LITTERER, NEGOTIATION 75–129 (1985).
44. Harter, Cure for Malaise, supra note 7, at 47. The legislature or courts could establish a perception of imminence by mandating agency action within a limited time period or the agency could set and publicize its own time frame for implementing regulatory programs.
45. Id. at 51. Professor Dunlop identified several of the same preconditions as being necessary for successful labor negotiations. Political scientists

have identified consensual decisionmaking as a way to reconcile majority and minority goals. See, e.g., T. LOWI, THE END OF LIBERALISM 31–41 (1969); R. DAHL, WHO GOVERNS? 315–24 (1961).
46. Note, supra note 1, at 1874–76. See also Dunlop, The Limits of Legal Compulsion, reprinted in 1975 D.S.H. REP. (BNA) 884, 886; Schuck, Litigation, Bargaining, and Regulation, REGULATION July–Aug. 1979, at 26.
47. Parties must at least do as well as their BATNA—Best Alternative to a Negotiated Agreement. Fisher and Ury argue that the BATNA provides a standard or floor against which any proposal should be measured. R. FISHER & W. URY, supra note 34, at 104.

tiation process—and perhaps a "hard look" by the courts.

The interests of the parties should be so well-reconciled that no possible joint gains are left unrealized. Changes which would help a party without harming another party should not be missed. If a more elegant method of reconciling the conflicting interests of the parties is possible, it will probably emerge once the draft agreement is publicized. Thus, it may take some time to evaluate fully negotiated rules relative to this criterion.

The agency should be able to demonstrate that it has upheld its statutory mandate, and the public-at-large should feel satisfied that both the process and the outcome were fair.[49] The perceptions of the parties who participated in the negotiations and the reactions of those they ostensibly represented ought to be a good preliminary indicator of success in this regard. Again, it may take some time to fully evaluate these perceptions.

Relationships among the participants in a negotiation should improve, not deteriorate, as a result of their interactions. The parties should be in a better position to deal with their differences in the future. Changed dynamics can be evaluated by questioning the participants and watching to see what happens in their subsequent dealings with each other.

The negotiated rule should take account of the best scientific and technical information available at the time of the negotiation. If, during the review and comment period, qualified experts testify that important scientific evidence has been ignored or misinterpreted, the result should clearly be judged an inferior or unwise rule. Although the wisdom of the negotiated rule will become clear once the rule has been implemented, it might be disastrous to delay evaluation until that point. . . .

III. EPA'S REGULATORY NEGOTIATION DEMONSTRATIONS

The notion of using a negotiated approach to rulemaking at EPA first emerged during the Carter Administration, when procedural reforms akin to negotiated rulemaking were tested.[50] A top EPA official strongly supported the idea at major Senate hearings

49. Cf. Note, supra note 1, at 1871, 1874–76 (alternative models of directing agency involvement in negotiated rulemaking and agency oversight without participation); Harter, Cure for Malaise, supra note 7, at 59–66 (advantages and disadvantages of agency participation). Some commentators have warned against agency participation. Since an agency has the final legal authority, parties might want to preserve their positions with the agency and therefore would negotiate less freely. Moreover, in its lead capacity, the agency might dominate the negotiations. However, these issues of inflexibility and posturing are endemic to all negotiations and not limited to instances where the agency is present.

50. N. Baldwin, Negotiated Rulemaking: A Case Study of Administrative Reform 25–26 (1983) (unpublished Master's Thesis, Department of Urban Studies and Planning, MIT). During the Carter Administration, two successful experiments

with procedural reforms illustrated that informal joint problem-solving could aid the progress of regulatory decision-making. The first of these reforms involved the creation of a technical panel which was responsible for making certain complex decisions regarding pesticides. The second was the adoption of an informal hearing procedure for the water pollution discharge permitting system, used to improve the efficiency of the existing, more cumbersome process. In both instances an informal participatory process was employed rather than the formal hearing method which tends to be more court-like and adversarial. See also Comment, An Alternative to the Traditional Rulemaking Process: A Case Study of Negotiation in the Development of Regulations, 29 VILL. L. REV. 1505, 1525–35 (1984) (describing the consultation procedure used by the Department of Labor's Office of Federal Contract Compliance Programs to gain public input prior to rulemaking).

held in 1980.[51] While the change of Administration slowed the momentum,[52] appointment of Joseph Cannon as Acting Associate Administrator of EPA's Office of Planning and Resource Management in 1981 brought renewed interest. Cannon and several other EPA officials had strong personal commitments to various regulatory reforms and worked diligently within EPA to develop backing for the idea of negotiated rulemaking.[53] In the fall of 1982, Cannon announced that the Agency would move ahead aggressively to demonstrate the concept. In a January 1983 address to the Conservation Foundation's National Conference on Environmental Dispute Resolution Cannon announced that EPA was ready to develop several rules using negotiation. . . .

V.   REFLECTIONS ON THE SUCCESS OF NEGOTIATED RULEMAKING

. . . In interviews after the demonstrations were completed, the participants in both negotiated rulemaking efforts indicated that they had become advocates of further demonstrations. Indeed, several urged EPA to proceed with further demonstrations (which, at this writing, the agency has done). The participants felt that the openness of meetings; the availability of minutes and written subcommittee reports, as well as drafts of the final agreement; and the presence of all the relevant stakeholders at the table ensured the legitimacy of the negotiated agreement. While it is too soon to make a final judgment and there are too few data

available to calculate formally the cost-effectiveness of negotiated rulemaking, the two demonstrations suggest that in a cooperative setting the pooling of views, experience, and knowledge can produce a rule that is considered by those directly involved to be more legitimate than what the Agency might otherwise have drafted on its own. In light of this clearly superior outcome of negotiated rules, the courts should be urged to evaluate the regulatory negotiation process in a more favorable light. Within the conventional rulemaking process, courts have undertaken an oversight role designed to induce agencies to conduct better research, pay attention to the concerns of those with a stake in the rule and exhibit analytical rigor in promulgating a final rule. The so-called "hard look" doctrine, adopted by the courts during the last decade, is intended to make sure that agencies provide a reasonable analytical justification for rules.

The products of negotiated rulemaking do not warrant the usual "hard look". The rationale behind the hard look doctrine will be satisfied during the negotiations themselves if the following key conditions are adhered to: 1) adequate notice; 2) availability of financial resources to disadvantaged groups to help them participate on an equal footing; 3) the keeping of a reasonable record of formal meetings; 4) ample opportunity for all parties to review the final draft; 5) an opportunity for all parties to discuss the results of the review and comment process; 6) a chance for all interested parties to shape the scope of the negotiation agenda, agree on the selection of a

---

51. Regulatory Negotiation Hearings, supra note 25, at 83–84, 94–95 (1980) (statement of Roy N. Gamse, Deputy Assistant Administrator, Planning and Evaluation, EPA).

52. N. Baldwin, supra note 50, at 25–26. Implementation of Regulatory Negotiation at EPA was slowed initially by the controversies associated with Administrator Ann Gorsuch.

53. Id. at 25–28. Cannon had been a lawyer involved in litigation prior to his appointment and

was deeply committed to the idea that many disputes were best resolved out of court. This personal commitment, coupled with the fact that many parties, including industry and the Reagan Administration's OMB and President's Task Force on Regulatory Relief, were supportive of the concept, prompted Cannon to make negotiated rulemaking his pet project.

facilitator, and receive access to the information they request; 7) a clear explanation by the agency of its obligation to the negotiating committee; and 8) an opportunity for all parties to sign off on a final version of the agreement. If these elements are incorporated in the negotiations process, the participants themselves will ensure that the Agency addresses their concerns, conducts adequate research, and carefully analyzes all proposals in choosing the best one. Thus, the judicial hard look doctrine would be redundant.

In short, a different standard of judicial review would help to ensure the efficiency and perceived legitimacy of the rulemaking process. Courts should insist on substantial reasons for granting judicial review of a rule that meets the eight conditions listed above. If information was falsified or the agency failed to promulgate the rule as negotiated, judicial review would certainly be justified. However, if a party were offered a chance to participate in a full-fledged negotiated rulemaking effort, but chose to remain aloof, the courts ought to respond skeptically to a request for judicial review. If the courts adopted this posture, the incentive to partici-

pate in negotiated rulemakings would be enhanced. This would, in turn, increase the odds of a workable consensus being reached and reduce the likelihood of legal challenges to subsequent rules. Of course, challenges to rules based on claims that fundamental rights have been abridged would still be heard as always.

Judge Patricia Wald of the U.S. Court of Appeals for the D.C. Circuit has suggested that the judicial role in reviewing negotiated regulations should not, and will not, be passive.[134] This is certainly a reasonable position, but once an active review has determined that the eight conditions suggested above have been met, the courts should realize that continued second-guessing of the results of negotiated rulemakings will undermine the prospects for using this particular regulatory reform to enhance the efficiency of the rulemaking process and to restore a measure of legitimacy to the outcomes of the process.

---

134. Wald, Negotiation of Environmental Disputes: A New Role for the Courts?, 10 COLUM. J. ENVTL. L. 1, 17–25 (1984).

■ **NOTES**

1. In the more than two decades since this article was written, negotiated rulemaking has become both more pervasive and more institutionalized within the United States. The following article, written some 15 years after Susskind and McMahon offered their relatively optimistic view of the potential for negotiated outcomes to transform the administrative system, presents a somewhat more sobering view of the performance to date, and attempts to offer a policy-directed framework for analysis.

2. Susskind and McMahon suggest here that the courts utilize a much more deferential standard of review when they are reviewing challenges to agency rules developed through negotiated rulemaking. Given that one of their overall goals in advocating negotiated rulemaking is to reduce the time and resources devoted to judicial review of agency decision making, this is perfectly understandable. Note, however, that this

could change the fundamental purpose of judicial review (which is discussed in more detail toward the end of this chapter) in these circumstances. Most significantly, it could elevate fealty to the compromise negotiated by the stakeholders above fealty to the policies dictated by Congress in the statutory mandate. As discussed in the following article, the Negotiated Rulemaking Act does not specify a different standard of judicial rule for negotiated rules.   ■

Negotiation as a Means of Developing and Implementing Environmental and Occupational Health and Safety Policy
Charles C. Caldart and Nicholas A. Ashford
Source: 23 *Harvard Environmental Law Review* 141 (1999), excerpted with permission.

III. NEGOTIATED RULEMAKING

Since the mid-1970s, many commentators in the United States have advocated the use of negotiated rulemaking as a more efficient, sensible alternative to the traditional "notice and comment" procedure typically followed by federal agencies in the development of regulations. Occasionally in the 1970s, and more often in the 1980s, EPA, OSHA, and other federal agencies used the negotiation process as an aid to the development of certain regulations. Often, such negotiations were held under the provisions of the Federal Advisory Committee Act ("FACA"), a 1972 statute governing the creation and operation of advisory committees convened to assist agency decisionmaking.[8] In 1990, Congress formally endorsed negotiated rulemaking with the passage of the federal Negotiated Rulemaking Act.[9] The Clinton Administration [was] a strong supporter of its use.[10]

A. Negotiated Rulemaking Within the U.S. Administrative System

The Negotiated Rulemaking Act specifies a set of procedures to be followed by an agency wishing to use negotiated rulemaking, although the Act cautions that these procedures "should [not] be construed as an attempt to limit innovation and experimentation with the negotiated rulemaking process...."[11] Under the Act, an agency may, but is not required to, use negotiated rulemaking to develop a proposed rule whenever the agency determines that it would be "in the public interest" to do so.[12] If the agency desires to use negotiated rulemaking, it must first identify the various interests that would be signifi-

---

8. See 5 U.S.C. App. 2 §§1–15 (1994). FACA requires, inter alia, that: (1) with certain exceptions, all groups convened by a federal agency to provide advice on agency decisionmaking be treated as "advisory committees" under FACA, id. §3(2) (1994); (2) the membership of advisory committees be "fairly balanced in terms of the points of view represented and the functions to be performed," id. §5(b)(2), 5(c); (3) the meetings of advisory committees be open to the public, see id. §10(a)(1); and (4) the records of advisory committee deliberations be open to the public, see id. §10(b).

9. 5 U.S.C. §§561–570 (1994). Congress permanently reauthorized the 1990 Act in the Administrative Dispute Resolution Act of 1996, Pub. L. No. 104–320, 110 Stat. 3870, 3873.
10. See, e.g., Exec. Order No. 12,866, 3 C.F.R. §638 (1993). This order directed each agency "to explore, and where appropriate, use consensual mechanisms for developing regulations, including negotiated rulemaking." Id.
11. 5 U.S.C. §561 (1994).
12. Id. §563(a).

cantly affected by a proposed rule and determine whether those interests could be represented adequately by a group of persons brought together to serve as a negotiated rulemaking committee. If so, the agency may then establish such a committee, which is treated as an advisory committee under FACA.[13] The negotiated rulemaking committee is to be made up of persons representing the various affected interests, as well as at least one member of the agency, who is to serve on the committee "with the same rights and responsibilities as other members of the committee."[14] The committee's goal is to determine whether its members can reach a "consensus" (which may be defined by the committee as something less than unanimity) on the wording of a draft rule.[15]

If the committee reaches consensus, the draft rule is published for public notice and comment, as is any other proposed rule. The agency retains authority over the wording of any proposed or final rule, and the agency is empowered to modify the rule drafted by the committee if it believes the draft rule is inconsistent with the applicable congressional mandate. Moreover, a rule drafted through negotiated rulemaking is not to be "accorded any greater deference by a court than a rule which is a product of other rulemaking procedures."[16]

B.   The Performance of Negotiated Rulemaking as a Means of Saving Time and Limiting Judicial Challenge

Those who advocate negotiated rulemaking, including Congress, tend to identify two primary benefits that are expected to flow from its use: (a) reduced rulemaking time, and (b) decreased litigation over the final rule.[17] Presumably, face-to-face meetings among the interested parties will avoid the various bureaucratic quagmires that can delay the drafting of a rule within an agency, and will produce a proposed rule more quickly on average. Further, since the interested parties have agreed on the wording of the proposed rule in advance, the notice and comment procedure presumably will be less contentious and time-consuming, and the incentive for anyone to file a judicial challenge to the final rule presumably will be slight.

In practice, however, it is not at all clear that negotiated rulemaking delivers on either of these promises. Of all the federal agencies in the United States, EPA has used negotiated rulemaking most often.[19] A recent study

---

13. See id. §562(7). Even without the Negotiated Rulemaking Act, any negotiated rulemaking committee convened by an agency would presumably be treated as an advisory committee under FACA, and thus would be required to have "balanced" representation. 5 U.S.C. App. 2 §5(b)(2)(c) (1994). See also supra note 8. For a discussion of FACA's fair balance requirement, see Nicholas A. Ashford, Advisory Committees in OSHA and EPA: Their Use in Regulatory Decisionmaking, 9 SCI. TECH. & HUM. VALUES 72, 76–77 (1984).

14. Id. §566(b).

15. See id. §§566(f), 562(2).

16. Id. §570.

17. The legislative history of the 1996 reauthorization of the Negotiated Rulemaking Act reflects almost unanimous support for negotiated rulemaking, and stresses these two presumed benefits of negotiated rulemaking. See The Reauthorization of the Negotiated Rulemaking Act, 1996: Hearings

Before the Subcomm. on Commercial and Admin. Law of the House Comm. on the Judiciary, 104th Cong. 52–82 (1996), 142 CONG. REC. H12303-04 (daily ed. Oct. 19, 1996).

19. Cary Coglianese reports that, through 1996, a total of "seventeen federal agencies had initiated at least one negotiated rulemaking process," and that the average number of negotiated rulemakings initiated by these agencies was four. Cary Coglianese, Assessing Consensus: The Promise and Performance of Negotiated Rulemaking, 46 DUKE L. J. 1255, 1273 (1997). EPA had initiated the most, and actually had finalized twelve. See id. at 1273–74. When one considers the hundreds of rules issued by EPA through 1996, however, it is clear that negotiated rulemaking has been used in a very small percentage of EPA rulemakings. See id. at 1299 n.197 (citing data indicating that EPA issued over 2100 rules from 1987 through 1991).

of EPA negotiated rulemakings has concluded that: (a) on average, the promulgation of EPA rules through negotiated rulemaking took no less time than did the promulgation of a "control" group of similar EPA rules through traditional notice and comment rulemaking,[20] and (b) fifty percent of EPA's twelve finalized negotiated rulemakings were the subject of legal challenge, compared with a litigation rate of twenty-six percent for all EPA rules issued during the period from 1987 through 1991.[21] To date, then, it has not been established that negotiated rulemaking actually provides the primary benefits touted by its proponents.[22]

C. The Performance of Negotiated Rulemaking as a Means of Securing a "Better" Rule

Despite an apparent failure to deliver its oft-cited benefits, negotiated rulemaking may offer other advantages. Significantly, because negotiated rulemaking facilitates face-to-face discussions among rulemaking "adversaries" that might not otherwise occur, there is the potential that creative solutions to difficult issues may be found as differences are understood and addressed, and that substantively better rules may emerge. Such a result might come, for example, through the identification

of opportunities for innovative technological responses within the regulated community.

As an initial attempt to determine whether this potential is being realized, this Article examines three negotiated rulemakings used by EPA to set emission standards under the Clean Air Act ("CAA")[23] ...

In addition to the limitations imposed by the small number of examples examined, the problem with an analysis of this nature is that any attempt to identify a "better" result is a qualitative exercise: depending on the context, it can mean quite different things to different people. For the purposes of this Article, the quality of the final rule produced by negotiated rulemaking is evaluated according to whether it produced a rule that was more protective of environmental or occupational health than might have been expected had negotiated rulemaking not been used. Further, the Article gives particular attention to the extent to which opportunities to promote technological change were seized upon by the negotiating committee.

1. Negotiated Rulemaking and Clean Air Act Emission Standards

Of the twelve negotiated rulemakings completed by EPA through 1996, this Article focuses on three that resulted in the promulgation of air emission standards under the

---

20. See id. at 1284–86.
21. See id. at 1298, 1301. If one looks only at all of the more significant EPA rules issued during this period, the overall litigation rate is 35%. See id. at 1300. Conversely, if one uses the Office of Management and Budget's data on the total number of EPA rules issued during this period, the overall litigation rate is only 19%. See id. at 1299. In a less comprehensive study, Laura Langbein and Cornelius Kerwin found a litigation rate of 33% for "significant" EPA rules promulgated through the conventional rulemaking process, as compared to a litigation rate of 29% for EPA rules formulated through negotiated rulemaking. See Laura Langbein & Cornelius Kerwin, Regulatory Negotiation Versus Conventional Rulemaking: Claims, Counter-claims, and Empirical Evidence 19–20

(Nov. 20, 1997) (unpublished manuscript, on file with the Harvard Environmental Law Review).
22. Interviews conducted by Cornelius Kerwin and Laura Langbein with participants in negotiated rulemakings at EPA have found general satisfaction with the procedure and the results. However, "[i]n terms of satisfaction with the process and their experience with it, certain classes of participants, notably environmental interests, gave lower ratings than did the others. Their ratings were positive, but marginally so." Cornelius Kerwin & Laura Langbein, An Evaluation of Negotiated Rulemaking at the Environmental Protection Agency Phase I: Report for the Administrative Conference of the U.S. 47 (September 1995) (unpublished manuscript, on file with the Harvard Environmental Law Review).
23. 42 U.S.C. §§7401–7767 (1994 & Supp. 1996).

CAA: (a) the setting of new source performance standards for the woodstove industry, (b) the setting of hazardous air pollutant standards for coke oven emissions, and (c) the setting of hazardous air pollutant standards for the wood furniture coatings industry. These three are used because they share a common set of features: a full committee remained with the negotiations to the end;[24] the rule negotiated was the rule eventually proposed by the agency;[25] and the rule set an air emission standard designed to protect the environment and/or public health.

a. The Woodstoves Rule One of EPA's early forays into negotiated rulemaking was the development of a national New Source Performance Standard ("NSPS") for "residential wood combustion units" (woodstoves). EPA came to regulate woodstoves as a result of lawsuits brought against the agency

by the Natural Resources Defense Council ("NRDC") and the State of New York.[27] These suits sought to force EPA to regulate polycyclic organic matter ("POM") as a hazardous air pollutant under section 112 of the CAA.[28] As part of its settlement of the POM litigation, EPA agreed to explore the possibility of regulating woodstoves, one of the primary contributors of POM,[29] as "stationary sources" of air pollution under section 111 of the Act.[30] Interestingly, such regulation was desired not only by environmental groups but also by woodstove manufacturers, who hoped that the promulgation of a national standard by EPA would discourage states from setting their own (likely differing) standards.[31]

Section 111 of the CAA requires that a NSPS reflect the level of emission limitation achievable through the application of the "best system of emission reduction . . . [that]

---

24. This distinguishes this group from the negotiations over EPA's worker protection standards for agricultural pesticides, where the farmworkers left the negotiating table early on and the rule was negotiated without their participation. See Worker Protection Standard, 57 Fed. Reg. 38,102 (1992) (codified at 40 C.F.R. pts. 156, 170).
25. This distinguishes this group from the negotiations over oxygenated and reformulated fuels under the CAA, where EPA chose to promulgate a rule different from the one negotiated by the negotiated rulemaking committee. See Regulation of Fuels and Fuel Additives: Standards of Reformulated and Conventional Gasoline, 59 Fed. Reg. 7716 (1994) (codified at 40 C.F.R. pt. 80).
27. See Natural Resources Defense Council v. Alm, No. 84-1473 (D.C. Cir. filed Sept. 18, 1984); New York v. Thomas, No. 84-1472 (D.C. Cir. filed Sept. 18, 1984). The lawsuits were brought to enforce §122(a) of the CAA, 42 U.S.C. §7422(a) (1994), which was added to the Act in 1977. Under this provision EPA was required to evaluate four designated substances, including "polycyclic organic matter" (POM), and to determine whether emissions of such material "into the ambient air will cause, or contribute to, air pollution which may reasonably be anticipated to endanger public health." Id. If EPA made an affirmative determination, it was then required under this section to list

POM under §7408(a)(1) as a "criteria" air pollutant or under §7412(b)(1)(A) as a "hazardous air pollutant." Concluding that there was uncertainty about whether POM endangered public health within the meaning of §7422, EPA stated that it could not make such a determination. See Final Decision, Regulation of Polycyclic Organic Matter Under the Clean Air Act, 49 Fed. Reg. 31,680 (1984) (codified at 40 C.F.R. ch. 1). The lawsuits followed.
28. See 42 U.S.C. §7412 (1994). POM contains chemicals that are known or believed to be carcinogenic. See Negotiated Agreement on Wood Stoves Would Cut Particulate Emissions by 70 Percent, 17 Env't. Rep. (BNA) 821 (1986).
29. POM is produced and released into the air by the partial combustion that is typical of the woodstove burning process. In 1987, EPA stated that "a growing number of areas [are] experiencing air quality problems because of particulate and polycyclic organic matter emissions from woodburning devices." EPA Announces Proposed Air Act Limits to Cut Wood Stove Particulate Emissions, 17 Env't. Rep. (BNA) 1740 (1987).
30. See 42 U.S.C. §7411 (1994).
31. See generally William Funk, When Smoke Gets in Your Eyes: Regulatory Negotiation and the Public Interest—EPA's Woodstove Standards, 18 ENVTL. L. J. 55, 61–62, 80–81 (1987).

has been adequately demonstrated."[32] To devise such a national emission standard, EPA convened an advisory committee consisting of representatives from industry, environmental groups, certain states, a consumer group, and the agency itself.[33]

Agreement on a single national standard was complicated, however, by the fact that there were two major categories of woodstoves on the market—those that incorporated catalytic combusters and those that did not. It was clear that, at least in the short term, the stoves with catalytic combusters were capable of meeting a lower, more protective emission standard than those without catalytic combusters. Because catalytic combusters require a higher degree of maintenance, however, there was some question as to whether they would continue to deliver this greater level of emission reduction over the long term. Rather than resolve this technical issue, the negotiating committee agreed rather early on to adopt the industry position on the matter and to propose two standards—one for stoves with catalytic combusters and the other for those without.[34] Thus, the opportunity to diffuse what may well be a superior emission-reduction technology throughout the woodstove industry was lost, as was an opportunity for innovation through the development of new woodstove technology.

This does not necessarily mean, however, that the woodstove rule was a "failure" from an environmental and public health perspective. It is questionable whether section 111 actually empowers EPA to regulate residential woodstoves as "stationary sources" of air pollution, especially since the rule governs the manufacturers and retailers who sell the

stoves rather than the individual homeowners who operate them.[35] Thus, it could be argued that the process of negotiated rulemaking—in which the various players were able to agree on a rule despite its legal infirmities—resulted in a giant step forward, in that it produced national emission standards which otherwise might not have been promulgated, or which might have been successfully challenged in court.

On the other hand, the CAA was not the only regulatory alternative available to address the woodstove issue. The Federal Consumer Products Safety Act ("CPSA"), which governs the design and sale of products "for use in or around" the home or school, clearly does cover woodstoves sold for residential use and contemplates regulation of both manufacturers and retailers.[36] It is not clear, however, that regulation under the CPSA would necessarily have produced a stricter emission standard for stoves without catalytic combusters. The CPSA requires that the benefits of a consumer products safety standard be justified by its costs, and the members of the non-catalytic stove industry doubtless would have argued that a stricter standard would have driven them out of the market. Further, unlike EPA, the Consumer Product Safety Commission, a chronically underfunded agency that is often reluctant to take on new issues, had no particular incentive to regulate woodstoves.

b.   The Coke Oven Emissions Rule   Coke ovens are used to convert coal to coke, which is then used to produce steel. Air emissions from coke ovens come largely from leaking oven doors and lids. In 1992, EPA estimated that some 3.5 million pounds of toxic chemi-

---

32. 42 U.S.C. §7411(a)(1) (1994).
33. See Intent to Form an Advisory Committee to Negotiate New Source Performance Standards for Residential Wood Stove Combustion Units, 51 Fed. Reg. 4800 (1986).

34. See Standards of Performance for New Stationary Sources, New Residential Wood Heaters, 53 Fed. Reg. 5860 (1988) (codified at 40 C.F.R. pt. 60); Funk, supra note 31, at 88.
35. See Funk, supra note 31, at 66–74.
36. 15 U.S.C. §§2051–2084 (1994).

cals, including benzene, phenol, toluene, and polyaromatic hydrocarbons, were emitted to the air annually from coke ovens operating in the United States. Based on this estimate, EPA put the cancer risk to exposed individuals at one in one hundred.[39]

Many of the materials emitted by coke ovens are subject to regulation as hazardous air pollutants under section 112 of the CAA, and the 1990 amendments to the Act specifically required that section 112 standards for coke oven emissions be promulgated by December 31, 1992.[40] In early 1992, after meeting with representatives of the steel industry, relevant labor unions, states, and environmental groups "to discuss available data to be used as the basis of a section 112 regulation," EPA convened a negotiated rulemaking committee that drew from all of these constituencies.[41] After several negotiating sessions, the committee agreed on a draft rule that was proposed by the agency in December 1992, and was published as a final rule in October 1993.[43]

In general, section 112 of the CAA as amended in 1990 takes a two-tiered approach to the regulation of hazardous air pollutants. EPA must first set technology-based emission standards, on an industry category-by-industry category basis. These standards must be set with reference to the application of the maximum achievable control technology ("MACT") that the industry category can afford.[44] Eight years later, the agency is to set a more stringent, health-based standard if further emission reductions are deemed necessary to provide "an ample margin of safety to protect public health."[45] A health-based standard for carcinogens must be set if the technology-based standard fails to "reduce life-time excess cancer risks to the individual most exposed to the emissions...to less than one in one million."[46] For coke oven emissions in particular, however, section 112 offers an alternative whereby a source may delay compliance with the health-based standard until 2020 if it meets a different, more stringent technology-based standard in the interim.[47] The committee followed this framework in drafting its proposed rule, and steel industry representatives said afterward that, because they viewed any likely health-based standard as "essentially a shut-down standard," they expected all plants except those that planned to go out of business in the near future to choose this "extended compliance" option.[48]

At the conclusion of the negotiated rulemaking process, participants from environmental groups, labor, industry, and state

---

39. See Year-Long Coke Oven Negotiations Yield Pact Between Steel Industry, Environmentalists, 23 Env't. Rep. (BNA) 1669 (1992) [hereinafter Year-Long Coke Oven Negotiations].

40. See 42 U.S.C. §7412(d)(8)(A) (1994).

41. EPA's description of the negotiated rulemaking committee and its work, and of the events leading up to the establishment of the committee, is found in the preamble to the proposed National Emission Standards for Hazardous Air Pollutants for Source Categories; Coke Oven Batteries, 57 Fed. Reg. 57,534, 57,536 (1992) (proposed Dec. 4, 1992) (codified at 40 C.F.R. pt. 63) [hereinafter Preamble].

43. See National Emission Standards for Coke Oven Batteries, 58 Fed. Reg. 57,911 (1993) (codified at 40 C.F.R. pt. 63(L)).

44. See 42 U.S.C. §7412(d) (1994). We use the term "technology-based standard" to mean an emission limit that is determined by reference to the level of emission reduction deemed attainable through the application of a particular technology or set of technologies. It can, but generally does not, actually require the adoption of the particular reference technology.

45. Id. §7412(f). The term "health-based standard" is used to mean an emission limit that is determined by reference to the level of emission reduction deemed necessary to attain a particular health goal (such as a particular level of risk).

46. Id. §7412(f)(2)(A).

47. See id. §7412(i)(8).

48. Coke Oven NESHAP Includes Two Options Based on Year-Long Negotiated Rule-Making, 23 Env't. Rep. (BNA) 1934 (1992).

governments all expressed satisfaction with the negotiated rule.[49] An EPA representative stated his belief that the negotiated rule would result in more emission reductions than would have been obtained through the conventional rulemaking process, and remarked that the agency had never before "been able to grapple with the economic and technological issues" addressed by the rule.[50] It is probably more accurate to say, however, that the rulemaking was made considerably easier because Congress had taken it upon itself to specify the dates by which, and the minimum amounts by which, the steel industry would be asked to reduce emissions. Indeed, the chief contribution of negotiation to the rulemaking process appears to have been to afford the industry the opportunity to negotiate a standard that actually is less stringent than that which was mandated by Congress.

For coke oven facilities choosing the "extended compliance" option, EPA was required to promulgate two sets of technology-based emission limits by December 31, 1992, to become effective in November 1993 and January 1998, respectively.[51]

Emission limits for coke ovens had traditionally been expressed in terms of a maximum permissible percentage of leaking doors, lids, and offtakes, and Congress adopted this approach in section 112. For the 1993 limits, Congress specified the precise percentages EPA was to require.[52] For the 1998 limits, Congress directed the agency to set percentages "reflecting the lowest achievable emission rate" ("LAER"), and also specified a set of percentages representing the least stringent permissible 1998 standard that EPA could set, and a second set representing a more stringent default 1998 standard that was to take effect if the agency failed to promulgate the 1998 limits by December 31, 1992.[53]

The negotiated rulemaking committee began with the 1993 limits specified in the statute, and with the least stringent permissible 1998 limits specified in the statute; however, it converted these limits to "statistically equivalent" limits based on thirty days' average performance in the rule promulgated by EPA.[54] Thus, while the statute specified a maximum percentage that was not to be exceeded, the negotiated rule specified an aver-

49. See Year-Long Coke Oven Negotiations, supra note 39.

50. Id. The EPA representative was William G. Rosenberg, Assistant Administrator for Air and Radiation. His comments were echoed by EPA Administrator William Reilly. In an EPA press release, Reilly stated that the negotiated rule "goes beyond the requirements of the Clean Air Act," and offered the rule as "another example ... of where EPA has successfully used cooperative problem-solving to find an environmentally and economically sound solution to a complex pollution problem." U.S. EPA Environmental News Press Release: EPA Announces Agreement on Coke Oven Rules (Oct. 28, 1992) at 1–2.

51. See 42 U.S.C. §7412(d)(8)(C),(i)(8)(B) (1994).

52. See id. §7412(d)(8)(C).

53. See id. §7412(i)(8)(B)(i) (least stringent permissible standard), id. §7412(i)(8)(B)(ii) (default standard). The two are identical except that the default standard has no exclusion for "emissions during the period after the closing of self-sealing doors." Id.

§7412(i)(8)(B)(ii). The negotiated rulemaking committee calculated that the presence of this exclusion added about two percent to the allowable percentage of leaking doors specified in the least stringent permissible standard. See Telephone Interview with Marvin Branscome, Technical Consultant on Coke Oven Negotiations, Research Triangle Institute, Research Triangle Park, N.C. (Dec. 15, 1997). In practical terms, then, this means that the default standard for leaking doors was, as specified in the statute, "three per centum leaking doors (five per centum leaking doors for six meter batteries)," while the least stringent permissible standard, after allowance for the two percent exclusion, was five percent leaking doors (seven percent leaking doors for six meter batteries). Id.

54. See Branscome Interview, supra note 53; see also Telephone Interview with Amanda Agnew, Office of Air Quality, Emission Standards Division, U.S. EPA, Research Triangle Park, N.C. (Dec. 1, 1997); Preamble, supra note 41.

age percentage that must be achieved over a thirty-day period. This allows a facility to exceed the percentage specified in the statute for certain periods, so long as it is sufficiently below that percentage for other periods to maintain the required thirty-day average.[55]

This change was made because the steel industry expressed concern that a straightforward application of the standards specified by Congress would necessitate the closure of most of the existing coke oven facilities throughout the country, as they would be unable to meet the specified maximum limits on a continual basis.[56] Union participants in the negotiations, who were interested both in preserving jobs and in reducing workplace emissions, apparently helped to persuade the environmental group participants that this concern of the steel industry was valid.[57] In addition, the statistical conversion to thirty-day averages allowed EPA and the environmental group representatives to point to regulatory limits expressed as numbers that were actually below the numbers specified by Congress in the statute. For example, the statute requires a maximum of eight percent leaking doors in the 1993 limits, while the regulation specifies seven percent leaking doors.[58] Even though this difference is simply an artifact of the statistical conversion of the statutory number to a thirty-day average value, it lends the appearance of a more stringent standard.

From a health perspective, however, the regulation may well be less protective than the standards specified in the statute. There is evidence that short-term exposure to a certain amount of carcinogenic materials is more harmful than exposure to the same amount of those materials, in smaller daily increments, spread out over a longer term.[59] The increased damage done on the individual days of high exposure levels allowed under the thirty-day average approach, then, may not be offset by the reductions in damage experienced on those days when emissions are below the required average.

---

55. As the statute itself does not specify any given period for which the limits must be maintained, the statutory limits appear on their face to be daily maximum requirements (i.e., numbers that may not be exceeded on any given day). According to EPA consultant Marvin Branscome, however, the negotiated rulemaking committee interpreted the legislative history of section 112's coke oven provisions as indicating that the intention was for the statutory numbers to apply as the average of three consecutive "runs" of the coke oven battery. A "run" is a period of time during which a visual observation of coke oven emissions is made according to EPA-prescribed methods. As there will typically be one run per day, a three-run average is effectively a three-day average, and a 30-run average is effectively a 30-day average. See Branscome Interview, supra note 53. The limits in EPA's negotiated rule are in terms of a 30-run average. See 40 C.F.R. §63.309(d)(1) (1998) (specifying a "30-run rolling average of the percent leaking coke oven doors, topside port lids, and offtake systems . . ."); see also id. §63.309(d)(2) (specifying a "logarithmic 30-day rolling average of the seconds of visible emissions per charge . . .").

56. See Branscome Interview, supra note 53; Telephone Interview with Michael Wright, negotiation participant, United Steelworkers of America, Washington, D.C., (Dec. 8, 1997); Telephone Interview with Roy Huntley, negotiation participant and Staff Engineer, Office of Air Quality, Emission Standards Division, U.S. EPA, Research Triangle Park, N.C. (Dec. 17, 1997).

57. Due to the nature of coke oven technology, there is a clear link between environmental and occupational emissions. The participants in the negotiations formed two separate caucuses, the industry caucus and the environmental caucus. According to Michael Wright of the Steelworkers union, who participated in the negotiations, the union representatives joined the environmental caucus, but served as a "bridge" between the environmental caucus and the industry caucus. See Wright Interview, supra note 56.

58. Compare 42 U.S.C. §7412(d)(8)(C) (1994) ("8 per centum leaking doors") with 40 C.F.R. §63.304(b)(1)(i) (1998) ("7.0 percent leaking coke oven doors").

59. See, e.g., Dale Hattis, Pharmacokinetic Principles for Dose-Rate Extrapolation of Carcinogenic Risk from Genetically Active Agents, 10 RISK ANALYSIS 303 (1990).

Moreover, it appears clear that the negotiated 1998 limits were not set according to LAER, which is defined in the CAA as "the most stringent emission limitation that is achieved in practice by [the] class or category of source," with no consideration of the cost of meeting that emission limitation.[60] That is, a LAER limit is to be based on the emission levels being attained by the best-performing existing plant within the particular industry class or category. The best-performing coke oven facility in operation in the United States at the time was the Jewell Smokeless plant, in Vansant, Virginia, owned by Sun Coal. This facility employs a nonrecovery coke oven technology, while all of the other coke oven plants in the country employ the older, and dirtier, by-product recovery technology.[61] A nonrecovery plant can achieve an emission limit of 0.0% leaking doors, and has no lids or offtakes.[62] Further, nonrecovery plants produce far less wastewater and hazardous waste than comparable by-product recovery plants, and also generate excess energy that can be utilized elsewhere in the facility.[63] From an environmental perspective, the nonrecovery technology is undeniably superior.

Although industry representatives reportedly were concerned that EPA would base the LAER limits on the performance of the Jewell Smokeless plant, the negotiated rulemaking committee decided instead to consider the performance of by-product recovery

plants only.[64] The committee apparently focused on the performance of a USX (United States Steel) plant in Clairton, Pennsylvania, which the committee appears to have deemed the best-performing by-product recovery facility.[65] Yet, as noted, the committee set the 1998 limits simply by specifying percentages that were calculated to be the "statistical equivalent" of the least stringent permissible limits specified in the statute. If the committee took this approach because it believed that this was the best that by-product recovery plants could do, this appears to have been a significant error in assessment.

The negotiated 1998 limits (expressed as thirty-day averages) are 4.3% leaking doors for all tall doors and foundry doors, and 3.8% leaking doors for all other doors.[66] As LAER limits, these limits were required by statute to be representative of the very best performance within the industry. An EPA survey of by-product recovery plants done six months after these limits were promulgated in 1993, however, found that most plants were easily meeting the 1998 limits, and that some plants were averaging one to two percent leaking doors.[67] In other words, the best performance in the industry was considerably better than what the 1998 limits allow. Subsequent EPA surveys of the industry revealed that the performance of many of the plants worsened somewhat thereafter, but was still comfortably in compliance with the legally applicable 1993 limits.[68] This suggests

---

60. 42 U.S.C. §7501(3)(B) (1994). The 1998 limits were to "reflect the lowest achievable emission rate as defined in section 7501 of this title for a coke oven battery that is rebuilt or a replacement at a coke oven plant for an existing battery." 42 U.S.C. §7412 (i)(8)(B)(i) (1994).
61. See Huntley Interview, supra note 56.
62. Accordingly, the MACT limit set by EPA for nonrecovery facilities specifies 0.0% leaking doors, lids, and offtakes. See 40 C.F.R. §63.303(b) (1998).
63. See Branscome Interview, supra note 53.
64. See Huntley Interview, supra note 56. EPA does have discretion under section 112 to

"distinguish among classes, types, and sources within a category or subcategory in establishing . . . standards. . . ." 42 U.S.C. §7412(d)(1) (1994).
65. See id. (noting that "most of the data used" came from the Clairton plant); Wright Interview, supra note 56 (noting that the Clairton facility was deemed the best-performing plant). The preamble to the proposed standard does not explain how the 1998 LAER limits were set. See Preamble, supra note 41.
66. See 40 C.F.R. §63.304(b)(2)(i) (1998).
67. See Huntley Interview, supra note 56.
68. See id.

that the plants may have initially been testing their technology to ensure that they could meet the 1998 limits.[69] In August 1997, with the 1998 limits due to become enforceable within a few months, most of the plants were again meeting the 1998 limits on a continuous basis, and roughly three out of every five of the plants had maximum (as opposed to thirty-day average) values of less than two percent leaking doors.[70]

The CAA also specifies that, by January 2007, EPA is to review the 1998 LAER limits for coke oven facilities, and "revise [them], as necessary... to reflect the lowest achievable emission rate as defined... at the time," with such revised limits to become effective on January 1, 2010.[71] Rather than waiting until later to set the revised LAER standard, so that it could assess technological improvements made in response to the 1993 and 1998 limits, EPA adopted the recommendation of the negotiated rulemaking committee to set the 2010 standard as part of the 1993 rule. Again based on performance data from the United States Steel plant in Clairton, the limits for 2010 are only slightly more stringent than their 1998 counterparts, and are considerably less stringent than what the current data indicate the best-performing by-product recovery plants could meet.[72] The

statutory criteria for LAER, then, simply were not met.

EPA was also required to promulgate section 112 emission limits for new coke oven sources. Once again, the negotiated rule appears to fall short of the statutory mark. The problem is one of scope as well as one of substance. Section 112 defines "new source" as "a stationary source the construction or reconstruction of which is commenced after the EPA first proposes regulations under this section establishing an emission standard applicable to such source."[74] By the terms of the statute, then, a "new" coke oven source includes both the construction of a wholly new coke oven plant and the reconstruction of an existing plant to install a new coke oven battery. Under the terms of the regulation, however, a reconstructed coke oven plant becomes a "new" source only if the new coke oven batteries "increase the design capacity" of the facility.[75] This removes an entire class of reconstructed facility from the ambit of the new source standard, and allows existing plants that do not expand their operations to replace coke oven batteries without making any improvements in technology.[76]

Moreover, new source limits under section 112 are to be "not less stringent than the emission control that is achieved in practice

---

69. This apparently was the opinion of many EPA field staff. See id.

70. See id.; Emission Factor & Inventory Group, U.S. EPA, Battery Performance Data Survey (August 1997) (unpublished data, on file with the Harvard Environmental Law Review). The survey included 23 of the 26 plants in operation, which represented 60 of the 66 operating coke oven batteries. Roy Huntley reported in the survey that 83% of the batteries surveyed were meeting the 1998 limits continuously, and that 62% had maximum values of two percent or less.

71. 42 U.S.C. §7412(i)(8)(C) (1994).

72. The 2010 standard is 4.0% leaking doors for tall doors and foundry doors, and 3.3% leaking doors for all other doors. The 2010 standard does not impose new limits for the other parts of the standard (percentage leaking lids, percentage leak-

ing offtakes, and number of seconds per charge). See 40 C.F.R. §63.304(b)(3) (1998).

74. Id. §7412(a)(4) (emphasis added).

75. 40 C.F.R. §63.300(b) (1998). Except for certain specified facilities which were under construction when the 1990 CAA amendments were passed, the date at which existing design capacity is deemed established under the regulation is November 15, 1990, the date of the 1990 amendments.

76. In contrast, EPA's general regulations for implementation of the pre-construction review requirements of section 112(i)(1) specify that "[u]pon reconstruction, an affected source is subject to relevant standards for new sources, including compliance dates, irrespective of any change in emissions of hazardous air pollutants from that source." 43 C.F.R. §63.5(b)(1) (1997).

by the best controlled similar source," without regard to cost.[77] As the Jewell Smokeless nonrecovery plant in Virginia was the best-performing coke oven plant in the United States, one would have expected it to have been the model for EPA's new source standards.[78] Indeed, Congress specified that, in setting new source limits for coke oven facilities, the agency "shall evaluate...the Jewell design Thompson non-recovery coke oven batteries and other non-recovery coke oven technologies."[79] Nonetheless, the negotiated rulemaking committee chose to set two new source standards, one for nonrecovery batteries and one for by-product recovery batteries.[80] New sources choosing nonrecovery technology must meet a limit of 0.0% leaking doors, lids, and offtakes, while new sources choosing by-product recovery technology need only outperform the 2010

limits: 4.0% leaking doors for tall and foundry doors, 3.3% leaking doors for other doors, 0.4% leaking lids, and 2.5% leaking offtakes.[81]

A final noteworthy feature of the negotiated rule is its requirement that compliance monitoring be done on a daily basis, by "certified observers" who are independent of the coke oven facility but whose funding comes from the industry.[82] Although there have been problems in securing the true "independence" of the observers,[83] there appears to be little question that the rule has enhanced both the frequency and the accuracy of the compliance monitoring. By all accounts, these monitoring improvements are a direct result of the negotiated rulemaking process.[84]

Overall, however, the rule fashioned by the negotiators was not designed to secure optimal environmental performance from coke

---

77. 42 U.S.C. §7412(d)(3) (1994).
78. The Jewell Smokeless plant certainly would seem to be a "similar source" within the meaning of section 112. Although the powerful by-product recovery faction of the industry argued to the negotiated rulemaking committee that the coke produced by the nonrecovery process was of inferior quality, they apparently did not convince the committee on this score. See Huntley Interview, supra note 56; Branscome Interview, supra note 53. And, while the two types of plants differ in the fact that one produces by-products while the other does not, the clear purpose of both is to produce coke.
79. 42 U.S.C. §7412(d)(8)(A) (1994).
80. Although section 112(d)(1) gives EPA general authority to "distinguish among classes, types, and sizes of sources within a category or subcategory," see 42 U.S.C. §7412(d)(1) (1994), the specific references to nonrecovery technology in section 112(d)(8)(A) would appear to indicate a congressional intent to move beyond by-product recovery technology for new coke ovens.
81. Compare 40 C.F.R. §63.303(b) (new source standards for nonrecovery batteries) with 40 C.F.R. §63.302(b)–(d) (1998) (new source standards for new by-product recovery batteries). A new by-product recovery source must either meet the limits for a new nonrecovery source or utilize "a new recovery technology, including but not limited to larger size ovens, operation under negative pres-

sure, and processes with emission points different from those regulated under this [regulation]," and meet emission limits that are "less than" the 2010 limits. 40 C.F.R. §63.302(b)–(d) (1998).
82. 40 C.F.R. §63.301 (defining "certified observer"), 63.309 (1998) (requiring observations to be done seven days a week when the plant is operating).
83. The rule calls for the observers to be employed by EPA, but the agency later concluded that it did not have the authority to act as an "employer" in this capacity. Reportedly, at least in some areas of the country, the "independent" observer thus is not only paid by the coke oven facility, but actually has an office at the plant, and effectively is a company employee. Apparently, there is a move afoot to have state and/or local government assume employment responsibility for the certified observers. See Huntley Interview, supra note 56.
84. EPA's Roy Huntley recalls that this was not an item that had been sought by EPA or environmental group representatives, but rather was something that the industry representatives simply offered to do at one negotiating session. See id. Presumably, industry representatives believed that this would help them achieve their broader goals at the negotiations. Michael Wright of the Steelworkers union recalls that this item was not viewed as a major concession by the industry. See Wright Interview, supra note 56.

oven facilities. The rule provides a framework wherein facilities are assured that, at least until the 2020 statutory target date for health-based limits, emission limits will be attainable through the use of inferior, pre-1993 technology.[85] Indeed, an EPA official noted at the time that companies choosing the "extension track" would be assured that any improvements made to their plants when the rule went into effect in 1993 would be the last they would be required to make for almost thirty years.[86] Although this could change if the agency decides to tighten the 2010 limits before the 2007 deadline,[87] the regulation clearly is not designed to encourage diffusion of the cleaner nonrecovery technology within the industry, much less to spur any further wholesale improvements in coke oven technology. Further, while EPA touted the negotiated rule as a triumph for "environmental justice" (because coke oven plants tend to be located in heavily industrialized, lower-income areas),[88] the effect of the negotiated new source standards will be to discourage the use of the cleaner technology in those areas until at least 2020.

This is not to say that the result achieved by the negotiated rule-making committee may not represent an appropriate balancing of environmental and economic concerns in its approach to a troubled industry. A major stumbling block to tying emission limits to the performance of nonrecovery technology, apparently, was the relatively high capital cost of replacing an existing by-product recovery battery with a new nonrecovery battery.[89] In addition, there was a concern about jobs. A nonrecovery facility typically employs fewer workers than a by-product recovery facility. Requiring improved performance at existing by-product recovery plants, however, actually created jobs.[90] Negotiated rulemaking appears to have been an ideal vehicle for the discussion of these issues, and for the sharing of information that appears to have been necessary to convince the environmental group representatives to accept the less stringent emission limitations favored by industry.[91]

However, had the goal instead been to "push" the industry toward markedly better technology, and thus to risk some short-term dislocation within the industry, it is not at all clear that negotiation would have been the best approach. The fact that EPA so grossly underestimated the performance capability of even the existing by-product recovery technology suggests that the agency's limited resources were directed more at ensuring a "successful" negotiation than at ensuring

---

85. Presumably, unless Congress relaxes the requirements of section 112 at the request of the steel industry, any meaningful health-based standard set by EPA (which, as noted, is required by section 112 to ensure that the cancer risk is no more than one in one million) would effectively require a move to nonrecovery technology.

86. This comment is attributed to William G. Rosenberg, Assistant Administrator for Air and Radiation. See Year-Long Coke Oven Negotiations, supra note 39.

87. The regulation leaves open this possibility. The specified limits for 2010 will apply "unless the Administrator [of EPA] promulgates more stringent limits." 40 C.F.R. §63.304(b)(3) (1998).

88. See, e.g., Final Rule on Coke Ovens Means Victory for 'Environmental Justice,' Browner Says, 24 Env't. Rep. (BNA) 1169–70 (1993).

89. Replacing a by-product recovery battery with a nonrecovery battery requires reconstruction of the entire surrounding structure. See Branscome Interview, supra note 53.

90. See Wright Interview, supra note 56.

91. EPA also credits negotiated rulemaking for having kept the coke oven rule out of the courts. See Agnew Interview, supra note 54. Most of the credit for this properly goes to Congress, however, for having devised a statutory "default" standard for the extension track, which would have gone into effect had a standard not been negotiated by December 31, 1992, that was more stringent than what the steel industry was able to obtain through negotiation. See supra note 52 and accompanying text.

that its technological and economic database was a reliable one.[92] Had EPA instead used those resources to take a hard look at what the industry could do, now and in the future, it is likely that the agency could have crafted a rule that met the environmental goals of the Clean Air Act and created meaningful incentives for the use of better technology.[93]

c. The Wood Furniture Coatings Rule Another section 112 regulation that was drafted largely through negotiated rulemaking was the hazardous air pollutant emission standard for the wood furniture industry. After a series of public meetings with representatives from industry, environmental groups, and state government in late 1992 and early 1993, EPA convened a negotiated rulemaking committee to attempt to formulate a rule governing wood furniture (surface coatings) nationwide. The committee held its first meeting in July 1993, and a proposed rule, largely drafted by the committee, was issued in December 1994. The timing of this promulga-

tion likely was influenced by (if not wholly determined by) the fact that the Sierra Club, a private, nonprofit environmental group, had sued EPA in 1993 to compel the issuance of several rules under section 112. A consent decree entered in that case called for the promulgation of this proposed rule by November 21, 1994.[94] The final rule—virtually unchanged from the proposed rule—was promulgated on December 7, 1995,[95] although portions of the rule were challenged in court by the chemical industry.[96]

Based on the committee's work, EPA determined that wood furniture manufacturers performed four basic operations in producing a finished product—finishing, gluing, cleaning, and washoff—and the proposed rule contained standards for each. All but the gluing operation standards were drafted by the committee. The standards for the gluing operations were developed "outside of the regulatory negotiation process, because adhesive suppliers were not represented on the Committee."[97] EPA estimated that more

---

92. Reportedly, the negotiated rulemaking process took an "immense" amount of agency resources. Huntley Interview, supra note 56. Most of the performance and cost data used in the negotiations apparently came from the steel industry and from the union. Throughout the negotiations, steel industry representatives insisted that the emission reductions under consideration would be extremely expensive and extremely difficult to meet. See id.; Branscome Interview, supra note 53; Wright Interview, supra note 56.

93. The potential economic viability of the nonrecovery technology, even in retrofitted existing plants, is highlighted by the fact that Inland Steel currently is replacing by-product recovery batteries with nonrecovery batteries at one of its plants. See Huntley Interview, supra note 56; Branscome Interview, supra note 53; Wright Interview, supra note 56. The key economic factor appears to be the energy savings that are available through the use of the nonrecovery technology. See Branscome Interview, supra note 53.

94. Sierra Club v. EPA, No. 93-0124 (D.D.C.) (consent decree entered Feb. 23, 1994).

95. See National Emission Standards for Hazardous Air Pollutants; Final Standards for

Hazardous Air Pollutant Emissions from Wood Furniture Manufacturing Operations, 60 Fed. Reg. 62,930, 62,936 (1995) (codified at 40 C.F.R. §63.800–.808).

96. In three separate actions filed in the United States Court of Appeals for the District of Columbia, the Chemical Manufacturer's Association, the Society of the Plastics Industry, and the Halogenated Solvents Industry Alliance challenged that portion of the rule that lists certain chemicals as Volatile Hazardous Air Pollutants ("VHAPs") of Potential Concern. See Coglianese, supra note 19, at 1305. The rule requires facilities to monitor their use of these designated VHAPs and establish a "baseline" annual usage. Any increase above this baseline that does not meet one of four designated criteria is to result in efforts by the facility to decrease its use of these chemicals, so long as the facility and the state agree that such reduction would be practical.

97. National Emission Standards for Hazardous Air Pollutants; Proposed Standards for Hazardous Air Pollutant Emissions From Wood Furniture Mfg. Operations, 59 Fed. Reg. 62,652, 62,654 (1994) (to be codified at 40 C.F.R. pt. 63) (proposed Dec. 6, 1994) [hereinafter "NESHAP"].

than 11,000 facilities were included within the wood furniture industrial source category, and that approximately 750 of these would be considered "major" (as defined by the rule), and thus subject to these regulations under section 112.[98]

As EPA noted in the preamble to the proposed regulation, "a regulatory negotiation process...often requires concessions from some parties in exchange for concessions from other parties...."[99] Considered as a whole, the wood furniture rule might well be viewed as a compromise on the stringency of emission levels in exchange for a clear focus on pollution prevention (as opposed to simply "end-of-pipe" emission control).

For example, section 112(d) specifies that EPA "may distinguish among classes, types, and sizes of sources within a category or subcategory in establishing [technology-based] standards" for the emission of hazardous air pollutants. Rather than distinguish among the technological and economic capabilities of particular wood furniture industry segments, however, the committee proposed —and EPA accepted—an industry-wide standard. Accordingly, EPA dismissed the suggestion that it require the use of "finishing materials with a very low- or zero-HAP hazardous air pollutant content," on the basis that such materials "have not been demonstrated to be feasible for all industry segments."[102] Had EPA divided the industry

into subcategories for regulatory purposes, however, it appears that lower emissions of hazardous air pollutants could have been achieved in certain sectors through the required use of these finishing materials where such use would be feasible.[103]

Further, in the part of the rule dealing with restrictions on certain work practices known to be associated with the release of hazardous air pollutants,[104] the committee specified a list of solvents to be forbidden from use in cleaning or "washoff" activities. Agency technical personnel believed that the committee's list of the chemicals to be so restricted was too narrow. As noted by EPA in the preamble:

> Some agency officials have expressed concern that the proposed rule only restricts the use of EPA type A and type B1/B2 carcinogens in cleaning and washoff solvents. They are concerned that restricting the use of only these chemicals implies that they are worse than other HAP.[105]

Despite the scientific arguments for including more chemicals on the list, however, EPA simply accepted the proposed rule as written by the negotiated rulemaking committee: "The Committee agreed to restrict the use of type A and type B sub1/B sub2 carcinogens only, so the EPA is proposing the rule using this approach."[106]

Nonetheless, while the rule drafted by the committee is less stringent than it likely could have been, it is designed to encourage

---

98. Id. at 62,664.

99. Id. at 62,654.

102. NESHAP, supra note 97, at 62,667 (emphasis added).

103. The preamble to the proposed rule indicates that the committee had divided the industry into several subcategories, such as kitchen cabinet manufacturers, residential furniture manufacturers, and upholstered furniture manufacturers, for other purposes. See id. at 62,666.

104. 42 U.S.C. §7412(h)(1) (1994) specifically allows EPA to promulgate work practice standards in lieu of emission standards for sources of hazardous air pollution for which an emission standard would not be feasible.

105. NESHAP, supra note 97, at 62,673. EPA further noted that these agency officials are also concerned that the rule draws a clear line between type B and type C carcinogens, although the scientific evidence does not suggest such a clear distinction. For example, some pollutants on the HAP list are designated type B/C because the data cannot clearly support a designation of type B or C. The proposed rule does not address these pollutants. Finally, the Agency is planning to update [its] risk assessment guidelines. Under these revised guidelines, the terms type A and type B carcinogens are likely to be meaningless. Id.

106. Id.

pollution prevention. Thus it could ultimately result in changes in technology and practices that reduce emissions below the levels required by the rule. Further, the emphasis on pollution prevention has the advantage of providing protection both to the environment and to workers, and is consistent with the goals of the Pollution Prevention Act. Rather than focusing on the use of control technology to reduce emissions, the committee endeavored to select a format that would "accommodate multiple compliance techniques for the various industry segments."[108] For finishing operations, the committee chose to express the required emission limit in terms of kilograms (or pounds) of volatile hazardous air pollutants emitted per kilogram (or pound) of solids contained in the finishing materials used. EPA noted this method of expressing the limit was chosen because "sources are encouraged to reduce the quantity of HAP through reformulation measures."[109]

Significant attention was paid to pollution prevention in the drafting of work practice rules as well. As mentioned above, the use of certain solvents is banned in cleaning and washoff operations. In addition, the use of solvents in spray booth cleaning is prohibited except in limited circumstances, and sources are required to maintain a "solvent accounting system" to track the use of solvents in cleaning and washoff.[110] As noted by the agency, "although it cannot be assumed that it will actually result in . . . reduction, the cleaning and washoff solvent accounting sys-

tem may prompt facilities to eliminate inefficient uses of solvent."[111]

The fact that this rule included a substantial emphasis on pollution prevention is not surprising. Both the decentralized industry profile, and the relatively straightforward and uncomplicated opportunities for chemical substitution and use reduction, made this industry an ideal candidate for pollution prevention.[112] Nonetheless, it does appear that the use of negotiated rulemaking facilitated the agency's focus on pollution prevention in the development of the rule. It seems likely that the active participation of industry representatives (who are in the best position to identify productive opportunities for pollution prevention) helped to both deepen and legitimize the committee's efforts to build pollution prevention into the rule.

Moreover, the committee negotiations produced an agreement, outside of the parameters of the rule, under which the industry agreed to prepare a semiannual "trends report," beginning in 1994,which would contain "a brief discussion of technologies being used by the industry to reduce emissions, and a discussion of evolving technologies including new finishing materials, adhesives, and improved application equipment."[113] This agreement reflects the belief—apparently shared by many committee members—that "new, lower emitting (both VOC volatile organic compound and HAP) technologies . . . are . . . on the threshold of demonstration."[114] In addition, to help determine whether the rule actually results in the tar-

---

108. NESHAP, supra note 97, at 62,668.
109. Id. at 62,675.
110. Id.
111. Id.
112. For example, the fact that input substitutions (such as using paints or solvents that are less toxic) can be done without major modifications to the production process makes pollution prevention easier to achieve here than in industries with more

inflexible processes. Further, the fact that the industry is comprised of hundreds of small shops, rather than a small number of large ones, makes it more difficult for the industry to exert collective economic pressure against change, and also means there will be considerably more opportunity for experimentation and variation.
113. NESHAP, supra note 97, at 62,680.
114. Id.

geted reductions in hazardous air pollutant emissions, and to determine whether those emission reductions are being met through the substitution of other hazardous chemicals that are not regulated as hazardous air pollutants, the trends report is to include a chemical use and emission survey from a representative sample of the industry.[115]

d. Evaluation The table reproduced below summarizes the results of these three negotiated rulemakings in terms of the substantive criteria suggested at the outset: environmental/public health protection and technological change.

The first two columns focus on the particular rulemaking's potential to effect technological change within the regulated industry, where "diffusion" refers to the diffusion of an environmentally superior existing technology within the industry, and "innovation" refers to the development of a new technology that either produces greater environmental gains than existing technology or produces equal gains at a lower cost. The second two columns refer to the rulemaking's potential to effect improvements in public health or the environment, where "short-term" gains are those that are achieved before new and better technology is developed, and "long-term" gains are those that are achieved when new and better technology is developed and fully implemented.

The woodstoves rulemaking did not seek to push the envelope of woodstove technology, and focused instead on the diffusion of existing control technology. It is assigned a "+/−" rating in the Diffusion column be-

cause it set a different emission standard for each of the two types of woodstove technologies on the market, rather than seeking to devise a standard that would diffuse the superior technology throughout the industry. This resulted in short-term environmental gain, but did not create a strong, consistent signal designed to encourage the kind of innovation in woodstove technology that might produce greater environmental gain in the long-term.

The profile for the coke oven rule is quite similar. Rather than seeking to diffuse the cleaner existing (nonrecovery) technology, the coke oven rule focused on the use of readily available control techniques to improve the performance of the dominant existing (by-product recovery) technology, and has resulted in short-term environmental gain. Further, by setting a standard for new facilities that is not tied to the performance of the cleaner existing technology, and by setting a 2010 standard for existing facilities that many firms were meeting easily in 1993, the negotiated rule provides clear incentives for keeping the dirtier technology in operation longer, thus actually reducing long-term environmental gain.

The wood furniture coatings rule, in contrast, has both a focus on pollution prevention—denoted as "+(PP)"—and a focus on innovation. It can be expected to diffuse existing pollution prevention technologies and, especially given industry's agreement to prepare the semiannual trends report, has a real potential to produce innovation (and, concomitantly, to produce long-term environmental gain). . . .

---

115. See id. at 62,679–80 (noting that "[b]ecause the emission limits for finishing materials can be met through substitution of non-HAP VOCs for HAP, and some non-HAP's can be as hazardous as the listed HAP's, [the committee] felt it was important to track emissions of other pollutants from the industry to ensure that materials of equal or greater toxicity were not being substituted for HAP. . . .").

Technological and Environmental Impact of Three Negotiated Air Emission Standards

	Diffusion	Innovation	Short-Term Env't. Gain	Long-Term Env't. Gain
Woodstoves	±	−	+	−
Coke Ovens	±	−	+	−
Wood Furniture	+(PP)	+(PP)	+	+

■ **NOTES**

1. It is interesting (and perhaps a tribute to the subtle power of myth) that the estimate by then-EPA Administrator William Ruckelshaus that a full 80% of administrative rules are taken to court—which appears not to be true—was cited again and again as an important justification for negotiated rulemaking.

2. Although, as noted, negotiated rules are still subject to judicial review, the Negotiated Rulemaking Act specifies that "agency action relating to establishing, assisting, or terminating a negotiated rulemaking committee under this subchapter shall not be subject to judicial review."

3. The reader should consult Sections 4, 7, 8, and 10 of the APA, together with the APA's negotiated rulemaking provisions. Many originating statues contain procedural requirements in addition to—or in lieu of—those specified in the APA. Close attention to the particular requirements of each statutory scheme is important.   ■

D. CITIZEN AND CORPORATE ACCESS TO THE ADMINISTRATIVE PROCESS

The affected public has considerable opportunity to influence agency rulemaking. At the very least, notice and an opportunity to comment must be provided before the promulgation of any substantive regulation. Although most people neither read the *Federal Register* nor take time to comment, those who do participate tend to reflect the broader populace. Typically, a *Federal Register* notice of proposed rulemaking in the area of workplace health or safety attracts the attention of labor unions, public interest groups, and representatives of the affected industries. They most likely will participate in the process, and in doing so they will present the views of their respective constituencies. Thus, although the outcome is still determined by the agency, a rough form of "administrative democracy" is at work.

Furthermore, other avenues of access provide additional opportunity to influence the outcome of administrative proceedings.

1. Initiation of Rulemaking

Section 4(e) of the APA requires every agency to "give an interested person the right to petition for the issuance, amendment, or repeal of a rule." Thus, although this section does not require the agency to actually take the requested action, it does give the interested public a formal opportunity to prod administrative consideration of a particular issue. Furthermore, unless the request is patently frivolous, the agency may be required to provide a statement of its rationale if it declines to act on the petition.

Some originating statutes provide even greater leverage to citizens seeking to initiate agency rulemaking. Section 21 of the Toxic Substances Control Act (15 U.S.C. §2620), for example, contains specific provisions authorizing citizen petitions. In addition, it requires EPA to "either grant or deny" the petition within 90 days, authorizes the agency to hold a public hearing on the petition if "appropriate," and requires it to publish its rationale in the *Federal Register* if it denies the petition. Finally, a citizen whose petition for rulemaking is denied has a right under Section 21 to appeal the matter to a federal district court for a de novo proceeding. In such an appeal, the court is required by the statute to evaluate the petition on its merits and may not simply defer to the discretion of the agency.

2. Access to Agency Proceedings and Records

Much of what an agency does is a matter of public record, and is generally accessible to the public. Three statutes, added to the APA in the 1970s, are particularly useful. The Government in the Sunshine Act, 5 U.S.C. §552b, requires that, except for certain enumerated exceptions, "every portion of every meeting of an agency shall be open to public observation." The exceptions are designed primarily to provide protection for personal privacy, trade secrets, agency enforcement efforts, and internal agency personnel rules and practices. A companion provision pertaining to agency records is the Freedom of Information Act (FOIA), 5 U.S.C. §552, which requires each agency to make all of its records "promptly available to any person," subject to a similar set of exceptions. Under the FOIA, an agency is required to respond to any request for records within 10 working days. Anyone who is denied access to records to which he or she is entitled under the FOIA may take the agency to federal district court to secure access and may recover attorneys' fees and the costs of the suit. Finally, there is the Privacy Act, 5 U.S.C. §552a, which provides broad access—with certain narrow exceptions—to agency records pertaining to oneself. The act provides a right to correct inaccurate references to oneself in agency records and limits an agency's disclosure of personal information.

3. Access to Advisory Committees

The proceedings and records of agency advisory committees also are generally open to the public. The Federal Advisory Committee Act (FACA), 5 U.S.C. App. 2, requires that, again with certain exceptions, the meetings of advisory committees be open to the general public and the records of these committees be made available to the general public. The exceptions generally follow those found in the Government in the Sunshine Act and the Freedom of Information Act. FACA also provides the public with some control over the composition of advisory committees. It requires the membership of an advisory committee to be "fairly balanced in terms of the points of view presented and the functions to be performed" [5 U.S.C. App. 2 §5(b)(2)]. This provision was designed to prevent advisory committees from being unduly biased toward any particular viewpoint on important policy or technical issues. In the words of the Supreme Court, the overriding purpose of FACA is to prevent "the wasteful expenditure of public funds for worthless committee meetings and biased proposals" [*Public Citizen v. United States Dept. of Justice*, 491 U.S. 440, 453 (1989)].

An important feature of FACA is that it does not apply only to advisory bodies specifically designated as FACA committees, such as negotiated rulemaking committees. FACA applies to almost all formal and informal advisory bodies convened by an agency, regardless of whether the agency refers to them as "advisory committees." Thus, if an agency meets with a group of industry scientists with regard to a proposed chemical regulation, but fails to include experts with other viewpoints (or, conversely, if it meets with a group of scientists from the public interest community without including representatives of industry), it may well be in violation of the fair balance requirement of FACA. Furthermore, if it holds such meetings and refuses admission to other interested parties, it may well be in violation of the public access provisions of the act. Careful attention to FACA, then, can be a useful tool for those seeking to have input to agency decision making, especially on issues of science and technology.

In addition to these general rights of access, the originating statute may provide other routes of access to agency proceedings or records. Conversely, in some cases the originating statute will contain provisions that limit the applicability of one or more of these laws.

▪ NOTES

1. Although the federal government has argued that FACA's "fair balance" requirement is so vague that the issue of whether a particular committee is fairly balanced is not "justiciable" (that is, that it is not a proper subject for judicial review) the courts

have disagreed. The federal courts will review the composition of federal advisory committees to determine whether the fair balance requirement has been satisfied, but they generally employ a deferential standard of review. See, for example, *Cargill, Inc. v. United States*, 173 F.3d 323, 334–338 (5th Cir. 1999), and the cases discussed therein.

2. One of the authors of this text has suggested that the fair balance requirement, when applied to scientific and technical advisory committees, logically requires that the committee be balanced as to relevant political outlook, as to outlook on the general type of scientific or technical issue before the committee, and as to relevant scientific or technical discipline. *See* N. Ashford (1984) "Advisory Committees in OSHA and EPA: Their Use in Regulatory Decisionmaking," *Science, Technology and Human Values* 9: 72.

3. After a court decision holding that FACA applied to a committee of the National Academy of Sciences, FACA was amended in 1997 to specify that committees established by the National Academy of Sciences or the National Academy of Public Administration are not advisory committees under FACA. Instead, the 1997 amendments added a new section to FACA governing such committees. See 5 U.S.C. App. 2 §15. ■

4. Access to the Courts

Finally, the public has a limited right of access to the courts to seek judicial review of agency performance. The standards by which courts evaluate agency decisions are discussed in the next section. To actually get into court, however, one must be able to jump through a few practical and procedural hoops.

In general, a court does not have the power to review an agency decision unless there is statutory authority for judicial review. To determine if a court is authorized to review an agency decision, one usually looks to the APA and the particular regulatory statute under which the agency decision was made.

Section 10 of the APA (5 U.S.C. §§701–706) provides for judicial review in situations in which the originating statute is silent on the point. (Technically, since the APA is not a jurisdictional provision, jurisdiction is secured in these situations under "federal question" jurisdiction, which is discussed earlier in this chapter.) However, not every agency decision is reviewable. To come under the ambit of Section 10 of the APA, the decision must be one that can be characterized as a "final agency action." The term "agency action" is defined elsewhere in the act as "the whole or a part of an agency rule, order, license, sanction, relief, or the equivalent or denial thereof, or failure to act" [5 U.S.C. §551(13)]. Importantly, then, an agency decision not to take regulatory action in a particular area is reviewable under this provision.

The word "final" is not defined in the APA, but the clear intent is to preclude review under this section before the regulatory issue in question has had an opportunity to make its way through the regulatory decision-making process.

Section 10 also provides that an agency decision that would be otherwise reviewable under the APA will not be reviewable if either another statute precludes judicial review or the decision is one that is "committed to agency discretion by law." Thus one must always look to the originating statute to determine whether it contains language that would place the decision in one of these categories. Originating statutes may also expand the availability of judicial review. Many health, safety, and environmental statutes have sections that specify direct access to the courts for review of certain agency decisions. Indeed, all of the environmental statutes discussed in the following chapters have such provisions.

Even where the right to judicial review regarding the subject matter is otherwise established by statute, there are certain threshold limitations on the availability of judicial review. Three doctrines of administrative law—commonly dubbed "exhaustion of administrative remedies," "ripeness," and "standing to sue"—sometimes pose threshold problems. The first two address the question of whether the administrative decision in question has "matured" sufficiently, whether it has reached that point in the administrative process at which it is deemed reviewable. Exhaustion of administrative remedies is the rule that all intraagency appeals must be utilized before one can seek judicial review. In large part this doctrine is consistent with that portion of the APA that provides review only for final agency actions. The exhaustion doctrine can be modified, however, if the court finds that additional proceedings in the agency would be futile or would work irreparable harm. Ripeness, a related doctrine, is a rule of constitutional derivation. As discussed, Article III of the Constitution empowers the federal courts to hear "Cases" and "Controversies." As interpreted by the Supreme Court, this means that federal courts may only entertain a case or controversy that is both real and present or imminent. Thus, if the agency is still considering the regulatory matter in question, or has not yet taken contemplated regulatory action, a court may find that the matter is not yet ripe for judicial review.

The third threshold limitation on jurisdiction, the standing doctrine, deals with the question of whether the person seeking judicial review is among those who are entitled to seek such review. Like the ripeness doctrine, the standing doctrine stems from the Supreme Court's interpretation of the "case or controversy" language of Article III. According to the Court, this language requires that the plaintiff in a case filed in federal court have a "personal stake in the outcome of the controversy" sought to be resolved [*Baker v. Carr*, 369 U.S. 186, 204 (1962)]. In cases seeking review of federal agency decision making, this means that the plaintiff must show that he or she will be injured by the agency action (or inaction) at issue. For those seeking review under the Administrative Procedure Act, this requirement is also imposed by Section 10 of the APA, which provides that "[a] person *suffering legal wrong* because of agency action, or *adversely affected* by agency action within the meaning of a relevant statute, is entitled to judicial review thereof" (5 U.S.C. §702, emphasis added). Thus, before one is entitled to judicial review of an agency decision—before one has standing to sue—one must be able to establish that one needs the intervention of the court to prevent injury to oneself. But what kind of "injury" is required, and how close must the nexus be between that injury and the person seeking review?

The first important environmental case on this issue was *Sierra Club v. Morton*, 405 U.S. 727 (1972). There, the Sierra Club (a nonprofit environmental group) brought suit under the Administrative Procedure Act in an effort to block the construction of a large resort in the Mineral King Valley in California, which is directly adjacent to Sequoia National Park. The group alleged that the secretary of interior's decisions to allow such construction "would destroy or otherwise affect the scenery, natural and historic objects and wildlife of the park and would impair the enjoyment of the park for future generations" (id. at 734). It did not allege that any of its members actually used the park, but rather alleged a general interest in protecting the environment on behalf of all members of the public. The Court agreed that the kind of injury alleged here—which it characterized as aesthetic rather than economic—"may amount to an 'injury in fact' sufficient to lay the groundwork for standing under Section 10 of the APA." However, the Court held that the Sierra Club did not have standing in this case because it had not alleged any specific aesthetic injury to any specific Sierra Club member. Standing, noted the Court, "requires that the party seeking review be himself among the injured" (id. at 734–735).

Although *Sierra Club v. Morton* dealt with the statutory requirements for standing under the APA, the Court has since made it clear that these same principles are applicable to any case brought in the federal courts. In *Lujan v. Defenders of Wildlife*, 504 U.S. 555 (1992), for example, the plaintiffs had sought to challenge a Department of Interior regulation that they alleged would threaten the habitats of endangered animal species in Egypt and Sri Lanka that they had an interest in observing. Although the Court acknowledged that the desire to observe an environmental amenity, "even for purely esthetic purposes, is undeniably a cognizable interest for purposes of standing," it held that the plaintiffs had not demonstrated an "actual or imminent" injury to such an interest, because none of them had any "concrete plans" to travel to Egypt or Sri Lanka in the foreseeable future (id. at 562–563). To have standing to sue under Article III of the Constitution, the Court held, the plaintiff must establish: (1) that he or she suffered an "injury in fact—an invasion of a legally-protected interest which is (a) concrete and particularized and (b) actual or imminent, not conjectural or hypothetical"; (2) that the injury is "fairly . . . trace[able] to the challenged action"; and (3) that it is "likely, as opposed to merely speculative, that the injury will be redressed by a favorable decision" (id. at 560–561). These three criteria—generally identified, in shorthand fashion, as injury in fact, traceability, and redressability—are the heart of the standing doctrine, and are deemed by the Supreme Court to be mandated by the Constitution. As such, they may not be relaxed by Congress.

In addition to these core standing criteria, the Court also has imposed a few "prudential" standing criteria. Because the prudential criteria are not based on the Court's interpretation of Article III, but rather have been developed by the Court "for its own governance," Congress is free to relax or eliminate them. See *Data Processing Service Organizations, Inc. v. Camp*, 397 U.S. 150, 153 (1970). The prudential criterion likely to be most important in cases seeking judicial review of agency action is known as the "zone of interests" requirement. To meet this requirement, the party seeking judicial review must show that the injury on which standing is based is to an interest that "is arguably within the zone of interests to be protected or regulated by the...statute in question" (id. at 153). That is, the injury claimed must be of the type, broadly speaking, sought to be prevented by the statute under which the challenged agency decision was made.

Some years ago, for example, OSHA promulgated a Hazard Communication Standard requiring, among other things, that employers using carcinogenic chemicals in their workplace label them as health hazards. The agency also issued a notice indicating that for the purposes of this requirement it would treat only certain types of lubricating oils as carcinogenic. Manufacturers of some of these lubricating oils sought judicial review of this notice. They did not claim that their oils were not carcinogenic, but rather that certain other lubricating oils made by competing manufacturers had been wrongly classified as noncarcinogenic. In an effort to establish the requisite injury in fact for standing, the plaintiff manufacturers claimed that they had been placed at a competitive disadvantage compared with the manufacturers whose oils had been designated as noncarcinogenic (because customers would prefer to purchase the "noncarcinogenic" oils). Although economic harm, properly alleged, can form the basis for standing, the District of Columbia Court of Appeals dismissed the case:

[T]he interest to be protected by the OSHAct is worker safety....As petitioners here do not come before us as protectors of worker safety, but instead as entrepreneurs seeking to protect their competitive interests, we think it plain they lack standing under...the zone of interests test. (*Calumet Industries v. Brock*, 807 F.2d 225, 228 (D.C. Cir. 1986))

The practical implications of the standing doctrine should be apparent. In general, if the administrative decision in question involves an environmental issue, at least one of the plaintiffs must be someone who has a direct health, economic, or aesthetic interest in the environmental amenity in question. If it involves a workplace issue, at least one of the plaintiffs should be an affected employer or employee, depending on the nature of the case. Once standing to sue is established by someone having a direct interest in the outcome, however, that party may raise the broader interests of the public at large. See *Sierra Club v. Morton*, 405 U.S. at 737–738 ("once review is properly invoked [by a party who has standing], that person may argue the public interest in support of his claim that the agency has failed to comply with its statutory mandate").

■ **NOTES**

1. It is important to emphasize that since standing and ripeness are doctrines of constitutional derivation, they are applicable to all cases brought in the federal courts, and not just to cases involving judicial review of agency decision making. As discussed in chapter 11, for example, standing has been a major battleground in "citizen suit" cases brought to enforce federal environmental statutes against alleged violators of those statutes. (These citizen suits are a form of congressionally sanctioned "private right of action," discussed later in this chapter.)

2. It should also be emphasized that this discussion of the standing and ripeness doctrines applies to federal court jurisdiction only. Standing to sue in the courts of any particular state will be determined by the statutes and/or constitution of that state, and may be broader or narrower than standing to sue in federal court.

3. The Supreme Court's standing doctrine has been criticized for straying too far from the simple "case or controversy" language of Article III. The Court has sometimes explained the standing doctrine with reference to the separation of powers inherent in the structure of the Constitution: if anyone (and not just those with a personal stake in the outcome) could seek federal court review of agency decision making, the judiciary, and not the executive, would effectively control the ways in which the laws of Congress are to be implemented. This, the Court has said, would run afoul of Article II of the Constitution, which gives responsibility for implementing federal laws to the president.

4. Congress has endorsed the zone of interest requirement for cases brought under the Administrative Procedure Act; Section 10 of the APA specifies that judicial review is available under the APA for persons adversely affected by agency action "within the meaning of a relevant statute." See *Sierra Club v. Morton*, 405 U.S. at 773.

5. Note that the plaintiff lubricating oil manufacturers in the *Calumet Industries* case would have satisfied the zone of interests test if they had challenged OSHA's designation of their own products as carcinogenic. In general, the subject of a particular regulatory action will always have standing to challenge that action. ■

5. Monetary Limitations on the Availability of Review

Legal considerations are not the only important factors in determining whether judicial review will be available. There are monetary limitations on the availability of review. Of primary practical concern is the fact that lawsuits cost money. Not only does one have to hire a lawyer to bring the case, but it is often also necessary to employ technical consultants to analyze the subject matter in question and to critique the agency's approach to technical issues. Fortunately, Congress has provided some assistance in this area. The Equal Access to Justice Act, 28 U.S.C. §2412, passed in 1984, provides for an award of "fees and other expenses" to any "prevailing party" in a lawsuit (other than a tort suit) with an agency of the United States, unless such an award is specifically prohibited by another statute. The act defines "fees and expenses" rather broadly. They include "the reasonable expenses of expert witnesses, the reasonable cost of any study, analysis, engineering report, test, or project which is found by the court to be necessary for the preparation of the party's case, and reasonable attorney fees." 28 U.S.C. §2412(d)(2)(A).

Thus, a person who is successful in securing judicial reversal or remand of an agency decision can obtain reimbursement for the principal costs of such litigation. In practice, this may make it possible for individuals to retain an attorney who will agree to defer the receipt of compensation on the expectation that it will be received from the government when the case is won. (This is often referred to as taking a case on a contingent fee basis.) There are limitations on the availability of fees and expenses under the Equal Access to Justice Act, however. For-profit corporations, and individuals with a net worth in excess of one million dollars, are not eligible under the act. Furthermore, one must be a "prevailing" party to qualify. In general, this means that one must be successful on at least one major part of the case. Moreover, the court may deny or reduce an award to the extent that it finds that the position of the agency was "substantially justified," that the party seeking the award "engaged in conduct which unduly and unreasonably protracted the final resolution of the matter in controversy," or that "special circumstances make an award unjust." Finally, compensation for attorneys under the act is limited to $125 per hour—which may, depending on the experience level of the attorney and the area of the country in which the case is heard, be well under the prevailing market rate—"unless the court determines that an increase in the cost of living or a special factor, such as the limited availability of qualified attorneys, justifies a higher fee."

In addition to the Equal Access to Justice Act, specific judicial review provisions found in some originating statutes also provide for an award of fees and expenses, generally at prevailing market rates. This is true for many environmental statutes. However, there is no such provision in Section 6(f) of the OSHAct, which governs judicial review of OSHA standards.

6. Bypassing the Agency: Citizen Enforcement Through the Private Right of Action

As discussed, the major functions of administrative agencies are to set regulatory standards and then to enforce them. What role does the citizen have when an agency does not follow through on its enforcement function, either because of a lack of resources or because of a lack of will? In the absence of a statute specifically authorizing citizen enforcement, that role probably is limited.

The Administrative Procedure Act authorizes citizens to seek a court order—a writ of mandamus—to compel the agency to carry out its responsibilities under the law. In general, however, the courts tend to defer to an agency's "prosecutorial discretion," and to give the agency wide latitude in determining when to enforce the law and whom to enforce it against.

A citizen may also seek to bypass the agency and to enforce the law directly against the violator. In doing so, the citizen must persuade the court that Congress intended that there be what is called a "private right of action" to enforce the statute in question. Where the statute is silent on the point, one must argue that there is an implied private right of action. This is an uphill battle, as the criteria for establishing such an implied right of action are difficult to meet. See *California v. Sierra Club*, 451 U.S. 287 (1981). However, the "citizen suit" provisions found in most federal environmental statutes contain specific authorization for private rights of action. In general, these provisions allow affected citizens to bring suit against violators of the act if certain preconditions are met, and to recover attorneys' fees and expenses if the suit is successful. These are extremely powerful tools for the citizen activist. Although the citizen's right of enforcement is clearly subordinate to that of the agency, these citizen suit provisions authorize aggressive private enforcement when agency enforcement has not been adequate. By coupling the private right of action with a specific authorization for the recovery of attorneys' fees and expenses from the violator, Congress here created real incentives for citizen participation in the environmental enforcement process. By and large, however, Congress has not chosen to create such incentives with regard to workplace health and safety and there is no private right of action to enforce the OSHAct. Enforcement under environmental citizen suit provisions is discussed in more detail in chapter 11.

E. THE ROLE OF THE COURTS IN REVIEWING AGENCY DECISION MAKING

Once one has secured access to the courts for review of an agency decision, the issue of the scope of judicial review remains. That is, to what extent will the courts delve into the actual details of the agency decision-making process in their review of that process? When one explores this issue, one is also exploring the broader issue of the nature of the agency's responsibilities under the law. For, without further action by Congress, the question of what an agency is authorized to do, or what an agency must or must not do, is up to the courts to decide.

1.   Five Judicial Limitations on Agency Authority

In general, there are five sources of law to which courts can turn in evaluating agency action. A court may reverse an agency's decision, or remand it to the agency for further consideration, if it finds that the agency has violated any of these sources of law. The first is *the originating statute* itself. Agencies must adhere to their statutory mandates. Thus, although it is never appropriate for the court to substitute its policy judgments for those of the agency, it is the court's duty in reviewing agency rulemaking to remand the agency's decision if the agency has taken policy positions that conflict with the choices made by Congress in the originating statute, or if the agency has failed to follow the rulemaking procedures specified in the originating statute. Second, the courts look to *other applicable legislation*, including the various procedural statutes such as the APA. To the extent that they apply to the agency's action, all other statutes must be followed as well. A third source of law is *the agency's own rules and procedures*. Although not always fatal, an agency's failure to adhere to the internal procedures it has developed for promulgating regulations may result in a court remand. A fourth limitation on agency behavior could be termed *administrative common law*—substantive or procedural requirements developed by the federal courts in their review of agency decisions. In theory, the courts have no authority to require more of the agencies than is required by statute. In practice, however, the courts take enough leeway in interpreting those statutes that they effectively impose requirements of their own. Finally, agency behavior is limited by *the Constitution*. Agency action that offends the Constitution is unlawful even when it is specifically authorized by statute. For example, when Congress passed the Occupational Safety and Health Act in 1970, it authorized OSHA to conduct random inspections of workplaces without first obtaining a search warrant. When an OSHA inspector attempted to utilize this authority by inspecting a workplace in the state of Idaho, however, the owner refused access, citing his Fourth Amendment right to be free of unreasonable government searches and seizures. The Supreme Court agreed with him, and declared this portion of the OSHAct to be unconstitutional. See *Marshall v. Barlow's, Inc.*, 436 U.S. 307 (1978), discussed in chapter 11.

2.   The Scope of Factual Review

Clearly, a court is empowered to strike down an agency decision that violates a relevant statutory or constitutional provision. But even when there is no strictly "legal" issue of this nature, courts play an important role in reviewing and ultimately shaping the decisions that agencies make. The Administrative Procedure Act, and in many cases the originating statute itself, direct the reviewing court to examine the factual basis for the agency's decision as well.

As discussed previously, the APA employs a twofold standard to define the scope of factual review. If the agency decision was made according to *informal notice and comment rulemaking*, the court is empowered to "hold unlawful and set aside agency action, findings, and conclusions found to be . . . arbitrary, capricious, [or] an abuse of discretion." This has come to be known as the "arbitrary and capricious" test (even though the statute itself uses "or" instead of "and"). If the agency decision was made according to *formal rulemaking*, the court is empowered to set the decision aside if it is "unsupported by substantial evidence." The original intention of Congress appears clear. If the agency employed a formal rulemaking process—with a full hearing, cross examination, and the other trappings of a trial-type proceeding—there would be an extensive record for the court to review. It thus made sense to Congress to require that the court examine that record carefully to ascertain that each important aspect of the agency's decision was supported by "substantial evidence" in the record. With the much sparser record expected to be generated by informal rulemaking, however, it made sense to require a less thorough review. Hence the less demanding arbitrary and capricious standard.

In practice, however, the distinction between the two standards of review has blurred considerably. There are two principal reasons for this, and both may be traced to the actions of Congress. The first is that Congress began sending mixed signals to the courts with the language of originating statutes passed well after the APA. In the 1970s, federal statutes were passed that required agencies to conduct their decision making according to informal rulemaking, but required the courts to review those decisions according to the substantial evidence standard. (This is true of both the Occupational Safety and Health Act and the Toxic Substances Control Act.) In conducting their review under these so-called hybrid rulemaking statutes, the courts began to require that the agencies develop more extensive administrative records under informal rulemaking than had been the accepted practice. Second, with the extensive delegation of policy-making authority to agencies that occurred during the 1970s, the federal courts found that they were spending considerably more of their time reviewing agency decision making. Perhaps because they recognized the importance of the social policy issues inherent in the decisions they were asked to review, the courts began to require more from the agencies than they had in the past, even when conducting review under the arbitrary and capricious standard.

The Supreme Court case that opened the proverbial floodgates was *Citizens to Preserve Overton Park v. Volpe*, 401 U.S. 402 (1971). Here, national and local environmental groups challenged a decision by the U.S. Department of Transportation to authorize the expenditure of federal funds to construct a six-lane highway through a public park in Memphis, Tennessee. Initial judicial review was secured in U.S. District Court under the Administrative Procedure Act, and the statutory scope of review was the APA's arbitrary and capricious standard. Concluding that the administrative record had not been reviewed in sufficient depth by the lower court, the Supreme Court sent the case back to the district court for further deliberation. In doing so, the Court noted that reviewing courts applying the arbitrary and capricious standard must engage in "a substantial inquiry . . . a thorough, probing, in-depth review." It directed reviewing courts to determine: (1) whether the agency acted within the scope of its statutory authority, (2) whether the agency's decision "was based on a consideration of the relevant factors and whether there has been a clear error of judgment", and (3) whether the agency "followed the necessary procedural requirements."

Overton Park enunciated a much broader standard for judicial review of informal agency decision making than had been assumed to exist at that time. Many courts, especially the influential District of Columbia Court of Appeals, took this as authorization to look much more closely at the factual basis for agency rulemaking and to remand agency decisions that appeared to the court to be at odds with the underlying factual record. What the courts must demand from agencies, the D.C. Circuit noted, was "reasoned decisionmaking." An agency practices reasoned decision making, said the court, when it (1) takes a "hard look . . . at the relevant issues", (2) deliberates "in a manner calculated to negate the danger of arbitrariness and irrationality", (3) violates "no law", and (4) provides an "articulated justification" that makes a "rational connection between the facts found and the choice made." See, for example, *Action for Children's Television v. FCC*, 564 F.2d 458, 472 n. 24, 479 (D.C. Cir. 1977).

However, the viability of *Overton Park*, and thus of the "reasoned decisionmaking" standard generally, was called into question by *Vermont Yankee Power Corp. v. Natural Resources Defense Council*, 435 U.S. 519 (1978), where the Supreme Court overturned the D.C. Circuit's reversal of a decision by the Atomic Energy Commission (AEC) to grant licenses for two nuclear power plants. The court of appeals had, in effect, required the AEC's successor, the Nuclear Regulatory Commission, to provide an opportunity for cross-examination in its informal rulemaking process. Since the relevant statutes contain no such requirement, the Supreme Court reversed, cautioning reviewing courts "against engrafting their own notions of proper procedures upon agencies entrusted with substantive functions by Congress." Some commentators read this case as a retreat from the "substantial inquiry" standard enunciated in *Overton Park*, and many interpreted it as a "slap on the wrist" to the D.C. Circuit for having taken an overly aggressive approach to judicial review.

This proved to be an overreaction. Five years later, in *Motor Vehicle Manufacturers' Association v. State Farm Mutual Automobile Insurance Company*, 463 U.S. 29 (1983), the Supreme court clarified its Vermont Yankee opinion and left little doubt that it had not intended in that case to signal a retreat from thoroughgoing judicial review. *State Farm* dealt with a decision by the Department of Transportation (through the National Highway Traffic Safety Administration, or NHTSA) to rescind its earlier regulation (Standard 208n) requiring "passive restraints" (airbags or detachable automatic seatbelts) in new model motor vehicles. The agency based this decision on its finding that the installation of detachable automatic seatbelts would not bring about "even a five percentage point increase" in seatbelt use. All nine members of the Court agreed that the rescission itself was arbitrary and capricious and a five-member majority held that the agency's factual finding was unsupported by the record.

Motor Vehicle Manufacturers' Association v. State Farm Mutual Automobile Insurance Company
Justice WHITE delivered the opinion of the Court
463 U.S. 29 (1983)
(United States Supreme Court)

... The Department of Transportation accepts the applicability of the "arbitrary and capricious" standard. It argues that under this standard, a reviewing court may not set aside an agency rule that is rational, based on consideration of the relevant factors and within the scope of the authority delegated to the agency by the statute. We do not disagree with this formulation. The scope of review under the "arbitrary and capricious" standard is narrow and a court is not to substitute its judgment for that of the agency. Nevertheless, the agency must examine the relevant data and articulate a satisfactory explanation for its action including a "rational connection between the facts found and the choice made." *Burlington Truck Lines v. United States*, 371 U.S. 156,168 (1962). In reviewing that explanation, we must "consider whether the decision was based on a consideration of the relevant factors and whether there has been a clear error of judgment." *Bowman Transp. Inc. v. Arkansas-Best Freight System*, 419 U.S. 281 (1974), *Citizens to Preserve Overton Park v. Volpe*, [402 U.S. 402], at 416. Normally, an agency rule would be arbitrary

and capricious if the agency has relied on factors which Congress has not intended it to consider, entirely failed to consider an important aspect of the problem, offered an explanation for its decision that runs counter to the evidence before the agency, or is so implausible that it could not be ascribed to a difference in view or the product of agency expertise. The reviewing court should not attempt itself to make up for such deficiencies: "We may not supply a reasoned basis for the agency's action that the agency itself has not given." *SEC v. Chenery Corp.*, 332 U.S. 194, 196 (1947). "We will, however, uphold a decision of less than ideal clarity if the agency's path may reasonably be discerned." *Bowman Transp. Inc. v. Arkansas-Best Freight Systems,* supra, at 286. See also *Camp v. Pitts*, 411 U.S. 138, 142–143 (1973) (per curiam).

V

The ultimate question before us is whether NHTSA's rescission of the passive restraint requirement of Standard 208 was arbitrary and capricious. We conclude, as did the

Court of Appeals, that it was. We also conclude, but for somewhat different reasons,
that further consideration of the issue by the
agency is therefore required. We deal separately with the rescission as it applies to airbags and as it applies to seatbelts.

A

The first and most obvious reason for finding
the rescission arbitrary and capricious is that
NHTSA apparently gave no consideration
whatever to modifying the Standard to require that airbag technology be utilized. Standard 208 sought to achieve automatic crash
protection by requiring automobile manufacturers to install either of two passive restraint
devices: airbags or automatic seatbelts. There
was no suggestion in the long rulemaking
process that led to Standard 208 that if only
one of these options were feasible, no passive
restraint standard should be promulgated. Indeed, the agency's original proposed standard
contemplated the installation of inflatable
restraints in all cars. Automatic belts were
added as a means of complying with the standard because they were believed to be as
effective as airbags in achieving the goal of
occupant crash protection. 36 Fed. Reg.
12,858, 12,859 (July 8, 1971). At that time,
the passive belt approved by the agency could
not be detached. Only later, at a manufacturer's behest, did the agency approve of the
detachability feature—and only after assurances that the feature would not compromise
the safety benefits of the restraint. Although
it was then foreseen that 60% of the new cars
would contain airbags and 40% would have
automatic seatbelts, the ratio between the
two was not significant as long as the passive
belt would also assure greater passenger
safety.

The agency has now determined that the
detachable automatic belts will not attain
anticipated safety benefits because so many
individuals will detach the mechanism. Even
if this conclusion were acceptable in its

entirety . . . standing alone it would not justify
any more than an amendment of Standard
208 to disallow compliance by means of the
one technology which will not provide effective passenger protection. It does not cast
doubt on the need for a passive restraint standard or upon the efficacy of airbag technology. In its most recent rule-making, the
agency again acknowledged the life-saving
potential of the airbag:

The agency has no basis at this time for changing
its earlier conclusions in 1976 and 1977 that basic
airbag technology is sound and has been sufficiently demonstrated to be effective in those
vehicles in current use. . . . NHTSA Final Regulatory Impact Analysis (RIA) at X14 (App. 264).

Given the effectiveness ascribed to airbag
technology by the agency, the mandate of the
Safety Act to achieve traffic safety would suggest that the logical response to the faults of
detachable seatbelts would be to require the
installation of airbags. At the very least this
alternative way of achieving the objectives of
the Act should have been addressed and adequate reasons given for its abandonment. . . .

Petitioners also invoke our decision in *Vermont Yankee Nuclear Power Corp. v. NRDC,*
435 U.S. 519 (1977), as though it were a talis-
man under which any agency decision is by
definition unimpeachable. Specifically, it is
submitted that to require an agency to consider an airbags-only alternative is, in essence, to dictate to the agency the procedures
it is to follow. Petitioners both misread Vermont Yankee and misconstrue the nature of
the remand that is in order. In Vermont Yankee, we held that a court may not impose
additional procedural requirements upon an
agency. We do not require today any specific
procedures which NHTSA must follow. Nor
do we broadly require an agency to consider
all policy alternatives in reaching decision. It
is true that a rulemaking "cannot be found
wanting simply because the agency failed to
include every alternative device and thought
conceivable by the mind of man . . . regardless
of how uncommon or unknown that alterna-

tive may have been. . . ." 435 U.S., at 551. But the airbag is more than a policy alternative to the passive restraint standard; it is a technological alternative within the ambit of the existing standard. We hold only that given the judgment made in 1977 that airbags are an effective and cost-beneficial life-saving technology, the mandatory passive-restraint rule may not be abandoned without any consideration whatsoever of an airbags-only requirement.

B

Although the issue is closer, we also find that the agency was too quick to dismiss the safety benefits of automatic seatbelts. NHTSA's critical finding was that, in light of the industry's plans to install readily detachable passive belts, it could not reliably predict "even a 5 percentage point increase as the minimum level of expected usage increase." 46 Fed. Reg., at 53,423. The Court of Appeals rejected this finding because there is "not one iota" of evidence that Modified Standard 208 will fail to increase nationwide seatbelt use by at least 13 percentage points, the level of increased usage necessary for the standard to justify its cost. Given the lack of probative evidence, the court held that "only a well-justified refusal to seek more evidence could render rescission non-arbitrary." 680 F.2d, at 232.

Petitioners object to this conclusion. In their view, "substantial uncertainty" that a regulation will accomplish its intended purpose is sufficient reason, without more, to rescind a regulation. We agree with petitioners that just as an agency reasonably may decline to issue a safety standard if it is uncertain about its efficacy, an agency may also revoke a standard on the basis of serious uncertainties if supported by the record and reasonably explained. Rescission of the passive restraint requirement would not be arbitrary and capricious simply because there was no evidence in direct support of the agency's con-

clusion. It is not infrequent that the available data [do] not settle a regulatory issue and the agency must then exercise its judgment in moving from the facts and probabilities on the record to a policy conclusion. Recognizing that policymaking in a complex society must account for uncertainty, however, does not imply that it is sufficient for an agency to merely recite the terms "substantial uncertainty" as a justification for its actions. The agency must explain the evidence which is available, and must offer a "rational connection between the facts found and the choice made." *Burlington Truck Lines, Inc. v. United States*, supra, at 168. Generally one aspect of that explanation would be a justification for rescinding the regulation before engaging in a search for further evidence.

In this case, the agency's explanation for rescission of the passive restraint requirement is not sufficient to enable us to conclude that the rescission was the product of reasoned decisionmaking. To reach this conclusion, we do not upset the agency's view of the facts, but we do appreciate the limitations of this record in supporting the agency's decision. We start with the accepted ground that if used, seatbelts unquestionably would save many thousands of lives and would prevent tens of thousands of crippling injuries. Unlike recent regulatory decisions we have reviewed, *Industrial Union Department v. American Petroleum Institute*, 448 U.S. 607 (1980) [striking down OSHA's benzene standard]; *American Textile Manufactures Inst., Inc. v. Donovan*, 452 U.S. 490 (1981) [upholding OSHA's cotton dust standard], the safety benefits of wearing seatbelts are not in doubt and it is not challenged that were those benefits to accrue, the monetary costs of implementing the standard would be easily justified. We move next to the fact that there is no direct evidence in support of the agency's finding that detachable automatic belts cannot be predicted to yield a substantial increase in usage. The empirical evidence on the record, consisting of surveys of drivers of automobiles equipped with passive belts, reveals more than a doubling of the usage rate experienced with manual belts. Much of the agency's rulemaking statement—and much of the controversy in this case—centers on the conclusions that should be drawn from these studies. The agency maintained that the doubling of seatbelt usage in these studies could not be extrapolated to an across-the-board mandatory standard because the passive seatbelts were guarded by ignition interlocks and purchasers of the tested cars are somewhat atypical. Respondents insist these studies demonstrate that Modified Standard 208 will substantially increase seat belt usage. We believe that it is within the agency's discretion to pass upon the generalizability of these field studies. This is precisely the type of issue which rests within the expertise of NHTSA, and upon which a reviewing court must be most hesitant to intrude.

But accepting the agency's view of the field tests on passive restraints indicates only that there is no reliable real-world experience that usage rates will substantially increase. To be sure, NHTSA opines that "it cannot reliably predict even a 5 percentage point increase as the minimum level of increased usage." Notice 25, 46 Fed. Reg., at 53,423. But this and other statements that passive belts will not yield substantial increases in seatbelt usage apparently take no account of the critical difference between detachable automatic belts and current manual belts. A detached passive belt does require an affirmative act to reconnect it, but—unlike a manual seat belt—the passive belt, once reattached, will continue to function automatically unless again disconnected. Thus, inertia—a factor which the agency's own studies have found significant in explaining the current low usage rates for seatbelts—works in favor of, not against, use of the protective device. Since 20 to 50% of motorists currently wear seatbelts on some occasions, there would seem to be grounds to believe that seatbelt use by occasional users will be substantially increased by the detachable passive belts. Whether this is in fact the case is a matter for the agency to decide, but it must bring its expertise to bear on the question.

[Concurring and dissenting opinion of REHNQUIST, J., in which BURGER, C. J., POWELL, J., and O'CONNOR, J. joined, omitted.]

This decision certainly can be read as a reaffirmation of the principles articulated in *Overton Park*. (Clearly, the Court was not shy about examining the factual basis for the agency's decision.) To borrow the Supreme Court's language from that earlier case, however, the question of just how "substantial" an inquiry, or how "in-depth" a review a court must conduct remains somewhat open today. This is especially true where, as is often the case with health, safety, and environmental issues, the agency's decision is based on the evaluation of highly technical data. Some commentators argue that lay judges are simply not qualified to understand and interpret such data. Thus, their argument runs, courts should defer to an agency's specialized expertise in these matters except in cases of obvious errors in reasoning. Others, however, argue that reviewing courts shirk their statutory responsibility if they do not carefully examine the factual basis for the regulatory choices made by the agency. If the underlying data and methodologies are complex, this argument proceeds, it is incumbent on the agency and the other parties to the litigation to elucidate them for the court. Support for both of these philosophies can be found in judicial decisions, and it remains rather difficult to predict which one of them will carry the day in any particular case. Suffice it to say that whenever an agency fails to provide a clear, well-reasoned factual analysis in support of a regulatory decision, it runs the risk of judicial reversal.

■ **NOTES**

1. It is important to reiterate that no matter how carefully a court scrutinizes the details of an agency's reasoning, the court is not empowered to overturn an administrative decision merely because it disagrees with the agency's policy determinations. In the administrative arena, policy decisions are the province of Congress, not the courts. Thus, policies are to be set in accordance with the statutory mandate.

2. The authors of this text have argued that in the area of health and safety regulation reviewing courts will fail to recognize the important policy decisions inherent in an agency's assessment of particular risks—and thus will be unable to determine whether the agency is carrying out the policy directives set forth in its statutory mandate—unless they look carefully at the risk assessment methodologies that lie behind the regulatory decision. See N. A. Ashford, C. W. Ryan, and C. C. Caldart (1983) "A Hard Look at Federal Regulation of Formaldehyde: A Departure from Reasoned Decisionmaking," 7 *Harvard Environmental Law Review* 297. For a somewhat different viewpoint, see T. McGarity (1986). "Beyond the Hard Look: A New Standard for Judicial Review?" *Natural Resources and the Environment* 2: 32.

3. One commentator, with tongue only partially in cheek, has described the tension between the two theories of factual review in practical, if cynical, terms: "As any practicing lawyer knows, file cabinets contain two form briefs for cases on judicial review of administrative action affecting technologies. One, for the losers below, bristles with irate talk about administrative caprice, urges exacting scrutiny, and cites *Overton Park*. The other, for the winners below, speaks dispassionately of administrative expertise, counsels deference, and cites *Vermont Yankee*. Often a party is both winner and loser below, and this calls for deft compartmentalization in the brief, simultaneously urging rigorous oversight on one issue while discouraging judicial overreaching on the other" [W. Rogers (1994) *Environmental Law*, 2nd ed. West Publishing, Eagan, Minn., p. 90].

4. The Clean Air Act cases excerpted in chapter 6 provide an excellent look at how far various courts have been willing to go in analyzing the technical data underlying agency decision making and at how well they have performed the analysis.

5. For a look at how various members of the D.C. Circuit Court of Appeals have addressed the issue of judicial review of "science-based" agency decision making through the years, see Patricia Wald (1982) "Making Informed Decisions on the District of Columbia Circuit," 50 *George Washington Law Review* 135; David Bazelon (1981) "Science and Uncertainty: A Jurist's View," 5 *Harvard Environmental Law Review* 211; David Bazelon (1977) "Coping with Technology Through the Legal Process," 62 *Cornell Law Review* 822; Harold Leventhal (1974) "Environmental Decisionmaking and the Role of the Courts," 122 *University of Pennsylvania Law Review* 511; J. Skelley Wright (1974) "The Courts and the Rulemaking Process: The Limits of Judicial Review," 59 *Cornell Law Review* 375.   ■

3. Judicial Review of Agency Decisions Not to Act

A final issue of importance is the scope of judicial review when an agency declines to take rulemaking action. Traditionally, courts have given greater deference to agency discretion in such situations. The D.C. Circuit Court of Appeals has set forth six principal reasons for affording such deference: (1) the issues involved may turn on "factors not inherently susceptible to judicial resolution," such as the management of budget and personnel and the balancing of competing policies within a broad statutory framework; (2) there may be "such rapid technological development that regulations would be outdated by the time they could become effective"; (3) the currently available data may be an inadequate basis for regulation; (4) "the circumstances in the regulated industry may be evolving in such a way that could vitiate the need for regulation"; (5) the agency may not yet possess "the expertise necessary for effective regulation" in the area in question; and (6) the record on review may not be "narrowly focused on the particular rule advocated by [the party seeking review]" [*Natural Resources Defense Council v. SEC*, 606 F.2d 1031, 1046, D.C. Cir. 1979].

Nonetheless, the courts clearly are empowered under Section 10 of the APA to review decisions not to act, and to "compel agency action unlawfully withheld or unreasonably delayed," and they have done so on several occasions. For example, despite the agency's protestations that it was already occupied with other regulatory priorities, the D.C. Circuit ordered the Occupational Safety and Health Administration to set a workplace exposure standard for ethylene oxide within 1 year. After reviewing OSHA's rather sparse regulatory agenda, the court concluded that the agency's failure to take action on ethylene oxide (for which the agency had ample evidence of human toxicity) could not be justified by the few pieces of pending regulation on which OSHA said it was working. See *Public Citizen v. Auchter*, 702 F.2d 1150 (D.C. Cir. 1983). Similarly, in *Public Citizen Health Research Group v. Chao*, 314 F.3d 143 (3rd Cir. 2002), the Third Circuit Court of Appeals ordered OSHA to promulgate new workplace standards for hexavalent chromium, concluding that the agency's 9-year delay in doing so could not be justified. But in *International Union v. Chao*, 361 F. 2d 249, 255 (3rd Cir. 2004) the same court declined to order OSHA to initiate rulemaking to regulate occupational exposure to machining fluids, noting that courts generally review decisions not to act "at the most deferential end of the arbitrary and capricious spectrum."

F. TWO GENERAL ENVIRONMENTAL MANDATES TO AGENCIES: THE NATIONAL ENVIRONMENTAL POLICY ACT AND THE ENDANGERED SPECIES ACT

In the early years of the "modern" environmental era—an era that might be described as beginning in the mid-1960s—Congress enacted two laws designed to imbue federal agency decision making with a systematic environmental ethos: the National Environmental Policy Act of 1969 and the Endangered Species Act of 1973. Both have had an important effect on the way in which federal agencies make many decisions regarding permits, projects, and regulations affecting the environment. Although a detailed discussion of these statutes is beyond the scope of this book, a general explication of each is set forth in the following sections.

■ NOTE

1. Although it is known as the National Environmental Policy Act of 1969, NEPA actually was signed into law on January 1, 1970. See Pub. L. 91-190.   ■

1. The National Environmental Policy Act

The National Environmental Policy Act (NEPA), 42 U.S.C. §4331, *et seq.*, which was spearheaded through Congress by Senate Democrat Henry Jackson of Washington and signed into law early in the Republican administration of President Richard Nixon, set the tone for the sweeping changes that would be wrought by the environmental legislation to follow. In its first sentence, NEPA acknowledges "the profound impact of man's activity on the interrelations of all components of the natural environment," extolls "the critical importance of restoring and maintaining environmental quality to the overall welfare and development of man," and declares it to be the national policy "to create and maintain conditions under which man and nature can live in productive harmony" [42 U.S.C. §4331(a)]. To this end, NEPA declares that it is "the continuing responsibility of the Federal Government to use all practicable means, consistent with other essential considerations of national policy, to improve and coordinate Federal plans, functions, programs, and resources" toward the satisfaction of six enumerated goals: (1) fulfilling "the responsibilities of each generation as trustee of the environment for succeeding generations"; (2) assuring "safe, healthful, productive, and esthetically and culturally pleasing surroundings" for all Americans; (3) attaining "the widest range of beneficial uses of the environment without . . . undesirable and unintended consequences"; (4) preserving "our national heritage" and maintaining "an environment which supports diversity and variety of individual choice"; (5) achieving "a balance between population and resource use which will permit high standards of living and a wide sharing of life's amenities"; and (6) enhancing "the quality of renewable resources" while working to achieve "the maximum attainable recycling of depletable resources" [42 U.S.C. §4331(b)]. Finally, NEPA declares that "each person should enjoy a healthful environment . . . and has a responsibility to contribute to the preservation and enhancement of the environment" [42 U.S.C. §4331(c)].

In short, in language both bold and broad, Congress declared in NEPA that the federal government, and federal agencies in particular, now had a programmatic responsibility to promote environmental restoration and preservation. The fact that most of this language is too general and too vague to be enforceable is almost beside the point, for here Congress was sounding the themes that would resonate through the more specific and more substantive legislation that would be enacted in the years to come: a concern for preserving environmental amenities, a concern for human health, a concern for economic equity and prosperity, and a concern for achieving the appropriate balance among these interests. More than this, however, the articulated overarching goal—a society in which humans and the environment "exist in productive harmony"—presupposes a gradual evolution toward a time when trade-offs between these interests are less and less necessary. In other words, NEPA envisions a move toward a *sustainable economy*. While there is no doubt that this goal oftentimes gets lost among the day-to-day minutiae of implementating environmental policy, it remains an important touchstone in our evaluation of the overall success of that policy.

a. The Environmental Impact Statement
Beyond its thematic importance, NEPA has had an important practical impact. Indeed, even if they have never read the statute, most people in (or affected by) the environmental field are familiar with the NEPA requirement for an environmental impact statement (EIS). The genesis of this requirement is found in Section 102:

The Congress authorizes and directs that, to the fullest extent possible . . . (2) all agencies of the federal government shall . . . (C) include in every recommendation or report on proposals for legislation and *other major federal actions significantly affecting the quality of the human environment, a detailed statement by the responsible official* on—

(i) the environmental impact of the proposed action,

(ii) any adverse environmental effects which cannot be avoided should the proposal be implemented,

(iii) alternatives to the proposed action,

(iv) the relationship between local short-term uses of man's environment and the maintenance and enhancement of long-term productivity, and

(v) any irreversible and irretrievable commitments of resources which would be involved in the proposed action should it be implemented. (42 U.S.C. §4332, emphasis added)

Thus, before certain federal actions are taken, a "detailed statement," commonly known as an environmental impact statement, must be performed. What does this mean? One way of approaching this inquiry is to divide it into four parts. First, when must an EIS be prepared? An EIS is required for "major federal actions significantly affecting the quality of the human environment." A "federal" action is one taken by the federal government, such as a federal highway project, or one taken pursuant to some formal authorization from the federal government, such as one for which a federal permit or license is required. That federal action must also be a "major" one that would "significantly" affect the environment. Intuitively, these would appear to be two separate criteria: the action must on the one hand be large enough to be major and on the other hand have enough potential to affect the environment that its impact can be deemed significant. In practice, however, the second criterion has been the driving factor. In general, if an action will have a significant effect on the environment, it will be considered major.

Given that an EIS is required, who must prepare it? The statute tells us that the EIS must be included in the recommendation for action "by the responsible official." This means that responsibility for the EIS lies with the federal agency or instrumentality taking or approving the action. In practice, however, the federal government often delegates the responsibility for preparing the EIS to a state agency or a private party (such as an environmental consulting firm). Indeed, where the proponent of the action is a private party (such as the proponent of a private development project for which a federal permit is required), the private party often funds the EIS. Nonetheless, ultimate responsibility for the sufficiency of the EIS remains with the federal agency or instrumentality whose approval is required for the project to proceed.

What must the EIS contain? The five basic topics to be addressed in an EIS are set forth in the statutory language quoted previously. More detailed criteria have been developed over time, both by practice and convention and by the Council on Environmental Quality. In broad brush, the projected environmental effects of the action (both short term and long term), as well as alternatives to the action that may involve lesser impacts, must be discussed in some detail. The "alternatives" analysis obviously is a critical component, because it has the potential for spurring reconfiguration or even wholesale reconsideration of the proposed action. In *Vermont Yankee*

Nuclear Power Corp. v. Natural Resources Defense Council, Inc. 435 U.S. 519 (1978), a case that we have already discussed in the context of the arbitrary and capricious standard, the Supreme Court addressed the important question of how wide the EIS must cast its net in considering alternatives. The case involved a challenge to a decision by the Atomic Energy Commission granting a federal license for the operation of a nuclear power plant. One of the challengers' arguments was that the environmental impact statement for the project was deficient because it did not include a consideration of energy conservation as an alternative to the construction of the power plant. The Supreme Court rejected this challenge and in doing so placed certain practical and conceptual limitations on the requirement for alternatives.

Noting that it was in the position of having to provide meaning to a term that "is not self-defining," the Court reasoned that "the concept of alternatives must be bounded by some notion of feasibility," and could not reasonably be expected to "include every alternative device and thought conceivable by the mind of man" (435 U.S. at 551). Moreover, reasoned the Court, "the concept of 'alternatives' is an evolving one, requiring the agency to explore more or fewer alternatives as they become better known and understood" (id. at 552–553). Applying these general principles of the case at hand, the Court found that at the time the decision to approve the plant was made (the early 1970s), the use of energy conservation as a means to reduce the need for power generation was neither well developed nor well understood. The Court also found that the opponents of the project had not, in their comments on the draft EIS, made a sufficient showing of the feasibility of energy conservation in this setting to have required the Atomic Energy Commission to revise the EIS to include consideration of that alternative. Although the Court did not provide a rubric for determining when a particular alternative must be considered in an EIS, it did endorse an AEC guideline stating that "the showing should be sufficient to require reasonable minds to inquire further" (id. at 554).

Finally, then, what is the function of the EIS? Clearly, it is intended to influence federal agency decision making, but is it directed only toward the manner of decision making, or is it also directed toward the kind of decision that is made? Although a credible argument can be made that the EIS requirement, especially when coupled with other language in NEPA, creates a substantive duty on the part of an agency to select the alternative that meets the agency's goals with the least adverse effect on the environment, the Supreme Court has repeatedly held that NEPA's mandate is a procedural one. NEPA does not require an agency to reach a particular result, but rather requires it to appropriately develop and consider certain types of information before making a decision. See, in particular, *Stryker's Bay Neighborhood Council, Inc. v. Karlen*, 444 U.S. 223, 227–228 (1980), and *Robertson v. Methow Valley Citizens Council*, 490 U.S. 332, 350 (1989) ("NEPA itself does not mandate particular results, but simply prescribes the necessary process").

This is not to say, however, that NEPA does not have an effect on the content of federal agency decision making. Obviously, there can be a meaningful relationship between the manner in which a decision is made and the content of that decision. Indeed, even as it was holding that NEPA is a procedural statute, the Supreme Court noted that "these procedures are almost certain to affect the agency's substantive decision" (*Robertson v. Methow Valley Citizens Council*, 490 U.S. at 350). And the courts have made it clear that the EIS must be given serious consideration in an agency's decision making. Perhaps the leading case on this point is *Calvert Cliffs Coordinating Committee v. Atomic Energy Commission*, 449 F.2d 1109 (D.C. Cir. 1971), which reviewed AEC rules purporting to implement NEPA in nuclear power plant licensing proceedings. The rules provided that where no party to a licensing proceeding raised an environmental issue, the EIS "will accompany the [license proposal] through the Commission's review processes, [but] will not be received in evidence, and the Commission's responsibilities under the National Environmental Policy Act of 1969 will be carried out in toto outside the hearing process" (449 F.2d at 1117). This, held the D.C. Circuit Court of Appeals, violated Section 102(2)(C) of NEPA, which provides that the EIS "shall accompany the proposal through the existing agency review processes" [42 U.S.C. §4332(2)(C)]. Rejecting what it termed the "crabbed" interpretation of this provision reflected in the AEC's rules, the court reasoned that Congress had intended that an EIS be integrated into the agency's decision making on the proposed course of action for which it is prepared:

What possible purpose could there be in the Section 102(2)(C) requirement (that the "detailed statement" accompany proposals through agency review processes) if "accompany" means no more than physical proximity—mandating no more than the physical act of passing certain folders and papers, unopened, to reviewing officials along with other folders and papers? What possible purpose could there be in requiring the "detailed statement" to be before hearing boards, if the boards are free to ignore entirely the contents of the statement? NEPA was meant to do more than regulate the flow of papers in the federal bureaucracy. The word "accompany" in Section 102(2)(C) must not be read so narrowly as to make the Act ludicrous. It must, rather, be read to indicate a congressional intent that environmental factors, as compiled in the "detailed statement," be *considered* through agency review processes. (449 F.2d at 1118)

In the words of the Supreme Court, NEPA "ensures that the agency, in reaching its decision, will have available, and will carefully consider, detailed information concerning significant environmental impacts," and it "require[s] that agencies take a 'hard look' at environmental consequences" (*Robertson v. Methow Valley Citizens Council*, 490 U.S. at 349–350).

b. The Council on Environmental Quality

NEPA is also noteworthy for its creation, within the Executive Office of the President, of the Council on Environmental Quality (CEQ). See 42 U.S.C. §§4341–4347.

Broadly speaking, CEQ performs two major functions. First, it acts as an advisor to the president, and a concomitant source of information for the public, on environmental matters. In carrying out this role, CEQ is to "gather timely and authoritative information" on environmental quality and provide it to the president, "review and appraise the various programs of the Federal Government" with regard to their achievement of NEPA's goals, and "develop and recommend to the President national policies to foster and promote the improvement of environmental quality" (42 U.S.C. §4344). Historically, CEQ's most visible task as presidential advisor has been in preparing and distributing the annual environmental quality report that NEPA requires the president to submit to Congress. See 42 U.S.C. §§4331 and 4344(1). Especially in its early years, the annual CEQ report has served as a comprehensive, authoritative source of information on environmental quality and trends, and on the efforts of federal agencies to carry out their environmental mandates. While it is fair to say that the importance of CEQ, both as policy advisor and source of information, has diminished in more recent years with the growing influence of EPA and the proliferation of nonprofit environmental policy and research organizations, CEQ retains its powers and duties under NEPA. Indeed, although President Clinton announced his intention to do away with CEQ, he could not find the votes in Congress to do so.

Moreover, CEQ performs a second major function that clearly has continuing importance. Acting pursuant to an executive order, CEQ has promulgated regulations setting forth guidelines for the preparation of environmental impact statements by federal agencies. These guidelines address when an EIS is to be prepared, who is to prepare it, how it is to be prepared, and what it is to contain. In general, the courts have deferred to these guidelines in lawsuits challenging an agency's compliance with NEPA. Thus, while the CEQ guidelines do not resolve the necessarily fact-specific questions raised by most NEPA litigation, they do provide a standardized procedure and a set of general benchmarks to which reviewing courts often refer. The regulations also give CEQ the role of advisor to federal agencies regarding these issues, and make it the arbiter of interagency disputes regarding the need for an EIS.

The CEQ regulations are found at 40 CFR Part 1500. See also "Forty Most Asked Questions Concerning CEQ's National Environmental Policy Act Regulations," 46 *Fed. Reg.* 18026 (March 23, 1981). The CEQ regulations have engendered a set of procedures that are now more or less routinely followed. First, an agency will determine whether a proposed activity has been categorically excluded from the EIS requirement (either because it is not a federal action or because it has been specifically excluded by another federal statute). If it is not, there will be an environmental assessment (EA) to determine whether an EIS is necessary. If it is determined not to be necessary, the agency will prepare a finding of no significant impact (FONSI). If an EIS is determined to be necessary, the agency will then usually place a notice in the *Federal Register* that an EIS will be prepared. The agency commonly will then engage in a "scoping" process to help identify who needs to be contacted, what needs to be considered, and what methods need to be used in preparing the EIS. Finally, once a draft EIS is prepared, it is commonly put out for public notice and comment.

■ NOTES

1. The first executive order directing CEQ to promulgate such regulations was issued by President Nixon. See Exec. Order No. 11575, 35 *Fed. Reg.* 4247 (1970). This mandate was modified seven years later by President Carter. See Exec. Order No. 11991, 42 *Fed. Reg.* 26967 (1977).

2. Congress has exempted certain federal actions from the EIS requirement. EPA's establishment of regulations under the Clean Water Act, for example, is exempted from the EIS requirement by Section 511(c)(1) of the Clean Water Act. See 33 U.S.C. §1371(c)(1).

3. Another way to look at the substantive-procedural issue under NEPA is that, at the very least, the EIS requirement provides a richer administrative record to which the agency must apply its decision-making responsibilities under the APA and/or the originating statute.

4. Even if no environmental impact statement is required, there still may be an obligation to consider alternatives to a proposed federal action under Section 102(E) of NEPA, which directs federal agencies to "study, develop, and describe appropriate alternatives to recommended courses of action in any proposal which involves unresolved conflicts concerning alternative uses of available resources" [42 U.S.C. §4332(E)].

5. The remedy for challenging a federal action where it is argued that a required EIS was not performed, or that the EIS performed was inadequate, is a court order directing a halt to the project until the NEPA requirements have been met. Since NEPA contains no provision for citizen suits, such a challenge would typically be brought under the APA, against the federal agency or instrumentality (or the applicable officer thereof) responsible for preparing the EIS. Neither NEPA nor the APA specifies a particular time period within which such a challenge must be filed. However, courts may not look favorably at a suit brought well after the federal action in question has begun to be implemented.

The equitable doctrine of *laches* (from the French term for "lax") can be invoked to bar suits where the plaintiff has unjustifiably delayed the filing of the action, and the delay has caused an undue burden to the defendant and/or related third parties. Although the use of the laches doctrine is generally disfavored in suits brought to enforce federal environmental statutes, because of the strong public benefit presumed to flow from the enforcement of those laws, the doctrine is invoked more often in NEPA cases. Thus, if the Forest Service granted a 100-year lease to a developer to construct a ski resort on old-growth forest land without first performing an EIS (an obvious violation of NEPA), but opponents waited to file suit until the developer spent millions of dollars on the project, committed construction crews to the site, and began advertising the new resort in ski journals, the opponents might find their NEPA claim barred by laches. In determining whether to invoke the laches doctrine, the court likely would consider (1) to what extent, if at all, the delay was justified; (2) the nature and extent of the burden to the developer caused by the delay if the NEPA challenge were allowed to go forward; and (3) the nature and extent of the public interest in having the NEPA challenge go forward in spite of the delay.

6. Many states have passed their own version of NEPA, applicable to certain actions taken or authorized by agencies or instrumentalities of state government. Depending on the state, these laws can be broader or narrower than NEPA. Some, such as the California Environmental Quality Act, have enforceable provisions that are clearly substantive in nature.

7. In 2007, underscoring both the growing concern about global warming and the potential power of NEPA, the Ninth Circuit Court of Appeals set aside prospective fuel economy standards for sport-utility vehicles and pickups and ordered the National Highway Traffic Safety Administration to prepare an EIS to determine the effect on carbon dioxide emissions of more stringent alterntive standard [*Center for Biological Diversity v. National Highway Transportation Safety Administration*, 508 F.3d 508 (9th Cir. 2007)].   ∎

2.   The Endangered Species Act

Another environmental statute that can have a significant impact on federal agency decision making is the Endangered Species Act. Against a backdrop of growing public concern over the fate of a few well-known animal species (such as the bald eagle), Congress first took systematic action designed to protect imperiled species in the 1960s with the passage of the Endangered Species Act of 1966 (80 Stat. 926) and the Endangered Species Conservation Act of 1969 (83 Stat. 275). A few years later Congress repealed these laws (see 87 Stat. 903) and replaced them with the stronger and more comprehensive Endangered Species Act of 1973 (ESA), which is codified at 16 U.S.C. §1531, *et seq.* Although certain of its effects have been blunted by subsequent amendment, the ESA has, no less than NEPA, fundamentally altered the way in which federal agencies conduct their activities. Indeed, although its programmatic scope, which extends only to threatened and endangered species, is not as wide as

NEPA's, the ESA can have a more dramatic impact in those cases in which it does apply because its enforceable mandates are substantive as well as procedural. Like NEPA, the ESA extends to those actions taken, funded, or authorized by the federal government. Moreover, unlike NEPA, the ESA has provisions that are directly applicable to private parties as well.

The ESA begins with a finding that "[imperiled] species of fish, wildlife, and plants are of esthetic, ecological, educational, historical, recreational, and scientific value to the Nation and its people," and goes on to declare that it is "the policy of Congress that all Federal departments and agencies shall seek to conserve endangered species and threatened species, and shall utilize their authorities in furtherance of the purposes of this chapter" [16 U.S.C. §§1531(a)(2) and (c)(1)]. Subsequent sections of the act give considerable "teeth" to this general policy pronouncement.

The various mandatory provisions of the Act are triggered by Section 4, which contains procedures for "listing" endangered or threatened species. A species may be proposed for listing under the ESA by the secretary of the interior or by any "interested person." See 16 U.S.C. §§1533(a) and (b)(3)(A). The U.S. Fish and Wildlife Service (USFWS), as the representative of the secretary of the interior, makes listing decisions for terrestrial species, and the National Marine Fisheries Service (NMFS, also known as NOAA Fisheries Service), as the representative of the secretary of commerce, makes listing decisions for marine species. See 16 U.S.C. §§1532(15) and 1533(a). (In ESA parlance, USFWS and NMFS often are collectively referred to as "the Services.") If a species is listed as endangered or threatened, the critical habitat of that species must also be identified. See 16 U.S.C. §§1533(b)(6)(C). Once this listing process has begun, Section 7 of the ESA comes into play. Section 7 applies to any federal agency, defined elsewhere in the act as "any department, agency, or instrumentality of the United States" [16 U.S.C. §1532(7)].

Section 7(c) requires that before a federal department, agency, or instrumentality takes certain actions, it must ask USFWS and/or NMFS, as appropriate, "whether any species which is listed or proposed to be listed may be present in the area of such proposed action" [16 U.S.C. §1536(c)(1)]. If either of the Services advises that any such species may be present, the department, agency, or instrumentality must then "conduct a biological assessment for the purpose of identifying any endangered species or threatened species which is likely to be affected by such action" [16 U.S.C. §§1536(c)(1)]. The regulations promulgated by the secretaries of interior and commerce to effectuate this provision specify that it applies only to those federal actions that are "major construction activities," which are defined as "construction projects[s] (or other undertaking[s] having similar physical impacts) which [are] major federal action[s] significantly affecting the quality of the human environment as referred to in the National Environmental Policy Act" [50 C.F.R. §§402.02 and 402.12(b)(1)].

The purpose of the biological assessment required by Section 7(c) is to assist the federal government in fulfilling its broader responsibilities under Section 7(a) of the ESA. That provision directs all federal departments, agencies, and instrumentalities to "utilize their authorities in furtherance of the purposes of this chapter by carrying out programs for the conservation of endangered species and threatened species" [16 U.S.C. §1536(a)(1)]. Furthermore, it specifies that:

Each Federal agency shall, in consultation with and with the assistance of the Secretary [of the Interior or Commerce, as appropriate], insure that any action authorized, funded, or carried out by such agency ... is not likely to jeopardize the continued existence of any endangered species or threatened species or result in the destruction or adverse modification of habitat of such species which is determined by the Secretary, after consultation as appropriate with affected States, to be critical. [16 U.S.C. §1536(a)(2)]

This directive—which, unlike that of Section 7(c), extends to all federal actions, and not just to those that also trigger the EIS requirement under NEPA—has two important consequences. First, it may require the federal agency to engage in formal consultation with "the Secretary" (USFWS and/or NMFS, as appropriate). If a listed species, or a species proposed for listing, is present, the responsible federal agency must determine [through the biological assessment, if one is required by Section 7(c), or otherwise] whether the action is likely to adversely affect such species. If the action is likely to have such an effect, then the federal agency must engage in formal consultation with USFWS and/or NMFS, as appropriate, under the procedures set forth in Section 7(b). See 16 U.S.C. §§1536(a)(3) and (4) and 1536(b). USFWS or NMFS must then prepare what has become known as a "biological opinion," a "written statement setting forth the [Service's] opinion, and a summary of the information on which the opinion is based, detailing how the agency action affects the species or its critical habitat" [16 U.S.C. §1536(b)(3)(A)]. "If jeopardy [to a listed species] or adverse modification [of a critical habitat] is found," the Service must "suggest those reasonable and prudent alternatives which [it] believes would not violate [Section 7(a)(2)] and can be taken by the Federal agency or applicant in implementing the agency action" (id.).

Second, independent of the consultation process, Section 7(a)(2) imposes an affirmative duty on federal departments, agencies, and instrumentalities to refrain from taking, funding, or authorizing actions that are likely to adversely affect the continued existence of an endangered or threatened species, or to destroy or adversely modify the critical habitat of such species. The Supreme Court dramatically affirmed the existence of this duty in *Tennessee Valley Authority v. Hill*, 437 U.S. 153 (1978). This case involved the snail darter, a rare species of perch that was placed on the endangered species list after the federal Tennessee Valley Authority (TVA) had substantially completed construction of a dam across the Little Tennessee River. As it turned out, the area of the river to be affected by the dam is also the only known habitat of the snail darter, and this area of the river was designated as critical habitat for the species. In making this listing, the secretary of the interior declared that completion and operation of the dam "would result in total destruction of the snail darter's habitat" (437 U.S. at 162). Invoking the ESA's citizen suit provision, 16 U.S.C. §1540(g), opponents of the dam brought suit to prevent its completion. They argued that operation of the dam would violate Section 7(a)(2).

Concluding that the operative language of this provision, quoted here, is clear on its face, the Supreme Court agreed, and held that an injunction should be issued forbidding the TVA from completing and operating the dam. Although it acknowledged the argument that "the burden on the public through the loss of millions of unrecoverable dollars [already spent on the dam] would greatly outweigh the loss of the snail darter" (id. at 187), the majority opinion pointedly noted that policy decisions of this nature are the province of the Congress, and not the courts:

[N]either the Endangered Species Act nor Article III of the Constitution provides federal courts with authority to make such fine utilitarian calculations. On the contrary, the plain language of the Act, buttressed by its legislative history, shows clearly that Congress viewed the value of endangered species as "incalculable." Quite obviously, it would be difficult for a court to balance the loss of a sum certain—even $100 million—against a congressionally declared "incalculable" value, even assuming we had the power to engage in such a weighing process, which we emphatically do not. (id. at 187–188)

In a vigorous dissent, Justice Powell, joined by Justice Blackmun, pointedly disagreed:

Under the Court's reasoning, the Act covers every existing federal installation, including great hydroelectric projects and reservoirs, every river and harbor project, and every national defense installation—however essential to the Nation's economic health and safety. The "actions" that an agency would be prohibited from "carrying out" would include the continued operation of such projects or any change necessary to preserve their continued usefulness. The only precondition . . . to thus destroying the usefulness of even the most important federal project in our country would be a finding by the Secretary of the Interior that a continuation of the project would threaten the survival or critical habitat of a newly discovered species of water spider or amoeba. (id. at 203–204)

Although Congress has left the operative language of Section 7(a)(2) intact, it has, consistent with Justice Powell's dissent, added other provisions to Section 7 to soften the impact of this language in certain circumstances. There is now an Endangered Species Committee (known colloquially as the God Committee), composed of six designated public officials and one representative of each affected state, which is authorized to grant an exemption, in whole or in part, from the Section 7(a)(2) mandate in certain circumstances and according to certain specified procedures and criteria. See 16 U.S.C. §§1536(e) through (o).

Placement of a species on the endangered species list also triggers the provisions of Section 9 of the ESA, which states that with respect to any endangered species of fish or wildlife listed pursuant to [Section 4 of the ESA], it is unlawful for any person subject to the jurisdiction of the United States to... take any such species within the United States or the territorial sea of the United States. [16 U.S.C. §1538(a)(1)]

This same prohibition can be, and often is, extended to species of fish or wildlife that have been listed as threatened under the act. See 16 U.S.C. §1533(d). This prohibition extends to any party, private or public. See 16 U.S.C. §1532(13) (defining "person"). The operative word, "take," is defined in the act to include, among other things, actions that "harass" or "harm" the species in question. See 16 U.S.C. §1532(19). The Services, in turn, have defined "harm" as including actions "significant habitat modification or degradation which actually kills or injures fish or wildlife by significantly impairing essential behavior patterns including breeding, spawning, rearing, migrating, feeding or sheltering" (50 C.F.R. §222.102), and have defined "harass" as including actions that "significantly disrupt normal behavior patterns which include, but are not limited to, breeding, feeding or sheltering" (50 C.F.R. §17.3). There are exceptions to the "take" prohibition. A federal action exempted from Section 7(a)(2) by the God Committee does not constitute a take. Moreover, Section 10 of the act allows the Services to grant an "incidental take permit," under which specified activities may go forward along with specified mitigation measures in certain circumstances. See 16 U.S.C. §1539.

■ **NOTES**

1. For a general discussion of the "take" prohibition, see *Babbit v. Sweet Home Chapter of Communities for a Great Oregon*, 515 U.S. 687 (1995).

2. Affected citizens may bring suit in federal court to enforce the requirements of Section 7 and Section 9 under Section 11(g), 33 U.S.C. §1540(g), the ESA's citizen suit provision.   ■

6 The Clean Air Act and the Regulation of Stationary Sources

A. Origins and Overview of the Clean Air Act
   1. Origins
   2. Structure and Overview of the Clean Air Act
B. National Ambient Air Quality Standards for Criteria Pollutants
C. State Implementation Plans
D. Additional Regulation of Stationary Sources
   1. Section 111 Standards
      a. New Source Performance Standards
         i. In General
         ii. What Is a "New" or "Major Modified" Source?
         iii. Alternative Standard-Setting Criteria
      b. Designated Pollutants
   2. Additional Emission Standards and Policies Designed to Achieve or Maintain Ambient Air Quality Standards: Nonattainment and the Prevention of Significant Deterioration
      a. Nonattainment Policy
         i. In General
         ii. Specific Requirements for Ozone, CO, and Particulates
      b. Nondegradation Policy (Prevention of Significant Deterioration)
         i. In General
         ii. Specific Requirements
      c. The Applicability of the Bubble Policy in Nonattainment and PSD Areas
   3. Visibility Protection
   4. Acid Rain Controls and the SO_2 Allowance Trading System
   5. Emission Standards for Hazardous Air Pollutants
      a. Section 112 before the 1990 Amendments
      b. Section 112 after the 1990 Amendments
         i. Designation of Specific Hazardous Air Pollutants
         ii. Distinguishing Between "Major" and "Area" Sources

iii. Specific Emission Standards According to a Specified Schedule
iv. Hazardous Air Pollutant Offsets
v. Reporting and Prevention of Accidental Chemical Releases
6. Enforcement and the Title VI Operating Permit Permits

This chapter and the following one address the Clean Air Act, the first of the five media-based regulatory systems (or "regimes") covered in this text. In chapter 8 we address the Clean Water Act and the Safe Drinking Water Act, and in chapter 9 we discuss the Resource Conservation and Recovery Act and the Comprehensive Environmental Response, Compensation, and Liability Act (the federal "Superfund" law). Together these five statutes were designed to protect public health and the environment from chemicals discharged from industrial, governmental, and mobile sources that pollute the air, water, and ground. The setting of standards and other legal requirements within these regulatory regimes is an ongoing process that is now well into its fourth decade. This period has seen significant changes in the way in which scientific and technical information is incorporated into the regulatory process, and in the way in which science, economics, and technological capability are viewed by the courts. The concepts of risk assessment, cost-benefit analysis, and technology forcing have evolved, both through the development of case law and through changes in the political environment. Often, changes in one of the regulatory regimes have affected the others as well.

Several themes run through the discussion of these regulatory systems: distinctions between performance and design or specification standards; differences between taking economics or costs into account in the setting of standards and doing so in the enforcement of standards; distinctions between interventions that encourage technological innovation and those that encourage diffusion of existing technologies; the role of polluters, environmental groups, and citizens in standard setting and enforcement; and shifts in the degree to which equity is taken into account, as reflected, for example, in the extent to which the Polluter Pays Principle and the Precautionary Principle are given legal embodiment.

Before beginning our discussion of these regulatory systems, it is useful to establish a common lexicon. Regulatory standards (what we will call "direct controls") can be classified in a number of ways. A *performance standard* is one that specifies a particular outcome, such as a specified emission level above which it is illegal to emit a specified air pollutant, but does not specify how that outcome is to be achieved. A *design* or *specification standard*, on the other hand, specifies a particular technology, such as a catalytic converter, that must be utilized. In either case, the standard can be based on (1) a desired level of protection for human health or environmental quality,

(2) some level of presumed technological feasibility, (3) some level of presumed economic feasibility, or (4) some balancing of social costs and social benefits. Within each of these options, there is a wide spectrum of possible approaches. A health-based standard, for example, might choose to protect only the average member of the population or it might choose to protect the most sensitive individual. Similarly, a technology-based standard might be based on what is deemed feasible for an entire industry or on what is deemed feasible for each firm within that industry. Moreover, some standards might be based on a combination of these factors. Many standards based on technological feasibility, for example, are also based on some concept of economic feasibility. Finally, the relevant regulatory requirements encompass more than simply placing a limit on pollution. Other requirements that could be considered "standards" include (1) information-based obligations, such as the disclosure of (and retention of, or provision of access to) exposure, toxicity, chemical content, and production data; and (2) requirements to conduct testing or screening of chemical products.

A.   ORIGINS AND OVERVIEW OF THE CLEAN AIR ACT

The Clean Air Act of 1970 addressed both stationary and mobile sources of air pollution and was amended in important ways thereafter. In 1977 the amendments were largely used to strengthen the existing structure. In 1990 some of the basic tenets of the original law were changed, and new major authorities (titles) were added covering acid rain (and the concomitant trading allowance system for oxides of sulfur and nitrogen), chlorofluorocarbon destruction of the ozone layer, chemical safety (related to sudden and accidental chemical releases), indoor air quality (radon), and new enforcement provisions. After a brief history of the origin of federal legislation leading to the 1970 Clean Air Act, we begin with a description of those provisions representing the act's original focus, and a discussion of the key court cases interpreting their reach and meaning.

1.   Origins

Significant federal involvement with air pollution did not begin until after the occurrence of serious air pollution episodes, such as a highly publicized episode in Donora, Pennsylvania, in 1948. There, a week-long inversion layer trapped a damp, suffocating, petrochemical smog. Twenty people died, scores more were hospitalized, and traffic was brought to a standstill by a lack of visibility. Pressure for regulatory action also came from California, because it had become clear by the 1950s that southern California had developed a chronic air pollution problem. In 1960, the

Division of Air Pollution was established within the U.S. Public Health Service, an arm of the Department of Health, Education, and Welfare (HEW, the forerunner of the current Department of Health and Human Services). In 1963 President Lyndon Johnson signed legislation authorizing the Public Health Service to undertake more intensive research, provide grants to the states, conduct studies on air pollution problems, and take action to abate air pollution by requesting the attorney general to bring abatement actions in federal court. In 1965, the statute was amended to authorize federal regulation of emissions from new automobiles.

Two years later, President Johnson signed the Air Quality Act of 1967 (AQA), which directed states to delineate air quality control regions (AQCRs), to establish ambient air quality standards for these regions based on federal criteria, and to submit state implementation plans (SIPs) for meeting and enforcing these ambient standards by placing emission limitations on polluting sources. Advisory ambient air quality standards were established by HEW, based on a set of criteria documents. Advisory standards were established for carbon monoxide (CO), sulfur dioxide (SO$_2$), nitrogen oxides (NO$_X$), large (inhalable) as opposed to small (respirable) particulate matter (PM), photochemical oxidants, and hydrocarbons (HCs). These (health-based) standards were grounded in the science at the time, which assumed there were safe "thresholds" of exposure below which no adverse effect was possible. These pollutants became known as the "criteria pollutants." Industry largely ignored these advisory standards, and states—who were charged with encouraging and monitoring compliance—were largely unsuccessful in securing compliance with these advisory standards. Industrial expansion, especially in urban areas, exacerbated the extent of exposure and hence the health risks from the criteria pollutants.

Angered and frustrated by the lack of state and industry commitment toward meeting the advisory standards, Senator Edmund Muskie of Maine (the Democratic vice presidential candidate in the 1968 Nixon-Humphrey presidential contest, and an aspirant to the 1972 Democratic presidential nomination), together with Representative Paul Rogers of Florida, co-authored the 1970 CAA amendments. The new legislation mandated compliance with federal standards, required the setting of new standards, and established the basic structure of the CAA that persists to this day.[1] The Environmental Protection Agency, which was created in 1970 by an executive order of President Richard Nixon, was charged with administering and enforcing the act.

---

1. Senator Muskie's original legislative proposal was somewhat weaker than a competing Clean Air proposal offered by President Nixon, but Muskie's desire to be considered a leader in the environmental field led to the stronger Senate bill that ultimately prevailed (see Arnold W. Reitze, Jr. (1999) "The Legislative History of U.S. Air Pollution Control," 36 *Houston Law Review* 679.

■ **NOTES**

1. For a description of the air pollution episode in Donora, Pennsylvania, as well as a history of pollution generally, see Devra Davis (2002) *When Smoke Ran Like Water: Tales of Environmental Deception and the Battle Against Pollution*. Basic Books, New York.

2. For a detailed legislative history of attempts to control air pollution, see Arnold W. Reitze, Jr. (1999) "The Legislative History of U.S. Air Pollution Control," 36 *Houston Law Review* 679. ■

2. Structure and Overview of the Clean Air Act

The Clean Air Act regulates both stationary and mobile sources of air pollution, taking into account the relative contributions of each (and the different kinds of sources within each category) to specific air pollution problems.

The five original criteria pollutants, and such other pollutants as are listed by EPA, are subject to concentration limitations known as National Ambient Air Quality Standards (NAAQS), which are to be met by a combination of federal and state emission limits on mobile and stationary sources. Beyond the criteria pollutants, federal limits are placed on emissions of identified toxic pollutants ("hazardous air pollutants") from stationary sources. Federal emission limits are established on criteria and toxic pollutants in exhaust from new motor vehicles (with California, and later other states, being able to set more stringent limits). In addition, there is federal regulation of motor vehicle fuels, and state regulation of motor vehicle maintenance and use.

The recognition that sources using newer technology might be able to achieve greater emission reductions than older sources with older technology, and likewise that different industry sectors may differ in their relative capacities to reduce pollution, led to the act's distinction—both in the stationary and mobile source provisions—between new and existing sources. Thus, newer models of cars and trucks are generally required to meet more stringent tailpipe emission standards than older models, and new stationary sources are required to meet federal emission standards. These distinctions were largely driven by equity concerns, stemming from a recognition that older sources generally face greater economic and technological hurdles in endeavoring to meet stringent emission limitations. However, especially in the case of stationary sources, an unintentional effect of this approach has been to discourage modernization or replacement of facilities, which has resulted in the operation of older (especially energy) facilities beyond their expected useful life. Thus, while for new sources there was a recognition of the need for uniformity and

the need to encourage technological innovation, this focus did not extend (at least not initially) to existing sources.

Congress directed EPA to set *primary* national ambient air quality standards at concentration levels that will protect "public health" with "an adequate margin of safety" [Section 109(b)(1)]. As discussed in some of the court decisions excerpted here, these standards are to be set on the basis of health considerations alone, without consideration of economic or technological feasibility. In the 1970 CAA, Congress specified that such standards for the original five criteria pollutants were to be attained by 1977. In addition, Congress directed that *secondary* ambient air quality standards be established at concentrations that will protect "the public welfare" [Section 109(b)(2)]. The NAAQS are expressed as concentrations—units of pollutant per volume of ambient air.

Both the federal and state governments have a role in securing compliance with these ambient air standards under the CAA. Emission limitations are placed on individual existing stationary source polluters through permits issued by the states as a part of their state implementation plans. See Section 110. Furthermore, EPA sets federal emission limitations for new sources, known as "new source performance standards," under Section 111 of the act. Finally, as discussed in detail in chapter 7, there are a variety of federal and state restrictions on new and existing mobile sources. In specifying compliance with federal emission standards for stationary and mobile sources, Congress expressed concern about "hot spots" of local intense pollution and also with intermittent versus continuous versus sudden and accidental releases of harmful substances. Emission standards, in contrast with ambient concentration standards, are expressed as a *rate* (milligrams emitted per 100 kg of product, or per hour, per day, per week, per quarter, per year, or per British thermal unit, per passenger-mile, etc.)

The 1970 CAA also carved out a special role for federal emission limitations in the control of "hazardous air pollutants," those recognized as extraordinarily toxic and eventually (though not at that time) regarded as non- or low-threshold pollutants. Under the 1970 act, these were to be regulated by emission limitations sufficient to protect public health with "an ample margin of safety" [Section 112]. Emission limitations were preferred to ambient standards for these pollutants because of their extraordinary toxicity, because the sources of these pollutants were relatively small in number (although significant), because emissions often occurred sporadically and at varying levels, and because of the desire to eliminate toxic hot spots.[2] (California,

---

2. Lead might have been considered a hazardous pollutant, but since its major urban source in many areas was originally the lead in gasoline, EPA did not regard a Section 112 emission standard appropriate for its control. Thus, as we will see, EPA designated lead as another criteria pollutant.

however, did establish a primary ambient standard for vinyl chloride in addition to an emission limitation.)

Subsequent amendments to the CAA added "nonattainment" requirements for air quality control regions that were out of compliance with an ambient standard for one or more criteria pollutants (see Sections 171–192), and added "prevention of significant deterioration" (PSD) provisions for pristine areas and other regions already in compliance with ambient standards (see Sections 169A and B), essentially addressing problems created by industrial and traffic growth, and welfare considerations (such as visibility) not reflected in secondary ambient air quality standards.

In the early stages of the implementation of the stationary source provisions of the Clean Air Act (approximately 1970–1975), EPA focused on the primary and secondary ambient air quality standards and on emission standards for *new* sources of criteria pollutants and for *all* sources emitting seven regulated hazardous air pollutants. Although our focus here will be on the actions of EPA, both in establishing federal standards and in encouraging the states to help implement these standards, it is important to note that except for certain limitations on new motor vehicles, Congress left the states free to promulgate ambient and emission standards more stringent than those set by EPA. See Section 116. Some states, especially California, took advantage of this enhanced authority.

California leader

B. NATIONAL AMBIENT AIR QUALITY STANDARDS FOR CRITERIA POLLUTANTS

As a part of its initial set of actions under the new Clean Air Act, EPA promulgated the prior advisory standards for CO, SO_2, NO_X, large particulate matter, and photochemical oxidants as mandatory ambient air quality standards. The agency has periodically modified the standards for photochemical oxidants and particulates since that time. In 1979, the standard for photochemical oxidants was narrowed to cover only ground-level ozone and was relaxed from 0.08 ppm to 0.12 ppm averaged over a 1-hour period. Almost two decades later, in 1997, the ozone standard was revised back to 0.08 ppm, averaged over an 8-hour period. The standard for particulate matter was revised to cover "inhalable" particulates up to 10 microns in diameter (PM_{10}) in 1987. Ten years later, the particulate standard was altered to place more stringent requirements on smaller "respirable" particles of less than 2.5 microns in diameter ($PM_{2.5}$). In 2006, the $PM_{2.5}$ standard was further lowered, from 65 to 35 $\mu g/m^3$ of air.

The CAA also authorizes EPA to expand the number of NAAQSs by listing additional air pollutants that "cause or contribute to air pollution which may reasonably be anticipated to endanger public health or the environment" [Section 108(a)(1)]. As held in *NRDC v. Train* 411 F. Supp. 864 (S.D.N.Y.), *affirmed* 545 F.2d 320 (2d Cir. 1976) (addressing airborne lead), such a listing is not discretionary if the agency finds sufficient endangerment to public health or the environment and the pollutant is emitted from numerous or diverse stationary or mobile sources. EPA is required to promulgate an appropriate standard within 12 months of listing. See Section 108(a)(2). As part of its strategy to control ozone, EPA adopted a NAAQS for hydrocarbons (HCs) in 1971. This national standard was withdrawn in 1983, but many states have promulgated their own standards for volatile organic compounds (VOCs) which cover hydrocarbons. In addition, since volatile organics contribute to photochemical smog, federal restrictions have been fashioned for reducing HCs in some ozone nonattainment areas. Lead was later added to the list of criteria pollutants, and a NAAQS for lead was promulgated in 1977. The current primary and secondary ambient air quality standards are listed in table 6.1.

Table 6.1
National Ambient Air Quality Standards

Carbon Monoxide	Primary (1970): 35 ppm averaged over 1 hr and 9.0 averaged over 8 hrs; neither to be exceeded more than once per year. Secondary: none.
Particulate Matter: PM$_{10}$	(note that 10 and 2.5 refer to particles equal to or less than 10 and 2.5 microns in diameter) Primary (1970): 150 $\mu g/m^3$ averaged over 24 hrs, with no more than one expected exceedance per calendar year; also, 50 $\mu g/m^3$ or less for the expected annual arithmetic mean concentration. Secondary: same as primary.
PM$_{2.5}$	Prior Primary (1997): 65 $\mu g/m^3$ averaged over 24 hrs; 15 $\mu g/m^3$ annual maximum. Revised Primary (2006): 35 $\mu g/m^3$ averaged over 24 hrs.
Ozone	Prior Primary (1979): 235 $\mu g/m^3$ (0.12 ppm) averaged over 1 hr, no more than one expected exceedance per calendar year (multiple violations in a day count as one violation). Revoked June 2005. Codified August 2005. Prior Secondary: same as primary. Revised Primary (1997): 0.08 ppm averaged over 8 hrs.
Nitrogen Dioxide	Primary (1970): 100 $\mu g/m^3$ (0.053 ppm) as an annual arithmetic mean concentration. Secondary: same as primary.
Sulfur Oxides	Primary (1970): 365 $\mu g/m^3$ (0.14 ppm) averaged over 24 hrs, not to be exceeded more than once per year; 80 $\mu g/m^3$ (0.03 ppm) annual arithmetic mean. Secondary: 1,300 $\mu g/m^3$ averaged over a 3-hr period, not to be exceeded more than once per year.
Lead	Primary (1977): 1.5 $\mu g/m^3$ arithmetic average over a calendar quarter. Secondary: same as primary.

■ **NOTES**

1. Initially, many stationary sources "complied" with the ambient standards by constructing tall emission stacks that dispersed pollutants over wide areas through meteorological mixing, thus allowing areas around the polluting sources to meet the NAAQS without actually reducing the emission of pollutants. In many cases these tall stacks would simply transport pollutants from one air quality control region to another. At one point, some 175 tall stacks higher than 500 feet had been constructed, 111 of which were used by utilities to emit SO_2 and NO_x, both of which contributed to the formation of acid rain in the eastern United States. See Robert B. Percival, Alan S. Miller, Christopher H. Schroeder, and James P. Leape (1992) *Environmental Regulation: Law Science and Policy*. Little Brown, Boston, p. 818. Thus in the 1977 amendments to the CAA, Congress gave EPA a specific directive to control stack heights (see Section 123), and EPA regulations specify that *continuous* emission controls, rather than less expensive approaches such as tall stacks or intermittent controls, must be the first method of complying with primary and secondary standards. The use of intermittent controls would have allowed air pollution sources to "tune" their level of pollutant control, employing a greater or lesser degree of control as meteorological conditions varied. This method, too, is disfavored under Section 123 of the act.

2. In 2005 EPA revoked its 1-hour ambient air quality standard for ozone in favor of the arguably more stringent 8-hour standard issued in 1997 (70 *Fed. Reg.* 44,470). Most of the areas that were in violation of the prior 1-hour standard were also out of attainment with the newer 8-hour standard [*Environment Reporter* 36(31): 1600 (2007)]. Further, EPA reported that 474 counties in 32 states (encompassing 159 million people) were out of compliance with the new 8-hour ozone standard, which is about twice the number out of compliance with the 1-hour standard [*Environment Reporter* 35(16): 805–806 (2004)]. The standard is expected to be further lowered. See note 8, p. 395.

3. In *South Coast Air Quality Management District v. EPA*, the Court of Appeals for the D.C. Circuit affirmed EPA's authority to impose the old 1-hour standard for ozone in nonattainment areas, even though it has been replaced by the new 8-hour standard to avoid "backsliding." [472 F.3rd 882 (D.C. Cir. 2006)].   ■

The first court challenge to a primary ambient air quality standard came when EPA moved beyond the original criteria pollutants by promulgating a standard for airborne lead.

Lead Industries Association, Inc. v. Environmental Protection Agency
Before WRIGHT, Chief Judge, and ROBINSON and MacKINNON, Circuit Judges
Opinion by Chief Judge J. SKELLY WRIGHT
647 F.2d 1130 (D.C. Cir. 1980)

I. BACKGROUND

...Acting pursuant to authority conferred on it by Congress in the Clean Air Act, as amended, 42 U.S.C. §7401 et seq., EPA has been involved in regulation of lead emissions almost since the Agency's inception.[5] Its initial approach to controlling the amount of lead in the ambient air was to limit lead emissions from automobiles by restricting the amount of lead in gasoline. To this end it promulgated the regulations which we upheld in *Amoco Oil Corp. v. EPA*, 163 U.S. App. D.C., 162, 501 F.2d 722 (D.C. Cir.1974) and *Ethyl Corp. v. EPA*, 176 U.S. App. D.C. 373, 541 F.2d 1 (D.C. Cir.) (en banc), cert. denied, 426 U.S. 941, 96 S. Ct. 2662, 49 L. Ed. 2d 394 (1976)...[I]n 1975 the Natural Resources Defense Council, Inc. (NRDC), and others brought suit against EPA claiming that the Agency was required by Section 108 of the Clean Air Act, 42 U.S.C. §7408, to list lead as a pollutant for which an air quality criteria document would be prepared, and for which national ambient air quality standards should be promulgated under Section 109 of the Act, 42 U.S.C. §7409. The District Court agreed with NRDC and directed the Administrator to list lead as a pollutant under Section 108 of the Act, by March 31, 1976. *Natural Resources Defense Council, Inc. v. Train*, 411 F. Supp. 864 (S.D.N.Y.1976). The Second Circuit affirmed, 545 F.2d 320 (2d Cir. 1976), and EPA initiated the proceedings outlined in the statute which are under review here.

II. THE STATUTORY SCHEME

The first step toward establishing national ambient air quality standards for a particular pollutant is its addition to a list, compiled by EPA's Administrator, of pollutants that cause or contribute to air pollution "which may reasonably be anticipated to endanger public health or welfare(.)" Section 108(a)(1), 42 U.S.C. §7408(a)(1). Within twelve months of the listing of a pollutant under Section 108(a) the Administrator must issue "air quality criteria" for the pollutant. Section 108 makes it clear that the term "air quality criteria" means something different from the conventional meaning of "criterion"; such "criteria" do not constitute "standards" or "guidelines," but rather refer to a document to be prepared by EPA which is to provide the scientific basis for promulgation of air quality standards for the pollutant. This criteria document must "accurately reflect the latest scientific knowledge useful in indicating the kind and extent of all identifiable effects on public health or welfare which may be expected from the presence of such pollutant in the ambient air, in varying quantities." Section 108(a)(2), 42 U.S.C. §7408(a)(2).

At the same time as he issues air quality criteria for a pollutant, the Administrator must also publish proposed national primary and secondary air quality standards for the pollutant. Section 109(a)(2), 42 U.S.C. §7409(a)(2). National primary ambient air quality standards are standards "the attain-

---

5. EPA and other federal agencies, including the Department of Housing and Urban Development, the Occupational Health and Safety Administra-

tion, and the Consumer Product Safety Commission, are involved in a variety of regulatory efforts aimed at controlling other sources of lead exposure.

ment and maintenance of which in the judgment of the Administrator, based on such criteria and allowing an adequate margin of safety, are requisite to protect the public health." Section 109(b)(1), 42 U.S.C. §7409(b)(1). Secondary air quality standards "specify a level of air quality the attainment and maintenance of which in the judgment of the Administrator, based on such criteria, is requisite to protect the public welfare from any known or anticipated adverse effects associated with the presence of such air pollutant in the ambient air." Section 109(b)(2), 42 U.S.C. §7409(b)(2). Effects on "the public welfare" include "effects on soils, water, crops, vegetation, man-made materials, animals, wildlife, weather, visibility, and climate, damage to and deterioration of property, and hazards to transportation, as well as effects on economic values and on personal comfort and well-being." Section 302(h), 42 U.S.C. §7602(h). The Administrator is required to submit the proposed air quality standards for public comment in a rulemaking proceeding, the procedure for which is prescribed by Section 307(d) of the Act, 42 U.S.C. §7607(d).

Within six months of publication of the proposed standards the Administrator must promulgate final primary and secondary ambient air quality standards for the pollutant. Section 307(d)(10), 42 U.S.C. §7607(d)(10). Once EPA has promulgated national ambient air quality standards, responsibility under the Act shifts from the federal government to the states. Within nine months of promulgation of the standards each state must prepare and submit to EPA for approval a state implementation plan [SIP]. Section 110(a)(1), 42 U.S.C. §7410(a)(1). These state implementation plans must contain emission limitations and all other measures necessary to attain the primary standards "as expeditiously as practicable," but no later than three years after EPA approval of the plan, and to attain the secondary standards within a reasonable period of time. Section 110(a)(2)(A) & (B), 42 U.S.C. §7410(a)(2)(A)

& (B). The Administrator is authorized to extend the deadline for attainment of the primary air quality standards by two years, but thereafter it must be met. Section 110(e), 42 U.S.C. §7410(e).

III. THE LEAD STANDARDS RULEMAKING PROCEEDINGS

. . .

A. The Lead Criteria Document

. . . EPA released its "Air Quality Criteria For Lead" on December 14, 1977. 42 Fed.Reg. 63076. The document was "prepared to reflect the current state of knowledge about lead specifically, those issues that are most relevant to establishing the objective scientific data base that will be used to recommend an air quality standard for lead that will adequately safeguard the public health." Accordingly, the Criteria Document examined a large number of issues raised by the problem of lead in the environment. One of these was the effects of lead exposure on human health. The Criteria Document concluded that, among the major organ systems, the hematopoietic (blood-forming) and neurological systems are the areas of prime concern. Its discussion of the effects of lead on these two organ systems is central to our review of the lead standards.[8]

The Criteria Document identified a variety of effects of lead exposure on the blood-forming system. We will discuss only the effects that played an important role in the Administrator's analysis. Anemia, which can be caused by lead-induced deformation and destruction of erythrocytes (red blood cells) and decreased hemoglobin synthesis, is often the earliest clinical manifestation of

---

8. Lead also affects the renal, reproductive, endocrine, hepatic, cardiovascular, immunologic, and gastrointestinal systems.

lead intoxication. Symptoms of anemia include pallor of the skin, shortness of breath, palpitations of the heart, and fatigability. The Criteria Document concluded, after a review of various studies, that in "children, a threshold level for anemia is about 40 μg Pb/dl, whereas the corresponding value for adults is about 50 μg Pb/dl." The concentration of lead in the blood is measured in micrograms of lead per deciliter of blood μg Pb/dl.

The Criteria Document also examined other more subtle effects on the blood-forming system, associated with lower levels of lead exposure. The most pertinent of these "subclinical"[11] effects for purposes of these cases is lead-related elevation of erythrocyte protoporphyrin (EP elevation). According to the Criteria Document, this phenomenon must, for a number of reasons, be regarded as an indication of an impairment of human health. First, EP elevation indicates an impairment in the functioning of the mitochondria, the subcellular units which play a crucial role in the production of energy in the body, and in cellular respiration. Second, it indicates that lead exposure has begun to affect one of the basic biological functions of the body production of heme within the red blood cells. Heme is critical to transporting oxygen to every cell in the body. Third, EP elevation may indicate that any reserve capacity there may be in the heme synthesis system has been reduced. Finally, the Criteria Document noted that lead's interference with the process of heme synthesis in the blood may suggest that lead interferes with produc-

tion of heme proteins in other organ systems, particularly the renal and neurological systems. The Criteria Document reported that the threshold for EP elevation in children and women is at blood lead levels of 15–20 μg Pb/dl, and 25–30 μg Pb/dl in adult males....

The Criteria Document also examined the effects of lead exposure on the central nervous system. Among the most deleterious effects of lead poisoning are those associated with severe central nervous system damage at high exposure levels. The Criteria Document noted that neurological and behavioral deficits have long been known to be among the more serious effects of lead exposure, but it pointed out that there is disagreement about whether these effects are reversible, and about what exposure levels are necessary to produce specific deleterious effects.

The Criteria Document also went on to consider the evidence on whether lower level lead exposures can affect the central nervous stem, particularly in children. It acknowledged that the issue is unsettled and somewhat controversial, but it was able to conclude, after a careful review of various studies on the subject,[14] that "a rather consistent pattern of impaired neural and cognitive functions appears to be associated with blood lead levels below those producing the overt symptomatology of lead encephalopathy." The Criteria Document reported that "(t)he blood lead levels at which neurobehavioral deficits occur in otherwise asymptomatic children appear to

---

11. According to the Criteria Document, "subclinical" effects "are disruptions in function, which may be demonstrated by special testing but not by the classic techniques of physical examination; using the term 'subclinical' in no way implies that those effects are without consequences to human health." Stedman's Medical Dictionary, supra note 10, defines "subclinical" as "(denoting) a period prior to the appearance of manifest symptoms in the evolution of a disease." Id. at 1433.

14. ...Some of these studies suggested that low level lead exposure may cause central nervous system deficits, resulting in impaired concept formation and altered behavioral profiles, may interfere with the normal intellectual development of lead-exposed children, and may cause subtle neurological damage.

start at a range of 50 to 60 µg/dl, although some evidence tentatively suggests that such effects may occur at slightly lower levels for some children."...

B. The Proposed Standards

Simultaneously with the publication of the Lead Criteria Document on December 14, 1977, the Administrator proposed a national primary ambient air quality standard for lead of 1.5 µg Pb/m^3 monthly average. 42 Fed.Reg. 63076. He also proposed that the secondary air quality standard be set at the same level as the primary standard because the welfare effects associated with lead exposure did not warrant imposition of a stricter standard. 42 Fed.Reg. 63081–63082. In the preamble to the proposed standards the Administrator explained the analysis EPA had employed in setting the standards.

The Administrator first pointed out that a number of factors complicate the task of setting air quality standards which will protect the population from the adverse health effects of lead exposure. First, some sub-groups within the population have a greater potential for, or are more susceptible to the effects of, lead exposure. Id. at 63077. Second, there are a variety of adverse health effects associated with various levels of lead exposure. Id. Third, the variability of individual responses to lead exposure, even within particular sub-groups of the population, would produce a range of blood lead levels at any given air lead level. Id. at 63079. Fourth, airborne lead is only one of a number of sources of lead exposure and the relative contribution from each source is difficult to quantify. Id. at

63080. Finally, the relationship between air lead exposure and blood lead levels is a complex one. Id. at 63079.

In response to the first problem the Administrator began by noting that protection of the most sensitive groups within the population had to be a major consideration in determining the level at which the air quality standards should be set. And he determined that children between the ages of 1 and 5 years are most sensitive to the effects of lead exposure both because the hematologic and neurologic effects associated with lead exposure occur in children at lower threshold levels than in adults, and because the habit of placing hands and other objects in the mouth subjects them to a greater risk of exposure. Id. at 63077–63078. Next, the Administrator examined the various health effects of lead exposure and proposed that EP elevation should be considered the first adverse health effect of lead exposure because it indicates an impairment of cellular functions, and should be the pivotal health effect on which the lead standards are based. Id. at 63078. Accordingly, he proposed that the air lead standards be designed to prevent the occurrence of EP elevation in children. In order to accomplish this, and to address the problem of variable responses to lead exposure, the Administrator selected 15 µg Pb/dl, the lowest reported threshold blood lead level for EP elevation in children, as the target mean population blood lead level.[17] He reasoned that setting the target mean population blood lead level at the lowest reported threshold blood lead level for EP elevation would ensure that most of the target population would be kept below blood lead levels at which

---

17. The target mean population blood lead level is the blood lead level that will ensure that the great majority of the target population is protected from the adverse health effects of lead. Given the variability in individual blood lead responses to lead exposure, a population with a mean blood lead

level of 15 µg Pb/dl will have individuals with blood lead levels higher and lower than 15 µg Pb/dl, but since 15 µg Pb/dl is the lowest blood lead level at which EP elevation has been detected, most children will be kept below blood lead levels at which adverse health effects occur.

adverse health effects occur. Id. at 63078. The Administrator also discussed the alternative approaches of basing the standard on more severe effects such as anemia, or attempting to decide the actual level of EP elevation which represents an adverse effect on health, and then making an adjustment to allow a margin of safety. Id. He specifically invited comments on these alternative approaches. Id. Finally, the Administrator outlined another approach to calculating the target mean population blood lead level involving the use of statistical techniques discussed in the Criteria Document.

Having selected a target mean population blood lead level, the Administrator's next step was to allow for the multiplicity of sources of lead exposure. He thus had to estimate the amount of blood lead that should be attributed to non-air sources. The Administrator admitted that any amount he selected could be no more than a theoretical national average, and on the basis of the evidence available he proposed that the lead standards should be based on the general assumption that 12 µg Pb/dl of blood lead should be attributed to non-air sources. Id. at 63080–63081. Given the target mean population blood lead level of 15 µg Pb/dl and the assumed contribution from non-air sources of 12 µg Pb/dl, the maximum allowable contribution from ambient air is 3 µg Pb/dl. The final step in his analysis was to determine what air lead level would prevent the ambient air contribution to blood lead levels from exceeding 3 µg Pb/dl. This step required determining the relationship between air lead exposure and blood lead levels, i.e., the air lead/blood lead ratio. On the basis of the information in the Criteria Document, the Administrator selected a ratio of 1:2 as appropriate for calculating the effect of air lead exposure on blood lead levels in children. Id. at 63079.

Thereafter, calculation of the air quality standard was a mathematical exercise....

C. Public Comments

A number of comments challenged the selection of EP elevation as the pivotal adverse health effect, insisting that EP elevation merely indicates a biological change or response which is in no way harmful to health, and in addition they criticized the Administrator's determination that the blood lead threshold for EP elevation in children is 15 µg Pb/dl. These comments suggested that a decrease in hemoglobin levels, which begins at blood lead levels no lower than 40 µg Pb/dl, should be the pivotal adverse health effect on which the standards are based. Other experts, however, agreed with the Administrator's conclusion that EP elevation must be considered an adverse health effect of lead exposure, and argued that using EP elevation as the pivotal adverse health effect would, in addition, allow an adequate margin of safety in protecting against the more serious health effects associated with higher levels of lead exposure. Finally, several industry experts appeared to indicate a preference for the lognormal statistical procedures that the Administrator had, in the proposed standards, suggested as an alternative method for determining the target mean population blood lead level.

D. The Final Air Quality Standards for Lead

The Administrator promulgated the final air quality standards on October 5, 1978, prescribing national primary and secondary ambient air quality standards for lead of 1.5 µg Pb/m^3, averaged over a calendar quarter. Although the final standards were the same as the proposed standards (with the exception of the change in the averaging period from 30 to 90 days), the Administrator arrived at the final standards through somewhat different analysis.... The Administrator's reexamination focused on two key questions: (1) What is the maximum safe individual blood lead level for children? and (2) what proportion of the target population should be kept below this blood lead level? Addressing the first issue required a review of the health effects of lead exposure discussed in the Criteria Document. The Administrator concluded that, although EP elevation beginning at blood lead levels of 15–20 µg Pb/dl is potentially adverse to the health of children, only when blood lead concentration reaches a level of 30 µg Pb/dl is this effect significant enough to be considered adverse to health. Accordingly, he selected 30 µg Pb/dl as the maximum safe individual blood lead level for children. The Administrator based this choice on three mutually supporting grounds. First, it is at this blood lead level that the first adverse health effect of lead exposure impairment of heme synthesis begins to occur in children. Second, a maximum safe individual blood lead level of 30 µg Pb/dl would allow an adequate margin of safety in protecting children against more serious effects of lead exposure anemia, symptoms of which begin to appear in children at blood lead levels of 40 µg Pb/dl, and central nervous system deficits which start to occur in children at blood lead levels of 50 µg Pb/dl. Third, the Administrator reasoned that the maximum safe individual blood lead level should be no higher than the blood lead level used by the Center for Disease Control in screening children for lead poisoning, 30 µg Pb/dl.

Having determined the maximum safe individual blood lead level for the target population, the Administrator next focused on the question of what percentage of children between the ages of 1 and 5 years the standard should attempt to keep below this blood lead level. According to the 1970 census, there are approximately 20 million children under the age of 5 years in the United States, 12 million

of them in urban areas and 5 million in inner cities where lead exposure may be especially high. The Administrator concluded that in order to provide an adequate margin of safety, and to protect special high risk subgroups, the standards should aim at keeping 99.5% of the target population below the maximum safe individual blood lead level of 30 µg Pb/dl. The next step in the analysis was to determine what target mean population blood lead level would ensure that 99.5% of the children below the age of 5 years would be kept below the maximum safe individual blood lead level of 30 µg Pb/dl. Using the lognormal statistical technique he had alluded to in the proposed standards, he calculated that a target mean population blood lead level of 15 µg Pb/dl (the same number as in the proposed standards, but arrived at through different analysis), would accomplish this task.[27] Thereafter, the Administrator used the same estimate of the contribution from non-air sources, 12 µg Pb/dl, and the same air lead/blood lead ratio, 1:2, that he had used in calculating the proposed standards, to compute the final ambient air quality standards for lead. The result was an ambient air quality standard of 1.5 µg Pb/m^3, the same as the proposed standard. The Administrator did, however, change the averaging period for the standards from one calendar month to one calendar quarter, because he felt that this change would significantly improve the validity of the data to be used in monitoring the progress toward attainment of the standards without rendering the standards less protective.

On December 8, 1978 LIA petitioned EPA for reconsideration and a stay of the lead standards. The Administrator denied the petition on February 2, 1979. These petitions for

27. The procedure involved determining the geometric mean blood lead level that would place 99.5% of the target population below a blood lead level of 30 µg Pb/dl (i.e., given the variability in individual responses to lead exposure, ... it was necessary to base the standards on a blood lead level of 15 µg Pb/dl in order to ensure that 99.5% of the children below the age of 5 years are kept under a blood lead level of 30 µg Pb/dl). In performing the calculation the Administrator used a geometric standard deviation of 1.3. 43 Fed.Reg. 46253.

review of the lead standards regulations followed. Before examining the petitioners' challenges to the regulations, we consider the limits of our reviewing function.

IV. STANDARD OF REVIEW

The scope of judicial review of the Administrator's decisions and actions is delineated by Section 307(d) of the Act, 42 U.S.C. §7607(d). We must uphold the Administrator's actions unless we find that they were: (1) "arbitrary, capricious, an abuse of discretion, or otherwise not in accordance with law"; (2) "contrary to constitutional right, power, privilege, or immunity"; (3) "in excess of statutory jurisdiction, authority, or limitations, or short of statutory right(.)" Section 307(d)(9), 42 U.S.C. §7607(d)(9). In addition, we may set aside any action found to be "without observance of procedure required by law," if (i) the failure to follow the prescribed procedure was arbitrary or capricious, (ii) the procedural objection was raised during the public comment period, or there were good reasons why it was not, and (iii) the procedural errors "were so serious and related to matters of such central relevance to the rule that there is a substantial likelihood that the rule would have been significantly changed if such errors had not been made." Id. Section 307(d)(8), 42 U.S.C. §7607(d)(8).

These statutory provisions and a considerable body of case law demonstrate that our role as a reviewing court is limited. The "arbitrary and capricious" standard of review is highly deferential, and presumes agency action to be valid. *Citizens to Preserve Overton Park, Inc. v. Volpe*, 401 U.S. 402, 415, 91 S. Ct. 814, 823, 28 L. Ed. 2d 136 (1971); *Ethyl Corp. v. EPA*, 541 F.2d at 34. Moreover, the reviewing court may not substitute its judgment for the agency's and must affirm the agency's decision if a rational basis for it is presented. Of course a reviewing court does not serve as a mere rubber stamp for agency decisions. Rather, the function of judicial review is to ensure that agency decisions are

"based on a consideration of the relevant factors." *Citizens to Preserve Overton Park, Inc. v. Volpe*.

In addition, the court must undertake a "substantial inquiry" into the facts, one that is "searching and careful." Id. at 415, 416, 91 S. Ct. at 823; *Ethyl Corp. v. EPA, supra*, 541 F.2d at 34. In cases such as the ones we have before us, cases which involve complex scientific and technical questions, conducting a "substantial inquiry" into the facts may require the court to delve into the scientific literature. The purpose of this scrutiny of the evidence in the record is to educate the court. . . . However, it is appropriate to sound some notes of caution about the limits of this exercise. First, we would be less than candid if we failed to acknowledge that we approach the task of examining some of the complex scientific issues presented in cases of this sort with some diffidence. More important, we stress that our review of the evidence is not designed to enable us to second-guess the Agency's expert decisionmaker. *Ethyl Corp. v. EPA, supra*, 541 F.2d at 36. Congress has entrusted the Agency with the responsibility for making these scientific and other judgments, and we must respect both Congress' decision and the Agency's ability to rely on the expertise that it develops. . . . 541 F.2d at 36–37 (citations and footnotes omitted; brackets in original).

It is also important to note that although the pertinent sections of the Clean Air Act outline the policy objectives to be sought and the procedural framework to be followed in promulgating ambient air quality standards, Congress left the formulation of the specific standards to EPA's Administrator. This task presents complex questions of science, law, and social policy under the Act. The record is lengthy (approximately 10,000 pages) and it is highly technical. The Administrator's task required both "a legislative policy determination and an adjudicative resolution of disputed facts." *Mobil Oil Corp. v. FPC*, 483 F.2d 1238, 1257 (D.C.Cir.1973).

These are conceptually distinct types of decisions, and it is important that we keep this in mind in reviewing the Administrator's decisions. *See Industrial Union Dep't., AFL-CIO v. Hodgson*, 162 U.S. App. D.C. 331, 499 F.2d 467, 474–475 (D.C.Cir.1974). Where factual determinations were necessary the Administrator often had to make decisions in the face of conflicting evidence. In some instances this merely required that he draw conclusions from the evidence in the record. In reviewing these conclusions we can examine the record to ascertain whether there is substantial evidence in the record when considered as a whole which supports the Administrator's determinations. Id. at 474. Other questions involved in the standard-setting process, however, are at the very "frontiers of scientific knowledge." Consequently, the information available may be insufficient to permit fully informed factual determinations. In such instances the Administrator's decisions necessarily had to rest largely on policy judgments. Policy choices of this sort "are not susceptible to the same type of verification or refutation by reference to the record as are (other) factual questions." 499 F.2d at 475. While we will indeed scrutinize such judgments carefully, we must adopt a different mode of judicial review. *Industrial Union Dep't., AFL-CIO v. Hodgson, supra*, 499 F.2d at 475–476. In short, "(t)he paramount objective is to see whether the agency, given an essentially legislative task to perform, has carried it out in a manner calculated to negate the dangers of arbitrariness and irrationality in the formulation of rules for general application in the future." *Automotive Parts & Accessories Ass'n., Inc. v. Boyd, supra*, 132 U.S. App. D.C. 200, 407 F.2d 330, 336, 338 (D.C.Cir.1968) at 338.

Finally, although we may set aside the Administrator's decisions if we find that he exceeded his authority under the statute, we note that EPA's construction of the Clean Air Act has been accorded considerable deference by the courts. *Union Electric Co. v. EPA*, 427 U.S. 246, 256, 96 S. Ct. 2518, 2525, 49 L. Ed. 2d 474 (1976); *Train v. Natural Resources Defense Council, Inc.*, 421 U.S. 60, 75, 95 (1975); *Ethyl Corp. v. EPA, supra*, 541 F.2d at 12 n.16.[32] Where different interpretations of the statute are plausible, so long as EPA's construction of the statute is reasonable we may not substitute our own interpretation for the Agency's. Deference to the Administrator's interpretation is particularly appropriate in construing a statute that invests him with a considerable amount of discretion. Unless it can be shown that the Administrator's construction of the statute is plainly unreasonable, we must uphold his interpretation.

Thus mindful of our restricted role, we turn to consider petitioners' claims. Petitioners posit three basic questions for decision. First, did the Administrator exceed his authority under the statute in promulgating the lead standards? Second, were key elements in the Administrator's analysis arbitrary or capricious? Third, do alleged procedural shortcomings in the lead standards rulemaking warrant a remand of the regulations to EPA?

V. STATUTORY AUTHORITY

The petitioners' first claim is that the Administrator exceeded his authority under the statute by promulgating a primary air quality standard for lead which is more stringent than is necessary to protect the public health because it is designed to protect the public against "sub-clinical" effects which are not harmful to health. According to petitioners, Congress only authorized the Administrator to set primary air quality standards that are aimed at protecting the public against health effects which are known to be clearly

---

32. Deference to EPA's interpretation is particularly warranted where, as here, the Act and its

amendments were enacted with the advice and cooperation of EPA and its predecessor agencies.

harmful. They argue that Congress so limited the Administrator's authority because it was concerned that excessively stringent air quality standards could cause massive economic dislocation.

In developing this argument St. Joe contends that EPA erred by refusing to consider the issues of economic and technological feasibility in setting the air quality standards for lead. St. Joe's claim that the Administrator should have considered these issues is based on the statutory provision directing him to allow an "adequate margin of safety" in setting primary air quality standards. In St. Joe's view, the Administrator must consider the economic impact of the proposed standard on industry and the technological feasibility of compliance by emission sources in determining the appropriate allowance for a margin of safety. St. Joe argues that the Administrator abused his discretion by refusing to consider these factors in determining the appropriate margin of safety for the lead standards, and maintains that the lead air quality standards will have a disastrous economic impact on industrial sources of lead emissions.

This argument is totally without merit. St. Joe is unable to point to anything in either the language of the Act or its legislative history that offers any support for its claim that Congress, by specifying that the Administrator is to allow an "adequate margin of safety" in setting primary air quality standards, thereby required the Administrator to consider economic or technological feasibility. To the contrary, the statute and its legislative history make clear that economic considerations play no part in the promulgation of ambient air quality standards under Section 109.

Where Congress intended the Administrator to be concerned about economic and technological feasibility, it expressly so provided. For example, Section 111 of the Act, 42 U.S.C. §7411, directs the Administrator to consider economic and technological feasibility in establishing standards of performance for new stationary sources of air pollution based on the best available control technology. In contrast, Section 109(b) speaks only of protecting the public health and welfare.[36] Nothing in its language suggests that the Administrator is to consider economic or technological feasibility in setting ambient air quality standards.[37]

The legislative history of the Act also shows the Administrator may not consider economic and technological feasibility in setting air quality standards; the absence of any provision requiring consideration of these factors was no accident; it was the result of a deliberate decision by Congress to subordinate such concerns to the achievement of health goals. Exasperated by the lack of significant progress toward dealing with the problem of air pollution under the Air Quality Act of 1967, 81 Stat. 485, and prior legislation, Congress

---

36. Section 302(h), 42 U.S.C. §7602(h), defines "welfare" to include "effects on economic values." This definition does not, however, include the cost of compliance with the air quality standards. It only refers to the economic costs of pollution.

37. Other provisions of the Act closely related to §109 confirm the view that the Administrator is not required or allowed to consider economic and technological feasibility in setting air quality standards. Section 108(a)(2), 42 U.S.C. §7408(a)(2), which outlines the criteria on which the air quality standards are to be based, makes no mention of such factors. Similarly, §110, 42 U.S.C. §7410, provides that once ambient air quality standards have been promulgated, each state must prepare and submit an implementation plan outlining the measures to be taken to ensure that the standards are met. It is these state implementation plans which actually impose pollution control requirements and, consequently, if Congress had wanted the economics of pollution control considered it would have so provided in §110. While states may consider economic and technological feasibility in selecting the mix of control devices, they may do so only insofar as this does not interfere with meeting the strict deadlines for attainment of the standards. Section 110(a)(2), 42 U.S.C. §7410(a)(2). Moreover, the Administrator, in reviewing a state implementation plan, may not consider economic or technological feasibility.

abandoned the approach of offering suggestions and setting goals in favor of "taking a stick to the States in the form of the Clean Air Amendments of 1970...." Congress was well aware that, together with Sections 108 and 110, Section 109 imposes requirements of a "technology-forcing" character. The Senate Report on the 1970 Amendments declared:

The protection of public health as required by the national ambient air quality standards...will require major action throughout the Nation. Many facilities will require major investments in new technology and new processes. Some facilities will need altered operating procedures.... Some may be closed. In the Committee discussions, considerable concern was expressed regarding the use of the concept of technical feasibility as the basis of ambient air standards. The Committee determined that 1) the health of people is more important than the question of whether the early achievement of ambient air quality standards protective of health is technically feasible; and, 2) the growth of pollution load in many areas, even with application of available technology, would still be deleterious to public health.

The Report concluded:

Therefore, the Committee determined that existing sources of pollutants either should meet the standard of the law or be closed down, and in addition that new sources should be controlled to the maximum extent possible to prevent atmospheric emissions.

It is difficult to reconcile these statements of legislative intent with St. Joe's claim that Congress wanted the Administrator to consider economic and technological feasibility in setting air quality standards. The "technology-forcing" requirements of the Act "are expressly designed to force regulated sources to develop pollution control devices that might at the time appear to be economically or technologically infeasible." *Union Electric Co. v. EPA, supra*, 427 U.S. at 257, 96 S. Ct. at 2525.

Furthermore, St. Joe's attempt to find a mandate for the Administrator to consider economic or technological feasibility in the Act's "adequate margin of safety" requirement is to no avail. The Senate Report explained the purpose of the margin of safety requirement:

Margins of safety are essential to any health-related environmental standards if a reasonable degree of protection is to be provided against hazards which research has not yet identified.

We are unable to discern here any congressional intent to require, or even permit, the Administrator to consider economic or technological factors in promulgating air quality standards. And when Congress directs an agency to consider only certain factors in reaching an administrative decision, the agency is not free to trespass beyond the bounds of its statutory authority by taking other factors into account. A policy choice such as this is one which only Congress, not the courts and not EPA, can make. Indeed, the debates on the Act indicate that Congress was quite conscious of this fact. For example, Senator Muskie, one of the prime architects of the Act, in speaking about the automobile emission standards and the automobile industry, noted:

...I think that we have an obligation to lay down the standards and requirements of this bill. I think that the industry has an obligation to try to meet them. If, in due course, it cannot, then it should come to Congress and share with the Congress the representatives of the people the need to modify the policy.

In the same manner, if there is a problem with the economic or technological feasibility of the lead standards, St. Joe, or any other party affected by the standards, must take its case to Congress, the only institution with the authority to remedy the problem.[39] ...

---

39. Indeed, at least some industry representatives have shown that they were aware of the fact that the Administrator may not consider economic or technological factors in setting air quality standards. At the time of the 1977 Amendments to the Act, industry spokesmen unsuccessfully attempted to persuade Congress to amend §109 to require the Administrator to consider these factors....

Section 109(b) does not specify precisely what Congress had in mind when it directed the Administrator to prescribe air quality standards that are "requisite to protect the public health." The legislative history of the Act does, however, provide some guidance. The Senate Report explains that the goal of the air quality standards must be to ensure that the public is protected from "adverse health effects." And the report is particularly careful to note that especially sensitive persons such as asthmatics and emphysematics are included within the group that must be protected. It is on the interpretation of the phrase "adverse health effects" that the disagreement between LIA and EPA about the limits of the Administrator's statutory authority appears to be based. LIA argues that the legislative history of the Act indicates that Congress only intended to protect the public against effects which are known to be clearly harmful to health, maintaining that this limitation on the Administrator's statutory authority is necessary to ensure that the standards are not set at a level which is more stringent than Congress contemplated. The Administrator, on the other hand, agrees that primary air quality standards must be based on protecting the public from "adverse health effects," but argues that the meaning LIA assigns to that phrase is too limited. In particular, the Administrator contends that LIA's interpretation is inconsistent with the precautionary nature of the statute, and will frustrate Congress' intent in requiring promulgation of air quality standards.

The Administrator begins by pointing out that the Act's stated goal is "to protect and enhance the quality of the Nation's air resources so as to promote the public health and welfare and the productive capacity of its population(.)" Section 101(b)(1), 42 U.S.C. §7401(b)(1). This goal was reaffirmed in the 1977 Amendments. For example, the House Report accompanying the Amendments states that one of its purposes is "(t)o emphasize the preventive or precautionary nature of the act, i.e., to assure that regulatory action can effectively prevent harm before it occurs; to emphasize the predominant value of protection of public health(.)" The Administrator notes that protecting the public from harmful effects requires decisions about exactly what these harms are, a task Congress left to his judgment. He notes that the task of making these decisions is complicated by the absence of any clear thresholds above which there are adverse effects and below which there are none. Rather, as scientific knowledge expands and analytical techniques are improved, new information is uncovered which indicates that pollution levels that were once considered harmless are not in fact harmless. Congress, the Administrator argues, was conscious of this problem, and left these decisions to his judgment partly for this reason.[43] In such situations the perspective that is brought to bear on the problem plays a crucial role in determining what decisions are made. Because it realized this, Congress, the Administrator maintains, directed him to err on the side of caution in making these judgments. First,

---

43. Section 109(b), 42 U.S.C. §7409(b), specifically states that the Administrator is to use his judgment in determining what air quality standards are necessary to protect the public health, a task which requires him to make factual determinations as well as policy judgments.

The Administrator notes that the issue of the uncertainty that surrounds attempts to set air quality standards which protect the public health featured prominently in the discussion about the 1977 Amendments. For example, noting that the primary standards are based on the assumption that

there is a discoverable no-effects threshold, the House Report on the Amendments observed:

However, in no case is there evidence that the threshold levels have a clear physiological meaning, in the sense that there are genuine adverse health effects at and above some level of pollution, but no effects at all below that level. On the contrary, evidence indicates that the amount of health damage varies with the upward and downward variations in the concentration of the pollutant, with no sharp lower limit. . . .

Congress made it abundantly clear that considerations of economic or technological feasibility are to be subordinated to the goal of protecting the public health by prohibiting any consideration of such factors. Second, it specified that the air quality standards must also protect individuals who are particularly sensitive to the effects of pollution. Third, it required that the standards be set at a level at which there is "an absence of adverse effect" on these sensitive individuals. Finally, it specifically directed the Administrator to allow an adequate margin of safety in setting primary air quality standards in order to provide some protection against effects that research has not yet uncovered. The Administrator contends that these indicia of congressional intent, the precautionary nature of the statutory mandate to protect the public health, the broad discretion Congress gave him to decide what effects to protect against, and the uncertainty that must be part of any attempt to determine the health effects of air pollution, are all extremely difficult to reconcile with LIA's suggestion that he can only set standards which are designed to protect against effects which are known to be clearly harmful to health.

We agree that LIA's interpretation of the statute is at odds with Congress' directives to the Administrator. As a preliminary matter, though it denies this, LIA does at times seem to be arguing, along with St. Joe, that the Administrator should have considered economic and technological feasibility in setting the standards, a claim that must be rejected for reasons we have already stated. Be that as it may, it is not immediately clear why LIA expects this court to impose limits on the Administrator's authority which, so far as we can tell, Congress did not. The Senate Report explains that the Administrator is to

set standards which ensure that there is "an absence of adverse effects." The Administrator maintains that the lead standards are designed to do just that, a claim we will examine in due course. But LIA would require a further showing that the effects on which the standards were based are clearly harmful or clearly adverse. We cannot, however, find the source of this further restriction that LIA would impose on the Administrator's authority. It may be that it reflects LIA's view that the Administrator must show that there is a "medical consensus that (the effects on which the standards were based) are harmful...." If so, LIA is seriously mistaken. This court has previously noted that some uncertainty about the health effects of air pollution is inevitable. And we pointed out that "(a)waiting certainty will often allow for only reactive, not preventive (regulatory action)." *Ethyl Corp. v. EPA*, 541 F.2d at 25. Congress apparently shares this view; it specifically directed the Administrator to allow an adequate margin of safety to protect against effects which have not yet been uncovered by research and effects whose medical significance is a matter of disagreement.[49] This court has previously acknowledged the role of the margin of safety requirement. In *Environmental Defense Fund v. EPA* 598 F.2d 62, 81 (D.C.Cir.1978), we pointed out that "(i)f administrative responsibility to protect against unknown dangers presents a difficult task, indeed, a veritable paradox calling as it does for knowledge of that which is unknown then, the term 'margin of safety' is Congress's directive that means be found to carry out the task and to reconcile the paradox." Moreover, it is significant that Congress has recently acknowledged that more often than not the "margins of safety" that are incorporated into air quality standards turn out to be very modest or

---

49. In Environmental Defense Fund v. EPA, 598 F.2d 62, 81 (D.C.Cir.1978), we discussed the significance of the margin of safety requirement, pointing out that "the use of the term...was...meant

by congress to take into account and compensate for uncertainties and lack of precise predictions in the are of forecasting the effects of toxic pollutants...."

nonexistent, as new information reveals adverse health effects at pollution levels once thought to be harmless. Congress' directive to the Administrator to allow an "adequate margin of safety" alone plainly refutes any suggestion that the Administrator is only authorized to set primary air quality standards which are designed to protect against health effects that are known to be clearly harmful.

Furthermore, we agree with the Administrator that requiring EPA to wait until it can conclusively demonstrate that a particular effect is adverse to health before it acts is inconsistent with both the Act's precautionary and preventive orientation and the nature of the Administrator's statutory responsibilities. Congress provided that the Administrator is to use his judgment in setting air quality standards precisely to permit him to act in the face of uncertainty. And as we read the statutory provisions and the legislative history, Congress directed the Administrator to err on the side of caution in making the necessary decisions. We see no reason why this court should put a gloss on Congress' scheme by requiring the Administrator to show that there is a medical consensus that the effects on which the lead standards were based are "clearly harmful to health." All that is required by the statutory scheme is evidence in the record which substantiates his conclusions about the health effects on which the standards were based. Accordingly, we reject LIA's claim that the Administrator exceeded his statutory authority and turn to LIA's challenge to the evidentiary basis for the Administrator's decisions.

VI. HEALTH BASIS FOR THE LEAD STANDARDS

. . .

A. Maximum Safe Individual Blood Lead Level

. . . Our review of the record persuades us that there is adequate support for each of the

Administrator's conclusions about the health effects of lead exposure and, consequently, that LIA's challenges to the evidentiary support for these findings must be rejected. Under the statutory scheme enacted by Congress, the Criteria Document prepared with respect to each pollutant is to provide the scientific basis for promulgation of air quality standards for the pollutant. We have already noted that the Lead Criteria Document was the product of a process that allowed the rigorous scientific and public review that are essential to the preparation of a document "accurately reflect(ing) the latest scientific knowledge useful in indicating the kind and extent of all identifiable effects (of lead exposure) on (the) public health. . . ." In our view, the Criteria Document provides ample support for the Administrator's findings. . . .

LIA's challenge to the Administrator's findings concerning the health significance of EP elevation also stresses that this phenomenon is only a "subclinical" effect. But the clinical/subclinical distinction has little to do with the question whether a particular effect is properly viewed as adverse to health. Rather, the distinction pertains to the means through which the particular effect may be detected: observation or physical examination in the case of clinical effects, and laboratory tests in the case of subclinical effects. Thus describing a particular effect as a "subclinical" effect in no way implies that it is improper to consider it adverse to health.[64] While EP elevation may not be readily identifiable as a sign of disease, the Administrator properly concluded that it indicates a lead-related interference with basic biological functions. Expert medical testimony in the record confirms that the modern trend in preventive medicine is to detect health problems in their "subclinical" stages, and thereupon to take corrective action. Moreover, as we

---

64. The Criteria Document suggests that death from lead poisoning may in fact occur without any prior clinical symptoms.

have already noted, the Center For Disease Control uses the same "subclinical" effect as the key indicator of the need for medical intervention in its lead poisoning screening program. The accepted use of this "subclinical" effect to determine the need for medical observation or intervention properly influenced the Administrator's decision. Thus the fact that the effects the Administrator relied on in setting the lead standards are "subclinical" does not detract from their significance for human health, or make them an improper basis for setting air quality standards. . . .

Finally, our examination of the record also reveals ample support for the Administrator's determination that lead-induced central nervous system deficits begin to occur in children at blood lead levels of 50 μg Pb/dl. The central nervous system damage about which the Administrator was concerned was not the severe brain damage that can occur at relatively high levels of lead exposure, 80–100 μg Pb/dl. Rather, his focus was on more subtle and largely irreversible neurological and behavioral impairment that has been detected in children at lower blood lead levels.[69] . . .

Our conclusion that there is ample support for the Administrator's determination that EP elevation at 30 μg Pb/dl is the first adverse health effect that children experience as a result of lead exposure is, of course, sufficient to sustain his selection of 30 μg Pb/dl as the maximum safe individual blood lead level. Given this, we cannot say that his further determination that a maximum safe individual blood lead level of 30 μg Pb/dl would in addition provide protection against the more serious adverse health effects of lead exposure was irrational.

To be sure, the Administrator's conclusions were not unchallenged; both LIA and the Administrator are able to point to an im-

pressive array of experts supporting each of their respective positions. However, disagreement among the experts is inevitable when the issues involved are at the "very frontiers of scientific knowledge," and such disagreement does not preclude us from finding that the Administrator's decisions are adequately supported by the evidence in the record. It may be that LIA expects this court to conclude that LIA's experts are right, and the experts whose testimony supports the Administrator are wrong. If so, LIA has seriously misconceived our role as a reviewing court. It is not our function to resolve disagreement among the experts or to judge the merits of competing expert views. . . . Our task is the limited one of ascertaining that the choices made by the Administrator were reasonable and supported by the record. *Ethyl Corp. v. EPA, supra*, 541 F.2d at 35–36. That the evidence in the record may also support other conclusions, even those that are inconsistent with the Administrator's, does not prevent us from concluding that his decisions were rational and supported by the record. . . .

Having determined that we must uphold the Administrator's decisions concerning the health effects that are the basis for the lead standards, we turn to petitioners' other challenges to the Administrator's analysis.

B. Margin of Safety

Both LIA and St. Joe argue that the Administrator erred by including multiple allowances for margins of safety in his calculation of the lead standards. Petitioners note that the statute directs the Administrator to allow an "adequate margin of safety" in setting primary air quality standards, and they maintain that as a matter of statutory construction the Administrator may not interpret "margin" of safety to mean "margins" of safety. In petitioners' view, the Administrator in fact did just this insofar as he made allowances for margins of safety at several points in his analysis. They argue that margin of safety

---

69. The manifestations of these impairments include diminished capacity to think, reason, and control behavior, and emotional instability.

allowances were reflected in the choice of the maximum safe individual blood lead level for children, in the decision to place 99.5 percent of the target population group below that blood lead level, in the selection of an air lead/blood lead ratio at 1:2, and in the Administrator's estimate of the contribution to blood lead levels that should be attributed to non-air sources. The net result of these multiple allowances for margins of safety, petitioners contend, was a standard far more stringent than is necessary to protect the public health. . . .

We agree with the Administrator that nothing in the statutory scheme or the legislative history requires him to adopt the margin of safety approach suggested by St. Joe. Adding the margin of safety at the end of the analysis is one approach, but it is not the only possible method. Indeed, the Administrator considered this approach but decided against it because of complications raised by the multiple sources of lead exposure. The choice between these possible approaches is a policy choice of the type that Congress specifically left to the Administrator's judgment. This court must allow him the discretion to determine which approach will best fulfill the goals of the Act. As we pointed out in *Hercules Inc. v. EPA*, 598 F.2d 91, 108 (D.C. Cir. 1978) "Decision between the alternatives is a quintessential policy judgment within the discretion of EPA. We cannot accept (the) notion that the administrator of the agency created to protect the environment lack(s) even the capability to exercise the discretion with which he was entrusted by Congress."[80] Where, as here, the Administrator has provided an explanation of why he chose one method rather than another, and this explanation and his choice are not irrational, we must accept his decision. See *Industrial Union*

Dep't., AFL-CIO v. Hodgson, supra, 499 F.2d at 475–476.

We also agree with the Administrator's suggestion that petitioners have ignored the distinction between scientific judgments based on the available evidence and allowances for margins of safety. In every instance in which the Administrator's judgment on a particular issue differed from petitioners' they attributed his decision to an allowance for a margin of safety. To be sure, there is no bright line that divides these two types of decisions, but they are nonetheless conceptually distinct. In any event, whatever the nature of the decision, the real test, as petitioners recognize, is whether the decision is reasonable when examined in light of the evidence in the record. We have already found that at least one of the decisions that the petitioners attribute to an allowance for a margin of safety (the selection of the maximum safe individual blood lead level for children) satisfies this test. Accordingly, we turn to petitioners' claims that the other steps in the Administrator's analysis cannot withstand critical scrutiny. . . .

XI. CONCLUSION

The national ambient air quality standards for lead were the culmination of a process of rigorous scientific and public review which permitted a thorough ventilation of the complex scientific and technical issues presented by this rulemaking proceeding. Interested parties were allowed a number of opportunities to participate in exploration and resolution of the issues raised by the standard-setting exercise. EPA, and ultimately the public whose health these air quality standards protect, have benefited from their contribution. To be sure, even the experts did not always agree about the

---

80. Thus, in contrast to the approach he adopted in the lead standards rulemaking, the Administrator, in setting air quality standards for ozone, decided that adjusting the final number was a rea-

sonable and feasible method of providing for an appropriate margin of safety. See 44 Fed.Reg. 8202, 8215–8217 (Feb. 8, 1979).

answers to the questions that were raised. Indeed, they did not always agree on what the relevant questions were. These disagreements underscore the novelty and complexity of the issues that had to be resolved, and both the EPA and the participants in the rulemaking proceeding deserve to be commended for the diligence with which they approached the task of coming to grips with these difficult issues.

We have accorded these cases the most careful consideration, combining as we must careful scrutiny of the evidence in the record with deference to the Administrator's judgments. We conclude that in this rulemaking proceeding the Administrator complied with the substantive and procedural requirements of the Act, and that his decisions are both adequately explained and amply supported by evidence in the record. Accordingly, we reject petitioners' claims of error. The regulations under review herein are

Affirmed.

■ **NOTES**

1. In this case, the District of Columbia Court of Appeals (known as the D.C. Circuit) delves deeply into the scientific evidence of lead's toxicity and EPA's treatment of science. While it is deferential to the EPA administrator's findings, the court provides guidance as to the meaning or importance of margins of safety, subclinical effects, thresholds, uncertainty, and the extent to which the courts should second-guess an agency's technical and policy determinations. Do these guidelines appear sensible? Do they appear to be in line with the intent of Congress in drafting the CAA?

2. Note that the *contributions* of air-based exposures to the total body load of lead from background exposures (reflected in the *national average* of 12 µg Pb/dl from nonair sources) is what counts and should be minimized. Does EPA adequately address air quality control regions with significantly higher backgrounds from nonair sources than the national average? In other words, is the lead standard stringent enough where higher nonair sources plus air sources result in a very high level of lead in the body? Could EPA have set a more stringent standard under the CAA to address this issue?

3. In proposing the lead standard, the EPA administrator relied on the Centers for Disease Control (CDC) recommendation that blood lead levels in children be no higher than 30 micrograms of lead per deciliter of blood (µg/dl) to prevent lead poisoning. Since then, the CDC has lowered the recommended maximum to 10 µg Pb/dl—lower than the then national average from nonair sources. If that recommendation had been in effect in 1978, what impact would it have had on the establishment of a NAAQS for lead? Does EPA have the authority under Section 109 of the CAA to ban all air sources of lead? Does another provision of the act (arguably) give the agency such authority?

4. The 1977 Clean Air Amendments require the EPA administrator to review the adequacy of the ambient air quality standards at least every 5 years [see Section 109(d)(1)]. In 2004, student environmental activists at Washington University in St. Louis, Missouri (the leading lead-producing state), brought a lawsuit against EPA seeking to compel the agency to exercise its "mandatory and non-discretionary" duty to review the primary ambient air quality standard for lead, which the agency had not reviewed since its promulgation in 1977. In 2005, the District Court for the Eastern District of Missouri ordered EPA to complete a review by September 1, 2008 of the adequacy of the standard to protect public health in light of increasing evidence that lead is harmful at lower and lower levels of exposure. See *Missouri Coalition for the Environment v. EPA*, No. 04-cv-00660 (E.D. Mo. 2005). With the phase-out of lead from gasoline, ambient air lead levels have been reduced by about 95% since the 1970s, with significant reductions in blood lead in humans as well. Compliance with a stricter standard thus should not find much resistance, except from the metals industries.

5. Note that the D.C. Circuit affords EPA flexibility in its application of the required "adequate margin of safety." Margins of safety may either be applied to various components of analysis, accumulating as it were into a final risk estimate, or alternatively, a margin of safety can be applied once at the end of a risk assessment.

6. Note the difference between using subclinical effects as a sentinel indicator of harm and viewing subclinical effects as part of the "adverse effect" to be avoided in determining permissible exposures.

7. Is the court clear on whether EPA views lead as having a finite threshold below which no adverse effects occur? Does the court conclude that lead does not have a finite threshold, or that it has one, but that this threshold cannot be determined owing to uncertainty?

8. Is the EPA target of protecting 99.5% of children (as a sensitive subgroup of the population) consistent with protecting the public health with an adequate margin of safety? The legislative history indicates that the primary ambient standards are intended to protect "sensitive populations" such as children, the elderly, and the asthmatic. Note, further, the D.C. Circuit's statement here (after footnote 43) that "Congress...specified that the air quality standards must also protect *individuals* who are particularly sensitive to the effects of pollution" (emphasis added). This language is at odds with a more recent EPA reinterpretation that states that the CAA does not require protection of all "sensitive individuals," but only sensitive *groups*. This is especially relevant to persons who might be chemically sensitive (see the discussion in chapter 2). Note that the D.C. Circuit again makes reference to "sensitive persons" in *American Petroleum Institute v. Costle*, excerpted below.

9. Note the court's explicit endorsement in the *Lead Industries* case of EPA's authority to promote the development of "pollution-control devices."

10. The court makes reference here to its earlier decisions under the Occupational Safety and Health Act regarding the deference to be afforded to agency decisions involving those scientific determinations that are "on the frontiers of scientific knowledge." OSHA case law has had a profound influence on the development of environmental law in general.

11. Note EPA's clear reliance on, and the court's finding of congressional support for, the Precautionary Principle—the notion that the EPA is expected to "err on the side of caution" in setting the NAAQS standards.

12. In 2007, the Clean Air Scientific Advisory Committee (CASAC) notified the EPA Administrator of its opinion that the air quality standard for lead should be reduced from the current 1.5 µg per cubic meter averaged quarterly to 0.2 µg per cubic meter or less averaged monthly.

Because of the difficulty of measuring the several and variable photochemical oxidants that make up photochemical smog, EPA simplified its photochemical oxidants standard in 1979 by placing restrictions only on ozone. One might have expected the restrictions on ozone to have been made more stringent to ensure the achievement of public health goals. However, as noted earlier, the NAAQS for ozone was actually relaxed from 0.08 ppm to 0.12 ppm averaged over a 1-hour period. Nonetheless, industry challenged the new standard, giving the D.C. Circuit a second opportunity to review an ambient air standard.

American Petroleum Institute v. Costle
Before ROBB, WALD, and MIKVA, Circuit Judges
Opinion by Judge ROBB
665 F.2d 1176 (D.C. Cir. 1981)

I

The standards challenged in this case establish restrictions on permissible levels of ozone. As with other photochemical oxidants, ozone is not emitted directly into the air, but is produced by complex chemical reactions between organic compounds (precursors) and nitrogen oxides in the presence of sunlight. Oxidant precursors are organic compounds which can occur naturally but are in large measure man-made. Sources of precursors include automobile emissions of hydrocarbons, chemical plant emissions, and gasoline vapors.... Although ozone is but one of many photochemical oxidants, total oxidant pollution has been measured by reference to the ozone level in the air since 1971.

Ozone is the primary cause of the ill effects associated with smog, of which it usually comprises 65–100%. At certain concentration levels, ozone irritates the respiratory system and causes coughing, wheezing, chest tightness, and headaches. Due to its irritating nature, ozone can aggravate asthma, bronchitis, and emphysema. Some studies indicate that chronic exposure to fairly low levels of ozone may reduce resistance to infection and alter blood chemistry or chromosome structure. Ozone can destroy vegetation, reduce crop yield, and damage exposed materials by causing cracking, fading, and weathering. . . .

EPA promulgated primary and secondary standards for photochemical oxidants (i.e., ozone) in 1971. Both standards were established at an 0.08 ppm hourly average not to be exceeded more than once a year. The method used to determine compliance with the 1971 standards measured only ozone. In 1976 EPA began to revise the 1971 standards and in April 1977 requested data and information relevant to the revision.

As part of the revision, EPA established a working group within the Criteria and Special Studies Office of its Office of Research and Development to develop a "criteria document." . . . In the early stages of preparing the ozone criteria document EPA retained a panel of expert environmental consultants (the Shy Panel) and sought their opinions on the ozone concentration levels at which adverse health effects might be experienced. The Shy Panel concluded that "short term exposures to ozone in the range of 0.15 to 0.25 ppm may impair mechanical function of the lung, and may induce respiratory and related symptoms in sensitive segments of the population." The panel recommended that the primary standard remain at 0.08 ppm. The panel's recommendations and conclusions were included in the draft criteria document.

In 1974 the Administrator of the EPA established a Science Advisory Board (SAB) to assist in establishing NAAQS, among other functions. During the revision of the ozone standards Congress passed the Environmental Research, Development, and Demonstration Authorization Act of 1978,

Pub. L. 95-155, 91 Stat. 1260 (1978) (ERD-DAA), which requires the Administrator to submit to the SAB any "proposed criteria document, standard, limitation, or regulation, together with relevant scientific and technical information in the possession of the (EPA). . . on which the proposed action is based." 42 U.S.C. §4365(e). During the revision of the ozone standard the SAB reviewed two full drafts and a third draft of the summary chapter of the ozone criteria document and offered comments on its content. After examining the summary of the third draft, six of the eleven SAB members voted to approve the criteria document, with reservations and recommended changes. Two members rejected the document, and three members offered no judgment. The parties dispute the effect of this "approval" under the Clean Air Act. Neither the final criteria document nor the final ozone standards were made available to the SAB for comment.

As a further aid to the Administrator in establishing the ozone standards, EPA conducted a "risk assessment study." This study combined medical opinions as to the necessary ozone levels for creation of certain adverse health effects (e.g., aggravation of emphysema) with predictions as to peak ozone levels in a five-year period. The study attempted to predict the probability of creating certain health problems under various possible standards. The Shy Panel relied on the results of this study in recommending that the primary standard remain at 0.08 ppm. Although the risk assessment study results were summarized in the preamble to the final regulations, the Administrator acknowledged that the method used in arriving at the results was not completely reliable. The parties dispute whether the results of the risk assessment study played a significant role in the establishment of the ozone standards. . . .

In February 1979 EPA published final primary and secondary standards for ozone, raising both to 0.12 ppm. The Administrator determined that "the most probable level for adverse health effects in sensitive persons, as well as in healthier (less sensitive) persons who are exercising vigorously, falls in the range of 0.15 to 0.25 ppm." He based his conclusion on the criteria document, the comments submitted on the proposed standards, the report of the Shy Panel, and medical opinions collected during the risk assessment study. The Administrator also concluded that the 0.12 ppm standard provides an adequate margin of safety. He raised the proposed secondary standard based on a determination that average daily maximum ozone concentrations of 0.12 ppm would not harm crop yields.

II. ISSUES PRESENTED BY THE PETITIONS

The petitions for review present both substantive and procedural challenges to the primary and secondary ozone standards promulgated by EPA. Some petitioners contend that the standards are irrational and unsupported by the record. Other petitioners argue that the standards do not contain an adequate margin of safety, are too stringent given naturally occurring ozone levels, and are not economically feasible. It is also argued that the measurement standards and control strategies promulgated by EPA are unreasonable and unsupported by the record. As to the procedural allegations, it is argued that the Administrator erred in his use of the Science Advisory Board, the Shy Panel, and the risk assessment study.... After discussing the standard of review which governs petitions for review under the Clean Air Act, we address each significant argument in turn....

III. STANDARD OF REVIEW

These provisions of the Act assign this court a restricted role in reviewing air quality standards. *Lead Industries Ass'n., Inc. v. EPA*, 647 F.2d 1130 (D.C. Cir. 1980). The Administrator's construction of the Act will be upheld if it is reasonable, and though it is our duty to undertake a "searching and careful" inquiry into the facts, our view of the evidence "is not designed to enable us to second-guess the agency's expert decisionmaker." Reversal for procedural defaults under the Act will be rare because the court must first find that the Administrator was arbitrary or capricious, that he overruled a relevant and timely objection on the point in question, and that the errors were so significant that the challenged rule would likely have been different without the error.

IV. SUBSTANTIVE CHALLENGES TO THE OZONE STANDARDS

Petitioner American Petroleum Institute contends that the primary ozone standard is not rational because, it alleges, no adverse health effects have been proven below 0.25 ppm with two hours exposure. API also argues that EPA must consider whether the 0.12 ppm standard is attainable and whether the anticipated costs of meeting that standard are justified when compared with the results to be achieved. Houston contends that the ozone standards are arbitrary and capricious because natural ozone levels and other physical phenomena in the Houston area prevent it from meeting the standards.

Petitioner Commonwealth of Virginia contends that EPA acted arbitrarily and capriciously in retaining the single hour averaging test for measuring compliance with the ozone standards. Virginia argues that the method chosen is not supported by logic or medical evidence, is costly, and will have no demonstrable beneficial effect on air quality. Petitioner Natural Resources Defense Council contends that the Administrator misinterpreted the Act in adopting standards for ozone alone and thus rescinding existing standards for other photochemical oxidants. NRDC also argues that the Administrator failed to establish an adequate margin of safety in the primary ozone standard.

API's argument that the Administrator erred in not considering attainability and cost justifications for the ozone standards was specifically rejected in the Lead Industries case. We stated there that under section 109 of the Act "the Administrator may not consider economic and technological feasibility in setting air quality standards...(because) of a deliberate decision by Congress to subordinate such concerns to the achievement of health goals." In a lengthy analysis of the Act and its legislative history we concluded that the "technology-forcing" requirements of the Act were expressly designed to force regulated sources to develop pollution control devices that might at the time appear to be economically or technologically infeasible.

API's other argument is that the standards are not supported by substantial evidence. We reject this argument because the record is replete with support for the final standards. The studies discussed in the criteria document constitute a rational basis for the finding that adverse health effects occur at ozone levels of 0.15 to 0.25 ppm for sensitive individuals. We need not find that each study discussed in the criteria document is accurate and reliable. The proper function of the court is not to weigh the evidence anew and make technical judgments; our role is limited to determining if the Administrator made a rational judgment. We find that the Administrator's conclusion that normal body functions are "disrupted" at low ozone levels, is supported by the studies.... The court finds no reason to hold that the Administrator abused his discretion in crediting the various studies relied on, even given the acknowledged uncertainties in some of the conclusions. The Administrator noted that "a clear threshold of adverse health effects cannot be identified with certainty for ozone." Because the Administrator acknowledged the uncertainty of his task and made a rational judgment, we cannot second-guess his conclusion. *Lead Industries, supra.*

Houston's argument that because natural factors make attainment impossible the Administrator acted arbitrarily and capriciously in setting the primary ozone standard at an "unattainable" level is addressed in part by our analysis of API's attainability argument. Attainability and technological feasibility are not relevant considerations in the promulgation of national ambient air quality standards. *Lead Industries, supra.* Further, the agency need not tailor national regulations to fit each region or locale. *NRDC v. EPA* 656 F.2d 768, 785 (D.C. Cir.1981). We also note that compliance extensions are available in some cases, 42 U.S.C. §7502(a)(2), and that Congress is aware that some regions are having difficulty in meeting the national standards.

Petitioner Commonwealth of Virginia challenges the method which EPA selected to measure compliance with the primary standard. The method chosen by EPA measures the highest average ozone level in any one hour to determine compliance. Virginia argues that it would be better to use a daily average ozone level to measure exposure. We find that the Administrator's selection of the maximum hourly average method is reasonable because it is calculated to measure the maximum exposure, which has been found to be a relevant factor in determining the likely consequences of ozone exposure.

Petitioner National Resources Defense Council argues that the Administrator has abdicated responsibility for regulation of photochemical oxidants other than ozone by relabeling the regulations here at issue. In 1971 when the first air quality standards were promulgated, the title of the regulation was "National primary and secondary ambient air quality standards for photochemical oxidants." The title was somewhat misleading because the 1971 standards applied only to ozone, which was the sole photochemical oxidant measured for compliance. The new standards challenged in this case expressly apply only to ozone and do not attempt to establish permissible levels for other photochemical oxidants.

Despite NRDC's characterization of the Administrator's action, it appears that EPA has not abandoned its statutory responsibility to regulate pollutants which "may reasonably be anticipated to endanger public health or welfare." Rather, the Administrator has chosen to regulate the photochemical oxidant (ozone) that, in his judgment presents a predictable danger. The setting of the ozone standard is not the only action taken by the agency with regard to photochemical oxidants; research concerning the less well known oxidants continues. The Administrator's approach to photochemical oxidants is reasonable, given the uncertain information concerning the class as a whole.

NRDC also argues that the Administrator failed to establish an adequate margin of safety in the primary standard. As required by the statute, the Administrator promulgated air quality standards that are calculated to "protect individuals who are particularly sensitive to the effects of pollution." *Lead Industries, supra.* In setting margins of safety the Administrator need not regulate only the known dangers to health, but may "err" on the side of overprotection by setting a fully adequate margin of safety. See *Environmental Defense Fund v. EPA* 598 F.2d 62, 80–81 (D.C. Cir. 1978). Of course the Administrator's conclusions must be supported by the record, and he may not engage in sheer guesswork. Where the Administrator bases his conclusion as to an adequate margin of safety on a reasoned analysis and evidence of risk, the court will not reverse. NRDC argues that the Administrator erred in setting a primary standard that does not protect sensitive individuals against easily predicted risks. In so arguing NRDC essentially ignores the mixed results of the medical studies evident in the record, choosing instead to rely only on the studies that favor its position. The Administrator, however, was required to take into account all the relevant studies revealed

in the record. Because he did so in a rational manner we will not overrule his judgment as to the margin of safety.

The Administrator concluded that the medical evidence "suggest(ed) the real possibility of significant human adverse health effects below 0.15 ppm. Consequently ... (he) determined that a standard of 0.12 ppm is necessary and is sufficiently prudent unless and until further studies demonstrate reason to doubt that it adequately protect public health." Having determined that the "probable level for adverse effects in sensitive persons is in the range of 0.15–0.25 ppm," the Administrator considered the evidence in the record that related to less predictable risks of ozone exposure, a relevant consideration in setting margins of safety. The Administrator considered the lack of medical evidence concerning especially sensitive persons, the possibility that ozone and other pollutants might combine to create cumulative effects, the significance of long-term exposure to otherwise safe ozone levels, inconclusive studies indicating very low ozone damage thresholds, and uncertainties arising from meteorological and calibration errors in measurements. The Administrator also indicated that the results of the risk assessment study did not support any safety margin above 0.12 ppm. Given the nature of the task assigned to the Administrator, which is to make an informed judgment based on available evidence, we find that the Administrator's selection of a margin of safety is rational.

V. PROCEDURAL CHALLENGES

Petitioners allege numerous procedural errors: EPA's relationship with the Science Advisory Board (SAB) and Advisory Panel on Health Effects of Photochemical Oxidants (Shy Panel). . . .

Under the procedural provisions of the Clean Air Act, 42 U.S.C. §7607(d), we may invalidate the ozone standard because of procedural error only if (1) the agency's failure to observe procedural requirements was arbitrary and capricious, (2) an objection was raised during the comment period, or, where the grounds for such an objection arose after the comment period and the objection is of "central relevance to the outcome of the rule," the objection was raised on a petition for reconsideration before the agency, and (3) "the errors were so serious and related to matters of such central relevance to the rule that there is a substantial likelihood that the rule would have been significantly changed if such errors had not been made." 42 U.S.C. §7607(d)(7) & (8). As we noted in *Sierra Club v. Costle* 657 F.2d 298, 391–92 (D.C. Cir. 1981), "(the) essential message of so rigorous a standard is that Congress was concerned that EPA's rulemaking not be casually overturned for procedural reasons, and we of course must respect that judgment."

1. Science Advisory Board (SAB)

API and Houston contend that in promulgating the ozone standards EPA violated section 8(e) of ERDDAA, 42 U.S.C. §4365(e) by failing to obtain approval of the criteria document from the SAB and to submit the proposed standards to the SAB for review. Section 8(e) provides, in relevant part, that

(e)(1) The Administrator, at the time any proposed criteria document, standard, limitation, or regulation under the Clean Air Act...is provided to any other Federal agency for formal review and comment, shall make available to the (Science Advisory) Board such proposed criteria document, standard, limitation, or regulation, together with relevant scientific and technical information....(2) The Board may make available to the Administrator, within the time specified by the Administrator, its advice and comments on the adequacy of the scientific and technical basis of the proposed criteria document, standard, limitation, or regulation, together with any pertinent information in the Board's possession.

The language of the statute indicates that making a proposed criteria document and standard available to the SAB for comment is mandatory but that SAB approval is not

required before proceeding to the final stage of rulemaking.

...The petitioners contend that the final criteria document, which was never submitted to the SAB, did not incorporate the changes requested by the Board, while EPA argues that the final criteria document adequately addressed the SAB's concerns.

The EPA action does not constitute a violation of section 8(e) of the ERDDAA. The Act requires only that the EPA submit the criteria document to the Board for advice and comment; it does not require that the Administrator obtain approval of the SAB or incorporate all suggested changes....

The proposed ozone standard, on the other hand, was never made available to the Board for advice and comment. Section 8(e) makes the submission of any proposed standard to the SAB mandatory. EPA contends that because the standard is based on the criteria document, submission of the standard to the SAB would have been redundant. This argument is unpersuasive; the statute explicitly mandates that standards be submitted to the Board for review. Accordingly, the failure to submit the standards was a violation of procedure required by law. We cannot find, however, that this error was "so serious and related to matters of such central relevance to the rule that there is a substantial likelihood that the rule would have been significantly changed" had the proposed standards been submitted to the SAB. 42 U.S.C. §7607(d)(8). The final standard of 0.12 ppm represents an allowance for a margin of safety in light of the adverse health effects range stated in the criteria document (0.15–0.25 ppm). Because any SAB review of the standard would have involved review of the criteria document, i.e., the scientific and technical basis for the standard, we cannot hold that the standard would likely have been significantly changed had it been submitted to the Board. The Administrator's final standard,...is rational and supported by the record. Although the failure to submit the proposed standards to the SAB was a violation of section 8(e) of the ERDDAA, the circumstances indicate that the error was not so central as to constitute grounds for invalidating the final standards.

2. Shy Health Effects Panel and Risk Assessment Study

API and Houston also argue that the EPA Advisory Panel on Health Effects of Photochemical Oxidants (Shy Panel) was an advisory committee within the meaning of the Federal Advisory Committee Act (FACA). Petitioners assert that because EPA failed to observe several requirements of FACA, the actions of the Shy Panel and the EPA reliance on the panel's risk assessment study require invalidation of the standard.

In early 1977 EPA officials responsible for developing the ozone standard asked Dr. Carl Shy of the Institute for Environmental Studies, University of North Carolina at Chapel Hill, to head a panel of paid environmental experts which would prepare "a detailed report on the translation of health data into an ambient air quality standard for photochemical oxidants." Dr. Shy was a leading advocate of the existing 0.08 ppm ozone standard. The panel met privately on June 7 and 8, 1977. A first draft of the panel report, co-authored by Shy and an EPA official, strongly endorsed the existing 0.08 standard. Following some minor revisions, the final draft of the Shy Panel report was submitted to the EPA in late 1977, made available for public comment in December 1977, and placed in the rulemaking docket on March 22, 1978. The report, which used a "risk assessment" technique to conclude that 0.08 ppm was the proper ozone standard, was made part of the criteria document and cited as one of the bases for the final 0.12 ppm standard.

The FACA defines an advisory committee, in relevant part, as "any...panel...which is...established or utilized by one or more agencies, in the interest of obtaining advice or recommendations for...one or more agencies...." Petitioners contend that because the Shy Panel clearly is an advisory committee within the meaning of this provision, the conduct of the panel violates several provisions of FACA and that EPA reliance on the panel's study as a basis for the final rule requires invalidation of the standard. For example, it is argued that the choice of a known partisan to chair the panel violates the FACA requirements that the committee be "fairly balanced" and that it not be "inappropriately influenced" by any "special interest." It is also asserted that the private meetings of the panel violate the FACA requirement that public notice and opportunity for public participation be given. EPA asserts, on the other hand, that the Shy Panel is not subject to FACA because the group consisted of paid consultants and the legislative history of FACA indicates that the Act was not intended to apply to persons having contractual relationships with the government. In any event, argues EPA, none of the Shy Panel actions violated FACA.

We need not reach the questions whether the Shy Panel was an advisory committee within the meaning of FACA and whether violations of FACA occurred. Even were we to find that the panel was subject to FACA, that violations of the Act occurred, and that reliance on the risk assessment study was therefore illegal, we would not be able to say that there is a substantial likelihood that the 0.12 ppm standard would have been significantly different if such errors not been made. The ultimate adoption of a 0.12 ppm standard constitutes a rejection of the Shy Panel's conclusion that the ozone standard should not be relaxed. Moreover, even though the Shy Report was cited as one of the bases for the final standards, the criteria document otherwise fully supports the 0.12 ppm standard as a figure representing a margin of safety below the 0.15–0.25 ppm danger zone. In short, absent the Shy Panel report, there is a substantial likelihood that the standard would have been the same. We therefore cannot invalidate the standard based on the alleged procedural irregularities....

VI. CONCLUSION

In summary, we hold that the primary and secondary standards for ozone emission are supported by a rational basis in the record. Although the EPA procedures were not a model of regulatory action, we hold that none of the alleged procedural errors warrants invalidation of the final standards. Affirmed.

■ **NOTES**

1. Note the statutorily required involvement of the EPA Science Advisory Board in offering comments on both the criteria document and the proposed standard, and also the use of a specially constituted advisory panel. Was the court correct in rejecting the petitioner's contention that this panel was subject to the Federal Advisory Committee Act (FACA)? Is the fact that the panel members were paid consultants necessarily dispositive of the issue?

2. EPA is not required to follow the advice of the SAB. The 1990 CAA Amendments established the Clean Air Science Advisory Committee (CASAC), a committee to guide the administrator specifically on the CAA. EPA is likewise required to consider, but not necessarily to adopt, its advice. Both the SAB and the CASAC clearly are subject to the requirements of FACA.

3. Even though it acknowledges procedural irregularities, the court is highly deferential to EPA's determinations, effectively noting that the procedural irregularities are not likely to have affected the content of the final standard.

4. The court underscored the national, health-based nature of the primary ambient air quality standards by noting that EPA "need not tailor national regulations to fit each region or locale," and that compliance extensions might be available to hard-pressed regions.   ■

As discussed, the 1977 CAA amendments required EPA to review the adequacy of all NAAQSs and revise them accordingly. The initial review was to be completed by the end of 1980, and subsequent reviews were to be done once every 5 years thereafter. See Section 109(d)(1). As a result of increasing evidence that serious health effects occurred at levels of ozone exposure lower than the ozone standard, that particulates less than 2.5 microns in diameter posed problems distinct from those posed by larger particles, and that these smaller particles and ozone *together* posed greater health risks than either alone, the American Lung Association went to federal district court in the early 1990s to compel EPA to promulgate a more protective particulate standard.

American Lung Association v. Environmental Protection Agency
ALFREDO C. MARQUEZ, Senior U.S. District Judge
884 F. Supp. 345 (D. Arizona 1994)

BACKGROUND

Underlying this law suit is the issue of whether the Defendant, United States Environmental Protection Agency (EPA), has established legitimate national ambient air quality standards (NAAQS) and particulate matter (PM) criteria. Plaintiff, American Lung Association, contends the EPA's current PM_{10} standard is too lax to protect the public health and welfare; interveners contend it is too strict.

In 1977 Congress directed the EPA to conduct formal reviews of ambient air quality standards, including PM, to ensure that EPA standards reflect the latest scientific knowledge and fully protect the public. Review and revisions, if appropriate, were to commence "not later than December 31, 1980, and at 5-year intervals thereafter...." 42 U.S.C. §7409(d)(1).[1] Thereby, Congress mandated fixed-date deadlines for the EPA to conduct the required reviews and if appropriate, to revise air quality criteria and ambient air quality standards. The EPA admittedly conducted only one review of PM criteria in December of 1982 and revised the NAAQS for PM in 1987 when it adopted the current standards.

Plaintiff filed this action to compel the EPA to perform its duty to review and, as appropriate, revise the national clean air standards for particulate matter. Defendant concedes it is in violation of the statutory mandate to review and revise NAAQS, including PM, at 5-year intervals. Summary judgment is appropriate where, as here, it remains only for the Court, acting in its discretion, to fashion an equitable remedy....

Plaintiff submits that the next 5-year review deadline is December 31, 1995 and urges this Court to require the EPA to complete the mandated review and any appropriate revision by that date. Alternatively, Plaintiff proposes an 18-month schedule. Defendants argue that a 4-year and 3-month schedule is necessary for it to conduct the review process to determine whether it is appropriate to revise the NAAQS, including PM criteria.[5]

LEGAL ANALYSIS: DISCUSSION

The Ninth Circuit has held that "when Congress has explicitly set an absolute deadline, congressional intent is clear.... The EPA cannot extract leeway from a statute that Congress explicitly intended to be strict." The Court cannot afford relief and is bound to order compliance until such time as Congress chooses to alter its directive.

---

1. The statute also provides that the Administrator may conduct earlier or more frequent review and revisions. 42 U.S.C. §7409(d)(1).

5. Defendant contends that the scientific and technical questions aimed at establishing PM criteria pose controversial issues at the frontiers of scientific knowledge and are necessarily time-consuming. Relevant to NAAQS revisions are certain key epidemiological studies which suggest that there is a statistical correlation between particulate pollution levels below the current NAAQS and injury to human health and welfare. Further, there is controversy regarding whether the reported health effects are caused by "coarse or fine" particles. The EPA contends that tightening or relaxing PM standards may or may not be appropriate depending on the reliability of the controversial studies.

Currently, there are several research initiatives underway which the EPA contends will help resolve some of the issues regarding PM standards....

Against this backdrop, exists the well-established principle that a district court has discretion to fashion equitable remedies other than injunctive relief. Accordingly, the equity court will "not embrace enforcement... of a party's duty to comply with an order that calls on him 'to do an impossibility'." *Sierra Club v. Ruckelshaus*, 602 F. Supp. 892, 898–99 (N.D. Cal. 1984) (quoting *N.R.D.C. v. Train*, 510 F.2d 692, 713, 166 U.S. App. D.C. 312 (D.C. Cir. 1975)).[6]

In such circumstances, the agency carries a heavy burden to show that compliance with statutory mandated deadlines is impossible or infeasible. Excuses for delay must go beyond the general proposition that further study and analysis of materials will make final agency action better, Id., because further study will always make everything better, and it is always easier to do something with more rather than less time.

This Court has broad latitude to devise its equitable scheme for relief. Foremost, relief will be tailored to bring about congressional objectives; but, this Court is mindful not to intrude upon the agency's realm of discretionary decision making.

Here, the statute involves an ongoing, periodic review and revision process set up by Congress to ensure that regulatory guidelines and standards which protect human safety and welfare are kept abreast of rapid scientific and technological developments. Congress mandated that review and any revisions should occur at 5-year intervals. Because almost 12 years have passed since 1982 when PM criteria were last reviewed and almost 7 years have passed since 1987 when NAAQS was last reviewed and revised, the EPA has not merely missed a deadline, it has nullified the congressional scheme for a fixed interval

review and revision process. The EPA further frustrates congressional intent by proposing a 4-year, 3-month review schedule with a final promulgation date of December 1, 1998. This schedule extends the mandated 5-year interval reviews and any possibility of revision to 11 years.

The EPA repeatedly argued, in its briefs and in open court, that any less time jeopardizes the review process and opens any decision it makes regarding NAAQS revision to judicial challenges of arbitrariness and capriciousness. The EPA's argument focuses on Congress's statutory language which requires that air quality criteria accurately reflect the latest scientific knowledge, 42 U.S.C. §7408(a)(2), to the exclusion of the 5-year mandate for interval reviews and any revisions. However, because both provisions are mandatory, the statutory purpose falls within the confines of both requirements. As the EPA recognized within the context of its ozone review, "at some point the process of incorporating new studies must end so that decisions can be made."

The EPA reports that since 1987, the date of the last NAAQS revision, it has engaged in an ongoing process of accumulating additional information on the effects of PM. On April 12, 1994, the EPA published notice in the Federal Register of its intent to commence the review process and to ultimately make its formal decision as to whether NAAQS should be revised. Thereafter, the EPA's proposed schedule includes approximately 3 more years for scientific review[7] and 2 years for regulatory development, to culminate in final agency action by promulgation in the Federal Register on December 1, 1998.

---

6. Accord, *Natural Resources Defense Council v. E.P.A.*, 797 F. Supp. 194, 198 (E.D.N.Y. 1983) (equitable modification of explicit statutorily mandated deadlines shall not issue short of EPA's showing impossibility or infeasibility; failing this,

EPA must persuade Congress to amend the statutory deadlines).

7. The EPA's proposed schedule does not reflect to what extent, if any, review activity has occurred either at the EPA or by CASAC.

The EPA's proposed schedule undoubtedly meets Congress's mandate that "air quality criteria for an air pollutant shall accurately reflect the latest scientific knowledge useful in indicating the kind and extent of all identifiable effects on public health or welfare...." 42 U.S.C. §7408. With equal certainty, this Court concludes that EPA's proposed schedule wholly defeats the mandate by Congress that "...at 5-year intervals, the Administrator shall complete a thorough review of the criteria published under section 7408 of this title and the national ambient air quality standards promulgated under this section and shall make such revisions in such criteria and standards and promulgate such new standards as may be appropriate in accordance with section 7408 of this title...." 42 U.S.C. §7409.[8] This forces the Court to develop a revised timetable.

While EPA's proposed schedule may be a commendable plan for involving the general public and the scientific community in the NAAQS review and revision process, it fails to meet the Congressional mandate. The Court recognizes that this laudable goal, aimed at building consensus and developing a more definitive scientific base for NAAQS revisions, might be desirable. Unfortunately, significant delays such as those occurring here serve to defeat the 5-year mandate for interval reviews. The Court finds that, under the circumstances,[9] the schedule must be adjusted to provide for only those review activities required by Congress and essential to ensuring that within the context of 5-year intervals, EPA standards reflect the latest scientific knowledge so as to fully protect the public.

Specifically, this Court finds that Congress provided for an independent scientific review committee (CASAC) to be appointed by the Administrator. 42 U.S.C. §7409(d)(2)(A). Congress required that CASAC, independent from the EPA, shall complete a review of criteria documents and air quality standards, at least every 5 years and make recommendations for appropriate changes to the Administrator. 42 U.S.C. §7409(d)(2)(B). "Congress created the Committee in order to provide an opportunity for objective evaluation of the scientific issues raised by the task of setting air quality standards." *Lead Industries Ass'n. v. E.P.A.*, (D.C. Cir. 1980). This Court finds that CASAC review of the criteria document and the "staff paper" (SP) is appropriate.

Review by the Office of Budget Management (OMB) serves no congressional purpose and is wholly discretionary. Therefore, it is not required, and the schedule shall exclude such review. *Natural Resources Defense Council v. E.P.A.*, 797 F. Supp. 194, 197 (E.D.N.Y. 1992); accord, *Environment[al] Defense Fund v. Thomas*, 627 F. Supp. 566, 571 (D.D.C. 1986) (after deadline expires, OMB review may not further delay rulemaking).

After considering the tasks and time allowances proposed by the EPA, the Court finds that the following tasks and corresponding estimates of time shall comprise the review and revision schedule with which the EPA shall comply. The Court adopts EPA's proposed schedule for preparation of the criteria document (CD) which sets forth the necessary activities from EPA's start date of October, 1993 to the end of April, 1995. The Court also adopts EPA's projection that CASAC review of the CD should be completed by the end of August, 1995.

Further, as the EPA estimates, running consecutively with the CD schedule, to the end of June, 1995, it shall complete a first

---

8. In 1990, Congress rejected a proposal by the EPA based on similar arguments raised here. Congress refused to amend section 109(d) of the Act to

extend the next fixed-date deadline for NAAQS review and revision to 1998.
9. The EPA's relief is with Congress, not with the courts.

draft of the SP setting forth the relevant criteria data and scientific analysis for determining whether NAAQS revision is appropriate. Commencing, thereafter, CASAC shall have 3 months, as estimated by the EPA, to complete its review of the SP draft. The Court excludes from its revised schedule, the EPA's provisions for interim CASAC review of various DC and SP drafts, including participation by CASAC in the development of methodologies for assessment of exposure/ risk analyses.

Also as proposed, after CASAC's review the EPA shall have 2 months to make any changes and to finalize the CD and SP. Thereafter, the EPA estimates that it can prepare the proposal packages in 5 months, this shall include publication of the proposed regulation in the Federal Register. The EPA set aside 90 days for public comment; but, the Court holds public comment to the statutory minimum of 60 days.[12] Following, the EPA shall have 5 months to make its administrative decision and prepare the final package so that promulgation of the new regulation can occur with publication in the Federal Register by January 31, 1997.

---

12. Section 307 of the Act provides for a 30 day public comment period, with an additional 30 days for filing rebuttals or supplements. 42 U.S.C. §§7607(h), 7607(d)(5).

■ NOTES

1. As was the case here, an action for a writ of mandamus—a court order directing a federal official to perform a statutory duty—usually is brought in the district courts, not the circuit courts of appeal. There are situations, however, in which the relevant statute specifies the filing of such an action in the court of appeals.

2. Ultimately, EPA promulgated the final rule in July 1997, some six months later than the court's deadline, but more than a year before the date the agency had originally proposed. What real power does the district court have in forcing a reluctant agency to accelerate its activities?

3. Note the reference to the important role played by the Clean Air Scientific Advisory Committee and its statutorily imposed duties.

4. Conscious of the increasingly political role played by OMB, the court prohibits any delay in the standard resulting from what it calls "discretionary" OMB review. Is compliance with an executive order requiring EPA to submit pending regulations to OMB for review "discretionary?" ■

As a result of the *American Lung Association* case, EPA promulgated a combined standard for ozone and small particulate matter ($PM_{2.5}$). The combined standard was immediately challenged by industry, and the case ultimately made its way to the United States Supreme Court. Before addressing the Supreme Court's disposition of the case, however, we first examine portions of the controversial intermediary opinion by the D.C. Circuit Court of Appeals. Carol Browner, then the EPA administrator, called the opinion "bizarre" on legal grounds.

American Trucking Associations, Inc. v. Environmental Protection Agency
Before WILLIAMS, GINSBURG, and TATEL, Circuit Judges
Per Curiam:
175 F.3d 1027 (D.C. Cir. 1999)

INTRODUCTION

... In July 1997 EPA issued final rules revising the primary and secondary NAAQS for particulate matter ("PM") and ozone. Numerous petitions for review have been filed for each rule.

In Part I we find that the construction of the Clean Air Act on which EPA relied in promulgating the NAAQS at issue here effects an unconstitutional delegation of legislative power. We remand the cases for EPA to develop a construction of the act that satisfies this constitutional requirement.

In Part II we reject the following claims: that §109(d) of the Act allows EPA to consider costs ... [and] that the NAAQS revisions violated the ... Unfunded Mandates Reform Act ("UMRA"), and Regulatory Flexibility Act ("RFA")....

The remaining issues cannot be resolved until such time as EPA may develop a constitutional construction of the act (and, if appropriate, modify the disputed NAAQS in accordance with that construction).

I. DELEGATION

Certain "Small Business Petitioners" argue in each case that EPA has construed §§108 & 109 of the Clean Air Act so loosely as to render them unconstitutional delegations of legislative power. We agree. Although the factors EPA uses in determining the degree of public health concern associated with different levels of ozone and PM are reasonable, EPA appears to have articulated no "intelligi-

ble principle" to channel its application of these factors; nor is one apparent from the statute. The nondelegation doctrine requires such a principle....

EPA regards ozone definitely, and PM likely, as nonthreshold pollutants, i.e., ones that have some possibility of some adverse health impact (however slight) at any exposure level above zero. See Ozone Final Rule ("Nor does it seem possible, in the Administrator's judgment, to identify [an ozone concentration] level at which it can be concluded with confidence that no 'adverse' effects are likely to occur."); National Ambient Air Quality Standards for Ozone and Particulate Matter (proposed rule) ("The single most important factor influencing the uncertainty associated with the risk estimates is whether or not a threshold concentration exists below which PM-associated health risks are not likely to occur."). For convenience, we refer to both as non-threshold pollutants; the indeterminacy of PM's status does not affect EPA's analysis, or ours.

Thus the only concentration for ozone and PM that is utterly risk-free, in the sense of direct health impacts, is zero. Section 109(b)(1) says that EPA must set each standard at the level "requisite to protect the public health" with an "adequate margin of safety." These are also the criteria by which EPA must determine whether a revision to existing NAAQS is appropriate. For EPA to pick any non-zero level it must explain the degree of imperfection permitted. The factors that EPA has elected to examine for this purpose in themselves pose no inherent nondelegation problem. But what EPA lacks is any determinate criterion for drawing lines. It has failed to state intelligibly how much is too much.

We begin with the criteria EPA has announced for assessing health effects in setting the NAAQS for non-threshold pollutants.[1] They are "the nature and severity of the health effects involved, the size of the sensitive population(s) at risk, the types of health information available, and the kind and degree of uncertainties that must be addressed." Although these criteria, so stated, are a bit vague, they do focus the inquiry on pollution's effects on public health. And most of the vagueness in the abstract formulation melts away as EPA applies the criteria: EPA basically considers severity of effect, certainty of effect, and size of population affected.

Read in light of these factors, EPA's explanations for its decisions amount to assertions that a less stringent standard would allow the relevant pollutant to inflict a greater quantum of harm on public health, and that a more stringent standard would result in less harm. Such arguments only support the intuitive proposition that more pollution will not benefit public health, not that keeping pollution at or below any particular level is "requisite" or not requisite to "protect the public health" with an "adequate margin of safety," the formula set out by §109(b)(1).

Consider EPA's defense of the 0.08 ppm level of the ozone NAAQS. EPA explains that its choice is superior to retaining the existing level, [0.12] ppm, because more people are exposed to more serious effects at [0.12] than at 0.08. In defending the decision not to go down to 0.07, EPA never contradicts the intuitive proposition, confirmed by data in its Staff Paper, that reducing the standard to that level would bring about comparable changes. Instead, it gives three other reasons. The principal substantive one is based on the criteria just discussed:

> The most certain O[3]-related effects, while judged to be adverse, are transient and reversible (particularly at O[3] exposures below 0.08 ppm), and the more serious effects with greater immediate and potential long-term impacts on health are less certain, both as to the percentage of individuals exposed to various concentrations who are likely to experience such effects and as to the long-term medical significance of these effects.

In other words, effects are less certain and less severe at lower levels of exposure. This seems to be nothing more than a statement that lower exposure levels are associated with lower risk to public health. The dissent argues that in setting the standard at 0.08, EPA relied on evidence that health effects occurring below that level are "transient and reversible," evidently assuming that those at higher levels are not. But the EPA language quoted above does not make the categorical distinction the dissent says it does, and it is far from apparent that any health effects existing above the level are permanent or irreversible.

In addition to the assertion quoted above, EPA cited the consensus of the Clean Air Scientific Advisory Committee ("CASAC") that the standard should not be set below 0.08. That body gave no specific reasons for its recommendations, so the appeal to its authority, also made in defense of other standards in the PM Final Rule, adds no enlightenment. The dissent stresses the undisputed eminence of CASAC's members, but the question whether EPA acted pursuant to lawfully delegated authority is not a scientific one. Nothing in what CASAC says helps us discern an intelligible principle derived by EPA from the Clean Air Act.

---

1. Technically, EPA describes the criteria as used only for setting the "adequate margin of safety." There might be thought to be a separate step in which EPA determines what standard would protect public health *without* any margin of safety, and that step might be governed by different criteria. But EPA did not use such a process, and it need not. Thus, the criteria mentioned in the text govern the whole standard-setting process.

Finally, EPA argued that a 0.07 standard would be "closer to peak background levels that infrequently occur in some areas due to nonanthropogenic sources of O[3] precursors, and thus more likely to be inappropriately targeted in some areas on such sources." But a 0.08 level, of course, is also *closer* to these peak levels than [0.12]. The dissent notes that a single background observation fell between 0.07 and 0.08, and says that EPA's decision "ensured that if a region surpasses the ozone standard, it will do so because of controllable human activity, not uncontrollable natural levels of ozone." EPA's language, coupled with the data on background ozone levels, may add up to a backhanded way of saying that, given the national character of the NAAQS, it is inappropriate to set a standard below a level that can be achieved throughout the country without action affirmatively *extracting* chemicals from nature. That may well be a sound reading of the statute, but EPA has not explicitly adopted it.

EPA frequently defends a decision not to set a standard at a lower level on the basis that there is greater uncertainty that health effects exist at lower levels than the level of the standard. And such an argument is likely implicit in its defense of the coarse PM standards. The dissent's defense of the fine particulate matter standard cites exactly such a justification. But the increasing-uncertainty argument is helpful only if some principle reveals how much uncertainty is too much. None does.

The arguments EPA offers here show only that EPA is applying the stated factors and that larger public health harms (including increased probability of such harms) are, as expected, associated with higher pollutant concentrations. The principle EPA invokes for each increment in stringency (such as for adopting the annual coarse particulate matter standard that it chose here)—that it is "possible, but not certain" that health effects exist at that level,—could as easily, for any non-

threshold pollutant, justify a standard of zero. The same indeterminacy prevails in EPA's decisions *not* to pick a still more stringent level.... [T]he agency rightly recognizes that the question is one of degree, but offers no intelligible principle by which to identify a stopping point.

... EPA cites prior decisions of this Court holding that when there is uncertainty about the health effects of concentrations of a particular pollutant within a particular range, EPA may use its discretion to make the "policy judgment" to set the standards at one point within the relevant range rather than another. *NRDC v. EPA*, 902 F.2d 962, 969 (D.C. Cir. 1990); *American Petroleum Inst. v. Costle*, 665 F.2d 1176, 1185 (D.C. Cir. 1981); *Lead Industries*, 647 F.2d at 1161 (D.C. Cir. 1980). We agree. But none of those panels addressed the claim of undue delegation that we face here, and accordingly had no occasion to ask EPA for coherence (for a "principle," to use the classic term) in making its "policy judgment." The latter phrase is not, after all, a self-sufficient justification for every refusal to define limits.

... What sorts of "intelligible principles" might EPA adopt? Cost-benefit analysis,... is not available under decisions of this court. Our cases read §109(b)(1) as barring EPA from considering any factor other than "health effects relating to pollutants in the air."

In theory, EPA could make its criterion the eradication of any hint of direct health risk. This approach is certainly determinate enough, but it appears that it would require the agency to set the permissible levels of both pollutants here at zero. No party here appears to advocate this solution, and EPA appears to show no inclination to adopt it....

... Alternatively, if EPA concludes that there is no principle available, it can so report to the Congress, along with such rationales as it has for the levels it chose, and seek legislation ratifying its choice....

II. OTHER GENERAL CLAIMS

The petitioners and amici contend that the EPA erroneously failed to consider a host of factors in revising the PM and ozone NAAQS. We reject each of these claims in turn.

A.   Consideration of Cost in Revising Standards

As this court long ago made clear, in setting NAAQS under §109(b) of the Clean Air Act, the EPA is not permitted to consider the cost of implementing those standards.…

D.   The Unfunded Mandates Reform Act

The State Petitioners in the particulate matter case and Congressman Bliley in the ozone case both contend that the EPA is required by the Unfunded Mandates Reform Act [UMRA], 2 U.S.C. §1501 *et seq.*, to prepare a Regulatory Impact Statement (RIS) when setting a NAAQS, and to choose the least burdensome from a range of alternative permissible NAAQS. Even if the petitioners and the amicus are correct regarding the interaction of the UMRA and the CAA—a point the EPA strongly contests—we can provide them with no relief. ("The inadequacy or failure to prepare [a RIS]…shall not be used as a basis for staying, enjoining, invalidating or otherwise affecting [an] agency rule"); (…"any compliance or noncompliance with the provisions of this chapter…shall not be subject to judicial review; and no provision of this chapter shall be construed to [be]…enforceable by any person in any…judicial action").

The State Petitioners, recognizing the limitations upon judicial review in §1571, contend that the EPA's failure to prepare a RIS can nonetheless render the NAAQS arbitrary and capricious.…No information in a RIS, however, could lead us to conclude that the EPA improperly set the PM and ozone NAAQS;

the only information such a statement would add to the rulemaking record for a NAAQS would pertain to the costs of implementation, and the EPA is precluded from considering those costs in setting a NAAQS. Accordingly, the failure to prepare a RIS does not render the NAAQS arbitrary and capricious.

E.   The Regulatory Flexibility Act

In both the ozone and particulate matter cases, the Small Business Petitioners argue that the EPA improperly certified that the revised NAAQS would not have a significant impact upon a substantial number of small entities. The Regulatory Flexibility Act, 5 U.S.C. §601 *et seq.*, as amended in 1996 by the Small Business Regulatory Enforcement Fairness Act, Pub. L. No. 104-121, tit. II, 110 Stat. 857–74 ("SBREFA"), requires an agency, when engaging in notice and comment rulemaking, to "prepare and make available for public comment an initial regulatory flexibility analysis.…[that] describes the impact of the proposed rule on small entities, including small businesses, small organizations, and small governmental jurisdictions. When promulgating a final rule, an agency must describe "the steps…taken to minimize the significant economic impact on small entities." According to the petitioners, if the EPA had complied with the RFA, it would likely have promulgated less stringent PM and ozone NAAQS than those actually chosen, which would have reduced the burden upon small entities.

A regulatory flexibility analysis is not required, however, if the agency "certifies that the rule will not, if promulgated, have a significant economic impact on a substantial number of small entities."…

The EPA certified that its revised NAAQS will "not have a significant economic impact on small entities within the meaning of the RFA." According to the EPA, the NAAQS themselves impose no regulations upon small entities. Instead, the several States regulate small entities through the state implementation plans (SIPs) that they are required by the Clean Air Act to develop. Because the NAAQS therefore regulate small entities only indirectly—that is, insofar as they affect the planning decisions of the States—the EPA concluded that small entities are not "subject to the proposed regulation."

The EPA's description of the relationship between NAAQS, SIPs, and small entities strikes us as incontestable. The States have broad discretion in determining the manner in which they will achieve compliance with the NAAQS. The EPA "is *required* to approve a state plan which provides for the timely attainment and subsequent maintenance of ambient air standards" and cannot reject a SIP based upon its view of "the wisdom of a State's choices of emission limitations," or of the technological infeasibility of the plan. See *Union Elec. Co. v. EPA*, 427 U.S. 246, 265 (1976). Therefore, a State may, if it chooses, avoid imposing upon small entities any of the burdens of complying with a revised NAAQS. Only if a State does not submit a SIP that complies with §110, 42 U.S.C. §7410, must the EPA adopt an implementation plan of its own, which would require the EPA to decide what burdens small entities should bear. The agency has stated, however, that it will do a regulatory flexibility analysis before adopting an implementation plan of its own, as it did in 1994 when proposing such a plan for Los Angeles....

We therefore conclude that the EPA properly certified that its NAAQS would not have a significant impact upon a substantial number of small entities....

IV. PARTICULATE MATTER

A. PM[10] as Coarse Particle Indicator

We now turn to petitioners' challenges to the Agency's regulation of coarse particulate pollution. Both the 1987 NAAQS and the proposed standards regulate all particles with diameters under 10 micrometers, signified by the indicator PM[10]. The PM[10] spectrum includes both coarse and fine particles. While the main distinction between coarse and fine particles is the process by which they are produced, EPA and epidemiologists who study the health effects of particulate pollution identify coarse and fine particles through rough approximations of those particles' diameters. Coarse particles, which become airborne usually from the crushing and grinding of solids, generally have diameters between 2.5 and 10 micrometers and can thus be identified by the indicator $PM_{[10-2.5]}$. Fine particles, indicated in these new NAAQS by $PM_{[2.5]}$, come mainly from combustion or gases and generally have diameters of 2.5 micrometers or less.

Despite EPA's conclusion that coarse and fine particles pose independent and distinct threats to public health, the Agency chose not to adopt an indicator, such as $PM_{[10-2.5]}$, that would measure only the coarse fraction of PM[10]. Petitioners make two arguments: that there is no scientific basis for regulating coarse particles at all, and that even if there were, retention of the PM[10] indicator simultaneously with the establishment of the new fine particle indicator is unsupported by evidence in the record and arbitrary and capricious. We agree with this latter argument....

CONCLUSION

We remand the cases to EPA for further consideration of all standards at issue. We do not vacate the new ozone standards.... We vacate the challenged coarse particulate matter standards because EPA will have to develop different standards when it corrects the arbitrarily chosen PM[10] indicator....

TATEL, *CIRCUIT JUDGE*, DISSENTING FROM PART I:

...In setting standards "requisite to protect the public health" EPA discretion is not unlimited. The Clean Air Act directs EPA to base standards on "air quality criteria" that "accurately reflect the latest scientific knowledge useful in indicating the kind and extent of all identifiable effects on public health or welfare which may be expected from the presence of such pollutant in the ambient air, in varying quantities." By directing EPA to set NAAQS at levels "requisite"—not reasonably requisite—to protect the public health with "an adequate margin of safety," the Clean Air Act tells EPA...[to] ensure a high degree of protection.

Although this court's opinion might lead one to think that section 109's language permitted EPA to exercise unfettered discretion in choosing NAAQS, the record shows that EPA actually adhered to a disciplined decisionmaking process constrained by the statute's directive to set standards "requisite to protect the public health" based on criteria reflecting the "latest scientific knowledge." To identify which health effects were "significant enough" to warrant protection, EPA followed guidelines published by the American Thoracic Society. It then set the ozone and fine particle standards within ranges recommended by CASAC, the independent scientific advisory committee created pursuant to section 109 of the Act. *See* 42 U.S.C. §7409(d)(2).

CASAC must consist of at least one member of the National Academy of Sciences, one physician, and one person representing state air pollution control agencies. In this case, CASAC also included medical doctors, epidemiologists, toxicologists and environmental scientists from leading research universities and institutions throughout the country. EPA must explain any departures from CASAC's recommendations. *See id.* §7607(d)(3). Bringing scientific methods to their evaluation of the Agency's Criteria Document and Staff Paper, CASAC provides an objective justification for the pollution standards the Agency selects. *Cf. Daubert v. Merrell Dow Pharmaceuticals, Inc.*, 113 S. Ct. 2786 (1993) ("Scientific methodology today is based on

generating hypotheses and testing them to see if they can be falsified; indeed, this methodology today is what distinguishes science from other fields of human inquiry.") (citation omitted). Other federal agencies with rulemaking responsibilities in technical fields also rely heavily on the recommendations, policy advice, and critical review that scientific advisory committees provide.

Beginning with CASAC's ozone recommendations—not one member recommended going below 0.08 ppm—EPA gave two perfectly rational explanations for the level it selected. First, it set the annual level based on the different types of health effects observed above and below 0.08 ppm. Particularly below 0.08, the Agency determined, "the most certain [ozone-]related effects, while judged to be adverse, are *transient and reversible.*" (emphasis added). Characterizing this explanation as saying nothing more than that "lower exposure levels are associated with lower risk to public health," Maj. Op. at 10, my colleagues find the Agency's reasoning unintelligible. But EPA did not find simply that public health risks decrease at lower levels. Instead, it found that public health effects *differ* below 0.08 ppm, i.e., that they are "transient and reversible."

Second, EPA explained that the level should not be set below naturally occurring background ozone concentrations. The Agency selected 0.08 ppm because it found that "a 0.07 ppm level would be closer to peak background levels that infrequently occur in some areas due to nonanthropogenic sources of [ozone] precursors, and thus more likely to be inappropriately targeted in some areas on such sources." Of course, any level of ozone pollution above background concentrations is closer to background levels than one just above it. *See* Maj. Op. at 11. But as I read EPA's explanation, the Agency found that peak background levels sometimes occur at 0.07 ppm, not at 0.08 ppm. Indeed, the data EPA provided in its "Responses to Significant Comments" show a range of background concentrations from a low of .042 ppm in Olympic National Park in Washington to a high of 0.075 ppm in Quachita National Forest in Arizona. No region registered background levels above 0.075 ppm. In other words, by setting the annual standard at 0.08 rather than 0.07 ppm, EPA ensured that if a region surpasses the ozone standard, it will do so because of controllable human activity, not because of uncontrollable natural levels of ozone.

EPA offered an equally reasonable explanation for the fine particle pollution standard. Again limiting itself to the range approved by CASAC, EPA set the annual standard for PM[2.5] pollution at the lowest level where it had confidence that the epidemiological evidence (filtered through peer-reviewed, published studies) displayed a statistically significant relationship between air pollution and adverse public health effects.

Recognizing that its decision must "accurately reflect the latest scientific knowledge useful in indicating the kind and extent of all identifiable effects on public health," EPA focused on three studies in the record that displayed a statistically significant relationship between fine particle pollution and adverse health effects[.] The Agency explained that "there is generally *greatest statistical confidence* in observed associations [between fine particle pollution and adverse health effects] for levels at and above the mean concentration [of pollution observed in the studies that showed a statistically significant relationship]." (emphasis added). Allowing "an adequate margin of safety," EPA then set the annual fine particle standard just below the lowest mean pollution levels observed in those studies, at 15 μg/m³.

In a passage directly answering this court's concerns, *see* Maj. Op. at 11–12, the Staff Paper explained why the longterm mean served

as a reasonable level for setting the fine particle NAAQS:

The mean (or median) concentration may serve as a reasonable cutpoint of increased PM health risk since at this point there is generally the *greatest confidence* (i.e., the smallest confidence intervals) in the association and the reported [relative risk] estimates. The mean concentration considered by staff as most informative to test implications of potential alternative concentration response functions is the *minimum mean concentration* associated with a study or studies reporting statistically significant increases in risk across a number of study locations. . . . (emphasis added).

EPA thus did not, as my colleagues charge, arbitrarily pick points on the ozone and particulate pollution continua indistinguishable from any other. Instead, acting pursuant to section 109's direction that it establish standards that, based on the "latest scientific knowledge" are "requisite" to protect the public health with "an adequate margin of safety," and operating within ranges approved by CASAC, the Agency set the ozone level just above peak background concentrations where the most certain health effects are not transient and reversible, and the fine particle level at the lowest long-term mean concentration observed in studies that showed a statistically significant relationship between fine particle pollution and adverse health effects. Whether EPA arbitrarily selected the studies it relied upon or drew mistaken conclusions from those studies (as petitioners argue), or whether EPA failed to live up to the principles it established for itself (as my colleagues believe), has nothing to do with our inquiry under the nondelegation doctrine. Those issues relate to whether the NAAQS are arbitrary and capricious. The Constitution requires that Congress articulate intelligible principles; Congress has done so here. . . .

■ **NOTES**

1. Note that this case was decided by a panel of three judges and was a 2 to 1 decision. A motion for an *en banc* (full court) rehearing was denied, but the Supreme Court accepted the case for review. That decision is excerpted below.

2. In setting the new ozone and particulate standards, EPA is alleged to have departed from its previous position that the criteria pollutants have finite thresholds. The (Wolfe) study upon which EPA relied in setting the new NAAQS stated that it is likely that ozone "may elicit a continuum of biological responses *down to background concentrations*" (emphasis added). Note that "background" concentrations are above zero, and that this study does not state whether there are likely to be effects below these background levels. In its proposed rule, EPA stated that it did not "seem possible, in the Administrator's judgment, to identify [an ozone concentration] level at which it can be concluded with confidence that no 'adverse' effects are likely to occur." In the final rule, EPA went on to say:

The core issue in this review of the primary $O_{[3]}$ standard, as stated by the Administrator at the time of proposal, is who is to be protected, and from what. Clearly, for pollutants, such as $O_{[3]}$, that have *no discernible thresholds* for health effects, no standard can be risk-free. The Administrator's task is to select a standard level that will reduce risks sufficiently to protect public health with an adequate margin of safety since a zero-risk standard is neither possible nor required by the Act. As CASAC and the Administrator recognize, the selection of a specific standard level for such pollutants requires public health policy judgments in addition to determinations of a strictly scientific nature (emphasis added).

Based on this language, was the court justified in characterizing EPA's position as being that ozone definitely is—and PM is likely to be—a nonthreshold pollutant? Concluding that there is "no discernible threshold" (i.e., that there is uncertainty about where a threshold might lie) is different from concluding that "no threshold exists." That is, we may not be able to discern a threshold, but one may nonetheless exist. This is a subtle but important difference and is relevant to how EPA carries out its mandate under Section 109.

3. Does EPA's assertion that "no standard can be [established that is] risk-free" really mean a there is no level that can be harm-free? Recall that "risk" means *probability* of harm. Does the inability to determine a "safe" level mean one does not exist? These semantic subtleties turn out to be important. An indeterminate risk is not necessarily either a zero or a nonzero risk. The concept of indeterminacy has importance beyond risk assessment. As discussed in chapter 3, one objection to using cost-benefit analysis as a means of establishing an "acceptable" risk is our inability to definitively measure the value of a human life. Some economists assert that this objection comes from those who are arguing that the value of human life is infinite,

but this is not the case. Rather, it is because the value of human life is *indeterminate* that cost-benefit analysis may not be inappropriate.

4. Note that, unlike the majority, the dissenting judge believes that EPA *did* articulate an intelligible principle in deciding that the standard should be set at 0.08 ppm instead of 0.07 ppm; namely, that effects at the latter concentration were *transient and reversible*. Isn't drawing a bright line between an effect and an *adverse* effect articulating an intelligible principle? Is this principle consistent with the statutory directive that an "adequate margin of safety" be maintained?

5. Note that two of the mid-1990s "regulatory reform" statutes, the Unfunded Mandates Reform Act and the Regulatory Flexibility Act (discussed in chapter 5), were invoked unsuccessfully here as grounds to invalidate the standard. Does this mean they did not, or could not be used to, influence the standard-setting process in the first place?   ∎

Environmental Protection Agency v. American Trucking Associations, Inc.
Justice SCALIA delivered the opinion of the court
United States Supreme Court
531 U.S. 457 (2001)

I

...The District of Columbia Circuit... agreed with the respondents (hereinafter respondents) that §109(b)(1) delegated legislative power to the Administrator in contravention of the United States Constitution, Art. I, §1, because it found that the EPA had interpreted the statute to provide no "intelligible principle" to guide the agency's exercise of authority. *American Trucking Assns., Inc. v. EPA*, 175 F.3d 1027, 1034 (1999). The court thought, however, that the EPA could perhaps avoid the unconstitutional delegation by adopting a restrictive construction of §109(b)(1), so instead of declaring the section unconstitutional the court remanded the NAAQS to the agency.... On the second issue that the Court of Appeals addressed, it unanimously rejected respondents' argument that the court should depart from the rule of *Lead Industries Assn., Inc. v. EPA*, 647 F.2d 1130 (CADC 1980), that the EPA may not

consider the cost of implementing a NAAQS in setting the initial standard....

II

In *Lead Industries Assn., Inc. v. EPA, supra*, the District of Columbia Circuit held that "economic considerations [may] play no part in the promulgation of ambient air quality standards under Section 109" of the CAA. In the present cases, the court adhered to that holding as it had done on many other occasions. See, *e.g., American Lung Assn. v. EPA*, 134 F.3d 388, 389 (3rd Cir. 1998) (1998); *NRDC v. Administrator, EPA*, 902, F.2d 962, 973, vacated in part on other grounds, *NRDC v. EPA*, 921, F.2d 326 (D.C. Cir. 1991), (CADC 1991); *American Petroleum Institute v. Costle*, 665 F.2d 1176, 1185 (D.C. Cir. 1981). Respondents argue that these decisions are incorrect. We disagree; and since the first step in assessing whether a statute delegates legislative power is to determine what authority the statute confers, we address that issue of interpretation first and reach respondents' constitutional arguments in Part III, *infra*.

Section 109(b)(1) instructs the EPA to set primary ambient air quality standards "the attainment and maintenance of which ... are requisite to protect the public health" with "an adequate margin of safety." Were it not for the hundreds of pages of briefing respondents have submitted on the issue, one would have thought it fairly clear that this text does not permit the EPA to consider costs in setting the standards. The language, as one scholar has noted, "is absolute." D. Currie, Air Pollution: Federal Law and Analysis 4–15 (1981). The EPA, "based on" the information about health effects contained in the technical "criteria" documents compiled under §108(a)(2), is to identify the maximum airborne concentration of a pollutant that the public health can tolerate, decrease the concentration to provide an "adequate" margin of safety, and set the standard at that level. Nowhere are the costs of achieving such a standard made part of that initial calculation.

... Other provisions explicitly permitted or required economic costs to be taken into account in implementing the air quality standards. Section 111(b)(1)(B), for example, commanded the Administrator to set "standards of performance" for certain new sources of emissions that as specified in §111(a)(1) were to "reflect the degree of emission limitation achievable through the application of the best system of emission reduction which (taking into account the cost of achieving such reduction) the Administrator determines has been adequately demonstrated." ... We have therefore refused to find implicit in ambiguous sections of the CAA an authorization to consider costs that has elsewhere, and so often, been expressly granted. See *Union Elec. Co. v. EPA* (1976). ...

... It should be clear from what we have said that the canon requiring texts to be so construed as to avoid serious constitutional problems has no application here. No matter how severe the constitutional doubt, courts may choose only between reasonably available interpretations of a text. The text of §109(b), interpreted in its statutory and historical context and with appreciation for its importance to the CAA as a whole, unambiguously bars cost considerations from the NAAQS-setting process, and thus ends the matter for us as well as the EPA.[4] We therefore affirm the judgment of the Court of Appeals on this point.

III

Section 109(b)(1) of the CAA instructs the EPA to set "ambient air quality standards the attainment and maintenance of which in the judgment of the Administrator, based on [the] criteria [documents of §108] and allowing an adequate margin of safety, are requisite to protect the public health." The Court of Appeals held that this section as interpreted by the Administrator did not provide an "intelligible principle" to guide the EPA's exercise of authority in setting NAAQS. "[The] EPA," it said, "lacked any determinate criteria for drawing lines. It has failed to state intelligibly how much is too much." The court hence found that the EPA's interpretation (but not the statute itself) violated the nondelegation doctrine. We disagree.

---

4. Respondents' speculation that the EPA is secretly considering the costs of attainment without telling anyone is irrelevant to our interpretive inquiry. If such an allegation could be proved, it would be grounds for vacating the NAAQS, because the Administrator had not followed the law. See, *e.g., Chevron U.S.A. Inc. v. Natural Resources Defense Council, Inc.*, 467 U.S. 837 (1984). It would not, however, be grounds for this Court's changing the law.

...The scope of discretion §109(b)(1) allows is in fact well within the outer limits of our nondelegation precedents....

We therefore reverse the judgment of the Court of Appeals....

IV

...To summarize our holdings in these unusually complex cases: (1) The EPA may not consider implementation costs in setting primary and secondary NAAQS under §109(b) of the CAA. (2) Section 109(b)(1) does not delegate legislative power to the EPA in contravention of Art. I, §1, of the Constitution....

The judgment of the Court of Appeals is affirmed in part and reversed in part, and the cases are remanded for proceedings consistent with this opinion.

It is so ordered....

Justice BREYER, concurring in part and concurring in the judgment

I join Parts I, III, and IV of the Court's opinion. I also agree with the Court's determination in Part II that the Clean Air Act does not permit the Environmental Protection Agency to consider the economic costs of implementation when setting national ambient air quality standards under §109(b)(1) of the Act. But I would not rest this conclusion solely upon §109's language or upon a presumption, such as the Court's presumption that any authority the Act grants the EPA to consider costs must flow from a "textual commitment" that is "clear." In order better to achieve regulatory goals—for example, to allocate resources so that they save more lives or produce a cleaner environment—regulators must often take account of all of a proposed regulation's adverse effects, at least where those adverse effects clearly threaten serious and disproportionate public harm. Hence, I believe that, other things being equal, we should read silences or ambiguities in the language of regulatory statutes as permitting, not forbidding, this type of rational regulation.

In this case, however, other things are not equal. Here, legislative history, along with the statute's structure, indicates that §109's language reflects a congressional decision not to delegate to the agency the legal authority to consider economic costs of compliance.

For one thing, the legislative history shows that Congress intended the statute to be "technology forcing." Senator Edmund Muskie, the primary sponsor of the 1970 amendments to the Act, introduced them by saying that Congress' primary responsibility in drafting the Act was not "to be limited by what is or appears to be technologically or economically feasible," but "to establish what the public interest requires to protect the health of persons," even if that means that *"industries will be asked to do what seems to be impossible at the present time."*

The Senate directly focused upon the technical feasibility and cost of implementing the Act's mandates. And it made clear that it intended the Administrator to develop air quality standards set independently of either. The Senate Report for the 1970 amendments explains:

"In the Committee discussions, considerable concern was expressed regarding the use of the concept of technical feasibility as the basis of ambient air standards. The Committee determined that 1) *the health of people is more important than the question of whether the early achievement of ambient air quality standards protective of health is technically feasible*; and, 2) the growth of pollution load in many areas, even with application of available technology, would still be deleterious to public health....

"Therefore, the Committee determined that *existing sources of pollutants either should meet the standard of the law or be closed down...."* [emphasis added]

Indeed, this Court, after reviewing the entire legislative history, concluded that the 1970 amendments were "expressly designed to force regulated sources to develop pollution control devices that *might at the time appear to be economically or technologically infeasible."*

Union Elec. Co. v. EPA, 427 U.S. 246, 257 (1976) (emphasis added). And the Court added that the 1970 amendments were intended to be a "drastic remedy to . . . a serious and otherwise uncheckable problem." Subsequent legislative history confirms that the technology-forcing goals of the 1970 amendments are still paramount in today's Act. See Clean Air Conference Report (1977): Statement of Intent; Clarification of Select Provisions, 123 Cong. Rec. 27070 (1977) (stating, regarding the 1977 amendments to the Act, that "this year's legislation retains and even strengthens the technology forcing . . . goals of the 1970 Act").

To read this legislative history as meaning what it says does not impute to Congress an irrational intent. Technology-forcing hopes can prove realistic. Those persons, for example, who opposed the 1970 Act's insistence on a 90% reduction in auto emission pollutants, on the ground of excessive cost, saw the development of catalytic converter technology that helped achieve substantial reductions without the economic catastrophe that some had feared. See §6(a) of the Clean Air Act Amendments of 1970, amending §§202(b)(1)(A), (B), (requiring a 90% reduction in emissions). . . .

At the same time, the statute's technology-forcing objective makes regulatory efforts to determine the costs of implementation both less important and more difficult. It means that the relevant economic costs are speculative, for they include the cost of unknown future technologies. It also means that efforts to take costs into account can breed time-consuming and potentially unresolvable arguments about the accuracy and significance of cost estimates. Congress could have thought such efforts not worth the delays and uncertainties that would accompany them. In any event, that is what the statute's history seems to say. See *Union Elec., supra*, at 256–259. And the matter is one for Congress to decide.

Moreover, the Act does not, on this reading, wholly ignore cost and feasibility. As the majority points out, the Act allows regulators to take those concerns into account when they determine how to implement ambient air quality standards. Thus, States may consider economic costs when they select the particular control devices used to meet the standards, and industries experiencing difficulty in reducing their emissions can seek an exemption or variance from the state implementation plan. See *Union Elec., supra*, at 266 ("The most important forum for consideration of claims of economic and technological infeasibility is before the state agency formulating the implementation plan").

The Act also permits the EPA, within certain limits, to consider costs when it sets deadlines by which areas must attain the ambient air quality standards. 42 U.S.C. §7502(a)(2)(A) (providing that "the Administrator may extend the attainment date . . . for a period no greater than 10 years from the date of designation as nonattainment, considering the severity of nonattainment and the availability and feasibility of pollution control measures"); §7502(a)(2)(C) (permitting the Administrator to grant up to two additional 1-year extensions); cf. §§7511(a)(1), (5) (setting more rigid attainment deadlines for areas in nonattainment of the ozone standard, but permitting the Administrator to grant up to two 1-year extensions). And Congress can change those statutory limits if necessary. Given the ambient air quality standards' substantial effects on States, cities, industries, and their suppliers and customers, Congress will hear from those whom compliance deadlines affect adversely, and Congress can consider whether legislative change is warranted.

Finally, contrary to the suggestion of the Court of Appeals and of some parties, this interpretation of §109 does not require the EPA to eliminate every health risk, however slight, at any economic cost, however great, to the point of "hurtling" industry over "the brink of ruin," or even forcing "deindustrialization." *American Trucking Assns., Inc. v. EPA*,

175 F.3d 1027, 1037 (CADC 1999); see also Brief for Cross-Petitioners in No. 99–1426, p. 25. The statute, by its express terms, does not compel the elimination of *all* risk; and it grants the Administrator sufficient flexibility to avoid setting ambient air quality standards ruinous to industry.

Section 109(b)(1) directs the Administrator to set standards that are "requisite to protect the public health" with "an adequate margin of safety." But these words do not describe a world that is free of all risk—an impossible and undesirable objective. See *Industrial Union Dept., AFL-CIO v. American Petroleum Institute*, 448 U.S. 607, 642 (1980) (plurality opinion) (the word "safe" does not mean "risk-free"). Nor are the words "requisite" and "public health" to be understood independent of context. We consider football equipment "safe" even if its use entails a level of risk that would make drinking water "unsafe" for consumption. And what counts as "requisite" to protecting the public health will similarly vary with background circumstances, such as the public's ordinary tolerance of the particular health risk in the particular context at issue. The Administrator can consider such background circumstances when "deciding what risks are acceptable in the world in which we live." *Natural Resources Defense Council, Inc. v. EPA*, 824 F.2d 1146, 1165 (CADC 1987).

The statute also permits the Administrator to take account of comparative health risks. That is to say, she may consider whether a proposed rule promotes safety overall. A rule likely to cause more harm to health than it prevents is not a rule that is "requisite to protect the public health." For example, as the Court of Appeals held and the parties do not contest, the Administrator has the authority to determine to what extent possible health risks stemming from reductions in tropospheric ozone (which, it is claimed, helps pre-

vent cataracts and skin cancer) should be taken into account in setting the ambient air quality standard for ozone.

The statute ultimately specifies that the standard set must be "requisite to protect the public health" "*in the judgment of the Administrator*," §109(b)(1), (emphasis added), a phrase that grants the Administrator considerable discretionary standard-setting authority.

The statute's words, then, authorize the Administrator to consider the severity of a pollutant's potential adverse health effects, the number of those likely to be affected, the distribution of the adverse effects, and the uncertainties surrounding each estimate. They permit the Administrator to take account of comparative health consequences. They allow her to take account of context when determining the acceptability of small risks to health. And they give her considerable discretion when she does so.

This discretion would seem sufficient to avoid the extreme results that some of the industry parties fear. After all, the EPA, in setting standards that "protect the public health" with "an adequate margin of safety," retains discretionary authority to avoid regulating risks that it reasonably concludes are trivial in context. Nor need regulation lead to deindustrialization. Preindustrial society was not a very healthy society; hence a standard demanding the return of the Stone Age would not prove "requisite to protect the public health."

Although I rely more heavily than does the Court upon legislative history and alternative sources of statutory flexibility, I reach the same ultimate conclusion. Section 109 does not delegate to the EPA authority to base the national ambient air quality standards, in whole or in part, upon the economic costs of compliance.

■ **NOTES**

1. Note the reference to EPA's authority under Section 111 to set emissions standards for new sources. (These new source performance standards are discussed more fully later.) There, unlike its role in setting Section 109 ambient standards, EPA is not only allowed, but required, to take feasibility into account. Are there reasons why it may be easier, from a political and practical perspective, to set health-based ambient standards than it is to set health-based emissions standards?

2. Note that the states *are* permitted to take costs into account in fashioning emissions restrictions on individual polluters in state implementation plans. See the discussion of the *Union Electric* case that follows.

3. The criteria pollutants regulated thus far are those that from a classical toxicology perspective have a threshold below which no harm is expected to occur. For this reason they are sometimes called "threshold pollutants." However, as discussed in chapter 2, the emerging science of endocrine disruption and chemical sensitivity raises questions as to whether the usual thresholds at the parts-per-million range are adequate to protect sensitive populations. The majority opinion here does not delve into the intricacies of zero or nonzero thresholds. Nor does the majority opinion address EPA's conclusion that protecting the public health with a "margin of safety" does not (necessarily) require a standard to ensure a risk-free outcome. Only Justice Breyer, reflecting his earlier writings (*Breaking the Vicious Circle: Toward Effective Risk Regulation* [1993] Harvard University Press; Cambridge), focuses on this issue in his concurring opinion, agreeing that "safe" does not mean "risk-free." He further argues that EPA "retains discretionary authority [under Section 109] to avoid regulating risks that it reasonably concludes are trivial in context." This view is consistent with the evolving concept in environmental law that *de minimis* risks need not be regulated, even where they come within the scope of the regulatory mandate. See, e.g., *Monsanto Co. v. Kennedy*, 613 F.2d 947 (D.C. Cir. 1979) (concluding that the Food and Drug Administration has implicit authority to ignore *de minimis* risks); and *Natural Resources Defense Council v. EPA*, 834 F.2d 1146 (D.C. Cir. 1987) (concluding that the term "ample margin of safety" in Section 112 of the CAA does not require a "risk-free" standard).

For critical appraisals of Justice Breyer's views on regulation, see Adam M. Finkel (1995) "A Second Opinion on an Environmental Misdiagnosis: The Risky Prescription of *Breaking the Vicious Circle,*" 3 *New York University Environmental Law Journal* 295; and David A. Wirth and Ellen K. Silbergeld (1995) "Book Review: Risky Reform," 95 *Columbia Law Review* 1857. For a discussion of the recent tendency of the courts to read considerations of cost and *de minimis* risk into legislative provisions, see William E. Kovacic (1991) "The Reagan Judiciary and Environmental Policy: The Impacts of Appointments to the Federal Courts of Appeal," 18 *Boston College Environmental Affairs Law Review* 669.

4. Notice Justice Breyer's affirmation of the technology-forcing authority given EPA in the Clean Air Act.

5. In 2004, EPA reported that 224 counties with 95 million people (roughly 50% of the U.S. population) were potentially in nonattainment with the fine particulate limitations, mostly in the eastern part of the country, owing to power plant emissions, and in California, owing to motor vehicles. See *Environment Reporter* 35(51): 2621–2622 (2004). And, as discussed, EPA also reported that a total of 474 counties in 32 states (covering some 159 million residents) were out of compliance with the 8-hour ozone standard. [*Environment Reporter* 35(16): 805 (2004)].

6. In 2005, EPA staff scientists issued a report indicating that the particulate standards should be tightened to better protect public health through adjustments to the annual and/or 24-hour $PM_{2.5}$ permissible levels. See *Environment Reporter* 36(27): 1384 (2005). In addition, they recommended replacing PM_{10} with a new 24-hour standard for "coarse thorasic" particulates between 2.5 and 10 microns. Also recommended was a lower secondary standard to reduce haze. A month earlier, the Clean Air Act Advisory Committee had endorsed the staff recommendations for revision of the $PM_{2.5}$ standard to a 24-hour standard of 30–35 $\mu g/m^3$, and an annual standard of 13–14 $\mu g/m^3$. See *Environment Reporter* 36(24): 1228; (50): 2621 (2005). On September 15, 2005, the CASAC issued a final report (available at http://www.epa.gov/sab/pdf/sab-casac-05-012.pdf) agreeing with the agency staff's recommendations for a coarse particulate standard as well. Those recommendations were a 24-hour allowable range of 65 to 85 $\mu g/m^3$ replacing the 24-hour PM_{10} standard of 150 $\mu g/m^3$ and an annual standard of 50 $\mu g/m^3$. The staff proposed eliminating the annual standard.

7. Ultimately, EPA proposed a final rule lowering the 24-hour fine particulate standard for $PM_{2.5}$ to 35 $\mu g/m^3$, while leaving the annual standard intact, and establishing a 24-hour coarse particulate standard of 70 $\mu g/m^3$, replacing both the daily and annual PM_{10} standards. Certain exemptions were also provided for rural areas, and for agricultural and mining facilities. See 71 *Fed. Reg.* 2620, January 17, 2006.

8. The EPA Children's Health Protection Advisory Committee has since recommended a tightening of the 8-hour ozone standards from 0.080 ppm to 0.060 ppm. The EPA Clean Act Scientific Advisory Committee (CASAC) and EPA staff recommended the standard be set somewhere between 0.060 and 0.070 ppm. Citing advancements in analytic measurement technology, both EPA staff and CASAC recommended standards specified to three decimal places [*Environment Reporter* 38(12): 663 (2007)]. Under agreement reached in a follow-up case [*American Lung Ass'n v. Leavitt*, No. 03-778 (D. D.C. 2004)], a revised standard must be set by March 12, 2008.

9. In 2007, in a 5-4 decision, the U.S. Supreme Court held that EPA has the authority under the Clean Air Act to regulate carbon dioxide and other greenhouse gases from new motor vehicles [*Massachusetts v. EPA*, 127 S.Ct. 1438 (2007)]. Although EPA had taken the position that it did have such authority, the agency had reversed course under the administration of President George W. Bush and had declined to regulate carbon dioxide under the CAA. While the case involved the regulation of mobile sources, it should be equally applicable to stationary sources. See the next chapter for an excerpt and discussion of the case. In response to this decision, EPA announced that it may regulate carbon dioxide from power plants and other stationary sources under the Clean Air Act's new source review requirements. However, since new source review requirements apply only in situations in which plants are modified, no carbon dioxide controls would be required of existing facilities unless they were sufficiently upgraded or otherwise changed. Options for more comprehensive regulation of greenhouse gas emissions from stationary sources are available under the CAA, although as this book goes to press, the agency has not given any indication it is moving in that direction [*Environment Reporter* 38(37): 2010 (2007)]. ▪

C. STATE IMPLEMENTATION PLANS

As discussed earlier, the states play a major role in securing compliance with the national ambient air quality standards through the promulgation and implementation of state implementation plans. Although Congress lacks the constitutional authority to *force* the states to develop and enforce such plans (or to develop *adequate* plans), it did authorize EPA to withhold federal highway funds from states that failed to do so, and directed EPA to assume responsibility for a state's plan if the state refused.

The following case demonstrates the interplay between the federal government and the states in the setting of ambient air quality standards and the permitting of existing facilities to achieve those standards. Note that here the Supreme Court addresses economic and technological feasibility in the context of *implementation*, long before the issue came before the Court (in the *American Trucking* case) in the context of *standard setting*. Nonetheless, the Court's discussion of the technology-forcing function of Section 109 standard setting is routinely cited in cases (such as those excerpted previously) reviewing national ambient air quality standards.

Big court case for exam.

Union Electric Co. v. Environmental Protection Agency
Justice MARSHALL delivered the opinion of the Court

United States Supreme Court
427 U.S. 246 (1976)

. . .

I

We have addressed the history and provisions of the Clean Air Amendments of 1970, in detail in *Train v. Natural Resources Defense Council (NRDC)*, 421 U.S. 60 (1975), and will not repeat that discussion here. Suffice it to say that the Amendments reflect congressional dissatisfaction with the progress of existing air pollution programs and a determination to "tak[e] a stick to the States," in order to guarantee the prompt attainment and maintenance of specified air quality standards. The heart of the Amendments is the requirement that each State formulate, subject to EPA approval, an implementation plan designed to achieve national primary ambient air quality standards—those necessary to protect the public health—"as expeditiously as practicable but . . . in no case later than three years from the date of approval of such plan." The plan must also provide for the attainment of national secondary ambient air quality standards—those necessary to protect the public welfare—within a "reasonable time." Ibid. Each State is given wide discretion in formulating its plan, and the Act provides that the Administrator "shall approve" the proposed plan if it has been adopted after public notice and hearing and if it meets eight specified criteria §110(a)(2).

On April 30, 1971, the Administrator promulgated national primary and secondary standards for six air pollutants he found to have an adverse effect on the public health and welfare. Included among them was sulfur dioxide, at issue here. After the promulgation of the national standards, the State of Missouri formulated its implementation plan and submitted it for approval. Since sulfur dioxide levels exceeded national primary standards in only one of the State's five air quality regions—the Metropolitan St. Louis Interstate region,—the Missouri plan concentrated on a control strategy and regulations to lower emissions in that area. The plan's emission limitations were effective at once, but the State retained authority to grant variances to particular sources that could not immediately comply. The Administrator approved the plan on May 31, 1972.

State authority to grant variances to specific sources (hot spots?)

Petitioner is an electric utility company servicing the St. Louis metropolitan area, large portions of Missouri, and parts of Illinois and Iowa. Its three coal-fired generating plants in the metropolitan St. Louis area are subject to the sulfur dioxide restrictions in the Missouri implementation plan. . . . [O]n May 31, 1974, the Administrator notified petitioner that sulfur dioxide emissions from its plants violated the emission limitations contained in the Missouri plan. Shortly thereafter petitioner filed a petition in the Court of Appeals for the Eighth Circuit for review of the Administrator's 1972 approval of the Missouri implementation plan.

Case sues EPA for approving State Plan

II

. . .

Administrator says tech feas not grounds to reject State Plan

B

. . . The Administrator's position is that he has no power whatsoever to reject a state implementation plan on the ground that it is economically or technologically infeasible. . . . After surveying the relevant provisions of the Clean Air Amendments of 1970 and their legislative history, we agree that

Congress intended claims of economic and technological infeasibility to be wholly foreign to the Administrator's consideration of a state implementation plan.

...[T]he 1970 Amendments to the Clean Air Act were a drastic remedy to what was perceived as a serious and otherwise uncheckable problem of air pollution. The Amendments place the primary responsibility for formulating pollution control strategies on the States, but nonetheless subject the States to strict minimum compliance requirements. These requirements are of a "technology-forcing character," *Train v. NRDC, supra,* U.S., at 91, and are expressly designed to force regulated sources to develop pollution control devices that might at the time appear to be economically or technologically infeasible.

This approach is apparent on the face of §110(a)(2). The provision sets out eight criteria that an implementation plan must satisfy, and provides that if these criteria are met and if the plan was adopted after reasonable notice and hearing, the Administrator "shall approve" the proposed state plan. The mandatory "shall" makes it quite clear that the Administrator is not to be concerned with factors other than those specified, and none of the eight factors appears to permit consideration of technological or economic infeasibility. Nonetheless, if a basis is to be found for allowing the Administrator to consider such claims, it must be among the eight criteria, and so it is here that the argument is focused.

It is suggested that consideration of claims of technological and economic infeasibility is required by the first criterion—that the primary air quality standards be met "as expeditiously as practicable but...in no case later than three years..." and that the secondary air quality standards be met within a "reasonable time." §110(a)(2)(A). The argument is that what is "practicable" or "reasonable" cannot be determined without assessing whether what is proposed is possible. This argument does not survive analysis.

Section 110(a)(2)(A)'s three-year deadline for achieving primary air quality standards is central to the Amendments' regulatory scheme and, as both the language and the legislative history of the requirement make clear, it leaves no room for claims of technological or economic infeasibility....As Senator Muskie, manager of the Senate bill, explained to his chamber:

"The first responsibility of Congress is not the making of technological or economic judgments—or even to be limited by what is or appears to be technologically or economically feasible. Our responsibility is to establish what the public interest requires to protect the health of persons. This may mean that people and industries will be asked to do what seems to be impossible at the present time."...

"In the Committee discussions, considerable concern was expressed regarding the use of the concept of technical feasibility as the basis of ambient air standards. The Committee determined that 1) the health of people is more important than the question of whether the early achievement of ambient air quality standards protective of health is technically feasible; and 2) the growth of pollution load in many areas, even with application of available technology, would still be deleterious to public health.

"Therefore, the Committee determined that existing sources of pollutants either should meet the standard of the law or be closed down...."

The Conference Committee and, ultimately, the entire Congress accepted the Senate's three-year mandate for the achievement of primary air quality standards, and the clear import of that decision is that the Administrator must approve a plan that provides for attainment of the primary standards in three years even if attainment does not appear feasible....The Conference Committee made clear that the States could not procrastinate until the deadline approached. Rather, the primary standards had to be met in less than three years if possible; they had to be met "as expeditiously as practicable." Whatever room there is for considering claims of infeasibility in the attainment of primary standards must lie in this phrase, which is, of course, relevant only in evaluating those implementation plans that attempt to achieve the primary standard in less than three years.

It is argued that when such a state plan calls for proceeding more rapidly than economics and the available technology appear to allow, the plan must be rejected as not "practicable." Whether this is a correct reading of §110(a)(2)(A) depends on how that section's "as expeditiously as practicable" phrase is characterized. The Administrator's position is that §110(a)(2)(A) sets only a minimum standard that the States may exceed in their discretion, so that he has no power to reject an infeasible state plan that surpasses the minimum federal requirements—a plan that reflects a state decision to engage in technology forcing on its own and to proceed more expeditiously than is practicable. On the other hand, petitioner and amici supporting its position argue that §110(a)(2)(A) sets a mandatory standard that the States must meet precisely, and conclude that the Administrator may reject a plan for being too strict as well as for being too lax. . . .

Section 116 of the Clean Air Act, provides that the States may adopt emission standards stricter than the national standards. Amici argue that such standards must be adopted and enforced independently of the EPA-approved state implementation plan. This construction of §§110 and 116, however, would not only require the Administrator to expend considerable time and energy determining whether a state plan was precisely tailored to meet the federal standards, but would simultaneously require States desiring stricter standards to enact and enforce two sets of emission standards, one federally approved plan and one stricter state plan. We find no basis in the

Amendments for visiting such wasteful burdens upon the States and the Administrator, and so we reject the argument of amici.

We read the "as may be necessary" requirement of §110(a)(2)(B) to demand only that the implementation plan submitted by the State meet the "minimum conditions" of the Amendments.[13] Beyond that if a State makes the legislative determination that it desires a particular air quality by a certain date and that it is willing to force technology to attain it—or lose a certain industry if attainment is not possible—such a determination is fully consistent with the structure and purpose of the Amendments, and §110(a)(2)(B) provides no basis for the EPA Administrator to object to the determination on the ground of infeasibility.[14]

In sum, we have concluded that claims of economic or technological infeasibility may not be considered by the Administrator in evaluating a state requirement that primary ambient air quality standards be met in the mandatory three years. And, since we further conclude that the States may submit implementation plans more stringent than federal law requires and that the Administrator must approve such plans if they meet the minimum requirements of §110(a)(2), it follows that the language of §110(a)(2)(B) provides no basis for the Administrator ever to reject a state implementation plan on the ground that it is economically or technologically infeasible. Accordingly, a court of appeals reviewing an approved plan under §307(b)(1) cannot set it aside on those grounds. . . .

---

13. Economic and technological factors may be relevant in determining whether the minimum conditions are met. Thus, the Administrator may consider whether it is economically or technologically possible for the state plan to require more rapid progress than it does. If he determines that it is, he may reject the plan as not meeting the requirement that primary standards be achieved "as expeditiously as practicable" or as failing to provide for attaining secondary standards within "a reasonable time."

14. In a literal sense, of course, no plan is infeasible since offending sources always have the option of shutting down if they cannot otherwise comply with the standard of the law. Thus, there is no need for the Administrator to reject an economically or technologically "infeasible" state plan on the ground that anticipated noncompliance will cause the State to fall short of the national standards. Sources objecting to such a state scheme must seek their relief from the State.

Summary
- *As long as State meets min fed req it can be as strict as it wants*
- *Admin can reject a Plan for 8 diff reasons*
- *econ & tech feas not one of the 8*

III

... Perhaps the most important forum for consideration of claims of economic and technological infeasibility is before the state agency formulating the implementation plan. So long as the national standards are met, the State may select whatever mix of control devices it desires, and industries with particular economic or technological problems may seek special treatment in the plan itself. Moreover, if the industry is not exempted from, or accommodated by, the original plan, it may obtain a variance, as petitioner did in this case; and the variance, if granted after notice and a hearing, may be submitted to the EPA as a revision of the plan. Lastly, an industry denied an exemption from the implementation plan, or denied a subsequent variance, may be able to take its claims of economic or technological infeasibility to the state courts.[16]

... Even if the State does not intervene on behalf of an emission source, technological and economic factors may be considered in at least one other circumstance. When a source is found to be in violation of the state implementation plan, the Administrator may, after a conference with the operator, issue a compliance order rather than seek civil or criminal enforcement. Such an order must specify a "reasonable" time for compliance with the relevant standard, taking into account the seriousness of the violation and "any good faith efforts to comply with applicable requirements." Claims of technological or

Possible for Admin Compliance order

economic infeasibility, the Administrator agrees, are relevant to fashioning an appropriate compliance order under §113(a)(4).[18]

In short, the Amendments offer ample opportunity for consideration of claims of technological and economic infeasibility. Always, however, care is taken that consideration of such claims will not interfere substantially with the primary goal of prompt attainment of the national standards. Allowing such claims to be raised by appealing the Administrator's approval of an implementation plan, as petitioner suggests, would frustrate congressional intent. It would permit a proposed plan to be struck down as infeasible before it is given a chance to work, even though Congress clearly contemplated that some plans would be infeasible when proposed. And it would permit the Administrator or a federal court to reject a State's legislative choices in regulating air pollution, even though Congress plainly left with the States, so long as the national standards were met, the power to determine which sources would be burdened by regulation and to what extent. Technology forcing is a concept somewhat new to our national experience and it necessarily entails certain risks. But Congress considered those risks in passing the 1970 Amendments and decided that the dangers posed by uncontrolled air pollution made them worth taking. Petitioner's theory would render that considered legislative judgment a nullity, and that is a result we refuse to reach.

Affirmed.

---

16. Of course, the Amendments do not require the States to formulate their implementation plans with deference to claims of technological or economic infeasibility, to grant variances on those or any other grounds, or to provide judicial review of such actions. Consistent with Congress' recognition of the primary role of the States in controlling air pollution, the Amendments leave all such decisions to the States, which have typically responded in the manner described in the text. Cf. 40 CFR §§51.2(b), (d) (1975).

18. If he chooses not to seek a compliance order, or if an order is issued and violated, the Administrator may institute a civil enforcement proceeding. §113(b). Additionally, violators of an implementation plan are subject to criminal penalties under §113(c) and citizen enforcement suits under §304. Some courts have suggested that in criminal or civil enforcement proceedings the violator may in certain circumstances raise a defense of economic or technological infeasibility. We do not address this question here.

■ **NOTE**

1. Thus, while economic and technological feasibility *may* be considered by the states, neither *must* be taken into account by the states in setting emission limitations (for specific sources or categories of sources) that are designed to meet primary ambient air quality standards. However, there is the potential that state courts may choose not to impose sanctions on firms that can establish economic hardship, especially if the judge views the emission restrictions as unreasonably stringent. Would this subvert the technology-forcing purpose of the CAA? If this state action prevented the achievement of a NAAQS, the state could be regarded as being in violation of its SIP, and EPA could apply sanctions or take over the state plan. Moreover, the federal government or (in the absence of a diligently prosecuted state suit) an affected citizen may bring a *federal court* action to enforce the provisions of a SIP. See Section 304.   ■

D. ADDITIONAL REGULATION OF STATIONARY SOURCES

In addition to the emission limitations imposed by the states to meet the NAAQS, the Clean Air Act mandates a variety of emission limitations for certain classes of stationary sources.

1. Section 111 Standards

a. New Source Performance Standards

i. In General   Recognizing that new sources would be in a better position than existing sources to adopt the latest, most effective pollution control technology, Congress fashioned Section 111 of the CAA to create uniform federal emission standards for a number of categories of new stationary sources. In specifying federal standards, Congress was motivated by a desire for uniformity of burden within any industrial class, to discourage the creation of "pollution havens" that would attract industry to a particular state or region.

Under Section 111, EPA is required to publish "from time to time" a list of categories of stationary sources that "cause, or contribute significantly to, air pollution which may be reasonably anticipated to endanger public health or welfare." See Section 111(b)(1)(A). Standards for the categories of sources are to be set within 1 year of listing. Unless it is not feasible to prescribe or enforce it, such a standard must be a performance standard "which reflects the degree of emission limitation achievable through the application of the best system of emission reduction which (taking into account the cost of achieving such reduction and any non-air quality health and environmental impact and energy requirements) the Administrator believes has been adequately demonstrated" [Section 111(a)(1)]. These new source performance standards must be reviewed at least every 8 years. Section 111(b)(1)(B). Moreover, it would appear that given the general requirement that these standards be set with reference to "the best system of emission reduction," they must be revised sooner than every 8 years if a technological advance increases an industry's capacity for reducing emissions.

■ **NOTE**

1. Section 111(j) contains waiver provisions and variance procedures designed to promote technological innovation. The owner or operator of a new source may request one or more waivers "to encourage the use of an innovative technological system or systems of *continuous* emission reduction" (emphasis added). A waiver may be granted for as long as 7 years or within 4 years after the date of the beginning of the operation of the source, whichever is earlier. Innovation waivers are discussed further in chapter 12 (as an example of negotiated implementation of a standard) and chapter 13 (as a means of promoting pollution prevention).   ■

ii.   What Is a "New" or "Major Modified" Source?   New source performance standards apply to newly constructed sources and to existing sources that have undergone substantial modification. An NSPS applies to all such sources within an industrial class, regardless of the air quality region in which they are located. Section 111(a)(4) defines a modification as "any physical change, or change in the method of operation of, a stationary source which increases the amount of any air pollutant emitted by such source or which results in the emission of any air pollutant not previously emitted." The process through which new construction is evaluated to determine whether an NSPS is applicable is known as preconstruction review.

EPA has devoted considerable effort to defining what constitutes a "new" source or "substantial modification" of an existing source that would trigger application of the NSPS, and much controversy has surrounded this definitional process. An innovation in regulatory policy, called the bubble concept, came about when EPA addressed the formulation of NSPS requirements for existing plants that were modified or expanded. Under the bubble concept, all of the individual sources of air pollution at a single facility—whether they be old or new—are envisioned as the component parts of a single emission emanating from an imaginary bubble placed over the entire facility. Thus, as long as the overall amount of the regulated pollutant emitted from this bubble did not increase, the facility did not become subject to the NSPS for that pollutant. This enabled the owners of the facility to alter individual polluting parts of the plant to minimize their overall cost by choosing different degrees or kinds of pollution control for the various components within the bubble. This bubble policy, with its plant-wide definition of "source," was upheld by the Supreme Court in a 1984 decision excerpted later in this chapter.

In 2002, at the urging of coal-fired power plants, EPA amended its new source review requirements with what was known as the equipment replacement rule. This rule specified that plants making modifications to improve their energy efficiency could do so without triggering the applicability of the NSPS. In effect, such modifications were not considered "substantial," and thus did not transform an existing source into a new source. Accordingly, under this rule, the plants could make changes to improve their energy efficiency without also improving their pollution reduction. Industry had argued that the previous requirements, under which such modification would have triggered NSPS applicability, inhibited innovation. Environmental activists, on the other hand, argued that the new rules discouraged innovation. Both were correct in a way. Under the old rules, innovations for more efficient energy production were discouraged because they would have triggered a requirement for potentially costly pollution control. On the other hand, allowing innovation for energy efficiency while not also forcing industry to reduce pollution discouraged innovation for pollution reduction. It also discouraged the development of innovative technology that both improves energy efficiency and reduces pollution. Under the new rules, newer, less polluting, energy-efficient sources did not enjoy the market advantage they would have had under the old rules, and older, dirtier, coal-fired plants had an increased incentive to continue to operate. This would appear to be contrary to the spirit of the CAA's new source policy.

In 2003 EPA issued a second rule exempting all "equipment replacement" projects for coal-fired power plants from new source review as long as the cost of the project was below 20% of the cost of the unit being repaired. While it could be argued that the old rules discouraged improving energy efficiency in old plants, and actually discouraged improving pollution per unit of fuel, it can also be argued that still greater energy efficiency and overall pollution reduction by newer installations were discouraged by this exemption.

These changes to long-standing new source review policies drew considerable opposition, and eventually fourteen states, thirty cities, and several environmental groups sued EPA seeking to have the new rues set aside. Eric Schaeffer, the former head of the EPA Enforcement Division who had resigned over his frustration with the George W. Bush administration's Clean Air Act enforcement policies, joined a coalition of environmentalists and northeastern states in an effort to have the equipment replacement rule reversed. New York Attorney General Eliot Spitzer led several states (among them New York, New Jersey, Connecticut, and California) in suing the EPA in the D.C. Circuit Court of Appeals, arguing that the new rule would increase air pollution. The D.C. Circuit stayed the equipment replacement rule in late 2003 in order to consider the challenge to both rules, and a unanimous three-judge panel of that court issued an opinion strking down the equipment replacement rule as "contrary to the plain language of section 111(a)(4) of the Clean Air Act." See *New York v. EPA*, 443 F.3rd 880 (D.C. Cir. 2006). The court's decision directly affects more than 100 old coal-fired power plants that were facing federal legal action before the new regulation was issued. Fifty of these plants emit 50% of the nation's sulfur dioxide emissions, but generate only 25% of the nation's electricity; fifty of these plants emit 40% of the nation's nitrogen oxides and 42% of the mercury, but generate only 29% of the nation's electricity (http://environmentalintegrity.org/pub314.cfm).

In 2007, the Supreme Court addressed another aspect of the meaning of "modification" under EPA rules. The Court held that EPA is authorized to define modification differently for different programs under the CAA and is free to calculate compliance with new source emissions limitations on an annual basis (for application in its prevention of signification deterioration policy discussed later in this chapter), in contrast to an hourly basis that EPA uses in the new source review rule [*Environmental Defense v. Duke Energy Corp.*, 127 S.Ct. 1423 (2007)]. Calculating compliance with new source emissions limitations on an hourly basis allows a plant to increase its capacity by operating longer hours at its original emissions rate without installing newer pollution control equipment, even though the annual emissions would increase. Despite having won the case, however, EPA may be moving forward with a rule allowing the calculations to be done on an hourly basis for PSD, putting them in line with the basis for new source review. See *Environment Reporter* 38(14): 789–790 (2007).

Another regulation proposed by EPA in 2006, known as the "aggregation, debottlenecking and netting" rule, would allow manufacturing plants, refineries, and other industrial sources to make modifications that expand production and increase emissions without triggering new source review requirements. See http://epa.gov/nsr/actions/html#sep06.

■ NOTES

1. As discussed later, additional restrictions are placed on growth in attainment versus nonattainment areas.

2. Another EPA action also affects the extent to which individual sources will reduce SO_2 and NO_X emissions. EPA has issued the Clean Air Interstate Rule (CAIR), 70 *Fed. Reg.* 44,154 (2005), which allows twenty-eight states and the District of Columbia to use tradable emissions allowances for ozone and fine particles (generated by sulfur dioxide and nitrogen oxides) and exempts power plants from the Clean Air Act Visibility Rule intended to control haze (discussed later). EPA has stated that it expects CAIR to achieve a 61% reduction in nitrogen oxide emissions and a 57% reduction in sulfur dioxide emissions by 2015. The emissions cap for sulfur dioxide

would not be fully met until 2025 because power companies hold excess trading allowances under the existing acid rain trading program. Environmental groups are ideologically split on the rule. The Environmental Defense Fund, which is generally supportive of economic incentives, favors the rule, while the National Resources Defense Council opposes it. The D.C. Circuit Court of Appeals has upheld the rule, rejecting challenges by environmental and industry groups [*Utility Air Regulatory Group v. EPA*, 471 F. 3rd 1333 (D.C. Cir. 2006)].

3. Even if planned new or modified sources within an installation were expected to be in technical compliance with NSPS emission requirements, they might not be allowed if they were located in an area that is not in attainment with NAAQS standards. As discussed later, EPA dealt with this "no growth" issue by extending its bubble policy to nonattainment areas.   ■

How certain does EPA have to be as to the capability of a particular technology before the agency may base a new source performance standard on that predicted capability? This is one of the issues addressed by the D.C. Circuit in the following case.

Portland Cement Association v. Ruckelshaus
LEVENTHAL, Circuit Judge
486 F.2d 375 (D.C. Cir. 1973)

Portland Cement Association seeks review[1] of the action of the Administrator of the Environmental Protection Agency (EPA) in promulgating stationary source standards for new or modified portland cement plants, pursuant to the provisions of Section 111 of the Clean Air Act. . . .

I. STATEMENT OF THE CASE

Section 111 of the Clean Air Act directs the Administrator to promulgate "standards of performance" governing emissions of air pol-

lutants by new stationary sources constructed or modified after the effective date of pertinent regulations.[3] The focus of dispute in this case concerns EPA compliance with the statutory language of Section 111(a) which defines "standard of performance" as follows:

(1) The term "standard of performance" means a standard for emissions of air pollutants which reflects the degree of emission limitation achievable through the application of the best system of emission reduction which (taking into account the cost of achieving such reduction) the Administrator determines has been adequately demonstrated.

---

1. Section 307(b)(1) of the Clean Air Act, 42 U.S.C. §1857h-5(b)(1), requires that a petition for review of the action of the Administrator in setting standards of performance under section 111 of the Act "be filed only in the United States Court of Appeals for the District of Columbia."
3. The term "new source" is defined as:

any stationary source, the construction or modification of which is commenced after the publication of

regulations (or, if earlier, proposed regulations) prescribing a standard of performance under this section which will be applicable to such source.

Modification is, in turn, defined as:

any physical change in, or change in the method of operation of, a stationary source which increases the amount of any air pollutant emitted by such source or which results in the emission of any air pollutant not previously emitted.

After designating portland cement plants as a stationary source of air pollution which may "contribute significantly to air pollution which causes or contributes to the endangerment of public health or welfare," under Section 111(b)(1)(A) of the Act, the Administrator published a proposed regulation establishing standards of performance for portland cement plants....

... The action of the Administrator has been challenged on the following grounds: ... (2) Economic costs were not adequately taken into account and the standards unfairly discriminate against portland cement plants, in comparison with standards promulgated for power plants and incinerators. (3) The achievability of the standards was not adequately demonstrated....

III. ECONOMIC COSTS

The objecting companies contend that the Administrator has not complied with the mandate of §111 of the Act, which requires him to "[take] into account the costs" of achieving the emission reductions he prescribes, a statutory provision that clearly refers to the possible economic impact of the promulgated standards....

Petitioners argue that ... the Administrator is required to prepare a quantified cost-benefit analysis, showing the benefit to ambient air conditions as measured against the cost of the pollution devices. However desirable in the abstract, such a requirement would conflict with the specific time constraints imposed on the Administrator. The difficulty, if not impossibility, of quantifying the benefit to ambient air conditions, further militates against the imposition of such an imperative on the agency. Such studies should be considered by the Administrator, if adduced in comments, but we do not inject them as a necessary condition of action.

The EPA contention that economic costs to the industry have been taken into account, derives substantial support from a study prepared for EPA, which was made part of the

rule-making record.... It concluded that the additional costs of control equipment could be passed on without substantially affecting competition with construction substitutes such as steel, asphalt and aluminum, because "demand for cement, derived for the most part from demand for public and private construction, is not highly elastic with regard to price and would not be very sensitive to small price changes." The study did note that individual mills may be closed in the years ahead, but observed that these plants were obsolete both from a cost and pollution point of view. Petitioners have not challenged these findings here. The Administrator has obviously given some consideration to economic costs....

Petitioners ... challenge the cement standards as unfair in light of lower standards mandated for fossil-fuel-fired steam generating power plants and incinerators....

First, we identify petitioner's mistake in making a comparison of the proposed standards, whereas the standards as finally adopted permitted pollution standards of only 0.08 for incinerators and 0.10 for power plants, compared with 0.03 for cement plants.

EPA, in response to comments from petitioners on this issue of discrepancy, stated in its supplemental statement in March 1972: "The difference between the particulate standard for cement plants and those for steam generators and incinerators is attributable to the superior technology available therefore (that is, fabric filter technology has not been applied to coal-fired steam generators or incinerators)."

... The core of our response to petitioners is that the Administrator is not required to present affirmative justifications for different standards in different industries. Inter-industry comparisons of this kind are not generally required, or even productive; and they were not contemplated by Congress in this Act. The essential question is whether the mandated standards can be met by a particular industry for which they are set, and this can typically be decided on the basis of information concerning that industry alone. This is not to say that evidence collected about the functioning of emission devices in one industry may not have implications for another. Certainly such information may bear on technological capability. But there is no requirement of uniformity of specific standards for all industries. The Administrator applied the same general approach, of ascertaining for each industry what was feasible in that industry....

IV. ACHIEVABILITY OF EMISSION STANDARD

Section 111 of the Act requires "the degree of emission limitation achievable [which]...the Administrator determines has been adequately demonstrated." Petitioners contend that the promulgated standard for new stationary sources has not been "adequately demonstrated," raising issues as to the interpretation to be given to this requirement, the procedures followed by the agency in arriving at its standard, and the scientific evidence upon which it was formulated....

B. Technology Available for New Plants

We begin by rejecting the suggestion of the cement manufacturers that the Act's requirement that emission limitations be "adequately demonstrated" necessarily implies that any cement plant now in existence be able to meet the proposed standards. Section 111 looks toward what may fairly be projected for the regulated future, rather than the state of the art at present, since it is addressed to standards for new plants—old stationary source pollution being controlled through other regulatory authority. It is the "achievability" of the proposed standard that is in issue.

...The Senate Report made clear that it did not intend that the technology "must be in actual routine use somewhere." The essential question was rather whether the technology would be available for installation in new plants. The House Report also refers to "available" technology. Its caution that "in order to be considered 'available' the technology may not be one which constitutes a purely theoretical or experimental means of preventing or controlling air pollution" merely reflects the final language adopted, that it must be "adequately demonstrated" that there will be "available technology."

The resultant standard is analogous to the one examined in *International Harvester v. EPA*, 478 F.2d 615, 629 (D.C. Cir. 1973). The Administrator may make a projection based on existing technology, though that projection is subject to the restraints of reasonableness and cannot be based on "crystal ball" inquiry. As there, the question of availability is partially dependent on "lead time," the time in which the technology will have to be available. Since the standards here put into effect will control new plants immediately, as opposed to one or two years in the future, the latitude of projection is correspondingly narrowed. If actual tests are not relied on, but instead a prediction is made, "its validity as applied to this case rests on the reliability of [the] prediction and the nature of [the] assumptions." *International Harvester....*

V. THE STANDARD OF JUDICIAL REVIEW AND CONCLUSIONS

We are quite aware that the standards promulgated and here under review are to be applied to *new* stationary sources. It would have been entirely appropriate if the Administrator had justified the standards, not on the basis of tests on existing sources or old test data in the literature, but on extrapolations from this data, on a reasoned basis responsive to comments, and on testimony from experts and vendors made part of the record. This course was not followed here. Instead, the Administrator in his statement of reasons relied on tests on existing plants and the literature, which EPA counsel now discounts without reference to other record support to take its place.

The Administrator's objectives are laudable, but the statute expressly requires, for the standards he promulgates, that technology be achievable. This record reveals a lack of an adequate opportunity of the manufacturers to comment on the proposed standards, due to the absence of disclosure of the detailed findings and procedures of the tests. . . .

We have identified a number of matters that require consideration and clarification on remand. While we remain diffident in approaching problems of this technical complexity, *see International Harvester, supra,* 478 F.2d at 648, the necessity to review agency decisions, if it is to be more than a meaningless exercise, requires enough steeping in technical matters to determine whether the agency "has exercised a reasoned discretion." We cannot substitute our judgment for that of the agency, but it is our duty to consider whether "the decision was based on a consideration of the relevant factors and whether there has been a clear error of judgment." *Citizens to Preserve Overton Park v. Volpe* 401 U.S. 402, 416 (1971). Ultimately, we believe, that the cause of a clean environment is best served by reasoned decision-making. The record is remanded for further proceedings not inconsistent with this opinion.

So ordered.

■ **NOTES**

1. In general, courts have upheld new source performance standards only if they had already or nearly been met by existing plants.

2. How does the court define "adequately demonstrated" technology? If it is "what may be fairly projected for the regulated future," how technology forcing is this likely to be?

3. Is EPA's authority to set the industry standard, in and of itself, a strong enough incentive for the designers of new source technology to innovate in order to establish their technology as the de facto industry standard? How much does this depend on industry's perception of how likely EPA is to base an NSPS on the new technology? ■

iii. Alternative Standard-Setting Criteria If performance standards for new sources are infeasible to prescribe or enforce, EPA may instead "promulgate a design, equipment, work practice, or operational standard, or combination thereof, which reflects the best technological system of *continuous* emission reduction, which (taking into account the cost of achieving such reduction and any non-air quality health and environmental impact and energy requirements) the Administrator determines has been adequately demonstrated" [Section 111(h)(1), emphasis added].

■ **NOTES**

1. See table 6.2 for NAAQS and NSPS as they apply to existing and new or modified sources, respectively.

Table 6.2
NAAQS and NSPS Requirements in NAAQS Attainment Areas

	NAAQS (§109) Primary and secondary ambient air quality (concentration) standards	NSPS (§111) (restrictions placed on individual sources)
Existing sources	CO, SO_2, NO_X, O_3, particulates (PM_{10}; $PM_{2.5}$), Pb Primary: to protect public health with an adequate margin of safety Secondary: to protect public welfare (implemented through state permitting of preferably continuous emission controls)	
New or modified sources		**NSPS:** Category-wide federal *emission standards* for pollutants based on "best system of emission reduction ... adequately demonstrated" [§111(a)(1)] or *a design standard* using the "best *technological* system of continuous emission reduction" [§111(h)(1)]—all enforced through state permits.

2. What impact does the addition of the word "continuous"—present in Section 111(h)(1), but not in Section 111(a)(1)—have on the type of standard that can be established under Section 111(h)(1)? Note also the reference to continuous emission reduction in the waiver provision of Section 111(j). Why do you suppose Congress believed continuous emission reduction to be preferable?

3. An individual source may secure a variance from a Section 111 specification standard if it establishes its use of an equivalent or better "alternative means of emission limitation," as provided by Section 111(h)(3).

4. Even though EPA is allowed to set alternative *specification* standards under this section, there is a congressional preference for *performance* standards. See Section 111(h)(4). ▪

b. Designated Pollutants

Even though the title to Section 111 mentions only new stationary sources, there is one provision, subsection (d), that addresses performance standards for existing sources. If EPA identifies an air pollutant for which air quality criteria have not been issued (or listed for development) under Section 109, and which is not emitted from a source category regulated under Section 112 (governing hazardous air pollutants), but for which a performance standard would be appropriate if the emitting source were new, EPA must promulgate regulations under which states will establish performance standards governing existing source emissions of that pollutant. If a state does not do so, EPA must set the standards for that state itself. Any such standard, whether set by the state or by EPA, must take into account, among other factors, the

Table 6.3
NAAQS and §111 Requirements in NAAQS Attainment Areas and Designated Pollutants

	NAAQS (§109) Primary and secondary ambient air quality (concentration) standards	NSPS (§111) + Designated Pollutants (§111d) (restrictions placed on individual sources)
Existing sources	CO, SO_2, NO_X, O_3, particulates (PM_{10}; $PM_{2.5}$), Pb Primary: to protect public health with an adequate margin of safety Secondary: to protect public welfare (implemented through state permitting of preferably continuous emission controls)	**Designated Pollutants:** Where no §109 or §112 standard does or would apply, and a performance standard under §111 would be appropriate if the source were new, EPA may set performance standards. Standards now exist for sulfuric acid mist, fluorides, and VOCs (§111d).
New or modified sources		**NSPS:** Category-wide federal *emission standards* for pollutants based on "best system of emission reduction ... adequately demonstrated" [§111(a)(1)] or *a design standard* using the "best *technological* system of continuous emission reduction" [§111(h)(1)]—all enforced through state permits.

remaining useful life of the existing source to which such standard applies. Pollutants qualifying for this action are called *designated pollutants*. Thus far, EPA has designated sulfuric acid mist, fluorides, and VOCs as such pollutants.

See table 6.3 for a NAAQS and NSPS requirements (as they apply to existing and new or modified sources, respectively) and of designated pollutants.

2.   Additional Emission Standards and Policies Designed to Achieve or Maintain Ambient Air Quality Standards: Nonattainment and the Prevention of Significant Deterioration

Initially, the new source performance standards were the most stringent requirements placed on new sources. However, both because of the failure of SIPs to achieve the NAAQS in many ambient air quality regions for one or more criteria pollutants, and because of the increased desire not to have even good air quality deteriorate further, in the 1977 CAA amendments Congress placed additional restrictions on growth. These new provisions defined the extent to which new industrial growth is allowed to take place in areas where one or more of the ambient air quality standards has not been attained, and in areas where further degradation of the environment has been deemed not to be desirable. The result was additional controls on both new and existing sources in certain areas of the country.

All air quality regions were henceforth to be classified as either "nonattainment" or "nondegradation," on a pollutant-by-pollutant basis (e.g., the same region may be nonattainment for particulates and nondegradation for CO), and new growth was permitted only if additional emission requirements were met. As discussed in detail later, in some regions new source performance standards became the minimum, rather than the maximum, requirements applicable to new major sources. In nonattainment areas, new sources are required to meet "lowest achievable emission reduction" (LAER) emissions standards, *and* to reduce overall emissions through "offsets" secured from existing sources. Existing sources in nonattainment areas are required to meet those emission levels deemed "reasonably achievable [by] control technology" (the so-called RACT standards), as set by the states according to federal criteria).

a. Nonattainment Policy

Nonattainment policy applies to regions where air quality does not meet primary and/or secondary standards.[3] See Sections 171–179B. There are general nonattainment regulations that apply to all criteria pollutants, and there are also pollutant-specific category designations. See Sections 186–192.

i. In General The 1977 amendments (as modified in 1979) established the following stringent requirements for new growth in nonattainment areas, to be imposed through the state permitting system:

1. Emissions from a new (or modified) major source—one that directly emits or has the potential to emit more than 100 tons per year of any pollutant, including fugitive emissions [see Section 302(j)]—must meet the "lowest achievable emission reduction" emissions standard established for the applicable source category. See Section 173(2). This LAER limit is to be based either on the most stringent requirement (regardless of cost) for the category of source found in *any* SIP, or on the lowest emission level achieved by any existing source, whichever is more stringent. See Section 171.

2. In addition, the source must demonstrate that there will be a net reduction in total emissions in the affected AQR as a result of the new growth, representing "reasonable further progress" toward achievement of the primary standard, as specified in Section 171(1). This is the "offset policy," under which the source must obtain emission reductions from existing sources that *more than offset* the emissions from the

---

3. Although the 1970 amendments required primary standards to be attained by 1975, regardless of economic or technological feasibility, EPA was reluctant to force existing plants to close where they had made good-faith efforts to comply. Thus, using its enforcement discretion under Section 113, EPA often issued compliance orders containing schedules that extended beyond 1975. These orders typically required the source to install controls deemed technologically and economically feasible. Congress approved this policy in the 1977 amendments through a specific provision [Section 113(d)] that authorized EPA to issue orders extending compliance until July 1979. After July 1979, compliance penalties were to be assessed in an amount equal to the cost of compliance. However, existing plants could also obtain a waiver for up to five additional years to implement innovative compliance technology.

Table 6.4
1990 CAA Nonattainment Requirements for Ozone

Marginal	Across-the-board application of RACT for existing major sources [cf. 42 U.S.C. §7511(a) (CAA §181(a)].
Moderate	RACT + 15% reductions in VOCs within 6 years.
Serious	The above + 3% annual reduction in VOCs thereafter—could substitute NO_x reduction, if effective in reducing ozone.
Severe	Attainment in 15–17 years; significant fees thereafter for major sources.
Extreme	Los Angeles: new source review + RACT applied to smaller stationary sources as well.

new source. Section 173(a)(1)(A). This can be achieved, for example, by retiring or cutting back on production from existing sources.

3. The applicant must also demonstrate that other facilities in the state subject to his or her ownership or control are in compliance with the CAA. Section 173(a)(3).

4. EPA will examine compliance schedules for other facilities controlled by the source to determine if any can comply more expeditiously than currently required; more stringent requirements on these other sources will be required if feasible. Section 173(a)(3).

5. Before growth is allowed in nonattainment AQRs, existing major sources must meet emissions limitations set with reference to "reasonably available control technology," taking cost into account, for the pollutant in question. Section 171c(1). Further, as discussed later, these sources must comply with other restrictions imposed by the nondegradation policy.

6. *All* sources in the AQR must be in compliance with the SIP. Section 173(a)(3).

In practice, LAER is determined by EPA and RACT is determined by the individual states for individual sources, according to statutory and EPA criteria that have become more precise over the years.

ii. Specific Requirements for Ozone, CO, and Particulates The 1990 CAA amendments specified special nonattainment requirements for ozone, PM_{10}, and CO. See Section 107(d)(4). Nonattainment areas were further classified according to these specific pollutants, with Congress specifying 96, 72, and 42 areas designated for ozone, PM_{10}, and CO, respectively.

The ozone areas were divided into five categories: *marginal, moderate, serious, severe*, and *extreme*. The control restrictions are shown in table 6.4. Areas that did not meet their restrictions in a timely matter were reclassified into the next worse category, with still greater requirements.

For PM_{10} particulates, all nonattainment areas were designated as moderate areas and required to apply RACT to existing sources. Those areas not in attainment by

Table 6.5
NAAQS/§111 Requirements in NAAQS Attainment and Nonattainment Areas

	NAAQS (§109) Primary and secondary ambient air quality (concentration) standards	NSPS (§111) + Designated Pollutants (§111d) (restrictions placed on individual sources)
Existing sources	CO, SO_2, NO_X, O_3, particulates (PM_{10}; $PM_{2.5}$), Pb Primary: to protect public health with an adequate margin of safety Secondary: to protect public welfare (implemented through state permitting of preferably continuous emission controls) **Additional Nonattainment Requirements:** Tiered reductions for CO, O_3, and PM_{10} particulates	**Designated Pollutants:** Where no §109 or §112 standard does or would apply, and a performance standard under §111 would be appropriate if the source were new, EPA may set performance standards. Standards now exist for sulfuric acid mist, fluorides, and VOCs (§111d). **Additional Nonattainment Requirements:** RACT [§172(c)(1)]
New or modified sources		**NSPS:** Category-wide federal *emission standards* for pollutants based on "best system of emission reduction . . . adequately demonstrated" [§111(a)(1)] or *a design standard* using the "best *technological* system of continuous emission reduction" [§111(h)(1)]—all enforced through state permits. **Additional Nonattainment Requirements:** LAER for major new sources + offsets §171(3)

the end of 1994 were to be classified as serious, with more stringent controls to be applied.

For CO, the designated regions were classified as either moderate or serious. Moderate areas were required to inventory automotive emissions, implement vehicle inspection and maintenance programs, and make oxygenated fuels available, with a goal of reaching attainment in 1995. Serious areas were required to adopt these measures and to adopt transportation controls as well. The latter refers to control of traffic and other administrative plans to reduce pollution from mobile sources. Table 6.5 depicts the additional requirements imposed in nonattainment areas.

b. Nondegradation Policy (Prevention of Significant Deterioration)

i. In General Nondegradation policy applies to air quality control regions where air quality meets or is cleaner than that required by primary and secondary standards for a specific pollutant. Pockets of clean air within an otherwise dirty region (i.e., in nonattainment areas) are also subject to the nondegradation policy. The policy, codi-fied at Sections 164–169, is also known by the acronym PSD (for prevention of sig-nificant deterioration) and its origin is the 1977 amendments to the CAA. Under the nondegradation policy, three classes are established for areas within the AQCRs that are in compliance with the NAAQS. Class I areas are subject to the most stringent standards of the three classes, and are permitted little growth. Class III areas are per-mitted the most new pollution of the three classes, but are not permitted to exceed the primary and secondary standards. National parks are classified as class I, while all other areas are statutorily designated class II. States have limited authority to redesignate class II areas as class I or III. Such redesignation may occur only after public notice of the health, environmental, economic, social, and energy effects of the redesignation.

PSD standards apply to any new major source regardless of where that source is located if its emissions affect a clean air area. The standards set uniform increments of permissible degradation, which are measured from the baseline air quality for each air quality control region (see Section 163). PSD requirements at present apply to SO_2, particulates, and NO_X.

ii. Specific Requirements Construction of new sources in PSD areas is allowed only if two requirements are met. First, the additional pollution from the new source must not cause the "increments of permissible degradation" to be exceeded for that area. Second, the new source must either keep emissions lower than levels deemed achievable by the application of the best available control technology, or comply through "netting" (reduction of emissions from existing sources at the plant so that there is no net increase in overall emissions from the plant). In contrast to the new source performance standards, which are set on an industry sector basis, the BACT limits are set by EPA or the state in case-by-case (source-by-source) determinations. Cost, energy, technology, and nonair quality environmental effects are all considered in these determinations, but in no case may a BACT standard be less stringent than the NSPS for the applicable industry sector. As with the nonattainment provisions, PSD requirements are pollutant specific. See Section 163. EPA may require BACT limits in PSD areas for pollutants other than those for which NAAQS have been established, as long as the pollutant is not listed or regulated as a hazardous air pol-lutant under Section 112. If the source is designated as a major source (determined by its volume of emissions with respect to *any* regulated pollutant) it is subject to PSD requirements for *all* qualifying emissions, even those that are below 100 tons per year. Table 6.6 depicts PSD requirements in addition to those discussed up to this point.

Table 6.6
NAAQS/§111 Requirements in NAAQS Attainment and Nonattainment Areas + PSD

	NAAQS (§109) Primary and secondary ambient air quality (concentration) standards		NSPS (§111) + Designated Pollutants (§111d) (restrictions placed on individual sources)	
Existing sources	CO, SO_2, NO_X, O_3, particulates (PM_{10}; $PM_{2.5}$), Pb Primary: to protect public health with an adequate margin of safety Secondary: to protect public welfare (implemented through state permitting of preferably continuous emission controls)	**PSD** requirements for SO_2, PM_{10} + NO_X	**Designated Pollutants:** Where no §109 or §112 standard does or would apply, and a performance standard under §111 would be appropriate if the source were new, EPA may set performance standards. Standards now exist for sulfuric acid mist, fluorides, and VOCs (§111d).	
	Additional Nonattainment Requirements: Tiered reductions for CO, O_3, and PM_{10} particulates		**Additional Nonattainment Requirements:** RACT [§172(c)(1)]	
New or modified sources			**NSPS:** Category-wide federal *emission standards* for pollutants based on "best system of emission reduction … adequately demonstrated" [§111(a)(1)] or *a design standard* using the "best *technological* system of continuous emission reduction" [§111(h)(1)]—all enforced through state permits.	**PSD:** (facility-specific) BACT or netting
			Additional Nonattainment Requirements: LAER for major new sources + offsets §171(3)	

c.   The Applicability of the Bubble Policy in Nonattainment and PSD Areas

The authority of EPA to implement its bubble policy in nonattainment and PSD areas was successfully challenged in the D.C. Circuit Court of Appeals, but was ultimately upheld by the Supreme Court.

Chevron U.S.A. Inc. v. Natural Resources Defense Council
Justice STEVENS delivered the opinion of the Court
United States Supreme Court
467 U.S. 837 (1984)

In the Clean Air Act Amendments of 1977, Congress enacted certain requirements applicable to States that had not achieved the national air quality standards established by the Environmental Protection Agency (EPA) pursuant to earlier legislation. The amended Clean Air Act required these "nonattainment" States to establish a permit program regulating "new or modified major stationary sources" of air pollution. Generally, a permit may not be issued for a new or modified major stationary source unless several stringent conditions are met. The EPA regulation promulgated to implement this permit requirement allows a State to adopt a plantwide definition of the term "stationary source."[2] Under this definition, an existing plant that contains several pollution-emitting devices may install or modify one piece of equipment without meeting the permit conditions if the alteration will not increase the total emissions from the plant. The question presented by these cases is whether EPA's decision to allow States to treat all of the pollution-emitting devices within the same industrial grouping as though they were encased within a single "bubble" is based on a reasonable construction of the statutory term "stationary source."

I

The EPA regulations containing the plantwide definition of the term stationary source were promulgated on October 14, 1981. Respondents filed a timely petition for review in the United States Court of Appeals for the District of Columbia Circuit. The Court of Appeals set aside the regulations.

The court observed that the relevant part of the amended Clean Air Act "does not explicitly define what Congress envisioned as a 'stationary source,' to which the permit program . . . should apply," and further stated that the precise issue was not "squarely addressed in the legislative history." In light of its conclusion that the legislative history bearing on the question was "at best contradictory," it reasoned that "the purposes of the non-attainment program should guide our decision here." Based on two of its precedents concerning the applicability of the bubble concept to certain Clean Air Act programs, the court stated that the bubble con-

---

2. "(i) 'Stationary source' means any building, structure, facility, or installation which emits or may emit any air pollutant subject to regulation under the Act.

"(ii) 'Building, structure, facility, or installation' means all of the pollutant-emitting activities which

belong to the same industrial grouping, are located on one or more contiguous or adjacent properties, and are under the control of the same person (or persons under common control) except the activities of any vessel."

cept was "mandatory" in programs designed merely to maintain existing air quality, but held that it was "inappropriate" in programs enacted to improve air quality. Since the purpose of the permit program—its *"raison d'etre,"* in the court's view—was to improve air quality, the court held that the bubble concept was inapplicable in these cases under its prior precedents. It therefore set aside the regulations embodying the bubble concept as contrary to law. We granted certiorari to review that judgment, and we now reverse.

II

...When a court reviews an agency's construction of the statute which it administers, it is confronted with two questions. First, always, is the question whether Congress has directly spoken to the precise question at issue. If the intent of Congress is clear, that is the end of the matter; for the court, as well as the agency, must give effect to the unambiguously expressed intent of Congress. If, however, the court determines Congress has not directly addressed the precise question at issue, the court does not simply impose its own construction on the statute, as would be necessary in the absence of an administrative interpretation. Rather, if the statute is silent or ambiguous with respect to the specific issue, the question for the court is whether the agency's answer is based on a permissible construction of the statute.

"The power of an administrative agency to administer a congressionally created... program necessarily requires the formulation of policy and the making of rules to fill any gap left, implicitly or explicitly, by Congress." If Congress has explicitly left a gap for the agency to fill, there is an express delegation of authority to the agency to elucidate a specific provision of the statute by regulation. Such legislative regulations are given controlling weight unless they are arbitrary, capricious, or manifestly contrary to the statute. Sometimes the legislative delegation to an agency on a particular question is implicit rather than explicit. In such a case, a court may not substitute its own construction of a statutory provision for a reasonable interpretation made by the administrator of an agency.

We have long recognized that considerable weight should be accorded to an executive department's construction of a statutory scheme it is entrusted to administer, and the principle of deference to administrative interpretations has been consistently followed by this Court whenever decision as to the meaning or reach of a statute has involved reconciling conflicting policies, and a full understanding of the force of the statutory policy in the given situation has depended upon more than ordinary knowledge respecting the matters subjected to agency regulations.

"... If this choice represents a reasonable accommodation of conflicting policies that were committed to the agency's care by the statute, we should not disturb it unless it appears from the statute or its legislative history that the accommodation is not one that Congress would have sanctioned."

In light of these well-settled principles it is clear that the Court of Appeals misconceived the nature of its role in reviewing the regulations at issue. Once it determined, after its own examination of the legislation, that Congress did not actually have an intent regarding the applicability of the bubble concept to the permit program, the question before it was not whether in its view the concept is "inappropriate" in the general context of a program designed to improve air quality, but whether the Administrator's view that it is appropriate in the context of this particular program is a reasonable one. Based on the examination of the legislation and its history which follows, we agree with the Court of Appeals that Congress did not have a specific intention on the applicability of the bubble concept in these cases, and conclude that the EPA's use of that concept here is a reasonable policy choice for the agency to make.

III

... Section 111(a) defined the terms that are to be used in setting and enforcing standards of performance for new stationary sources. It provided: "For purposes of this section:..." (3) The term 'stationary source' means any building, structure, facility, or installation which emits or may emit any air pollutant."

In the 1970 Amendments that definition was not only applicable to the NSPS program required by §111, but also was made applicable to a requirement of §110 that each state implementation plan contain a procedure for reviewing the location of any proposed new source and preventing its construction if it would preclude the attainment or maintenance of national air quality standards....

IV

... The Clean Air Act Amendments of 1977 are a lengthy, detailed, technical, complex, and comprehensive response to a major social issue. A small portion of the statute expressly deals with nonattainment areas. The focal point of this controversy is one phrase in that portion of the Amendments.[22]

Basically, the statute required each State in a nonattainment area to prepare and obtain approval of a new SIP...[T]he SIP's were required to contain a number of provisions designed to achieve the goals as expeditiously as possible.

Most significantly for our purposes, the statute provided that each plan shall "(6) require permits for the construction and operation of new or modified major stationary sources in accordance with section 173...."

Before issuing a permit, §173 requires (1) the state agency to determine that there will be sufficient emissions reductions in the region to offset the emissions from the new source and also to allow for reasonable further progress toward attainment, or that the increased emissions will not exceed an allowance for growth established pursuant to §172(b)(5); (2) the applicant to certify that his other sources in the State are in compliance with the SIP, (3) the agency to determine that the applicable SIP is otherwise being implemented, and (4) the proposed source to comply with the lowest achievable emission rate (LAER).[24]

The 1977 Amendments contain no specific reference to the "bubble concept." Nor do they contain a specific definition of the term "stationary source," though they did not disturb the definition of "stationary source" contained in §111(a)(3), applicable by the terms of the Act to the NSPS program. Section 302(j), however, defines the term "major stationary source" as follows: "(j) Except as otherwise expressly provided, the terms 'ma-

---

22. Specifically, the controversy in these cases involves the meaning of the term "major stationary sources."

24. Section 171(3) provides:

"(3) The term 'lowest achievable emission rate' means for any source, that rate of emissions which reflects—

"(A) the most stringent emission limitation which is contained in the implementation plan of any State for such class or category of source, unless the owner or operator of the proposed source demonstrates that such limitations are not achievable, or

"(B) the most stringent emission limitation which is achieved in practice by such class or category of source, whichever is more stringent.

"In no event shall the application of this term permit a proposed new or modified source to emit any pollutant in excess of the amount allowable under applicable new source standards of performance."

The LAER requirement is defined in terms that make it even more stringent than the applicable new source performance standard developed under §111 of the Act, as amended by the 1970 statute.

jor stationary source' and 'major emitting facility' mean any stationary facility or source of air pollutants which directly emits, or has the potential to emit, one hundred tons per year or more of any air pollutant (including any major emitting facility or source of fugitive emissions of any such pollutant, as determined by rule by the Administrator)."

V

The legislative history of the portion of the 1977 Amendments dealing with nonattainment areas does not contain any specific comment on the "bubble concept" or the question whether a plantwide definition of a stationary source is permissible under the permit program. It does, however, plainly disclose that in the permit program Congress sought to accommodate the conflict between the economic interest in permitting capital improvements to continue and the environmental interest in improving air quality....

VI

As previously noted, prior to the 1977 Amendments, the EPA had adhered to a plantwide definition of the term "source" under a NSPS program....

...In April, and again in September 1979, the EPA published additional comments in which it indicated that revised SIP's could adopt the plantwide definition of source in nonattainment areas in certain circumstances. On the latter occasion, the EPA made a formal rulemaking proposal that would have permitted the use of the "bubble concept" for new installations within a plant as well as for modifications of existing units.... The use of offsets inside the same source is called the

"bubble."... Significantly, the EPA expressly noted that the word "source" might be given a plantwide definition for some purposes and a narrower definition for other purposes. It wrote:

"Source means any building structure, facility, or installation which emits or may emit any regulated pollutant. 'Building, structure, facility or installation' means plant in PSD areas and in nonattainment areas except where the growth prohibitions would apply or where no adequate SIP exists or is being carried out."[28]

In August 1980, however... EPA adopted a dual definition of "source" for nonattainment areas that required a permit whenever a change in either the entire plant, or one of its components, would result in a significant increase in emissions even if the increase was completely offset by reductions elsewhere in the plant. The EPA expressed the opinion that this interpretation was "more consistent with congressional intent" than the plantwide definition because it "would bring in more sources or modifications for review,"...

In 1981 a new administration took office and initiated a "Government-wide reexamination of regulatory burdens and complexities." In the context of that review, the EPA reevaluated the various arguments that had been advanced in connection with the proper definition of the term "source" and concluded that the term should be given the same definition in both nonattainment areas and PSD areas.

In explaining its conclusion, the EPA first noted that the definitional issue was not squarely addressed in either the statute or its legislative history and therefore that the issue involved an agency "judgment as how to best carry out the Act." It then set forth several

---

28. In its explanation of why the use of the "bubble concept" was especially appropriate in preventing significant deterioration (PSD) in clean air areas, the EPA stated: "In addition, application of the bubble on a plant-wide basis encourages voluntary upgrading of equipment, and growth in productive capacity."

reasons for concluding that the plantwide definition was more appropriate. It pointed out that the dual definition "can act as a disincentive to new investment and modernization by discouraging modifications to existing facilities" and "can actually retard progress in air pollution control by discouraging replacement of older, dirtier processes or pieces of equipment with new, cleaner ones." Moreover, the new definition "would simplify EPA's rules by using the same definition of 'source' for PSD, nonattainment new source review and the construction moratorium. This reduces confusion and inconsistency." Finally, the agency explained that additional requirements that remained in place would accomplish the fundamental purposes of achieving attainment with NAAQS's as expeditiously as possible. These conclusions were expressed in a proposed rulemaking in August 1981 that was formally promulgated in October.

VII

In this Court, respondents expressly reject the basic rationale of the Court of Appeals' decision. That court viewed the statutory definition of the term "source" as sufficiently flexible to cover either a plantwide definition, a narrower definition covering each unit within a plant, or a dual definition that could apply to both the entire "bubble" and its components. It interpreted the policies of the statute, however, to mandate the plantwide definition in programs designed to maintain clean air and to forbid it in programs designed to improve air quality. Respondents place a fundamentally different construction on the statute. They contend that the text of the Act requires the EPA to use a dual definition—if either a component of a plant, or the plant as a whole, emits over 100 tons of pollutant, it is a major stationary source. They thus contend that the EPA rules adopted in 1980, insofar as they apply to the

maintenance of the quality of clean air, as well as the 1981 rules which apply to nonattainment areas, violate the statute.

Statutory Language

The definition of the term "stationary source" in §111(a)(3) refers to "any building, structure, facility, or installation" which emits air pollution. This definition is applicable only to the NSPS program by the express terms of the statute; the text of the statute does not make this definition applicable to the permit program. Petitioners therefore maintain that there is no statutory language even relevant to ascertaining the meaning of stationary source in the permit program aside from §302(j), which defines the term "major stationary source." We disagree with petitioners on this point.

The definition in §302(j) tells us what the word "major" means—a source must emit at least 100 tons of pollution to qualify—but it sheds virtually no light on the meaning of the term "stationary source." It does equate a source with a facility—a "major emitting facility" and a "major stationary source" are synonymous under §302(j). The ordinary meaning of the term "facility" is some collection of integrated elements which has been designed and constructed to achieve some purpose. Moreover, it is certainly no affront to common English usage to take a reference to a major facility or a major source to connote an entire plant as opposed to its constituent parts. Basically, however, the language of §302(j) simply does not compel any given interpretation of the term "source."

Respondents recognize that, and hence point to §111(a)(3). Although the definition in that section is not literally applicable to the permit program, it sheds as much light on the meaning of the word "source" as anything in the statute. As respondents point out, use of the words "building, structure, facility, or installation," as the definition of source, could be read to impose the permit conditions on an individual building that is a part of a plant.[33]

...We are not persuaded that parsing of general terms in the text of the statute will reveal an actual intent of Congress. We know full well that this language is not dispositive; the terms are overlapping and the language is not precisely directed to the question of the applicability of a given term in the context of a larger operation. To the extent any congressional "intent" can be discerned from this language, it would appear that the listing of overlapping, illustrative terms was intended to enlarge, rather than to confine, the scope of the agency's power to regulate particular sources in order to effectuate the policies of the Act.

Legislative History

In addition, respondents argue that the legislative history and policies of the Act foreclose the plantwide definition, and that the EPA's interpretation is not entitled to deference because it represents a sharp break with prior interpretations of the Act.

Based on our examination of the legislative history, we agree with the Court of Appeals that it is unilluminating.

More importantly, that history plainly identifies the policy concerns that motivated the enactment; the plantwide definition is fully consistent with one of those concerns—the allowance of reasonable economic growth—and, whether or not we believe it most effectively implements the other, we must recognize that the EPA has advanced a reasonable explanation for its conclusion

that the regulations serve the environmental objectives as well. Indeed, its reasoning is supported by the public record developed in the rulemaking process, as well as by certain private studies.[37]

Our review of the EPA's varying interpretations of the word "source"—both before and after the 1977 Amendments—convinces us that the agency primarily responsible for administering this important legislation has consistently interpreted it flexibly—not in a sterile textual vacuum, but in the context of implementing policy decisions in a technical and complex arena. The fact that the agency has from time to time changed its interpretation of the term "source" does not, as respondents argue, lead us to conclude that no deference should be accorded the agency's interpretation of the statute. An initial agency interpretation is not instantly carved in stone. On the contrary, the agency, to engage in informed rulemaking, must consider varying interpretations and the wisdom of its policy on a continuing basis. Moreover, the fact that the agency has adopted different definitions in different contexts adds force to the argument that the definition itself is flexible, particularly since Congress has never indicated any disapproval of a flexible reading of the statute....

Policy

The arguments over policy that are advanced in the parties' briefs create the impression that respondents are now waging in a judicial forum a specific policy battle which they ultimately lost in the agency and in the 32 jurisdictions opting for the "bubble concept," but

---

33. Since the regulations give the States the option to define an individual unit as a source, petitioners do not dispute that the terms can be read as respondents suggest.

37. "Economists have proposed that economic incentives be substituted for the cumbersome administrative-legal framework. The objective is to make the profit and cost incentives that work so

well in the marketplace work for pollution control....[The 'bubble' or 'netting' concept] is a first attempt in this direction. By giving a plant manager flexibility to find the places and processes within a plant that control emissions most cheaply, pollution control can be achieved more quickly and cheaply."

one which was never waged in the Congress. Such policy arguments are more properly addressed to legislators or administrators, not to judges.

In these cases the Administrator's interpretation represents a reasonable accommodation of manifestly competing interests and is entitled to deference: the regulatory scheme is technical and complex, the agency considered the matter in a detailed and reasoned fashion, and the decision involves reconciling conflicting policies. Congress intended to accommodate both interests, but did not do so itself on the level of specificity presented by these cases. Perhaps that body consciously desired the Administrator to strike the balance at this level, thinking that those with great expertise and charged with responsibility for administering the provision would be in a better position to do so; perhaps it simply did not consider the question at this level; and perhaps Congress was unable to forge a coalition on either side of the question, and those on each side decided to take their chances with the scheme devised by the agency. For judicial purposes, it matters not which of these things occurred.

Judges are not experts in the field, and are not part of either political branch of the Government. Courts must, in some cases, reconcile competing political interests, but not on the basis of the judges' personal policy preferences. In contrast, an agency to which Congress has delegated policymaking responsibilities may, within the limits of that delegation, properly rely upon the incumbent administration's views of wise policy to inform its judgments. While agencies are not directly accountable to the people, the Chief Executive is, and it is entirely appropriate for this political branch of the Government to make such policy choices—resolving the competing interests which Congress itself either inadvertently did not resolve, or intentionally left to be resolved by the agency charged with the administration of the statute in light of everyday realities.

When a challenge to an agency construction of a statutory provision, fairly conceptualized, really centers on the wisdom of the agency's policy, rather than whether it is a reasonable choice within a gap left open by Congress, the challenge must fail. In such a case, federal judges—who have no constituency—have a duty to respect legitimate policy choices made by those who do. The responsibilities for assessing the wisdom of such policy choices and resolving the struggle between competing views of the public interest are not judicial ones: Our Constitution vests such responsibilities in the political branches.

We hold that the EPA's definition of the term "source" is a permissible construction of the statute which seeks to accommodate progress in reducing air pollution with economic growth. "The Regulations which the Administrator has adopted provide what the agency could allowably view as...[an] effective reconciliation of these twofold ends...."

The judgment of the Court of Appeals is reversed.

It is so ordered.

Justice MARSHALL and Justice REHNQUIST took no part in the consideration or decision of these cases.

Justice O'CONNOR took no part in the decision of these cases.

■ **NOTES**

1. In footnote 11 of the published case, the Court cautions reviewing courts to defer to "reasonable" agency interpretations of statutory language even when these interpretations are not "the reading the court would have reached." Is this in effect an ab-

dication of the Article III responsibility of the federal judiciary to determine the cases and controversies that come before it? (See discussion of the *"Chevron* deference" concept in chapter 5.)

2. The bubble policy is clearly an attempt by EPA to insert considerations of cost-effectiveness into the implementation of the ambient air quality standards, and it is a mechanism for allowing growth where it otherwise might not be permissible. Further, as the Court observes in footnote 37, the bubble policy allows EPA to utilize economic incentives in the implementation of the act.

3. The bubble concept has given rise to a few related terms of art under the CAA. Bubbles can involve multiplant facilities under common ownership. *Netting*, on the other hand, involves at least *no increase* in emissions from a single plant (using the bubble concept). In contrast, *offsetting* means a significant *net reduction* in emissions—on the order of 20–25%—as a result of trading among facilities. Under some circumstances, offsetting may be permitted within the same source or among commonly controlled sources, but the use of the bubble must always result in a net reduction in pollution in nonattainment areas. *Banking* is a related concept allowing states or firms to accumulate (and then sell or use) unused emission reduction credits (e.g., from plants going out of business) for offsetting pollution from future new sources or sources in the future. However, banking may have been restricted by limitations on the use of "old growth allowances" in the 1990 CAAA. See Section 173(b); J. Gordon Arbuckle, G. William Frick, Marshall Lee Miller, Thomas F. P. Sullivan, and Timothy A. Vanderver (1979) *Environmental Law Handbook*, 6th ed. Government Institutes, Washington, D.C., p. 546, footnote 48.   ∎

3. Visibility Protection

As part of its nondegradation policy, EPA has developed a policy to preserve the visual aesthetics in national parks (class I areas). EPA adopted a "phased" approach to protecting visibility. Phase I is aimed at reducing visibility impairment that is attributable to a particular source (known as "reasonably attributable" impairment) through the application of best available retrofit technology (BART) and a long-term strategy. Phase II is intended to address regional haze. Under the phase I controls, adopted in 1980, most states were required to revise their implementation plans to ensure that visibility is protected. In determining emissions reductions required for individual sources—both new and existing—these states were to consider the economic, energy, and environmental costs of compliance, the remaining useful life of existing sources, and the environmental benefits of compliance. As with other aspects of the SIP, if the states do not implement the required controls, EPA may take over the SIP. This happened in Arizona, and a challenge to the resultant EPA regulations put the agency's visibility policy to the test.

Central Arizona Water Conservation District v. United States Environmental Protection Agency
GOODWIN, Circuit Judge
990 F.2d 1531 (9th Cir. 1993)

I. BACKGROUND

This case involves regulations promulgated by EPA in an attempt to remedy, at least partially, visibility impairment at the Grand Canyon. In a final rule entitled "Approval and Promulgation of Implementation Plans: Revision of the Visibility FIP for Arizona," EPA required a 90% reduction in SO_2 emissions at NGS, a power plant situated approximately twelve miles from the Grand Canyon, near Page, Arizona. The Final Rule limits SO_2 emissions from NGS to 0.10 pound per million British thermal units (lb/MMBtu), with an estimated 7% winter average visibility improvement in the Grand Canyon. The estimated cost of the improvement, following an initial capital cost estimated at $430 million, is $89.6 million per year....

A.   Regulatory Framework

1.   The Clean Air Act, Visibility Impairment, and the Grand Canyon

In 1977, Congress substantially amended the Clean Air Act (the "Act"). Included in the 1977 amendments was section 169A, which declared "as a national goal the prevention of any future, and the remedying of any existing, impairment of visibility in mandatory class I Federal areas which impairment results from manmade air pollution." Congress required EPA to promulgate regu-

lations to assure "reasonable progress toward meeting this national goal." EPA was further directed to require each state with a class I Federal area to revise its state implementation plan ("SIP") "to contain such emission limits, schedules of compliance and other measures as may be necessary to make reasonable progress toward meeting the national goal." Measures for achieving "reasonable progress" generally include best available retrofit technology ("BART")[4] and a long-term strategy. 42 U.S.C. §§7491(b)(2)(A), (B). If an individual state fails to fulfill its obligations under the Act, EPA is directed to take such measures as are required to achieve "reasonable progress" pursuant to a federal implementation plan ("FIP") under section 110(c) of the Act.

The Act defines class I Federal areas as international parks, national wilderness areas or memorial parks which exceed 5,000 acres in size, and national parks which exceed 6,000 acres in size. The Grand Canyon has been classified as a class I Federal area. Congress recorded its concern with the visibility impairment at the Grand Canyon caused by NGS.

2.   EPA's 1980 Regulations

In 1980, EPA promulgated visibility regulations under section 169A of the Act. The regulations adopted a "phased approach to visibility protection." Phase I was directed at controlling visibility impairment "that can be

---

4. The regulations provide the following definition of BART: Best Available Retrofit Technology (BART) means an emission limitation based on the degree of reduction achievable through the application of the best system of continuous emission reduction for each pollutant which is emitted by an existing stationary facility. The emission limitation must be established, on a case-by-case basis, taking into consideration the technology available, the costs of compliance, the energy and nonair quality environmental impacts of compliance, any pollution control equipment in use or in existence at the source, the remaining useful life of the source, and the degree of improvement in visibility which may reasonably be anticipated to result from the use of such technology.

traced to a single existing stationary facility or small group of existing stationary facilities." EPA refers to this type of impairment as "reasonably attributable" impairment. EPA deferred addressing other types of impairment such as "regional haze" for future phases due to the heightened complexity and the scientific and technical limitations inherent in attempts to identify, measure, and control such broadscale visibility impairment.

Generally, EPA's "Phase I" regulations require affected states to coordinate the development of SIPs with the appropriate Federal land managers, to develop programs to assess and remedy visibility impairment from new and existing sources, and to develop a long-term strategy to assure reasonable progress toward section 169A's national visibility goal. The regulations specifically require states to identify those existing sources "which may reasonably be anticipated to cause or contribute" to any visibility impairment which is "reasonably attributable to that existing stationary facility." Once the source is identified, the affected state is required to take such measures as are required to attain "reasonable progress"; such measures generally include determination of emissions limitations for that source under BART and the development of a long-term strategy.

The regulations define the term "visibility impairment" as "any humanly perceptible change in visibility (visual range, contrast, coloration) from that which would have existed under natural conditions." The term "reasonably attributable" is defined as "attributable by visual observation or any other technique the State deems appropriate." The states, or EPA under §7910(c), thus have broad discretion in determining how and whether impairment may be attributed to an individual source.

B. Prior Proceedings and the Rulemaking History

In its implementation of Phase I, EPA required all states containing class I Federal areas to submit revised visibility SIPs within a nine-month period. Arizona was one of thirty-five states failing to submit a revised SIP to EPA. In 1982, the Environmental Defense Fund and other environmental groups brought a citizen suit against EPA to compel performance of the agency's nondiscretionary duty under §7410(c)(1)(A) to promulgate visibility FIPs when states fail to submit SIPs pursuant to the 1980 regulations. The parties reached a settlement agreement which the court approved in an April 20, 1984 consent decree. This consent decree required EPA to review existing SIPs for deficiencies and allow states to cure those deficiencies. If states remained deficient, the consent decree required EPA to issue visibility FIPs.

The Department of Interior subsequently certified the existence of visibility impairment in all class I Federal areas, and specifically declared NGS as a probable source of impairment at the Grand Canyon. Following this certification, the National Park Service ("Park Service") conducted the Winter Haze Intensive Tracer Experiment ("WHITEX"), a winter visibility attribution study. In part, WHITEX involved the release from NGS of a unique "tracer" gas, CD4; because CD4 is not found in the ambient air, its use "fingerprinted" NGS emissions when detected downwind.

In November 1987, EPA disapproved the SIPs of twenty-nine states, including Arizona, for failing to comply with the visibility regulations. Over the next few years, EPA further investigated visibility impairment at Grand Canyon and other class I Federal areas. While acting on many of the areas, EPA delayed action on the Grand Canyon to allow the Park Service time to analyze the data obtained from the WHITEX study. The Park Service issued an April 1989 draft report which attributed to NGS 70% of the sulfates in the Grand Canyon during the WHITEX experiment period.

Relying on the Park Service's April 1989 draft report, EPA preliminarily attributed to NGS several episodes of wintertime visibility impairment at the Grand Canyon. EPA solicited public comment on the merits of its preliminary attribution finding, and began the informal rulemaking process to determine the appropriate action to be taken.

... In the Final Rule, dated October 3, 1991, EPA issued its final determination that certain visibility impairment episodes at the Grand Canyon were "traceable to NGS and that NGS is a dominant contributor to certain visibility impairment episodes," and promulgated revisions to the Arizona visibility FIP to address the impairment. The revisions adopted a regulatory approach consistent with the memorandum of understanding's proposal, reducing SO_2 emissions 90% to a level of 0.10 lb/MMBtu. EPA determined that this approach would more adequately achieve "reasonable progress" toward the national visibility goal under section 169A(b)(2) of the Act, than would the alternative provided by BART analysis. As required by section 307(d) of the Act, EPA's action was "accompanied by a response to each of the significant comments, criticisms, and new data submitted in written or oral presentations during the comment period." ...

IV.   DISCUSSION

. . .

B.   The Final Rule as the Product of "Reasoned Decisionmaking"

Petitioners proffer various arguments that the Final Rule is not the product of "reasoned decisionmaking." They assert that EPA has acted arbitrarily and capriciously by overestimating the improvements in visibility expected from the Final Rule's emission controls at NGS, by purportedly failing to address criticisms to the scientific data and analyses on which it relied, and by allegedly ignoring certain evidence while placing undue reliance on other evidence. At bottom, however, Petitioners' real complaint appears to be that the Final Rule will most likely lead to minimal visibility improvement at the Grand Canyon while imposing a substantial financial burden on them. Nonetheless, we find unsupported Petitioners' legal claim that EPA acted arbitrarily and capriciously in promulgating the Final Rule. The Final Rule makes "reasonable progress" toward the national goal of remedying visibility impairment at the Grand Canyon, and is the product of reasoned decisionmaking.

1.   The Final Rule as "Reasonable Progress" toward the National Goal of Remedying Visibility Impairment at the Grand Canyon

In reviewing whether the agency's action in promulgating the Final Rule was arbitrary and capricious, this court "is not to substitute its judgment for that of the agency." Instead, we inquire whether the agency has "examined the relevant data and articulated a satisfactory explanation for its action, including a 'rational connection between the facts found and the choice made.'" In this case, the relevant factors are provided by Congress's definition of "reasonable progress" in §7491(g)(1). Additionally, as the D.C. Circuit recently noted in discussing a similar provision of the Act, "because Congress did not assign the specific weight the Administrator should accord each of these factors, the Administrator is free to exercise his discretion in this area."[10]

a.   The "Reasonable Progress" Provisions
In the Act, Congress directed EPA to promulgate regulations to assure "reasonable

---

10. Petitioners incorrectly suggest that EPA was required to engage in "cost-benefit" analysis. Congress has not required "cost-benefit" analysis in the Act. *Cf. American Textile Mfrs. Inst., Inc. v. Dono-* *van*, 452 U.S. 490 (1981) ("When Congress has intended that an agency engage in cost-benefit analysis, it has clearly indicated such intent on the face of the statute.").

progress toward meeting the national goal" of preventing future, and remedying existing visibility impairment in Class I federal areas like the Grand Canyon. Congress chose not to define the term "reasonable progress," but instead set forth several factors for the agency to consider:

In determining reasonable progress there shall be taken into consideration the costs of compliance, the time necessary for compliance, and the energy and nonair quality environmental impacts of compliance, and the remaining useful life of any existing source subject to such requirements[.]

In promulgating the Final Rule, EPA relied on the "reasonable progress" provisions as its statutory authority.

Generally, the Act and its regulations require the application of BART once it has been determined that visibility impairment is "reasonably attributable" to an existing source like NGS. Under the unique circumstances of this case, however, EPA chose not to adopt the emission control limits indicated by BART analysis, but instead to adopt an emission limitations standard that would produce greater visibility improvement at a lower cost. Congress's use of the term "including" in §7491(b)(2) prior to its listing BART as a method of attaining "reasonable progress" supports EPA's position that it has the discretion to adopt implementation plan provisions other than those provided by BART analyses in situations where the agency reasonably concludes that more "reasonable progress" will thereby be attained. Since the Act itself is ambiguous on the specific issue, we apply the Supreme Court's deferential standard from *Chevron* and hold that the agency's reliance on the "reasonable progress" provisions is a "permissible construction of the statute," since "reasonable

progress" is the overarching requirement that implementation plan revisions under §7491(b)(2) must address.

b. EPA Reasonably Considered the Relevant Factors The administrative record reveals that EPA adequately considered the relevant factors in promulgating the Final Rule.[11] Petitioners' essential argument does not claim that EPA failed to consider the relevant factors, but instead contends that EPA erred in its consideration of those factors. This court is not to substitute Petitioners' judgment, or its own, for that of EPA, as long as the agency's interpretation is reasonable. In fact, this is just the type of case in which the Supreme Court has stated that judicial review should "be at its most deferential," because the agency is "making predictions, within its area of special expertise, at the frontiers of science." We therefore find that the agency's interpretation of the evidence, and its weighing of the relevant factors, are reasonable, and that the Final Rule is the product of "reasoned decisionmaking." ...

V. CONCLUSION

In the final analysis, Petitioners simply adhere to a different interpretation of the rather disparate and equivocal scientific data in the record. While Petitioners may not be satisfied with EPA's responses, it is not EPA's duty to satisfy all of the concerns of potentially affected or aggrieved parties. EPA conducted an extensive and involved notice and comment period, and adequately met its statutory obligation of responding to significant comments and criticisms under §7607(d)(6)(B). Notwithstanding Petitioners' challenge, the Final Rule is the result of a site-specific informal rulemaking process that included

---

11. Actually, EPA not only considered the "reasonable progress" factors, but also considered expected visibility improvement under the Final Rule, as required by BART analysis.

virtually unprecedented cooperation between the governmental agency and the directly affected parties. Petitioners' arguments afford no reason for this court disruptively to interject itself into the picture. Because Congress delegated to EPA the power to "regulate on the borders of the unknown," this court will not interfere with the agency's "reasonable interpretations of equivocal evidence." Even if this case highlights how hard it is to engage in "reasoned decisionmaking" in cases involving scientific uncertainty, EPA's actions in promulgating the Final Rule were reasonable and within the bounds of its statutory authority, and not arbitrary and capricious.

The Districts' petition for review and motion to supplement the administrative record are accordingly DENIED.

■ **NOTE**

1. This case is yet another example of the many attempts to impose the cost-benefit criterion on EPA's administration of the CAA, and of the corresponding insistence by the courts that unless Congress has authorized cost-benefit analysis, it is not permitted (see footnote 10 in the case).   ■

In 2005, in response to a consent agreement with Environmental Defense, EPA promulgated a regulation known as The Clean Air Act Visibility Rule (40 C.F.R. §51). This rule aims to reduce emissions by a total of one million tons a year in 156 parks and nature or wilderness areas by requiring power plants and other sources that contribute to haze in those areas to meet emission limitations based on BART. The rule also exempts from this requirement power plants located in those areas (28 states and the District of Columbia) covered by the Clean Air Interstate Rule (CAIR), the allowance-trading rule for ozone and fine particulates discussed earlier. According to EPA, CAIR will achieve greater reductions in haze-forming nitrogen oxide and sulfur dioxide emissions from power plants than would the visibility rule. Nonetheless, some fear that buying up pollution reduction credits will slow the achievement of haze reductions in their area. See *Environment Reporter* 36(28): 1446 (2005).

4. Acid Rain Controls and the SO₂ Allowance Trading System

Acid rain is created by the hydrolysis (addition of water) to SO_2 and NO_X, usually involving oxidation as well, resulting in sulfurous, sulfuric, nitrous, and nitric acids. In addition to causing subsequent acidification of rain and receiving waters, acid aerosols contribute to serious lung damage. The 1990 CAA amendments require significant reduction in both SO_2 and NO_X emissions. The 1990 amendments set a national ceiling on SO_2 emissions from power plants and require a nearly 40% reduction (amounting to a 10-million-ton reduction from 1980 levels) by 2010 in two phases: 1995–1999 and 2000 and beyond. Of this reduction, 8.5 million tons are to come from power plants. The 1990 amendments also call for a 2-million-ton reduction in NO_X emissions by 2010, representing a 10% reduction from 1980 levels.

A noteworthy feature of the reduction program for SO_2 is that it incorporates an allowance trading system. Allowances are allocated to owners of affected units free of charge for 30 years, generally in proportion to each unit's average annual heat input during the baseline period of 1985–1987. A small percentage of the allowances allocated to affected units are withheld for sale through an annual auction conducted by EPA to encourage trading and to ensure that some allowances will be available for new generating units. Allowances not used in the year for which they are allocated can be sold or banked for future use by the original owner or by any party to whom the banked allowance is sold. Under this system, affected sources are permitted to trade their SO_2 emission allowances. Rather than employ expensive pollution reduction measures, high-cost pollution abaters can purchase reduction credits from low-cost abaters who abate more than they are required to by law. This results in a total lower cost of pollution abatement. (See chapter 12 and the sources cited there for an evaluation of the SO_2 trading program; see chapters 3 and 12 for a discussion of pollution trading generally.)

The Clean Air Act does not contain a similar authorization for trading NO_X emission allowances. However, NO_X emissions may be reduced in lieu of VOC reductions in certain ozone nonattainment areas if that approach is effective in reducing ozone concentrations. See the discussion of the Northeastern NO_x Budget Program in A. Denny Ellerman (2003) "Are Cap and Trade Programs More Effective in Meeting Environmental Goals than Command-and Control Alternatives?" at http://web.mit.edu/ceepr/www/2003-015.pdf. Also available in *Moving to Markets in Environmental Regulation: Lessons from Twenty Years of Experience*, Jody Freeman and Charles Kolstad (eds.), Oxford University Press, 2006.

■ NOTES

1. As discussed earlier, EPA's Clean Air Interstate Rule calls for a 65% reduction in NO_X emissions and a 70% reduction in SO_2 from coal-fired power plants by 2015, to be achieved through cap-and-trade provisions. Both pollutants contribute to the formation of acid rain. As discussed later in this chapter, the agency has also proposed to employ the cap-and-trade concept to mercury emissions. Because mercury is a highly toxic pollutant, however, this has engendered considerable controversy. (Ironically, sulfates in acid rain have been found to speed up the production of methyl mercury, which bioaccumulates in fish and then may lead to human exposure.

Environmental Science and Technology Online: http://pubs.acs.org/subscribe/journals/esthag-w/2006/may/science/nl-methylmercury.html.)

2. A GAO report issued in 1997 found that trading had reduced compliance costs and emissions. *Air Pollution: Overview and Issues on Emissions Allowance Trading Programs*. GAO/RCED-97-183, GAO, Washington, D.C. See also R. Schmalensee, P. Joskow, A. D. Ellerman, and J. P. Montero (1998) "Emission Trading Under the US Acid Rain Program: Evaluation of Compliance Costs and Allowance Market Performance," Center for Energy and Environmental Policy Research MIT. For a more recent evaluation, see A. Danny Ellerman (2003). See James Salzman and Barton Thompson, Jr. (2003) *Environmental Law and Policy*. Foundation Press, New York, ch. 4, section D, for a descriptive treatment of the workings of the trading system.   ■

5. Emission Standards for Hazardous Air Pollutants

a. Section 112 before the 1990 Amendments

In crafting the 1970 Clean Air Act, Congress distinguished between the criteria pollutants and a set of other, more hazardous air pollutants. These latter pollutants, Congress determined, were sufficiently dangerous to preclude any reliance on atmospheric dispersion and mixing as a means of reducing their ambient concentrations. Local "hot spots" (pockets of high concentrations of these pollutants) were deemed to pose a serious threat to public health. Thus, in Section 112, Congress directed the EPA administrator to set national emission standards for hazardous air pollutants (NESHAPS) at a level that protects public health "with an ample margin of safety." This phraseology reflected an early assumption that although they were very dangerous, hazardous pollutants exhibited a finite threshold (a nonzero level of exposure below which no harm would occur). As the 1970s progressed, however, there was a growing recognition that this assumption might be wrong, and that for many hazardous pollutants there was no level of exposure (at least at levels within the limits of detection) below which one could confidently predict that no harmful or irreversible effects (especially cancer or birth defects) would occur.

This presented an implementation challenge for EPA. Arguably, given its mandate to protect public health "with an ample margin of safety," the agency might have been required to ban the *emissions* of several hazardous substances. This would as a practical matter essentially ban the *use* of these substances in many industries, although an alternative view was that the agency would have been required only to prohibit any detectable level of the substance. Seeking to avoid having to ban the use of many widely used chemicals, EPA adopted a policy of setting Section 112 emission standards at the level that could be achieved by available technology.[5] Using this approach, EPA set finite (nonzero) standards for arsenic, asbestos, benzene, beryllium, coke-oven emissions, mercury, vinyl chloride, and radionuclides. The standard-setting process was slow and had to be forced by litigation; the agency took 4 to 7 years to establish a final standard for each of these substances. Had EPA continued to set standards for other substances, and had it used the technological feasibility approach to spur the development of cleaner technology, the environmental groups may well have been content to allow the implementation of Section 112 to proceed in this fashion. When the setting of new Section 112 standards all but stalled during the Reagan administration, however, the Natural Resources Defense Council decided to press the issue in court.

Natural Resources Defense Council, Inc. v. Environmental Protection Agency
BORK, Circuit Judge
824 F.2d 1146 (D.C. Cir. 1987)

Current scientific knowledge does not permit a finding that there is a completely safe level of human exposure to carcinogenic agents. The Administrator of the Environmental Protection Agency, however, is charged with regulating hazardous pollutants, including carcinogens, under section 112 of the Clean Air Act by setting emission standards "at the level which in his judgment provides an ample margin of safety to protect the public health." §7412(b)(1)(B). We address here the question of the extent of the Administrator's authority under this delegation in setting emission standards for carcinogenic pollutants.

Petitioner Natural Resources Defense Council ("NRDC") contends that the Administrator must base a decision under section 112 exclusively on health-related factors and, therefore, that the uncertainty about the effect of carcinogenic agents requires the Administrator to prohibit all emissions. The Administrator argues that in the face of this

uncertainty he is authorized to set standards that require emission reduction to the lowest level attainable by best available control technology whenever that level is below that at which harm to humans has been demonstrated. We find no support for either position in the language or legislative history of the Clean Air Act. We therefore grant the petition for review and remand to the Administrator for reconsideration in light of this opinion.

I

Section 112 of the Clean Air Act provides for regulation of hazardous air pollutants, which the statute defines as "air pollutant[s] to which no ambient air quality standard is applicable and which in the judgment of the Administrator cause, or contribute to, air pollution which may reasonably be anticipated to result in an increase in mortality or

5. This was the approach then followed by the Occupational Safety and Health Administration in setting standards for exposure to workplace chemicals. In the case of carcinogens, at that time OSHA considered no levels to be safe, and established control requirements at the limit of technological and economic feasibility. OSHA's statutory mandate, which requires such standards to be based on considerations of technological and economic feasibility, facilitated this approach.

an increase in serious irreversible, or incapacitating reversible, illness." §7412(a)(1). The statute requires the Administrator to publish a list containing each hazardous pollutant for which he intends to adopt an emission standard, to publish proposed regulations and a notice of public hearing for each such pollutant, and then, within a specified period, either to promulgate an emission standard or to make a finding that the particular agent is not a hazardous air pollutant. *See* §7412(b)(1)(B). The statute directs the Administrator to set an emission standard promulgated under section 112 "at the level which in his judgment provides an ample margin of safety to protect the public health."

This case concerns vinyl chloride regulations. Vinyl chloride is a gaseous synthetic chemical used in the manufacture of plastics and is a strong carcinogen. In late 1975, the Administrator issued a notice of proposed rulemaking to establish an emission standard for vinyl chloride. In the notice, the EPA asserted that available data linked vinyl chloride to carcinogenic, as well as some noncarcinogenic, disorders and that "reasonable extrapolations" from this data suggested "that present ambient levels of vinyl chloride may cause or contribute to...[such] disorders." The EPA also noted that vinyl chloride is "an apparent non-threshold pollutant," which means that it appears to create a risk to health at all non-zero levels of emission. Scientific uncertainty, due to the unavailability of dose-response data and the twenty-year latency period between initial exposure to vinyl chloride and the occurrence of disease, makes it impossible to establish any definite threshold level below which there are no adverse effects to human health. The notice also stated the "EPA's position that for a carcinogen it should be assumed, in the absence of strong evidence to the contrary, that there is no atmospheric concentration that poses absolutely no public health risk."

Because of this assumption, the EPA concluded that it was faced with two alternative interpretations of its duty under section 112. First, the EPA determined that section 112 might require a complete prohibition of emissions of non-threshold pollutants because a "zero emission limitation would be the only emission standard which would offer absolute safety from ambient exposure." The EPA found this alternative "neither desirable nor necessary" because "complete prohibition of all emissions could require closure of an entire industry," a cost the EPA found "extremely high for elimination of a risk to health that is of unknown dimensions."

The EPA stated the second alternative as follows:

An alternative interpretation of section 112 is that it authorizes setting emission standards that require emission reduction to the lowest level achievable by use of the best available control technology in cases involving apparent non-threshold pollutants, where complete emission prohibition would result in widespread industry closure and EPA has determined that the cost of such closure would be grossly disproportionate to the benefits of removing the risk that would remain after imposition of the best available control technology.

The EPA adopted this alternative on the belief that it would "produce the most stringent regulation of hazardous air pollutants short of requiring a complete prohibition in all cases."

On October 21, 1976, the EPA promulgated final emission standards for vinyl chloride which were based solely on the level attainable by the best available control technology. The EPA determined that this standard would reduce unregulated emissions by 95 percent. With respect to the effect of the standard on health, the EPA stated that it had assessed the risk to health at ambient levels of exposure by extrapolating from dose-response data at higher levels of exposure and then made the following findings:

EPA found that the rate of initiation of liver angiosarcoma among [the 4.6 million] people living around uncontrolled plants is expected to range from less than one to ten cases of liver angiosarcoma per year of exposure to vinyl chloride.... Vinyl chloride is also estimated to produce an equal number of primary cancers at other sites, for a total of somewhere between less than one and twenty cases of cancer per year of exposure among residents around plants. The number of these effects is expected to be reduced at least in proportion to the reduction in the ambient annual average vinyl chloride concentration, which is expected to be 5 percent of the uncontrolled levels after the standard is implemented.

The EPA did not state whether this risk to health is significant or not. Nor did the EPA explain the relationship between this risk to health and its duty to set an emission standard which will provide an "ample margin of safety."

The Environmental Defense Fund ("EDF") filed suit challenging the standard on the ground that section 112 requires the Administrator to rely exclusively on health and prohibits consideration of cost and technology. The EDF and the EPA settled the suit, however, upon the EPA's agreement to propose new and more stringent standards for vinyl chloride and to establish an ultimate goal of zero emissions.

The EPA satisfied its obligations under the settlement agreement by proposing new regulations on June 2, 1977. While the proposal sought to impose more strict regulation by requiring sources subject to a 10 parts per million ("ppm") limit to reduce emissions to 5 ppm, and by establishing an aspirational goal of zero emissions, the EPA made it clear that it considered its previous regulations valid and reemphasized its view that the inability scientifically to identify a threshold of adverse effects did not require prohibition of all emissions, but rather permitted regulation at the level of best available technology. The EPA received comments on the proposal, but took no final action for more than seven years. On January 9, 1985, the EPA withdrew the proposal. Noting that certain aspects of the proposed regulations imposed "unreason-

able" costs and that no control technology "has been demonstrated to significantly and consistently reduce emissions to a level below that required by the current standard," the EPA concluded that it should abandon the 1977 proposal and propose in its place only minor revisions to the 1976 regulations.

This petition for review followed....

III

The NRDC's challenge to the EPA's withdrawal of the 1977 amendments is simple: because the statute adopts an exclusive focus on considerations of health, the Administrator must set a zero level of emissions when he cannot determine that there is a level below which no harm will occur....

Section 112 commands the Administrator to set an "emission standard" for a particular "hazardous air pollutant" which in his "judgment" will provide an "ample margin of safety." Congress' use of the term "ample margin of safety" is inconsistent with the NRDC's position that the Administrator has no discretion in the fac[e] of uncertainty. The statute nowhere defines "ample margin of safety." The Senate Report, however, in discussing a similar requirement in the context of setting ambient air standards under section 109 of the Act, explained the purpose of the "margin of safety" standard as one of affording "a *reasonable* degree of protection... against hazards which research has not yet identified." (emphasis added). This view comports with the historical use of the term in engineering as "a safety factor... meant to compensate for uncertainties and variabilities." Furthermore, in a discussion of the use of identical language in the Federal Water Pollution Control Act, this court has recognized that, in discharging the responsibility to assure "an ample margin of safety," the Administrator faces "a difficult task, indeed, a veritable paradox—calling as it does for knowledge of that which is unknown—

[but]...the term 'margin of safety' is Congress's directive that means be found to carry out the task and to reconcile the paradox." And while Congress used the modifier "ample" to exhort the Administrator not to allow "the public [or] the environment...to be exposed to anything resembling the maximum risk" and, therefore, to set a margin "greater than 'normal' or 'adequate'," Congress still left the EPA "great latitude in meeting its responsibility."

Congress' use of the word "safety," moreover, is significant evidence that it did not intend to require the Administrator to prohibit all emissions of non-threshold pollutants. As the Supreme Court has recently held, "safe" does not mean "risk-free." *Industrial Union Dep't. AFL-CIO v. American Petroleum Inst.*, 448 U.S. 607, 642, 65 L. Ed. 2d 1010, 100 S. Ct. 2844 (1980). Instead, something is "unsafe" only when it threatens humans with "a significant risk of harm."

Thus, the terms of section 112 provide little support for the NRDC's position. The uncertainty about the effects of a particular carcinogenic pollutant invokes the Administrator's discretion under section 112. In contrast, the NRDC's position would eliminate any discretion and would render the standard "ample margin of safety" meaningless as applied to carcinogenic pollutants.[1] Whenever *any* scientific uncertainty existed about the ill effects of a nonzero level of hazardous air pollutants—and we think it unlikely that science will ever yield *absolute* certainty of safety in an area so complicated and rife with problems of measurement, modeling, long latency, and the like—the Administrator would have no discretion but would be required to prohibit all emissions. Had Congress intended that result, it could very easily have said so by writing a statute that states that no level of emissions shall be allowed as to which there is any uncertainty. But Congress chose instead to deal with the pervasive nature of scientific uncertainty and the inherent limitations of scientific knowledge by vesting in the Administrator the discretion to deal with uncertainty in each case.

The NRDC also argues that the legislative history supports its position. To the contrary, that history strongly suggests that Congress did not require the Administrator to prohibit emissions of all non-threshold pollutants; Congress considered and rejected the option of requiring the Administrator to prohibit all emissions....

The only arguable support for the NRDC's position is a passage in the summary of the provisions of the conference agreement attached to Senator Muskie's statement during the post-conference debate on the Clean Air Act:

The standards must be set to provide an ample margin of safety to protect the public health. This could mean, effectively, that a plant could be required to close because of the absence of control techniques. It could include emission standards which allow for no *measurable* emissions, [emphasis added].

...To accept the petitioner's contention that section 112 *requires* the Administrator to prohibit all emissions of non-threshold pollutants, we would have to conclude that, without even discussing the matter, Congress mandated massive economic and social dislocations by shutting down entire industries. That is not a reasonable way to read the legislative history....It is simply not possible that Congress intended such havoc in the American economy and not a single representative or senator mentioned the fact....

IV

We turn now to the question whether the Administrator's chosen method for setting emission levels above zero is consistent with congressional intent. The Administrator's position is that he may set an emission level for

---

1. With the exception of mercury, every pollutant the Administrator has listed or intends to list under §112 is a non-threshold carcinogen....

non-threshold pollutants at the lowest level achievable by best available control technology when that level is anywhere below the level of demonstrated harm and the cost of setting a lower level is grossly disproportionate to the benefits of removing the remaining risk. The NRDC argues that this standard is arbitrary and capricious because the EPA is never permitted to consider cost and technological feasibility under section 112 but instead is limited to consideration of health-based factors. Thus, before addressing the Administrator's method of using cost and technological feasibility in this case, we must determine whether he may consider cost and technological feasibility at all.

A

On its face, section 112 does not indicate that Congress intended to preclude consideration of any factor. Though the phrase "to protect the public health" evinces an intent to make health the primary consideration, there is no indication of the factors the Administrator may or may not consider in determining, in his "judgment," what level of emissions will provide "an ample margin of safety." Instead, the language used, and the absence of any specific limitation, gives the clear impression that the Administrator has some discretion in determining what, if any, additional factors he will consider in setting an emission standard.

B

The petitioner argues that the legislative history makes clear Congress' intent to foreclose reliance on non-health-based considerations in setting standards under section 112....
... The legislative history is simply ambiguous with respect to the question of whether the Administrator may permissibly consider cost and technological feasibility under section 112.... The resulting standard neither

permits nor prohibits consideration of any factor. Thus, we cannot find a clear congressional intent in the language, structure, or legislative history of the Act to preclude consideration of cost and technological feasibility under section 112.

C

The petitioner argues next that a finding that section 112 does not preclude consideration of cost and technological feasibility would render the Clean Air Act structurally incoherent and would be inconsistent with the Supreme Court's interpretation of section 110 of the Act, *see Union Electric Co. v. EPA*, 427 U.S. 246 (1976), and this court's interpretation of section 109 of the Act, *see Lead Indus. Ass'n. v. EPA*, 647 F.2d 1130 (D.C. Cir. 1980), as precluding consideration of these factors. We do not believe that our decision here is inconsistent with either the holding or the statutory interpretation in either case.

First, as discussed below, the court in each case rejected an argument that the EPA must consider cost and technological feasibility as factors equal in importance to health. We reject the same argument here. In this case, however, we must also address the question of whether the Administrator may consider these factors if necessary to further *protect* the public health. This issue was not addressed in either *Union Electric* or *Lead Industries*.

Second, these decisions do not provide precedential support for the petitioner's position that, as a matter of statutory interpretation, cost and technological feasibility may never be considered under the Clean Air Act unless Congress expressly so provides. In each case there was some indication in the language, structure, or legislative history of the specific provision at issue that Congress intended to preclude consideration of cost and technological feasibility. As discussed

above, we find no such indication with respect to section 112.[4]

In *Union Electric*, the Court addressed the
issue of whether the Administrator could reject a state implementation plan submitted
for approval under section 110 of the Clean
Air Act on the ground that the plan was not
economically or technologically feasible. The
Court noted that section 110 sets out eight
criteria that a state plan must meet and further provides that if these criteria are met,
and if the state adopted the plan after notice
and a hearing, the Administrator "shall" approve the plan. The Court then held that "the
mandatory 'shall' makes it quite clear that

the Administrator is not to be concerned
with factors other than those specified,... and
none of the eight factors appears to permit
consideration of technological or economic
infeasibility." In a footnote to this statement,
the Court found its position bolstered by
a "comparison of the eight criteria of
§110(a)(2)" with other provisions of the Act
which expressly permit consideration of cost
and technological feasibility. The Court concluded that "where Congress intended the
Administrator to be concerned about economic and technological infeasibility, it
expressly so provided." We simply do not, as
the NRDC does, read these statements

---

4. The NRDC also argues that the structure of §112
itself supports its contention; Congress expressed a
clear intent to preclude consideration of cost and
technological feasibility in setting an emission standard under §112(b)(1) by specifically directing the
EPA to consider these factors in three other subsections of §112. These provisions, the NRDC contends, would be superfluous if the EPA could
consider cost and technological feasibility in setting
an emission standard under §112(b)(1).

The NRDC's argument fails because the cited
provisions continue to have significance if the
Administrator is permitted to consider cost and
technological feasibility under §112(b)(1). Section
112(c)(1)(B)(ii) authorizes the EPA to grant an
existing source a waiver from an emission standard
for up to two years if "necessary for the installation
of controls." This provision could be utilized to
grant a waiver to a source that is not able to comply with a standard which was based upon cost and
technological feasibility because it does not have
the appropriate control technology.

Section 112(c)(2) allows the President to exempt
any stationary source from emission standards "if
he finds that the technology to implement such
standards is not available and the operation of
such source is required for reasons of national security." This provision would be necessary if the
Administrator considered cost and technological
feasibility in setting an emission level for non-
threshold pollutants and then set the level below
that achievable by the best available control technology because the balance favored the elimination
of the risk. This provision would also be necessary
when the known threshold level for a hazardous

pollutant is below the level that current technology
can attain.

Finally, §112(e) authorizes the EPA to set a "design, equipment, work practice, or operational
standard" if in the Administrator's judgment "it is
not feasible to prescribe or enforce an emission
standard for control of a hazardous air pollutant."
For the purpose of this subsection, the term "feasible," however, relates only to the ability to *measure*
emissions. Thus, this subsection has no relevance to
the Administrator's ability to consider cost and
technological feasibility in setting an emission
standard.

We also reject the contention that because Congress explicitly directed the Administrator to consider cost and technology in these provisions it
intended to preclude the Administrator from considering these factors under §112(b)(1). Petitioner
in effect asserts that Congress knew how to designate such factors and did so expressly where it intended their application. We do not agree. That
Congress explicitly provided for certain specific
considerations in these limited and detailed subsections does not seem to us a persuasive reason to
conclude that failure to specify such considerations
when employing a generalized standard in
§112(b)(1) forecloses reliance on those factors in
fleshing out that standard. If elsewhere in §112
Congress had exhorted the Administrator "to provide an ample margin of safety to protect the public
health," or had stated some similarly broad delegation, and then had specifically noted that he could
or should consider cost or technological feasibility
in making his determination, only then would the
failure to so specify in §112(b)(1) arguably foreclose
consideration of such factors.

as announcing the broad rule that an agency may never consider cost and technological feasibility, under any delegation of authority, and for any purpose, unless Congress specifically provides that the agency is authorized to consider these factors. At most, we believe that these statements stand for the proposition that when Congress has specifically directed an agency to consider certain factors, the agency may not consider unspecified factors. Because Congress chose not to limit specifically the factors the Administrator may consider in section 112, this discussion in *Union Electric* is not in point here. The factors that the Administrator may consider under section 112 could conceivably include all of the specific factors listed in other parts of the Act if necessary "to protect the public health."

A similar analysis distinguishes this court's reasoning in *Lead Industries*. In *Lead Industries*, we held that the Administrator is not required to consider cost and technology under the mandate in section 109 of the Clean Air Act to promulgate primary air quality standards which "allow[ ] an adequate margin of safety... to protect the public health." The NRDC argues that the decision in *Lead Industries*, which involved the more permissive language "adequate," rather than "ample," "margin of safety," compels the conclusion that section 112 precludes consideration of economic and technological feasibility. We think not.

The *Lead Industries* court did note that the statute on its face does not allow consideration of technological or economic feasibility, but the court based its decision that section 109 does not allow consideration of these factors in part on structural aspects of the ambient air pollution provisions that are not present here. First, besides "allowing an adequate margin of safety," ambient air standards set under section 109(b) must be based on "air quality criteria," which section 108 defines as comprising several elements, all related to health. The court reasoned that the

exclusion of economic and technological feasibility considerations from air quality criteria also foreclosed reliance on such factors in setting the ambient air quality standards based on those criteria. The court also relied on the fact that state implementation plans, the means of enforcement of ambient air standards, could not take into account economic and technological feasibility if such consideration interfered with the timely attainment of ambient air standards, and that the Administrator could not consider such feasibility factors in deciding whether to approve the state plans. This provided further grounds for the court to believe that Congress simply did not intend the economics of pollution control to be considered in the scheme of ambient air regulations.

In *Lead Industries*, moreover, the relevant Senate Report stated flatly that "existing sources of pollutants either should meet the standard of the law or be closed down." 647 F.2d at 1149. This is a far clearer statement than anything in the present case that Congress considered the alternatives and chose to close down sources or even industries rather than to allow risks to health.

The substantive standard imposed under the hazardous air pollutants provisions of section 112, by contrast with sections 109 and 110, is not based on criteria that enumerate specific factors to consider and pointedly exclude feasibility. Section 112(b)(1)'s command "to provide an ample margin of safety to protect the public health" is self-contained, and the absence of enumerated criteria may well evince a congressional intent for the Administrator to supply reasonable ones. Further, section 112, in marked contrast to the regime of ambient air standards, operates through nationally enforced standards; the state plans are permissive and may not interfere with national enforcement of any hazardous pollutant standard. No detailed provisions preclusive of technological and economic considerations govern the state plans allowed under section 112; indeed, the

Administrator must delegate enforcement and implementation authority to the state (subject to his continuing ability to enforce national standards) if he finds the state plan "adequate." Thus, nothing in the scheme of state implementation plans under section 112 demonstrates disfavor for feasibility considerations, and this further distinguishes section 112 from the *Lead Industries* court's interpretation of section 109.

Thus, in *Lead Industries*, the court found clear evidence that Congress intended to limit the factors the Administrator is permitted to consider in setting a "margin of safety" under section 109. The "margin of safety" standard in section 112 is not so adorned. For that reason, *Lead Industries* does not control this case. . . .

V

Since we cannot discern clear congressional intent to preclude consideration of cost and technological feasibility in setting emission standards under section 112, we necessarily find that the Administrator may consider these factors. We must next determine whether the Administrator's use of these factors in this case is "based on a permissible construction of the statute." *Chevron U.S.A. Inc. v. NRDC*, 467 U.S. 837 (1984). We must uphold the Administrator's construction if it represents "a reasonable policy choice for the agency to make." We cannot, however, affirm an agency interpretation found to be "arbitrary, capricious, or manifestly contrary to the statute." Nor can we affirm if "it appears from the statute or its legislative history that the accommodation [chosen] is not the one that Congress would have sanctioned."

Our role on review of an action taken pursuant to section 112 is generally a limited one. Because the regulation of carcinogenic agents raises questions "on the frontiers of scientific knowledge," *Industrial Union Dep't., AFL-CIO v. Hodgson*, 499 F.2d 467 (D.C. Cir. 1974), we have recognized that the Administrator's decision in this area "will depend to a greater extent upon policy judgments" to which we must accord considerable deference. We have also acknowledged that "EPA, not the court, has the technical expertise to decide what inferences may be drawn from the characteristics of . . . substances and to formulate policy with respect to what risks are acceptable," and we will not second-guess a determination based on that expertise. Our only role is to determine whether "the agency has exercised a reasoned discretion, with reasons that do not deviate from or ignore the ascertainable legislative intent." Despite this deferential standard, we find that the Administrator has ventured into a zone of impermissible action. The Administrator has not exercised his expertise to determine an acceptable risk to health. To the contrary, in the face of uncertainty about risks to health, he has simply substituted technological feasibility for health as the primary consideration under Section 112. Because this action is contrary to clearly discernible congressional intent, we grant the petition for review.

Given the foregoing analysis of the language and legislative history of section 112, it seems to us beyond dispute that Congress was primarily concerned with health in promulgating section 112. Every action by the Administrator in setting an emission standard is to be taken "to protect the public health." In setting an emission standard for vinyl chloride, however, the Administrator has made no finding with respect to the effect of the chosen level of emissions on health. Nor has the Administrator stated that a certain level of emission is "safe" or that the chosen level will provide an "ample margin of safety." Instead, the Administrator has substituted "best available technology" for a finding of the risk to health.

In the decision withdrawing the proposed 1977 amendments, the Administrator mentioned the risks to health, but based his decision solely on the finding that "there is no improved or new control technology that has been demonstrated to significantly and consistently reduce emissions to a level below that required by the current standard." Nowhere in the decision did the Administrator state that the 1976 emission standards provide an "ample margin of safety" such that revisions to those standards are not necessary.

In the 1977 proposal to decrease the level of emissions, the Administrator did not determine the risk to health under the then existing standard or under the proposed new standard. Nor did the Administrator explain why one standard was "safe" and the other was not.

The absence of any finding regarding the relationship between the risk to health at a certain level of emissions and the "ample margin of safety" standard is also evident in the Administrator's decision adopting the 1976 standards. Again, the Administrator mentioned the risks to health before and after regulation, but did not provide any explanation as to whether the risk was significant, or whether the chosen standard provided an "ample margin of safety."

In the three decisions regarding emission standards for vinyl chloride, the Administrator has made one finding regarding the duty to set emission standards that will provide an "ample margin of safety." The Administrator has determined that he is not required to determine on a case-by-case basis the risk to health at a particular level of emissions or to determine the relationship between that risk and "safety." Instead, the Administrator has adopted a generic rule, which when met, will always result in an "ample margin of safety." The Administrator has determined that this standard is met whenever he sets "emission standards that require emission reduction to the lowest level achievable by use of the best available control technology in cases involving apparent non-threshold pollutants where complete emission prohibition

would result in widespread industry closure and EPA has determined that the cost of such closure would be grossly disproportionate to the benefits of removing the risk that would remain after imposition of the best available control technology."

Thus, in setting emission standards for carcinogenic pollutants, the Administrator has decided to determine first the level of emissions attainable by best available control technology. He will then determine the costs of setting the standard below that level and balance those costs against the risk to health below the level of feasibility. If the costs are greater than the reduction in risk, then he will set the standard at the level of feasibility. This exercise, in the Administrator's view, will always produce an "ample margin of safety."

If there was any doubt that the Administrator has substituted technological feasibility for health as the primary consideration in setting emission standards under section 112, that doubt was dispelled by counsel for the EPA at oral argument. In response to a question from the court regarding a carcinogenic pollutant known to cause certain harm at 100 ppm, counsel stated that the Administrator could set an emission level at 99 ppm if that was the lowest feasible level and the costs of reducing the level below 99 ppm would be grossly disproportionate to the reduction in risk to health. Given the strong inference that harm would also certainly result at 99 ppm, the Administrator appears to have concluded that the "ample margin of safety" standard does not require any finding that a level of emissions is "safe." Instead, the Administrator need only find that the costs of control are greater than the reduction in risk to health. We disagree.

We find that the congressional mandate to provide "an ample margin of safety" "to protect the public health" requires the Administrator to make an initial determination of what is "safe." This determination must be based exclusively upon the Administrator's determination of the risk to health at a particular emission level. Because the Administrator in this case did not make any finding of the risk to health, the question of how that determination is to be made is not before us. We do wish to note, however, that the Administrator's decision does not require a finding that "safe" means "risk-free," *see Industrial Union Dep't.*, 448 U.S. at 642, or a finding that the determination is free from uncertainty. Instead, we find only that the Administrator's decision must be based upon an expert judgment with regard to the level of emission that will result in an "acceptable" risk to health. *Environmental Defense Fund v. EPA*, 194 U.S. App. D.C. 143, 598 F.2d 62, 81 (D.C. Cir. 1978) at 83–84. In this regard, the Administrator must determine what inferences should be drawn from available scientific data and decide what risks are acceptable in the world in which we live. *See Industrial Union Dep't. v. American Petroleum Institute*, 448 U.S. 607 642 (1980) ("There are many activities that we engage in every day—such as driving a car or even breathing city air—that entail some risk of accident or material health impairment; nevertheless, few people would consider those activities 'unsafe'."); *Alabama Power Co. v. Costle*, 204 U.S. App. D.C. 51, 636 F.2d 323, 360–61 (D.C. Cir. 1979). This determination must be based solely upon the risk to health. The Administrator cannot under any circumstances consider cost and technological feasibility at this stage of the analysis. The latter factors have no relevance to the preliminary determination of what is safe. Of course, if the Administrator cannot find that there is an acceptable risk at any level, then the Administrator must set the level at zero.

Congress, however, recognized in section 112 that the determination of what is "safe" will always be marked by scientific uncertainty and thus exhorted the Administrator to set emission standards that will provide an "ample margin" of safety. This language permits the Administrator to take into account scientific uncertainty and to use expert discretion to determine what action should be taken in light of that uncertainty. *Environmental Defense Fund*, 598 F.2d at 83 ("by requiring EPA to set standards providing an 'ample margin of safety,' Congress authorized and, indeed, required EPA to protect against dangers before their extent is conclusively ascertained"); *Hercules, Inc. v. EPA*, 194 U.S. App. D.C. 172, 598 F.2d 91 (D.C. Cir. 1978) at 104 ("Under the 'ample margin of safety' directive, EPA's standards must protect against incompletely understood dangers to public health and the environment, in addition to well-known risks."). In determining what is an "ample margin" the Administrator may, and perhaps must, take into account the inherent limitations of risk assessment and the limited scientific knowledge of the effects of exposure to carcinogens at various levels, and may therefore decide to set the level below that previously determined to be "safe." This is especially true when a straight line extrapolation from known risks is used to estimate risks to health at levels of exposure for which no data is available. This method, which is based upon the results of exposure at fairly high levels of the hazardous pollutants, will show some risk at every level because of the rules of arithmetic rather than because of any knowledge. In fact the risk at a certain point on the extrapolated line may have no relationship to reality; there is no particular reason to think that the actual line of the incidence of harm is represented by a straight line. Thus, by its nature the finding of risk is uncertain and the Administrator must use his discretion to meet the statutory mandate. It is only at this point of the regulatory process that the Administrator may set the emission standard at the lowest level that is technologically feasible. In fact, this is, we believe, precisely the type of policy choice that Congress envisioned when it directed the Administrator to provide an "ample margin of safety." Once "safety" is assured, the Administrator should be free to diminish as much of the statistically determined risk as possible by setting the standard at the lowest feasible level. Because consideration of these factors at this stage is clearly intended "to protect the public health," it is fully consistent with the Administrator's mandate under section 112.[11]

We wish to reiterate the limited nature of our holding in this case because it is not the court's intention to bind the Administrator to any specific method of determining what is "safe" or what constitutes an "ample margin." We hold only that the Administrator cannot consider cost and technological feasibility in determining what is "safe." This determination must be based solely upon the risk to health. The issues of whether the Administrator can proceed on a case-by-case basis, what support the Administrator must provide for the determination of what is "safe," or what other factors may be considered, are issues that must be resolved after the Administrator has reached a decision upon reconsideration of the decision withdrawing the proposed 1977 amendments.

For the foregoing reasons, the petition for review is granted, the decision withdrawing the 1977 proposed rule is vacated, and this case is hereby remanded for timely reconsideration of the 1977 proposed rule consistent with this opinion.

It is so ordered.

---

11. In response to the facts presented in this case we have analyzed this issue by using a two-step process. We do not mean to indicate that the Administrator is bound to employ this two-step process in setting every emission standard under §112. If the Administrator finds that some statistical methodology removes sufficiently the scientific uncertainty present in this case, then the Administrator could conceivably find that a certain statistically determined level of emissions will provide an ample margin of safety. If the Administrator uses this methodology, he cannot consider cost and technological feasibility: these factors are no longer relevant because the Administrator has found another method to provide an "ample margin" of safety.

■ **NOTES**

1. To the extent that the court relies on the nonthreshold nature of chemical carcinogenesis as a means of gaining insight into the intent of the congressional drafters of Section 112, the opinion is on shaky historical ground. As discussed earlier, environmental science had not yet recognized the existence of nonthreshold pollutants in 1970, and Congress therefore did not (and could not have) distinguished threshold pollutants from nonthreshold pollutants in drafting the provisions of the 1970 CAA. The recognition that carcinogens were likely not to exhibit a finite threshold came from later understanding of the mechanisms of carcinogenesis, not from the difficulty in ascertaining a threshold (see chapter 2). In the 1970 CAA, hazardous air pollutants were regulated separately from criteria pollutants, not because the former were nonthreshold pollutants, but because hazardous pollutants were those considered extraordinarily toxic, those resulting in "an increase in mortality or an increase in irreversible, or incapacitating reversible illness" [§112(a)], and toxic hot spots were therefore to be avoided. Furthermore, there are important practical differences. For example, unlike the case for criteria pollutants, there may be a relatively small

number of sources emitting a particular hazardous air pollutant within any given geographic area; establishing an NAAQS standard based on meteorological mixing of the emissions from those few sources would yield an extremely stringent standard, possibly below measurable levels and hence difficult to enforce.

2. There is a distinction between requiring *zero exposure* (i.e., disallowing *any* exposure) by banning the use of a substance in commerce, and requiring *no permissible exposure* by ensuring that the exposure be below detectable limits (by, for example, requiring closed production processes). In fact, the OSHA vinyl chloride workplace standard set a limit of 1 ppm over 8 hours because it represented the limits of detection, not because it was safe. The NRDC was not motivated by a desire to shut down vinyl chloride operations, but rather to modernize them. While the court acknowledges these two alternatives in citing Senator Muskie's statement during the postconference debate on the CAA (see the text above footnote 1 in the opinion), it proceeds to take up only the more onerous restriction. Can this be explained by the differences between the operative statutory mandate here ("ample margin of safety") and in the OSHAct (economic and technological feasibility)?

3. The court concludes that "ample margin of safety" does not mean "risk-free," that EPA must determine in each case what a "safe" level is, and that this determination "must be based upon an expert judgment with regard to the level of emission that will result in an 'acceptable' risk to health." What might enter into a determination of a "safe level"? Is it the size of the estimated risk alone? Does it involve a (necessarily covert) consideration of costs in making what appears to be a purely risk-based decision? Is an "acceptable" risk the same thing as *de minimis* risk? Is it the same as a "reasonable" risk? In other contexts, reasonable risk usually involves a consideration of social costs and benefits. However, since the court disavows the consideration of costs in determining the "acceptable" level of risk, presumably the cost-benefit criterion was not to be used here.

4. Note that Justice Breyer's concurring opinion in the *American Trucking* case, discussed previously, also endorses the notion that "safe" does not mean "risk-free." (See note 3 following that case for a further discussion of the judicial trend toward recognizing an inherent authority among regulatory bodies to ignore *de minimis* risks.)

5. Is the court convincing in drawing a distinction between the operational application of the similar mandates of Section 109 and Section 112 based on the extent of congressional specification of the criteria to be considered in each? Recall that the Section 109 standards for criteria pollutants are to be set at a level that is low enough to protect sensitive populations (even perhaps sensitive individuals) as well as the average person. Does an adequate (or ample) *margin* of safety mean the same thing

as an adequate (or ample) *degree* of safety? Are the cases interpreting Section 109 helpful here?

6. Is the court's recommended two-tiered approach, in which EPA is allowed to take technological feasibility into account in the face of scientific uncertainty, but only after determining "acceptable risk," consistent with the language of Section 112 at that time? Arguably, the court's heroic attempt to rationalize the "ample margin of safety" mandate with the regulation of nonthreshold pollutants in a way that avoided requiring no permissible exposure was effectively a rewriting of the statutory language. The reaction of Congress to the court's decision, and to EPA's slow pace in regulating hazardous air pollutants, was to conform EPA's mandate to new scientific knowledge about thresholds by significantly revising Section 112.

b. Section 112 after the 1990 Amendments

By the end of the 1980s, EPA had identified twenty-five substances for which Section 112 standards were contemplated, but little action had been taken beyond the standards for the eight hazardous air pollutants originally designated by the agency. As we have seen, the D.C. Circuit's 1987 decision in *NRDC v. EPA* had placed new limitations on EPA's approach to regulating hazardous air pollutants, and was likely to delay the process even further. Thus, to revitalize the moribund standard-setting process, Congress fundamentally reconceptualized Section 112 as part of the 1990 amendments to the Clean Air Act. Under the revised provisions, stationary sources of designated hazardous air pollutants are to be governed by numeric emission limits that are initially technology based (at least for nonthreshold pollutants), but which ultimately must ensure protection of the public health with an ample margin of safety. The amended Section 112 is voluminous and complicated, spanning eighteen often lengthy subsections; selected highlights are discussed here.

i. Designation of Specific Hazardous Air Pollutants

Rather than continue to leave the designation of hazardous air pollutants to EPA, Congress specified an "initial list" of 189 substances for which Section 112 standards were required to be set. See Section 112(b)(1). As we will see, this is the same approach that Congress had taken in 1977 in the regulation of toxic water pollutants under the Clean Water Act, and in 1984 in the regulation of hazardous wastes under the Resource Conservation and Recovery Act. The agency was further directed to conduct periodic reviews of this list, to remove substances from the list when appropriate, and to add substances to the list if they "present or may present . . . a threat of adverse human effects (including, but not limited to, substances which are known to be or may be reasonably anticipated to be, carcinogenic, mutagenic, teratogenic, neurotoxic, which cause reproductive dysfunction, or which are acutely or chronically toxic) or adverse environmental effects whether through ambient concentration, bioaccumulation, deposition or otherwise . . ." Moreover, interested persons are given the explicit right to petition to have particular substances added to or removed from the list. See Section 112(b)(2), (3). The current list stands at 188 after one chemical was "delisted" under Section 112(b)(3)(C). The addition of other substances is anticipated.

ii. Distinguishing between "Major" and "Area" Sources The 1990 amendments also singled out the larger stationary sources of hazardous air pollutants for more stringent regulation. "Major" sources—generally, those with annual emissions of more than 10 tons of any single hazardous air pollutant, or of more than 25 tons of two or more hazardous air pollutants combined—are to meet a clearly delineated set of national technology-based emission limitations established by EPA according to a specified 10-year schedule. Smaller stationary sources of hazardous air pollutants, referred to in the revised Section 112 as "area" sources, are also subject to technology-based emission limits, but these limits are expressly permitted to be less stringent than the limits for major sources. EPA was directed to establish categories (and subcategories) of major and area sources, and these categorizations define the industry groupings for which specific emission limits are established. See, generally, Sections 112(a)(1), (2), and 112(c). The listing of major source categories and subcategories must be updated at least every 8 years, and the listing of area source categories may also be revised. Once a new category is listed, an emission limitation for that category must be promulgated within 2 years. See Section 112(c)(5). EPA may also remove a source category from the list so long as specified health-based criteria are satisfied. See Section 112(c)(9).

Given the greater degree of regulation to be applied to major sources, companies generally prefer to have their facilities classified as area sources instead. Thus, when EPA issued a rule that announced a relatively broad interpretation of the statute's major source designation, industry appealed. The D.C. Circuit addressed industry's arguments in the following decision.

National Mining Association v. Environmental Protection Agency
Before SILBERMAN, GINSBURG, and RANDOLPH, Circuit Judges
Opinion Per Curiam
59 F.3d 1351 (D.C. Cir. 1995)

I

In 1990, as part of its comprehensive overhaul of the Clean Air Act, Congress revised §112 of the Act, which regulates emissions of hazardous air pollutants. Dissatisfied with EPA's health-based regulation of hazardous air pollutants under the 1970 program,[1] Congress replaced this approach with a detailed, technology-based regulatory scheme. The 1990 amendments to §112 establish an initial list, which EPA may periodically revise, of 189 hazardous air pollutants. EPA must publish a list of "categories and subcategories" of "major sources" and certain "area sources" that emit these pollutants. §7412(c). For each listed "category or subcategory of major sources and area sources" of hazardous air pollutants, §112(d) of the Act directs EPA to promulgate emission standards.

Under the Act, "major sources" of hazardous air pollutants are potentially subject to stricter regulatory control than are "area sources."[2] For example, major sources must comply with technology-based emission standards requiring the maximum degree of reduction in emissions EPA deems achievable, often referred to as "maximum achievable control technology" or MACT standards.[3] 42 U.S.C. §7412(d)(1)–(2). In order to obtain an operating permit under title V of the Act,

§§501–507, major sources must comply with extensive monitoring, reporting and record-keeping requirements. §§7661–7661f. Further, §112(g) generally conditions the modification, construction or reconstruction of a major source on the source's meeting MACT emission limitations. §7412(g).

"Area sources" of hazardous air pollutants are not necessarily subject to such stringent regulation. EPA need not list all "categories and subcategories" of area sources, §7412(c)(3),[4] and it does not have to establish emission standards for unlisted area sources, §7412(d)(1). For listed area sources, EPA may choose to promulgate emission standards requiring only "generally available control technologies or management practices." §7412(d)(5). These standards can be less rigorous than those required for major sources under §7412(d)(1). Area sources are not subject to title V permitting requirements, or to §112(g)'s restrictions on modification, construction and reconstruction of their facilities.

---

1. The previous version of §112 directed EPA to list those hazardous air pollutants that it intended to regulate because they might "cause, or contribute to, an increase in mortality or an increase in serious irreversible or incapacitating reversible, illness." For such pollutants, EPA was to institute emission standards that provided for "an ample margin of safety to protect the public health." Over 18 years, EPA listed only 8 pollutants as hazardous, and regulated only some sources of 7 of these chemicals.
2. Section 112(a)(1) provides:

The term "major source" means any stationary source or group of stationary sources located within a contiguous area and under common control that emits or has the potential to emit considering controls, in the aggregate, 10 tons per year or more of any hazardous air pollutant or 25 tons per year or more of any combination of hazardous air pollutants. The Administrator may establish a lesser quantity... for a major source... on the basis of the potency of the air pollutant, persistence, potential for bioaccumulation, other characteristics of the air pollutant, or other relevant factors.

An "area source" is "any stationary source . . . that is not a major source," and does not include "motor vehicles or nonroad vehicles subject to regulation under [§§7521–7590]."
3. EPA develops such standards "taking into consideration the cost of achieving such emission reduction, and any non-air quality health and environmental impacts and energy requirements." §7412(d)(2). For new sources, the maximum achievable reduction in emissions must be at least as stringent as the emission control achieved in practice by the best controlled similar source. §7412(d)(3). For existing sources in a category of 30 or more such sources, the maximum achievable reduction in emissions must be at least as stringent as the average emission limitation achieved by the 12 [percent] best-performing sources in that category.
4. EPA is directed to list only those "area sources" that present "a threat of adverse effects to human health or the environment." §7412(c)(3). No later than five years after November 15, 1990, EPA shall have listed sufficient categories of area sources to ensure regulation of 90 percent of area source emissions of the 30 hazardous air pollutants presenting the greatest threat to public health in the largest number of urban areas. §7412(k).

In July 1992, pursuant to §112(c)(1), EPA published an initial list of categories of sources that emit hazardous air pollutants, and almost seventeen months later, it published a schedule for promulgation of emission standards for these listed source categories, as required by §112(e). In August 1993, in order to "eliminate the need to repeat general information and requirements within each [emission] standard," EPA proposed a rule codifying the "procedures and criteria needed to implement" emission standards for hazardous air pollutants. It promulgated a final rule, which is the subject of this dispute, adopting these general provisions on March 16, 1994.

Among other things, the general provisions rule implements §112(a)(1)'s definition of "major source." The rule defines "major source" in terms nearly identical to those in §112(a)(1) of the Clean Air Act:

Major source means any stationary source or group of stationary sources located within a contiguous area and under common control that emits or has the potential to emit considering controls, in the aggregate, 10 tons per year or more of any hazardous air pollutant or 25 tons per year or more of any combination of hazardous air pollutants, unless the Administrator establishes a lesser quantity, or in the case of radionuclides, different criteria from those specified in this sentence.

A "stationary source" is "any building, structure, facility or installation which emits or may emit any air pollutant." An "area source [is] any stationary source . . . that is not a major source." The preambles to the proposed and final rules, and other definitions adopted in the final rule explain in greater detail how EPA plans to identify major sources.

Petitioners challenge . . . aspects of EPA's implementation of the definition of "major source." First, National Mining Association and American Forest and Paper Association (collectively referred to as "National Mining Association") and General Electric question EPA's requiring the aggregation of all hazardous air emissions within a plant site—instead of only those emissions from equip-

ment in similar industrial categories—in a §112 major source determination. Second, National Mining Association challenges EPA's requiring the inclusion of "fugitive emissions" in a source's aggregate emissions in determining whether the source is major. . . .

II

. . .

A

General Electric and National Mining Association have similar arguments against the final rule's implementation of §112(a)(1). Both maintain that EPA may not, in determining whether a site is a major source, include emissions from all facilities on a contiguous plant site under common control. These petitioners assert that, for purposes of major source determinations, EPA may aggregate emissions from different facilities on a contiguous plant site under common control only when the facilities fall within a similar industrial classification. General Electric says EPA must aggregate emissions on a "source category" basis; National Mining Association contends that EPA may combine emissions only if the emitting facilities fall within the same two-digit Standard Industrial Classification (SIC) Code.

In the preamble to the final rule, EPA made clear that in determining whether a source is major, emissions from all sources of hazardous air pollutants within a plant site must be aggregated, so long as the sources are geographically adjacent and under common control. As a result, if the total annual emissions of hazardous air pollutants from a plant site exceed the designated thresholds, each source emitting pollutants at the site must comply with the stricter MACT emission standards applicable to sources under §112(d)(2), and with other requirements applicable to major sources.

Petitioners read §112(a)(1) more restrictively. In their view, EPA's approach will impermissibly regulate "minor facilities" that happen to be located at an industrial site with annual emissions of hazardous air pollutants that, in the aggregate, exceed the major source thresholds. They contend that EPA may require aggregation of emissions from sources only if those sources fall within a single source category—General Electric's argument, or the same two-digit SIC Code—National Mining Association's contention. It follows, according to petitioners, that a source must comply with regulatory requirements applicable to major sources only if it belongs to some group of sources at an industrial site emitting, in the aggregate, more than the major source threshold. Under petitioners' theories, it is possible that only some of a site's sources would have to comply with the regulatory requirements applicable to major sources, including the stricter emission limitations of §112(d)(2). Other sources of hazardous air pollutants would be regulated as area sources, possibly subject to less stringent emission standards or to none at all. §7412(c)(5).

EPA rejected petitioners' methods of implementing "major source." With respect to General Electric's source category definition, EPA acknowledged that "more than one source category on the EPA's source category list may be represented within a plant that is a major source" of hazardous air pollutants, as is the case for a large chemical manufacturing complex. ("a large plant... would clearly be a 'major source,' but would also comprise multiple source categories"). Congress intended, according to EPA, "that all portions of a major source be subject to MACT [emission standards] regardless of the number of source categories into which the facility is divided." "Thus, the EPA will set one or more MACT standards for a major source, and sources within that major source will be covered by the standard(s), regardless of whether, when standing alone, each one

of those regulated sources would be major." EPA also rejected the SIC Code approach to implementing "major source," advanced here by National Mining Association. Because §112(a)(1) does not refer to SIC Codes, EPA reasoned that Congress intended major sources of hazardous air pollutants to "encompass entire contiguous... plant sites without being subdivided according to industrial classifications." A separation of emission sources by SIC Codes "would be an artificial division of sources that, in reality, all contribute to public exposure around a plant site."

If §112(a)(1) is viewed in isolation, EPA's reading of the provision is not simply consistent with the provision; it is nearly compelled by the statutory language. Section 112(a)(1) states that a "group of stationary sources" need meet only three conditions to be termed a "major source": (1) sources within the group must be "located within a contiguous area"; (2) they must be "under common control"; and (3) in the aggregate, they must emit or, considering controls, have the potential to emit 10 or more tons per year of a single hazardous air pollutant or 25 or more tons per year of any combination of hazardous air pollutants. Section 112(a)(1) says nothing about combining emissions only from sources within the same source categories or SIC Codes. In this respect, EPA's definition of "major source," set forth in the preamble to the final rule, is faithful to the language of §112(a)(1)....

B

National Mining Association also thinks EPA erred in deciding to count "fugitive emissions" of hazardous air pollutants in determining whether a "source" is a "major source," without first conducting a rulemaking pursuant to §302(j). "Fugitive emissions" are defined in the final rule as:

those emissions from a stationary source that could not reasonably pass through a stack, chimney, vent or other functionally equivalent opening. Under section 112 of the Act, all fugitive emissions are to be considered in determining whether a stationary source is a major source.[16]

...We conclude that EPA may require the inclusion of fugitive emissions in a site's aggregate emissions without conducting any special rulemaking, even if "major source" and "major stationary source" mean the same thing. Section 112(a)(1) expressly provides that a "major source" is any stationary source or group of stationary sources *"located within a contiguous area and under common control"* and emitting more than 10 tons per year of a single hazardous air pollutant or 25 tons per year of such pollutants combined. An emission may be fugitive, but it is still an emission from a stationary source. And so the italicized language certainly may be read as EPA reads it—that *all* emissions are to be counted in determining whether a source is major, subject only to the qualification that they emanate from a contiguous site under common control. So read, §112(a)(1) satisfies §302(j)'s "except as otherwise expressly provided" clause such that fugitive emissions may be counted in a source's aggregate emissions without a special rulemaking....

In sum, EPA's definition of "major source" without respect to source categories or two-digit SIC codes is reasonable, as is its requirement that fugitive emissions be included in a source's aggregate emissions in determining whether the source is major. We therefore deny the petition for review with respect to these issues....

---

16. In contrast to fugitive emissions, emissions emanating from a stack, chimney or vent are often called "point source" emissions.

■ **NOTE**

1. What classification is appropriate when a major source reduces its emissions of hazardous air pollutants to a level that is below the threshold for the "major" source designation? Under the Clinton administration, EPA adopted a policy under which such a source remained subject to the requirements applicable to major sources, in deference to Section 112's ultimate goal of ensuring the protection of public health from hazardous air pollutants with an ample margin of safety. Under the G. W. Bush administration, however, EPA proposed a rule that would allow a major source that reduced its emissions of hazardous air pollutants to below 25 tons per year would be reclassified as an "area source" and would thus be exempt from MACT requirements. See *Environment Reporter* 38(1): 5 (2007).   ■

iii.   Specific Emission Standards According to a Specified Schedule   The revised Section 112 embodies a two-phase approach to emission standards for hazardous air pollutants.

Phase 1 Standards   The first phase is largely technology based. Section (d)(1) directs EPA to "promulgate regulations establishing emission standards for each category and subcategory of major and area sources of hazardous air pollutants." As discussed in the *National Mining Association* case excerpted here, Section 112(d)(2) specifies that such regulations

shall require the *maximum degree of reduction* in emissions of the hazardous pollutants subject to this section (including a prohibition of such emissions, where achievable) that the Administrator [of EPA], taking into consideration the cost of achieving such emission reduction, and any non-air quality health and environmental impacts, determines is *achievable*. . . . [42 U.S.C. §7412(d)(2), emphasis added]

In setting these standards, EPA is to consider pollution control *and* pollution prevention methods and technologies. See Section 112(d)(2)(A)–(E). These standards are commonly referred to as the *maximum achievable control technology* (MACT) standards. MACT standards for *new* sources in any given category or subcategory "shall not be less stringent than the emission control that is achieved in practice by the best controlled similar source." MACT standards for *existing* sources in any given category or subcategory may be less stringent than those for new sources, "but shall not be less stringent than, and may be more stringent than . . . the average emission limitation achieved by the best performing 12 percent of the existing sources" in that category or subcategory (or, for categories or subcategories with less than 30 sources, "the average emission limitation achieved by the best performing 5 sources") [Section 112(d)(3)].

There are two potential exceptions to these specific, technology-based MACT standards. First, EPA may instead promulgate health-based emission limits for "pollutants for which a health threshold has been established," if those limits are adequate to ensure "an ample margin of safety" [Section 112(d)(4)]. Thus, for hazardous air pollutants with known threshold exposure levels (below which adverse health effects do not occur), Congress essentially permitted EPA to revert to its standard-setting authority under the original version of Section 112. Second, EPA need not promulgate MACT standards for categories or subcategories of *area* sources, and may instead "elect to promulgate standards or requirements . . . which provide for the use of generally available control technologies or management practices" [Section 112(d)(5)]. These less stringent emission limits for categories and subcategories of area sources are commonly referred to as the *generally available control technology* (GACT) standards.

Just as it did not leave the designation of hazardous air pollutants to the discretion of EPA, the revised Section 112 did not leave the timing of standard setting to EPA. Instead, Congress established a set of statutory deadlines for both major source and area source emission standards. MACT standards (or alternative health-based standards for threshold pollutants) for all major source categories and subcategories were to be set within 10 years, with standards for "not less than" forty categories and subcategories to be set by November 1992, standards for 25% of all of the categories and subcategories to be set by November 1994, standards for 50% to be set by November

1997, and standards for 100% to be set by November 2000. See Section 112(e). While EPA often missed these statutory deadlines, it generally promulgated the required number of standards within 18 months of the specified date. To the extent that EPA had not promulgated a required standard for a source category or subcategory within 18 months of the specified date, sources within that category or subcategory were required to apply for an operating permit. (The permit program for stationary sources—another feature of the 1990 amendments—is discussed in more detail later.) The permit for that source in turn was to contain an emission limit deemed by the issuer of the permit (EPA or the state) to be equivalent to the limit that would have been applicable to that source had EPA issued the required Section 112 standard in a timely fashion. See Section 112(j).

There are also specific timelines for area source standards. EPA was to (1) identify "not less than 30 hazardous air pollutants which, as the result of emissions from area sources, present the greatest threat to public health in the largest number of urban areas"; (2) identify the categories or subcategories of sources "accounting for 90 per centum or more of the aggregate emissions" of each of these identified pollutants; and (3) issue emissions standards for those source categories within 10 years from the date of the 1990 amendments (i.e., by November 15, 2000). See Sections 112(c)(3) and (k)(3)(B). In addition, Section 112(c)(6) calls for the regulation of area sources of seven specific hazardous air pollutants, without regard to their inclusion on EPA's list of the thirty most dangerous pollutants, also by November 15, 2000. Although the agency has identified source categories under these provisions, it has promulgated emission standards for only a fraction of the area source categories identified. In 2006, after concluding that "EPA has been grossly delinquent in making serious efforts to comply" with the statutory timetable for area sources, the United States District Court for the District of Columbia ordered EPA to complete its promulgation of the required Section 112 emission standards for the remaining categories of area sources by 2009, in stages beginning December 2006. *Sierra Club v. Johnson*, 444 F.Supp.2d. 46, 58–61 (D. D.C. 2006).

Phase 2 Standards   The revised Section 112 envisions that emission limits for major and area sources ultimately will be made more stringent if that is necessary to protect public health or the environment. To facilitate an eventual reconsideration of the hazardous air pollutant standards, Section 112(f)(1) directed EPA to submit a report to Congress by the end of 1996 detailing the nature and extent of any health risks likely to remain from stationary sources of hazardous air pollutants once the Phase 1 standards are fully implemented, and to make a recommendation to Congress regarding legislation to address these risks. The agency submitted such a report in 1999 and recommended that Congress not pass any new legislation [U.S. EPA (1999), *Residual Risk: Report to Congress* EPA-453/R-99-001, Washington, D.C.]. In this re-

Table 6.7
NAAQS and NSPS Requirements in NAAQS Attainment and Nonattainment Areas + PSD + NESHAPS

	NAAQS (§109) Primary and secondary ambient air quality (concentration) standards	PSD requirements for SO_2, PM_{10} + NO_X	NSPS (§111) + Designated Pollutants (§111d) (restrictions placed on individual sources)	NESHAPS §112 (restrictions placed on individual sources)
Existing sources	CO, SO_2, NO_X, O_3, particulates (PM_{10}; $PM_{2.5}$), Pb Primary: to protect public health with an adequate margin of safety Secondary: to protect public welfare (implemented through state permitting of preferably continuous emission controls) **Additional Nonattainment Requirements:** Tiered reductions for CO, O_3, and PM_{10} particulates		**Designated Pollutants:** Where no §109 or §112 standard does or would apply, and a performance standard under §111 would be appropriate if the source were new, EPA may set performance standards. Standards now exist for sulfuric acid mist, fluorides, and VOCs (§111d). **Additional Nonattainment Requirements:** RACT [§172(c)(1)]	189 MACT (major sources) or GACT (area sources) [if not feasible, design standard under §112(h)(1) *or* health-based standards for threshold pollutants] §112(d)(4) Offsets ok between pollutants Risk report with recommendations for legislation in 6 years; if no action within 8 years, EPA must protect with ample margin of safety ($<10^{-6}$ for carcinogens) [§112(f)(2)]
New or modified sources		**PSD:** (facility-specific) BACT or netting	**NSPS:** Category-wide federal *emission standards* for pollutants based on "best system of emission reduction ... adequately demonstrated" [§111(a)(1)] or a *design standard* using the "best technological system of continuous emission reduction" [§111(h)(1)]—all enforced through state permits. **Additional Nonattainment Requirements:** LAER for major new sources + offsets §171(3)	For both major and area sources, more stringent standards permissible than MACT, taking cost into account [§112(d)(3)]

port EPA explained that it intended to use various methodologies "for making final risk management decisions under section 112(f) for carcinogens rather than adopting any bright line." See David M. Friedland and James R. Greene (2005), "Residual Risk Standards: 'Phase Two' of Clean Air Act's Air Toxics Provisions" *Environment Reporter* 36(23): 1206.

If Congress does not act on the report recommendations, EPA must revise the Section 112 emission standard applicable to a particular category or subcategory of sources within 8 years of the promulgation of the initial standard if it finds that such revision

is required in order to provide an ample margin of safety to protect public health in accordance with this section (as in effect before November 15, 1990) or to prevent, taking into consideration cost, energy, safety, and other relevant factors, an adverse environmental effect. [Section 112(f)(2)(A)]

Any such revised emission standard must be set at the level deemed sufficient to provide an ample margin of safety to protect public health, unless a more stringent standard is deemed necessary to prevent an adverse environmental effect, "taking into consideration costs, energy, safety, and other relevant factors" [id.]. Moreover, if any Phase 1 standard for a category or subcategory of sources emitting one or more pollutants "classified as a known, probable, or suspected human carcinogen" fails to "reduce lifetime cancer risks *to the individual most exposed* to emissions from a source in the category or subcategory to less than one in one million," EPA *must* promulgate such a revised standard for that category or subcategory [id., emphasis added]. Although these provisions are broadly applicable to both major sources and area sources, EPA need not promulgate such a standard for those area sources that have already been regulated under a Phase 1 emission standard. See Section 112(f)(5). EPA proposal the first of these revised "residual risk" rules in 2004 (69 Fed. Reg. 48,342) and issued the final standard in 2005 (70 Fed. Reg. 19,993). This standard, applicable to emissions from coke oven batteries, is estimated to reduce the lifetime cancer risk to exposed persons to 200 chances in one million, which is considerably higher than the one-in-one-million lifetime cancer risk anticipated by Section 112(f). [*Environment Reporter* 36(23): 1206 (2005)] Table 6.7 summarizes the emission requirements established by the revised Section 112.

■ **NOTES**

1. For a history of EPA's first 10 years implementing the revised Section 112, and for a detailed evaluation of the hazardous air pollutants program generally, see Arnold W. Reitze, Jr. and Randy Lowell (2001) "Control of Hazardous Air Pollution," 28 *Boston College Environmental Affairs Law Review* 229.

2. If EPA concludes that it is not feasible to "prescribe or enforce" a Section 112 emission standard in a particular situation, the agency may instead promulgate a "design, equipment, work practice, [and/]or operational standard" [Section 112(h)(1)]. For an emission standard to be deemed "not feasible" under this provision, one or more of three conditions must be met: (1) the hazardous air pollutant(s) in question "cannot be emitted through a conveyance designed and constructed to emit or capture such pollutant[s]," (2) use of such a conveyance would be inconsistent with applicable law, or (3) the measurement technology or methodology necessary to confirm compliance with an emission standard "is not practicable due to technological and economic limitations" [Section 112(h)(2)].

3. Existing sources are generally given 3 years to meet a Section 112 standard and may be granted an extension for an additional year. Section 112(j)(3). Thereafter, the president may grant additional extensions of up to two years at a time. Section 112(i)(4). New sources (which are subject to more stringent MACT standards) generally have 10 years from the date of their construction to meet a later promulgated health-based standard established under Section 112(f) [see Section 112(i)(7)], and existing sources may be granted a waiver of up to 2 years to meet such standards [see Section 112(f)(4)(B)].

4. Mercury emissions from power plants are of increasing concern and are thought to be inadequately covered by a prior proposed MACT standard for such plants. EPA estimates that 630,000 children are born annually with unsafe levels of mercury in their blood, raising their risk of delayed development, neurological effects, and retardation [*Environment Reporter* 35(7): 339–340 (2004)]. In March 2005, 5 days after it promulgated the Clean Air Interstate Rule for NO_X and SO_2 emissions from coal-fired energy plants, EPA also issued the Clean Air Act Mercury rule (http://www.epa.gov/oar/mercuryrule), withdrawing a proposed MACT standard for mercury scheduled to go into effect in 2008, and instead instituting a cap-and-trade policy with a target of achieving a 69% reduction in mercury emissions by 2018. This may create "hot spots" of local high-level exposures, which is no longer thought to be an issue with NO_X and SO_2. (See a study by the Hubbard Brook Research Foundation cited in *Environment Reporter* 38(1): 7 (2007).) In July 2005, both the Senate and the House responded to the mercury rule by introducing resolutions to disapprove the rule under the Congressional Review Act. In the same month, a coalition of environmental organizations asked the D.C. Circuit Court of Appeals to block the mercury rule, and five environmental groups have filed suit in that court to halt the trading provisions of the mercury rule [*Environment Reporter* 36(28): 1446 (2005)]. On September 13, 2005 the Senate narrowly rejected (51–47) the resolution, leaving the rule intact. In October 2005, EPA agreed to reconsider parts of the mercury cap-and-trade rule, as well as the appropriateness of regulating mercury under the mandate

of Section 112. On May 15, 2006, Acting U.S. Attorney General Bill Roderick questioned EPA's assertion that emissions trading will not lead to hot spots [*Environment Reporter* 37(20): 1051 (2006)].

5. Many states have developed or are developing mercury emissions programs that are more stringent than the federal standard. Most prohibit interstate mercury emissions trading [*Environment Reporter* 37(29): 1501 (2006)]. Some states are suing the federal government to compel the issuance of a more stringent federal standard for mercury. See Cheryl Hogue (2007) "Mercury Battle: States are demanding faster cuts in mercury emissions than EPA requires" *Chemical & Engineering News* 85(14): 52–55.

6. The EPA's Inspector General has questioned the propriety of adopting a cap-and-trade approach for mercury in place of a MACT standard. See *Environment Reporter* 36(6): 273 (2005). In withdrawing its proposed MACT standard for mercury, EPA cited an absence of commercially available technological controls, and expressed optimism that the cap-and-trade program would provide incentives to develop the needed technology. See *Environment Reporter* 36(11): 525 (2005). See chapter 12 for a discussion of incentives for innovation under a cap-and-trade program compared with technology-forcing regulation.

7. On January 13, 2005, the National Research Council (NRC) issued a congressionally mandated interim report on these and other Bush administration efforts, otherwise known as the "Clear Skies Initiative," first proposed in 2002, in which power plant emissions of sulfur dioxide, nitrogen oxides, and mercury were to have been reduced 70% by 2018 through cap-and-trade provisions. The interim report concluded that the proposed new initiatives were unlikely to achieve more stringent reductions that the traditional new source review provisions of the CAA (see http://www.nap.edu/books/0309095786/htmv/). The nonpartisan Congressional Research Service was openly critical of the initiative. The final NRC report was more equivocal because of court rulings that have struck down many features of the initiative. The report concluded: "because current models shed little light on the expected effects of EPA's rule changes on particular plants and geographic locations and local populations with varying characteristics, no conclusions can be drawn about how the revisions would affect human health." See The National Academies News, "Report Recommends Broader Approach to Assessing Changes to New Sources Review Rules for Air Pollution" July 21, 2006. (http://www8.nationalacademies.org/onpinews/newsitem.aspx?RecordID=11701)

8. EPA's penchant for placing its own extraregulatory priorities, such as the Clear Skies Initiative, above the regulatory agenda established by Congress in the Clean Air Act also drew the ire of United States District Court Judge Paul Friedman in

his analysis of the agency's failure to meet the statutory deadlines for establishing Section 112 standards for area sources. EPA had sought to justify its delay in setting those standards by pointing to the other regulatory work in which it was engaged. However, Judge Friedman noted that the agency "currently devotes substantial resources to discretionary rulemakings, many of which make existing regulations more congenial to industry, and several of which since have been found unlawful" [*Sierra Club v. Johnson*, 444 F. Supp. 2d. 46, 57 (D. D.C. 2006)]. "By all appearances," Judge Friedman went on to note, "EPA's failure to promulgate the required standards owes less to the magnitude of the task at hand than to the footdragging efforts of a delinquent agency, or an attempt by EPA to prioritize its own regulatory agenda over that set by Congress in the 1990 Clean Air Act amendments. It is emphatically not within an agency's authority to set regulatory priorities that clearly conflict with those established by Congress" [id. at 58, internal citation omitted].

9. Section 183(e) of the act, 42 U.S.C. §7511b(e), calls on EPA to "conduct a study of the emissions of volatile organic compounds into the ambient air from consumer and commercial products" in order to "determine their potential to contribute to ozone levels" that violate EPA limits on ambient ozone levels, and to "establish criteria for regulating consumer and commercial products...which shall be subject to control under this subsection" [42 U.S.C. §7511b(e)(2)(A)]. After completing the study, EPA is to (1) list the categories of products that account for 80% or more of VOC emissions in areas that violate EPA ambient standards for ozone; (2) divide the list into four priority categories, based on specified criteria; and (3) every 2 years after the list is promulgated, regulate one group of categories until all four categories are regulated [42 U.S.C. §7511b(e)(3)(A)]. Finding that EPA had lagged significantly behind in completing this task as well, Judge Friedman also ordered the agency to promulgate the remaining required regulations under this section according to an implementation schedule culminating in September 2008. *Sierra Club v. Johnson*, 444 F. Supp. 2d. at 46.   ■

iv. Hazardous Air Pollutant Offsets   No major source may be modified in any way that "results in a greater than de minimis increase in actual emissions of a hazardous air pollutant" unless that source, once modified, will meet the applicable MACT standard (or the equivalent limitation, if no such standard has yet been set) [Section 112(g)(1), (2)]. The owner of the source cannot escape this requirement by offering to reduce emissions of hazardous air pollutants at another source. However, the owner may choose to offset the increase by reducing other, more hazardous pollutant emissions at the *same* source because no modification is deemed to have occurred at a source if the increase in emissions is "offset by an equal or greater decrease in the quantity of emissions of *another* hazardous air pollutant (or pollutants) from such source which is deemed *more hazardous*" [Section 112(g)(1)(A)]. Thus, if the net effect is to reduce the overall risk from hazardous air pollutants, the modification requirements are avoided.

v.   Reporting and Prevention of Accidental Chemical Releases   Subsection (r) of the revised Section 112—the last of the section's numerous subsections—creates a federal program designed to reduce chemical accidents at industrial facilities. Section 112(r) directs EPA to develop regulations regarding the prevention and detection of accidental chemical releases, and to publish a list of at least 100 chemical substances (with associated threshold quantities) to be covered by the regulations. The regulations must include requirements for the development of risk management plans by facilities using any of the regulated substances in amounts above the relevant threshold. These risk management plans must include a hazard assessment, an accident prevention program, and an emergency release program. See Sections 112(r)(3) and 112(r)(7)(ii). In addition, Section 112(r)(1) imposes a "general duty" on the owners and operators of stationary sources producing, processing, handling, or storing hazardous chemicals "to design and maintain a safe facility[,] taking such steps as are necessary to prevent releases, and to minimize the consequences of accidental releases that do occur." Section 112(r), and chemical accident prevention generally, are discussed in greater detail in chapter 13 of this text.

6.   Enforcement and the Title V Operating Permits

As with implementation of the act generally, enforcement of the Clean Air Act against individual stationary sources is a shared federal and state responsibility. This federal-state structure was put in place with the 1970 amendments, and it became the enforcement model for the federal water pollution and hazardous waste programs that followed. In practice, much of the day-to-day enforcement of Clean Air Act standards—conducting inspections, issuing notices of noncompliance and compliance orders, assessing administrative penalties, and bringing judicial actions seeking court-ordered penalties and/or injunctive relief—is done by the states. However, enforcement of the act is ultimately a federal responsibility, and state enforcement is subject to federal oversight. EPA has independent, overriding enforcement authority, and has a clear mandate from Congress to take federal enforcement when state enforcement has not been adequate to secure compliance. See Section 113(a). Moreover, Congress chose to augment the federal enforcement scheme by giving private citizens the right to bring their own enforcement actions in federal district court when EPA and the state have been unable (or unwilling) to secure compliance. In general, subject to certain limitations and restrictions, citizens are authorized to bring such actions—commonly known as "citizen suits"—against those (including departments and instrumentalities of the federal government) who are in violation of an applicable emission limit or other air pollution requirement specified in EPA regulation, in the relevant SIP, or in the facility's operating permit (discussed below). See Section 304 (the act's provision for citizen suits).

In the 1990 amendments to the act, Congress sought to strengthen enforcement of air pollution regulations in two important ways. First, it sought to increase the emphasis on federal enforcement, both by expanding EPA's authority to seek and assess penalties and by redirecting the use of penalties assessed in citizen suit litigation. With these amendments, EPA now has the authority to impose civil penalties administratively (i.e., without going to court). The EPA administrator may assess administrative penalties of up to $25,000 per day (not to exceed $200,000 in any one assessment), and EPA inspectors may issue "field citation" penalties of up to $5,000 per day for minor violations [see Section 113(d)]. (In either situation, the alleged violator has a right to seek federal court review of the penalty assessment.) EPA also has the authority to issue administrative compliance orders—directing the alleged violator to take specified steps to attain compliance by a specified date—and to enlist the aid of the Department of Justice to file suit in federal district court to seek court-ordered compliance and other appropriate injunctive relief. In any such lawsuit, the court may impose a civil penalty of up to $25,000 per day per violation (see Section 113b). Citizens may also seek penalties and injunctive relief in enforcement actions filed under the act. However, Congress amended the citizen suit provision in 1990 to specify that civil penalties awarded in Clean Air Act citizen suit actions must either be placed into a special fund within the U.S. Treasury to be used by EPA "to finance air compliance and enforcement activities," or be used to finance "beneficial mitigation projects which are consistent with this chapter and enhance the public health or the environment" [see Sections 304(g)(1) and (2)]. This second option is available at the discretion of the court, and is limited to the first $100,000 of any penalty imposed. Finally, the act authorizes the federal government to seek *criminal* sanctions—penalties and/or imprisonment—for certain specified egregious violations [see Section 113(c)].

The second, and potentially far more significant, step taken in the 1990 amendments to strengthen enforcement was the establishment of a *permitting* program for most stationary sources. This addressed a long-standing set of problems with Clean Air Act implementation and enforcement. Given the myriad federal and state standards that were promulgated to implement the act, it was often difficult—for the regulators, for the regulated sources, and for interested citizens—to know just exactly which regulations applied to a particular facility. Quite often this required laborious research, not only of the Code of Federal Regulations, but also of the relevant SIP. The cumbersome nature of this task was exacerbated by the fact that many SIPs are not kept as self-contained documents but are interspersed through the state's various statutory and regulatory codes. In addition, even when the applicable standards were known, it often was difficult to determine whether the source was in compliance with those standards because of the paucity of reliable monitoring data.

This same set of issues did not arise under the federal Clean Water Act, however. This is because (as we will see in chapter 8) that act has long required that all facilities discharging pollutants to the surface waters obtain, and comply with, a discharge permit that (1) incorporates all applicable Clean Water Act discharge limits, (2) requires periodic self-monitoring to determine whether those limits are being met, and (3) requires the results of this monitoring to be supplied to the permitting agency (EPA or the state) on a regular basis. Drawing from this comparatively successful model, the 1990 Clean Air Act amendments created a similar permitting program for stationary sources of air pollution. See Sections 501–507. Since the permitting program was added as a separate subchapter—Title V—of the Clean Air Act, the permits are often referenced as "Title V permits."

The criteria for the Title V permits are set forth in the statute, as supplemented by EPA regulation. It is anticipated that the states will, in conformance with these criteria, issue and administer the permits to the individual sources, but EPA is directed to do so where a state does not. Each permit is to contain "enforceable emission limitations and standards, a schedule of compliance, a requirement that the permittee submit to the permitting authority, no less often than every 6 months, the results of any required monitoring, and such other conditions *as are necessary to ensure compliance with applicable requirements of this chapter, including the requirements of the applicable implementation plan*" [see Section 504(a), emphasis added]. As required by Title V, EPA has promulgated regulations specifying various monitoring requirements, and the states and EPA are slowly implementing Title V by issuing permits to individual facilities. If the experience under the Clean Water Act is any indication, the existence of these permits, and the concomitant monitoring and reporting requirements, should make enforcement of the act less cumbersome.

■ **NOTES**

1. See chapter 11 for a more detailed discussion of enforcement of federal environmental statutes, including the role of penalties, injunctive relief, and citizen enforcement.

2. As we have seen, in addition to authorizing private rights of action against violators of the act, the Clean Air Act's citizen suit provision authorizes citizens to bring suit against EPA to compel the agency to perform "any act or duty under this chapter which is not discretionary" [Section 304(a)(2)]. However, it is the states that are responsible for issuing the act's Title V permits. What can citizens do to ensure that

states issue (and revise) permits in conformance with the act? A state's failure to issue permits in conformance with the directives of the act may give rise to a mandamus action against the state (in state court) under state law. Moreover, state administrative law may well provide citizens who comment on a draft permit (or permit revision) a right to appeal the permit through a state administrative (and, ultimately, judicial) process.

3. Title V permits must either require immediate compliance with all applicable CAA standards or contain a compliance schedule that requires such compliance by a specified date. In *New York Public Interest Group, Inc. v. Johnson*, 426 F.3d 172 (2d Cir. 2002), the Second Circuit Court of Appeals ordered EPA to veto the Title V operating permits of two large coal-fired power plants in New York City because they were out of compliance with PSD requirements and their permits contained no compliance schedule designed to bring them into compliance. ∎

7 The Regulation of Mobile Sources Under the Clean Air Act

The one thing we need to do to solve our transportation problems is to stop thinking that there is one thing we can do to solve our transportation problems.
—Robert Liberty, Executive Director, 1000 Friends of Oregon

The automobile has become synonymous with mobility and accessibility in the United States and throughout much of the developed world. Mobility—the ability to move people and goods—has continued to increase as vehicle ownership and vehicle-miles traveled have risen. Accessibility—the relative ease with which people and business can reach different locations—is also determined largely by vehicle ownership in most areas of the United States. In this country, vehicle ownership has meant access to work, to markets, and to recreation. Culturally, the automobile and the system of automobility have become icons for flexibility, individuality, and freedom. See, generally, James P. Womack, Daniel T. Jones, and Daniel Roos (1991) *The Machine That Changed the World: The Story of Lean Production.* Harper and Row, New York.

At the same time, automotive transport gives rise to a well-known set of social concerns. They include a variety of air pollutants (such as toxic emissions, acid rain precursors, and greenhouse gases), fuel consumption and fuel efficiency (and the concomitant issues that arise from our dependence on petroleum-based fuels obtained from foreign sources), and driver and passenger safety. Because the technical challenges posed by these issues are interrelated, workable solutions are likely to require coordination and integration. For example, some fuel efficiency gains can be achieved by lowering vehicle weight, but this could have negative implications for passenger safety. Fuel efficiency gains may result in a "rebound" effect, encouraging motorists to use their cars more often because of the lower per-mile cost of fuel. And implementing efficient hybrids in sports utility vehicles (SUVs) may encourage a fleet mix that further deemphasizes smaller cars. Unfortunately, as is often the case with evolving problems, legislative and political initiatives in this area have tended to be fragmented.

This chapter focuses primarily on the mobile source provisions of the Clean Air Act, but also briefly discusses other avenues for government intervention. Thus, we describe government efforts to address the social costs associated with health and environmental effects of emissions from mobile sources. It is clear that many of these efforts have had a significant impact.[1] Total automobile emissions have largely decreased since the 1970s, despite a doubling in the number of vehicle-miles trav-

---

1. Office of Information and Regulatory Affairs, Office of Management and Budget, *Informing Regulatory Decisions: 2003 Report to Congress on the Costs and Benefits of Federal Regulations and Unfunded Mandates on State, Local, and Tribal Entities.* September 22, 2003. Available at http://www.whitehouse.gov/omb/inforeg/2003_cost-ben_final_rpt.pdf (viewed on 11/20/03).

eled.[2] Moreover, automobile energy use per kilometer fell by 30% in the United States from 1970 to 1990, largely owing to the establishment of fuel economy standards.[3] Ambient air quality has improved in many urban areas, thanks in no small part to the combined effect of regulations of fuel efficiency, tailpipe emissions, engine performance, and fuel content. In addition, technology-forcing standards such as the California Zero Emission Vehicle program, while politically contentious, have spurred manufacturers to seriously consider and produce alternatively powered vehicles and alternative fuel sources. The past two decades have also seen federal efforts to tackle both congestion and pollution problems by funding transportation control measures aimed at reducing dependence on the automobile.

A. OUR ONGOING LOVE AFFAIR WITH THE AUTOMOBILE

As one scholar has noted, "the automobile achieved dominance remarkably swiftly —in a single generation—and has then extended that dominance."[4] The tremendous economic growth and urban expansion in the United States during the twentieth century both fueled and was fed by automobile consumption. By 1930, more than 25 million cars were registered to drive on 830,000 miles of paved highways.[5] By 1989 there were more than 210 million passenger cars and light trucks on the road in the United States. These vehicles consumed 85% of all the energy used for transporting people.[6] Worldwide, there were roughly 700 million cars on the road in 2002, and that figure is expected to double by 2030 (see figure 7.1).[7] Not only has the number of vehicles grown over the past several decades, but the distance traveled by each has increased as well. The distances traveled by car, bus, train, and aircraft have risen by

---

2. Annual emissions of NO_x from vehicles have increased slightly. The transportation sector's CO_2 emissions, an unregulated pollutant at the federal level, increased by 15% from 1990 to 2000.

3. This energy use, however, has reached a plateau more recently through the shift in vehicle mix to larger vehicles such as light trucks and SUVs.

4. Deborah Gordon (1991) *Steering a New Course: Transportation, Energy, and the Environment*. Island Press, Washington, DC, quoting J. Davis, *Unregulated Potential Sources of Groundwater Contamination Involving the Transport and Storage of Liquid Fuels: Technical and Policy Issues*. Argonne National Laboratory, Argonne, Ill. Available from National Technical information Services, Springfield, Va., August 1989.

5. The U.S. Census Bureau estimated that the U.S. population was about 123 million at that time.

6. Figures updated from the Bureau of Transportation Studies (U.S. Department of Transportation), *Transportation Statistics Annual Report 2000*, which estimates that the number of registered motor vehicles (autos, buses, private and commercial trucks, and publicly owned trucks) on the highways was 221.3 million in 2000, up from 188.3 million in 1990 (BTS01-02, Department of Transportation, Washington, D.C., 2001).

7. Note that in 1985 this figure was closer to 500 million cars worldwide. See Intergovernmental Panel on Climate Change (2001) *Climate Change 2001: Mitigation*. Organization for Cooperation and Development, Paris.

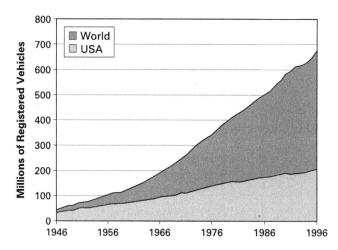

Figure 7.1
Growth of world motor vehicle population, 1946–1996. (Source: Intergovernmental Panel on Climate Change (2001), *Climate Change 2001: Mitigation.* Organization for Economic Cooperation and Development, Paris.)

roughly the same proportion as average income in the United States and in other countries.[8]

The U.S. economy is interlinked with its transportation system. In general, at least one in ten jobs in industrialized countries is linked to the automobile industry, and the United States is no exception.[9] Overall, transportation-related goods and services make up one-tenth of the U.S. economy ($990 billion in 1999) and contribute roughly one in eight jobs.[10] Transportation makes up the largest segment (18.9%) of household expenditures after housing (32.6%), amounting to $7,000 annually per household on average, with the majority going to vehicle purchase, maintenance, insurance, and gas consumption.[11] In addition, our nation's highways carry roughly 89% of the total dollar value of freight transport. The number of ton-miles moved on highways is second only to that of rail transport.[12]

As of 1995, privately owned vehicles were used for a whopping 91.2% of all trips taken for personal travel in the United States, while public transportation (bus,

8. Andreas Schafer and David Victor (1997) "The Past and Future of Global Mobility," *Scientific American* October, pp. 58–61.

9. "Living with the car," *The Economist*, June 22, 1996, pp. 3–18.

10. U.S. Dept. of Transportation, Bureau of Transportation Statistics, *Transportation Statistics Annual Report 2000.* BTS01-02 (Washington, DC, 2001).

11. Federal Highway Administration, *Our Nation's Highways* (2000).

12. Bureau of Transportation Statistics, *National Transportation Statistics 2000.*

Public used only

streetcar, commuter train, subway) was used for only 2.1%.[13] In fact, public transit's overall market share has been declining since the 1970s, despite the fact that more people are using it.[14] The dominance of car use has been attributed to the greater convenience and comfort associated with personal vehicles, to low gas prices, to the availability of subsidized or free parking, and to land use patterns affording accessibility by cars but not by other modes of transportation.[15]

■ **NOTE**

1. In the 1960s a French cartoon lampooned the American preoccupation with the automobile by depicting a Martian's-eye view of the United States. What the Martians saw was a society run by and for elongated, four-wheeled beings whose every need was met by a service class of compliant bipeds. Would this view seem out of place today?   *Good*   ■

B. THE DOWNSIDE OF AUTOMOBILITY

The catalog of ills that the system of automobility has brought with its obvious benefits is staggering to consider. Roughly 42,000 traffic-related fatalities occurred in the United States in 2000, while the number of persons with reported injuries from traffic accidents totaled nearly 3,200,000.[16] Motor vehicle crashes remain the leading cause of death for persons 4 to 33 years old.[17] Worldwide, the figures are equally dramatic,

---

13. Federal Highway Administration, *1995 Nationwide Personal Transportation Survey.*

14. For instance, the use of mass transit in the United States (in terms of revenue-miles) grew by 30%, to over 3 billion miles. Also see Jennifer L. Dorn, Federal Transit Administration administrator, in remarks to American Public Transportation Association, annual meeting, Las Vegas, Nev., September 23, 2002, at http://www.fta.dot.gov/library/intro/st/092302.html.

Although critics question the costs per rider of mass transit and the federal subsidies it receives, the benefits would appear to clearly outweigh the costs. This was the conclusion of a 1999 report sponsored by the Federal Transit Administration. See David Lewis and Fred Laurence Williams (1999) *Policy and Planning as Public Choice: Mass Transit in the United States.* Ashgate, Aldershot, UK. The use of mass transit and highways is linked because in many cases mass transit prevents added congestion on the nation's highways; in addition, it provides access for those who cannot afford vehicles (8% of households do not own vehicles, with the majority making less than $25,000) or who are unable to drive (the elderly, children, and the disabled).

15. This topic lies in the realm of transportation planning, which is beyond the scope of this chapter. For an interesting discussion, see Bradford Snell, "The Conspiracy Explained," *New Electric Railway Journal* Autumn 1995, pp. 26–29, which describes the efforts by General Motors and National City Lines to eliminate streetcars in the late 1940s.

16. These figures remained roughly constant through the 1990s. Nearly one half million deaths were attributed to vehicle accidents in the 1990s.

17. "Traffic Safety Facts 2000: Overview," U.S. Department of Transportation, National Highway Traffic Safety Administration (2000). The death rate for 2000 (fatalities per 100 million vehicle-miles traveled) actually represented a historic low of 1.5 (down from 1.6 from 1997 to 1999). The decrease was due mainly to increased use of seat belts and a reduction in drunk driving. While most of the deaths involved occupants of vehicles, 13% were pedestrians, pedal-cyclists, and other nonoccupants.

with more than 20 million individuals injured or crippled and more than 1 million killed annually in automobile-related accidents.[18]

Automobiles, and the industries that support them, also have a significant adverse effect on human health and the environment. Familiar health effects include the respiratory ailments caused by carbon monoxide, particulate matter, carcinogenic compounds, or smog. Environmental impacts on the local, regional, and global level are also clear. They include the risks of climate change caused by CO_2 emissions; impacts associated with urban and suburban sprawl made possible by vehicles; visibility problems in national parks and urban areas; and ground, air, and water pollution from exploration, extraction, transportation, and refining of fuels. Finally, our steadfast dependence on petroleum to fuel our transportation system has created great economic costs as well as political risks. Various estimates of the air pollution costs in the United States alone are between $30 billion and $200 billion.[19] The World Resources Institute places the total U.S. social cost of driving (not paid directly by motorists) at $300 billion a year, or 5.3% of the gross domestic product (GDP), while other estimates range up to 12% of GDP for the United States and 4.6% for Europe.[20] If one included the political and military spending associated with protecting U.S. oil interests, these figures would be higher, although difficult to measure.[21]

Human health effects that are due to exposure to airborne pollutants were addressed generally in chapter 2. For a review of the relative contribution of outdoor and traffic-related air pollution to public health, see N. Künzli et al. (2000) "Public-health Impact of Outdoor and Traffic-related Air Pollution: A European Assessment," *Lancet* 356: 795–801, September. As discussed in chapter 6, national primary ambient air quality standards were established to protect public health with "an adequate margin of safety." The primary ambient standards relevant to the major criteria pollutants emanating from mobile sources are listed in table 7.1.

---

18. *Report of the Road Traffic Injuries and Health Equity Conference*, April 10–12, 2002, Cambridge, Mass., Harvard Center for Population and Development Studies.

19. Senate Report 105-95. Intermodal Surface Transportation Efficiency Act of 1997, October 1, 1997.

20. "Living with the car," *The Economist* June 22, 1996, pp. 3–27. Also see "'Social Costs' of Motor Vehicle Pollution Pegged at $40 Billion in DOT First Estimate," *Environment Reporter* 31(33): 1710 (2000). Most of the costs were associated with premature death and illness caused by exposure to particulate matter, including both direct particulate emissions and secondary formation of particulates from other emissions.

21. If links between dependence on the Middle East for oil and terrorism are assumed, the added potential security risks would pose a growing cost related to automobility. See Gawdat Bahgat (2004) "Terrorism and Energy," *World Affairs* 167(2): 51 (Fall); Michael T. Klare (2002) "The Deadly Nexus: Oil, Terrorism, and America's National Security," *Current History: A Journal of Contemporary World Affairs* vol. 101, issue 659: 414; Marianne Lavelle, "Living without Oil; As War Looms, the Search for New Energy Alternatives is All the More Urgent," *U.S. News & World Report*, February 17, 2003, pp. 32–39.

Table 7.1
Primary Air Quality Standards for Transportation-Related Pollutants

Pollutant	Type of Average	Concentration
CO	8-hour	9 ppm (10 mg/m^3)
	1-hour	35 ppm (40 mg/m^3)
O$_3$	1-hour	0.08 ppm (157 mg/m^3)
PM$_{2.5}$	24-hour	35 μg/m^3
PM$_{10}$	24-hour	150 μg/m^3
NO$_2$	Annual	100 μg/m^3 (0.053 ppm)

Notes: ppm = parts per million; mg/m^3 = milligrams (10^{-3} g) per cubic meter; μg/m^3 = micrograms (10^{-6} g) per cubic meter.

Hazardous air pollutants ("air toxics") from mobile sources also present a major health concern. While major stationary sources accounted for 24% of 3.7 million tons of emissions of air toxics and area (stationary) sources accounted for 34%, mobile sources accounted for 42% of air toxics as of 1993. Highway vehicle emissions of benzene, 1,3-butadiene, and directly emitted formaldehyde (all carcinogens) are of special concern. Emissions from diesel engines are reported to account for 78% of the cancer risk associated with all hazardous air pollutants. See *Environment Reporter* 32(29): 1397 (2001).

▪ NOTES

1. Small particulates (PM$_{2.5}$) are implicated in increased heart attacks that are due to an increased pulmonary load. See: http://walshcarlines.com, no. 45 "Heart Attack Risk Seen from Small Particles," issue 2001-4, August 2001, pp. 44–45.

2. External emissions are not the only concern. The automobile or truck cabin is a confined space and therefore can accumulate toxic emissions from upholstery, electrical equipment, and the internal combustion engine. See Ian A. Greaves (2000) "The Automobile as a Confined Space for Toxic Chemical Hazards: Letter to the Editor," *American Journal of Industrial Medicine* 38: 481–482.

3. Mercury contamination is of special concern when cars are discarded or destroyed. The bulk of mercury is released when contaminated scrap steel is melted in electric arc furnaces. In total, more than 175 metric tons of mercury are present in cars on the road today, primarily in mercury switches in hood and trunk lighting and antilock braking systems. See "Vehicles Major Source of Mercury Emissions," *American Public Health Association Newsletter*, 2001. Available at http://www.cleancarcampaign.org/mercury.html. ▪

Figure 7.2
Typical smog conditions during the 1940s and 1950s in Los Angeles. (Source: Federal Highway Administration, ⟨http://www.fhwa.dot.gov⟩.)

C. THE EMERGENCE OF AIR POLLUTION LEGISLATION FOR MOBILE SOURCES

California was the first to act against the mounting environmental hazard from U.S. automobile use. In 1947, that state attempted to address its severe air quality problems by forming the first Air Pollution Control District, in Los Angeles (see figure 7.2).[22] Continued growth stymied that effort, however, and by 1954 smog levels were causing frequent shutdowns of industry and schools in the Los Angeles basin. These smog episodes, and others like them throughout the country, prompted Congress to enact the Air Pollution Control Act of 1955, which was the first federal legislation addressing air pollution.[23] The act called for the Department of Health, Education, and Welfare (HEW) to provide assistance to local and state governments in addressing air pollution problems.[24] While doing little to prevent pollution, the act provided the rationale for subsequent statutes addressing motor vehicle emissions.[25]

---

22. Los Angeles County passed regulations requiring major industries to obtain pollution permits and install smog control equipment.

23. Pollution problems were also prevalent elsewhere, with similar incidents on the East Coast (e.g., New York City). As discussed in chapter 6, a 1948 smog episode in Donora, Pennsylvania, left half the population ill and 20 dead. In one particularly infamous episode in December 1952, London's "killer smog" led to 4,000 excess deaths. While the latter two episodes were due mainly to SO_x and PM from stationary sources, they helped call national attention to air pollution in general.

24. A subsequent amendment, the Federal Motor Vehicle Act of 1960, specifically called for research on the health effects caused by motor vehicle emissions.

25. H.R. Rep. No. 89-899 (1965), reprinted in 1965 U.S.C.C.A.N. 3608, 3611.

California was also the first to actually establish regulatory controls on automobile emissions. State legislation enacted in 1959 directed the California Department of Public Health to establish air quality standards and controls for motor vehicle emissions.[26] By 1961, the state had both established emission standards for new vehicles sold in California and mandated the installation of emissions control technology (positive crankcase ventilation valves) in those vehicles.[27] Four years later, Congress passed the 1965 Clean Air Act Amendments, Title II of which authorized control of air pollution from mobile sources. Known as the Motor Vehicle Air Pollution Control Act, Title II directed HEW to set vehicle emission standards "giving appropriate consideration to technological feasibility and economic costs."[28] Shortly thereafter, HEW promulgated standards requiring 1968 model year vehicles to achieve a 72% reduction in emissions of hydrocarbons (HCs), a 56% reduction in emissions of carbon monoxide (CO), and a 100% reduction in crankcase HC emissions, compared with 1963 models.[29]

Five years later, however, a Congress that had become sorely displeased with the auto industry's performance ushered in the "modern era" of mobile source regulation with the Clean Air Act Amendments of 1970. As with stationary sources, the basic framework established for mobile sources in the 1970 amendments is still in force today. Nonetheless, after 20 years of gradual implementation, occasional refinements, and some considerable backtracking, Congress refocused the act's mobile source provisions in 1990. Accordingly, we will first take a detailed look at the structure and implementation of the 1970 amendments and then examine the changes brought about by the 1990 amendments.

D. THE 1970 CLEAN AIR ACT AMENDMENTS

In the period leading up to the 1970 Clean Air Act Amendments, public concern over health, safety, and the environment grew steadily.[30] The publication of Rachel Carson's *Silent Spring* in 1962 had called attention to the threat of chemical pollution, and Ralph Nader's *Unsafe at Any Speed* in 1965 had heightened concerns over

---

26. See http://www.arb.ca.gov/html/brochure/history.htm (viewed on 4/27/04).

27. The emission standards were required for new vehicles sold in model year 1966.

28. *Motor Vehicle Air Pollution Control Act of 1965*, Pub. L. No. 89-272, §202(a), 1965 U.S.C.C.A.N. (79 Stat. 992) 983, 984. (codified at 42 U.S.C. 3251).

29. Information from the American Meteorological Society. Available at http://www.ametsoc.org/sloan/cleanair/ (viewed on 4/22/04).

30. The environmental movement gained strength in response to decades of worsening air quality. The year 1970 saw the signing of the National Environmental Policy Act, the first "Earth Day" celebration, and the creation of EPA under the Nixon administration.

the safety of the American automobile. An environmental and consumer movement was forming, represented by newly formed organizations such as the Sierra Club, the Environmental Defense Fund, and the World Wildlife Fund. As noted at the time by Warren Burger, who had recently been tapped by President Richard Nixon to serve as Chief Justice of the Supreme Court,

not a week passes without speeches in Congress and elsewhere, and editorials, demanding new laws, new laws to control pollution, new laws to change the environment, new laws to allow class actions by consumers to protect the public.... [Senator Dole of Kansas, quoting then Chief Justice Burger, who was expressing concern that the Court would become overburdened with the new laws. *National Air Quality Standards Act of 1970*, SR 4358, 91st Cong., 2d sess., *Cong. Rec.* 116 (Sept. 22, 1970): S. 330078]

Much of the public concern focused on air pollution:

[P]eople living in smoggy cities wanted clean air—air that did not aggravate respiratory problems, burn the eyes, smell acidic, or restrict visibility. They wanted industries to stop pumping plumes of black smoke out of tall chimneys. They wanted automobile manufacturers to build cars that neither created nor contributed to the smog problem. They wanted clean air immediately and painlessly. [Dennis C. Williams (1993) *The Guardian: EPA's Formative Years, 1970–1973.* EPA 202-K-93-002, Environmental Protection Agency, Washington, D.C.]

Congressional hearings on air pollution in 1967 revealed that little progress was being made to reduce automobile emissions.[31] Moreover, tests performed in 1968 and 1969 found that more than half of the vehicles for these model years failed to meet the new standards required by HEW. By 1969, the Department of Justice had charged the four largest automakers with conspiracy to delay development of emission control devices.[32]

Congress responded with what was designed to be strong medicine for automakers and drivers alike. As noted in the House report for the 1970 Clean Air Act Amendments, Congress had decided that a different approach was needed:

A review of achievements to date... make abundantly clear that the strategies which we have pursued in the war against air pollution have been inadequate in several important respects, and the methods employed in implementing those strategies often have been slow and less effective than they might have been.... [*Clean Air Act Amendments of 1960*, H. Rep. No. 91-1146, at 1 (1970), reprinted in 1970 U.S.C.C.A.N., 5356, 5356]

Further, several members of the House of Representatives were decidedly blunt in their dismissal of the arguments raised by automobile manufacturers in opposition to the tougher new strategy chosen by Congress:

---

31. Senate Hearings on Air Pollution—1967, Hearings before the Subcomm. on Air and Water Pollution, Sen. Comm. on Public Works, 90th Cong., 1st sess., pt. 3, 1155–6 (1967).

32. The case was resolved by consent decree. *United States v. Automobile Manufacturers Ass'n.*, 307 F. Supp. 617 (C.D. Cal. 1969), aff'd. sub nom. *City of New York v. United States*, et al., 397 U.S. 248, 90 S. Ct. 1105, 25 L. Ed. 2d 280 (1970).

We are not impressed by the wails of the auto industry that meaningful improvements in their product pose insurmountable cost and engineering problems. We listened to the same complaints back in 1967, when Congress agreed to permit California to depart from national auto emission norms in setting and enforcing more stringent controls. The industry demonstrated then that it has the expertise and the know-how to make just about any change for the better when the public demand is great enough. [Additional views of Hon. Lionel V. Deerlin et al., *Clean Air Act Amendments of 1960*, H. Rep. No. 91-1146, (1970), reprinted in 1970 U.S.C.C.A.N., 5356, 5371]

The 1970 amendments embodied and set in motion a three-pronged approach to auto pollution. First, they imposed national emission standards on new motor vehicles. Significantly, the specific standards and timetable for new light-duty gasoline-powered motor vehicles were established by Congress itself and explicitly set forth in the statute. Other emission standards were to be set by HEW (whose role was soon given to the newly formed Environmental Protection Agency). Second, in what was initially an effort to reduce airborne lead concentrations, the 1970 amendments authorized the regulation of the content of motor vehicle fuels. Third, as part of the state implementation plan (SIP) program, Congress encouraged the states to develop "transportation control" initiatives to influence how, when, where, and in what condition motor vehicles were driven. We address each part of this three-pronged attack on auto pollution in turn.

1. Emission Standards for New Motor Vehicles

a. Limits Set by Congress

The 1970 amendments called for a reduction of at least 90% in emissions of HC, CO, and NO_x from light-duty motor vehicles. The first two of these were to be attained by the 1975 model year and the latter by the 1976 model year.[33] A 90% reduction was specified as a goal because it represented the level deemed necessary to attain ambient air quality standards. The deadlines, however, reflected more a political calculus than a technical judgment. With the political tide turning against them, the heads of the major automakers had met with President Nixon in early 1970 and proposed two sets of emission reductions, the first for 1975 and the second for 1980.[34] President Nixon later recommended a more stringent set of standards for 1975 and a 90%

---

33. The 90% reductions for CO and HC were to be achieved in comparison with 1970 model year vehicle standards. The 90% reduction for NO_x was to be achieved in comparison with the average emissions measured from 1971 model year vehicles [CAAA 1970, §202(b), Dec. 18, 1970]. Note that the earlier standards promulgated by HEW under the 1965 Clean Air Act were considered attainable by the auto industry. (See the statements of Senator Griffin of Michigan in the *Congressional Record*, Senate, Sept. 22, 1970, 33082.)

34. The proposed 1980 achievement was half that eventually mandated by Congress in the 1970 amendments. "Individual View by Senator Edward Gurney," Senate Committee of Public Works, *National Air Quality Standards Act of 1970*, 91st Cong., 2d sess., 1970, S. Rep. 91-1196, at 50–51.

reduction as a research target for 1980. Senator Edmund Muskie of Maine moved to outflank the president by making the 1980 research target an actual requirement and by advancing the schedule 5 years, to 1975. See David Gerard and Lester Lave (2005) "Implementing Technology-Forcing Policies: The 1970 Clean Air Act Amendments and the Introduction of Advanced Automotive Emissions Controls." *Technological Forecasting and Social Change* 72: 761–778.

In specifying a flat 90% reduction, Congress made a conscious decision to attempt to force automakers to develop and implement the necessary technology despite their avowed disinclination to do so. As a key part of this strategy, Congress chose to establish the standards itself rather than delegating the task to an administrative agency.[35] On the Senate floor, Republican Senator Robert Dole of Kansas noted that the Senate Public Works Committee had determined that establishing motor vehicle emission standards was "a policy decision so important to public health that it should be made by the Congress, rather than the Secretary of Health, Education, and Welfare."[36] On a more practical level, Senator Muskie reportedly believed "that a bureaucrat would always extend the deadline, so he wanted Congress to make the decision."[37]

The gauntlet, then, had been thrown down, but not without certain misgivings. During the Senate debate, there was considerable discussion as to what could, and should, happen if the required 90% reduction proved to be unattainable within the specified time frame, and which branch of government should provide "redress" if Congress had miscalculated. As noted by Republican Senator Howard Baker of Tennessee:

That redress can come from three sources. It can come from the executive department; it can come from the legislative department; or it can come from the judiciary. That really is the question that confronts us.... Where do we put it? [*Congressional Record* 116 (Sept. 22, 1970): S. 33084]

Ultimately, Congress chose to place this responsibility in the hands of the judiciary. However, Congress endeavored to circumscribe the role of the judiciary by limiting the court's review to the single question of whether the automakers had satisfied specific statutory criteria for a 1-year extension of the deadlines. The limitation was

---

35. Although the statute specified that the act was to be administered by the secretary of HEW, the HEW effectively became a part of the EPA during this time. The EPA was established in the executive branch as an independent agency, pursuant to the Reorganization Plan No. 3 of 1970, and came into formal being on December 2, 1970, just days before the Clean Air Act Amendments were passed on December 18, 1970.

36. *National Air Quality Standards Act of 1970*, SR 4358, 91st Cong., 2d sess., *Cong. Rec.* 116 (Sept. 22, 1970): S. 33078.

37. Comments by Senator Muskie's aide, Leon Billings, as quoted in Gerard and Lave, "Implementing Technology-Forcing Policies," citing Doyle, Jack (2000), *Taken for a Ride: Detroit's Big Three and the Politics of Pollution*. New York: Four Walls Eight Windows.

made because Congress was concerned that the courts might insert themselves into policy-making determinations that are properly the province of Congress. This redress mechanism, and the overall technology-forcing scheme embodied in the 1970 amendments, was rather quickly put to the test.

International Harvester Co., et al., v. Environmental Protection Agency
LEVENTHAL, Circuit Judge
478 F.2d 615 (D.C. Cir. 1973)

These consolidated petitions of International Harvester and the three major auto companies, Ford, General Motors and Chrysler, seek review of a decision by the Administrator of the Environmental Protection Agency denying petitioners' applications, filed pursuant to Section 202 of the Clean Air Act, for one year suspensions of the 1975 emission standards prescribed under the statute for light duty vehicles in the absence of suspension.

I. STATEMENT OF THE CASE

The tension of forces presented by the controversy over automobile emission standards may be focused by two central observations:

(1) The automobile is an essential pillar of the American economy. Some 28 per cent of the nonfarm workforce draws its livelihood from the automobile industry and its products.

(2) The automobile has had a devastating impact on the American environment. As of 1970, authoritative voices stated that "automotive pollution constitutes in excess of 60% of our national air pollution problem" and more than 80 per cent of the air pollutants in concentrated urban areas. . . .

Congress was aware that these 1975 standards were "drastic medicine," designed to "force the state of the art." There was, naturally, concern whether the manufacturers would be able to achieve this goal. Therefore, Congress provided, in Senator

Baker's phrase, a "realistic escape hatch": the manufacturers could petition the Administrator of the EPA for a one-year suspension of the 1975 requirements, and Congress took the precaution of directing the National Academy of Sciences to undertake an ongoing study of the feasibility of compliance with the emission standards. The "escape hatch" provision addressed itself to the possibility that the NAS study or other evidence might indicate that the standards would be unachievable despite all good faith efforts at compliance. This provision was limited to a one-year suspension, which would defer compliance with the 90% reduction requirement until 1976. Under section 202(b)(5)(D) of the Act, 42 U.S.C. §1857f-1(b)(5)(D), the Administrator is authorized to grant a one-year suspension only if he determines that (i) such suspension is essential to the public interest or the public health and welfare of the United States, (ii) all good faith efforts have been made to meet the standards established by this subsection, (iii) the applicant has established that effective control technology, processes, operating methods, or other alternatives are not available or have not been available for a sufficient period of time to achieve compliance prior to the effective date of such standards, and (iv) the study and investigation of the National Academy of Sciences conducted pursuant to subsection (c) of this section and other information available to him has not indicated that such technology, processes, or other alternatives are available to meet such standards. . . .

B.   Initial Decision of the Administrator

The data available from the concerned parties related to 384 test vehicles run by the five applicants and the eight other vehicle manufacturers subpoenaed by the Administrator. In addition, 116 test vehicles were run by catalyst and reactor manufacturers subpoenaed by the Administrator. These 500 vehicles were used to test five principal types of control systems: noble metal monolithic catalysts, base metal pellet catalysts, noble metal pellet catalysts, reactor systems, and various reactor/catalyst combinations.

At the outset of his Decision, the Administrator determined that the most effective system so far developed was the noble metal oxidizing catalyst. Additionally, he stated that the "most effective systems typically include: improved carburetion; a fast-release choke; a device for promoting fuel vaporization during warm-up; more consistent and durable ignition systems; exhaust gas recirculation; and a system for injecting air into the engine exhaust manifold to cause further combustion of unburned gases and to create an oxidizing atmosphere for the catalyst." It was this system to which the data base was initially narrowed: only cars using this kind of system were to be considered in making the "available technology" determination.

The problem the Administrator faced in making a determination that technology was available, on the basis of these data, was that actual tests showed only one car with actual emissions which conformed to the standard prescribing a maximum of .41 grams, per mile, of HC and 3.4 grams per mile of CO. No car had actually been driven 50,000 miles, the statutory "useful life" of a vehicle and the time period for which conformity to the emission standards is required. . . .

In light of these difficulties, the Administrator "adjusted" the data of the auto companies by use of several critical assumptions.

First, he made an adjustment to reflect the assumption that fuel used in 1975 model year cars would either contain an average of .03 grams per gallon or .05 grams per gallon of lead. This usually resulted in an increase of emissions predicted, since many companies had tested their vehicles on lead free gasoline.

Second, the Administrator found that the attempt of some companies to reduce emissions of nitrogen oxides below the 1975 Federal standard of 3.0 grams per vehicle mile resulted in increased emissions of hydrocarbons and carbon monoxide. This adjustment resulted in a downward adjustment of observed HC and CO data, by a specified factor.

Third, the Administrator took into account the effect the "durability" of the preferred systems would have on the emission control obtainable. This required that observed readings at one point of usage be increased by a deterioration factor (DF) to project emissions at a later moment of use. The critical methodological choice was to make this adjustment from a base of emissions observed at 4000 miles. Thus, even if a car had actually been tested over 4000 miles, predicted emissions at 50,000 miles would be determined by multiplying 4000 mile emissions by the DF factor.

Fourth, the Administrator adjusted for "prototype-to-production slippage." This was an upward adjustment made necessary by the possibility that prototype cars might have features which reduced HC and CO emissions, but were not capable of being used in actual production vehicles. Finally, in accord with a regulation assumed, as to substance, in the text of the Decision, but proposed after the suspension hearing, a downward adjustment in the data readings was made on the basis of the manufacturers' ability, in conformance with certification procedures, to replace the catalytic converter "once during 50,000 miles of vehicle operation," a change they had not used in their testing.

With the data submitted and the above assumptions, the Administrator concluded that no showing had been made that requisite technology was not available. The EPA noted that this did not mean that the variety of vehicles produced in 1975 would be as extensive as before. According to EPA, "Congress clearly intended to require major changes in the kinds of automobiles produced for sale in the United States after 1974" and there "is no basis, therefore, for construing the Act as authorizing suspension of the standards simply because the range of performance of cars with effective emission control may be restricted as compared to present cars." As long as "basic demand" for new light duty motor vehicles was satisfied, the applicants could not establish that technology was not available....

C. This Court's December 1972 Remand

After oral argument to this court on December 18, 1972, in a *per curiam* order issued December 19, 1972, we remanded the record to the Administrator, directing him to supplement his May 12, 1972 decision by setting forth:

(a) the consideration given by the Administrator to the January 1, 1972 Semiannual Report on Technological Feasibility of the National Academy of Sciences; and (b) the basis for his disagreement, if any, with the findings and conclusion in that study concerning the availability of effective technology to achieve compliance with the 1975 model year standards set forth in the Act.... We were... troubled by arguments advanced by petitioners that the methodology used by the Administrator in reaching his conclusion, and indeed the conclusion itself, was inconsistent with that of the Academy. It was our view that if and to the extent such differences existed they should be explained by EPA, in order to aid us in determining whether the Administrator's conclusion under (iii) rested on a reasoned basis.

D. Supplement to the Decision of the Administrator

Our remand of the record resulted in a "Supplement to Decision of the Administrator" issued December 30, 1972. The Administrator in his Supplement stated that "In general I consider the factual findings and technical conclusions set forth in the NAS report and in the subsequent Interim Standards Report dated April 26, 1972... to be consistent with my decision of May 12, 1972."

The Report made by the NAS, pursuant to its obligation under 202(b)(5)(D) of the Clean Air Act, had concluded: "The Committee finds that the technology necessary to meet the requirements of the Clean Air Act Amendments for 1975 model year light-duty motor vehicles is not available at this time."

The Administrator apparently relied, however, on the NAS Report to bolster his conclusion that the applicants had not established that technology was unavailable. The same NAS Report had stated:

... the status of development and rate of progress made it possible that the larger manufacturers will be able to produce vehicles that will qualify, provided that provisions are made for catalyst replacement and other maintenance, for averaging emissions of production vehicles, and for the general availability of fuel containing suitably low levels of catalyst poisons.

The Administrator pointed out that two of NAS's provisos—catalytic converter replacement and low lead levels—had been accounted for in his analysis of the auto company data, and provision therefor had been insured through regulation. As to the third, "averaging emissions of production vehicles," the Administrator offered two reasons for declining to make a judgment about this matter: (1) The significance of averaging related to possible assembly-line tests, as distinct from certification test procedure, and such tests had not yet been worked out. (2) If there were an appropriate assembly-line test it would be expected that each car's emissions could be in conformity, without a need for averaging, since the assembly line vehicles "equipped with fresh catalysts can be expected to have substantially lower emissions at zero miles than at 4000 miles." ...

The Administrator did refer to the "severe driveability problems" underscored by the NAS Report, which in the judgment of NAS "could have significant safety implications," stating that he had not been presented with any evidence of "specific safety hazard" nor knew of any presented to the NAS. He did not address himself to the issue of performance problems falling short of specific safety hazards.

II. REJECTION OF MANUFACTURERS' GENERAL CONTENTIONS

We begin with consideration, and rejection, of the broad objections leveled by petitioners against EPA's over-all approach.

A. Future Technological Developments

We cannot accept petitioners' arguments that the Administrator's determination whether technology was "available," within the meaning of section 202(b)(5)(D) of the Act, must be based solely on technology in being as of the time of the application, and that the requirement that this be "available" precludes any consideration by the Administrator of what he determines to be the "probable" or likely sequence of the technology already experienced. ...

While we reject the contention as broadly stated, principally by General Motors, we hasten to add that the Administrator's latitude for projection is subject to the restraints of reasonableness, and does not open the door to "'crystal ball' inquiry." The Administrator's latitude for projection is unquestionably limited by relevant considerations of lead time needed for production. Implicit also is a requirement of reason in the reliability of the EPA projection. In the present case, the

Administrator's prediction of available technology was based on known elements of existing catalytic converter systems. This was a permissible approach subject, of course, to the requirement that any technological developments or refinements of existing systems, used as part of the EPA methodology, would have to rest on a reasoned basis.

B. Claimed Right of Cross-Examination

Chrysler has advanced a due process claim based upon two principal features of the proceeding, the inability to engage in cross-examination and the inability to present arguments against the methodology used in the Technical Appendix of the Administrator, which served as a basis for his decision.

[The Court rejected the due process claim, but acknowledged that it was troubled by EPA's failure to afford the manufacturers an opportunity to comment on its methodology.] ...

While we do not say that the failure to provide reasonable opportunity to comment on EPA methodology invalidates the EPA Decision for lack of procedural due process, or similar contention, we must in all candor accompany that ruling with the comment that the lack of such opportunity has had serious implications for the court given the role of judicial review.

We shall subsequently develop the legal questions, primarily questions of EPA's burden of proof, that arise with respect to EPA methodology. We preface these with admission of our doubts and diffidence. We are beset with contentions of petitioners that bear indicia of substantiality. ...

III. OVERALL PERSPECTIVE OF SUSPENSION ISSUE

This case ultimately involves difficult issues of statutory interpretation, as to the showing required for applicants to sustain their burden that technology is not available. It also taxes our ability to understand and evaluate technical issues upon which that showing, however it is to be defined, must rest. At the same time, however, larger questions are at stake. As Senator Baker put it, "This may be the biggest industrial judgment that has been made in the United States in this century." 116 Cong. Rec. 33,085 (1970). This task of reviewing the suspension decision was not assigned to us lightly. It was the judgment of Congress that this court, isolated as it is from political pressures, and able to partake of calm and judicious reflection would be a more suitable forum for review than even the Congress. . . .

Two principal considerations compete for our attention. On the one hand, if suspension is not granted, and the prediction of the EPA Administrator that effective technology will be available is proven incorrect, grave economic consequences could ensue. This is the problem Senator Griffin described as the "dangerous game of economic roulette." 116 Cong. Rec. 33,081 (1970). On the other hand, if suspension is granted, and it later be shown that the Administrator's prediction of feasibility was achievable in 1975 there may be irretrievable ecological costs. It is to this second possibility which we first turn.

A. Potential Environmental Costs

The most authoritative estimate in the record of the ecological costs of a one-year suspension is that of the NAS Report. . . . NAS concluded that:

. . . the effect on total emissions of a one-year suspension with no additional interim standards appears to be small. The effect is not more significant because the emission reduction now required of model year 1974 vehicles, as compared with uncontrolled vehicles (80 percent for HC and 69 percent for CO), is already so substantial. . . .

Other considerations may diminish the costs even further. There seems to be agreement that there are performance costs for automobiles in employing pollution control devices, even if the effects on performance cannot fairly be characterized as constituting safety hazards. The NAS Report summarized the problem, as follows:

Three areas of vehicle performance are likely to be adversely affected by the 1975 emission control systems. These are fuel economy, vehicle-acceleration capability, and vehicle driveability (or ability to perform adequately in all normal operating modes and ambient conditions).

The question in this context is not whether these are costs the consumer should rightly bear if ecological damage is to be minimized, but rather the general effect on consumer purchasing of 1975 model year cars in anticipation of lower performance. A drop-off in purchase of 1975 cars will result in a prolonged usage of older cars with *less* efficient pollution control devices. If the adverse performance effect deterred purchasing significantly enough, resulting in greater retention of "older" cars in the "mix" of cars in use, it might even come to pass that total actual emissions (of all cars in use) would be greater under the 1975 than the 1974 standards. . . .

Many of the anticipated performance problems are traceable to the systems introduced to conform cars to control of nitrogen oxides to achieve prescribed 1975 standards, by use of exhaust-gas recycle (EGR). Such systems affect vehicle-acceleration capability because the power output for a given engine displacement, engine speed, and throttle setting is reduced. The NAS Report indicates that such systems could result in direct fuel-economy penalties of up to 12 percent compared with 1973 prototype vehicles. . . .

The NAS Report states that the effects of emission controls on vehicle driveability are difficult to quantify, but nevertheless makes the following qualitative evaluation:

Driveability after a cold-engine start, and especially with cold ambient conditions, is likely to be impaired. To reduce HC and CO emissions during engine warmup, the choke is set to release quickly, and the fuel-air mixture is leaned out as early as possible after engine startup. Under these conditions, problems of engine stall, and vehicle stumble and hesitation on rapid acceleration, have been prevalent.

The willingness of the consumer to buy 1975 model year cars may also be affected, to some degree, by the anticipated significant costs of pollution control devices. The problem is further bedeviled by the possibility that consumers, albeit rightly assigned the cost burden of pollution devices, may seek to avoid that burden, however modest, and to exercise, at least in some measure, an option to use older cars. Again, this would have the thrust of increasing actual total emissions of cars in use....

We may also note that it is the belief of many experts—both in and out of the automobile industry—that air pollution cannot be effectively checked until the industry finds a substitute for the conventional automotive power plant—the reciprocating internal combustion (*i.e.*, "piston") engine. According to this view, the conventional unit is a "dirty" engine. While emissions from such a motor can be "cleaned" by various thermal and catalytic converter devices, these devices do nothing to decrease the production of emissions in the engine's combustion chambers. The automobile industry has a multi-billion-dollar investment in the conventional engine, and it has been reluctant to introduce new power plants or undertake major modifications of the conventional one.[62] Thus the bulk of the industry's work on emission control has focused narrowly on converter devices. It is clear from the legislative history that Congress expected the Clean Air Amendments to force the industry to broaden the scope of its research—to study new types of engines and new control systems. Perhaps even a one-year suspension does not give the industry sufficient time to develop a new approach to emission control and still meet the absolute deadline of 1976. If so, there will be ample time for the EPA and Congress, between now and 1976 to reflect on changing the statutory approach. This kind of cooperation, a unique three-way partnership between the legislature, executive and judiciary, was contemplated by the Congress[64] and is apparent in the provisions of the Act.

The NAS estimated that there would be a small environmental cost to suspension of 1975 standards even if 1974 standards were retained, but further recommended intermediate standards that would dilute even such modest environmental cost. [The table] shows the various standards, and one put forward by Ford for 1975:

Maximum Emissions (grams per mile)

	HC	CO
1974 Standards	3.4	39.0
Ford Proposal	1.6	19.0
NAS Recommendations for intermediate standards:		
No catalyst change	1.1	8.2
One catalyst change	0.8	6.3
1975 Standards	0.41	3.4

62. The General Accounting Office reported in 1972 that the industry was "entrenched" in efforts to retain the conventional engine.

64. Congress made clear that it would be ready to exercise its right to intervene if it did not agree with the results its statutory "shock treatment" produced. *See* 116 Cong. Rec. 32,905 (1970) (Senator Muskie). Congress, through Oversight Hearings conducted by the Subcommittee on Air and Water Pollution of the United States Senate, continues to keep a watchful eye on the implementation of the Act. *See* Implementation of the Clean Air Act Amendments of 1970, Hearings before the Subcomm. on Air and Water Pollution, Senate Comm. on Public Works, 92d Cong., 2d Sess., pts. 1–3 (1972).

Our concern that the 1975 standards may possibly be counter-productive, due to decreased driveability and increased cost, is not to be extrapolated into a caution against any improvement, and concomitant reduction in permitted emissions. In such matters, as the NAS recommendation for interim standards implicitly suggests...the insistence on absolute 1975 standards, without suspension or intermediate level, may stretch for the increment that is essentially counter-productive.

On balance the record indicates the environmental costs of a one-year suspension are likely to be relatively modest. This must be balanced against the potential economic costs—and ecological costs—if the Administrator's prediction on the availability of effective technology is incorrect.

B. Potential Economic Costs

Theoretical Possibility of Industry Shutdown

If in 1974, when model year 1975 cars start to come off the production line, the automobiles of Ford, General Motors and Chrysler cannot meet the 1975 standards and do not qualify for certification, the Administrator of EPA has the theoretical authority, under the Clean Air Act, to shut down the auto industry, as was clearly recognized in Congressional debate. We cannot put blinders on the facts before us so as to omit awareness of the reality that this authority would undoubtedly never be exercised, in light of the fact that approximately 1 out of every 7 jobs in this country is dependent on the production of the automobile. Senator Muskie, the principal sponsor of the bill, stated quite clearly in the debate on the Act that he envisioned the Congress acting if an auto industry shutdown were in sight.

The Economic Consequence of an Approach Geared to Stringency, Relying on Relaxation as a Safety Valve

A more likely forecast, and one which enlightens what influenced the EPA decision to deny the suspension, was articulated by George Allen, Deputy Assistant Administrator for General Enforcement and a member of EPA's Hearing Panel:

The problem really comes down to this: A decision has to be made next month, early next month. If the decision is to suspend the standards and adopt an interim standard...and in 1975 it turns out that technology exists to meet the statutory standard, today's decision turns out to be wrong....

If, on the other hand, a decision is made today that the standards cannot lawfully be suspended, and we go down to 1975 and nobody can meet the standard, today's decision was wrong.

In [the first] case, there is not much to do about the wrong decision; it was made, many people relied on it; it turns out the standard could have been met, but I doubt if we could change it.

In the second case, if a wrong decision is made, there is probably a remedy, a re-application and a recognition by the agency that it is not technically feasible to meet the standards. You can correct the one; you probably can't correct the other. Grave problems are presented by the assumption that if technical feasibility proves to be a "wrong decision" it can be remedied by a relaxation....

The record before us suggests that there already exists a technological gap between Ford and General Motors, in Ford's favor. General Motors did not make the decision to concentrate on what EPA found to be the most effective system at the time of its decision—the noble metal monolithic catalyst. Instead it relied principally on testing the base metal catalyst as its first choice system. In predicting that General Motors could meet the 1975 standards, EPA employed a unique methodological approach. Instead of taking emissions at 4000 miles of cars with preferred systems—with which none of the General Motors cars was equipped—and applying against this adjustments for lead levels and deterioration, as had been done in the case of Ford and Chrysler, EPA took emissions at 4000 miles of GM cars which had no converters of any kind, and predicted how they would function with an Engelhard monolithic catalytic converter, based on auto manufacturers' use of this device in a number of cars—principally Ford's—when testing it for durability....

The case is haunted by the irony that what seems to be Ford's technological lead may operate to its grievous detriment, assuming the relaxation-if-necessary approach voiced by Mr. Allen. If in 1974, when certification of production vehicles begins, any one of the three major companies cannot meet the 1975 standards, it is a likelihood that standards will be set to permit the higher level of emission control achievable by the laggard. This will be the case whether or not the leader has or has not achieved compliance with the 1975 standards. Even if the relaxation is later made industry-wide, the Government's action, in first imposing a standard not generally achievable and then relaxing it, is likely to be detrimental to the leader who has tooled up to meet a higher standard than will ultimately be required.

In some contexts high achievement bestows the advantage that rightly belongs to the leader, of high quality. In this context before us, however, the high achievement in emission control results, under systems presently available, in lessened car performance—an inverse correlation. The competitive disadvantage to the ecological leader presents a forbidding outcome—if the initial assumption of feasibility is not validated, and there is subsequent relaxation—for which we see no remedy.

C. Light Weight Trucks

We now take up the serious contention of International Harvester (IH) that the EPA decision effectively rules out the production of 1975 model year IH light weight trucks and multi-purpose passenger vehicles (MPVs). This requires us to focus on the Administrator's conception that the 1970 Clean Air Act envisioned restricting production of vehicles to that necessary to fill "basic demand."

The Administrator does not dispute International Harvester's claim that it will not be able to produce the vehicles in question, and indeed the limited testing of one of its MPVs

showed, even as evaluated by EPA methodology, that such standards could not be achieved. Yet a suspension was not granted, presumably for the reasons advanced by EPA to this court, that International Harvester was "required to alter the performance characteristics of its vehicles in the interest of meeting the 1975 emission standards." The inability of IH vehicles to meet the standards seems accountable by the uses to which they are put, hauling large loads or towing heavy trailers.... Therefore, for all practical purposes a redesign of performance characteristics will preclude the present uses to which IH vehicles are put.

The Administrator, nonetheless, takes the position that International Harvester can be denied a suspension because he has found that "new car demand" will be satisfied by the production of the major auto companies, and thus apparently posits that the absence from the 1975 market of all light weight trucks and MPVs is fully consistent with the Act. We cannot agree.

Section 202(b)(1) of the Act applies its drastic standards to 1975 models of "light duty vehicles." It is our view that the legislative history reveals this term to mean "passenger cars." In the Report of the Senate Committee on Public Works on S.4358, the Committee clearly distinguished between the automobile, which must "meet a rigid timetable and a high degree of emission control compliance," and other vehicles, such as "trucks and buses and other commercial vehicles,"...

This is not to say that the modification of the "light duty vehicles" definition must exclude MPVs, which largely overlap in their usage with passenger cars. We merely hold the present regulation contrary to legislative intent....

E. Balancing of Risks

This case inevitably presents, to the court as to the Administrator, the need for a perspective on the suspension that is informed by an analysis which balances the costs of a "wrong decision" on feasibility against the gains of a correct one. These costs include the risks of grave maladjustments for the technological leader from the eleventh-hour grant of a suspension, and the impact on jobs and the economy from a decision which is only partially accurate, allowing companies to produce cars but at a significantly reduced level of output. Against this must be weighed the environmental savings from denial of suspension. The record indicates that these will be relatively modest. There is also the possibility that failure to grant a suspension may be counter-productive to the environment, if there is significant decline in performance characteristics.

Another consideration is present, that the real cost to granting a suspension arises from the symbolic compromise with the goal of a clean environment. We emphasize that our view of a one-year suspension, and the intent of Congress as to a one-year suspension, is in no sense to be taken as any support for further suspensions. This would plainly be contrary to the intent of Congress to set an absolute standard in 1976. On the contrary, we view the imperative of the Congressional requirement as to the significant improvement that must be wrought no later than 1976, as interrelated with the provision for one-year suspension. The flexibility in the statute provided by the availability of a one-year suspension only strengthens the impact of the absolute standard. Considerations of fairness will support comprehensive and firm, even drastic, regulations, provided a "safety valve" is also provided—ordinarily a provision for waiver, exception or adjustment, in this case a provision for suspension. "The limited safety valve permits a more rigorous adherence to an effective regulation." *WAIT Radio v. FCC*, 418 F.2d 1153, 1159 (D.C. Cir. 1969). To hold the safety valve too rigidly is to interfere with the relief that was

contemplated as an integral part of the firmness of the overall, enduring program.

We approach the question of the burden of proof on the auto companies with the previous considerations before us.

IV. THE REQUIRED SHOWING ON "AVAILABLE TECHNOLOGY"

It is with utmost diffidence that we approach our assignment to review the Administrator's decision on "available technology." The legal issues are intermeshed with technical matters, and as yet judges have no scientific aides. Our diffidence is rooted in the underlying technical complexities, and remains even when we take into account that ours is a judicial review, and not a technical or policy redetermination, our review is channeled by a salutary restraint, and deference to the expertise of an agency that provides reasoned analysis. Nevertheless we must proceed to the task of judicial review assigned by Congress.

The Act makes suspension dependent on the Administrator's determination that:

the applicant has established that effective control technology, processes, operating methods, or other alternatives are not available or have not been available for a sufficient period of time to achieve compliance prior to the effective date of such standards. . . .

A. Requirement of Observed Data from Manufacturers

Clearly this requires that the applicants come forward with data which showed that they could not comply with the contemplated standards. The normal rules place such a burden on the party in control of the relevant information. It was the auto companies who were in possession of the data about emission performance of their cars.

The submission of the auto companies unquestionably showed that no car had actually been driven 50,000 miles and achieved conformity of emissions to the 1975 standards. The Administrator's position is that on the basis of the methodology outlined, he can predict that the auto companies can meet the standards, and that the ability to make a prediction saying the companies can comply means that the petitioners have failed to sustain their burden of proof that they cannot comply.

B. Requisite Reliability of Methodology Relied on by EPA to Predict Feasibility Notwithstanding Lack of Actual Experience

We agree with the Administrator's proposition in general. Its validity as applied to this case rests on the reliability of his prediction, and the nature of his assumptions. One must distinguish between prediction and prophecy. *See EDF v. Ruckelshaus*, 439 F.2d 584, 597 (D.C. Cir. 1971). In a matter of this importance, the predictor must make a showing of reliability of the methodology of prediction, when that is being relied on to overcome this "adverse" actual test data of the auto companies. The statute does not contemplate use of a "crystal ball." . . .

Additionally, our perspective on the interests furthered by a sound EPA decision, and jeopardized by a "wrong decision," are material to the issue of standard of proof. This is a situation where, as we have stated, the risks of an erroneous denial of suspension outweigh the risks of an erroneous grant. On the issue of burden of proof, the standard adopted must take into account the nature and consequences of risk of error. . . .

The underlying issue is the reasonableness and reliability of the Administrator's methodology, for it alone offsets the data adduced by petitioners in support of suspension. It is the Administrator who must bear the burden on this matter, because the development and use of the methodology are attributable to his knowledge and expertise. When certain material "lies particularly within the knowledge"

of a party he is ordinarily assigned the burden of adducing the pertinent information. This assignment of burden to a party is fully appropriate when the other party is confronted with the often-formidable task of establishing a "negative averment." *United States v. Denver & R.G.R. Co.*, 191 U.S. 84, 92 (1903). In the context of this proceeding, this requires that EPA bear a burden of adducing a reasoned presentation supporting the reliability of its methodology.

C. Analysis of EPA Assumptions

[The Court then analyzed in detail the scientific and engineering reliability and the statistical validity of the technical assumptions used by the Administrator to adjust the manufacturer's data. The Court concluded that in several respects the EPA had failed to adequately respond to manufacturer criticism of these assumptions and methodologies.]

V. CONCLUSION AND DISPOSITION

We may sensibly begin our conclusion with a statement of diffidence. It is not without diffidence that a court undertakes to probe even partly into technical matters of the complexity of those covered in this opinion. It is with even more diffidence that a court concludes that the law, as judicially construed, requires a different approach from that taken by an official or agency with technical expertise. Yet this is an inescapable aspect of the judicial condition, though we stay mindful of the overarching consideration that a court's role on judicial review embraces that of a constructive cooperation with the agency involved in furtherance of the public interest.

A court does not depart from its proper function when it undertakes a study of the record, hopefully perceptive, even as to the evidence on technical and specialized matters, for this enables the court to penetrate to the underlying decisions of the agency, to satisfy itself that the agency has exercised a reasoned discretion, with reasons that do not deviate from or ignore the ascertainable legislative intent.

... In approaching our judicial task we conclude that the requirement of a "reasoned decision" by the Environmental Protection Agency means, in present context, a reasoned presentation of the reliability of a prediction and methodology that is relied upon to overcome a conclusion, of lack of available technology, supported prima faciely by the only actual and observed data available, the manufacturers' testing.

The number of unexplained assumptions used by the Administrator, the variance in methodology from that of the Report of the National Academy of Science, and the absence of an indication of the statistical reliability of the prediction, combine to generate grave doubts as to whether technology is available to meet the 1975 statutory standards. We think the vehicle manufacturers established by a preponderance of the evidence, in the record before us, that technology was not available, within the meaning of the Act, when they adduced the tests on actual vehicles; that the Administrator's reliance on technological methodology to offset the actual tests raised serious doubts and failed to meet the burden of proof which in our view was properly assignable to him, in the light of accepted legal doctrine and the intent of Congress discerned, in part, by taking into account that the risk of an "erroneous" denial of suspension outweighed the risk of an "erroneous" grant of suspension. We do not use the burden of proof in the conventional sense of civil trials, but the Administrator must sustain the burden of adducing a reasoned presentation supporting the reliability of EPA's methodology.

... The agency was presented with a prickly task, but has acted expeditiously to carry out what it perceived to be a drastic mandate from Congress. This statute was, indeed, deliberately designed as "shock treatment" to the industry. Our central difference with the Administrator, simply put, stems from our view concerning the Congressional intent underlying the one year suspension provision. That was a purposeful cushion—with the twin purpose of providing "escape hatch" relief for 1975, and thus establishing a context supportive of the rigor and firmness of the basic standards slated for no later than 1976. In our view the overall legislative firmness does not necessarily require a "hard-nosed" approach to the application for suspension, as the Administrator apparently supposed. ...

Our decision is also responsive to the differences between the EPA decision and the NAS Report. Although in some instances "the factual findings and technical conclusions" are consistent with those of the Administrator, the NAS conclusion was that technology was not available to meet the standards in 1975. Congress called on NAS, with presumed reliance on the knowledge and objectivity of that prestigious body, to make an independent judgment. The statute makes the NAS conclusion a necessary but not sufficient condition of suspension. While in consideration of the other conditions of suspension, EPA was not necessarily bound by NAS's approach, particularly as to matters interlaced with policy and legal aspects, we do not think that it was contemplated that EPA could alter the conclusion of NAS by revising the NAS assumptions, or injecting new ones, unless it states its reasons for finding reliability—possibly by challenging the NAS approach in terms of later-acquired research and experience.

These factors combine to convince us that, under our view of Congressional intent, we cannot affirm the EPA's denial of suspension as stated. That is not necessarily to assume, as at least some petitioners do, that the EPA's process must be brought to nullity.

[The Court concluded that a remand for further proceedings was appropriate.]

...the Administrator may consider possible use of interim standards short of complete suspension.

The case is remanded for further proceedings not inconsistent with this opinion.

BAZELON, CHIEF JUDGE (CONCURRING IN RESULT)

Socrates said that wisdom is the recognition of how much one does not know. I may be wise if that is wisdom, because I recognize that I do not know enough about dynamometer extrapolations, deterioration factor adjustments, and the like to decide whether or not the government's approach to these matters was statistically valid. Therein lies my disagreement with the majority.

The court's opinion today centers on a substantive evaluation of the Administrator's assumptions and methodology. I do not have the technical know-how to agree or disagree with that evaluation—at least on the basis of the present record. My grounds for remanding the case rest upon the Administrator's failure to employ a reasonable decision-making process for so critical and complex a matter. At this time I cannot say to what extent I could undertake an evaluation of the Administrator's findings if they were based on an adequate decisional process.

I cannot believe that Congress intended this court to delve into the substance of the mechanical, statistical, and technological disputes in this case. Senator Cooper, the author of the judicial review provision, stated repeatedly that this court's role would be to "determine the question of due process." Thus the court's proper role is to see to it that the agency provides "a framework for principled decision-making." Such a framework necessarily includes the right of interested parties to confront the agency's decision and the requirement that the agency set forth with clarity the grounds for its rejection of opposing views.

The majority's interpretation of the present statute and the administrative precedents would give us no right to establish these procedural guidelines. Their opinion maintains that the strict deadlines in the Clean Air Act preclude any right to challenge the Administrator until after the decision has been made. It indicates that, since this hearing was "rule-making" rather than "adjudicatory," cross-examination and confrontation are not required under traditional rules of administrative law.

I understand this viewpoint, but I do not share it. I do not think the authors of the Clean Air Act intended to put such strict limits on our review of the Administrator's decision-making process. Further, the interests at stake in this case are too important to be resolved on the basis of traditional administrative labels. We recognized two years ago that environmental litigation represents a "new era" in administrative law. We are dealing here not with an airline's fares or a broadcaster's wattage, but with all humanity's interest in life, health, and a harmonious relationship with the elements of nature.

This "new era" does not mean that courts will dig deeper into the technical intricacies of an agency's decision. It means instead that courts will go further in requiring the agency to establish a decision-making process adequate to protect the interests of all "consumers" of the natural environment. In some situations, traditional rules of "fairness"—designed only to guard the interests of the specific parties to an agency proceeding—will be inadequate to protect these broader interests. This is such a case. Whether or not traditional administrative rules require it, the critical character of this decision requires at the least a carefully limited right of cross-examination at the hearing and an opportunity to challenge the assumptions and methodology underlying the decision....

Outside of the foregoing differences, I agree with much of the majority opinion.

I would have preferred to make the "public interest" factor—the considerations set forth in Part III of that opinion—an independent ground for suspension. The court today deals with the public interest indirectly, through the device of burden of proof. I do not fully understand this approach, but I suspect it leads to essentially the same result I favor.

■ NOTES

1. After the issue was remanded to EPA, the agency granted the requested 1-year extension to all of the manufacturers and imposed less stringent interim standards over the period of the extension.

2. Judge Leventhal's majority opinion notes that Congress, in adopting the 1975 standards, was aware that it was administering "drastic medicine," designed to "force the state of the art." Did including the escape hatch of the 1-year extension serve to undermine, or to strengthen, the integrity of this statutory scheme? In general, how is the absence of an escape hatch likely to affect a firm's willingness to engage in radical innovation in the face of stringent environmental regulation? What factors are likely to be important, in any given situation, in influencing whether a stringent regulation is likely to produce the desired technological change? An agency's historical response to pressures by industry may determine whether firms decide to radically innovate or attempt to obstruct and delay implementation of regulatory requirements. What signal(s) may this extension have given to the auto industry?

3. Who had the statutory burden of proof here, the manufacturers or EPA? What did the court do with the burden of proof? Did the manufacturers prevail because they had established that EPA's assumptions and projections were incorrect, or because EPA failed to establish that they were not? Note that the court states that it "approaches" the question of the burden of proof in light of its assessment of the broader economic considerations at stake.

4. The statute provided that only those manufacturers that had made "all good faith efforts . . . to meet the standards" were entitled to an extension. In his findings on this issue, EPA Administrator William Ruckelshaus cited a "disturbing and frustrating" absence of diligence on the part of U.S. automakers in their pursuit of alternatives to catalyst controls. He also noted that Chrysler had sacrificed emissions control in favor of cost considerations, and had spent (as a percentage of overall sales) only a third of what Ford and General Motors had on control technology. Ruckelshaus nonetheless concluded, "with serious reservations," that Chrysler had acted in good faith. In so doing, he acknowledged that his decision was colored by the fact that thousands of jobs depended on Chrysler's continued financial health. What would the likely consequences have been for Chrysler had EPA granted an extension to the

other manufacturers but not to Chrysler? Is it significant that Detroit's "big three" automakers—Chrysler, Ford, and General Motors—effectively wielded oligopoly power within the U.S. automobile market at the time?

5. In general, how does the granting of extensions (or other relaxing of a regulatory standard or deadline) affect the "first-mover" advantage enjoyed by the technological leaders (such as the one originally enjoyed here by Ford)? Note that, instead of focusing on the desirability of "rewarding" Ford for (apparently) having met the technological goals set by Congress, the court instead focuses on the need to avoid "punishing" Ford by granting extensions to the other manufacturers but not to Ford. Could Ford's apparent success with the catalytic converter have been seen as a decisive rebuttal to the argument that the necessary emissions reduction technology was not yet available? Could it have been seen as evidence of a *lack* of good faith on the part of Chrysler and General Motors?

6. The NAS report highlighted the presumed trade-offs between specific emission control systems and vehicle performance, fuel economy, "driveability" (i.e., relevant to safety), and customer willingness to pay. How much discretion, if any, was given to the administrator to consider these other factors when deciding whether to grant an extension? Would they, as Judge Bazelon implied in his concurring opinion, come in under a consideration of the "public interest?"

7. The court cites the administrator's determination "that the most effective system so far developed was the noble metal oxidizing catalyst," and that "only cars using this kind of system were to be considered in making the 'available technology' determination." The court acknowledges, however, that "the automobile industry has a multi-billion-dollar investment in the conventional engine, and ... has been reluctant to introduce new power plants or undertake major modifications of the conventional one. Thus the bulk of the industry's work on emission control has focused narrowly on converter devices." Would the factors identified by NAS (discussed in note 6) necessarily have been trade-offs had these other technologies been pursued? Note that there is a clear technological potential for reducing (if not wholly eliminating) these trade-offs even assuming the continued dominance of the internal combustion engine. Indeed, despite the potential trade-offs, all of the factors cited by the NAS—safety, fuel economy, and performance—have been steadily improved over the past 30 years through innovation, even as automobile emissions have been dramatically reduced.

8. In general, what is the risk that "technology-forcing" regulations become merely "technology-diffusing" (i.e., simply prompting the "diffusion" of an existing technology within the regulated industry, rather than prompting more far-reaching technological change)? Had the automakers been given more lead time, is it likely that the 90% emission reduction standards would have prompted them, in the court's

words, to "introduce new power plants or undertake major modifications of the conventional one," rather than to turn to the catalytic converter? Conversely, had the administrator's initial decision to deny the extension been upheld, would the "shock" of this regulatory signal have been sufficient to prompt a true commitment to improving the technology, or would it have prompted a massive campaign by the industry to lobby Congress for a relaxation of the standard? In any event, as discussed below, such a lobbying campaign was mounted successfully a few years later. And automakers have only recently begun marketing new types of power plants (e.g., hybrid battery-gasoline systems), some 30 years later than Congress had originally envisioned. Does this mean that the technology-forcing scheme devised by Congress was a failure?

9. As the court's discussion of "light-duty vehicles" suggests, the designations for the various categories of vehicles regulated under the Clean Air Act is somewhat confusing. An overly simplified description is that "light-duty," "medium-duty," and "heavy-duty" refer to specific weight ranges. The court concluded that Congress intended the standards for "light-duty vehicles" to apply only to passenger cars and not to trucks, buses, or other commercial vehicles, and this is the approach EPA has taken since that time. (Accordingly, light-duty vehicles do *not* include light-duty trucks.) Nonetheless, the court acknowledged that, as EPA had found, the (heavier) multipurpose passenger vehicles largely overlap in use with the passenger car. As discussed later in this chapter, EPA later established separate but more lenient standards for light-duty trucks and multipurpose vehicles. This led to what many have seen as a "loophole": SUVs and light-duty trucks have been subject to less stringent emission requirements than light-duty passenger vehicles, despite the similarity in use. This discrepancy has only recently been addressed, and only to a certain extent, by the Tier II standards put in place by the 1990 Clean Air Act Amendments.

10. Finally, note that (as was their wont) Judge Leventhal and Judge Bazelon carried on a spirited debate as to the appropriate role of judicial review when the underlying agency determination is grounded in complex scientific and engineering determinations. ▪

Perhaps predictably, the *International Harvester* case was only the beginning of a long battle over the implementation of the standards, one that would continue into the early 1980s. After EPA issued the first 1-year extension in 1973, Congress issued another 1-year extension in 1974, citing concerns over sulfuric acid emissions from cars with catalytic converters, and EPA granted a third 1-year reprieve in 1975, citing fuel economy considerations. This pushed the deadline for meeting the HC and CO standards to the 1978 model year. However, during congressional hearings held over the course of 1975 to 1977, automakers and representatives of the United Auto

Extended deadlines

Workers union testified that the standards could not be met and that the industry needed more time. President Ford—in a move strongly supported by the auto industry—proposed to continue the moratorium on implementation of the standards until 1981. Thus, in 1977 Congress amended the Clean Air Act to permit EPA to extend the deadlines for HC and CO to 1980, and to extend the deadline for NO_x to 1981, 5 years later than specified in the 1970 amendments. In additional, the required emission reduction for NO_x was loosened from 90% to 75%. Ironically, these deadlines and standards were virtually identical to the reduction targets that President Nixon had originally proposed in 1970. Finally, the 1977 amendments gave EPA the authority to grant limited waivers from the CO and NO_x standards to manufacturers who lacked the technological and economic capacity to comply on their own and depended on emission control technology developed by other manufacturers.

According to the Senate report, the 1977 extensions were necessary to ensure that the statutory goals would be more "closely related to the performance of the auto industry" (Senate Committee on Environment and Public Works, *Clean Air Act Amendments of 1977*, 95th Cong., 1st sess., 1977, S. Rep. 95–127, at 3). Moreover, the threat of an industry shutdown loomed in the background.

In August 1977, U.S. producers began manufacturing 1978 model cars that did not meet the new standards. Because the law prohibited introducing cars into commerce without certification, the manufacturers could not ship them to dealers. GM filled every parking lot within a 3-mile radius of their plants with cars that could not meet the standards (Leonard, 2001). EPA had exhausted its allotted delays, and Congress was forced either to push the standards back further or prohibit U.S. producers from selling automobiles. Faced with the prospect of an industry shutdown, Congress passed the 1977 amendments to the Clean Air Act. [David Gerard and Lester Lave, "Implementing Technology-Forcing Policies."]

The implementation timeline for the 1970 HC, CO, and NO_x standards is summarized in table 7.2. Although this presents a clear picture of delay and retrenchment, it also masks the overall progress made during this period in reducing emissions from new motor vehicles. That story is told in table 7.3, which tracks the gradual strengthening of the federal standards for new light-duty motor vehicles. In this table, the numbers in parentheses are the standards set by Congress in 1970 Clean Air Act Amendments, while the numbers in bold represent the eventual implementation of those standards.

Congress had made, in its words, a "balancing judgment," acquiescing in the short term to political pressure and industry foot dragging, in exchange for long-term progress and overall adherence to the program's goals. And it is clear that the program both forced and accelerated the development and diffusion of several innovations, beginning with the catalytic converter, followed by the three-way catalyst and

Table 7.2
Timeline of Delays

December 31, 1970	Clean Air Act Amendments direct EPA to set standards and federal test procedure to be met by 1975 model year
June 23, 1971	EPA sets standards for 1975 model year
January 1, 1972	NAS issues report suggesting technology to meet standards is not yet available
March 13, 1972	Volvo requests delay of standards. Other automakers follow suit, including the Big Three on April 5
May 12, 1972	EPA denies extension
December 18–19, 1972	D.C. Court of Appeals hears automakers appeal and remands the case back to EPA for further investigation (*International Harvester v. Ruckelshaus*)
December 30, 1972	EPA issues supplement to decision of the administrator
February 1973	D.C. Court of Appeals again remands (*International Harvester v. Ruckelshaus*)
April 1973	EPA grants 1-year delay in HC, CO standards, and imposes interim standards
June 1973	EPA grants 1-year delay in NO_x standards, and imposes interim standards
June 1974	Congress extends interim HC and CO standards to 1977 and NO_x to 1978
February, March 1975	EPA extends interim HC, CO standards to 1978
August 1977	Clean Air Act Amendments extend interim HC and CO standards to 1980, and NO_x to 1981 (and weaken ultimate NO_x standards)

Source: Adopted from David Gerard and Lester Lave (2003) *Implementing Technology-Forcing Policies: The 1970 Clean Air Act Amendments and the Introduction of Advanced Automotive Emissions Controls.* Center for the Study and Improvement of Regulation, Carnegie-Mellon University, Pittsburgh, Pa. Reprinted with permission.

Table 7.3
Federal Emissions Standards, 1968–1981

Model Year	HC (g/mile)	CO (g/mile)	NO_x (g/mile)
Uncontrolled Vehicle	8.7	87	4.4
1968	6.2	51	—
1970	4.1	34	—
1972	3.0	28	—
1973			3.1
1975	1.5 (0.41)	15 (3.4)	
1976			(0.41)
1977			2.0
1980	**0.41**	7.0	
1981		**3.4**	1.0

Source: Reproduced from David Gerard and Lester Lave (2003) *Implementing Technology-Forcing Policies: The 1970 Clean Air Act Amendments and the Introduction of Advanced Automotive Emissions Controls.* Center for the Study and Improvement of Regulation, Carnegie-Mellon University, Pittsburgh, Pa. Reprinted with permission.

on-board electronics (e.g., to optimize air to oxygen ratios). By 1981, 70% of new vehicles were equipped with these control devices. See David Gerard and Lester Lave, "Implementing Technology-Forcing Policies."

■ **NOTE**

1. In 1977, Congress also authorized EPA to grant limited waivers from the NO_x standards (not to exceed 5% of the manufacturer's total production, or 50,000 vehicles, whichever was greater) to manufacturers who used the waiver to develop and use an innovative emission control device. See Section 202(b)(3).   ■

b.   Additional Limits Set by EPA

Beyond the congressionally mandated standards for light-duty vehicles, the 1970 Clean Air Act Amendments called for additional emission standards, for other pollutants and vehicle categories, to be set by EPA. In general, these standards were to be established for pollutants that endangered public health or welfare, and were to be based on the agency's assessment of technological and economic feasibility. The agency did set a number of such standards, although all of them were considerably more lenient than the standards established by Congress for light-duty vehicles. In the 1977 amendments to the act, Congress called for stricter regulations for both gasoline and diesel-powered heavy-duty vehicles (heavy-duty trucks and buses). Until then, EPA had regulated gasoline-powered (but not diesel-powered) heavy-duty vehicles. The 1977 amendments directed EPA to establish standards for heavy-duty vehicles reflecting "the greatest degree of emission reduction achievable through the application of technology which the Administrator determines will be available for the model year to which such standards apply, giving appropriate consideration to the cost of applying such technology...and to noise, energy, and safety factors." Congress further specified that these standards "shall be promulgated and shall take effect as expeditiously as practicable" [42 U.S.C. §7521(a)(3)(A)(iii) (1977) (this provision was superceded by the 1990 Clean Air Act Amendments)].

In addition to setting standards for heavy-duty vehicles under this authority, EPA used its authority under the 1970 amendments to set technology-based standards governing the emission of particulate matter from light-duty diesel vehicles and light-duty diesel trucks. These latter standards were promulgated in 1980 and were challenged both by automakers and by the Natural Resources Defense Council. This case gave the D.C. Circuit an opportunity to revisit the "technology forcing" issue, albeit in a different context.

Natural Resources Defense Council v. Environmental Protection Agency
MIKVA, Circuit Judge
655 F.2d 318 (D.C. Cir. 1981)

These consolidated cases present a variety of challenges to actions of the Environmental Protection Agency (EPA) in setting standards to govern emissions of particulate matter and oxides of nitrogen from diesel vehicles. The Natural Resources Defense Council (NRDC) argues that the agency's actions do not adequately protect the public health; General Motors Corporation (GM) and Intervenors Mercedes-Benz of North America, Inc., and Volkswagen of America, Inc., assert that the EPA did not give adequate consideration to safety factors, and that, in a variety of ways, the standards are too strict. Finding that the agency has stated adequate reasons for its decisions, and that its actions are consistent with statute, we uphold the challenged regulations in their entirety.

I. THE REGULATORY FRAMEWORK

The EPA is authorized by the Clean Air Act to regulate emissions of harmful pollutants from motor vehicles. The Act itself specifies the quantity of acceptable emissions from light-duty vehicles for three classes of pollutants: carbon monoxide, hydrocarbons, and oxides of nitrogen. Act §202(b)(1). Section 202(a)(1) of the Act confers on the EPA Administrator the general power to prescribe by regulation "standards applicable to the emission of any air pollutant from any class or classes of new motor vehicles or new motor vehicle engines, which in his judgment cause, or contribute to, air pollution which may reasonably be anticipated to endanger public health or welfare." These provisions are supplemented and qualified by various specific provisions relating to particular classes of vehicles or pollutants. E.g., Act §§202(a)(3)(A)(i), 202(a)(3)(F), 202(b)(6)(A).

The statutory standard for hydrocarbon emissions from light-duty vehicles is an absolute one. For models manufactured from 1977 to 1979, hydrocarbon emissions may not exceed 1.5 grams per vehicle mile; for those manufactured from 1980 on, the standards must require a reduction of at least ninety percent from the emission standards applying in 1970. Act §202(b)(1)(A). The statutory standards for carbon monoxide and oxides of nitrogen are also absolute, but they are subject to a variety of waivers for certain manufacturers who lack the technological capacity to comply. See Act §§202(b)(1)(B), 202(b)(5), 202(b)(6).

The emission standards set by the EPA under its general regulatory power, in contrast, are "technology-based"—the levels chosen must be premised on a finding of technological feasibility. Section 202(a)(2) of the Act provides that standards promulgated under section 202(a)(1) shall not take effect until "after such period as the Administrator finds necessary to permit the development and application of the requisite technology."

The requirement that emission standards be technologically achievable highlights the need for the EPA's power to divide the broad spectrum of motor vehicles into classes or categories. See Act §§202(a)(1), 202(a)(3)(A)(iv). Manufacturers produce a wide variety of motor vehicles of different sizes, some using different engine technologies resulting in unusual emission characteristics. In particular, diesel engines use a different fuel, emit exhaust at a lower temperature, and produce a different distribution of pollutants than traditional gasoline engines. For example, diesel carbon monoxide levels are typically lower than those from gasoline vehicles, see 45 Fed.Reg. 5480, 5493 (1980), but diesel vehicles produce particulate emissions at thirty to seventy times the rate of gasoline vehicles, see 45 Fed.Reg. 14,496 (1980), and also produce higher levels of the unregulated pollutants sulfur dioxide and benzo[*a*]pyrene, see 45 Fed.Reg. 5480, 5489 (1980).

The present challenges concern the EPA's promulgation of standards governing particulate emissions from light-duty diesel vehicles and light-duty diesel trucks, and the EPA's waiver of the statutory standard for oxides of nitrogen for light-duty vehicles. The EPA's particulate standard and NO_x decisions are appropriately linked in the present proceeding because current technology creates an unfortunate trade-off between particulate control and control of oxides of nitrogen. The primary technique used today for reducing NO_x emissions is exhaust gas recirculation (EGR). While lowering the NO_x content of the exhaust, EGR increases the particulate content, and "the greater the EGR rate, the greater the increase in particulate emissions." Environmental Protection Agency, Regulatory Analysis (of) Light-Duty Diesel Particulate Regulations 33 (1980) (hereinafter cited as Regulatory Analysis), Joint Appendix (J.A.) 510. Thus the stringency of a technology-based particulate standard depends on the level of the NO_x standard concurrently applied. We consider the EPA's actions and the NRDC and industry challenges in turn.

II. THE PARTICULATE STANDARDS

The EPA announced its intention to promulgate standards for particulate emissions from light-duty diesels on February 1, 1979. The proposed standards would have limited diesel particulates to 0.60 grams per vehicle mile (gpm) in model year 1981, and to 0.20 gpm in model year 1983. The agency concluded that a single standard, governing all light-duty vehicles, was the preferable regulatory strategy, although 1979 certification data

indicated that diesel particulate performance among those vehicles ranged from the 0.23 gpm achieved by the Volkswagen Rabbit to the 0.84 gpm emitted by the Oldsmobile 350. Furthermore, these restrictions would have applied equally to light-duty vehicles and light-duty trucks....

After analyzing the comments elicited by its notice of proposed rulemaking, the EPA promulgated as final standards a modification of the rules originally announced. See 45 Fed.Reg. 14,496 (1980). The limit of 0.60 gpm was retained, but its effective date was postponed to model year 1982, because the rulemaking process had absorbed so much time that testing and certification of 1981 models was no longer feasible. Id. at 14,497. The agency concluded that the technology necessary to make the 0.20 gpm standard feasible would probably not be developed in time for implementation in 1983 model vehicles; 1984 was a more likely goal, but the effective date was postponed to model year 1985 to give sufficient margin for error. Id. at 14,498. Finally, the EPA believed that light-duty trucks would not be able to perform as well as light-duty vehicles, and the 1985 standard for light-duty trucks was therefore adjusted to 0.26 gpm. Id. at 14,497.

The auto industry petitioners do not challenge the 1982 standard of 0.60 gpm, but they vigorously deny the likelihood that technology will be available to meet the lower standards in 1985. In setting the 1985 standards, the EPA predicted that a currently experimental particulate control device, known as a "trap-oxidizer," would be perfected early enough to allow its mass production and installation in 1985 model diesel vehicles. The manufacturers argue that this prediction lacked a sufficient evidentiary basis, and that the agency's action must therefore be invalidated as failing to meet the requirement of reasoned decisionmaking. They also argue that the EPA gave inadequate consideration to the safety risks involved in trap-oxidizer technology.

NRDC insists that the EPA's entire regulatory strategy is an inadequate response to the agency's statutory mandate to protect the public health. The EPA deliberately set a single standard for all light-duty diesel vehicles, predicting that even the worst performing diesel could meet it. NRDC argues that that regulatory choice is inconsistent with the EPA's statutory responsibilities; it urges a variable standard, imposing more rigorous requirements on better performing vehicles. NRDC also urges that the agency failed to consider the risks posed by diesel particulate as a carcinogen, and that in giving "appropriate consideration" to cost as a factor in standard-setting, it should have tried to discourage purchase of polluting vehicles through economic disincentives. Finally, NRDC attacks the postponement of the 0.20 gpm standard from 1984 to 1985 as unnecessary and irresponsible....

B. Technological Feasibility

The EPA's choice of the 0.20 gpm standard for light-duty diesels in 1985 was the result of adjusting current diesel particulate emission data by the percentage of reduction expected from certain technological improvements, most notably the trap-oxidizer. The manufacturers' attack on the standard focuses on the EPA's prediction concerning the probable pace of development of trap-oxidizer technology. Before examining the details of the agency's reasoning and the industry challenges, however, we find it useful to discuss the legal standard that governs our inquiry.

1. The Standard of Review

The standard of review in this case is the traditional one for judicial scrutiny of agency rulemaking: we are to set aside any action found to be "arbitrary, capricious, an abuse of discretion, or otherwise not in accordance with law." Act §307(d)(9)(A). As nonscientists, we must recall that "(o)ur 'expertise' is not in setting standards for emission control but in determining if the standards as set are the result of reasoned decisionmaking." *Essex Chemical Corp. v. Ruckelshaus*, 486 F.2d 427, 434 (D.C.Cir.1973), cert. denied, 416 U.S. 969 (1974). Despite this limited role, our examination of the record must be searching, for the necessity to review agency decisions, if it is to be more than a meaningless exercise, requires enough steeping in technical matters to determine whether the agency "has exercised a reasoned discretion." ... We cannot substitute our own judgment for that of the agency, but it is our duty to consider whether "the decision was based on a consideration of the relevant factors and whether there has been a clear error of judgment." *Portland Cement Ass'n. v. Ruckelshaus*, 486 F.2d 375, 402 (D.C.Cir.1973), cert. denied, 417 U.S. 921 (1974).

In the present case, GM attacks the EPA's estimation of the period of time "necessary to permit the development and application of the requisite technology" to achieve compliance with the 1985 particulate standards, see Act §202(a)(2). The agency has determined that the technology will be available in time, and now seeks to defend its conclusion as a product of reasoned decisionmaking. Such predictions inherently involve a greater degree of uncertainty than estimations of the effectiveness of current technology. If we judge the EPA's action by the standard of certainty appropriate to current technology, the agency will be unable to set pollutant levels until the necessary technology is already available.

The legislative history of both the 1970 and the 1977 amendments demonstrates that Congress intended the agency to project future advances in pollution control capability. It was "expected to press for the development and application of improved technology rather than be limited by that which exists today." S.Rep.No.1196, 91st Cong., 2d Sess. 24 (1970), reprinted in 1 Legislative History 424; H.R.Rep.No.294, 95th Cong., 1st Sess. 273 (1977), reprinted in (1977) U.S.Code Cong.

& Ad.News 1077, 1352, 4 Legislative History 2740. In designing the particulate standard, the EPA recognized the uncertainty necessarily accompanying its duty to predict:

When projecting a near-term standard when little time exists for technological advances, it is relatively simple for a regulatory agency to predict what the best available control technology will be, and to set a standard based on its application. It is more difficult to regulate on this basis in the long-term because of the uncertainty that inevitably surrounds expected technological improvements. Nevertheless, . . . EPA has concluded that it is absolutely necessary to issue standards which motivate the private sector to maximize its efforts in reducing particulate emissions from light-duty vehicles.

Regulatory Analysis at 32, J.A. 511.

This court has upheld the agency's power to make such projections, while recognizing that it is "subject to the restraints of reasonableness, and does not open the door to 'crystal ball' inquiry." *International Harvester Co. v. Ruckelshaus*, 478 F.2d 615, 629 (D.C.Cir.1973). The Clean Air Act requires the EPA to look to the future in setting standards, but the agency must also provide a reasoned explanation of its basis for believing that its projection is reliable. This includes a defense of its methodology for arriving at numerical estimates. Id.

The thoroughness and persuasiveness of the explanation we can expect from the agency will, of course, vary with the nature of the prediction undertaken. "Where existing methodology or research in a new area of regulation is deficient, the agency necessarily enjoys broad discretion to attempt to formulate a solution to the best of its ability on the basis of available information." *Industrial Union Dep't. v. Hodgson*, 499 F.2d 467, 474 n.18 (D.C.Cir.1974). At one extreme, this court has recognized that the EPA's decision to regulate potentially harmful pollutants involves a large element of policy choice that cannot be demonstrably "correct," although it must have a genuine scientific basis. . . . At the other extreme, this court's inquiry into agency methodology in the physical sciences has been far more exacting "where the facts

pertinent to (a) standard's feasibility are available and easily discoverable by conventional technical means." *National Lime Ass'n. v. EPA*, 627 F.2d 416, 454 (D.C.Cir.1980).

The present case lies between those two extremes. It does not involve questions at the frontier of physiological knowledge, but it does require a determination by the EPA of the likely sequence of further technological development. There is no known scientific technique for calculating when an as yet unsolved design problem will be ironed out. Thus, unlike the short-term feasibility assessments scrutinized in *National Lime Association*, the present determination presents the court with "the question how much deference is owed a judgment predicated on limited evidence when additional evidence cannot be adduced or adduced in the near future," id. at 454.

The time element in the EPA's prediction affects our reviewing task in three distinct ways. First, it introduces uncertainties in the agency's judgment that render that judgment vulnerable to attack. At the same time, however, the time element gives the EPA greater scope for confidence that theoretical solutions will be translated successfully into mechanical realizations, for "the question of availability is partially dependent on a 'lead time', the time in which the technology will have to be available." *Portland Cement Ass'n. v. Ruckelshaus*, 486 F.2d 375, 391 (D.C.Cir.1973), cert. denied, 417 U.S. 921 (1974). Finally, the presence of substantial lead time for development before manufacturers will have to commit themselves to mass production of a chosen prototype gives the agency greater leeway to modify its standards if the actual future course of technology diverges from expectation.

The relevance of lead time, and of the ability to modify standards in light of future developments, to the degree of justification the agency must offer may be seen in this court's opinion in *International Harvester Co. v. Ruckelshaus*, 478 F.2d 615 (D.C.Cir.1973). That case, despite numerous dissimilarities to the present one, provides a useful point of reference, and all the parties seek to claim it as their own. In *International Harvester*, the court reversed the EPA's refusal to suspend for one year strict new 1975 model year emission standards that had been set by Congress in the 1970 amendments. This court, reviewing in early 1973 an EPA decision of May 1972, stressed the harm that would result from "a relaxation of standards, and promulgation of an interim standard, at a later hour after the base hour for 'lead time' has been passed, and the production sequence set in motion." Too late a relaxation would penalize technologically advanced firms, like Ford, which would already have begun manufacture of vehicles that achieved better emission control at the expense of road performance. For this and other reasons, the hardship resulting if a suspension were mistakenly denied outweighed the risks from a suspension needlessly granted. Because of that balance of hardships, the court probed deeply into the reliability of the EPA's methodology. The present case is quite different; the "base hour" for commencement of production is relatively distant, and until that time the probable effect of a relaxation of the standard would be to mitigate the consequences of any excessive strictness in the initial rule, not to create new hardships.

The significance of the time factor in *International Harvester* was increased by the fact that the EPA was not predicting future technological advances, but rather was imposing an interpretation on current industry data. That data uniformly indicated that the standards were not being met, yet the EPA claimed that "adjustments" of the data demonstrated the likelihood of compliance. But the court concluded that the agency had failed to demonstrate the reliability of its methodology sufficiently to defend its reinterpretation of apparently adverse data.

International Harvester has been cited frequently in cases involving presently-available-technology standards, as well as in other cases in which the agency's "central argument is that the standard is achievable because it has been achieved," *National Lime Association*, 627 F.2d at 432–33 (emphasis in original). The defense of a projection methodology in such cases has required "that variables be accounted for, that the representativeness of test conditions be ascertained, that the validity of tests be assured and the statistical significance of results determined." *National Lime Association*, 627 F.2d at 452–53 (footnotes omitted). But statistically-based techniques for reviewing the methodology of contemporary projections do not translate well into rules for reviewing predictions of future progress. If the agency is to predict more than the results of merely assembling preexisting components, it must have some leeway to deduce results that are not represented by present data.

The EPA has generally been granted "considerable latitude in extrapolating from today's technology" when it predicts future technological developments for the purposes of the Clean Water Act, 33 U.S.C. §§1251–1376 (1976 & Supp. II 1978). See *California & Hawaiian Sugar Co. v. EPA*, 553 F.2d 280, 288 (2d Cir. 1977). The courts have had numerous occasions to review EPA determinations that a given control technique constitutes the "best available technology economically achievable" in the 1980s. Most of the opinions, including our own *American Paper Institute v. Train*, 543 F.2d 328, 352–53 (D.C.Cir.1976), cert. dismissed, 429 U.S. 967 (1976), steer close by the shores of their factual contexts and yield little in the way of explicit doctrine. But their essential requirement is that the agency provide "a reasonable basis for belief that a new technology will be available and economically achievable."[21]

---

21. The last three words, of course, reflect the statutory language of the Clean Water Act, 33 U.S.C. §1311(b)(2)(A) (Supp. II 1978), rather than a general principle of judicial review.

Hooker Chemicals & Plastics Corp. v. Train, 537 F.2d 620, 635 (2d Cir. 1976). When a technology is already in use in other industries, the court often expects more solid evidence that the technology can be transferred to the industry in question, or at least that relevant dissimilarities have been considered. *American Meat Institute v. EPA*, 526 F.2d 442, 465 (7th Cir. 1975).

To apply these general considerations to our task of review in the present case, we must examine the nature of the EPA's determination. The agency has predicted that the manufacturers will be able to develop a satisfactory version of the trap-oxidizer in the time remaining. This device was designed specifically for the purpose for which EPA intends it, and prototypes have achieved partial success. GM itself has characterized trap-oxidizers as "the most promising particulate traps," and has admitted that "current program status (would) indicate a possibility of 1985 model year production." General Motors Response to EPA Notice of Proposed Rulemaking 132, 175 (1979) (hereinafter GM Response), J.A. 279, 284. The EPA's decision must be judged in terms of record evidence available in early 1980, allowing a "time frame of 2-21/2 years for completion of the design development phase (and) 2-21/2 years of production lead time." 45 Fed.Reg. 48,133, 48,139 (1980).

Given this time frame, we feel that there is substantial room for deference to the EPA's expertise in projecting the likely course of development. The essential question in this case is the pace of that development, and absent a revolution in the study of industry, defense of such a projection can never possess the ines-

capable logic of a mathematical deduction. We think that the EPA will have demonstrated the reasonableness of its basis for prediction if it answers any theoretical objections to the trap-oxidizer method, identifies the major steps necessary in refinement of the device, and offers plausible reasons for believing that each of those steps can be completed in the time available. If the agency can make this showing, then we cannot say that its determination was the result of crystal ball inquiry, or that it neglected its duty of reasoned decisionmaking.

2. The Time "Necessary to Permit the Development and Application of the Requisite Technology"

Applying the standard described in the preceding section to the challenged particulate regulations, we can determine whether the EPA has presented an adequate exposition of its reasons for believing that the necessary technology will be available for 1985 model year light-duty diesels to comply with the standard. The EPA bases its prediction that the 1985 standard will be achieved on two factors: modifications decreasing the particulate output of diesel engines, and development of "aftertreatment" technology, that is, means by which the vehicle will remove particulate matter from its own exhaust. The larger proportion of the expected reduction in particulate emissions depends on aftertreatment, and it is the availability of that technology that provokes the major controversy in this case.

The EPA has identified a number of strategies for extracting particulates from diesel exhaust,[25] but the 1985 standard was set in

---

25. The agency also explored the possibility of using continuously operating catalytic converters, or simple replaceable trapping filters. It never ruled out the possibility that these would become feasible alternatives, but it concentrated its discussion on trap-oxidizers, which it expected "to be the preferred aftertreatment technology." 45 Fed.Reg. 14,496, 14,497 (1980). We do not rely on these al-

ternative technologies in upholding the particulate standard. Of course, should catalytic converters prove effective, the manufacturers are free to implement them. An EPA emission standard under the Clean Air Act dictates only the level of emissions permitted, not the technology required for achieving that level.

reliance on one preferred method and must stand or fall with the agency's prediction that that method will be available in time. This favored device is the trap-oxidizer, a mechanism that filters out particulates and then periodically incinerates its catch in order to maintain the trapping capacity of the filter.

The trap-oxidizer is essentially a compromise between two other particulate reduction strategies. At one extreme, the vehicle could rely on a mechanical filter alone but unless that filter were somehow able to maintain its trapping efficiency indefinitely, it would periodically need either replacement or cleaning. At the other extreme, particulates could be continuously incinerated in a catalytic converter but difficult engineering problems accompany the resulting need to maintain sufficient temperature in the converter (c. 1000°F.) and to keep the particulate matter inside the converter long enough to be burned. Citing the technical barriers to continuous incineration and the behavioral barriers to periodic restoration of a filter by car owners, the EPA recognized the trap-oxidizer as "the preferred method" of particulate control. Regulatory Analysis at 47–50, J.A. 526–29. The trap-oxidizer combines the short-term technical superiority of a filter with the long-term usefulness of a converter.

The EPA has predicted that trap-oxidizers will be available for use in model year 1985 vehicles. As the agency has repeatedly observed, the trap-oxidizer is familiar and unobjectionable as a concept. It is not only theoretically sound[;] experimental data demonstrate that periodic incineration can maintain efficiency for over 10,000 miles. But to date, no filter material has been found

that can withstand periodic incineration of the accumulated particulates throughout the 50,000-mile useful life of the vehicle[26] while maintaining a high level of trapping efficiency. The agency noted that

the best durability of a trap reported to EPA was a metal mesh trap on an Opel vehicle, run on a modified AMA driving schedule with no hard accelerations, hills, or speeds above 45 mph. The trap survived 12,800 miles and at that time had a collection efficiency similar to its zero-mile efficiency of 55 percent.

Regulatory Analysis at 51, J.A. 530.

Understandably, the EPA has concluded that further research is needed before devices with the appropriate characteristics will be available for use:

Clearly, more basic research still needs to be done in the areas of regeneration initiation and control, and trap durability. Enough progress has been achieved to convince EPA that a successful trap-oxidizer can be developed, but as of this time, no design has proven to have the required collection efficiency over the desired length of time.

Id. at 52. Nevertheless, the agency concludes that it is merely a question of time before the trap-oxidizer is perfected. "The improvements that are necessary are engineering problems, and are more a function of the resources allocated to the problem than any scientific or technical breakthrough." 45 Fed.Reg. 14,496, 14,498 (1980). Based on the routine nature of most of the remaining problems, the rapid pace of progress in the field since 1978, and the industry's own forecasts of 1985 as a potential completion date, the agency has determined that the lead time remaining is sufficient for application of the requisite technology.

---

26. Section 202(d)(1) of the Act sets the useful life of light-duty vehicles and their engines at "five years or fifty thousand miles (or the equivalent), whichever first occurs." In determining compliance with the emission standard, the EPA analyzes the exhaust of vehicles that have accumulated 50,000 miles. See 45 Fed.Reg. 14,496, 14,506 (1980). The EPA believes, however, that a trap-oxidizer should last at least 100,000 miles. See Regulatory Analysis at 51, J.A. 530, 45 Fed.Reg. 48,133, 48,137 n.36 (1980).

GM dismisses the agency's conclusion as baseless speculation and charges the EPA with naive optimism about the solution of myriad uncertainties, ranging from the development of a durable filter material to the proper location of the trap on the vehicle itself. GM regards the gaps in present knowledge as vitiating the entire standard-setting endeavor:

Until further experimental knowledge on these major development needs is obtained, it is totally impossible to specify when a successful system will be developed for passenger cars and light-duty trucks. Thus, any particulate standard which contemplates use of a regenerative trap-oxidizer must be judged premature and not technologically feasible.

GM Petition for Reconsideration of Standard at 8 (hereinafter GM Petition) J.A. 812. Thus, GM believes that no standard can be promulgated, regardless of its effective date, on the current record.

Before analyzing GM's technical objections, we must reiterate the standard of review that governs this case. The EPA is not obliged to provide detailed solutions to every engineering problem posed in the perfection of the trap-oxidizer. In the absence of theoretical objections to the technology, the agency need only identify the major steps necessary for development of the device, and give plausible reasons for its belief that the industry will be able to solve those problems in the time remaining. The EPA is not required to rebut all speculation that unspecified factors may hinder "real world" emission control.

The EPA has identified as the necessary remaining steps in development of trap-oxidizer technology the choice of a durable, efficient filter material, the selection of an incineration method, and the refinement of a control mechanism to bring about automatic initiation of the regeneration process. GM agrees with the agency's specification of these aspects of the trap-oxidizer as the

ones requiring further research. GM Brief at 22 ("Three critical issues concerning trap oxidizer feasibility remain unresolved: trap durability, regeneration, and collection efficiency.").

a. Development of a Durable Filter The most vigorously controverted issue in this case concerns durability, which the EPA has recognized as the key remaining problem....

The EPA has predicted that the necessary work can be accomplished in time for 1985 model year production. The agency points to the wide variety of materials that have demonstrated appropriate initial efficiencies; several of these are hybrids, suggesting that new combinations of present candidates, rather than hitherto untested substances, may provide the answer....

We conclude that these are plausible reasons for a determination that the industry is capable of solving the durability problem in the allotted time. The EPA could reasonably refuse to be discouraged by the limited initial success, as the project is relatively young. The rapidity of recent progress is a factor that the agency may consider in making a prediction of future capabilities. See *Society of the Plastics Industry, Inc. v. OSHA*, 509 F.2d 1301, 1309 (2d Cir. 1975), cert. denied, 421 U.S. 992 (1975)....We conclude that the EPA's durability prediction, though uncertain, is no more uncertain than such estimates inherently must be, and that the EPA has met the requirement of "reasoned decisionmaking."...

c. Regeneration Initiation and Control ...GM insists that the agency has no basis for believing that a control mechanism for initiating and regulating the incineration process can be developed. This argument is without merit. GM's own prototype throttling vehicle "utilize(d) a microprocessor controller to set the position of the throttle in the air intake as a function of engine speed and rack angle."...the EPA is not obliged to establish that no unknown parameters will later prove relevant to proper control.[30]

d. Conclusion In summary, we find sufficient support for the EPA's necessarily predictive judgment and therefore uphold the EPA's particulate standard. The agency has given the manufacturers substantial lead time, and there is room for interim adjustments to the standard without significant hardship. Under those circumstances, the applicable standard of review allows the EPA considerable latitude to exercise its expertise through reasoned projections. We find that the agency has given an adequate explanation of its reasons for believing that the necessary steps in improving trap-oxidizer technology can be completed in the time remaining.[31] ...

D. Light-Duty Trucks

As we have had occasion to observe, some light-duty trucks come within the "heavy-duty vehicle" category for which particulate emissions standards are authorized by section 202(a)(3)(A)(iii), while others remain in a residual category, neither heavy-duty vehicles nor light-duty vehicles, governed by section 202(a)(1). ... This distinction does not affect our analysis of the present challenges to the particulate standard for light-duty trucks, however, because petitioners' objections are too general to implicate the varying nuances of the separate statutory provisions. NRDC essentially repeats its claims against the light-duty vehicle standard, while GM's attack focuses on the adequacy of the support in the record.

The EPA originally proposed the same particulate standards for light-duty trucks and light-duty vehicles, for both 1981 and 1983, see 44 Fed. Reg. 6650 (1979). The agency subsequently explained this proposal as reflecting the frequent congruity between light-duty truck and light-duty vehicle emission control:

It has been established in previous EPA rulemakings that manufacturers usually apply passenger car emission control technologies to light-duty trucks in order to comply with similar standards, since the engine configurations and type of use are very similar. For instance, GM's diesel light-duty trucks utilize the same diesel engines that are used in the GM 4,500 pound light-duty vehicles.

The meager relevant data submitted in comments on the proposed rulemaking, however, suggested that light-duty trucks emit substantially more particulates than do passenger vehicles.

---

30. We similarly reject GM's argument that the EPA failed to consider the question of where the trap-oxidizer would be placed under the automobile. None of the drawbacks GM sees in various positions raises insuperable barriers to the trap-oxidizer system, and we agree with the EPA that location and configuration are problems for individual manufacturers to deal with at the appropriate time.

31. GM also makes a health-related argument, claiming that the EPA failed to give adequate consideration to safety factors in relying on trap-oxidizers. This complaint is based on the wording of section 202(a)(3)(A)(iii), which requires the EPA to give "appropriate consideration to ... safety factors associated with the application of such technology," but we believe that safety considerations are equally relevant in evaluating the technological feasibility of standards promulgated under section 202(a)(1). GM's argument is essentially that, in its current state of development, the trap-oxidizer is not safe because the incineration of particulate sometimes gets out of hand, posing a possible danger to the rest of the car. GM insists that its pessimism about its ability to cure this problem should preclude the EPA from imposing particulate standards that assume the use of a trap-oxidizer. We fully approve the EPA's response to this claim: "EPA would not require a particulate control technology that was known to involve serious safety problems. If during the development of the trap-oxidizer safety problems are discovered, EPA would reconsider the control requirements implemented by this rulemaking." 45 Fed.Reg. 14,496, 14,503 (1980). GM has not presented any theoretical reason why trap-oxidizers cannot be made safe, and it would be premature to rule them out at present.

See Regulatory Analysis at 53–58, J.A. 532–37.

The EPA analyzed these data, and concluded that the "higher inertia weight and aerodynamic drag" of light-duty trucks would necessarily result in higher particulate levels. 45 Fed.Reg. 14,496, 14,497 (1980). The higher road load horsepower of the trucks also contributed to greater emission levels. See 45 Fed.Reg. 48,133, 48,138 (1980); Regulatory Analysis at 54–55, J.A. 533–34. Furthermore, the expected improvements in light-duty vehicle emissions due to downsizing of vehicles and their engines would not be equalled by light-duty trucks. Regulatory Analysis at 58, J.A. 537. Finally, the increasing stringency over the next decade of the oxides of nitrogen standard for light-duty trucks would exacerbate particulate emissions.[34] Taking into account all these factors, the EPA concluded that the particulate emissions from light-duty trucks, before aftertreatment, would be thirty percent greater than those from light-duty vehicles. Therefore, the appropriate particulate standard, after trap-oxidizer treatment, would be 0.26 gpm rather than 0.20 gpm. 45 Fed. Reg. 14,496, 14,497 (1980)....

[In a portion of the opinion not reproduced here, the court upheld EPA's grant of a waiver of the NO_x standard for light-duty vehicles.]

V.   CONCLUSION

In the Clean Air Act, Congress encouraged the EPA to set standards for the future without specifying the methodology the agency must follow to determine the probable course of future technological growth. In these circumstances, a reviewing court's role is to make sure that the agency has acted responsibly in formulating a reasoned prediction. It is not our task to decide whether the agency is correct, or to require proof to a mathematical certainty. We must be satisfied if the agency has undertaken its analysis with the degree of precision and clarity that the subject inherently permits. The EPA has done so in this case.

We find no merit in the NRDC's allegations that the EPA granted NO_x waivers unlawfully, at undue risk to the public health. We similarly reject the NRDC's challenges to the particulate standards as inconsistent with the statutory mandate. We uphold the EPA's hydrocarbon testing procedure, and accept as sufficiently reasoned the EPA's prediction of technological availability and the particulate standards based thereupon. The regulations reviewed in this proceeding, in their entirety, are

Affirmed.

ROBB, CIRCUIT JUDGE, CONCURRING IN PART AND DISSENTING IN PART:

I concur in Part III of the court's opinion, upholding the EPA's grant of NO_x waivers to various diesel manufacturers. I must dissent, however, from that part of the opinion in which the court sustains the particulate standards for 1985. In my view the record does not support the EPA's prediction that the necessary technology will be available in time to meet the 1985 standard. My doubts focus in particular on the inability of the auto manufacturers to develop a filtering material for trap-oxidizers that possesses the durability needed to withstand periodic incineration of collected particulates for the useful life of the vehicle.

The majority states that "the EPA will have demonstrated the reasonableness of its basis for prediction if it answers any theoretical objections to the trap-oxidizer method, identifies the major steps necessary in refinement of the device, and offers plausible reasons for believing that each of those steps

---

34. This result is due to the trade-off between particulate control and NO_x control caused by exhaust gas regeneration technology.

can be completed in the time available." I have no quarrel with this standard, but I do not agree that the EPA has offered plausible reasons for believing that the critical step of achieving the required level of trap durability can be completed in the time available.

The record demonstrates that General Motors (GM) alone, which began its particulate control research program in 1974, has tested many different trap materials provided by at least 16 different manufacturers. Of these materials, 22 are characterized by GM as "the best materials" available, based on tests conducted with an Opel 2.1 liter diesel engine and an Oldsmobile 5.7 liter diesel engine. (J.A. 237) Yet the durability of even the best of these materials...is far below what will be needed to meet the standard. The most successful test results were obtained by installing a metal mesh trap in a GM Opel, which was then driven on a non-typical schedule with no hard accelerations, hills, or speeds above 45 miles per hour. The filtering material survived only 12,800 miles, at which time it had a collection efficiency of 55 percent. GM also reported some particulate "blow-off" (i.e., particulate matter escaping through the exhaust system) and self-incineration. (J.A. 530) The statute, however, establishes a useful life for light duty vehicles and light duty vehicle engines of "five years or fifty thousand miles (or the equivalent),

whichever first occurs." 42 U.S.C. §7521(d)(1) (Supp. I 1977). Furthermore, the EPA stated in its Regulatory Analysis of the particulate standards that the trapping material "should last at least 100,000 miles." (J.A. 530)

After acknowledging the shortcomings of the Opel test, the EPA summarized the status of trap-oxidizer research as follows:

Clearly, more basic research still needs to be done in the areas of regeneration initiation and control, and trap durability. Enough progress has been achieved to convince EPA that a successful trap-oxidizer can be developed, but as of this time, no design has proven to have the required collection efficiency over the desired length of time. With the research that has been, and is, going on with regards to trap-oxidizer development, and a determined broad-based effort by the manufacturers to comply with the final standards, EPA's technical staff has concluded that it is very likely that a successful trap-oxidizer design can be optimized within the next 11/2 to 2 years.

(J.A. 531) In my opinion, these exhortations to the manufacturers and the EPA's vaguely articulated faith that a "design can be optimized" soon do not amount to "plausible reasons for believing that each of (the necessary) steps can be completed in the time available," within the meaning of the majority's standard. Pious hope and speculation cannot take the place of evidence. Accordingly, I must dissent from Part II of the court's opinion.

■ NOTES

1. Uncertainty about the rate of future innovation is an issue throughout the case. If EPA were to wait, as GM suggests, until further experimental knowledge demonstrates that the technology is feasible, what incentive would GM have to further develop the technology? Are there any incentives for firms to share "positive" data regarding technological innovation with EPA in the future?

2. Note that Judge Mikva's majority opinion affords EPA "considerable latitude to exercise its expertise through reasoned projections." The majority states that the reasonableness of EPA's prediction as to the availability of the targeted control

technology is demonstrated when the agency identifies the major steps necessary for the innovation to occur and the time needed to complete those steps. Judge Robb's dissent, on the other hand, argues that EPA's expectations regarding likely improvements in trap durability were unreasonable. Is the court's view of technological innovation more in line with innovation of an incremental nature or of a radical nature? Given that the technology trajectories for radical (or disruptive) innovations are discontinuous and nonlinear, what does this imply for standards seeking to "force" more radical innovation? Would the court's approach to the issue of technological feasibility necessarily invalidate standards designed to encourage radical innovation, or would that depend on the nature of the authority given to the agency by Congress?

3. In this case, as in *International Harvester*, EPA had focused on a specific technology, arguing that the technology could be developed and that the challenged standards thus could be met. The process reflects the agency's response to the information asymmetry that arises when, as is often the case, the agency has less technical knowledge than the industry regarding potential technological solutions. Both to establish credibility and to provide counterarguments to industry's protestations of technical *in*feasibility, the agency limits the asymmetry by selecting and targeting one type of technology. How does this in turn limit the "problem space" of the industry in its research efforts and outlays to meet the standards?

4. At least at first glance, the statutory provisions under which these standards were set might be said to be less favorable to EPA than those at play in the *International Harvester* case. Here, the statutory burden of proof was squarely on the agency. Furthermore, the standards at issue here, as the court notes at the beginning of the opinion, are technology based (i.e., set according to the level of emission reduction deemed attainable by the application of a particular technology). In contrast, the congressionally mandated standards at issue in *International Harvester* were health based (i.e., they were, in the words of the court here, "absolute" emission limits, not set with reference to the level of emission reduction attainable by the application of any particular technology). Despite these factors, the agency's decision to implement emission standards clearly fares better with the court in this case than in *International Harvester*. If one were to generalize solely on the basis of these two cases, then, could one say that technology-based standards are more likely to force technological development than health-based standards? Or is the better view that the *context* within which the standards are set, and within which a court reviews the standards, is likely to be an important factor in determining the outcome?

5. What are some of the key differences between the respective contexts within which this case and *International Harvester* arise? The court distinguishes *International Har-*

vester on the basis of the longer lead time available to the regulated automakers here. How persuasive is this distinction? Beyond the issue of lead time, are there different economic and political considerations at stake? What is the nature of the vehicles being regulated? What percentage of the overall U.S. vehicle market did diesel vehicles likely represent in the early 1980s? Had EPA's technological assessments been inaccurate, were the potential societal consequences of the same level of significance as those facing the court in *International Harvester*?

6. Two other distinctions from *International Harvester* may also have been important here. First, in the years since that case had been decided, the federal courts, and the D.C. Circuit Court of Appeals in particular, had seen a number of cases in which they were asked to review agency decisions based on scientific and engineering determinations that had necessarily been made in the face of technical uncertainty. (The *Ethyl Corp.* case, discussed later in this chapter, was one significant example.) It is likely that this court was somewhat more sanguine about such decisions than it had been at the time of *International Harvester*. Further, the court was not limited here to the viewpoints and arguments raised in an adversary battle between the regulator and the regulated over whether the proposed standards should be relaxed. Rather, the court's view of the issues was also shaped by the arguments of the NRDC, which urged the court to order the agency to *strengthen* the standards at issue.

7. The court upholds EPA's decision to promulgate more lenient particulate standards for light-duty trucks because of the nature of these vehicles (i.e., their drag and weight). Given that most of today's light-duty trucks are used for the same general purposes as light-duty cars, it could be argued that EPA made a poor choice for the long run. Could EPA have categorized vehicles into different classes based on characteristics *other* than weight? As discussed later, the Tier II standards put in place by the 1990 Clean Air Act Amendments reversed EPA's approach and established similar standards for all light- and medium-duty vehicles. Note, however, that this reversal did not begin to take effect until more than 20 years after EPA's initial decision, and will take even longer to have a real impact. ■

c. Federal Preemption (and the California Exception)

When it began regulating motor vehicle emissions in 1967, Congress generally precluded the states from setting their own emission standards for new vehicles to ensure that manufacturers would not have to face the prospect of fifty different sets of standards. However, in recognition of California's leadership role in addressing auto pollution and the severe air quality problems that the state faced as a result of auto pollution, the act gave California, alone among the states, the right to continue to set and enforce its own emission standards for new motor vehicles. The 1970 amendments continued this explicit preemption of state standards for new motor vehicles and also continued the exemption for California. See CAA Section 209.

In the ensuing years, many argued that restricting state regulation in this manner interfered with the states' long-standing exercise of their "police power" to protect public health. Congress addressed this concern in part in the 1977 amendments. It authorized states with air quality control regions that exceeded primary air quality standards to adopt California's standards for new motor vehicle emissions. See CAA Section 177.

This federal preemption exemption, and the concomitant right of certain states to "piggyback" on California's standards, has helped keep California at the forefront of mobile source regulation. The state has served, in effect, as a test bed, setting the precedent for future federal standards. In recent years, California was the first to develop a low emission vehicle program and the first to announce a regulatory program to cut the emission of greenhouse gases (chiefly CO_2) from motor vehicles. If the "California standards" have not always been popular with automakers, the automakers have largely acquiesced to California's special role under the Clean Air Act, perhaps in no small part because the state represents a large enough market for motor vehicles to warrant the economic investment necessary to comply with its standards.

2.   Regulation of Fuel Content—Product Ban as Technology Forcing

Another important component of the motor vehicle program put in place by the 1970 Clean Air Act Amendments was the authority given to EPA to regulate motor vehicle fuels and their additives. The 1967 Air Quality Act had simply required manufacturers to *register* fuels and additives with the HEW. The legislative history of the 1970 amendments shows that Congress was especially concerned about lead additives in gasoline. Growing evidence suggested that airborne lead absorbed into the body posed a health hazard to adults and children, especially in the inner city. Moreover, Congress recognized that lead would have deleterious effects on the catalytic converters being used to reduce emissions. Thus, the 1970 amendments authorized EPA to regulate or prohibit the sale of fuels and additives deemed to impair the performance of emission control devices, and to prohibit the sale of fuel or fuel additives found to "endanger the public health or welfare" [CAA Section 211(c)(1)(A)].

Acting on this latter authority, EPA promulgated regulations in November 1973 directing gasoline refiners to reduce the lead content of gasoline over a 5-year period, beginning in 1975. An appeal was filed by manufacturers of lead additives and gasoline refiners, and was heard by a three-judge panel of the District of Columbia Court of Appeals. By a 2-to-1 vote (Judge Malcolm Wikey joined by Judge Edward Tamm), the court set aside the standard. The "will endanger" criterion, reasoned the majority, is a rigorous one requiring a substantial quantum of proof. Moreover, the majority reasoned, that proof must establish "that the lead from auto emissions by itself or alone contributes a measurable increment of lead to the human body, and that this increment causes a significant health hazard." Finding that the evidence did not rise to this level, the majority concluded that the standard was invalid. See *Ethyl Corp. v. EPA*, 7 Env't. Rep. Cases (BNA) 1353, 1357 (D.C. Cir. 1975). EPA appealed and was granted a rehearing by the full D.C. Circuit. The resulting majority opinion, authored by Judge J. Skelly Wright, made *Ethyl Corp. v. EPA* a landmark case, both for its explication of the precautionary approach in regulation and for its treatment of the role of judicial review in the face of scientific evidence (and scientific uncertainty).

Ethyl Corp. v. Environmental Protection Agency
WRIGHT, Circuit Judge
541 F.2d 1 (D.C. Cir. 1976)

Man's ability to alter his environment has developed far more rapidly than his ability to foresee with certainty the effects of his alterations. It is only recently that we have begun to appreciate the danger posed by unregulated modification of the world around us, and have created watchdog agencies whose task it is to warn us, and protect us, when technological "advances" present dangers unappreciated—or unrevealed—by their supporters. Such agencies, unequipped with crystal balls and unable to read the future, are nonetheless charged with evaluating the effects of unprecedented environmental modifications, often made on a massive scale. Necessarily, they must deal with predictions and uncertainty, with developing evidence, with conflicting evidence, and, sometimes, with little or no evidence at all. Today we address the scope of the power delegated one such watchdog, the Environmental Protection Agency (EPA). We must determine the certainty required by the Clean Air Act before EPA may act to protect the health of our populace from the lead particulate emissions of automobiles.

Section 211(c)(1)(A) of the Clean Air Act authorizes the Administrator of EPA to regulate gasoline additives whose emission products "will endanger the public health or welfare. . . ." 42 U.S.C. §1857f-6c(c)(1)(A). Acting pursuant to that power, the Administrator, after notice and comment, determined that the automotive emissions caused by leaded gasoline present "a significant risk of harm" to the public health. Accordingly, he promulgated regulations that reduce, in stepwise fashion, the lead content of leaded gasoline. We must decide whether the Administrator properly interpreted the meaning of Section 211(c)(1)(A) and the scope of his power thereunder, and, if so, whether the evidence adduced at the rule-making preceeding supports his final determination. Finding in favor of the Administrator on both grounds, and on all other grounds raised by petitioners, we affirm his determination.

I. THE FACTS, THE STATUTE, THE PROCEEDINGS AND THE REGULATIONS

Hard on the introduction of the first gasoline-powered automobiles came the discovery that lead "antiknock" compounds, when added to gasoline, dramatically increase the fuel's octane rating. Increased octane allows for higher compression engines, which operate with greater efficiency. Since 1923 antiknocks have been regularly added to gasoline, and a large industry has developed to supply those compounds. Today, approximately 90 percent of motor gasoline manufactured in the United States contains lead additives, even though most 1975 and 1976 model automobiles are equipped with catalytic converters, which require lead-free gasoline. From the beginning, however, scientists have questioned whether the addition of lead to gasoline, and its consequent diffusion into the atmosphere from the automobile emission, poses a danger to the public health. . . .

Human body lead comes from three major sources. In most people, the largest source is the diet. Absorption of dietary lead . . . is generally regarded as, for all practical purposes, uncontrollable.

A second major source of the body's lead burden, at least among urban children, *is* regarded as controllable, although effective control may be both difficult and expensive to achieve. Ingestion of lead paint by children with pica (the abnormal ingestion of non-food substances, a relatively common trait in pre-school children, particularly ages 1–3) is generally regarded as "the principal environmental source in cases of severe acute lead poisoning in young children." NAS Report at 140.

The last remaining major source of lead exposure for humans is the ambient air. This source is easily the most controllable, since approximately 90 percent of lead in the air comes from automobile emissions, and can be simply eliminated by removing lead from gasoline. . . .

The multiple sources of human exposure to lead explain in part why it has been difficult to pinpoint automobile lead emissions as a danger to public health. . . . For years the lead antiknock industry has refused to accept the developing evidence that lead emissions

contribute significantly to the total human lead body burden. In the Clean Air Act Amendments of 1970, Pub. L. 91-604, December 31, 1970, 84 STAT. 1698–1700, however, Congress finally set up a legal mechanism by which that evidence could be weighed in a more objective tribunal. It gave the newly-created EPA authority to control or prohibit the sale or manufacture of any fuel additive whose emission products "will endanger the public health or welfare. . . ." 42 U.S.C. §1857f-6c(c)(1)(A) (1970). It is beyond question that the fuel additive Congress had in mind was lead.

Given this mandate, EPA published on January 31, 1971 advance notice of proposed rule-making. The Administrator announced he was considering possible controls on lead additives in gasolines, both because of their possible danger to health and because of their incompatibility with the newly-developed catalytic converter emission control system. 36 FED. REG. 1486 (1971).

Proposed regulations were issued a year later, February 23, 1972, supported by a document *Health Hazards of Lead* (hereinafter First Health Document), prepared by the EPA scientific staff. Comments were invited for a 90-day period, later reopened for an additional 30 days. 37 FED. REG. 11786–11787 (1972). . . .

On January 10, 1973 the Administrator, while issuing final regulations requiring availability of some lead-free gasoline to allow implementation of the catalytic converter system, 38 FED. REG. 1254; *approved in Amoco Oil Co.* v. *EPA*, 501 F.2d 722 (D.C. Cir. 1974), reproposed the health-based regulations now at issue. 38 FED. REG. 1258. The reproposal was supported by a second health document, *EPA's Position on the Health Effects of Airborne Lead* (hereinafter Second Health Document), JA 158, and was necessitated by a modification of EPA's analysis of the health effects of lead emissions. . . .

On October 28, 1973, as a result of a motion filed in *Natural Resources Defense Council, Inc.* v. *EPA*, D.C. Cir. No. 72-2233, this court ordered EPA to reach within 30 days a final decision on whether lead additives should be regulated for health reasons. EPA published its final health document, entitled *EPA's Position on the Health Implications of Airborne Lead*, on November 28, 1973. JA 27. This document, the Third Health Document, extensively details and reviews the state of knowledge of the health effects of airborne lead. It candidly discusses the various scientific studies, both pro and con, underlying this information, and ultimately concludes that lead from automobile emissions will endanger the public health. The same day, based largely on the conclusions of the Third Health Document, EPA promulgated its final regulations, accompanied by a thorough discussion of its health conclusions, the impact of the regulations, and the alternative courses of action considered and rejected. 38 FED. REG. 33734.... Under the final regulations, lead in all gasoline would be reduced over a five-year period to an average of 0.5 grams per gallon.[12]

Petitioners, various manufacturers of lead additives and refiners of gasoline, appealed the promulgation of low-lead regulations to this court under Section 307 of the Clean Air Act, 42 U.S.C. §1857h-5. The appeal was heard by a division of the court on September 9, 1974. On December 20, 1974, the division, one judge dissenting, ordered the regulations set aside. The majority and dissenting opinions were published on January 28, 1975.[13] Because of the importance of the issues presented, we granted EPA's petition for rehearing *en banc* on March 17, 1975, vacating the judgment and opinions of the division and setting the case for reargument on May 30, 1975. All parties were invited to submit supplementary briefs addressing the issues raised by the division opinions....

II. THE STATUTORY REQUIREMENTS

Under Section 211(c)(1)(A) the Administrator may, on the basis of all the information available to him, promulgate regulations that "control or prohibit the manufacture, introduction into commerce, offering for sale, or sale of any fuel or fuel additive for use in a motor vehicle or motor vehicle engine (A) if any emission products of such fuel or fuel additive will endanger the public health or welfare...."

...The Administrator cannot act under Section 211(c)(1)(A), however, until after "consideration of all relevant medical and scientific evidence available to him, including consideration of other technologically or economically feasible means of achieving emission standards under [Section 202]." Section 211(c)(2)(A). Section 202 of the Act allows the Administrator to set standards for emission of pollutants from automobiles (as opposed to standards for the composition of the gasoline that produces the emissions), and is thus the preferred—although not the mandatory—alternative under the statutory

---

12. The reduction would proceed in the following steps:
1.7 g/gal. after Jan. 1, 1975
1.4 g/gal. after Jan. 1, 1976
1.0 g/gal. after Jan. 1, 1977
0.8 g/gal. after Jan. 1, 1978
0.5 g/gal. after Jan. 1, 1979
40 C.F.R. §80.20 (1975).
13. Commentators have been uniformly critical of the majority opinion. *See* Gardner, *Federal Courts and Agencies: An Audit of the Partnership Books*, 75 COLUM. L. REV. 800, 801 & n.77 (1975); Note, *Judicial Review of the Facts in Informal Rulemaking: A Proposed Standard*, 84 YALE L.J. 1750, 1767–68 & nn. 81–82 (1975); Note, *Reserve Mining—The Standard of Proof Required to Enjoin an Environmental Hazard to the Public Health*, 58 MINN. L. REV. 893, 918–19 n.116 (1975). *See also Reserve Mining Co.* v. *EPA*, 514 F.2d 492, 519–520 (8th Cir. 1975) (*en banc*).

scheme, presumably because it minimizes Agency interference with manufacturer prerogatives.[14]

The Administrator is also required, before prohibiting a fuel or fuel additive under Section 211(c)(1)(A), to find, and publish the finding, that in his judgment any fuel or fuel additive likely to replace the prohibited one will not "endanger the public health or welfare to the same or greater degree...." Section 211(c)(2)(C), 42 U.S.C. §1857f-6c(c)(2)(C). It is significant that this is the *only* conclusion the Administrator is expressly required to "find" before regulating a fuel or fuel additive for health reasons.

A. The Threshold Determination

In making his threshold determination that lead particulate emissions from motor vehicles "will endanger the public health or welfare," the Administrator provided his interpretation of the statutory language by couching his conclusion in these words: such emissions "present a significant risk of harm to the health of urban populations, particularly to the health of city children." 38 FED. REG. 33734. By way of further interpretation, he added that it was his view "that the statutory language...does not require a determination that automobile emissions alone create the endangerment on which controls may be based. Rather, the Administrator believes that in providing this authority, the Congress was aware that the public's exposure to harmful substances results from a number of sources which may have varying degrees of susceptibility to control." *Id....*

Petitioners argue that the "will endanger" standard requires a high quantum of factual proof, proof of actual harm rather than of a "significant risk of harm." *See* Supplemental brief of petitioner Ethyl Corporation (hereinafter Ethyl Supp. Br.) at 20. Since, according to petitioners, regulation under Section 211(c)(1)(A) must be premised upon factual proof of actual harm, the Administrator has, in their view, no power to assess risks or make policy judgments in deciding to regulate lead additives. Moreover, petitioners argue, regulation must be based on the danger presented by lead additives "in and of themselves," so it is improper to consider, as the Administrator did, the cumulative impact of lead additives on all other sources of human exposure to lead. We have considered these arguments with care and find them to be without merit. It is our view that the Administrator's interpretation of the standard is the correct one.

The Precautionary Nature of "Will Endanger"
Simply as a matter of plain meaning, we have difficulty crediting petitioners' reading of the "will endanger" standard. The meaning of "endanger" is not disputed. Case law and dictionary definition agree that endanger means something less than actual harm. When one is endangered, harm is *threatened*; no actual injury need ever occur. Thus, for example, a town may be "endangered" by a threatening plague or hurricane and yet emerge from the danger completely unscathed.[18] A statute allowing for regulation in the face of danger is, necessarily, a precautionary statute. Regulatory action may be

---

14. When EPA acts under §211(c)(1)(A) it is essentially telling manufacturers how to make their fuels, a task Congress felt the Agency should enter upon only with trepidation. *See, e.g.*, 116 CONG. REC. 32920 (1970) (remarks of Sen.Baker); *id.* at 19229 (remarks of Reps. Rogers & Waggoner). On the other hand, when the Agency acts under §202, it is only mandating an end product—regulated emissions. The method for achieving the required result is entirely in the hands of the manufacturers.

18. Petitioner Ethyl suggests that while these may indeed be examples of endangerment, they differ from the threat from automotive lead emissions in that plagues do cause death and illness; violent storms do cause damage—known facts that may be experienced by the threatened community. We may preliminarily observe that the absorption of lead does cause lead poisoning, a known fact that may be evaluated by the public and the EPA. However, in so far as Ethyl is complaining that the

taken before the threatened harm occurs; indeed, the very existence of such precautionary legislation would seem to *demand* that regulatory action precede, and, optimally, prevent, the perceived threat. As should be apparent, the "will endanger" language of Section 211(c)(1)(A) makes it such a precautionary statute....

...While cases interpreting the meaning of "endanger" are few in number, at least one recent case is directly on point and fully in accord with our view.

In *Reserve Mining Co.* v. *EPA*, 514 F.2d 492 (8th Cir. 1975) (*en banc*), the Eighth Circuit addressed, among other issues, the meaning of the phrase "endangering the health or welfare of persons" under Section 1160 of the Federal Water Pollution Control Act of 1970 (FWPCA), 33 U.S.C. §1160. FWPCA and the Clean Air Act together constitute the bulk of this nation's substantive environmental protection legislation. As such, and because of their contemporaneous enactment, interpretations of provisions of one Act have frequently been applied to comparable provisions of the other. *See, e.g., Natural Resources Defense Council, Inc.* v. *Train*, 166 U.S. App. D.C. 312, 321–322, 510 F.2d 692, 701–702 (1975). Thus *Reserve Mining's* interpretation of "endangering" is relevant to the meaning of the term "endanger" in the Clean Air Act. Indeed, it is particularly relevant because in construing the language before it the Eighth Circuit borrowed extensively from the interpretation of the "will endanger" language of Section 211 expressed in the dissent from the division opinion in this case, the

same interpretation we adopt here. *See Reserve Mining Co.* v. *EPA, supra,* 514 F.2d at 528–529. After analysis of the plain meaning of the FWPCA provision, comparison with other sections of that Act, and reference to our division's dissent, the Eighth Circuit's unanimous conclusion fully supports our view of the "will endanger" standard:

In the context of this environmental legislation, we believe that Congress used the term "endangering" in a precautionary or preventive sense, and, therefore, evidence of potential harm as well as actual harm comes within the purview of that term.

Id. at 528.

In sum, based on the plain meaning of the statute, the juxtaposition of Section 211 with Sections 108 and 202, and the *Reserve Mining* precedent, we conclude that the "will endanger" standard is precautionary in nature and does not require proof of actual harm before regulation is appropriate.

Perhaps because it realized that the above interpretation was the only possible reading of the statutory language, petitioner Ethyl addresses this interpretation and argues that even if actual harm is not required for action under Section 211(c)(1)(A), the occurrence of the threatened harm must be "probable" before regulation is justified. Ethyl Supp. Br. 12. While the dictionary admittedly settles on "probable" as its measure of danger, we believe a more sophisticated case-by-case analysis is appropriate. *See* note 17 *supra.* Danger, the Administrator recognized, is set not by a fixed probability of harm, but rather is composed of reciprocal elements of risk

---

mechanism by which plagues and storms cause damage is well known while the question of the relation between lead automobile emissions and the absorption of lead is less certain, Ethyl's observation only supports the reading of §211(c)(1)(A) as a precautionary statute. The massive diffusion of airborne lead is a gross environmental modification never before experienced. Of course, there are no past disasters of the kind anticipated by the Administrator on which the community's experience may

be based. This, however, is inherent in such a threat and does not imply that no danger is posed by it. We believe the precautionary language of the Act indicates quite plainly Congress' intent that regulation should precede any threatened, albeit unprecedented, disaster. Ethyl is correct that we have not had the opportunity to learn from the consequences of an environmental overdose of lead emissions; Congress, however, sought to spare us that communal experience by enacting §211(c)(1)(A).

and harm, or probability and severity. *Cf. Carolina Environmental Study Group* v. *United States*, 510 F.2d 796, 799 (D.C. Cir. 1975); *Reserve Mining Co.* v. *EPA, supra*, 514 F.2d at 519–520. That is to say, the public health may properly be found endangered both by a lesser risk of a greater harm and by a greater risk of a lesser harm.[32] Danger depends upon the relation between the risk and harm presented by each case, and cannot legitimately be pegged to "probable" harm, regardless of whether that harm be great or small. . . .

In *Reserve Mining* the issue was whether asbestiform wastes flushed into Lake Superior by the Reserve Mining Company endangered health. The polluted lake waters formed the drinking supply of several surrounding communities, while a medical theory, bolstered only by inconclusive evidence, suggested that ingestion of the wastes caused cancer. Applying the "endangering the health or welfare of persons" standard of the FWPCA, the court found the wastes to be a danger cognizable under the Act. The court did not find that the danger was probable; rather it found the wastes to be "potentially harmful," 514 F.2d at 528, and potential harm to be embraced by the "endangering" standard. The court concluded:

The record shows that Reserve is discharging a substance into Lake Superior waters, which under *an acceptable but unproved medical theory* may be considered as carcinogenic. As previously discussed, this discharge gives rise to a *reasonable medical concern* over the public health. We sustain the district court's determination that Reserve's discharge into Lake Superior constitutes pollution of waters "endangering the health or welfare of persons"

within the terms of §§1160(c)(5) and (g)(1) of the Federal Water Pollution Control Act and is subject to abatement.

514 F.2d at 529 (footnote omitted) (emphasis added). The court thus allowed regulation of the effluent on only a "reasonable" or "potential" showing of danger, hardly the "probable" finding urged by Ethyl as the proper reading of the "endanger" language in Section 211. The reason this relatively slight showing of probability of risk justified regulation is clear: the harm to be avoided, cancer, was particularly great. However, because the risk was somewhat remote, the court did not order the immediate cessation of asbestiform dumping, but rather ordered such cessation within "a reasonable time." *Id.* at 538.

Reserve Mining convincingly demonstrates that the magnitude of risk sufficient to justify regulation is inversely proportional to the harm to be avoided. *Cf. Carolina Environmental Study Group* v. *United States, supra.* It would be a bizarre exercise in balancing horrors to determine whether cancer or lead poisoning is a greater harm to be avoided, but fortunately such balancing is unnecessary in this case. Undoubtedly, the harm caused by lead poisoning is severe; nonetheless, the Administrator does not rely on a "potential" risk or a "reasonable medical concern" to justify the regulations before us. Instead, he finds a "significant" risk of harm to health. While this finding may be less than the "probable" standard urged by Ethyl, it is considerably more certain than the risk that justified regulation in *Reserve Mining* of a comparably "fright-laden" harm. . . .

---

32. This proposition must be confined to reasonable limits, however. In *Carolina Environmental Study Group* v. *United States*, 510 F.2d 796 (D.C. Cir. 1975), a division of this court found the possibility of a Class 9 nuclear reactor disaster, a disaster of ultimate severity and horrible consequences, to be so low that the Atomic Energy Commission's minimal consideration of the effects of such a disaster in an environmental impact statement prepared

for a new reactor was sufficient. Likewise, even the absolute certainty of *de minimis* harm might not justify government action. Under §211 the threatened harm must be sufficiently significant to justify health-based regulation of national impact. Ultimately, of course, whether a particular combination of slight risk and great harm, or great risk and slight harm, constitutes a danger must depend on the facts of each case.

This conclusion follows not only from the language of Section 211(c)(1)(A) and its legislative history, but from the nature of the Administrator's charge: to protect the public from danger. Regulators such as the Administrator must be accorded flexibility, a flexibility that recognizes the special judicial interest in favor of protection of the health and welfare of people, even in areas where certainty does not exist. *Environmental Defense Fund, Inc.* v. *Ruckelshaus*, 439 F.2d 584, 598 (1971).

Questions involving the environment are particularly prone to uncertainty. Technological man has altered his world in ways never before experienced or anticipated. The health effects of such alterations are often unknown, sometimes unknowable. While a concerned Congress has passed legislation providing for protection of the public health against gross environmental modifications, the regulators entrusted with the enforcement of such laws have not thereby been endowed with a prescience that removes all doubt from their decision-making. Rather, speculation, conflicts in evidence, and theoretical extrapolation typify their every action. How else can they act, given a mandate to protect the public health but only a slight or nonexistent data base upon which to draw? . . . Yet the statutes and common sense demand regulatory action to prevent harm, even if the regulator is less than certain that harm is otherwise inevitable . . .[52]

The problems faced by EPA in deciding whether lead automotive emissions pose a threat to the public health highlight the limitations of awaiting certainty. First, lead concentrations are, even to date, essentially low-level, so that the feared adverse effects would not materialize until after a lifetime of exposure. Contrary to petitioners' suggestion, however, we have not yet suffered a lifetime of exposure to lead emissions. At best, emissions at present levels have been with us for no more than 15–20 years. Second, lead exposure from the ambient air is pervasive, so that valid control groups cannot be found against which the effects of lead on our population can be measured. Third, the sources of human exposure to lead are multiple, so that it is difficult to isolate the effect of automobile emissions. Lastly, significant exposure to lead is toxic, so that considerations of decency and morality limit the flexibility of experiments on humans that would otherwise accelerate lead exposure from years to months, and measure those results. *Cf. Environmental Defense Fund, Inc.* v. *EPA* (*Shell*), 510 F.2d 1292, 1299 (D.C. Cir. 1975).

The scientific techniques for attempting to overcome these limitations are several: toxicology can study the distribution and effect of lead in animals; epidemiological techniques can analyze the effects of lead emissions on entire populations; clinical studies can reproduce in laboratories atmospheric conditions and measure under controlled circumstances the effects on humans. All of these studies are of limited usefulness, however. . . .

Propriety of the Cumulative Impact Approach
In addition to demanding that the Administrator act solely on facts, petitioner Ethyl insists that those facts convince him that the emission product of the additive to be

---

52. Even scientific "facts" are not certain, but only theories with high probabilities of validity. Scientists typically speak not of certainty, but of probability; they are trained to act on probabilities that statistically constitute "certainties." *See generally* T. KUHN, THE STRUCTURE OF SCIENTIFIC REVOLUTIONS. While awaiting such statistical certainty may constitute the typical mode of scientific behavior, its appropriateness is questionable in environmental medicine, where regulators seek to prevent harm that often cannot be labeled "certain" until after it occurs. . . . The uncertainty of scientific fact parallels the uncertainty of all fact. In a metaphysical sense, at least, facts are themselves nothing more than risks, or statistical probabilities. *See* D. HUME, A TREATISE OF HUMAN NATURE, bk. I, pt. III, §6, at 87 (L. A. Selby-Bigge ed. 1958).

regulated "in and of itself," *i.e.*, considered in isolation, endangers health. The Administrator contends that the impact of lead emissions is properly considered together with all other human exposure to lead. We agree....

... Airborne lead, in and of itself, may not be a threat. But the realities of human lead exposure show that no one source *in and of itself* (except possibly leaded paint) is a threat. Thus, under Ethyl's tunnel-like reasoning, even if parallel legislation permitted regulation of other sources of lead exposure, which it does not, no regulation could ever be justified.

Such cannot be the case. Congress understood that the body lead burden is caused by multiple sources. It understood that determining the effect of lead automobile emissions, by themselves, on human health is of no more practical value than finding the incremental effect on health of the fifteenth sleeping pill swallowed by a would-be suicide.[62] It did not mean for "endanger" to be measured only in incremental terms.[63] This the Administrator also understood. He determined that absorption of lead automobile emissions, when added to all other human exposure to lead, raises the body lead burden to a level that will endanger health. He realized that lead automobile emissions were, far and away, the most readily reduced significant source of environmental lead. And he deter-

mined that the statute authorized him to reduce those emissions on such a finding. We find no error in the Administrator's use of the cumulative impact approach.

Summary of the "Will Endanger" Determination

In sum, we must reject petitioners' cramped and unrealistic interpretation of Section 211(c)(1)(A). Their reading would render the statute largely useless as a basis for health-related regulation of lead emissions. Petitioners' arguments are rebuffed by the plain meaning of the statute and the Administrator's interpretation of it, by the legislative history and the implications that can be drawn from other sections of the same statute, by the relevant precedents, and by the established maxim that health-related legislation is liberally construed to achieve its purpose....

III.   THE EVIDENCE

A.   The Standard of Review

In promulgating the low-lead regulations under Section 211, EPA engaged in informal rule-making. As such, since the statute does not indicate otherwise, its procedures are conducted pursuant to Section 4 of the APA, 5 U.S.C. §553, and must be reviewed under Section 10 of the Act, 5 U.S.C. §706(2)(A)–

---

62. While the incremental effect of lead emissions on the total body lead burden is of no practical value in determining whether health is endangered, it is of value, of course, in deciding whether the lead exposure problem can fruitfully be attacked through control of lead additives. Moreover, even under the cumulative impact theory emissions must make more than a minimal contribution to total exposure in order to justify regulation under §211(c)(1)(A). We accept the Administrator's determination that the contribution must be "significant" before regulation is proper. *See* 38 FED. REG. 33734.

63. Congress had before it a complete explanation of the multiple sources of human lead exposure. It understood that lead is ubiquitous in nature, that

trace elements of lead are present in everyone, and that only when lead concentration reaches higher levels would the public be endangered. It could not have thought that lead automobile emissions could, by themselves, endanger the public, although it clearly did think they could be regulated only if they provided a significant increment to the total human lead burden. *See, e.g.*, Hearings on S. 3229, S. 2466 & S. 3546 before the Subcommittee on Air & Water Pollution of the Senate Committee on Public Works, 91st Cong., 2d Sess., pt. 1, at 433–434 (1970) (answers to Sen. Muskie's questions, supplied by the Dept. of Health, Education & Welfare); *id.*, pt. 3, at 1177; 116 CONG. REC. 32920 (1970) (remarks of Sen. Baker).

(D). Our review of the evidence is governed by Section 10(e)(2)(A), which requires us to strike "agency action, findings, and conclusions" that we find to be "arbitrary, capricious, an abuse of discretion, or otherwise not in accordance with law...." 5 U.S.C. §706(2)(A). This standard of review is a highly deferential one. It presumes agency action to be valid. *Citizens to Preserve Overton Park* v. *Volpe*, 401 U.S. 402, 415 (1971); *Pacific States Box & Basket Co.* v. *White*, 296 U.S. 176, 185–186 (1935); *United States* v. *Chemical Foundation*, 272 U.S. 1, 14–15 (1926). Moreover, it forbids the court's substituting its judgment for that of the agency, *Citizens to Preserve Overton Park* v. *Volpe, supra*, 401 U.S. at 416, and requires affirmance if a rational basis exists for the agency's decision....

This is not to say, however, that we must rubber-stamp the agency decision as correct. To do so would render the appellate process a superfluous (although time-consuming) ritual. Rather, the reviewing court must assure itself that the agency decision was "based on consideration of the relevant factors...." Moreover, it must engage in a "substantial inquiry" into the facts, one that is "searching and careful." *Citizens to Preserve Overton Park* v. *Volpe, supra*, 401 U.S. at 415, 416. This is particularly true in highly technical cases such as this one.

A court does not depart from its proper function when it undertakes a study of the record, hopefully perceptive, even as to evidence on technical and specialized matters, for this enables the court to penetrate to the underlying decisions of the agency, to satisfy itself that the agency has exercised a reasoned discretion, with reasons that do not deviate from or ignore the ascertainable legislative intent.

Greater Boston Television Corp. v. *FCC*, 143 U.S. App. D.C. 383, 392, 444 F.2d 841, 850 (1970), *cert. denied*, 403 U.S. 923 (1971).

There is no inconsistency between the deferential standard of review and the requirement that the reviewing court involve itself in even the most complex evidentiary matters; rather, the two indicia of arbitrary and capricious review stand in careful balance. The close scrutiny of the evidence is intended to educate the court. It must understand enough about the problem confronting the agency to comprehend the meaning of the evidence relied upon and the evidence discarded; the questions addressed by the agency and those bypassed; the choices open to the agency and those made. The more technical the case, the more intensive must be the court's effort to understand the evidence, for without an appropriate understanding of the case before it the court cannot properly perform its appellate function. But that function must be performed with conscientious awareness of its limited nature. The enforced education into the intricacies of the problem before the agency is not designed to enable the court to become a superagency that can supplant the agency's expert decision maker. To the contrary, the court must give due deference to the agency's ability to rely on its own developed expertise. *Market Street Railway* v. *Railroad Commission*, 324 U.S. 548, 559–561 (1945). The immersion in the evidence is designed *solely* to enable the court to determine whether the agency decision was rational and based on consideration of the relevant factors. It is settled that we must affirm decisions with which we disagree so long as this test is met.

Thus, after our careful study of the record, we must take a step back from the agency decision. We must look at the decision not as the chemist, biologist or statistician that we are qualified neither by training nor experience to be, but as a reviewing court exercising our narrowly defined duty of holding agencies to certain minimal standards of rationality. "Although [our] inquiry into the facts is to be searching and careful, the ultimate standard of review is a narrow one." *Citizens to Preserve Overton Park* v. *Volpe, supra*, 401 U.S. at 416. We must affirm unless the agency decision is arbitrary or capricious.

With the "arbitrary and capricious" standard firmly in mind, we now turn to the evidence supporting the regulations before us.

B. Overview of the Evidence

Petitioners vigorously attack both the sufficiency and the validity of the many scientific studies relied upon by the Administrator, while advancing for consideration various studies allegedly supportive of their position. The record in this case is massive—over 10,000 pages. Not surprisingly, evidence may be isolated that supports virtually any inference one might care to draw. Thus we might well have sustained a determination by the Administrator *not* to regulate lead additives on health grounds. That does not mean, however, that we cannot sustain his determination to so regulate. . . .

. . . Contrary to the apparent suggestion of some of the petitioners, we need not seek a single dispositive study that fully supports the Administrator's determination. Science does not work that way; nor, for that matter, does adjudicatory fact-finding. Rather, the Administrator's decision may be fully supportable if it is based, as it is, on the inconclusive but suggestive results of numerous studies. By its nature, scientific evidence is cumulative: the more supporting, albeit inconclusive, evidence available, the more likely the accuracy of the conclusion. . . .

. . . [W]e should note that some things appear to be uncontested. Thus petitioners seem to concede the following: that lead serves no known purpose in the human body; that lead in sufficiently high quantity is destructive to the body, causing anemia, severe intestinal cramps, paralysis, neurologic damage, and, in sufficient dosage, death, Third Health Document at III-1, 2, JA 54–55; that more than 250,000 tons of lead per year are used in production of lead additives, accounting, according to EPA, for approximately 90 percent of all airborne lead, *id.* at Table II-1, JA 46; that lead concentrations in the air over our largest cities are 2,000 times greater than lead concentrations in the air over the mid-Pacific, NAS Report at 205; that lead in the ambient air contributes to body blood lead levels, Nalco Supp. Br. at 37; supplemental brief of petitioners PPG Industries and E.I. duPont de Nemours & Company (hereinafter PPG/duPont Supp. Br.) at 23; and that blood lead levels are a reasonable indication of the body's lead burden. Stripped of their generalized and largely unsubstantiated claims of "bias" and "distortion of the evidence," petitioners principally challenge three EPA conclusions: (1) that, based on a preliminary determination that blood lead levels of 40 μg are indicative of danger to health, elevated blood lead levels "exist to a small but significant extent in the general adult population, and to a very great extent among children," Third Health Document at VII-3, JA at 144; (2) that airborne lead is directly absorbed in the body through respiration to a degree that constitutes a significant risk to public health; and (3) that airborne lead falls to the ground where it mixes with dust and poses a significant risk to the health of urban children.

1. Blood Lead Levels Are Elevated Among the General Public

a. Blood Lead Levels of 40 μg Are Indicative of Danger to Health. Although recognizing that a blood lead level of 40 μg "does not represent a sharp demarcation between health and disease," the Administrator found] it "prudent to regard blood lead levels over 40 μg/100 g as indicators of lead intake that should be prevented." Third Health Document at III-11, JA 64. . . .

. . . Petitioners do not contest the recommendation of the United States Public Health Service that 80 μg be taken as the standard of unequivocal lead poisoning, or the Service's recommendation that blood lead levels of 50–79 μg justify immediate evaluation for possible lead poisoning. Medical Aspects of Childhood Lead Poisoning, HSMHA Health Reports, 86 (2), 140–143 (1971), *cited in* Third Health Document at IV-3, JA 71. What draws petitioners' fire is only the last of the Service's recommendations, adopted by EPA, that for older children and adults "a blood lead concentration of 40 µg or more per 100 ml of whole blood . . . be considered evidence suggestive of undue absorption of lead, either past or present." *Id.* . . . Such a "prudent" determination is well within the Administrator's discretion under the "will endanger" standard. We have examined the evidence relied upon carefully and, while it is not necessary to summarize it here, we find that it provides a rational basis for the Administrator's determination.

b. Blood Lead Levels Are Elevated among a Small, but Significant, Number of Adults and a Considerable Number of Children. Again, petitioners challenge the Administrator's determination as unsupported by the evidence. The problem here is one of choosing among the items of evidence. Petitioners rely heavily on the results of the so-called Seven Cities Study, which found a very small percentage of adults with elevated (in excess of 40 µg) blood levels. PPG/duPont brief at 12–15; Nalco brief at 16. The Administrator, on the other hand, finds serious methodological flaws in the Seven Cities Study that limit its usefulness, 38 FED. REG. 33735, and relies instead on studies which concededly support his conclusion, Third Health Document at Tables VII-1, 2 & 3, JA 145–147, but which petitioners score as representative only of certain occupational groups. PPG/duPont brief at 15; Nalco brief at 15–16.

Having analyzed this evidence and the arguments of the parties, we would again defer to the Administrator's judgment. First we note that, while contesting the source of lead exposure, petitioners do not challenge at all the Agency's conclusion that blood lead levels are elevated in a large number of children, including a possible 25 percent of all preschool children living in substandard housing.[88] Third Health Document at Table VII-3, JA 147.

Next, while the studies relied on by the Administrator are largely of various occupational groups, they are frequently occupations whose only exposure to lead is through the ambient air in which their workers— policemen, mailmen, service station employees, parking lot attendants, and the like—are forced to spend their working hours. Third Health Document at Table VII-1, JA 145. Contrary to the arguments of petitioners, studies of occupational groups are often particularly valuable in acting as an early warning system of possible effects on the public at large. . . .

2. Automobile Lead Emission Products Are Directly Absorbed in the Body to a Significant Extent

Since it is apparent from the face of his decision and the Third Health Document that the Administrator considered all the evidence before him, the only issue is whether he treated that evidence in a rational manner.

---

88. Petitioners PPG Industries, Inc. (PPG) and E.I. duPont de Nemours & Company (duPont) charge that this conclusion has no bearing on whether there is undue lead exposure among the general adult population. Of course it does not. It does have bearing, however, on whether blood lead levels are elevated among children and among the general population, both adult and child. It is for this purpose that the conclusion is cited. Ethyl argues that these children have high blood lead levels primarily because of exposure to lead-based paint. The Administrator does not disagree. 38 FED. REG. 33735. What is important for his purpose is that blood lead levels are elevated in the general public; under the cumulative impact theory the source of the elevation is irrelevant in determining whether the public health is endangered by exposure to lead. *See* pages 56–61 *supra.* The source becomes relevant only when deciding whether the emission products of lead additives make a significant contribution to that exposure, thereby justifying regulation under §211(c)(1)(A).

Petitioners have now conceded that lead emissions are directly absorbed in the body from the ambient air, and they challenge only whether the extent of absorption is significant enough to justify these regulations. The Administrator's conclusion that lead absorption from the air is significant is amply supported by the record in this rule-making.

The Administrator relied on three types of evidence: theoretical, epidemiological, and clinical studies. The theoretical evidence consisted of a set of calculations designed to estimate the amount of lead in the air which, when added to an average dietary intake, would suffice to bring the blood lead burden of a "standard man" up to 40 µg. These calculations indicated that the 40 µg level can be reached by exposure to ambient air lead concentrations no greater than those now found in parts of our larger cities. Significantly, the results of two clinical experiments support the estimates derived from these theoretical calculations....

The second type of evidence relied upon by the Administrator in reaching his conclusion that airborne lead contributes significantly to the human lead body burden consisted of epidemiological research.... Since diet accounts for a major portion of the body lead burden, an individual's blood lead level varies not only according to his exposure to lead in the ambient air, but according to his daily dietary intake of lead. Wide variations in dietary lead intake, which are common, can completely mask the effects of air lead absorption. Nonetheless, none of the epidemiological studies could control or measure dietary lead intake. This uncertainty in the data severely limited the usefulness of the broadly conceived epidemiological studies and led the Administrator to rely instead on data limited to situations in which dietary exposure could roughly be termed constant.

Following this rationale, the Administrator focused on the consistent relationship found between air and blood lead levels within particular metropolitan areas, rather than on the lack of such a relationship between areas. The Administrator also drew support for his conclusion that lead in the air significantly affects lead in the blood from studies conducted in single neighborhoods. There, too, confounding factors were minimized by proximity, and there, too, a clear direct relationship was found. Thus the epidemiological studies, although perhaps insufficient to justify the Administrator's decision if considered singly or even collectively, were reasonably relied on as part of the basis for the low-lead rules.

The conclusions the Administrator drew from theoretical calculations and the epidemiological studies are significantly bolstered by two important clinical studies.... Both studies found that airborne lead provided a significant portion of the lead in the blood of the experiments' subjects. Moreover, the amount of lead actually absorbed from the air during these studies corresponded closely with the amount EPA's theoretical calculations predicted would be absorbed....

3. Lead Exposure from Dustfall Threatens the Health of Children

While we would have no difficulty in sustaining the low-lead regulations solely on the basis of the evidence and conclusions discussed above, the Administrator based his decision to regulate on other evidence as well. He presented a hypothesis, which he found consistent with known information, that urban children are particularly threatened by lead additives in that they are prone to ingest lead emissions that have fallen to the ground and mixed with dust. While the hypothesis is admittedly not proved as fact, we need not decide whether it would be sufficient by itself to support the low-lead regulations, for it is offered only in support of the evidence already presented....

...[A]s we have demonstrated above, the "will endanger" standard is a precautionary standard that embraces a wide range of permissible proof. It is therefore no objection to the dustfall hypothesis that it is merely a hypothesis. A supportable and reasonable hypothesis may well form the basis for regulations under Section 211(c)(1)(A). Indeed, the totality of evidence relied upon in the *Reserve Mining* case constituted no more than such a hypothesis....

... The logical steps to the Administrator's conclusion are these:

a. High lead concentrations in dust and dirt are prevalent in urban areas.
b. In most circumstances, lead from exhausts and not lead paint or lead from stationary sources is the primary source of lead in urban dust and dirt.
c. Children prone to pica, about 50 percent of those between the ages of one and three, eat nonfood objects, including dust and dirt.
d. As a result of ingesting dust and dirt contaminated with lead fallout, children can be expected to absorb lead into their bodies.

38 FED. REG. 33736. If the intermediate steps are supported by the evidence, the validity of the Administrator's conclusion as a reasonable hypothesis is unassailable. Our study of the underlying evidence convinces us that it is firm and convincing, and certainly sufficient to support the Administrator's hypothesis as reasonable....

V. CONCLUSION

...

Because of the importance of the issues raised, we have accorded this case the most careful and exhaustive consideration. We find that in this rule-making proceeding the EPA has complied with all the statutory procedural requirements and that its reasons as stated in its opinion provide a rational basis for its action. Since we reject all of petitioners' claims of error, the Agency may enforce its low-lead regulations.

Affirmed.

...

BAZELON, *C.J., WITH WHOM* MCGOWAN, *J. JOINS, CONCURRING:*

I concur in Judge Wright's opinion for the court, and wish only to further elucidate certain matters.

I agree with the court's construction of the statute that the Administrator is called upon to make "essentially legislative policy judgments" in assessing risks to public health. But I cannot agree that this automatically relieves the Administrator's decision from the "procedural . . . rigor proper for questions of fact." Quite the contrary, this case strengthens my view that[4]

... [I]n cases of great technological complexity, the best way for courts to guard against unreasonable or erroneous administrative decisions is not for the judges themselves to scrutinize the technical merits of each decision. Rather, it is to establish a decisionmaking process that assures a reasoned decision that can be held up to the scrutiny of the scientific community and the public.

This record provides vivid demonstration of the dangers implicit in the contrary view, ably espoused by Judge Leventhal, which would have judges "steeping" themselves "in technical matters to determine whether the agency has exercised a reasoned discretion."[5] It is one thing for judges to scrutinize FCC judgments concerning diversification of media ownership to determine if they are rational. But I doubt judges contribute much to

---

4. *International Harvester Co. v. Ruckelshaus*, 155 U.S. App. D.C. 411, 448, 478 F.2d 615, 652 (1973) (Bazelon, C.J., concurring).
5. *Portland Cement Ass'n v. Ruckelshaus*, 158 U.S. App. D.C. 308, 335, 486 F.2d 375, 402 (1973), *cert.* denied, 417 U.S. 921 (1974) (Leventhal, J.), *citing Greater Boston TV v. FCC*, 143 U.S. App. D.C. 383, 392, 444 F.2d 841, 850, *cert. denied*, 403 U.S. 923 (1971).

improving the quality of the difficult decisions which must be made in highly technical areas when they take it upon themselves to decide, as did the panel in this case, that "in assessing the scientific and medical data the Administrator made clear errors of judgment." The process of making a de novo evaluation of the scientific evidence inevitably invites judges of opposing views to make plausible-sounding, but simplistic, judgments of the relative weight to be afforded various pieces of technical data.[7]

It is true that, where, as here, a panel has reached the result of invalidating agency action by undue involvement in the uncertainties of the typical informal rulemaking record, the court *en banc* will be tempted to justify its affirmation of the agency by confronting the panel on its own terms. But this is a temptation which, if not resisted, will not only impose severe strains upon the energies and resources of the court but also compound the error of the panel in making legislative policy determinations alien to its true function. We would be wiser to heed the admonition of the Supreme Court that: "[e]xperience teaches...that the affording of procedural safeguards, which by their nature serve to illuminate the underlying facts, in itself often operates to prevent erroneous decisions on the merits from occurring."

Because substantive review of mathematical and scientific evidence by technically illiterate judges is dangerously unreliable, I continue to believe we will do more to im-

prove administrative decision-making by concentrating our efforts on strengthening administrative procedures:[9]

When administrators provide a framework for principled decision-making, the result will be to diminish the importance of judicial review by enhancing the integrity of the administrative process, and to improve the quality of judicial review in those cases where judicial review is sought.

It does not follow that courts may never properly find that an administrative decision in a scientific area is irrational. But I do believe that in highly technical areas, where our understanding of the import of the evidence is attenuated, our readiness to review evidentiary support for decisions must be correspondingly restrained.

As I read the court's opinion, it severely limits judicial weighing of the evidence by construing the Administrator's decision to be a matter of "legislative policy," and consequently not subject to review with the "substantive rigor proper for questions of fact." Since this result would bar the panel's close analysis of the evidence, it satisfies my concerns....

STATEMENT OF CIRCUIT JUDGE LEVENTHAL:

I concur without reservation in the excellent opinion for the court.

I write an additional word only because of observations in the concurring opinion au-

---

7. For example, Judge Wright states little weight is to be given the absence of studies documenting actual harm from lead in auto emissions with the observation, among several others that "...lead exposure from the ambient air is pervasive, so that valid control groups cannot be found against which the effects of lead on our population can be measured."

Similarly, Judge Wilkey, in his original panel opinion, discounts the value of a particular study with the observation: "Realistically, it is impossible to say that any definite scientific or medical conclu-

sion can be drawn from the observation of one or two subjects."

I do not know whether or not these observations are valid, although it was my impression that techniques had been devised which minimized these problems in certain cases. Be that as it may, these overt examples of homespun scientific aphorisms indicate that on more subtle, and less visible, matters of scientific judgment we judges are well beyond our institutional competency.

9. *Environmental Defense Fund, Inc. v. Ruckelshaus*, 142 U.S. App. D.C. 74, 88, 439 F.2d 584, 598 (1971) (Bazelon, C.J.).

thored by Chief Judge Bazelon. I would not have thought they required airing today, since they in no way relate, so far as I can see, to the court's en banc opinion. But since they have been floated I propose to bring them to earth, though I can here present only the highlights of analysis.

What does and should a reviewing court do when it considers a challenge to technical administrative decisionmaking? In my view, the panel opinion in this case overstepped the bounds of proper judicial supervision in its willingness to substitute its own scientific judgments for that of the EPA. In an effort to refute that approach convincingly the panel dissent may have overreacted and responded too much in kind. In a kind of sur-rebuttal against such overzealousness, Judge Bazelon has also over-reacted. His opinion—if I read it right—advocates engaging in no substantive review at all, whenever the substantive issues at stake involve technical matters that the judges involved consider beyond their individual technical competence.

If he is not saying that, if he agrees there must be some substantive review, then I am at a loss to discern its significance. Certainly it does not help those seeking enlightenment to recognize when the difference in degree of substantive review becomes a difference in kind.

Taking the opinion in its fair implication, as a signal to judges to abstain from any substantive review, it is my view that while giving up is the easier course, it is not legitimately open to us at present. In the case of legislative enactments, the sole responsibility of the courts is constitutional due process review. In the case of agency decision-making the courts have an additional responsibility set by Congress. Congress has been willing to delegate its legislative powers broadly— and courts have upheld such delegation—because there is court review to assure that the agency exercises the delegated power within statutory limits, and that it fleshes out objectives within those limits by an administration

that is not irrational or discriminatory. Nor is that envisioned judicial role ephemeral, as *Overton Park* makes clear.

Our present system of review assumes judges will acquire whatever technical knowledge is necessary as background for decision of the legal questions. It may be that some judges are not initially equipped for this role, just as they may not be technically equipped initially to decide issues of obviousness and infringement in patent cases. If technical difficulties loom large, Congress may push to establish specialized courts. Thus far, it has proceeded on the assumption that we can both have the important values secured by generalist judges and rely on them to acquire whatever technical background is necessary.

The aim of the judges is not to exercise expertise or decide technical questions, but simply to gain sufficient background orientation. Our obligation is not to be jettisoned because our initial technical understanding may be meager when compared to our initial grasp of FCC or freedom of speech questions. When called upon to make de novo decisions, individual judges have had to acquire the learning pertinent to complex technical questions in such fields as economics, science, technology and psychology. Our role is not as demanding when we are engaged in review of agency decisions, where we exercise restraint, and affirm even if we would have decided otherwise so long as the agency's decisionmaking is not irrational or discriminatory.

The substantive review of administrative action is modest, but it cannot be carried out in a vacuum of understanding. Better no judicial review at all than a charade that gives the imprimatur without the substance of judicial confirmation that the agency is not acting unreasonably. Once the presumption of regularity in agency action is challenged with a factual submission, and even to determine whether such a challenge has been made, the agency's record and reasoning has to be looked at. If there is some factual support for the challenge, there must be either evidence or judicial notice available explicating the agency's result, or a remand to supply the gap.

Mistakes may mar the exercise of any judicial function. While in this case the panel made such a mistake, it did not stem from judicial incompetence to deal with technical issues, but from confusion about the proper stance for substantive review of agency action in an area where the state of current knowledge does not generate customary definitiveness and certainty. In other cases the court has dealt ably with these problems, without either abandoning substantive review or

ousting the agency's action for lack of factual underpinning.

On issues of substantive review, on conformance to statutory standards and requirements of rationality, the judges must act with restraint. Restraint, yes, abdication, no.

[The dissenting opinions of Judge Mac-KINNON and Judge WILKEY (the latter of which Judges TAMM and ROBB joined, and Judge MaKINNON joined in part) are omitted. Judge Wilkey's dissent, which is every bit as comprehensive and detailed as Judge Wright's majority opinion, reasserts the positions taken in his earlier panel decision in this case.]

- **NOTES**

1. The court finds that the agency acted well within its statutory authority in taking a precautionary approach—that is, by erring on the side of caution in the face of scientific uncertainty. "Precautionary legislation," notes the court, "would seem to *demand* that regulatory action would precede, and, optimally, prevent, the perceived threat." Indeed, the court notes that even a "supportable and reasonable hypothesis may well form the basis for regulations" under a statutory "endangerment" standard. Where "endangerment" is the criterion, the agency need not show proof of actual harm. Nor does the agency need to show that harm is "probable." In the court's formulation, danger is the product of risk times harm (i.e., impact = probability × severity). Is the court implicitly encouraging agencies to apply risk assessment in the face of scientific uncertainty? Does the use of probability and severity to measure potential danger contradict the precautionary approach? Consider cases in which both the true probability and the severity of the potential harm are unknown, such as is arguably the case with global climate change. Does this rise to the level of an "endangerment"?

2. Brian Wynne distinguishes four different kinds of "uncertainty" that are relevant here: risk, uncertainty, ignorance, and indeterminacy. Wynne describes *risk* as knowing the odds, *uncertainty* as not knowing the odds but knowing the main parameters, *ignorance* as not knowing what we don't know, and *indeterminacy* as uncertainty in the outcome(s) attributable to unpredictable or unquantifiable (though identifiable) social factors such as human interventions, differences in regulatory regimes and actors, and culture. See Brian Wynne (1992) "Uncertainty and Environmental

Learning: Reconceiving Science and Policy in the Preventive Paradigm," *Global Environmental Change* 2: 111 (June).

3. The court envisions a kind of "sliding scale" as a means of gauging "endangerment." On the one hand, a high risk of a relatively smaller harm may well be an endangerment. On the other hand, a low risk of a much more significant harm may also be an endangerment. The courts have relied upon this formulation in interpreting the "endangerment" concept in other federal environmental statutes, most notably in the two hazardous waste laws, the Resource Conservation and Recovery Act and the Comprehensive Environmental Compensation, Response, and Liability Act (the federal "Superfund" law). Note, however, that this sliding scale is limited by a commonsense understanding of "danger." Thus, the court notes, even "absolute certainty of *de minimis* harm might not justify government action." (See footnote 32 in the opinion.)

4. Judge Wright's majority opinion states that judicial review must incorporate a "substantial inquiry" into the facts, because the court "must understand enough of the problem . . . to comprehend the meaning of the evidence relied upon and evidence discarded." In practice, is there any guarantee that the judiciary will be able to understand the evidence? Judge Bazelon's concurring opinion questions whether the judiciary can reliably review scientific evidence without relying on "plausible-sounding, but simplistic, judgments. . . ." On the other hand, as Judge Leventhal notes in his concurring opinion, the failure of the reviewing court to sufficiently engage the facts may well mean that it effectively turns a blind eye to agency error or malfeasance. The risk that a court will make mistakes in its review of the facts, he suggests, is a necessary price to pay for ensuring that there is an effective "check" on agency decision making.

5. The controversy surrounding the initial ruling of the court's three-judge panel, and the significance of the subsequent decision of the full court, led Congress to clarify the "endangerment" standard when it amended the Clean Air Act in 1977. The legislative history of those amendments reveals strong support for the full court's opinion. In the words of the House Committee on Interstate and Foreign Commerce, "the *Ethyl* case posed fundamental policy questions concerning the future of measures for protection of public health from environmental contaminants."[38] Consistent with the majority opinion in *Ethyl Corp.*, Congress broadened the "will endanger" language in the Clean Air Act to read "may reasonably be anticipated to endanger public health or welfare." This "may reasonably be anticipated" phrase was not only added to the provisions of Section 211 on fuel additives, but also

---

38. *Clean Air Act Amendments of 1977*, Pub. L. No. 95-95, Legislative History, page 48, reprinted in 1977 U.S.C.C.A.N. 1126.

to Sections 108 (ambient air quality criteria), 111 (new source performance standards for stationary sources), 112 (hazardous air pollutant standards for stationary sources), 202 (emission standards for mobile sources), and 231 (aircraft emission standards). According to the House committee, this was done to "emphasize the precautionary or preventive purpose of the act (and, therefore, the Administrator's duty to assess risks rather than wait for proof of actual harm)" and to

[1] authorize the Administrator to weigh risks and make reasonable projections of future trends...[2] assure consideration of the cumulative impact of all sources...in setting ambient and emission standards...[3] require consideration of cumulative or synergistic effects of multiple pollutants...[4] provide the same standard of proof for regulation of any air pollutant...[5] assure that the health of susceptible individuals, as well as healthy adults, will be encompassed in the term "public health," regardless of the section of the act under which the Administrator proceeds...[6] reflect awareness of the uncertainties and limitations in the data which will be available to the Administrator in the foreseeable future...[and] [7] provide for adequate judicial review of the reasonableness of the Administrator's judgment...while restraining the courts from attempting to act "as the equivalent of a combined Ph.D. in chemistry, biology, and statistics" or from applying a standard of review which is appropriate only to review of adjudications or formal fact finding. [Ibid. (numbering added for clarification)]

As discussed later in this chapter, this amendment proved instrumental to the Supreme Court's remand of EPA's refusal to address "greenhouse gas" emissions from motor vehicles.

6. What would have been the result if EPA had decided not to regulate lead in gasoline in 1973? Judge Wright's majority opinion in *Ethyl Corp.* notes that "we might well have sustained a determination by the Administrator *not* to regulate lead additives on health grounds," suggesting that the majority found the evidence on the health effects of leaded gasoline to be equivocal. As discussed below, it does appear that EPA's projections were generally correct.

As discussed in chapter 6, two years after the *Ethyl Corp.* decision, and after considerable prompting from environmentalists, EPA listed lead as a criteria pollutant under Section 108(a)(1) of the Clean Air Act.[39] Meanwhile, the removal of lead from gasoline proceeded slowly and haltingly. In the early 1980s, the Task Force on Regulatory Relief, established by President Ronald Reagan and headed by then Vice President George H. W. Bush, proposed relaxing or abandoning the phaseout of leaded gasoline. This announcement, coupled with the comments of EPA Adminis-

---

39. For a more complete description of these events, see Arnold W. Reitze Jr. (1994) "The Regulation of Fuels and Fuel Additives Under Section 211 of the Clean Air Act," 29 *Tulsa Law Journal* 485. The EPA listed lead as a criteria air pollutant on October 5, 1978; National Primary and Secondary Ambient Air Quality Standards for Lead, 43 *Fed. Reg.* 46,246, 46,258 (1978) (final rule). See also *Natural Resources Defense Council v. Train*, 411 F. Supp. 864, 867–69 (S.D.N.Y. 1976), aff'd, 545 F.2d 320 (2d Cir. 1976), and *Lead Industries Ass'n., Inc. v. EPA*, 647 F.2d 1130 (D.C. Cir. 1980) (excerpted earlier in chapter 6).

trator Anne Gorsuch that existing lead limits would not be enforced because the regulations would soon be repealed, coursed an uproar in the press.[40] In the face of mounting criticism, the Reagan administration reversed course and actually accelerated the phaseout. By 1986, lead levels in most gasoline supplies were reduced to 0.1 grams per gallon. In the 1990 Clean Air Act Amendments, Congress flatly prohibited the use of any amount of lead in gasoline after 1995. See CAA Section 211(n). The U.S. Center for Disease Control (CDC) reports that average blood lead levels for adults and children have dropped more than 80% since the late 1970s.[41] Indeed, it appears clear that EPA was correct in its assessment of the relationship between blood lead levels of children and the levels of lead in gasoline. Figure 7.3 summarizes the results of numerous studies correlating decreases in blood lead level in cities throughout the world after lead was removed from gasoline. The body of scientific evidence continues to mount that blood lead levels previously thought to be safe could cause ill health. Currently, lead levels greater than 10 micrograms per deciliter of blood are considered potentially damaging to a child's ability to learn.[42]

3. Transportation Controls and Inspection and Maintenance Programs

The deadlines set by Congress for achieving the national ambient air quality standards effectively required many regions to limit emissions from mobile sources as part of their Clean Air Act state implementation plans. States without adequate mobile source provisions in their SIPs faced the possible loss of federal highway funds.[43] In the 1970 amendments, Congress specified that land-use and transportation controls were to be included in the SIPs if such measures were necessary to enable the state to meet ambient air quality standards. The initial SIP regulations issued by EPA, however, failed to include such requirements, and they were set aside in *NRDC v. EPA*, 475 F.2d 968 (D.C. Cir. 1973). The court ordered EPA to require transportation control measures of this nature for areas that were expected to exceed the NAAQS after June 30, 1975[44] and EPA subsequently determined that twenty-nine metropolitan areas would need them.

---

40. See, generally, Richard E. Cohen (1995) *Washington at Work: Back Rooms and Clean Air*, 2nd ed. Upper saddle River, N.J.: Prentice Hall. Gorsuch's remarks to a visiting gas refiner were soon leaked and appeared in newspapers, including in the comic strip *Doonesbury*. Gorsuch soon resigned under pressure.

41. http://www.cdc.gov/od/oc/media/pressrel/lead.htm (last visited 8/17/2004).

42. http://www.cdc.gov/exposurereport/2nd/lead_factsheet.htm (last viewed 8/17/2004). Also see http://aspe.hhs.gov/hsp/97trend/hc2-9.htm.

43. The first federal withholding (of federal highway construction and sewage treatment funding) occurred in March 14, 1982, when Colorado lost funding after failing to implement an auto emission control plan.

44. "Transportation Controls Established in Major Urban Areas to Lower Air Pollution Levels," EPA press release, Oct. 15, 1973 (available at http://www.epa.gov/history/topics/caa70/10.htm). Also see H. Rep. 95-294 (1977) at 227.

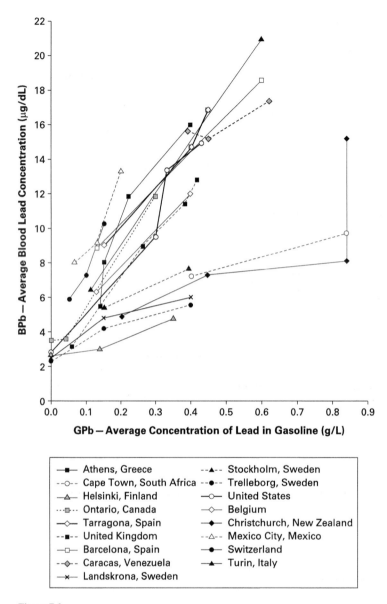

Figure 7.3

Seventeen studies of changes in population blood levels concentrations with changes in the concentration of lead in gasoline. (Reprinted with permission from: V. M. Thomas, R. H. Socolow, J. J. Fanelli, and T. G. Spiro (1999) "Effects of Reducing Lead in Gasoline: An Analysis of the International Experience," *Environmental Science and Technology* 33, 3942. Copyright 1999, American Chemical Society.)

The resulting transportation control plans proposed by the EPA contained many controversial measures, including restrictions on gas sales, partial traffic bans, traffic-free zones, parking restrictions, and the "retrofitting" of older vehicles through the mandatory installation of air pollution control devices. Los Angeles, for instance, was found to need potential restrictions on 80% of the vehicle-miles traveled within its borders, and would almost have had to ban driving altogether to meet the primary ambient air quality standards in a timely fashion. The perceived harshness of some of the measures was necessitated, from a regulatory perspective, both by the severity of the air pollution plaguing many cities and by the Clean Air Act's 1977 deadline for achieving the ambient standards. Some of these measures, such as the parking restrictions, stirred a virtual hornet's nest of opposition and were limited by Congress in the 1977 amendments. The House report for the 1977 amendments voiced the assessment that

> the implementation of many of these measures is impracticable within the time frame permitted.... Some of the measures may never be practicable.... On the other hand, the Committee still believes many transportation related measures are feasible and can be implemented.... Construction of ... freeways may be required to take second place to rapid and mass transit ... in certain areas. [H. Rep. 95-294 (1977) at 229]

The 1977 amendments called for EPA to evaluate the reasonableness of transportation control measures according to their relative effectiveness, their effect on transportation services, and their impacts on the economy, energy use, and the environment. In addition, Congress removed EPA's authority to require the regulation of "indirect sources": installations, such as shopping centers, airports, apartment complexes, and major parking lots, that do not emit pollution themselves but attract significant motor vehicle traffic. Congress left the decision of whether, and to what extent, to regulate indirect sources to state and local governments, who could choose to submit such regulations as part of their SIPs, or not, as they saw fit. However, EPA was forbidden from requiring controls on indirect sources as a condition of SIP approval.[45]

On the other hand, the 1977 amendments included measures to strongly encourage the states to develop and implement inspection and maintenance (I/M) programs. These programs, now familiar to most drivers across the nation, require the periodic testing of motor vehicles to determine whether they meet certain emission limits (and thus determine whether emission control devices are working properly).

---

45. Originally, EPA had proposed regulations requiring a "preconstruction" review of indirect sources. However, after congressional and administrative action twice delayed these regulations, the agency suspended the parking portions of the regulations to allow Congress to review the issue. Further background on this topic can be found in H. Rep. 95-294 (1977) at 220.

Congress specified that states which were unable to meet the air quality standards by 1982 must either implement I/M programs as part of their SIPs, or lose federal highway funds. Much research had shown that many in-use vehicles were in noncompliance with the standards, and I/M programs were expected to correct this problem by forcing noncompliant vehicles to be either repaired or removed from the fleet.

Today, many states have incorporated I/M programs as part of their annual licensing of motor vehicles. Other transportation control measures, such as high-occupancy vehicle (HOV) lanes and park-and-ride lots, are also a familiar part of the highway infrastructure in many states. Indeed, in many cases, transportation control measures are among the few viable options available at the state and local level to offset both the congestion and the pollution caused by driving.

E.   THE CLEAN AIR ACT AMENDMENTS OF 1990

In the 1980s, the Clean Air Act program became ensnared in political controversy and was the subject of skirmishing within and among Congress and the executive branch. Bills to reduce the regulatory burden on the auto industry and coal industry through the relaxation of air quality standards and mobile source regulations were pushed forward in Congress.[46] The Clean Air Act was not reauthorized in 1981, and the air pollution program remained in operation only through annual congressional appropriations. Regional politics led to the defeat of most bills designed to further reduce air pollution as members of Congress from states with electric, coal, and automotive industries posed a formidable opposition. By the late 1980s, less than half the population lived in areas where primary air quality standards had been attained. Despite previous improvements in passenger vehicle emissions of particulate matter, carbon monoxide, and nonmethane organic gases (NMOG), progress was being offset by increases in vehicle-miles traveled and by shifts to SUVs and light-duty trucks (see figures 7.4 and 7.5).[47] Political gridlock prevented a comprehensive response to these issues until an administration generally more supportive of environmental protection took office in 1988[48] and several proponents of air pollution legislation took key committee positions in Congress.[49] Two years later, Congress passed the most far-reaching air pollution legislation since 1970.

---

46. For a review of these efforts, see Arnold W. Reitze, Jr. (1999) "The Legislative History of U.S. Air Pollution Control," 36 *Houston Law Review* 679.

47. NMOGs consist mostly of hydrocarbons (HCs) and volatile organic compounds (VOCs).

48. President (1989–1993) George H. W. Bush made environmental protection a more significant priority than had his predecessor, Ronald Reagan.

49. Arnold W. Reitze, Jr., "The Legislative History of U.S. Air Pollution Control."

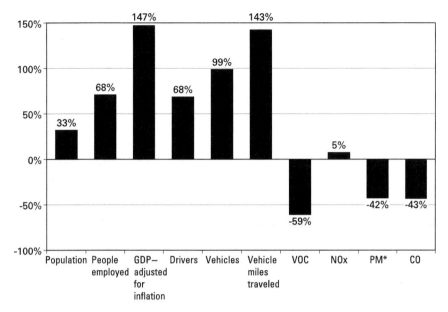

Figure 7.4
Mobile vehicle emissions and selected national statistics (1970–1999). (Sources: Federal Highway Administration, ⟨http://www.fhwa.dot.gov⟩. Compiled from the Bureau of Economic Analysis. *Survey of Business*, August 2000, table 2A; U.S. Census Bureau. *Statistical Abstract of the United States, 2000*, December 2000, table 1; Federal Highway Administration. *Highway Statistics Summary to 1995*, July 1997, tables VM-201, DL-201, MV-200; *Highway Statistics 1999*, October 2000, tables VM-3, DL-22, MV-1; U.S. Environmental Protection Agency, *National Air Pollutant Emissions Trends*, June 2001. Note: Consistent data not available through 1970.)

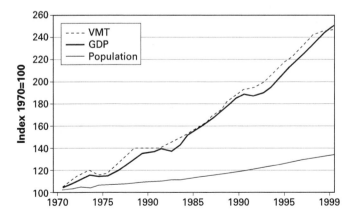

Figure 7.5
Travel, economic growth, and population (1970–1999). (Sources: Federal Highway Administration, ⟨http://www.fhwa.dot.gov⟩. Compiled from the Federal Highway Administration, Highway Statistics Summary to 1995, July 1997; table VM-20, Highway Statistics 1997; October 1998, table VM-3; Highway Statistics 1999, October 2000; table VM-3, Bureau of Economic Analysis; Survey of Current Business, August 2000, table 2A.)

Representative Henry Waxman of California, one of the primary sponsors of the 1990 amendments, described the political dynamics as follows:[50]

When President Bush signed the 1990 Amendments into law on November 15, 1990, he ended one of the longest—and hardest fought—legislative battles in recent congressional history. Throughout the 1980s, thousands of hours were spent developing, debating, and blocking legislative proposals; hundreds of witnesses testified at hearings; and millions of dollars were spent on lobbying by interest groups. Eventually, the Speaker of the House and the Senate Majority Leader both had to personally participate in negotiations to resolve specific issues. The product of all this effort is a sweeping collection of programs that dwarfs previous environmental laws. Any one of the 1990 Amendments' five major titles would ordinarily be an act in itself. [21 *Environmental Law* 1721 (1991)]

Enactment of new air pollution legislation came partly in response to the fact that mobile sources had remained the largest source of HC, NO_x, CO, and toxic emissions.[51] In Congress, supporters of stricter standards also argued that reductions from motor vehicles were in many cases more cost-effective than further reductions from stationary sources.

The 1990 amendments to the mobile source provisions, and to the Clean Air Act generally, were shaped from bills that had been proposed (but defeated) in the 1980s. This time around, a combination of concerted effort and political pressure ensured their passage. Key factors included the Bush administration's own introduction of a clean air bill, Senate proponent George Mitchell's ascendancy into the position of Majority Leader (and his staff's extensive negotiations on the bill's behalf), and the compromise reached by Representative Waxman and Representative John Dingell of Michigan on mobile source controls.[52]

The basic structure of the new mobile source provisions was largely that which had been put in place in 1970. However, the 1990 provisions were, as Representative Waxman noted, "unusually prescriptive and far reaching," and they collectively tripled the length of the mobile sources section of the act. Congress expanded requirements in four broad program areas: (1) conventional vehicles, (2) motor vehicle fuels, (3) clean-fuel vehicles, and (4) nonroad vehicles. Major new strategies introduced by the 1990 amendments included:

• Stricter tailpipe standards for light-duty cars and trucks (implemented as Tier I and Tier II standards)

---

50. Henry A. Waxman, "Overview and Critique: An Overview of the Clean Air Act Amendments of 1990," 21 *Environmental Law* 1721 (1991). Waxman presents an insider's review of the political climate and an analysis of the resulting statutes. Unless otherwise noted, quotations from Representative Waxman appearing in the remainder of this chapter are drawn from this source.

51. Michael P. Walsh, *Toxic Air Pollution Handbook*, p. 470.

52. The Bush administration sent its own air pollution control bill to Congress in July 1989. However, the Waxman-Dingell compromise was largely adopted as the final version.

- New programs to reduce refueling, evaporative, and "running loss" emissions
- Reformulated gasoline to reduce CO and HCs in the smoggiest areas
- Reduced sulfur content provisions for diesel fuel
- Regulation of nonroad engines (e.g., construction machinery, lawn devices, farm equipment, offroad vehicles)
- Revised heavy-duty truck and bus standards, including the authority to regulate engines
- Control of air toxics
- Enhanced I/M programs and stronger transportation control measures, including surcharges on parking fees
- Initiation of a clean fuel car pilot program in California
- Encouragement of alternative fuels
- Procurement of cleaner vehicle fleets for twenty-six nonattainment areas

We take a closer look at some of these programs in the remainder of this section.[53]

1. Tier I Standards

The 1990 amendments established two "tiers" of tailpipe emission standards for passenger vehicles, the first to be phased in from 1994 to 1998, and the second from 2004 to 2008. Congress chose once again to specify the performance standards themselves [see CAA Section 202(g)]. Different sets of standards were applied to passenger vehicles and to light-duty trucks, which included SUVs.

Tier I standards were based on those previously enacted by the state of California. Standards for light-duty trucks remained more lenient than for passenger vehicles, while standards for heavy-duty vehicles remained largely unchanged until 1998, when permissible NO_x emissions were reduced. For passenger vehicles, nonmethane hydrocarbons (NMHC) were reduced further by roughly 30%[54] while the NO_x standard was tightened by 60%. Cold-temperature emissions of carbon monoxide, a particular problem in the winter, were also regulated, effectively reducing CO emission overall by an estimated 25% [CAA Section 202(j)]. Ironically, the Tier I NO_x standard amounted to a 90% NO_x reduction over 1971 levels, the same level specified in the 1970 amendments.

Diesel vehicles received a more lenient NO_x standard (until 2004), owing to perceived limitations in the available technology. Diesel particulate matter, however,

---

53. For a more complete analysis of all the major programs (mobile source and stationary source) put in place by the 1990 amendments, by one of the principal authors of those amendments, see Henry A. Waxman, "Overview and Critique: An Overview of the Clean Air Act Amendments of 1990." Some of the material in this section of this text summarizes programmatic descriptions found in that article.

54. Methane was found to be relatively insignificant in contributing to ozone formation and thus was not included in the new standards.

had to be reduced by 80% from previous levels. Further reductions in CO emissions were also sought via standards for cold-temperature emissions.

2.   Tier II Standards—Uniform Standards for Light-Duty Cars, Trucks, and SUVs

Congress directed EPA to begin implementing a second level of standards—known as the Tier II standards—in 2004, to further reduce NMHC, NO_x, and CO by a minimum of 50%. EPA was given leave to adjust these statutory minima, as appropriate, based on its assessment of (1) the need for further emission reductions to meet the national ambient air quality standards, (2) the availability and cost of technology for meeting the statutory Tier II requirements, and (3) the cost-effectiveness of obtaining the necessary emission reductions from cars. As a strategy to help make the technology feasible in time, Congress included in Title II a new Part C, which called for the introduction of "clean-fuel vehicles" in nonattainment areas. These vehicles were to meet the statutory Tier II requirements by 2001 as opposed to 2004. The program was expected to create new technologies that could be transferred to more conventional vehicles. EPA promulgated the Tier II requirements in 2000. See 64 *Fed. Reg.* 26004–26142 (1999); 65 *Fed. Reg.* 6698 (2000). The Tier II regulation calls for a phase in of the standards over the period from 2004 to 2008 for most vehicles, but allows an additional 2 years for larger vehicles. The Tier II program includes new mechanisms designed to afford manufacturers greater flexibility in the manner in which they achieve compliance. Chief among these are provisions allowing automakers to meet emission requirements through "fleet averaging," and a banking and trading scheme.

Under fleet averaging, manufacturers may choose from sets of emission "bins," or different sets of emission standards, for their various vehicle models. A larger vehicle may be placed in a less restrictive emission bin while a smaller vehicle may fall into a very restrictive emission bin, so long as the average across the automaker's fleet is below the overall standard. The bins are set so that the overall fleet average standard for NO_x will be at or below 0.07 gram per mile. The standards for nonmethane hydrocarbons, CO, and PM emissions depend on which averaging bin is selected. Overall, however, fleet emissions will be less for all categories.

The banking and trading system allows automobile manufacturers to buy and sell NO_x credits from other automakers. The use of credits establishes one of the first mobile-source emissions trading programs, paralleling the SO_2 trading program for stationary sources. The corporate-average NO_x emission level approach is in some ways similar to the corporate-average fuel economy (CAFE) standard for manufacturers (discussed later in this chapter) and the "bubble" approach used for stationary sources, both of which allow firms to decide on the most cost-effective mix of emission reductions. Introduction of banking and trading mechanisms allows, in

Table 7.4
Federal Standards for Gasoline-Fueled Passenger Cars

	Nonmethane hydrocarbon emissions (g/mile)		Carbon monoxide (g/mile)		Nitrogen oxides (g/mile)		Particulate Matter (g/miles)	
	<50,000 miles old	<100,000 miles old	<50,000 miles old	<100,000 miles old	<50,000 miles old	<100,000 miles old	<50,000 miles old	<100,000 miles old
Pre-Tier	0.390	none	7.000	none	1.000	none	0.080	none
Federal Tier I	0.250	0.310	3.400	4.200	0.400	0.600	—	0.100
NLEV								
TLEV	0.125	0.156	3.400	4.200	0.400	0.600	—	0.080
LEV	0.075	0.090	3.400	4.200	0.200	0.300	—	0.040
Federal Tier II*	—	0–0.125	—	2.1–4.2	—	0.07**	—	0–0.02

Sources: Dyerson, R. and A. Pilkington (2004) "Expecting the Unexpected: Disruptive Technological Change Processes and the Electric Vehicle," *International Journal of Innovation and Technology Management* 1(2): 165–183. Reproduced from *The ABCs of AFVs*: A Guide to Alternative Fuel Vehicles, California Energy Commission, April 1996. US Environmental Protection Agency, EPA420-B-00-001, Feb 2000; 65 F.R. 6698, February 10, 2000. Sacramento, California.
Notes: NLEV = national low-emission vehicle.
The values shown for the federal Tier I standards are for light-duty vehicles (0–3,750 lbs).
The values shown for federal Tier II standards apply to light and medium vehicles, weighing up to 10,000 lbs.
*expands the useful life to <120,000 miles or 10 years, whichever is first. Values represent the range allowed by emission bins.
**Value represents the fleet average standard (values range between 0 to 0.2 g/mile).

theory, cost reductions for manufacturers as well as credit for earlier-than-required reductions.

The Tier II rules also require that the same set of emission standards apply to light-duty passenger vehicles, light-duty trucks, and medium-duty passenger vehicles (which include larger SUVs and passenger vans).[55] Tier II standards were also broadened to be "fuel-neutral," applying to vehicles operating on any fuels, including diesel. EPA determined that even for large vehicles, the new standards would not necessarily be technology forcing because their own laboratory tests showed achievement using conventional technology. In fact, by 2000 more than fifty vehicle models were at or below Tier II levels. See 65 *Fed. Reg.* 6704 (2000). Comparisons of the emission requirements for pre-Tier I, Tier I, NLEV, and Tier II are shown in table 7.4.

Finally, the Tier II program calls for lowered sulfur levels in gasoline, both to help meet the new vehicle emission standards and to maintain the effectiveness of emission

---

55. Light-duty vehicles encompass passenger vehicles below 8,500 pounds gross vehicle weight (GVWR). The category is further subdivided into passenger cars and two truck categories based on weight. Medium duty encompasses passenger vehicles between 8,500 and 10,000 GVWR.

control technology.[56] The gasoline-sulfur rules, which took effect in 2006, effectively require refiners to add additional equipment to further remove sulfur. Similar requirements for low-sulfur diesel were promulgated in a separate rulemaking for heavy-duty engine vehicles, discussed later.

3.   New Measures Regulating Gasoline

Another significant feature of the 1990 amendments was the mandated use of reformulated gasoline (RFG).[57] The term refers to gasoline in which certain fuel properties and chemical compounds are limited, modified, or added to reduce emissions of specific pollutants while maintaining the same performance characteristics.

Except for the phaseout of lead, regulation of fuel had been largely omitted from the overall emissions reduction strategy.[58] Indeed, lead aside, gasoline actually became "dirtier" from 1970 to 1990, producing higher emissions of toxic air pollutants such as benzene. As noted by Representative Waxman in his critique, "Ironically, it appears that much of the degradation of gasoline can be attributed to the lead phasedown, because oil companies compensated for the elimination of lead by increasing smog-forming and toxic constituents in gasoline."

As a result of the 1990 amendments, requirements for reduced volatility in gasoline during summer months were applied nationwide by the summer of 1992. See CAA Section 211(h). These standards helped reduce evaporative emissions (caused by the evaporation of gasoline). Congress also directed EPA to promulgate new regulations requiring that gasoline sold in certain areas be reformulated to reduce vehicle emissions of toxic and ozone-forming compounds. See CAA Section 211(k)(1). These sale mandates applied to nine nonattainment cities with the worst ozone air quality records, which together represented 20% of the national market.[59] In addition, areas in nonattainment for ozone could opt into the RFG program. California, with severe urban smog problems, took the lead in using RFG by enacting stricter gasoline spec-

---

56. EPA also found that reduced-sulfur gasoline would be necessary to enable new advanced technologies (such as gasoline-direct injection engines) that provide higher fuel economy but can be harmed by sulfur.

57. One justification for the reformulated fuels program was that it would reduce auto emissions without raising costs. As noted by Waxman, "Analyses of costs of clean fuels vary widely. However, EPA predicts no net cost to the economy through the use of clean fuels, because lower fuel costs and maintenance expenses will offset upfront capital costs." U.S. EPA (1990) *Ozone Nonattainment Analysis: A Comparison of Bills.* EPA, Washington, D.C., p. 5. Furthermore, the estimates of the California Air Resources Board (CARB) show actual cost savings from the use of natural gas and electricity in vehicles. California Air Resources Board, "Proposed Regulations for Low-Emission Vehicles and Clean Fuels: Staff Report 70-71" (Aug. 13, 1990).

58. Although actual requirements for RFG were first set forth in the 1990 CAAA, it is important to note that both the California Air Resources Board and the EPA had set regulations on gas properties as early as 1959 and 1974, respectively.

59. Some regions also have voluntarily adopted RFG.

ifications than the federal government's standards and requiring them several years earlier. Also, diesel fuel manufacturers were required to reduce the sulfur content of their fuels, thus reducing the formation of particulate matter in diesel exhaust. The fuels strategy was effective in immediately improving emissions from gasoline and diesel vehicles. New vehicle emission requirements, in contrast, required the turnover of the entire vehicle fleet—a delay of at least 10 years—to achieve maximum benefit.

Both the California and the federal approach involved two phases of RFGs (with the federal program known as Phase I RFG and Phase II RFG). The rules are somewhat complex, and include both performance standards and minimum fuel specification standards. The RFGs were required to meet performance standards calling for specified reductions in VOCs, NO_x, and emissions of air toxics (i.e., benzene and aromatics). The fuel specification requirements called for limits on the content of aromatics, benzene, olefins, and sulfur; specified the Reid vapor pressure; increased the oxygen content; and reduced the gasoline evaporation rates at 200° and 300°F.[60] Refineries were allowed to certify their gasoline as RFG on a per-gallon basis or on an average basis, with the latter requiring slightly more stringent requirements. The RFGs also reduced both exhaust and evaporative emissions for CO, sulfur dioxide, formaldehyde, 1,3-butadiene, and polycyclic organic compounds.[61]

One unintentional environmental consequence of the new fuels program was groundwater contamination resulting from the use of the chemical methyl *tert*-butyl ether (MTBE) in gasoline. EPA began requiring the addition of oxygenates to gasoline in 1992 to reduce ambient air CO levels in nonattainment regions during the winter months.[62] Oxygenates are fuel additives (alcohols and ethers) containing oxygen. They help boost gasoline's octane quality, enhance combustion, and reduce exhaust emissions, particularly during warm up of the vehicle. The term "oxygenated gasoline" is most commonly associated with the wintertime program to reduce CO emissions from motor vehicles.

MTBE has been the most commonly used oxygenate, with roughly 8.0 billion kilograms produced in 1995 in the United States (almost all of it going into fuel oxygenation). Ethanol (EtOH) is the second most widely used, with 4.3 billion kilograms produced in 1994.[63] Ironically, however, the use of MTBE and EtOH to reduce vehicle emissions resulted in a shift of pollution from the air to the groundwater

---

60. See F. M. Bowman and J. H. Seinfeld (1985) "Atmospheric Chemistry of Alternative Fuels and Reformulated Gasoline Components," *Progress in Energy Combustion Science* 21: 387.

61. W. Keesom and M. Humbach (1994) "Effective Gasoline Reformulation," *ASTM Standardization News* 22: 26.

62. The actual standard requires a 2% by weight oxygen content. The Clean Air Act does not specify what type of oxygenate is to be used, only the content.

63. J. S. Zogoroski et al. (1997) "Fuel Oxygenates and Water Quality," ch. 2 in *Interagency Assessment of Oxygenated Fuels.* July 2, prepared by the White House Office of Science and Technology Policy.

through leaks and spills of gasoline at filling stations. See P. M. Franklin et al. (2000) "Cleaning the Air: Using Scientific Information to Regulate Reformulated Fuels," *Environmental Science and Technology* 34: 3857.

■ **NOTES**

1. Wide evidence of groundwater contamination by MTBE has been reported in several areas. Former California Governor Gray Davis ordered the removal of MTBE from gasoline sold in California by the end of 2003. Arizona, Colorado, Connecticut, Iowa, Michigan, Minnesota, Nebraska, New York, and South Dakota have followed suit. The Oxygenated Fuels association filed a lawsuit seeking to block California's impending ban on MTBE, but the Ninth Circuit Court of Appeals rejected the association's argument that the Clean Air Act preempts California's phaseout of MTBE use. See *Oxygenated Fuels Ass'n. Inc. v. Davis*, 331 F.3d 665 (9th Cir. 2003).

2. In November 1998, the South Tahoe Public Utility District in California filed suit against MTBE producers, refineries, oil companies, and several local gas stations and distributors.[64] A settlement was reached in which Shell, Texaco, and Equilon will pay $28 million to clean up South Lake Tahoe's groundwater supply. The jury found that MTBE and gasoline containing MTBE were defective products and found clear and convincing evidence that Shell and Lyondell Chemical Co. acted with malice. The groundwater was contaminated by MTBE during delivery of the gasoline.

3. The most likely replacement for MTBE is ethanol. However, EPA has reported that ethanol production facilities may be a significant source of VOCs, CO, and hazardous air pollutants such as acetaldehyde, formaldehyde, and acrolein.[65] Moreover, large-scale increases in corn production bring with them the attendant risks of pesticide and fertilizer runoff. Nonetheless, ethanol has powerful friends in Congress from corn-growing states.   ■

4. Encouraging the Use of Alternative Fuels

Although one clear goal of the 1990 amendments was to improve the performance of conventional gasoline-powered vehicles, Congress also recognized that such improvements were not likely to be sufficient to meet air quality goals. Many nonattainment areas, for example, were not expected to be able to meet the ambient standards without greater emission reductions than deemed possible through improvements to conventional vehicles. Thus, Congress sought to promote the longer-term development

---

64. Information from http://tahoe.ceres.ca.gov/stpud/shellsettlement080502.html.
65. C. Hogue (2002) "Air Pollution from Ethanol," *CENEAR* 80(19): 6, May 13.

of a new, cleaner generation of vehicles. Alternatively *fueled* vehicles (AFVs), such as those powered by natural gas, ethanol, or methanol, and alternatively *powered* vehicles (APVs), such as electric vehicles, were both considered desirable.

Prior to the 1990 amendments, Congress had passed the Alternative Motor Fuel Act (AMFA) of 1988 (Pub. L. 100-494). This law directed the Department of Energy (DOE) to encourage the development and use of methanol, ethanol, and natural gas as transportation fuels. The AMFA called on DOE to purchase the maximum practicable number of AFVs to complement its fleet of vehicles, to develop programs to aid in the commercialization of AFVs, and to conduct studies relating to the feasibility and promotion of AFVs.

Building on the AMFA, the Clean Air Act Amendments of 1990 mandated the use of alternative fuels (fuels other than conventional gasoline) in certain metropolitan areas having serious or extreme air quality problems. The 1990 amendments also created a Clean-Fuel Fleet Vehicle Program, under which 30% of new vehicle purchases for centrally fueled fleets in twenty-three nonattainment areas were to be "clean-fueled vehicles" by 1998, and 70% were to be clean-fueled by 2000. Under this program, a "fleet" comprises ten or more vehicles, such as delivery vans, taxicabs, or school buses, which are commonly fueled at a central location. To qualify as a clean-fuel vehicle, a vehicle must both rely on an alternative fuel and produce emissions of NO_x and VOCs in amounts no greater than 20% of the allowable 1990 levels for comparable gasoline-powered vehicles. The list of acceptable alternative fuels under this program goes beyond those targeted by the AMFA, and includes reformulated gasoline, diesel, electricity, and propane, as well as methanol, ethanol, and natural gas. See 42 U.S.C. §7581(2). Accordingly, the major impact of the Clean-Fuel Fleet Vehicle Program has been to increase the use of reformulated gasoline, as most fleet operators preferred this "alternative" fuel because of its relatively lower cost.

In the Energy Policy Act of 1992 (Pub. L. 102-486), Congress went a step further. The Energy Policy Act established a program that required specific entities operating fleets of light-duty vehicles—including federal agencies, state and local governments, alternative fuel providers, and certain private entities—to procure AFVs. The federal government was required to take the lead: a full 75% of all new light-duty vehicle purchases by federal agencies are to be AFVs. Moreover, the Energy Policy Act defines "alternative fuels" more narrowly than the Clean Air Act, requiring mixtures that contain 85% or more (by volume) of alcohols, natural gas, propane, electricity, hydrogen, coal-derived liquid fuels, or biologically derived fuels (such as biodiesel).

The environmental performance of AFVs has thus far been something of a mixed bag. Although the use of alternative fuels can reduce the emission of criteria pollutants, it may also increase the emission of toxic air pollutants, as is the case with the use of ethanol and methanol (whether as fuels or as oxygenates in reformulated gasoline). Studies have shown increased benzene, formaldehyde, acetaldehyde, and

1,3-butadiene from ethanol and methanol AFVs.[66] Natural gas APVs, however, were found to have lower toxic emissions than comparable gasoline-powered vehicles.[67]

■ NOTES

1. The Web site for DOE's Alternative Fuels Data Center can be found at www.afdc.doe.gov/documents/amfa.html.

2. In the years since the events of September 11, 2001, the issue of energy independence has been brought sharply into focus, and the calls for the increased use of ethanol and biodiesel fuels have become louder. A potentially significant problem with heeding these calls, however, is that we may be trading off energy security for environmental health. Research—and probably technology development—regarding the use of these fuels likely would be preferable to their cavalier adoption.

3. The Energy Policy Act of 2005, 42 USC 15801, et seq., creates additional incentives for the production and use of ethanol-based fuels. For a brief description of the provisions in the 2005 act designed to stimulate the use of alternative fuels and renewable energy sources in mobile sources, see James A. Duffield and Keith Collins (2006) "Evolution of Renewable Energy Policy," *Choices*, pp. 9–14 available at http://www.choicesmagazine.org/2006-1/biofuels/2006-1-02.pdf.   ■

5. Diesel Sulfur, Heavy-Duty Engine, Heavy-Duty Vehicle Rule

Emissions from heavy-duty vehicles have become an increasing portion of overall U.S. vehicle emissions over the past three decades, owing both to increases in freight transportation and to decreases in the emissions from cars and light-duty trucks. While emissions of HCs, NO_x, and CO from cars declined by 80–95% in the period from 1967 to 1998, emissions from heavy-duty diesel trucks declined much more slowly (by 47% for HC, 74% for NO_x, and 13% for CO).[68] At present, heavy-duty trucks and buses account for roughly one-third of all NO_x emissions and roughly one-fourth of all PM emissions from mobile sources.

EPA did not establish aggressive standards to curb pollution by heavy-duty vehicles until some 10 years after the passage of the 1990 amendments. These regula-

---

66. J. J. Winebrake and M. L. Deaton (1999) "Hazardous Air Pollution from Mobile Sources: A Comparison of Alternative Fuel and Reformulated Gasoline Vehicles," *Journal of the Air and Waste Management Association* (49)5: 576.

67. F. Black, S. Tejada, and M. Gurevich (1998) "Alternative Fuel Motor Vehicle Tailpipe and Evaporative Emissions Composition and Ozone Potential," *Journal of the Air and Waste Management Association* (48)7: 578.

68. U.S. Environmental Protection Agency, *AP-42: Compilation of Air Pollutant Emission Factors.* November 24, 2000. Tables 7.1.1 and 1.1A.1.

tions grew out of the 1998 settlement of the agency's enforcement action against Caterpillar Inc., Cummins Engine Company, Detroit Diesel Corporation, Mack Trucks, Inc., Navistar International Transportation Corporation, Renault Vehicles Industries, and Volvo Truck Corporation, all of whom were charged with having violated the Clean Air Act by installing devices to defeat diesel emission controls, and thus having caused millions of tons of additional NO_x emissions. The resulting consent decree, which represented the largest enforcement settlement in Clean Air Act history, cost the companies nearly $1 billion, including $83.4 million in civil penalties. The settlement caused something of a political stir. A subsequent congressional report, although critical of the companies' malfeasance, also criticized the EPA for what it termed "a pattern of gross negligence and striking indifference ... throughout the early and mid-1990s to the very real possibility—now a known certainty—that diesel truck engines were emitting pollutants far in excess of regulatory standards." See *Asleep at the Wheel: The EPA's Failure to Enforce Pollution Standards for Heavy-Duty Diesel Trucks*, Staff report prepared for Committee of Commerce, U.S. House of Representatives, March 2000.

Within a year thereafter, EPA had promulgated new exhaust performance standards for heavy-duty engines, increasing the stringency of the standards for NO_x, PM, and NMHC by 95, 90, and 90%, respectively.[69] Heavy-duty diesel engines meeting these standards are to be phased in from 2007 to 2010, and heavy-duty gasoline engines meeting these standards are to be in use by 2009. During the phase-in period, manufacturers will be allowed to participate in an averaging, banking, and trading (ABT) program similar to the federal Tier II program. The ABT program allows a manufacturer to obtain credits for engines that outperform the standards. These credits can then be applied to engines that are unable to meet the 2007 standards.[70] Banking these credits and trading them to other firms is also allowed, albeit only within the specific engine category.

In parallel with these engine performance requirements, EPA also promulgated exhaust emission standards for heavy-duty vehicles. Heavy-duty vehicles having a gross vehicle weight rating between 8,500 and 10,000 lbs will be required to emit less than 0.2 gram per mile (g/mi) of NO_x, 0.02 g/mi of PM, 0.195 g/mi of NMHC, and 0.032 g/mi of formaldehyde. For vehicles between 10,000 and 14,000 pounds, the standards increase to 0.4 g/mi for NO_x, 0.02 g/mi for PM, 0.230 g/mi for NMHC, and 0.04

---

69. These engine performance standards are 0.01 grams per brake-horsepower-hour (g/bhp-hr) for PM, 0.20 g/bhp-hr for NO_x, and 0.14 g/bhp-hr for NMHC (66 *Fed. Reg.* 5001, January 18, 2001). A set of rules for 2004 to 2007 were also promulgated on October 6, 2000 (65 *Fed. Reg.* 59895–59978) which called for engine performance standards of 2.4 g/bhp-hr for NO_x and HC (combined), versus the previous 4 g/bhp-hr NO_x and 1.3 g/bhp-hr HC standard. The rule also required on-board diagnostic (OBD) systems for engines between 8,500 and 14,000 pounds to be phased in beginning in 2005. These systems identify the failure of emissions control system components.

70. 66 *Fed. Reg.* at 5109–11; 40 C.F.R. §86.007–15.

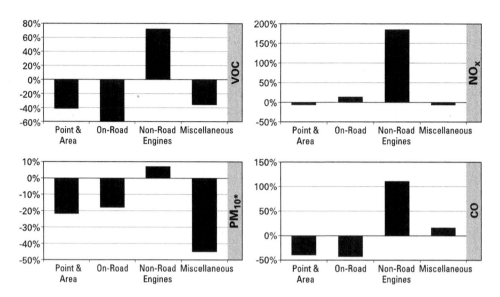

Figure 7.6
Percent of change in emissions from 1970 to 1999 for various sources. (Source: "Emission Trends Part I—Air Quality Fact Book." Federal Highway Administration ⟨http/www.fhwa.dot.gov/environment/aqfactbk/factbk8.htm⟩.)

g/mi for formaldehyde. Stricter evaporative standards were also promulgated, specifying evaporation rates more than 50% below previous standards.

In addition, EPA has extended the regulation of fuel content to diesel fuels. The requirements call for significantly lower levels of sulfur (from a then-current maximum level of 500 ppm to 15 ppm), to allow advanced exhaust emission controls on diesel vehicles. Refiners were to begin producing low-sulfur highway diesel fuel by June 1, 2006, although they are given flexibility in making this transition through 2009.

6.   Emissions Rules for Nonroad Engines

While emissions from on-road mobile sources and point and area sources have markedly declined since the 1970 Clean Air Act Amendments, emissions from non-road engines have grown significantly (see figure 7.6).[71] Nonroad emissions come from a number of engine types, including those found in forklifts, electric generators, airport baggage transport vehicles, construction vehicles, farm equipment, recreational vehicles (principally all-terrain vehicles, off-road motorcycles, and snowmobiles), and diesel marine engines (yachts and cruisers). Emissions from this category

---

71. "Emission Trends Part I—Air Quality Fact Book," Federal Highway Administration. Available at ⟨http/www.fhwa.dot.gov/environment/aqfactbk/factbk8.htm⟩.

were virtually unregulated until the mid-1990s. The 1990 amendments directed EPA to study the contribution of nonroad engines to air pollution and to regulate them if necessary. In a startling finding, EPA reported that total emissions from this category were nearly as high as those from highway motor vehicles, making it one of the largest sources of air emissions.[72] Indeed, nonroad mobile sources were found to emit significantly higher amounts of diesel particulate matter than all highway motor vehicles combined.

Because many nonroad engines operate in warehouses or other enclosed areas, worker exposure to high levels of CO and other pollutants is also an issue. A 2003 report by the Northeast States for Coordinated Air Use Management (NESCAUM) found substantially increased PM exposures for workers and nearby residents in all locations studied, with as many as 200,000 workers potentially exposed to harmful concentration levels in the Northeast region alone. Measured concentrations of acetaldehyde, benzene, and formaldehyde around the tested nonroad equipment operations were also found to be substantially high.[73] For instance, particle levels inside the cabins of heavy-duty equipment can be as much as sixteen times the national ambient air quality standards.[74]

EPA began to promulgate regulations for a variety of off-road vehicles in the mid-1990s. The categories regulated include land-based diesel engines; land-based, spark-ignition engines (mostly gas powered); marine engines and vessels (gas and diesel); locomotives; and aircraft.[75] The diversity of sources poses an especially difficult regulatory challenge. The first set of emission standards (Tier 1), promulgated in 1994, targeted NO_x emissions from new, nonroad diesel engines greater than 50 horsepower and was phased in between 1996 and 2000. Tier 2 standards (phased in from 2001 to 2006) cover all engine sizes and impose more stringent standards. Tier 3 standards (to be phased in from 2006 to 2008) will further reduce allowable NO_x and PM emissions for 50–750-horsepower engines. In 2003, EPA proposed Tier 4 emission standards to further reduce PM and NO_x (by as much as 90%) over the period from 2008 to 2014. All four tiers of off-road regulations include provisions for averaging, banking, and trading emission credits, and for emission averaging through maximum "family emission limits."[76] Like the diesel engine standards for road trucks and

---

72. "Nonroad Engine and Vehicle Emission Study Report," EPA-21A-2001 or EPA460/3-91-01, November 1991. See http://www.epa.gov/otaq/nonroad.htm for access to the document (last accessed on 8/17/04).

73. NESCAUM (June 2003) *Evaluating the Occupational and Environmental Impact of Nonroad Diesel Equipment in the Northeast* (Interim Report).

74. "Off-Road Equipment Operators Exposed to High Levels of Particulates, Report Says," *Environment Reporter* 34(24): 1328 (2003).

75. Interested readers are referred to EPA (April 2003) "Program Update: Reducing Air Pollution from Nonroad Engines," EPA420-F-03-011, for further information on all regulated categories. Available at http://www.epa.gov/otaq/nonroad.htm (last viewed on 10/7/03).

76. Source: www.dieselnet.com/standards/us/offroad.html.

buses, the nonroad engine standards require the use of diesel particulate filters and NO_x control catalysts. A fuel program was added to the standards, limiting sulfur content in nonroad diesel fuel (500 ppm for 2007, 15 ppm for 2010) to preserve the effectiveness of the emission control devices.

7. The Mobile Source Air Toxics Program

Motor vehicle emissions may contain a host of carcinogens and potential carcinogens, such as particulate matter, benzenes, acetaldehyde, butadiene, aromatic hydrocarbons, and dioxins. EPA estimates that toxic pollutants emitted from mobile sources (not including nonroad vehicles) account for roughly half of all cancers from outdoor sources of airborne toxicants. In 2005, EPA indicated that motor vehicles are the primary source of hazardous air pollution in the United States, emitting an estimated 168,000 tons of benzene, 83,000 tons of formaldehyde, 23,500 tons of 1,3-butadiene, and 28,700 tons of acetaldehyde annually. See *Environment Reporter* 36(26): 1341 (2005). Both the nature of motor vehicle toxicants and their proximity to human population centers make them a significant risk to human health. Diesel particulate emissions, for example, can adsorb a wide variety of toxic chemicals, including carcinogens and mutagens, and they are easily inhaled into the lungs of drivers, passengers, and passersby.

Until the 1990 amendments, no specific provision of the Clean Air Act regulated the emission of toxic air pollutants from mobile sources as a separate category of pollutants. In 1990, Congress added provisions to Section 202 of the act to address "mobile source-related air toxics" [42 U.S.C. §7521(l)]. In these provisions, EPA was directed to establish "reasonable requirements to control hazardous air pollutants from motor vehicles and motor vehicle fuels" by 1995. These requirements were to reflect "the greatest degree of emission reduction achievable using technology that will be available," taking into account cost, lead time, noise, energy needs, and safety, and were, "at a minimum," to apply to emissions of benzene and formaldehyde. Although EPA did not meet this statutory deadline, studies performed by the agency over the 1990s did lead to a Mobile Source Air Toxics (MSAT) rule in 2001. See 55 *Fed. Reg.* 17230 (2001). The MSAT rule identified a list of twenty-one compounds emitted from mobile sources that are known to cause serious health effects. The MSAT rule also established "antibacksliding" requirements for gasoline refiners, which are designed to cap toxic emissions at 1998–2000 levels. See http://www.epa.gov/otaq/toxics.htm. While this rule raised awareness of the risks posed by mobile source toxicants, it did not satisfy the "air toxics" mandate given to the agency by Congress.

Thus, the Sierra Club and the U.S. Public Interest Research Group sued EPA in 2004 to compel the issuance of an air toxics rule for motor vehicles and motor vehicle fuels. See *Environment Reporter* 36(26): 1341 (2005). In response, EPA proposed a rule in 2006 that it estimated would reduce air toxics emissions from cars and trucks by 80% (compared with 1999 levels) by 2030. See *Environment Reporter* 37(9): 430 (2006). Commenting on the proposed rule, a coalition of persons with high-level ties to the administrations of George H. W. Bush and Bill Clinton urged a further lowering of the benzene content of fuels and a concomitant increase in the ethanol content. See *Environment Reporter* 37(24): 1262 (2006). The final rule, issued in 2007, includes somewhat tighter controls on benzene. Refiners will be required to meet a national average benzene concentration in gasoline of 0.62%, a reduction of approximately one third from the current national average of 0.97%. Although refiners will be able to comply by buying and selling benzene reduction credits, thus creating the likelihood that gasoline will be below the standard in some locales and above it in others, the regulation also sets a 1.3% maximum cap on the annual average benzene concentration in the gasoline from any refinery. In addition, the regulation imposes limits on automotive emissions of a number of toxic substances, including benzene and other NMHCs. The limits will be phased in over a number of years, with smaller vehicles (less than 6,000 pounds) required to meet an emission standard of 0.3 grams per mile by 2013, and larger vehicles (over 6,000 pounds) required to meet a standard of 0.5 grams per mile by 2015. The emission standards will be measured as sales-weighted averages. Finally, the rule imposes as a national standard the State of California's 2007 limits on evaporative air toxic emissions from vehicles. Overall, EPA estimates that implementation of the rule will reduce annual toxic air emissions by 330,000 tons by 2030. See Steven D. Cook (2007) "EPA to Reduce Benzene in Gasoline By One-Third in Mobile Source Rule," *Environment Reporter* 38(7): 357.

F. REGULATION OF FUEL EFFICIENCY

A desire to reduce U.S. dependence on foreign oil, brought on by the 1973 Arab oil embargo, led to the passage of the 1975 Energy Policy and Conservation Act. See 42 USC §6274. Congress sought in this law to curb highway fuel consumption, and it thus established fuel efficiency requirements for new motor vehicles. The resulting Corporate Average Fuel Economy (CAFE) program[77] established sales-weighted, average fuel efficiency standards for passenger cars and light-duty truck fleets. Congress itself set the passenger vehicle CAFE standards at 18 miles per gallon (mpg) in 1978 and subsequently elevated them to 27.5 in 1985, where they have remained since. The National Highway Traffic Safety Administration (NHTSA) was given the authority to set the light-duty truck CAFE standard.

---

77. National Academy of Sciences (2002) *Effectiveness and Impact of Corporate Average Fuel Economy (CAFE) Standards.*

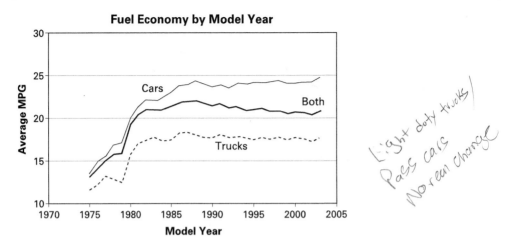

Figure 7.7
Fuel economy by model year, United States. (Source: *Light-Duty Automotive Technology and Fuel Economy Trends 1975 Through 2001*. Environmental Protection Agency, EPA420-S-01-001. Washington, D.C., September 2001.)

Ironically, while average fuel economy improved over the 1980s, the combined average fuel economy for model year 2002 reached a 22-year low of 20.4 mpg (for light-duty and passenger vehicles combined).[78] See figure 7.7. The growth in popularity of larger minivans and sport utility vehicles over smaller passenger vehicles was the main reason for the decline in fuel efficiency. Together, light-duty trucks, SUVs, and minivans made up nearly 50% of all new car sales in 2000, compared with only 25% in 1985 (see figure 7.8). In 2001, new SUVs averaged 17.2 mpg, pickup trucks 16.5 mpg, vans and minivans 19.3 mpg, and passenger vehicles 24.2 mpg.[79] A 2002 report by the National Academy of Sciences (NAS) suggested that automakers could, on average, increase the fuel efficiency of cars, pickups, SUVs, and vans from 16 to 47% over 10 to 15 years.[80] Despite the NAS report, Congress declined to raise the CAFE standards, deciding instead to allow NHTSA to establish appropriate rules. NHTSA chose to raise the light-duty truck standard by only 1.5 mpg (from 20.7 to 22.2 mpg) over the period from 2005 to 2007.[81] In late 2007, Con-

78. The peak occurred in model year 1987, with 22.1 mpg combined.

79. Environmental Protection Agency (2001) *Light-Duty Automotive Technology and Fuel Economy Trends 1975 Through 2001*. EPA420-S-01-001. EPA, Washington, D.C.

80. National Academy of Sciences (2002) *Effectiveness and Impact of Corporate Average Fuel Economy (CAFE) Standards*; "Popularity of Light Trucks in U.S. Blamed for Drop in Fleet Fuel Economy," *Environment Reporter* 32(40): 1955 (2001).

81. In 2002, the Senate adopted the Levin-Bond amendment, granting NHTSA 2 years to recommend and complete increased fuel economy standards for passenger vehicles. NHTSA was given 15 months to in-

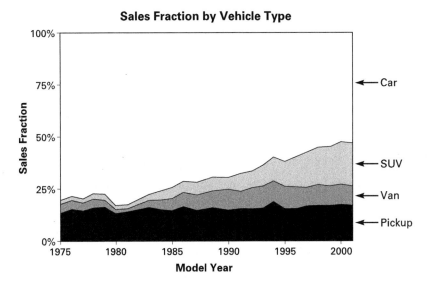

Figure 7.8
Change in new vehicle mix, United States. (Source: *Light-Duty Automotive Technology and Fuel Economy Trends 1975 Through 2001*. Environmental Protection Agency, EPA420-S-01-001. Washington, D.C., September 2001.)

gress enacted new CAFÉ legislation that raises the standard for cars, SUVs, and light-duty trucks to an average of 35 mpg by 2020 and paves the way for fuel economy standards for heavy-duty trucks.

■ **NOTES**

1. One of the factors cited by the National Academy of Sciences report relied on by the court in the 1973 *International Harvester* case was a projected trade-off between reduced automobile emissions and fuel efficiency. Overall, however, use of the catalytic converter was not a detriment to fuel economy.

Operation of the catalyst proved more trouble free than many had anticipated. Because the catalyst was efficient in oxidizing HC and CO engine emissions, it enabled manufacturers to "retune" engines, relaxing various ignition and fuel adjustments that had previously been utilized to reduce HC and CO emissions at the expense of fuel economy and operating

crease the CAFE standards for light trucks. Congressional efforts to increase the CAFE standards for both light trucks and passenger vehicles to 36 mpg by 2015 were defeated. Appropriations bills had prohibited NHTSA from spending funds to study CAFE standards for the previous 6 years. "Senate Refuses to Set New CAFE Level; Proponents of Higher Standard Admit Defeat," *Environment Reporter* 33(11): 574 (2002).

characteristics. (Such adjustments had resulted in a 6 to 15% fuel penalty for 1973–74 models compared to 1970 models.) The less stringent 1975 standard applicable outside California permitted a considerable degree of retuning. The resulting gains in fuel economy and performance resulted in widespread use of catalysts by domestic manufacturers on cars sold outside as well as inside California. However, these performance and fuel economy gains were purchased at an increased capital cost of $130 to $225 for catalyst-equipped 1975 models in comparison with comparable 1974 models. Moreover, even with catalysts, the more stringent California standards required finer operating tolerances that exacted a 5 percent fuel penalty over catalyst-equipped cars tuned to meet the standards governing the remaining forty-nine states. [Robert V. Percival, Alan S. Miller, Christopher H. Schroeder, and James P. Leape (1992) *Environmental Regulation: Law, Science, and Policy*. Little, Brown, Boston]

A 1977 Senate report cited data showing that additional weight and horsepower were the main reasons for declines in fuel economy, and that the biggest improvement in fuel economy occurred in 1975 as auto emission standards became more stringent. "In the past, industry estimates have consistently overstated the adverse effect of emissions controls on fuel economy" (Senate Committee on Environment and Public Works, *Clean Air Act Amendments of 1977*, 95th Cong., 1st sess., 1977, S. Rep. 95-127, at 5). Ten months before 1975 models were introduced for sale, GM and Chrysler executives stated that fuel economy penalties would occur because of the standards. The 1975 model vehicles, however, had increased fuel economy—a fact that Congress noted.

2. Another concern has been the potential for trade-offs between fuel economy and safety. As the 2002 NAS fuel efficiency report explains, increasing fuel economy requires either improving the power-train efficiency through the use of new technologies, or reducing the amount of work required by the engine to move the car, normally by reducing wind resistance or reducing car size and weight. The latter approach, however, may be associated with decreased driver and passenger safety. The NAS committee estimated that the costs of downsizing automobiles in the 1970s and 1980s, regardless of CAFE or market-induced changes, may have contributed to an additional 1,300 to 2,600 fatalities in 1993. (There were 40,716 traffic-related fatalities in the United States in 1994.) However, the concept of a safety versus fuel economy trade-off is controversial, and many argue that it need not be the case. There is a body of work suggesting that it is not average car weight that is the determinitive safety factor, but rather the distribution of weight in the vehicle fleet.[82] A dissenting opinion in the NAS report argued that higher fuel economy standards may have reduced the size and weight of larger vehicles more than smaller

---

82. Fatality Analysis Reporting System (FARS), National Center for Statistics and Analysis, NHTSA. A strong critique of the CAFE program in general is provided by Pietro Nivola and Robert Crandall (1995) *The Extra Mile: Rethinking Energy Policy for Automotive Transportation*. Brookings Institution, Washington D.C., chs. 1 and 2.

vehicles, thus on average diminishing the vulnerability rate of smaller vehicles during two-car collisions. The GAO has concluded that with sufficient lead time, auto-makers could use fuel-saving technologies rather than simply building lighter, smaller cars.[83]

G. REGULATION OF GREENHOUSE GAS EMISSIONS

As global climate change progresses and its detrimental impacts become clearer, it seems likely that reductions and even sequestration of global greenhouse gases (GHGs) will be necessary to stabilize the earth's climate system.[84] The transportation sector remains among the largest emitters of GHGs, contributing roughly 27% of such emissions in the United States and 21% worldwide.[85]

To date, there has been no formal regulatory activity at the federal level to address greenhouse gas emissions in the United States. Several voluntary programs have been initiated, but these have been addressed principally toward stationary sources of carbon dioxide (CO_2). These voluntary programs have included the first President Bush's National Energy Strategy, Green Lights Program, and Energy Star Program (1991), President Clinton's Climate Change Action Plan (1993), the Bush-Cheney National Energy Plan (2001), and a national goal, announced by the Bush administration in 2002, of reducing greenhouse gas intensity (the ratio of emissions to economic output) by 18% by 2012. Success of the latter effort will depend on voluntary programs such as the Climate RESOLVE (Responsible Environmental Steps, Opportunities to Lead by Voluntary Efforts) initiative. Skeptics noted, however, that because the economy would continue to grow, the targeted reduction in greenhouse gas intensity actually would allow for a 12% increase in GHG emissions, essentially the same rate as in previous years.

No federal program has been created that imposes binding requirements, enforceable mandates, or the trading of permits to reduce greenhouse gases. Several bills addressing GHGs have been filed in Congress during the George W. Bush

---

83. For alternative viewpoints, also see Danny Hakim (2003) "Pitting Fuel Economy Against Safety," *New York Times*, June 28, p. B1; J. D. Khazzoom (1994) "Fuel Efficiency and Automobile Safety—Single-Vehicle Highway Fatalities for Passenger Cars," *Energy Journal* 15(4): 49–101; and J. M. Yun (2002) "Offsetting Behavior Effect of the Corporate Average Fuel Economy Standards," *Economic Inquiry* 40(2): 260–270.

84. Reports of changes in the Arctic climate have already been studied and thoroughly documented. See Andrew C. Revkin (2004) "Big Arctic Perils Seen in Warming, Survey Finds," *New York Times* science section, October 20; ACIA (2004) *Impacts of a Warming Arctic: Arctic Climate Impact Assessment.* Cambridge University Press. Available at http://www.acia.uaf.edu.

85. Estimates represent direct tailpipe GHG emissions relative to total energy-related GHG emissions, and do not include emissions generated from the extraction, production, or transport of fuels. See U.S. EPA (2006) *Greenhouse Gas Emissions from the U.S. Transportation Sector, 1990–2003*, Office of Transportation and Air Quality (http://epa.gov/otaq/greenhousegases.htm).

administration, but all have been opposed by the White House, and none has garnered sufficient support for passage. Given the uncertain prospects for passage of specific GHG legislation in Congress, many suggested that the present Clean Air Act already provides authority for regulation of CO_2.

Perhaps predictably, EPA's response to that suggestion has varied with the politics of the administration it serves. During the Clinton administration, EPA determined that the Clean Air Act authorizes the regulation of CO_2 emissions. In support of this position, the agency cited the act's broad definition of "air pollutant." Thus, the agency told Congress in 1999, it had clear authority to regulate CO_2, although it had not yet determined whether to exercise that authority.[86] Four years later, however, EPA reversed course under the George W. Bush administration. In a 2003 memorandum, EPA's general counsel advised the agency's acting administrator that "CO_2 and other GHGs cannot be considered 'air pollutants' subject to the CAA's regulatory provisions." Rather than proceeding from an analysis of the language of the statute, this conclusion appears to have rested on the assumption that Congress did not intend with the Clean Air Act to address issues of global climate change.

An administrative agency properly awaits congressional direction before addressing a fundamental policy issue such as global climate change, instead of searching for authority in an existing statute that was not designed or enacted to deal with the issue. . . .

Because EPA lacks CAA regulatory authority to address global climate change, the term "air pollution" as used in the regulatory provisions cannot be interpreted to encompass global climate change. Thus, CO_2 and other GHGs are not "agents" of air pollution and do not satisfy the [act's] definition of "air pollutant." [Robert E. Fabricant, EPA general counsel, memorandum to Marianne L. Horinko, EPA acting administrator, August 28, 2003. Obtained from http://www.eesi.org/publications/Fact%20Sheets/co2petitiongcmemo8-28.pdf (last viewed on 8/23/2004)]

Accordingly, the agency denied a petition by environmental groups requesting that it regulate greenhouse gas emissions from motor vehicles.

Subsequently, nearly a dozen states, three major metropolitan areas, and several advocacy groups filed petitions in the D.C. Circuit challenging this decision. They argued that EPA is obligated to address CO_2 emissions from motor vehicles under Section 202(a)(1) of the Clean Air Act.

Although they acknowledged that there is uncertainty about the nature and extent of the link between GHGs and climate change, the plaintiffs invoked the D.C. Circuit's *Ethyl Corp.* case, and the precautionary approach taken there to the statutory

---

86. Testimony of Gary S. Guzy, EPA general counsel, before a Joint Hearing of the Subcommittee on National Economic Growth, Natural Resources and Regulatory Affairs of the Committee on Government Reform and the Subcommittee on Energy and Environment of the Committee on Science. U.S. House of Representatives, on October 6, 1999, citing the previous EPA general counsel Jonathan Z. Cannon's memorandum to the administrator on April 10, 1998.

term "endanger." In a 2 to 1 opinion, the D.C. Circuit denied the petitions, with only one member of the majority reaching the substance of the case. The plaintiffs sought review in the Supreme Court, and that Court issued its opinion in 2007.

Massachusetts, et al. v. Environmental Protection Agency
Justice STEVENS delivered the opinion of the Court
United States Supreme Court
127 S. Ct. 1438 (2007)

A well-documented rise in global temperatures has coincided with a significant increase in the concentration of carbon dioxide in the atmosphere. Respected scientists believe the two trends are related. For when carbon dioxide is released into the atmosphere, it acts like the ceiling of a greenhouse, trapping solar energy and retarding the escape of reflected heat. It is therefore a species—the most important species—of a "greenhouse gas."

Calling global warming "the most pressing environmental challenge of our time," a group of States, local governments, and private organizations, alleged in a petition for certiorari that the Environmental Protection Agency (EPA) has abdicated its responsibility under the Clean Air Act to regulate the emissions of four greenhouse gases, including carbon dioxide. Specifically, petitioners asked us to answer two questions concerning the meaning of §202(a)(1) of the Act: whether EPA has the statutory authority to regulate greenhouse gas emissions from new motor vehicles; and if so, whether its stated reasons for refusing to do so are consistent with the statute.

In response, EPA, supported by 10 intervening States and six trade associations, correctly argued that we may not address those two questions unless at least one petitioner has standing to invoke our jurisdiction under Article III of the Constitution. Notwithstanding the serious character of that jurisdictional argument and the absence of any conflicting decisions construing §202(a)(1), the unusual importance of the underlying issue persuaded us to grant the writ.

I

Section 202(a)(1) of the Clean Air Act, as added by Pub.L. 89-272, §101(8), 79 Stat. 992, and as amended by, *inter alia*, 84 Stat. 1690 and 91 Stat. 791, 42 U.S.C. §7521(a)(1), provides:

"The [EPA] Administrator shall by regulation prescribe (and from time to time revise) in accordance with the provisions of this section, standards applicable to the emission of any air pollutant from any class or classes of new motor vehicles or new motor vehicle engines, which in his judgment cause, or contribute to, air pollution which may reasonably be anticipated to endanger public health or welfare ...."[7]

---

7. The 1970 version of §202(a)(1) used the phrase "which endangers the public health or welfare" rather than the more-protective "which may reasonably be anticipated to endanger public health or welfare." See §6(a) of the Clean Air Amendments of 1970, 84 Stat. 1690. Congress amended §202(a)(1) in 1977 to give its approval to the decision in *Ethyl Corp. v. EPA*, 541 F.2d 1, 25 (C.A.D.C.1976) (en banc), which held that the Clean Air Act "and common sense ... demand regulatory action to prevent harm, even if the regulator is less than certain that harm is otherwise inevitable." See §401(d)(1) of the Clean Air Act Amendments of 1977, 91 Stat. 791; see also H.R.Rep. No. 95-294, p. 49 (1977), U.S. Code Cong. & Admin.News 1977, p. 1077.

The Act defines "air pollutant" to include "any air pollution agent or combination of such agents, including any physical, chemical, biological, radioactive...substance or matter which is emitted into or otherwise enters the ambient air." §7602(g). "Welfare" is also defined broadly: among other things, it includes "effects on...weather...and climate." §7602(h).

When Congress enacted these provisions, the study of climate change was in its infancy.[8] In 1959, shortly after the U.S. Weather Bureau began monitoring atmospheric carbon dioxide levels, an observatory in Mauna Loa, Hawaii, recorded a mean level of 316 parts per million. This was well above the highest carbon dioxide concentration—no more than 300 parts per million—revealed in the 420,000-year-old ice-core record. By the time Congress drafted §202(a)(1) in 1970, carbon dioxide levels had reached 325 parts per million.[10]

In the late 1970's, the Federal Government began devoting serious attention to the possibility that carbon dioxide emissions associated with human activity could provoke climate change. In 1978, Congress enacted the National Climate Program Act, 92 Stat. 601, which required the President to establish a program to "assist the Nation and the world to understand and respond to natural and man-induced climate processes and their implications," *id.*, §3. President Carter, in turn, asked the National Research Council, the working arm of the National Academy of Sciences, to investigate the subject. The Council's response was unequivocal: "If carbon dioxide continues to increase, the study group finds no reason to doubt that climate changes will result and no reason to believe that these changes will be negligible....A wait-and-see policy may mean waiting until it is too late."

Congress next addressed the issue in 1987, when it enacted the Global Climate Protection Act, Title XI of Pub.L. 100-204, 101 Stat. 1407, note following 15 U.S.C. §2901. Finding that "manmade pollution-the release of carbon dioxide, chlorofluorocarbons, methane, and other trace gases into the atmosphere-may be producing a long-term and substantial increase in the average temperature on Earth," §1102(1), 101 Stat. 1408, Congress directed EPA to propose to Congress a "coordinated national policy on global climate change," §1103(b), and ordered the Secretary of State to work "through the channels of multilateral diplomacy" and coordinate diplomatic efforts to combat global warming, §1103(c). Congress emphasized that "ongoing pollution and deforestation may be contributing now to an irreversible process" and that "[n]ecessary actions must be identified and implemented in time to protect the climate." §1102(4).

Meanwhile, the scientific understanding of climate change progressed. In 1990, the Intergovernmental Panel on Climate Change (IPCC), a multinational scientific body organized under the auspices of the United

---

8. The Council on Environmental Quality had issued a report in 1970 concluding that "[m]an may be changing his weather." Environmental Quality: The First Annual Report 93. Considerable uncertainty remained in those early years, and the issue went largely unmentioned in the congressional debate over the enactment of the Clean Air Act. But see 116 Cong. Rec. 32914 (1970) (statement of Sen. Boggs referring to Council's conclusion that "[a]ir pollution alters the climate and may produce global changes in temperature").

10. A more dramatic rise was yet to come: In 2006, carbon dioxide levels reached 382 parts per million, see Dept. of Commerce, National Oceanic & Atmospheric Administration, Mauna Loa CO_2 Monthly Mean Data, www.esrl.noaa.gov/gmd/ccgg/trends/co2_mm_mlo.dat (all Internet materials as visited Mar. 29, 2007, and available in Clerk of Court's case file), a level thought to exceed the concentration of carbon dioxide in the atmosphere at any point over the past 20-million years. See Intergovernmental Panel on Climate Change, Technical Summary of Working Group I Report 39 (2001).

Nations, published its first comprehensive report on the topic. Drawing on expert opinions from across the globe, the IPCC concluded that "emissions resulting from human activities are substantially increasing the atmospheric concentrations of . . . greenhouse gases [which] will enhance the greenhouse effect, resulting on average in an additional warming of the Earth's surface."

Responding to the IPCC report, the United Nations convened the "Earth Summit" in 1992 in Rio de Janeiro. The first President Bush attended and signed the United Nations Framework Convention on Climate Change (UNFCCC), a nonbinding agreement among 154 nations to reduce atmospheric concentrations of carbon dioxide and other greenhouse gases for the purpose of "prevent[ing] dangerous anthropogenic [*i.e.*, human-induced] interference with the [Earth's] climate system." S. Treaty Doc. No. 102-38, Art. 2, p. 5 (1992). The Senate unanimously ratified the treaty.

Some five years later—after the IPCC issued a second comprehensive report in 1995 concluding that "[t]he balance of evidence suggests there is a discernible human influence on global climate"—the UNFCCC signatories met in Kyoto, Japan, and adopted a protocol that assigned mandatory targets for industrialized nations to reduce greenhouse gas emissions. Because those targets did not apply to developing and heavily polluting nations such as China and India, the Senate unanimously passed a resolution expressing its sense that the United States should not enter into the Kyoto Protocol. See S. Res. 98, 105th Cong., 1st Sess. (July 25, 1997) (as passed). President Clinton did

not submit the protocol to the Senate for ratification.

II

On October 20, 1999, a group of 19 private organizations[15] filed a rulemaking petition asking EPA to regulate "greenhouse gas emissions from new motor vehicles under §202 of the Clean Air Act." App. 5. Petitioners maintained that 1998 was the "warmest year on record"; that carbon dioxide, methane, nitrous oxide, and hydrofluorocarbons are "heat trapping greenhouse gases"; that greenhouse gas emissions have significantly accelerated climate change; and that the IPCC's 1995 report warned that "carbon dioxide remains the most important contributor to [man-made] forcing of climate change." *Id.*, at 13 (internal quotation marks omitted). The petition further alleged that climate change will have serious adverse effects on human health and the environment. *Id.*, at 22–35. As to EPA's statutory authority, the petition observed that the agency itself had already confirmed that it had the power to regulate carbon dioxide. See *id.*, at 18, n. 21. In 1998, Jonathan Z. Cannon, then EPA's General Counsel, prepared a legal opinion concluding that "CO_2 emissions are within the scope of EPA's authority to regulate," even as he recognized that EPA had so far declined to exercise that authority. *Id.*, at 54 (memorandum to Carol M. Browner, Administrator (Apr. 10, 1998) (hereinafter Cannon memorandum)). Cannon's successor, Gary S. Guzy, reiterated that opinion before a congressional committee just two weeks before the rulemaking petition was filed. See *id.*, at 61.

---

15. Alliance for Sustainable Communities; Applied Power Technologies, Inc.; Bio Fuels America; The California Solar Energy Industries Assn.; Clements Environmental Corp.; Environmental Advocates; Environmental and Energy Study Institute; Friends of the Earth; Full Circle Energy Project, Inc.; The Green Party of Rhode Island; Greenpeace USA; International Center for Technology Assessment; Network for Environmental and Economic Responsibility of the United Church of Christ; New Jersey Environmental Watch; New Mexico Solar Energy Assn.; Oregon Environmental Council; Public Citizen; Solar Energy Industries Assn.; The SUN DAY Campaign. See App. 7-11.

Fifteen months after the petition's submission, EPA requested public comment on "all the issues raised in [the] petition," adding a "particular" request for comments on "any scientific, technical, legal, economic or other aspect of these issues that may be relevant to EPA's consideration of this petition." 66 Fed. Reg. 7486, 7487 (2001). EPA received more than 50,000 comments over the next five months. See 68 Fed.Reg. 52924 (2003).

Before the close of the comment period, the White House sought "assistance in identifying the areas in the science of climate change where there are the greatest certainties and uncertainties" from the National Research Council, asking for a response "as soon as possible." App. 213. The result was a 2001 report titled Climate Change: An Analysis of Some Key Questions (NRC Report), which, drawing heavily on the 1995 IPCC report, concluded that "[g]reenhouse gases are accumulating in Earth's atmosphere as a result of human activities, causing surface air temperatures and subsurface ocean temperatures to rise. Temperatures are, in fact, rising." NRC Report 1.

On September 8, 2003, EPA entered an order denying the rulemaking petition. 68 Fed.Reg. 52922. The agency gave two reasons for its decision: (1) that contrary to the opinions of its former general counsels, the Clean Air Act does not authorize EPA to issue mandatory regulations to address global climate change, see *id.*, at 52925–52929; and (2) that even if the agency had the authority to set greenhouse gas emission standards, it would be unwise to do so at this time, *id.*, at 52929–52931.

In concluding that it lacked statutory authority over greenhouse gases, EPA observed that Congress "was well aware of the global climate change issue when it last comprehensively amended the [Clean Air Act] in 1990," yet it declined to adopt a proposed amendment establishing binding emissions limitations. *Id.*, at 52926. Congress instead chose to authorize further investigation into climate

change. *Ibid.* (citing §§103(g) and 602(e) of the Clean Air Act Amendments of 1990, 104 Stat. 2652, 2703, 42 U.S.C. §§7403(g)(1) and 7671a(e)). EPA further reasoned that Congress' "specially tailored solutions to global atmospheric issues," 68 Fed.Reg. 52926-in particular, its 1990 enactment of a comprehensive scheme to regulate pollutants that depleted the ozone layer, see Title VI, 104 Stat. 2649, 42 U.S.C. §§7671-7671q-counseled against reading the general authorization of §202(a)(1) to confer regulatory authority over greenhouse gases. . . .

EPA reasoned that climate change had its own "political history": Congress designed the original Clean Air Act to address *local* air pollutants rather than a substance that "is fairly consistent in its concentration throughout the *world's* atmosphere," 68 Fed.Reg. 52927 (emphasis added); declined in 1990 to enact proposed amendments to force EPA to set carbon dioxide emission standards for motor vehicles, *ibid.* (citing H.R. 5966, 101st Cong., 2d Sess. (1990)); and addressed global climate change in other legislation, 68 Fed.Reg. 52927. Because of this political history, and because imposing emission limitations on greenhouse gases would have even greater economic and political repercussions than regulating tobacco, EPA was persuaded that it lacked the power to do so. *Id.*, at 52928. In essence, EPA concluded that climate change was so important that unless Congress spoke with exacting specificity, it could not have meant the agency to address it.

Having reached that conclusion, EPA believed it followed that greenhouse gases cannot be "air pollutants" within the meaning of the Act. See *ibid.* ("It follows from this conclusion, that [greenhouse gases], as such, are not air pollutants under the [Clean Air Act's] regulatory provisions . . ."). The agency bolstered this conclusion by explaining that if carbon dioxide were an air pollutant, the only feasible method of reducing tailpipe emissions would be to improve fuel economy. But because Congress has already created detailed mandatory fuel economy standards subject to Department of Transportation (DOT) administration, the agency concluded that EPA regulation would either conflict with those standards or be superfluous. *Id.*, at 52929.

Even assuming that it had authority over greenhouse gases, EPA explained in detail why it would refuse to exercise that authority. The agency began by recognizing that the concentration of greenhouse gases has dramatically increased as a result of human activities, and acknowledged the attendant increase in global surface air temperatures. *Id.*, at 52930. EPA nevertheless gave controlling importance to the NRC Report's statement that a causal link between the two "'cannot be unequivocally established.'" *Ibid.* (quoting NRC Report 17). Given that residual uncertainty, EPA concluded that regulating greenhouse gas emissions would be unwise. 68 Fed.Reg. 52930.

The agency furthermore characterized any EPA regulation of motor-vehicle emissions as a "piecemeal approach" to climate change, *id.*, at 52931, and stated that such regulation would conflict with the President's "comprehensive approach" to the problem, *id.*, at 52932. That approach involves additional support for technological innovation, the creation of nonregulatory programs to encourage voluntary private-sector reductions in greenhouse gas emissions, and further research on climate change-not actual regulation. *Id.*, at 52932–52933. According to EPA, unilateral EPA regulation of motor-vehicle greenhouse gas emissions might also hamper the President's ability to persuade key developing countries to reduce greenhouse gas emissions. *Id.*, at 52931.

III

Petitioners, now joined by intervenor States and local governments, sought review of EPA's order in the United States Court of Appeals for the District of Columbia Circuit. Although each of the three judges on the panel wrote a separate opinion, two judges agreed "that the EPA Administrator properly exercised his discretion under §202(a)(1) in denying the petition for rule making." 415 F.3d 50, 58 (2005). The court therefore denied the petition for review....

IV

Article III of the Constitution limits federal-court jurisdiction to "Cases" and "Controversies." Those two words confine "the business of federal courts to questions presented in an adversary context and in a form historically viewed as capable of resolution through the judicial process." *Flast v. Cohen*, 392 U.S. 83, 95, 88 S.Ct. 1942, 20 L.Ed.2d 947 (1968). It is therefore familiar learning that no justiciable "controversy" exists when parties seek adjudication of a political question, *Luther v. Borden*, 7 How. 1, 12 L.Ed. 581 (1849), when they ask for an advisory opinion, *Hayburn's Case*, 2 Dall. 409, 1 L.Ed. 436 (1792), see also *Clinton v. Jones*, 520 U.S. 681, 700, n. 33, 117 S.Ct. 1636, 137 L.Ed.2d 945 (1997), or when the question sought to be adjudicated has been mooted by subsequent developments, *California v. San Pablo & Tulare R. Co.*, 149 U.S. 308, 13 S.Ct. 876, 37 L.Ed. 747 (1893). This case suffers from none of these defects.

The parties' dispute turns on the proper construction of a congressional statute, a question eminently suitable to resolution in federal court. Congress has moreover authorized this type of challenge to EPA action. See 42 U.S.C. §7607(b)(1). That authorization is of critical importance to the standing inquiry: "Congress has the power to define injuries and articulate chains of causation that will give rise to a case or controversy where none existed before." *Lujan*, 504 U.S., at 580, 112 S.Ct. 2130 (KENNEDY, J., concurring in part and concurring in judgment). "In exercising this power, however, Congress must at the very least identify the injury it seeks to vindicate and relate the injury to the class of persons entitled to bring suit." *Ibid.* We will not, therefore, "entertain citizen suits to vindicate the public's nonconcrete interest in the proper administration of the laws." *Id.*, at 581, 112 S.Ct. 2130.

EPA maintains that because greenhouse gas emissions inflict widespread harm, the doctrine of standing presents an insuperable jurisdictional obstacle. We do not agree. At bottom, "the gist of the question of standing" is whether petitioners have "such a personal stake in the outcome of the controversy as to assure that concrete adverseness which sharpens the presentation of issues upon which the court so largely depends for illumination." *Baker v. Carr*, 369 U.S. 186, 204, 82 S.Ct. 691, 7 L.Ed.2d 663 (1962). As Justice KENNEDY explained in his *Lujan* concurrence:

"While it does not matter how many persons have been injured by the challenged action, the party bringing suit must show that the action injures him in a concrete and personal way. This requirement is not just an empty formality. It preserves the vitality of the adversarial process by assuring both that the parties before the court have an actual, as opposed to professed, stake in the outcome, and that the legal questions presented . . . will be resolved, not in the rarified atmosphere of a debating society, but in a concrete factual context conducive to a realistic appreciation of the consequences of judicial action." 504 U.S., at 581, 112 S.Ct. 2130 (internal quotation marks omitted).

To ensure the proper adversarial presentation, *Lujan* holds that a litigant must demonstrate that it has suffered a concrete and particularized injury that is either actual or imminent, that the injury is fairly traceable to the defendant, and that it is likely that a favorable decision will redress that injury. See *id.*, at 560–561, 112 S.Ct. 2130. However, a litigant to whom Congress has "accorded a procedural right to protect his concrete interests," *id.*, at 572, n. 7, 112 S.Ct. 2130-here, the right to challenge agency action unlawfully withheld, §7607(b)(1)-"can assert that

right without meeting all the normal standards for redressability and immediacy," *ibid.* When a litigant is vested with a procedural right, that litigant has standing if there is some possibility that the requested relief will prompt the injury-causing party to reconsider the decision that allegedly harmed the litigant. *Ibid.*; see also *Sugar Cane Growers Cooperative of Fla. v. Veneman*, 289 F.3d 89, 94–95 (C.A.D.C.2002) ("A [litigant] who alleges a deprivation of a procedural protection to which he is entitled never has to prove that if he had received the procedure the substantive result would have been altered. All that is necessary is to show that the procedural step was connected to the substantive result").

Only one of the petitioners needs to have standing to permit us to consider the petition for review. See *Rumsfeld v. Forum for Academic and Institutional Rights, Inc.*, 547 U.S. 47, 52, n. 2, 126 S.Ct. 1297, 164 L.Ed.2d 156 (2006). We stress here, as did Judge Tatel below, the special position and interest of Massachusetts. It is of considerable relevance that the party seeking review here is a sovereign State and not, as it was in *Lujan*, a private individual.

Well before the creation of the modern administrative state, we recognized that States are not normal litigants for the purposes of invoking federal jurisdiction. As Justice Holmes explained in *Georgia v. Tennessee Copper Co.*, 206 U.S. 230, 237, 27 S.Ct. 618, 51 L.Ed. 1038 (1907), a case in which Georgia sought to protect its citizens from air pollution originating outside its borders:

"The case has been argued largely as if it were one between two private parties; but it is not. The very elements that would be relied upon in a suit between fellow-citizens as a ground for equitable relief are wanting here. The State owns very little of the territory alleged to be affected, and the damage to it capable of estimate in money, possibly, at least, is small. This is a suit by a State for an injury to it in its capacity of *quasi*-sovereign. In that capacity the State has an interest independent of and behind the titles of its citizens, in all the earth and air within its domain. It has the last word as to whether its mountains shall be stripped of their forests and its inhabitants shall breathe pure air."

Just as Georgia's "independent interest...in all the earth and air within its domain" supported federal jurisdiction a century ago, so too does Massachusetts' well-founded desire to preserve its sovereign territory today. Cf. *Alden v. Maine*, 527 U.S. 706, 715, 119 S.Ct. 2240, 144 L.Ed.2d 636 (1999) (observing that in the federal system, the States "are not relegated to the role of mere provinces or political corporations, but retain the dignity, though not the full authority, of sovereignty"). That Massachusetts does in fact own a great deal of the "territory alleged to be affected" only reinforces the conclusion that its stake in the outcome of this case is sufficiently concrete to warrant the exercise of federal judicial power.

When a State enters the Union, it surrenders certain sovereign prerogatives. Massachusetts cannot invade Rhode Island to force reductions in greenhouse gas emissions, it cannot negotiate an emissions treaty with China or India, and in some circumstances the exercise of its police powers to reduce instate motor-vehicle emissions might well be pre-empted. See *Alfred L. Snapp & Son, Inc. v. Puerto Rico ex rel. Barez*, 458 U.S. 592, 607, 102 S.Ct. 3260, 73 L.Ed.2d 995 (1982) ("One helpful indication in determining whether an alleged injury to the health and welfare of its citizens suffices to give the State standing to sue *parens patriae* is whether the injury is one that the State, if it could, would likely attempt to address through its sovereign lawmaking powers").

These sovereign prerogatives are now lodged in the Federal Government, and Congress has ordered EPA to protect Massachusetts (among others) by prescribing standards applicable to the "emission of any air pollutant from any class or classes of new motor vehicle engines, which in [the Administrator's] judgment cause, or contribute to, air pollution which may reasonably be antici-

pated to endanger public health or welfare." 42 U.S.C. §7521(a)(1). Congress has moreover recognized a concomitant procedural right to challenge the rejection of its rulemaking petition as arbitrary and capricious. §7607(b)(1). Given that procedural right and Massachusetts' stake in protecting its quasi-sovereign interests, the Commonwealth is entitled to special solicitude in our standing analysis.

With that in mind, it is clear that petitioners' submissions as they pertain to Massachusetts have satisfied the most demanding standards of the adversarial process. EPA's steadfast refusal to regulate greenhouse gas emissions presents a risk of harm to Massachusetts that is both "actual" and "imminent." *Lujan*, 504 U.S., at 560, 112 S.Ct. 2130 (internal quotation marks omitted). There is, moreover, a "substantial likelihood that the judicial relief requested" will prompt EPA to take steps to reduce that risk. *Duke Power Co. v. Carolina Environmental Study Group, Inc.*, 438 U.S. 59, 79, 98 S.Ct. 2620, 57 L.Ed.2d 595 (1978).

The Injury

The harms associated with climate change are serious and well recognized. Indeed, the NRC Report itself—which EPA regards as an "objective and independent assessment of the relevant science," 68 Fed.Reg. 52930—identifies a number of environmental changes that have already inflicted significant harms, including "the global retreat of mountain glaciers, reduction in snow-cover extent, the earlier spring melting of rivers and lakes, [and] the accelerated rate of rise of sea levels during the 20th century relative to the past few thousand years...." NRC Report 16.

Petitioners allege that this only hints at the environmental damage yet to come. According to the climate scientist Michael MacCracken, "qualified scientific experts involved in climate change research" have reached a "strong consensus" that global warming threatens (among other things) a precipitate rise in sea levels by the end of the century, MacCracken Decl. ¶15, Stdg.App. 207, "severe and irreversible changes to natural ecosystems," *id.*, ¶5(d), at 209, a "significant reduction in water storage in winter snowpack in mountainous regions with direct and important economic consequences," *ibid.*, and an increase in the spread of disease, *id.*, ¶28, at 218–219. He also observes that rising ocean temperatures may contribute to the ferocity of hurricanes. *Id.*, ¶¶23–25, at 216–217.[18]

That these climate-change risks are "widely shared" does not minimize Massachusetts' interest in the outcome of this litigation. See *Federal Election Comm'n v. Akins*, 524 U.S. 11, 24, 118 S.Ct. 1777, 141 L.Ed.2d 10 (1998) ("[W]here a harm is concrete, though widely shared, the Court has found 'injury in fact'"). According to petitioners' unchallenged affidavits, global sea levels rose somewhere between 10 and 20 centimeters over the 20th century as a result of global warming. MacCracken Decl. ¶5(c), Stdg.App. 208. These rising seas have already begun to swallow Massachusetts' coastal land. *Id.*, at 196 (declaration of Paul H. Kirshen ¶5), 216 (MacCracken Decl. ¶23). Because the Commonwealth "owns a substantial portion of the state's coastal property," *id.*, at 171 (declaration of Karst R. Hoogeboom ¶4), it has alleged a particularized injury in its capacity

as a landowner. The severity of that injury will only increase over the course of the next century: If sea levels continue to rise as predicted, one Massachusetts official believes that a significant fraction of coastal property will be "either permanently lost through inundation or temporarily lost through periodic storm surge and flooding events." *Id.*, ¶6, at 172. Remediation costs alone, petitioners allege, could run well into the hundreds of millions of dollars. *Id.*, ¶7, at 172; see also Kirshen Decl. ¶12, at 198.[21]

Causation

EPA does not dispute the existence of a causal connection between man-made greenhouse gas emissions and global warming. At a minimum, therefore, EPA's refusal to regulate such emissions "contributes" to Massachusetts' injuries.

EPA nevertheless maintains that its decision not to regulate greenhouse gas emissions from new motor vehicles contributes so insignificantly to petitioners' injuries that the agency cannot be haled into federal court to answer for them. For the same reason, EPA does not believe that any realistic possibility exists that the relief petitioners seek would mitigate global climate change and remedy their injuries. That is especially so because predicted increases in greenhouse gas emissions from developing nations, particularly

---

18. In this regard, MacCracken's 2004 affidavit-drafted more than a year in advance of Hurricane Katrina-was eerily prescient. Immediately after discussing the "particular concern" that climate change might cause an "increase in the wind speed and peak rate of precipitation of major tropical cyclones (i.e., hurricanes and typhoons)," MacCracken noted that "[s]oil compaction, sea level rise and recurrent storms are destroying approximately 20–30 square miles of Louisiana wetlands each year. These wetlands serve as a 'shock absorber' for storm surges that could inundate New Orleans, significantly enhancing the risk to a major urban population." ¶¶24–25, Stdg.App. 217.

21. In dissent, THE CHIEF JUSTICE dismisses petitioners' submissions as "conclusory," presumably because they do not quantify Massachusetts' land loss with the exactitude he would prefer. He therefore asserts that the Commonwealth's injury is "conjectur[al]." Yet the likelihood that Massachusetts' coastline will recede has nothing to do with whether petitioners have determined the precise metes and bounds of their soon-to-be-flooded land. Petitioners maintain that the seas are rising and will continue to rise, and have alleged that such a rise will lead to the loss of Massachusetts' sovereign territory. No one, save perhaps the dissenters, disputes those allegations. Our cases require nothing more.

China and India, are likely to offset any marginal domestic decrease.

But EPA overstates its case. Its argument rests on the erroneous assumption that a small incremental step, because it is incremental, can never be attacked in a federal judicial forum. Yet accepting that premise would doom most challenges to regulatory action. Agencies, like legislatures, do not generally resolve massive problems in one fell regulatory swoop. See *Williamson v. Lee Optical of Okla., Inc.*, 348 U.S. 483, 489, 75 S.Ct. 461, 99 L.Ed. 563 (1955) ("[A] reform may take one step at a time, addressing itself to the phase of the problem which seems most acute to the legislative mind"). They instead whittle away at them over time, refining their preferred approach as circumstances change and as they develop a more-nuanced understanding of how best to proceed. Cf. *SEC v. Chenery Corp.*, 332 U.S. 194, 202, 67 S.Ct. 1575, 91 L.Ed. 1995 (1947) ("Some principles must await their own development, while others must be adjusted to meet particular, unforeseeable situations"). That a first step might be tentative does not by itself support the notion that federal courts lack jurisdiction to determine whether that step conforms to law.

And reducing domestic automobile emissions is hardly a tentative step. Even leaving aside the other greenhouse gases, the United States transportation sector emits an enormous quantity of carbon dioxide into the atmosphere. . . .

The Remedy

While it may be true that regulating motor-vehicle emissions will not by itself *reverse* global warming, it by no means follows that we lack jurisdiction to decide whether EPA has a duty to take steps to *slow* or *reduce* it. See also *Larson v. Valente*, 456 U.S. 228, 244, n. 15, 102 S.Ct. 1673, 72 L.Ed.2d 33 (1982) ("[A] plaintiff satisfies the redressability requirement when he shows that a favorable decision will relieve a discrete injury to himself. He need not show that a favorable decision will relieve his *every* injury"). Because of the enormity of the potential consequences associated with man-made climate change, the fact that the effectiveness of a remedy might be delayed during the (relatively short) time it takes for a new motor-vehicle fleet to replace an older one is essentially irrelevant. Nor is it dispositive that developing countries such as China and India are poised to increase greenhouse gas emissions substantially over the next century: A reduction in domestic emissions would slow the pace of global emissions increases, no matter what happens elsewhere. . . .

V

The scope of our review of the merits of the statutory issues is narrow. As we have repeated time and again, an agency has broad discretion to choose how best to marshal its limited resources and personnel to carry out its delegated responsibilities. See *Chevron U.S.A. Inc. v. Natural Resources Defense Council, Inc.*, 467 U.S. 837, 842–845, 104 S.Ct. 2778, 81 L.Ed.2d 694 (1984). That discretion is at its height when the agency decides not to bring an enforcement action. Therefore, in *Heckler v. Chaney*, 470 U.S. 821, 105 S.Ct. 1649, 84 L.Ed.2d 714 (1985), we held that an agency's refusal to initiate enforcement proceedings is not ordinarily subject to judicial review. Some debate remains, however, as to the rigor with which we review an agency's denial of a petition for rulemaking.

There are key differences between a denial of a petition for rulemaking and an agency's decision not to initiate an enforcement action. See *American Horse Protection Assn., Inc. v. Lyng*, 812 F.2d 1, 3–4 (C.A.D.C.1987). In contrast to nonenforcement decisions, agency refusals to initiate rulemaking "are less frequent, more apt to involve legal as opposed to factual analysis, and subject to special formalities, including a public explanation." *Id.*, at 4; see also 5 U.S.C. §555(e). They moreover arise out of denials of petitions for rulemaking which (at least in the circumstances here) the affected party had an undoubted procedural right to file in the first instance. Refusals to promulgate rules are thus susceptible to judicial review, though such review is "extremely limited" and "highly deferential." *National Customs Brokers & Forwarders Assn. of America, Inc. v. United States*, 883 F.2d 93, 96 (C.A.D.C.1989).

EPA concluded in its denial of the petition for rulemaking that it lacked authority under 42 U.S.C. §7521(a)(1) to regulate new vehicle emissions because carbon dioxide is not an "air pollutant" as that term is defined in §7602. In the alternative, it concluded that even if it possessed authority, it would decline to do so because regulation would conflict with other administration priorities. As discussed earlier, the Clean Air Act expressly permits review of such an action. §7607(b)(1). We therefore "may reverse any such action found to be . . . arbitrary, capricious, an abuse of discretion, or otherwise not in accordance with law." §7607(d)(9).

VI

On the merits, the first question is whether §202(a)(1) of the Clean Air Act authorizes EPA to regulate greenhouse gas emissions from new motor vehicles in the event that it forms a "judgment" that such emissions contribute to climate change. We have little trouble concluding that it does. In relevant part, §202(a)(1) provides that EPA "shall by regulation prescribe . . . standards applicable to the emission of any air pollutant from any class or classes of new motor vehicles or new motor vehicle engines, which in [the Administrator's] judgment cause, or contribute to, air pollution which may reasonably be anticipated to endanger public health or welfare." 42 U.S.C. §7521(a)(1). Because EPA believes that Congress did not intend it to regulate substances that contribute to climate change, the agency maintains that carbon dioxide is not an "air pollutant" within the meaning of the provision.

The statutory text forecloses EPA's reading. The Clean Air Act's sweeping definition of "air pollutant" includes "*any* air pollution agent or combination of such agents, including *any* physical, chemical . . . substance or matter which is emitted into or otherwise enters the ambient air . . . ." §7602(g) (emphasis added). On its face, the definition embraces all airborne compounds of whatever stripe, and underscores that intent through the repeated use of the word "any." Carbon dioxide, methane, nitrous oxide, and hydrofluorocarbons are without a doubt "physical [and] chemical . . . substance [s] which [are] emitted into . . . the ambient air." The statute is unambiguous.[26] . . .

EPA finally argues that it cannot regulate carbon dioxide emissions from motor vehicles because doing so would require it to tighten

---

26. In dissent, Justice SCALIA maintains that because greenhouse gases permeate the world's atmosphere rather than a limited area near the earth's surface, EPA's exclusion of greenhouse gases from the category of air pollution "agent[s]" is entitled to deference under *Chevron U.S.A. Inc. v. Natural Resources Defense Council, Inc.* 467 U.S. 837, 104 S.Ct. 2778, 81 L.Ed.2d 694 (1984). EPA's distinction, however, finds no support in the text of the statute, which uses the phrase "the ambient air" without distinguishing between atmospheric layers. Moreover, it is a plainly unreasonable reading of a sweeping statutory provision designed to capture

"*any* physical, chemical . . . substance or matter which is emitted into or otherwise enters the ambient air." 42 U.S.C. §7602(g). Justice SCALIA does not (and cannot) explain why Congress would define "air pollutant" so carefully and so broadly, yet confer on EPA the authority to narrow that definition whenever expedient by asserting that a particular substance is not an "agent." At any rate, no party to this dispute contests that greenhouse gases both "ente[r] the ambient air" and tend to warm the atmosphere. They are therefore unquestionably "agent[s]" of air pollution.

mileage standards, a job (according to EPA) that Congress has assigned to DOT. See 68 Fed.Reg. 52929. But that DOT sets mileage standards in no way licenses EPA to shirk its environmental responsibilities. EPA has been charged with protecting the public's "health" and "welfare," 42 U.S.C. §7521(a)(1), a statutory obligation wholly independent of DOT's mandate to promote energy efficiency. See Energy Policy and Conservation Act, §2(5), 89 Stat. 874, 42 U.S.C. §6201(5). The two obligations may overlap, but there is no reason to think the two agencies cannot both administer their obligations and yet avoid inconsistency.

While the Congresses that drafted §202(a)(1) might not have appreciated the possibility that burning fossil fuels could lead to global warming, they did understand that without regulatory flexibility, changing circumstances and scientific developments would soon render the Clean Air Act obsolete. The broad language of §202(a)(1) reflects an intentional effort to confer the flexibility necessary to forestall such obsolescence. See *Pennsylvania Dept. of Corrections v. Yeskey*, 524 U.S. 206, 212, 118 S.Ct. 1952, 141 L.Ed.2d 215 (1998) ("[T]he fact that a statute can be applied in situations not expressly anticipated by Congress does not demonstrate ambiguity. It demonstrates breadth" (internal quotation marks omitted)). Because greenhouse gases fit well within the Clean Air Act's capacious definition of "air pollutant," we hold that EPA has the statutory authority to regulate the emission of such gases from new motor vehicles.

VII

The alternative basis for EPA's decision— that even if it does have statutory authority to regulate greenhouse gases, it would be unwise to do so at this time—rests on reasoning divorced from the statutory text. While the statute does condition the exercise of EPA's authority on its formation of a "judgment,"

42 U.S.C. §7521(a)(1), that judgment must relate to whether an air pollutant "cause[s], or contribute[s] to, air pollution which may reasonably be anticipated to endanger public health or welfare," *ibid.* Put another way, the use of the word "judgment" is not a roving license to ignore the statutory text. It is but a direction to exercise discretion within defined statutory limits.

If EPA makes a finding of endangerment, the Clean Air Act requires the agency to regulate emissions of the deleterious pollutant from new motor vehicles. *Ibid.* (stating that "[EPA] shall by regulation prescribe . . . standards applicable to the emission of any air pollutant from any class of new motor vehicles"). EPA no doubt has significant latitude as to the manner, timing, content, and coordination of its regulations with those of other agencies. But once EPA has responded to a petition for rulemaking, its reasons for action or inaction must conform to the authorizing statute. Under the clear terms of the Clean Air Act, EPA can avoid taking further action only if it determines that greenhouse gases do not contribute to climate change or if it provides some reasonable explanation as to why it cannot or will not exercise its discretion to determine whether they do. *Ibid.* To the extent that this constrains agency discretion to pursue other priorities of the Administrator or the President, this is the congressional design.

EPA has refused to comply with this clear statutory command. Instead, it has offered a laundry list of reasons not to regulate. For example, EPA said that a number of voluntary executive branch programs already provide an effective response to the threat of global warming, 68 Fed.Reg. 52932, that regulating greenhouse gases might impair the President's ability to negotiate with "key developing nations" to reduce emissions, *id.*, at 52931, and that curtailing motor-vehicle emissions would reflect "an inefficient, piecemeal approach to address the climate change issue," *ibid.*

Although we have neither the expertise nor the authority to evaluate these policy judgments, it is evident they have nothing to do with whether greenhouse gas emissions contribute to climate change. Still less do they amount to a reasoned justification for declining to form a scientific judgment. In particular, while the President has broad authority in foreign affairs, that authority does not extend to the refusal to execute domestic laws. In the Global Climate Protection Act of 1987, Congress authorized the State Department-not EPA-to formulate United States foreign policy with reference to environmental matters relating to climate. See §1103(c), 101 Stat. 1409. EPA has made no showing that it issued the ruling in question here after consultation with the State Department. Congress did direct EPA to consult with other agencies in the formulation of its policies and rules, but the State Department is absent from that list. §1103(b).

Nor can EPA avoid its statutory obligation by noting the uncertainty surrounding various features of climate change and concluding that it would therefore be better not to regulate at this time. See 68 Fed.Reg. 52930–52931. If the scientific uncertainty is so profound that it precludes EPA from making a reasoned judgment as to whether greenhouse gases contribute to global warming, EPA must say so. That EPA would prefer not to regulate greenhouse gases because of some residual uncertainty—which, contrary to Justice SCALIA's apparent belief, is in fact all that it said, see 68 Fed.Reg. 52929 ("We do not believe . . . that it would be either effective or appropriate for EPA *to establish [greenhouse gas] standards for motor vehicles* at this time" (emphasis added))—is irrelevant. The statutory question is whether sufficient information exists to make an endangerment finding.

In short, EPA has offered no reasoned explanation for its refusal to decide whether greenhouse gases cause or contribute to climate change. Its action was therefore "arbitrary, capricious, . . . or otherwise not in accordance with law." 42 U.S.C. §7607(d)(9)(A). We need not and do not reach the question whether on remand EPA must make an endangerment finding, or whether policy concerns can inform EPA's actions in the event that it makes such a finding. Cf. *Chevron U.S.A. Inc. v. Natural Resources Defense Council, Inc.*, 467 U.S. 837, 843–844, 104 S.Ct. 2778, 81 L.Ed.2d 694 (1984). We hold only that EPA must ground its reasons for action or inaction in the statute.

VIII

The judgment of the Court of Appeals is reversed, and the case is remanded for further proceedings consistent with this opinion.

CHIEF JUSTICE ROBERTS, WITH WHOM JUSTICE SCALIA, JUSTICE THOMAS, AND JUSTICE ALITO JOIN, DISSENTING:

Global warming may be a "crisis," even "the most pressing environmental problem of our time." Pet. for Cert. 26, 22. Indeed, it may ultimately affect nearly everyone on the planet in some potentially adverse way, and it may be that governments have done too little to address it. It is not a problem, however, that has escaped the attention of policymakers in the Executive and Legislative Branches of our Government, who continue to consider regulatory, legislative, and treaty-based means of addressing global climate change.

Apparently dissatisfied with the pace of progress on this issue in the elected branches, petitioners have come to the courts claiming broad-ranging injury, and attempting to tie that injury to the Government's alleged failure to comply with a rather narrow statutory provision. I would reject these challenges as nonjusticiable. Such a conclusion involves no judgment on whether global warming exists, what causes it, or the extent of the problem. Nor does it render petitioners without recourse. This Court's standing jurisprudence simply recognizes that redress of grievances of the sort at issue here "is the function of Congress and the Chief Executive," not the federal courts. *Lujan v. Defenders of Wildlife*, 504 U.S. 555, 576, 112 S.Ct. 2130, 119 L.Ed.2d 351 (1992). I would vacate the judgment below and remand for dismissal of the petitions for review.

I

Article III, §2, of the Constitution limits the federal judicial power to the adjudication of "Cases" and "Controversies." "If a dispute is not a proper case or controversy, the courts have no business deciding it, or expounding the law in the course of doing so." *Daimler-Chrysler Corp. v. Cuno*, 547 U.S. ----, ----, 126 S.Ct. 1854, 1860–1861, 164 L.Ed.2d 589 (2006)....

Relaxing Article III standing requirements because asserted injuries are pressed by a State, however, has no basis in our jurisprudence, and support for any such "special solicitude" is conspicuously absent from the Court's opinion....

On top of everything else, the Court overlooks the fact that our cases cast significant doubt on a State's standing to assert a quasi-sovereign interest-as opposed to a direct injury-against the Federal Government. As a general rule, we have held that while a State might assert a quasi-sovereign right as *parens patriae* "for the protection of its citizens, it is no part of its duty or power to enforce their rights in respect of their relations with the Federal Government. In that field it is the United States, and not the State, which represents them." *Massachusetts v. Mellon*, 262 U.S. 447, 485–486, 43 S.Ct. 597, 67 L.Ed. 1078 (1923) (citation omitted); see also *Alfred L. Snapp & Son, supra*, at 610, n. 16, 102 S.Ct. 3260....

II

It is not at all clear how the Court's "special solicitude" for Massachusetts plays out in the standing analysis, except as an implicit concession that petitioners cannot establish standing on traditional terms. But the status of Massachusetts as a State cannot compensate for petitioners' failure to demonstrate injury in fact, causation, and redressability.

When the Court actually applies the three-part test, it focuses, as did the dissent below, see 415 F.3d 50, 64 (C.A.D.C.2005) (opinion of Tatel, J.), on the State's asserted loss of coastal land as the injury in fact. If petitioners rely on loss of land as the Article III injury, however, they must ground the rest of the standing analysis in that specific injury. That alleged injury must be "concrete and particularized," *Defenders of Wildlife*, 504 U.S., at 560, 112 S.Ct. 2130, and "distinct and palpable," *Allen*, 468 U.S., at 751, 104 S.Ct. 3315 (internal quotation marks omitted). Central to this concept of "particularized" injury is the requirement that a plaintiff be affected in a "personal and individual way," *Defenders of Wildlife*, 504 U.S., at 560, n. 1, 112 S.Ct. 2130, and seek relief that "directly and tangibly benefits him" in a manner distinct from its impact on "the public at large," *id.*, at 573–574, 112 S.Ct. 2130. Without "particularized injury, there can be no confidence of 'a real need to exercise the power of judicial review' or that relief can be framed 'no broader than required by the precise facts to which the court's ruling would be applied.'" *Warth v. Seldin*, 422 U.S. 490, 508, 95 S.Ct. 2197, 45 L.Ed.2d 343 (1975) (quoting *Schlesinger v. Reservists Comm. to Stop the War*, 418 U.S. 208, 221–222, 94 S.Ct. 2925, 41 L.Ed.2d 706 (1974)).

The very concept of global warming seems inconsistent with this particularization requirement. Global warming is a phenomenon "harmful to humanity at large," 415 F.3d, at 60 (Sentelle, J., dissenting in part and concurring in judgment), and the redress petitioners seek is focused no more on them than on the public generally-it is literally to change the atmosphere around the world.

If petitioners' particularized injury is loss of coastal land, it is also that injury that must be "actual or imminent, not conjectural or hypothetical," *Defenders of Wildlife, supra*, at 560, 112 S.Ct. 2130 (internal quotation marks omitted), "real and immediate," *Los Angeles v. Lyons*, 461 U.S. 95, 102, 103 S.Ct. 1660, 75 L.Ed.2d 675 (1983) (internal quotation marks omitted), and "certainly impending," *Whitmore v. Arkansas*, 495 U.S. 149, 158, 110 S.Ct. 1717, 109 L.Ed.2d 135 (1990) (internal quotation marks omitted).

As to "actual" injury, the Court observes that "global sea levels rose somewhere between 10 and 20 centimeters over the 20th century as a result of global warming" and that "[t]hese rising seas have already begun to swallow Massachusetts' coastal land." *Ante*, at 1456. But none of petitioners' declarations supports that connection. One declaration states that "a rise in sea level due to climate change is occurring on the coast of Massachusetts, in the metropolitan Boston area," but there is no elaboration. Petitioners' Standing Appendix in No. 03-1361, etc. (CADC), p. 196 (Stdg.App.). And the declarant goes on to identify a "significan[t]" *non*-global-warming cause of Boston's rising sea level: land subsidence. *Id.*, at 197; see also *id.*, at 216. Thus, aside from a single conclusory statement, there is nothing in petitioners' 43 standing declarations and accompanying exhibits to support an inference of actual loss of Massachusetts coastal land from 20th century global sea level increases. It is pure conjecture. . . .

III

Petitioners' reliance on Massachusetts's loss of coastal land as their injury in fact for standing purposes creates insurmountable problems for them with respect to causation and redressability. To establish standing, petitioners must show a causal connection between that specific injury and the lack of new motor vehicle greenhouse gas emission standards, and that the promulgation of such standards would likely redress that injury. As is often the case, the questions of causation and redressability overlap. See *Allen*, 468 U.S., at 753, n. 19, 104 S.Ct. 3315 (observing that the two requirements were "initially articulated by this Court as two facets of a single causation requirement" (internal quotation marks omitted)). And importantly, when a party is challenging the Government's allegedly unlawful regulation, or lack of regulation, of a third party, satisfying the causation and redressability requirements becomes "substantially more difficult." *Defenders of Wildlife, supra*, at 562, 112 S.Ct. 2130 (internal quotation marks omitted); see also *Warth, supra*, at 504–505, 95 S.Ct. 2197. . . .

The Court ignores the complexities of global warming, and does so by now disregarding the "particularized" injury it relied on in step one, and using the dire nature of global warming itself as a bootstrap for finding causation and redressability. First, it is important to recognize the extent of the emissions at issue here. Because local greenhouse gas emissions disperse throughout the atmosphere and remain there for anywhere from 50 to 200 years, it is global emissions data that are relevant. See App. to Pet. for Cert. A-73. According to one of petitioners' declarations, domestic motor vehicles contribute about 6 percent of global carbon dioxide emissions and 4 percent of global greenhouse gas emissions. Stdg.App. 232. The amount of global emissions at issue here is smaller still; §202(a)(1) of the Clean Air Act covers only *new* motor vehicles and *new* motor vehicle engines, so petitioners' desired emission standards might reduce only a fraction of 4 percent of global emissions. . . .

Petitioners are never able to trace their alleged injuries back through this complex web to the fractional amount of global emissions that might have been limited with EPA standards. In light of the bit-part domestic new motor vehicle greenhouse gas emissions have played in what petitioners describe as a 150-year global phenomenon, and the myriad additional factors bearing on petitioners' alleged injury—the loss of Massachusetts coastal land—the connection is far too speculative to establish causation.

IV

Redressability is even more problematic. To the tenuous link between petitioners' alleged injury and the indeterminate fractional domestic emissions at issue here, add the fact that petitioners cannot meaningfully predict what will come of the 80 percent of global greenhouse gas emissions that originate outside the United States. As the Court acknowledges, "developing countries such as China and India are poised to increase greenhouse gas emissions substantially over the next century," so the domestic emissions at issue here may become an increasingly marginal portion of global emissions, and any decreases produced by petitioners' desired standards are likely to be overwhelmed many times over by emissions increases elsewhere in the world. . . .

V

Petitioners' difficulty in demonstrating causation and redressability is not surprising given the evident mismatch between the source of their alleged injury-catastrophic global warming-and the narrow subject matter of the Clean Air Act provision at issue in this suit. The mismatch suggests that petitioners' true goal for this litigation may be more symbolic than anything else. The constitutional role of the courts, however, is to decide concrete cases-not to serve as a convenient forum for policy debates. See *Valley Forge Christian College v. Americans United for Separation of Church and State, Inc.*, 454 U.S. 464, 472, 102 S.Ct. 752, 70 L.Ed.2d 700 (1982) ("[Standing] tends to assure that the legal questions presented to the court will be resolved, not in the rarified atmosphere of a debating society, but in a concrete factual context conducive to a realistic appreciation of the consequences of judicial action").

When dealing with legal doctrine phrased in terms of what is "fairly" traceable or "likely" to be redressed, it is perhaps not surprising that the matter is subject to some debate. But in considering how loosely or rigorously to define those adverbs, it is vital to keep in mind the purpose of the inquiry. The limitation of the judicial power to cases and controversies "is crucial in maintaining the tripartite allocation of power set forth in the Constitution." *DaimlerChrysler*, 547 U.S., at ----, 126 S.Ct., at 1860–1861 (internal quotation marks omitted). In my view, the Court today—addressing Article III's "core component of standing," *Defenders of Wildlife, supra*, at 560, 112 S.Ct. 2130—fails to take this limitation seriously.

To be fair, it is not the first time the Court has done so. Today's decision recalls the previous high-water mark of diluted standing requirements, *United States v. Students Challenging Regulatory Agency Procedures (SCRAP)*, 412 U.S. 669, 93 S.Ct. 2405, 37 L.Ed.2d 254 (1973). *SCRAP* involved "[p]robably the most attenuated injury conferring Art. III standing" and "surely went to the very outer limit of the law"-until today. *Whitmore*, 495 U.S., at 158–159, 110 S.Ct. 1717; see also *Lujan v. National Wildlife Federation*, 497 U.S. 871, 889, 110 S.Ct. 3177, 111 L.Ed.2d 695 (1990) (*SCRAP* "has never since been emulated by this Court"). In *SCRAP*, the Court based an environmental group's standing to challenge a railroad freight rate surcharge on the group's allegation that increases in railroad rates would cause an increase in the use of non-recyclable goods, resulting in the increased need for natural resources to produce such goods. According to the group, some of these resources might be taken from the Washington area, resulting in increased refuse that might find its way into area parks, harming the group's members. 412 U.S., at 688, 93 S.Ct. 2405.

Over time, *SCRAP* became emblematic not of the looseness of Article III standing requirements, but of how utterly manipulable they are if not taken seriously as a matter of judicial self-restraint. *SCRAP* made standing seem a lawyer's game, rather than a fundamental limitation ensuring that courts function as courts and not intrude on the politically accountable branches. Today's decision is *SCRAP* for a new generation.

Perhaps the Court recognizes as much. How else to explain its need to devise a new doctrine of state standing to support its result? The good news is that the Court's "special solicitude" for Massachusetts limits the future applicability of the diluted standing requirements applied in this case. The bad news is that the Court's self-professed relaxation of those Article III requirements has caused us to transgress "the proper-and-properly limited-role of the courts in a democratic society." *Allen*, 468 U.S., at 750, 104 S.Ct. 3315 (internal quotation marks omitted). I respectfully dissent.

JUSTICE SCALIA, WITH WHOM THE CHIEF JUSTICE, JUSTICE THOMAS, AND JUSTICE ALITO JOIN, DISSENTING:

I join THE CHIEF JUSTICE's opinion in full, and would hold that this Court has no jurisdiction to decide this case because petitioners lack standing. The Court having decided otherwise, it is appropriate for me to note my dissent on the merits.

I

A

The provision of law at the heart of this case is §202(a)(1) of the Clean Air Act (CAA), which provides that the Administrator of the Environmental Protection Agency (EPA) "shall by regulation prescribe...standards applicable to the emission of any air pollutant from any class or classes of new motor vehicles or new motor vehicle engines, which *in his judgment* cause, or contribute to, air pollution which may reasonably be anticipated to endanger public health or welfare." 42 U.S.C. §7521(a)(1) (emphasis added). As the Court recognizes, the statute "condition[s] the exercise of EPA's authority on its formation of a 'judgment.'" There is no dispute that the Administrator has made no such judgment in this case...

The question thus arises: Does anything *require* the Administrator to make a "judgment" whenever a petition for rulemaking is filed? Without citation of the statute or any other authority, the Court says yes. Why is that so? When Congress wishes to make private action force an agency's hand, it knows how to do so. See, *e.g., Brock v. Pierce County*, 476 U.S. 253, 254–255, 106 S.Ct. 1834, 90 L.Ed.2d 248 (1986) (discussing the Comprehensive Employment and Training Act (CETA), 92 Stat. 1926, 29 U.S.C. §816(b) (1976 ed., Supp. V), which "provide[d] that the Secretary of Labor 'shall' issue a final determination as to the misuse of CETA funds by a grant recipient within 120 days after receiving a complaint alleging such misuse"). Where does the CAA say that the EPA Administrator is required to come to a decision on this question whenever a rulemaking petition is filed? The Court points to no such provision because none exists.

Instead, the Court invents a multiple-choice question that the EPA Administrator must answer when a petition for rulemaking is filed. The Administrator must exercise his judgment in one of three ways: (a) by concluding that the pollutant *does* cause, or contribute to, air pollution that endangers public welfare (in which case EPA is required to regulate); (b) by concluding that the pollutant *does not* cause, or contribute to, air pollution that endangers public welfare (in which case EPA is *not* required to regulate); or (c) by "provid[ing] some reasonable explanation as to why it cannot or will not exercise its discretion to determine whether" greenhouse gases endanger public welfare (in which case EPA is *not* required to regulate).

I am willing to assume, for the sake of argument, that the Administrator's discretion in this regard is not entirely unbounded— that if he has no reasonable basis for deferring judgment he must grasp the nettle at once. The Court, however, with no basis in text or precedent, rejects all of EPA's stated "policy judgments" as not "amount[ing] to a reasoned justification," *ante*, at 1463, effectively narrowing the universe of potential reasonable bases to a single one: Judgment can be delayed *only* if the Administrator concludes that "the scientific uncertainty is [too] profound." *Ibid*. The Administrator is precluded from concluding *for other reasons* "that it would...be better not to regulate at this time." *Ibid*.[1] Such other reasons— perfectly valid reasons—were set forth in the agency's statement....

...When the Administrator *makes* a judgment whether to regulate greenhouse gases, that judgment must relate to whether they are air pollutants that "cause, or contribute to, air pollution which may reasonably be anticipated to endanger public health or welfare." 42 U.S.C. §7521(a)(1). But the statute says *nothing at all* about the reasons for which the Administrator may *defer* making a judgment-the permissible reasons for deciding

not to grapple with the issue at the present time. Thus, the various "policy" rationales that the Court criticizes are not "divorced from the statutory text," except in the sense that the statutory text is silent, as texts are often silent about permissible reasons for the exercise of agency discretion. The reasons the EPA gave are surely considerations executive agencies *regularly* take into account (and *ought* to take into account) when deciding whether to consider entering a new field: the impact such entry would have on other Executive Branch programs and on foreign policy. There is no basis in law for the Court's imposed limitation.

EPA's interpretation of the discretion conferred by the statutory reference to "its judgment" is not only reasonable, it is the most natural reading of the text. The Court nowhere explains why this interpretation is incorrect, let alone why it is not entitled to deference under *Chevron U.S.A. Inc. v. Natural Resources Defense Council, Inc.*, 467 U.S. 837, 104 S.Ct. 2778, 81 L.Ed.2d 694 (1984). As the Administrator acted within the law in declining to make a "judgment" for the policy reasons above set forth, I would uphold the decision to deny the rulemaking petition on that ground alone.

B

Even on the Court's own terms, however, the same conclusion follows. As mentioned above, the Court gives EPA the option of determining that the science is too uncertain to allow it to form a "judgment" as to whether greenhouse gases endanger public welfare. Attached to this option (on what basis is unclear) is an essay requirement: "If," the Court says, "the scientific uncertainty is so profound that it precludes EPA from making a reasoned judgment as to whether

---

1. The Court's way of putting it is, of course, not quite accurate. The issue is whether it would be better *to defer the decision about whether to exercise*

judgment. This has the *effect* of deferring regulation but is quite a different determination.

greenhouse gases contribute to global warming, EPA must say so." But EPA *has* said precisely that—and at great length, based on information contained in a 2001 report by the National Research Council (NRC) entitled Climate Change Science: An Analysis of Some Key Questions:

"...The science of climate change is extraordinarily complex and still evolving. Although there have been substantial advances in climate change science, there continue to be important uncertainties in our understanding of the factors that may affect future climate change and how it should be addressed.... The NRC noted, in particular, that '[t]he understanding of the relationships between weather/climate and human health is in its infancy and therefore the health consequences of climate change are poorly understood.' Substantial scientific uncertainties limit our ability to assess each of these factors and to separate out those changes resulting from natural variability from those that are directly the result of increases in anthropogenic GHGs. Reducing the wide range of uncertainty inherent in current model predictions will require major advances in understanding and modeling of the factors that determine atmospheric concentrations of greenhouse gases and aerosols, and the processes that determine the sensitivity of the climate system." 68 Fed.Reg. 52930.

I simply cannot conceive of what else the Court would like EPA to say.

II

A

Even before reaching its discussion of the word "judgment," the Court makes another significant error when it concludes that "§202(a)(1) of the Clean Air Act *authorizes* EPA to regulate greenhouse gas emissions from new motor vehicles in the event that it forms a 'judgment' that such emissions contribute to climate change." For such authorization, the Court relies on what it calls "the Clean Air Act's capacious definition of 'air pollutant.'"

"Air pollutant" is defined by the Act as "any air pollution agent or combination of such agents, including any physical, chemical,...substance or matter which is emitted into or otherwise enters the ambient air." 42 U.S.C. §7602(g). The Court is correct that "[c]arbon dioxide, methane, nitrous oxide, and hydrofluorocarbons," *ante*, at 1462, fit within the second half of that definition: They are "physical, chemical,...substance[s] or matter which [are] emitted into or otherwise ente[r] the ambient air." But the Court mistakenly believes this to be the end of the analysis. In order to be an "air pollutant" under the Act's definition, the "substance or matter [being] emitted into...the ambient air" must also meet the *first* half of the definition—namely, it must be an "air pollution agent or combination of such agents." The Court simply pretends this half of the definition does not exist....

It is perfectly reasonable to view the definition of "air pollutant" in its entirety: An air pollutant *can* be "any physical, chemical,...substance or matter which is emitted into or otherwise enters the ambient air," but only if it retains the general characteristic of being an "air pollution agent or combination of such agents." This is precisely the conclusion EPA reached...

B

Using (as we ought to) EPA's interpretation of the definition of "air pollutant," we must next determine whether greenhouse gases are "agent[s]" of "air pollution." If so, the statute would authorize regulation; if not, EPA would lack authority.

Unlike "air pollutants," the term "air pollution" is not itself defined by the CAA; thus, once again we must accept EPA's interpretation of that ambiguous term, provided its interpretation is a "permissible construction of the statute." *Chevron*, 467 U.S., at 843, 104 S.Ct. 2778. In this case, the petition for rulemaking asked EPA for "regulation of [greenhouse gas] emissions from motor vehicles to reduce the risk of global climate change." 68 Fed.Reg. 52925. Thus, in deciding whether it had authority to regulate, EPA had to determine whether the concentration of greenhouse gases assertedly responsible for "global climate change" qualifies as "air pollution." EPA began with the common-sense observation that the "[p]roblems associated with atmospheric concentrations of CO_2," *id.*, at 52927, bear little resemblance to what would naturally be termed "air pollution" ... [because] regulating the buildup of CO_2 and other greenhouse gases in the upper reaches of the atmosphere, which is alleged to be causing global climate change, is not akin to regulating the concentration of some substance that is *polluting* the *air*.

We need look no further than the dictionary for confirmation that this interpretation of "air pollution" is eminently reasonable. The definition of "pollute," of course, is "[t]o make or render impure or unclean." Webster's New International Dictionary 1910 (2d ed. 1949). And the first three definitions of "air" are as follows: (1) "[t]he invisible, odorless, and tasteless mixture of gases which surrounds the earth"; (2) "[t]he body of the earth's atmosphere; esp., the part of it near the earth, as distinguished from the upper rarefied part"; (3) "[a] portion of air or of the air considered with respect to physical characteristics or as affecting the senses." *Id.*, at 54. EPA's conception of "air pollution"—

focusing on impurities in the "ambient air" "at ground level or near the surface of the earth"—is perfectly consistent with the natural meaning of that term.

In the end, EPA concluded that since "CAA authorization to regulate is generally based on a finding that an air pollutant causes or contributes to air pollution," 68 Fed.Reg. 52928, the concentrations of CO_2 and other greenhouse gases allegedly affecting the global climate are beyond the scope of CAA's authorization to regulate. "[T]he term 'air pollution' as used in the regulatory provisions cannot be interpreted to encompass global climate change." *Ibid.* Once again, the Court utterly fails to explain why this interpretation is incorrect, let alone so unreasonable as to be unworthy of *Chevron* deference.

The Court's alarm over global warming may or may not be justified, but it ought not distort the outcome of this litigation. This is a straightforward administrative law case, in which Congress has passed a malleable statute giving broad discretion, not to us but to an executive agency. No matter how important the underlying policy issues at stake, this Court has no business substituting its own desired outcome for the reasoned judgment of the responsible agency.

■ **NOTES**

1. Through its first six years, the administration of President George W. Bush compiled a record of steadfast refusal to address global warming as a serious issue. In fact, the Bush administration instead became known for having disputed the notion that there *is* a global warming problem, and for having attempted to silence federal government scientists who insisted that global warming is occurring. See, e.g., Andrew Revkin (2005) "Bush Aide Softened Greenhouse Gas Links to Global Warming," *New York Times*, June 8, p. 1; A. Regalado and J. Carlton (2006) "NOAA Scientists Say Hurricanes, Warming Linked," *Wall Street Journal*, Feb. 16, p. 1.

2. President Bush responded to the Supreme Court's decision by issuing an executive order directing the Environmental Protection Agency and the departments of Transportation, Energy, and Agriculture to cooperate on writing regulations to cut gasoline use and control greenhouse gas emission [*Environment Reporter* 38(20): 113 (2007)]. He directed EPA, in conjunction with the National Highway Traffic Safety Administration, the Department of Energy, the Department of Agriculture, and other agencies, to issue a rulemaking to implement his "20-in-10" program to reduce projected gasoline consumption 20 percent by 2017. EPA also announced that by the end of 2008, it would issue a final rule to boost the use of biofuels, including coal-to-liquids, and other alternative fuels to 35 billion gallons by 2017 from its requirement of 4.7 billion gallons of biofuels in 2007 [*Environment Reporter* 38(37): 2011 (2007)].

3. What alternatives are available to EPA in responding to the Supreme Court's decision? What *must* the agency do in response to this decision?

4. In addition to being a primer on global warming, this case also is a primer on the law of Article III standing to sue (discussed in detail in chapter 5). Under the view of Article III standing articulated in the dissent of Chief Justice Roberts, would anyone other than a federal regulatory agency be able to invoke the jurisdiction of the federal courts to address complex, widespread environmental issues such a global warming? As discussed in both the majority and dissenting opinions, the doctrine of standing was developed by the Supreme Court as a means of ensuring that the federal courts decide real, concrete "cases or controversies" rather than abstract, hypothetical, or purely political issues. Does the analysis conducted by Justice Stevens in the majority opinion satisfy that purpose? Does the issue turn on whether one believes that carbon dioxide emissions from motor vehicles contribute to ongoing climate change?

5. The case is also a primer on the degree of deference due to federal agency decision making. The concept of "*Chevron* deference" stressed by Justice Scalia in his dissent refers to the court's decision in *Chevron U.S.A. Inc. v. Natural Resources Defense Council, Inc.*, 467 U.S. 837 (1984). As discussed in chapter 5, that case affirms the principle that a federal agency may not interpret a federal statute it administers in a manner that conflicts with the plain statutory language or clear legislative history. Where the statute and legislative history are ambiguous, however, the agency is to be afforded deference in construing the statute, so long as the agency's interpretation is reasonable in light of the language, purpose, and history of the statute. Was the situation before the court here one that afforded EPA the discretion to take no action under the Clean Air Act to reduce CO_2 emission from mobile sources? In other words, does the plain language of section 202(a)(1) compel EPA to take action? If not, was the agency's interpretation of that provision reasonable in light of the evi-

dence on the relationship between CO_2 emissions and global warming? Does Justice Scalia's deference to the agency's interpretation give appropriate consideration to the precautionary nature of section 202(a)(1)? (See footnote 7 in the opinion.)

6. Note that the plaintiffs here sought review of EPA's (in)action directly in the circuit court of appeals, rather than going first to the federal district court as would be the usual process under the Administrative Procedure Act. They were able to do this because section 307(b) of the Clean Air Act specifies that the circuit courts have jurisdiction to review "any...final action taken" by EPA under the act [42 U.S.C. §7607(b)]. ▪

In the absence of a comprehensive federal program, there have been a variety of regional, state, and local initiatives to address GHGs. Almost two-thirds of the states, often with the assistance of EPA, have conducted their own emission inventories. Many states have used inventory data to develop action plans to reduce their GHG emissions, and some have implemented programs to reduce GHG emissions. By May 2001, 19 states had completed greenhouse gas reduction plans, with several others initiating such plans, while 134 cities and counties were participating in commitments to reduce contributions. See "State Officials Want Bush to Act on Global Warming," *Car Lines*, August 2002, http://walshcarlines.com. Eight states in the Northeast, including New York, have collaborated to establish a regional greenhouse gas registry under the Northeast States for Coordinated Air Use Management (NESCAUM). The states under NESCAUM have committed to establishing a regional CO_2 cap-and-trade program for power plants.[87] This program, known as the Regional Greenhouse Gas Initiative, is to begin in 2009. Overall, a variety of state and local initiatives, such as the establishment of climate change commissions, the development of GHG inventories, the mapping of action plans to identify GHG reduction opportunities, and the implementation of energy efficiency standards, are currently being pursued throughout the country.

In the West, California enacted legislation in 2002 directing the California Air Resources Board to adopt regulations that "achieve the maximum feasible reduction of greenhouse gases" from passenger vehicles and light-duty trucks.[88] The California plan calls for CARB to implement such regulations beginning with model year 2009 vehicles. An auto industry lawsuit challenging these regulations was rejected in late 2007 [*Central Valley Chrysler-Jeep, Inc. v. Goldstone*, No. 04-6663 (E.D. Cal. Dec. 11, 2007)], but EPA subsequently denied California's request for the federal waiver that would allow their implementation. As this book goes to press, several states

---

87. Governor George Pataki, "Governor Announces Cooperation on Clean Air Initiative" (press release, July 24, 2003). www.state.ny.us/governor/press/year03/july24_03.htm (last viewed on 12/10/2004).

88. Assembly Bill No. 1493, June 22, 2002 California Legislature, 2001–02 Regular Session.

have announced their intention to join California in a lawsuit seeking to overturn EPA's decision. In 2007, Governor Arnold Schwarzenneger issued an executive order establishing a low carbon fuel standard under which California petroleum refiners and importers will be required to reduce the "GHG intensity" of the fuels brought into the state by 10% by 2010.

H.   BEYOND THE TRADITIONAL INTERNAL COMBUSTION ENGINE

Facing stricter federal and state regulations, international concerns over global climate change, and public pressure for more sustainable transportation, the auto industry has invested in a range of pollution-reducing technologies. These include incremental innovations in traditional gasoline and diesel engines and emission control equipment, as well as more radical innovations such as alternatively powered vehicles. In general, the latter approach implies a shift away from a fossil fuel-based infrastructure, while the former represents an attempt to make improvements within the confines of that infrastructure.[89] Considerable research effort has been devoted to finding replacements for the traditional internal combustion engine (ICE). The alternatives explored range from lightweight vehicles integrating advanced ICEs to alternatively powered vehicles such as the hybrid electric and fuel-cell vehicles.

Perhaps the most ambitious regulatory program pushing for alternatives to the traditional ICE has been California's Zero Emission Vehicle (ZEV) Program. Begun in 1990, the ZEV program mandates that an increasing percentage of the vehicles sold in California be zero or partial-zero emission vehicles.[90] The program has proven to be one of the more technology-forcing in history and, correspondingly, one of the more contentious. Legal challenges from the auto industry, coupled with slow development of vehicle technology, caused the ZEV requirements to be substantially

---

89. It should be noted, however, that most current efforts to transition to a hydrogen economy are based on obtaining hydrogen from traditional fossil fuels such as gasoline, diesel, and natural gas, and are thereby dependent on the current infrastructure.

90. The ZEV program is part of a larger low-emission vehicle program in California. The state has established several categories of low- to zero-emission vehicles. Low-emission vehicles (LEVs) are those that meet only the basic, least stringent emission standard applicable to all new cars sold in California in 2004 and beyond. Ultra low-emission vehicles (ULEVs) are 50% cleaner than the average new 2004 model year vehicle. Super ultra-low-emission vehicles (SULEVs) are 90% cleaner than the average new 2004 model year vehicle. Partial zero-emission vehicles (PZEVs) meet SULEV tailpipe emission standards, have a 15-year or 150,000-mile warranty on some parts, and have zero evaporative emissions. More than thirty models reportedly meet this standard, including some Ford Focus, Honda Accord, and BMW 325i models. Advanced technology PZEVs (AT PZEV) are hybrids or compressed natural gas vehicles that meet PZEV emission standards. Examples include the Toyota Prius, Honda Civic Hybrid, and Honda Insight. Finally, zero-emission vehicles (ZEVs) have zero tailpipe emissions. They include electric cars and fuel cell cars. Very few of these exist at present. See "New Cars Meet Strict Pollution Standard, Hit Road in Big Numbers," *San Jose Mercury News*, August 6, 2004.

relaxed and delayed from 1998 to 2005.[91] Moreover, the Supreme Court ruled in 2004 that certain "fleet rules" promulgated by California's South Coast Air Quality Management District—which required operators of specified motor vehicle fleets to purchase alternative-fueled vehicles or vehicles that met specified emission limitations—were preempted by Section 209(a) of the Clean Air Act. See *Engine Manufacturers Ass'n. v. South Coast Air Quality Management District*, 541 U.S. 246 (2004). Nonetheless, the ZEV program has pushed industry to seriously research and develop the technologies that are now appearing in hybrid and fuel cell vehicles.

In the next section we briefly explore some of the incremental innovations being pursued with ICE vehicles, and examine one of the more fundamental innovations, the electric-drive vehicle.

Cali forcing innovation, hybrid electric

1. The New Breed of ICEs

The internal combustion engine represents a mature technology. ICEs are normally classified as reciprocating or rotary, spark ignition or compression ignition, and two- or four-stroke. At present, most passenger vehicles on the roads in the United States are fueled by gasoline and powered by reciprocating, spark-ignited, four-stroke engines.[92] Gasoline-powered engines rely on a spark from a spark plug to ignite an injected mixture of air and fuel. Diesel-powered engines, more commonly found in heavy-duty vehicles and in the passenger cars of Europe, rely on the heat generated during compression to cause combustion. Diesel-powered ICEs typically operate at higher temperatures and compression ratios. As a consequence, the diesel engine's combustion process is 15 to 20% more efficient than that of the gas engine, and this improved engine efficiency results in greater fuel economy.[93] On the other hand, diesels historically generate higher levels of particulate and NO_x emissions than their gasoline counterparts. All four-stroke engines, whether gasoline or diesel, emit

---

91. Automakers challenged the authority of the California Air Resources Board to promulgate part of the ZEV program, arguing that the agency was effectively attempting to regulate fuel economy. A federal judge placed a 2-year injunction on the program in June 2002. The California Air Resources Board settled with automakers after an appeal was heard.

92. The fuel intake, compression, power, and exhaust cycles comprise the "four strokes" of the piston.

93. "Efficiency" here is measured as the amount of useful work generated by a given amount of fuel. The overall fuel economy improvements can be somewhat complex because diesel contains more energy per gallon than its gasoline counterpart. Thus, while diesels may traditionally have a 15–20% better fuel economy (miles/gallon) than gasoline vehicles, on a fuel efficiency basis (miles/unit of energy such as a British thermal unit), diesels have only a 6–8% advantage. In addition, the energy required to process low-sulfur diesel fuels is higher than that for reformulated gasoline, which reduces the efficiency of the fuel over the complete life cycle. For more details, see Patricia Monahan and David Friedman (2004) *The Diesel Dilemma: Diesel's Role in the Race for Clean Cars*, Union of Concerned Scientists, Cambridge, MA, and K. Stork et al. (1997) "Another Way to Go? Some Implications of a Light-Duty Diesel Strategy." Argonne National Laboratory, 76th Annual Meeting of the Transportation Research Board, Washington D.C.

nitrogen oxides, carbon monoxide, carbon dioxide, and unburned hydrocarbons as by-products of combustion. Strategies to reduce emissions from gasoline and diesel engine vehicles have largely been incremental,[94] and have focused on three general approaches.

The first approach has involved improvements to the efficiency of the engine and/or transmission to reduce emissions emanating from the engine itself (i.e., the "engine-out" exhaust streams). The focus here has been on optimizing the combustion process and on minimizing the losses that occur during the conversion of chemical combustion energy (from the engine) to mechanical energy (to turn the wheels). These improvements can lead to increased fuel economy (miles traveled per gallon) as well as reduced emissions. Engine and transmission improvements that are currently available for diesel- and gasoline-powered vehicles[95] include direct fuel injection, variable valve lift and timing, and cylinder deactivation.[96] Direct injection allows a precise amount of fuel to be injected directly into the engine cylinders where combustion occurs. It removes the need to mix fuel and air prior to combustion, essentially eliminating the need for a carburetor and improving engine efficiency. Variable valve lift and timing refers to the ability to better control the intake and exhaust valves on an engine, resulting in more efficient and complete utilization of engine cylinders across different speeds. This added control produces greater engine efficiency and power. Cylinder deactivation (also known as a variable displacement engine) switches off engine cylinders when their power is not needed, thus improving fuel economy. All of these innovations have been enabled by the incorporation of on-board diagnostic systems (also known as engine management systems) that use microprocessors, sensors to monitor conditions, and software to provide real-time control and optimization of engine performance. Other examples of this approach are measures that reduce friction and those that reduce overall weight.

The second general approach has been the refinement of exhaust control equipment (or "aftertreatment" technologies) to treat engine-out exhaust. This can lead to reductions in emissions, but may also reduce fuel economy because of the additional energy losses from the exhaust conversion process. Exhaust control technologies that are at present available for both gasoline- and diesel-powered vehicles

94. U.S. EPA (2005) *Progress Report on Clean and Efficient Automotive Technologies Under Development at EPA: Interim Technical Report*, EPA 420-R-04-002, Washington, D.C.; U.S. EPA Office of Transportation and Air Quality (2004) *Interim Report: New Powertrain Technologies and Their Projected Costs*, Washington, D.C.

95. Note that while these technologies are commercially available, they are not applied to all models or classes of vehicles. In many cases, the diffusion of the technology takes more than 10–15 years to become ubiquitous. Some technologies are not aimed at exclusively reducing emissions but may also be designed to enhance performance or improve efficiency. For instance, the use of lightweight materials results in greater fuel efficiency and, as a result, a decrease in overall emissions.

96. See *EPA's Progress Report on Clean and Efficient Automotive Technologies* for more depth.

include the catalytic converter (which converts CO and HCs to CO_2 and water),[97] on-board computers and electronic sensors that allow exhaust gas conditions to be continuously monitored and optimized, and exhaust gas recirculation, which returns a portion of the exhaust back into the engine to reduce peak combustion temperatures (which in turn lowers NO_x formation).

The third approach has been to make changes to the fuel or oil used in the vehicle.[98] This can decrease overall emissions while only marginally affecting performance. As discussed previously, innovations on the fuel side, such as reformulated gasoline and low-sulfur fuel, have allowed cleaner engine combustion and fewer resultant evaporative emissions. Moreover, because these elements impair the functioning of catalytic converters, the removal of lead (from gasoline) and sulfur (from diesel) has allowed innovation on aftertreatment technologies to continue.

Many future innovations are likely to focus on improvements to, and variations on, some of these strategies. Incremental changes of this nature will be required if diesel-powered vehicles are to meet federal Tier II standards for NO_x and PM. Improvements in aftertreatment technology appear to be the way in which diesels will meet the new emission limits. Such technologies that are currently in the optimization stage include improved trap systems, which capture particulate matter and oxidize (burn) particles through ignition; NO_x catalytic converters, which trap and convert NO_x to nitrogen gas; and turbochargers, which use a turbine to return exhaust gas to the engine, increasing the air pressure and the resulting power.[99] Turbochargers, which can also be applied to gasoline vehicles, have demonstrated a 20 to 40% reduction in PM and a 30 to 65% reduction in CO.[100] Plasma treatment, a more radical innovation that incorporates a pulsing electric field to ionize (or charge) the exhaust gases, would allow catalytic converters to better capture NO_x.[101] Gasoline-powered vehicles, on the other hand, are expected to be able to meet federal Tier II standards without further innovation. For example, by model year

---

97. The three-way catalytic converter is typical for gasoline engines and also reduces NO_x to N_2. Diesel-powered vehicles commonly use an oxidation catalyst, which is not as effective at converting NO_x emissions.

98. Patricia Monahan and David Friedman, *The Diesel Dilemma*, p. 41.

99. Patricia Monahan and David Friedman, *The Diesel Dilemma*, pp. 45–48. These NO_x traps are known as lean nitrogen oxide catalysts, NO_x adsorbers, or selective catalytic reduction. Turbocharged, spark-ignition (SI) engines powered by gasoline are increasingly popular in Europe; see for instance, Stefan Pischinger (2004) "The Future of Vehicle Propulsion—Combustion Engines and Alternatives," *Topics in Catalysis* 30/31: 5–16, July.

100. Patricia Monahan and David Friedman, *The Diesel Dilemma*, p. 43, citing Manufacturers of Emission Control Association (MECA) (2000) "Emission Control Retrofit of Diesel-Fueled Vehicles." March.

101. David Talbot (2002) "Next Stop: Clean Diesel," March. http://www.technologyreview.com/ articles/ 02/03/innovation20302.asp?p=1 (last viewed on 4/21/04).

2005, nineteen models of gas ICE vehicles were already certified to meet California's even stricter super ultra-low-emission vehicle standards.[102]

The more fundamental technological challenge will be to develop automotive technologies that can both reduce greenhouse gas emissions and improve fuel efficiency (thus reducing dependence on foreign oil). More radical innovations, such as hybrid vehicles and electric-drive vehicles, currently surpass ICE vehicles in these two performance measures (among others metrics). However, many of the technologies that were developed to reduce the emission of criteria pollutants from ICE vehicles, such as direct fuel injection, turbocharging, cylinder deactivation, and variable valve lift and timing, can also reduce CO_2 emissions and improve fuel efficiency.[103] Other developments, such as 42-volt battery systems (compared with the current 12-volt battery now used in most vehicles), allow a number of CO_2-reducing options, such as turning off the engine while idling at a stoplight. A 2004 study by the Northeast States Center for a Clean Air Future identified more than thirty currently available technologies that would reduce GHGs.[104] A majority of these technologies are already in full-volume production. It was estimated that by using various combinations of these technologies, GHG emissions from ICE vehicles could be reduced by up to 47% (compared with 2002 values) within 5–10 years. Moreover, it was predicted that these technology scenarios would result in decreased consumer costs through lower fuel use.[105] The largest potential reductions in GHG emissions came from vehicles using hybrid technologies, which are discussed below.

2. Electric-Drive Vehicles

Broadly described, electric-drive vehicles are propelled by an electric motor that is in turn powered by an energy storage device or fuel cell. A number of battery systems have been used in electric-drive vehicles, including lead-acid, nickel metal hydride, nickel cadmium, zinc-air, and lithium-based systems. A variety of hydrogen fuel cell

---

102. Federal Tier II standards were modeled after California's super ultra-low emission vehicle standards and are largely similar. Vehicle model information is from California Air Resources Board, "2005 Zero Emission and PZEV Credit Vehicles," http://www.arb.ca.gov/msprog/ccvl/2005sulevpzevlist.htm (last viewed on 4/21/05). A comparison between the two sets of standards can be found in Northeast States for Coordinated Air Use Management (2003) *Comparing the Emissions Reductions of the LEV II Program to the Tier 2 Program*. October.

103. Note that most of the technologies focus on CO_2 reduction. However, the GHGs methane (CH_4), nitrous oxide (N_2O), and hydrofluorocarbons (used in air conditioning refrigerants), are also emitted from ICE vehicles (both diesel and gasoline) and are also of concern.

104. For the complete description of technologies available, see Northeast States Center for a Clean Air Future (2004) *Reducing Greenhouse Gas Emissions from Light-Duty Motor Vehicles*. September, Appendix A: Technology Descriptions.

105. Ibid. p. xii–xx. Costs were based on assumed gas and diesel fuel prices of $1.58 and $2.00 per gallon; projected savings would be greater at higher costs.

systems, utilizing a number of different fuel sources and designs, have also been developed.

Electric-drive vehicles typically are more efficient than gasoline-powered vehicles. This is due not only to the higher efficiency of the electric motor, but also to its direct connection with the wheels and its ability to harness energy from regenerative braking schemes. Tank-to-wheels efficiency (TTW), or the efficiency of converting fuel in the tank into vehicle motion at the wheels, is approximately 16% for conventional gasoline ICEs, but jumps to 44% for battery-electric and fuel-cell electric vehicles.[106]

However, these differences are reduced when one considers the well-to-wheels efficiency, which compares the energy use over the whole life cycle. This efficiency metric includes the efficiency of fuel production, fuel transport, vehicle production, and vehicle operation. Life-cycle emissions for electric-drive vehicles for criteria pollutants and GHGs will also vary with the type of power plant(s) from which the energy is produced. Energy generated from sources other than fossil fuels—such as solar power, hydroelectric, geothermal, wind, and nuclear power—will lead to lower emissions. For fuel cells, life-cycle emissions depend on how the hydrogen is produced. Currently, the major focus is on obtaining hydrogen by converting diesel, methanol, and gasoline. Although this process can reduce overall emissions, the conversion is never truly perfect and emission by-products (including CO_2) are created. It should be noted, however, that the potential emission reductions likely to be achievable over the life cycle of electric-drive vehicles exceed those of current ICE-powered vehicles. Table 7.5, reproduced from an MIT study of technological options for vehicles by 2020, shows this trend.[107] For instance, it is estimated that a battery electric vehicle will use only 29% of the energy during operation that a baseline gasoline ICE will use in 2020. Accounting for the total life cycle, however, the value increases to 80%. A similar relationship is seen for reductions in GHC emissions.

Hybrid electric vehicles have recently come onto the market with the successful commercialization of such vehicles as the Toyota Prius, Honda Insight, and hybrid versions of the Honda Civic and Accord. In general, a hybrid joins an energy storage device with a power source. Such storage devices can include batteries, flywheels, or capacitors, while the power source might be a traditional ICE, a set of fuel cells,

---

106. ICE TTW efficiency information is from http://www.toyota.co.jp/en/tech/environment/fchv/fchv12 .html. Other values are from Frank Kreith and R. E. West (2003) "Gauging Efficiency, Well to Wheel," *Mechanical Engineering Power*. Available at http://www.memagazine.org/supparch/mepower03/gauging/ gauging.html (last viewed on 4/22/05).

107. Note that there are large error bars inherent in these technological assessments. M. Weiss et al. (2000) *On the Road in 2020: A Life-Cycle Analysis of New Automobile Technologies.* MIT Energy Laboratory Report MIT EL 00-003, Massachusetts Institute of Technology, Cambridge, Mass. Also see "Well-to-Wheel Energy Use and Greenhouse Gas Emissions of Advanced Fuel/Vehicle System, North American Analysis." Argonne National Laboratories/GM, June 2001. Available at http://www.transportation.anl.gov/ software/GREET/publications.html.

Table 7.5
Comparison of Energy Consumption and GHG Emissions on a Life-Cycle Basis and Vehicle Operation Only Basis

2020 Technologies	Relative Energy Consumption		Relative GHG Emissions	
	Life Cycle Basis	Vehicle Operation Only	Life Cycle Basis	Vehicle Operation Only
Baseline gasoline ICE	100	100	100	100
Advanced gasoline ICE	89	88	89	88
Advanced diesel ICE	76	77	78	82
Hybrid gasoline ICE	65	61	63	61
Hybrid petrol. diesel ICE	55	53	56	56
Hybrid CNG ICE	62	59	51	45
Hybrid F-T diesel	86	53	66	54
Hybrid gasoline FC	104	102	104	102
Hybrid methanol FC	99	76	80	73
Hybrid hydrogen FC	72	46	72	0
Battery electric	80	29	69	0

Source: Reproduced with permission from Weiss, M., J. Heywood, E. Drake, A. Schafer, and F. AuYeung (2000) On the road in 2020: A life-cycle analysis of new automobile technologies, October 2000, Energy Laboratory Report # MIT EL 00-003, Massachusetts Institute of Technology, Cambridge, MA.
Notes: The *baseline gasoline ICE* refers to a midsize passenger vehicle in 2020 that has reduced GHG and fuel consumption by a third relative to a 1996 model vehicle.
CNG = compressed natural gas, FC = fuel cell, F-T = Fischer-Tropsch synthetic diesel from remote natural gas.

or even solar panels. Various configurations are possible. In the "parallel" configuration, for example, the engine can run at a more constant speed (leading to more optimum run conditions and fewer emissions), but can draw assistance from the battery when more power is required (for example, during acceleration or uphill driving). The motor (powered by the ICE or fuel cell) serves to recharge the battery as needed, while simultaneously providing torque to the drive shaft, thus obviating the need for a generator. The parallel configuration can also be designed to be externally charged and to run on batteries alone.

One of the more promising near to mid-term technologies is the plug-in hybrid electric vehicle (PHEV), which uses a larger battery pack and can be plugged into a standard electrical outlet for charging. Although the PHEV can be run on traditional petroleum fuels, the larger battery pack allows the vehicle to be driven greater distances running only on electricity. Several preliminary studies and initial testing in government fleets suggest that PHEVs are capable of efficiencies exceeding 90 miles per gallon when the battery is fully charged.

Table 7.6
Comparison of Technology Paths based on Air Pollutants, Range, Power, and Infrastructure

Type	HC	CO	NO$_x$	PM	CO$_2$	Pwr	Rng	IS	Issues
Gasoline SI	o	o	o	o	o	o	o	++	—
Diesel	o	o	−	−	+	−	+	++	—
Otto-type methanol	o	o	o	o	o	o	−	−	Aldehydes
Diesel-type methanol	o	o	o	o	+	o	−	−	Aldehydes
LPG	o	o	o	o	o	−	o	+	—
CNG	o	o	o	o	+	−	−	+	Range
Battery-electric	++	++	++	++	+	−	−	o	Range, cost
Hybrid-electric	+	+	+	o	+	o	+	++	Battery, complexity
Fuel cell (H$_2$)	++	++	++	++	++	−	−	−−	Fuel supply
Fuel cell (HC)	o	o	++	++	+	−	+	+	Complexity, cost
Gas turbine	o	o	−	o	o	o	−	o	Thermal efficiency

Source: Adapted from Dearing, A. (2000) Technologies supportive of sustainable transportation, *Annual Review of Energy and the Environment*, 25, 89–113.
Notes: LPG = liquid petroleum gases, CNG = compressed natural gas. Pwr = power, Rng = range, IS = infrastructure.
o, good or improving; +/++, very good/compelling; −/−−, inadequate/nonexistent.

■ NOTES

1. Like the electric vehicle, hybrid electrics have been known for some time, with H. Piper being the first to patent the idea beginning in 1905. See A. Dearing (2000) "Technologies Supportive of Sustainable Transportation," *Annual Review of Energy and the Environment* 25: 89. For a more in-depth description of hybrid vehicles, see V. Wouk (1997) "Hybrid Electric Vehicles," *Scientific American* October.

2. Comparisons based on emissions, power, range, and infrastructure (a measure of the degree of dependence on fossil fuels) for various systems are shown in table 7.6. Models comparing the life-cycle energy efficiency of hybrids, fuel cells, battery electric, and traditional ICE-powered vehicles have shown hybrids to be the most efficient—more so than even the advanced fuel cell vehicle. See N. Demirdöven and J. Deutch (2004) "Hybrid Cars Now, Fuel Cell Cars Later," *Science* 305: 974. However, when one considers vehicle emissions rather than energy efficiency, the results are more mixed. See M. Weiss, J. Heywood, E. Drake, A. Schafer, and F. AuYeung (2000) *On The Road in 2020: A Life-Cycle Analysis of New Automobile Technologies*. Energy Laboratory Report, MIT EL 00-003, Massachusetts Institute of Technology, Cambridge, Mass.

3. Note that, in this context, the fuel efficiency will be a function of the driving cycle, the size of the battery pack, the type of control strategy utilized, and the design of the emission control system. ■

There is a general consensus that the technological potential for reducing life-cycle emissions from motor vehicles—either through incremental improvements to the internal combustion engine or through more fundamental innovations—has not been exhausted, and most would agree that a technology-forcing strategy should remain a major component of any program designed to achieve a more sustainable transportation system. Nonetheless, this is only one among a suite of strategies available to policymakers, and many of these other strategies are likely to be necessary as well. Technology forcing can be congruous with a larger portfolio of government actions, including the promotion of mass transit, the use of economic approaches (such as congestion pricing), the application of transportation control measures (such as operational restrictions), and better land-use planning and development. See, e.g., Joseph F. Coughlin (1994) "The Tragedy of the Concrete Commons: Defining Traffic Congestion as a Public Problem," in *The Politics of Problem Definition: Shaping the Policy Agenda*, David A. Rochefort and Roger W. Cobb (eds.). University Press of Kansas, Lawrence, pp. 138–158.

I. THE LEGACY OF THE CLEAN AIR ACT

With the Clean Air Act Amendments of 1970, Congress built the foundation for a comprehensive approach to the nation's air pollution problems from mobile sources. While regulations have often been fiercely opposed by industry, forced through the courts by citizen groups, or simply implemented in a protracted time frame, emission standards have been steadily ratcheted downward, pushing an often reluctant auto industry to improve the underlying technology. Continued growth in vehicle use, the prominence of other mobile source categories, and the multitude of pollutant species led Congress to strengthen the act's mobile source provisions in the 1990 amendments.

Other transportation modes and mobile sources beyond the passenger car are now being addressed in serious fashion, and the act's mobile source strategy is becoming increasingly multimodal. EPA has relied upon a variety of increasingly sophisticated regulatory strategies, including simultaneous regulation (e.g., targeting fuel and emission standards), incentive programs, and emission market mechanisms. However, some efforts—particularly those addressing multimedia-based problems—have been less successful, due in part to institutional and political resistance within Congress and EPA. See National Academy of Public Administration (1997) *Resolving the Paradox of Environmental Protection: An Agenda for Congress, EPA and the States* (Report to Congress) and *Panel Encourages EPA to Build Capacity for Foresight in Office of Research and Development*. Available at http://www.napawash.org/resources/news/news_10_10_99.html (last viewed on 12/10/2004).

Problems of a transboundary nature are also becoming a greater challenge. Not only do emissions of greenhouse gases from mobile sources in the United States contribute to worldwide global warming, but air pollution plumes from Asia have been shown to travel along transoceanic air currents to North America.[108] Increasing levels of toxic and criteria pollutants from factories and power plants in Asia could one day stymie domestic efforts to meet the goals of the Clean Air Act. One researcher estimates, for example, that one-third of the ambient mercury in the United States comes from the burning of fossil fuels in Asia.[109] While EPA has established cooperation and demonstration initiatives with Asian countries, the United States currently lacks an institutional framework to deal with transboundary pollutants. It appears that domestic programs addressing mobile sources may need to be coordinated with international programs if ambient air standards are to be reached in the United States. It remains to be seen whether the Clean Air Act will provide the framework for new efforts to control transboundary pollutants and greenhouse gases from mobile sources.

Acknowledgment

The authors are indebted to Simon Mui for his contributions to the writing of this chapter.

---

108. http://usinfo.state.gov/gi/Archive/2004/May/04-385774.html (last viewed on 8/21/2004).
109. http://www.al.noaa.gov/ITCT/2k2/2k2News.html (last viewed on 8/21/2004).

8 Protection of Surface Waters, Wetlands, and Drinking Water: The Clean Water Act and the Safe Drinking Water Act

A. The Clean Water Act: Regulation of Point Source Discharges of Pollutants to Surface Waters, Wetlands, and Sewage Treatment Plants
  1. The History and Development of the Federal Regulations
    a. The 1972 Federal Water Pollution Control Act Amendments
      i. Setting the National Goals
      ii. The Absolute Prohibition Against Nonconforming Discharges
      iii. Broad (but Shrinking?) Definition of Navigable Waters
      iv. The National Pollutant Discharge Elimination System (NPDES) Permit
      v. National Technology-Based Effluent Limits for Industry
      vi. Health-Based Effluent Limits for Toxic Pollutants, Set on a Pollutant-by-Pollutant Basis
      vii. Technology-Based Effluent Limitations and Public Financing for Public Sewage Treatment Plants
      viii. Federal Pretreatment Standards for Discharges into Public Sewage Treatment Plants
      ix. Ambient Water Quality Standards Set by the States
      x. Data Generation and Data Disclosure
      xi. A Strong Emphasis on Public Participation
      xii. State Involvement in Implementation and Enforcement
    b. The 1977 Clean Water Act Amendments
      i. The Division of Pollutants into Three Categories
      ii. Technology-Based Effluent Limits for Toxic Pollutants
      iii. Relaxation of Deadlines
    c. The 1987 Water Quality Act Amendments
      i. A Renewed Emphasis on Water Quality-Based Limitations for Toxic Pollutants
      ii. An Increased Emphasis on Penalties
      iii. Relaxation of Deadlines

Concern with water pollution is nearly as old as human civilization. When the philosopher Plato drafted a model code of behavior for the ancient Greeks, he included the following provisions:

Water is easily polluted by the use of any kind of drug. It therefore needs the protection of a law, as follows: Whoever purposely pollutes water shall be obliged, in addition to paying an indemnity, to purify the spring or receptacle of the water, using whatever method of purification is prescribed by ordinance, at all times and to everyone. (Plato, Law 845)

That this language appears directed toward the protection of drinking water, and not toward the broader protection of all surface waters, simply reflects the concerns of the times. The basic principle—that protection of our waters is serious business requiring a strong law—has endured.

Congress passed a strong law protecting surface waters in 1972. Although it stops far short of requiring the payment of an "indemnity" (penalty) whenever someone introduces pollution into the waters of the United States, the Clean Water Act has sent a clear signal that reductions in water pollution are a national priority. The act has had a profound and largely positive effect on the nation's waters. In the years before its passage, water pollution in the United States had been steadily increasing. As the provisions of the act began to be implemented in the mid-1970s, however, this trend was reversed; by 1980, water pollution had dropped to 1970 levels. More recently, especially as it has become clearer that reductions in certain *types* of pollutants can be more important than reducing the overall *amount* of pollutants, gains (though nonetheless real) have been slower in coming.

Some of this can be attributed to the early availability of "low hanging fruit." In the early years, relatively large reductions in pollution could be achieved through the straightforward application of existing (and largely end-of-pipe) technologies. Subsequent reductions, however, often have required changes in production processes, innovative control technologies, or changes in manufacturing or waste control practices. While implementation of the Clean Water Act has prompted all of these responses, it has also been slowed by the resistance of many industries to making these changes.

The lack of a broader success in reducing water pollution can also be attributed to the structure of the Clean Water Act itself. For a host of practical and political reasons, Congress chose to draw important distinctions in the act between point sources of water pollution—"discrete conveyances" such as industrial and sewage treatment plant discharge pipes—and nonpoint sources—diffuse sources such as runoff of pesticides and fertilizers from a farmer's field. To date the bulk of the meaningful federal regulatory structure for addressing water pollution has been directed toward point sources. The result has been increasingly stringent regulation of industrial and other commercial enterprises, public sewage treatment plants, and federal and state government installations. Meaningful federal attention toward nonpoint sources, however, has been slow in coming. At present there is no comprehensive program of federal regulation of nonpoint sources, and these sources remain a significant cause of water pollution. Because it is the primary focus of the Clean Water Act, we look first in this chapter at the regulatory program governing point source discharges of pollutants, and then at the emerging program for nonpoint sources. We also look at the act's provisions governing the discharge of materials from dredging and filling operations, which have become the primary federal mechanism for protecting wetlands.

Finally, we turn to the topic that most likely spurred the law of Plato quoted at the outset: the safety of drinking water. Although ensuring the quality of surface waters that are used as drinking water is a central goal of the Clean Water Act, that statute does not directly regulate the quality of the water actually delivered to people's homes (from surface waters and underground aquifers) by public water systems. That task—often a Herculean one—is left to the Safe Drinking Water Act. Enacted in 1974 amid growing concern over the presence of industrial chemicals in public drinking water, the Safe Drinking Water Act is the primary mechanism by which EPA and the states attempt to keep chemical and biological contaminants out of public water supplies. While the act cannot be called an unqualified success, especially in light of the funding gaps that have plagued its implementation, it nonetheless has gone a long way toward ensuring a baseline level of drinking water safety.

A. THE CLEAN WATER ACT: REGULATION OF POINT SOURCE DISCHARGES OF POLLUTANTS TO SURFACE WATERS, WETLANDS, AND SEWAGE TREATMENT PLANTS

The present Clean Water Act was fashioned in three major stages: the act's basic framework and scope were established in 1972; several important revisions (and the name "Clean Water Act") were introduced in 1977; and a few important refinements were added in 1987. We explore the features of the act by first examining its progression through these three stages—stopping along the way to ask whether a 2006 decision of the Supreme Court has narrowed the scope originally intended by Congress—and then we turn to a closer examination of how the act's key point source provisions have been implemented.

1. The History and Development of the Federal Regulations

The Clean Water Act has its historical origins in two different federal statutes: the Federal Water Pollution Control Act of 1948, and the Rivers and Harbors Appropriation Act of 1899 (also known as the Refuse Act). As amended in 1965, the Federal Water Pollution Control Act required each state, subject to federal approval, to classify its waterways according to intended use (e.g., for drinking water, fishing, or waste disposal), to set ambient water quality standards for each waterway consistent with its use designation, and to adopt implementation plans to ensure that the ambient standards were met. Like the Clean Air Act program for criteria air pollutants, then, the regulatory scheme was to begin with ambient standards and to work backward to the establishment of discharge limitations to meet those standards. This program proved cumbersome and ineffectual. As might be expected, there was considerable delay in basic implementation. Although the act set a 1967 deadline for the submission of state water quality standards for federal approval, only about half of the states had federally approved standards by 1971. See S. Rep. No. 92-414, 92d Cong., 1st sess. 4 (1971). More important, it proved difficult—especially with the lack of adequate databases for several important water quality considerations—to determine the discharge limitations that would be necessary to meet the water quality standards that had been approved. The result, concluded the Senate Committee on Public Works in 1971, was "an almost total lack of enforcement" (id.).

Thus, in late 1970 the federal government began a comprehensive federal permitting program under the Rivers and Harbors Act. That statute prohibits the discharge of any "refuse matter" into the navigable waters of the United States unless it is authorized by the secretary of the army. Although it had originally been thought that the act was limited only to the regulation of refuse discharges that actually impeded navigation, two Supreme Court cases in the 1960s construed the act as applying to almost all discharges of waste or other materials into navigable waters. See *United States v. Republic Steel Corp.*, 362 U.S. 482 (1960), and *United States v. Standard Oil Co.*, 384 U.S. 224 (1966). Under the authority of these decisions, the secretary of the army and the newly created federal Environmental Protection Agency began a joint program under which the secretary would issue permits to industrial sources of water pollution, subject to water quality-based discharge limits determined by EPA on a case-by-case basis. See 35 *Fed. Reg.* 19,627 (1970). Evaluating the fledging permit program in 1971, the Senate Committee on Public Works concluded that it "may be as cumbersome" to implement as the Federal Water Pollution Control Act. "Estimates of the number of permit applications to be received run as high as 300,000," noted the committee, while "estimates of the time required to process the applications run as long as four years" [S. Rep. No. 92-414, 92d Cong., 1st sess. 4 (1971)].

a. The 1972 Federal Water Pollution Control Act Amendments

Given this background of regulatory stagnation, Congress decided in 1972 to take decisive action. With some important exceptions, the basic structure of today's Clean Water Act was put in place in that year, with the passage of sweeping amendments to the Federal Water Pollution Control Act.

1972 Federal Water Pollution Control act (handwritten annotation)

i. Setting the National Goals   Faced with what it perceived as massive and pervasive pollution of the nation's waters, Congress formulated a bold and far-reaching response. "The objective of this chapter," Congress declared in the opening section of the new act, would be nothing less than "to restore and maintain the chemical, physical, and biological integrity of the Nation's waters" [Section 101(a), 33 U.S.C. §1251(a)]. To accomplish this formidable task, the act specified two national goals: (1) "that the discharge of pollutants into the navigable waters be eliminated by 1985;" and (2) "that wherever attainable, an interim goal of water quality which provides for the protection and propagation of fish, shellfish, and wildlife and provides for recreation in and on the water be achieved by July 1, 1983." (This is colloquially referred to as the act's "fishable and swimmable" goal.) [Section 101(a)(1) and (2)]. The act further specified that it would thereafter be the national policy that "the discharge of toxic pollutants in toxic amounts be prohibited" [Section 101(a)(3)].

This core language of Section 101, which has remained intact in the subsequent major revisions to the act, not only articulates a clear set of long-range goals for the reduction of water pollution, but also forms the conceptual basis for the wide array of ambient standards and discharge limitations to which the act has given rise. If these goals seemed ambitious in 1972, they seem, with the benefit of hindsight, even more so today. Far from attaining the "no discharge" goal of Section 101(a)(1) by 1985, for example, in 1985 EPA had not even completed the task of promulgating the basic set of technology-based limitations designed to regulate the discharge of water pollutants by industry. Today, more than two decades later, the discharge of pollutants—toxic and otherwise—into the nation's waterways remains commonplace.

This gap between goal and reality does not mean that Section 101 has lost its meaning within the act's regulatory scheme, however. Especially because Congress has seen fit to leave them intact when it has revised the statute, these goals and policies remain the standard against which the Clean Water Act's implementation is to be measured. Significantly, when there is a question in the courts as to the interpretation of one of the act's provisions, that interpretation is to be done against the backdrop of the act's ultimate purpose. Indeed, Congress itself has used the failure to attain the goals of Section 101 as a reason for strengthening the act in subsequent revisions. The House and Senate floor debates on the 1987 amendments to the act, for example, reflected a keen awareness of these goals:

The Clean Water Act, when developed in 1972, was based on two concepts and a compromise. A national goal was adopted calling for a twofold objective: to eliminate the discharge of pollutants, and maintain the biological integrity of our water. Then, as a compromise, an interim goal was added: To assure that water quality would at least support fish, shellfish, wildlife, body contact sports, and drinking water. The first goal is as poignant and relevant today as it was when it was adopted in 1972. We have made progress, but even the compromise goal euphemistically referred to as "fishable, swimmable" has not been fully achieved.

These goals are the real issues confronting us today. These are the goals for which the American public will hold us accountable. [133 *Cong. Rec.* S743 (daily ed., Jan 14, 1987) (statement of Sen. Baucus)]

See also, e.g., 133 *Cong. Rec.* H169 (Jan. 8, 1987) (statement of Rep. Hammerschmidt) ("we have not reached our goal...to achieve, wherever attainable, fishable and swimmable water quality").

ii. The Absolute Prohibition Against Nonconforming Discharges   Perhaps the most significant feature of the 1972 Federal Water Pollution Control Act Amendments was the addition of Section 301(a), which imposes an absolute prohibition against nonconforming discharges of pollutants to the waters of the United States. In keeping with the national "no discharge" goal, Section 301(a) flatly states that "[e]xcept as in compliance with [various specified sections of the Clean Water Act] *the discharge of any pollutant by any person shall be unlawful*" [33 U.S.C. §1311(a), emphasis added]. The sections of the act enumerated in this provision are Section 301 (dealing with federal technology-based and state water quality-based effluent limitations); Section 302, 33 U.S.C. §1312 (dealing with federal water quality-based effluent limitations); Section 306, 33 U.S.C. §1316 (dealing with federal technology-based effluent limitations for new sources); Section 307, 33 U.S.C. §1317 (dealing with federal limitations on the discharge of toxic pollutants); 318, 33 U.S.C. §1328 (dealing with the issuance of permits for discharges associated with aquaculture projects); Section 402, 33 U.S.C. §1342 (dealing with the issuance of permits for the discharge of pollutants to the navigable waters); and Section 404, 33 U.S.C. §1344 (dealing with the issuance of permits for the discharge of dredged or fill material to the navigable waters). Under Section 301(a), discharges in violation of one or more of the requirements imposed by these various sections of the act are "unlawful."

With the inclusion of this simple prohibition, Congress brought about a fundamental change in the rules of the game. No longer could companies, governmental entities, or others claim a right to discharge to the nation's waters unless they were told not to do so. Under Section 301(a), no one has a right to "discharge" pollutants to the waters of the United States *except in compliance with the Clean Water Act.*

As suggested by the quotation marks in the preceding sentence, the term *discharge* has a special meaning under the act. As set forth in Section 502, the act's definitional section, "discharge of a pollutant" means "any addition of any pollutant to navigable waters from any point source" [33 U.S.C. §1362(12)]. *Point source*, in turn,

means any discernible, confined and discrete conveyance, including but not limited to any pipe, ditch, channel, tunnel, conduit, well, discrete fissure, container, rolling stock, concentrated animal feeding operation, or vessel or other floating craft, from which pollutants are or may be discharged. The term does not include agricultural stormwater discharges and return flows from irrigated agriculture. [Section 502(14); see also 40 C.F.R. §122]

In essence—with the exception of the specific agricultural discharges excluded by the definition—any defined, nondiffuse path by which pollutants are deposited into surface waters is regulated as a point source under the Clean Water Act. In prohibiting all nonconforming point source discharges, then, the act casts its net rather widely.

However, by specifically limiting this prohibition to point source pollution, the act excludes from direct federal regulation the wide variety of diffuse sources of water pollution—such as uncollected runoff from farming and forestry operations—that currently account for an estimated 50% of all surface water pollution. This is compounded by the act's specific exclusion of agricultural stormwater discharges and return flows from irrigated agriculture, even where they would otherwise come within the definition of point source.

▪ NOTES

1. The term "pollutant" also has a specialized definition under the act, although that definition is a broad one. As specified in Section 502(6), pollutant "means dredged spoil, solid waste, incinerator residue, sewage [other than from an armed forces vessel], garbage, sewage sludge, munitions, chemical wastes, biological materials, radioactive materials, heat, wrecked or discarded equipment, rock, sand, cellar dirt and industrial, municipal, and agricultural waste discharged into water." Munitions fired from aircraft as part of navy training exercises have been held to be pollutants [*Weinberger v. Romero-Barcelo*, 456 U.S. 306 (1982)], as has sand and silt carried off a construction site by stormwater [*Driscoll v. Adams*, 181 F.3d 1288, 1290 (11th Cir. 1999)]. Farm-raised Atlantic salmon escaping through holes in their rearing pens into open water (where they can breed with, and dilute the stock of, wild native salmon) have been treated as pollutants [*USPIRG v. Atlantic Salmon of Maine, L.L.C.*, 215 F. supp. 2d 239 (D. Me. 2002)], although shells and feces from farm-raised mussels have been held not to be where the mussels are native to the receiving waters and the discharges cause no identifiable harm to the receiving waters [*Assoc. to Protect Hammersley, Eld, and Totten Inlets v. Taylor Resources, Inc.*, 299 F.3d 1007, 1017–18, and n. 9] ("these materials come from the natural growth and development of the mussels and not from a transformative human process").

2. A wide variety of "conveyances" have been held to be point sources of pollution within the meaning of the Clean Water Act. See, for example *Weinberger v. Romero-Barcelo*, 456 U.S. 305 (1982) (aircraft firing munitions into the water); *United States v. West Indies Transport, Inc.*, 127 F.3d 299 (3rd Cir. 1996) (a barge from which portions of a dismantled vessel were dumped); *Avovelles Sportsmen's League v. Marsh*, 715 F.2d 897 (5th Cir. 1993) (bulldozers and backhoes dropping dredged vegetation into a wetland); *Sierra Club v. Abston Construction Co.*, 620 F.2d 41 (5th Cir. 1980) (pile of mining waste from which pollutants were eroded by rainwater).

3. Note that concentrated animal feeding operations (CAFOs)—"factory farm" operations in which livestock are housed and fed in quantities that exceed criteria specified by EPA regulation—are specifically enumerated in the statute as one type of point source. Large fish farms—called concentrated aquatic animal production facilities (CAAPFs)—are also included within EPA's CAFO regulations. In contrast, at least one court has held that individual animals are not point sources. See *Oregon Natural Desert Ass'n. v. Dombeck*, 172 F.3d 1092 (9th Cir. 1998). Another court has held that individual humans are not point sources, at least if they are not involved in a systematic discharge by, say, their employer. See *United States v. Plaza Health Labs*, 3 F.3d 643 (2nd Cir. 1993).

4. May point source discharges into the groundwater, which then are carried by the groundwater to surface waters, be regulated as point source discharges under the act? See *Rice v. Harken Exploration Co.*, 250 F.3d 264 (5th Cir. 2001) (a point source discharge to land that then seeps into groundwater is not a discharge to navigable waters where the connection to those waters is "indirect, remote, and attenuated").

5. Is the application of pesticides to the surface waters—either intentionally, to kill aquatic pests, or unintentionally, because of drift from nearby spraying—the discharge of a pollutant requiring a Clean Water Act permit? The Ninth Circuit Court of Appeals has held that it is, so long as pesticide residues remain in the water after application to the target pests [*Headwaters, Inc. v. Talent Irrigation Dist.*, 243 F.3d 526 (9th Cir. 2001), *League of Wilderness Defenders v. Forsgren*, 309 F.3d 1181 (9th Cir. 2002), and *Fairhurst v. Hagener*, 422 F.3d 1146 (9th Cir. 2005)]. Accordingly, some states within the Ninth Circuit have implemented permit programs for such discharges. In response to a rulemaking petition filed by the pesticide industry, however, EPA issued a regulation in 2006 exempting certain pesticide applications from Clean Water Act coverage so long as they are done in compliance with the Federal Insecticide, Fungicide, and Rodenticide Act. EPA's rationale for this exemption, which is codified at 40 C.F.R. §122.3(h), is that the pesticides are not "pollutants" when they are applied because they are being used for a beneficial purpose. Thus, the agency reasons, although the pesticide residues that remain in the water are pollutants, they were not "discharged" as such by a point source. See 71 *Fed. Reg.* 68,483, 68,486–487 (Nov. 27, 2006). As this book goes to press, a coalition of environmental groups is challenging this pesticide exemption in the courts. ∎

iii. Broad (but Shrinking?) Definition of Navigable Waters Another limitation on the prohibition against nonconforming discharges is the definition of navigable waters. Section 502 defines "navigable waters" as "the waters of the United States, including the territorial seas," and it further defines "territorial seas" as all the seas up to 3 miles from United States shores [Section 502(7) and (8)]. EPA has indicated in regulation that "the waters of the United States" include not only creeks, streams, rivers, lakes, bays, and the like, but also interstate wetlands and, to the extent that they have a potential relationship with interstate commerce, *intrastate* wetlands as well (40 C.F.R. §122). More than two decades after these regulations were first promulgated, the Supreme Court called EPA's expansive interpretation into question in the case excerpted below. Although the case came to the Supreme Court as a result of a challenge to a regulation issued by the United States Army Corps of Engineers under the "dredge and fill" provisions of Section 404 of the act (discussed in section C of this chapter), the Court's interpretation of the act's use of the term "navigable waters" extends broadly to all parts of the act. Because this was a fractured decision, with no majority opinion, portions of the four-justice plurality, the two concurring opinions, and the four-justice dissent are all reproduced here. At the outset, however, it should be noted that even with the narrowing interpretation (apparently) applied by the Court in this case, the Clean Water Act still covers the bulk of the surface waters in or near the United States.

Rapanos v. United States
Justice SCALIA announced the judgment of the Court and delivered an opinion in which the Chief Justice, Justice THOMAS, and Justice ALITO join
United States Supreme Court
126 S.Ct. 2208 (2006)

In April 1989, petitioner John A. Rapanos backfilled wetlands on a parcel of land in Michigan that he owned and sought to develop. This parcel included 54 acres of land with sometimes-saturated soil conditions. The nearest body of navigable water was 11 to 20 miles away. 339 F.3d 447, 449 (C.A.6 2003) *(Rapanos I)*. Regulators had informed Mr. Rapanos that his saturated fields were "waters of the United States," 33 U.S.C. §1362(7), that could not be filled without a permit. Twelve years of criminal and civil litigation ensued.

The burden of federal regulation on those who would deposit fill material in locations denominated "waters of the United States" is not trivial. In deciding whether to grant or deny a permit, the U.S. Army Corps of Engineers (Corps) exercises the discretion of an enlightened despot, relying on such factors as "economics," "aesthetics," "recreation," and "in general, the needs and welfare of the people," 33 CFR §320.4(a) (2004). The average applicant for an individual permit spends 788 days and $271,596 in completing the process, and the average applicant for a nationwide permit spends 313 days and $28,915—not counting costs of mitigation or design changes. Sunding & Zilberman, The Economics of Environmental Regulation by Licensing: An Assessment of Recent Changes to the Wetland Permitting Process, 42 Natural Resources J. 59, 74–76 (2002). "[O]ver $1.7 billion is spent each year by the private and public sectors obtaining wetlands permits." *Id.*, at 81. These costs cannot be avoided, because the Clean Water Act "impose[s] criminal liability," as well as steep civil fines, "on a broad range of ordinary industrial and commercial activities." *Hanou-*

sek v. United States, 528 U.S. 1102, 1103, 120 S.Ct. 860, 145 L.Ed.2d 710 (2000) (THOMAS, J., dissenting from denial of certiorari). In this litigation, for example, for backfilling his own wet fields, Mr. Rapanos faced 63 months in prison and hundreds of thousands of dollars in criminal and civil fines. See *United States v. Rapanos*, 235 F.3d 256, 260 (C.A.6 2000).

The enforcement proceedings against Mr. Rapanos are a small part of the immense expansion of federal regulation of land use that has occurred under the Clean Water Act, without any change in the governing statute, during the past five Presidential administrations. In the last three decades, the Corps and the Environmental Protection Agency (EPA) have interpreted their jurisdiction over "the waters of the United States" to cover 270-to-300 million acres of swampy lands in the United States-including half of Alaska and an area the size of California in the lower 48 States. And that was just the beginning. The Corps has also asserted jurisdiction over virtually any parcel of land containing a channel or conduit-whether man-made or natural, broad or narrow, permanent or ephemeral-through which rainwater or drainage may occasionally or intermittently flow. On this view, the federally regulated "waters of the United States" include storm drains, roadside ditches, ripples of sand in the desert that may contain water once a year, and lands that are covered by floodwaters once every 100 years. Because they include the land containing storm sewers and desert washes, the statutory "waters of the United States" engulf entire cities and immense arid wastelands. In fact, the entire land area of the United States lies in some drainage basin, and an endless network of visible channels furrows the entire surface, containing water ephemerally wherever the rain falls. Any plot of land containing such a channel may potentially be regulated as a "water of the United States."

I

Congress passed the Clean Water Act (CWA or Act) in 1972. The Act's stated objective is "to restore and maintain the chemical, physical, and biological integrity of the Nation's waters." 86 Stat. 816, 33 U.S.C. §1251(a). The Act also states that "[i]t is the policy of Congress to recognize, preserve, and protect the primary responsibilities and rights of States to prevent, reduce, and eliminate pollution, to plan the development and use (including restoration, preservation, and enhancement) of land and water resources, and to consult with the Administrator in the exercise of his authority under this chapter." §1251(b).

One of the statute's principal provisions is 33 U.S.C. §1311(a), which provides that "the discharge of any pollutant by any person shall be unlawful." "The discharge of a pollutant" is defined broadly to include "any addition of any pollutant to navigable waters from any point source," §1362(12), and "pollutant" is defined broadly to include not only traditional contaminants but also solids such as "dredged spoil, . . . rock, sand, [and] cellar dirt," §1362(6). And, most relevant here, the CWA defines "navigable waters" as "the waters of the United States, including the territorial seas." §1362(7).

The Act also provides certain exceptions to its prohibition of "the discharge of any pollutant by any person." §1311(a). Section 1342(a) authorizes the Administrator of the EPA to "issue a permit for the discharge of any pollutant, . . . notwithstanding section 1311(a) of this title." Section 1344 authorizes the Secretary of the Army, acting through the Corps, to "issue permits . . . for the discharge of dredged or fill material into the navigable waters at specified disposal sites." §1344(a), (d). It is the discharge of "dredged or fill material," which, unlike traditional water pollutants, are solids that do not readily wash downstream, that we consider today.

For a century prior to the CWA, we had interpreted the phrase "navigable waters of the United States" in the Act's predecessor statutes to refer to interstate waters that are "navigable in fact" or readily susceptible of being rendered so. *The Daniel Ball*, 10 Wall. 557, 563, 19 L.Ed. 999 (1871); see also *United States v. Appalachian Elec. Power Co.*, 311 U.S. 377, 406, 61 S.Ct. 291, 85 L.Ed. 243 (1940). After passage of the CWA, the Corps initially adopted this traditional judicial definition for the Act's term "navigable waters." See 39 Fed.Reg. 12119, codified at 33 CFR §209.120(d)(1) (1974); see also *Solid Waste Agency of Northern Cook Cty. v. Army Corps of Engineers*, 531 U.S. 159, 168, 121 S.Ct. 675, 148 L.Ed.2d 576 (2001) *(SWANCC)*. After a District Court enjoined these regulations as too narrow, *Natural Resources Defense Council, Inc. v. Callaway*, 392 F.Supp. 685, 686 (DC 1975), the Corps adopted a far broader definition. See 40 Fed.Reg. 31324–31325 (1975); 42 Fed.Reg. 37144 (1977). The Corps' new regulations deliberately sought to extend the definition of "the waters of the United States" to the outer limits of Congress's commerce power. See *id.*, at 37144, n. 2.

The Corps' current regulations interpret "the waters of the United States" to include, in addition to traditional interstate navigable waters, 33 CFR §328.3(a)(1) (2004), "[a]ll interstate waters including interstate wetlands," §328.3(a)(2); "[a]ll other waters such as intrastate lakes, rivers, streams (including intermittent streams), mudflats, sandflats, wetlands, sloughs, prairie potholes, wet meadows, playa lakes, or natural ponds, the use, degradation or destruction of which could affect interstate or foreign commerce," §328.3(a)(3); "[t]ributaries of [such] waters," §328.3(a)(5); and "[w]etlands adjacent to [such] waters [and tributaries] (other than waters that are themselves wetlands)," §328.3(a)(7). The regulation defines "adjacent" wetlands as those "bordering, contig-

uous [to], or neighboring" waters of the United States. §328.3(c). It specifically provides that "[w]etlands separated from other waters of the United States by man-made dikes or barriers, natural river berms, beach dunes and the like are 'adjacent wetlands.'" *Ibid.*

We first addressed the proper interpretation of 33 U.S.C. §1362(7)'s phrase "the waters of the United States" in *United States v. Riverside Bayview Homes, Inc.*, 474 U.S. 121, 106 S.Ct. 455, 88 L.Ed.2d 419 (1985). That case concerned a wetland that "was adjacent to a body of navigable water," because "the area characterized by saturated soil conditions and wetland vegetation extended beyond the boundary of respondent's property to . . . a navigable waterway." *Id.*, at 131, 106 S.Ct. 455; see also 33 CFR §328.3(b) (2004). Noting that "the transition from water to solid ground is not necessarily or even typically an abrupt one," and that "the Corps must necessarily choose some point at which water ends and land begins," 474 U.S., at 132, 106 S.Ct. 455, we upheld the Corps' interpretation of "the waters of the United States" to include wetlands that "actually abut[ted] on" traditional navigable waters. *Id.*, at 135, 106 S.Ct. 455. . . .

In *SWANCC*, we considered the application of the Corps' "Migratory Bird Rule" to "an abandoned sand and gravel pit in northern Illinois." 531 U.S., at 162, 121 S.Ct. 675. Observing that "[i]t was the *significant nexus* between the wetlands and 'navigable waters' that informed our reading of the CWA in *Riverside Bayview*," *id.*, at 167, 121 S.Ct. 675 (emphasis added), we held that *Riverside Bayview* did not establish "that the jurisdiction of the Corps extends to ponds that are not adjacent to open water." 531 U.S., at 168, 121 S.Ct. 675 (emphasis deleted). On the contrary, we held that "nonnavigable, isolated, intrastate waters," *id.*, at 171, 121 S.Ct. 675—which, unlike the wetlands at issue in *Riverside Bayview*, did not "actually abu[t] on a navigable waterway," 531 U.S., at 167, 121 S.Ct. 675—were not included as "waters of the United States."

Following our decision in *SWANCC*, the Corps did not significantly revise its theory of federal jurisdiction under §1344(a). The Corps provided notice of a proposed rulemaking in light of *SWANCC*, 68 Fed.Reg.1991 (2003), but ultimately did not amend its published regulations. Because *SWANCC* did not directly address tributaries, the Corps notified its field staff that they "should continue to assert jurisdiction over traditional navigable waters...and, generally speaking, their tributary systems (and adjacent wetlands)." 68 Fed.Reg.1998. In addition, because *SWANCC* did not overrule *Riverside Bayview*, the Corps continues to assert jurisdiction over waters "'neighboring'" traditional navigable waters and their tributaries. 68 Fed.Reg.1997 (quoting 33 CFR §328.3(c) (2003)).

Even after *SWANCC*, the lower courts have continued to uphold the Corps' sweeping assertions of jurisdiction over ephemeral channels and drains as "tributaries." For example, courts have held that jurisdictional "tributaries" include the "intermittent flow of surface water through approximately 2.4 miles of natural streams and manmade ditches (paralleling and crossing under I-64)," *Treacy v. Newdunn Assoc.*, 344 F.3d 407, 410 (C.A.4 2003); a "roadside ditch" whose water took "a winding, thirty-two-mile path to the Chesapeake Bay," *United States v. Deaton*, 332 F.3d 698, 702 (C.A.4 2003); irrigation ditches and drains that intermittently connect to covered waters, *Community Assn. for Restoration of Environment v.*

Henry Bosma Dairy, 305 F.3d 943, 954–955 (C.A.9 2002); *Headwaters, Inc. v. Talent Irrigation Dist.*, 243 F.3d 526, 534 (C.A.9 2001); and (most implausibly of all) the "washes and arroyos" of an "arid development site," located in the middle of the desert, through which "water courses...during periods of heavy rain," *Save Our Sonoran, Inc. v. Flowers*, 408 F.3d 1113, 1118 (C.A.9 2005).[2] ...

III

The Rapanos petitioners contend that the terms "navigable waters" and "waters of the United States" in the Act must be limited to the traditional definition of *The Daniel Ball*, which required that the "waters" be navigable in fact, or susceptible of being rendered so. See 10 Wall., at 563, 19 L.Ed. 999. But this definition cannot be applied wholesale to the CWA. The Act uses the phrase "navigable waters" as a *defined* term, and the definition is simply "the waters of the United States." 33 U.S.C. §1362(7). Moreover, the Act provides, in certain circumstances, for the substitution of state for federal jurisdiction over "navigable waters...*other than* those waters which are presently used, or are susceptible to use in their natural condition or by reasonable improvement as a means to transport interstate or foreign commerce...including wetlands adjacent thereto." §1344(g)(1) (emphasis added). This provision shows that the Act's term "navigable waters" includes something more than traditional navigable waters. We have twice stated that the meaning of "navigable waters" in the Act is broader than the

---

2. We are indebted to the *Sonoran* court for a famous exchange, from the movie *Casablanca* (Warner Bros. 1942), which portrays most vividly the absurdity of finding the desert filled with waters:

"'Captain Renault [Claude Rains]: "What in heaven's name brought you to Casablanca?"

"'Rick [Humphrey Bogart]: "My health. I came to Casablanca for the waters."

"'Captain Renault: "The waters? What waters? We're in the desert."

"'Rick: "I was misinformed."' 408 F.3d, at 1117.

traditional understanding of that term, *SWANCC*, 531 U.S., at 167, 121 S.Ct. 675; *Riverside Bayview*, 474 U.S., at 133, 106 S.Ct. 455. We have also emphasized, however, that the qualifier "navigable" is not devoid of significance, *SWANCC, supra*, at 172, 121 S.Ct. 675.

We need not decide the precise extent to which the qualifiers "navigable" and "of the United States" restrict the coverage of the Act. Whatever the scope of these qualifiers, the CWA authorizes federal jurisdiction only over "waters." 33 U.S.C. §1362(7). The only natural definition of the term "waters," our prior and subsequent judicial constructions of it, clear evidence from other provisions of the statute, and this Court's canons of construction all confirm that "the waters of the United States" in §1362(7) cannot bear the expansive meaning that the Corps would give it.

The Corps' expansive approach might be arguable if the CSA defined "navigable waters" as "water of the United States." But "the waters of the United States" is something else. The use of the definite article ("the") and the plural number ("waters") show plainly that §1362(7) does not refer to water in general. In this form, "the waters" refers more narrowly to water "[a]s found in streams and bodies forming geographical features such as oceans, rivers, [and] lakes," or "the flowing or moving masses, as of waves or floods, making up such streams or bodies." Webster's New International Dictionary 2882 (2d ed.1954) (hereinafter Webster's Second).[4] On this definition, "the waters of the United States" include only relatively permanent, standing or flowing bodies of water.[5] The definition refers to water as found in "streams," "oceans," "rivers," "lakes," and "bodies" of water "forming geographical features." *Ibid.* All of these terms connote continuously present, fixed bodies of water, as opposed to ordinarily dry channels through which water occasionally or intermittently flows. Even the least substantial of the definition's terms, namely "streams," connotes a continuous flow of water in a permanent channel—especially when used in company with other terms such as "rivers," "lakes," and "oceans." None of these terms encompasses transitory puddles or ephemeral flows of water.

The restriction of "the waters of the United States" to exclude channels containing merely

---

4. Justice KENNEDY observes that the dictionary approves an alternative, somewhat poetic usage of "waters" as connoting "[a] flood or inundation; as the *waters* have fallen. 'The peril of *waters*, wind, and rocks.' *Shak.*" Webster's Second 2882. It seems to us wholly unreasonable to interpret the statute as regulating only "floods" and "inundations" rather than traditional waterways—and strange to suppose that Congress had waxed Shakespearean in the definition section of an otherwise prosaic, indeed downright tedious, statute. The duller and more commonplace meaning is obviously intended. 5. By describing "waters" as "relatively permanent," we do not necessarily exclude streams, rivers, or lakes that might dry up in extraordinary circumstances, such as drought. We also do not necessarily exclude *seasonal* rivers, which contain continuous flow during some months of the year but no flow during dry months—such as the 290-day, continuously flowing stream postulated by Justice STEVENS' dissent. Common sense and common usage distinguish between a wash and seasonal river.

Though scientifically precise distinctions between "perennial" and "intermittent" flows are no doubt available, see, *e.g.*, Dept. of Interior, U.S. Geological Survey, E. Hedman & W. Osterkamp, Streamflow Characteristics Related to Channel Geometry of Streams in Western United States 15 (1982) (Water-Supply Paper 2193), we have no occasion in this litigation to decide exactly when the drying-up of a stream bed is continuous and frequent enough to disqualify the channel as a "wate[r] of the United States." It suffices for present purposes that channels containing permanent flow are plainly within the definition, and that the dissent's "intermittent" and "ephemeral" streams, (opinion of STEVENS, J.)—that is, streams whose flow is "[c]oming and going at intervals...[b]roken, fitful," Webster's Second 1296, or "existing only, or no longer than, a day; diurnal...short-lived," *id.*, at 857—are not.

intermittent or ephemeral flow also accords with the commonsense understanding of the term. In applying the definition to "ephemeral streams," "wet meadows," storm sewers and culverts, "directional sheet flow during storm events," drain tiles, man-made drainage ditches, and dry arroyos in the middle of the desert, the Corps has stretched the term "waters of the United States" beyond parody. The plain language of the statute simply does not authorize this "Land Is Waters" approach to federal jurisdiction.

In addition, the Act's use of the traditional phrase "navigable waters" (the defined term) further confirms that it confers jurisdiction only over relatively *permanent* bodies of water. The Act adopted that traditional term from its predecessor statutes. See *SWANCC*, 531 U.S., at 180, 121 S.Ct. 675 (STEVENS, J., dissenting). On the traditional understanding, "navigable waters" included only discrete *bodies* of water. For example, in *The Daniel Ball*, we used the terms "waters" and "rivers" interchangeably. 10 Wall., at 563, 19 L.Ed. 999. And in *Appalachian Electric*, we consistently referred to the "navigable waters" as "waterways." 311 U.S., at 407–409, 61 S.Ct. 291. Plainly, because such "waters" had to be navigable in fact or susceptible of being rendered so, the term did not include ephemeral flows. As we noted in *SWANCC*, the traditional term "navigable waters"— even though defined as "the waters of the United States"—carries *some* of its original substance: "[I]t is one thing to give a word limited effect and quite another to give it no effect whatever." 531 U.S., at 172, 121 S.Ct. 675. That limited effect includes, at bare minimum, the ordinary presence of water....

Absent a plausible ground in our case law for its sweeping position, the dissent relies heavily on "Congress' deliberate acquiescence in the Corps' regulations in 1977," noting that "[w]e found [this acquiescence] significant in *Riverside Bayview*," and even "acknowledged in *SWANCC*" that we had

done so. *SWANCC* "acknowledged" that *Riverside Bayview* had relied on congressional acquiescence only to criticize that reliance. It reasserted in no uncertain terms our oft-expressed skepticism towards reading the tea leaves of congressional inaction:

"Although we have recognized congressional acquiescence to administrative interpretations of a statute in some situations, we have done so with extreme care. Failed legislative proposals are a particularly dangerous ground on which to rest an interpretation of a prior statute.... The relationship between the actions and inactions of the 95th Congress and the intent of the 92d Congress in passing [§1344(a)] is also considerably attenuated. Because subsequent history is less illuminating than the contemporaneous evidence, respondents face a difficult task in overcoming the plain text and import of [§1344(a)]." 531 U.S., at 169, 121 S.Ct. 675 (citations, internal quotation marks, and footnote omitted).

Congress takes no governmental action except by legislation. What the dissent refers to as "Congress' deliberate acquiescence" should more appropriately be called Congress's failure to express any opinion. We have no idea whether the Members' failure to act in 1977 was attributable to their belief that the Corps' regulations were correct, or rather to their belief that the courts would eliminate any excesses, or indeed simply to their unwillingness to confront the environmental lobby. To be sure, we have sometimes relied on congressional acquiescence when there is evidence that Congress considered and rejected the "*precise* issue" presented before the Court, *Bob Jones Univ. v. United States*, 461 U.S. 574, 600, 103 S.Ct. 2017, 76 L.Ed.2d 157 (1983) (emphasis added). However, "[a]bsent such *overwhelming evidence* of acquiescence, we are loath to replace the plain text and original understanding of a statute with an amended agency interpretation." *SWANCC, supra*, at 169, n. 5, 121 S.Ct. 675 (emphasis added)....

VIII

Because the Sixth Circuit applied the wrong standard to determine if these wetlands are covered "waters of the United States," and because of the paucity of the record in both of these cases, the lower courts should determine, in the first instance, whether the ditches or drains near each wetland are "waters" in the ordinary sense of containing a relatively permanent flow; and (if they are) whether the wetlands in question are "adjacent" to these "waters" in the sense of possessing a continuous surface connection that creates the boundary-drawing problem we addressed in *Riverside Bayview....*

We vacate the judgments of the Sixth Circuit in both No. 04-1034 and No. 04-1384, and remand both cases for further proceedings.

It is so ordered.

CHIEF JUSTICE ROBERTS, CONCURRING:

Five years ago, this Court rejected the position of the Army Corps of Engineers on the scope of its authority to regulate wetlands under the Clean Water Act, 86 Stat. 816, as amended, 33 U.S.C. §1251 *et seq. Solid Waste Agency of Northern Cook Cty. v. Army Corps of Engineers*, 531 U.S. 159, 121 S.Ct. 675, 148 L.Ed.2d 576 (2001) *(SWANCC)*. The Corps had taken the view that its authority was essentially limitless; this Court explained that such a boundless view was inconsistent with the limiting terms Congress had used in the Act. *Id.*, at 167–174, 121 S.Ct. 675.

In response to the *SWANCC* decision, the Corps and the Environmental Protection Agency (EPA) initiated a rulemaking to consider "issues associated with the scope of waters that are subject to the Clean Water Act (CWA), in light of the U.S. Supreme Court decision in *[SWANCC]*." 68 Fed.Reg.1991 (2003). The "goal of the agencies" was "to develop proposed regula-

tions that will further the public interest by clarifying what waters are subject to CWA jurisdiction and affording full protection to these waters through an appropriate focus of Federal and State resources consistent with the CWA." *Ibid.*

Agencies delegated rulemaking authority under a statute such as the Clean Water Act are afforded generous leeway by the courts in interpreting the statute they are entrusted to administer. See *Chevron U.S.A. Inc. v. Natural Resources Defense Council, Inc.*, 467 U.S. 837, 842–845, 104 S.Ct. 2778, 81 L.Ed.2d 694 (1984). Given the broad, somewhat ambiguous, but nonetheless clearly limiting terms Congress employed in the Clean Water Act, the Corps and the EPA would have enjoyed plenty of room to operate in developing *some* notion of an outer bound to the reach of their authority.

The proposed rulemaking went nowhere. Rather than refining its view of its authority in light of our decision in *SWANCC*, and providing guidance meriting deference under our generous standards, the Corps chose to adhere to its essentially boundless view of the scope of its power. The upshot today is another defeat for the agency.

It is unfortunate that no opinion commands a majority of the Court on precisely how to read Congress' limits on the reach of the Clean Water Act. Lower courts and regulated entities will now have to feel their way on a case-by-case basis. This situation is certainly not unprecedented. See *Grutter v. Bollinger*, 539 U.S. 306, 325, 123 S.Ct. 2325, 156 L.Ed.2d 304 (2003) (discussing *Marks v. United States*, 430 U.S. 188, 97 S.Ct. 990, 51 L.Ed.2d 260 (1977)). What is unusual in this instance, perhaps, is how readily the situation could have been avoided.

JUSTICE KENNEDY, CONCURRING IN THE JUDGMENT:

...The statutory term to be interpreted and applied in the two instant cases is the term "navigable waters." The outcome turns on whether that phrase reasonably describes certain Michigan wetlands the Corps seeks to regulate. . . .

Contrary to the plurality's description, wetlands are not simply moist patches of earth. They are defined as "those areas that are inundated or saturated by surface or ground water at a frequency and duration sufficient to support, and that under normal circumstances do support, a prevalence of vegetation typically adapted for life in saturated soil conditions. Wetlands generally include swamps, marshes, bogs, and similar areas." §328.3(b). The Corps' Wetlands Delineation Manual, including over 100 pages of technical guidance for Corps officers, interprets this definition of wetlands to require: (1) prevalence of plant species typically adapted to saturated soil conditions, determined in accordance with the United States Fish and Wildlife Service's National List of Plant Species that Occur in Wetlands; (2) hydric soil, meaning soil that is saturated, flooded, or ponded for sufficient time during the growing season to become anaerobic, or lacking in oxygen, in the upper part; and (3) wetland hydrology, a term generally requiring continuous inundation or saturation to the surface during at least five percent of the growing season in most years. . . .

Twice before the Court has construed the term "navigable waters" in the Clean Water Act. In *United States v. Riverside Bayview Homes, Inc.*, 474 U.S. 121, 106 S.Ct. 455, 88 L.Ed.2d 419 (1985), the Court upheld the Corps' jurisdiction over wetlands adjacent to navigable-in-fact waterways. *Id.*, at 139, 106 S.Ct. 455. The property in *Riverside Bayview*, like the wetlands in the *Carabell* case now before the Court, was located roughly one mile from Lake St. Clair, see *United States v. Riverside Bayview Homes, Inc.*, 729 F.2d 391, 392 (C.A.6 1984) (decision on review in *Riverside Bayview*), though in that case, unlike *Carabell*, the lands at issue formed part of a wetland that directly abutted a navigable-in-

fact creek, 474 U.S., at 131, 106 S.Ct. 455. In regulatory provisions that remain in effect, the Corps had concluded that wetlands perform important functions such as filtering and purifying water draining into adjacent water bodies, 33 CFR §320.4(b)(2)(vii), slowing the flow of runoff into lakes, rivers, and streams so as to prevent flooding and erosion, §§320.4(b)(2)(iv), (v), and providing critical habitat for aquatic animal species, §320.4(b)(2)(i). 474 U.S., at 134–135, 106 S.Ct. 455. Recognizing that "[a]n agency's construction of a statute it is charged with enforcing is entitled to deference if it is reasonable and not in conflict with the expressed intent of Congress," *id.*, at 131, 106 S.Ct. 455 (citing *Chemical Mfrs. Assn. v. Natural Resources Defense Council, Inc.*, 470 U.S. 116, 125, 105 S.Ct. 1102, 84 L.Ed.2d 90 (1985), and *Chevron U.S.A. Inc. v. Natural Resources Defense Council, Inc.*, 467 U.S. 837, 842–845, 104 S.Ct. 2778, 81 L.Ed.2d 694 (1984)), the Court held that "the Corps' ecological judgment about the relationship between waters and their adjacent wetlands provides an adequate basis for a legal judgment that adjacent wetlands may be defined as waters under the Act," 474 U.S., at 134, 106 S.Ct. 455. The Court reserved, however, the question of the Corps' authority to regulate wetlands other than those adjacent to open waters. See *id.*, at 131–132, n. 8, 106 S.Ct. 455.

In *SWANCC*, the Court considered the validity of the Corps' jurisdiction over ponds and mudflats that were isolated in the sense of being unconnected to other waters covered by the Act. 531 U.S., at 171, 121 S.Ct. 675. The property at issue was an abandoned sand and gravel pit mining operation where "remnant excavation trenches" had "evolv[ed] into a scattering of permanent and seasonal ponds." *Id.*, at 163, 121 S.Ct. 675. Asserting jurisdiction pursuant to a regulation called the "Migratory Bird Rule," the Corps argued that these isolated ponds were "waters of the United States" (and thus "navigable waters" under the Act) because they were used as habitat by migratory birds. *Id.*, at 164–165, 121 S.Ct. 675. The Court rejected this theory. "It was the significant nexus between wetlands and 'navigable waters,'" the Court held, "that informed our reading of the [Act] in *Riverside Bayview Homes.*" *Id.*, at 167, 121 S.Ct. 675. Because such a nexus was lacking with respect to isolated ponds, the Court held that the plain text of the statute did not permit the Corps' action. *Id.*, at 172, 121 S.Ct. 675.

Riverside Bayview and *SWANCC* establish the framework for the inquiry in the cases now before the Court: Do the Corps' regulations, as applied to the wetlands in *Carabell* and the three wetlands parcels in *Rapanos*, constitute a reasonable interpretation of "navigable waters" as in *Riverside Bayview* or an invalid construction as in *SWANCC?* Taken together these cases establish that in some instances, as exemplified by *Riverside Bayview*, the connection between a nonnavigable water or wetland and a navigable water may be so close, or potentially so close, that the Corps may deem the water or wetland a "navigable water" under the Act. In other instances, as exemplified by *SWANCC*, there may be little or no connection. Absent a significant nexus, jurisdiction under the Act is lacking. Because neither the plurality nor the dissent addresses the nexus requirement, this separate opinion, in my respectful view, is necessary.

A

The plurality's opinion begins from a correct premise. As the plurality points out, and as *Riverside Bayview* holds, in enacting the Clean Water Act Congress intended to regulate at least some waters that are not navigable in the traditional sense. *Riverside Bayview*, 474 U.S., at 133, 106 S.Ct. 455; see also *SWANCC, supra*, at 167, 121 S.Ct. 675. This conclusion is supported by "the evident

breadth of congressional concern for protection of water quality and aquatic ecosystems." *Riverside Bayview, supra*, at 133, 106 S.Ct. 455; see also *Milwaukee v. Illinois*, 451 U.S. 304, 318, 101 S.Ct. 1784, 68 L.Ed.2d 114 (1981) (describing the Act as "an all-encompassing program of water pollution regulation"). It is further compelled by statutory text, for the text is explicit in extending the coverage of the Act to some nonnavigable waters. In a provision allowing States to assume some regulatory functions of the Corps (an option Michigan has exercised), the Act limits States to issuing permits for: "the discharge of dredged or fill material into the navigable waters (other than those waters which are presently used, or are susceptible to use in their natural condition or by reasonable improvement as a means to transport interstate or foreign commerce shoreward to their ordinary high water mark, including all waters which are subject to the ebb and flow of the tide shoreward to their ordinary high water mark, or mean higher high water mark on the west coast, including wetlands adjacent thereto) within its jurisdiction." 33 U.S.C. §1344(g)(1).

Were there no Clean Water Act "navigable waters" apart from waters "presently used" or "susceptible to use" in interstate commerce, the "other than" clause, which begins the long parenthetical statement, would overtake the delegation of authority the provision makes at the outset. Congress, it follows, must have intended a broader meaning for navigable waters. The mention of wetlands in the "other than" clause, moreover, makes plain that at least some wetlands fall within the scope of the term "navigable waters." See *Riverside Bayview, supra*, at 138–139, and n. 11, 106 S.Ct. 455.

From this reasonable beginning the plurality proceeds to impose two limitations on the Act; but these limitations, it is here submitted, are without support in the language and purposes of the Act or in our cases interpreting it. First, because the dictionary defines "waters" to mean "water '[a]s found in streams and bodies forming geographical features such as oceans, rivers, [and] lakes,' or 'the flowing or moving masses, as of waves or floods, making up such streams or bodies,'" (quoting Webster's New International Dictionary 2882 (2d ed. 1954) (hereinafter Webster's Second)), the plurality would conclude that the phrase "navigable waters" permits Corps and EPA jurisdiction only over "relatively permanent, standing or flowing bodies of water," a category that in the plurality's view includes "seasonal" rivers, that is, rivers that carry water continuously except during "dry months," but not intermittent or ephemeral streams. Second, the plurality asserts that wetlands fall within the Act only if they bear "a continuous surface connection to bodies that are 'waters of the United States' in their own right"—waters, that is, that satisfy the plurality's requirement of permanent standing water or continuous flow.

The plurality's first requirement—permanent standing water or continuous flow, at least for a period of "some months," makes little practical sense in a statute concerned with downstream water quality. The merest trickle, if continuous, would count as a "water" subject to federal regulation, while torrents thundering at irregular intervals through otherwise dry channels would not. Though the plurality seems to presume that such irregular flows are too insignificant to be of concern in a statute focused on "waters," that may not always be true. Areas in the western parts of the Nation provide some examples. The Los Angeles River, for instance, ordinarily carries only a trickle of water and often looks more like a dry roadway than a river. Yet it periodically releases water volumes so powerful and destructive that it has been encased in concrete and steel over a length of some 50 miles. Though this particular waterway might satisfy the plurality's test, it is illustrative of what often-dry

watercourses can become when rain waters flow.

To be sure, Congress could draw a line to exclude irregular waterways, but nothing in the statute suggests it has done so. Quite the opposite, a full reading of the dictionary definition precludes the plurality's emphasis on permanence: The term "waters" may mean "flood or inundation," Webster's Second 2882, events that are impermanent by definition. Thus, although of course the Act's use of the adjective "navigable" indicates a focus on waterways rather than floods, Congress' use of "waters" instead of "water," does not necessarily carry the connotation of "relatively permanent, standing or flowing bodies of water." (And contrary to the plurality's suggestion, there is no indication in the dictionary that the "flood or inundation" definition is limited to poetry.) In any event, even granting the plurality's preferred definition—that "waters" means "water '[a]s found in streams and bodies forming geographical features such as oceans, rivers, [and] lakes,'" (quoting Webster's Second 2882)—the dissent is correct to observe that an intermittent flow can constitute a stream, in the sense of "'a current or course of water or other fluid, flowing on the earth,'" (quoting Webster's Second 2493), while it is flowing. It follows that the Corps can reasonably interpret the Act to cover the paths of such impermanent streams. . . .

The plurality's second limitation—exclusion of wetlands lacking a continuous surface connection to other jurisdictional waters—is also unpersuasive. To begin with, the plurality is wrong to suggest that wetlands are "*indistinguishable*" from waters to which they bear a surface connection. Even if the precise boundary may be imprecise, a bog or swamp is different from a river. The question is what circumstances permit a bog, swamp, or other nonnavigable wetland to constitute a "navigable water" under the Act—as §1344(g)(1), if nothing else, indicates is sometimes possible. *Riverside Bayview* addressed that question and its answer is inconsistent with the plurality's theory. There, in upholding the Corps' authority to regulate "wetlands adjacent to other bodies of water over which the Corps has jurisdiction," the Court deemed it irrelevant whether "the moisture creating the wetlands...find[s] its source in the adjacent bodies of water." 474 U.S., at 135, 106 S.Ct. 455. The Court further observed that adjacency could serve as a valid basis for regulation even as to "wetlands that are not significantly intertwined with the ecosystem of adjacent waterways." *Id.*, at 135, n. 9, 106 S.Ct. 455. "If it is reasonable," the Court explained, "for the Corps to conclude that in the majority of cases, adjacent wetlands have significant effects on water quality and the aquatic ecosystem, its definition can stand." *Ibid.* . . .

SWANCC, likewise, does not support the plurality's surface-connection requirement. *SWANCC*'s holding that "nonnavigable, isolated, intrastate waters," 531 U.S., at 171, 121 S.Ct. 675, are not "navigable waters" is not an explicit or implicit overruling of *Riverside Bayview's* approval of adjacency as a factor in determining the Corps' jurisdiction. In rejecting the Corps' claimed authority over the isolated ponds in *SWANCC*, the Court distinguished adjacent nonnavigable waters such as the wetlands addressed in *Riverside Bayview*. 531 U.S., at 167, 170–171, 121 S.Ct. 675.

As *Riverside Bayview* recognizes, the Corps' adjacency standard is reasonable in some of its applications. Indeed, the Corps' view draws support from the structure of the Act, while the plurality's surface-water-connection requirement does not.

As discussed above, the Act's prohibition on the discharge of pollutants into navigable waters, 33 U.S.C. §1311(a), covers both the discharge of toxic materials such as sewage, chemical waste, biological material, and radioactive material and the discharge of dredged spoil, rock, sand, cellar dirt, and the like. All these substances are defined as pollutants whose discharge into navigable waters violates the Act. §§1311(a), 1362(6), (12). One reason for the parallel treatment may be that the discharge of fill material can impair downstream water quality. The plurality argues otherwise, asserting that dredged or fill material "does not normally wash downstream." As the dissent points out, this proposition seems questionable as an empirical matter. It seems plausible that new or loose fill, not anchored by grass or roots from other vegetation, could travel downstream through waterways adjacent to a wetland; at the least this is a factual possibility that the Corps' experts can better assess than can the plurality. Silt, whether from natural or human sources, is a major factor in aquatic environments, and it may clog waterways, alter ecosystems, and limit the useful life of dams. See, *e.g.*, Fountain, Unloved, But Not Unbuilt, N.Y. Times, June 5, 2005 section 4, p. 3, col. 1; DePalma, Dam to Be Demolished to Save an Endangered Species, N.Y. Times, Apr. 26, 2004, section B, p. 1, col. 2; MacDougall, Damage Can Be Irreversible, Los Angeles Times, June 19, 1987, pt. 1, p. 10, col. 4.

Even granting, however, the plurality's assumption that fill material will stay put, Congress' parallel treatment of fill material and toxic pollution may serve another purpose. As the Court noted in *Riverside Bayview*, "the Corps has concluded that wetlands may serve to filter and purify water draining into adjacent bodies of water, 33 CFR §320.4(b)(2)(vii) (1985), and to slow the flow of surface runoff into lakes, rivers, and streams and thus prevent flooding and erosion, see §§320.4(b)(2)(iv) and (v)." 474 U.S., at 134, 106 S.Ct. 455. Where wetlands perform these filtering and runoff-control functions, filling them may increase downstream pollution, much as a discharge of toxic pollutants would. Not only will dirty water no longer be stored and filtered but also the act of filling and draining itself may cause the release of nutrients, toxins, and pathogens that were trapped, neutralized, and perhaps amenable to filtering or detoxification in the wetlands. See U.S. Congress, Office of Technology Assessment, Wetlands: Their Use and Regulation, OTA-O-206 pp. 43, 48–52 (Mar.1984), http://govinfo.library.unt.edu/ota/OTA_4/DATA/1984/8433.pdf (hereinafter OTA). In many cases, moreover, filling in wetlands separated from another water by a berm can mean that flood water, impurities, or runoff that would have been stored or contained in the wetlands will instead flow out to major waterways. With these concerns in mind, the Corps' definition of adjacency is a reasonable one, for it may be the absence of an interchange of waters prior to the dredge and fill activity that makes protection of the wetlands critical to the statutory scheme.

In sum the plurality's opinion is inconsistent with the Act's text, structure, and purpose....

It bears mention also that the plurality's overall tone and approach—from the characterization of acres of wetlands destruction as "backfilling...wet fields," to the rejection of Corps authority over "man-made drainage ditches" and "dry arroyos" without regard to how much water they periodically carry, to the suggestion, seemingly contrary to Congress' judgment, that discharge of fill material is inconsequential for adjacent waterways, seems unduly dismissive of the interests asserted by the United States in these cases. Important public interests are served by the Clean Water Act in general and by the protection of wetlands in particular. To give just one example, *amici* here have noted that nutrient-rich runoff from the Mississippi River has created a hypoxic, or oxygen-depleted, "dead zone" in the Gulf of Mexico that at times approaches the size of Massachusetts and New Jersey. Brief for Association of State Wetland Managers et al. 21–23;

Brief for Environmental Law Institute 23. Scientific evidence indicates that wetlands play a critical role in controlling and filtering runoff. See, *e.g.*, OTA 43, 48–52; R. Tiner, In Search of Swampland: A Wetland Sourcebook and Field Guide 93–95 (2d ed. 2005); Whitmire & Hamilton, Rapid Removal of Nitrate and Sulfate in Freshwater Wetland Sediments, 34 J. Env. Quality 2062 (2005). It is true, as the plurality indicates, that environmental concerns provide no reason to disregard limits in the statutory text, but in my view the plurality's opinion is not a correct reading of the text. The limits the plurality would impose, moreover, give insufficient deference to Congress' purposes in enacting the Clean Water Act and to the authority of the Executive to implement that statutory mandate....

B

While the plurality reads nonexistent requirements into the Act, the dissent reads a central requirement out—namely, the requirement that the word "navigable" in "navigable waters" be given some importance. Although the Court has held that the statute's language invokes Congress' traditional authority over waters navigable in fact or susceptible of being made so, *SWANCC*, 531 U.S., at 172, 121 S.Ct. 675 (citing *Appalachian Power*, 311 U.S., at 407–408, 61 S.Ct. 291), the dissent would permit federal regulation whenever wetlands lie alongside a ditch or drain, however remote and insubstantial, that eventually may flow into traditional navigable waters. The deference owed to the Corps' interpretation of the statute does not extend so far.

Congress' choice of words creates difficulties, for the Act contemplates regulation of certain "navigable waters" that are not in fact navigable. Nevertheless, the word "navigable" in the Act must be given some effect. See *SWANCC, supra*, at 172, 121 S.Ct. 675. Thus, in *SWANCC* the Court rejected the

Corps' assertion of jurisdiction over isolated ponds and mudflats bearing no evident connection to navigable-in-fact waters. And in *Riverside Bayview*, while the Court indicated that "the term 'navigable' as used in the Act is of limited import," 474 U.S., at 133, 106 S.Ct. 455, it relied, in upholding jurisdiction, on the Corps' judgment that "wetlands adjacent to lakes, rivers, streams, and other bodies of water may function as integral parts of the aquatic environment even when the moisture creating the wetlands does not find its source in the adjacent bodies of water," *id.*, at 135, 106 S.Ct. 455. The implication, of course, was that wetlands' status as "integral parts of the aquatic environment"—that is, their significant nexus with navigable waters—was what established the Corps' jurisdiction over them as waters of the United States.

Consistent with *SWANCC* and *Riverside Bayview* and with the need to give the term "navigable" some meaning, the Corps' jurisdiction over wetlands depends upon the existence of a significant nexus between the wetlands in question and navigable waters in the traditional sense. The required nexus must be assessed in terms of the statute's goals and purposes. Congress enacted the law to "restore and maintain the chemical, physical, and biological integrity of the Nation's waters," 33 U.S.C. §1251(a), and it pursued that objective by restricting dumping and filling in "navigable waters," §§1311(a), 1362(12). With respect to wetlands, the rationale for Clean Water Act regulation is, as the Corps has recognized, that wetlands can perform critical functions related to the integrity of other waters—functions such as pollutant trapping, flood control, and runoff storage. 33 CFR §320.4(b)(2). Accordingly, wetlands possess the requisite nexus, and thus come within the statutory phrase "navigable waters," if the wetlands, either alone or in combination with similarly situated lands in the region, significantly affect the chemical, physical, and biological integrity of other

covered waters more readily understood as "navigable." When, in contrast, wetlands' effects on water quality are speculative or insubstantial, they fall outside the zone fairly encompassed by the statutory term "navigable waters." . . .

In these consolidated cases I would vacate the judgments of the Court of Appeals and remand for consideration whether the specific wetlands at issue possess a significant nexus with navigable waters.

JUSTICE STEVENS, WITH WHOM JUSTICE SOUTER, JUSTICE GINSBURG, AND JUSTICE BREYER JOIN, DISSENTING:

In 1972, Congress decided to "restore and maintain the chemical, physical, and biological integrity of the Nation's waters" by passing what we now call the Clean Water Act. 86 Stat. 816, as amended, 33 U.S.C. §1251 *et seq.* The costs of achieving the Herculean goal of ending water pollution by 1985, see §1251(a), persuaded President Nixon to veto its enactment, but both Houses of Congress voted to override that veto by overwhelming margins. To achieve its goal, Congress prohibited "the discharge of any pollutant"—defined to include "any addition of any pollutant to navigable waters from any point source"—without a permit issued by the Army Corps of Engineers (Army Corps or Corps) or the Environmental Protection Agency (EPA). §§1311(a), 1362(12)(A). Congress further defined "navigable waters" to mean "the waters of the United States." §1362(7).

The narrow question presented in No. 04-1034 is whether wetlands adjacent to tributaries of traditionally navigable waters are "waters of the United States" subject to the jurisdiction of the Army Corps; the question in No. 04-1384 is whether a manmade berm separating a wetland from the adjacent tributary makes a difference. The broader question is whether regulations that have protected the quality of our waters for decades, that were implicitly approved by Congress, and that have been repeatedly enforced in case after case, must now be revised in light of the creative criticisms voiced by the plurality and Justice KENNEDY today. Rejecting more than 30 years of practice by the Army Corps, the plurality disregards the nature of the congressional delegation to the agency and the technical and complex character of the issues at stake. Justice KENNEDY similarly fails to defer sufficiently to the Corps, though his approach is far more faithful to our precedents and to principles of statutory interpretation than is the plurality's.

In my view, the proper analysis is straightforward. The Army Corps has determined that wetlands adjacent to tributaries of traditionally navigable waters preserve the quality of our Nation's waters by, among other things, providing habitat for aquatic animals, keeping excessive sediment and toxic pollutants out of adjacent waters, and reducing downstream flooding by absorbing water at times of high flow. The Corps' resulting decision to treat these wetlands as encompassed within the term "waters of the United States" is a quintessential example of the Executive's reasonable interpretation of a statutory provision. See *Chevron U.S.A. Inc. v. Natural Resources Defense Council, Inc.*, 467 U.S. 837, 842–845, 104 S.Ct. 2778, 81 L.Ed.2d 694 (1984).

Our unanimous decision in *United States v. Riverside Bayview Homes, Inc.*, 474 U.S. 121, 106 S.Ct. 455, 88 L.Ed.2d 419 (1985), was faithful to our duty to respect the work product of the Legislative and Executive Branches of our Government. Today's judicial amendment of the Clean Water Act is not....

II

Our unanimous opinion in *Riverside Bayview* squarely controls these cases. There, we eval-

uated the validity of the very same regulations at issue today. These regulations interpret "waters of the United States" to cover all traditionally navigable waters; tributaries of these waters; and wetlands adjacent to traditionally navigable waters or their tributaries. 33 CFR §§328.3(a)(1), (5), and (7) (2005); §§323.2(a)(1), (5), and (7) (1985). Although the particular wetland at issue in *Riverside Bayview* abutted a navigable creek, we framed the question presented as whether the Clean Water Act "authorizes the Corps to require landowners to obtain permits from the Corps before discharging fill material into wetlands adjacent to navigable bodies of water and their tributaries." 474 U.S. at 123 (emphasis added).

We held that, pursuant to our decision in *Chevron*,

"our review is limited to the question whether it is reasonable, in light of the language, policies, and legislative history of the Act for the Corps to exercise jurisdiction over wetlands adjacent to but not regularly flooded by rivers, streams, and other hydrographic features more conventionally identifiable as 'waters.'" 474 U.S., at 131, 106 S.Ct. 455.

Applying this standard, we held that the Corps' decision to interpret "waters of the United States" as encompassing such wetlands was permissible. We recognized the practical difficulties in drawing clean lines between land and water, *id.*, at 132, 106 S.Ct. 455, and deferred to the Corps' judgment that treating adjacent wetlands as "waters" would advance the "congressional concern for protection of water quality and aquatic ecosystems," *id.*, at 133, 106 S.Ct. 455.

Contrary to the plurality's revisionist reading today, *Riverside Bayview* nowhere implied that our approval of "adjacent" wetlands was contingent upon an understanding that "adjacent" means having a "continuous surface connection" between the wetland and its neighboring creek. Instead, we acknowledged that the Corps defined "adjacent" as including wetlands "'that form the border of or are in reasonable proximity to other waters'" and found that the Corps reasonably concluded that adjacent wetlands are part of the waters of the United States. 474 U.S., at 134, 106 S.Ct. 455 (quoting 42 Fed.Reg. 37128 (1977)). Indeed, we explicitly acknowledged that the Corps' jurisdictional determination was reasonable even though

"not every adjacent wetland is of great importance to the environment of adjoining bodies of water.... If it is reasonable for the Corps to conclude that in the majority of cases, adjacent wetlands have significant effects on water quality and the ecosystem, its definition can stand. That the definition may include some wetlands that are not significantly intertwined with the ecosystem of adjacent waterways is of little moment, for where it appears that a wetland covered by the Corps' definition is in fact lacking in importance to the aquatic environment... the Corps may always allow development of the wetland for other uses simply by issuing a permit." 474 U.S., at 135, n. 9, 106 S.Ct. 455.

In closing, we emphasized that the scope of the Corps' asserted jurisdiction over wetlands had been specifically brought to Congress' attention in 1977, that Congress had rejected an amendment that would have narrowed that jurisdiction, and that even proponents of the amendment would not have removed wetlands altogether from the definition of "waters of the United States." *Id.*, at 135–139, 106 S.Ct. 455.

Disregarding the importance of *Riverside Bayview*, the plurality relies heavily on the Court's subsequent opinion in *Solid Waste Agency of Northern Cook Cty. v. Army Corps of Engineers*, 531 U.S. 159, 121 S.Ct. 675, 148 L.Ed.2d 576 (2001) *(SWANCC)*. In stark contrast to *Riverside Bayview*, however, *SWANCC* had nothing to say about wetlands, let alone about wetlands adjacent to traditionally navigable waters or their tributaries. Instead, *SWANCC* dealt with a question specifically reserved by *Riverside Bayview*, see n. 3, *supra*, namely, the Corps' jurisdiction over isolated waters—"'waters that are *not* part of a tributary system to in-

terstate waters or to navigable waters of the United States, the degradation or destruction of which could affect interstate commerce.'" 531 U.S., at 168–169, 121 S.Ct. 675 (quoting 33 CFR §323.2(a)(5) (1978); emphasis added); see also 531 U.S., at 163, 121 S.Ct. 675 (citing 33 CFR §328.2(a)(3) (1999), which is the later regulatory equivalent to §323.2(a)(5) (1978)). At issue in *SWANCC* was "an abandoned sand and gravel pit... which provide[d] habitat for migratory birds" and contained a few pools of "nonnavigable, isolated, intrastate waters." 531 U.S., at 162, 166, 121 S.Ct. 675. The Corps had asserted jurisdiction over the gravel pit under its 1986 Migratory Bird Rule, which treated isolated waters as within its jurisdiction if migratory birds depended upon these waters. The Court rejected this jurisdictional basis since these isolated pools, unlike the wetlands at issue in *Riverside Bayview*, had no "significant nexus" to traditionally navigable waters. 531 U.S., at 167, 121 S.Ct. 675. In the process, the Court distinguished *Riverside Bayview's* reliance on Congress' decision to leave the Corps' regulations alone when it amended the Act in 1977, since "'[i]n both Chambers, debate on the proposals to narrow the definition of navigable waters centered largely on the issue of wetlands preservation'" rather than on the Corps' jurisdiction over truly isolated waters. 531 U.S., at 170, 121 S.Ct. 675 (quoting 474 U.S., at 136, 106 S.Ct. 455).

Unlike *SWANCC* and like *Riverside Bayview*, the cases before us today concern wetlands that are adjacent to "navigable bodies of water [or] their tributaries," 474 U.S., at 123, 106 S.Ct. 455. Specifically, these wetlands abut tributaries of traditionally navigable waters. As we recognized in *Riverside Bayview*, the Corps has concluded that such wetlands play important roles in maintaining the quality of their adjacent waters, see *id.*, at 134–135, 106 S.Ct. 455, and consequently in the waters downstream. Among other things, wetlands can offer "nesting, spawning, rearing and resting sites for aquatic or land species"; "serve as valuable storage areas for storm and flood waters"; and provide "significant water purification functions." 33 CFR §320.4(b)(2) (2005); 474 U.S., at 134–135, 106 S.Ct. 455. These values are hardly "*independent*" ecological considerations as the plurality would have it—instead, they are integral to the "chemical, physical, and biological integrity of the Nation's waters," 33 U.S.C. §1251(a). Given that wetlands serve these important water quality roles and given the ambiguity inherent in the phrase "waters of the United States," the Corps has reasonably interpreted its jurisdiction to cover nonisolated wetlands. See 474 U.S., at 131–135, 106 S.Ct. 455.

This conclusion is further confirmed by Congress' deliberate acquiescence in the Corps' regulations in 1977. *Id.*, at 136, 106 S.Ct. 455. Both Chambers conducted extensive debates about the Corps' regulatory jurisdiction over wetlands, rejected efforts to limit this jurisdiction, and appropriated funds for a "'National Wetlands Inventory'" to help the States "'in the development and operation of programs under this Act.'" *Id.*, at 135–139, 106 S.Ct. 455 (quoting 33 U.S.C. §1288(i)(2)). We found these facts significant in *Riverside Bayview*, see 474 U.S., at 135–139, 106 S.Ct. 455, as we acknowledged in *SWANCC*. See 531 U.S., at 170–171, 121 S.Ct. 675 (noting that "*[b]eyond Congress' desire to regulate wetlands adjacent to 'navigable waters,'* respondents point us to no persuasive evidence" of congressional acquiescence (emphasis added))....

III

... Most importantly, the plurality disregards the fundamental significance of the Clean Water Act. As then-Justice Rehnquist explained when writing for the Court in 1981, the Act was "not merely another law" but rather was "viewed by Congress as a 'total restructuring' and 'complete rewriting' of the existing water pollution legislation." *Milwaukee v. Illinois*, 451 U.S. 304, 317, 101 S.Ct. 1784, 68 L.Ed.2d 114. "Congress' intent in enacting the [Act] was clearly to establish an all-encompassing program of water pollution regulation," and "the most casual perusal of the legislative history demonstrates that . . . views on the comprehensive nature of the legislation were practically universal." *Id.*, at 318, and n. 12, 101 S.Ct. 1784; see also 531 U.S., at 177–181, 121 S.Ct. 675 (STEVENS, J., dissenting). The Corps has concluded that it must regulate pollutants at the time they enter ditches or streams with ordinary high-water marks—whether perennial, intermittent, or ephemeral—in order to properly control water pollution. 65 Fed.Reg. 12823 (2000). Because there is ambiguity in the phrase "waters of the United States" and because interpreting it broadly to cover such ditches and streams advances the purpose of the Act, the Corps' approach should command our deference. Intermittent streams can carry pollutants just as perennial streams can, and their regulation may prove as important for flood control purposes. The inclusion of all identifiable tributaries that ultimately drain into large bodies of water within the mantle of federal protection is surely wise....

- **NOTES**

1. Is it likely that Congress could avoid the result in this case (and in the *SWANCC* case on which the plurality relies) simply by amending the Clean Water Act to

specify that the act's provisions apply to all bodies of water and wetlands regardless of their size or location? What issue of constitutional law hovers at the edges of the Court's decision here?

2. It is interesting to compare the contrasting views of wetlands regulation embodied in Justice Scalia's plurality opinion, on the one hand, and in Justice Kennedy's concurring opinion and Justice Stevens' dissent. Is it fair to say that the differing views reflect differing *policy preferences* with regard to the strength and scope of environmental regulation? Should a judge's policy preferences have any bearing on his or her interpretation of a congressional statute? In this case, which view of wetlands regulation appears to be most faithful to the policy preferences of Congress, as expressed in the Clean Water Act? The impact of this decision on wetlands protection is revisited later in this chapter.

3. The dissenting opinion makes much of the fact that Congress never amended the statute in response to the more expansive definition employed by the Corps of Engineers, while the plurality opinion argues that congressional inaction is an inherently untrustworthy indication of congressional intent. As a general matter of statutory construction, does the plurality's caution on this point appear sound? Is there nonetheless sufficient evidence here that the failure of Congress to amend the statute was a purposeful decision?

4. Note that while Justice Scalia's plurality opinion is the lead opinion, five of the nine Justices disagree with that opinion. What value, if any, does Justice Scalia's opinion have as a precedent for future cases? Does Justice Kennedy's opinion—with its "substantial nexus" test—now become the standard by which future questions regarding the scope of the Clean Water Act will be evaluated?

5. The act's definition of "discharge of a pollutant" extends the prohibition against nonconforming discharges to "any addition of any pollutant to the waters of the contiguous zone or the ocean from any point source other than a vessel or other floating craft" [Section 502(12)]. The contiguous zone is "the entire zone established or to be established by the United States under . . . the Convention of the Territorial Sea and the Contiguous Zone" [Section 502(9)].

6. In addition to the waters of the fifty states, the waters of other territories associated with the United States, such as the District of Columbia, Puerto Rico, and Guam, are also covered by the act. See Section 502(3).   ■

iv. The National Pollutant Discharge Elimination System (NPDES) Permit   Another significant change brought about by the 1972 amendments was a comprehensive permit program governing discharges to the navigable waters. The specifications for this permit program are set forth in Section 402. Consistent with

Permits to Pollute

the national "no discharge" goal, this section is titled "National Pollutant Discharge Elimination System." Accordingly, the permits issued under the authority of this section are known as National Pollutant Discharge Elimination System (NPDES) permits. The NPDES permit is the central implementation mechanism for most of the Clean Water Act's requirements for point sources. Generally speaking, discharge to the navigable waters without a permit is unlawful under Section 301(a). This requirement applies to all point sources, including industrial plants and other commercial enterprises, public sewage treatment plants, and a wide variety of other government facilities (such as military bases, prisons, and energy facilities) discharging pollutants to the navigable waters.

The NPDES permit performs two important functions. First, it is the principal means by which EPA ensures that the various requirements of the Clean Water Act have been imposed on the individual discharger, and by which those requirements are applied to the particular circumstances of the individual discharger. Second, the NPDES permit is the principal means by which the individual discharger may ensure that it does not run afoul of the Section 301(a) prohibition against noncomplying discharges. For, as specified in Section 402(k), which is commonly known as the act's "permit shield" provision, adherence to the discharge limitations specified in its NPDES permit protects the discharger from liability under Section 301, unless the discharge limitations in the permit are inconsistent with a Section 307 standard "for a toxic pollutant injurious to human health" [33 U.S.C. §1342(k)].

adherence Protects Polluter

v. National Technology-Based Effluent Limits for Industry In keeping with the specified national goals of the act, the 1972 amendments directed EPA to develop a series of specific *national* limitations on point source discharges of pollutants. In Section 301(b), Congress specified a timetable by which these limitations were to be promulgated, and in Section 304 it specified the criteria that EPA was to take into account in developing them. The central feature of this congressional scheme was a two-stage program for the reduction of discharges from existing industrial facilities. By 1977, EPA was to promulgate "effluent limitations for point sources [other than public sewage treatment plants]...which shall require the application of the best practicable control technology currently available" [Section 301(b)(1)(A)(i)]. In the second stage, to be completed by 1983, EPA was to promulgate "effluent limitations for point sources [other than public sewage treatment plants]...which shall require the application of the best available technology economically achievable" [Section 301(b)(2)(A)]. In addition, the 1972 amendments directed EPA to promulgate within 15 months a separate set of national effluent limitations, called "standards of performance," for new industrial sources of water pollution [Section 306(b)(1)(A) and (B)]. These effluent limitations are to require "the greatest degree of effluent reduction which...[is] achievable through application of the best available demonstrated

Best tech avail

control technology, processes, operating methods, or other alternatives" [Section 306(a)(1)].

The key feature uniting these three types of national effluent standards is that they are set primarily according to certain considerations of cost and technological feasibility. This, too, marked a departure from the earlier versions of the Federal Water Pollution Control Act. Rather than working from the bottom up—directing EPA to assess the quality of the receiving waters and to determine the kinds and amounts of effluent reductions necessary to meet water quality criteria—Congress instead chose to work from the top down, by directing EPA to simply determine the kinds and amounts of effluent reduction industry could afford within the confines of available technology. Although, as discussed later, this proved to be far from an easy task for the agency, it nonetheless did not require the agency to prove either that a particular level of water quality was required or that a particular level of effluent reduction was necessary to meet a particular water quality goal. Congress had effectively made these policy choices already.

Congress also specified in the 1972 amendments that these national regulations are to include technology-based requirements governing the *intake* of surface waters by point source facilities that utilize these waters to cool their industrial processes. The intake of cooling water—which can occur on a massive scale at the larger facilities—routinely kills or maims fish and other aquatic life. Thus, section 316(b) of the act specifies that "[a]ny standard" promulgated by EPA under section 301 or 306 "shall require that the location, design, construction, and capacity of cooling water intake structures reflect the best technology available for minimizing adverse environmental consequences" [33 U.S.C. § 1326(b)]. For years, EPA simply applied this requirement to individual sources on a case-by-case basis. After being sued by a coalition of environmental groups in the mid-1990s, however, the agency began issuing national cooling water intake standards for specified categories of facilities. *See Riverkeeper v. EPA*, 358 F.3d 174 (2nd Cir. 2004).

vi. Health-Based Effluent Limits for Toxic Pollutants, Set on a Pollutant-by-Pollutant Basis   For a particular set of pollutants, Congress chose to retain the water quality-based approach inherent in previous versions of the act. The 1972 amendments directed EPA to publish a list of "toxic pollutants" within 90 days. 33 U.S.C. §1317(a)(1) (1972). Toxic pollutants are defined in the act as

those pollutants, or combination of pollutants, including disease-causing agents, which after discharge and upon exposure, ingestion, inhalation or assimilation into any organism, either directly from the environment or indirectly by ingestion through food chains, will, on the basis of information available to the Administrator [of EPA], cause death, disease, behavioral abnormalities, cancer, genetic mutations, physiological malfunctions (including malfunctions in reproduction) or physical deformations, in such organisms or their offspring. [Section 502(13)]

Within 180 days after listing a pollutant as a toxic pollutant, EPA was to promulgate a proposed standard limiting the discharge of the pollutant into the navigable waters. That standard, applicable to all point sources regardless of age or cost of compliance, was to "take into account the toxicity of the pollutant, its persistence, degradability, the usual or potential presence of the affected organisms in any waters, the importance of the affected organisms and the nature and extent of the toxic pollutant on such organisms," and was to provide "an ample margin of safety." EPA was to hold a public hearing on the proposed standard, and was to promulgate the final standard within 6 months. 33 U.S.C. §1317(a)(1) and (4) (1972).

The Clean Water Act's definition of "toxic pollutant" is a broad one, and the act's toxic pollutant provisions clearly are not limited to those substances that cause toxic effects in humans. Any substance capable of causing one or more of the enumerated toxic effects to *some organism* after discharge to the water, through one or more of the enumerated exposure routes, satisfies the statutory definition.

vii.   Technology-Based Effluent Limitations and Public Financing for Public Sewage Treatment Plants   Consistent with their approach to other point sources, the 1972 amendments directed EPA to set a technology-based standard for all public sewage treatment plants, which are referred to in the act as "publicly owned treatment works" (POTWs). By July 1, 1977, all POTWs were to meet "effluent limitations based on secondary treatment," as defined by EPA [Section 301(b)(1)(B)]. Secondary treatment refers to biological treatment of the wastewater (the use of microorganisms to remove the organic matter), while primary treatment (which is commonly a necessary precursor to biological treatment) is simply the removal of solids. By July 1, 1983, all POTWs were to apply "the best practicable waste treatment technology over the life of the works" [Sections 301(b)(2)(B) and 201(g)(2)(A)].

Recognizing that many communities had antiquated sewage treatment plants that did not provide secondary treatment, and that some communities had no sewage treatment plant at all, Congress created a massive federal grant program in Title II of the revised act, and allocated several billion dollars to be given to local communities for the construction and improvement of sewage treatment facilities. Initially, this set in place a confrontation between Congress and the executive, as President Nixon impounded the allocated funds and refused to allow EPA to make the grants called for by the statute. Ultimately, the Supreme Court held that the president had overstepped the bounds of his authority, and the grant program moved forward.

viii.   Federal Pretreatment Standards for Discharges into Public Sewage Treatment Plants   Recognizing that many industrial facilities discharged all or a portion of their waste to public sewer systems, and that such discharges can be both an additional source of pollution to the surface waters and a means of disrupting the treatment efficiency of the POTW, the amendments also directed EPA to develop pretreatment standards for introduction of pollutants into treatment works...which are publicly owned for those pollutants which are determined not to be susceptible to treatment by such treatment works or which would interfere with the operation of such treatment works. [Section 307(b)(1)]

Such regulations were to be proposed within 180 days of the passage of the amendments, "and from time to time thereafter."

ix. Ambient Water Quality Standards Set by the States   Retained from the previous version of the act was a system of ambient water quality standards to be set by the states, subject to EPA approval. Section 303, 33 U.S.C. §1313, added in 1972, specified that state water quality standards previously adopted would remain in effect unless EPA specifically disapproved them by a specified date, and it directed states who did not have such standards to promulgate them. Section 303(a). If a state did not promulgate such standards, EPA was to promulgate standards for that state; similarly, if EPA rejected a state standard, EPA was to promulgate an appropriate replacement standard. Section 303(b). As discussed more fully later, Section 303 also mandates a process for the periodic revision of ambient water quality standards, and requires that certain steps be taken to facilitate the promulgation of water quality-based effluent limitations in individual NPDES permits. Section 303(c) and (d).

x. Data Generation and Data Disclosure   Another key feature of the act is its reliance on mandatory data generation and disclosure. Section 308, 33 U.S.C. §1318, put in place by the 1972 amendments, gives EPA broad authority to:

...require the owner or operator of any point source to (i) establish and maintain such records, (ii) make such reports, (iii) install, use, and maintain such monitoring equipment or methods (including, where appropriate, biological monitoring methods), (iv) sample such effluents (in accordance with such methods, at such locations, at such intervals, and in such manner as the Administrator [of EPA] may prescribe), and (v) provide such other information as [the Administrator] may reasonably require [in carrying out the purposes of the act]. [Section 308(a)(A)]

As was clearly intended by the act, EPA has used this authority through the years to require dischargers to develop an increasingly sophisticated database on what (and how much) they are discharging to the surface waters, on the impact of those discharges on water quality, and on the processes that led to those discharges. As discussed later, the development and reporting of such information is essential to the NPDES permitting process.

Further, Section 308(b) specifies that "[a]ny records, reports, or information obtained under this section ... shall be available to the public...." This, then, creates a right of public access that is independent of the Freedom of Information Act (see chapter 5). In essence, copies of any document, computer file, or other data expression submitted to EPA or the state pursuant to the requirements of the act may be obtained from the agency to which it was submitted. The only exception to this broad right of public access is a provision against disclosures that "would divulge methods or processes entitled to protection as trade secrets." This trade secret exception is not applicable to "effluent data," however, reflecting an apparent congressional conclusion that the value of making such data available to the public outweighs any harm that would ensue from the relatively rare circumstance in which such data would reveal legitimate trade secrets.

- **NOTE**

1. The 1972 amendments also established procedures for the generation of information on the quality of the nation's surface waters. See, for example, Section 305, 33 U.S.C. §1315, which directs the states to do biennial reports on water quality within their borders, and Section 314, 33 U.S.C. §1324, which calls for biennial state reports on lakes.   ■

xi. A Strong Emphasis on Public Participation

Congress not only made considerable information available to the public under the revised act, but it took pains to give the public meaningful opportunities to use that information. As revised in 1972, the Clean Water Act's statement of purpose establishes citizen participation as one of the cornerstones on which the act's implementation and enforcement rest:

Public participation in the development, revision, and enforcement of any regulation, standard, effluent limitation, plan, or program established by the Administrator [of EPA] or any State under this [act] shall be provided for, encouraged, and assisted by the Administrator and the States. The Administrator, in cooperation with the States, shall develop and publish regulations specifying minimum guidelines for such programs. [Section 101(e)]

The legislative history of the 1972 amendments fully supports the strength and breadth of this language. The Senate report stated that "[a] high degree of informed public participation in the control process is essential to the accomplishment of the goal we seek—a restored and protected natural environment" [S. Rep. No. 414, 92d Cong., 2d sess. (1971), reprinted in Senate Committee on Public Works, *A Legislative History of the Federal Water Pollution Control Act Amendments of 1972*, vol. 2 (1973) at 1430]. Indeed, as noted by Representative John Dingell of Michigan during the House debates on the conference bill, "the bill requires that its provisions be administered and enforced in a fishbowl-like atmosphere. This is excellent" [Statement of Rep. Dingell (Oct. 14, 1972), reprinted in Senate Committee on Public Works, *A Legislative History of the Federal Water Pollution Control Act Amendments of 1972*, vol. 1 (1973) at 249].

The act provides several specific opportunities for public participation. As discussed later, the public has a right to participate in the NPDES permitting process, and steps are taken as part of that process to facilitate such involvement. Further, Section 505 of the act, 33 U.S.C. §1365, also added in 1972, is a relatively broad provision for citizen suits. As noted in the House report on the 1972 amendments, this provision was designed "to restore the public's confidence and to open wide the opportunities for the public to participate in a meaningful way in the decisions of government" [H. Rep. No. 911, 92d Cong., 2d sess. 132, reprinted in *A Legislative History of the Federal Water Pollution Control Act Amendments of 1972*, vol. 1 (1973) at 819]. Originally modeled on a similar provision added to the Clean Air Act 2 years previously, Section 505 authorizes two types of citizen suits.

Section 505(a)(2) authorizes suits against EPA to compel the agency to perform "any act or duty under this [act] which is not discretionary." This gives the federal courts specific jurisdiction over *mandamus* actions seeking to make EPA do what it is required to do under the statute, and the federal courts are given express authority to "order the Administrator to perform such act or duty." To be susceptible to such a suit, however, the EPA action that is sought to be compelled must be nondiscretionary. Thus, while citizens may use this provision to secure an order directing EPA to comply with a clear statutory mandate, such as to issue a particular regulation by a particular date, citizens may not use this provision to second-guess agency decisions clearly committed by Congress to EPA's discretion. Thus, for example, this provision could not be used to force the agency to take enforcement action against a particular facility.

In certain circumstances, however, citizens are authorized to bring such enforcement actions themselves. Section 505(a)(1) grants affected citizens a *private right of action*, in federal court, "against any person (including . . . any governmental instrumentality or agency to the extent permitted by the eleventh amendment to the Constitution) who is alleged to be in violation of [various provisions of the act or an order or permit issued thereunder]." Although their enforcement authority is not coextensive with that of the agency, persons or groups bringing such actions "effectively stand in the shoes of EPA" for the purpose of enforcing the act [*Sierra Club v. Chevron U.S.A., Inc.*, 834 F.2d 1517, 1522 (9th Cir. 1988)].

■ **NOTES**

1. Persons seeking to use the mandamus provisions of Section 505 must first give 60 days' written notice to EPA of the act or duty allegedly not performed. Similarly, except for alleged violations of Section 306 or 307(a), persons seeking to invoke the act's private right of action must give 60 days' notice of the alleged violation to EPA, to the state, and to the alleged violator. If either EPA or the state files and diligently prosecutes a suit against the violator in the interim, the right to bring a citizen action is extinguished.

2. To facilitate citizen enforcement actions, each EPA region prepares a quarterly noncompliance report (QNCR) every 3 months, listing those facilities deemed to be in significant noncompliance with the act. The QNCRs are available from the regional offices under the Freedom of Information Act.

3. Chapter 11 contains a more detailed discussion of citizen enforcement suits.

4. Sections 509(b) and (c) contain special provisions governing judicial review of certain specified forms of EPA rulemaking under the act. Suits requesting such review must be filed in the appropriate U.S. Court of Appeals within 120 days. Challenges to the various effluent limitations set by EPA under the act must be brought under these provisions. Judicial review of EPA actions not specified in Section 509 must be sought in the federal district courts under the Administrative Procedure Act.

xii. State Involvement in Implementation and Enforcement   Like many federal statutes, the 1972 amendments were an exercise in federalism. Although the program they created was undeniably a federal one, the new provisions also carved out an important role for the states. Congress clearly wanted to enlist the aid of the states in meeting the act's pollution reduction goals, and was careful not to extinguish all state sovereignty over issues of water pollution control. Thus, the list of federal goals and policies in Section 101 is followed by a congressional recognition of "the primary responsibilities and rights of States to prevent, reduce, and eliminate pollution, to plan the development and use . . . of land and water resources, and to consult with the Administrator [of EPA] in the exercise of his [or her] authority under this chapter" [33 U.S.C. §1251(b)]. Moreover, Congress provided significant opportunities for the states to implement and enforce the new federal water pollution program, subject to EPA's right of oversight and ultimate control. As discussed, the states are given the first opportunity to set ambient water quality standards. Furthermore, any state may administer the NPDES program if it meets the criteria established by EPA, thus assuming primary responsibility for issuing and enforcing NPDES permits within its borders, and most states have chosen to do this.

While the states' role is significant, however, there is no question that the 1972 amendments created a federal program designed to serve a set of clearly articulated federal interests, and that they gave EPA the authority, and the responsibility, to override state decisions that do not meet the federal criteria established under the act. Indeed, as noted by the Supreme Court in comparing the 1972 Federal Water Pollution Control Act Amendments with the 1970 Clean Air Act, "in comparison with the Clean Air Act, the Amendments give the EPA a more prominent role in relation to the States" [*EPA v. State Water Resources Control Board*, 426 U.S. 200, 214 (1976)]. As a practical matter, of course, EPA does not second-guess state

States less of a role than w/ CAA

implementation or enforcement of the act on a daily basis. Furthermore, respective federal administrations tend to vary in the degree of deference they choose to give to state decision making in these areas. Nonetheless, EPA retains broad authority to strengthen state water quality standards, to strengthen state-issued NPDES permits, and to take enforcement action against violators of such permits.

■ **NOTE: SPECIAL REGULATION OF OIL SPILLS**

With large oil spills very much in the public consciousness, Congress in 1970 created a comprehensive program to remediate, and assign liability for, spills of oil and hazardous substances to the surface waters of the United States. Slightly revised in 1972, this became Section 311 of the Clean Water Act. As currently phrased, Section 311 applies to "any spilling, leaking, pumping, pouring, emitting, emptying or dumping" of oil, or of certain hazardous substances, in quantities above a minimum amount specified by regulation. It does not, however, apply to the more routine discharge of these pollutants by a facility governed by an NPDES permit. See Section 311(a)(2). Administered by EPA and the Coast Guard, Section 311 authorizes the United States to compel a responsible party to pay for the cost of cleaning up a spill. This section served as a model for the 1980 "Superfund" statute for hazardous waste remediation, which is discussed in chapter 9.   ■

b.   The 1977 Clean Water Act Amendments
Having had 5 years to evaluate the regulatory scheme it put in place with the 1972 amendments, and after reviewing the report of the National Committee on Water Quality that had been created by those amendments, in 1977 Congress decided to revise the act once again. The overall goals, philosophy, and structure of the 1972 act were retained, but certain important adjustments were made in an attempt to strengthen implementation. These amendments were dubbed the "Clean Water Act of 1977," and the statute—while still formally titled the Federal Water Pollution Control Act—has been known as the Clean Water Act ever since.

i.   The Division of Pollutants into Three Categories   One significant change made by the 1977 amendments was the creation of a separate category of pollutants, to be known as *"conventional pollutants."* These are defined in the statute as biological oxygen demand (BOD), suspended solids, fecal coliform bacteria, pH, and any other pollutant so designated by EPA. Section 304(a)(4). Since the passage of the 1977 amendments, EPA has added oil and grease to this list. See 40 C.F.R. §401.16. These pollutants can be considered "conventional" in at least two senses. They are commonly found in the effluents of a wide variety of dischargers (both industrial and nonindustrial), and they are among the first types of pollutants for which control technology was developed. Congress was apparently satisfied that conventional pollutants from industrial sources often could be effectively controlled through application of the first-tier "best practicable" technology (BPT) and was concerned that requiring application of the second-tier "best available" technology (BAT) for conventional pollutants might constitute "treatment for treatment's sake." See 123 Cong. Rec. 38961, 39171 (1977) (statements of Rep. Roberts and Sen. Muskie), reprinted in Senate Comm. on Env't. and Pub. Works, 95th Cong., 2d sess, *Legislative History of the Clean Water Act of 1977* (1978) at 329, 427–428. Thus, Congress specified in the 1977 amendments that the second-tier effluent limitations for conventional pollutants were to be based on the application of the "best conventional pollution control technology" (BCT), which requires improvements over best practicable technology only in certain circumstances. In designating this class of "conventional" pollutants, Congress had effectively created three categories of industrial water pollutants: conventional, toxic, and all others (known, rather inelegantly, as "nonconventional," or "nonconventional/nontoxic").

■ **NOTES**

1. Section 304(a)(4) defines the initial list of conventional pollutants as "pollutants *classified as* biological oxygen demanding, suspended solids, fecal coliform, and ph" [33 U.S.C. §1314(a)(4) (emphasis added)]. They are defined in this way because they are not particular substances, but rather are particular conditions (or measures) that can be caused by a variety of substances. For example, a number of different acidic substances will cause low pH, just as a number of alkaline (basic) substances will cause high pH.

2. Although it is identified as *biological* oxygen demand in the statute, BOD is usually expressed (both in common parlance and in Clean Water Act permits) as *biochemical* oxygen demand. BOD is a proxy for the amount of organic matter in the wastewater; it is the measured amount of oxygen required by microorganisms to biologically degrade the organic matter in the wastewater. Thus, it provides a prediction of the extent to which the wastewater will remove dissolved oxygen form the receiving waters as the organic matter is degraded.

3. Fecal coliform identifies a family of bacteria, and is used a proxy for the measurement of pathogens.   ■

ii. Technology-Based Effluent Limits for Toxic Pollutants Another significant change written into the act in 1977 concerned the manner in which EPA was to regulate discharges of toxic pollutants. Taking its cue from the settlement negotiated between EPA and environmental groups in a suit brought to enforce the toxic pollutant provisions of the 1972 amendments, Congress abandoned its attempt to compel health-based standards, and instead directed EPA to adopt a technology-based approach.

The Regulation of Toxic Pollutants Under the Clean Water Act: EPA's Ten-Year Rulemaking Nears Completion

Bradford W. Wyche

Source: 15 *Natural Resources Lawyer* 511 (1983). Copyright © 1983 by the American Bar Association. Reprinted in part with permission.

One notable, if not dubious, distinction of the U.S. Environmental Protection Agency (EPA) is its inability to issue regulations in accordance with statutory deadlines.[1] EPA maintains that compliance with the timetables is usually impossible,[2] while environmental groups charge that the agency is engaged in deliberate footdragging and delay.[3] Whatever the reason, there is no doubt that EPA has failed to meet most of its deadlines for issuing regulations, affording environmental lawyers the happy prospect of first litigating the question of when EPA must issue the regulations and later challenging the rules themselves after they are promulgated.[4]

This article focuses on perhaps the best known "deadline case"—EPA's ten-year struggle to establish regulatory controls on toxic pollutants under the federal Clean Water Act....

I. STATUTORY FRAMEWORK

Although enacted in 1948, the Clean Water Act did not become an effective piece of environmental regulation until 1972. In that year, Congress passed sweeping amendments to the act that merged the traditional (and unsuccessful) "ambient" approach of controlling water pollution with direct "end-of-the-pipe" controls of the discharge itself....

In [the 1972 amendments] Congress recognized that industrial wastewater often contains not only the well-known conventional pollutants (such as suspended solids and oxygen-demanding wastes) but also many

---

1. See, e.g. *Natural Resources Defense Council v. Train*, S10 F.2d 692 (D.C. Cir. 1975) (issuance of effluent limitations guidelines under Clean Water Act), *New York v. Gorsuch*, 18 Env't. Rep. Cas. (BNA) 1585 (S.D.N.Y. 1982) (issuance of regulations for inorganic arsenic under Clean Air Act); *Sierra Club v. Gorsuch*, 18 Env't. Rep. Cas. (BNA) 1549 (N.D. Calif. 1982) (issuance of regulations for radionuclides under Clean Air Act); *Environmental Defense Fund, Inc. v. Gorsuch*, 17 ERC 1099 (D.D.C. 1982) (republication of National Contingency Plan under Comprehensive Environmental Response, Compensation and Liability Act of 1980, Pub. L. No. 96-510, §105, 94 Stat. 2767, to be codified at 42 U.S.C. §9605; *Illinois v. Gorsuch*, 16 ERC 2021 (D.D.C. 1981) (issuance of hazardous waste regulations under Resource Conservation and Recovery Act, 42 U.S.C. §§6901–6987 (1981)).

2. See, e.g., *Weyerhaeuser Co. v. Costle*, 590 F.2d 1011, 1020 n.2 (D.C. Cir. 1978) ("[T]he Agency found its task too overwhelming to complete in so short a time."); *E.I. DuPont de Nemours & Co. v. Train*, 541 F.2d 1018, 1025 (4th Cir. 1976), modi-

fied, 430 U.S. 112 (1977) ("The Administrator did not act within the one-year requirements of §304. Compliance was not within the realm of reality.").

3. Plaintiffs' Memorandum in Opposition to Defendants' Cross Motion to Modify Consent Decree (March 29, 1982) at 2, 17–19 in *Natural Resources Defense Council v. Gorsuch*, Nos. 2153-73, 75-0172, 75-1267 and 75-1698 (D.D.C. May 7, 1982).

4. Under the Clean Water Act alone, industry has brought dozens of suits challenging EPA's pollutant control regulations. See, e.g., *Association of Pacific Fisheries v. EPA*, 615 F.2d 794 (9th Cir. 1980) (seafood processing industry); *BASF Wyandotte Corp. v. Costle*, 598 F.2d 637 (1st Cir. 1979), cert. denied, 444 U.S. 1096 (1980) (pesticides manufacturing industry); *Weyerhauser Co. v. Costle*, supra note 2 (pulp and paper industry); *American Iron & Steel Institute v. EPA*, 526 F.2d 1027 (3d Cir. 1975), cert. denied, 435 U.S. 914 (1978) (iron and steel manufacturing industry); *American Meat Institute v. EPA*, 526 F.2d 442 (7th Cir. 1975) (slaughterhouse and packinghouse industry).

"toxic pollutants." With respect to these pollutants, Congress adopted a strategy based on the issuance of "toxic pollutant effluent standards." The key features of this approach were short deadlines and stringent control. EPA was directed to publish by January 16, 1973, pollutants for which toxic effluent standards would be established and to issue the standards six months thereafter.[26] Compliance was required within one year from the date the standards were issued.

The overriding factor in setting such standards was the protection of human health and the environment. In contrast to its mandate in issuing effluent limitations, EPA was not required to give any consideration to technological feasibility or economic factors in establishing toxic pollutant effluent standards.[28]

II. COMMENCEMENT OF THE TOXICS CONSENT DECREE LITIGATION

Congress's vision of a swiftly established and effective toxic pollutant control program proved illusory. Faced with large gaps in scientific information on toxic pollutants, EPA failed to meet the ninety-day deadline for publishing its list of toxic pollutants. The agency then missed the 180-day deadline for issuing pretreatment standards and the one-year deadline for promulgating the section 304(b) effluent limitations guidelines.

As a result, from 1973 to 197S, environmental organizations brought five suits against the agency. One action involved issuance of the effluent limitations guidelines and resulted in the entry of a court order requiring EPA to promulgate its regulations by no later than December 31, 1974.[31] Acting under this order, EPA by 1976 had established regulations for 418 industrial subcategories.[32]

The other four suits comprise the Toxics Consent Decree Litigation. One action sought an order requiring the agency to expand its list of toxic pollutants.[33] Two others asked that EPA be ordered to promulgate toxic effluent standards for the toxic pollutants already listed.[34] The final action demanded that the agency promulgate pretreatment standards for indirect dischargers.[35]

All four suits were consolidated before Judge Thomas A. Flannery of the U.S. District Court for the District of Columbia. Several industries were permitted to intervene in the suit.[36] While the case was pending, EPA and the environmental groups, led by Natural

---

26. 33 U.S.C. §1317(a)(1) (1976). This strategy incorporates features of both the "ambient" and "effluent limitations" approaches, since the standards are based on protecting in-stream quality but apply only to dischargers designated by EPA. To date EPA has issued toxic pollutant effluent standards for aldrin/dieldrin; DDT, DDD and DDE; endrin; toxaphene; benzidine; and PCBs. 40 C.F.R. Part 129 (1982).

28. *Hercules, Inc. v. EPA*, 598 F.2d 91, 111 (D.C. Cir. 1978) (upholding toxic effluent standards for endrin and toxaphene). In practice, however, EPA has given some consideration to technological and economic factors in establishing such standards. 598 F.2d at 114.

31. *Natural Resources Defense Council, Inc. v. Train*, 510 F.2d 692 (D.C. Cir. 1975).

32. Hall, *The Evolution and Implementation of EPA's Regulatory Program to Control the Discharge of Toxic Pollutants to the Nation's Waters,*

10 NAT. RESOURCES LAW 507 (1977) [hereinafter cited as Hall, *Evolution and Implementation*].

33. *Natural Resources Defense Council, Inc. v. Train*, No. 2153-73 (D.D.C. 1973). At the time EPA had listed only nine pollutants as toxic.

34. *Environmental Defense Fund, Inc. v. Train*, NO. 75-0172 (D.D.C. 1975) and *Citizens for a Better Environment, Inc. v. Train*, No. 75-1698 (D.D.C. 1975).

35. *Natural Resources Defense Council, Inc. v. Agee*, No. 75-1267 (D.D.C. 1975).

36. The interveners consisted of numerous companies in the steel, chemical, petroleum and mining industries and several trade associations. The district court had denied the motion of some of these industries to intervene but this decision was reversed by the court of appeals. *Natural Resources Defense Council v. Costle*, 561 F.2d 904 (D.C. Cir. 1977).

Resources Defense Council, Inc. (NRDC), settled their differences and presented a proposed agreement to the court. Before considering the settlement, the court allowed the interveners and other interested persons to submit comments. Over the objections of the interveners and several of the commenters, the court approved the settlement agreement with certain modifications.[37]

This agreement, or the "Toxics Consent Decree" as it became known, established a comprehensive program for controlling the discharge of toxic pollutants into the nation's waters.[38] Most important, it authorized EPA to regulate toxic pollutants on an industry-by-industry basis through the establishment and enforcement of technology-based effluent limitations, an approach that the agency found far superior to regulation on a pollutant-by-pollutant basis through the issuance of toxic effluent standards. As the D.C. Circuit Court of Appeals later explained:

Adoption of the industry-by-industry, technology-based approach, using statutory authority conferred by various sections of the FWPCA [Clean Water Act], marked a change in EPA's regulatory strategy. Its previous efforts to control discharge of toxic pollutants had relied on authority conferred by Section 307 of the FWPCA in developing health-based standards on a pollutant-by-pollutant basis. The new strategy offered substantial advantages over the old. First, it allowed EPA to cover far more substances and emission sources than could have been handled under the old approach.

Second, it allowed the Agency to develop a single regulatory package which would apply to all of the problem pollutants in the discharge of a particular industry, enabling the industry to predict the entire cost of pollution control. Third, the Agency could allow consideration of cost and technology to enter into its decisionmaking and industry was allowed a longer compliance period. Finally, EPA also expected that the new program would be easier to administer.[39]

The Toxics Consent Decree, in short, required EPA to promulgate by no later than December 31, 1979, BAT effluent limitations guidelines, new source performance standards, and pretreatment standards for sixty-five toxic pollutants, known as the "Priority Pollutants,"[40] for each of twenty-one major industrial categories, the so-called "Primary Industries."[41]

The decree, however, included more than simply a schedule for issuing regulations. EPA also agreed to identify point sources discharging toxic pollutants not included on the priority pollutant list, to regulate at least 95 percent of all point sources within each industrial category for which national regulations would be issued, to publish water quality criteria for each priority pollutant, to establish a "specific and substantial program" to determine whether additional measures would be necessary to control toxic pollutants, and to include "reopener" clauses in NPDES permits providing that upon promulgation of

37. *Natural Resources Defense Council, Inc. v. Train*, 8 ERC 2120 (D.D.C. 1976).

38. For historical accounts of the Toxics Consent Decree, see K. Hall, *The Control of Toxic Pollutants Under the Federal Water Pollution Control Act Amendments of 1972*, 63 IOWA L. REV. 609 (1977); Hall, *Evolution and Implementation*, supra note 32.

39. *Environmental Defense Fund, Inc. v. Costle*, 636 F.2d 1229, 1235–36 (D.C. Cir. 1980).

40. The 65 "Priority Pollutants" are listed in Appendix A to the Consent Decree. *Natural Resources Defense Council, Inc. v. Train*, 8 ERC 2120 at 2129. Because the priority pollutants actually represent compounds or classes of compounds (such as chro-

mium, copper and lead) and thereby include potentially thousands of pollutants, EPA is concentrating at this time on 126 specific toxic pollutants. See 44 Fed. Reg. 34361–62, 34395 (June 14, 1979); 49 Fed. Reg. 2266 (Jan. 8, 1981); 46 Fed. Reg. 10723 (Feb. 4, 1981).

41. The primary industries are listed in Appendix B to the Consent Decree. *Natural Resources Defense Council, Inc. v. Train*, 8 ERC at 2130. These are the industries believed to be the major contributors of toxic pollutants to the nation's waters. The list of 21 primary industries was later subdivided to include 34 industrial categories. See *Natural Resources Defense Council, Inc. v. Costle*, 12 ERC 1833, 1841–42 (D.D.C. 1979).

the toxic pollutant regulations, the permit would be revised or modified to require compliance with any limitation or standard more stringent than the conditions of the permit. . . .

[When it amended the Clean Water Act in 1977], Congress endorsed the Consent Decree's approach to the control of toxic pol-

lutants. In fact, several parts of the decree were written into the act. The list of the sixty-five priority pollutants was codified, and EPA was given clear authority to regulate toxic pollutants on the basis of technology-based effluent limitations. . . .

Under the revised Section 301, EPA was directed to set, "for categories and classes of point sources [other than POTWs]," best available technology standards for toxic pollutants. For the sixty-five chemicals specifically listed by Congress (as taken from the Toxics Consent Decree), the standards were to be promulgated by July 1, 1980, and compliance was to be achieved 4 years thereafter. For any additional chemical later designated as a toxic pollutant by EPA under Section 307, compliance was to be achieved 3 years after EPA promulgated regulations for such chemicals. See 33 U.S.C. §1311(b)(2)(A), (C), and (D) (1977).

Although it might appear at first glance that the move from health-based to technology-based standards represented a retreat from Section 101's goal of no "toxic pollutants in toxic amounts," the plain fact was that EPA had managed to set health-based standards for only six classes of toxic chemicals, most of which were pesticides. The 1977 mandate to set technology-based standards for a considerably longer list of designated toxic pollutants, then, represented a clear effort by Congress to move closer to the statutory goal by putting toxic pollutant limitations in effect across a wide range of industries.

▪ NOTES

1. The list of the 65 designated toxic pollutants is found at 40 C.F.R. §401.15. Because many of the chemicals listed refer to more than one compound or class of compound, there actually are some 129 chemical compounds for which toxic pollutant effluent standards have been issued.

2. EPA retains its original authority, under Section 307(a), to set pollutant-specific, health-based effluent standards for toxic pollutants. Nonetheless, the agency has not added to the six health-based standards that it promulgated before the 1977 amendments were passed. See 40 C.F.R. §§129.100 (standard for aldrin and dieldrin), 129.101 (standard for DDT, DDD, and DDE), 129.102 (standard for endrin), 129.103 (standard for toxaphene), 129.104 (standard for benzidine), and 129.105 (standard for PCBs).

3. One of the reasons that the parties to the Toxics Consent Decree, and ultimately Congress, decided to move to a technology-based approach is that EPA found such an approach easier to implement than the health-based approach envisioned under the 1972 amendments. There were several reasons why this was the case. First, the health-based approach required EPA to prove, for each chemical it chose to so regulate, that discharge of the chemical above the amount of the proposed standard would result in sufficient harm to warrant the limitation in question. Second, the health-based approach, which set a single standard applicable to all industries, did not permit EPA to make allowances for the differing technological and economic capabilities of the various industries discharging the chemical in question. This virtually ensured that any broad-based attempt to regulate toxic pollutants would meet heavy opposition and would be a difficult task both practically and politically. The revised technology-based approach, however, allowed EPA to make adjustments on an industry-by-industry basis. Third, the procedural requirements for setting a health-based standard under Section 307 (which include a public hearing with cross-examination and transcription of a verbatim record, and a number of health-oriented inquiries that EPA must undertake) tend to make the rulemaking, and the likely appeal from the rulemaking, more complicated and time-consuming. (This may be why the majority of chemicals for which EPA did set the health-based standards were pesticide chemicals—known toxicants for which a detailed toxicity database had already been developed.)

4. Note also that the switch here from a primary reliance on health-based standards for toxic pollutants to a primary reliance on technology-based standards foreshadowed the similar approach that Congress eventually took to hazardous air pollutants from stationary sources. ∎

iii. Relaxation of Deadlines Perhaps not surprisingly, given the magnitude of the task, EPA had failed to meet a number of its deadlines for promulgating the effluent limitations mandated by the 1972 amendments. And, as discussed above, when the agency did issue regulations under the act, affected industries often challenged them in court. Thus it was clear when Congress revised the act in 1977 that many firms were not yet operating at the best practicable technology level that was to be the norm by that year, and that even if EPA were to manage to promulgate all the requisite regulations in time, widespread compliance with best available technology standards was not likely to be achieved by 1983. Accordingly, along with the division of industrial pollutants into three categories, Congress extended the industry compliance deadlines somewhat. Although the 1977 deadline for compliance with best practicable technology standards was retained, the 1977 amendments specified that (1) compliance with best conventional technology standards for conventional pollutants was to be attained by July 1, 1984; (2) compliance with best available technology standards for the toxic pollutants specifically listed by Congress was to be attained by July 1, 1984; and (3) compliance with best available technology standards for nonconventional pollutants was to be attained 3 years after the applicable regulations were established, but no earlier than July 1, 1984, and no later than July 1, 1987.

c. The 1987 Water Quality Act Amendments

Ten years after revising the structure of the act in 1977, Congress made a set of smaller, but still significant, changes. Called the Water Quality Act Amendments of 1987, these revisions were noteworthy, not only for their substance, but also for their manner of passage. The 1987 amendments began as a Senate bill in early 1985 and as a House of Representatives bill later that year. A compromise bill was reported out of the House and Senate conference committee in late 1986, and was passed unanimously by both houses of Congress. President Reagan subsequently vetoed the bill twice, but both vetoes were overridden by nearly unanimous votes in the Senate and House, first in January 1987 and a second time in early February 1987. See *The Clean Water Act Amendments of 1987, BNA Reports*, vol. 18, no. 19 (Sept. 4, 1987), pp. 37–38.

i. A Renewed Emphasis on Water Quality-Based Limitations for Toxic Pollutants

True to their title, the 1987 amendments did infuse the act with a more direct emphasis on the quality of the receiving waters. Since the 1972 amendments, water quality-based effluent limitations had been a required part of the NPDES permit program. Section 301(b)(1)(C), placed in the act in 1972, requires that, "not later than July 1, 1977," dischargers must meet

… any more stringent limitation, including those necessary to meet water quality standards … established pursuant to any State law or regulations … or any other Federal law or regulation, or required to implement any applicable water quality standard established pursuant to [the Clean Water Act]. [33 U.S.C. §1311(b)(1)(C)]

As of July 1977, then, whenever the discharge of a pollutant from a point source contributed to a violation of an ambient water quality standard, and the ambient standard could not be attained through the source's compliance with applicable technology-based standards, a water quality-based effluent limitation (that is, for any pollutant, a limitation derived from a calculation of the maximum effluent loading or concentration of that pollutant deemed to be consistent with the desired level of water quality in the receiving waters) was to have been placed into the NPDES permit for that source. As a practical matter, however, the primary Clean Water Act focus in the 1970s and early 1980s was on setting, and then implementing, the national technology-based limitations. Thus, it was not at all uncommon in the mid-1980s to find permits that were not meeting the additional water quality-based requirements of Section 301(b)(1)(C). In an effort to address this issue for toxic pollutants, Congress in 1987 added subsection (l) to Section 304 of the act. 33 U.S.C. §1314(l). This new Section 304(l) established a procedure for identifying and attempting to remedy water quality problems caused by toxic pollutants. Section 304(l)—which became known colloquially as the "toxic hot spot" provision of the Clean Water Act—mandates the imposition of water quality-based discharge limits for toxic pollutants when such limits are necessary to bring the receiving waters into compliance with ambient water quality standards. This provision is described more fully in the section on water quality-based effluent limitations.

ii.   An Increased Emphasis on Penalties   When Congress reexamined the Clean Water Act in 1987, it found enforcement to be wanting. Thus, in an effort to toughen the act's enforcement scheme, Congress (1) increased the maximum civil penalty from $10,000 per day per violation to $25,000 per day per violation, (2) added language specifying that a court must consider certain deterrence factors in assessing those penalties, (3) gave EPA the added power to impose penalties administratively (and specified similar factors to be considered in assessing those penalties), and (4) toughened the act's criminal penalties. See, generally, 33 U.S.C. §1319(d), (g), and (c), respectively. The legislative history reflects a strong conviction as to the importance of penalties in motivating compliance. See, for example, S. Rep. No. 50, 99th Cong., 1st sess. 25 (1985) ("The increase in the maximum daily penalty . . . reflects the seriousness of these violations"); 133 *Cong. Rec.* H175 (daily ed., Jan. 8, 1987) (statement of Rep. Novak) (the increased penalty focus should "reduce violations of the Act and discourage those parties who would choose to violate the Act with little fear of punishment").

iii.   Relaxation of Deadlines   As it had done in 1977, in 1987 Congress again extended the final deadline for meeting the second-stage federal technology-based standards. This was in part a recognition of the fact that EPA had not yet promulgated BAT and BCT standards for all relevant industry categories. In the 1987 amendments, the date for compliance with these effluent limitations was specified as 3 years after EPA promulgated the applicable regulation, or March 31, 1989, whichever came first. See Section 301(b)(2) and (3).

2.   The Technology-Based Effluent Limitations in Detail

Broadly speaking, the Clean Water Act establishes two sets of national technology-based effluent limitations: one for industrial facilities (whether privately or publicly

Facilities & waste treatment

owned) and one for public sewage treatment plants. We focus first on the limitations applicable to industrial point sources.

a.   Industrial Source Limitations in General

As discussed earlier, the act envisioned a phased-in compliance schedule for industrial sources. By 1977, all existing industrial sources were expected to be in compliance with best practicable technology limitations. By 1983 (extended to 1989 by the 1987 amendments), these sources were expected to be in compliance with best available technology limitations (or, later, best conventional technology limitations, as applicable). And by 1974, *new* industrial sources were expected to be in compliance with best available demonstrated technology (BADT) limitations. A key feature of all of these limitations is that they were in each instance to be set by EPA according to the agency's determination of technological and economic feasibility. As one might imagine, the prospect of this system of federal effluent limitations created considerable apprehension, and considerable opposition, within the business community. In two key legal challenges, industry found several ways of raising a single critical issue: to what extent was EPA required to take the particular financial and technological situation of the individual firm into account when establishing and implementing these limitations? In each case, the Supreme Court ultimately provided the answer.

Dupont v. Train
Mr. Justice STEVENS delivered the opinion of the Court
United States Supreme Court
430 U.S. 112 (1977)

Inorganic chemical manufacturing plants operated by the eight petitioners in Nos. 75-978 and 75-1473 discharge various pollutants into the Nation's waters and therefore are "point sources" within the meaning of the Federal Water Pollution Control Act (Act), as added and amended by §2 of the Federal Water Pollution Control Act Amendments of 1972, 86 Stat. 816, 33 U.S.C. §1251 et seq.

(1970 ed., Supp. V).[1] The Environmental Protection Agency[2] has promulgated industry wide regulations imposing three sets of precise limitations on petitioners' discharges. The first two impose progressively higher levels of pollution control on existing point sources after July 1, 1977, and after July 1, 1983, respectively. The third set imposes limits on

---

1. A "point source" is "any discernible, confined and discrete conveyance, . . . from which pollutants are or may be discharged." §502(14), 33 U.S.C. §1362(14) (1970 ed., Supp. V).

2. Throughout this opinion we will refer interchangeably to the Administrator of the EPA and to the Agency itself.

"new sources" that may be constructed in the future.[3]

These cases present three important questions of statutory construction: (1) whether EPA has the authority under §301 of the Act to issue industry wide regulations limiting discharges by existing plants; (2) whether the Court of Appeals, which admittedly is authorized to review the standards for new-sources, also has jurisdiction under §509 to review the ' regulations concerning existing plants; and (3) whether the new-source standards issued under §306 must allow variances for individual plants.

As a preface to our discussion of these three questions, we summarize relevant portions of the statute and then describe the procedure which EPA followed in promulgating the challenged regulations.

The Statute

The statute, enacted on October 18, 1972, authorized a series of steps to be taken to achieve the goal of eliminating all discharges of pollutants into the Nation's waters by 1985, §101(a)(1).

The first steps required by the Act are described in §304, which directs the Administrator to develop and publish various kinds of technical data to provide guidance in carrying out responsibilities imposed by other sections of the Act. Thus, within 60 days, 120 days, and 180 days after the date of enactment, the Administrator was to promulgate a series of guidelines to assist the States in developing and carrying out permit programs pursuant to §402. §§304(h), (f), (g). Within 270 days, he was to develop the information to be used in formulating standards for new plants pursuant to §306. §304(c). And within one year he was to publish regulations providing guidance for effluent limitations on existing point sources. Section 304(b)[4] goes into great detail concerning the contents of these regulations. They must identify the degree of effluent reduction attainable through use of the best practicable or best available

---

3. The reasons for the statutory scheme have been described as follows:

"Such direct restrictions on discharges facilitate enforcement by making it unnecessary to work backward from an overpolluted body of water to determine which point sources are responsible and which must be abated. In addition, a discharger's performance is now measured against strict technology-based effluent limitations—specified levels of treatment—to which it must conform, rather than against limitations derived from water quality standards to which it and other polluters must collectively conform." *EPA V. California ex rel. State Water Resources Control Board*, 426 U.S. 200, 204–205 (footnotes omitted).

4. Section 304(b) provides:

"(b) For the purpose of adopting or revising effluent limitations under this Act the Administrator shall, after consultation with appropriate Federal and State agencies and other interested persons, publish within one year of enactment of this title, regulations, providing guidelines for effluent limitations, and, at least annually thereafter, revise, if

appropriate, such regulations. Such regulations shall—

"(1)(A) identify, in terms of amounts of constituents and chemical, physical, and biological characteristics of pollutants, the degree of effluent reduction attainable through the application of the best practicable control technology currently available for classes and categories of point sources (other than publicly owned treatment works); and

"(B) specify factors to be taken into account in determining the control measures and practices to be applicable to point sources (other than publicly owned treatment works) within such categories or classes. Factors relating to the assessment of best practicable control technology currently available to comply with subsection (b)(1) of section 301 of this Act shall include consideration of the total cost of application of technology in relation to the effluent reduction benefits to be achieved from such application, and shall also take into account the age of equipment and facilities involved, the process employed, the engineering aspects of the application of various types of control techniques, process changes, non-water quality environmental impact (including energy requirements), and such other factors as the Administrator deems appropriate;

technology for a class of plants. The guidelines must also "specify factors to be taken into account" in determining the control measures applicable to point sources within these classes. A list of factors to be considered then follows. The Administrator was also directed to develop and publish, within one year, elaborate criteria for water quality accurately reflecting the most current scientific knowledge, and also technical information

on factors necessary to restore and maintain water quality. §304(a). The title of §304 describes it as the "information and guidelines" portion of the statute.

Section 301 is captioned "effluent limitations."[5] Section 301(a) makes the discharge of any pollutant unlawful unless the discharge is in compliance with certain enumerated sections of the Act. The enumerated sections which are relevant to this case are

---

"(2)(A) identify, in terms of amounts of constituents and chemical, physical, and biological characteristics of pollutants, the degree of effluent reduction attainable through the application of the best control measures and practices achievable including treatment techniques, process and procedure innovations, operating methods, and other alternatives for classes and categories of point sources (other than publicly owned treatment works); and

"(B) specify factors to be taken into account in determining the best measures and practices available to comply with subsection (b)(2) of section 301 of this Act to be applicable to any point source (other than publicly owned treatment works) within such categories or classes. Factors relating to the assessment of best available technology shall take into account the age of equipment and facilities involved, the process employed, the engineering aspects of the application of various types of control techniques, process changes, the cost of achieving such effluent reduction, non-water quality environmental impact (including energy requirements), and such other factors as the Administrator deems appropriate; and

"(3) identify control measures and practices available to eliminate the discharge of pollutants from categories and classes of point sources, taking into account the cost of achieving such elimination of the discharge of pollutants." 86 Stat. 851, 33 U.S.C. §1314(b) (1970 ed., Supp. V).

5. Section 301 provides in pertinent part:

"SEC. 301. (a) Except as in compliance with this section and sections 302, 306, 307, 318, 402, and 404 of this Act, the discharge of any pollutant by any person shall be unlawful.

"(b) In order to carry out the objective of this Act there shall be achieved—

"(1)(A) not later than July 1, 1977, effluent limitations for point sources, other than publicly owned treatment works, (i) which shall require the applica-

tion of the best practicable control technology currently available as defined by the Administrator pursuant to section 304(b) of this Act....

"(2)(A) not later than July 1, 1983, effluent limitations for categories and classes of point sources, other than publicly owned treatment works, which (i) shall require application of the best available technology economically achievable for such category or class, which will result in reasonable further progress toward the national goal of eliminating the discharge of all pollutants, as determined in accordance with regulations issued by the Administrator pursuant to section 304(b)(2) of this Act, which such effluent limitations shall require the elimination of discharges of all pollutants if the Administrator finds, on the basis of information available to him (including information developed pursuant to section 315), that such elimination is technologically and economically achievable for a category or class of point sources as determined in accordance with regulations issued by the Administrator pursuant to section 304(b)(2) of this Act....

"(c) The Administrator may modify the requirements of subsection (b)(2)(A) of this section with respect to any point source for which a permit application is filed after July 1, 1977, upon a showing by the owner or operator of such point source satisfactory to the Administrator that such modified requirements (1) will represent the maximum use of technology within the economic capability of the owner or operator; and (2) will result in reasonable further progress toward the elimination of the discharge of pollutants.

"(d) Any effluent limitation required by paragraph (2) of subsection (b) of this section shall be reviewed at least every five years and, if appropriate, revised pursuant to the procedure established under such paragraph.

"(e) Effluent limitations established pursuant to this section or section 302 of this Act shall be applied to all point sources of discharge of pollutants in accordance with the provisions of this Act." 86 Stat. 844, 33 U.S.C. §1311 (1970 ed., Supp. V).

§301 itself, §306, and §402.[6] A brief word about each of these sections is necessary.

Section 402[7] authorizes the Administrator to issue permits for individual point sources, and also authorizes him to review and approve the plan of any State desiring to administer its own permit program. These permits serve "to transform generally applicable effluent limitations...into the obligations (including a timetable for compliance) of the individual discharger[s]...." *EPA v. California ex rel. State Water Resources Control Board*, 426 U.S. 200, 205. Petitioner chemical companies' position in this litigation is that §402 provides the only statutory authority for the issuance of enforceable limitations on the discharge of pollutants by existing plants. It is noteworthy, however, that although this section authorizes the imposition of limitations in individual permits, the section itself does not mandate either the Administrator or the States to use permits as the method of prescribing effluent limitations.

Section 306[8] directs the Administrator to publish within 90 days a list of categories of sources discharging pollutants and, within one year thereafter, to publish regulations establishing national standards of performance for new sources within each category. Section 306 contains no provision for exceptions from the standards for individual plants; on the contrary, subsection (e) expressly makes it unlawful to operate a new source in violation of the applicable standard of performance after its effective date. The statute provides that the new-source standards shall reflect the greatest degree of effluent reduction achievable through application of the best available demonstrated control technology.

Section 301(b) defines the effluent limitations that shall be achieved by existing point

---

6. There is no provision for compliance with §304, the guideline section.

7. Section 402(a)(1) provides:

"Except as provided in sections 318 and 404 of this Act, the Administrator may, after opportunity for public hearing, issue a permit for the discharge of any pollutant, or combination of pollutants, notwithstanding section 301(a), upon condition that such discharge will meet either all applicable requirements under sections 301, 302, 306, 307, 308, and 403 of this Act, or prior to the taking of necessary implementing actions relating to all such requirements, such conditions as the Administrator determines are necessary to carry out the provisions of this Act." 86 Stat. 880, 33 U.S.C. §1342(a)(1) (1970 ed., Supp. V).

Under §402(b), the Administrator may delegate this authority to the States, but retains the power to withdraw approval of the state program, §402(c)(3), and to veto individual state permits, §402(d). Finally, under §402(k), compliance with the permit is generally deemed compliance with §301. Twenty-seven States now administer their own permit programs.

8. The pertinent provisions of §306, 86 Stat. 854, 33 U.S.C. §1316 (1970 ed., Supp. V), are as follows:

"(a) For purposes of this section:

"'(1) The term 'standard of performance' means a standard for the control of the discharge of pollutants which reflects the greatest degree of effluent reduction which the Administrator determines to be achievable through application of the best available demonstrated control technology, processes, operating methods, or other alternatives, including, where practicable, a standard permitting no discharge of pollutants....

"(b)(1)...

"(B) As soon as practicable, but in no case more than one year, after a category of sources is included in a list under subparagraph (A) of this paragraph, the Administrator shall propose and publish regulations establishing Federal standards of performance for new sources within such category....

"(2) The Administrator may distinguish among classes, types, and sizes within categories of new sources for the purpose of establishing such standards and shall consider the type of process employed (including whether batch or continuous).

"(3) The provisions of this section shall apply to any new source owned or operated by the United States....

"(e) After the effective date of standards of performance promulgated under this section, it shall be unlawful for any owner or operator of any new source to operate such source in violation of any standard of performance applicable to such source."

sources in two stages. By July 1, 1977, the effluent limitations shall require the application of the best practicable control technology currently available; by July 1, 1983, the limitations shall require application of the best available technology economically achievable. The statute expressly provides that the limitations which are to become effective in 1983 are applicable to "categories and classes of point sources"; this phrase is omitted from the description of the 1977 limitations. While §301 states that these limitations "shall be achieved," it fails to state who will establish the limitations.

Section 301(c) authorizes the Administrator to grant variances from the 1983 limitations. Section 301(e) states that effluent limitations established pursuant to §301 shall be applied to all point sources.

To summarize, §301(b) requires the achievement of effluent limitations requiring use of the "best practicable" or "best available" technology. It refers to §304 for a definition of these terms. Section 304 requires the publication of "regulations, providing guidelines for effluent limitations." Finally, permits issued under §402 must require compliance with §301 effluent limitations. Nowhere are we told who sets the §301 effluent limitations, or precisely how they relate to §304 guidelines and §402 permits.

The Regulations

The various deadlines imposed on the Administrator were too ambitious for him to meet. For that reason, the procedure which

he followed in adopting the regulations applicable to the inorganic chemical industry and to other classes of point sources is somewhat different from that apparently contemplated by the statute. Specifically, as will appear, he did not adopt guidelines pursuant to §304 before defining the effluent limitations for existing sources described in §301(b) or the national standards for new sources described in §306. This case illustrates the approach the Administrator followed in implementing the Act.

EPA began by engaging a private contractor to prepare a Development Document. This document provided a detailed technical study of pollution control in the industry. The study first divided the industry into categories. For each category, present levels of pollution were measured and plants with exemplary pollution control were investigated. Based on this information, other technical data, and economic studies, a determination was made of the degree of pollution control which could be achieved by the various levels of technology mandated by the statute. The study was made available to the public and circulated to interested persons. It formed the basis of "effluent limitation guideline" regulations issued by EPA after receiving public comment on proposed regulations. These regulations divide the industry into 22 subcategories. Within each subcategory, precise numerical limits are set for various pollutants.[9] The regulations for each subcategory contain a variance clause, applicable only to the 1977 limitations.[10]

---

9. Some subcategories are required to eliminate all discharges by 1977. E.g., 40 CFR §§415.70–415.76 (1976). Other subcategories are subject to less stringent restrictions. For instance, by 1977 plants producing titanium dioxide by the chloride process must reduce average daily discharges of dissolved iron to 0.72 pounds per thousand pounds of product. This limit is cut in half for existing plants in 1983 and for all new plants. 40 CFR §§415.220–415.225 (1976).

10. These limitations may be made "either more or less stringent" to the extent that "factors relating to the equipment or facilities involved, the process applied, or other such factors related to such discharger are fundamentally different from the factors considered" in establishing the limitations. See, e.g., for the two subcategories discussed in n. 9, supra, 40 CFR §§415.72 and 415.222 (1976), respectively.

Eight chemical companies filed petitions in the United States Court of Appeals for the Fourth Circuit for review of these regulations.[11] The Court of Appeals rejected their challenge to EPA's authority to issue precise, single-number limitations for discharges of pollutants from existing sources. It held, however, that these limitations and the new plant standards were only "presumptively applicable" to individual plants. We granted the chemical companies' petitions for certiorari in order to consider the scope of EPA's authority to issue existing-source regulations. 425 U.S. 933; 426 U.S. 947. We also granted the Government's cross-petition for review of the ruling that new-source standards are only presumptively applicable. Ibid. For convenience, we will refer to the chemical companies as the "petitioners."

The Issues

The broad outlines of the parties' respective theories may be stated briefly. EPA contends that §301 (b) authorizes it to issue regulations establishing effluent limitations for classes of plants. The permits granted under §402, in EPA's view, simply incorporate these across-the-board limitations, except for the limited variances allowed by the regulations themselves and by §301(c). The §304(b) guidelines, according to EPA, were intended to guide it in later establishing §301 effluent-limitation

regulations. Because the process proved more time consuming than Congress assumed when it established this two-stage process, EPA condensed the two stages into a single regulation.[13]

In contrast, petitioners contend that §301 is not an independent source of authority for setting effluent limitations by regulation. Instead, §301 is seen as merely a description of the effluent limitations which are set for each plant on an individual basis during the permit-issuance process. Under the industry view, the §304 guidelines serve the function of guiding the permit issuer in setting the effluent limitations.

The jurisdictional issue is subsidiary to the critical question whether EPA has the power to issue effluent limitations by regulation. Section 509(b)(1), 86 Stat. 892, 33 U.S.C. 1369(b)(1), provides that "[r]eview of the Administrator's action...(E) in approving or promulgating any effluent limitation... under section 301" may be had in the courts of appeals. On the other hand, the Act does not provide for judicial review of §304 guidelines. If EPA is correct that its regulations are "effluent limitation[s] under section 301," the regulations are directly reviewable in the Court of Appeals. If industry is correct that the regulations can only be considered §304 guidelines, suit to review the regulations could probably be brought only in the District Court, if anywhere.[14] Thus, the issue of

---

11. Because EPA's authority to issue the regulations is closely tied to the question whether the regulations are directly reviewable in the Court of Appeals, see infra, at 124–125, some of the companies also filed suit in District Court challenging the regulations. The District Court held that EPA had the authority to issue the regulations and that exclusive jurisdiction was therefore in the Court of Appeals. 383 F. Supp. 1244 (WD Va. 1974), aff'd., 528 F.2d 1136 (CA4 1975) (Du Pont I).

13. Section 304(b) calls for publication of guideline regulations within one year of the Act's passage. EPA failed to meet this deadline and was ordered to issue the regulations on a judicially imposed timetable. *Natural Resources Defense Council, Inc.*

v. Train, 166 U.S. App. D.C. 312, 510 F. 2d 692 (1975).

14. Although the Act itself does not provide for review of guidelines, the Eighth Circuit has held that they are reviewable in the district court, apparently under the Administrative Procedure Act. *CPC Int'l., Inc. v. Train*, 515 F. 2d 1032, 1038 (1975) (CPC I). It has been suggested, however, that even if the EPA regulations are considered to be only §304 guidelines, the Court of Appeals might still have ancillary jurisdiction to review them because of their close relationship with the §301 effluent limitations, and because they were developed on the same record as the §306 standards of performance for new plants, which are directly reviewable in the Court of Appeals.

jurisdiction to review the regulations is intertwined with the issue of EPA's power to issue the regulations.[15]

I

We think §301 itself is the key to the problem. The statutory language concerning the 1983 limitations, in particular, leaves no doubt that these limitations are to be set by regulation. Subsection (b)(2)(A) of §301 states that by 1983 "effluent limitations for categories and classes of point sources" are to be achieved which will require "application of the best available technology economically achievable for such category or class." (Emphasis added.) These effluent limitations are to require elimination of all discharges if "such elimination is technologically and economically achievable for a category or class of point sources." (Emphasis added.) This is "language difficult to reconcile with the view that individual effluent limitations are to be set when each permit is issued." *American Meat Institute v. EPA*, 526 F. 2d 442, 450 (CA7 1975). The statute thus focuses expressly on the characteristics of the "category or class" rather than the characteristics of individual point sources.[16] Normally, such class wide determinations would be made by regulation, not in the course of issuing a permit to one member of the class.[17]

Thus, we find that §301 unambiguously provides for the use of regulations to establish the 1983 effluent limitations. Different language is used in §301 with respect to the 1977 limitations. Here, the statute speaks of "effluent limitations for point sources," rather than "effluent limitations for categories and classes of point sources." Nothing elsewhere in the Act, however, suggests any radical difference in the mechanism used to impose limitations for the 1977 and 1983 deadlines. See *American Iron & Steel Institute v. EPA*, 526 F. 2d 1027, 1042 n. 32 (CA3 1975). For instance, there is no indication in either §301 or §304 that the §304 guidelines play a different role in setting 1977 limitations. Moreover, it would be highly anomalous if the 1983 regulations and the new-source standards[18] were directly reviewable in the Court of Appeals, while the 1977 regulations based on the same administrative record were reviewable only in the District Court. The magnitude and highly technical character of the administrative record involved with these regulations makes it

---

15. The Courts of Appeals have resolved these issues in various ways. Only the Eighth Circuit, the first to consider the issues, has accepted the industry position.

16. The Court of Appeals noted that "[t]he 1983 and new source requirements are on the basis of categories." Du Pont II, 541 F. 2d, at 1029.

17. Furthermore, §301(c) provides that the 1983 limitations may be modified if the owner of a plant shows that "such modified requirements (1) will represent the maximum use of technology within the economic capability of the owner or operator; and (2) will result in reasonable further progress toward the elimination of the discharge of pollutants." This provision shows that the §301 (b) limitations for 1983 are to be established prior to consideration of the characteristics of the individual plant. Moreover, it shows that the term "best technology economically achievable" does not refer to any individual plant. Otherwise, it would be impos-

sible for this "economically achievable" technology to be beyond the individual owner's "economic capability."

18. Section 509 (b)(1)(A) makes new-source standards directly reviewable in the court of appeals. The Court of Appeals in this litigation did not believe that Congress "intended for review to be bifurcated," with the new-source standards reviewable in a different forum than regulations governing existing sources. 528 F. 2d, at 1141. The Eighth Circuit has acknowledged the practical problems and potential for inconsistent rulings created by bifurcated review. CPC II, supra, at 1332 n. 1. We consider it unlikely that Congress intended such bifurcated review, and even less likely that Congress intended regulations governing existing sources to be reviewable in two different forums, depending on whether the regulations require compliance in 1977 or 1983.

almost inconceivable that Congress would have required duplicate review in the first instance by different courts. We conclude that the statute authorizes the 1977 limitations as well as the 1983 limitations to be set by regulation, so long as some allowance is made for variations in individual plants, as EPA has done by including a variance clause in its 1977 limitations.[19]

The question of the form of §301 limitations is tied to the question whether the Act requires the Administrator or the permit issuer to establish the limitations. Section 301 does not itself answer this question, for it speaks only in the passive voice of the achievement and establishment of the limitations. But other parts of the statute leave little doubt on this score. Section 304(b) states that "[f]or the purpose of adopting or revising effluent limitations...the Administrator shall" issue guideline regulations; while the judicial-review section, §509(b)(1), speaks of "the Administrator's action...in approving or promulgating any effluent limitation or other limitation under section 301...." See infra, at 136–137. And §101 (d) requires us to resolve any ambiguity on this score in favor of the Administrator. It provides that "[e]xcept as otherwise expressly provided in this Act, the Administrator of the Environmental Protection Agency...shall administer this Act." (Emphasis added.) In sum, the language of the statute supports the view that §301 limitations are to be adopted by the Administrator, that they are to be based primarily on classes and categories, and that they are to take the form of regulations.

The legislative history supports this reading of §301. The Senate Report states that "pur-suant to subsection 301 (b)(1) (A), and Section 304(b)" the Administrator is to set a base level for all plants in a given category, and "[i]n no case...should any plant be allowed to discharge more pollutants per unit of production than is defined by that base level." S. Rep. No. 92-414, p. 50 (1971), Leg. Hist. 1468.[20] The Conference Report on §301 states that "the determination of the economic impact of an effluent limitation [will be made] on the basis of classes and categories of point sources, as distinguished from a plant by plant determination." Sen. Conf. Rep. No. 92-1236, p. 121 (1972), Leg. Hist. 304. In presenting the Conference Report to the Senate, Senator Muskie, perhaps the Act's primary author, emphasized the importance of uniformity in setting §301 limitations. He explained that this goal of uniformity required that EPA focus on classes or categories of sources in formulating effluent limitations. Regarding the requirement contained in §301 that plants use the "best practicable control technology" by 1977, he stated:

"The modification of subsection 304(b)(1) is intended to clarify what is meant by the term 'practicable.' The balancing test between total cost and effluent reduction benefits is intended to limit the application of technology only where the additional degree of effluent reduction is wholly out of proportion to the costs of achieving such marginal level of reduction for any class or category of sources.

"The Conferees agreed upon this limited cost-benefit analysis in order to maintain uniformity within a class and category of point sources subject to effluent limitations, and to avoid imposing on the Administrator any requirement to consider the location of sources within a category or to ascertain water quality impact of effluent controls, or to determine the economic impact of controls on any individual plant in a single community." 118 Cong. Rec. 33696 (1972), Leg. Hist. 170 (emphasis added).

---

19. We agree with the Court of Appeals, 541 F. 2d, at 1028, that consideration of whether EPA's variance provision has the proper scope would be premature.

20. All Citations to the legislative history are to Senate Committee on Public Works, A Legislative History of the Water Pollution Control Act Amendments of 1972, prepared by the Environmental Policy Division of the Congressional Research Service of the Library of Congress (Comm. Print 1973).

He added that:

"The Conferees intend that the factors described in section 304 (b) be considered only within classes or categories of point sources and that such factors not be considered at the time of the application of an effluent limitation to an individual point source within such a category or class." 118 Cong. Rec. 33697 (1972), Leg. Hist. 172.I

This legislative history supports our reading of §301 and makes it clear that the §304 guidelines are not merely aimed at guiding the discretion of permit issuers in setting limitations for individual plants.

What, then, is the function of the §304 (b) guidelines? As we noted earlier, §304 (b) requires EPA to identify the amount of effluent reduction attainable through use of the best practicable or available technology and to "specify factors to be taken into account"

in determining the pollution control methods "to be applicable to point sources... within such categories or classes." These guidelines are to be issued "[f]or the purpose of adopting or revising effluent limitations under this Act."[21] As we read it, §304 requires that the guidelines survey the practicable or available pollution-control technology for an industry and assess its effectiveness. The guidelines are then to describe the methodology EPA intends to use in the §301 regulations to determine the effluent limitations for particular plants. If the technical complexity of the task had not prevented EPA from issuing the guidelines within the statutory deadline,[22] they could have provided valuable guidance to permit issuers, industry, and the public, prior to the issuance of the §301 regulations.[23]

---

21. Petitioners rely heavily on selected portions of the following passage from the Senate Report to support their view of §301:

"It is the Committee's intention that pursuant to subsection 301(b)(1)(A), and Section 304(b) the Administrator will interpret the term 'best practicable' when applied to various categories of industries as a basis for specifying clear and precise effluent limitations to be implemented by January 1, 1976 [now July 1, 1977]. In defining best practicable for any given industrial category, the Committee expects the Administrator to take a number of factors into account. These factors should include the age of the plants, their size and the unit processes involved and the cost of applying such controls. In effect, for any industrial category, the Committee expects the Administrator to define a range of discharge levels, above a certain base level applicable to all plants within that category. In applying effluent limitations to any individual plant, the factors cited above should be applied to that specific plant. In no case, however, should any plant be allowed to discharge more pollutants per unit of production than is defined by that base level.

"The Administrator should establish the range of best practicable levels based upon the average of the best existing performance by plants of various sizes, ages, and unit processes within each industrial category." S. Rep. No. 92-414, p. 50 (1971), Leg. Hist. 1468.

If construed to be consistent with the legislative history we have already discussed, and with what we

have found to be the clear statutory language, this language can be fairly read to allow the use of subcategories based on factors such as size, age, and unit processes, with effluent limitations for each subcategory normally based on the performance of the best plants in that subcategory.

22. As the Court of Appeals held, 541 F. 2d, at 1027, EPA's response to this problem was within its discretion. Even if we considered this course to constitute a procedural error, it would not invalidate the §301 regulations themselves since the purposes for issuing the guidelines were substantially achieved, see n. 23, infra, and no prejudice has been shown.

23. The guidelines could have served at least three functions. First, they would have provided guidance to permit issuers prior to promulgation of the §301 effluent limitation regulations. Second, they would have given industry more time to prepare to meet the §301 regulations. Third, they would have afforded a greater opportunity for public input into the final §301 regulations, by giving notice of the general outlines of those regulations. These functions were substantially served by EPA's practice of obtaining public comment on the development document and proposed regulations. In addition, the guidelines could furnish technical guidance to companies lacking expertise in pollution control by informing them of appropriate control methods. See S. Rep. No. 92-414, p. 45 (1971), Leg. Hist. 1463. This function is served by the Development Document and supporting materials.

Our construction of the Act is supported by §501(a), which gives EPA the power to make "such regulations as are necessary to carry out" its functions, and by §101(d), which charges the agency with the duty of administering the Act. In construing this grant of authority, as Mr. Justice Harlan wrote in connection with a somewhat similar problem:

"'[C]onsiderations of feasibility and practicality are certainly germane' to the issues before us. *Bowles v. Willingham*, [321 U.S. 503,] 517. We cannot, in these circumstances, conclude that Congress has given authority inadequate to achieve with reasonable effectiveness the purposes for which it has acted." Permian Basin Area Rate Cases, 390 U.S. 747, 777.I

The petitioners' view of the Act would place an impossible burden on EPA. It would require EPA to give individual consideration to the circumstances of each of the more than 42,000 dischargers who have applied for permits, Brief for Respondents in No. 75-978, p. 30 n. 22, and to issue or approve all these permits well in advance of the 1977 deadline in order to give industry time to install the necessary pollution-control equipment. We do not believe that Congress would have failed so conspicuously to provide EPA with the authority needed to achieve the statutory goals.

Both EPA and petitioners refer to numerous other provisions of the Act and fragments of legislative history in support of their positions. We do not find these conclusive, and little point would be served by discussing them in detail. We are satisfied that our reading of §301 is consistent with the rest of the legislative scheme.

Language we recently employed in another case involving the validity of EPA regulations applies equally to this case:

"We therefore conclude that the Agency's interpretation . . . was 'correct,' to the extent that it can be said with complete assurance that any particular interpretation of a complex statute such as this is the 'correct' one. Given this conclusion, as well as the facts that the Agency is charged with administration of the Act, and that there has undoubtedly been reliance upon its interpretation by the States and other parties affected by the Act, we have no doubt whatever that its construction was sufficiently reasonable to preclude the Court of Appeals from substituting its judgment for that of the Agency." *Train v. Natural Resources Def. Council*, 421 U.S. 60, 87.I

When, as in this litigation, the Agency's interpretation is also supported by thorough, scholarly opinions written by some of our finest judges, and has received the overwhelming support of the Courts of Appeals, we would be reluctant indeed to upset the Agency's judgment. Here, on the contrary, our independent examination confirms the correctness of the Agency's construction of the statute.[25,26]

---

25. Petitioners contend that the administrative construction should not receive deference because it was not contemporaneous with the passage of the Act. They base this argument primarily on the fact that EPA's initial notices of its proposed rulemaking refer to §304(b), rather than §301, as the source of authority. But this is merely evidence that the Administrator originally intended to issue guidelines prior to issuing effluent limitation regulations. In fact, in a letter urging the President to sign the Act, the Administrator stated that "[t]he Conference bill fully incorporates as its central regulatory point the Administration's proposal concerning effluent limitations in terms of industrial categories and groups ultimately applicable to individual dischargers through a permit system." 118 Cong. Rec. 36777 (1972), Leg. Hist. 149 (emphasis added).

26. This litigation exemplifies the wisdom of allowing difficult issues to mature through full consideration by the courts of appeals. By eliminating the many subsidiary, but still troubling, arguments raised by industry, these courts have vastly simplified our task, as well as having underscored the reasonableness of the agency view.

Consequently, we hold that EPA has the authority to issue regulations setting forth uniform effluent limitations for categories of plants.

II

Our holding that §301 does authorize the Administrator to promulgate effluent limitations for classes and categories of existing point sources necessarily resolves the jurisdictional issue as well. For, as we have already pointed out, §509(b)(1) provides that "[r]eview of the Administrator's action...in approving or promulgating any effluent limitation or other limitation under section 301, 302, or 306,...may be had by any interested person in the Circuit Court of Appeals of the United States for the Federal judicial district in which such person resides or transacts such business...."

Petitioners have argued that the reference to §301 was intended only to provide for review of the grant or denial of an individual variance pursuant to §301(c). We find this argument unpersuasive for two reasons in addition to those discussed in Part I of this opinion. First, in other portions of §509, Congress referred to specific subsections of the Act and presumably would have specifically mentioned §301(c) if only action pursuant to that subsection were intended to be reviewable in the court of appeals. More importantly, petitioners' construction would produce the truly perverse situation in which the court of appeals would review numerous individual actions issuing or denying permits pursuant to §402 but would have no power of direct review of the basic regulations governing those individual actions. See *American Meat Institute v. EPA*, 526 F. 2d, at 452.

We regard §509(b)(1)(E) as unambiguously authorizing court of appeals review of EPA action promulgating an effluent limitation for existing point sources under §301. Since those limitations are typically promulgated in the same proceeding as the new-source standards under §306, we have no doubt that Congress intended review of the two sets of regulations to be had in the same forum.[27]

III

The remaining issue in this case concerns new plants. Under §306, EPA is to promulgate "regulations establishing Federal standards of performance for new sources...." §306(b)(1)(B). A "standard of performance" is a "standard for the control of the discharge of pollutants which reflects the greatest degree of effluent reduction which the Administrator determines to be achievable through application of the best available demonstrated control technology,...including, where practicable, a standard permitting no discharge of pollutants." §306(a)(1). In setting the standard, "[t]he Administrator may distinguish among classes, types, and sizes within categories of new sources...and shall consider the type of process employed (including whether batch or continuous)." §306(b)(2). As the House Report states, the standard must reflect the best technology for "that category of sources, and for class, types, and sizes within categories." H.R. Rep. No. 92-911, p. 111 (1972), Leg. Hist. 798.

27. It should be noted that petitioners' principal arguments are directed to the proposition that §301 did not mandate the promulgation of industry wide regulations for existing point sources. But that ultimate proposition is not necessarily inconsistent with EPA's position that it was authorized to proceed by regulation if the aggregate effect of thousands of individual permit proceedings would not achieve the required effluent limitations by the 1977 and 1983 deadlines. Even with respect to the permit programs authorized by §402, it is clear that EPA can delegate responsibilities to the States without surrendering its ultimate authority over such programs as well as over individual permit actions.

The Court of Appeals held:

"Neither the Act nor the regulations contain any variance provision for new sources. The rule of presumptive applicability applies to new sources as well as existing sources. On remand EPA should come forward with some limited escape mechanism for new sources." *Du Pont II*, 541 F. 2d, at 1028.

The court's rationale was that "[p]rovisions for variances, modifications, and exceptions are appropriate to the regulatory process." Ibid.

The question, however, is not what a court thinks is generally appropriate to the regulatory process; it is what Congress intended for these regulations. It is clear that Congress intended these regulations to be absolute prohibitions. The use of the word "standards" implies as much. So does the description of the preferred standard as one "permitting no discharge of pollutants." (Emphasis added.)

It is "unlawful for any owner or operator of any new source to operate such source in violation of any standard of performance applicable to such source." §306(e) (emphasis added). In striking contrast to §301(c), there is no statutory provision for variances, and a variance provision would be inappropriate in a standard that was intended to insure national uniformity and "maximum feasible control of new sources." S. Rep. No. 92-414, p. 58 (1971), Leg. Hist. 1476.[28]

That portion of the judgment of the Court of Appeals in 541 F. 2d 1018 requiring EPA to provide a variance procedure for new sources is reversed. In all other aspects, the judgments of the Court of Appeals are affirmed.

It is so ordered.

Mr. Justice POWELL took no part in the consideration or decision of these cases.

---

28. Petitioners attach some significance to the fact that compliance with a §402 permit is "deemed compliance, for purposes of sections 309 [the federal enforcement section] and 505 [the citizen suit section], with sectio[n]...306...." §402(k). This provision plainly cannot allow deviations from §306 standards in issuing the permit. For, after standards of performance are promulgated, the permit can only be issued "upon condition that such discharge will meet...all applicable requirements under sectio[n]...306...." §402(a)(1); and one of the requirements of §306 is that no new source may operate in violation of any standard of performance. §306(e). The purpose of §402(k) seems to be to insulate permit holders from changes in various regulations during the period of a permit and to relieve them of having to litigate in an enforcement action the question whether their permits are sufficiently strict. In short, §402(k) serves the purpose of giving permits finality.

■ NOTES

1. As discussed previously, EPA failed to meet its statutory deadlines for promulgation of the effluent limitations for several industrial categories. How would the implementation of the act have been affected had the Court accepted the chemical manufacturers' argument that the technology-based limitations were instead to be set on a plant-by-plant basis? Does the reference to "categories and classes of point sources" in the statutory language describing the 1983 limitations, coupled with the concomitant absence of such a reference in the language describing the 1977 limitations, create an inference that supports their argument? How does the Court deal with this inference?

2. Note that the Court comes to different conclusions on the implied variance issue for the 1977 limitations for existing sources, on the one hand, and for the limitations for new sources, on the other. Can the seemingly divergent conclusions be reconciled with the language and policy of the statute? ∎

EPA v. National Crushed Stone Association
Justice WHITE delivered the opinion of the Court
United States Supreme Court
449 U.S. 64 (1980)

In April and July 1977, the Environmental Protection Agency (EPA), acting under the Federal Water Pollution Control Act (Act), as amended, 86 Stat. 816, 33 U. S. C. §1251 *et seq.*, promulgated pollution discharge limitations for the coal mining industry and for that portion of the mineral mining and processing industry comprising the crushed-stone, construction-sand, and gravel categories. Although the Act does not expressly authorize or require variances from the 1977 limitation, each set of regulations contained a variance provision.[2] Respondents sought review of the regulations in various Courts of Appeals, challenging both the substantive standards and the variance clause.[3] All of the petitions for review were transferred to the Court of Appeals for the Fourth Circuit. In *National Crushed Stone Assn. v. EPA*, 601 F.2d 111 (1979), and in *Consolidation Coal*

---

2. The variance provision reads as follows:

"In establishing the limitations set forth in this section, EPA took into account all information it was able to collect, develop and solicit with respect to factors (such as age and size of plant, raw materials, manufacturing processes, products produced, treatment technology available, energy requirements and costs) which can affect the industry subcategorization and effluent levels established. It is, however, possible that data which would affect these limitations have not been available and, as a result, these limitations should be adjusted for certain plants in this industry. An individual discharger or other interested person may submit evidence to the Regional Administrator (or to the State, if the State has the authority to issue NPDES permits) that factors relating to the equipment or facilities involved, the process applied, or other such factors related to such discharger are fundamentally different from the factors considered in the establishment of the guidelines. On the basis of such evidence or other available information, the Regional Administrator (or the State) will make a written finding that such factors are or are not fundamentally different for that facility compared to those specified in the Development Document. If

such fundamentally different factors are found to exist, the Regional Administrator or the State shall establish for the discharger effluent limitations in the NPDES permit either more or less stringent than the limitations established herein, to the extent dictated by such fundamentally different factors. Such limitation must be approved by the Administrator of the Environmental Protection Agency. The Administrator may approve or disapprove such limitations, specify other limitations, or initiate proceedings to revise these regulations."

See 40 CFR §434.22 (1980) (coal preparation plants); §434.32 (acid mine drainage); §434.42 (alkaline mine drainage); §436.22 (crushed stone) and §436.32 (construction sand and gravel).

3. The actions were brought under §509 (b)(1)(E), which, as set forth in 33 U. S. C. §1369 (b)(1)(E), gives the courts of appeals jurisdiction to review "the Administrator's action...in approving or promulgating any effluent limitation or other limitation under section 1311...of this title...." Plaintiffs in *National Crushed Stone* were three producers and their trade association. Plaintiffs in *Consolidation Coal* were 17 coal producers, their trade association, 5 citizens' environmental associations, and the Commonwealth of Pennsylvania.

Co. v. *Costle*, 604 F.2d 239 (1979), the Court of Appeals set aside the variance provision as "unduly restrictive" and remanded the provision to EPA for reconsideration.[4]

To obtain a variance from the 1977 uniform discharge limitations a discharger must demonstrate that the "factors relating to the equipment or facilities involved, the process applied, or other such factors relating to such discharger are fundamentally different from the factors considered in the establishment of the guidelines." Although a greater than normal cost of implementation will be considered in acting on a request for a variance, economic ability to meet the costs will not be considered.[5] A variance, therefore, will not be granted on the basis of the applicant's economic inability to meet the costs of implementing the uniform standard.

The Court of Appeals for the Fourth Circuit rejected this position. It required EPA to "take into consideration, among other things, the statutory factors set out in §301 (c)," which authorizes variances from the more restrictive pollution limitations to become effective in 1987 and which specifies economic capability as a major factor to be taken into account.[6] The court held that

"if [a plant] is doing all that the maximum use of technology within its economic capability will per-

mit and if such use will result in reasonable further progress toward the elimination of the discharge of pollutants...no reason appears why [it] should not be able to secure such a variance should it comply with any other requirements of the variance." 601 F.2d, at 124, quoting from *Appalachian Power Co.* v. *Train*, 545 F.2d 1351, 1378 (CA4 1976).

We granted certiorari to resolve the conflict between the decisions below and *Weyerhaeuser Co.* v. *Costle*, 191 U. S. App. D. C. 309, 590 F.2d 1011 (1978), in which the variance provision was upheld. 444 U.S. 1069.

I

We shall first briefly outline the basic structure of the Act, which translates Congress' broad goal of eliminating "the discharge of pollutants into the navigable waters," 33 U. S. C. §1251(a)(1), into specific requirements that must be met by individual point sources.[7]

Section 301 (b) of the Act, 33 U. S. C. §1311(b) (1976 ed. and Supp. III), authorizes the Administrator to set effluent limitations for categories of point sources.[8] With respect to existing point sources, the section provides for implementation of increasingly stringent effluent limitations in two steps. The first step to be accomplished by July 1, 1977, requires all point sources to meet standards

---

4. In *National Crushed Stone*, the Court of Appeals also vacated and remanded the substantive regulations. That action is not before the Court. In *Consolidation Coal*, the substantive regulations were upheld.

5. EPA has explained its position as follows:

"Thus a plant may be able to secure a BPT variance by showing that the plant's own compliance costs with the national guideline limitation would be x times greater than the compliance costs of the plants EPA considered in setting the national BPT limitation. A plant may not, however, secure a BPT variance by alleging that the plant's own financial status is such that it cannot afford to comply with the national BPT limitation." 43 Fed. Reg. 50042 (1978).

6. Section 301 (c), 86 Stat. 844, 33 U. S. C. §1311 (c), allows the Administrator to grant a variance "upon a showing by the owner or operator...that such modified requirements (1) will represent the maximum use of technology within the economic capability of the owner or operator; and (2) will result in reasonable further progress toward the elimination of the discharge of pollutants."

7. A "point source" is defined as "any discernible, confined and discrete conveyance,...from which pollutants are or may be discharged." §502 (14), 33 U. S. C. §1362(14) (1976 ed., Supp. III).

8. Throughout this opinion "Administrator" refers to the Administrator of EPA. In *E. I. du Pont de Nemours & Co.* v. *Train*, 430 U.S. 112 (1977), we sustained the Administrator's authority to issue the 1977 effluent limitations.

based on "the application of the best practicable control technology currently available [BPT] as defined by the Administrator...." §301 (b)(1) (A). The second step, to be accomplished by July 1, 1987, requires all point sources to meet standards based on application of the "best available technology economically achievable [BAT] for such category or class...."[9] §301 (b)(2) (A). Both sets of limitations—BPT's followed within 10 years by BAT's—are to be based upon regulatory guidelines established under §304 (b).

Section 304 (b) of the Act, 33 U. S. C. §1314(b), is again divided into two sections corresponding to the two levels of technology, BPT and BAT. Under §304 (b)(1) the Administrator is to quantify "the degree of effluent reduction attainable through the application of the best practicable control technology currently available [BPT] for classes and categories of point sources...." In assessing the BPT the Administrator is to consider

"the total cost of application of technology in relation to the effluent reduction benefits to be achieved from such application, ... the age of equipment and facilities involved, the process employed, the engineering aspects of the application of various types of control techniques, process changes, non-water quality environmental impact (including energy requirements), and such other factors as the Ad-

ministrator deems appropriate." 33 U. S. C. §1314 (b)(1)(B).

Similar directions are given the Administrator for determining effluent reductions attainable from the BAT except that in assessing BAT total cost is no longer to be considered in comparison to effluent reduction benefits.[10]

Section 402 authorizes the establishment of the National Pollutant Discharge Elimination System (NPDES), under which every discharger of pollutants is required to obtain a permit. The permit requires the discharger to meet all the applicable requirements specified in the regulations issued under §301. Permits are issued by either the Administrator or state agencies that have been approved by the Administrator.[11] The permit "[transforms] generally applicable effluent limitations ... into the obligations (including a timetable for compliance) of the individual discharger...." *EPA* v. *California ex rel. State Water Resources Control Board*, 426 U.S. 200, 205 (1976).

Section 301 (c) of the Act explicitly provides for modifying the 1987 (BAT) effluent limitations with respect to individual point sources. A variance under §301 (c) may be obtained upon a showing "that such modified requirements (1) will represent the maximum

---

9. The Federal Water Pollution Control Act Amendments of 1972, 86 Stat. 816, required that the second-stage standards be met by 1983. This deadline was extended in the Clean Water Act of 1977, 91 Stat. 1567. Depending on the nature of the pollutant, the deadline for the more stringent limitations now falls between July 1, 1984, and July 1, 1987. The 1977 Act also replaced the BAT standard with a new standard, "best conventional pollutant control technology [BCT]," for certain so-called "conventional pollutants." 33 U. S. C. §1311(b)(2)(E) (1976 ed., Supp. III). The distinction between BCT and BAT is not relevant to the issue presented here.

10. Senator Muskie, the principal Senate sponsor of the Act, described the "limited cost-benefit analysis" employed in setting BPT standards as being intended to "limit the application of technology

only where the additional degree of effluent reduction is wholly out of proportion to the costs of achieving such marginal level of reduction...." Remarks of Senator Muskie reprinted in Legislative History of the Water Pollution Control Act Amendments of 1972 (Committee Print compiled for the Senate Committee on Public Works by the Library of Congress) Ser. No. 93-1, p. 170 (1973) (hereafter Leg. Hist.). Section 304 (b)(2)(B) lists "cost" as a factor to consider in assessing BAT, although it does not state that costs shall be considered in relation to effluent reduction.

11. Establishment of state permit programs is authorized by §402 (b), 33 U. S. C. §1342 (b) (1976 ed., Supp. III). At present, over 30 States and covered territories operate their own NPDES programs.

use of technology within the economic capability of the owner or operator; and (2) will result in reasonable further progress toward the elimination of the discharge of pollutants." Thus, the economic ability of the individual operator to meet the costs of effluent reductions may in some circumstances justify granting a variance from the 1987 limitations.

No such explicit variance provision exists with respect to BPT standards, but in *E. I. du Pont de Nemours & Co.* v. *Train*, 430 U.S. 112 (1977), we indicated that a variance provision was a necessary aspect of BPT limitations applicable by regulations to classes and categories of point sources. *Id.*, at 128. The issue in this case is whether the BPT variance provision must allow consideration of the economic capability of an individual discharger to afford the costs of the BPT limitation. For the reasons that follow, our answer is in the negative.

II

The plain language of the statute does not support the position taken by the Court of Appeals. Section 301 (c) is limited on its face to modifications of the 1987 BAT limitations. It says nothing about relief from the 1977 BPT requirements. Nor does the language of the Act support the position that although §301 (c) is not itself applicable to BPT standards, it requires that the affordability of the prescribed 1977 technology be considered in

BPT variance decisions.[13] This would be a logical reading of the statute only if the factors listed in §301 (c) bore a substantial relationship to the considerations underlying the 1977 limitations as they do to those controlling the 1987 regulations. This is not the case.

The two factors listed in §301 (c)— "maximum use of technology within the economic capability of the owner or operator" and "reasonable further progress toward the elimination of the discharge of pollutants"— parallel the general definition of BAT standards as limitations that "require application of the best available technology economically achievable for such category or class, which will result in reasonable further progress toward... eliminating the discharge of all pollutants...." §301 (b)(2). A §301 (c) variance, thus, creates for a particular point source a BAT standard that represents for it the same sort of economic and technological commitment as the general BAT standard creates for the class. As with the general BAT standard, the variance assumes that the 1977 BPT standard has been met by the point source and that the modification represents a commitment of the maximum resources economically possible to the ultimate goal of eliminating all polluting discharges. No one who can afford the best available technology can secure a variance.

There is no similar connection between §301 (c) and the considerations underlying the establishment of the 1977 BPT limita-

---

13. It is true that in *Du Pont* we said there "[was no] radical difference in the mechanism used to impose limitations for the 1977 and the 198[7] deadlines" and that "there is no indication in either §301 or §304 that the §304 guidelines play a different role in setting 1977 limitations." 430 U.S., at 127. But our decision in *Du Pont* was that the 1977 limitations, like the 1987 limitations, could be set by regulation and for classes of point sources. It dealt with the power of the Administrator and the procedures he was to employ. There was no suggestion, nor could there have been, that the 1977 BPT and the 1987 BAT limitations were to have iden-

tical purposes or content. It follows that no proper inference could be drawn from *Du Pont* that the grounds for issuing variances from the 1987 limitations should also be the grounds for permitting individual point sources to depart from 1977 standards. Indeed, our opinion recognized that §301 (c) was designed for BAT limitations. Had we thought that §301 (c) governed variances from both the BAT and BPT standards, there would have been no need to postpone to another day, as we did, the question whether the variance clause contained in the 1977 regulations had the proper scope. That scope would have been defined by §301 (c).

tions. First, §301 (c)'s requirement of "reasonable further progress" must have reference to some prior standard. BPT serves as the prior standard with respect to BAT. There is, however, no comparable, prior standard with respect to BPT limitations.[14] Second, BPT limitations do not require an industrial category to commit the maximum economic resources possible to pollution control, even if affordable. Those point sources already using a satisfactory pollution control technology need take no additional steps at all. The §301 (c) variance factor, the "maximum use of technology within the economic capability of the owner or operator," would therefore be inapposite in the BPT context. It would not have the same effect there that it has with respect to BAT's, *i.e.*, it would not apply the general requirements to an individual point source.

More importantly, to allow a variance based on the maximum technology affordable by the point source, even if that technology fails to meet BPT effluent limitations, would undercut the purpose and function of BPT limitations. Rather than the 1987 requirement of the best measures economically and technologically feasible, the statutory provisions for 1977 contemplate regulations prohibiting discharges from any point source in excess of the effluent produced by the best practicable technology currently available in the industry. The Administrator was referred to the industry and to existing practices to de-

termine BPT. He was to categorize point sources, examine control practices in exemplary plants in each category, and, after weighing benefits and costs and considering other factors specified by §304, determine and define the best practicable technology at a level that would effect the obvious statutory goal for 1977 of substantially reducing the total pollution produced by each category of the industry.[15] Necessarily, if pollution is to be diminished, limitations based on BPT must forbid the level of effluent produced by the most pollution-prone segment of the industry, that segment not measuring up to "the average of the best existing performance." So understood, the statute contemplated regulations that would require a substantial number of point sources with the poorest performances either to conform to BPT standards or to cease production. To allow a variance based on economic capability and not to require adherence to the prescribed minimum technology would permit the employment of the very practices that the Administrator had rejected in establishing the best practicable technology currently in use in the industry.

To put the matter another way, under §304, the Administrator is directed to consider the benefits of effluent reductions as compared to the costs of pollution control in determining BPT limitations. Thus, every BPT limitation represents a conclusion by the Administrator that the costs imposed on

---

14. Also, the ultimate goal expressed in §301 (c), "the elimination of the discharge of pollutants," reflects the "national goal" specified in §301 (b) (2)(A) of "eliminating the discharge of all pollutants." This is not the aim of a BPT limitation; its more modest purpose is to effect a first step toward this goal. Thus, while BAT limitations may be regarded as falling between a level of effluent reduction already achieved and the ultimate goal, the frame of reference within which BPT limitations are established contains neither the prior nor the subsequent measure.
15. EPA defines BPT as "the average of the best existing performance by plants of various sizes,

ages and unit processes within each industrial category or subcategory. This average is not based upon a broad range of plants within an industrial category or subcategory, but is based upon performance levels achieved by exemplary plants." 39 Fed. Reg. 6580 (1974). See also EPA, Effluent Guidelines Div., Development Document for Mineral Mining and Processing Point Source Category 409 (1979) and Development Document for Coal Mining 225 (1976). Support for this definition is found in the legislative history, Leg. Hist. 169–170 (remarks of Sen. Muskie); *id.*, at 231 (remarks of Rep. Jones).

the industry are worth the benefits in pollution reduction that will be gained by meeting those limits. To grant a variance because a particular owner or operator cannot meet the normal costs of the technological requirements imposed on him, and not because there has been a recalculation of the benefits compared to the costs, would be inconsistent with this legislative scheme and would allow a level of pollution inconsistent with the judgment of the Administrator.[16]

In terms of the scheme implemented by BPT limitations, the factors that the Administrator considers in granting variances do not suggest that economic capability must also be a determinant. The regulations permit a variance where "factors relating to the equipment or facilities involved, the process applied, or such other factors relating to such discharger are fundamentally different from the factors considered in the establishment of the guidelines." If a point source can show that its situation, including its costs of compliance, is not within the range of circumstances considered by the Administrator, then it may receive a variance, whether or not the source could afford to comply with the minimum standard.[17] In such situations, the variance is an acknowledgment that the uniform BPT limitation was set without reference to the full range of current practices, to which the Administrator was to refer. Insofar as a BPT limitation was determined without consideration of a current practice fundamentally different from those that were considered by the Administrator, that limitation is incomplete. A variance based on economic capability, however, would not have this character: it would allow a variance simply because the point source could not afford a compliance cost that is not fundamentally different from those the Administrator has already considered in determining BPT. It would force a displacement of calculations already performed, not because those calculations were incomplete or had unexpected effects, but only because the costs happened to fall on one particular operator, rather than on another who might be economically better off.

Because the 1977 limitations were intended to reduce the total pollution produced by an industry, requiring compliance with BPT standards necessarily imposed additional costs on the segment of the industry with the least effective technology. If the statutory goal is to be achieved, these costs must be borne or the point source eliminated. In our view, requiring variances from otherwise valid regulations where dischargers cannot afford normal costs of compliance would un-

---

16. Respondents fail to consider this tension between a general calculation of costs and benefits and a particularized consideration of costs when they argue that because EPA only has authority to promulgate industrywide BPT regulations by analogy to its authority to promulgate industrywide BAT regulations, the same kind of economic capability/effluent reduction balancing relevant to a BAT variance must apply as well to a BPT variance.

17. Respondents argue that precluding consideration of economic capability in determining whether to grant a variance effectively precludes consideration of the "total costs" for the individual point source. Respondents rely upon a statement by Representative Jones as to the meaning of "total cost" in §304 (b)(1)(B):

"internal, or plant, costs sustained by the owner or operator and those external costs such as potential, unemployment, dislocation and rural area economic development sustained by the community, area, or region." Leg. Hist. 231.

Unless economic capability is considered, it is argued, it will be impossible to consider the potential external costs of meeting a BPT limitation, caused by a plant closing. Although there is some merit to respondents' contention, we do not believe it supports the decision of the Court of Appeals. The court did not hold that economic capability is relevant only if it discloses "fundamentally different" external costs from those considered by EPA in establishing the BPT limitation; rather, the court held that the factors included in §301 (c) *must* be taken into consideration. Section 301 (c) makes economic capability, regardless of its effect on external costs, a ground for a variance. It is this position that we reject.

dermine the purpose and the intended operative effect of the 1977 regulations.

III

The Administrator's present interpretation of the language of the statute is amply supported by the legislative history, which persuades us that Congress understood that the economic capability provision of §301 (c) was limited to BAT variances; that Congress foresaw and accepted the economic hardship, including the closing of some plants, that effluent limitations would cause; and that Congress took certain steps to alleviate this hardship, steps which did not include allowing a BPT variance based on economic capability.[18]

There is no indication that Congress intended §301 (c) to reach further than the limitations of its plain language. The statement of the House managers of the Act described §301 (c) as "not intended to justify modifications which would not represent an upgrading over the July 1, 1977, requirements of 'best practicable control technology.'" Leg. Hist. 232. The Conference Report noted that a §301 (c) variance could only be granted after the effective date of BPT limitations and could only be applied to BAT limitations. Similarly, the Senate Report on the Conference action emphasized that one of the purposes of the BPT limitation was to avoid imposing on the "Administrator any requirement . . . to determine the economic impact of controls on any individual plant in a single community." Leg. Hist. 170.

Nor did Congress restrict the reach of §301 (c) without understanding the economic hardships that uniform standards would impose. Prior to passage of the Act, Congress had before it a report jointly prepared by EPA, the Commerce Department, and the Council on Environmental Quality on the impact of the pollution control measures on industry.[19] That report estimated that there would be 200 to 300 plant closings caused by the first set of pollution limitations. Comments in the Senate debate were explicit: "There is no doubt that we will suffer some disruptions in our economy because of our efforts; many marginal plants may be forced to close." Leg. Hist. 1282 (Sen. Bentsen).[20] The House managers explained the Conference position as follows:

"If the owner or operator of a given point source determines that he would rather go out of business than meet the 1977 requirements, the managers clearly expect that any discharge issued in the interim would reflect the fact that all discharges not in compliance with such 'best practicable technology currently available' would cease by June 30, 1977." Id., at 231.

Congress did not respond to this foreseen economic impact by making room for variances based on economic impact. In fact, this

---

18. Since any variance provision will permit non-uniformity with the general BPT standard for a given category, we cannot attribute much weight to those passages in the legislative history, to which EPA points, that express a desire and expectation that "each polluter within a category or class of industrial sources . . . achieve nationally uniform effluent limitations based on 'best practicable' technology no later than July 1, 1977." See Leg. Hist. 162 (statement of Sen. Muskie). See also, e.g., id., at 170; id., at 302, 309 (Conference Report); id., at 787 (Report of House Committee on Public Works). Moreover, EPA has itself stated that a variance does not represent an exception to BPT or BAT limitations, but rather sets an individualized BPT or BAT limitation for that point source:

"No discharger . . . may be excused from the Act's requirement to meet BPT [and] BAT . . . through this variance clause. A discharger may instead receive an individualized definition of such a limitation or standard where the nationally prescribed limit is shown to be more or less stringent than appropriate for the discharger under the Act." 44 Fed. Reg. 32893 (1979). Therefore, expressions of an intent that "all" point sources meet BPT standards by 1977 do not necessarily support EPA's argument.

19. U.S. Council on Environmental Quality, Dept. of Commerce, & EPA, The Economic Impact of Pollution Control (Mar. 1972). See Leg. Hist. 156, 523.

20. See also remarks quoted in n. 22, infra.

possibility was specifically considered and rejected:

"The alternative [to a loan program] would be waiving strict environmental standards where economic hardship could be shown. But the approach of giving variances to pollution controls based on economic grounds has long ago shown itself to be a risky course: All too often, the variances become a tool used by powerful political interests to obtain so many exemptions for pollution control standards and timetables on the filmsiest [*sic*] of pretenses that they become meaningless. In short, with variances, exceptions to pollution cleanup can become the rule, meaning further tragic delay in stopping the destruction of our environment." *Id.*, at 1355 (Sen. Nelson).

Instead of economic variances, Congress specifically added two other provisions to address the problem of economic hardship.

First, provision was made for low-cost loans to small businesses to help them meet the cost of technological improvements. 86 Stat. 898, amending §7 of the Small Business Act, 15 U. S. C. §636. The Conference Report described the provision as authorizing the Small Business Administration "to make loans to assist small business concerns...if the Administrator determines that the concern is likely to suffer substantial economic injury without such assistance." Leg. Hist.

153. Senator Nelson, who offered the amendment providing for these loans, saw the loans as an alternative to the dangers of an economic variance provision that he felt might otherwise be necessary.[21] Several Congressmen understood the loan program as an alternative to forced closings: "It is the smaller business that is hit hardest by these laws and their enforcement. And it is that same class of business that has the least resources to meet the demands of this enforcement.... Without assistance, many of these businesses may face extinction." *Id.*, at 1359 (Sen. McIntyre).[22]

Second, an employee protection provision was added, giving EPA authority to investigate any plant's claim that it must cut back production or close down because of pollution control regulations. §507 (e), 86 Stat. 890, 33 U. S. C. §1367 (e).[23] This provision had two purposes: to allow EPA constantly to monitor the economic effect on industry of pollution control rules and to undercut economic threats by industry that would create pressure to relax effluent limitation rules.[24] Representative Fraser explained this second purpose as follows:

"[The] purpose of the amendment is to provide for a public hearing in the case of an industry claim

---

21. See quotation above.
22. Similar remarks were made by Representative Harrington ("No one in Congress wishes to legislate so irresponsibly that we drive out of business those who sincerely wish to abide by the new pollution laws but who, because of a bad state of the economy, will be forced to close. The $800 million authorized by this section may not be completely adequate. But it is a start," Leg. Hist. 450).
23. Section 507 (e) provides in pertinent part: "The Administrator shall conduct continuing evaluations of potential loss or shifts of employment which may result from the issuance of any effluent limitation or order under this chapter, including, where appropriate, investigating threatened plant closures or reductions in employment allegedly resulting from such limitation or order. Any employee who is discharged or laid-off, threatened with discharge or lay-off...because of the alleged results of any effluent limitation or order issued under this chapter...may request the Administrator to conduct a full investigation of the matter.... [The] Ad-

ministrator shall make findings of fact as to the effect of such effluent limitation or order on employment and on the alleged discharge, lay-off, or discrimination and shall make such recommendations as he deems appropriate. Such report, findings, and recommendations shall be available to the public." 33 U. S. C. §1367 (e).
24. See Leg. Hist. 654–659. Representative Abzug emphasized the first purpose of the provision: "This amendment will allow the Congress to get a close look at the effects on employment of legislation such as this, and will thus place us in a position to consider such remedial legislation as may be necessary to ameliorate those effects." *Id.*, at 658. Representative Miller noted that "some economic hardship, especially in smaller communities who rely on single, older plants, may result from the requirements of the pending bill," but opposed this provision because he thought that economic hardships caused by the Act should be addressed systematically by modifying the Economic Development Act. *Ibid.*

that enforcement of these water-control standards will force it to relocate or otherwise shut down operations.... I think too many companies use the excuse of compliance, or the need for compliance, to change operations that are going to change anyway. It is this kind of action that gives the whole antipollution effort a bad name and causes a great deal of stress and strain in the community." Leg. Hist. 659.

The only protection offered by the provision, however, is the assurance that there will be a public inquiry into the facts behind such an economic threat. The section specifically concludes that "[nothing] in this subsection shall be construed to require or authorize the Administrator to modify or withdraw any effluent limitation or order issued under this chapter." §507 (e), 33 U. S. C. §1367 (e).

As we see it, Congress anticipated that the 1977 regulations would cause economic hardship and plant closings: "[The] question . . . is not what a court thinks is generally appropriate to the regulatory process; it is what Congress intended for *these* regulations." *Du Pont*, 430 U.S., at 138.

IV

It is by now a commonplace that "when faced with a problem of statutory construction, this Court shows great deference to the interpretation given the statute by the officers or agency charged with its administration." *Udall* v. *Tallman*, 380 U.S. 1, 16 (1965). The statute itself does not provide for BPT variances in connection with permits for indi-

vidual point sources, and we had no occasion in *Du Pont* to address the adequacy of the Administrator's 1977 variance provision. In the face of §301 (c)'s explicit limitation and in the absence of any other specific direction to provide for variances in connection with permits for individual point sources, we believe that the Administrator has adopted a reasonable construction of the statutory mandate.

In rejecting EPA's interpretation of the BPT variance provision, the Court of Appeals relied on a mistaken conception of the relation between BPT and BAT standards. The court erroneously believed that since BAT limitations are to be more stringent than BPT limitations, the variance provision for the latter must be at least as flexible as that for the former with respect to affordability.[26] The variances permitted by §301 (c) from the 1987 limitations, however, can reasonably be understood to represent a cost in decreased effluent reductions that can only be afforded once the minimal standard expressed in the BPT limitation has been reached.

We conclude, therefore, that the Court of Appeals erred in not accepting EPA's interpretation of the Act. EPA is not required by the Act to consider economic capability in granting variances from its uniform BPT regulations.

The judgments of the Court of Appeals are *Reversed*.

Justice POWELL took no part in the consideration or decision of these cases.

---

26. ... The Court of Appeals also believed that because there will be situations in which the BPT and the BAT standards are identical, see Development Document for Mineral Mining, *supra* n. 15, at 438, it would be illogical to allow a variance based on economic capability for the latter but not for the former. The result would be to "close a plant in 1979 which would be allowed to operate under a variance in 1983." 601 F.2d, at 124. This assumes, however, that a variance would be available even though BPT standards had not been met, an as-

sumption which EPA rejects, Brief for Petitioners 27, and which is questionable in light of the legislative history. Leg. Hist. 232 ("This provision [§301 (c)] is not intended to justify modifications which would not represent an upgrading over the July 1, 1977, requirements of 'best practicable control technology'." (Rep. Jones, chairman of the House Conferees)). The suggested contradiction is accordingly unlikely to appear. In any event, it is of minor significance in considering the facial validity of the 1977 variance provisions.

■ **NOTES**

1. How does the variance from BPT standards that EPA authorized by regulation (see footnote 5) differ from the cost variance that the mining industry was seeking? The former—known as a "fundamentally different factors" (FDF) variance—is discussed in more detail in the following sections. In the 1987 amendments to the act, Congress wrote the FDF variance into the statute itself and made this type of variance available for the BAT and BCT standards as well. See Section 301(n), 33 U.S.C. §1311(n).

2. Two years before this decision, the D.C. Circuit Court of Appeals had rejected the argument that EPA should take the condition of the receiving waters into account when setting the BPT and BAT effluent limitations. See *Weyerhaeuser Co. v. Costle*, 590 F.2d 1011 (D.C. Cir. 1978). Weyerhaeuser's goal in this suit had been to require EPA to set standards less stringent than the requisite technology-based limits where compliance with the technology-based limits was not necessary to meet water quality standards. Although the Supreme Court did not directly address this issue in either *DuPont* or *National Crushed Stone*, it is clear from the Court's fealty in these cases to the language and purpose of the statute that it, too, would have rejected this argument.   ■

With the clarifications provided by these two Supreme Court cases, and with the further delineation provided by Congress in the 1987 amendments, the Clean Water Act's program of technology-based limitations took on much clearer shape. Perhaps the most important point to emerge from these cases was the affirmation of EPA's industry category-by-industry category approach to setting these standards. That is, the determination of economic and technological feasibility on which the limit is based is made for the delineated industry category (or subcategory) as a whole, and not for each plant or facility on an individual basis. This is the case for all of the various "B-acronym" technology-based limitations.

Keep in mind, however, that, these technology-based standards do *not* explicitly require the use of particular control or process technology. Although they are calculated on the basis of EPA's determination of the level of pollution reduction that can be achieved through the use of a particular technology (or group of technologies), the standards themselves are expressed in terms of numeric limits. Typically, there is a *loading* limit (which restricts the amount of a particular pollutant that may lawfully be discharged over a given period) and/or a *concentration* limit (which limits the concentration of a particular pollutant that may lawfully be discharged in the effluent). Quite often, there is both a *daily maximum* limit and a *monthly (or weekly) average* limit for the same pollutant. (Note that where a concentration limit is coupled with a limit on the overall flow—that is, on the number of gallons of effluent per day—it is effectively a loading limit as well.)

b. First-Tier Limitations for Existing Sources: BPT

Best practicable control technology currently available is defined in Section 304 (b)(1)(B). In setting these limits, EPA was to look to *existing industry practices* (as opposed to existing or available technology generally), and to consider "the total cost of application of technology in relation to the effluent reduction benefits to be achieved from such application, ... the age of equipment and facilities involved, the process employed, the engineering aspects of the application of various types of control techniques, process changes, [and] non-water quality environmental impact" [33 U.S.C. §1314(b)(1)(B)]. Thus, in establishing a BPT effluent limit, EPA was to consider not simply the economic feasibility of the limit, but rather the overall costs of the limit in relationship to its pollution reduction benefits. As noted in the *National Crushed Stone* case (see footnote 15), EPA defined BPT performance as "the average of the best existing performance by plants of various sizes, ages and unit processes" within each industrial category [39 *Fed. Reg.* 6850 (1974)].

Once the BPT limit was established for a particular industry segment, individual firms within that segment were not allowed to seek a waiver from the limit based on their inability to afford the costs of compliance. However, as discussed, EPA did allow a fundamentally different factors variance from the BPT limit for those dischargers that could demonstrate that "factors relating to the equipment or facilities involved, the process applied, or other such factors relating to such discharger are *fundamentally different* from the factors considered in the establishment of [the limit]" [43 *Fed. Reg.* 50042 (1978), emphasis added]. Under this provision, a discharger could qualify for a variance from the standard if, for example, its process technology differed from those of most other firms within its industry category, and if, because of these differences, its cost of compliance was meaningfully higher than those of these other firms.

In contrast to the procedure for the BCT and BAT standards, the Clean Water Act does not divide water pollutants into different classifications for the BPT standards. Indeed, the statute does not specify the pollutants for which the BPT standards are to be set. In practice, the selection of the pollutants to be covered by the BPT standards for any given industry was driven by the nature of the existing pollution reduction technology used by the industry. In the main, these were end-of-pipe technologies, and the pollutants they removed or controlled were those that were historically recognized as posing water pollution concerns, such as suspended solids, pH, BOD, metals, and a few toxic chemicals.

c. Second-Tier Limitations for Existing Sources: BCT and BAT

Best conventional pollution control technology which is applicable to those few pollutants designated as "conventional" pollutants, is defined in Section 304(b)(4). As with the BPT limits, EPA must give consideration in setting these limits to "the age of equipment and facilities involved, the process employed, the engineering aspects of the application of various types of control techniques, process changes, [and any] non-water quality environmental impact." In addition, the agency must consider "the reasonableness of the relationship between the cost of attaining a reduction in effluents and the effluent reduction benefits derived, and the comparison of the cost and level of reduction of such pollutants from the discharge from publicly owned treatment works to the cost and level of reduction of such pollutants from a class or category of industrial sources" [33 U.S.C. §1314(b)(4)(B)]. This latter requirement reflects a recognition of the fact that the four pollutants initially designated as conventional in the 1977 amendments—BOD, suspended solids, fecal coliform, and pH—are amenable to treatment by the types of pollution control technologies typically employed at sewage treatment plants.

Once the BCT standard has been established for a particular industry category, individual dischargers within that category have limited opportunities to seek an exemption from the standard. An individual modification of the BCT limitations for BOD and pH is available for discharges into the "deep waters of the territorial seas" under Section 301(m). In addition, individual dischargers may seek an FDF variance under the provisions of Section 301(n).

Best available control technology economically achievable is defined in Section 304(b)(2) and is applicable to both "nonconventional" and toxic pollutants. The BAT standards are to "result in reasonable further progress toward the national goal of eliminating the discharge of all pollutants," and are to require "the elimination of discharges of all pollutants [where] such elimination is technologically and economically achievable" [Section 301(b)(2)(A)]. In setting these limits, EPA is to consider the usual factors relating to age, process, engineering, and nonwater quality impact. In addition, the agency is to consider "the cost of achieving such effluent reduction," although it is not to do a cost-benefit analysis [Section 304(b)(2)(B)]. Further, EPA's consideration of "available" pollution reduction technology is not limited to existing industry practices. In essence, then, the BAT standard is to be based on economic and technological feasibility within the regulated industry sector.

There are a number of potential avenues of relief for individual dischargers seeking an exemption from a BAT standard for a nonconventional pollutant. Most significantly, Section 301(c) allows a modification of BAT requirements for dischargers who can demonstrate that they lack the financial wherewithal to meet the standard. Under this provision, EPA may modify the standard so that it requires "the maximum use of technology within the economic capability of the discharger" (as noted by the Supreme Court in the *National Crushed Stone* case, "no one who can afford" BAT can secure this modification) as long as the modified standard represents "reasonable further progress" toward the goal of no discharge. In addition, an FDF variance is available under Section 301(n), and, under Section 301(k), a time extension of up to 2 years from the date the standard becomes effective is available to dischargers who propose to meet the standard through the use of an innovative technology that EPA determines has the potential for industry-wide use. (A more detailed discussion of innovation waivers appears in chapters 12 and 13.) Finally, Section 301(g) allows a modification from BAT to BPT for discharges of ammonia, chlorine, color, iron, total phenols, and other nonconventional pollutants listed by EPA, in situations where certain water quality and other conditions can be met, and Section 316(a) affords dischargers an opportunity to demonstrate that a less stringent thermal standard would be adequate to protect water quality.

The opportunities for individual exceptions to the BAT standards for *toxic* pollutants are far more limited. Section 301(l) specifies that, other than granting an FDF variance under the provisions of Section 301(n), EPA "may not modify any requirement of this section as it applies to any specific pollutant which is on the toxic pollutant list."

Both because it was allowed to look beyond the technologies already in use within an industry, and because it could give companies a longer lead time before requiring compliance, in setting the BAT limits EPA gave consideration to changes in production processes as well as to end-of-pipe technology. Section 301(e) requires that the BCT and BAT standards "be reviewed at least every five years and, if appropriate, revised." Presumably, this requirement for a 5-year review was designed to ensure that as the technological capability to reduce pollution improves or becomes cheaper within a particular industry category, EPA would strengthen the (technology-based) limits for that category. The agency has revised some of its BAT standards and has in some cases placed a greater emphasis on improvements in production processes. BAT standards for pulp and paper mills, for example, have been revised to limit the types of chlorine that may be used in the bleaching process because the use of chlorine is known to create dioxins and other harmful pollutants in pulp and paper mill effluent. See 63 *Fed. Reg.* 18504 (April 15, 1998), and 63 *Fed. Reg.* 42238 (August 7, 1998). These regulations, known as the "Pulp and Paper Cluster Rule," are also noteworthy because they combine Clean Water Act standards and Clean Air Act standards in a single rule.

▪ NOTES

1. A study of the combined effect on industry of Clean Water Act standards and Clean Air Act standards for the period from 1972 through 1977 found that in those industry sectors with the highest compliance costs, the number of plants had been reduced, with a concomitant increase in average plant size. After controlling for

other factors, the study concluded that this effect had been attributable in substantial part to the environmental regulations. See B. Peter Pashigian (1984) "How Large and Small Plants Fare Under Environmental Regulation," 27 *Journal of Law and Economics* 1. EPA promulgated its first round of regulations setting BPT and BAT limits for a number of industry categories (upheld by the Supreme Court in the *DuPont* decision) in 1974. This study suggests that one effect of these regulations (and contemporaneous Clean Air Act regulations) was to cause some companies to shut down their smaller plants rather than pay the cost of retrofitting them for compliance. As between the BPT standards and the BAT standards, which were likely to have been the driving force in producing this result?

2. Does the availability of an FDF variance tend to discourage the movement within an industry sector to "cleaner" technology (especially where one production process within that sector is less polluting than another)? Can the variance nonetheless be justified on fairness grounds?

3. As discussed in the *DuPont* decision, EPA's practice has been to promulgate all of the technology-based limits for a particular industry category (BPT, BAT, and BADT and, after the 1977 amendments, BPT, BCT, BAT, and BADT) in one regulation. As also discussed in *DuPont*, EPA has relied heavily on outside consultants to help it develop these limits. Given the enormity of the task of learning enough about the technological and economic capabilities of a large number of industry categories in a relatively short period of time, this is not surprising. If your goal were to ensure the most accurate possible assessment of each sector's capability, whom would you want to use as consultants to investigate that sector?   ∎

d. Limitations for New Sources: BADT

Best available demonstrated control technology is applicable to new sources and is defined in Section 306. A BADT limit is to be

a standard for the control of the discharge of pollutants which reflects the greatest degree of effluent reduction which ... [is] achievable through application of the best available demonstrated control technology, processes, operating methods, or other alternatives, including, where practicable, a standard permitting no discharge of pollutants. [Section 306(a)(1)]

In setting these limits, EPA is to consider "the cost of achieving such effluent reduction, and any non-water quality environmental impact and energy requirements" [Section 306(b)(1)(B)]. As with the BPT, BCT, and BAT standards, these limitations are set on an industry-segment basis. "New sources" subject to a BADT standard include "any building, structure, facility, or installation from which there is or may be the discharge of pollutants [to the navigable waters]," the construction of which was begun after the applicable standard was promulgated [Section 306(2) and (3)]. EPA is

Table 8.1
Second Tier (POST-BPT) Direct Discharge Effluent Limitations Applicable to Industrial Point Sources Under the Clean Water Act

Pollutant Type	Existing Source	New Source	New or Existing Source
Conventional	BCT (Subject to FDF variance, innovative technology time extension); potential relaxation for pH and BOD discharges to deep waters of the territorial seas under 301(m)	BADT	Any more stringent limitation necessary to meet water quality criteria [via 303(d) or otherwise], including nondegradation requirements and possible WET limitation
Nonconventional	BAT (subject to cost waiver, FDF variance, innovative technology time extension); potential relaxation to BPT under 301(g)	BADT	Any more stringent limitation necessary to meet water quality criteria [via 303(d) or otherwise], including nondegradation requirements and possible WET limitation
Toxic	BAT (subject to FDF variance, innovative technology time extension)	BADT	Any more stringent limitation necessary to meet water quality criteria [via 303(d), 304(l), or otherwise], including nondegradation requirements and possible WET limitation

required to revise BDAT standards "from time to time, as technology and alternatives change," but a new source is entitled to rely for up to 10 years on the standard to which it was originally subject [Section 306(b)(1)(B) and (d)]. No variances are available from a BADT standard. Table 8.1 summarizes the effluent limitations governing pollutant discharges from industrial point sources to the waters of the United States.

■ **NOTES**

1. Both the BAT standards (for existing sources) and the BADT standards (for new sources) are to be based on "best available" technology and cost. Why are the new source standards nonetheless likely to be more stringent (at least in their practical impact) than the existing source standards?

2. In addition to being required to meet applicable technology-based limitations, industrial sources (whether new or existing) are subject to such water quality-based limitations as are necessary to meet ambient water quality criteria. The mechanism for establishing these limitations is discussed in detail in a later section.

3. EPA's obligation to consider the pollution reduction attainable through substitution of chemical inputs and other industrial process changes when it formulates and

revises the BAT standards was strengthened by the passage of the Pollution Prevention Act of 1990. This omnibus statute, discussed in detail in chapter 13, requires agencies to give preference to regulations that reduce pollution at its source.   ■

e. Limitations for Public Sewage Treatment Plants

Until roughly the late 1980s, most of the regulatory attention given to sewage treatment plants was focused on the more conventional types of pollutants (BOD, solids, fecal coliform, and pH). POTWs are required to meet emission limitations for these pollutants that are consistent with secondary treatment, which requires, inter alia, 85% removal of BOD and total suspended solids (TSS). The 1987 amendments, however, placed increased attention on the toxic pollutants that are contained in POTW discharges. POTWs are now required to test more comprehensively for toxic substances in their discharges, and can expect to have limitations for some of these pollutants placed in their permits. In addition, as discussed later, the 1987 amendments added provisions to Section 405 that required EPA to set health-based standards designed to limit the concentrations of toxic substances in sewage sludge. Finally, as also discussed later, POTWs are required to have a pretreatment program to regulate any industrial sources that discharge wastes into the sewage system. The Clean Water Act requirements for POTWs thus can be summarized as follows:

• Meet effluent limitations consistent with secondary treatment (85% reduction in BOD and TSS) for conventional pollutants
• Meet any more stringent limitation necessary to meet water quality criteria [via 303(d), 304(l), or otherwise], including nondegradation requirements and possible WET limitation (discussed later in this chapter)
• Develop and implement an EPA-approved pretreatment program for industrial indirect dischargers; meet EPA standards for the disposal of sewage sludge

3. Water Quality-Based Effluent Limitations

Unlike the system for technology-based standards, in which federal standards set by EPA are the driving force, the Clean Water Act's system for water quality-based standards is primarily state driven. EPA does have the authority to set federal discharge standards based on water quality considerations, but this authority is rarely used. As discussed earlier, Section 307 authorizes EPA to set health-based discharge standards for toxic pollutants, and the agency did set a handful of these standards (mostly for discharges of pesticide chemicals) before the shift to a technology-based approach for toxic pollutants in the 1977 amendments. Further, Section 302 authorizes EPA to set water quality-based effluent limitations for individual point sources whose discharges "interfere with the attainment or maintenance of [water quality goals] in a specific portion of the navigable waters. . . ." [33 U.S.C. §1312(a)]. Rather than use this authority, however, EPA has preferred to rely on the process described in the next section, in which the states take the lead in setting water quality-based discharge limits, subject to EPA backup and oversight. This process is a throwback to the pre-1972 era Federal Water Pollution Control Act. The states are to establish ambient water quality standards, and effluent limitations sufficient to meet those standards are then to be applied to individual dischargers.

a. The State and Federal Roles in Setting and Revising Ambient Water Quality Standards

The centerpiece of the Clean Water Act's program of ambient water quality standards is Section 303, 33 U.S.C. §1333. As amended in 1972, this provision directed each state to set "water quality standards"—limitations on the ambient level or concentration of pollutants permitted to be in a particular body of water—for all navigable waters within its borders, and to submit these standards for EPA approval by mid-1973. See Section 303(a). If a state chose not to participate in this process (recall that the Constitution does not empower Congress to compel a state to take regulatory action), or if a state declined to revise a standard found wanting by EPA, the agency was directed to set the appropriate ambient standard(s) for that state itself. See Section 303(b). The states are also directed to review their water quality standards and to revise them as necessary every 3 years. See Section 303(c). Any such revised standard is to be submitted to EPA for approval. If EPA finds the revised standard to be inadequate to protect water quality, it must promulgate its own revised standard for the state unless the state modifies the standard to meet EPA's objections. Moreover, if a state does not revise its standards, and EPA finds that a revised standard will be necessary to protect water quality, the agency must promulgate the revised standard for the state. See Section 303(c)(4).

All the states eventually promulgated water quality standards that have been approved under this program, although EPA has found it necessary to promulgate standards for certain water bodies in certain states. It has, for example, promulgated numeric toxic pollutant criteria for designated waterways in several states. See 40 CFR §§131.36–131.38. The states (and EPA) have also worked to periodically revise the ambient standards, although the statutory goal of revisions at regular 3-year intervals has not been widely attained.

■ NOTES

1. The rationale behind the requirement for a periodic review of water quality standards, of course, is that additional information (about the effects of a particular pollutant, for example, or about the nature of the aquatic life inhabiting a particular

body of water) will become available over time as new research and experiential data are accumulated. The review process is designed to provide an orderly mechanism for integrating this new information into an assessment of the adequacy of current standards.

2. Sometimes the need for a revised water quality standard can be suggested by regulatory action taken under another statute. When the U.S. Fish and Wildlife Service declared the bull trout to be a threatened species under the Endangered Species Act in 1999, for example, it noted that the state of Washington's current standards for ambient water temperature "are likely inadequate to protect bull trout spawning, rearing, or migration" [64 *Fed. Reg.* 58296 (Nov. 1, 1999)]. This in turn prompted the Washington State Department of Ecology to begin a review of its temperature standards.

3. EPA regulations regarding review and revision of water quality standards, and the water quality standards promulgated by EPA, are found at 40 CFR §§131.20–131.22.

4. In addition to establishing criteria for the ambient waters some states have established *sediment* criteria for some water bodies. In 1998, EPA released an analysis of sediments in U.S. lakes, rivers, and coastal waters. Drawing on a database that reportedly included more than 21,000 sampling stations located in 1,363 of the nation's 2,111 watersheds, the agency estimated that contaminated sediments were likely to be causing adverse effects to humans, fish, and/or wildlife in 7% of U.S. waters. See Bette Hileman, "EPA Finds 7% of Watersheds Have Polluted Sediments," *Chemical and Engineering News*, January 26, 1998, p. 27.

5. Under Section 303(I), added to the act in 2000, each state having "coastal recreation waters" was to submit to EPA proposed water quality standards for those "pathogen and pathogen indicators" for which EPA has promulgated criteria under Section 304(a). If any such state fails to adopt standards that are "as protective of human health" as the criteria promulgated by EPA, the agency is to adopt the required standards within 6 months.   ■

b. The Mechanics of Establishing Water Quality Standards

As specified in EPA regulations (40 CFR §131), ambient water quality standards are to be established under a two-step process. The first step is the *classification* of the waters of the state. Each state is to "specify appropriate water uses to be achieved and protected," according to a set of criteria specified by EPA that reflect the water quality goals articulated in Section 101 of the act, and is then to classify state waterways (or the various portions thereof) according to which of these uses they are deemed to support. 40 CFR §131.10(a). "In no case," however, "shall a state adopt waste transport or waste administration as a designated use" (id.).

Thus, for example, a state might adopt a classification system in which class A waters are those used for drinking water and other highest quality uses, class B waters are those that protect sensitive species of aquatic life, class C waters are those that are generally "fishable and swimmable," and class D waters are those that do not meet Clean Water Act goals. EPA regulation allows waters to be classified under this latter category, however, only if the state demonstrates that attainment of a higher use category "is not feasible" because of natural conditions, because of human-caused conditions that "cannot be remedied or would cause more environmental damage to correct than to leave in place," because of dams or other hydrologic modifications, or because the application of effluent limitations beyond the national technology-based limits to point sources discharging to these waters "would result in substantial and widespread economic and social impact" [40 CFR §131.10(g)]. Moreover, any waterway that has been so classified is to be reexamined every 3 years, and if any new information has become available that "indicates that the uses specified in section 101(a)(2) of the [Clean Water Act] are attainable," the waterway must be reclassified accordingly [40 CFR §131.20(a)].

(2) do what it takes

Once the waters of the state have been classified, the states are to "adopt those water quality criteria that protect the designated use," and, for those waters "with multiple use designations," those criteria "shall support the most sensitive use" [40 CFR §131.11(a)]. These criteria, then, are the ambient water quality standards. In setting these standards, the states are to (1) establish "numerical values" based on EPA guidance documents or other "scientifically defensible methods," and (2) establish "narrative criteria or criteria based on biomonitoring methods" in situations where "numerical criteria cannot be established" or "to supplement numerical criteria" [40 CFR §131.11(b)]. In general, such criteria are to be established for those pollutants and other indicia of water quality (such as dissolved oxygen) deemed relevant to maintaining the designated uses at the particular waterway in question. The states are afforded some flexibility in determining the pollutants for which water quality criteria will be established, and the manner by which those criteria will be established. However, Section 303 requires the establishment of "specific numerical criteria" for each toxic pollutant for which EPA has published criteria under Section 304(a), "as necessary to support...designated uses," so long as the presence of that pollutant in the affected waters "could reasonably be expected to interfere with those designated uses" [33 U.S.C. §1313(c)(1)(B)].

EPA regulations also specify that each state must have a "statewide antidegradation policy" that ensures that existing water uses are "maintained and protected." These regulations specify that high-quality waters may be downgraded to reflect existing uses only if it is determined, after opportunity for public participation, "that allowing lower water quality is necessary to accommodate important economic or social development in the area in which the waters are located." However, if the high-quality waters in question "constitute an outstanding National resource," no such downgrading is permitted. See 40 CFR §§131.12(a)(1)–(3).

■ **NOTES**

1. In 1981, to encourage states to revise their water quality standards in accordance with Section 303(c), Congress specified that any state whose revision process was not completed by December 29, 1984 would not be eligible for federal grants under Title II of the act until it had completed its obligations under the revision process. See Section 303a, 33 U.S.C. §1313a.

2. Where the numeric criterion for a toxic pollutant is designed to protect aquatic life, both an acute exposure criterion and a chronic exposure criterion will be set. The aquatic criterion is the criteria maximum concentration (CMC), which is defined as "the highest concentration of a pollutant to which aquatic life can be exposed for a short period of time without deleterious effects" [40 C.F.R. §131.38(b)(1) fn. d]. The referenced "short period of time" is usually 1 hour. The chronic criterion is the criteria continuous concentration (CCC), which is defined as "the highest concentration of a pollutant to which aquatic life can be exposed for an extended period of time (4 days) without deleterious effects" (id.).

3. Where a state contains both freshwater and saltwater waterways, acute and chronic criteria are to be set for each for those pollutants whose toxicity is affected by relative salinity. Similarly, for pollutants whose aquatic toxicity is influenced by hardness (i.e., the concentration of calcium carbonate) or pH, the numeric criteria commonly will be adjusted according to the relative hardness and pH of the receiving water. See, e.g., the hardness-dependent criteria for certain metals found at 40 C.F.R. §131.38(b)(1).

4. Where the numeric criterion for a toxic pollutant is designed to protect human life, two criteria are set: one for waterways that are used as drinking water supplies (where it is assumed that humans will be exposed to the pollutant both through consumption of fish and other aquatic organisms and through consumption of the water), and one for waterways that are not used as drinking supplies (where it is assumed that humans will be exposed only through consumption of fish and other aquatic organisms). As with the health-based standards for hazardous air pollutants under Section 112 of the Clean Air Act, criteria for carcinogens are designed to achieve a cancer risk of less than one in one million. See, e.g., the list of human health criteria found at 40 C.F.R. §131.36(b).

5. For a detailed discussion of EPA's rationale for its numeric water quality standards for several toxic pollutants, see the preamble to EPA's standards for the state of California, 65 *Fed. Reg.* 31682 (May 18, 2000).   ■

c. Translating Ambient Standards into Effluent Limitations

As discussed earlier, Section 301 requires each discharger to comply not only with applicable technology-based effluent limitations, but also with "any more stringent limitation . . . necessary to meet water quality standards" [Section 301(b)(1)(C)]. However, because the "permit shield" protections of Section 402(k) generally insulate the discharger from the mandates of Section 301 as long as the discharger complies with its NPDES permit, this requirement is meaningful in practice only if the necessary water quality-based limitations are placed in the discharger's permit. Two Clean Water Act programs were designed to encourage the incorporation of specific water quality considerations into NPDES permits.

i. The Total Maximum Daily Load

The first of these is the total maximum daily load (TMDL). For any particular body of water, the TMDL for a particular pollutant is defined as the total amount of that pollutant that may be discharged to the water body (from point and nonpoint sources) on any given day without violating the relevant ambient water quality standard. To facilitate the calculation of these TMDLs, EPA was directed to publish, by October 1973, "information . . . on and the identification of pollutants suitable for maximum daily load measurement correlated with the achievement of water quality objectives" [Section 304(a)(2)(D)]. Thereafter, each state was to "identify those waters within its boundaries for which the [national technology-based] effluent limitations . . . are not stringent enough to implement any water quality standard applicable to such waters," and to "establish a priority ranking for such waters, taking into account the severity of the pollution and the uses to be made of such waters" [Section 303(d)(1)(A)]. The states were then to calculate, for each pollutant identified by EPA under 304(a)(2)(D), "the total maximum daily load" for these waters. See Section 303(d)(1)(C). The TMDL is to be "established at a level necessary to implement the applicable water quality standards with seasonal variations and a margin of safety which takes into account any lack of knowledge concerning the relationship between effluent limitations and water quality" (id.).

The lists of waters, and the corresponding TMDL calculations, were to be submitted to EPA within 180 days after EPA published its identification of TMDL pollutants under 304(a)(2)(D), and revisions are to be submitted "from time to time" thereafter. EPA was to approve or disapprove the state submissions within 30 days. To the extent that EPA disapproved of a particular state's submission, the agency was to publish its own list and TMDLs for that state within 30 days thereafter. See Section 303(d)(2).

Development of the TMDLs was slow in coming. Indeed, it was not until the mid- to late 1990s, as environmental and citizen groups across the country brought suits to compel EPA to establish TMDLs for waters where the states had failed to do so, that they began to play an important role in the implementation of the Clean Water Act's water quality program. For a discussion of these lawsuits and other aspects of the TMDL program see Oliver Houck (2000) *The Clean Water Act TMDL Program: Law, Policy, and Implementation.* Environmental Law Institute, Washington, D.C.

Calculation of a TMDL often leads naturally to a reassessment of permitted discharges. Suppose, for example, that the TMDL for biochemical oxygen demand for a small river is calculated to be 4,000 pounds per day. This would represent a determination that at daily BOD loadings at or below this level, the level of dissolved oxygen in the river would be sufficient to break down this material without falling below the water quality standard for dissolved oxygen. At daily BOD loadings above 4,000 pounds, however, the amount of oxygen required to assimilate this loading would be such that the level of dissolved oxygen in the river would fall below the water quality standard. Suppose now that there are three point sources discharging to the river, each of which is permitted to discharge 1,500 pounds per day of BOD. The total permitted BOD loading to the river (4,500 pounds per day) would thus exceed the calculated maximum daily loading deemed to be consistent with the relevant ambient water quality standard. This would rather straightforwardly suggest a need to tighten the BOD limits in the permits of these dischargers.

The clear expectation of the act is that the calculation of the TMDLs *will* lead to more stringent effluent limitations where such limitations are necessary to meet water quality standards. Section 303(e) directs the states to submit for EPA approval, and to periodically update, a "continuing planning process" that ensures, among other things, that point sources are subject to "effluent standards and schedules of compliance at least as stringent as those required [to meet water quality standards]." If a state fails to implement or update this planning process, EPA is empowered to revoke the state's authority to administer the NPDES program within its borders, and to set such effluent limitations as are necessary to meet water quality standards.

■ **NOTES**

1. Section 303 also creates a similar program for thermal discharges, which is designed "to assure protection and propagation of a balanced indigenous population of shellfish, fish, and wildlife" [Sections 303(d)(1)(B) and (d)(1)(D)].

2. "For the specific purpose of developing information," states also are directed to "estimate" the TMDLs for all waters within the state for which a TMDL (or thermal discharge TMDL) is not required [Section 303(d)(3)].

3. A TMDL may have the effect of triggering state-imposed limits on the contribution of pollutants from nonpoint sources. The calculation of TMDLs can also bring

about interesting interplays between point and nonpoint sources of pollution. Although nonpoint sources are not subject to the NPDES program, the incentives that the TMDL process adds to that program can serve as an indirect mechanism for reducing the pollution emanating from those sources. Suppose, for example, that a company owns an industrial facility that discharges phosphorus to a lake. The company would like to expand its operations at this facility, but knows that this expansion would result in a substantial enough increase in its phosphorus discharge to cause the overall phosphorus loading to the lake to exceed the lake's TMDL for that pollutant. Suppose also, however, that a major portion of the loading of phosphorus to the lake comes from fertilizers that contaminate the runoff from a large community golf course. If the company offers to finance a program of fertilizer management and runoff control at the golf course, and the owner of the golf course is amenable, the company may be able to achieve sufficient reduction in the phosphorus loadings to the lake to proceed with its expansion plans without exceeding the TMDL. (See the discussion of EPA's watershed-based pollutant trading program in the section on nonpoint sources later in this chapter.)   ■

ii.   The Section 304(l) Program for "Toxic Hot Spots"   The second major provision of the Clean Water Act designed to place water quality considerations into NPDES permits is Section 304(l), which, as discussed earlier, was part of the Water Quality Act Amendments of 1987. This provision focuses solely on the water quality effects of toxic pollutants. Section 304(l) gave the states 2 years to submit to EPA (1) a list of "all navigable waters" in the state that were not expected to meet applicable ambient water quality standards, even after compliance with all applicable national technology-based effluent limitations, because of point source discharges of toxic pollutants; (2) for "each segment" of the navigable waters so identified, a list of the point source dischargers "believed to be preventing or impairing such water quality" and "the amount of each such toxic pollutant discharged by each such source"; and (3) for each such segment, an "individual control strategy" determined to be sufficient to reduce the discharge of toxic pollutants from the identified point source or sources to the extent necessary to "achieve the applicable water quality standard … not later than 3 years after the establishment of the strategy" [Section 304(l)(1)(B), (C), and (D)]. EPA was to approve or disapprove the individual control strategies within 120 days of their submission, and the strategies were to be implemented once approved. Section 304(l)(2). To the extent that any state failed to carry out these tasks, and to the extent that EPA disapproved of any state's submittal, the agency was directed to take the necessary actions itself. Section 304(l)(3).

Perhaps because it came as a midcourse correction in which Congress expressed its clear desire that EPA pay closer attention to the effects of toxic pollutants, Section

304(l) had a much more immediate impact than the more broadly focused TMDL requirements. Considerable fanfare accompanied the passage of this new program to address "toxic hot spots," and indications are that EPA and the states took these responsibilities seriously. States did submit their proposed 304(l) lists and individual control strategies on a more-or-less timely basis, and in many cases EPA did step in with its own actions where the states faltered. Not surprisingly, the individual control strategies devised to reduce point source discharges of toxic pollutants under the 304(l) program have almost always involved a tightening of the applicable discharge limits of the point sources identified.

To the extent that it results in the imposition of discharge limitations deemed sufficient to attain water quality standards, of course, Section 304(l) does nothing that was not already mandated by Section 301(b)(1)(C), which has been a part of the statute since the 1972 amendments. The key to the relative success of 304(l) in making this mandate a reality is that it specifies a mechanism for identifying individual point sources that are compromising water quality, imposes a specific deadline for reducing their discharges, and requires EPA to take action if the states do not. For toxic pollutants, then, Section 304(l) has operated to give "teeth" to the oft-ignored directive of Section 301(b)(1)(C) that no point source should be permitted to discharge pollution that causes or contributes to a violation of ambient water quality standards.

One should not infer from this, however, that there are no longer any waterways in the United States that are not being impaired by point source discharges of toxic pollutants. Either because ambient standards are not protective, discharge limits aren't strong enough, or both, many waterways (and their resident aquatic life) are still being affected by point source toxic discharges.

iii. The Mechanics of Establishing Water Quality-Based Effluent Limitations In theory, the application of ambient water quality criteria to an individual discharger might appear relatively straightforward. If, for example, the ambient standard for copper in a particular waterway is 17 micrograms per liter, a point source discharging to that waterway might logically be deemed in violation of that standard *at the point of discharge* unless the concentration of copper in its effluent is less than 17 micrograms per liter. However, presumably because it views such a result as overly stringent, EPA has included the following language in its regulations on water quality standards:

States may, at their discretion, include in their State standards, policies generally affecting their application and implementation, such as mixing zones, low flows and variances. Such policies are subject to EPA review and approval. (40 CFR §131.13)

In practice, this means that states may, subject to EPA approval, build features into their water quality standards that allow individual sources to violate water quality criteria under certain circumstances. The most widely used of such features is the *mixing zone* concept. Generally speaking, a mixing zone is a designated area (defined by length, width, and depth) within the receiving waters in which violation of ambient water quality criteria is allowed. If both acute (for short-term exposure) and chronic (for longer-term exposure) water quality criteria have been established for the pollutant at issue, both a (smaller) acute and a (larger) chronic mixing zone typically will be designated.

The scientific rationale behind the use of mixing zones is that once the effluent has been discharged, the receiving water will dilute it. The mixing zone allows the discharger to take advantage of this dilution. So long as the concentration of the pollutant in the discharge is such that the water quality standard is achieved at the edge of the mixing zone, no violation is said to have occurred. The resultant effluent limit, then, is determined by the amount of dilution calculated to be available within the mixing zone.

▪ NOTES

1. Is the use of mixing zones authorized (explicitly or implicitly) by the Clean Water Act? If so, are they authorized under all circumstances?

2. Assuming that the ambient water quality criteria are sufficiently protective, is there nonetheless a risk of harm within the mixing zone?

3. EPA has promulgated regulations for the Great Lakes that phase out (over a 10-year period) the use of mixing zones for certain bioaccumulative toxic chemicals. Does EPA have the authority to make such a regulation generally applicable to all waterways in all states? Does EPA have the authority to disallow the use of mixing zones in their entirety? Would such a move be *politically* viable?   ▪

d.   Whole Effluent Toxicity Standards

In addition to containing numeric discharge limitations for particular pollutants (or classes of pollutants), many permits now have *whole effluent toxicity* (WET) limitations as well. WET limitations generally require the discharger to test the toxicity of samples of its effluent with regard to certain specified reference species. There generally is an *acute* WET limit, usually based on the LC_{50} (the concentration of the tested effluent in water at which half of the test organisms die) and a *chronic* WET limit, often based on the no observed chronic effects level (the NOEL, the concentration of the tested effluent in water at which no effects are observed in the test organisms over a specified period of time). EPA regulations encourage the use of WET limitations for discharges that are likely to exhibit acute or chronic toxicity.

4. The Permitting Process in Detail

Section 402 (a)(1) provides as follows:

Except as provided in [Sections 318 and 404, which deal, respectively, with the issuance of permits for discharges associated with aquaculture projects and with the issuance of permits for the discharge of dredged or fill material], *the Administrator [of EPA] may, after opportunity for public hearing, issue a permit for the discharge of any pollutant, or combination of pollutants, notwithstanding [Section 301(a)], upon condition that such discharge will meet either (A) all applicable requirements* under [Sections 301, 302, 306, and 307, section 308 (dealing with data gathering and reporting requirements), and section 403 (dealing with discharges to the ocean)], *or (B) prior to the taking of necessary implementing actions relating to all such requirements, such conditions as the Administrator determines are necessary* to carry out the provisions of [the Clean Water Act]. [33 U.S.C. §1342(a)(1), emphasis added]

Section 402(k) in turn specifies that compliance with such a permit "shall be deemed compliance with" Sections 301, 302, 306, 307, and 403, "except any standard imposed under [Section 307] for a toxic pollutant injurious to human health."

Although ultimate responsibility for the NPDES program always rests with the EPA, Section 402(b) specifies that EPA must delegate NPDES permitting authority to any state that—by meeting a number of specified conditions—demonstrates that it is capable of implementing and enforcing the various requirements of the Clean Water Act. In practice, almost all states have asked for, and received, such authority. Thus within most states the NPDES program is administered by the state, with EPA oversight. This means that the NPDES permits are issued by the state, subject to the right of EPA to object to a permit if it does not meet federal requirements, and subject to the right of EPA to take over the issuance of a permit under certain circumstances. It also means that the state assumes the primary responsibility for enforcing those permits, although EPA retains enforcement authority as well. If the state does not administer the program in accordance with the requirements of the act, Section 402(c) specifies a procedure by which EPA must withdraw its authorization of the state program if the deficiencies are not rectified. EPA has from time to time withdrawn authorization for state programs under this section.

As specified in Section 402(a)(1), the NPDES permit is to contain discharge and monitoring requirements sufficient to satisfy "all applicable requirements" imposed by a number of specified sections of the act. In general, this will mean compliance with applicable EPA regulations, and/or with any applicable state regulations that are more stringent. Where there are no regulations implementing a specified provision of the act, Section 402(a)(1)(B) directs EPA (or the state) to impose "such conditions as [EPA or the state] determines are necessary to carry out the provisions of [the act]." In these circumstances, the permit writer (an agency employee, often an engineer) commonly is said to be exercising his or her "best professional judgment"

(BPJ) in specifying a discharge limitation (or monitoring requirement) for the discharger in question. In the popular parlance, then, permit requirements designed by the permit writer in the absence of specific regulatory guidance have become known as *BPJ* standards. BPJ standards were especially important in the early years of the Clean Water Act, when permits were being issued before EPA had promulgated even the most basic discharge limitations required by the act.

To obtain a permit, a discharger must submit a permit application containing information about the kinds and amount of pollutants discharged and (if the discharger is an industrial facility) the types of industrial processes employed. Based on this information, the permit writer is then to determine which regulations and other requirements imposed by the act are applicable, and to design a permit that applies those requirements to the particular circumstances of this discharger. As EPA has acquired a more sophisticated understanding of the kinds of information needed to design an effective permit, the requirements for the permit application have become more numerous and detailed. At a minimum, the permit application generally must contain baseline effluent monitoring data on a host of specified pollutants, the results of specified toxicity testing of the discharger's effluent, the results of any studies done to determine the quality of the receiving waters, and (where applicable) production data regarding the facility's industrial output.

Because Section 402(b)(1)(B) specifies that permits are to be "for fixed terms not exceeding five years," most NPDES permits are issued for 5-year terms, with the formal expectation that a revised (reissued) permit (incorporating newly promulgated regulations and newly acquired data) will be issued 5 years later. To obtain a revised permit, the permitee must submit a new, updated permit application, which typically will require more information than the previous application. In practice, the permit revision process often extends well beyond the expiration date of the previous permit. Typically, the "old" permit remains in force until the revised permit is issued.

In an attempt to ensure that the issuance or revision of an NPDES permit is more than simply a negotiation between the permit writer and the discharger, the Clean Water Act requires that the process be a public one. Section 402(b)(3) requires that the public "receive notice of each application for a permit," and that there be "an opportunity for a public hearing before a ruling on each such application." Further, Section 402(j) requires that all NPDES permits and permit applications be available for public inspection and copying. By EPA regulation, the permitting agency (EPA or the state) issues a draft permit for public comment, together with a fact sheet describing the nature of the permitee and its discharge and explaining the basis for the provisions in the draft permit. After a public comment period of at least 30 days, the agency then issues the final permit, together with written responses to any written comments received from the public. Although it is not uncommon to find that the permitee is the only member of the "public" to have provided comment, meaningful public participation in the permitting process is far from an exceptional occurrence and has in many cases had an impact on the content of the final permit. Any person (including the permitee) who provides comments during the public comment period has a right to file an administrative appeal of the final permit if those comments are not adopted by the agency.

To demonstrate compliance (or noncompliance, as the case may be) with their NPDES permits, dischargers are required to submit "discharge monitoring reports" (DMRs), on a monthly basis, to the permitting authority (EPA and/or the state). The DMRs are preprinted forms that list the various numeric limitations imposed by the permit, and include spaces for the discharger to record the actual discharge(s) for the given month. The NPDES reporting system relies in large part on the assumption that the discharger will provide honest monitoring information. In an attempt to ensure that the information provided is indeed accurate, EPA requires that a responsible company official sign the DMRs, under penalty of perjury.

▪ NOTES

1. Section 402(l) prohibits EPA from requiring—and from requiring "directly or indirectly" any *state* to require—an NPDES permit for "discharges composed entirely of return flows from irrigated agriculture," or for certain uncontaminated "discharges of stormwater runoff from mining operations or oil and gas exploration, processing, or treatment operations or transmission facilities."

2. Often a new EPA or state standard will be promulgated and go into effect before an affected source's NPDES permit is revised. To address this eventuality, most permits are now written with reopener clauses, which allow specific revision of the permit, before it would otherwise be revised, to include applicable new standards. Since these provisions generally are not self-effectuating, however, their use tends to vary with the will and the resources of the permitting agency.

3. NPDES permits can be lengthy and detailed documents. In addition to specific discharge limits and monitoring requirements, permits usually contain several pages of narrative requirements (covering topics such as sampling and analytical procedures, reporting and record-keeping requirements, and best management practices) and "general conditions" (covering topics such as signatory requirements, permit modification, and permit transfer).

4. Section 402(o), added in 1987, specifies that (with some exceptions) no modified permit may be less stringent than previous BPJ requirements in that permit, and that no modified permit may be less stringent than previous requirements in that permit based on 301(b)(1)(C) or 303(d) (water quality-based effluent limitations), except as provided in 303(d)(4). This is known as the act's "antibacksliding" provision.

5. In the language of NPDES permits, the various regulated aspects of a discharge (e.g., the amount of copper discharged in the wastewater, the pH of the wastewater discharge, the flow of the discharge) are called the regulated "parameters." ■

5.   Regulation of Stormwater Discharges

Prior to the 1987 amendments to the act, some NPDES permits contained limits on storm drain discharges, while many others did not. Section 402(p) was added in 1987 to specifically address storm drain discharges. This provision gave EPA 2 years to "establish regulations setting forth permit application requirements" for stormwater discharges "associated with industrial activity," and for municipal storm sewer systems serving 250,000 or more persons, and two additional years to establish such regulations for municipal storm sewer systems serving from 100,000 to 250,000 persons. See 33 U.S.C. §§1342(p)(2), (3) and (4).

EPA's approach has been to require that at a minimum, facilities subject to the stormwater requirements of Section 402(p) obtain coverage under a regulation that is known as a "general" (nonindividualized) NPDES permit, and to follow the requirements of that regulation. See 40 CFR §122.26 (for states where the stormwater program is administered by EPA) and §123.25 (for state stormwater programs). Broadly speaking, the general permits require that stormwater discharges be identified and that they be subjected to baseline monitoring for certain parameters in circumstances where those parameters are deemed to be relevant. In addition, the discharger must devise and implement a "best management practices" (BMP) program to minimize the extent to which pollutants get into stormwater discharges. (This might involve, e.g., procedures to prevent or contain spills of toxic chemicals.) In practice, there is considerable variation in the comprehensiveness and stringency of the stormwater general permits among the states.

Many permit writers continue to add coverage of stormwater discharges to individual NPDES permits when the permits are revised. The discharge and monitoring requirements placed on storm drain discharges in individual permits tend to be more specific and stringent than those in the general permit. To the extent that stormwater discharge causes a violation of an ambient water quality standard, additional restrictions of this nature are required by Section 301(b)(1)(C).

6.   Limitations on Discharges to Public Sewage Treatment Plants

To the extent that they discharge into a public sewer system instead of directly into the surface waters, industrial sources are known as "indirect" dischargers. Under Section 307 of the act, new and existing indirect dischargers must meet "pretreatment" standards (so termed because they often require treatment of the wastewater before it is discharged into the sewer system, where presumably it is subjected to further treatment by the POTW itself). See, generally, 33 U.S.C. §§1317(b), (c) and (d). There are three classes of pretreatment standards that may be applicable to an indirect discharger. Colloquially, these are known as general pretreatment standards, categorical pretreatment standards, and local limits.

The *general* pretreatment standards are narrative (rather than numeric) standards, promulgated by EPA, that are applicable to all indirect dischargers. See 40 CFR §403.5. These standards prohibit the discharge of pollutants that (alone or in combination with pollutants from other sources) either (1) "interfere" with treatment or sludge disposal at the POTW and cause a violation of the POTW's NPDES permit or of sludge disposal requirements, or (2) "pass through" the POTW and cause a violation of the POTW's NPDES permit. See 40 CFR §403.3(i) and (n) for the definition of interference and pass through.

The *categorical* pretreatment standards are numeric standards for specific pollutants that are set by EPA on an industry category-by-industry category basis. The general criteria for these standards are set forth in 40 CFR §403.6, but the specific standards for any given industrial category are found in the same regulation as the direct discharger limitations for that category. The categorical standards are applicable to all sources within the given category, although individual indirect dischargers may seek a fundamentally different factors variance from these limits. See Section 301(n) and 40 CFR §403.13. EPA regulations specifically prohibit the use of dilution in lieu of treatment as a means of meeting the categorical standards. See 40 CFR §403.6(d).

Local limits are pretreatment standards set by the POTW itself. Under EPA regulation (40 CFR §403.8), most POTWs with a total design flow of more than 5 million gallons per day, and some smaller POTWs, must have an approved pretreatment program if they receive significant discharges from industrial sources. The pretreatment program is the POTW's regulatory program for indirect dischargers, and it is to include numeric "local limits" that at a minimum are sufficient to prevent interference, pass through, and other conditions specifically enumerated by EPA. See 40 CFR §§403.8(f)(4) and 403.5(c)(1). If they are part of an approved pretreatment program, local limits are enforceable by EPA and citizens as Section 307 pretreatment standards. See 40 CFR §403.5(d).

In a state that has received EPA approval to administer the pretreatment program, the state is the approval authority for such programs. Otherwise, they must be approved by EPA. Upon approval of its pretreatment program, the operator of the POTW—usually a municipal or county government—assumes primary responsibility for enforcing the pretreatment standards. Often the general, categorical, and local limits are applied to individual indirect dischargers in an *indirect discharge permit*, which is similar in concept to a NPDES permit. Typically, the indirect discharger is required to monitor its discharge to the sewer system on a quarterly basis and to report the results. (See 40 CFR §403.12 for a delineation of minimum monitoring requirements.)

■ **NOTES**

1. Under section 307(b)(1), POTWs are authorized in certain circumstances to grant "removal credits" to industrial sources that would otherwise perform duplicative treatment of a particular pollutant. The effect of such a credit, if granted, is to allow the industrial source to ignore the usual pretreatment requirements to the extent that the POTW treats that pollutant. See 40 CFR §403.7.

2. POTWs with design capacities greater than 5 million gallons per day are required to have an approved pretreatment program if they "receiv[e] from Industrial Users pollutants which Pass Through or Interfere with the operation of the POTW or are otherwise subject to Pretreatment Standards" [40 CFR §403.8(a)]. Smaller POTWs can be required to have a pretreatment program if "the nature or volume of the industrial influent, treatment process upsets, violations of POTW effluent limitations, contamination of municipal sludge, or other circumstances warrant in order to prevent Interference with the POTW or Pass Through" (id.).

3. Where a POTW does not yet have an approved pretreatment program, EPA or the state is responsible for administering pretreatment requirements at the POTW. Moreover, under 40 CFR §403.10(e), a state that has been authorized by EPA to administer the pretreatment program may opt to administer the Section 307 pretreatment program at a particular POTW within its jurisdiction in lieu of the POTW. In EPA parlance, the governmental body administering the pretreatment program at a particular POTW is known as the "control authority" for that POTW.

4. One potential ramification of industrial discharges to sewer systems can be the creation of toxic gases. Although EPA regulations prohibit the discharge of "pollutants which result in the presence of toxic gases, vapor, or fumes within the POTW in a quantity that may cause acute worker health and safety problems" [40 CFR §403.5(b)(7)], they do not specifically address exposures that may cause chronic worker health problems. Nor do they address exposures of surrounding neighborhoods (through leaking pipes, surface covers, or the like).

5. Industrial dischargers are not the only potential source of toxicants in POTW effluents. A study by the United States Geological Survey (USGS) of waters downstream of sewage treatment plants found "traces of dozens of drugs, disinfectants, hormones, chemicals excreted by smokers[,] and other contaminants" apparently excreted by humans [Andrew C. Revkin (2002) "Stream Tests Show Traces of Array of Contaminants," *New York Times*, March 13]. ■

7. Regulation of Toxic Chemicals in Sewage Sludge

As part of the 1987 amendments to the act, Congress directed EPA to identify "toxic pollutants which, on the basis of available information on their toxicity, persistence, concentration, mobility, or potential for exposure, may be present in sewage sludge in concentrations which may adversely affect public health or the environment" [Section 405(d)(2)]. EPA was then to set "numerical limitations" specifying safe concentrations of each such toxic substance for a variety of uses, including disposal in landfills, unless it was not "feasible to prescribe or enforce" such limitations, in which case the agency was permitted to substitute "a design, equipment, management practices, or operational standard" [Section 405(d)(2) and (3)]. Under this authority, EPA declined to set numeric standards for toxic substances in sludge deposited in municipal solid waste landfills. Instead, it promulgated regulations establishing general federal criteria for the location, design, and operation of such landfills. See 40 CFR §503. These provisions were upheld by the D.C. Circuit Court of Appeals in a challenge brought by environmental groups. See *Sierra Club v. EPA*, 992 F.2d 337 (D.C. Cir. 1993). However, the sludge regulations do set numeric criteria limiting the presence of ten metals (arsenic, cadmium, chromium, copper, lead, mercury, molybdenum, nickel, selenium, and zinc) in sewage sludge that is applied to agricultural, forest, or other lands, and the regulations also impose numeric criteria for sludge that is incinerated. See 40 CFR §§503.13 and 503.43. Moreover, sewage sludge that meets the definition of hazardous waste under the Resource Conservation and Recovery Act (see chapter 9) must be handled in accordance with the requirements of that law.

B. THE CLEAN WATER ACT: PROTECTION OF SURFACE WATERS AND WETLANDS FROM NONPOINT SOURCE POLLUTION

Under the Clean Water Act, the term "nonpoint source" pollution refers to any pollution of the waters of the United States that does not meet the act's definition of "point source" pollution. In practice, this includes pollution from a diverse array of locations and activities. According to a 1999 report issued by the United States General Accounting Office (now the Government Accountability Office), the three largest contributors to nonpoint source pollution are agricultural runoff (much of which could be regulated as a point source discharge if the act did not specifically exempt it), which can contain pesticide chemicals and fertilizers; runoff from silviculture (tree cutting and cultivation), which often contains high concentrations of sediments; and uncollected urban runoff (such as "sheet" runoff from roads and parking lots), which can contain petroleum-based compounds, metals, and a variety of other pollutants.

The continuing nonpoint source threat to aquatic life and human health was high-lighted in a U.S. Geological Survey analysis of data from 1991 to 2000 for sixteen major river basins and aquifers. In rural waterways, the major contaminants attributable to nonpoint sources are nutrients (from fertilizers) and herbicides. A nationwide study conducted by EPA between 2000 and 2004 concluded that 47% of stream miles are in poor condition, and 25% in fair condition, as the result of nonpoint source runoff. This study, which examined 1,392 streams randomly selected to represent a variety of ecological conditions in the 48 contiguous states, found that nearly a third of the streams had high concentrations of phosphorus and nearly a third had high concentrations of nitrogen. See Amena H. Sailyd (2006) "Nitrogen, Phosphorus, Sediment Runoff Said to Pollute Nearly Half of U.S. Streams," *Environment Reported* 37(19): 357.

Pesticides and nutrients were also found to be a problem in urban waterways. Indeed, the levels of insecticides in urban waterways (presumably stemming both from mosquito abatement efforts and from individual lawn applications) were found to be higher than the levels of herbicides in rural areas. Moreover, the levels of polycyclic aromatic hydrocarbons and zinc (thought to be from motor vehicle tires) were found to be on the rise in urban waterways. See Susan Bruninga (2001) "Pesticide Levels Higher in Urban Waters than Agricultural Waters, USGS Report Says," *Environment Reporter* 26: 1283. See also Richard Wiles, Brian Cohen, Chris Campbell, and Susan Elderkin (1994) *Tap Water Blues: Herbicides in Drinking Water*, Physicians for Social Responsibility and Environmental Working Group. This report describes levels of herbicides in surface waters in rural and urban communities and assesses the cancer risks they pose.

There is no shortage of evidence that nonpoint sources are an important contributor to water pollution. Nor is there serious disagreement that given adequate effort and investment, pollution from nonpoint source could be significantly reduced. Some types of nonpoint pollution are easier to address than others, of course, and some are not amenable to an easy fix. In many cases, however, the use of measures such as erosion control, best management practices (to reduce the extent to which pollutants are allowed to contaminate runoff), and collection and treatment systems would cut nonpoint pollution dramatically. Thus far, however, there is no effective nationwide program to bring about the widespread implementation of these measures.

This is not to say that the Clean Water Act does not address the issue. The 1972 amendments included a lengthy provision, codified as Section 208 of the act, which envisions regional (water basin-wide) planning and control for nonpoint sources. See 33 U.S.C. §1288. Under Section 208, states were to develop "areawide waste treatment management plans," in which they were to identify and assess those areas facing "substantial water quality control problems" because of "urban-industrial

Section 208 for non-Point

concentrations or other factors," and to recommend measures for addressing non-point sources contributing to those problems. These plans were then to be reviewed by EPA (and to be revised if they did not meet EPA approval). EPA was then to develop, in coordination with the states, a priority list of measures to be taken. Finally, federal funding was to be made available to the states to carry out measures selected from this list. In theory, then, EPA would assist the states in ameliorating their most important water quality problems from nonpoint sources. In practice, however, the state plans were late in coming, the federal funding was much less than had been anticipated, and the number of projects actually funded and completed under Section 208 were far fewer than had been contemplated. See, e.g., Kathy Barton (1978) "The Other Water Pollution," *Environment* June, p. 12.

By the early 1980s there was general agreement that the Section 208 program had largely been a failure. Thus, as Congress prepared to reauthorize the act, considerable attention was focused on strengthening the controls on nonpoint sources. The result was Section 319, which was added as part of the 1987 amendments. See 33 U.S.C. §1329. Under this provision, the states were to prepare a report to EPA identifying those waterways within their borders that cannot reasonably be expected to attain or maintain water quality criteria or other goals or requirements of the act without further controls on nonpoint sources. The states were also to submit a "management program for controlling pollution added from nonpoint sources to the navigable waters." Among other things, the program was to include "[a]n identification of the best management practices and measures which will be undertaken to reduce pollutant loadings from each category, subcategory, or particular nonpoint source" identified in the management program [Section 319(b)(1) and (2)]. If a state did not submit a program meeting EPA's approval, the agency was directed to propose its own program for that state. Federal funding was then to be made available to finance the implementation of approved programs.

Section 319 is more clearly focused on nonpoint sources than is Section 208. Also, with its emphasis on problem-specific management plans, it is more action oriented. In overall concept, however, it is in many ways a rehash of the earlier provision. Not surprisingly, it has suffered much the same fate. Some state nonpoint source management projects have been funded with Section 319 monies, and EPA has an active nonpoint source division that endeavors to provide assistance and expertise to the states. Moreover, as discussed below, Section 319 contains certain limitations on grant funding that give EPA greater authority to encourage the states to require nonpoint source controls. Nonetheless, the states have encountered both political and financial barriers to taking widespread, effective measures to control nonpoint sources of water pollution.

Conspicuous in its absence from the Clean Water Act's nonpoint source provisions is anything giving EPA the authority to directly regulate nonpoint sources. As noted by the Ninth Circuit Court of Appeals, the act "provides no direct mechanism to control nonpoint source pollution but rather uses the 'threat and promise' of federal grants to accomplish this task" [*Oregon Natural Desert Assoc. v. Dombeck*, 172 F. 3d 1092, 1096 (9th Cir. 1998), citations omitted]. If the agency had the authority to require the adoption of nonpoint source control measures, it could fashion a meaningful implementation program. While any such program would still have to rely on federal and state cooperation and a healthy dose of federal funding, the regulatory "hammer" of mandatory compliance would be available to move recalcitrant actors forward. Without direct regulatory authority, EPA has been left to try to fashion indirect incentives for the owners of nonpoint sources to reduce the runoff of pollution from those sources.

One such effort is EPA's watershed-based pollutant trading program. See U.S. EPA (1996) *Draft Framework for Watershed-Based Pollutant Trading*, EPA 800-R-96 001, Washington, D.C.: U.S. EPA. Under this program, a point source discharging pollutants into a waterway may be able to avoid having to invest in further pollution reduction of its own if it finances a reduction in nonpoint source pollution to that waterway. As with the offset program under the Clean Air Act, the overall pollution reduction attained must be greater than that which would otherwise be required of the point source.

EPA has also used its authority under the Section 303(d) TMDL program to "leverage" states into requiring reductions in nonpoint source pollution. This approach has survived its first major test in the courts. In *Pronsolino v. EPA*, 291 F.3d 1123 (9th Cir. 2002), the Ninth Circuit Court of Appeals upheld EPA's designation of the Garcia River in California as impaired—and thus in need of a TMDL—owing to pollution from nonpoint sources alone. The establishment of this TMDL in turn led the state of California to impose limitations on the harvesting of trees in the Garcia River watershed, because nonpoint source runoff from silviculture contributed to the river's inability to meet water quality standards. Although the act did not (and, under the Tenth Amendment, could not) compel the state to impose these limitations—as noted by the court, "California chose both *if* and *how* it would implement the Garcia River TMDL,"—EPA encouraged their imposition by conditioning grant funding (presumably under Section 319) on the adequacy of the state's TMDL compliance (id. at 1140). EPA has general authority under Section 319(h)(1) to attach to Section 319 grants "such terms and conditions as [the agency] considers appropriate." Moreover, Section 319(h)(8) forbids EPA from making grants for 2 years in succession to any state unless the agency determines that the state has "made satisfactory progress" in implementing its Section 319 management program. Although the effectiveness of these provisions depends both on the willingness of EPA to use them and the desire of the state to obtain funding for nonpoint source control, they do hold the promise, as with the Garcia River, of real progress with nonpoint source pollution.

■ **NOTES**

1. What likely are some of the chief reasons that Congress has been unwilling to give EPA wider authority over nonpoint sources? Would regulation of farmers and the forestry industry be less popular than regulating the various entities subject to the NPDES program? What about the regulation of pesticide and fertilizer applications on golf courses, cemeteries, or individual residences? Would the cost to municipalities of implementing nonpoint source controls be deemed unacceptable? Would federal regulation of nonpoint sources smack too much of federal control over land use practices? Could Congress choose to subject certain categories of nonpoint sources to regulation while leaving others to state control?

2. Short of direct federal regulation of nonpoint sources, should Congress consider conditioning a state's right to administer the NPDES program on the state's willingness to control nonpoint source pollution?

3. Note that because the federal technology-based effluent limitations are to be uniformly attained within each industrial category, EPA has discretion to allow pollutant trading with nonpoint sources only as a means of attaining the applicable water quality criteria. Would it be good policy, in your opinion, to amend the act to allow such pollutant trading on a wider basis?

4. As discussed earlier, runoff of animal wastes from ranches and farmlots *is* treated as a point source discharge if it is from a concentrated animal feeding operation (CAFO).   ■

C. THE CLEAN WATER ACT: PROTECTION OF SURFACE WATERS AND WETLANDS FROM THE DISCHARGE OF DREDGED AND FILL MATERIAL

In addition to the NPDES permit program of Section 402, the Clean Water Act has a separate permit program for the discharge of "dredged" or "fill" material. This program, created by Section 404, is overseen jointly by the EPA and the United States Army Corps of Engineers (the Corps), with the Corps taking the lead in matters of implementation and enforcement. The choice of the Corps of Engineers for this function reflects the fact that it had historically been concerned (under the Rivers and Harbors Act and other statutes) with protecting the navigability of the nation's waters. Since waterways are sometimes dredged to improve navigability, and since the discharge of dredged or fill materials into waterways can affect navigability, the involvement of the Corps most likely seemed only natural to Congress. At the same time, because the focus of the Clean Water Act is the preservation and restoration of the environmental quality of the nation's waters, EPA was given a prominent role as well. Accordingly, to understand the mechanics of the Section 404 permit program, one must look both to regulations promulgated by the Corps and to those promulgated by EPA.

Although the Clean Water Act contains no definition of "dredged" or "fill" materials, EPA and the Corps have defined these terms in regulations. Dredged material is "material that is excavated or dredged from the waters of the United States" [33 C.F.R. §323.2(c) (Corps of Engineers) and 40 C.F.R. §232.2 (EPA)]. Fill material is defined by the Corps as "any material used for the primary purpose of replacing an aquatic area with dry land or changing the bottom elevation of [a] waterbody" [33 C.F.R. §323.2(e)], and is defined by EPA as any pollutant that has either of these effects (40 C.F.R. §232.2). In colloquial terms, then, dredged material consists of soil, rocks, vegetation, and the like *taken from the waters of the United States*, while fill material is anything added to the waters of the United States to *"fill them in"* (i.e., to make them more shallow or to create dry land in their place).

Since the definition of "pollutant" in Section 502 of the Clean Water Act includes, among other enumerated items, "dredged spoil," "rock," "sand," and "cellar dirt," it seems likely that most, and perhaps all, dredged and fill materials are also "pollutants" under the statute. See 33 U.S.C. §1362(6). There thus is a conceptual opportunity for overlap between the Section 402 permit program for the discharge of pollutants and the Section 404 permit program for dredged or fill materials. As a practical matter, however, the discharge of dredged material is usually governed by Section 404. Further, consistent with the Corps of Engineers definition, the discharge of fill materials "for the primary purpose" of filling in the waters of the United States is governed by Section 404. But when fill materials are discharged as a means of disposing waste to the waters of the United States, their discharge will be governed by Section 402. As explained in the Corps' permitting regulations, "[t]he term [fill material] does not include any pollutant discharged into the water primarily to dispose waste, as that activity is regulated under Section 402 of the Clean Water Act" [33 C.F.R. §323.2(e)].

Nonetheless, to the extent that dredged materials and fill materials are pollutants under the Clean Water Act, their discharge to waters of the United States is covered by the Section 301(a) prohibition against nonconforming discharges. Section 301(a) provides, in pertinent part, that, "[e]xcept as in compliance with...section...1344 [404] of this title, the discharge of any pollutant by any person shall be unlawful" [33 U.S.C. §1311(a)]. Thus, unless it is exempted from the permit process under the terms of Section 404, any discharge of dredged or fill material from a point source to the waters of the United States will be in violation of Section 301(a) unless it is covered by, and in compliance with, a Section 404 permit.

1.   The Section 404 Permit Program

Unlike the Section 402 permit program, which is "fed" by standards set under other provisions of the act, the Section 404 program is largely self-contained. Its operative standards and conditions are set by Section 404 itself, and by regulations adopted thereunder. The major substantive standards for a Section 404 permit are set by EPA, after consultation with the Corps of Engineers, under Section 404(b)(1). The current regulations, promulgated in 1980, specify four basic conditions that must be met before a Section 404 permit will be issued.

First, a permit is not to be granted if there is a "practicable alternative" to the proposed discharge that "would have less adverse impact on the aquatic ecosystem," provided that the alternative would not cause "other significant adverse environmental consequences" [40 C.F.R. §230.10(a)]. For the purposes of this requirement, an alternative is to be deemed "practicable" if "it is available and capable of being done after taking into consideration costs, existing technology, and logistics in light of overall project purposes" [40 C.F.R. §230.10(a)(2)].

Second, the proposed discharge of dredged or fill material must not cause or contribute to a violation of a water quality standard, violate a Section 307 toxic pollutant standard, jeopardize the continued existence of an endangered or threatened species, cause the destruction or adverse modification of critical habitat within the meaning of the Endangered Species Act, or violate any requirement under Title III of the Marine Protection, Research, and Sanctuaries Act. See 40 C.F.R. §230.10(b).

Third, the proposed discharge must not "cause or contribute to significant degradation of the waters of the United States" [40 C.F.R. §230.10(c)]. The regulations specify certain tests and factual determinations that must be made as part of the analysis of whether "significant" degradation would occur, and make it clear that the effects on the health of humans, aquatic life, and other wildlife, as well as the effects on recreational, aesthetic, and economic values, are to be considered (id.).

Fourth, no Section 404 permit is to be granted "unless appropriate and practicable steps have been taken which will minimize potential adverse impacts of the discharge on aquatic ecosystems" [40 C.F.R. §230.10(d)]. The regulations specify a number of potential mitigation measures to be considered as appropriate to the particular project. Among others, these include changes in the location of the discharge or the material to be discharged, measures to control the material after it is discharged, and habitat development and restoration. See 40 C.F.R. §230.70–230.77.

In an effort to streamline the permitting process in certain circumstances, Congress provided in Section 404(e)(1) that general permits may be issued under these guidelines "on a State, regional, or nationwide basis for [a] category of activities." The Corps has issued such permits, which principally apply to smaller projects, and the activity under these general permits represents a substantial portion of Section 404 permitting.

As with the NPDES program, Congress has made the policy choice in Section 404 to exempt certain activities known to be a substantial source of adverse environmental effects. Section 404(f) specifies that discharges of dredged or fill material associated with "normal farming, silviculture, and ranching activities" are not required to have Section 404 permits. This section also exempts certain other farm-related activities, certain construction activities, and certain temporary and emergency projects.

Although the Section 404 program was solely federal when it was first placed into the act in 1972, the 1977 amendments added provisions allowing the states to take over the permitting function for certain waters. These provisions, Sections 404(g)–(l), track the state NPDES provisions of Section 402 in allowing a state to apply for permitting authority, and in conditioning such authority on compliance with federal regulations specifying the minimum requirements for the maintenance of a state program. These regulations, promulgated by EPA, are found at 40 C.F.R. §233. As with the NPDES programs, the states are free to impose additional permitting conditions beyond those required by the EPA regulations.

States always allowed to make it more strict

■ **NOTES**

1. Under Section 404(c) EPA has the authority to withdraw an area from consideration for a Section 404 permit if the issuance of such permit would have "unacceptable adverse effects" on municipal water supplies, fish or shellfish, wildlife, or recreation. Thus far, EPA has used this authority sparingly.

2. Conversely, Section 404(b)(2) specifies that the Corps may grant a permit where an application of the Section 404(b)(1) guidelines would otherwise prohibit it, if such action is warranted by "the economic impact of the site on navigation and anchorage."

3. Section 404(m) provides a procedure by which the U.S. Fish and Wildlife Service may comment on proposed individual and general permits.   ■

2.   The Application of the Section 404 Program to Wetlands

As defined by EPA in the context of the Section 404 program, wetlands are

those areas that are inundated or saturated by surface or ground water at a frequency and duration sufficient to support, and that under normal circumstances do support, a prevalence of vegetation typically adapted for life in saturated soil conditions. Wetlands generally include swamps, marshes, bogs and similar areas. [40 C.F.R. §230.3(t)]

Wetlands play a number of important roles in the environment. They help preserve the quality of adjacent waters by removing nutrients such as nitrogen and phosphorus, and by filtering chemical pollutants such as pesticides and heavy metals. They also serve as breeding and feeding grounds for fish and birds. Moreover, wetlands assist in flood control (by absorbing peak flows and releasing the water slowly), and serve as buffer against heavy storms in coastal areas.

Valuable though they may be, however, that value commonly is not reflected in the price of the wetland on the real estate market. (This is a classic case of a positive externality. Because the true value of the wetland is enjoyed by society at large, and is not sufficiently captured by the owner of the wetland, the market does not accurately calculate the wetland's value.) Indeed, to many persons a wetland is something of a nuisance—an undesirable place to recreate, much less to live. The owners of wetland property, then, often have a market-driven incentive to transform that property into something more valuable, which usually means dry land on which development can occur. [As a U.S. Fish and Wildlife Service employee in Florida reportedly told a *New York Times* reporter, "The feeling around here is: we've got plenty of wetlands, but we don't have very many Wal-Marts." John H. Cushman, Jr. (1996) "From Wetlands to Asphalt, a Parcel at a Time," *New York Times*, October 27, p. 1.] If one accepts that wetlands should be preserved, governmental intervention to "correct" the market will be necessary.

For more than three decades, in the absence of a federal regulatory program more specifically focused on wetlands preservation, Section 404 of the Clean Water Act has been the primary federal law regulating the development of wetlands. Since EPA and the Corps have treated most wetlands as "waters of the United States" under the act, and since one method of converting a wetland into more commercially valuable property is to "dig it out and fill it in," many wetlands development projects involve a discharge of dredged or fill material for which a permit must be obtained under the applicable regulations. Although this applies to only a fraction of the projects that destroy wetlands, there is evidence that the Section 404 program, along with state and local laws (and a somewhat heightened awareness in society of the importance of wetlands), has had a positive impact on wetlands preservation. According to a report issued by the U.S. Fish and Wildlife Service, the nation lost 1.2 million acres of wetlands (and about 1% of the remaining wetlands in the lower 48 states) in the decade from 1985 to 1995. While this is undeniably a substantial loss, it compares favorably with the loss of almost 3 million acres recorded in the previous decade. See John H. Cushman, Jr. (1997) "Million Wetland Acres Lost in 1985–1995," *New York Times*, September 18, p. 1. Further, a more recent report issued by the Fish and Wildlife Service indicates that the rate of wetlands loss continued to decline into the next decade. See U.S. Department of the Interior, U.S. Fish and Wildlife Service (2001) *Report to Congress on the Status and Trends of Wetlands in the Coterminous United States 1986 to 1997.*

This is not to say that the Section 404 program is uniformly praised by wetlands advocates. As many have pointed out, the record of the Section 404 program is largely one of approving permits rather than denying them. Special criticism has been reserved for the Corps of Engineers' nationwide permit program. The problem with this "general" permitting program, environmentalists argue, is that it loses sight of the proverbial forest for the trees. That is, while each of the smaller projects approved under the nationwide permit may have a relatively small impact, the aggregate impact, even within a local geographic area, can be significant. One example of this phenomenon was reported as follows:

When a health clinic sought Federal approval to build on one of the wetlands nestled among the malls, homes and hotels of [Panama City, Florida], the Army Corps of Engineers had no objection. At a loss of less than six acres of swamp, the project was deemed to do little environmental harm to the local watershed, which drains into a sensitive estuary of Gulf Coast bays and bayous.

But when the Corps notified another Federal agency, the United States Fish and Wildlife Service, that it would issue a routine quick [national] permit, the wildlife agency sought a more rigorous examination, complaining that the project was one of several that, while individually innocuous, were together destroying 70 acres of wetlands within a two-mile radius of the site.

As often happens, the Corps disregarded the wildlife agency's objections, and today the swamp has been filled. . . . [John H. Cushman, Jr., "From Wetlands to Asphalt, a Parcel at a Time"]

But if the Section 404 wetlands program is criticized by environmentalists, it is roundly condemned by many in the development community, and they have increasingly turned to the courts to challenge aspects of the program. And, as reportedly stated by Lance Wood, assistant chief counsel for environmental law and regulatory programs at the Corps, "many judges view Section 404 as an 'evil, communistic' provision that infringes on the rights of property owners" ["Federal Jurisdiction Attacked by Courts, Rules Needed to Clarify Issues, Official Says," 17 *Toxics Law Reporter* 541 (June 6, 2002)]. The Supreme Court's *Rapanos* decision, discussed earlier in this chapter, can be expected to provide fodder for wetlands litigation into the foreseeable future. It appears clear from that decision that at least under the current wording of the Clean Water Act, the Section 404 program does not extend to "isolated" wetlands. Future litigation likely will determine, on a case-by-case basis, which categories of wetlands will be treated as having a sufficient nexus to navigable waters to be subject to the Clean Water Act.

■ NOTES

1. President George H. W. Bush declared a national "no net loss" goal for wetlands (implying that any loss of wetlands would have to be compensated by the creation of

a new wetland), and the Clinton administration continued this policy. Obviously, the goal has not been achieved.

2. After the Supreme Court's 2001 decision in the *SWANCC* case (discussed in *Rapanos*), the George W. Bush administration embarked on a policy of reducing the number of wetlands it deems to be subject to regulation under the Clean Water Act. For example, the regional office of the Army Corps of Engineers in Galveston, Texas, reported that the coastal wetland acreage over which it asserted jurisdiction in 2003 was only 60% of the coastal wetland acreage over which it had asserted jurisdiction in 2000. See Douglas Jehl (2003) "Chief Protector of Wetlands Redefines Them and Retreats," *New York Times*, February 11, p. 1. Following the *Rapanos* decision, EPA and the Corps of Engineers issued a guidance document that would reduce the acreage over which the federal government asserts jurisdiction under the Clean Water Act. See John M. Broder (2007) "After Lobbying, Wetlands Rules Are Narrowed," *New York Times*, July 6, p. A13. The June 5, 2007 guidance document, *Clean Water Act Jurisdiction Following the U.S. Supreme Court's Decision in Rapanos v. United States & Carabell v. United States*, is available on EPA's website.

3. In addition to their current disagreement as to the scope of the Clean Water Act, the justices of the Supreme Court also appear to hold divergent views on wetlands regulation. Justice Stevens' four-justice dissent in *Rampanos* stresses the ecological importance of protecting wetlands, while the four-justice plurality opinion by Justice Scalia characterizes the role of the Corps under section 404 as that of "an enlightened despot."   ■

D. THE PROTECTION OF PUBLIC WATER SYSTEMS: THE SAFE DRINKING WATER ACT

Obviously, one purpose of the Clean Water Act is to protect drinking water. As discussed earlier, if a waterway is used as a source of public drinking water, it generally is afforded the highest classification for the establishment of ambient water quality standards. In many waterways, however, these standards are not being met, and the standards are not always adequate to ensure healthful drinking water. Moreover, not all public drinking water comes from surface waters; wells and underground aquifers also play an important role. In an effort to ensure healthful drinking for all who take their water from public water systems, then, Congress passed the Safe Drinking Water Act in 1974. Rather than focus on the various *sources* of public drinking water, this law focuses on the water systems themselves. In essence, it regulates the quality of the water delivered by the water system to the consumer. To begin our study of this legislation, we turn first to a city that featured prominently in its passage.

1.   The City of New Orleans and the Origins of the Safe Drinking Water Act

As reported in the June 11, 1984 edition of the *New York Times*, the citizens of New Orleans were justifiably proud of their drinking water.

With bombast, poetry and some Olympic-class hoopla, eight bottles of crystalline and not-so-crystalline water—the pride of eight cities—were gurgled, sniffed and slurped by a trio of judges... today in a Great North American Taste-Off.

Amid oooohs, aaaahs, smacking lips and a moue or two, judges from Munich, London, and Dallas rated the water samples for clarity, aroma, flavor, and the wine taster's sixth sense of "feel."

They tried clear mountain water from New York.

They tried Lake Michigan water from Chicago.

They tried kitchen sink water from Toronto.

And they tried water from the municipal systems of Los Angeles, Miami, Dallas and Seattle.

But as the last glassful was swirled and quaffed and New York City officials looked on glumly, the judges awarded the first prize to New Orleans' Mississippi River Water....

[I]n a similar test, sponsored with different samples from the same cities last week by The Dallas Morning News, New Orleans also was the clear winner....

"The winner was a jolly good drink of water," Mr. Fish [the London judge] said. "It doesn't taste of anything but water, and it's refreshing to the palate."

("A Sip of Mississippi River Water Takes Prize," *New York Times*, June 11, 1984, pp. A1, B2)

In that same year, however, the *Wall Street Journal* published an article that offered another picture of the city's Mississippi River water.

New Orleans's main source of water, the Mississippi River, is a dumping place for Tenneco [the operator of a hazardous waste disposal site for oil refinery wastes] and more than 100 other refiners, sewage plants, petrochemical producers and other industrial operators in Louisiana. It isn't known whether the river dumping is related, but a National Cancer Institute study in the mid-1970's showed New Orleans' cancer death rate to be 21% above the U.S. average and the highest among 11 metropolitan areas surveyed. More recently, state water specialists began finding evidence of carcinogens in the river water. [Thomas Petzinger, Jr. and George Getschow (1984) "In Louisiana, Pollution and Cancer are Rife in the Petroleum Area," *Wall Street Journal*, October 23, pp. 1, 24]

Taste buds alone, it seemed, would not be enough to protect the consumer.

Indeed, petrochemicals in the city's drinking water had been an issue since at least 1970. In that year, the director of the citizen-based Ecology Center of Louisiana had mentioned in a radio interview that he would not drink tap water in New Orleans because it came from the Mississippi River. This brought public assurances from the New Orleans Sewer and Water Board that the city's tap water was perfectly safe. The next year, however, EPA tested a sample of New Orleans drinking water and found forty organic chemicals, three of which were known or suspected carcinogens. There years later, in 1974, the magazine *Consumer Reports* ran an article on the safety of the nation's drinking water that highlighted the reported contamination of the water in New Orleans. The city's Sewer and Water Board denounced the article, noting that its author, Dr. Robert Harris of the nonprofit Environmental Defense Fund, had never seen the city's water treatment plant. The Ecology Center of Louisiana then asked the Sewer and Water Board for permission to have Harris tour the plant. During the subsequent (and well-publicized) visit by Harris to New Orleans, a New Orleans city councilman asked whether there was any relationship between cancer in the region and the city's drinking water. Harris then did a quick epidemiologic study that showed excess cancer mortality among those areas drawing their drinking water from the Mississippi River. A few days later, EPA released a second study on New Orleans, identifying additional suspected carcinogens in the drinking water. All of this was featured prominently in a CBS television special on drinking water, and shortly thereafter, in December 1974, Congress passed the Safe Drinking Water Act.

■ **NOTES**

1. For a discussion of New Orleans' role in the passage of the Safe Drinking Water Act (told from the point of view of the Environmental Defense Fund), see *Environment* 26(10) (December 1984). For a more detailed discussion of the act's history (which does not mention the role of New Orleans, but which highlights the role of the Environmental Defense Fund's cancer study), see Thomas J. Douglas (1976) "Safe Drinking Water Act of 1974—History and Critique," *Environmental Affairs* 5: 501.

2. One response to the apparent disparity between taste and quality highlighted by the *New York Times* and *Wall Street Journal* articles, of course, is that the City of New Orleans may have removed all of the troublesome chemicals from the river water before supplying it to city residents. As discussed later, however, it was not until after the 1986 amendments to the Safe Drinking Water Act that public water supplies were compelled to treat their water for many of the more common synthetic organic chemicals.

3. Unfortunately, water has again brought New Orleans into the news, this time via the tragic flooding precipitated by Hurricane Katrina in 2005. Although much of the initial attention from Katrina centered on the widespread displacement and loss of life, increasing attention is being paid to the enormous release of toxic materials that accompanied the breaching of the dikes and the flooding of the city.   ■

2.   The 1974 Act: Establishing the Framework

The Safe Drinking Water Act was enacted on December 16, 1974 as a new subchapter to the Public Health Service Act of 1944. Although the Safe Drinking Water Act

[handwritten: All major acts receive Framework in 70's]

has been significantly amended since that time, the 1974 act established the basic framework that is still in place today. As with the Clean Air Act and Clean Water Act, the U.S. Environmental Protection Agency is responsible for the overall implementation and setting of standards under the act.

■ **NOTE**

1. Although it was added as a series of new sections to the Public Health Service Act, the entire Safe Drinking Water Act was codified within Section 300 of Title 42 of the United States Code. The act can be found at 42 U.S.C. §300f through 42 U.S.C. §300j-26. As one might imagine, this often makes the citations for the individual provisions of the act annoyingly cumbersome. One the bright side, however, is the fact that the section numbers of the act are the same as the section numbers assigned to them with the United States Code. Thus, Section 300g of the act is 42 U.S.C. §300-g.

a. Coverage: Public Water Systems

[handwritten: only regulates Non-Private & larger sources]

In general, the Safe Drinking Water Act applies to any "public water system," which is defined as "a system for the provision to the public of water for human consumption through pipes or other constructed conveyances," so long as the system has at least fifteen service connections or regularly serves at least twenty-five persons [Section 300f(4)]. Smaller systems and most private wells are not covered. Moreover, the standards set under the act do not apply to water systems that do not have collection and treatment facilities, that obtain all of their water from another entity that is subject to these standards, or that do not sell water to any person. See Section 300g. Thus, for example, a large company that supplies water to the employees in its building is not subject to Safe Drinking Water Act standards.

In 1993, EPA estimated that 44% of the population of the United States is served by water systems with more than 100,000 customers (which represent 1% of the total number of public water systems in the country), and that 35% of the population is served by systems with 10,000 to 1,000,000 customers (which represent 5% of the total number of systems). At the other end of the spectrum, an estimated 2% of the population is served by systems with 25 to 500 customers (which represent 62% of the total number of systems). *See* U.S. EPA, Office of Water, Technical and Economic Capacity of States and Public Water Systems to Implement Drinking Water Regulations: Report to Congress, EPA 810-R-93-001, Washington, D.C. (September 1993).

b. Federal Standards: Primary and Secondary Drinking Water Standards

Like the Clean Air Act, the Safe Drinking Water Act employs the concept of *primary* standards for the protection of public health and *secondary* standards for the

Primary — health
Secondary — appearance

protection of public welfare (in this instance, the taste, odor, and appearance of drinking water). See Section 300f(1) and (2). The backbone of the act is the establishment of national primary drinking water standards for "contaminants," which are defined as "any physical, chemical, biological, or radiological substance or matter in water" [Section 300f(6)]. The following explanation from a 1987 opinion of the Court of Appeals for the District of Columbia Circuit (the remainder of which is excerpted later in this chapter) accurately describes the general process for the primary standards under the 1974 act.

[Section 301g-1] requires the Administrator of the EPA to regulate the level of contaminants in drinking water using a three-step process. The first step is the immediate promulgation of "interim primary drinking water regulations." In the second step...the Administrator must establish recommended levels for certain contaminants. To be precise, the Administrator is required to promulgate rules establishing recommended levels "for each contaminant, which in his judgment based on the report [of an independent scientific organization], may have an adverse effect on the health of persons." If the Administrator determines that a recommended level is necessary for a particular contaminant, "such recommended maximum contaminant level shall be set at a level at which, in the Administrator's judgment based on such report, no known or anticipated adverse effects on the health of persons occur and which allows an adequate margin of safety." The recommended levels thus promulgated are non-enforceable health goals. They serve, however, as the benchmark for the third step of the regulatory process—the promulgation of maximum contaminant levels (MCLs), which are federally enforceable standards. Under the Drinking Water Act, a MCL must be set "as close to the [recommended level] as is feasible." Thus, whereas recommended levels are aspirational levels set without regard to practical impediments, MCLs are set at the lowest level feasible, taking into account considerations of cost and available technology and treatment techniques. [*Natural Resources Defense Council v. EPA*, 824 F.2d 1211, 1213–14 (D.C. Cir. 1987)]

As we will see, relevant portions of this framework were changed twice by Congress, first in 1986, and then again in 1996. Nonetheless, the maximum contaminant level (MCL)—representing the maximum allowable concentration of a contaminant in the drinking water that is supplied to customers by a public water system—remains the primary regulatory feature of the act. Moreover, Congress has continued to specify that the MCLs be set with reference to a health-based recommended level. In the 1986 amendments to the act, these recommended levels were renamed "MCL goals." Where EPA finds that "it is not economically or technologically feasible to ascertain the level of [a] contaminant" in water in public water systems, the agency is instructed to specify a treatment technology for that contaminant, rather than set an MCL. See Sections 300f(1)(C) and 300g-1(b)(7)(A).

■ **NOTES**

1. Currently (as of the 1996 amendments) the act defines an MCL goal as "the level at which no known or anticipated adverse effects on the health of persons occur and

which allows an adequate margin of safety" [Section 300g-1(b)(4)(A)]. EPA is to request comments from its Science Advisory Board before proposing an MCL goal, although the board is under no duty to respond [id. §300g-1(e)].

2. "Feasible," when used in the context of setting MCLs, "means feasible with the
use of the best technology, treatment techniques and other means which the Administrator [of EPA] finds, after examination for efficacy under field conditions and not
solely under laboratory conditions, are available (taking cost into consideration)"
[Section 300g-1(b)(4)(E)]. This section further specifies that "granular activated carbon is feasible for the control of synthetic organic chemicals" (id.).

3. Although the MCLs are set at a level deemed technologically and economically
feasible, many water systems have had difficulty affording the cost of meeting, and
monitoring for, the MCLs. To attempt to ameliorate the financial burden associated
with compliance, the 1974 act, and the two subsequent amendments, have made federal funding available—through grants and low-interest loans—to many public
water systems. The financial challenge, however, remains large. In 2002, the General
Accounting Office cited an EPA estimate "that nearly $151 billion will be needed
over the next 20 years to repair, replace, and upgrade the nation's 55,000 community
water systems." About 80% of this total is estimated to be needed for "the basic
infrastructure needed to deliver safe drinking water to the public," while the remaining 20% ($31 billion) is estimated to be needed to comply with proposed and existing
regulations. See General Accounting Office, *Drinking Water Infrastructure: Information on Estimated Needs and Financial Assistance*, GAO-02-592T, Washington, D.C.
(April 11, 2002), at 1, 4.

4. States that are granted primary enforcement authority under the act (see later discussion) are authorized to grant individual variances from a particular MCL to public water systems within their borders that, "because of the characteristics of the raw
water sources which are reasonably available to these systems," are unable to meet
the MCL. Such a variance may be conditioned on the requirement that the public
water system implement the best available treatment techniques as determined by
EPA. Similar variances may be granted for standards requiring specific treatment
technologies. See Section 300g-4(a)(i). In states that have not assumed primary enforcement authority for the act, EPA may grant such variances. Sections 300g-
4(a)(2)–(3). In addition, under provisions added to the law in 1996, states may grant
a variance to water systems serving 3,300 or fewer persons, and may with EPA approval grant variance to water systems serving between 3,300 and 10,000 persons,
where the water systems cannot afford to meet the MCL, and "the terms of the variance ensure adequate protection of human health" [Section 300g-4(e)]. If EPA concludes that a state has "in a substantial number of instances, abused its discretion in

granting variances," the agency is to take action to rescind variances granted by that state [Section 300g-4(a)(1)(G)].

5. The act requires public water systems to comply with monitoring requirements established by EPA to gauge compliance with the MCLs. See Section 300j-4(a). In addition, under the 1996 amendments to the act, every 5 years EPA must designate "not more than thirty" unregulated contaminants for required monitoring [Section 300j-4(a)(2)].   ∎

c. Notification to Consumers

Another prominent feature of the 1974 act is the requirement that public water systems notify their customers (1) when they violate an MCL, (2) when they are operating under a variance for an MCL, and (3) when they fail to perform required monitoring. In the 1996 amendments, Congress added the requirement that public water systems also notify their customers of the concentrations of any unregulated contaminants that they are required to monitor under Section 300j-4(a)(2). See Section 300g-3(c). These provisions, which are effectively a mandatory labeling requirement for public drinking water, serve at least two functions. First, they afford risk-averse consumers who would prefer to switch to an alternative source of drinking water (such as bottled water) an opportunity to do so. Second, they may motivate the more activist members of the water supplier's customer base to lobby (or litigate) for safer water. Moreover, since most large water systems are financed through charges to its customers, such notification may help the system gain acceptance for the increased user charges that may be necessary to attain safer water. In essence, then, the notification provisions are a means to create public pressure for compliance with MCLs.

d. State Implementation

Drawing again from the Clean Air and Clean Water Act models, the act establishes a process by which states may apply to EPA for authority to administer the Safe Drinking Water Act within their borders. Assuming they meet the minimum criteria established by EPA under the statute, such as an agreement to enforce regulations that are no less stringent than the primary drinking water standards established by EPA, states "have primary enforcement responsibility for public water systems" [Section 300g-2]. As with the Clean Air and Clean Water programs, EPA retains statutory oversight authority and may enforce the act where the state does not. See Section 300g-2. Almost all states have sought and been granted authority to administer their own drinking water programs in accordance with these provisions of the act.

e. Regulation of Underground Injection Wells

The Safe Drinking Water Act of 1974 also created a separate program designed to address one of the causes of drinking water contamination: the injection of wastes into deep underground wells, and the attendant potential that these wastes could migrate to aquifers. The impetus for these provisions was explained in an EPA publication of the time:

In hearings prior to enacting the Safe Drinking Water Act, Congress found that numerous public and private agencies had become concerned about the hazards associated with deep well injection of contaminants. A number of States already had been rejecting or discouraging applications for injection systems, and the U.S. Geological Survey and the Bureau of Mines had expressed worry about the indiscriminate "sweeping of our wastes underground."

Both industry and government had been using this method of waste disposal. Cities were engaging in underground injection of sewage sludge, and other wastes. Industries were injecting chemicals and by-products. Even government agencies, including the military, were disposing of wastes in this manner.

Congress therefore provided in the Act for the protection of underground sources of drinking water, including aquifers, by means of a regulatory program similar to that governing public water systems. [U.S. EPA (1975) *An Environmental Law: Highlights of the Safe Drinking Water Act of 1974* (July)]

The program for the protection of underground drinking water sources is found at Sections 300h–300h-8. Under these provisions of the act, EPA was directed to identify certain states for which an underground injection control program is necessary, and establish minimum standards for the establishment and implementation of such a program. The states were then required to submit their own programs for EPA approval, and EPA was directed to establish a federal program in those states for which no state program was approved. After an initial delay, EPA issued underground injection well control regulations. After a second delay, in which EPA was sometimes compelled to operate its own program in certain states, state programs became operative. At a minimum, the programs must prohibit the underground injection of waste not specifically authorized by permit or regulation, and no such permit or regulation is to be issued if underground injection would "endanger" drinking water sources. See Section 300-h(b)(1).

▪ NOTE

1. The Safe Drinking Water Act has a citizen suit provision, Section 300j-8, which affords affected citizens the right to bring suit in federal court to enforce the provisions of the act, including the requirement to meet MCLs. Indeed, citizen suits were a primary force in pushing EPA to establish the underground injection well program.   ▪

3. The 1986 Amendments: Mandating the Maximum Contaminant Levels

When the Safe Drinking Water Act was amended in 1986 "with no fanfare or press coverage," one commentator mused that "the lack of attention shouldn't be surprising: The Safe Drinking Water Act always has been the Rodney Dangerfield of federal environmental laws." See Kenneth F. Gray (1986) "Drinking Water Act Amendments Tap New Sources of Strength," *National Law Journal*, Sept. 1. The reference to Dangerfield, a popular comedian of the time whose well-known tag line was "I don't get no respect," was a reflection of the fact that the Safe Drinking Water Act had not made a major impression in the first 12 years of its existence. Implementation had lagged far behind promise. By 1986 only twenty-three federal drinking water standards were in force, and the underground injection well program had just gotten off the ground. Dissatisfied with the pace of implementation, Congress took dramatic action. In the 1986 amendments to the act, it directed EPA to set standards for eighty-three specified contaminants within 3 years. Moreover, it commanded EPA to establish standards for twenty-five additional contaminants (to be selected by the agency in accordance with the act), *every 3 years* thereafter. See Pub. L. 99-339, June 19, 1986.

Thus EPA found itself under a clear and specific mandate to determine recommended levels (renamed "MCL goals" in the 1986 amendments) and set mandatory MCLs for a host of contaminants. As the following case illustrates, the specification by Congress of eighty-three contaminants for which regulation was required made it easier for EPA to promulgate these standards over industry opposition.

Natural Resources Defense Council v. EPA
MIKVA, Circuit Judge
824 F.2d 1211 (D.C. Cir. 1987)

Three sets of petitioners seek review of a final rule of the Environmental Protection Agency (EPA or the agency) that promulgated recommended maximum contaminant levels (recommended levels) for eight volatile organic compounds (VOCs). The rule established recommended levels of zero for five VOCs that the EPA found to be known or probable carcinogens, a recommended level above zero for one compound the agency found to be a possible carcinogen, and recommended levels above zero for two compounds the agency determined to be non-

carcinogens. Several petitioners challenge the EPA's general determination to set recommended levels for known or probable carcinogens at zero. In addition, two industrial petitioners challenge the inclusion of a particular VOC in the category of known or probable carcinogens, while petitioner Natural Resources Defense Council (NRDC) contests EPA's decision to set a recommended level above zero for the compound determined to be a possible carcinogen. Finding the agency's determinations to be well within the bounds of its authority under the Safe Drinking Water Act (the Drinking Water Act), we affirm the rule in all respects and deny the petitions for review.

I. BACKGROUND

The Drinking Water Act provides the statutory framework for the rule under review. Congress amended the Act in June 1986, after the agency action under review, but, with one exception which we detail below, the amendments do not bear on this case, and we refer in this opinion to the provisions in the pre-1986 version of the Act on which the agency relied....

EPA began the process that culminated in the rule under review in March of 1982, when the agency published an advance notice of proposed rulemaking for regulation of certain VOCs that had been detected in drinking water. In the notice, the agency requested comment on whether to set recommended levels for carcinogenic VOCs at zero or at "some finite relative risk level." *See* 47 Fed.Reg. 9356 (March 4, 1982). In June of 1984, the agency issued a proposed rulemaking, in which it announced a plan to regulate nine of the VOCs listed in the advance notice. The agency proposed recommended levels above zero for the noncarcinogenic VOCs, on the theory that an organism can tolerate and detoxify a certain threshold level of such compounds. For the carcinogenic VOCs, the agency tentatively determined to set the recommended levels at zero, reasoning that any exposure to these compounds would present a risk to human health.

The agency rulemaking here under review followed in November of 1985. The rulemaking assigned recommended levels to eight VOCs according to a three-category scheme. Category I comprised known or probable carcinogens, which the agency concluded should have recommended levels of zero. EPA determined that five of the VOCs properly belonged in this category. One of these five was trichloroethylene, or "TCE." EPA

acknowledged that the evidence of TCE's carcinogenicity was more equivocal than was the evidence for the other four VOCs in this category, but the agency nevertheless decided to regulate TCE as a probable carcinogen. The EPA placed one VOC, vinylidene chloride, in Category II—VOCs for which there is some equivocal evidence of carcinogenicity. EPA decided not to treat vinylidene chloride as a carcinogen, and it did not set a recommended level of zero for the compound. Rather, the agency decided to establish a recommended level for vinylidene chloride based on the compound's risk of causing noncancerous liver and kidney damage. In setting the actual recommended level, however, the agency factored in the equivocal evidence of vinylidene chloride's carcinogenicity. The EPA placed the remaining two VOCs in Category III—contaminants for which there is inadequate or no evidence of carcinogenicity—and assigned recommended levels above zero to these compounds....

II. DISCUSSION

A. Recommended Levels of Zero for Known or Probable Carcinogens

Faced with the unenviable task of challenging the goal of a total absence of known or probable carcinogens in the nation's drinking water, industrial petitioners offer two arguments. The first of these is the contention by petitioners Chemical Manufacturers Association and American Petroleum Institute that the EPA's decision to set recommended levels of zero for the five Category I VOCs was based solely on a misconception that the Drinking Water Act compelled such a result. In support of this claim, petitioners cite language in the order in which the agency refers to a "mandate" from Congress. Petitioners also maintain that the agency placed undue reliance on a passage from the Drinking Water Act's legislative history that states that in cases where there is no safe threshold for a contaminant, the recommended level "should be set at the zero level." *See* H.R.Rep. No. 1185, 93rd Cong., 2d Sess. 20 (1974) U.S.Code Cong. & Admin.News 1974, pp. 6454, 6473. In petitioners' view, the agency considered itself bound to set a recommended level of zero for all known or probable carcinogens, overlooking the possibility that such contaminants do have a tolerably safe threshold within the meaning of the Drinking Water Act.

The record soundly contradicts petitioners' characterization of the EPA's decisionmaking. The rule under review noted that the agency had requested comments on three distinct options for setting recommended levels for carcinogens, including nonzero levels based on a calculation of the finite relative risk of each compound. The final rule itself, far from revealing an abdication of judgment, evidences a reasoned determination by EPA that known and probable carcinogens have no safe threshold. The agency wrote, for example:

"EPA believes that the zero level is necessary to prevent known or anticipated effects from human or probable human carcinogens including a margin of safety. No other margin of safety would be adequate since EPA does not believe a threshold for carcinogens exists."

50 Fed. Reg. at 46,896. The agency did state that "it believed a [recommended level] of zero was more consistent with the [Drinking Water Act] mandate and the legislative history." *Id.* at 46,881. The mandate to which this passage refers, however, as the final rule later makes clear, is not a perceived congressional directive to set recommended levels for carcinogens at zero, but rather, "the direction of Congress that EPA set [recommended levels] to prevent known or anticipated effects with a margin of safety." *Id.* at 46,896. The Drinking Water Act clearly does impose this obligation on the agency. Thus, there is no indication that the agency misconstrued or failed to meet its responsibilities under the Drinking Water Act, or that it failed to adequately consider alternatives to the approach it ultimately adopted. Rather, EPA made an expert judgment that there is no safe threshold level for known or probable carcinogens, and set recommended levels of zero for those compounds accordingly.

Petitioners' second argument is that under the Drinking Water Act, the agency is required to make a predicate finding of "significant risk" before it can regulate a VOC at all. Petitioners contend that the Drinking Water Act must be interpreted to encompass this requirement, because otherwise the statute would confer unfettered discretion to regulate on the EPA, in violation of the delegation doctrine set out by the Supreme Court in *A.L.A. Schecter Poultry Corp. v. United States*, 295 U.S. 495 (1935). In advancing this argument, petitioners rely on the Supreme Court's decision in *Industrial Union Department, AFL-CIO v. American Petroleum Institute*, 448 U.S. 607 (1980), popularly known as the "*Benzene*" decision. In *Benzene*, the Court construed the Occupational Safety and Health Act (OSHA) as prohibiting the Secretary of Labor from issuing standards to provide safe or healthful employment without a threshold determination "that a place of employment is unsafe—in the sense that significant risks are present and can be eliminated or lessened by changing practices." *Id.* at 642. Three members of the plurality opinion suggested that one reason for favoring such a construction of OSHA was to avoid any concern of an unconstitutionally broad delegation of legislative power. Petitioners seize upon this language to claim that the EPA lacked authority to regulate the five Category I VOCs unless it first found that even negligible amounts of the compounds in drinking water presented a significant risk to human health.

The Court based its decision in *Benzene* on a close reading of the statutory language of OSHA, which we note differs significantly from the statutory scheme that we confront in this case. The OSHA language that the Supreme Court interpreted as incorporating a requirement of a finding of significant risk directed the Secretary to set standards "reasonably necessary and appropriate to provide safe or healthful employment." 29 U.S.C. §652(8). The Drinking Water Act, by contrast, directs the Administrator to establish a recommended level for "each contaminant which, in his judgment . . . *may have any* adverse effect on the health of persons." 42 U.S.C. §300g-1(b)(1)(B) (emphasis added). This language is inconsistent with a requirement that the Administrator make a threshold finding of significant risk; a contaminant may have some adverse effect on the health of persons without posing a significant risk to human health.

Petitioners' reliance on *Benzene* is unwarranted not only because of the differences between the two statutory schemes. Whatever the impact of the decision on statutory schemes other than OSHA, *Benzene* applies only if Congress has not specifically set the agency's regulatory agenda. *Benzene* could not possibly apply in this case because Congress in fact has now told the EPA to regulate the VOCs that are the subject of the rule under review. The 1986 amendments to the Drinking Water Act specifically direct EPA to establish national primary drinking water regulations for 83 enumerated VOCs, including the eight compounds which the EPA regulated in this rule. *See* Section 101, Safe Drinking Water Act Amendments of 1986, Pub.L. No. 99-339, 100 Stat. 642 (1986). Petitioners point out that the amendments also permit the EPA to substitute a specific contaminant for one of the contaminants enumerated by Congress if, in the judgment of the agency, regulation of the substitute contaminant is more likely to be protective of public health. This added measure of discretion, however, in no way alters the fact that Congress has given a preliminary directive to the EPA to regulate the VOCs at issue here. Thus, we need not determine whether the *Benzene* decision might have applied by anal-

ogy to the unamended Drinking Water Act. Congress now has issued precise marching orders instructing the EPA to regulate these VOCs, and that is all the agency needs to know. *See American Mining Congress v. Thomas*, 772 F.2d 617, 627–28 (10th Cir. 1985) (significant risk determination by EPA inappropriate and unnecessary where Congress had indicated its desire for regulation).

B. Promulgation of a Recommended Level of Zero for TCE

Petitioners Halogenated Solvent Industry Alliance and Diamond Shamrock Chemicals Company protest at length the EPA's decision to categorize TCE as a probable carcinogen, which resulted in the agency's promulgation of a recommended level of zero for TCE. Petitioners argue that the EPA miscategorized TCE because any risk presented by the compound is at most *de minimus*. TCE's carcinogenicity has been the subject of at least six scientific studies on mice, which have produced varying results. Petitioners belittle the two studies that have indicated that TCE may be a human carcinogen, while they trumpet the studies that point the other way. In brief, petitioners argue that the positive studies are unreliable because they involved suspect dosage levels, dosage methods, TCE grades, mice strains, and mice housing.

Happily, it is not for the judicial branch to undertake comparative evaluations of conflicting scientific evidence. Our review aims only to discern whether the agency's evaluation was rational. EPA provided ample explanation for its decision to classify TCE as a probable carcinogen. It received and replied to extensive comments on the issue, and it detailed its reasons for giving greater weight to the positive studies than to the negative or inconclusive studies. *See* 50 Fed.Reg. 46,886–87. To summarize the EPA's reasoning, the agency was particularly impressed by finding in two different studies that TCE caused a significant increase in the incidence of liver tumors in mice. Although we gather there is some disagreement in the scientific community as to the relevance of evidence of mouse tumors, EPA's proposed guidelines for carcinogen risk-assessment reasonably take such findings as sufficient evidence of carcinogenicity in the absence of certain contraindications, none of which was present in the studies in question. Moreover, the agency identified concrete flaws in the negative studies. The agency also took note of the consensus among scientists that where cancer is concerned, positive results in one study are not necessarily negated by negative results in another. EPA, in sum, made a reasonable choice to categorize TCE as a probable carcinogen based on a rational evaluation of somewhat conflicting scientific evidence. As we previously have stated, "in an area characterized by scientific and technological uncertainty [w]here administrative judgment plays a key role, . . . this court must proceed with particular caution, avoiding all temptation to direct the agency in a choice between rational alternatives." *Environmental Defense Fund v. Costle* 578 F.2d 337, 339 (D.C. Cir. 1978). We are satisfied that the alternative for which the agency opted was rational, and we therefore have no cause to disturb the EPA's choice.

C. Failure to Promulgate a Zero Recommended Level for Vinylidene Chloride

NRDC does not dispute EPA's finding that vinylidene chloride is a possible—rather than a known or probable—human carcinogen. NRDC instead contends that Congress intended that EPA treat possible carcinogens no differently from known or probable ones. NRDC argues that EPA's regulatory scheme in effect imposes a requirement that a compound be found to be carcinogenic by a preponderance of the evidence before the agency will establish a recommended level of zero for it. Such a threshold requirement,

NRDC contends, violates EPA's obligation to resolve uncertainty on the side of protecting public health.

We agree with NRDC that a preponderance-of-the-evidence threshold test would probably be inconsistent with Congress' directions in the Drinking Water Act. If the evidence established, for example, a 40% probability that a compound was carcinogenic, the agency's decision not to regulate would be difficult to square with the Drinking Water Act's instruction to the agency to establish a recommended level for each contaminant which, in its judgment, may have any adverse effect on health. Such a decision might well constitute an abuse of the discretion the agency is granted under the Drinking Water Act. But that situation in no way describes the instant case, and certainly there is no indication in the final rule that the agency has adopted a general policy not to establish a recommended level for a VOC unless a preponderance of the evidence demonstrates that it is a carcinogen. NRDC perhaps has taken too much to heart the agency's use of the word "possible" in its categorization of different VOCs. Although that label on its face could augur a preponderance-of-the-evidence test, the agency's explication of the Category II— compounds for which there is *some equivocal evidence* of carcinogenicity—makes it clear that the EPA has no such test in mind. Nor does the EPA's treatment of vinylidene chloride suggest that the agency employed a threshold preponderance-of-the-evidence test. The EPA here reasonably concluded that the evidence of vinylidene chloride's carcinogenicity was not even close to being in equipoise. The agency pointed out that no fewer than a dozen long-term animal studies had not demonstrated that vinylidene chloride has any carcinogenic effect. *See* 50 Fed.Reg. 46,888, J.A. 9. Against this data EPA weighed two studies that revealed a possibility of carcinogenic or protocarcinogenic effects, and it noted that the results in both of these studies had limitations that made their applicability to humans highly questionable. The agency therefore had adequate support for its conclusion that the evidence of TCE's carcinogenicity was sparse and equivocal.

Whether the EPA, having reached such a conclusion, properly declined to set a zero recommended level for vinylidene chloride involves essentially a question of statutory interpretation. The Drinking Water Act provides that the Administrator shall establish recommended levels for each contaminant which, "in his judgment . . . may have any adverse effect on the health of persons." By its terms, the statute grants discretion to the Administrator to determine whether there is sufficient evidence to justify establishing a recommended level for a particular compound. Unless the agency must regulate as a carcinogen every VOC whose carcinogenicity it cannot conclusively disprove, an interpretation that would read the concept of administrative judgment out of the Act, the EPA has discretion not to treat a compound as a carcinogen notwithstanding some equivocal evidence to the contrary. *See Environmental Defense Fund v. EPA*, 598 F.2d 62, 88 (D.C. Cir. 1978) (where evidence of a chemical's carcinogenicity is inconclusive, Administrator has discretion whether to regulate). EPA's decision not to establish a recommended level for vinylidene chloride based on the compound's carcinogenicity thus does not violate the statutory scheme of the Drinking Water Act.

Although EPA did not set a recommended level for vinylidene chloride based on the compound's carcinogenicity, the agency decided that the compound's other toxic effects did warrant the establishment of a recommended level. In then calculating the actual recommended level for vinylidene chloride, EPA divided by ten in order to take account of vinylidene chloride's possibly carcinogenic effects. NRDC argues that it was arbitrary

and capricious for the agency to refuse to establish a recommended level of zero based on vinylidene chloride's risk of carcinogenicity but then to take account of the very same risk in setting the recommended level for the compound. We disagree. A careful parsing of the statutory language provides ample support for EPA's action. The Drinking Water Act provides for promulgation of recommended levels in two steps. In the first, the Administrator determines whether a contaminant may have any adverse effect on the health of persons. If a contaminant may have an adverse effect (for example, in the case of vinylidene chloride, because of its noncarcinogenic risks), the Administrator is directed to set the recommended level at a level at which "*no* known or anticipated adverse effects on the health of persons occur *and* which allows an adequate margin of safety." The statute thus leaves room for the EPA to consider in its actual setting of the recommended level risks other than those that catalyzed the preliminary decision to establish a recommended level. Here, the EPA did just that, concluding that the equivocal evidence of vinylidene chloride's carcinogenicity, although not sufficient to justify establishing a recommended level on that ground alone, was palpable enough to be accounted for at the "adequate margin of safety" stage. This is neither an unreasonable interpretation of the statute nor an unwise choice of policy. . . .

III. CONCLUSION

The coincidental opposition to EPA's rule by public-interest forces *and* industrial representatives is not relevant to the reviewing process and is not a factor for our consideration, except that it reflects EPA's careful efforts to carry out its regulatory obligations. The rule under review is measured and well within the regulatory contours established by Congress under the Drinking Water Act. Accordingly, for the foregoing reasons, the petitions for review are denied and the final rule under review is affirmed.

It is so ordered.

WILLIAMS, CIRCUIT JUDGE, CONCURRING:

In view of Congress's clear mandate in the Safe Drinking Water Act Amendments of 1986, I see no need to consider whether the language of the Safe Drinking Water Act, directing the Administrator to establish a recommended level for "each contaminant which, in his judgment . . . , may have any adverse effect on the health of persons," requires a threshold finding of significant risk under *Benzene*.

- **NOTES**

1. Is the D.C. Circuit's approach to the "significant risk" issue in this case consistent with the approach it took to this issue in its treatment of Section 112 of the Clean Air Act in *Natural Resources Defense Council v. EPA*, 824 F.2d 1146 (D.C. Cir. 1987), a case (coincidentally enough) with the same name, decided in the same year, and reported in the same volume of the *Federal Reporter*? In the Clean Air Act case, discussed in chapter 6, the court interpreted the mandate of Section 112 that emission standards for hazardous air pollutants be set at a level that ensures "an ample margin of safety" as nonetheless requiring a threshold finding that the standard is necessary to avoid a "significant risk" of harm (because, in the court's words, "safe" does not mean "risk free"). Are there differences between the Safe Drinking Water Act (as it existed after the 1986 amendments) and Section 112 of the Clean Air Act (as it existed prior to the 1990 Clean Air Act Amendments) that justify the differing approaches taken in these two cases? Does it matter that the standard at issue under the Safe Drinking Water Act was an "aspirational" recommended level, rather than a mandatory compliance level?

2. The 1986 amendments to the Safe Drinking Water Act were reminiscent of the changes that Congress had effectuated in the regulatory structure for hazardous wastes 2 years earlier. In the 1984 amendments to the Resource Conservation and Recovery Act, discussed in chapter 9, Congress ordered EPA to establish regulations for specified hazardous wastes according to a specified timetable.

3. The ramifications of the mandatory schedule for promulgation of drinking water standards extended beyond the drinking water tap. In the 1986 amendments to the Comprehensive Environmental Response, Compensation, and Liability Act, Congress specified that maximum contaminant level goals be designated, where appropriate, as cleanup standards for hazardous waste sites. As the promulgation of drinking water standards progressed, then, CERCLA cleanup requirements accordingly became more stringent.   ■

4.   The 1996 Amendments: Scaling Back

Ten years after the 1986 amendments—with scores of MCLs and MCL goals now on the books—Congress again changed the rules of the game. In a 1996 compromise endorsed by environmental groups and water suppliers alike, Congress amended the act in a way that effectively ensured both that the standards (MCL goals and MCLs) that had been set would largely be allowed to remain in place, and that new standards would be far slower in coming (and most likely would be relatively weaker).

The requirement that twenty-five standards be set every 3 years was eliminated, as was the general directive to EPA to set standards for those contaminants that "may have an adverse effect on the health of persons." Instead, EPA is now directed to set standards for a contaminant when (1) "the contaminant may have an adverse effect on the health of persons," (2) there is "a substantial likelihood that the contaminant will occur in public water systems with a frequency and at levels of public health concern," and (3) in the "sole judgment" of EPA, regulation of the contaminant "presents a meaningful opportunity for health risk reduction for persons served by public water systems" [Section 300g-1(b)(A)]. As a means of targeting contaminants that may meet these criteria, EPA is directed to compile, once every 5 years, a list of contaminants that are not subject to any proposed or promulgated national primary drinking water regulation, that are known or anticipated to occur in public water systems, and that "may require regulation" under the act. In compiling this list, EPA must consider hazardous substances under CERCLA and pesticides registered under the Federal Insecticide, Fungicide, and Rodenticide Act. EPA's determination as to which contaminants to include on this list "shall not be subject to judicial review" [Section 300g-1(b)(1)(B)(i)]. Within $3\frac{1}{2}$ years thereafter, the agency must select at least five contaminants from the list and determine for each contaminant whether it meets the three criteria for regulation in Section 300g-1(b)(A). See Section 300g-1(b)(1)(B)(ii).

In making this determination, EPA must base its findings on "the best available public health information," including information on the levels and frequency at which the contaminant is found in public water systems. The agency may also choose to regulate contaminants that do not appear on the list, so long as this determination is made in accordance with these provisions. See Sections 300g-1(b)(1)(B)(ii)(II)–(III). If EPA determines that a contaminant meets the statutory criteria for regulation, the agency must propose an MCL goal and primary drinking water standard for that contaminant within 24 months, and must publish a final goal and standard within 18 months thereafter. See Section 300g-1(b)(1)(E).

In establishing new MCLs, EPA is no longer bound solely to considerations of technological and economic feasibility. Although the 1996 amendments retain the general directive that standards be set "as close to the maximum contaminant level goal as is feasible" [Section 300g-1(b)(4)(B)], there are two important exceptions. EPA may choose a less protective standard if it finds that the feasible level "would result in an increase in the health risk for drinking water" by increasing the concentration of other contaminants or by interfering with the techniques or processes used to meet other primary drinking water standards [Section 300g-1(b)(5)]. EPA may also choose a less protective standard if "the benefits of a maximum contaminant level promulgated [at the level of feasibility] would not justify the costs of complying with [that] level," excluding any costs associated with small water systems that are eligible for cost variances under the act [Section 300g-1(b)(6)]. To provide the basis for this cost-benefit determination, EPA must "publish, seek public comment on, and use" an analysis of the "quantifiable and unquantifiable" benefits and costs associated with an MCL based on feasibility, the "quantifiable and unquantifiable" benefits and costs associated with any alternative less-stringent MCLs being considered, the "incremental costs and benefits" associated with each alternative MCL being considered, the effects of the contaminants on the general population and on identifiable subgroups "likely to be at greater risk of adverse health effects," any increased health risk "that may occur as a result of compliance," and other "relevant factors," including "the quality and extent of the information, the uncertainties in the analysis...and factors with regard to the degree and nature of the risk" [Section 300g-1(b)(3)(C)].

In addition, "to the degree that [its] action is based on science," EPA is required to base its standard-setting determinations under the act on:

(i) the best available, peer-reviewed science and supporting studies conducted in accordance with sound and objective scientific practices; and
(ii) data collected by accepted methods or best available methods (if the reliability of the method and the nature of the decision justifies use of the data). [Section 300g-1(b)(3)(A)]

These new provisions were not made immediately applicable to MCLs promulgated prior to the 1996 amendments, but EPA was directed to "review and revise, as appropriate, each national primary drinking water regulation" at least once every 6 years, and to promulgate any revised standards "in accordance with" the provisions of the 1996 amendments. However, any such revision must "maintain, or provide for greater, protection of the health of persons" [Section 300g-1(b)(9)]. With this language, Congress placed a health-based "overlay" on existing standards that should prevent them from being significantly weakened.

■ **NOTES**

1. In her public statements about the 1996 amendments, then-EPA Administrator Carol Browner called attention to "the role that the Natural Resources Defense

Council, U.S. Public Interest Research Group, and other environmental and citizen groups played in writing" the revised law ["Clinton Signs Drinking Water Act: Says Law Is 'First Line of Defense' in Health," *Environment Reporter* 27: 822 (1996)]. At the same time, the executive director of the Association of Municipal Water Agencies praised the amendments, noting that "We can now expect EPA to develop responsible regulations that rely on good science and health effects data" [id.].

2. Are standards set under the provisions of the 1996 amendments more, or less, likely to be the type that stimulates the development of innovative water treatment techniques than standards set under the previous versions of the act? Why?

3. The 1996 amendments also required EPA to set standards for arsenic, sulfate, and radon according to specified timetables. See Sections 300g-1(b)(12) and (13). In addition, EPA was directed to complete the rulemaking it had already begun on disinfectants (such as chlorine) and disinfectant by-products [Sections 300g-1(b)(2)(C) and (8)] and the agency was prohibited from using cost-benefit considerations to weaken the MCL for such contaminants in surface water sources of drinking water [id. §300g-1(b)(C)]. The agency was also forbidden to use cost-benefit considerations in setting an MCL for the biological contaminant cryptosporidium. See Section 300g-1(b)(C).

4. To provide information on the levels and frequency at which contaminants are found in public water systems, the 1996 amendments required EPA to assemble and maintain a "national drinking water contaminant occurrence data base." This compilation is to include data on "both regulated and unregulated contaminants," which are to be drawn both from the monitoring required under the act and from "reliable information from other public and private sources" [Section 300j-4(g)(1)].

5. Although both the House and Senate versions of the 1996 amendments would have established a program within EPA to screen chemicals for their endocrine-disruption potential, such a program was instead established under 1996 amendments to the Food, Drug, and Cosmetic Act. The EPA was, however, given the responsibility of conducting the program. See, e.g., U.S. Environmental Protection Agency (2000) *Endocrine Disrupter Screening Program Report to Congress*. EPA, Washington, D.C.   ■

9 Regulation of Hazardous Wastes: RCRA, CERCLA, and Hazardous Waste Facility Siting

A. OVERVIEW

1. Nowhere to Hide: The Relationship Between Hazardous Waste Regulation and Pollution Prevention

Viewing pollution as a media-based phenomenon, one can divide pollution of the outdoor environment into three general categories: the discharge of pollutants to the air, the discharge of pollutants to the water, and the discharge of pollutants to the land. This chapter addresses the last of these. The order in which we have chosen to address these three topics is not coincidental. Rather, it follows the order in which Congress chose to deal with them in the 1970s: the Clean Air Act Amendments of 1970; the Water Pollution Control Act Amendments of 1972; and, for land disposal, the 1976 amendments to the Solid Waste Disposal Act (also known as the Resource Conservation and Recovery Act, or RCRA), and the Comprehensive Environmental Response, Compensation, and Liability Act of 1980 (CERCLA, commonly known as the federal Superfund law). With the media-based regulatory systems progressing in this order, one saw a general shift in the discharge of pollutants from medium to medium as the respective systems were implemented.

As air pollution regulation became more restrictive, industrial facilities began to install control technology to reduce the emission of the various regulated pollutants. Because this often was accomplished by trapping and collecting the pollutants just before they were to be emitted to the air, and disposing of the materials thus collected, one effect of the increased control of air pollutants was the creation of additional water pollution and/or hazardous waste. Where a wet scrubber technology was employed to keep pollutants from going out the top of a smokestack, for example, the pollutants often would simply be diverted to the facility's wastewater discharge. Thereafter, when the Clean Water Act's effluent limitations began to regulate wastewater discharges, a common response was the installation of end-of-pipe water pollution control technologies, such as filtering systems or oil and water separators. While these technologies removed regulated pollutants from the wastewater, they also often created hazardous residues, and most of these residues were simply placed in the unlined landfills that were utilized by industry at the time.

When, in the 1980s, the federal regulatory system began to put meaningful restrictions on the disposal of hazardous wastes, many industrial facilities found themselves facing an undeniable fact of nature: there was no fourth environmental medium to which they could transfer their hazardous residues. Given that they could not lawfully discharge those residues to the air or water, these facilities thus faced a choice: they could comply with the increasingly stringent restrictions imposed by RCRA, they could violate the law, or they could find a way to reduce their generation of hazardous residues in the first place. This, then, might be viewed as the birth of the modern federal regulatory incentive toward the implementation of pollution prevention. For, with the lawful disposal of hazardous wastes becoming more expensive, there was now a greater financial incentive to explore the feasibility of process changes, input substitution, product reformulation, and other strategies that held the promise, not just of reducing the production of hazardous waste, but of simultaneously reducing the discharge of residues into all three environmental media. An additional incentive for pollution prevention came from the newly passed Superfund law, which sent the message that even lawful disposal of hazardous waste did not insulate generators from potential liability for future costs of remediation.

■ **NOTES**

1. The contribution of pollution control technologies to the creation of solid waste was cited by Congress in the opening provisions of RCRA as one of the reasons for the passage of that law. Section 1002(b)(3) of RCRA states that, "as a result of the Clean Air Act, the Water Pollution Control Act, and other Federal and State laws respecting public health and the environment, greater amounts of solid waste (in the form of sludge and other pollution treatment residues) have been created" [42 U.S.C. §6901(b)(3)].

2. The three environmental media—air, water, and land—are not the only potential receptacles for hazardous residues, of course. Hazardous residues are routinely discharged into the workplace environment every day, just as they routinely leave manufacturing facilities as components of certain products. Moreover, it is true that one response to the increasingly stringent regulation of hazardous discharges into the environment has been a shifting of pollutants to these two "closed" media. While this has not happened on the scale of the more widespread shifting of pollutants seen among environmental media, it nonetheless can result in significant human exposure to toxic substances, and should be addressed in the design of any comprehensive pollution prevention policy.

3. Two of the first expressions of the pollution prevention concept in the language of hazardous waste reduction are Charles C. Caldart and C. William Ryan (1985) "Waste Generation Reduction: A First Step Toward Developing a Regulatory Policy to Encourage Hazardous Substance Management Through Production Process Change," *Hazardous Waste and Hazardous Materials* 2: 309–351; and Joel S. Hirschhorn (1988) "Cutting Production of Hazardous Waste" *Technology Review* 91: 52.

4. For a more detailed discussion of the combined use of environmental, workplace, and consumer protection regulation to promote pollution prevention, see chapter 13. ■

2.   Activist Suburbs: The Revitalization of the Environmental Movement and the Resulting Difficulty in Siting Hazardous Waste Treatment, Storage, and Disposal Facilities

As we discuss later in this chapter, EPA promulgated its first comprehensive RCRA regulations in 1980, and Congress upped the ante in its 1984 amendments to RCRA by commanding the agency to significantly strengthen those regulations. This congressional directive was in turn spurred by a growing grass-roots political movement, born in communities throughout the country, calling for increased controls on hazardous waste. The highly publicized misfortunes of the ironically named Love Canal, New York—where more than 1,000 families were evacuated from their homes after being inundated by toxic chemicals from a leaking industrial landfill—personalized the hazardous waste issue for the nation, and helped spawn a network of activists concerned about hazardous waste risks in their own communities. The following description from a 1981 *Boston Globe* article captures the early days of this movement.

They live in ranch houses alive with children and dogs. They work hard—for other people. And until recently, they always have espoused the philosophy that you don't rock the boat that's taking you from where you were to where you are.

No More.

Perhaps the least publicized political force today, at least in New England, is peopled by once-tame suburbanites who have become radicalized over the danger of hazardous wastes....

The people speak in arcane vocabularies about soil permeability, ground water tables, aquifers and the relative toxicity of chemicals such as trichloroethylene.

Most of the suburbanites have never before been politically active. But they have been goaded into almost monomaniacal devotion by a common mistrust of industry and the government bureaucracies they thought would protect them, their homes, children, their drinking water—but haven't. (Andrew Blake (1981) "Silent No Longer: The Fear of Toxic Wastes Produces Activist Suburbs," *Boston Globe*, January 27, p. 1)

In addition to advocating stronger regulation of hazardous wastes, these activists fought the siting of new hazardous waste facilities in their communities. Indeed, often it was the news of the pending construction of a hazardous waste landfill or treatment facility that galvanized local residents and prompted them to take political action. See, e.g., Bill Sproat (1982) "OUCH: A Pain in the Dump in Pennsylvania," *Everyone's Backyard* (Citizen's Clearinghouse for Hazardous Wastes), vol. 1, no. 1, p. 2 (Fall) (discussing the community group "OUCH"—Opposing Unnecessary Chemical Hazards—which was formed to fight a proposal to place chemical wastes in a former sanitary landfill in York County, Pennsylvania). Although such groups were often derided by industry, and by some in the public policy community, as having fallen prey to the "NIMBY syndrome" (a pejorative term based on the acronym for "not in my back yard," and usually intended to signify irrationality), local opposition to the siting of hazardous waste facilities was another important factor in creating and maintaining incentives for pollution prevention.

With the promulgation of EPA's first comprehensive RCRA regulations in 1980, disposal of hazardous waste anywhere but in a RCRA-approved facility became illegal. Especially with the increased wastes being created by newly installed air and water pollution control technology, hazardous waste generators wishing to comply with RCRA began demanding new treatment or disposal facilities to which they could send their wastes. Indeed, John Berwick, then the secretary of environmental affairs for the Commonwealth of Massachusetts, told the *Boston Globe* in 1981 that the siting of a new hazardous waste facility was "the single most important goal" of his administration (Andrew Blake, "Silent No Longer"). With local opposition to such facilities far stronger than anticipated, however, hazardous waste generators found it more and more to their advantage to invest in technologies and practices that could reduce the amount of waste they had to dispose.

(handwritten margin note: Shows benefit of taking a firm stance)

■ **NOTES**

1. One spirited defense of local opposition to hazardous waste facilities was supplied by the Citizen's Clearinghouse for Hazardous Waste, a national organization started by Lois Gibbs, the self-described "housewife turned activist" from Love Canal, New York:

> People across the country are being accused of having "NIMBY." What is it?... NIMBY, of course, is not a dreaded disease, but rather government's term for most communities' reaction to the placement of a new landfill in their neighborhood. To make matters worse, government and industry have even successfully made people feel guilty about having the NIMBYs. Yet NIMBY can be one of the best things you'll ever acquire in your lifetime. It's not only OK to feel that way; it's also very justifiable....
>
> ... According to the EPA, 90% of the hazardous wastes generated today can be disposed of safely without landfilling. There *are* many alternatives to land disposal of toxic wastes that are currently available, feasible, affordable, and safe.... The ideal solution is to reduce waste at the source by changing the industrial processes so that hazardous by-products are not produced. ["I've Got NIMBY and I'm Glad I Do," *Everyone's Backyard*, vol. 1, no. 4, p. 1 (Fall 1983)]

2. A somewhat different view of the NIMBY phenomenon was offered by the Fourth Circuit Court of Appeals in *Geo-Tech Reclamation Industries, Inc. v. Hamrick*, 886 F.2d 662 (4th Cir. 1989). At issue in that case was a West Virginia law that authorized the state's Department of Natural Resources to deny a permit for any solid waste disposal facility found to be "significantly adverse to the public sentiment of the area where the solid waste facility is or will be located" (id. at 663). In response to a challenge brought under the due process clause of the Fourteenth Amendment, the state argued that the law promoted community pride, spirit, and quality of life. While acknowledging the legitimacy of these interests, the court noted that, "with commendable candor, the state also recognizes that many who may speak out against a landfill may do so because of self-interest, bias, or ignorance" (id. at 666). These, the court commented, "are but a few of the less than noble motivations commonly referred to as the 'Not-in-My-Backyard' syndrome" (id.). Finding that "[t]he potential that, by virtue of [the siting law], sensitive administrative decisions regarding waste disposal will be made by mob rule is too great to ignore" (id. at 667), the court declared the law to be unconstitutional.   ■

[handwritten: Both Sides See other as irrational.]

3. The "Breakthrough" that Wasn't: Constitutional Limitations on Local Control of Hazardous Waste Shipment and Treatment

Spirited opposition to such facilities did not mean, of course, that the search for new hazardous waste treatment and storage facilities came to an end. The siting issue was the subject of considerable attention in public policy circles throughout the 1980s. Predictably, the issue often elicited polarized views. Industry spokespeople routinely characterized the problem as one of overcoming a largely irrational public opposition to the siting of treatment facilities that were far safer than the unlined landfills that had been used in the past, while community groups generally characterized the problem as one of overcoming industry opposition to technologies that would reduce the generation of waste.

The paucity of new hazardous waste facilities also created a predictable dynamic among states. Each state was worried that if it approved a new facility, that facility would become the "dumping ground" for generators in neighboring states, thus relieving those states of the need to develop their own facilities. This was a troubling proposition even for those who believed there was a need for new hazardous waste facilities. Accordingly, one approach that was seriously discussed in many states was the idea of creating a facility solely for the use of in-state generators. The notion that a state should be responsible for the waste it created—but for no more—had an equitable appeal to many. As it turned out, that equitable appeal was no match for the "dormant commerce clause" when the issue was reviewed by the Supreme Court.

Chemical Waste Management, Inc., v. Guy Hunt, Governor of Alabama, et al.
Justice WHITE delivered the opinion of the Court
United States Supreme Court
504 U.S. 334 (1992)

Alabama imposes a hazardous waste disposal fee on hazardous wastes generated outside the State and disposed of at a commercial facility in Alabama. The fee does not apply to such waste having a source in Alabama. The Alabama Supreme Court held that this differential treatment does not violate the Commerce Clause. We reverse.

I

Petitioner, Chemical Waste Management, Inc., a Delaware corporation with its principal place of business in Oak Brook, Illinois, owns and operates one of the Nation's oldest commercial hazardous waste land disposal facilities, located in Emelle, Alabama. Opened in 1977 and acquired by petitioner in 1978, the Emelle facility is a hazardous waste treatment, storage, and disposal facility operating pursuant to permits issued by the Environmental Protection Agency (EPA) under the Resource Conservation and Recovery Act of 1976 (RCRA), 90 Stat. 2795, as amended, 42 U. S. C. §6901 *et seq.*, and the Toxic Substances Control Act, 90 Stat. 2003, as amended, 15 U. S. C. §2601 *et seq.* (1988 ed. and Supp. II), and by the State of

Alabama under Ala. Code §22-30-12(i) (1990). Alabama is 1 of only 16 States that have commercial hazardous waste landfills, and the Emelle facility is the largest of the 21 landfills of this kind located in these 16 States. Brief for National Governors' Assn. et al. as *Amici Curiae* 3, citing E. Smith, EI Digest 26–27 (Mar. 1992).

The parties do not dispute that the wastes and substances being landfilled at the Emelle facility "include substances that are inherently dangerous to human health and safety and to the environment. Such waste consists of ignitable, corrosive, toxic and reactive wastes which contain poisonous and cancer causing chemicals and which can cause birth defects, genetic damage, blindness, crippling and death." 584 So. 2d 1367, 1373 (Ala. 1991). Increasing amounts of out-of-state hazardous wastes are shipped to the Emelle facility for permanent storage each year. From 1985 through 1989, the tonnage of hazardous waste received per year has more than doubled, increasing from 341,000 tons in 1985 to 788,000 tons by 1989. Of this, up to 90% of the tonnage permanently buried each year is shipped in from other States.

Against this backdrop Alabama enacted Act No. 90-326 (Act). Ala. Code §§22-30B-1 to 22-30B-18 (1990 and Supp. 1991). Among other provisions, the Act includes a "cap" that generally limits the amount of hazardous wastes or substances[2] that may be disposed of in any 1-year period, and the amount of hazardous waste disposed of during the first year under the Act's new fees becomes the permanent ceiling in subsequent years. Ala. Code §22-30B-2.3 (1990). The cap applies to commercial facilities that dispose of over 100,000 tons of hazardous wastes or substances per year, but only the Emelle facility, as the only commercial facility operating within Alabama, meets this description. The Act also

imposes a "base fee" of $25.60 per ton on all hazardous wastes and substances disposed of at commercial facilities, to be paid by the operator of the facility. Ala. Code §22-30B-2(a) (Supp. 1991). Finally, the Act imposes the "additional fee" at issue here, which states in full:

"For waste and substances which are generated outside of Alabama and disposed of at a commercial site for the disposal of hazardous waste or hazardous substances in Alabama, an additional fee shall be levied at the rate of $72.00 per ton." §22-30B-2(b).

Petitioner filed suit in state court requesting declaratory relief against respondents and seeking to enjoin enforcement of the Act. In addition to state-law claims, petitioner contended that the Act violated the Commerce, Due Process, and Equal Protection Clauses of the United States Constitution, and was pre-empted by various federal statutes. The trial court declared the base fee and the cap provisions of the Act to be valid and constitutional; but, finding the only basis for the additional fee to be the origin of the waste, the trial court declared it to be in violation of the Commerce Clause. App. to Pet. for Cert. 83a-88a. Both sides appealed. The Alabama Supreme Court affirmed the rulings concerning the base fee and cap provisions but reversed the decision regarding the additional fee. The court held that the fee at issue advanced legitimate local purposes that could not be adequately served by reasonable nondiscriminatory alternatives and was therefore valid under the Commerce Clause. 584 So. 2d at 1390.

Chemical Waste Management, Inc., petitioned for writ of certiorari, challenging all aspects of the Act. Because of the importance of the federal question and the likelihood that it had been decided in a way conflicting with applicable decisions of this Court, this

---

2. "Hazardous substance(s)" and "hazardous waste(s)" are defined terms in the Act, §§22-30B-1(3) and 22-30B-1(4), but these definitions largely parallel the meanings given under federal law.

Court's Rule 10.1(c), we granted certiorari limited to petitioner's Commerce Clause challenge to the additional fee. 502 U.S. 1070 (1992). We now reverse.

II

No State may attempt to isolate itself from a problem common to the several States by raising barriers to the free flow of interstate trade.[3] Today, in *Fort Gratiot Sanitary Landfill, Inc.* v. *Michigan Dept. of Natural Resources*, 504 U.S. 353 (1992), we have also considered a Commerce Clause challenge to a Michigan law prohibiting private landfill operators from accepting solid waste originating outside the county in which their facilities operate. In striking down that law, we adhered to our decision in *Philadelphia* v. *New Jersey*, 437 U.S. 617, 57 L. Ed. 2d 475, 98 S. Ct. 2531 (1978), where we found New Jersey's prohibition of solid waste from outside that State to amount to economic protectionism barred by the Commerce Clause:

"The evil of protectionism can reside in legislative means as well as legislative ends. Thus, it does not matter whether the ultimate aim of ch. 363 is to reduce the waste disposal costs of New Jersey residents or to save remaining open lands from pollution, for we assume New Jersey has every right to protect its residents' pocketbooks as well as their environment. And it may be assumed as well that

New Jersey may pursue those ends by slowing the flow of *all* waste into the State's remaining landfills, even though interstate commerce may incidentally be affected. But whatever New Jersey's ultimate purpose, it may not be accompanied by discriminating against articles of commerce coming from outside the State unless there is some reason, apart from their origin, to treat them differently. Both on its face and in its plain effect, ch. 363 violates this principle of nondiscrimination.

The Court has consistently found parochial legislation of this kind to be constitutionally invalid, whether the ultimate aim of the legislation was to assure a steady supply of milk by erecting barriers to allegedly ruinous outside competition, *Baldwin* v. *G. A. F. Seelig, Inc.*, 294 U.S. [511,] 522–524 [(1935)]; or to create jobs by keeping industry within the State, *Foster-Fountain Packing Co.* v. *Haydel*, 278 U.S. 1, 10, 73 L. Ed. 147, 49 S. Ct. 1 [(1928)]; *Johnson* v. *Haydel*, 278 U.S. 16, 73 L. Ed. 155, 49 S. Ct. 6 [(1928)]; *Toomer* v. *Witsell*, 334 U.S. [385,] 403–404 [(1948)]; or to preserve the State's financial resources from depletion by fencing out indigent immigrants, *Edwards* v. *California*, 314 U.S. 160, 173–174, 86 L. Ed. 119, 62 S. Ct. 164 [(1941)]." *Fort Gratiot Sanitary Landfill*, 504 U.S. at 360 (quoting *Philadelphia* v. *New Jersey, supra*, at 626–627).

To this list may be added cases striking down a tax discriminating against interstate commerce, even where such tax was designed to encourage the use of ethanol and thereby reduce harmful exhaust emissions, *New Energy Co. of Ind.* v. *Limbach*, 486 U.S. 269, 279, 100 L. Ed. 2d 302, 108 S. Ct. 1803 (1988), or to support inspection of foreign

---

3. The Alabama Supreme Court assumed that the disposal of hazardous waste constituted an article of commerce, and the State does not explicitly argue here to the contrary. In *Fort Gratiot Sanitary Landfill, Inc.* v. *Michigan Dept. of Natural Resources*, 504 U.S. 353, 359 (1992), we have reaffirmed the idea that "solid waste, even if it has no value, is an article of commerce." As stated in *Philadelphia* v. *New Jersey*, 437 U.S. 617, 622–623, 57 L. Ed. 2d 475, 98 S. Ct. 2531 (1978): "All objects of interstate trade merit Commerce Clause protection; none is excluded by definition at the outset. . . . Just as Congress has power to regulate the interstate movement of these wastes, States are not free from constitutional scrutiny when they restrict that movement." The definition of "hazardous waste"

makes clear that it is simply a grade of solid waste, albeit one of particularly noxious and dangerous propensities, but whether the business arrangements between out-of-state generators of hazardous waste and the Alabama operator of a hazardous waste landfill are viewed as "sales" of hazardous waste or "purchases" of transportation and disposal services, "the commercial transactions unquestionably have an interstate character. The Commerce Clause thus imposes some constraints on [Alabama's] ability to regulate these transactions." *Fort Gratiot Sanitary Landfill*, 504 U.S. at 359. See *National Solid Wastes Management Assn.* v. *Alabama Dept. of Environmental Mgmt.*, 910 F.2d 713, 718–719 (CA11 1990), modified, 924 F.2d 1001, cert. denied, 501 U.S. 1206 (1991).

cement to ensure structural integrity, *Hale* v. *Bimco Trading, Inc.*, 306 U.S. 375, 379–380, 83 L. Ed. 771, 59 S. Ct. 526 (1939). For in all of these cases, "a presumably legitimate goal was sought to be achieved by the illegitimate means of isolating the State from the national economy." *Philadelphia* v. *New Jersey, supra*, at 627.

The Act's additional fee facially discriminates against hazardous waste generated in States other than Alabama, and the Act overall has plainly discouraged the full operation of petitioner's Emelle facility.[4] Such burdensome taxes imposed on interstate commerce alone are generally forbidden: "[A] State may not tax a transaction or incident more heavily when it crosses state lines than when it occurs entirely within the State." *Armco Inc.* v. *Hardesty*, 467 U.S. 638, 642, 81 L. Ed. 2d 540, 104 S. Ct. 2620 (1984); see also *Walling* v. *Michigan*, 116 U.S. 446, 455, 29 L. Ed. 691, 6 S. Ct. 454 (1886); *Guy* v. *Baltimore*, 100 U.S. 434, 439, 25 L. Ed. 743 (1880). Once a state tax is found to discriminate against out-of-state commerce, it is typically struck down without further inquiry. See, *e.g., Westinghouse Electric Corp.* v. *Tully*, 466 U.S. 388, 406–407, 80 L. Ed. 2d 388, 104 S. Ct. 1856 (1984); *Maryland* v. *Louisiana*, 451 U.S. 725, 759–760, 68 L. Ed. 2d 576, 101 S. Ct. 2114 (1981); *Boston Stock Exchange* v. *State Tax Comm'n*, 429 U.S. 318, 336–337, 50 L. Ed. 2d 514, 97 S. Ct. 599 (1977).

The State, however, argues that the additional fee imposed on out-of-state hazardous waste serves legitimate local purposes related to its citizens' health and safety. Because the additional fee discriminates both on its face and in practical effect, the burden falls on the State "to justify it both in terms of the local benefits flowing from the statute and the unavailability of nondiscriminatory alternatives adequate to preserve the local interests at stake." *Hunt* v. *Washington State Apple Advertising Comm'n*, 432 U.S. 333, 353, 53 L. Ed. 2d 383, 97 S. Ct. 2434 (1977); see also *Fort Gratiot Sanitary Landfill*, 504 U.S. at 359; *New Energy Co., supra*, at 278–279. "At a minimum such facial discrimination invokes the strictest scrutiny of any purported legitimate local purpose and of the absence of nondiscriminatory alternatives." *Hughes* v. *Oklahoma*, 441 U.S. 322, 337, 60 L. Ed. 2d 250, 99 S. Ct. 1727 (1979).[5]

The State's argument here does not significantly differ from the Alabama Supreme Court's conclusions on the legitimate local purposes of the additional fee imposed, which were:

"The Additional Fee serves these legitimate local purposes that cannot be adequately served by reasonable nondiscriminatory alternatives:

(1) protection of the health and safety of the citizens of Alabama from toxic substances;
(2) conservation of the environment and the state's natural resources;
(3) provision for compensatory revenue for the costs and burdens that out-of-state waste generators impose by dumping their hazardous waste in Alabama;

---

4. The Act went into effect July 15, 1990. The volume of hazardous waste buried at the Emelle facility fell dramatically from 791,000 tons in 1989 to 290,000 tons in 1991.

5. To some extent the State attempts to avail itself of the more flexible approach outlined in, *e.g., Brown-Forman Distillers Corp.* v. *New York State Liquor Authority*, 476 U.S. 573, 579, 90 L. Ed. 2d 552, 106 S. Ct. 2080 (1986), and *Pike* v. *Bruce Church, Inc.*, 397 U.S. 137, 142, 25 L. Ed. 2d 174, 90 S. Ct. 844 (1970), but this lesser scrutiny is only available "where other legislative objectives are

credibly advanced *and* there is *no* patent discrimination against interstate trade." *Philadelphia* v. *New Jersey*, 437 U.S. at 624 (emphasis added). We find no room here to say that the Act presents "effects upon interstate commerce that are only incidental," *ibid.* for the Act's additional fee on its face targets *only* out-of-state hazardous waste. While no "clear line" separates close cases on which scrutiny should apply, "this is not a close case." *Wyoming* v. *Oklahoma*, 502 U.S. 437, 455, n. 12, 117 L. Ed. 2d 1, 112 S. Ct. 789 (1992).

(4) reduction of the overall flow of wastes traveling on the state's highways, which flow creates a great risk to the health and safety of the state's citizens." 584 So. 2d at 1389.

These may all be legitimate local interests, and petitioner has not attacked them. But only rhetoric, and not explanation, emerges as to why Alabama targets *only* interstate hazardous waste to meet these goals. As found by the trial court, "although the Legislature imposed an additional fee of $72.00 per ton on waste generated outside Alabama, there is absolutely no evidence before this Court that waste generated outside Alabama is more dangerous than waste generated in Alabama. The Court finds under the facts of this case that the only basis for the additional fee is the origin of the waste." App. to Pet. for Cert. 83a–84a. In the face of such findings, invalidity under the Commerce Clause necessarily follows, for "whatever [Alabama's] ultimate purpose, it may not be accomplished by discriminating against articles of commerce coming from outside the State unless there is some reason, apart from their origin, to treat them differently." *Philadelphia* v. *New Jersey*, 437 U.S. at 626–627; see *New*

Energy Co., 486 U.S. at 279–280. The burden is on the State to show that "the *discrimination* is demonstrably justified by a valid factor unrelated to economic protectionism,"[6] *Wyoming* v. *Oklahoma*, 502 U.S. 437, 454, 117 L. Ed. 2d 1, 112 S. Ct. 789 (1992) (emphasis added), and it has not carried this burden. Cf. *Fort Gratiot Sanitary Landfill, post*, at 361.

Ultimately, the State's concern focuses on the volume of the waste entering the Emelle facility.[7] Less discriminatory alternatives, however, are available to alleviate this concern, not the least of which are a generally applicable per-ton additional fee on *all* hazardous waste disposed of within Alabama, cf. *Commonwealth Edison Co.* v. *Montana*, 453 U.S. 609, 619, 69 L. Ed. 2d 884, 101 S. Ct. 2946 (1981), or a per-mile tax on *all* vehicles transporting hazardous waste across Alabama roads, cf. *American Trucking Assns., Inc.* v. *Scheiner*, 483 U.S. 266, 286, 97 L. Ed. 2d 226, 107 S. Ct. 2829 (1987), or an evenhanded cap on the total tonnage landfilled at Emelle, see *Philadelphia* v. *New Jersey, supra*, at 626, which would curtail volume from all sources.[8] To the extent

---

6. The Alabama Supreme Court found no "economic protectionism" here, and thus purported to distinguish *Philadelphia* v. *New Jersey*, based on its conclusions that the legislature was motivated by public health and environmental concerns. 584 So. 2d 1367, 1388–1389 (1991). This narrow focus on the intended consequence of the additional fee does not conform to our precedents, for "[a] finding that state legislation constitutes 'economic protectionism' may be made on the basis of either discriminatory purpose, see *Hunt* v. *Washington Apple Advertising Comm'n.*, 432 U.S. 333, 352–353, 53 L. Ed. 2d 383, 97 S. Ct. 2434 (1977), or discriminatory effect, see *Philadelphia* v. *New Jersey, supra*." *Bacchus Imports, Ltd.* v. *Dias*, 468 U.S. 263, 270, 82 L. Ed. 2d 200, 104 S. Ct. 3049 (1984). The "virtually *per se* rule of invalidity," *Philadelphia* v. *New Jersey, supra*, at 624, applies "not only to laws motivated solely by a desire to protect local industries from out-of-state competition, but also to laws that respond to legitimate local concerns by discriminating arbitrarily against interstate trade."

Maine v. *Taylor*, 477 U.S. 131, 148, n. 19, 91 L. Ed. 2d 110, 106 S. Ct. 2440 (1986).

7. "The risk created by hazardous waste and other similarly dangerous waste materials is proportional to the *volume* of such waste materials present, and may be controlled by controlling that volume." Brief for Respondents 38 (citation omitted; emphasis in original).

8. The State asserts: "An equal fee, at any level, would necessarily fail to serve the State's purpose. An equal fee high enough to provide any significant deterrent to the importation of hazardous waste for landfilling in the State would amount to an attempt by the State to avoid its responsibility to deal with its own problems, by tending to cause in-state waste to be exported for disposal. An equal fee not so high as to amount to an attempt to force Alabama's own problems to be borne by citizens of other states would fail to provide any significant reduction in the enormous volumes of imported hazardous waste being dumped in the State. At the point where an equal fee would become effective to

Alabama's concern touches environmental conservation and the health and safety of its citizens, such concern does not vary with the point of origin of the waste, and it remains within the State's power to monitor and regulate more closely the transportation and disposal of *all* hazardous waste within its borders. Even with the possible future financial and environmental risks to be borne by Alabama, such risks likewise do not vary with the waste's State of origin in a way allowing foreign, but not local, waste to be burdened.[9] In sum, we find the additional fee to be "an obvious effort to saddle those outside the State" with most of the burden of slowing the flow of waste into the Emelle facility. *Philadelphia* v. *New Jersey*, 437 U.S. at 629. "That legislative effort is clearly impermissible under the Commerce Clause of the Constitution." *Ibid.*

Our decisions regarding quarantine laws do not counsel a different conclusion. The Act's additional fee may not legitimately be deemed a quarantine law because Alabama permits both the generation and landfilling of hazardous waste within its borders and the importation of still more hazardous waste subject to payment of the additional fee. In any event, while it is true that certain quarantine laws have not been considered forbidden protectionist measures, even though directed against out-of-state commerce, those laws "did not discriminate against interstate commerce as such, but simply prevented traffic in noxious articles, whatever their origin." *Philadelphia* v. *New Jersey, supra*, at 629.[11] As the Court stated in *Guy* v. *Baltimore*, 100 U.S. at 443: "In the exercise of its police powers, a State may exclude from its territory, or prohibit the sale therein of any

---

serve the State's purpose in protecting public health and the environment from uncontrolled volumes of imported waste, that equal fee would also become an avoidance of the State's responsibility to deal with its own waste problems." *Id.*, at 46. These assertions are without record support and in any event do not suffice to validate plain discrimination against interstate commerce. See *New Energy Co. of Ind.* v. *Limbach*, 486 U.S. 269, 280, 100 L. Ed. 2d 302, 108 S. Ct. 1803 (1988); *Hale* v. *Bimco Trading, Inc.*, 306 U.S. 375, 380, 83 L. Ed. 771, 59 S. Ct. 526 (1939): "That no Florida cement needs any inspection while all foreign cement requires inspection at a cost of fifteen cents per hundredweight is too violent an assumption to justify the discrimination here disclosed." The additional fee is certainly not a "'last ditch' attempt" to meet Alabama's expressed purposes "after nondiscriminatory alternatives have proved unfeasible. It is rather a choice of the most discriminatory [tax] even though nondiscriminatory alternatives would seem likely to fulfill the State's purported legitimate local purposemore effectively." *Hughes* v. *Oklahoma*, 441 U.S. 322, 338, 60 L. Ed. 2d 250, 99 S. Ct. 1727 (1979).
9. The State presents no argument here, as it did below, that the additional fee makes out-of-state generators pay their "fair share" of the costs of Alabama waste disposal facilities, or that the additional fee is justified as a "compensatory tax." The trial court rejected these arguments, App. to Pet.

for Cert. 88a, n. 6, finding the former foreclosed by *American Trucking Assns. Inc.* v. *Scheiner*, 483 U.S. 266, 287–289, 97 L. Ed. 2d 226, 107 S. Ct. 2829 (1987), and the latter to be factually unsupported by a requisite "substantially equivalent" tax imposed solely on in-state waste, as required by, *e.g., Tyler Pipe Industries, Inc.* v. *Washington State Dept. of Revenue*, 483 U.S. 232, 242–244, 107 S. Ct. 2810, 97 L. Ed. 2d 199 (1987). Various *amici* assert that the discrimination patent in the Act's additional fee is consistent with congressional authorization. We pretermit this issue, for it was not the basis for the decision below and has not been briefed or argued by the parties here.
11. "The hostility is to the thing itself, not to merely interstate shipments of the thing; and an undiscriminating hostility is at least nondiscriminatory. But that is not the case here. The State of Illinois is quite willing to allow the storage and even the shipment for storage of spent nuclear fuel in Illinois, provided only that its origin is intrastate." *Illinois* v. *General Elec. Co.*, 683 F.2d 206, 214 (CA7 1982), cert. denied, 461 U.S. 913, 77 L. Ed. 2d 282, 103 S. Ct. 1891 (1983); cf. *Oregon-Washington Co.* v. *Washington*, 270 U.S. at 96: Inspection followed by quarantine of hay from fields infested with weevils is "a real quarantine law, and not a mere inhibition against importation of alfalfa from a large part of the country without regard to the condition which might make its importation dangerous."

articles which, in its judgment, fairly exercised, are prejudicial to the health or which would endanger the lives or property of its people. But if the State, under the guise of exerting its police powers, should make such exclusion or prohibition applicable solely to articles, of that kind, that may be produced or manufactured in other States, the courts would find no difficulty in holding such legislation to be in conflict with the Constitution of the United States."

See also *Reid* v. *Colorado*, 187 U.S. 137, 151, 47 L. Ed. 108, 23 S. Ct. 92 (1902); *Railroad Co.* v. *Husen*, 95 U.S. 465, 472, 24 L. Ed. 527 (1878).

The law struck down in *Philadelphia* v. *New Jersey* left local waste untouched, although no basis existed by which to distinguish interstate waste. But "if one is inherently harmful, so is the other. Yet New Jersey has banned the former while leaving its landfill sites open to the latter." 437 U.S. at 629. Here, the additional fee applies only to interstate hazardous waste, but at all points from its entrance into Alabama until it is landfilled at the Emelle facility, every concern related to quarantine applies perforce to local hazardous waste, which pays no additional fee. For this reason, the additional fee does not survive the appropriate scrutiny applicable to discriminations against interstate commerce.

Maine v. *Taylor*, 477 U.S. 131, 91 L. Ed. 2d 110, 106 S. Ct. 2440 (1986), provides no additional justification. Maine there demonstrated that the out-of-state baitfish were subject to parasites foreign to in-state baitfish. This difference posed a threat to the State's natural resources, and absent a less discriminatory means of protecting the environment—and none was available—the importation of baitfish could properly be banned. *Id.*, at 140. To the contrary, the record establishes that the hazardous waste at issue in this case is the same regardless of its point of origin. As noted in *Fort Gratiot Sanitary Landfill*, "our conclusion would be different if the imported waste raised health or other concerns not presented by [Alabama] waste." *Post*, at 367. Because no unique threat is posed, and because adequate means other than overt discrimination meet Alabama's concerns, *Maine* v. *Taylor* provides the State no respite.

III

The decision of the Alabama Supreme Court is reversed, and the cause is remanded for proceedings not inconsistent with this opinion, including consideration of the appropriate relief to petitioner. See *McKesson Corp.* v. *Division of Alcoholic Beverages and Tobacco, Fla. Dept. of Business Regulations*, 496 U.S. 18, 31, 110 S. Ct. 2238, 110 L. Ed. 2d 17 (1990); *Tyler Pipe Industries, Inc.* v. *Washington State Dept. of Revenue*, 483 U.S. 232, 251–253, 107 S. Ct. 2810, 97 L. Ed. 2d 199 (1987).

So ordered.

CHIEF JUSTICE REHNQUIST, DISSENTING:

I have already had occasion to set out my view that States need not ban all waste disposal as a precondition to protecting themselves from hazardous or noxious materials brought across the State's borders. See *Philadelphia* v. *New Jersey*, 437 U.S. 617, 629, 57 L. Ed. 2d 475, 98 S. Ct. 2531 (1978) (REHNQUIST, J., dissenting). In a case also decided today, I express my further view that States may take actions legitimately directed at the preservation of the State's natural resources, even if those actions incidentally work to disadvantage some out-of-state waste generators. See *Fort Gratiot Sanitary Landfill, Inc.* v. *Michigan Dept. of Natural Resources*, 504 U.S. 353, 368 (1992) (REHNQUIST, C. J., dissenting). I dissent today, largely for the reasons I have set out in those two cases. Several additional comments that pertain specifically to this case, though, are in order.

Taxes are a recognized and effective means for discouraging the consumption of scarce commodities—in this case the safe environment that attends appropriate disposal of hazardous wastes. Cf. 26 U. S. C. §§4681, 4682 (1988 ed., Supp. III) (tax on ozone-depleting chemicals); 26 U. S. C. §4064 (gas guzzler excise tax). I therefore see nothing unconstitutional in Alabama's use of a tax to discourage the export of this commodity to other States, when the commodity is a public good that Alabama has helped to produce. Cf. *Fort Gratiot*, 504 U.S. at 372 (REHNQUIST, C. J., dissenting). Nor do I see any significance in the fact that Alabama has chosen to adopt a differential tax rather than an outright ban. Nothing in the Commerce Clause requires Alabama to adopt an "all or nothing" regulatory approach to noxious materials coming from without the State. See *Mintz* v. *Baldwin*, 289 U.S. 346, 77 L. Ed. 1245, 53 S. Ct. 611 (1933) (upholding State's *partial* ban on cattle importation).

In short, the Court continues to err by its failure to recognize that waste—in this case admittedly *hazardous* waste—presents risks to the public health and environment that a State may legitimately wish to avoid, and that the State may pursue such an objective by means less Draconian than an outright ban. Under force of this Court's precedent, though, it increasingly appears that the only avenue by which a State may avoid the importation of hazardous wastes is to ban such waste disposal altogether, regardless of the waste's source of origin. I see little logic in creating, and nothing in the Commerce Clause that requires us to create, such perverse regulatory incentives. The Court errs in substantial measure because it refuses to acknowledge that a safe and attractive environment is the commodity really at issue in cases such as this. See *Fort Gratiot*, 504 U.S. at 369, n. (REHNQUIST, C. J., dissenting). The result is that the Court today gets it exactly backward when it suggests that Alabama is attempting to "isolate itself from a

problem common to the several States." *Ante*, at 339. To the contrary, it is the 34 States that have no hazardous waste facility whatsoever, not to mention the remaining 15 States with facilities all smaller than Emelle, that have isolated themselves.

There is some solace to be taken in the Court's conclusion, *ante*, at 344–345, that Alabama may impose a substantial fee on the disposal of all hazardous waste, or a per-mile fee on all vehicles transporting such waste, or a cap on total disposals at the Emelle facility. None of these approaches provide Alabama the ability to tailor its regulations in a way that the State will be solving only that portion of the problem that it has created. See *Fort Gratiot*, 504 U.S. at 370–371 (REHNQUIST, C. J., dissenting). But they do at least give Alabama some mechanisms for requiring waste-generating States to compensate Alabama for the risks the Court declares Alabama must run.

Of course, the costs of any of the proposals that the Court today approves will be less than fairly apportioned. For example, should Alabama adopt a flat transportation or disposal tax, Alabama citizens will be forced to pay a disposal tax equal to that faced by dumpers from outside the State. As the Court acknowledges, such taxes are a permissible effort to recoup compensation for the risks imposed on the State. Yet Alabama's general tax revenues presumably already support the State's various inspection and regulatory efforts designed to ensure the Emelle facility's safe operation. Thus, Alabamians will be made to pay twice, once through general taxation and a second time through a specific disposal fee. Permitting differential taxation would, in part, do no more than recognize that, having been made to bear all the risks from such hazardous waste sites, Alabama should not in addition be made to pay *more* than others in supporting activities that will help to minimize the risk.

Other mechanisms also appear open to Alabama to achieve results similar to those that are seemingly foreclosed today. There seems to be nothing, for example, that would prevent Alabama from providing subsidies or other tax breaks to domestic industries that generate hazardous wastes. Or Alabama may, under the market participant doctrine, open its own facility catering only to Alabama customers. See, *e.g., White* v. *Massachusetts Council of Constr. Employers, Inc.*, 460 U.S. 204, 206–208, 75 L. Ed. 2d 1, 103 S. Ct. 1042 (1983); *Reeves, Inc.* v. *Stake*, 447 U.S. 429, 436–437, 65 L. Ed. 2d 244, 100 S. Ct. 2271 (1980); *Hughes* v. *Alexandria Scrap Corp.*, 426 U.S. 794, 810, 49 L. Ed. 2d 220, 96 S. Ct. 2488 (1976). But certainly we have lost our way when we require States to perform such gymnastics, when such performances will in turn produce little difference in ultimate effects. In sum, the only sure by-product of today's decision is additional litigation. Assuming that those States that are currently the targets for large volumes of hazardous waste do not simply ban hazardous waste sites altogether, they will undoubtedly continue to search for a way to limit their risk from sites in operation. And each new arrangement will generate a new legal challenge, one that will work to the principal advantage only of those States that refuse to contribute to a solution.

For the foregoing reasons, I respectfully dissent.

■ NOTES

1. For a discussion of Waste Management's transition from the garbage collection business to the business of hauling and disposing of hazardous waste, see Charles G. Burk (1980) "There's Big Business in All that Garbage," *Fortune*, April 7.

2. Is Chief Justice Rehnquist's quarrel with the majority's application of the dormant commerce clause to this case, or with the concept of the dormant commerce clause itself? How persuasive is his argument that the citizens of Alabama should be able to impose the disproportionate tax because they pay for the regulatory infrastructure to deal with the wastes? Are there ways of addressing that concern that do not discriminate against interstate commerce?

3. Could Congress authorize the states to exclude out-of-state wastes from their hazardous waste facilities? (Recall the "interstate compact" system created to deal with low-level nuclear waste, as discussed in *New York v. U.S.* in chapter 5.) Even without authorization from Congress, could a state exclude out-of-state waste from a facility that was state owned and state financed?

4. The Emelle, Alabama, landfill is one example cited by those in what has come to be called the "environmental justice" movement in their call for a greater concern for socioeconomic equity in the siting of facilities posing public health and environmental risks. That the largest active hazardous waste landfill in the country is located in a relatively poor area such as Emelle, they say, is no mere coincidence. In fact, the apparent inequity of this situation was one of the arguments cited by those seeking new hazardous waste facilities in the Northeast. Without new capacity closer to home,

they argued, companies in the Northeast would have to ship more of their wastes to
Emelle.   ▪

B. THE RESOURCE CONSERVATION AND RECOVERY ACT (SOLID WASTE DISPOSAL ACT)

The primary federal statute for the regulation of hazardous waste is officially known
as the Solid Waste Disposal Act. As originally enacted in 1965, the statute provided
federal assistance to municipalities to aid them in the transition from open dumps to
"sanitary landfills" for the disposal of solid waste. In 1970, the year of the first Earth
Day, Congress amended the statute with the Resource Conservation and Recovery
Act. The 1970 act called for a number of studies on the recovery and reuse of solid
waste, and for a series of studies on the nation's hazardous waste management practices. Based in part on the results of these studies, Congress completely revised the
statute with the Resource Conservation and Recovery Act (RCRA) Amendments of
1976, which added a principal focus on the regulation of hazardous waste. The statute has been more commonly known as RCRA since that time.

1. The History and Development of the Federal Regulations

The 1976 amendments gave EPA until mid-1978 to promulgate regulations implementing the hazardous waste provisions that comprised the new Subtitle C of
RCRA. The agency did not meet its deadline, and in October 1978, shortly after the
situation at Love Canal had risen to national prominence, a subcommittee of
the House Interstate and Commerce Committee began a series of hearings on hazardous waste. The subcommittee released a report in October 1979 condemning
both government and industry for enumerated lapses in hazardous waste management, and calling for the expeditious promulgation of comprehensive RCRA regulations. Meanwhile, environmental groups joined the state of Illinois in bringing suit to
compel EPA to issue the regulations, and a court-imposed deadline followed. That
deadline was missed as well, but in the spring of 1980 EPA was ready to propose its
comprehensive RCRA regulations. However, even this long-awaited event was not
without its mishaps.

The site chosen for the unveiling, a chemical waste dump in New Jersey, had to be changed
when the dump blew up shortly before the invited dignitaries and the press were scheduled to
arrive. [Mary Worobec (1980) "An Analysis of the Resource Conservation and Recovery
Act," *Environment Reporter*, Special Report, Part II, p. 7]

Unfortunately, this proved to be a fitting metaphor for EPA's experience with the
hazardous waste issue over the next 4 years.

[handwritten: interesting how people act when it is something they see]

As had been noted by then-EPA Administrator Douglas M. Costle a few months earlier (reportedly in October 1979), public pressure for a more aggressive approach to hazardous waste had been mounting:

The ticking time bombs were primed. Then Love Canal went off, followed by other explosions around the country. Industry's failings—both careless and callous—were exposed. Government's shortcomings also became evident. The public is concerned and frightened, and it is demanding action. (id. at 5)

However, while EPA's 1980 regulations did contain the basics of the "cradle-to-grave" hazardous waste management program discussed in this chapter, the agency's implementation of those regulations lagged far behind public expectations. The new EPA administrator, Anne M. Gorsuch (later Anne Gorsuch Burford), came into office in 1981 as a champion of newly elected President Reagan's deregulatory agenda, and she slowed the agency's fledgling hazardous waste activities to a virtual crawl. *[handwritten: Reagan EPA]* By 1982, EPA had not yet established permitting requirements for hazardous waste treatment and disposal facilities, and had cut back on the implementation of other regulations. See, e.g., Marjorie Sun (1982) "EPA Relaxes Hazardous Waste Rules," *Science* 216, April 16, p. 275. Nor had the agency taken action to discourage the disposal of hazardous waste in landfills, even though many were operated without liners. See, e.g., "Panel Told All Landfills Leak, EPA Rules on Hazardous Waste Land Disposal Inadequate," *Environment Reporter* 13: 1276 (1982). Predictably, this incurred the wrath of many in Congress. "The Administration has set disgracefully low goals for itself," stated then-Senator James Florio of New Jersey in 1982, "and it is meeting them" (Marjorie Sun, "EPA Relaxes Rules").

The congressional reaction culminated 2 years later in the passage of the Hazardous and Solid Waste Amendments of 1984, which dramatically changed RCRA in several important respects. While the 1976 act had set broad general standards, and had largely left it to EPA to formulate the specific regulations to implement those standards, the 1984 amendments gave the agency a series of rather specific directives, and imposed a clear timetable for their implementation. Perhaps the most prominent feature of the 1984 revisions were the so-called land-ban provisions, which effectively prohibit the land disposal of certain specified wastes unless EPA has promulgated regulations specifying health-based treatment standards that must be met before the wastes may be placed in a landfill. For the purpose of these provisions, Congress divided hazardous wastes into five categories: a group of specified solvents and dioxins; a group of specified wastes known as the "California wastes"; and a long list of wastes to be divided into thirds, which are known as the "first-third," "second-third," and "third-third" wastes, respectively. Then, beginning with the solvent and dioxin wastes and moving in order through the five categories, Congress specified a date by which the land disposal of any waste within that category would be illegal unless either (1) EPA had promulgated treatment standards for that waste and those standards were met prior to land disposal, or (2) the person seeking to dispose of the wastes could prove that land disposal would be protective of human health and the environment. See RCRA Section 3004(d) (California wastes), (e) (solvents and dioxins), and (g) (First, Second, and Third-Third wastes), 42 U.S.C. §§6924(d), (e), and (g). With these land-ban provisions, Congress brought about a veritable sea change in hazardous waste disposal practices, which up until then had involved little more than simple landfilling.

■ **NOTES**

1. What incentive did the land-ban provisions create for hazardous waste-generating industries with regard to EPA's promulgation of treatment standards for the land disposal of their wastes? The nature of these treatment standards, and their practical relationship to the land-ban provisions, are discussed in more detail later in this chapter.

2. Note that the land-ban provisions share a set of common features with the 1977 revisions to the toxic pollutant provisions of Section 307 of the Clean Water Act and the 1990 revisions to the hazardous air pollutant provisions of Section 112 of the Clean Air Act. In all three cases, Congress moved away from giving a general grant of authority to EPA to formulate regulations at its discretion, and instead imposed a set of specific directives that were to be accomplished according to a specified timetable.

3. Although they kept the basic structure of RCRA intact, the 1984 amendments were an extensive rewrite of the act. In general, they added stringency and specificity throughout the statute, especially in the Subtitle C provisions for hazardous wastes. Among other things, the 1984 amendments banned the landfilling of noncontainerized liquid hazardous wastes; imposed new restrictions on hazardous waste treatment, storage, and disposal facilities; strengthened the financial responsibility requirements for these facilities; strengthened the act's enforcement provisions; placed provisions in the act designed to encourage waste minimization; and created a program to clean up leaking underground storage tanks. For a comprehensive description of the various changes introduced by the 1984 amendments, see U.S. Environmental Protection Agency, EPA Staff Summary of 1984 Amendments to Resource Conservation and Recovery Act (Oct. 9, 1984), reprinted at *Environment Reporter* 15: 1136 (1984).

4. One of the changes EPA sought, and was given, in the 1984 amendments was authorization for the attorney general to deputize EPA employees to act as special U.S. marshals in RCRA criminal investigations. This authority came after EPA rep-

resentatives testified at congressional hearings about the experiences of agency field personnel in attempting to investigate hazardous waste violations. Among the stories told at these hearings were those of the EPA inspector in Ohio who was told that "guys with jobs like yours can get shot," and the target of a hazardous waste investigation in Oregon who attempted to discourage his employees from cooperating with investigators by "threaten[ing] to cut up and stuff disloyal employees into [a] 55 gallon drum" ["EPA Asks for Firearm, Arrest Power; Violence Seen in Environmental Enforcement," *Environment Reporter* 14: 578 (1983)].

2.   The Broad Impact: A Federal "Tax" on Hazardous Waste Generation

Before we delve into the details of RCRA's regulatory system, it is useful to pause for a moment to consider the broader picture. Unlike the Clean Air Act and the Clean Water Act, RCRA does not place limits on the quantities or concentrations of hazardous residues that may be discharged from waste-generating facilities. Rather, RCRA's approach has simply been to impose conditions designed to ensure that the handling, transportation, and disposal of hazardous waste is done safely. Indeed, as long as one complies with the various conditions imposed by RCRA, one may ship as much hazardous waste for disposal (and keep as much for on-site disposal) as one chooses. It would be wrong to conclude from this, however, that RCRA has had no effect on the generation of hazardous waste. The conditions imposed by RCRA come with a price tag, and—as the conditions have become more stringent—that price tag has grown over time.

One way of thinking of RCRA, then, is as a federal tax on the generation of hazardous waste. The analogy is not a perfect one, of course. Unlike a true tax, the amount of the charge is not set by the government, but by the market. For example, the RCRA "tax" on a waste that must be incinerated before disposal is determined by the cost of the required incineration (plus the costs of meeting any other RCRA requirements that are relevant to that waste). Nonetheless, this charge works like a tax by creating an ongoing financial incentive for the generator to reduce the amount of such waste it generates. And while the Clean Air Act, Clean Water Act, and all other environmental statutes that require the treatment of residues before disposal also create this kind of financial incentive, RCRA is distinct in that it relies on this financial incentive as the means of reducing the quantities of residues actually discharged from a regulated facility.

3.   The Regulated Materials: Solid and Hazardous Waste

Consistent with its origins as an amendment to the Solid Waste Disposal Act, RCRA regulates "solid waste." The statute places certain limitations on the disposal of any solid waste, and more stringent limitations on the handling, transportation, and disposal of those solid wastes that are classified as "hazardous."

a.   Solid Waste

The statute defines solid waste as:

> ... any garbage, refuse, sludge from a waste treatment plant, water supply treatment plant, or air pollution control facility and any other discarded material, including *solid, liquid, semisolid, or contained gaseous material* resulting from industrial, commercial, mining, and agricultural operations, and from community activities. ... [42 U.S.C. §6903(27), emphasis added]

EPA regulations state that solid waste is "any *discarded material* that is not excluded by [EPA regulation]" (40 C.F.R. §261.2, emphasis added). The regulations define "discarded material" as any material that is "abandoned," "recycled," or "inherently waste-like" (as those terms are defined in the regulations) [40 C.F.R. §261.2(a)].

The statutory definition sets forth a number of exclusions, and EPA repeats and expands upon these in its regulations. Among those materials *excluded* from the definition of "solid waste" under EPA regulations are

1. domestic sewage, and any mixture of domestic sewage and other wastes that passes through a sewer system to a POTW;
2. industrial wastewater discharges that are point source discharges subject to regulation under Section 402 (the permitting section) of the Clean Water Act;
3. irrigation return flows;
4. radioactive materials regulated under the Atomic Energy Act;
5. materials subjected to in situ mining techniques that are not removed from the ground as part of the extraction process;
6. "secondary materials that are reclaimed and returned to the original process or processes in which they were generated where they are used in the production process," provided that certain criteria are met; and
7. certain other specified recycled materials, provided that certain criteria are met [40 C.F.R. §261.4(a)].

In addition, EPA regulations specify that materials are *not* solid waste:

> when they can be shown to be recycled by being (i) Used or reused as ingredients in an industrial process to make a product, provided the materials are not being reclaimed; or (ii) Used or reused as effective substitutes for commercial products; or (iii) Returned to the original process from which they are being generated, without first being reclaimed or land disposed [so long as certain criteria are met]. [40 C.F.R. §261.2(e)]

However, such recycled materials *are* treated as solid waste if they are "used in a manner constituting disposal," "used to produce products that are applied to the land," "burned for energy recovery," "used to produce a fuel," "contained in fuels," or "accumulated speculatively." (Regulations governing the management of hazardous recyclable material "used in a manner constituting disposal" are found at 40 C.F.R. §266.) In the *American Petroleum Institute* case excerpted later in this chapter, the D.C. Circuit Court of Appeals draws a distinction between materials that are reclaimed and reused in the industrial process from which they were generated, and those that are reclaimed and used as an input to another process at another facility. Consistent with exemption (6) from the list above, the former are not treated as waste but the latter are.

b. Hazardous Waste

"Hazardous" wastes are a subset of solid wastes (i.e., if a material is not a solid waste, it cannot be a hazardous waste). The differentiation between hazardous wastes and other solid wastes is significant because hazardous wastes are subject to more stringent regulations. Section 3001 of RCRA sets forth requirements for the identification and listing of hazardous wastes. In general, a solid waste is "hazardous" under RCRA if it falls into one or more of four categories.

i. Characteristic Waste

In the first category are the so-called characteristic hazardous wastes. In 40 C.F.R. §§261.20–24, EPA specifies four tests designed to determine whether a waste has a particular hazardous characteristic. Wastes testing positive in one (or more) of these tests are classified as hazardous under RCRA.

The first characteristic is *ignitability*. In general, a waste is deemed "ignitable" if it is a liquid with a flashpoint below 140°F (or with other severe ignitability properties), if it is an ignitable compressed gas meeting certain criteria, or if it is an oxidizer meeting certain criteria. The second characteristic is *corrosivity*. In general, a liquid waste is deemed "corrosive" if it has a pH of 2 or lower, or of 12.5 or higher, or if it meets certain other specified criteria. The third characteristic is *reactivity*. EPA's regulation sets forth a number of alternative criteria for determining whether a waste is to be deemed "reactive." The fourth and final characteristic is *toxicity*. If a waste contains one or more of a number of specified contaminants, it is deemed hazardous if the regulatory concentration level for that contaminant is exceeded upon application of the toxicity characteristic leaching procedure (TCLP) analytical test to the waste. EPA has assigned a separate hazardous waste number to each of these contaminants, and "[a] solid waste that exhibits the characteristic of toxicity has the EPA Hazardous Waste Identification Number . . . which corresponds to the toxic contaminant causing it to be hazardous" [40 CFR 261.24(b)].

ii. Criteria (Listed) Waste

40 C.F.R. §§261.30–35 contains a lengthy list of specific wastes that have been designated as "hazardous" by EPA. These are hazardous

regardless of whether they meet any of the "characteristic" tests outlined above. EPA has given each of these wastes, which are known collectively as the "criteria" wastes, a separate hazardous waste identification number.

iii. RCRA Definition Waste   Even if it is neither a characteristic nor a criteria waste, a solid waste will be hazardous if it meets the definition of "hazardous waste" set forth in Section 1004(5) of the statute, which provides as follows:

The term "hazardous waste" means a solid waste, or combination of solid wastes, which because of its quantity, concentration, or physical, chemical, or infectious characteristics may—

(A) cause, or significantly contribute to, an increase in mortality, or an increase in serious irreversible, or incapacitating reversible illness; or
(B) pose a substantial present or potential hazard to human health or the environment when improperly treated, stored, transported, or disposed of, or otherwise managed. [42 U.S.C. §6903(5)]

iv. State Definition Waste   Finally, states are free to define "hazardous waste" more expansively than Congress and EPA have done in RCRA. Section 3006 of RCRA authorizes states to administer and enforce their own hazardous waste program in lieu of RCRA if they meet and maintain a set of requirements specified by EPA. See 42 U.S.C. §6926. Where a broader definition of hazardous waste is adopted by a state that has been authorized by EPA to operate a hazardous waste program under Section 3006, wastes meeting that definition are treated as RCRA hazardous wastes within that state.

v. Ash Generated by Municipal Solid Waste Incinerators   When it promulgated its first round of hazardous waste regulations in 1980, EPA exempted certain kinds of waste from the regulatory definition of hazardous waste, even though they would otherwise qualify. Congress explicitly removed some of these regulatory exemptions in the 1984 amendments. One regulatory exemption retained by EPA after the 1984 amendments was an exemption for the ash produced by municipal resource recovery facilities—solid waste incinerators that "converted" the solid waste into energy. Apparently EPA had fashioned this exemption because it wanted to encourage the construction of such facilities, and thus did not want to impose the additional cost of hazardous waste disposal on the municipalities that operated them. The Supreme Court set the exemption aside in 1994.

City of Chicago v. Environmental Defense Fund
Justice SCALIA delivered the opinion of the Court
United States Supreme Court
511 U.S. 328 (1994)

We are called upon to decide whether, pursuant to §3001(i) of the Solid Waste Disposal Act (Resource Conservation and Recovery Act of 1976 (RCRA)), as added, 98 Stat. 3252, 42 U.S.C. §6921(i), the ash generated by a resource recovery facility's incineration of municipal solid waste is exempt from regulation as a hazardous waste under Subtitle C of RCRA.

I

Since 1971, petitioner City of Chicago has owned and operated a municipal incinerator, the Northwest Waste-to-Energy Facility, that burns solid waste and recovers energy, leaving a residue of municipal waste combustion (MWC) ash. The facility burns approximately 350,000 tons of solid waste each year and produces energy that is both used within the facility and sold to other entities. The city has disposed of the combustion residue—110,000 to 140,000 tons of MWC ash per year—at landfills that are not licensed to accept hazardous wastes.

In 1988, respondent Environmental Defense Fund (EDF) filed a complaint against petitioners, the City of Chicago and its mayor, under the citizen suit provisions of RCRA, 42 U.S.C. §6972, alleging that they were violating provisions of RCRA and of implementing regulations issued by the Environmental Protection Agency (EPA). Respondent alleged that the MWC ash generated by the facility was toxic enough to qualify as a "hazardous waste" under EPA's regulations, 40 CFR pt. 261 (1993). It was uncontested that, with respect to the ash, petitioners had not adhered to any of the requirements of Subtitle C, the portion of RCRA addressing hazardous wastes. Petitioners contended that RCRA §3001(i), 42 U.S.C. §6921(i), excluded the MWC ash from those requirements. The District Court agreed with that contention, see *Environmental Defense Fund, Inc.* v. *Chicago*, 727 F. Supp. 419, 424 (1989), and subsequently granted petitioners' motion for summary judgment.

The Court of Appeals reversed, concluding that the "ash generated from the incinerators of municipal resource recovery facilities is subject to regulation as a hazardous waste under Subtitle C of RCRA." *Environmental Defense Fund, Inc.* v. *Chicago*, 948 F.2d 345, 352 (CA7 1991). The city petitioned for a writ of certiorari, and we invited the Solicitor General to present the views of the United States. *Chicago* v. *Environmental Defense Fund, Inc.*, 504 U.S. 906, 118 L. Ed. 2d 539, 112 S. Ct. 1932 (1992). On September 18, 1992, while that invitation was outstanding, the Administrator of EPA issued a memorandum to EPA Regional Administrators, directing them, in accordance with the agency's view of §3001(i), to treat MWC ash as exempt from hazardous waste regulation under Subtitle C of RCRA. Thereafter, we granted the city's petition, vacated the decision, and remanded the case to the Court of Appeals for the Seventh Circuit for further consideration in light of the memorandum. *Chicago* v. *Environmental Defense Fund*, 506 U.S. 982, 121 L. Ed. 2d 426, 113 S. Ct. 486 (1992).

On remand, the Court of Appeals reinstated its previous opinion, holding that, because the statute's plain language is dispositive, the EPA memorandum did not affect its analysis. 985 F.2d 303, 304 (CA7 1993).

Petitioners filed a petition for writ of certiorari, which we granted. 509 U.S. 903 (1993).

II

RCRA is a comprehensive environmental statute that empowers EPA to regulate hazardous wastes from cradle to grave, in accordance with the rigorous safeguards and waste management procedures of Subtitle C, 42 U.S.C. §§6921–6934. (Nonhazardous wastes are regulated much more loosely under Subtitle D, 42 U.S.C. §§6941–6949.) Under the relevant provisions of Subtitle C, EPA has promulgated standards governing hazardous waste generators and transporters, see 42 U.S.C. §§6922 and 6923, and owners and operators of hazardous waste treatment, storage, and disposal facilities (TSDF's), see §6924. Pursuant to §6922, EPA has directed hazardous waste generators to comply with handling, recordkeeping, storage, and monitoring requirements, see 40 CFR pt. 262 (1993). TSDF's, however, are subject to much more stringent regulation than either generators or transporters, including a 4- to 5-year permitting process, see 42 U.S.C. §6925; 40 CFR pt. 270 (1993); U.S. Environmental Protection Agency Office of Solid Waste and Emergency Response, The Nation's Hazardous Waste Management Program at a Crossroads, The RCRA Implementation Study 49–50 (July 1990), burdensome financial assurance requirements, stringent design and location standards, and, perhaps most onerous of all, responsibility to take corrective action for releases of hazardous substances and to ensure safe closure of each facility, see 42 U.S.C. §6924; 40 CFR pt. 264 (1993). "[The] corrective action requirement is one of the major reasons that generators and transporters work diligently to manage their wastes so as to avoid the need to obtain interim status or a TSD permit." 3 Environmental Law Practice Guide §29.06[3]d (M. Gerrard ed. 1993) (hereinafter Practice Guide).

RCRA does not identify which wastes are hazardous and therefore subject to Subtitle C regulation; it leaves that designation to EPA. 42 U.S.C. §6921(a). When EPA's hazardous waste designations for solid wastes appeared in 1980, see 45 Fed. Reg. 33084, they contained certain exceptions from normal coverage, including an exclusion for "household waste," defined as "any waste material... derived from households (including single and multiple residences, hotels and motels)," id., at 33120, codified as amended at 40 CFR §261.4(b)(1) (1993). Although most household waste is harmless, a small portion— such as cleaning fluids and batteries—would have qualified as hazardous waste. The regulation declared, however, that "household waste, including household waste that has been collected, transported, stored, treated, disposed, recovered (e.g., refuse-derived fuel) or reused" is not hazardous waste. *Ibid.* Moreover, the preamble to the 1980 regulations stated that "residues remaining after treatment (*e.g.* incineration, thermal treatment) [of household waste] are not subject to regulation as a hazardous waste." 45 Fed. Reg. 33099. By reason of these provisions, an incinerator that burned only household waste would not be considered a Subtitle C TSDF, since it processed only nonhazardous (*i.e.*, household) waste, and it would not be considered a Subtitle C generator of hazardous waste and would be free to dispose of its ash in a Subtitle D landfill.

The 1980 regulations thus provided what is known as a "waste stream" exemption for household waste, *ibid., i.e.*, an exemption covering that category of waste from generation through treatment to final disposal of residues. The regulation did not, however, exempt MWC ash from Subtitle C coverage if the incinerator that produced the ash burned anything *in addition to* household waste, such as what petitioners' facility burns: nonhazardous industrial waste. Thus, a facility like petitioners' would qualify as a Subtitle C hazardous waste generator if the MWC ash it produced was sufficiently toxic, see 40 CFR §§261.3, 261.24 (1993)—though it would still not qualify as a Subtitle C TSDF, since all the waste it took in would be characterized as nonhazardous. (An ash can be hazardous, even though the product from which it is generated is not, because in the new medium the contaminants are more concentrated and more readily leachable, see 40 CFR §§261.3, 261.24, and pt. 261, App. II (1993).)

Four years after these regulations were issued, Congress enacted the Hazardous and Solid Waste Amendments of 1984, Pub. L. 98-616, 98 Stat. 3221, which added to RCRA the "Clarification of Household Waste Exclusion" as §3001(i), §223, 98 Stat. 3252. The essence of our task in this case is to determine whether, under that provision, the MWC ash generated by petitioners' facility—a facility that would have been considered a Subtitle C generator under the 1980 regulations—is subject to regulation as hazardous waste under Subtitle C. We conclude that it is.

Section 3001(i), 42 U.S.C. §6921(i), entitled "Clarification of household waste exclusion," provides:

"A resource recovery facility recovering energy from the mass burning of municipal solid waste shall not be deemed to be treating, storing, disposing of, or otherwise managing hazardous wastes for the purposes of regulation under this subchapter, if

"(1) such facility—
"(A) receives and burns only—
"(i) household waste (from single and multiple dwellings, hotels, motels, and other residential sources), and
"(ii) solid waste from commercial or industrial sources that does not contain hazardous waste identified or listed under this section, and

"(B) does not accept hazardous wastes identified or listed under this section, and
"(2) the owner or operator of such facility has established contractual requirements or other appropriate notification or inspection procedures to assure that hazardous wastes are not received at or burned in such facility."

The plain meaning of this language is that so long as a facility recovers energy by incineration of the appropriate wastes, it (the *facility*) is not subject to Subtitle C regulation as a facility that treats, stores, disposes of, or manages hazardous waste. The provision quite clearly does *not* contain any exclusion for the *ash itself*. Indeed, the waste the facility produces (as opposed to that which it receives) is not even mentioned. There is thus no express support for petitioners' claim of a waste-stream exemption.[1]

Petitioners contend, however, that the practical effect of the statutory language is to exempt the ash by virtue of exempting the facility. If, they argue, the facility is not deemed to be treating, storing, or disposing of hazardous waste, then the ash that it treats, stores, or disposes of must itself be considered nonhazardous. There are several problems with this argument. First, as we have explained, the only exemption provided by the terms of the statute is for the *facility*. It is the facility, *not the ash*, that "shall not be deemed" to be subject to regulation under Subtitle C. *Unlike* the preamble to the 1980 regulations, which had been in existence for four years by the time §3001(i) was enacted, §3001(i) does not explicitly exempt MWC ash generated by a resource recovery facility from regulation as a hazardous waste. In

---

1. The dissent is able to describe the provision as exempting the ash itself only by resorting to what might be called imaginative use of ellipsis: "even though the material being treated and disposed of contains hazardous components before, during, and after its treatment[,] that material 'shall not be deemed to be...hazardous'." *Post*, at 346. In the full text, quoted above, the subject of the phrase "shall not be deemed...hazardous" is *not* the ma-

terial, but the *resource recovery facility*, and the complete phrase, including (italicized) the ellipsis, reads "shall not be deemed to be *treating, storing, disposing of, or otherwise managing* hazardous *wastes*." Deeming a facility not to be engaged in these activities with respect to hazardous wastes is of course quite different from deeming the output of that facility not to be hazardous.

light of that difference, and given the statute's express declaration of national policy that "waste that is...generated should be treated, stored, or disposed of so as to minimize the present and future threat to human health and the environment," 42 U.S.C. §6902(b), we cannot interpret the statute to permit MWC ash sufficiently toxic to qualify as hazardous to be disposed of in ordinary landfills.

Moreover, as the Court of Appeals observed, the statutory language does not even exempt the *facility* in its capacity as a *generator* of hazardous waste. RCRA defines "generation" as "the act or process of producing hazardous waste." 42 U.S.C. §6903(6). There can be no question that the creation of ash by incinerating municipal waste constitutes "generation" of hazardous waste (assuming, of course, that the ash qualifies as hazardous under 42 U.S.C. §6921 and its implementing regulations, 40 CFR pt. 261 (1993)). Yet although §3001(i) states that the exempted facility "shall not be deemed to be treating, storing, disposing of, or otherwise managing hazardous wastes," it significantly omits from the catalog the word "*generating*." Petitioners say that because the activities listed as exempt encompass the full scope of the facility's operation, the failure to mention the activity of generating is insignificant. But the statute itself refutes this. Each of the three specific terms used in §3001(i)—"treating," "storing," and "disposing of"—is separately defined by RCRA,

and none covers the production of hazardous waste.[2] The fourth and less specific term ("otherwise managing") is also defined, to mean "collection, source separation, storage, transportation, processing, treatment, recovery, and disposal," 42 U.S.C. §6903(7)—just about every hazardous waste-related activity *except* generation. We think it follows from the carefully constructed text of §3001(i) that while a resource recovery facility's management activities are excluded from Subtitle C regulation, its generation of toxic ash is not.

Petitioners appeal to the legislative history of §3001(i), which includes, in the Senate Committee Report, the statement that "all waste management activities of such a facility, including the *generation*, transportation, treatment, storage and disposal of waste shall be covered by the exclusion." S. Rep. No. 98-284, p. 61 (1983) (emphasis added). But it is the statute, and not the Committee Report, which is the authoritative expression of the law, and the statute prominently *omits* reference to generation. As the Court of Appeals cogently put it: "Why should we, then, rely upon a single word in a committee report that did not result in legislation? Simply put, we shouldn't." 948 F.2d at 351.[3] Petitioners point out that the activity by which they "treat" municipal waste is the very same activity by which they "generate" MWC ash, to wit, incineration. But there is nothing extraordinary about an activity's being exempt for some purposes and nonexempt for others.

---

2. "Treatment" means "any method, technique, or process, including neutralization, designed to change the physical, chemical, or biological character or composition of any hazardous waste so as to neutralize such waste or so as to render such waste nonhazardous, safer for transport, amenable for recovery, amenable for storage, or reduced in volume. Such term includes any activity or processing designed to change the physical form or chemical composition of hazardous waste so as to render it nonhazardous." 42 U.S.C. §6903(34).

"Storage" means "the containment of hazardous waste, either on a temporary basis or for a period

of years, in such a manner as not to constitute disposal of such hazardous waste." §6903(33).

"Disposal" means "the discharge, deposit, injection, dumping, spilling, leaking, or placing of any solid waste or hazardous waste into or on any land or water so that such solid waste or hazardous waste or any constituent thereof may enter the environment or be emitted into the air or discharged into any waters." §6903(3).

3. Nothing in the dissent's somewhat lengthier discourse on §3001(i)'s legislative history, see *post*, at 343–345, convinces us that the statute's omission of the term "generation" is a scrivener's error.

The incineration here is exempt from TSDF regulation, but subject to regulation as hazardous waste generation. (As we have noted, see *supra*, at 331–332, the latter is much less onerous.)

Our interpretation is confirmed by comparing §3001(i) with another statutory exemption in RCRA. In the Superfund Amendments and Reauthorization Act of 1986, Pub. L. 99-499, §124(b), 100 Stat. 1689, Congress amended 42 U.S.C. §6921 to provide that an "owner and operator of equipment used to recover methane from a landfill shall not be deemed to be managing, generating, transporting, treating, storing, or disposing of hazardous or liquid wastes within the meaning of" Subtitle C. This provision, in contrast to §3001(i), provides a complete exemption by including the term "generating" in its list of covered activities. "It is generally presumed that Congress acts intentionally and purposely" when it "includes particular language in one section of a statute but omits it in another," *Keene Corp.* v. *United States*, 508 U.S. 200, 208, 124 L. Ed. 2d 118, 113 S. Ct. 2035 (1993) (internal quotation marks omitted). We agree with respondents that this provision "shows that Congress knew how to draft a waste stream exemption in RCRA when it wanted to." Brief for Respondents 18.

Petitioners contend that our interpretation of §3001(i) turns the provision into an "empty gesture," Brief for Petitioners 23, since even under the pre-existing regime an incinerator burning household waste and nonhazardous industrial waste was exempt from the Subtitle C TSDF provisions. If §3001(i) did not extend the waste-stream exemption to the product of such a combined household/nonhazardous-industrial treatment facility, petitioners argue, it did nothing at all. But it is not nothing to codify a household waste exemption that had previously been subject to agency revision; nor is it nothing (though petitioners may value it as less than nothing) to *restrict* the exemption that the agency previously provided—which is what the provision here achieved, by withholding all waste-stream exemption for waste processed by resource recovery facilities, even for the waste stream passing through an exclusively household waste facility.[4]

We also do not agree with petitioners' contention that our construction renders §3001(i) ineffective for its intended purpose of promoting household/nonhazardous-industrial resource recovery facilities, see 42 U.S.C. §§6902(a)(1), (10), (11), by subjecting them "to the potentially enormous expense of managing ash residue as a hazardous waste." Brief for Petitioners 20. It is simply not true that a facility which is (as our interpretation says these facilities are) a hazardous waste "generator" is also deemed to be "managing" hazardous waste under RCRA. Section 3001(i) clearly exempts these facilities from Subtitle C TSDF regulations, thus enabling them to avoid the "full brunt of EPA's enforcement efforts under RCRA." Practice Guide §29.05[1]. . . .

RCRA's twin goals of encouraging resource recovery and protecting against contamination sometimes conflict. It is not unusual for legislation to contain diverse purposes that must be reconciled, and the most reliable guide for that task is the enacted text. Here that requires us to reject the Solicitor General's plea for deference to the EPA's interpretation, cf. *Chevron U. S. A. Inc.* v. *Natural Resources Defense Council, Inc.*, 467 U.S. 837, 843–844, 81 L. Ed. 2d 694, 104 S.

---

4. We express no opinion as to the validity of EPA's household waste regulation as applied to resource recovery facilities *before* the effective date of §3001(i). Furthermore, since the statute in question addresses only resource recovery facilities, not household waste in general, we are unable to reach any conclusions concerning the validity of EPA's regulatory scheme for household wastes *not* processed by resource recovery facilities.

Ct. 2778 (1984), which goes beyond the scope of whatever ambiguity §3001(i) contains. See *John Hancock Mut. Life Ins. Co. v. Harris Trust & Sav. Bank*, 510 U.S. 86, 109, 126 L. Ed. 2d 524, 114 S. Ct. 517 (1993). Section 3001(i) simply cannot be read to contain the cost-saving waste-stream exemption petitioners seek.

For the foregoing reasons, the judgment of the Court of Appeals for the Seventh Circuit is *Affirmed*.

[Dissenting opinion by Justice STEVENS and Justice O'CONNOR omitted.]

---

4. The "Cradle-to-Grave" System for Hazardous Waste

Hazardous wastes are subject to regulation under Subtitle C (Subchapter III) of RCRA (Sections 3001–3023). These provisions, and the EPA regulations promulgated thereunder, establish what is commonly known as the "cradle-to-grave" regulatory program for hazardous waste. The basic features of this program were put in place with EPA's 1980 regulations and were strengthened by the 1984 amendments to RCRA. The cradle-to-grave program has four basic components, which are described briefly below.

a. Notification and Identification

In general, anyone who generates, transports, treats, stores, or disposes of hazardous waste above certain minimum quantities must so notify the appropriate RCRA regulatory authority (EPA or the state), and must be assigned a RCRA identification (ID) number. It is illegal to handle or manage such waste without a RCRA ID number. Further, a generator of waste is under an obligation to determine whether its waste is in fact "hazardous" under RCRA.

[handwritten margin note: "If you make haz waste, must notify"]

b. The Manifest System

All containers of hazardous waste going from a generator to a treatment, storage, or disposal facility (TSD facility, or TSD) must be accompanied by a written manifest meeting certain specifications. Section 1004(12) of RCRA defines the manifest as:

… the form used for identifying the quantity, composition, and the origin, routing, and destination of hazardous waste during its transportation from the point of generation to the point of disposal, treatment, or storage. [42 U.S.C. §6904(12)]

Each party handling the waste must sign the manifest and a copy must be retained by the generator and the TSD.

c. The Permit Program

TSD facilities that were not in existence as of November 19, 1980 (the date the relevant EPA regulation was promulgated) must have a RCRA permit. TSD facilities in operation as of that date were allowed to continue to operate as "interim status" facilities, pending issuance of a final permit. The 1984 amendments contain provisions designed to spur the issuance of final permits to these facilities (or to spur their closure, if they cannot meet the permitting requirements). The permit program is described in Section 3005 of RCRA. Permitted facilities must meet all RCRA requirements, and interim status facilities must meet certain specified minimum requirements (which are in some cases less stringent).

d. Performance and Monitoring Standards

The core substantive provisions of the cradle-to-grave program are contained in Sections 3002 through 3004 and the regulations promulgated thereunder. Section 3002 applies to generators of hazardous waste; Section 3003 to transporters of hazardous waste; and Section 3004 to treatment, storage, and disposal facilities. By far the most important of these, from a practical perspective, is Section 3004. As amended in 1984, this section not only imposes the aforementioned land-ban restrictions and hazardous waste treatment standards, but also sets forth minimum technological and other requirements for TSD facilities and details a number of other restrictions on the disposal of hazardous wastes.

Among other things, Section 3004 (and EPA's implementing regulations):

1. bans the placement of "bulk or noncontainerized liquid hazardous waste or free liquids contained in hazardous waste" in landfills [Section 3004(c)];

2. bans the placement of bulk or noncontainerized liquid hazardous wastes in salt dome formations, salt bed formations, underground mines, or caves unless EPA finds that it is "protective of human health and the environment" to do so; promulgates performance standards governing such disposal; and issues a permit to the facility performing such disposal [Section 3004(b)];

3. requires single liners, and a leachate collection system, at all *permitted* landfills (new or old), except for those portions of the landfill that were in use as of November 19, 1980, unless EPA finds that "alternative design and operating practices . . . will prevent the migration of any hazardous constituent . . . into the groundwater or surface water at any future time" [40 C.F.R. §§264.301(a) and (b)];

4. requires double liners, and a leachate collection system, at all portions added to a landfill (permitted or interim status) after January 29, 1992 [40 C.F.R. §264.301(c); 40 C.F.R. §265.301(a)];

5. requires the promulgation of air emission standards for TSDs [Section 3004(n)], which, as discussed later, EPA has done in conjunction with the issuance of MACT standards under Section 112 of the Clean Air Act;

6. establishes record-keeping, monitoring, financial responsibility, closure, and post-closure monitoring requirements for TSDs;

7. specifies that a generator becomes a TSD for RCRA purposes if it stores its waste on-site for more than 90 days; and

8. establishes minimum management, storage, and record-keeping requirements for generators who store waste onsite for less than 90 days (40 C.F.R. §262.34).

▪ NOTES

1. Although the 1980 regulations that first established the cradle-to-grave program were often maligned by the environmental movement—both for being late in coming and for being insufficiently protective of human health and the environment—their importance should not be underestimated. As Redmond H. ("Red") Clark, hazardous waste director for the Massachusetts Department of Environmental Management in the early 1980s, was fond of saying, the significance of the identification and tracking requirements imposed by these regulations was that they brought the relevant actors "within the RCRA envelope," where their actions could then be subjected to regulatory control. If it took the 1984 RCRA amendments to put the necessary "teeth" into that regulatory control, the 1980 regulations were nonetheless important for having laid the requisite groundwork.

2. Prior to the 1984 amendments, Section 3004 gave a general grant of authority to EPA and largely left it to the agency to promulgate specific requirements. The relevant statutory language, which was retained when the act was amended in 1984, is found in Section 3004(a):

Not later than [April, 1978], and after opportunity for public hearings . . . the Administrator shall promulgate regulations establishing such performance standards, applicable to owners and operators of facilities for the treatment, storage, or disposal of hazardous waste identified or listed under this subchapter, as may be necessary to protect human health and the environment. Such standards shall include . . . requirements respecting . . .

(3) . . . such operating methods, techniques, and practices as may be satisfactory to the Administrator; [and]

(4) the location, design, and construction of such treatment, storage, or disposal facilities. . . . [42 U.S.C. §6924(a)]

Using the authority provided in these provisions, could EPA, prior to 1984, have banned the disposal of (noncontainerized) liquid hazardous wastes in landfills? Could it have required liners in all landfills? Was it *required* to take one or both of these actions? What difficulties would the agency likely have encountered had it attempted one or both of these?

3. Section 3004(a)(6) requires EPA to maintain standards "requiring such additional qualifications as to ownership, continuity of operation . . . and financial responsibility . . . as may be necessary or desirable. . . ." These provisions are intended to ensure that those responsible for the TSD will have the financial wherewithal to

stand behind its performance. The act also provides that the requisite financial responsibility may be demonstrated through "insurance, guarantee, surety bond, letter of credit, or qualification as a self-insurer" [Section 3004(t)(1)], and states that "[n]o private entity shall be precluded" from authorization to operate a TSD under these requirements "where such entity can provide assurances of financial responsibility and continuity consistent with the degree and duration of risks associated with the treatment, storage, or disposal of specified hazardous waste" [Section 3004(a)]. As discussed in chapter 12, enforcement of sufficiently stringent financial responsibility requirements for the handlers of hazardous chemicals can help both to internalize the environmental risks of such substances and sustain a market for hazardous waste insurance.

4. An operating TSD facility must have a closure plan that describes how each hazardous waste management unit (e.g., each separate landfill cell) at the facility will be closed after it stops receiving wastes, and must fulfill certain "postclosure" monitoring and maintenance requirements after the unit is closed. Moreover, the owner or operator of the facility must demonstrate the requisite financial capacity to comply with all closure and postclosure requirements. See 40 C.F.R. Part 264 Subpart H.

5. As discussed in *City of Chicago v. EDF*, resource recovery (i.e., electricity-generating) incinerators that receive only household waste and nonhazardous industrial waste are exempt from Subchapter C requirements under Section 3001(i).

6. EPA has established somewhat less cumbersome regulations for the handling of "hazardous wastes that are recycled" (which are known as "recyclable materials"). 40 C.F.R. §261.6 specifies that recyclable materials "are subject to the requirements for generators, transporters, and storage facilities" to the extent set forth therein, and 40 C.F.R. Part 266 specifies management standards for certain classes of recyclable materials.

7. The 1984 amendments added certain record-keeping requirements designed to encourage generators to minimize the amount and toxicity of the wastes they generate. Section 3002(a)(6) requires generators to submit a report to EPA (or to the state, if it has been authorized to administer the RCRA program under Section 3006) once every 2 years detailing the quantities and nature of wastes it has generated, the disposition of those wastes, the efforts taken "to reduce the volume and toxicity of waste generated," and any "changes in the volume and toxicity" compared with previous years. Further, Section 3002(b) requires that the hazardous waste manifest signed by the generator contain a certification that the generator "has a program in place to reduce the volume or quantity and toxicity of such waste to the degree determined by the generator to be economically practicable."

8. As with the definition of hazardous waste, state requirements may be more stringent that those specified in RCRA (or by EPA in regulation). Where the state has

been authorized under Section 3006 to administer its own hazardous waste program in lieu of RCRA, those more stringent state regulations are enforceable in the state as RCRA standards.

9. In its 1980 regulations, EPA had exempted from the cradle-to-grave program those facilities that generated less than 1,000 kilograms (2,200 pounds) of hazardous waste per month, as long as they did not generate more than 1 kilogram per month of certain acutely hazardous wastes. At the time, EPA estimated that these "small-quantity generators" contributed less than 10% of the overall hazardous waste stream. In the 1984 amendments to RCRA, Congress endorsed the general approach of treating small-quantity generators somewhat differently, but lowered the threshold level. New Section 3001(d) directed EPA to promulgate standards for generators that generate more than 100 kilograms (220 pounds) but less than 1,000 kilograms of hazardous waste per month. Under the current regulatory program, generators whose monthly output of hazardous waste is between these amounts are called small-quantity generators. They are not obligated to meet all of the requirements applicable to large-quantity generators (those who generate more than 1,000 kilograms a month), but they are required to meet a number of requirements, including use of an assigned RCRA identification number and compliance with the land disposal restrictions discussed below.

Those who generate less than 100 kilograms of hazardous waste per month are called conditionally exempt small-quantity generators. EPA does not require these generators to meet the requirements of the cradle-to-grave program, as long as they meet the requirements set forth in 40 C.F.R. §261.5. For example, if they generate more than 1 kilogram of certain acutely hazardous wastes per month (or if they store more than 1 kilogram of such wastes on site for any period of time), they must meet the standards applicable to large-quantity generators for such wastes. For a general discussion of the regulations applicable to small-quantity generators, see U.S. EPA (2001) *Managing Your Hazardous Waste: A Guide for Small Businesses.* EPA530-K-01-005, Washington, D.C.

10. EPA has promulgated a Universal Waste Rule to specify handling and disposal requirements for certain wastes (batteries, agricultural pesticides, lamps, and equipment containing mercury) generated in small quantities by large numbers of businesses. See 40 C.F.R. §273. All generators, including conditionally exempt small-quantity generators, must comply with the Universal Waste Rule.   ∎

5. The "Land Ban" and the Hazardous Waste Treatment Standards

As noted, the centerpiece of the 1984 RCRA Amendments was a restriction on the types of wastes that may be placed into hazardous waste landfills. As set out in Section 3004, the "land-ban" concept can be divided into two parts; the first has to do with who bears the burden of uncertainties in assessing the risk of land disposal, and the second with the technologies to be used to reduce those risks.

a.   A Shift in the Burden of Proof

Under the statutory scheme as it existed prior to the 1984 amendments, the ultimate burden was on EPA to prove that any land disposal regulations it promulgated were necessary to protect human health or the environment. Under the revised Section 3004, however, land disposal of any hazardous waste listed under RCRA is prohibited

unless the Administrator [of EPA] determines the prohibition on one or more methods of land disposal of such waste is not required in order to protect human health and the environment for as long as the waste remains hazardous, taking into account (A) the long-term uncertainties associated with land disposal, (B) the goal of managing hazardous waste in an appropriate manner in the first instance, and (C) the persistence, toxicity, mobility, and propensity to bio-accumulate of such hazardous wastes and their hazardous constituents.

This language is found in Subsections (d), (e), and (g) of Section 3004, 42 U.S.C. §§6924(d)(1), (e)(1), and (g)(1). Moreover, unless the waste meets applicable EPA treatment standards, land disposal of the waste "may not be determined to be protective of human health and the environment . . . unless, upon application by an interested person, it has been demonstrated to the Administrator, to a reasonable degree of certainty, that there will be no migration of hazardous constituents [from the land disposal facility] for as long as the wastes remain hazardous" (id.). Not only does this clearly place the burden of proving the safety of land disposal of untreated wastes on the party seeking to dispose of wastes in this fashion, but it also represents a congressional assumption that migration of hazardous waste will be harmful. Given the difficulty, in most circumstances, of making the showing necessary to obviate the need to meet the treatment standards prior to utilizing land disposal, compliance with those treatment standards became the only legal option (short of not generating the waste in the first place) for most generators.

b.   The BDAT Standards

The treatment standards are described in Section 3004(m), which directs EPA to

promulgate regulations specifying those levels or methods of treatment, if any, which substantially diminish the toxicity of waste or substantially reduce the likelihood of migration of hazardous constituents from the waste so that short-term and long-term threats to human health and the environment are minimized. [42 U.S.C. §6924(m)]

Although this language unquestionably calls for health-based standards, EPA determined that because of uncertainties about the risks posed by various wastes in various types of landfills, it would instead set technology-based standards that seek to ensure no migration of the waste from the land disposal facility. Thus, the agency has promulgated a series of what it terms "best demonstrated available technology" (BDAT) standards. These standards are a mixture of performance and specification standards. Usually they offer a choice: Either (1) meet specified performance levels deemed achievable through the use of a treatment technology that has been designated BDAT (e.g., reduce the concentration of the hazardous constituent to below a specified level), or (2) actually use the designated BDAT treatment technology (e.g., incinerate the waste at a specified temperature and under specified conditions). Sometimes, however, application of the designated technology is required. As a group, these BDAT standards are commonly known as the land disposal restrictions, or LDRs.

EPA promulgated the BDAT standards in accordance with the timetable specified by Congress: the standards for the specified solvent and dioxin wastes on November 8, 1986; the standards for the California wastes on July 8, 1987; and the standards for the first-third, second-third, and third-third wastes on August 8, 1988, June 8, 1989, and May 8, 1990, respectively. The regulations were subjected to a variety of court challenges, but were largely upheld. Perhaps the most significant of these challenges, because it went to the very heart of the congressional land-ban scheme, was brought against EPA's regulations for the first-third wastes. Judicial review of these regulations was sought by eighteen business groups and companies, and by one environmental group, and the various cases were consolidated into one proceeding.

American Petroleum Institute v. United States EPA
Per curiam opinion by WALD, Chief Judge, and EDWARDS and RUTH B. GINSBURG, Circuit Judges
906 F.2d 729 (D.C. Cir. 1990)

These consolidated petitions for review challenge various aspects of a final Environmental Protection Agency ("EPA" or "agency") rule promulgated under the authority of the Resource Conservation and Recovery Act of 1976 ("RCRA") §3004, 42 U.S.C. §6924. The rule sets out land disposal prohibitions and treatment standards for "First-Third" scheduled wastes ("First-Third Rule"), 53 Fed.Reg. 31,138 (Aug. 17, 1988).[1]

The American Petroleum Institute, the American Iron and Steel Institute, the Chemical Manufacturers Association and the National Association of Metal Finishers (col-

---

1. 42 U.S.C. §6924(g) required EPA to promulgate final regulations governing the disposal of all scheduled hazardous wastes. Section 6924(g)(4) required EPA to promulgate a schedule dividing such wastes into "thirds." In 1986, EPA established a three-part schedule for setting treatment standards for the §6924(g) hazardous wastes. 51 Fed.Reg. 19,300 (May 28, 1986). Land disposal restrictions for First-Third scheduled wastes took effect on August 8, 1988.

lectively "Industry Petitioners") challenge EPA's conclusion that the RCRA precludes the agency from considering land treatment, in conjunction with pretreatment, as an authorized method of treating hazardous wastes. Industry Petitioners also challenge EPA's abandonment of comparative risk analysis as a means of determining authorized treatment standards for hazardous wastes, claiming that the agency did not provide adequate reasons for abandoning this type of risk assessment.

The Natural Resources Defense Council, Chemical Waste Management, Inc. and the Hazardous Waste Treatment Council (collectively "NRDC") challenge the part of the First-Third Rule that establishes treatment standards for K061 hazardous waste. NRDC claims that EPA has unlawfully exempted the slag residues that result from the "treatment" of K061 in zinc smelters from the RCRA's restrictions on land disposal of hazardous wastes.

We agree with EPA that the RCRA does preclude land treatment in conjunction with pretreatment as a method of treating hazardous wastes. Additionally, we find that EPA provided adequate reasons for abandoning comparative risk analysis. However, because we find that EPA unlawfully exempted the residue produced from smelting K061 waste from the RCRA's restrictions on land disposal of hazardous wastes, we vacate that portion of the rule and remand to the agency for further rulemaking consistent with this opinion.

I. BACKGROUND

A. Overview

. . .

In the 1984 amendments to the RCRA, Congress shifted the focus of hazardous waste management away from land disposal to treatment alternatives, determining that:

Certain classes of land disposal facilities are not capable of assuring long-term containment of certain hazardous wastes, and to avoid substantial risk to human health and the environment, reliance on land disposal should be minimized or eliminated. . . . Land disposal . . . should be the least favored method for managing hazardous wastes.

42 U.S.C. §6901(b)(7). Consistent with this finding, Subtitle C of the RCRA now prohibits hazardous wastes from being disposed of on the land unless one of two conditions is satisfied: (1) the Administrator of EPA determines, "to a reasonable degree of certainty, that there will be no migration of hazardous constituents from the disposal unit or injection zone for as long as the wastes remain hazardous." 42 U.S.C. §6924(d), (e), (g), (m); or (2) the waste is treated to meet standards established by EPA pursuant to 42 U.S.C. §6924(m). Section 6924(m)(1), which sets forth treatment requirements, provides:

the Administrator shall, after notice and opportunity for hearings . . . , promulgate regulations specifying those levels or methods of treatment, if any, which substantially diminish the toxicity of the waste or substantially reduce the likelihood of migration of hazardous constituents from the waste so that short-term and long-term threats to human health and the environment are minimized.

42 U.S.C. §6924(m)(1).

To satisfy this directive, EPA required that the hazardous wastes subject to the standards be treated to levels that are achievable by performance of the "best demonstrated available technology" ("BDAT") or be treated by methods that constitute BDAT. *See* 51 Fed. Reg. 40,572, 40,578 (Nov. 7, 1986). EPA also explained that in setting BDATs it would compare the risk of various treatments for a particular waste with the risk of land disposal of that waste ("comparative risk" assessment).

B. EPA's First-Third Rule

1. Land Treatment
EPA's First-Third Rule established BDATs for the petroleum refining wastes with the

waste codes K048-K052, as set forth in 40 C.F.R. §§268.41.[2] The standards chosen by EPA are based on incineration and solvent extraction technology. 53 Fed.Reg. 31,159–60 (Aug. 17, 1988).

Notwithstanding the requests of Industry Petitioners, the agency refused to consider land treatment (in conjunction with certain forms of pretreatment) as a potential BDAT for petroleum wastes. In responses to comments advocating such treatment, the agency explained that "Congress had specifically voided the consideration of land treatment as BDAT by defining it to be land disposal in [§6924(k)] as amended.... Land treatment is a type of land disposal, and prohibited wastes must meet a treatment standard *before* they are land disposed, unless they are disposed in no-migration units." Response to Comments Related to the First-Third Wastes Treatment Technologies and Associated Performance, vol. V, Doc. No. LDR7-S001E, p. 01621 (emphasis added); vol. VI, Doc. No. LDR9-S001F, pp. 01755, 01758.

2. K061 Hazardous Waste

The final First-Third Rule also established BDATs for K061, a zinc-bearing listed hazardous waste that emanates from the primary production of steel in electric furnaces. 40 C.F.R. §261.32. The rule established separate treatment standards for two subcategories of K061: a high zinc subcategory (K061 that is at least 15% zinc in composition) and a low zinc subcategory (K061 that is less than 15% zinc in composition). Only the treatment standard for the high zinc subcategory is at issue in this case.

EPA determined that high temperature metals recovery was the BDAT for treating high zinc K061 hazardous wastes. It selected this treatment method on the ground that mandatory recycling of recoverable metals

would reduce the amount of hazardous wastes ultimately treated and disposed. 53 Fed.Reg. 31,162 (1988).

Nonetheless, EPA determined that it lacked authority to establish any treatment standards for the slag residue that results from the metals reclamation process. As the agency explained in the notice of proposed rulemaking, the furnaces used for metals reclamation "are normally...essential components of the industrial process, and when they are actually burning secondary materials for material recovery[,] [they] can be involved in the very act of production, an activity normally beyond the Agency's RCRA authority." 53 Fed.Reg. 11,753 (1988). Consequently, EPA felt constrained to view K061 as no longer being "waste" within the meaning of the RCRA once the K061 enters a reclamation furnace. *See id.* In the preambles to the final rule, EPA related this analysis to the agency's so-called "indigenous principle," under which EPA disclaims the power to regulate any material generated by the same type of furnace in which the material is being reclaimed. *See* 53 Fed.Reg. 31,162.

3. Comparative Risk

In addition to establishing BDATs for various hazardous wastes, the First-Third Rule discussed certain general principles that the agency would follow in establishing treatment standards. As part of this discussion, EPA stated that it would no longer compare the risks of treatment technologies with the risks of land disposal in determining treatment technologies. 53 Fed.Reg. 31,190–91 (Aug. 17, 1988). EPA found that such assessments had been of negligible benefit to the agency in previous rulemakings and concluded that the continued use of the assessments would have no influence on the treatment standards chosen under the First-

---

2. Petroleum refining wastes K048–K052 are listed, respectively, as dissolved air flotation float, slop oil emulsion solids, heat exchanger bundle cleaning

sludge, API separator sludge and tank bottoms. *See* 40 C.F.R. §261.32.

Third Rule and subsequent rulemakings and could lead to environmentally counterproductive results. *Id.*

II. ANALYSIS

A. Land Treatment

Prior to the final First-Third rulemaking, Industry Petitioners asked EPA to consider land treatment in conjunction with pretreatment as a BDAT for K048-K052, which are "listed" hazardous wastes that emerge from the petroleum refining process. *See* 40 C.F.R. §261.32. While EPA made no mention of these comments in either the proposed or final rule on First-Third wastes, the agency responded to them in a document entitled "Response to Comments Related to the First-Third Wastes Treatment Technologies and Associated Performance" ("Response to Comments"). EPA explained that the RCRA precluded the agency from considering land treatment methods as BDATs because "land treatment is a type of land disposal, and prohibited wastes must meet a treatment standard before they are land disposed, unless they are disposed in no-migration units.... Congress has *specifically* voided the consideration of land treatment as BDAT by defining it to be land disposal in §[6924(k)] of RCRA as amended."[5] Response to Comments, vol. V, Doc. No. LDR7-S001E, p. 01621 (emphasis added); vol. VI, Doc. No. LDR9-S001F, pp. 01755, 01758.

Industry Petitioners take issue with EPA's finding that the RCRA precludes consideration of land treatment as a BDAT. They maintain that the RCRA permits EPA to consider land treatment and that we must vacate the portion of the agency's rule that established BDATs for petroleum wastes because the agency misinterpreted the RCRA in determining those BDATs. *See Securities and Exchange Commission v. Chenery Co.*, 318 U.S. 80, 95, 87 L. Ed. 626, 63 S. Ct. 454 (1943) ("An administrative order cannot be upheld unless the grounds upon which the agency acted in exercising its powers were those upon which its action can be sustained."). *See also International Brotherhood of Electrical Workers, Local Union No. 474 v. NLRB (St. Francis Hospital)*, 259 U.S. App. D.C. 168, 814 F.2d 697, 708 (D.C.Cir. 1987) ("when [an agency] bases a decision on a standard it unjustifiably believes was mandated by Congress, [its] decision must not be enforced, even though [it] might be able to adopt the very same standard in the exercise of its discretion"). We find, however, that EPA properly interpreted the RCRA as precluding consideration of land treatment.

Section 6924(k) of the RCRA specifically includes the placement of hazardous waste in a "land treatment facility" within its definition of land disposal. *See* n. 5 *supra.* Consequently, land treatment is subject to all of the statutory restrictions applicable to land disposal generally. In simple terms, land treatment is a form of land disposal involving the placement of hazardous waste directly on the ground (rather than, for example, in a landfill or surface impoundment) with the expectation that the hazardous constituents will eventually become less hazardous.[6] Thus, in a "land treatment facility," the treatment of

---

5. 42 U.S.C. §6924(k) provides in relevant part that:

the term "land disposal" [ ]... shall be deemed to include but not be limited to, any placement of such hazardous waste in a... land treatment facility.
6. EPA has described the land treatment of hazardous waste as:

the application of waste on the soil surface or the incorporation of waste into the upper layers of the soil... in order to degrade, transform, or immobilize hazardous constituents present in the waste. As such, land treatment is both a treatment and a disposal operation. 51 Fed.Reg. 1,602, 1,702 (Jan. 14, 1986) (proposed "solvents and dioxins" rule).

hazardous wastes occurs only *after* the waste has been land disposed.

The RCRA clearly specifies, however, that hazardous wastes must be treated *before* being land disposed. Unless a waste is disposed of in a unit demonstrated to meet the "no migration" test of 42 U.S.C. §§6924(g)(5) and (d)(1),[7] the waste may not be land disposed unless the waste "*has complied* with the pretreatment regulations promulgated under" §6924(m) of the RCRA. 42 U.S.C. §6924(g)(5) (emphasis added).

Sections 6924(m)(1) and (2) are equally explicit. In pertinent part they provide that when a

Hazardous waste *has been treated* [in a manner] which substantially diminish[es] the toxicity of the waste or substantially reduce[s] the likelihood of migration of hazardous constituents from the waste so that the short-term and long-term threats to human health and the environment are minimized…[,] such waste or residue thereof… may be disposed of in a land disposal facility which meets the requirements of this subchapter.

(Emphasis added.) These provisions are unambiguous: treatment, *i.e.*, a BDAT, must substantially diminish the toxicity of a waste or substantially reduce the likelihood of the migration of its hazardous constituents *prior* to land disposal.

While there is one instance in which Congress allowed hazardous wastes to be treated in nonprotective land disposal units without first being treated to meet the §6924(m) treatment standards, this is the exception that proves the rule. Pursuant to 42 U.S.C §6925(j)(11), Congress allowed surface impoundments (a type of land disposal unit under §6924(k)) to receive, on an interim basis, hazardous wastes that have not been treated to meet §6924(m) standards. Such surface impoundments must, however, meet certain "minimum technological requirements" specified in §6924(o)(1), including double liners and leachate collection systems. 42 U.S.C. §6925(j)(11)(A). Moreover, the hazardous treatment residues from such surface impoundments must be removed for subsequent management within a year after the hazardous waste has been placed in the impoundment. 42 U.S.C. §6925(j)(11)(B).

If Industry Petitioners' interpretation of §6924(m) were correct, §6925(j)(11) would be surplusage since EPA would already have been authorized to permit the treatment of hazardous wastes *subsequent* to land disposal. Moreover, §6925(j)(11) shows that when Congress intended to allow the land disposal of untreated hazardous wastes in units not meeting the "no migration" standard, it did so explicitly and placed numerous restrictions upon such disposal.

In sum, then, because we find no indication in the record that the pretreatment component of the BDAT that Industry Petitioners asked EPA to consider—land treatment in conjunction with some form of pretreatment—would *by itself* meet the strictures of §6924(m), we find that EPA was correct in concluding that the BDAT suggested by Industry Petitioners was precluded from consideration by §6924(m).

---

7. The "no migration test" operates as follows. Where the Administrator determines that a method of land disposal of a hazardous waste "will be protective of human health and the environment for as long as the waste remains hazardous," §6924(g)(5), the RCRA allows land disposal of the waste pursuant to that method. The Administrator may not determine a method of land disposal of a hazardous waste to be protective of health and the environment unless:

it has been demonstrated to the Administrator, to a reasonable degree of certainty, that there will be *no migration* of hazardous constituents from the disposal unit…for as long as the waste remains hazardous.

42 U.S.C. §6924(d)(1) (emphasis added). The "no migration" provision is not in issue here, however, because Industry Petitioners do not argue that the BDAT they are requesting meets the "no migration" test.

Of course, if Industry Petitioners had asserted that the pretreatment they were contemplating in conjunction with land treatment *by itself* met either the "substantially diminish" or "substantially reduce" requirement of §6924(m), we would agree that EPA erred in concluding that the RCRA precluded consideration of the recommended BDAT.[8]

The record, however, is not only barren of any such suggestions, it contains indications to the contrary. *See, e.g.*, Comments of the American Petroleum Institute ("API") on the Proposed Rule "Land Disposal Restrictions For the First Third of Scheduled Wastes," Docket No. LDR7-FFFFF, 53 Fed.Reg. 11742 (April 8, 1988), J.A. 287 ("API Comments") ("API believes that the agency... should consider whether such land treatment is a method that satisfies the requirements of §[6924](m) for oily wastes.... Record evidence suggests that land treatment *combined* with a pretreatment step may be effective in meeting Section [6924](m) requirements.") (emphasis added). Indeed, a report by the API relied upon by some commenters requesting consideration of land treatment in conjunction with pretreatment explicitly emphasizes the value of land treatment and discusses pretreatment only peripherally.[9] Thus, it was eminently reasonable for EPA to conclude that Industry Petitioners were requesting the agency to consider a BDAT that clearly contravened the strictures of the RCRA.

B. Comparative Risk

1. Standing

In the First-Third Rule, EPA announced that it would no longer engage in comparative risk assessment—comparing the risks to human health and the environment of treatment of a waste by a particular BDAT with those inherent in land disposal of the same waste. Industry Petitioners challenge this decision. EPA claims, however, that Industry Petitioners lack standing to raise their challenge because Industry Petitioners have alleged no harm flowing from EPA's decision to abandon comparative risk assessment. We disagree.

In their comments on EPA's Proposed First-Third rulemaking, Industry Petitioners identified several techniques for the treatment of refinery wastes. *See, e.g.*, API Comments, J.A. 277-92. In the final rule, however, without performing comparative risk analyses, EPA rejected several of these methods in establishing treatment levels for the wastes, and limited standards for the listed petroleum refining wastes essentially to three technologies (incineration, a three-cycle solvent extraction process and fixation). 53 Fed.Reg. 31,160 (Aug. 17, 1988). Consequently, the alternative and allegedly cheaper technologies recommended by Industry Petitioners were precluded from use. Industry Petitioners claim that had comparative risk assessments been made, these alternative technologies

---

8. Unlike Industry Petitioners, however, we would not interpret §6924(m) as giving EPA the *discretion* to allow land treatment, *i.e.*, land disposal, of wastes that have been pretreated to either the "substantially reduce" or "substantially diminish" level. Rather, if a party meets the pretreatment standard set out by §6924 *and* requests permission to subsequently place the treated waste in a land treatment facility, we would interpret §6924(m) as *compelling* EPA to grant that request. *See* §6924(m)(2) ("If such waste has been treated to the level or by a method specified in regulations promulgated under this subsection, such waste...*shall* not be subject

to any [land disposal] prohibition and may be disposed of in a land disposal facility....") (emphasis added).

9. *See* "Evaluation of Treatment Technologies for Listed Petroleum Refinery Wastes," Final Report, J.A. 000233, 000238, 000304-05 ("Land treatment is the most widely used waste treatment process in the petroleum industry today.... [L]and treatment significantly reduces the concentration of waste constituents in the leachate, to levels which are as low or lower than those from TCLP extracts of the residual solids from other treatment technologies.").

would not have been rejected by EPA. *See* API Comments, J.A. 278-91. Preclusion of such technologies in many cases may increase the cost of waste treatment for refiners and may compel refiners to make expensive changes in the manner in which they manage hazardous wastes. Thus, Industry Petitioners have alleged an "actual or threatened injury as a result of the putatively illegal conduct of the defendants." *Gladstone Realtors v. Village of Bellwood*, 441 U.S. 91, 99, 60 L. Ed. 2d 66, 99 S. Ct. 1601 (1979).

2. Merits

Industry Petitioners contend that EPA's decision to abandon comparative risk analysis was arbitrary and capricious. In reviewing an agency's action under the arbitrary and capricious standard, we must affirm the agency if it has articulated a satisfactory explanation for its action including a "rational connection between the facts found and the choice made." *Motor Vehicle Manufacturers Association v. State Farm Mutual Automobile Ins. Co.*, 463 U.S. 29, 43, 103 S. Ct. 2856, 77 L. Ed. 2d 443 (1983); *ALLTEL Corp. v. FCC*, 267 U.S. App. D.C. 253, 838 F.2d 551, 556 (D.C.Cir. 1988). EPA has done so here. In the final First-Third rulemaking, EPA offered two reasons for its decision to abandon comparative risk analysis. We think both reasons are in and of themselves satisfactory.

First, EPA explained that if a comparative risk assessment resulted in ruling out all treatments as riskier than land disposal (in terms of the potential danger it posed to human health and the environment), then treatment standards could not be set for a given waste *and* that waste could not be land disposed.

53 Fed.Reg. 31,190 (Aug. 17, 1988).[10] Industry Petitioners take issue with this justification for abandonment of comparative risk. They argue that it is highly unlikely that comparative risk assessments will result in a lack of treatment standards because as applied by EPA so far, comparative risk has rarely precluded consideration of technologies as potential BDATs. This argument, however, is not an attack on the soundness of EPA's reasoning but rather speculation that the scenario envisioned by the agency is unlikely to occur. But to suggest that the scenario is unlikely to occur is not to demonstrate that it will not, and EPA is certainly entitled to take into account worst-case scenarios in dealing with issues of such staggering environmental significance.

The second reason EPA offered for abandoning comparative risk was that the methodology had not proven to be particularly useful because it does not compare equally viable options since land disposal is presumptively disfavored by the RCRA. 53 Fed.Reg. 31,190 (Aug. 17, 1988). Industry Petitioners also reject this reason, arguing that comparing the risks inherent in treatments with those attendant to land disposal serves the useful purpose of helping the agency eliminate consideration of treatments that are riskier than land disposal.

The ultimate goal of comparative risk assessment, however, is not to eliminate consideration of individual treatment technologies, but to arrive at treatments that can be used as BDATs. EPA has noted that comparative risk assessment has not been helpful in that regard. *See id.* ("the use of [comparative risk in prior rulemakings] [has] not affect[ed] the

---

10. The reason for this potentially ironic result is that Congress has written timetables for developing BDATs into the RCRA. If EPA does not meet these timetables, land disposal of the waste in issue is forever foreclosed. Thus, for example, if there are no treatment standards for "Third-Third" hazardous wastes by May 8, 1990, then a "hard ham-

mer" will fall: such hazardous wastes will be prohibited from land disposal. *See* 42 U.S.C. §6924(g)(6)(C).

While the "hammer" date for "First-Third" wastes—August 8, 1988—has already passed, EPA's reasoning is not "moot" since "hammers" for "Third-Third" and other wastes have yet to fall.

determination as to whether a specific treatment technology was available"). Thus we agree with EPA that rather than continuing to expend resources on comparative risk analyses which have in the past proven relatively useless to the agency, it is considerably more efficient for the agency's time to focus on comparing "the net risk posed by alternative [treatment] practices [as a way to]... identif[y the] [ ] 'best' treatment technologies." *Id.*

In sum, then, we find that EPA's decision to abandon comparative risk analysis was not arbitrary and capricious, and that the agency articulated a more than satisfactory explanation for its action.[11]

C. K061 Hazardous Waste

1. Overview

Ordinarily, once EPA determines that a particular substance is a hazardous waste, the agency continues to treat as a hazardous waste any product "derived from" that substance in the course of waste treatment. *See* 40 C.F.R. §261.3(c)(2). EPA declined to apply the "derived-from" rule in this case on the belief that the RCRA prevents the agency from treating K061 as a "solid waste" once it reaches a metals reclamation facility. *See* 53 Fed.Reg. 11,753. Consequently, EPA declined to prescribe treatment standards for K061 slag pursuant to the land disposal prohibition contained in Subtitle C of the RCRA. Thus, but for EPA's determination that it lacked *authority* to regulate the K061 slag, the slag would automatically be treated

as a hazardous waste as a product "derived from" a listed hazardous waste.[12]

NRDC argues that EPA's failure to prescribe treatment standards derives from a flawed interpretation of the scope of EPA's statutory authority. We agree. We conclude that the EPA failed to give a reasoned explanation for its construction of the RCRA and therefore remand for further consideration of this issue.

2. Ripeness

As a threshold matter, we consider EPA's claim that NRDC's challenge should be dismissed as unripe. Our primary concern in assessing the ripeness of a pre-enforcement challenge to agency action is "the fitness of the issue[ ] for judicial decision." *Abbott Labs. v. Gardner*, 387 U.S. 136, 149, 87 S. Ct. 1507, 18 L. Ed. 2d 681 (1967).[13] To determine fitness, we ask first whether the issue raised in the petition for review presents a "purely legal question," in which case it is "presumptively reviewable." *Better Gov't. Ass'n. v. Department of State*, 250 U.S. App. D.C. 424, 780 F.2d 86, 92 (D.C.Cir. 1986). Next we consider "whether the agency or court will benefit from deferring review until the agency's policies have crystallized" through the application of the policy to particular facts. *Eagle-Picher Indus. v. EPA*, 759 F.2d 905, 915 (D.C.Cir. 1985).

Applying these criteria, we have no difficulty concluding that NRDC's challenge is ripe. Whether EPA has the statutory authority to prescribe treatment standards for K061 slag is a purely legal question, one that can

---

11. Industry Petitioners additionally contend that EPA's explanations are arbitrary and capricious because the agency had "resolved or rejected" the problems associated with comparative risk in its earlier "Framework Rulemaking." Even if this were so, an agency is certainly entitled to change course so long as it does so for adequately explained reasons.

12. EPA maintains that it would prescribe treatment standards only in the event that the slag

possessed properties making it a hazardous waste by "characteristic" for purposes of 40 C.F.R. §261.20–.24.

13. A secondary concern under the ripeness doctrine is "the hardship to the parties of withholding court consideration." *Id.* We reach the issue of hardship, however, only if the fitness of the issue for judicial resolution is in doubt. *See Consolidated Rail Corp. v. United States*, 283 U.S. App. D.C. 47, 896 F.2d 574, 577 (D.C.Cir. 1990).

be answered solely by consulting the text, legislative history and judicial interpretations of the RCRA. *See Better Gov't. Ass'n.*, 780 F.2d at 92. Nor will EPA have occasion to refine its conclusion that it lacks statutory authority to regulate K061 slag in the course of applying the standards that the agency has promulgated for the treatment of K061.

EPA challenges this analysis on the ground that the agency's so-called "indigenous principle" is not yet final. EPA notes that this principle—which the agency uses to identify the general characteristics of materials that fall outside the range of the RCRA by virtue of being reclaimed in an industrial furnace—is the subject of pending rulemakings. *See* 54 Fed.Reg. 43,731–32 (1989); 52 Fed.Reg. 16,989–91 (1987). EPA suggests that we defer review of the First-Third Rule until those rulemakings are concluded.

We see no merit in this suggestion. The rulemakings in which EPA is currently developing and applying the indigenous principle are entirely separate from the First-Third Rule. If these proceedings result in a conception of the agency's authority consistent with that reflected in the First-Third Rule—as EPA expects, *see* 53 Fed.Reg. 31,162—they will not furnish a new opportunity to challenge the agency's refusal to prescribe standards for K061 slag. Nor would a change in position initiated in these rulemakings undo the agency's failure to issue such standards in the First-Third rulemaking. It is true that the agency could at that point amend the First-Third Rule. But an agency *always* retains the power to revise a final rule through additional rulemaking. If the possibility of unforeseen amendments were sufficient to render an otherwise fit challenge unripe, review could be deferred indefinitely.

3. The Merits

EPA concluded that it lacked authority to regulate K061 slag because the material is not a "solid waste," and thus not a "hazardous waste," for purposes of the RCRA. *See* 42 U.S.C. §6903(5) (defining "hazardous waste" to be a subset of "solid waste"). The RCRA defines "solid waste" as

any garbage, refuse, sludge from a waste treatment plant, water supply treatment plant, or air pollution control facility *and other discarded material....*

Id. §6903(27) (emphasis added). Although it is undisputed that K061 is a "solid waste" when it leaves the electric furnace in which it is produced,[14] EPA concluded that K061 ceases to be a "solid waste" when it arrives at a metal reclamation facility because at that point it is no longer "discarded material."

Review of the EPA's interpretation of the RCRA is governed by *Chevron U.S.A. Inc. v. Natural Resources Defense Council, Inc.*, 467 U.S. 837, 81 L. Ed. 2d 694, 104 S. Ct. 2778 (1984). Under *Chevron's* familiar two-step analysis, we ask first "whether Congress has directly spoken to the precise question at issue"; if so, we "must give effect to the unambiguously expressed intent of Congress." *Id.* at 842–43. If not, we defer to the agency's interpretation so long as it is "permissible," *id.* at 843, that is, "so long it is *reasonable* and consistent with the statutory purpose." *Ohio v. Department of the Interior*, 279 U.S. App. D.C. 109, 880 F.2d 432, 441 (D.C.Cir. 1989) (emphasis added).

Our application of the *Chevron* test is necessarily influenced by the agency's own explanation of its action. In this case, EPA concluded that the terms of the RCRA left it *no choice* but to disclaim authority to prescribe treatment standards for K061 slag.

---

14. K061 is produced when particulate matter in the gasses emitted by electric furnaces is removed by air pollution control equipment. It therefore constitutes "sludge" from an "air pollution control facility." *See* 53 Fed.Reg. 11,752; 40 C.F.R. §260.10 (defining "sludge" as "any solid, semi-solid, or liquid waste generated from a[n]...air pollution control facility").

See 53 Fed.Reg. 11,753; *see also* 53 Fed.Reg. 31,162. It follows that we can uphold EPA's construction of the statute *only* if the agency's exercise of authority over the slag was indeed foreclosed by the RCRA under *Chevron* step one. For an agency's conclusion that a particular course is compelled by a statute that is actually ambiguous does not display the caliber of reasoned decisionmaking necessary to warrant *Chevron* step two deference. *See, e.g., King Broadcasting Co. v. FCC*, 860 F.2d 465, 470 (D.C.Cir. 1988). Because a reviewing court is powerless to remedy this defect in reasoning, *see Chenery*, 318 U.S. at 95, the proper course in such a situation is to remand so that the agency can pursue a reasoned interpretation of the statute. *See St. Francis Hosp.*, 814 F.2d at 707–08; *Prill v. NLRB*, 244 U.S. App. D.C. 42, 755 F.2d 941, 942 (D.C.Cir.), *cert. denied*, 474 U.S. 948, 106 S. Ct. 313, 88 L. Ed. 2d 294 (1985).

"Employing traditional tools of statutory construction," *Chevron*, 467 U.S. at 843 n. 9, we find that the answer to the question regarding EPA's authority to prescribe treatment standards for K061 slag is at best ambiguous. EPA contends that K061 "discarded" by producers of steel is no longer "discarded" under section 6903(5) when it arrives at a facility for metal reclamations. An at least equally plausible reading of the statute, however, is that K061 remains "discarded" *throughout* the "waste treatment" process dictated by the agency. Indeed, EPA does not seriously contend that this reading of the statute is *foreclosed* by the text of the statute, nor does it refer us to anything in

the legislative history that prohibits such a construction.[15]

Rather, EPA bases its reading of the RCRA almost entirely on our decision in *American Mining Congress v. EPA*, 263 U.S. App. D.C. 197, 824 F.2d 1177 (D.C. Cir. 1987) ("*AMC*"). The issue in *AMC* was whether the EPA could, under the RCRA, treat as "solid wastes" "materials that are recycled and reused in an *ongoing* manufacturing or industrial process." *Id.* at 1186. We held that it could not because

these materials have not yet become part of the waste disposal problem; rather, *they are destined for beneficial reuse or recycling in a continuous process by the generating industry itself.*

Id. Materials subject to such a process were not "discarded" because they were never "disposed of, abandoned, or thrown away." *Id.* at 1193.

AMC is by no means dispositive of EPA's authority to regulate K061 slag. Unlike the materials in question in *AMC*, K061 is indisputably "discarded" *before* being subject to metals reclamation. Consequently, it *has* "become part of the waste disposal problem"; that is why EPA has the power to require that K061 be subject to mandatory metals reclamation. *See* 53 Fed.Reg. 11,752–53 (recognizing this point). Nor does anything in *AMC* require EPA to cease treating K061 as "solid waste" once it reaches the metals reclamation facility. K061 is delivered to the facility not as part of an "*ongoing* manufacturing or industrial process" within "the generating industry," but as part of a mandatory waste treatment plan prescribed by EPA. As such, the resulting slag appears to remain within

---

15. EPA notes that Congress consciously decided to forego regulation of the generation of hazardous waste on the ground that doing so might "in many instances...amount to interference with the productive process itself." H.R.Rep. No. 1491, 94th Cong., 2d Sess. 26 (1976). Regulating furnaces used to recover metals from hazardous waste as a form of waste treatment, EPA argues, "would be like directly regulating the industrial production of

zinc from ore." Brief of Respondent at 57. The two forms of regulation might be "like" each other, but they are by no means one and the same. The cited report simply does not address the issue of whether the agency retains the authority to prescribe treatment standards for the slag produced when metal reclamation facilities are used to treat discarded hazardous wastes.

the scope of the agency's authority as "sludge from a *waste treatment plant*." 42 U.S.C. §6903(27); *see also* 42 U.S.C. §6903(34) (defining "treatment" as "any method, technique, or process ... designed to change the physical [or] chemical ... character or composition of any hazardous waste so as to ... render such waste ... amendable for recovery. ...").[16] Because the EPA mistakenly concluded that our case law left it no discretion to interpret the relevant statutory provisions, we are constrained to remand. *See Phillips Petroleum Co. v. FERC*, 253 U.S. App. D.C. 211, 792 F.2d 1165, 1171 (D.C.Cir. 1986).

We add, however, that the scope of the agency's interpretive discretion on remand is far from unbounded. First, although we conclude that Congress has not spoken precisely on the question of EPA's authority to regulate the slag produced from the treatment of K061, any "permissible" construction of the relevant provisions must comport with the broader "statutory purpose" of the RCRA. *See Ohio v. Department of Interior*, 880 F.2d at 441. Thus, it appears unlikely that EPA can simply readopt the conclusion that its authority to regulate K061 ends at the door of the reclamation facility. To reach such a conclusion, EPA would have to reconcile this position with the RCRA's acknowledged objective to "establish[ ] a 'cradle-to-grave' regulatory structure" for the safe handling of hazardous wastes. *United*

Technologies Corp., 821 F.2d 714, 716 (D.C.Cir. 1987).

Second, the agency's interpretive discretion is limited by its *previous* interpretations of the RCRA. EPA has expressly defined "solid waste" to include any *listed hazardous waste* (including K061) subject to reclamation, 40 C.F.R. §261.2(c)(3), and "hazardous waste" to include "any solid waste generated *from the treatment* ... of a hazardous waste," *id.* §261.3(c)(2)(i) (emphasis added). Thus, it would appear that EPA must prescribe treatment standards for the disposal of K061 slag, for "it is axiomatic that an agency must adhere to its own regulations. ..." *Brock v. Cathedral Bluffs Shale Oil Co.*, 254 U.S. App. D.C. 242, 796 F.2d 533, 536 (D.C.Cir. 1986) (Scalia, J.). However, because an agency is entitled to construe its own regulations in the first instance, we offer no view at this point on whether these rules can be reconciled with a disavowal of authority to regulate K061 slag. But clearly, this is a matter that will have to be addressed on remand should EPA again seriously consider whether it is without such authority.[17]

After reconsidering these matters with *AMC* in correct focus, it appears likely that EPA will recognize that it must comply with its statutory mandate to prescribe treatment standards for the disposal of K061 slag. And, if as we expect, this is the result on remand, then EPA must enforce the RCRA's ban on land disposal of K061 slag unless the agency

---

16. Contrary to what the intervenors suggest, it is also immaterial under *AMC* that the method of waste treatment prescribed by the agency results in the production of something of value, namely, reclaimed metals. Indeed, the *AMC* decision expressly *disavowed* a reading of the statute that would prevent EPA from regulating processes for extracting valuable products from *discarded* materials that qualify as hazardous wastes:

Oil recyclers typically collect discarded used oils, distill them, and sell the resulting material for use as fuel in boilers. *Regulation of those activities is*

likewise consistent with an everyday reading of the term "discarded." It is only when EPA attempts to extend the scope of [the RCRA] to include the recycling of *undiscarded* oils at petroleum refineries that conflict [with the statute] occurs.

Id. at 1187 n. 14 (first emphasis added).

17. In the notice of proposed rulemaking, EPA explained its failure to apply 40 C.F.R. §261.2(c) on the ground that K061 slag is not a "solid waste." *See* 53 Fed. Reg. 11,753. Insofar as 40 C.F.R. §261.2(c) *defines* "solid waste," we find this argument circular.

determines that one of the statutory exceptions of Subtitle C is satisfied. *See* 42 U.S.C. §6924(d), (e), (g), (m).[18]

III. CONCLUSION

EPA was correct in concluding that the RCRA's land disposal and hazardous waste treatment provisions preclude consideration of land treatment of hazardous wastes. Consequently, we deny the petition to review EPA's interpretation of the RCRA's land disposal and hazardous waste treatment provisions. Additionally, because EPA provided adequate reasons for abandoning comparative risk assessment, we deny the petition to review its decision in this regard. However, because EPA unlawfully exempted the K061 residues from the RCRA's land disposal restrictions, we grant the petition to review EPA's rulemaking on K061 wastes, vacate that part of the rule, and remand for further rulemaking consistent with this opinion.

---

18. In its brief to this court, EPA argues that it need not prescribe treatment standards for K061 slag because it has determined that high temperature metals reclamation by itself satisfies section 6924(m)(1)'s directive to "promulgate regulations specifying those...methods of treatment" that minimize "threats to human health and the environment." But as we have explained, in the notice of proposed rulemaking and preambles to the final rule, the agency declined to prescribe treatment standards solely because it *lacked authority* to do so. We therefore reject as "appellate counsel's *post hoc* rationalization[ ] for agency action," *Motor Vehicle Mfrs. Ass'n. v. State Farm Mutual Automobile Ins. Co.*, 463 U.S. 29, 50, 77 L. Ed. 2d 443, 103 S. Ct. 2856 (1983), the suggestion that such standards are *unnecessary* under the statute.

■ **NOTES**

1. While it may not have been consistent with the language of Section 3004, EPA's move from health-based standards to technology-based standards for hazardous wastes is similar to the approach taken by Congress to toxic water pollutants (in Section 307 of the Clean Water Act) and hazardous air pollutants (in Section 112 of the Clean Air Act).

2. In limited circumstances, a generator or treatment facility may obtain a variance from the LDRs. See 40 C.F.R. §268.44. Such a variance may be granted—on a general basis [40 C.F.R. §268.44(a)] or a site-specific basis [40 C.F.R. §268.44(h)]—if the petitioner can demonstrate: (1) that it "is not physically possible" to meet the applicable treatment standard "because the physical or chemical properties of the waste differ significantly from wastes analyzed in developing the treatment standard"; or (2) that it is "inappropriate" to meet the treatment standard (although possible to do so), either because technical difficulties make it "technically inappropriate (for example, resulting in combustion of large quantities of mildly contaminated environmental media)," or because it is "environmentally inappropriate because it would likely discourage aggressive remediation." Any such variance (known colloquially

as a "treatability" variance) must include specific additional controls that are "sufficient to minimize threats to human health and the environment posed by land disposal of the waste" [40 C.F.R. §268.44(k)], and must first be put out for public comment.

3. Note that the "impossibility" prong of this variance provision is analogous to the "fundamentally different factors" variance available under the Clean Water Act. The "environmentally inappropriate" prong is available in those circumstances where a variance is necessary to promote "aggressive remediation" of past contamination. This would most likely be done as a site-specific variance. It might, for example, allow placement of partially treated remediation wastes (wastes taken from a contaminated site) into a RCRA landfill when the time it would take to provide the full treatment necessary to meet the LDRs would endanger health, safety, or the environment by delaying removal of the wastes from the contaminated site. In general, this type of variance may provide an alternative mechanism for the disposal of remediation wastes where use of the CAMU regulation (discussed later) is unavailable or otherwise inappropriate.

4. Strictly from a policy perspective (rather than as a matter of statutory construction), does it make sense to distinguish between materials that are reclaimed and reused in the process from which they were generated and those that are reclaimed for use as an input elsewhere? Note that the first of these—involving what is sometimes called "closed loop recycling"—is generally consistent with a waste reduction philosophy, while the second is not. The second is, however, consistent with many common formulations of what has come to be called "industrial ecology." We explore industrial ecology in more detail in chapters 12 and 13.

5. Recall that EPA regulations exempt from the definition of solid waste materials that are "(i) used or reused as ingredients in an industrial process to make a product, provided the materials are not being reclaimed; or (ii) used or reused as effective substitutes for commercial products" [40 C.F.R. §261.2(e)]. Are these exemptions consistent with the court's discussion of the K061 wastes? Is any inconsistency cured by EPA's caveat in the regulation that these exemptions do not apply when the materials are "used in a manner constituting disposal?" Does this caveat create circularity in the definition?   ∎

6. Standards for Hazardous Waste Incinerators

One result of the implementation of the land disposal treatment standards has been an increase in the incineration of hazardous wastes; quite often the LDRs either require, or are based on, the use of incineration to "treat" the waste before it is deposited in a landfill. Indeed, even without the LDRs, the gradual tightening of hazardous waste and solid waste regulations over the past three decades has caused an increase in the use of incineration. See Thomas McKone and Katharine Hammond (2000) "Managing the Health Impacts of Waste Incineration," *Environmental Science and Technology News* September 1, p. 380A. This is one obvious instance where waste regulation has caused a shift of pollutants back to another environmental medium. This has been, at best, a mixed bag from an environmental and public health perspective. While state-of-the-art incinerators will do a good job of destroying many types of waste, other chemicals, such as dioxins, can survive (or even be created by) the incineration process in amounts that may still pose public health risks. And many older incineration facilities do a much poorer job of destruction and can result in the dispersion of significant amounts of toxicants into the air (id.).

In 1999, under Section 112 of the Clean Air Act and Section 3004(n) of RCRA, EPA promulgated air emission standards for hazardous waste incinerators, hazardous waste-burning cement kilns, and hazardous waste-burning lightweight aggregate kilns. See 64 *Fed. Reg.* 52,828 (Sept. 30, 1999). According to EPA, this covered 172 separate facilities that together burn approximately 80% of the hazardous waste combusted in the United States. See U.S. EPA (1999) *Environmental Fact Sheet: Revised Technical Standards for Hazardous Waste Combustion Facilities*, Washington, D.C.

Recognizing the overlap between the Clean Air Act and RCRA on this issue, EPA chose to set the standards as technology-based MACT standards under the Clean Air Act, although it set the standard for dioxin emissions at a level more stringent than MACT. However, the standards were immediately challenged in the District of Columbia Court of Appeals by a variety of industry and environmental groups. Agreeing with the Sierra Club that EPA had not based the MACT standards on the performance of the best-performing facilities as required by Section 112 of the Clean Air Act, and that the standards may thus have been too lenient, the court remanded the regulations to the agency for further deliberation. At the same time, the court declined the Sierra Club's suggestion that the standards be kept in place during the remand, noting that industry had also raised many arguments against the standards that may have validity. See *Cement Kiln Recycling Coalition v. Environmental Protection Agency*, 255 F.3d 855 (D.C. Cir. 2001).

EPA issued the revised standards in 2005, and as this book goes to print the revised rule is under review in the D.C. Circuit. If they are substantially upheld on appeal, the standards will increase the costs of sending wastes to cement kilns. Historically, cement kilns (which burn hazardous waste as fuel to produce energy for the cement-making process) have been cheaper to operate, and have produced considerably more air emissions, than newer hazardous waste incinerators. The new MACT standards will require emission controls at cement kilns that should make it substantially more expensive to burn wastes at these facilities. EPA has estimated that the revised standards will impose an overall cost on industry of $40 million per year. EPA also estimates that the standards will reduce emissions of dioxins, heavy metals, and other hazardous air pollutants by up to 3,380 tons per year, from a baseline of 12,650 tons. The Sierra Club, however, faults the rule for neglecting certain toxic pollutants, and for not requiring greater reductions in certain circumstances. See "Sierra Club Sues EPA Over Emission Limits for Hazardous Waste Combustor Operations," 20 *Toxics Law Reporter* 1088 (Dec. 15, 2005). The rule is codified at 40 *C.F.R.* §63.1200, et seq.

7.   Corrective Action and the CAMU

The Comprehensive Environmental Response, Compensation, and Liability Act, discussed later in this chapter, is the primary federal statute governing the remediation ("cleanup") of environmental contamination caused by hazardous waste sites. However, cleanup at operating TSD facilities is governed, in the first instance, by what are known as the "corrective action" provisions of RCRA. Corrective action at RCRA-permitted facilities is covered by Section 3004(u), which requires that any permit issued to a TSD include provisions to ensure "corrective action for all releases of hazardous waste or constituents from any sold waste management unit" at the facility. In addition, EPA is authorized to order corrective action at interim status facilities under Section 3008(h). In either case, corrective action is to be performed by the owner or operator of the facility, and is not necessarily limited to contaminated areas within the facility boundaries. Section 3004(v) specifies that corrective action shall "be taken beyond the facility boundary where necessary to protect human health and the environment unless the owner or operator... demonstrates to the satisfaction of the Administrator that, despite the owner or operator's best efforts, the owner or operator was unable to obtain the necessary permission to undertake such action."

In general, corrective action under these provisions follows the same steps—from site investigation, to selection of remedies, to performing remediation—as are required for CERCLA cleanups. One noteworthy feature of the corrective action program is an EPA regulation authorizing the designation, in certain circumstances, of a "corrective action management unit" (CAMU) (40 C.F.R. §264.552). A CAMU is "an area within a facility [in general, a landfill or designated portion of a landfill] that is used only for managing CAMU-eligible wastes for implementing corrective action or cleanup at the facility" [id. at §264.552(a)]. "CAMU-eligible wastes," in turn, are wastes "that are managed for implementing cleanup" [id. at

§264.552(a)(1)]. Wastes generated "from ongoing industrial operations" at the site are not CAMU-eligible (id.). That is, CAMU-eligible wastes are wastes taken from a contaminated area of the site during remediation of that site. Placement of such wastes into a CAMU "does not constitute land disposal of hazardous wastes" [id. at 264.552(a)(4)], which means that the LDRs do not apply. Moreover, CAMUs are not subject to the full panoply of technological requirements applicable to licensed hazardous waste landfills, although they must meet the technological requirements of the CAMU regulation.

Unless alternative requirements are approved, these requirements include a composite liner and a leachate collection system for any CAMU that is a "new, replacement, or laterally expanded unit" [id. at §264.552(e)(3)(i)]. In addition, CAMU-eligible wastes containing certain "principal hazardous constituents" must meet specified (less stringent) treatment standards [id. at §264.552(e)(4)], although these standards may be relaxed under certain circumstances if the adjusted standard is "protective of human health and the environment" [id. at §264.552(3)(v)]. Where wastes are to remain in a CAMU after its closure, such wastes "shall be managed and contained so as to minimize future releases, to the extent practicable" [id. at §264.552(c)(4)]. An area may not be designated as a CAMU without "public notice and a reasonable opportunity for public comment," and the public must be provided with a specific opportunity to comment on any proposed relaxation of the minimum treatment standards [id. at §264.552(h)].

■ **NOTES**

1. At the close of 2001, EPA reported that a total of 47 CAMUs had been approved or scheduled for approval. See Paul Balserak, EPA Office of Solid Waste, Corrective Action Management Unit (CAMU) Site Background Document (December 21, 2001), at 3.

2. Both the regulation authorizing CAMUs and the regulation authorizing treatability variances (discussed earlier) create the potential for relaxing the LDRs (and, in the case of the CAMU, other RCRA requirements) to the detriment of the environment or public health. Are the provisions for public notice and comment likely to be sufficient to keep this from happening? If not, can these regulations nonetheless be justified on policy grounds? Are there good reasons for allowing remediation wastes to be handled differently from wastes that are generated from ongoing industrial processes? Is there a difference from a pollution prevention perspective?

3. By requiring EPA to provide for "corrective action" at TSD facilities, did Congress necessarily authorize the agency to relax the LDRs for wastes removed from

those sites? Can the CAMU regulations (as summarized here) be read to extend to remediation wastes from sites other than those at which RCRA corrective action is being performed (such as CERCLA sites)? Is this consistent with EPA's corrective action authority under RCRA?   ∎

8. Underground Storage Tanks

For years, storage of oil and other hazardous substances in underground tanks was rather commonplace. Predictably, when the (usually metallic) storage vessels were allowed to remain in the ground for a long period of time, they tended to develop leaks. The leaking of petroleum products from tanks placed under gas stations, for example, became a nationwide problem. Underground storage tanks are addressed under Subchapter IX of RCRA (42 U.S.C. §§6991–6991i), which was added to the statute in 1984. EPA's program for leaking underground storage tanks (originally called the "LUST" program, but now known, perhaps somewhat more decorously, as the "UST" program) is designed to be both preventive and remedial in nature.

Regulated under this program as "underground storage tanks" are "any one or a combination of tanks (including underground pipes connected thereto) which is used to contain an accumulation of regulated substances," where at least 10% of the structure is located beneath the surface of the ground [42 U.S.C. §6991(1)]. "Regulated substances" include petroleum and anything (other than a RCRA hazardous waste) that is defined as a "hazardous substance" under CERCLA [42 U.S.C. §6991(2)]. Underground storage of RCRA hazardous waste is exempted from this program because it is already regulated under Subchapter III of RCRA. A number of enumerated types of containers, including storage tanks for residential heating oil, tanks for storing farm or residential motor fuel that have a capacity of 1,100 gallons or less, septic tanks, and certain pipeline facilities, are also exempted from the program.

The owner or operator of an "underground storage tank" is required to meet minimum requirements for leak detection, leak prevention, and financial responsibility (to cover the cost of any necessary corrective action), and to take corrective action in the case of a leak. EPA may also take corrective action in response to a petroleum leak from an underground storage tank, and (much in the manner of the CRECLA program discussed later) may recover the costs of that corrective action from the owner or operator so long as it was performed in accordance with applicable regulations. Such corrective action may include (in addition to removal or treatment of contaminated material) temporary or permanent relocation of affected residents, provision of alternative household water supplies, and exposure assessments. See 42 U.S.C. §6991b(h).

To facilitate regulatory oversight, the 1984 RCRA amendments required the owners or operators of underground storage tanks that had not been taken out of operation before January 1, 1974 to provide notification to EPA ("specifying the age, size, type, location, and uses" of the tank) within 18 months. Those who put such tanks into operation after the effective date of the 1984 amendments have been required to provide such notification within 30 days. See 42 U.S.C. §6991a(a). Moreover, new tanks are required to conform to new tank performance standards promulgated by EPA. See 42 U.S.C. §6991b(e).

States may receive authorization from EPA both to administer the UST program generally and to conduct corrective actions in response to petroleum leaks. See 42 U.S.C. §§6991b(7) and 6991c.

9. The Regulation of Other Solid Waste

Solid wastes that are not hazardous wastes [these are specifically listed at 40 CFR §261.4(b)] are governed by Subtitle D (Subchapter IV) of RCRA (Sections 4001 through 4010). Minimum requirements for municipal solid waste landfills (including those that are used for the disposal of sewage sludge under the Clean Water Act) are set forth in 40 CFR 258. All other solid waste disposal facilities that are not regulated under Subtitle C (Subchapter III) of RCRA (i.e., that are not regulated as hazardous waste facilities) are subject to the regulations set forth in 40 CFR §257. Disposal of solid wastes that are not hazardous wastes in a manner that does not satisfy the criteria of 40 CFR §257 or §258 (whichever is applicable) constitutes "open dumping" in violation of Section 4005 of RCRA.

10. The Citizen Suit and Imminent and Substantial Endangerment Provisions

Like the Clean Air and Clean Water acts, RCRA has a citizen suit provision that authorizes affected citizens both to sue EPA to compel the performance of a nondiscretionary act and, provided certain conditions are met, to sue those who are in violation of the act or its regulations. See Section 7002, 42 U.S.C. §6972. Moreover, affected citizens and EPA are authorized, under certain circumstances, to bring suit against "any person . . . who has contributed or is contributing to the past or present handling, storage, treatment, transportation, or disposal of any solid or hazardous waste which may present an imminent and substantial endangerment to health or the environment" [42 U.S.C. §§6972(a)(1)(B) (citizens) and 6973(a) (EPA)]. As the following case illustrates, these are potentially powerful provisions that can be used to address solid waste even if it is not hazardous, and to address hazards caused by past practices.

Dague v. City of Burlington
Opinion: PRATT, Circuit Judge
935 F.2d 1343 (2d Cir. 1991)

Plaintiffs are owners of land adjacent to the Burlington Municipal Disposal Grounds (the "landfill"). They brought this action against the City of Burlington for alleged violations of state and federal laws arising out of the operation of the landfill. Plaintiffs alleged that the operation of the landfill generally harmed the environment, and specifically damaged their properties, by generating methane gas, wind-blown debris, and hazardous waste. The city closed the landfill on December 31, 1989.

The plaintiffs' ten-count complaint sought injunctive relief, civil penalties, compensatory damages, and punitive damages, plus costs and attorneys' fees. Judge Billings held a bench trial on the first five counts of the complaint. Counts I, II, and III were brought pursuant to the citizen-suit provision of the Resource Conservation and Recovery Act ("RCRA"), 42 U.S.C. §6972; count IV was brought pursuant to the citizen-suit provision of the Clean Water Act ("CWA"), 33 U.S.C. §1365; and count V was brought pursuant to the Vermont Groundwater Protection Law, 10 Vt. Stat. Ann. §1410.

The district court found that the City of Burlington had operated the landfill in violation of prohibitions against open dumping practices found in 42 U.S.C. §6945(a); that the landfill may have presented an imminent and substantial endangerment to health or the environment in violation of 42 U.S.C. §6972(a)(1)(B); and that the landfill had discharged pollutants from a point source into waters of the United States in violation of 33 U.S.C. §1311. Liability under the remaining common law claims, counts VI through X, and the issue of damages on count V, were reserved for trial by jury at a later date. . . .

The city appeals all of these rulings.

BACKGROUND

The City of Burlington has owned and operated the landfill since the early 1960s. The landfill is rectangular in shape and is located on approximately eleven acres of land to the north of the commercial-residential center of the city. It is bounded to the east and south by properties owned by the plaintiffs, to the north by a railroad embankment, and to the west and northwest by a marsh area called the Intervale, which has been designated a wetland, as well as by Beaver Pond, which is actually the southeast portion of the marsh. A large stone culvert runs under the railroad and connects the Beaver Pond portion of the marsh with the northeast quadrant of the Intervale.

The Intervale is in the flood plain of the Winooski River. It is inundated or saturated by surface water sufficient to support a variety of vegetation typically adapted for life in saturated soil conditions. The Intervale occasionally floods, leaving the entire area covered with surface water, including parts of the landfill itself. At normal times, water in the culvert is either in equilibrium or flows from south to north through the culvert. During times of high water, however, surface water may flow from north to south through the culvert.

Trash is buried in the landfill to a depth of approximately nine feet below the ground water table on the northern edge of the landfill. Historically, rain water and run-off from the land have been able to percolate into the landfill mass. As a result, groundwater mixes with and flows through contaminants in the landfill.

The landfill contains typical domestic and municipal wastes as well as materials deposited over the years by local industries. When groundwater infiltrates the landfill, the water mixes with the material in the landfill and forms leachate. Leachate is a liquid that has passed through or emerged from solid waste and contains soluble, suspended, or miscible materials removed from such wastes. The leachate is generated both by percolation of precipitation into the landfill mass and by the flow of groundwater through the refuse in the landfill. The leachate produced in the landfill contains chemicals and compounds found on toxic and hazardous lists under RCRA and the CWA. Because the landfill is unlined, the leachate enters the upper gradients or "flow tubes" of ground water under the landfill. The ground water then flows north beyond the landfill boundaries, and the flow tubes of the leachate-contaminated groundwater all surface in the Intervale, north of and within 300 feet of the railroad embankment.

Leachate has also emerged from the sides of the landfill via seeps. From there, it flows into Beaver Pond and thence through the culvert under the railroad embankment and into the Intervale. The fact that leachate from the landfill is toxic to a small fish called the fathead minnow demonstrates that the leachate can kill a vertebrate in the food chain. The leachate also kills Daphnia (water fleas) and algae.

In the early 1980s, the State of Vermont began to closely scrutinize the landfill. As a result of the state's investigation, the state and the city entered into an Assurance of Discontinuance on December 15, 1981, which nominally required the city by July 1, 1984, to cease disposing of any refuse in the landfill, with the exception of residue from a planned resource recovery facility. When the city did not comply, the terms of the Assurance were amended several times, the most pertinent amendment ("Amended Assurance") occurring on January 31, 1985. It required that the city install and make operational a leachate

collection system at the landfill by September 1, 1985, and that the city install and make operational a methane gas control system by December 1, 1985. It also gave the city two options: (1) select another landfill site and close the current landfill by January 1, 1988, or (2) begin operating a resource recovery facility ("RRF") and close the landfill by January 1, 1990. This Amended Assurance was entered as an order of the Chittenden Superior Court on March 7, 1985.

The city did not timely comply, however, even with the terms of the Amended Assurance. It did not install the leachate collection system or the methane gas control system until March of 1986, after the State of Vermont, on December 18, 1985, had brought an action against the city to enforce the March 7th order. Moreover, the city never notified the state in writing of its choice between the two closure options, despite its obligation to do so. While the city's board of aldermen did adopt a resolution to pursue the RRF option, the mayor vetoed the resolution.

During the years 1985 and 1986, the state performed its own environmental assessment of the landfill, conducting substantial monitoring and testing of the area in and around the landfill, and collecting both leachate data and biological data. While the state concluded, as a result of its investigation, that the landfill did not, at that time, present an imminent and substantial endangerment to human health or the environment, it did determine that January 1, 1990, was the appropriate closure date in view of the environmental concerns presented by the landfill.

Plaintiffs filed their complaint in this matter on October 9, 1985. . . .

Plaintiffs moved for a preliminary injunction seeking immediate closing of the landfill. The case was initially referred to the Honorable Jerome J. Niedermeier, United States Magistrate for the District of Vermont, to hear and determine the motion. The city moved to dismiss the complaint primarily on the basis of failure to comply with the notice prerequisites of 42 U.S.C. §6972(a) and 33 U.S.C. §1365(a)....

In February of 1986, the magistrate issued a Report and Recommendation, finding for purposes of the preliminary injunction motion that the city was in violation of §6945(a) of RCRA and §1311(a) of the CWA. However, the magistrate recommended that the court deny plaintiffs' motion at that time and order the city to take certain specific steps toward remedying the violations. Adopting the magistrate's Report and Recommendation *in toto*, the district court denied plaintiffs' motion for a preliminary injunction and ordered the city, within sixty days, to make fully operational both a gas ventilation system and a leachate collection system for the landfill. At this point, the city complied.

After a bench trial, the district court issued its Findings of Fact, Opinion and Order. 732 F. Supp. 458. As to count I, it concluded that the city had not violated the hazardous waste permit and notification requirements of 42 U.S.C. §§6925(a) and 6930(a). It based this holding on the fact that the State of Vermont had authorization to implement its own solid and hazardous waste program pursuant to 42 U.S.C. §6926(b), and that the state's regulations superseded the requirements under RCRA. Accordingly, the court found that a direct action to enforce the RCRA regulations was not available to the plaintiffs. *See Williamsburgh-Around-the-Bridge Block Assn., et al. v. Jorling, et al.*, No. 89-CV-471, slip op. at 10, 1989 U.S. Dist. LEXIS 9961 (N.D.N.Y. August 21, 1989); *Thompson v. Thomas*, 680 F. Supp. 1, 3 (D.D.C. 1987).

As to count II, which alleged three separate open dumping practices in violation of 42 U.S.C. §6945(a), the court found that (a) the city had generated methane gas, in violation of 40 C.F.R. §257.3-8(a)(2), but had abated that practice on or about December 27, 1985, and since then had not violated this provision; (b) the city had, through a point

source, discharged pollutants into waters of the United States without a permit, in violation of 40 C.F.R. §257.3-3(a); and (c) the city had not contaminated an underground drinking water source beyond the landfill boundary, and therefore had not violated 40 C.F.R. §257.3-4(a).

As to count III, the court held that the city had violated subchapter III (hazardous waste management provisions) and subchapter IV (solid waste management provisions) of RCRA because the landfill may have presented an imminent and substantial endangerment to health or the environment, and therefore, its continued operation violated 42 U.S.C. §6972(a)(1)(B).

As to count IV, the court found that the city had violated the CWA by discharging pollutants from a point source (the railroad culvert) into the Intervale without authorization. Finally, as to count V, the court held that the city had violated Vermont's Groundwater Protection Law, 10 Vt. Stat. Ann. §1410, by altering the character and quality of the groundwater beneath and north of the landfill.

Subsequently, the district court entered an Opinion and Order denying the city's motion to dismiss counts II, III, and part of IV, and it also entered an Opinion and Order granting the plaintiffs' motion for attorney's fees. The district court then entered judgment with respect to its holdings on counts I through IV, and pursuant to Fed. R. Civ. P. 54(b), certified for appeal the judgment on the federal issues presented by these four counts. The court deferred for future action the damage issues under state law that were presented by count V.

DISCUSSION

[The court's discussion of whether the plaintiffs provided adequate pre-suit notice as required by the citizen suit provisions of RCRA and the Clean Water Act, and of whether the city had discharged pollutants through a point source within the meaning of the Clean Water Act, is omitted.]

C. Imminent and Substantial Endangerment

The city next challenges the district court's conclusion that the landfill may present an imminent and substantial endangerment to health or the environment. It asserts that there is no evidence to support the court's conclusion, because (1) the mere presence of chemicals found on the list of toxins, without regard to their concentrations, does not evidence an endangerment; (2) the state environmental investigation concluded that the landfill and its leachate did not present an imminent and substantial endangerment to the environment; and (3) plaintiffs' expert, Dr. Reed, did not cite evidence in support of his opinion. We disagree with the city's contention that the district court erred.

Section 6972(a)(1)(B) authorizes citizens to sue an owner or operator of a disposal facility which has contributed or is contributing to the past or present "disposal of any solid or hazardous waste which may present an imminent and substantial endangerment to health or the environment." 42 U.S.C. §6972(a)(1)(B). When congress enacted RCRA in 1976, it sought to close "the last remaining loophole in environmental law, that of unregulated land disposal of discarded materials and hazardous wastes." H.R.Rep. No. 1491, 94th Cong., 2d Sess. 4, *reprinted in* 1976 U.S.C.C.A.N. 6238, 6241. RCRA's waste management requirements for disposal facilities are designed not only to prevent, but also to mitigate, endangerments to public health and the environment. *See id.*

Significantly, Congress used the word "may" to preface the standard of liability: "present an imminent and substantial endangerment to health or the environment." *United States v. Price*, 688 F.2d 204, 213 (3d Cir. 1982); *United States v. Waste Industries, Inc.*, 734 F.2d 159, 166 (4th Cir. 1984). This

is "expansive language," which is "intended to confer upon the courts the authority to grant affirmative equitable relief to the extent necessary to eliminate *any risk* posed by toxic wastes." *Price*, 688 F.2d at 213–14 (emphasis added). *See also Middlesex County Board of Chosen Freeholders v. New Jersey*, 645 F. Supp. 715, 722 (D.N.J. 1986); *United States v. Ottati & Goss, Inc.*, 630 F. Supp. 1361, 1393 (D.N.H. 1985).

The statute is "basically a prospective act designed to prevent improper disposal of hazardous wastes in the future." *Waste Industries*, 734 F.2d at 166 (quoting H.R. Committee Print No. 96-IFC 31, 96th Cong., 1st Sess. at 32 (1979) ("the Eckhardt Report")). It is not specifically limited to emergency-type situations. *Waste Industries*, 734 F.2d at 165. A finding of "imminency" does not require a showing that actual harm will occur immediately so long as the risk of threatened harm is present: "An 'imminent hazard' may be declared at any point in a chain of events which may ultimately result in harm to the public." *Environmental Defense Fund v. Environmental Protection Agency*, 150 U.S. App. D.C. 348, 465 F.2d 528, 535 (D.C. Cir. 1972) (quoting EPA Statement of Reasons Underlying the Registration Decisions); *Ottati & Goss*, 630 F. Supp. at 1394. Imminence refers "to the nature of the threat rather than identification of the time when the endangerment initially arose." *Price*, 688 F.2d at 213 (quoting the Eckhardt Report); *Waste Industries, Inc.*, 734 F.2d at 166.

In addition, a finding that an activity may present an imminent and substantial endangerment does not require actual harm. *United States v. Waste Industries, Inc.*, 734 F.2d 159 (4th Cir. 1984). Courts have consistently held that "endangerment" means a threatened or potential harm and does not require proof of actual harm. *Ottati & Goss*, 630 F. Supp. at 1394; *United States v. Vertac Chemical Corp.*, 489 F. Supp. 870, 885 (E.D. Ark. 1980). *See also Ethyl Corp. v. EPA*, 176 U.S. App. D.C. 373, 541 F.2d 1, 13 (D.C. Cir.) (en banc), *cert. denied*, 426 U.S. 941, 96 S. Ct. 2662, 49 L. Ed. 2d 394 (1976) ("case law and dictionary definition agree that endanger means something less than actual harm").

The evidence presented at trial supports the district court's finding that the landfill presented an imminent and substantial endangerment to health and the environment. The landfill had been leaking hazardous chemicals into the soil, into groundwater beneath and to the north of the landfill, and into surface waters of the Intervale wetland. Even after installation and operation of the leachate collection system in 1986, at least 10 percent of the leachate, which contains toxic and hazardous chemicals, was still migrating from the landfill into the groundwater and surface water in and around the landfill. Standard bioassay techniques revealed that leachate from the landfill was toxic to freshwater aquatic life, including at least one vertebrate in the food chain. At the time it last assessed the landfill on September 21, 1988, the state determined that "the Burlington Landfill has inadequate separation distance to groundwater and inadequate isolation distance to surface water. Monitoring of both groundwater and surface water has indicated impacts to water quality."

The amount and presence of toxic chemicals, including lead, found in groundwater wells have increased over time, and are bio-accumulating in the Intervale. Some of these toxic chemicals, which continue to migrate from the landfill, may have a dramatic, adverse impact on the food chain in the Intervale. While the cattails in the Intervale tend to be resistant to toxic chemicals, the marsh is a "climax" system, *i.e.*, cattails can stand in the face of chemical insult, but when deterioration of them finally can be seen, they will degrade quickly, and that will be "long past the point . . . of saving the system."

In addition, the district court based its finding on (1) the fact that leachate which escaped from the landfill contained chemicals and compounds found on the EPA toxic list; (2) the fact that the state, on the basis of its independent environmental investigation in and around the landfill, had concluded that January 1, 1990, was an appropriate closing date for the landfill; and (3) "other evidence in this case, such as Dr. Reed's expert opinion."

Based on all of the foregoing, the district court properly concluded that there were sufficient circumstances that may present an imminent and substantial endangerment to health or the environment.

[The court's discussion upholding the district court's award of attorneys' fees to the plaintiffs under RCRA and the Clean Water Act is omitted.]

CONCLUSION

We affirm the judgment of the district court in all respects.

■ **NOTES**

1. Note that the D.C. Circuit's *Ethyl Corp* case (dealing with EPA's first regulations limiting the lead content of gasoline) served as authority for the Second Circuit's determination in this case as to the meaning of "endangerment" under the RCRA provision.

2. Although they can be powerful tools in an appropriate case, the imminent and substantial endangerment provisions of RCRA generally may not be invoked at a

site on which EPA is proceeding with a cleanup under CERCLA. See 42 U.S.C. §6972(b)(2)(B) (pertaining to suits filed by private citizens) and Section 113(h) of CERCLA, 42 U.S.C. §9613(h) (pertaining to suits filed by anyone, including the federal government).

3. In the *Dague* case, the plaintiffs were not able to enforce the provisions of Subtitle C of RCRA, because Vermont had received authorization from EPA, under Section 3006 of RCRA, to operate its own hazardous waste program in lieu of RCRA. However, they could have invoked RCRA's citizen suit provision to enforce the state's hazardous waste laws, because the RCRA provision gives affected citizens the right to bring suit in federal court for violation of "any . . . standard, regulation, condition, requirement, prohibition, or order which has become effective pursuant to [RCRA]" [42 U.S.C. §6972(a)(1)(A)]. When a state hazardous waste program is approved by EPA under the provisions of Section 3006, it has "become effective" under RCRA. ∎

C. THE COMPREHENSIVE ENVIRONMENTAL RESPONSE, COMPENSATION, AND LIABILITY ACT (THE SUPERFUND LAW)

If the 1984 RCRA amendments were the ultimate congressional reaction to the firestorm of community concern that had been set off by the events at Love Canal in the late 1970s, the more immediate reaction was the passage of the Comprehensive Response, Compensation, and Liability Act in 1980. Widely known as the "Superfund" law because of its creation of a large federal fund earmarked for use in cleaning up hazardous waste sites, the statute was, consistent with the imagery evoked by its name, hailed at the time as something of a "caped crusader" of federal policy, on a mission that would set the nation's hazardous waste problems to right. While most would agree that the law has not lived up to these expectations, it is nonetheless true that CERCLA, along with RCRA, has had a profound effect on environmental policy.

1. Looking Both Ways: The Policy Impact of CERCLA

A useful way to think of CERCLA is as a federal statutory embodiment of the tort system. Like tort law, CERCLA looks backward, focusing on the remediation of harm caused, and risks posed, by past practices. At the same time, because those who deal with hazardous substances today would prefer not to be subjected to CERCLA liability in the future, the statute looks forward as well. That is, the threat of future CERCLA liability, like the threat of future tort liability, provides an incentive to engage in safer behavior today.

The scope of CERCLA liability is narrower than that of the tort system. CERCLA does not provide monetary damages for personal injury or private property damage. Rather, CERCLA liability extends only to the cost of remediation and (in some circumstances) to monetary damages for harm to natural resources owned by the government. Within this scope, however, CERCLA liability is considerably stronger than tort liability. For one thing, CERCLA imposes strict liability; if the statutory conditions for liability have been met, the parties specified in the statute (known colloquially as "responsible parties") are liable regardless of whether their behavior would have been deemed negligent (or otherwise actionable) under common law. Moreover, responsible parties (most notably, industrial facilities that shipped hazardous waste to the contaminated site in question) can be held liable for paying cleanup costs and/or monetary damages under CERCLA even if it has not been proven that they actually caused or contributed to the particular release of hazardous substances at issue. In contrast to common law, where the burden of proof is always on the plaintiff, the burden of proof under CERCLA shifts to the responsible parties to prove that their actions did not contribute to the problem. As discussed more fully later, if they prove this, they *may* be able to escape liability for cleanup costs. But if they cannot prove this, and if they also cannot prove that the portion of the harm attributable to them is divisible from the portion of the harm attributable to others, they may find themselves liable for all costs and damages assessed at the site (subject to their right to seek contribution from other responsible parties).

■ NOTES

1. CERCLA was substantially amended in 1986 with the Superfund Amendment and Reauthorization Act (SARA, or SARA amendments), and the following discussion addresses the law as it is following those amendments. Title III of SARA created the Emergency Planning and Community Right-to-Know Act (EPCRA), 42 U.S.C. §11001, *et seq.*, which is discussed in chapter 10.

2. Unwilling to give certain exposure monitoring, health assessment, and toxicological tasks to EPA, Congress also used CERCLA to create the Agency for Toxic Substances and Disease Registry (ATSDR). See Section 104(i), 42 U.S.C. §9604(i). ATSDR's responsibilities were significantly increased by the 1986 SARA amendments. The statute directs ATSDR to (1) maintain a national registry of serious diseases and conditions and a national registry of persons exposed to toxic substances; (2) maintain an inventory of literature, research, and studies on the health effects of toxic substances; (3) maintain a listing of all areas closed to the public or otherwise restricted in use because of contamination by toxic substances; (4) provide medical care and testing (including, as appropriate, tissue sampling, chromosomal testing, and epidemiological studies) to exposed individuals in cases of public health emergencies caused by exposure to toxic substances; (5) conduct periodic survey and screening programs to determine relationships between exposure to toxic substances

and illness; (6) prepare toxicological profiles of substances that are commonly found at CERCLA cleanup sites; (7) provide information to EPA or states, as requested, on health issues related to exposure to hazardous substances; and (8) conduct preliminary health risk assessments at individual sites.　■

2. The President's Authority to Take, Order, or Contract for the Performance of Cleanup Action under CERCLA

a. Section 104

Section 104(a) of CERCLA gives broad powers to the president to take "response action" (defined later) when there is, or threatens to be, a "release" of certain substances into the environment. The president, in turn, has delegated this authority to EPA, and has delegated specific authority to other federal departments for certain kinds of cleanups on their own property. Section 104 authorizes response action when "any hazardous substance is released or there is a substantial threat of such release into the environment," or when "there is a release or substantial threat of release into the environment of any pollutant or contaminant which may present an imminent and substantial danger to the public health or welfare" [42 U.S.C. §§9604(a)(1)(A) and (a)(1)(B)].

The term "hazardous substance" is defined as any of the substances specifically listed by EPA under CERCLA, as well as any other substances identified as hazardous or toxic under certain other federal statutes (including RCRA). Specifically excluded from the definition, however, are petroleum (including any crude oil fraction that is not specifically listed under one or more of the other enumerated federal statutes) and "natural gas, natural gas liquids, liquefied natural gas, [and] synthetic gas usable for fuel" [Section 101(14), 42 U.S.C. §9601(14)].

The term "pollutant or contaminant" is defined generically (without regard to any particular statute) as any substance which, "upon exposure, ingestion, inhalation, or assimilation . . . will or may reasonably be anticipated to cause death, disease, behavioral abnormalities, cancer, genetic mutation, physiological malfunctions (including malfunctions in reproduction) or physical deformations." Here again, however, petroleum, natural gas, and synthetic gas usable for fuel are specifically excluded from the definition. See Section 101(33), 42 U.S.C. §9601(33).

The term "release" is rather broadly defined, but excludes (1) exhaust emissions from motor vehicles, airplanes, or boats; (2) most releases of nuclear material; and (3) "the normal application of fertilizer" [Section 101(22), 42 U.S.C. §9601(22)].

If EPA determines that the necessary response action "will be done properly and promptly" by one or more responsible party, the agency is authorized to enter into a contract with those parties, under Section 122 of CERCLA, to perform the action. See Section 104(a)(1), 42 U.S.C. §9604(a)(1).

Petroleum Natural gas excludes

All Section 104 response action, whether done by EPA or a third party, is to be done in a manner "consistent with the national contingency plan" promulgated by EPA under Section 105 of CERCLA. See Section 104(a), 42 U.S.C. §9604(a).

Under Section 104(b), EPA is authorized, either in conjunction with a Section 104(a) response action or in other specified circumstances involving actual or threatened releases, "to undertake such investigations, monitoring, surveys, testing, and other information gathering activities as [the agency] may deem necessary or appropriate to identify the existence and extent of the release or threat thereof, the source and nature of the hazardous substances, pollutants or contaminants involved, and the extent of the danger to the public health or welfare or the environment" [42 U.S.C. §9604(b)].

Much of the remainder of Section 104 deals with the manner in which actions taken under 104(a) and 104(b) are to be funded. In general, funding can come from the Hazardous Substance Superfund created contemporaneously with CERCLA, from the state in which the cleanup occurs (but only up to 10% of the total), and from responsible parties. The manner in which CERCLA apportions funding for cleanup is discussed in more detail later.

b.   Section 106

When "there may be an imminent and substantial endangerment to the public health or welfare or the environment because of an actual or threatened release of a hazardous substance from a facility"—which is defined as anything other than a consumer product or a vessel [see Section 101(9)]—EPA is authorized under Section 106(a) to either go to federal district court to seek injunctive relief or to issue "such orders as may be necessary to protect public health and welfare and the environment." This, then, serves as an additional means for EPA to secure cleanup. Actions secured under Section 106(a) need not be consistent with the national contingency plan.

A party ordered to take cleanup actions under Section 106 may, upon compliance with the order, recover the costs of such actions in federal court upon a showing that either (1) it is not a "responsible party" under Section 107 or (2) "the President's decision in selecting the response action was arbitrary and capricious or was otherwise not in compliance with the law" [Section 106(b)(2)(C) and (D), 42 U.S.C. §9606(b)(2)(C) and (D)].

■ NOTES

1. In an effort to ensure that EPA has early warning of situations necessitating response action, CERCLA requires that releases of hazardous substances in amounts above thresholds designated by EPA (called "reportable quantities") be reported to

the National Response Center. See Section 103(a), 42 U.S.C. §9603(a). This does not apply to the application of a pesticide registered under the Federal Insecticide, Fungicide, and Rodenticide Act, or to the handling or storage of such a pesticide by an agricultural producer. See Section 103(e), 42 U.S.C. §9603(e).

2. Note that if there is an imminent and substantial danger involving a "pollutant or contaminant," Section 104 response action also is authorized, but if there is an imminent and substantial endangerment involving a hazardous substance, a Section 106 order is authorized.

3. Standardization and Prioritization

a. The National Contingency Plan

In order to foster general consistency in the development and implementation of cleanup methodology, Congress directed the president to revise the "national contingency plan" (NCP) that had been promulgated by EPA under Section 311 of the Clean Water Act to address spills of oil and other hazardous substances into navigable waters. The revised NCP was to include a "national hazardous substance response plan," setting forth "procedures and standards for responding to releases of hazardous substances, pollutants, and contaminants" [Section 105(a), 42 U.S.C. §9605(a)]. The NCP was so revised by EPA, and was substantially revised again in accordance with the SARA amendments of 1986. The present regulation sets out detailed criteria for the conduct of response actions under CERCLA. See 40 C.F.R. §300.

The national contingency plan actually predates both the formation of EPA and the passage of the 1972 Federal Water Pollution Control Act Amendments. The original NCP was a multiagency strategy developed in 1968 for dealing with environmental disasters. It was first put into formal published form to comply with the requisites of Section 311 of the Clean Water Act. See *Ohio v. EPA*, 907 F.2d 1520, 1525 (D.C. Cir. 1993). At present, the NCP governs both the implementation of Section 311 of the Clean Water Act and the implementation of CERCLA.

b. The National Priorities List

One of the points that Congress directed the president to address in the NCP was the prioritization of sites for cleanup. Section 105 requires the president to delineate "criteria for determining priorities among releases or threatened releases throughout the United States," and to publish, and periodically revise, a list of priority sites for cleanup. To the extent practicable, at least one site from each state must be included among the top 100 priority sites. See Section 105(a)(8)(A) and (B), 42 U.S.C. §9605(a)(8)(A) and (B). This list, which is published by EPA, has become known as the national priorities list (NPL), and is referenced by that name in other provisions of CERCLA. If EPA is considering a site for inclusion on the NPL, the agency typically will conduct a *preliminary assessment and site inspection* (PA/SI) to determine whether the contamination at the site is serious enough to warrant such inclusion. See, generally, 42 U.S.C. §9616(b).

4. The Nature of Response Actions Under CERCLA

CERCLA defines "response" as "removal...[a]nd remedial action," and all "enforcement activities related thereto" [Section 101(25), 42 U.S.C. §9601(25)]. A useful, though imperfect, way of conceptualizing the difference between removal and remedial action is that *removal* actions tend to be short-term measures taken to stabilize a situation and/or respond to an emergency, while *remedial* actions are long-term measures designed to achieve a permanent remedy. Thus, while a removal action might be completed in a few days, a few months, or a year, a remedial action usually takes years to complete. In general, if a site has been included on the NPL, it has been slated for remedial action.

a. Removal Action

As defined in CERCLA, removal includes the following categories of action: (1) "the cleanup or removal of released hazardous substances from the environment"; (2) "such actions as may be necessary...in the event of the threat of release of hazardous substances into the environment"; (3) "such actions as may be necessary to monitor, assess, and evaluate the release or threat of release of hazardous substances," including all actions taken under Section 104(b); (4) "the disposal of removed material"; or (5) "the taking of such other actions as may be necessary to prevent, minimize, or mitigate damage to public health or welfare or to the environment which may otherwise result from a release or threat of release" [Section 101(23)]. Significantly, the definition of removal also specifically includes "provision of alternative water supplies, temporary evacuation and housing of threatened individuals not otherwise provided for...[a]nd any emergency assistance which may be provided under the Disaster Relief and Emergency Assistance Act [42 U.S.C. §5121, *et seq.*]" [id.].

b. Remedial Action

Remedial action is defined as "those actions *consistent with permanent remedy* taken *instead of or in addition to removal actions* in the event of a release or threatened release of a hazardous substance into the environment, to prevent or minimize the release of hazardous substances so that they do not migrate to cause substantial danger to present or future public health or welfare or the environment" [Section 101(24), 42 U.S.C. §9601(24), emphasis added]. A number of examples of remedial activities are specifically listed in the definition, including "provision of alternative

[handwritten: Long term]

water supplies," "any monitoring reasonably required to ensure" that the remedial actions taken "protect the public health and welfare and the environment," and, where certain criteria are met, "permanent relocation of residents and businesses and community facilities" (id.).

i. The Steps of a Remedial Action As the definition indicates, remedial action is to be taken "instead of or in addition to" removal action. At some sites, removal action alone will be sufficient to address the problem. If remedial action is being considered, the first step in determining what kinds of remedial action, if any, will be appropriate at a particular site is the performance of a *remedial investigation and feasibility study* (RI/FS). As specified in the NCP, the function of the RI/FS is to identify and evaluate both the nature and extent of the risks posed by the release or threatened release at issue, and the various alternative strategies that could be used to eliminate or substantially reduce those risks. After preparation of the RI/FS, EPA (and the responsible federal department or agency if the site is a federal facility) is to select the remedial actions to be taken at the site. The selection is to be based on a set of findings set forth in a *record of decision* (ROD), and is to result in the preparation of a *remedial action plan* (RAP). Where several cleanup sites are all located on the same property (such as, for example, three leaking landfills located in different parts of a single large industrial site), it is not uncommon for there to be a separate RI/FS, ROD, and RAP for each of the cleanup sites, especially when the nature of the releases differs from site to site.

[handwritten right margin: RAP]

ii. Cleanup Standards The standards governing the selection and performance of remedial action are set forth in Section 121, which was added as part of the 1986 SARA amendments. Remedial actions—whether selected under Section 104, under Section 106, or (as discussed later) under the Section 120 program for high-priority federal facilities—are to be "appropriate," "necessary," and "cost-effective" [Section 121(a), 42 U.S.C. §9621(a)]. The determination of the relative cost-effectiveness of particular actions is to "take into account the total short- and long-term costs of such actions" (id.). In addition, the remedial actions selected are to be, "to the extent practicable," "in accordance with...the national contingency plan" (id.).

The level of cleanup to be attained by the remedial action is specified in Section 121(d). "[A]t a minimum," remedial actions must "attain a degree of cleanup...and of control of further release...which assures protection of human health and the environment" [Section 121(d)(1), 42 U.S.C. §9621(d)(1)]. More specifically, any residues of a hazardous substance, pollutant, or contaminant remaining on the site after completion of the remedial action must, with limited exceptions, meet "any standard, requirement, criteria [sic], or limitation under any Federal environmental law," and any *more stringent* "promulgated standard, requirement, criteria [sic], or limitation under a State environmental or facility siting law," that is "legally applicable to the

[handwritten right margin: must Clean up to normal acceptable standard]

hazardous substance or pollutant or contaminant concerned or is relevant and appropriate under the circumstances of the release or threatened release" [Sections 121(d)(2)(A)(i) and (ii), 42 U.S.C. §§9621(d)(2)(A)(i) and (ii)]. Such standards, requirements, criteria, and limitations are known colloquially as ARARs (legally *applicable* or *relevant* and *appropriate requirements*). To comply with the statute, the remedial actions selected must be sufficient to attain, and must actually attain, all ARARs. Depending on the nature of the site, water quality criteria and effluent standards set under the Clean Water Act, MCL goals and drinking water standards set under the Safe Drinking Water Act, treatment and design standards set under RCRA, ambient air quality standards and emission limitations set under the Clean Air Act, and other standards set under federal law may be designated as ARARs. Moreover, in states with additional or more stringent standards, state laws or regulations may also become ARARs.

- **NOTES**

1. Section 122 of CERCLA specifies that the remedial action selected "shall require a level or standard of control which at least attains the Maximum Contaminant Level Goals established under the Safe Drinking Water Act and water quality criteria established under section 304 or 303 of the Clean Water Act, where such goals or criteria are relevant and appropriate under the circumstances of the release or threatened release" [Section 122(d)(2)(A), 42 U.S.C. §9622(d)(2)(A)]. Why might a party found liable for CERCLA response costs be gratified by the 1996 amendments to the Safe Drinking Water Act?

2. The statute contains provisions designed to prevent a state from using the ARAR process either as a pretext to keep a site from being remediated or as a way of imposing especially stringent standards at a particular site or group of sites. See Section 121(d)(2)(B)(iii) (requiring a finding that the state ARAR is "of general applicability," was "adopted by formal means," and was "not adopted for the purpose of precluding onsite remedial action or other land disposal for reasons unrelated to the protection of human health and the environment").

3. EPA is allowed to deviate from ARARs in certain limited circumstances, but the state must be allowed to participate in that decision. See Section 121(d)(4) and (f)(E)(5) and (G), 42 U.S.C. §§9621(d)(4) and (f)(E)(5).

4. The NCP provides as follows:

Each remedial action selected shall be cost-effective, provided that it first satisfies the threshold criteria set forth in §300.430(f)(1)(ii)(A) and (B) [which require the cleanup to be protective of human health and the environment and to attain ARARs]. Cost-effectiveness is determined by evaluating the following three...criteria...to determine overall effectiveness: long-term effectiveness and permanence, reduction of toxicity, mobility, or volume through treatment, and short-term effectiveness. Overall effectiveness is then compared to cost to ensure that the remedy is cost-effective. A remedy shall be cost-effective if its costs are proportional to its overall effectiveness. [40 C.F.R. §300.430(f)]

By thus defining cost-effectiveness as meaning that the costs of a cleanup are proportional to its overall effectiveness, has EPA imposed a cost-benefit overlay on the language of the statute? Why or why not? See *Ohio v. EPA*, 907 F.2d 1520, 1531 (D.C. Cir. 1993).   ∎

5. The Hazardous Substance Superfund

To help fund cleanup taken under Section 104 of CERCLA, Congress created a Hazardous Substance Response Fund financed by general appropriations and taxes on certain activities. It is this fund that gave CERCLA the "Superfund" moniker by which it is commonly known. Thus, when Congress amended the act in 1986, it formally changed the name of the fund to the Hazardous Substance Superfund. The fund itself was created as part of the Internal Revenue Code. See 26 U.S.C. §9507. As amended in 1986, CERCLA appropriated some $13 billion out of general federal revenues for the fund over an 8-year period. See Section 111(a), 42 U.S.C. §9611(a). Congress also directed money to the fund by imposing a 9.7 cent tax on crude oil and petroleum products, to be capped at a total of $12 billion, and a variable tax on the sale of enumerated feedstock chemicals, ranging from $0.22 per ton for potassium hydroxide to $4.87 per ton for benzene. See 26 U.S.C. §§4611 and 4661. The fund was also financed through an "environmental tax" of 0.12% on annual corporate taxable income above $2 million. See 26 U.S.C. §59A. These three taxes were imposed for 9 years, beginning in 1987 and ending in 1995. As CERCLA has not been reauthorized, however, there has been no regular source of federal financing for the Superfund since that time. Instead, the fund has been replenished by a series of periodic congressional resolutions, and by monies recovered from responsible parties.

Now funded through resolutions & responsive Parties

Ultimately, funding for the cleanup at any given CERCLA site is to come from responsible parties to the extent that they can be identified and are still solvent, and then from the Superfund. However, EPA is authorized, and quite often does, take response action before it is determined whether, or to what extent, responsible parties will be contributing to the cleanup. However, because the financing for such action comes, in the first instance, from the fund, the lack of a regular funding source has served to retard the pace of cleanup. See, e.g., Jennifer Lee (2003) "Superfund Job, Not Quite Finished, Frustrates a Town," *New York Times*, November 10, p. 1.

Q w/out appropriated funds do responsible Parties Pay more now? is this good?

■ **NOTES**

1. Beyond their use in generating funds for CERCLA cleanups, is it likely that the taxes discussed here have had any effect in reducing pollution?

2. Was it fair to single out these parties for the imposition of the Superfund taxes?

3. In the administration of President George W. Bush, EPA has taken the position before Congress that reinstatement of the Superfund taxes would both be unnecessary and poor public policy. See Amena H. Saiyid (2006) "EPA Continues to Oppose Reinstatement of Corporate Taxes to Replenish Trust Fund," *Environment Reporter* 37(10): 498. Nonetheless, congressional attempts to resurrect the industry taxes continue as this book goes to press. See Linda Roeder (2007) "Rep. Hinchley Reintroduces Legislation to Reinstate Industry Fees for Site Cleanups," *Environment Reporter* 38(16): 914.   ■

6.   The Liability of Responsible Parties to Pay the Cost of Response Action

The nature and extent of the liability of responsible parties under CERCLA is set forth in Section 107. In general, responsible parties at a particular site are liable for "all costs of removal and remedial action" incurred by the federal government, a state, or an Indian tribe at that site, so long as the action is "not inconsistent with the national contingency plan" [Section 107(a)(4)(A), 42 U.S.C. §9607(a)(4)(A)]. In addition, they are liable for "any other necessary costs of response incurred by any other person" at the site, so long as the response is "consistent with the national contingency plan" [Section 107(a)(4)(B), 42 U.S.C. §9607(a)(4)(B)]. Further, if "health assessment or health effects" studies are carried out at the site under Section 104(i)—which, as discussed earlier, creates the Agency for Toxic Substances and Disease Registry and authorizes it to perform studies of this nature—the responsible parties are liable for the costs of those studies as well. See Section 107(a)(4)(D), 42 U.S.C. §9607(a)(4)(D).

a.   Who Is Liable?

The statute assigns liability for such costs at a given cleanup site to the following parties:

1. the current "owner and operator" of the site;

2. any prior owner who owned the site "at the time of disposal of any hazardous substance";

3. any party (such as a generator of hazardous waste) who "by contract, agreement, or otherwise arranged for disposal or treatment, or arranged with a transporter for transport for disposal or treatment, of hazardous substances" to the site; and

[handwritten: Whole Process "cradle to grave" responsible]

4. any party "who accepts or accepted any hazardous substance for transport" to the site for disposal or treatment, provided the site was "selected by such person" [Section 107(a)(1)–(4), 42 U.S.C. §9607(a)(1)].

Subject to a few specified exceptions, these parties are all "responsible parties" under CERCLA, and the president is authorized to file suit against them in federal court to obtain reimbursement of cleanup costs. Important parties specifically exempted from the foregoing definition are *lenders* who do not actively manage the site, Section 101(20); *innocent purchasers* of the property who meet certain criteria, Section 101(35); and *consultants* who assist in cleanup, so long as they are not negligent, Section 107(d)(1). See 42 U.S.C. §§9601(20)(E), (F), and (G). 9601(35), and 9607(d)(1). In addition, there is no liability under Section 107 "for any response costs or [natural resource] damages resulting from the application of a pesticide product regulated under the Federal Insecticide, Fungicide, and Rodenticide Act," or for any such costs or damages resulting from a "federally permitted release" (such as discharges to the navigable waters in compliance with a NPDES permit) [42 U.S.C. §§9607(l), 9607(j) and 9601(10)]. Finally, the generators and transporters of certain municipal solid wastes are exempted from liability. See 42 U.S.C. §9607(p).

In practice, EPA commonly identifies a number of parties (chiefly generators and past and present owners) who are associated with a particular site, and notifies them that they are potentially responsible parties (PRPs) for the cleanup at the site. EPA then negotiates and/or litigates with the PRPs, either collectively or individually, to determine which (if any) among them will contribute to response costs at the site, and the amount each will contribute.

■ **NOTES**

[handwritten: amount each pays determined through negotiation / litigation.]

1. The Supreme Court has held that parent corporations may be held liable as "operators" of a facility owned by one of their subsidiary corporations if they actually take a role in managing the environmental affairs of the facility. It is not enough, however, that they take a role in managing the general business affairs of the subsidiary. Rather, noted the Court, "an operator must manage, direct, or conduct operations specifically related to pollution, that is, operations having to do with the leakage or disposal of hazardous waste, or decisions about compliance with environmental regulations" [*U.S. v. Bestfoods*, 524 U.S. 51, 67 (1998)].

2. The innocent purchaser exemption was modified as part of the Small Business Liability Relief and Brownfields Revitalization Act of 2002 (the brownfields amendments). Rather loosely defined, the term "brownfields" has come to be used to refer to partially contaminated sites that most likely would be developed but for concerns about hazardous waste liability. The brownfields amendments were designed

to remove some of the legal, institutional, and economic barriers to development at these sites. In amending the criteria defining an innocent purchaser, however, Congress may actually have made it more difficult for entities to qualify under this exemption. See, for example, Larry Schnapf (2002) "Congress Enacts Sweeping Amendments to CERCLA: Is the Wicked Witch Dead?" 17 *Toxics Law Reporter* 109. Nonetheless, other provisions added by the 2002 amendments are likely to aid brownfields development. For example, the amendments increased the federal monetary support for brownfields development, raising federal appropriations from $96 million to $250 million for fiscal years 2002 through 2006. See 42 U.S.C. §9628(i). The amendments also authorized EPA to defer placement of an eligible brownfields site on the NPL (thus avoiding the stigma of a Superfund site designation) at the request of the state, provided that a state or private cleanup meeting certain criteria is under way. See 42 U.S.C. §9605(h)(1). ∎

b. Defenses to Liability

The explicit statutory defenses to liability are minimal. Section 107(b) specifies that an otherwise responsible party can avoid or limit CERCLA liability by establishing, "by a preponderance of the evidence," that "the threat or release of a hazardous substance" at the site was "caused solely" by (1) an "act of God," (2) an "act of war," or (3) an "act or omission of a third party other than an employee or agent of the defendant, or than one whose act or omission occurs in connection with a contractual relationship . . . with the defendant," provided the defendant "exercised due care with respect to the hazardous substance concerned" and "took precautions against foreseeable acts or omissions of any such third party."

In 2002, as part of the brownfields amendments, Congress added a "de micromis" defense to Section 107 liability. Under this provision, a generator or transporter that contributed less than 100 gallons of liquid material, or less than 200 pounds of solid materials, to an NPL site prior to April 1, 2001 is relieved of liability unless those materials "have contributed significantly or could contribute significantly, either individually or in the aggregate, to the cost of the response action or natural resource restoration" at the site [42 U.S.C. §9617(o)]. Beyond this, the statute does not specifically provide a "causation" defense. However, some courts have held that a generator (or transporter) may be able to avoid liability by demonstrating by a preponderance of the evidence that the hazardous substances that it sent (or transported) to the site did not cause or contribute to any release or threatened release being addressed by the CERCLA response action. See *United States v. Alcan Aluminum Corp.*, 990 F.2d 711 (2d Cir. 1993), and related cases, discussed below.

A party may not "contract away" its CERCLA liability. For example, a generator may not escape liability by entering into a contract with a transporter wherein the transporter agrees to assume all liability if the hazardous substance being transported

[handwritten note: This happened in love canal when Hooker tried to absolve itself of future liability]

is later associated with an actionable "release." However, a party may agree with another party to be *indemnified* for the costs of CERCLA liability. See Section 107(e).

c. The Nature of the Liability

At most sites, responsible parties are liable for the full cost of the remedial actions taken, as long as these actions are consistent with the NCP, and for up to $50,000,000 for damage to natural resources owned by the government. See Section 107(c)(1)(D). For remedial action taken with regard to releases from motor vehicles, aircraft, hazardous liquid pipeline facilities, and certain types of vessels, however, the liability of responsible parties is limited to a specified dollar amount. See Section 107(c)(1)(A)–(C). *[handwritten: weird]* The statutory limitations on liability are inapplicable if "the release or threat of release . . . was the result of willful misconduct or willful negligence within the privity or knowledge" of the responsible party, if "the primary cause of the release was a violation (within the privity or knowledge of [the responsible party]) of applicable safety, construction, or operating standards or regulations," or if the responsible party "fails or refuses to provide all reasonable cooperation and assistance" as requested by a "responsible public official" under the NCP [Section 107(c)(2)]. Moreover, any responsible party who "fails without sufficient cause" to comply with an order issued under Section 104 or 106 "may be liable to the United States for punitive damages in an amount at least equal to, and not more than three times, the amount of any costs incurred by the Fund [the Hazardous Substance Superfund] as a result of such failure to take proper action" [Section 107(c)(3)].

The liability of a responsible party under Section 107 is strict, retroactive, and (at least presumptively) joint and several. Each of these is deserving of emphasis.

Liability is *strict* because it attaches (subject to the potential causation defense discussed here) upon proof that the party in question is a "responsible party" under the statutory definition. Since liability attaches without proof of negligence, exercise of due care is *not* a defense.

Liability is *retroactive* because it applies to the costs of remedial actions taken to address releases and threatened releases resulting from activities occurring *at any time*, whether before or after the passage of CERCLA on December 11, 1980. *[handwritten: interesting concept]*

Finally, the courts have held that liability is *joint and several*. This is a concept borrowed from common law torts. In tort law, joint and several liability is sometimes applied when there is more than one defendant. In general, it means that *all* of the defendants are liable for the plaintiff's damages ("joint" liability), and that any *one* of them can be made to pay *all* of those damages ("several" liability), subject to the caveat that the plaintiff is not entitled to recover his or her damages more than once. Although CERCLA does not explicitly provide for joint and several liability, Congress confirmed when passing the SARA amendments in 1986 that this was its intention. Accordingly, all of the responsible parties at a cleanup site are said to be jointly

[handwritten note: do they try to determine percent of contribution of more of a ?? list]

*like when
Costs distant
based on
Market
Share*

and severally liable for the response costs incurred at the site. The practical import of this is that if, say, only five of twenty responsible parties are meaningfully solvent at the time that response costs are sought under Section 107, these five may be liable for the entire cost of the cleanup. However, a responsible party has an opportunity to avoid (or at least blunt) the effect of joint and several liability if it can demonstrate that its contribution to the release or threatened release is *divisible* from the contributions of other responsible parties at the site. If, say, a company can demonstrate that it sent only lead-contaminated hazardous wastes to a hazardous waste landfill, and that 90% of the response costs at that site were incurred in conjunction with contaminants other than lead, it may be able to limit its liability to no more than 10% of the total cost. The nature of the divisibility defense, and thus the nature of joint and several liability under CERCLA, is discussed in the following decision by the Eighth Circuit Court of Appeals.

U.S. v. Hercules, Inc.
Opinion by WOLLMAN, Circuit Judge
247 F.3d 706 (8th Cir. 2001)

…One aspect of CERCLA that has long vexed courts is the role of causation in the statutory scheme. This is because, "although the simplistic slogan 'make the polluter pay' may have helped propel CERCLA into law, the statutory scheme does not take a simplistic view of who is and who is not a 'polluter'." *Westfarm Assoc. Ltd. Partnership v. Washington Suburban Sanitary Comm'n.*, 66 F.3d 669, 681 (4th Cir. 1995) (citation omitted). Indeed, at least at the liability stage, the language of the statute does not require the government to prove as part of its prima facie case that the defendant caused any harm to the environment. *Control Data v. S.C.S.C.*

Corp., 53 F.3d 930, 935 (8th Cir. 1995). Rather, once the requisite connection between the defendant and a hazardous waste site has been established (because the defendant fits into one of the four categories of responsible parties), it is enough that response costs resulted from "a" release or threatened release—not necessarily the defendant's release or threatened release.[8] 42 U.S.C. §9607(a)(4). Thus, the government need not trace or "fingerprint" a defendant's wastes in order to recover under CERCLA. *United States v. Monsanto*, 858 F.2d 160, 169–70 (4th Cir. 1988). Considerations of causation explicitly enter into the statutory liability

---

8. Although we have stated that "CERCLA focuses on whether the defendant's release or threatened release caused harm to the plaintiff in the form of response costs," *Control Data*, 53 F.3d at 935 (emphasis added), the case we cited for that proposition referred not to the defendant's release but merely to "a" release, *General Electric Company v. Litton Industrial Automation Systems, Inc.*, 920 F.2d 1415, 1417 (8th Cir. 1990) abrogated on other grounds, *Key Tronic Corp. v. United States*,

511 U.S. 809, 814, 819, 128 L. Ed. 2d 797, 114 S. Ct. 1960 (1994). The argument that the government must prove a direct causal link between the incurrence of response costs and an actual release caused by a particular defendant has been rejected by "virtually every court" that has directly considered the issue. *United States v. Alcan Alum. Corp. (Alcan I)*, 964 F.2d 252, 264–65 (3d Cir. 1992) (citing cases); see 42 U.S.C. §9607(a)(4).

scheme only as part of the three statutory defenses not at issue in this case. *Id.* at 170; 42 U.S.C. §9607(b).

Many courts, however, have recognized the defense of divisibility of harm, a "special exception to the absence of causation requirement" that in effect brings causation principles "back into the case—through the backdoor, after being denied entry at the front door." *United States v. Alcan Alum. Corp. (Alcan II)*, 990 F.2d 711, 722 (2d Cir. 1993); see *United States v. Township of Brighton*, 153 F.3d 307, 317–19 (6th Cir. 1998); *Matter of Bell Petroleum, Inc.*, 3 F.3d 889, 894–902 (5th Cir. 1993); *Alcan I*, 964 F.2d at 268–69; *O'Neil v. Picillo*, 883 F.2d 176, 178–79 (1st Cir. 1989); *Monsanto*, 858 F.2d at 171–73. Although we have not been squarely presented with the question whether a divisibility defense should be allowed under CERCLA, we have expressed our approval of the doctrine on several occasions. . . .

The parties in this case do not dispute the general validity of the divisibility doctrine, and we find it to be both compatible with the text and the overall statutory scheme of CERCLA[9] and a sensible way to avoid imposing on parties excessive liability for harm that is not fairly attributable to them. See *Alcan I*, 964 F.2d at 269. We thus proceed to a more detailed discussion of the doctrine.

The universal starting point for divisibility of harm analyses in CERCLA cases is the Restatement (Second) of Torts, which provides for the apportionment of damages among two or more parties when at least one is able to show either (1) "distinct harms" or (2) a "reasonable basis for determining the contribution of each cause to a single harm."

Restatement (Second) of Torts §433A (1965); see *Township of Brighton*, 153 F.3d at 318; *Bell*, 3 F.3d at 895; *Chem-Dyne*, 572 F. Supp. at 810. We will follow the Restatement, however, only to the extent that it is compatible with the provisions of CERCLA. See *O'Neil*, 883 F.2d at 179 n. 4 (describing the Restatement as "one source for us to consult"). Thus, for example, although the Restatement contemplates that plaintiffs bear the burden of proving causation, in a CERCLA case, once the government has established the four essential elements of liability the burden shifts to the defendant to demonstrate, by a preponderance of the evidence, that there exists a reasonable basis for divisibility. *Township of Brighton*, 153 F.3d at 318; *O'Neil*, 883 F.2d at 182. Divisibility generally limits the scope of, but does not entirely eliminate, CERCLA liability since the doctrine is essentially a defense only to joint and several liability. *Control Data*, 53 F.3d at 934 n. 4; *Bell*, 3 F.3d at 895.

We have previously observed that proving divisibility is a "very difficult proposition," *Control Data*, 53 F.3d at 934 n. 4, and the Restatement recognizes that some harms, "by their nature, are normally incapable of any logical, reasonable, or practical division." Restatement (Second) of Torts §433A cmt. to subsection (2) (1965), quoted in *Bell*, 3 F.3d at 896. Where this is the case, the Restatement cautions against making an "arbitrary apportionment for its own sake." Id.; see also *United States v. Colorado & Eastern R. Co.*, 50 F.3d 1530, 1535 (10th Cir. 1995) (noting that "the courts have been reluctant to apportion costs" and that "responsible parties rarely escape joint and several liability");

---

9. Other courts have persuasively argued, based on the legislative history surrounding CERCLA and its 1986 Superfund amendments, that the divisibility of harm doctrine is consistent with the intent of Congress that "'traditional and evolving common law principles' should define the scope of liability under CERCLA." *Redwing Carriers, Inc. v. Saraland Apts.* 94 F.3d 1489, 1513 (11th Cir. 1996) (quoting *Bell*, 3 F.3d at 895); see *O'Neil*, 883 F.2d at 178–79; *Monsanto*, 858 F.2d at 171 n. 23; *United States v. Chem-Dyne Corp.*, 572 F. Supp. 802, 805–08 (S. D. Ohio 1983).

O'Neil, 883 F.2d at 183 (defendants hoping to escape joint and several liability must satisfy the "stringent burden placed on them by Congress"). When a defendant is successful in demonstrating a reasonable basis for apportionment, approaches to divisibility will vary tremendously depending on the facts and circumstances of each case. Evidence of divisibility will focus on determining the amount of harm caused by the defendant. *Bell*, 3 F.3d at 903. Our description below of some of the most common approaches is by no means intended to be exhaustive, for "we know that we cannot define for all time what is a reasonable basis for divisibility and what is not." *Township of Brighton*, 153 F.3d at 319.

"Distinct harms" are those that may properly be regarded as separate injuries. See Restatement (Second) of Torts §433A (1965); *Bell*, 3 F.3d at 895. Defendants may be able to demonstrate that harms are distinct based on geographical considerations, such as where a site consists of "non-contiguous" areas of soil contamination, Akzo *Coatings, Inc. v. Aigner Corp.*, 881 F. Supp. 1202, 1210 (N. D. Ind. 1994), clarified on reconsid., 909 F. Supp. 1154 (N. D. Ind. 1995), or separate and distinct subterranean "plumes" of groundwater contamination, *United States v. Broderick Investment Co.*, 862 F. Supp. 272, 277 (D. Colo. 1994).

Other cases, by contrast, involve a "single harm" that is nonetheless divisible because it is possible to discern the degree to which different parties contributed to the damage. Id. The basis for division in such situations is that "it is clear that each [defendant] has caused a separate amount of harm, limited in time, and that neither has any responsibility for the harm caused by the other," such as where "two defendants, independently operating the same plant, pollute a stream over successive periods of time." Bell, 3 F.3d at 895. Single harms may also be "treated as divisible in terms of degree," based, for ex-

ample, on the relative quantities of waste discharged into the stream. Id. at 895–96. Divisibility of this type may be provable even where wastes have become cross-contaminated and commingled, for "commingling is not synonymous with indivisible harm." *Alcan II*, 990 F.2d at 722; see also *Bell*, 3 F.3d at 903.

Evidence supporting divisibility must be concrete and specific. *See United States v. Alcan Alum. Corp.*, 892 F. Supp. 648, 657 (M. D. Penn. 1995) (*Alcan III*) (rejecting divisibility argument on remand because defendant took "all or nothing approach," presenting no new evidence beyond what court of appeals had already considered), aff'd, 96 F.3d 1434 (3d Cir. 1996) (table). The preliminary issue of whether the harm to the environment is capable of apportionment among two or more causes is a question of law. *Bell*, 3 F.3d at 902. Then, "once it has been determined that the harm is capable of being apportioned among the various causes of it, the actual apportionment of damages is a question of fact." Id. at 896.

We also observe that the divisibility doctrine is conceptually distinct from contribution or allocation of damages. See *Redwing*, 94 F.3d at 1513. At the allocation phase, the only question is the extent to which a defendant's liability may be offset by the liability of another; the inquiry at this stage is an equitable one and courts generally take into account the so-called "Gore factors." See 42 U.S.C. §9613(f) (providing that a court "may allocate response costs among liable parties using such equitable factors as the court determines are appropriate"); *Township of Brighton*, 153 F.3d at 318; Control *Data*, 53 F.3d at 935. The divisibility of harm inquiry, by contrast, is guided not by equity—specifically, not by the Gore factors—but by principles of causation alone. *United States v. Rohm & Haas Co.*, 2 F.3d 1265, 1280–81 (3d Cir. 1993). Thus, where causation is unclear, divisibility is not an opportunity for courts to "split the difference" in an attempt to achieve equity.[10] *Township of Brighton*, 153 F.3d at 319. Rather, "if they are in doubt, district courts should not settle on a compromise amount that they think best

approximates the relative responsibility of the parties." Id. In such circumstances, courts lacking a reasonable basis for dividing causation should avoid apportionment altogether by imposing joint and several liability. Id....

---

10. Accordingly, we reject any suggestion that the financial condition of the parties should play a role in a CERCLA divisibility analysis. But see *Bell*, 3 F.3d at 896 (noting that the Restatement allows courts to consider insolvency); id. at 902 n. 13

("There may be exceptional cases in which it would be unjust to impose several liability, such as when one of the defendants is so hopelessly insolvent that the plaintiff will be unable to recover any damages from it.").

■ NOTES

1. In the *Alcan II* case cited here by the Eighth Circuit, the Second Circuit enunciated the following standard for responsible parties:

Alcan [a generator that sent wastes to a site now subject to remediation under CERCLA] may escape any liability for response costs if it either succeeds in proving that its oil emulsion, when mixed with other hazardous wastes, did not contribute to the release and the clean-up costs that followed, or contributed at most to only a divisible portion of the harm. Alcan as the polluter bears the ultimate burden of establishing a reasonable basis for apportioning liability. The government has no burden of proof with respect to what caused the release of hazardous waste and triggered response costs. It is the defendant that bears that burden. [*United States v. Alcan Aluminum Corp.*, 990 F.2d 711, 722 (2nd Cir. 1993) (citations omitted)]

Thus, in contrast to the clear line drawn by the Eighth Circuit between liability and divisibility, the Second Circuit would effectively allow a PRP to raise a causation defense to Section 107 liability itself. If a generator can prove that it did not cause or contribute to any part of the release being remediated (even though it sent other hazardous wastes to the site), wouldn't the generator escape liability even under the Eighth Circuit's divisibility defense? In other words, aren't the "divisibility" and "causation" defenses the same thing under these circumstances? Both the Sixth and Seventh Circuits have effectively held as much, reasoning that a finding that a party is potentially liable under Section 107 because it contributed waste to a site does not preclude a finding that the contribution was too small to warrant the imposition of cleanup costs. See *Kalamazoo River Study Group v. Rockwell International Corp.*, 274 F. 3d 1043 (6th Cir. 2001) (upholding the district court's refusal to allocate PCB cleanup costs to a company that contributed less than one hundredth of 1% of the PCBs to the site); and *PMC Inc. v. Sherwin-Williams Co.*, 151 F.3d 610, 616 (7th Cir. 1998) (upholding the district court's refusal to allocate cleanup costs to a company whose contribution to the site was deemed to be "too inconsequential to affect the costs of cleaning up significantly"). In these cases, however, the parties found to be responsible for the great bulk of the contamination were also before the court. Is the addition of the explicit de micromis defense likely to have an impact on this line of authority?

2. Consistent with the overwhelming weight of judicial authority, both the Eighth and Second Circuits make clear (in the cases discussed here) that joint and several liability will be applied under CERCLA unless the defendant can carry the factual burden of proving otherwise.

3. Does the imposition of retroactive liability under CERCLA violate the due process or "takings" provision of the Fifth Amendment? That is, does it violate the Constitution to impose liability today on someone for activities carried out decades ago, especially where that liability is strict and (at least potentially) joint and several? Thus far the courts have answered this question in the negative. See, for example, *Franklin County Convention Facilities Auth. v. Am. Premier Underwriters, Inc*, 240 F.3d 534, 552 (6th Cir. 2001); *United States v. Alcan Aluminum Corp.*, 49 F. Supp. 2d 96 (N.D. N.Y. 1999); and *Combined Props./Greenbriar Ltd. P'ship v. Morrow*, 58 F. Supp. 2d 675, 681 (E.D. Va. 1999). The Supreme Court has not addressed the issue, however, and Fifth Amendment challenges to CERCLA liability can be expected to continue. Such challenges might also be expected to cleanup actions brought under RCRA's imminent and substantial endangerment provisions.

4. A key argument in the constitutional challenges to CERCLA is that it is fundamentally unfair to impose financial liability for cleanup costs stemming from waste disposal activities that were perfectly legal at the time they were conducted. How strong is this argument? Would the argument apply with equal force to common law rules of tort liability that became more stringent over time? If so, would the Fourteenth Amendment (which imposes due process requirements on state governmental actions) effectively prevent state tort law from applying retroactively? Would this have an effect on the usefulness of tort law as a social policy tool? Is it relevant to the discussion of CERCLA's constitutionality that those engaging in potentially harmful activities, such as the disposal of hazardous wastes, have long done so with the knowledge that they could later be subjected to a tort suit if harm actually results? ■

As discussed in the *Hercules* case excepted here, a party made to pay response costs under CERCLA (whether under Section 107 or under Section 106) may seek *contribution* (reimbursement for some portion of the amounts paid) from other responsible parties that have not yet satisfied their obligation for such costs. See Section 113(f). Thus, it is not uncommon for one PRP to bring a cost recovery action against other PRPs to compel them to share in the costs of cleanup. Indeed, one of the policy advantages of joint and several liability is that it encourages responsible parties who have been identified by EPA to search for other PRPs. In 2004, the Supreme Court held that contribution suits for costs incurred in a voluntary cleanup (i.e., one initiated by a PRP instead of in response to an administrative or court order) are not authorized under section 113 of CERCLA [*Cooper Industries, Inc. v. Aviall Services, Inc.*, 543 U.S. 157 (2004)]. However, the court later held that such actions are permissible under section 107 [*U.S. v. Atlantic Research Corp.*, 127 S. Ct. 2331 (2007)], and several courts have allowed contribution actions for voluntary cleanup costs to go forward under that provision.

7. The Special Program for Remediating Federal Facilities

Concerned that hazardous waste sites at federal facilities were not being adequately remediated, Congress added special provisions to CERCLA in 1986 specifically addressing cleanup at federal facilities. These provisions are set forth in Section 120. In addition to confirming (as had been the case previously) that all departments, agencies, and instrumentalities of the United States are subject to the requirements of CERCLA "to the same extent . . . as any nongovernmental entity," this section also creates a separate program for the remediation of high-priority federal sites [42 U.S.C. §§9620(a) and (e)]. When a federal facility is placed on the NPL, the responsible federal department must—according to a specified timetable—commence an RI/FS, select (together with EPA) appropriate remedial action, and complete that remedial action in accordance with the standards set forth in Section 121 (id.). As with response action taken under Section 104, remedial action taken under Section 120 must be consistent with the NCP. See 42 U.S.C. §9620(a)(2).

8. The Search for Innovative Cleanup Technologies

In 1997 EPA estimated that there were approximately 217,000 sites nationwide requiring clean-up because of contamination with hazardous substances. Included on this list were private NPL sites, Department of Defense, Department of Energy, and other federal agency sites, RCRA corrective action sites, RCRA underground storage tank sites, and sites identified under state cleanup programs [U.S. EPA (1997) *Cleaning Up the Nation's Waste Sites: Markets and Technology Trends.* EPA 542-A-96-005, Washington, D.C., Ex. 1-1]. The total cost of remediating these sites, in 1996 dollars, was estimated to be $187 billion (id., Ex. 1-2). Given the high cost of clean-up, one would think that there would be an ample market for cheaper, more efficient cleanup technologies. To a certain extent this has been true. The use at NPL sites of technologies deemed "innovative" by EPA increased from 0% in 1983 to almost 20% in 1993, and largely ranged between 20% and 40% in the 12 years thereafter, with a low of 15% in 2003 and a high of 48% in 2005. [U.S. EPA (2007) *Treatment Technologies for Site Cleanup: Annual Status Report* (12th ed.). EPA-542-R-07-12, Washington, D.C., p. 3-10, fig. 13.]

In 2000, EPA analyzed ten studies that had attempted to identify the key factors restricting the development and use of innovative technologies at hazardous waste sites. The agency found that almost 70% of the barriers cited could be classified as either institutional (those that "stem from the internal workings or functions of entities that seek to regulate, develop, or select" innovative cleanup technologies) or economic and financial (those that "tend to reduce or eliminate financial incentives" for development, use, or marketing of such technologies) [U.S. EPA (2000) *An Analysis of Barriers to Innovative Treatment Technologies: Summary of Existing Studies and Current Initiatives*, EPA-542-B-00-003, p. 7.] In contrast, technical barriers to development and use, including issues regarding the performance of particular technologies, represented only 14% of all barriers cited (id.). Although earlier studies had cited community resistance to the use of innovative technologies, and a failure by EPA to systematically assess the opportunities for innovative technology use at existing sites, more recent studies suggest that these factors are no longer extant (id., p. 17).

■ **NOTES**

1. As one might expect, there is no single definition of "innovative" cleanup technology that is accepted in all quarters. According to a study by the GAO, the most commonly used "innovative" technologies through 1991 were soil vapor extraction (the use of vapor extraction wells to remove volatile organic constituents from the soil), thermal desorption (heating waste in a controlled environment to volatilize organic compounds, usually as a means of isolating them for further treatment), ex situ bioremediation (the use of microorganisms to degrade organic contaminants in excavated soil), and in situ bioremediation (the use of microorganisms to degrade organic contaminants in the soil or in an aquifer) [U.S. General Accounting Office (1992) *Superfund: EPA Needs to Better Focus Cleanup Technology Development*. GA)/T-RCED-92-92, Washington, D.C., pp. 13–15.] EPA now considers soil vapor extraction an established technology, but treats multiphase extraction technologies (which extract VOCs from soil vapor and groundwater simultaneously) as innovative. Through 2005, the three most common "innovative" treatment technologies used at NPL sites were bioremediation (47% of innovative applications), multiphase extraction (19%), and chemical treatment (12%). [U.S. EPA (2007) *Treatment Technologies for Site Cleanup*, p. 3-9, fig. 12; see also www.epa.gov/tio/databases.]

2. How might Congress amend CERCLA to better encourage the development and use of innovative cleanup technologies? Are the types of incentives that are likely to promote the desired innovation likely to be different from those that will spur the kinds of innovations in production processes that are consistent with pollution prevention? Is the target "audience" (the entities that are expected to develop the innovative technologies) likely to be different?

3. Another form of technological innovation spurred by CERCLA has been the development of "tagging" technologies that will assist hazardous waste generators in establishing a defense to joint and several liability (by enabling them to establish that their wastes did not contribute to the contamination in question). See "Fingering Pollution," *The Economist*, November 27, 1993, p. 91.   ■

9.   The Liability of Responsible Parties to Pay for Damage to Natural Resources

Under Section 107(a)(4)(C), responsible parties are also liable for monetary damages for natural resource harm caused by the release in question. "Natural resource" has a specialized meaning under the statute, and is limited to resources (including wildlife) owned, managed, or held in trust by the United States, a state or local government, a foreign government, or an Indian tribe. Subject to statutory limitations on the amount of the liability, the nature of the liability for harm to natural resources is the same as that for response costs, except that it is *not* retroactive. That is, responsible parties are not liable for natural resource harm occurring before the statute was passed on December 11, 1980. See Section 107(a)(1), 42 U.S.C. §9607(a)(1). Actions to recover monetary damages for natural resource harm also are subject to the 3-year statute of limitations set forth in Section 113(g).

10.   The Citizen's Role   *Wonder how economists assess this*

The 1986 SARA amendments expanded the opportunities for public oversight of the cleanup process. For example, the public has a right to comment on a proposed remedial action plan before it is finalized (see Section 117), and to comment on any consent decree under which responsible parties propose to undertake cleanup [see Section 122(i)]. Further, the NCP requires that the various steps of a remedial action, and certain types of removal actions, be subject to public review and comment before they are taken. To assist citizen and community groups in evaluating both the nature of the releases at issue and the nature of the remedial actions being considered, CERCLA also provides for technical assistance grants (known as TAG grants). Moreover, states are to be given opportunities for "substantial and meaningful involvement" in CERCLA cleanups occurring within their borders. See Section 121(f)(1), 42 U.S.C. §9621(f)(1).

Congress also added a citizen suit provision to CERCLA in 1986. See Section 310, 42 U.S.C. §9659. The impact of this addition was substantially muted, however, by the concomitant addition of Section 113(h), which prohibits, with limited exceptions, the filing of *any* action in federal court, under state or federal law (including RCRA), "to review any challenges to removal or remedial action selected under [Section 104], or to review any order issued under [Section 106]." Section 113(h)(4) exempts CERCLA citizen suits from this jurisdictional bar, but specifies that such suits may be brought only *after* removal and remedial action for a specific release or threatened release has been completed. The Ninth Circuit Court of Appeals has held that the Section 113(h) bar does *not* apply to challenges to Section 120(e) remedial actions at federal facilities because those actions are selected under Section 120, rather than under Section 104. See *Fort Ord Toxics Project v. California EPA*, 189 F. 3d 828 (9th Cir. 1999).

Further, Section 113(h) specifies that the jurisdictional bar does not apply to actions brought to compel payment of response costs, monetary damages for harm to natural resources, or contributions under Sections 106 or 107. See 42 U.S.C. §§9613(h)(1), (2), (3), and (5). Responsible parties are authorized to challenge the response actions selected (arguing, for example, that they were not the most cost-effective alternative available) in defending such actions.

11.   Monetary Damages for Personal Injury and Damage to Private Property

When the Superfund bill was first debated in Congress, there was much discussion of establishing a statutory compensation scheme for those harmed by hazardous substances, but no consensus was reached on whether or how to fashion such a system. Thus, as noted at the beginning of this chapter, CERCLA does not provide private parties a separate means for recovering monetary damages for injury to persons or property caused by the release of hazardous substances. However, the statute disavows any intent to preempt state tort law suits seeking such relief (except that it prevents recovery of compensation for "the same removal costs or damages or claims" under both CERCLA and another federal or state law). See Section 114(a) and (b), 42 U.S.C. §§9614(a) and (b).

Moreover, as part of the 1986 SARA amendments, Congress liberalized the "limitations period" for such suits (the period of time within which such suits must be filed) by specifying that no state may impose a starting date for the limitations period that is sooner than "the date the plaintiffs knew (or reasonably should have known) that the personal injury or property damages . . . were caused or contributed to by the hazardous substance or pollutant or contaminant concerned" [Section 309(a) and (b)(4)(A), 42 U.S.C. §§9658(a) and (b)(4)(A)]. Since this provision applies only to suits alleging damage from a "hazardous substance, or pollutant or contaminant, released into the environment" [Section 309(a)], and since the definition of "release" excludes "any release which results in exposure to persons solely within a workplace, with respect to a claim which such persons may assert against [their] employer" [42 U.S.C. §9601(22)], this federal liberalization of the limitations period does not apply to workers' compensation claims, or to worker lawsuits against an employer.

10 The Right to Know: Mandatory Disclosure of Information Regarding Chemical Risks

A. Worker Right to Know
　1. The OSHAct
　2. TSCA
　3. The NLRA
B. Community Right to Know
　1. EPCRA Reporting Generally
　2. Chemical Release Reporting Under the TRI Program
C. Community Right to Know as a Spur to Risk Reduction

As should be clear by this point, the various media-based environmental laws incorporate a number of *information disclosure* requirements. Under the Clean Air and Clean Water acts, for example, pollution sources are required to monitor discharges of pollutants and report the results to EPA or the state. Similarly, those who generate, transfer, treat, store, or dispose of hazardous waste must maintain records of the types and amounts of wastes involved, and must supply these records to the appropriate agency. In fact, the existence of adequate and accurate information of this nature is essential to the optimal operation of both the command-and-control approaches to risk reduction discussed in previous chapters and the so-called market-based approaches discussed in chapter 12. Without such information, neither class of policies can succeed.

Beyond the particular informational requirements attached to the various regulatory regimes, however, there is a class of more broadly based information disclosure requirements popularly known as "right-to-know" laws. In essence, these laws give workers and citizens a general statutory right to be apprised of the substances to which they are (or may be) exposed, as well as to obtain information about the hazardous nature of those substances. These laws have a twofold risk-reduction purpose. The first is to give potentially exposed persons information that may enable them to take action to avoid or limit such exposure. The second is to encourage those who create such exposures—the manufacturers and users of toxic chemicals—to take actions to reduce or eliminate the exposure. In this chapter we examine these laws and evaluate their actual and potential effectiveness.

Political and legislative initiatives focusing on the right to know came to the fore in the early 1980s during a time when the direct regulation of toxic substances was being deemphasized by the federal agencies. Workplace information disclosure and reporting requirements under the 1970 Occupational Safety and Health Act (the OSHAct) and at the state and local level preceded the more general community right-to-know requirements embodied in the 1986 Emergency Planning and Community Right to Know Act (EPCRA), and these worker right-to-know initiatives greatly influenced the evolution of the community right to know.

Worker and community right-to-know laws largely focus on scientific information about chemicals: (1) the ingredients of chemical products and the specific composition of pollution in air, water, and waste; (2) the toxicity and safety hazards posed by the related chemicals, materials, and industrial processes; and (3) information related to exposure of various vulnerable groups to harmful substances and processes. However, disseminating (or providing access to) legal and technological information may be even more important for empowering workers and citizens to facilitate a transformation of hazardous industries and their practices. Legal information refers to statements (or explanations) of the rights and obligations of producers, employers, consumers, workers, and the general public with regard to potential or actual chemical exposures. Technological information includes information regarding (1) monitoring technologies; (2) options for controlling or minimizing pollution, waste, or chemical accidents; and (3) available substitutes or alternative inputs, products, and processes that may prevent pollution, waste, and chemical accidents. Dissemination of such technological information, especially, tends to have a far greater potential to induce technological change than simply collecting and disseminating scientific information about chemical risks and exposures. See, e.g., Lars Koch and Nicholas Ashford (2006) "Rethinking the Role of Information in Chemicals Policy: Implications for TSCA and REACH," *Journal of Cleaner Production* 14(1): 31–46 for a discussion of the role of different kinds of information in minimizing or eliminating the risks due to the production, use, and disposal of chemical substances. See also the discussion in chapter 13 on the importance of technological information for pollution and accident *prevention*, as opposed to pollution and accident *control*.

A.   WORKER RIGHT TO KNOW

The dissemination of information regarding workplace exposure to toxic substances has received considerable public attention. It is generally agreed that workers need an accurate picture of the nature and extent of probable chemical exposures to make a meaningful decision as to whether to enter or remain in a particular workplace. Workers also need to have knowledge regarding past or current exposures to be alert to the onset of occupational disease. Regulatory agencies must have timely access to such information if they are to devise effective strategies to reduce disease and death from occupational exposures to toxic substances. Accordingly, laws designed to facilitate the flow of such information have been promulgated at the federal, state, and local levels. In the 1980s, the right to know became a political battleground in many states and communities and was the subject of intensive organizing efforts by business, labor, and citizen-action groups.

In essence, the right to know embodies a democratization of the workplace. It is the mandatory sharing of information between management and labor. Through a variety of laws, manufacturers and employers are directed to disclose information regarding workers' exposure to toxic substances, to unions in their capacity as workers' representatives, and to governmental agencies charged with the protection of public health. The underlying rationale for these directives is the assumption that this transfer of information will prompt activity that will improve workers' health.

Although the phrase *right to know* is a useful generic designation, it is an inadequate description of the legal rights and obligations that govern the communication of workplace information on toxic substances. A person will not have a meaningful *right* to information unless someone else has a corresponding *duty* to provide that information. Thus, a worker's right to know is secured by requiring a manufacturer or employer to disclose information. The disclosure requirement can take a variety of forms, and the practical scope of that requirement may depend on the nature of the form chosen. In particular, a duty to disclose only such information as has been requested may result in a narrower flow of information than a duty to disclose all information, regardless of whether it has been requested. The various rights and obligations in the area of imparting information on toxics may be grouped into three categories. Although they share a number of similarities, each category is conceptually distinct:

1. *The duty to generate or retain information* refers to the obligation to compile a record of certain workplace events or activities or to maintain such a record for a specified period of time if it has been compiled. An employer may, for example, be required to undertake workplace measurements (of toxic substances, noise, or radiation) or to monitor its workers regularly for evidence of toxic exposures (biological monitoring) and to keep written records of the results of such monitoring.

2. *The right of access* (and the corresponding duty to disclose information on request) refers to the right of a worker, a union, or an agency to request and secure access to information held by a manufacturer or employer. Such a right of access

would provide workers with a means of obtaining copies of environmental and bio-logical monitoring records pertaining to their own exposure to toxic substances.

3. Finally, *the duty to inform* refers to an employer's or manufacturer's obligation to disclose, without request, information pertaining to toxic substance exposures in the workplace. An employer may, for example, have a duty, independent of any worker's exercise of a right to access, to inform workers whenever environmental or biological monitoring reveals that their exposure to a toxic substance has produced bodily con-centrations of that substance above a specified level.

The scope of a particular right or duty depends on many factors. The first, and perhaps most important, is the nature of the information that must be supplied. As discussed earlier, the main categories of information are *scientific*, *technological*, and *legal*. In the context of the workplace, scientific information can be further divided into three subcategories:

1. *Ingredients information* provides the worker with the identity of the substances to which he or she is exposed. Depending on the circumstances, this information may constitute only the generic classifications of the various chemicals involved or may include the specific chemical identities of all chemical exposures and the specific contents of all chemical mixtures.

2. *Exposure information* encompasses all data regarding the amount, frequency, du-ration, and route of workplace exposures. This information may be of a general na-ture, such as the results of ambient air monitoring at a central workplace location, or may take individual forms, such as the results of personal environmental or bio-logical monitoring of a specific worker.

3. *Health effects information* indicates known or potential health effects of workplace exposures. This may be limited to general data regarding the effects of chemical exposure, usually found in a material safety data sheet (MSDS) or a published or unpublished workplace epidemiological study, but it may also include individual data, such as workers' medical records compiled as a result of medical surveillance.

Rights and duties governing provision of information on toxics in the workplace can originate from a variety of sources. Some are grounded in state common law, whereas others arise out of specific state statutes or local ordinances. Although the states have been active in this field, the primary source of regulation is federal law. Most federal regulation in this area emanates from three statutes: the OSHAct, 29 U.S.C. §§651, *et seq.*, the Toxic Substances Control Act (TSCA), 15 U.S.C. §§2601, *et seq.*, and the National Labor Relations Act (NLRA), 29 U.S.C. §§151, *et seq.*, the last of which is administered by the National Labor Relations Board (NLRB). In general, the broadest coverage is found in rights and duties emanating from the OSHAct. By its terms, that act is applicable to all *private* employers and thus covers the bulk of workplace exposures to toxic substances. Most private industrial workplaces are also subject to the NLRA. Farm workers and workers subject to the Railway Labor Act, however, are exempt from NLRA coverage. TSCA provides a generally narrower scope. Although many of the act's provisions apply broadly to the manufacture and use of chemicals, its informational requirements extend only to chemical manufacturers, processors, and importers. On the state level, the relevant coverage of the various rights and duties depends on the specifics of the particular state and local law defining them. In general, common-law rights and duties show much less variation than those created by state statute or local ordinance.

1. The OSHAct

Under OSHA's Hazard Communication Standard, 29 C.F.R. §1910.1200, employers have an affirmative duty to inform their workers of the identity of the chemical substances with which they work. Employers must ensure that chemical product containers are properly labeled, and must make MSDSs on the various chemicals available to the workers. Employers are under no obligation under the Hazard Communication Standard to amend inadequate, insufficient, or incorrect information provided to them by the chemical manufacturer. They must, however, transmit information to their employees regarding the nature of the standard and its requirements, the operations in their work areas where hazardous chemicals are present, and the location and availability of the employer's hazard communication program. The standard also requires that workers be trained in (1) methods to detect the presence or release of the hazardous chemicals; (2) the physical and health hazards of the chemicals; (3) protective measures, such as appropriate work practices, emergency procedures, and personal protective equipment; and (4) the details of the hazard communication program developed by the employer, including an explanation of the labeling system and the MSDSs, and an explanation of how employees can obtain and use information on hazards.

Under OSHA's Medical Access Rule, 29 C.F.R. §1910.20, an employer may not limit or deny an employee access to his or her own medical or exposure records. The regulation grants employees a general right of access to medical and exposure records kept by their employer. Furthermore, it requires the employer to preserve and maintain these records for 30 years. There appears to be some overlap in the definitions of *medical* and *exposure* records, because both may include the results of biological monitoring. Medical records, however, are in general defined as those pertaining to "the health status of an employee," whereas the exposure records are defined as those pertaining to "employee exposure to toxic substances or harmful physical agents." The employer's duty to make these records available is a broad one. Upon any employee request for access to a medical or exposure record, the employer *shall* ensure that access is provided in a reasonable time, place, and manner, but in no event later than 15 days after the request for access is made.

An employee's right of access to medical records is limited to records pertaining specifically to that employee. The regulations allow physicians some discretion as well in limiting employee access. Similar constraints do not apply to employee access to exposure records. Not only is the employee ensured access to records of his or her own exposure to toxic substances, but the employee is also ensured access to the exposure records of other employees "with past or present job duties or working conditions related to or similar to those of the employee." In addition, the employee has access to all general exposure information pertaining to the employee's workplace or working conditions and to any workplace or working condition to which he or she is to be transferred. All information in exposure records that cannot be correlated with a particular employee's exposure is accessible.

One criticism of the OSHA regulation is that it does not require an employer to compile medical or exposure information, but merely requires employee access to such information if it is compiled. The scope of the regulation, however, should not be underestimated. The term "record" is meant to be "all-encompassing," and the access requirement appears to extend to all information gathered on employee health or exposure, no matter how it is measured or recorded. Thus, if an employer embarks on any program of human monitoring, no matter how it is conducted, he or she must provide the subjects access to the results. This access requirement may serve as a disincentive for employers to monitor employees' exposure or health, if it is not clearly in the employer's interest to do so.

The regulations permit an employer to deny access to "trade secret data which discloses manufacturing processes or . . . the percentage of a chemical substance in a mixture," provided that the employer (1) notifies the party requesting access of the denial; (2) if relevant, provides alternative information sufficient to permit identification of when and where exposure occurred; and (3) provides access to all "chemical or physical agent identities including chemical names, levels of exposure, and employee health status data contained in the requested records." The key feature of this provision is that it ensures employees access to the precise identities of chemicals and physical agents. This access is especially critical for chemical exposures. Within each generic class of chemicals, there are a variety of specific chemical compounds, each of which may have its own particular effect on human health. The health effects can vary widely within a particular family of chemicals. Accordingly, the medical and scientific literature on chemical properties and toxicity is indexed by specific chemical name, not by generic chemical class. To discern any meaningful correlation between a chemical exposure and a known or potential health effect, an employee must know the precise chemical identity of that exposure. Furthermore, in the case of biological monitoring, the identity of the toxic substance or its metabolite is itself the information monitored. Particularly in light of the public health emphasis inherent in the OSHAct, disclosure of such information would not appear to constitute an unreasonable infringement on the trade secret interests of the employer. In general, of all the proprietary information relevant to a particular manufacturing process, chemical health and safety data are the least valuable to an employer.

2. TSCA

The Toxic Substances Control Act imposes substantial requirements on chemical manufacturers, processors, and distributors to develop health effects data relating to chemical exposures. TSCA requires testing, premarket manufacturing notification, and reporting and retention of information. Although TSCA is broadly focused on all risks from chemical exposure, workers will often be the most direct beneficiaries of the act's chemical reporting requirements. TSCA imposes no specific medical surveillance or biological monitoring requirements. However, to the extent that human monitoring is used to meet more general requirements of assessing occupational health or exposure to toxic substances, the data resulting from such monitoring are subject to an employer's recording and retention obligations.

Under TSCA, EPA has promulgated regulations requiring general reporting on several hundred chemicals, including information related to occupational exposure. EPA has also promulgated rules under TSCA requiring the submission of health and safety studies for several hundred substances (40 C.F.R. §712). A health and safety study includes "[a]ny data that bear on the effects of chemical substance on health." Examples are "[m]onitoring data, when they have been aggregated and analyzed to measure the exposure of humans . . . to a chemical substance or mixture." Only data that are "known" or "reasonably ascertainable" need be reported [15 U.S.C. §2607(a)(2)].

Section 8(a) of TSCA also requires that records of "significant adverse reactions to health or the environment" be retained for 30 years. See 15 U.S.C. §2607(c). A rule implementing this section defines significant adverse reactions as those "that may indicate a substantial impairment of normal activities, or long-lasting or irreversible damage to health or the environment" [40 C.F.R. §717.3(i)]. Under the rule, human monitoring data, especially if derived from a succession of tests, would seem especially reportable. Genetic monitoring of employees, if some basis links the results with increased risk of cancer or other disease, also seems to fall within the rule. Section 8(e) of TSCA imposes a further duty to report "immediately . . . information which supports the conclusion that [a] substance or mixture presents a substantial risk of injury to health." See 15 U.S.C. §2607(e). In a policy statement issued in 1978, EPA interpreted "immediately" in this context to require receipt by the agency within 15 working days after the reporter obtains the information. Substantial risk is defined exclusive of economic considerations. Evidence can be provided by either designed, controlled studies or undesigned, uncontrolled studies, including "medical and health surveys" or evidence of effects in workers. From 1978 to 2003, EPA received more than 25,000 such submissions. During the years 2001 and 2002 the percentage of these reports addressing reproductive and developmental toxicity, eco-toxicity, cancer, and mutagenicity ranged from 21 to 19%, 7.5 to 14%, 11 to 9%, and 5 to 11%, respectively. See Myra L. Karstadt (2003) "The Toxic Substances Control Act Section 8(e) Database: A Rich Source of Data for Studies of Occupational Carcinogenesis," *European Journal of Oncology* 8: 159.

Section 14(b) of TSCA gives EPA authority to disclose from health and safety studies the data pertaining to chemical identities, except for the proportion of chemicals in a mixture. In addition, EPA may disclose information otherwise classified as a trade secret "if the Administration determines it necessary to protect...against an unreasonable risk of injury to health" [15 U.S.C. §2613(b)]. Human monitoring data thus seem subject to full disclosure.

3. The NLRA

In addition to the access provided by OSHA regulations, individual employees may have a limited right of access to their medical and exposure records under federal labor law. Logically, the right to refuse hazardous work, which is inherent in U.S. labor law, carries with it the right of access to the information necessary to determine whether a particular condition is hazardous. In the case of exposure to toxic substances, this right of access may mean access to all information relevant to the health effects of the exposure and may include access to both medical and exposure records. Any such individual right is not an adequate substitute for the OSHA access regulations, however, because there is no systematic mechanism for enforcing this right.

Collective employee access is available to unionized employees through the collective bargaining process. In four cases the NLRB has held that unions have a right of access to exposure and medical records so that they may bargain effectively with an employer regarding conditions of employment. Citing the general proposition that employers are required to bargain on health and safety conditions when requested to do so, the NLRB adopted a broad policy favoring union access: "Few matters can be of greater legitimate concern to individuals in the workplace, and thus to the bargaining agent representing them, than exposure to conditions potentially threatening their health, well-being, or their very lives" [*Minnesota Mining & Mfg, Co.* 261 N.L.R.B. 27, 29 (1982)]. The NLRB did not grant an unlimited right of access, however. The union's right of access is constrained by the individual employee's right of personal privacy. Furthermore, the NLRB acknowledged an employer's interest in protecting trade secrets. Although ordering the employer in each of the four cases to disclose the chemical identities of substances to which the employer did not assert a trade secret defense, the NLRB indicated that employers are entitled to take reasonable steps to safeguard "legitimate" trade secret information. The NLRB did not delineate a specific mechanism for achieving the balance between union access and trade secret disclosure. Instead, it ordered the parties to attempt to resolve the issue through collective bargaining.

Over the years, the legal avenues for worker and agency access to information relevant to exposures to toxic substances in the workplace have been expanded substantially. Despite certain gaps in the current laws, and despite recent attempts by OSHA to narrow the scope of some of these laws even further, access to data on workplace chemicals remains broader than it has ever been. By itself, however, this fact is of little significance. The mere existence of information transfer laws means little unless those laws are used aggressively to further the objective of the right to know: the protection of workers' health. The various rights and duties governing dissemination of information in the workplace present workers, unions, and agencies with an important opportunity. The extent to which they seize this opportunity is a measure of their resolve to bring about meaningful improvement in the health of the American worker.

In general, worker right-to-know laws do not require the disclosure of *technological* information, as we use that term here. This is unfortunate, because shifting the focus of the discussion between workers and management from the *risks* in the workplace to technological *solutions* may offer a fruitful avenue for collective bargaining and could hasten a movement to cleaner, safer production technologies. See, e.g., Nicholas A. Ashford and Christine Ayers (1987) "Changes and Opportunities in the Environment for Technology Bargaining," 62 *Notre Dame Law Review* 810; Lars Koch and Nicholas Ashford (2006) "Rethinking the Role of Information in Chemicals Policy: Implications for TSCA and REACH," *Journal of Cleaner Production* 14(1): 31–46. As discussed later, access to certain information regarding available alternatives for reducing exposure to toxic substances and the chances of sudden and accidental releases of chemicals *is* available under federal community right-to-know laws.

■ **NOTES**

1. For a more detailed discussion of worker right-to-know laws, see Nicholas A. Ashford and Charles C. Caldart (1996) *Technology, Law and the Working Environment*, 2nd ed., Island Press, Washington, D.C., ch. 7; and Nicholas A. Ashford, Christine J. Spadafor, and Charles C. Caldart (1984) "Human Monitoring: Scientific, Legal, and Ethical Considerations," 8 *Harvard Environmental Law Review* 263.

2. Although the Emergency Planning and Community Right to Know Act, discussed in the next section, is not a workplace right-to-know law per se, it provides an alternative means through which many employees can learn about the use of toxic

substances, not only in their own workplaces, but also in other places in which they may wish to work.

3. In December 2005, a $16.5 million penalty—the highest administrative penalty in EPA history—was imposed upon E.I. du Pont de Nemours and Company as part of a settlement of allegations that DuPont had violated both TSCA and RCRA by failing to disclose its data indicating (1) the rate at which a carcinogenic component of Teflon, perflurooctanoic acid, migrated through the placenta of a pregnant woman into her fetus, (2) the deaths of test animals who inhaled the chemical, and (3) the presence of the chemical in community drinking water. See *Environment Reporter* 36(49): 2581 (2005).   ■

B. COMMUNITY RIGHT TO KNOW

In 1986, Congress amended the federal Superfund statute with the Superfund Amendment and Reauthorization Act of 1986 (known as SARA). Beyond strengthening certain provisions governing the clean-up of hazardous waste sites, Congress took in SARA what has proven to be a significant step toward reducing the likelihood of new hazardous substance contamination in the future. Title III of SARA created the Emergency Planning and Community Right to Know Act (EPCRA), now codified at 42 U.S.C. §§11001, *et seq.* EPCRA is a comprehensive federal community right-to-know program implemented by the states under guidelines promulgated by EPA. The central feature of this federal program is broad public dissemination of information pertaining to the nature and identity of chemicals used at commercial facilities.[1]

---

1. On its web page, EPA describes the impetus for this reauthorization as follows: "In 1984 a deadly cloud of methyl isocyanate killed thousands of people in Bhopal, India. Shortly thereafter, there was a serious chemical release at a sister plant in West Virginia. These incidents underscored demands by industrial workers and communities in several states for information on hazardous materials. Public interest and environmental organizations around the country accelerated demands for information on toxic chemicals being released "beyond the fence line"—outside of the facility. Against this background, the Emergency Planning and Community Right-to-Know Act (EPCRA) was enacted in 1986" (http://www.epa.gov/tri/). Others, however, credit passage of the legislation not so much to the established national environmental groups, but rather to a burgeoning cadre of citizen activists from communities (such as Love Canal) who grew increasingly concerned about hazardous substances in their midst. See Bradley C. Karkkainen (2001) "Information as Environmental Regulation: TRI and Performance Benchmarking, Precursor to a New Paradigm?" 89 *Georgetown Law Journal* 257, text accompanying notes 268–269. (See chapter 9 for a discussion of how concern about hazardous waste spurred community activism in the 1980s.) As to how proponents of SARA's community right-to-know provisions were able to overcome the substantial opposition of the business community, a congressional staffer explained to one of the authors of this text that industry lobbyists were preoccupied with the debate of the law's hazardous waste cleanup provisions, and were unable to mount as strong an offensive against the right-to-know provisions as they most likely would have had those provisions been offered on their own.

1. EPCRA Reporting Generally

EPCRA has four major provisions:

- Emergency planning (Sections 301–303; 42 U.S.C. §§11001–11003)
- Emergency release notification (Section 304; 42 U.S.C. §11004)
- Hazardous chemical storage reporting (Sections 311–312; 42 U.S.C. §§11011–12), and
- The Toxic Chemical Release Inventory (TRI) (Section 313; 42 U.S.C. §11013)

The essential requirements put in place by the 1986 SARA Amendments are summarized in table 10.1.

The implementation of EPCRA began with the creation of state and local bodies to implement this community right-to-know program. Section 301 required the governor of each state to appoint a "state emergency response commission" (SERC), to be staffed by "persons who have technical expertise in the emergency response field." In practice, these state commissions have tended to include representatives from the various environmental and public health and safety agencies in the state. Each state commission in turn was required to divide the state into various "local emergency planning districts" and to appoint a "local emergency planning committee" (LEPC) for each of these districts. These state and local entities are responsible for receiving, coordinating, maintaining, and providing access to the various types of information required to be disclosed under the act.

EPCRA established four principal requirements for reporting information about hazardous chemicals. Section 304 requires all facilities that manufacture, process, use, or store certain "extremely hazardous substances" in excess of certain quantities to provide "emergency" notification to the SERC and the LEPC of an unexpected release of one of these substances. Section 311 requires facilities covered by the OSHA Hazard Communication Standard to prepare and submit to the LEPC and the local fire department material safety data sheets for chemicals covered by the OSHA standard. Under Section 312, many of these same firms are required to prepare and submit to the LEPC an "emergency and hazardous substance inventory form" that describes the amount and location of certain hazardous chemicals on their premises. Finally, Section 313 requires firms in the manufacturing sector to provide to EPA an annual reporting of certain routine releases of hazardous substances. These reports comprise what is known as the Toxics Release Inventory (TRI). In addition, Section 303 requires certain commercial facilities to cooperate with their respective LEPCs in preparing emergency response plans for dealing with major accidents involving hazardous chemicals. The applicability of these provisions to any particular facility depends on the amount of the designated chemicals that it uses or stores during any given year.

Table 10.1
EPCRA Chemicals, Reportable Actions, and Reporting Thresholds

	Section 302 Emergency Planning	Section 304 Unexpected Releases	Sections 311/312 Chemicals in Storage	Section 313 (TRI) Routine Emissions
Chemicals covered	356 extremely hazardous substances	>1,000 substances	500,000 products with MSDSs* (required under OSHA regulations)	650 toxic chemicals and categories**
Reportable actions and thresholds	Threshold planning quantity: 1–10,000 pounds *present on site at any one time* requires notification of the SERC and LEPC within 60 days upon on-site production or receipt of shipment.	Reportable quantity, 1–5,000 pounds, *released at any time in a 24-hour period*; reportable to the SERC and LEPC	TPQ or 500 pounds for Section 302 chemicals; 10,000 pounds *present on site at any one time* for other chemicals. Copy if requested to SERC/LEPC; annual inventory Tier I/Tier II report to SERC/LEPC/local fire department by March 1.	25,000 pounds per year *manufactured or processed*; 10,000 pounds a year *used*; certain persistent bioaccumulative toxics have lower thresholds; annual report to EPA and the state by July 1.

Notes: EPCRA = Emergency Planning and Community Right to Know Act; SERC = state emergency response commission; LEPC = local emergency planning committee; TRI = toxics release inventory; TPQ = threshold planning quantity.
*MSDSs on hazardous chemicals are maintained by a number of universities and can be accessed through http://www.hazard.com.
**The TRI reporting requirement applies to all federal facilities that have 10 or more full-time employees, and those that manufacture (including importing), process, or otherwise use a listed toxic chemical above threshold quantities, and that are in one of the following sectors: Manufacturing (Standard Industrial Classification (SIC) codes 20 through 39), Metal mining (SIC code 10, except for SIC codes 1011, 1081, and 1094), Coal mining (SIC code 12, except for 1241 and extraction activities), Electrical utilities that combust coal and/or oil (SIC codes 4911, 4931, and 4939), Resource Conservation and Recovery Act (RCRA), Subtitle C hazardous waste treatment and disposal facilities (SIC code 4953), Chemicals and allied products wholesale distributors (SIC code 5169), Petroleum bulk plants and terminals (SIC code 5171), and Solvent recovery services (SIC code 7389).
Source: Adapted from *The Community Planning and Right-to-Know Act*, EPA 550-F-00-004, March 2000.

In 1990 Congress added two more chemical reporting requirements to federal law. The Pollution Prevention Act (PPA) of 1990, 42 U.S.C. §§13101, *et seq.*, which seeks to encourage a general shift from pollution control to pollution prevention, amended EPCRA to require firms subject to TRI reporting to also report their "source reduction" (pollution prevention) and waste management practices on an annual basis. In addition, the 1990 Clean Air Act Amendments directed EPA and OSHA to issue regulations governing prevention of chemical accidents. Under these regulations, facilities that use certain chemicals above specified threshold quantities are required to develop a risk management program to identify, evaluate, and manage chemical safety hazards, to submit a risk management plan (RMP) summarizing their program to EPA or the state, and to report accidental chemical releases above specified thresholds. Furthermore, chemical manufacturers and refineries must file start-up, shut-down, and malfunction (SSM) plans with EPA or state air regulators. Some RMP information is available to the public through RMP*Info, which can be accessed through www.epa.gov/enviro. Worst-case chemical accident scenarios—called "offsite consequence analyses" (OCA)—are now available for reading, but not for copying, in locally designated reading rooms.

Taken as a whole, these requirements constitute a broad federal declaration that firms choosing to rely heavily on hazardous chemicals in their production processes may not treat information regarding their use of those chemicals as their private domain. Indeed, except for trade secrecy protections that generally parallel those available under the OSHA Hazard Communication Standard, there are no statutory restrictions on the disclosure of EPCRA information to the general public.[2] Section 324 of the act mandates that most of the information subject to EPCRA reporting requirements "be made available to the general public" upon request, and requires that each local emergency planning committee publicize this fact in a local newspaper. However, as a result of the terrorist attacks of September 11, 2001, EPA has been reassessing the proper balance to strike between the public's right to know and the possible increased security risk of disseminating data collected under the informational provisions of various federal statutes. The most contentious issue has been the reporting required under the chemical safety provisions of the Clean Air Act (discussed in chapter 13). Industry representatives have argued that allowing the public access to SSM plans increases the vulnerability of the reporting facilities to terrorist attacks, and they have asked to be relieved of the obligation to submit such plans. In response, EPA has proposed that the information be screened before it is disseminated to the public.

---

2. EPCRA Section 322 addresses trade secrets as they apply to reporting under EPCRA Sections 303, 311, 312, and 313; a facility may not claim trade secrets under Section 304 of the statute. Only specific chemical identity may be claimed as a trade secret, and the generic class for the chemical must then be provided. The criteria a facility must meet to claim chemical identity as a trade secret are set forth in 40 CFR Part 350. Less than 1% of facilities have filed such claims. Even if chemical identity information can be legally withheld from the public, EPCRA Section 323 allows the information to be disclosed to health professionals who need the information for diagnostic or treatment purposes or to local health officials who need the information for prevention or treatment activities. In nonemergency cases, the health professional must sign a confidentiality agreement with the facility and provide a written statement of need. In medical emergencies, the health professional, if requested by the facility, provides these documents as soon as circumstances permit. Any person may challenge trade secret claims by petitioning EPA. The agency must then review the claim and rule on its validity. See EPA, *The Community Planning and Right-to-Know Act* (550-F-00-004, March 2000).

■ **NOTES**

1. The Pollution Prevention Act and the chemical safety provisions of the Clean Air Act are discussed in detail in chapter 13. For a general discussion of the value of chemical safety information, see Thomas C. Beierle (2003) "The Benefits and Costs of Environmental Information Disclosure: What Do We Know About Right-to-Know?" RFF discussion paper 03-05, Resources for the Future, Washington, D.C.

2. For a discussion of the tension between community right to know and security concerns, see Kathryn E. Durham-Hammer (2004) "Left to Wonder: Reevaluating, Reforming, and Implementing the Emergency Planning and Community Right-to-Know Act of 1986," 29 *Columbia Journal of Environmental Law* 323, 349–352. The use of the "inherent safety" approach as a means of reducing both the risk of chemical accidents and the risk of "chemical terrorism" is discussed in chapter 13.

3. Section 325 of EPCRA authorizes civil and administrative penalties ranging up to $75,000 per day of violation for facilities that fail to comply with the act's reporting requirements. Criminal sanctions of up to $50,000 and/or 5 years in prison may be assessed against persons who knowingly and willfully fail to provide the required notification of emergency releases. Criminal sanctions of up to $20,000 and/or 1 year in prison may be assessed against persons who knowingly and willfully disclose any information entitled to protection as a trade secret under the act.

4. Section 326 of EPCRA authorizes citizens to initiate civil actions against EPA, SERCs, and the owner or operator of a facility for failure to meet the EPCRA requirements. A SERC, LEPC, and state or local government may institute actions against facility owners or operators for failure to comply with EPCRA requirements. In addition, states may sue EPA for failure to provide trade secret information.

5. The Oil Pollution Act (OPA) of 1990, 33 U.S.C. §§2701, *et seq.*, includes national planning and preparedness provisions for oil spills that are similar to EPCRA provisions for extremely hazardous substances. Plans are developed at the local, state, and federal levels. This offers an opportunity for LEPCs to coordinate their plans with area and facility oil spill plans covering the same geographical area.   ■

2.   Chemical Release Reporting Under the TRI Program

As noted, EPCRA requires certain industries to report the releases and transfers of certain chemical substances to air, water, or land, and to report any other amounts of these chemicals that are transferred off-site. Each firm must enter the required data on a standardized form. The data from all reporting firms are then compiled by EPA in the Toxics Release Inventory, which is publicly available. (The data can be found on EPA's web page: http://www.epa.gov/tri/.) Currently about 650 chemicals are subject to TRI reporting, roughly double the number covered in 1987.

The TRI reporting system imposes its requirements on any firm with more than ten employees that annually *manufactures or processes*[3] more than 25,000 pounds or *uses* over 10,000 pounds of the designated chemicals. In 1999, EPA lowered the reporting threshold to 100 pounds for six persistent, bioaccumulative toxic chemicals (PBTs), to 10 pounds for eleven highly persistent and highly bioaccumulative toxic chemicals, and to 0.1 gram for dioxin and dioxin-like compounds. Altogether, some 6,100 facilities are required to report, including all facilities in the manufacturing sector and facilities in several other designated industries, such as metal and coal mining, electrical power generation, and commercial hazardous waste treatment.

The potential power of TRI as a tool to stimulate risk reduction depends on the quality and representativeness of the data reported, as well as the capacity of the public to understand and interpret the data. On both scores, the TRI system leaves much to be desired. The inventory focuses only on the releases of chemicals and does not include releases that occur during the whole life cycle of a product (such as releases during extraction activities of the basic starting materials delivered to chemical facilities, or releases associated with the disposal of products sold by the facilities to other operations or to consumers). Moreover, only some 6–7% of all chemical releases are covered. Further, a reduction in a reported release does not necessarily mean a real reduction in chemical releases because the reported reduction could simply represent a shift from the use of a chemical that is subject to TRI reporting to one that is not. And because firms are not required to provide information about the risks posed by the releases reported, the public may have an inadequate picture of whether, and to what extent, a change in reported releases means a reduction (or an increase) in overall risk. In addition, except for the lowered reporting thresholds discussed earlier, no attempt is made to distinguish among the differing severities (i.e., the potential health or environmental consequences) of the various reported releases. Unless interested observers account for the differential hazardousness of the various releases, however, they may not be able to make a meaningful assessment of changes in overall risk. Finally, many reported reductions in releases to air or water simply reflect transfers to the solid waste stream, which makes it extremely difficult to evaluate the resulting consequences for overall risk.

Despite these limitations, however, the publication of TRI data appears to have led to an enormous initial reduction of reported releases. During the period from

---

3. The term "manufacture" means to produce, prepare, import, or compound a toxic chemical. The term "process" means the preparation of a toxic chemical, after its manufacture, for distribution in commerce. See 42 U.S.C. §11023 (b)(1)(C). See also 42 U.S.C. §§11023 (a)(b)(1) and (g)(2).

1988 to 2001, on- and off-site releases of the core TRI chemicals were reduced by 54.5%, even though the overall production of chemicals increased. Almost 40% of this decrease had been attained by 1995. However, while emissions to air and water decreased, there were corresponding large increases in the generation of hazardous waste. Thus, it is far from clear at this stage that TRI reporting has led to a reduction in the overall risk from the industrial use of toxic chemicals.

▪ NOTES

1. Responding to demands from communities that the agency share TRI data sooner and in the basic format received, EPA is now releasing the information as it is reported to the agency. In the past, the data were quality checked and analyzed by EPA before being released in the annual Toxics Release Inventory report. Beginning with reporting year 2003 TRI data, however, EPA launched its Electronic-Facility Data Release (e-FDR) program. In the e-FDR format, the data are presented for each facility received by EPA, one reporting form for each chemical. In a press release announcing the e-FDR, the agency credited the earlier release of the data to the ease and accuracy afforded by electronic reporting: "Increased electronic reporting allowed EPA to publish the earlier e-FDR, and is part of EPA's initiative to modernize and streamline the TRI program. Electronic reporting also supports data accuracy with built-in quality checks and makes reporting easier for industry" ["Early Release of 2003 TRI Data" (press release issued by Suzanne Ackerman of EPA (202) 564-7819, ackerman.suzanne@epa.gov)]. The e-FDR is available at http://www.epa.gov/tri-efdr. Somewhat ironically, the early release of the TRI data received mixed reviews from many environmental and public interest groups, who questioned the utility of releasing data without at least some initial EPA analysis. See *Environment Reporter* 35(48): 2498 (2004).

2. For reporting year 2003, the TRI report included for the first time a focus on five selected chemicals of particular interest: mercury, lead and lead compounds, dioxins, trichloroethylene, and toluene. Also included was a focus on trends in recycling, recovery, and treatment, as well as a focus on trends in waste management from 1998 through 2003 by industry sector and by chemical sector.

3. In September 2005, EPA announced its intention to modify TRI reporting requirements in two major ways: (1) to shift annual reporting requirements to every-other-year (biennial) reporting; and (2) to increase the reporting threshold from 500 pounds to 5,000 pounds, except for those substances, such as lead, mercury, dioxins and PCBs, classified as PBTs. Firms under the new threshold would be able to use a new reporting form, Form A, which is considerably shorter than form R, requires reporting only the names of the chemicals released, and not the amounts released.

At the 5,000 pound threshold, one-third of all TRI reporting facilities would be entitled to use the shorter form A. As expected, environmental groups were critical of these proposed changes, arguing that they would make it more difficult to assess the seriousness of the releases from many facilities and to track releases of substances such as mercury. In December 2006, EPA issued a proposed rule that would raise the threshold from 500 pounds to 2000 pounds, but would leave the annual reporting intact (71 Fed. Reg. 76,932). As this book goes to press, legislation (known as the Toxic Right-to-Know Protection Act) has been introduced in the House and Senate to disallow the proposed rule.

4. Information on releases of toxic chemicals can be accessed over the Internet at http://www.epa.gov/triexplorer; http://www.epa.gov/enviro; http://www.scorecard .org; and http://www.rtk.net. These websites provide access to specific data and trend information on individual facilities, counties, states, and the nation as whole. In addition, one can analyze the data by industry, by specific media (e.g., air, water, or land), and by chemical.

5. As of fall 2007, EPA is posting on its website toxicity data volunteered by industry for 101 high-production-volume chemicals in excess of 1 million pounds per year: http://www.iaspub.epa.gov/oppthpv/hpv_hc_characterization.get_report. EPA plans to produce toxicity data for more chemicals and link toxicity data with exposure information in the future [*Chemical & Engineering News*, p. 10, September 17, 2007, available at http://www.cen-online.org].

6. Originally, some had recommended that formal "materials accounting"—a quantitative assessment of materials flow from inputs and feedstocks to final products—be included as part of EPCRA's reporting requirements. Strong industry resistance, articulated as a concern for the possible divulgence of trade secret information, was successful in eliminating this provision from the final law. Nonetheless, as discussed in the following excerpt from a Congressional Research Service report, Congress did commission a study of the potential usefulness of such reporting.

Prior to enactment of EPCRA, Congress considered whether manufacturers also should be required to report the amount of chemical present at each point in the manufacturing process. However, because the issue was contentious, Congress directed the Administrator [in Section 313(1) of EPCRA] to arrange for the National Academy of Sciences (NAS) to study the value of collecting data to permit "mass balance" analysis of toxic chemicals manufactured, processed, or used by manufacturing facilities. Congress defined "mass balance" to include quantities of chemicals transported to, produced, consumed, used, or accumulated at, or released or transported from a facility, including any toxic chemical in waste, commercial products, or byproducts. The resulting NAS study was published in 1990. [National Academy of Sciences, *Tracking Toxic Substances at Industrial Facility*. National Academy Press, Washington, D.C.] It distinguished reporting of precisely measured quantities of chemicals that would permit calculation of "mass balance" for a facility from less precise information suitable for "materials accounting" and production planning purposes. The NAS concluded that although "mass balance" data might be useful for engineering purposes, "materials accounting" data would be more useful for informing the general public about potential exposure. [Linda-Jo Schierow (1997) *Toxics Release Inventory: Do Communities Have a Right to Know More?* Congressional Research Service Report 97-970 ENR, October 26]

The Massachusetts Toxics Use Reduction Act, discussed in chapter 13, does require industry to undertake a form of materials accounting, and to report the results to state officials, but the data are regarded as "confidential business information" under the legislation and hence are not disseminated to the public.

7. For a highly critical view of the TRI program, see Alexander Volokh (2002) "The Pitfalls of the Environmental Right-to-Know," 2 *Utah Law Review* 805. Citing many of the deficiencies discussed here, Volokh characterizes TRI data as "irredeemably misleading," and concludes that expanding the law's informational requirements would not cure the inadequacies inherent in this type of reporting system. For a more sympathetic, constructive, and prescriptive critical analysis, see Kathryn E. Durham-Hammer (2004) "Left to Wonder: Reevaluating, Reforming, and Implementing the Emergency Planning and Community Right-to-Know Act of 1986," 29 *Columbia Journal of Environmental Law* 323. Durham-Hammer notes that only 1% of the chemicals in use are covered; that the reports often are neither accurate nor complete; and that communities often lack awareness of, access to, and a meaningful understanding of the TRI data. For an optimistic view of TRI reporting as a successful alternative to command-and-control regulation, see Archon Fung and Dara O'Rourke (2000) "Reinventing Environmental Regulation from the Grassroots Up: Explaining and Expanding the Success of the Toxics Release Inventory," *Environmental Management* 15: 115.

8. The nature of the required reporting of "source reduction" activities under the TRI program can be seen in the TRI reporting form included at the end of this chapter. The Pollution Prevention Act defines source reduction as any practice that "reduces the amount of any hazardous substance, pollutant, or contaminant entering any waste stream or otherwise released into the environment (including fugitive emissions) and reduces the hazards to public health and the environment associated with the release of such substances, pollutants, or contaminants" [42 U.S.C. §13102(5)(A)]. ■

C. COMMUNITY RIGHT TO KNOW AS A SPUR TO RISK REDUCTION

The following article provides an insightful analysis of the potential of the TRI program to promote pollution reduction through both corporate responsibility and citizen activism.

Information as Environmental Regulation: TRI and Performance Benchmarking, Precursor to a New Paradigm?
Bradley C. Karkkainen

Source: 89 *Georgetown Law Journal* 257 (2001), excerpted with permission.

. . .

III. WHAT DRIVES PERFORMANCE IMPROVEMENTS

Information bottlenecks and administrative costs aside, however, the crucial question remains: How can simple information disclosure like that required under TRI drive improvements in pollution performance? After all, the skeptic might regard TRI as the quintessential "paperwork" requirement— the only formal demand it makes of the regulated entity is the production and disclosure of information. Although firms have the flexibility to choose their own improvement targets, why should they bother to do so at all? How, in other words, can TRI spur firms to reduce pollution?

This Article argues that TRI works by establishing an objective, quantifiable, standardized (and therefore comparable), and broadly accessible metric that transforms the firm's understanding of its own environmental performance, while facilitating unprecedented levels of transparency and accountability. Firms and facilities are compelled to self-monitor and, therefore, to "confront disagreeable realities" concerning their environmental performance "in detail and early on," even prior to the onset of market, community, or regulatory reactions to the information they are required to make public. Simultaneously, they are subjected to the scrutiny of a variety of external parties, including investors, community residents, and regulators, any of whom may desire improved environmental performance and exert powerful pressures on poor performers

to upgrade their performance as measured by the TRI yardstick.

A. Self-Monitoring: "You Manage What You Measure"

TRI mandates a sharply focused form of environmental self-monitoring, compelling firms to produce a stream of periodic, quantified reports on releases of listed pollutants at each reporting facility. This information becomes available, inter alia, to the firm itself, which may use it to evaluate its own performance and production processes. General availability of detailed, comparable TRI performance data further allows the firm to place each of its required reports in a variety of interpretive contexts. The firm can identify its own top-performing and underperforming facilities and processes, establish performance baselines and track process-, facility-, and firm-level performance trends over time. It can also compare its performance against that of its peers and competitors and set specific, objective performance targets to which it may hold itself and each of its operating units accountable. Analysis of TRI-derived comparative rankings of process- and facility-level performance may also facilitate the identification of environmentally superior processes and technologies and hasten their diffusion within and across firms. Very little of this information can be generated through conventional, fragmentary, frequently non-standardized, compliance-oriented environmental reporting.

TRI places information in the hands of corporate managers in the first instance. Consequently, it might be analogized to a private sector version of the National Environmental Policy Act (NEPA), requiring a process—the production and disclosure of environmental information relevant to decisionmaking—rather than substantive outcomes. In neither case does the regulatory approach require that anything in particular be done with the information once it is produced. But by compelling managers to examine environmental outcomes, it may influence their decisionmaking. Just as NEPA-generated information may prompt some governmental managers to mitigate the worst environmental consequences of their proposed actions, or even to choose less environmentally harmful alternatives, the performance monitoring mandated by TRI might also alert corporate managers to performance problems and opportunities for improvement that might otherwise have escaped their notice.

Many top corporate managers, previously unaware of the volumes of toxic pollutants their firms were generating, were indeed surprised by the information produced in the first rounds of TRI. In many cases, that knowledge prompted a swift and decisive response, as firms adopted ambitious improvement targets far above the levels required for compliance with regulatory requirements, often in the range of fifty, seventy, or even ninety percent reductions from initial TRI-reported levels. Beyond jarring firms into action, TRI also establishes the objective metric by which managers set firm-wide improvement targets and gauge progress toward their achievement.

Managers can also use TRI data as an internal metric, exercising control over the firm's environmental performance by requiring operational subunits to set their own improvement targets and monitor and report their progress. This establishes the internal transparency and accountability necessary to achieve firm-wide objectives. . . .

This kind of careful self-monitoring may well be a necessary step toward improving the environmental performance of facilities and firms. As the well-worn adage has it, "what you don't know about, you can't manage," or yet more precisely, "you manage what you measure." And not only is the information generated by TRI valuable to managers in its own right, but in some cases TRI's reporting requirements may inspire broader improvements in a firm's internal management of environmental information. Many firms now deploy a broader set of TRI-like performance metrics to monitor and manage a variety of environmental problems.

Finally, as corporate boards and institutional investors, in particular, reinvent themselves as independent monitors of corporate performance and evaluate environmental performance in assessing overall firm performance, objective metrics like TRI take on added significance as tools of corporate governance. TRI data offer directors a window on firm- and facility-level environmental trends, as well as comparative yardsticks by which to judge the firm's performance against that of its peers and competitors. In some cases, board committees may monitor TRI and similar performance data directly. In other cases, they rely on independent third-party monitoring and analysis provided by organizations like the Investor Responsibility Research Center (IRRC), which typically incorporate TRI data into their own corporate environmental profiles. Exercise of this board-level internal monitoring function may itself spur management to set specific TRI performance improvement goals, or to address environmental problems revealed through TRI data.

TRI's basic approach—performance monitoring and benchmarking—is congruent with emerging paradigms of corporate management and governance at the leading edge of innovation. Unlike conventional regulatory rules, TRI is not a costly, flexibility-impeding, externally imposed constraint. Rather, it is a familiar kind of information tool that enables managers, directors, and employees to measure and control performance outcomes. Many of the most successful and innovative firms have already made rigorous performance monitoring, benchmarking, and a "continuous improvement" approach to product quality and process efficiency foundational elements in their management philosophy, often under the rubric of "Total Quality Management" (TQM) or "Total Quality Environmental Management" (TQEM). These firms can seamlessly integrate environmental metrics (including, but not limited to, TRI) into a broader set of corporate performance indicators and they frequently find the resulting environmental performance gains compatible with their larger efficiency objectives. And, as with product quality and process efficiency in general, once a firm adds environmental metrics to its package of self-evaluative tools, there is no logical stopping point to the performance gains that may result. However much performance improves, at every stage both central management and operational subunits can (and under the TQM/TQEM "continuous improvement" ethos are encouraged to) aim for "better," whether the revised improvement targets are derived from comparative benchmarking against "best in class," or simply represent some measurable incremental gain from their own previous best.

This improvement-by-monitoring approach is also broadly congruent with the new ISO 14001 environmental management systems (EMS) standard. ISO 14001 is a voluntary international consensus standard recently promulgated by the International Organization for Standardization. It establishes a common framework for systems to identify, evaluate, and manage environmental outcomes and aims to produce "continuous improvement" toward self-identified goals. Within the prescribed EMS framework, firms retain complete discretion to devise their own environmental policies, objectives, and metrics. While enthusiastically embraced by some firms and policy analysts, ISO 14001 has

been criticized by some environmentalists for focusing exclusively on management processes rather than environmental performance outcomes, and for failing to provide public accountability and transparency. But ISO 14001 requires that firms select performance metrics and establish improvement targets based upon those metrics. By handing them a ready-made, publicly reported performance metric and simultaneously creating a range of external pressures to improve performance against that yardstick, TRI challenges ISO-compliant firms to incorporate TRI into their EMS as an internal performance metric. Of course, nothing in either TRI or ISO 14001 requires firms to wed the two. But by dovetailing TRI into the ISO 14001 framework, the firm would simultaneously satisfy ISO's procedural mandate that it establish a performance metric, create a management infrastructure capable of generating the TRI-reported performance improvements it may need to satisfy its external monitors and critics, and generate the transparency and public accountability that ISO 14001 alone would lack.

Because TRI compels polluting firms to monitor their own volumes of waste—in effect, to engage in a limited form of materials accounting—it may spur them to investigate pollution prevention options that may reduce materials and waste disposal costs, increase effective utilization of productive capacity, and simultaneously improve environmental performance. In some cases, investments in pollution prevention may be profitable even in the short run. But even when they are not, many leading firms now believe that their long-term competitive advantage lies in continuously pushing the envelope of innovation in both products and process efficiency, including pollution efficiency. These firms, and others, may find that the net financial costs of pollution prevention are low after reduced materials and waste disposal costs are taken into account. This means that "soft" or deferred payoffs in the form of reputational benefits, relaxed regulatory scrutiny, improved community and employee relations, and reduced likelihood of future environmental liabilities or compliance costs can be purchased quite cheaply. These external drivers of performance improvement are taken up in the sections that follow.

Pollution prevention is not uniformly profitable or cheap, of course. Even where it is, investments in pollution prevention might be crowded out by more attractive investment alternatives, or the firm may lack the necessary capital, know-how, or commitment to make pollution prevention part of its overall business strategy. And for a variety of reasons, firms may not be equally responsive to the community, regulatory, and market pressures that figure into the long-range planning of the most sophisticated practitioners of pollution prevention. Put differently, the value of gains in these areas will vary by firm, depending on firm-specific circumstances. Consequently, we should expect that performance gains from TRI will be uneven across facilities, firms, and industries, generating a pattern of "leaders and laggards." . . .

Meanwhile, at the top end of the performance scale, TRI will often prove to be an inadequate indicator of environmental performance for the most advanced practitioners of corporate environmentalism. . . . TRI is, at best, a narrow, one-dimensional metric, covering only releases and transfers of listed toxic pollutants. It is not a very sophisticated metric, measuring only total pounds of listed pollutants released without regard to their relative toxicity, environmental fate, potentially affected populations, or other relevant risk factors. For those reasons, many leading firms supplement TRI with other, typically self-devised, environmental performance metrics. Yet the fact that some leading firms have voluntarily elected to expand and refine environmental self-monitoring beyond TRI's legally mandated minimum can hardly stand as evidence against TRI's usefulness. Instead, it appears to reaffirm the vitality of

TRI's underlying performance-monitoring-and-benchmarking approach, as well as its fit with emerging trends in corporate management among the nation's most successful and innovative firms. This, in turn, begins to suggest tantalizing possibilities as to how TRI-style performance monitoring might be improved and extended into other areas of environmental performance.

B. Industry Self-Regulation Through Peer Monitoring Responsible Care and Beyond

Buffeted by public reaction to the Bhopal tragedy and anticipating further adverse publicity upon the release of the first round of TRI data, the Chemical Manufacturers Association (CMA) (now known as the American Chemistry Council) launched its Responsible Care program in 1988. Its explicit goal was to repair the chemical industry's reputation by "promoting continuous improvement in member company environmental, health, and safety performance" and "assisting members' demonstration of improvements in performance to critical public audiences."

The core idea animating Responsible Care is that by establishing a regime of peer monitoring and mutual accountability to industry "best practice" standards, the industry can regulate itself effectively but flexibly. Peer pressure would cause laggards to come up to industry-wide norms, while continuously raising the "best practice" bar through innovation, benchmarking, and inter-firm competition. As implemented to date, however, the Responsible Care regime falls short of that ideal. Responsible Care enlisted member firms to comply voluntarily with six industry-written codes of best environmental management practices. But the Responsible Care codes were expressed in quite general narrative language and initially lacked mechanisms to ensure transparency and accountability. For example, the pollution prevention code simply called on participating firms to establish management systems that would produce "continuous improvement" in pollution prevention. Responsible Care neither established industry-wide performance goals, nor required participating firms to report their own improvement targets or performance metrics.

CMA amended Responsible Care in 1999 to require participating firms to establish and submit individual performance improvement targets. It also adopted the ambitious (and possibly unattainable) ultimate goal of zero environmental impact for the industry as a whole. CMA is also considering further measures to revise and upgrade Responsible Care's performance metrics, identify and publicize top performers to provide industry-wide benchmarks, and include independent audits of performance data in the management systems verification that already occurs.

Given this checkered history, it is not surprising that the performance gains achieved through Responsible Care to date are also quite ambiguous. The latest available TRI data show that, in the aggregate, chemical manufacturers have reduced TRI pollutant releases and transfers significantly more (in percentage terms) than the average for all industries since TRI reporting began, despite increases in chemical production over this period. And in volumetric terms, the industry's reductions dwarf those of any other industry because they begin from a much larger base. However, a recent empirical study concluded that chemical firms participating in Responsible Care showed no greater performance improvement than other firms in the chemical sector.* Moreover, there are wide variations in the levels of improvement achieved by participating firms. Yet given CMA's dominant position in the chemical industry, it is difficult to draw clear lines demarcating where Responsible Care's influence leaves off.

These results may suggest to some that Responsible Care has added little value beyond the improvements that would have been otherwise achieved though TRI and the pressures it generates. A more charitable interpretation is that by promoting TRI as the industry-wide metric of pollution performance and spurring its members to set ambitious improvement targets against that metric, Responsible Care has set the pace for the entire chemical industry and perhaps for other industries as well. Specifically, leading chemical firms have established performance benchmarks that other industries may emulate, whether through Responsible Care-style industrial self-regulation, or through individual firm-by-firm efforts. Although the jury is still out on whether Responsible Care will evolve into a vibrant and durable form of industry self-regulation, it is at a minimum an intriguing experiment.

Most significantly for our purposes, however, Responsible Care operates in an experimental space that is largely created and sustained by TRI. TRI simultaneously unleashed and amplified the external pressures that made Responsible Care necessary, and provided the tool of transparency and accountability that made its core elements of self- and peer-monitoring, intra-industry bench-marking, and continuous performance improvement possible. No less significantly, it is the TRI performance metric that provides the yardstick of accountability that allows both the industry and its critics to evaluate the success of Responsible Care and similar experiments in each successive iteration. Finally, TRI offers a rough prototype for the succeeding generations of performance metrics that will be necessary if Responsible Care-style industrial self-regulation is to succeed.

C. Regulators as Monitors

1. Regulatory Monitoring and Anticipatory Self-Regulation

TRI-generated performance data are readily available to regulators, as well as to environmentalists and other citizen-critics of

---

* [The reader is referred to chapter 12 for further discussion of industry self-regulation.]

regulatory policy. Regulators can use TRI data to establish baselines, profiles, and trends in the pollution performance of facilities, firms, industrial sectors, communities, and states, and to make benchmarking comparisons among them. Moreover, the data provide some indication of the effectiveness of regulatory and non-regulatory environmental policies, providing the basis for comparative analysis and benchmarking of program outcomes. TRI data thus help regulators identify regulatory gaps and shortcomings, set research and enforcement priorities, and identify the most effective programs so as to replicate or expand them. In perhaps the most widely cited instance, early rounds of TRI data revealed that much larger volumes of hazardous air pollutants were being released than had been previously recognized. This led Congress to amend the Clean Air Act in 1990 to strengthen its hazardous air pollutant (HAP) provisions, and to bypass and amend the cumbersome HAP regulatory listing procedure, which had resulted in the listing of only a small handful of pollutants.

Simultaneously, citizen-critics of governmental policies can use TRI-derived information to criticize or support current policies and programs, propose new ones, and benchmark and evaluate the achievements of regulated entities and regulators alike. Thus, TRI-generated information holds great potential to alter the level of political demand for environmental regulation, and to redirect that demand toward perceived "problem" firms, industries, pollutants, or communities as identified by TRI-generated criteria.

Adverse facility-, firm-, or industry-level TRI data thus carry the implicit threat that regulatory action may follow, whether at the initiative of regulators themselves or in response to rising political demand for regulatory action. But precisely because forward-thinking firms and investors anticipate that additional regulatory requirements may prove burdensome and costly, firms may come under self-imposed and market-driven pressures to undertake cost-effective, voluntary, pollution prevention measures....

This phenomenon of anticipatory self-regulation is not unique to the environmental arena. Other successfully self-regulated industries recognize that the background threat of potentially costly and inefficient government regulation causes industry members to regulate themselves, despite the obvious short-term costs of doing so....

The regulatory threats are manifold. In the absence of effective industry self-regulation, legislators might enact more stringent or expansive regulatory statutes. Agencies might exercise discretionary authority to expand regulatory coverage to additional pollutants, industries, or industrial processes; strengthen existing regulatory standards; or concentrate their research, rulemaking, compliance monitoring, and enforcement efforts on sectors, firms, facilities, and pollutants identified as priorities on the basis of TRI data.... TRI-style performance monitoring carries the potential to inform, empower, and redirect that process in response to the changing and sometimes surprising patterns of performance revealed through the reported data. Because these new regulatory directions may be either favorable or unfavorable to the interests of regulated or potentially regulated entities, TRI creates powerful incentives for firms to reduce their TRI-measured emissions "voluntarily" as a precautionary and preemptive step.

2. Local Regulatory Monitoring, Locally Tailored Rules

Although a nationally uniform program, TRI also informs and facilitates environmental policymaking at the state, local, and regional ecosystem levels. TRI reduces the cost of making informed decisions at sub-national levels while achieving scale efficiencies for governments and reporting firms. Most states now maintain their own TRI databases, and many combine TRI with other data or incorporate it into GIS mapping programs. Like their federal counterparts, state and local governments and regional ecosystem management authorities use TRI-generated information to assess and monitor local and regional environmental baselines and trends, evaluate the effectiveness of their own environmental programs, develop proposals to fill regulatory gaps, and identify and monitor the performance of individual polluting facilities and firms within their jurisdictions.

These authorities typically have a battery of regulatory and non-regulatory tools at their disposal.... TRI data also assist in the administration of non-regulatory programs; for example, the data allow states to identify leading polluters for purposes of offering technical assistance in pollution prevention planning....

D. Community Monitoring and "Informal Regulation"

...Community residents...can deploy a variety of costly, disruptive, and, therefore, frequently effective countermeasures, including boycotts and pickets, social ostracism of the firm's employees and managers, adverse publicity, lawsuits or the threat of lawsuits, and political pressure on regulators and elected officials to enforce existing regulatory standards, enact new requirements, or exercise discretionary governmental authority against the offending firm....

...[M]andatory provision of TRI data might advance informal regulation in several ways. First, it lowers the barriers to acquisition of firm- and facility-specific information. Information provided at virtually no direct cost to citizens through mechanisms like TRI may trigger initial community awareness of local pollution problems, or confirm claims or suspicions that otherwise might have been difficult to substantiate, leading to more frequent and more robust attempts at informal regulation.

Second, by strengthening the community's informational hand, TRI may level the ground on which negotiations with the polluting firm occur. Community residents armed with objective TRI data are less likely to be outmaneuvered or misled by better-informed corporate negotiators. And because TRI information is both self-reported and imprinted with the stamp of regulatory approval, it is less easily dismissed as ill-founded or erroneous in negotiations and in the crucial court of public opinion. Third, the required disclosures and the ensuing dialogue may themselves bring to the attention of plant managers information they might otherwise have overlooked and thereby improve the information base upon which they make crucial decisions.... And because community residents can use TRI data to benchmark performance across facilities and time periods, it may pressure managers to make fuller use of TRI's benchmarking opportunities, if only to verify, qualify, or respond to community-produced information. Thus, whether or not "informal regulation" results in formal negotiations between managers and community representatives, the local disclosure of TRI data may prompt a dynamic, information-rich dialogue between the firm and those most directly affected by its environmental performance, revealing new information at each successive stage while reshaping preferences, informing decisions, and influencing performance outcomes.

Finally, by establishing baselines and an objective metric for evaluating the firm's subsequent performance, and by facilitating community monitoring of compliance with the informal standard, ongoing TRI disclosures will help the community enforce any formal agreement, unilateral pledge, or informal understanding that is reached. All these effects, then, would tend to push in the direction of increasing the frequency and effectiveness of informal regulation in raising environmental performance levels as measured by TRI.

There is ample evidence that this kind of "informal regulation" is widespread in the

United States, and that TRI-generated information plays an important role in much of it. Environmental and community organizations are among the principal users of TRI data, employing it in conscious efforts to pressure firms to raise environmental standards. At the national level, environmental organizations use TRI data to generate reports and profiles of toxic pollution and leading polluters, and to direct reputation-damaging publicity campaigns against polluting firms. TRI data are also used by both national and local organizations to produce community-level reports and profiles, and to single out the leading local sources of toxic pollution. Community groups use this information to educate and recruit community residents into local anti-pollution efforts, and to organize local campaigns seeking "good neighbor agreements" and similar commitments from polluting firms to reduce releases. And even where community residents do not explicitly put forth such demands, firms may self-regulate to preempt potentially costly and damaging attempts at informal regulation.

Indeed, TRI owes its very existence to community-based "informal regulation" of toxic polluters, tracing its ancestry to the Love Canal incident. Isolated local efforts later evolved into a robust, nationwide, locally based "right-to-know" movement that had already won dozens of mandatory disclosure measures at the state and local level prior to TRI's enactment. TRI was a direct lineal descendent of these state and local measures whose purpose was, in the words of the New Jersey statute, to assist communities and workers by providing information on the "full range of the risks they face so that they can make reasoned decisions and take informed action concerning their employment and their living conditions." ...

The consequences of TRI were not surprising to the Congress that enacted it.... Both supporters and opponents understood that by requiring reporting of routine releases and chronic pollutants, TRI reached well beyond Bhopal-type accidental releases of acutely toxic substances. TRI's sponsors emphasized that it would encourage pollution prevention and enable communities to engage in local self-help—central themes of the "right-to-know" movement. The statute itself identifies informing the local citizenry and facilitating local action among TRI's core purposes. TRI has fulfilled those expectations, facilitating local organizing aimed at improving the environmental performance of polluting facilities. In recent years, TRI has taken on an "environmental justice" flavor as low-income and minority communities add complaints of disparate impact, backed by TRI-derived inter-community comparisons, to underlying concerns about toxic exposures.

The role of an informed citizenry in a democratic polity, and the consequent need to maintain a free flow of information, are familiar and well-rehearsed themes in democratic discourse. But the emergence of local informal regulation of toxic polluters, aided and inspired by the mandatory production of environmental performance data, begins to recast these themes in a distinctive new light. It opens new avenues of direct, localized, and distinctly participatory democratic expression. No longer content to be merely the passive beneficiary of regulatory protection offered by a distant rulemaking elite, the citizen as informal regulator is empowered to participate directly in setting effective environmental standards, tailored to local needs and conditions. The role of the central regulatory agency is simultaneously recast, from that of expert and paternalistic protector of the citizenry, to guarantor of the minimum flow of information necessary for local self-governance. The result is a two-fold "de-centering" of the locus of environmental standard-setting: from national center to localities, and from the exclusive competence of an expert regulatory state to multi-party processes, in which regulator, regulated, and regulatory beneficiary alike are active participants....

IV. SOME LIMITATIONS

A. Scope and Data Quality: TRI as Flawed Proxy for Environmental Performance

1. A Narrow and Potentially Misleading Metric

In the absence of a broader and more comprehensive set of metrics, many users of TRI information are tempted to use it as a proxy for the overall environmental performance of a facility or firm simply because it is the most visible and accessible source of comparable, quantifiable data. But TRI information provides, at best, one narrow and potentially highly misleading indicator of environmental performance, measuring releases from major point sources of substances on a short and far-from-complete EPA-compiled list of toxic pollutants.

A firm with superior TRI data might nonetheless produce large volumes of conventional pollutants or solid waste, or recklessly despoil valuable wildlife habitats—all beyond TRI's purview—while a firm with poor TRI data could nonetheless be a superior environmental performer along these other dimensions. Nor can we safely assume that every improvement in TRI data counts as an environmental gain because, in some cases, it might reflect a shift to activities that cause equal or greater environmental harm that is not reflected in TRI data. To that extent, TRI's very power to drive performance improvements as measured by the TRI metric makes it potentially misleading and possibly counterproductive if it is not matched and counterbalanced by a set of equally powerful metrics for other important dimensions of environmental performance.

Similarly, because all reported TRI releases are measured uniformly in pounds, regardless of the relative toxicity of the pollutant, a firm or facility might cut its reported emissions and transfers without reducing—and possibly even while increasing—health and environmental risks by substituting lower-volume, higher-toxicity pollutants. Because sulfuric acid, a relatively low-toxicity, high-volume pollutant, represented a large fraction of total TRI releases in the early rounds of reporting, some firms found they could achieve large TRI improvements by cutting their bulk sulfuric acid releases, although the net health and environmental benefits were in many cases thought to be quite modest. It appears, however, that while a few individual firms or facilities may "game" TRI reporting in this way, the general pattern is one of substantial reductions in releases of almost every listed TRI substance, regardless of relative toxicity. Unsurprisingly, slightly larger percentage reductions have been recorded for higher-volume TRI substances as firms have sought to improve their overall TRI rankings. These reductions include, however, highly toxic substances as well as less toxic ones.

In addition, because TRI measures only the quantity of the pollutant released without factoring in proximity to population, exposure route, dispersion, persistence, sensitivity of exposed populations, or other important risk-related factors, it does not provide a very good guide to actual human and environmental risks. While TRI data may be combined with other information to provide a richer and more nuanced picture of risk, such information is often not available, and is rarely provided in a form readily accessible to non-expert users.[4] Many users are tempted

---

4. The most ambitious effort to date to provide risk-relevant data is Environmental Defense's Scorecard, which combines TRI data with relative toxicity rankings, GIS mapping, and population estimates. See Environmental Defense, Scorecard, at http://www.scorecard.org (last visited Oct. 15, 2000). Scorecard is not without its shortcomings and critics, but it nonetheless represents an admirable first attempt at broad integration of TRI data with other risk-relevant information, thus attempting to cure TRI's information deficiencies through more and better information, rather than less as suggested by some of TRI's critics.

to rely on TRI data as a handy proxy for the environmental and health risks associated with toxic pollutants. In short, they use TRI as an indicator of environmental quality (which it is not), rather than as an indicator of the environmental performance of a limited class of sources (the only use the data can fairly support). But to do so may lead to serious overestimation or underestimation of risk.

Even understood narrowly as an indicator of toxic pollution performance, TRI has severe shortcomings. Although TRI's coverage extends to more toxic pollutants than are regulated under conventional standards, the TRI list is incomplete.[5] While a final, comprehensive list of toxic pollutants is almost certainly an unattainable goal, our current level of toxic ignorance should be sobering.* EPA acknowledges that even for the highest-volume organic chemicals, "the majority... lack the basic information needed to determine whether they should be listed on the TRI."[6] As with other forms of regulation, EPA bears the burden of identifying candidate substances and producing sufficient information to justify their listing under TRI. Because the information threshold for TRI listing determinations is generally lower than for other kinds of regulatory action, EPA is able to adjust its TRI lists relatively rapidly. But EPA is ordinarily not the party in the best position to identify the toxic risks of the tens of thousands of chemicals used and manufactured.[7] Consequently, TRI goes only part way toward solving the information bottleneck problem.... Specifically, the information demands placed on the central regulator to identify toxic substances in the first instance remain a critical limitation on TRI's reach and effectiveness.

A related problem is that arbitrary volumetric reporting thresholds keep some toxic pollutants off the TRI list, and in other cases understate the aggregate effects of numerous small releases that may cause serious cumulative harm. As elsewhere in environmental regulation, no consideration is given to the problem of co-causation—the synergistic, interactive, or cumulative effects of multiple toxic pollutants, each of which may escape reporting if it falls below reporting thresholds. Moreover, TRI requires reporting only by selected classes of pollution sources. Generally, these include manufacturers and other large point sources in specified SIC codes, excluding most small businesses (those with fewer than ten employees), non-regulated sectors, and diffuse sources like automobiles and farms. As a result, TRI provides a radically underinclusive and consequently distorted picture of the extent, nature, and causes of toxic pollution and its associated health and environmental risks. Small "area sources" like dry cleaners are often an important source of local exposures. In large metropolitan areas automobiles are the leading source of many forms of airborne toxic pollution.

---

5. See GAO, TOXIC SUBSTANCES: EPA NEEDS MORE RELIABLE SOURCE REDUCTION DATA AND PROGRESS MEASURES, GAO/RCED-94-93, at 14 (1994)... (of seventy thousand chemicals used commercially in the United States, TRI requires reporting on only a small fraction, so that firms may maintain or even increase toxic pollution by substituting non-TRI chemicals). EPA has twice expanded the list of TRI chemicals, from around 300 initially to nearly 650 currently.

* [However, the reader is reminded that the Toxic Substances Inventory compiled under the Toxic Substances Control Act is a source of important information.]

6. ... (no toxicity data is available for forty-six percent of high production volume organic chemicals not currently listed on the TRI, and less than four percent of these chemicals have been subjected to a full battery of toxicity screening tests).

7. EPA has recently negotiated an agreement with chemical manufacturers calling for manufacturers to voluntarily test 2,800 high production volume chemicals by 2004.... However, that still leaves tens of thousands of chemicals still untested.

Pesticide run-off is a leading contributor to groundwater and surface water contamination. Exclusion of these sources from community-level toxic profiles understates the aggregate and cumulative risks of toxic pollution, while feeding the commonplace but erroneous assumption that large industrial polluters are solely responsible for toxic risks faced by the public. Although small and diffuse sources may be more difficult to monitor, and are frequently less able to bear the costs of self-monitoring, sample monitoring combined with statistical extrapolations and modeling could provide the public with improved information about toxic pollution from these sources.

Finally, TRI has important limitations as a comparative measure of facility- or firm-level pollution performance because release volumes are not normalized to reflect production levels. Consequently, a single large plant may appear to have a "worse" level of TRI releases than a series of smaller plants producing more toxic pollution per unit of output. In addition, fluctuations attributable to the business cycle, changes in industrial composition, or changes in a facility's operating levels will be reflected in rising or falling TRI data, where they may be erroneously attributed to improvement or backsliding in performance.

▪ NOTES

1. Not all commentators attribute the reduction of toxic releases to TRI. Based on a statistical study of petroleum refineries, Linda Bui concludes that, "although TRI public disclosure may have contributed to the decline in reported releases, . . . [t]he evidence is strong that changes in toxic emissions intensity is a byproduct of more traditional command and control regulation of emissions of *non*-toxic [i.e., criteria] pollutants." See Linda Bui (2005) "Public Disclosure of Private Information as a Tool for Regulating Environmental Emissions: Firm-level Responses by Petroleum Refineries to the Toxics Release Inventory" CES 05-13 October (available at http://webserver01.ces.census.gov/index.php/ces/1.00/cespapers?limit=30 or http://webserver01.ces.census.gov/index.php/ces/1.00/cespapers?down_key=101723).

2. The Massachusetts Toxics Use Reduction Act (TURA), which is discussed in chapter 13, not only requires the reporting of toxic releases, but also requires firms to report the efforts they are taking to reduce those releases and to undertake assessments of technological alternatives (a state-of-the-art review) of pollution prevention options. For a discussion of the potential for TURA to stimulate technology development, see Dara O'Rourke and Lee Eungkyoon (2004) "Mandatory Planning for Environmental Innovation: Evaluating Regulatory Mechanisms for Toxic Use Reduction," *Journal of Environmental Planning and Management* 47(2): 181–200.

3. For an interesting comparison of right-to-know reporting, outcomes, and implications for governance in England, Wales, and Scotland, see Andy Gouldson (2004) "Risk, Regulation and the Right to Know: Exploring the Impacts of Access

to Information on the Governance of Environmental Risk," *Sustainable Development* 12: 136–149.

4. In August 2006, EPA revised its form R, the form on which facilities report total releases. The revised TRI Reporting form R is found at the end of this chapter.

5. The involvement of workers in community right-to-know activities is reported to yield significant reductions in risks. An analysis of the 1991–1992 TRI database found statistically relevant evidence that manufacturers using a combination of three formal employee participation practices tripled the reduction of emissions compared with those manufacturers using none of those practices. See John Bunge, Edward Cohen-Rosenthal, and Antonio Ruiz-Quintanilla (1996) "Employee Participation in Pollution Reduction: Preliminary Analysis of the TRI," *Journal of Cleaner Production* 4(1): 9. The source reduction methods identified for reporting in Section 8.10 of form R by the EPA are listed in table 10.2. The methods involving employee participation identified by the authors are in bold type in the table and include worker involvement in audits of internal opportunities to prevent pollution, participative team management, and employee recommendations. Manufacturers combining these practices with external pollution prevention assistance obtained results comparable to or better than those of manufacturers who did not.

6. While EPCRA does not require the reporting of violations of environmental laws and regulations to the public, shareholder reaction to a firm violating standards and incurring liability costs might be an effective spur to undertake better practices. Jason Johnston has argued that capital markets do in fact respond adversely to objection-

Table 10.2
TRI Form R Source Reduction Methods

Code	Source Reduction Method	Group
TO1	**Internal pollution prevention opportunity audit(s)**	Audits
TO2	External pollution prevention opportunity audit(s)	
TO3	Materials balance audits	
TO4	**Participative team management**	Employee-based strategies
TO5	Employee recommendation (independent of a formal company program)	
TO6	**Employee recommendation (under a formal company program)**	
TO7	State government technical assistance program	External assistance
TO8	Federal government technical assistance program	
TO9	Trade association/industry technical assistance program	
TlO	Vendor assistance	
T11	Other	

Source: John Bunge, Edward Cohen-Rosenthal, and Antonio Ruiz-Quintanilla (1996) "Employee Participation in Pollution Reduction: Preliminary Analysis of the TRI," *Journal of Cleaner Production* 4(1): 9. Reprinted with permission.

able environmental, health, safety, and labor practices by publicly owned firms, and that better enforced and expanded Security and Exchange Commission disclosure laws would facilitate a even larger market response. See Jason Scott Johnston (2005) "Signaling Social Responsibility: On the Law and Economics of Market Incentives for Corporate Environmental Performance." (Paper presented May 11, 2005 at the John F. Kennedy School of Government, Harvard University, and available at http://www.ksg.harvard.edu/cbg/CSR%20and%20the%20Law.pdf.) For a contrary view, see Linda Bui's study of oil refineries, discussed in note 1. Also see Linda Bui and Christopher Mayer (2003) "Regulation and Capitalization of Environmental Amenities: Evidence from the Toxics Release Inventory," *Review of Economics and Statistics* 85(3): 693–708.

7. Another federal "right-to-know" program for toxic substances—this one aimed at consumer products—is the Federal Hazardous Substances Act, 15 U.S.C. §§1261, *et seq.* This act requires any "hazardous substance" (as defined in the statute) that is "intended, or packaged in a form suitable, for use in the household or by children," to exhibit a label that sufficiently warns consumers of its risks. Failure to comply with the statute's labeling requirements is likely to be treated by the courts as evidence of negligence in a common-law products liability action. See, e.g., *Milanese v. Rust-Oleum Corp.*, 244 F. 3d 104 (2d. Cir. 2001). ■

Form Approved OMB Number: 2070-0093

(IMPORTANT: Type or print; read instructions before completing form)   Approval Expires: 01/31/2008   **Page 1 of 5**

		FORM R	TRI Facility ID Number
EPA United States Environmental Protection Agency	Section 313 of the Emergency Planning and Community Right-to-Know Act of 1986, also Known as Title III of the Superfund Amendments and Reauthorization Act		Toxic Chemical, Category or Generic Name

WHERE TO SEND COMPLETED FORMS: 1. TRI Data Processing Center	2. APPROPRIATE STATE OFFICE	Enter "X" here if this is a revision
P. O. Box 1513 Lanham, MD 20703-1513 ATTN: TOXIC CHEMICAL RELEASE INVENTORY	(See instructions in Appendix F)	For EPA use only

IMPORTANT: See instructions to determine when "Not Applicable (NA)" boxes should be checked.

PART 1. FACILITY IDENTIFICATION INFORMATION

SECTION 1. REPORTING YEAR _____

SECTION 2. TRADE SECRET INFORMATION

2.1 Are you claiming the toxic chemical identified on page 2 trade secret?

☐ Yes (Answer question 2.2; Attach substantiation forms)   ☐ No (Do not answer 2.2; Go to Section 3)

2.2 Is this copy ☐ Sanitized   ☐ Unsanitized

(Answer only if "YES" in 2.1)

SECTION 3. CERTIFICATION   (Important: Read and sign after completing all form sections.)

I hereby certify that I have reviewed the attached documents and that, to the best of my knowledge and belief, the submitted information is true and complete and that the amounts and values in this report are accurate based on reasonable estimates using data available to the preparers of this report.

Name and official title of owner/operator or senior management official:	Signature:	Date Signed:

SECTION 4. FACILITY IDENTIFICATION

4.1		TRI Facility ID Number	
Facility or Establishment Name		Facility or Establishment Name or Mailing Address (If different from street address)	
Street		Mailing Address	
City/County/State/Zip Code		City/State/Zip Code	Country (Non-US)

4.2 This report contains information for: ☐ a. An entire facility   ☐ b. Part of a facility   ☐ c. A Federal facility   ☐ d. GOCO
(Important: Check a or b; check c or d if applicable)

4.3	Technical Contact Name		Telephone Number (include area code)
	Email Address		

4.4	Public Contact Name		Telephone Number (include area code)

4.5	NAICS Code (s) (6 digits)	Primary a.	b.	c.	d.	e.	f.

4.7	Dun & Bradstreet Number (s) (9 digits)	a.
		b.

SECTION 5. PARENT COMPANY INFORMATION

5.1	Name of Parent Company	NA ☐	
5.2	Parent Company's Dun & Bradstreet Number	NA ☐	

EPA Form 9350 -1 (Rev. 08/2006) - Previous editions are obsolete.

Form Approved OMB Number: 2070-0093
Approval Expires: 01/31/2008 **Page 2 of 5**

(IMPORTANT: Type or print; read instructions before completing form)

FORM R

PART II. TOXIC CHEMICAL RELEASE INVENTORY REPORTING FORM

TRI Facility ID Number

Toxic Chemical, Category or Generic Name

SECTION 1. TOXIC CHEMICAL IDENTITY   (Important: DO NOT complete this section if you completed Section 2 below.)

1.1	CAS Number (Important: Enter only one number exactly as it appears on the Section 313 list. Enter category code if reporting a chemical category.)

1.2	Toxic Chemical or Chemical Category Name (Important: Enter only one name exactly as it appears on the Section 313 list.)

1.3	Generic Chemical Name (Important: Complete only if Part 1, Section 2.1 is checked "yes". Generic Name must be structurally descriptive.)

1.4 **Distribution of Each Member of the Dioxin and Dioxin-like Compounds Category.**
(If there are any numbers in boxes 1-17, then every field must be filled in with either 0 or some number between 0.01 and 100. Distribution should
be reported in percentages and the total should equal 100%. If you do not have speciation data available, indicate NA.)

	1	2	3	4	5	6	7	8	9	10	11	12	13	14	15	16	17
NA																	

SECTION 2. MIXTURE COMPONENT IDENTITY   (Important: DO NOT complete this section if you completed Section 1 above.)

2.1	Generic Chemical Name Provided by Supplier (Important: Maximum of 70 characters, including numbers, letters, spaces and punctuation.)

SECTION 3. ACTIVITIES AND USES OF THE TOXIC CHEMICAL AT THE FACILITY
(Important: Check all that apply.)

3.1 Manufacture the toxic chemical:	3.2 Process the toxic chemical:	3.3 Otherwise use the toxic chemical:
a. ☐ Produce b. ☐ Import If produce or import c. ☐ For on-site use/processing d. ☐ For sale/distribution e. ☐ As a byproduct f. ☐ As an impurity	a. ☐ As a reactant b. ☐ As a formulation component c. ☐ As an article component d. ☐ Repackaging e. ☐ As an impurity	a. ☐ As a chemical processing aid b. ☐ As a manufacturing aid c. ☐ Ancillary or other use

SECTION 4. MAXIMUM AMOUNT OF THE TOXIC CHEMICAL ONSITE AT ANY TIME DURING THE CALENDAR YEAR

4.1		(Enter two digit code from instruction package.)

SECTION 5.   QUANTITY OF THE TOXIC CHEMICAL ENTERING EACH ENVIRONMENTAL MEDIUM ONSITE

		A. Total Release (pounds/year*) (Enter a range code** or estimate)	B. Basis of Estimate (enter code)	C. % From Stormwater
5.1	Fugitive or non-point air emissions	NA ☐		
5.2	Stack or point air emissions	NA ☐		
5.3	Discharges to receiving streams or water bodies (enter one name per box)			
	Stream or Water Body Name			
5.3.1				
5.3.2				
5.3.3				

If additional pages of Part II, Section 5.3 are attached, indicate the total number of pages in this box
and indicate the Part II, Section 5.3 page number in this box.   (example: 1,2,3, etc.)

EPA Form 9350-1 (Rev. 08/2006) - Previous editions are obsolete.

*For Dioxin or Dioxin-like compounds, report in grams/year.
** Range Codes: A= 1-10 pounds; B= 11-499 pounds; C= 500-999 pounds.

(IMPORTANT: Type or print; read instructions before completing form)

FORM R
PART II. CHEMICAL - SPECIFIC INFORMATION (CONTINUED)

TRI Facility ID Number

Toxic Chemical, Category or Generic Name

SECTION 5. QUANTITY OF THE TOXIC CHEMICAL ENTERING EACH ENVIRONMENTAL MEDIUM ONSITE (continued)

		NA	A. Total Release (pounds/year*) (enter range code ** or estimate)	B. Basis of Estimate (enter code)
5.4.1	Underground Injection onsite to Class I Wells	☐		
5.4.2	Underground Injection onsite to Class II-V Wells	☐		
5.5	Disposal to land onsite			
5.5.1A	RCRA Subtitle C landfills	☐		
5.5.1B	Other landfills	☐		
5.5.2	Land treatment/application farming	☐		
5.5.3A	RCRA Subtitle C surface impoundments	☐		
5.5.3B	Other surface impoundments	☐		
5.5.4	Other disposal	☐		

SECTION 6. TRANSFERS OF THE TOXIC CHEMICAL IN WASTES TO OFF-SITE LOCATIONS

6.1 DISCHARGES TO PUBLICLY OWNED TREATMENT WORKS (POTWs)

6.1.A Total Quantity Transferred to POTWs and Basis of Estimate

6.1.A.1 Total Transfers (pounds/year*) (enter range code ** or estimate)	6.1.A.2 Basis of Estimate (enter code)

6.1.B _____ POTW Name

POTW Address

City		State		County		Zip	

6.1.B _____ POTW Name

POTW Address

City		State		County		Zip	

If additional pages of Part II, Section 6.1 are attached, indicate the total number of pages in this box ☐ and indicate the Part II, Section 6.1 page number in this box ☐ (example: 1,2,3, etc.)

SECTION 6.2 TRANSFERS TO OTHER OFF-SITE LOCATIONS

6.2. _____ Off-Site EPA Identification Number (RCRA ID No.)

Off-Site Location Name

Off-Site Address

City		State		County		Zip		Country (Non-US)

Is location under control of reporting facility or parent company?   ☐ Yes   ☐ No

* For Dioxin or Dioxin-like compounds, report in grams/year
** Range Codes: A=1-10 pounds; B=1-499 pounds; C=500 - 999 pounds.

Form Approved OMB Number: 2070-0093
Approval Expires: 01/31/2008

(IMPORTANT: Type or print; read instructions before completing form)   Page 4 of 5

FORM R
PART II. CHEMICAL-SPECIFIC INFORMATION (CONTINUED)

TRI Facility ID Number

Toxic Chemical, Category or Generic Name

SECTION 6.2 TRANSFERS TO OTHER OFF-SITE LOCATIONS (CONTINUED)

A. Total Transfers (pounds/year*) (enter range code** or estimate)	B. Basis of Estimate (enter code)	C. Type of Waste Treatment/Disposal/ Recycling/Energy Recovery (enter code)
1.	1.	1. M
2.	2.	2. M
3.	3.	3. M
4.	4.	4. M

6.2 ____ Off-Site EPA Identification Number (RCRA ID No.)

Off-Site Location Name

Off-Site Address

City	State	County	Zip	Country (Non-US)

Is location under control of reporting facility or parent company?   Yes ☐   No ☐

A. Total Transfers (pounds/year*) (enter range code** or estimate)	B. Basis of Estimate (enter code)	C. Type of Waste Treatment/Disposal/ Recycling/Energy Recovery (enter code)
1.	1.	1. M
2.	2.	2. M
3.	3.	3. M
4.	4.	4. M

SECTION 7A. ON-SITE WASTE TREATMENT METHODS AND EFFICIENCY

☐ Not Applicable (NA) - Check here if no on-site waste treatment is applied to any waste stream containing the toxic chemical or chemical category.

a. General Waste Stream [enter code]	b. Waste Treatment Method(s) Sequence [enter 3- or 4- character code(s)]		d. Waste Treatment Efficiency [enter 2 character code]
7A.1a	7A.1b 1 2	3 4 5 / 6 7 8	7A.1d
7A.2a	7A.2b 1 2	3 4 5 / 6 7 8	7A.2d
7A.3a	7A.3b 1 2	3 4 5 / 6 7 8	7A.3d
7A.4a	7A.4b 1 2	3 4 5 / 6 7 8	7A.4d
7A.5a	7A.5b 1 2	3 4 5 / 6 7 8	7A.5d

If additional pages of Part II, Section 6.2/7A are attached, indicate the total number of pages in this box ☐ and indicate the Part II, Section 6.2/7 page number in this box: ☐ (example: 1,2,3,etc.)

EPA Form 9350 -1 (Rev. 08/2006) - Previous editions are obsolete.

*For Dioxin or Dioxin-like compounds, report in grams/year
**Range Codes: A=1 - 10 pounds; B=11 - 499 pounds C= 500-999 pounds.

(IMPORTANT: Type or print; read instructions before completing form) Form Approved OMB Number: 2070-0093   **Page 5 of 5**
                                                                       Approval Expires: 01/31/2008

FORM R

PART II. CHEMICAL-SPECIFIC INFORMATION (CONTINUED)

TRI Facility ID Number

Toxic Chemical, Category or Generic Name

SECTION 7B. ON-SITE ENERGY RECOVERY PROCESSES

☐ Not Applicable (NA) - Check here if no on-site energy recovery is applied to any waste stream containing the toxic chemical or chemical category.

Energy Recovery Methods [enter 3-character code(s)]

1 ☐   2 ☐   3 ☐

SECTION 7C. ON-SITE RECYCLING PROCESSES

☐ Not Applicable (NA) - Check here if no on-site recycling is applied to any waste stream containing the toxic chemical or chemical category.

Recycling Methods [enter 3-character code(s)]

1 ☐   2 ☐   3 ☐

SECTION 8. SOURCE REDUCTION AND RECYLING ACTIVITIES

		Column A Prior Year (pounds/year*)	Column B Current Reporting Year (pounds/year*)	Column C Following Year (pounds/year*)	Column D Second Following Year (pounds/year*)
8.1					
8.1a	Total on-site disposal to Class I Underground InjectionWells, RCRA Subtitle C landfills, and other landfills				
8.1b	Total other on-site disposal or other releases				
8.1c	Total off-site disposal to Class I Underground Injection Wells, RCRA Subtitle C landfills, and other landfills				
8.1d	Total other off-site disposal or other releases				
8.2	Quantity used for energy recovery onsite				
8.3	Quantity used for energy recovery offsite				
8.4	Quantity recycled onsite				
8.5	Quantity recycled offsite				
8.6	Quantity treated onsite				
8.7	Quantity treated offsite				
8.8	Quantity released to the environment as a result of remedial actions, catastrophic events, or one-time events not associated with production processes (pounds/year)*				
8.9	Production ratio or activity index				
8.10	Did your facility engage in any source reduction activities for this chemical during the reporting year? If not, enter "NA" in Section 8.10.1 and answer Section 8.11.				

	Source Reduction Activities [enter code(s)]	Methods to Identify Activity (enter codes)		
8.10.1		a.	b.	c.
8.10.2		a.	b.	c.
8.10.3		a.	b.	c.
8.10.4		a.	b.	c.
8.11	If you wish to submit additional optional information on source reduction, recycling, or pollution control activities, check "Yes."		Yes ☐	

EPA Form 9350 -1 (Rev. 08/2006) - Previous editions are obsolete.   *For Dioxin or Dioxin-like compounds, report in grams/year

11 Enforcement: Encouraging Compliance with Environmental Statutes

A. OVERVIEW

Without a meaningful "enforcement presence"—i.e., without a meaningful sense within the regulated community that the law means what it says—implementation of environmental laws is a hit-or-miss proposition. Enforcement takes in a broad range of activities, from quite informal to quite formal. Although we focus in this chapter on the more formal forms of enforcement—in part because it is these activities that set the parameters within which the more informal forms of enforcement will operate—it is important to remember that much of the real "enforcement" of environmental laws happens behind the scenes. It may come, for example, with a phone call or a visit from an agency engineer, asking a plant manager why his or her facility has been out of compliance over the past 3 months. Or it may come with a call from a member of a community group, asking to discuss the plant's latest TRI reporting data. Or it may come from the plant manager, hoping to fix a compliance problem in time to forestall a call from an agency or environmental group.

Early on, Congress recognized that enforcement of the nation's environmental laws would require myriad actors. Thus, starting with the Clean Air and Clean Water acts, Congress invoked what is essentially a tripartite enforcement model, which gives important roles to the federal government, the state government, and private citizens. Moreover, in certain areas, such as the Clean Water Act's "indirect discharger" program, local government is given a role as well.

B. THEORIES OF ENFORCEMENT: COMPLIANCE, DETERRENCE, AND RESTITUTION

Any enforcement action—from the most formal to the most informal—can be evaluated against three distinct goals. The first is *compliance*: Has the enforcement action brought the violator into compliance with the applicable law (and, if not, will it do so within a reasonable time frame)? The second is *deterrence*: Will the enforcement action deter violations of the law in the future? This concept has two components. *Specific* deterrence refers to the deterrent effect on a particular violator, while *general* deterrence refers to the deterrent effect on a broader class of would-be violators (within the relevant industry, within the region, or among all who are regulated by this law). The third potential goal is *restitution*: Does the enforcement action recover anything (through the payment of penalties into the public fisc, the performance of environmental remediation or enhancement projects, or some other means) that can be said to help repay the public for the damage caused by the violations?

Although not all enforcement efforts will—or necessarily should—address all three of these goals, attention to each of them generally is an appropriate step in evaluating the extent of the enforcement action to be taken. Lack of attention to these three goals often will cause an enforcement system to fail. For example, an agency that simply identified noncompliant facilities and ordered them to come into compliance would most likely be doomed to repeat this exercise time and again. If a noncompliant facility knows that the only consequence of its violations will be to eventually be forced to attain compliance, it will have no economic incentive to attain compliance before it is made to do so. Rather (assuming that compliance costs money), there will actually be an economic *disincentive* for the facility to attain compliance any earlier because noncompliance "frees up" the compliance money so that it can be used for other purposes in the interim.

C. THE ENFORCERS AND THEIR ROLES

Most of the major environmental pollution statutes—including the Clean Air Act, the Clean Water Act, RCRA, and the Safe Drinking Water Act—utilize a similar enforcement scheme. Ultimate responsibility for enforcing an act rests with EPA, which sets broad federal enforcement policies and often makes adherence to such policies a condition of delegating the day-to-day implementation of the statute to the state. If a state seeks (and is granted) delegation of a particular federal regulatory program, the state becomes the primary (i.e., frontline) enforcer of that program. However, EPA retains the statutory right (and obligation) to monitor the state's enforcement efforts, to rescind the delegation if it finds the state's performance to be far short of the mark, and to bring its own enforcement actions (administrative or judicial) when it believes them to be warranted. Moreover, all of these statutes grant jurisdiction to the federal courts to hear enforcement cases brought by interested citizens in situations where EPA and the state lack either the resources or the political will to diligently enforce the act themselves.

■ **NOTES**

1. Not all federal environmental statutes provide for delegation of administrative authority to the states. The program for regulating nuclear power plants under the Atomic Energy Act, for example, is strictly the province of the Nuclear Regulatory Commission. Similarly, the "Superfund" program created under CERCLA, and the chemical regulatory program created by the Toxic Substances Control Act (TSCA), are both administered at the federal level, by EPA.

2. Nor do all federal environmental statutes provide for citizen enforcement suits. CERCLA and TSCA both do, but the Atomic Energy Act does not; nor does the Federal Insecticide, Fungicide, and Rodenticide Act, the primary statute regulating the manufacture, sale, and use of pesticides. Furthermore, most statutes regulating chemical exposures in other than an environmental context—such as the Occupational Safety and Health Act and the Food, Drug, and Cosmetic Act—do not contain provisions for citizen suits.

3. There is a special set of "threshold" issues governing the right to bring citizen enforcement suits; these are discussed later in this chapter.

4. When we speak of "citizen enforcement suits" in this chapter, we are referring to suits brought against a member of the regulated community—i.e., against a party alleged to be in violation of a regulatory standard (or of an agency permit or order issued pursuant to such a standard)—as distinguished from suits brought against an

agency to compel it to implement or enforce the law. That is, these are suits brought under an explicit *private right of action* (discussed in section D.6 in chapter 5). For a general discussion of suits brought to compel agency action or to seek review of agency rulemaking, see sections D.4 and E in chapter 5.   ▪

D. ENFORCEMENT IN PRACTICE: THE PROVERBIAL NUTS AND BOLTS

1. Monitoring, Reporting, and Record-keeping Requirements

In general, an enforcement action depends for its success on the availability of reliable evidence of noncompliance. To this end, the major environmental pollution statutes all require regulated entities to monitor certain specified outputs (such as pollution levels), and to report the results of this monitoring to the oversight agency and/or retain the monitoring records for a specified period. The most well-developed self-monitoring program is that put in place under the Clean Water Act. As discussed in chapter 8, anyone desiring to discharge pollutants to surface waters must first obtain an NPDES permit. This permit in turn must incorporate all relevant pollutant discharge limits and must require the discharger to monitor for those pollutants (and report the results to EPA or the state) on a specified regular basis. The act further requires the agencies to make these monitoring records freely available to the public. In short, the act has mandated the creation and maintenance of a comprehensive, self-reported compliance database, which can be used by the agencies and by citizen plaintiffs as a means of identifying and mounting an enforcement action against noncompliant facilities.

It is because of this comprehensive database that the majority of the early citizen enforcement suits were brought under the Clean Water Act. Seeking to repeat this success in the field of air pollution, Congress included the Title V permitting requirements in the 1990 Clean Air Act Amendments. As these requirements are (slowly) being implemented, the number of Clean Air Act citizen suits is on the rise.

2. Inspections

Marshall v. Barlow's Inc.
Mr. Justice WHITE delivered the opinion of the Court
United States Supreme Court
436 U.S. 307 (1978)

Section 8(a) of the Occupational Safety and Health Act of 1970 (OSHA) empowers agents of the Secretary of Labor (the Secretary) to search the work area of any employment facility within the Act's jurisdiction. The purpose of the search is to inspect for safety hazards and violations of OSHA regulations. No search warrant or other process is expressly required under the Act.

On the morning of September 11, 1975, an OSHA inspector entered the customer service area of Barlow's, Inc., an electrical and plumbing installation business located in Pocatello, Idaho. The president and general manager, Ferrol G. "Bill" Barlow, was on hand; and the OSHA inspector, after showing his credentials, informed Mr. Barlow that he wished to conduct a search of the working areas of the business. Mr. Barlow inquired whether any complaint had been received about his company. The inspector answered no, but that Barlow's, Inc. had simply turned up in the agency's selection process. The inspector again asked to enter the nonpublic area of the business; Mr. Barlow's response was to inquire whether the inspector had a search warrant. The inspector had none. Thereupon, Mr. Barlow refused the inspector admission to the employee area of his business. He said he was relying on his rights as guaranteed by the Fourth Amendment of the United States Constitution.

Three months later, the Secretary petitioned the United States District Court for the District of Idaho to issue an order compelling Mr. Barlow to admit the inspector. The requested order was issued on December 30, 1975, and was presented to Mr. Barlow on January 5, 1976. Mr. Barlow again refused admission, and he sought his own injunctive relief against the warrantless searches assertedly permitted by OSHA. A three-judge court was convened. On December 30, 1976, it ruled in Mr. Barlow's favor. 424 F. Supp. 437. Concluding that *Camara v. Municipal Court*, 387 U.S. 523, 528–529 (1967), and *See v. City of Seattle*, 387 U.S. 541, 543 (1967), controlled this case, the court held that the Fourth Amendment required a warrant for the type of search involved here and that the statutory author-

ization for warrantless inspections was unconstitutional. An injunction against searches or inspections pursuant to §8(a) was entered. The Secretary appealed, challenging the judgment, and we noted probable jurisdiction. 430 U.S. 964.

I

The Secretary urges that warrantless inspections to enforce OSHA are reasonable within the meaning of the Fourth Amendment. Among other things, he relies on §8(a) of the Act, 29 U.S.C. §657(a), which authorizes inspection of business premises without a warrant and which the Secretary urges represents a congressional construction of the Fourth Amendment that the courts should not reject. Regretfully, we are unable to agree.

The Warrant Clause of the Fourth Amendment protects commercial buildings as well as private homes. To hold otherwise would belie the origin of that Amendment, and the American colonial experience. An important forerunner of the first 10 Amendments to the United States Constitution, the Virginia Bill of Rights, specifically opposed "general warrants, whereby an officer or messenger may be commanded to search suspected places without evidence of a fact committed." The general warrant was a recurring point of contention in the colonies immediately preceding the Revolution. The particular offensiveness it engendered was acutely felt by the merchants and businessmen whose premises and products were inspected for compliance with the several Parliamentary revenue measures that most irritated the colonists'. "[T]he Fourth Amendment's commands grew in large measure out of the colonists' experience with the writs of assistance... [that] granted sweeping power to customs officials and other agents of the King to search at large for smuggled goods." *United States v. Chadwick*, 433 U.S.1,78 (1977). See also *G.M. Leasing Corporation v. United States*, 429 U.S. 338, 355 (1977). Against this background, it is untenable that the ban on warrantless searches was not intended to shield places of business as well as of residence. This Court has already held that warrantless searches are generally unreasonable, and that this rule applies to commercial premises as well as homes. In *Camara v. Municipal Court*, 387 U.S.523, 528–529 (1967), we held:

[E]xcept in certain carefully defined classes of cases, a search of private property without proper consent is 'unreasonable' unless it has been authorized by a valid search warrant.

On the same day, we also ruled:

"As we explained in *Camara*, a search of private houses is presumptively unreasonable if conducted without a warrant. The businessman, like the occupant of a residence, has a constitutional right to go about his business free from unreasonable official entries upon his private commercial property. The businessman, too, has that right placed in jeopardy if the decision to enter and inspect for violation of regulatory laws can be made and enforced by the inspector in the field without official authority evidenced by a warrant."

See v. City of Seattle, 387 U.S. 541,543 (1967). These same cases also held that the Fourth Amendment prohibition against unreasonable searches protects against warrantless intrusions during civil as well as criminal investigations. *See v. City of Seattle*, supra, at 543. The reason is found in the "basic purpose of this Amendment . . . [which] is to safeguard the privacy and security of individuals against arbitrary invasions by governmental officials." *Camara*, supra, at 528. If the government intrudes on a person's property, the privacy interest suffers whether the government's motivation is to investigate violations of criminal laws or breaches of other statutory or regulatory standards. It therefore appears that unless some recognized exception to the warrant requirement applies, *See v. City of Seattle*, supra, would require a warrant to conduct the inspection sought in this case.

The Secretary urges that an exception from the search warrant requirement has been recognized for "pervasively regulated business[es]," *United States v. Biswell*, 406 U.S. 311, 316 (1972), and for "closely regulated" industries "long subject to close supervision and inspection." *Colonnade Catering Corp. v. United States*, 297 U.S. 72, 74, 77, (1970). These cases are indeed exceptions, but they represent responses to relatively unique circumstances. Certain industries have such a history of government oversight that no reasonable expectation of privacy, see *Katz v. United States*, 380 U.S. 347, 351–352 (1967), could exist for a proprietor over the stock of such an enterprise. Liquor (*Colonnade*) and firearms (*Biswell*) are industries of this type; when an entrepreneur embarks upon such a business, he has voluntarily chosen to subject himself to a full arsenal of governmental regulation.

Industries such as these fall within the "certain carefully defined classes of cases" referenced in *Camara*, supra, at 528. The element that distinguishes these enterprises from ordinary businesses is a long tradition of close government supervision, of which any person who chooses to enter such a business must already be aware. "A central difference between those cases [*Colonnade* and *Biswell*] and this one is that businessmen engaged in such federally licensed and regulated enterprises accept the burdens as well as the benefits of their trade, whereas the petitioner here was not engaged in any regulated or licensed business. The businessman in a regulated industry in effect consents to the restrictions placed upon him." *Almeida-Sanchez v. United States*, 413 U.S. 266, 271 (1973).

The clear import of our cases is that the closely regulated industry of the type involved in *Colonnade* and *Biswell* is the exception. The Secretary would make it the rule. Invoking the Walsh-Healy Act of 1936, 41 U.S.C. §35 et seq., the Secretary attempts to support a conclusion that all businesses involved in interstate commerce have long been subjected to close supervision of employee safety and health conditions. But the degree of federal involvement in employee working circumstances has never been of the order of specificity and pervasiveness that OSHA mandates. It is quite unconvincing to argue that the imposition of minimum wages and maximum hours on employers who contracted with the government under the Walsh-Healy Act prepared the entirety of American interstate commerce for regulation of working conditions to the minutest detail. Nor can any but the most fictional sense of voluntary consent to later searches be found in the single fact that one conducts a business affecting interstate commerce; under current practice and law, few businesses can be conducted without having some effect on interstate commerce.

The Secretary also attempts to derive support for a *Colonnade-Biswell*-type exception by drawing analogies from the field of labor law. In Republic *Aviation Corp. v. NLRB*, 324 U.S. 793 (1945), this Court upheld the rights of employees to solicit for a union during nonworking time where efficiency was not compromised. By opening up his property to employees, the employer had yielded so much of his private property rights as to allow those employees to exercise §7 rights under the National Labor Relations Act. But this Court also held that the private property rights of an owner prevailed over the intrusion of non-employee organizers, even in nonworking areas of the plant and during nonworking hours. *NLRB v. Babcock & Wilcox Co.*, 351 U.S. 105 (1956).

The critical fact in this case is that entry over Mr. Barlow's objection is being sought by a Government agent. Employees are not being prohibited from reporting OSHA violations. What they observe in their daily functions is undoubtedly beyond the employer's reasonable expectation of privacy. The Government inspector, however, is not an employee. Without a warrant he stands in no better position than a member of the public.

What is observable by the public is observable, without a warrant, by the Government inspector as well. The owner of a business has not, by the necessary utilization of employees in his operation, thrown open the areas where employees alone are permitted to the warrantless scrutiny of Government agents. That an employee is free to report, and the Government is free to use, any evidence of noncompliance with OSHA that the employee observes furnishes no justification for federal agents to enter a place of business from which the public is restricted and to conduct their own warrantless search.

II

The Secretary nevertheless stoutly argues that the enforcement scheme of the Act requires warrantless searches, and that the restrictions on search discretion contained in the Act and its regulations already protect as much privacy as a warrant would. The secretary thereby asserts the actual reasonableness of OSHA searches, whatever the general rule against warrantless searches might be. Because "reasonableness is still the ultimate standard," *Camara v. Municipal Court*, supra, at 539, the Secretary suggests that the Court decide whether a warrant is needed by arriving at a sensible balance between the administrative necessities of OSHA inspections and the incremental protection of privacy of business owners a warrant would afford. He suggests that only a decision exempting OSHA inspections from the Warrant Clause would give "full recognition to the competing public and private interests here at stake." *Camara v. Municipal Court*, supra, at 539.

The Secretary submits that warrantless inspections are essential to the proper enforcement of OSHA because they afford the opportunity to inspect without prior notice and hence to preserve the advantages of surprise. While the dangerous conditions outlawed by the Act include structural defects that cannot be quickly hidden or remedied, the Act also regulates a myriad of safety details that may be amenable to speedy alteration or disguise. The risk is that during the interval between an inspector's initial request to search a plant and his procuring a warrant following the owner's refusal or permission, violations of this latter type could be corrected and thus escape the inspector's notice. To the suggestion that warrants may be issued ex parte and executed without delay and without prior notice, thereby preserving the element of surprise, the Secretary expresses concern for the administrative strain that would be experienced by the inspection system, and by the courts, should ex parte warrants issued in advance become standard practice.

We are unconvinced, however, that requiring warrants to inspect will impose serious burdens on the inspection system or the courts, will prevent inspections necessary to enforce the statute, or will make them less effective. In the first place, the great majority of businessmen can be expected in normal course to consent to inspection without warrant; the Secretary has not brought to this Court's attention any widespread pattern of refusal. In those cases where an owner does insist on a warrant, the Secretary argues that inspection efficiency will be impeded by the advance notice and delay. The Act's penalty provisions for giving advance notice of a search, 29 U.S.C. §666(f), and the Secretary's own regulations, 29 CFR §1903.6, indicate that surprise searches are indeed contemplated. However, the Secretary has also promulgated a regulation providing that upon refusal to permit an inspector to enter the property or to complete his inspection, the inspector shall attempt to ascertain the reasons for the refusal and report to his superior, who shall "promptly take appropriate action, including compulsory process, if necessary." 29 CE:R §1903.4. The regulation represents

a choice to proceed by process where entry is refused and on the basis of evidence available from present practice, the Act's effectiveness has not been crippled by providing those owners who wish to refuse an initial requested entry with a time lapse while the inspector obtains the necessary process. Indeed, the kind of process sought in this case and apparently anticipated by the regulation provides notice to the business operator. If this safeguard endangers the efficient administration of OSHA, the Secretary should never have adopted it, particularly when the Act does not require it. Nor is it immediately apparent why the advantages of surprise would be lost if, after being refused entry, procedures were available for the Secretary to seek an ex parte warrant and to reappear at the premise without further notice to the establishment being inspected.

Whether the Secretary proceeds to secure a warrant or other process, with or without prior notice, his entitlement to inspect will not depend on his demonstrating probable cause to believe that conditions in violation of OSHA exist on the premises. Probable cause in the criminal law sense is not required. For purposes of an administrative search such as this, probable cause justifying the issuance of a warrant may be based not only on specific evidence of an existing violation but also on a showing that "reasonable legislative or administrative standards for conducting an . . . inspection are satisfied with respect to a particular [establishment]," *Camara v. Municipal Court*, supra, at 538. A warrant showing that a specific business has been chosen for an OSHA search on the basis of a general administrative plan for the enforcement of the Act derived from neutral sources such as, for example, dispersion of employees in various types of industries across a given area, and the desired frequency of searches in any of the lesser divisions of the area, would protect an employer's Fourth Amendment rights. We doubt that the consumption of enforcement energies in the obtaining of such warrants will exceed manageable proportions.

Finally, the Secretary urges that requiring a warrant for OSHA inspectors will mean that, as a practical matter, warrantless search provisions in other regulatory statutes are also constitutionally infirm. The reasonableness of a warrantless search, however, will depend upon the specific enforcement needs and privacy guarantees of each statute. Some of the statutes cited apply only to a single industry, where regulations might already be so pervasive that a *Colonnade-Biswell* exception to the warrant requirement could apply. Some statutes already envision resort to federal court enforcement when entry is refused, employing specific language in some cases and general language in others. In short, we base today's opinion on the facts and law concerned with OSHA and do not retreat from a holding appropriate to that statute because of its real or imagined effect on other, different administrative schemes.

Nor do we agree that the incremental protections afforded the employer's privacy by a warrant are so marginal that they fail to justify the administrative burdens that may be entailed. The authority to make warrantless searches devolves almost unbridled discretion upon executive and administrative officers, particularly those in the field, as to when to search and whom to search. A warrant, by contrast, would provide assurance from a neutral officer that the inspection is reasonable under the Constitution, is authorized by statute, and is pursuant to an administrative plan containing specific neutral criteria. Also, a warrant would then and there advise the owner of the scope and objects of the search, beyond which limits the inspector is not expected to proceed. These are important functions for a warrant to perform, functions which underlie the Court's prior decisions that the Warrant Clause applies to inspections for compliance with regulatory statutes. *Camara v. Municipal Court*, supra; *See v. City of Seattle*, supra. We conclude that the concerns expressed by the Secretary do not suffice to justify warrantless inspections under OSHA or vitiate the general constitutional requirement that for a search to be reasonable a warrant must be obtained.

III

We hold that Barlow was entitled to a declaratory judgment that the Act is unconstitutional insofar as it purports to authorize inspections without warrant or its equivalent and to an injunction enjoining the Act's enforcement to that extent. The judgment of the District Court is therefore affirmed.
[Dissenting opinion of STEPHENS, J. (in which BLACKMUN, J. and REHNQUIST, J., joined) omitted. BRENNAN, J., took no part in the case.]

■ **NOTES**

1. While this is an OSHAct case, the basic Fourth Amendment principle applies broadly to all agencies seeking to enforce environmental or public health laws. What does such an agency have to demonstrate in order to perform an unannounced inspection? Why are unannounced inspections important to the enforcement of a given statutory scheme?

2. In a later case, the Supreme Court held that EPA did not violate the Fourth Amendment by "inspecting" Dow Chemical Company's hazardous waste management practices from an airplane flying in the airspace above Dow's property. See *Dow Chemical Co. v. U.S.*, 476 U.S. 227 (1986). Nonetheless, the Court has read the Fourth Amendment as placing limits on the government's right to use technology to perform searches (or inspections). For example, the Court has held that the use of heat-sensing technology to locate basements housing marijuana "farms" (which rely on heat lamps to help the plant grow) is an unreasonable search under the Fourth Amendment. *See Kyllo v. United States*, 533 U.S. 27 (2001).   ■

3. Injunctions

The "big stick" in the enforcer's compliance arsenal is the injunction—a court order directing the violator to take and/or refrain from taking particular actions. Under the common law, the decision as to whether to grant an injunction, as well as the decision as to what the content of any injunction should be, is said to be within the court's *equitable* jurisdiction, which leaves these decisions largely to the sound discretion of the court. When Congress transformed environmental law from a common-law concern to a federal statutory concern, did it circumscribe the traditional discretion of the federal courts in administering injunctive relief? The Supreme Court addressed this question in a rather unusual pollution case arising under the Clean Water Act.

Weinberger, Secretary of Defense, et al. v. Romero-Barcelo et al.
Justice WHITE delivered the opinion of the Court
United States Supreme Court
456 U.S. 305 (1982)

The issue in this case is whether the Federal Water Pollution Control Act (FWPCA or Act), 86 Stat. 816, as amended, 33 U.S.C. §1251 et seq. (1976 ed. and Supp. IV), requires a district court to enjoin immediately all discharges of pollutants that do not comply with the Act's permit requirements or whether the district court retains discretion to order other relief to achieve compliance. The Court of Appeals for the First Circuit held that the Act withdrew the courts' equitable discretion. *Romero-Barcelo v. Brown*, 643 F.2d 835 (1981). We reverse.

I

For many years, the Navy has used Vieques Island, a small island off the Puerto Rico coast, for weapons training. Currently all Atlantic Fleet vessels assigned to the Mediterranean Sea and the Indian Ocean are required to complete their training at Vieques because it permits a full range of exercises under conditions similar to combat. During air-to-ground training, however, pilots sometimes miss land-based targets, and ordnance falls into the sea. That is, accidental bombings of the navigable waters and, occasionally, intentional bombings of water targets occur. The District Court found that these discharges have not harmed the quality of the water.

In 1978, respondents, who include the Governor of Puerto Rico and residents of the island, sued to enjoin the Navy's operations on the island. Their complaint alleged violations of numerous federal environmental statutes and various other Acts. After an extensive hearing, the District Court found that under the explicit terms of the Act, the Navy had violated the Act by discharging ordnance into the waters surrounding the island without first obtaining a permit from the Environmental Protection Agency (EPA). *Romero-Barcelo v. Brown*, 478 F.Supp. 646 (PR 1979).

Under the FWPCA, the "discharge of any pollutant" requires a National Pollutant Discharge Elimination System (NPDES) permit....

As the District Court construed the FWPCA, the release of ordnance from aircraft or from ships into navigable waters is a discharge of pollutants, even though the EPA, which administers the Act, had not promulgated any regulations setting effluent levels or providing for the issuance of an NPDES permit for this category of pollutants. Recognizing that violations of the Act "must be cured," 478 F.Supp., at 707, the District Court ordered the Navy to apply for an NPDES permit. It refused, however, to enjoin Navy operations pending consideration of the permit application. It explained that the Navy's "technical violations" were not causing any "appreciable harm" to the

environment.[4] Id., at 706. Moreover, because of the importance of the island as a training center, "the granting of the injunctive relief sought would cause grievous, and perhaps irreparable harm, not only to Defendant Navy, but to the general welfare of this Nation." Id., at 707. The District Court concluded that an injunction was not necessary to ensure suitably prompt compliance by the Navy. To support this conclusion, it emphasized an equity court's traditionally broad discretion in deciding appropriate relief and quoted from the classic description of injunctive relief in *Hecht Co. v. Bowles*, 321 U.S. 321, 329–330 (1944): "The historic injunctive process was designed to deter, not to punish."

The Court of Appeals for the First Circuit vacated the District Court's order and remanded with instructions that the court order the Navy to cease the violation until it obtained a permit. 643 F.2d 835 (1981). Relying on *TVA v. Hill*, 437 U.S. 153 (1978), in which this Court held that an imminent violation of the Endangered Species Act required injunctive relief, the Court of Appeals concluded that the District Court erred in undertaking a traditional balancing of the parties' competing interests. "Whether or not the Navy's activities in fact harm the coastal waters, it has an absolute statutory obligation to stop any discharges of pollutants until the permit procedure has been followed and the Administrator of the Environmental Protection Agency, upon review of the evidence, has granted a permit." 643 F.2d, at 861. The court suggested that if the order would interfere significantly with military preparedness, the Navy should request that the President

---

4. The District Court wrote:

"In fact, if anything, these waters are as aesthetically acceptable as any to be found anywhere, and Plaintiff's witnesses unanimously testified as to their being the best fishing grounds in Vieques." 478 F.Supp., at 667. "[If] the truth be said, the control of large areas of Vieques [by the Navy]

probably constitutes a positive factor in its over all ecology. The very fact that there are in the Navy zones modest numbers of various marine species which are practically non-existent in the civilian sector of Vieques or in the main island of Puerto Rico, is an eloquent example of res ipsa loquitur." Id., at 682 (footnote omitted).

grant it an exemption from the requirements in the interest of national security."[6]

Because this case posed an important question regarding the power of the federal courts to grant or withhold equitable relief for violations of the FWPCA, we granted certiorari, 454 U.S. 813 (1981). We now reverse.

II

It goes without saying that an injunction is an equitable remedy. It "is not a remedy which issues as of course," *Harrisonville v. W. S. Dickey Clay Mfg. Co.*, 289 U.S. 334, 337–338 (1933), or "to restrain an act the injurious consequences of which are merely trifling." *Consolidated Canal Co. v. Mesa Canal Co.*, 177 U.S. 296, 302 (1900). An injunction should issue only where the intervention of a court of equity "is essential in order effectually to protect property rights against injuries otherwise irremediable." *Cavanaugh v. Looney*, 248 U.S. 453, 456 (1919). The Court has repeatedly held that the basis for injunctive relief in the federal courts has always been irreparable injury and the inadequacy of legal remedies.

Where plaintiff and defendant present competing claims of injury, the traditional function of equity has been to arrive at a "nice adjustment and reconciliation" between the competing claims, *Hecht Co. v. Bowles*, [321 U.S. 321, 329 (1944)]. In such cases, the court "balances the conveniences of the parties and possible injuries to them according as they may be affected by the granting or withholding of the injunction." *Yakus v. United States*, 321 U.S. 414, 440 (1944). "The essence of equity jurisdiction has been the power of the Chancellor to do equity and to mould each decree to the necessities of the particular case. Flexibility rather than rigidity has distinguished it." *Hecht Co. v. Bowles*, supra, at 329.

In exercising their sound discretion, courts of equity should pay particular regard for the public consequences in employing the extraordinary remedy of injunction. *Railroad Comm'n. v. Pullman Co.*, 312 U.S. 496, 500 (1941). Thus, the Court has noted that "[the] award of an interlocutory injunction by courts of equity has never been regarded as strictly a matter of right, even though irreparable injury may otherwise result to the plaintiff," and that "where an injunction is asked which will adversely affect a public interest for whose impairment, even temporarily, an injunction bond cannot compensate, the court may in the public interest withhold relief until a final determination of the rights of the parties, though the postponement may be burdensome to the plaintiff." *Yakus v. United States*, supra, at 440 (footnote omitted). The grant of jurisdiction to ensure compliance with a statute hardly suggests an absolute duty to do so under any and all circumstances, and a federal judge sitting as chancellor is not mechanically obligated to grant an injunction for every violation of law. *TVA v. Hill*, 437 U.S., at 193; *Hecht Co. v. Bowles*, 321 U.S., at 329.

These commonplace considerations applicable to cases in which injunctions are sought in the federal courts reflect a "practice with a

---

6. Title 33 U.S.C. §1323(a) provides, in relevant part:

"The President may exempt any effluent source of any department, agency, or instrumentality in the executive branch from compliance with any such a requirement if he determines it to be in the paramount interest of the United States to do so.... No such exemptions shall be granted due to lack of appropriation unless the President shall have specifically requested such appropriation as part of the budgetary process and the Congress shall have failed to make available such requested appropriation. Any exemption shall be for a period not in excess of one year, but additional exemptions may be granted for periods of not to exceed one year upon the President's making a new determination. The President shall report each January to the Congress all exemptions from the requirements of this section granted during the preceding calendar year, together with his reason for granting such exemption."

background of several hundred years of history," *Hecht Co. v. Bowles*, supra, at 329, a practice of which Congress is assuredly well aware. Of course, Congress may intervene and guide or control the exercise of the courts' discretion, but we do not lightly assume that Congress has intended to depart from established principles. *Hecht Co. v. Bowles*, supra, at 329. As the Court said in Porter v. Warner Holding Co., 328 U.S. 395, 398 (1946):

"Moreover, the comprehensiveness of this equitable jurisdiction is not to be denied or limited in the absence of a clear and valid legislative command. Unless a statute in so many words, or by a necessary and inescapable inference, restricts the court's jurisdiction in equity, the full scope of that jurisdiction is to be recognized and applied. 'The great principles of equity, securing complete justice, should not be yielded to light inferences, or doubtful construction.' *Brown v. Swann*, 10 Pet. 497, 503...."

In *TVA v. Hill*, we held that Congress had foreclosed the exercise of the usual discretion possessed by a court of equity. There, we thought that "[one] would be hard pressed to find a statutory provision whose terms were any plainer" than that before us. 437 U.S., at 173. The statute involved, the Endangered Species Act, 87 Stat. 884, 16 U.S.C. §1531 et seq., required the District Court to enjoin completion of the Tellico Dam in order to preserve the snail darter, a species of perch. The purpose and language of the statute under consideration in *Hill*, not the bare fact of a statutory violation, compelled that conclusion. Section 7 of the Act, 16 U.S.C. §1536, requires federal agencies to "insure that actions authorized, funded, or carried out by them do not jeopardize the continued existence of [any] endangered species . . . or re-

sult in the destruction or modification of habitat of such species which is determined . . . to be critical." The statute thus contains a flat ban on the destruction of critical habitats.

It was conceded in *Hill* that completion of the dam would eliminate an endangered species by destroying its critical habitat. Refusal to enjoin the action would have ignored the "explicit provisions of the Endangered Species Act." 437 U.S., at 173. Congress, it appeared to us, had chosen the snail darter over the dam. The purpose and language of the statute limited the remedies available to the District Court; only an injunction could vindicate the objectives of the Act.

That is not the case here. An injunction is not the only means of ensuring compliance. The FWPCA itself, for example, provides for fines and criminal penalties. 33 U.S.C. §§1319(c) and (d). Respondents suggest that failure to enjoin the Navy will undermine the integrity of the permit process by allowing the statutory violation to continue. The integrity of the Nation's waters, however, not the permit process, is the purpose of the FWPCA.[7] As Congress explained, the objective of the FWPCA is to "restore and maintain the chemical, physical, and biological integrity of the Nation's waters." 33 U.S.C. §1251(a).

This purpose is to be achieved by compliance with the Act, including compliance with the permit requirements.[8] Here, however, the discharge of ordnance had not polluted the waters, and, although the District Court declined to enjoin the discharges, it neither ignored the statutory violation nor undercut the purpose and function of the permit system. The court ordered the Navy to apply for a permit. It temporarily, not permanently,

7. The objective of this statute is in some respects similar to that sought in nuisance suits, where courts have fully exercised their equitable discretion and ingenuity in ordering remedies. E.g., *Spur Industries, Inc. v. Del E. Webb Development Co.*, 108 Ariz. 178, 494 P. 2d 700 (1972); *Boomer v. Atlantic Cement Co.*, 26 N. Y. 2d 219, 257 N. E. 2d 870 (1970).

8. Federal agencies must comply with the water pollution abatement requirements "in the same manner, and to the same extent as any nongovernmental entity...." 33 U.S.C. §1323(a) (1976 ed., Supp. IV). S. Rep. No. 92-414, p. 80 (1971), pointed to "[federal] agencies such as the Department of Defense" for failing to abate pollution.

allowed the Navy to continue its activities without a permit.

In Hill, we also noted that none of the limited "hardship exemptions" of the Endangered Species Act would "even remotely apply to the Tellico Project." 437 U.S., at 188. The prohibition of the FWPCA against discharge of pollutants, in contrast, can be overcome by the very permit the Navy was ordered to seek. The Senate Report to the 1972 Amendments explains that the permit program would be enacted because "the Committee recognizes the impracticality of any effort to halt all pollution immediately." S. Rep. No. 92-414, p. 43 (1971). That the scheme as a whole contemplates the exercise of discretion and balancing of equities militates against the conclusion that Congress intended to deny courts their traditional equitable discretion in enforcing the statute.

Other aspects of the statutory scheme also suggest that Congress did not intend to deny courts the discretion to rely on remedies other than an immediate prohibitory injunction. Although the ultimate objective of the FWPCA is to eliminate all discharges of pollutants into the navigable waters by 1985, the statute sets forth a scheme of phased compliance. As enacted, it called for the achievement of the "best practicable control technology currently available" by July 1, 1977, and the "best available technology economically achievable" by July 1, 1983. 33 U.S.C. §1311(b). This scheme of phased compliance further suggests that this is a statute in which Congress envisioned, rather than curtailed, the exercise of discretion.[11]

The FWPCA directs the Administrator of the EPA to seek an injunction to restrain immediately discharges of pollutants he finds to be presenting "an imminent and substantial endangerment to the health of persons or to the welfare of persons." 33 U.S.C. §1364(a)

(1976 ed., Supp. IV). This rule of immediate cessation, however, is limited to the indicated class of violations. For other kinds of violations, the FWPCA authorizes the Administrator of the EPA "to commence a civil action for appropriate relief, including a permanent or temporary injunction, for any violation for which he is authorized to issue a compliance order...." 33 U.S.C. §1319(b). The provision makes clear that Congress did not anticipate that all discharges would be immediately enjoined. Consistent with this view, the administrative practice has not been to request immediate cessation orders. "Rather, enforcement actions typically result, by consent or otherwise, in a remedial order setting out a detailed schedule of compliance designed to cure the identified violation of the Act." Brief for Petitioners 17. See *Milwaukee v. Illinois*, 451 U.S. 304, 320–322 (1981). Here, again, the statutory scheme contemplates equitable consideration....

Like the language and structure of the Act, the legislative history does not suggest that Congress intended to deny courts their traditional equitable discretion. Congress passed the 1972 Amendments because it recognized that "the national effort to abate and control water pollution has been inadequate in every vital aspect." S. Rep. No. 92-414, p. 7 (1971). The past failings included enforcement efforts under the Rivers and Harbors Appropriation Act of 1899 (Refuse Act), 33 U.S.C. §401 et seq. The "major purpose" of the 1972 Amendments was "to establish a comprehensive long-range policy for the elimination of water pollution." S. Rep. No. 92-414, supra, at 95. The permit system was the key to that policy. "The Amendments established a new system of regulation under which it is illegal for anyone to discharge pollutants into the Nation's waters except pursuant to a permit." *Milwaukee v. Illinois*, supra, at 310–311; see

---

11. ... But, as we have also observed in construing this Act: "The question... is not what a court thinks is generally appropriate to the regulatory process, it is what Congress intended...." E. I. *du*

Pont de Nemours & Co. v. Train, 430 U.S., at 138. Here we do not read the FWPCA as intending to abolish the courts' equitable discretion in ordering remedies.

generally *EPA v. California ex rel. State Water Resources Control Board*, 426 U.S. 200 (1976). Nonetheless, "[in] writing the enforcement procedures involving the Federal Government the Committee drew extensively . . . upon the existing enforcement provisions of the Refuse Act of 1899." S. Rep. No. 92-414, *supra*, at 63. Violations of the Refuse Act have not automatically led courts to issue injunctions.

III

This Court explained in *Hecht Co. v. Bowles*, 321 U.S. 321 (1944), that a major departure from the long tradition of equity practice should not be lightly implied. As we did there, we construe the statute at issue "in favor of that interpretation which affords a full opportunity for equity courts to treat enforcement proceedings . . . in accordance with their traditional practices, as conditioned by the necessities of the public interest which Congress has sought to protect." Id., at 330. We do not read the FWPCA as foreclosing completely the exercise of the court's discretion. Rather than requiring a district court to issue an injunction for any and all statutory violations, the FWPCA permits the district court to order that relief it considers necessary to secure prompt compliance with the Act. That relief can include, but is not limited to, an order of immediate cessation.

The exercise of equitable discretion, which must include the ability to deny as well as grant injunctive relief, can fully protect the range of public interests at issue at this stage in the proceedings. The District Court did not face a situation in which a permit would very likely not issue, and the requirements and objective of the statute could therefore not be vindicated if discharges were permitted to continue. Should it become clear that no permit will be issued and that compliance with the FWPCA will not be forthcoming, the statutory scheme and purpose would require the court to reconsider the balance it has struck.

Because Congress, in enacting the FWPCA, has not foreclosed the exercise of equitable discretion, the proper standard for appellate review is whether the District Court abused its discretion in denying an immediate cessation order while the Navy applied for a permit. We reverse and remand to the Court of Appeals for proceedings consistent with this opinion.

It is so ordered.

JUSTICE POWELL, CONCURRING:

I join the opinion of the Court. In my view, however, the record clearly establishes that the District Court in this case did not abuse its discretion by refusing to enjoin the immediate cessation of all discharges. Finding that the District Court acted well within the equitable discretion left to it under the Federal Water Pollution Control Act (FWPCA), I would remand the case to the Court of Appeals with instructions that the decision of the District Court should be affirmed.* . . .

---

* The District Court's thorough opinion demonstrates the reasonableness of its decision in light of all pertinent factors, including of course the evident purpose of the statute. The District Court concluded as matters of fact that the Navy's violations have caused no "appreciable harm," *Romero-Barcelo v. Brown*, 478 F.Supp. 646, 706 (PR 1979), and indeed that the Navy's control of the area "probably constitutes a positive factor in its over all ecology," id., at 682. Moreover, the District Court found it "abundantly clear from the evidence in the record . . . that the training that takes place in Vieques is vital to the defense of the interests of the United States." Id., at 707. Balancing the equities as they then stood, the District Court declined to order an immediate cessation of all violations but nonetheless issued affirmative orders aimed at securing compliance with the law. See id., at 708. As I read its opinion, the District Court did not foreclose the possibility of ordering further relief that might become appropriate under changed circumstances at a later date.

JUSTICE STEVENS, DISSENTING:

The appropriate remedy for the violation of a federal statute depends primarily on the terms of the statute and the character of the violation. Unless Congress specifically commands a particular form of relief, the question of remedy remains subject to a court's equitable discretion. Because the Federal Water Pollution Control Act does not specifically command the federal courts to issue an injunction every time an unpermitted discharge of a pollutant occurs, the Court today is obviously correct in asserting that such injunctions should not issue "automatically" or "mechanically" in every case. It is nevertheless equally clear that by enacting the 1972 Amendments to the FWPCA Congress channeled the discretion of the federal judiciary much more narrowly than the Court's rather glib opinion suggests. Indeed, although there may well be situations in which the failure to obtain an NPDES permit would not require immediate cessation of all discharges, I am convinced that Congress has circumscribed the district courts' discretion on the question of remedy so narrowly that a general rule of immediate cessation must be applied in all but a narrow category of cases. The Court of Appeals was quite correct in holding that this case does not present the kind of exceptional situation that justifies a departure from the general rule.

The Court's mischaracterization of the Court of Appeals' holding is the premise for its essay on equitable discretion. This essay is analytically flawed because it overlooks the limitations on equitable discretion that apply in cases in which public interests are implicated and the defendant's violation of the law is ongoing. Of greater importance, the Court's opinion grants an open-ended license to federal judges to carve gaping holes in a reticulated statutory scheme designed by Congress to protect a precious natural resource from the consequences of ad hoc judgments about specific discharges of pollutants.

I

Contrary to the impression created by the Court's opinion, the Court of Appeals did not hold that the District Court was under an absolute duty to require compliance with the FWPCA "under any and all circumstances," ante, at 313, or that it was "mechanically obligated to grant an injunction for every violation of law." The only "absolute duty" that the Court of Appeals mentioned was the Navy's duty to obtain a permit before discharging pollutants into the waters off Vieques Island.[2] In light of the Court's opinion the point is worth repeating—the Navy, like anyone else, must obey the law.

The Court of Appeals did not hold that the District Court had no discretion in formulating remedies for statutory violations. It merely "[concluded] that the district court erred in undertaking a traditional balancing of the parties' competing interests." *Romero-Barcelo v. Brown*, 643 F.2d 835, 861 (CA1 1981). The District Court was not free to disregard the "congressional ordering of priorities" and "the judiciary's 'responsibility to

---

2. "Whether or not the Navy's activities in fact harm the coastal waters, it has an absolute statutory obligation to stop any discharges of pollutants until the permit procedure has been followed and the Administrator of the Environmental Protection Agency, upon review of the evidence, has granted a permit." *Romero-Barcelo v. Brown*, 643 F.2d 835, 861 (CA1 1981).

This statement by the Court of Appeals is entirely consistent with the comments in the Senate Report on the legislation that "[enforcement] of violations...should be based on relatively narrow fact situations requiring a minimum of discretionary decision making or delay," and that "the issue before the courts would be a factual one of whether there had been compliance." S. Rep. No. 92-414, pp. 64, 80 (1971).

protect the integrity of the...process mandated by Congress'." Ibid. (quoting *Jones v. Lynn*, 477 F.2d 885, 892 (CA1 1973)). The Court of Appeals distinguished a statutory violation that could be deemed merely "technical" from the Navy's "[utter disregard of] the statutory mandate." 643 F.2d, at 861–862. It then pointed out that an order prohibiting any discharge of ordnance into the coastal waters off Vieques until an NPDES permit was obtained would not significantly affect the Navy's training operations because most, if not all, of the Navy's targets were landbased. Id., at 862, n. 55. Finally, it noted that the statute authorized the Navy to obtain an exemption from the President if an injunction would have a significant effect on national security. Id., at 862; see 33 U.S.C. §1323(a) (1976 ed., Supp. IV).

Under these circumstances—the statutory violation is blatant and not merely technical, and the Navy's predicament was foreseen and accommodated by Congress—the Court of Appeals essentially held that the District Court retained no discretion to deny an injunction. The discretion exercised by the District Court in this case was wholly at odds with the intent of Congress in enacting the FWPCA. In essence, the District Court's remedy was a judicial permit exempting the Navy's operations in Vieques from the statute until such time as it could obtain a permit from the Environmental Protection Agency or a statutory exemption from the President. The two principal bases for the temporary judicial permit were matters that Congress did not commit to judicial discretion. First, the District Court was persuaded that the pollution was not harming the quality of the coastal waters, see *Romero-Barcelo v. Brown*, 478 F.Supp. 646, 706–707 (PR 1979); and second, the court was concerned that compliance with the Act might adversely affect national security, see id., at 707–708. The Court of Appeals correctly noted that the first consideration is the business of the EPA and the second is the business of the President....

II

Our cases concerning equitable remedies have repeatedly identified two critical distinctions that the Court simply ignores today. The first is the distinction between cases in which only private interests are involved and those in which a requested injunction will implicate a public interest. Second, within the category of public interest cases, those cases in which there is no danger that a past violation of law will recur have always been treated differently from those in which an existing violation is certain to continue....

In that case, the public interest, reflected in an Act of Congress, was in opposition to the availability of injunctive relief. The Court stated, however, that the public interest factor would have the same special weight if it favored the granting of an injunction:...

Hecht Co. v. Bowles, 321 U.S. 321, which the Court repeatedly cites, did involve an attempt to obtain an injunction against future violations of a federal statute. That case fell into the category of cases in which a past violation of law had been found and the question was whether an injunction should issue to prevent future violations. Cf. *United States v. W. T. Grant Co.*, 345 U.S. 629, 633–636; *United States v. Oregon Medical Society*, 343 U.S. 326, 332–334. Because the record established that the past violations were inadvertent, that they had been promptly terminated, and that the defendant had taken vigorous and adequate steps to prevent any recurrence, the Court held that the District Court had discretion to deny injunctive relief. But in reaching that conclusion, the Court made it clear that judicial discretion "must be exercised in light of the large objectives of the Act. For the standards of the public interest, not the requirements of private litigation, measure the propriety and need for injunctive relief in these cases." 321 U.S., at 331. Indeed, the Court emphasized that any exercise of discretion "should reflect an acute awareness of the Congressional admonition" in the statute at issue. Ibid.

In contrast to the decision in Hecht, today the Court pays mere lip service to the statutory mandate and attaches no weight to the fact that the Navy's violation of law has not been corrected. The Court cites no precedent for its holding that an ongoing deliberate violation of a federal statute should be treated like any garden-variety private nuisance action in which the chancellor has the widest discretion in fashioning relief. . . .

III

The Court's discussion of the FWPCA creates the impression that Congress did not intend any significant change in the enforcement provisions of the Rivers and Harbors Appropriation Act of 1899. The Court goes so far as to suggest that the FWPCA is little more than a codification of the common law of nuisance. . . .

In *Milwaukee v. Illinois* the Court described the FWPCA in these terms:

"The statutory scheme established by Congress provides a forum for the pursuit of such claims before expert agencies by means of the permit-granting process. It would be quite inconsistent with this scheme if federal courts were in effect to 'write their own ticket' under the guise of federal common law after permits have already been issued and permittees have been planning and operating in reliance on them." Id., at 326.

Ironically, today the Court holds that federal district courts may in effect "write their own ticket" under the guise of federal common law before permits have been issued.

The Court distinguishes *TVA v. Hill*, 437 U.S. 153, on the ground that the Endangered Species Act contained a "flat ban" on the destruction of critical habitats. Ante, at 314. But the statute involved in this case also contains a flat ban against discharges of pollutants into coastal waters without a permit. Surely the congressional directive to protect the Nation's waters from gradual but possibly irreversible contamination is no less clear than the command to protect the snail darter.[14] To assume that Congress has placed a greater value on the protection of vanishing forms of animal life than on the protection of our water resources is to ignore the text, the legislative history,[15] and the previously consistent interpretation of this statute.

It is true that in *TVA v. Hill* there was no room for compromise between the federal project and the statutory objective to preserve an endangered species; either the snail darter or the completion of the Tellico Dam had to be sacrificed. In the FWPCA, the Court tells us, the congressional objective is to protect the integrity of the Nation's waters, not to protect the integrity of the permit process. Therefore, the Court continues, ante, at 315, a federal court may compromise the process chosen by Congress to protect our waters as long as the court is content that the waters are not actually being harmed by the particular discharge of pollutants.

On analysis, however, this reasoning does not distinguish the two cases. Courts are in no better position to decide whether the permit process is necessary to achieve the objectives of the FWPCA than they are to decide whether the destruction of the snail darter is an acceptable cost of completing the Tellico Dam. Congress has made both decisions, and there is nothing in the respective statutes

---

14. "Congress' intent in enacting the Amendments was clearly to establish an all-encompassing program of water pollution regulation. Every point source discharge is prohibited unless covered by a permit, which directly subjects the discharger to the administrative apparatus established by Congress to achieve its goals." *Milwaukee v. Illinois,*

supra, at 318 (emphasis in original; footnote omitted).
15. The Senate Report emphasized that "if the timetables established throughout the Act are to be met, the threat of sanction must be real, and enforcement provisions must be swift and direct." S. Rep. No. 92-414, p. 65 (1971).

or legislative histories to suggest that Congress invited the federal courts to second-guess the former decision any more than the latter.

A disregard of the respective roles of the three branches of government also tarnishes the Court's other principal argument in favor of expansive equitable discretion in this area. The Court points out that Congress intended to halt water pollution gradually, not immediately, and that "the scheme as a whole contemplates the exercise of discretion and balancing of equities." In the Court's words, Congress enacted a "scheme of phased compliance." Equitable discretion in enforcing the statute, the Court states, is therefore consistent with the statutory scheme.

The Court's sophistry is premised on a gross misunderstanding of the statutory scheme. Naturally, in 1972 Congress did not expect dischargers to end pollution immediately.[18] Rather, it entrusted to expert administrative agencies the task of establishing timetables by which dischargers could reach that ultimate goal. These timetables are determined by the agencies and included in the NPDES permits; the conditions in the permits constitute the terms by which compliance with the statute is measured. Quite obviously, then, the requirement that each discharger subject itself to the permit process is crucial to the operation of the "scheme of phased compliance." By requiring each discharger to obtain a permit before continuing its discharges of pollutants, Congress demonstrated an intolerance for delay in compliance with the statute. It is also obvious that the "exercise of discretion and balancing of equities" were tasks delegated by Congress to expert agencies, not to federal courts, yet the Court simply ignores the difference.

IV

The decision in *TVA v. Hill* did not depend on any peculiar or unique statutory language. Nor did it rest on any special interest in snail darters. The decision reflected a profound respect for the law and the proper allocation of lawmaking responsibilities in our Government. There we refused to sit as a committee of review. Today the Court authorizes free-thinking federal judges to do just that. Instead of requiring adherence to carefully integrated statutory procedures that assign to non-judicial decisionmakers the responsibilities for evaluating potential harm to our water supply as well as potential harm to our national security, the Court unnecessarily and casually substitutes the chancellor's clumsy foot for the rule of law.

I respectfully dissent.

---

18. "The Committee believes that the no-discharge declaration in Section 13 of the 1899 Refuse Act is useful as an enforcement tool. Therefore, this section [§301] declares the discharge of pollutants unlawful. The Committee believes it is important to clarify this point: No one has the right to pollute.

"But the Committee recognizes the impracticality of any effort to halt all pollution immediately. Therefore, this section provides an exception if the discharge meets the requirements of this section, Section 402, and others listed in the bill." S. Rep. No. 92-414, *supra*, at 43.

■ **NOTES**

1. Both the majority opinion and Justice Stevens' dissenting opinion acknowledge that the decision as to the appropriate role of the federal courts in such circumstances is one for which the judgment of Congress will control. This means that each

regulatory statute must be analyzed separately to determine the intent of Congress on this issue. Do this decision and *TVA v. Hill* (discussed by the Supreme Court here, and briefly excerpted in chapter 5), taken together, provide a reasonable guide for determining when Congress will be deemed to have foreclosed the exercise of the courts' equitable discretion, and when it will be deemed (as in this case) to have left it to the courts to decide when and how a violation of the law should be brought to an end?

2. Does this case mean that EPA or a citizen plaintiff seeking to enjoin conduct that is in violation of the Clean Water Act will fare no better than did the plaintiffs seeking an injunction against the cement plant in the *Boomer* case, discussed in chapter 4?

3. Suppose you live alongside a small river, just downstream of a factory that is discharging toxic chemicals into the water without an NPDES permit. Suppose further that you bring suit in federal court under the Clean Water Act's citizen suit provision seeking to stop the factory from discharging until it obtains and complies with an NPDES permit. The owner of the factory agrees to apply for a permit, but cites *Weinberger* to the court for the proposition that no injunction need be issued. As in *Weinberger*, the owner argues, the factory should be allowed to continue to discharge during the period of time it takes to obtain the necessary permit. What is your best response to this argument? (Does this situation differ from the situation in *Weinberger*? Is the permit ultimately issued to the factory likely to be more, or less, substantive than the one likely issued to the Navy? Is the balancing of the equities likely to be different here?)

4. The general rule in *Weinberger*—that a federal court retains its equitable discretion to decide when (and under what conditions) to impose an injunction, unless Congress has chosen to circumscribe that discretion—applies to all cases endeavoring to enforce federal environmental laws in federal court, whether brought by a citizen or the enforcement agency.

5. On the other hand, the Court has also stated that "[e]nvironmental injury, by its nature, can seldom be adequately remedied by money damages and is often permanent or at least of long duration, i.e., irreparable. If such injury is sufficiently likely, therefore, the balance of harms will usually favor the issuance of an injunction to protect the environment" [*Amoco Prod. Co. v. Gambell*, 480 U.S. 531, 545 (1987)]. ■

Unless Congress has specifically constrained their authority, federal courts will have their traditionally broad discretion in fashioning the injunctive relief that they find to be appropriate to the case before them. They are not limited to ordering compliance with the applicable statute, regulation, or permit. Nor are they bound by the relief deemed appropriate by the administrative agencies. And, as the following case illustrates, they may order the violator to remediate the harm caused by the violations.

United States Public Interest Research Group, et al. v. Atlantic Salmon of Maine, LLC, et al.
BOUDIN, Chief Judge
339 F.3d 23 (1st Cir. 2003)

This is an appeal by two companies ("the companies") engaged in operating salmon farms in Maine: Atlantic Salmon of Maine, LLC, and Stolt Sea Farm, Inc. In a citizen-suit civil action under the Clean Water Act, 33 U.S.C. §1365 (2000), the district court found the companies liable for polluting Maine waters, *USPIRG v. Atl. Salmon, LLC*, 215 F. Supp. 2d 239 (D. Me. 2002) ("Atlantic Salmon I"), and granted injunctive relief, *USPIRG v. Atl. Salmon, LLC*, 257 F. Supp. 2d 407 (D. Me. 2003) ("Atlantic Salmon II"). The companies claim that the district court's authority to grant injunctive relief has been superceded by a subsequent state permit.

We recount only what is needed to frame the legal issues before us. The two companies are engaged in sea farming or "aquaculture." Its key feature is that young salmon, called "smolts," are transferred from freshwater hatcheries to sea cages called "net pens," the net pens being submerged in ocean water. The smolts are held in these net pens for 18 months or so while they mature and the salmon are then harvested. The origin of this case is the pollution that occurs in various forms incident to the net pen operations.

Atlantic Salmon began operating salmon farms along the Maine coast in 1988 and currently operates four farms (previously five) in Machias Bay and two in Pleasant Bay. It also owns two other companies that together operate seven more farms. Stolt, which began operating in Maine in 1987, runs three farms in Cobscook Bay and has a subsidiary operating two more salmon farms. Both parent companies hold aquaculture leases from the Maine Department of Marine Resources

and site permits from the Army Corps of Engineers.

The Clean Water Act provides that, except as otherwise authorized, "the discharge of any pollutant [into navigable waters] by any person shall be unlawful." 33 U.S.C. §§1311(a), 1362(12) (2000). One of the exceptions allows discharge where the person holds a discharge permit from the Environmental Protection Agency ("EPA") or, if the state has been authorized by EPA to conduct its own program, a state discharge permit. 33 U.S.C. §§1342(a)(1) & (b) (2000).... [W]hile a permit is in effect, it protects the holder (with exceptions not here relevant) against claims that the holder is violating the Clean Water Act, thus providing a kind of safe harbor or shield. 33 U.S.C. §1342(k) (2000).

The companies in this case say that in the late 1980s EPA told them that they did not need a permit under the Clean Water Act; but indisputably in 1990 EPA told the companies that they did need permits. In the same year the companies began to seek permits for one or more sites, and further applications (and entreaties for action) followed but EPA never issued permits for any of the companies' sites. Instead, EPA began what appears to have been a leisurely process of consultation, ending in January 2001 with EPA delegating to Maine the authority to issue permits.

On September 25, 2000, the United States Public Interest Research Group and two of its members (collectively, "USPIRG"), filed suit against the companies in district court to enjoin the discharge of pollutants without a permit....

On June 17, 2002, the district judge issued a decision [declaring] that the companies had violated the Clean Water Act, and ordered a hearing on injunctive relief and civil penalties. *Atlantic Salmon I*, 215 F. Supp. 2d at 241. After a lengthy evidentiary hearing in October 2002 followed by more briefing, the district court on May 28, 2003, issued a decision making further fact findings, rejecting various legal defenses by the companies, imposing a statutory civil penalty of $50,000 on each of the two companies, and ordering injunctive relief. *Atlantic Salmon II*, 257 F. Supp. 2d at 416–27, 434–36 n2.

The two injunctive provisions of principal concern here required specified periods of fallowing (that is, temporary idling) of net pens after the next harvest and prohibited the future stocking of any of the companies' net pens with non-native strains of salmon. *Atlantic Salmon II*, 257 F. Supp. 2d at 435–36. The court also ordered that each pen be stocked with only a one-year class of fish at any time. Id. at 435. However, the court did allow fish currently in the pens to be harvested, both to avoid irreparable loss and because the environmental harm would be reparable. Id. at 435–36.

While the district court was considering this case, the Maine Board of Environmental Protection was conducting proceedings looking to the issuance of a general permit covering all Maine salmon farming operations. Draft permit provisions were made known to the district court during its deliberations. *Atlantic Salmon II*, 257 F. Supp. 2d at 430 n.19. On June 19, 2003, the Maine Board issued its general permit, which is currently being challenged in the Maine Superior Court by USPIRG. The permit is currently effective but provides protection for individual companies only after a notice period.

The companies have now appealed to this court to challenge the injunction. Because of the impact on their ongoing operations, they sought expedited briefing and oral argument, which we granted, and a stay of the injunction pending our decision, a request that we denied immediately after the oral argument on July 29, 2003. The companies have primarily focused on a single claim, namely, that the district court's injunction is beyond its "jurisdiction" insofar as the terms of the injunction differ from those of the Maine general permit. Maine regulators have filed an amicus brief supporting this position.

The companies do not challenge the district court's ruling that they have been violating the Clean Water Act for over a decade or its rejection of their various defenses (e.g., laches, estoppel, de minimus effects). Yet the liability ruling is a necessary backdrop for demarcating the district court's authority vis-a-vis that of EPA and Maine. Congress set out in the Clean Water Act to solve a set of practical problems, and any useful construction of the statute must be responsive to this objective. See, e.g., *Chapman v. United States*, 500 U.S. 453, 473, 114 L. Ed. 2d 524, 111 S. Ct. 1919 (1991).

In this case, the district court found that both companies had discharged into navigable waters, in violation of the statute, five types of pollutants: non-North American salmon that escape from the pens; large quantities of salmon feces and urine that exit the pens; uneaten salmon feed containing a range of chemicals for combating infection and providing coloring; other chemicals to fight sea lice; and copper that flakes from the net pens themselves. *Atlantic Salmon I*, 215 F. Supp. 2d at 247–49; *USPIRG v. Stolt Sea Farm, Inc.*, 2002 U.S. Dist. LEXIS 2757, Civ. No. 00-149-B-C, 2002 WL 240386, at *5–*7 (D. Me. Feb. 19, 2002), aff'd *USPIRG v. Stolt Sea Farm, Inc.*, 2002 U.S. Dist. LEXIS 12589, Civ. No. 00-1490B0C, 2002 WL 1552165, at *1 (D. Me. June 17, 2002).

That the wastes and chemicals should be classified as pollutants of the sea floor and waters is hardly surprising; but the district court also found that non-native strains of salmon are pollutants under the statute and regulations. *Atlantic Salmon II*, 257 F. Supp.

2d at 420–22. The reason is that through a variety of causes, some of the penned salmon tend to escape and to interbreed with native North Atlantic salmon;[3] and through competition from the non-native salmon and the genetic effects of interbreeding, the native strain's survival is threatened. Id. North Atlantic salmon is currently listed as an endangered species. Id. at 420. Just how serious and immediate this threat may be is a matter of dispute. But the companies do not challenge the ultimate finding that non-native species are a pollutant and can be banned. The Maine Board's general permit also has a ban on non-native species, although one more flexible than that adopted by the district court. The companies do not dispute that the other pollutants are regularly released by their operations nor do they now claim that their past operations complied with the statute.

Instead, the companies argue that in three respects the injunction, as applied to their future operations, is at odds with more lenient regulation limned by the Maine Board general permit. The areas of alleged conflict are the treatment of non-native salmon, the fallowing schedule, and (potentially) the limits on one-class year stocking—all matters described more fully below. However, the threshold question is whether it is premature for us to consider this so-called jurisdictional attack at all.

At the time the injunction was issued, the general permit itself had not been issued. . . .

[O]rdinarily, the proper course would be for the appellants to seek a modification by the district court before raising the conflict issue with us.

[However,] on the two main issues—fallowing and non-native species—the district court's decision adopting the injunction makes clear that the obligations imposed by the injunction are intended to apply notwithstanding any less stringent regulation of the same topics that might be imposed by the state permit. *Atlantic Salmon II*, 257 F. Supp. 2d at 435–36. In short, the district court in issuing the injunction considered and rejected the companies' present claim that the injunction should be qualified by the permit. The district court reaffirmed this position when, on June 25, 2003, it denied the companies' motion for a stay of the injunction pending this appeal. *USPIRG v. Atl. Salmon*, LLC, Civ. No. 00-151-B-C (D. Me. July 25, 2003), 273 F. Supp. 2d 126.

This brings us to the merits of the so-called jurisdictional objection that the companies assert. The term "jurisdiction" has several reasonably distinct usages in relation to court authority (e.g., subject matter jurisdiction, personal jurisdiction), although it is sometimes used simply as an epithet meaning little more than that an issue is fundamental or important. The more specific usages entail specific consequences: here, the companies urge that their objection is based on subject matter jurisdiction and therefore (among other consequences) requires de novo review of everything but raw factual findings. *Francis v. Goodman*, 81 F.3d 5, 7 (1st Cir. 1996).

The companies' characterization of their objection is doubtful. The Clean Water Act expressly grants the district court authority—that is, subject matter jurisdiction—to enforce the statute against violators and to provide equitable relief, and the companies do not contest that they violated the statute. Their main argument is essentially a substantive claim, based on language in the statute, that in granting relief the district court must refrain from ordering conduct that an effective permit would allow. Still, this is an issue

---

3. The escapes, well documented in the case of *Atlantic Salmon* and less so as to *Stolt*, result from natural wear or injury to the pens, accidents in delivering the fish, submergence of the open pen tops in bad conditions, and other documented causes. *Atlantic Salmon II*, 257 F. Supp. 2d at 412, 414.

of law even if non-jurisdictional so in any event we review the issue de novo.

The companies' statutory argument is straightforward. Although the statute authorizes the court to enforce the Clean Water Act against violators, it also provides—in the so-called shield provision—that compliance with an effective permit is compliance with the statute. 33 U.S.C. §1342(k) (2000); *Atl. States Legal Found. v. Eastman Kodak, Co.*, 12 F.3d 353, 357 (2d Cir. 1993). Thus, say the companies, the injunction must give way to the permit wherever they "conflict"— a concept they construe generously. Otherwise, the district court would be overriding the substantive protection granted by the shield provision.

The supposed conflicts between court and agency authority in this case are several. The sharpest contrast between what is required by the injunction and by the permit concerns the stocking of non-native species. Up to now, the companies have included in their pens non-native species of salmon which are apparently bred for economically desirable characteristics. *Atlantic Salmon II*, 257 F. Supp. 2d at 420–22. Such non-native salmon were in the pens when the injunction issued. The district court did not require removal of those salmon already in the pens but did ban outright any future introduction of non-native species. Id. at 435–36.

The Maine general permit, by contrast, says that non-native salmon can be re-stocked until July 31, 2004; thereafter the stocking must be of native salmon unless the permit holder proves that native stock is not available in sufficient quantities to match the farm's prior stocking level based on historical data. Maine Permit 24. The injunction thus provides a flat ban for future stocking effective immediately, preventing the companies from transferring smolts due to be placed into the pens this summer (July–August 2003); the permit by contrast would permit this stocking.

The second supposed conflict is slightly less direct. The district court ordered that the companies' pens once emptied remain fallow for fixed periods: 24 months for most, 36 months for one badly degraded site, and 6 months for the least afflicted site. *Atlantic Salmon II*, 257 F. Supp. 2d at 435. The Maine permit requires fallowing only "for a sufficient time to avoid harboring or spread of diseases from one class year to the next," allowing retention of carryover stock for reproduction purposes of up to 10 percent of the prior fish in the last year class, unless otherwise directed. Maine Permit 30.

Lastly both the injunction and the Maine permit seek to reduce the risk of pathogens inside the pens, which can also infect fish outside the pens, by requiring that operators stock individual pens with only a single-year class of salmon at any one time. Thus a net pen stocking salmon of the 2003 year class would have to be emptied before 2004 salmon were introduced. *Atlantic Salmon II*, 257 F. Supp. 2d at 435; Maine Permit 30. The companies see a potential conflict because the district court ban would apply— unless modified—even if the Maine Board were in the future to relax this restriction.

It is evident that the conflict in all three instances is of a specific kind, namely, that the district court's restriction is more demanding than the state permit. Hypothetically, the vaguely phrased state fallowing restriction might turn out to be more stringent in a specific case; but this would probably be rare. In all events, the injunction in this case would be unlikely to impair a stricter permit because the injunction explicitly requires compliance with federal and state requirements as well as the more specific requirements of the injunction. *Atlantic Salmon II*, 257 F. Supp. 2d at 435.

Accordingly, our concern here is with an injunction that requires more of the companies than an agency permit sanctioned by the federal statute. And, if the companies had never violated the statute and now held a valid state permit, the shield provision in the statute would protect the companies as to future operations, 33 U.S.C. §1342(k) (2000). In such a case we would agree that the district court could not substitute its view as to what the Clean Water Act required for that of the agency.

Here, however, the companies have violated the statute; and, despite the companies' argument to the contrary, nothing in the shield provision's language directly addresses the question whether and when in such a situation the district court's authority gives way to the agency's. This is hardly unique: overlapping grants of authority are the common stuff of statutes and the fare of judicial decisions. *2 Pierce*, Administrative Law Treatise §14-1 (4th ed. 2002). Here Congress may never have thought about the precise issue of how the shield provision should affect a district court order issued before a permit and designed to remedy pre-permit violations. Certainly nothing definitive is cited to us.

Sensibly reconciling court and agency power is not very difficult. In our view, the fact that violations have occurred in the past does not generally strip the violator of the shield's protection as to future operations; but so long as a district court does not reduce the environmental protection provided by the permit, the court may grant additional injunctive relief governing the post-permit operations of the companies insofar as the court is remedying harm caused by their past violations. This is a loose formulation, but it is sufficient for the present case.

This premise gives meaning to the statute's grant of enforcement authority to the court without undercutting the ability of the agency to regulate generally through the permitting process. Conventionally, a court's equitable power to enforce a statute includes the power to provide remedies for past violations—an area in which the courts have settled authority and competence, *Weinberger v. Romero-*

Barcelo, 456 U.S. 305 (1982), and "the comprehensiveness of this equitable jurisdiction is not to be denied or limited in the absence of a clear and valid legislative command." Id. at 313 (quoting *Porter v. Warner Holding Co.*, 328 U.S. 395, 398, 90 L. Ed. 1332, 66 S. Ct. 1086 (1946)); accord *United States v. Mass. Water Res. Auth.*, 256 F.3d 36, 48 (1st Cir. 2001).

The language of the enforcement provision is generous: it says that the district court has authority "to enforce [ ] an effluent standard or limitation," 33 U.S.C. §1365(a), a phrase that encompasses the pollution ban in this case. *Atlantic Salmon I*, 215 F. Supp. 2d at 245–46, 256–57. Nothing in this language precludes, as part of this enforcement authority, measures remediating the harm caused by an existing violation, nor have we been cited to any legislative history or circuit precedent imposing such a limitation. Cf. *United States v. Alcoa*, 98 F. Supp. 2d 1031 (N.D. Ind. 2000).

This view does not disregard the shield provision, which still fully protects non-violators and also protects violators except so far as more may be required of them than of others until they have repaired the damage they have done. True, for this limited purpose, the agency's judgment that less is necessary will not control; but it is hardly inevitable that the agency's general permit calculus will focus on the special remediation that may be required by a violator's individual past transgressions. In any case the statute gives the district court authority to make this judgment so far as it is remedial.

Of course, if the district court thought that the agency's general permit requirements were themselves adequate to remedy past violations, it might defer to the agency's solution. But, so far as authority goes, the remedying of past violations, so long as it does not reduce protection ordered by the agency, is a matter of district court judgment reviewed for abuse of discretion. *United States v. Deaton*, 332 F.3d 698, 714 (4th Cir.

2003). That does not mean that a district court's judgment is untrammeled but only that it is not ousted by the later grant of a permit.

There is not much direct precedent but the closest case in point comports with our own reading. In *National Resources Defense Council v. Southwest Marine, Inc.*, 236 F.3d 985 (9th Cir. 2000), the district court was concerned with a company that had a permit but had been violating its terms—not a situation identical to our case but somewhat analogous. On appeal, the question was whether the district court was confined to merely ordering that the permit be observed or whether it could impose additional obligations to remedy the violation. The court rejected the more restrictive view, saying (id. at 1000 (quoting *Alaska Ctr. for Env't. v. Browner*, 20 F.3d 981, 986 (9th Cir. 1994))):

According to Defendant, a court may do little more than tell the violator to comply with the applicable [state plan] requirements.

We do not agree that a district court's equitable authority is so cramped. The authority to "enforce" an existing requirement is more than the authority to declare that the requirement exists and repeat that it must be followed. So long as the district court's equitable measures are reasonably calculated to "remedy an established wrong," they are not an abuse of discretion.

The companies say that in Southwest Marine there was less or no "conflict" between the plan and the injunctive relief. But the Ninth Circuit's broad proposition—that the court may go where the agency's plan did not in order to remedy a past violation—is what is relevant. As we have seen, the "conflict" in this case is not a dangerous one. It is confined to injunctive measures that do or may go beyond state protections for the purpose of remedying past violations and vindicating the statutory prohibition on non-permitted pollution.

Whether this last proposition governs the present case is debated by the companies, and this is not surprising. The district court's injunction, after all, was framed before the general permit became effective. Thus, the district court was not at the time necessarily confined to remedying past violations (as opposed to preventing new ones based on its own view of the Clean Water Act). Nevertheless, as we will see, the district court's remedial aim is sufficiently clear as to the three contested provisions that a remand merely to make the court spell out this remedial purpose even more clearly would be a waste of time.

The district court's decision as to all three of the contested requirements had a remedial purpose. This is borne out by statements of the district court, *Atlantic Salmon II*, 257 F. Supp. 2d at 414, 419–21, 419 n.3, 420 n.5, 428–30, and by ample, if originally disputed, evidence as to the ongoing harm to the ocean and the native fish population caused by past violations. The varying periods set for fallowing further evidence a purpose to remedy past violations and not just to set general standards for the future based on a different view of how all companies should operate.

In what is really a legal argument rather than one concerned with actual intent, the companies say that the purpose cannot be remedial because the injunction—like a permit—regulates future conduct. This is a classic non sequitur. Injunctive remedies for past harm commonly dictate future conduct so as to mitigate past harm. *Lovell v. Brennan*, 728 F.2d 560, 562–63 (1st Cir. 1984). To say that the injunction looks to the future does not alter the fact that it is rooted in past violations, nor prevent its aims or its effects from being remedial.

Conceivably, the companies could have challenged the substantive findings linking the admitted past violations to the remedial provisions of the injunction. They do so only in one respect, namely, by arguing at the very end of their main brief that escaping non-native salmon do not degrade the native species and so the remedial provision is without support even if it is otherwise within the district court's authority. They point to gaps in the testimony of USPIRG's expert, along with testimony by their own expert at the remedy hearing that non-native salmon do not cause genetic damage to native salmon.

This is a permissible attack but hopeless on the facts. The companies' expert may or may not take a minority view among experts, but in any event USPIRG presented an expert who took the opposite view and specifically refuted the companies' expert. The district court credited USPIRG's expert and was satisfied "beyond any reasonable doubt that use of [non-native salmon] stocks imperils the survival of wild salmon." *Atlantic Salmon II*, 257 F. Supp. 2d at 428 n.16. This conclusion was neither clearly erroneous nor irrational. That the Maine Board's own general permit severely limits non-native stocking further undermines the position urged by the companies.

In their reply brief, the companies now offer a further quite different legal argument against treating the injunction as a remedial measure. They say that, whether so intended or supported, any remedial injunction is barred by statutory language that precludes citizen suits where there is no current violation but only a past violation that has ceased. Specifically, the citizen suit provision says: "Any citizen may commence a civil action on his own behalf... against any person... who is alleged to be in violation of... an effluent standard or limitation.... The district courts shall have jurisdiction... to enforce such an effluent standard or limitation...." 33 U.S.C. §1365(a) (2000) (emphasis added).

This argument may be forfeit because not presented in the opening brief, *Rivera-Muriente v. Agosto-Alicea*, 959 F.2d 349, 354 (1st Cir. 1992), but it is useful to lay it to rest. The statute's use of the present tense does limit the district court's authority; only citizen suits alleging that defendants are in violation of the Clean Water Act at the time suit is brought are cognizable. *Gwaltney v. Chesapeake Bay Found.*, 484 U.S. 49, 64–67, 98 L.

Ed. 2d 306, 108 S. Ct. 376 (1987). Accordingly, if the suit alleges a past violation but no present violation, it is subject to dismissal, at least assuming a timely objection (whether the requirement is jurisdictional or can be waived need not be decided here). Id. at 57–64.

But once a citizen suit is brought and establishes a present violation, there is nothing in the statute or in *Gwaltney* that prevents a court from ordering equitable relief to remedy the harm done in the past. See *Romero-Barcelo*, 456 U.S. at 313, 318, & related discussion above. Nor would it make policy sense to allow such a suit or remedy, if legitimate when brought, to be defeated by having the offender cease the violation as soon as the suit is filed while leaving the past harm unremedied. *Gwaltney*, 484 U.S. at 69 (Scalia, J., concurring).

We turn, finally, to two arguments that the companies have not made on this appeal. Notably, in the district court, the companies invoked the doctrine of primary jurisdiction. They were unsuccessful, *Atlantic Salmon II*, 257 F. Supp. 2d at 426, and have not pursued the issue in this court. Nevertheless, the interests served by the doctrine are such that a court may choose to invoke it on its own even if neither side raises the concern. So something ought to be said about an issue implicit in the controversy and one that could easily arise in future cases.

In a nutshell, the primary jurisdiction doctrine permits and occasionally requires a court to stay its hand while allowing an agency to address issues within its ken. *Ass'n. of Int'l. Auto. Mfrs. v. Comm'r., Mass. Dep't. of Envt'l. Prot.*, 196 F.3d 302, 304 (1st Cir. 1999); 2 *Pierce*, supra, §14-1. Although sometimes treated as a mechanical and rigid requirement, the modern view is more flexible, *United States v. W. Pac. R.R. Co.*, 352 U.S. 59, 64, 1 L. Ed. 2d 126, 77 S. Ct. 161, 135 Ct. Cl. 997 (1956) ("No fixed formula exists...."), and the decision usually depends on whether a reference will advance the sound disposition of the court case and whether failure to refer will impair the statutory scheme or undermine the agency to which the reference might be made. *Pejepscot Indus. Park, Inc. v. Maine Cent. R.R. Co.*, 215 F.3d 195, 205 (1st Cir. 2000) (listing relevant factors).

In this instance, the underlying scientific issues are clearly technical ones—a factor that encourages a reference to an agency—but expert testimony was employed in the court proceeding. Weighing against a reference were inter alia the need for reasonable dispatch—matched against a decade of delay by the pertinent agencies—and the necessary focus upon the actions of two particular companies. Indeed, we were advised at oral argument that USPIRG's efforts to broaden the Maine general permit proceeding to include special concerns raised by the companies' past violations were rejected.

Conversely, because the district court's injunction does no more than impose additional constraints, it cannot undermine the central thrust of the Maine general permit regime; and, the court proceedings having now been completed, invoking the assistance of the agency would be a waste of time. Accordingly, a refusal in this case to make a primary jurisdiction reference prior to the state's issuance of the permit was neither a mistake of law nor an abuse of discretion. See also *Student Pub. Interest Research Group v. Fritzsche, Dodge & Olcott, Inc.*, 579 F. Supp. 1528, 1537 (D.N.J. 1984) (suggesting that primary jurisdiction should be invoked sparingly where it would preempt a citizen suit under the Clean Water Act).

A second issue not squarely raised by appellants also deserves mention. The injunction is inherently time limited as to one aspect of relief; the fallowing periods prescribed are only for one cycle beginning after the injunction. But the prohibitions on non-native stocking and inclusion of more than a single-year class of salmon in a pen appear to be permanent. Yet there may be doubt whether such specific provisions are permanently needed to remedy past harms which, in the nature of things, are likely to be assuaged with the passage of time. Cf. *Swann v. Charlotte-Mecklenburg Bd. of Ed.*, 402 U.S. 1, 32, 28 L. Ed. 2d 554, 91 S. Ct. 1267 (1971); *Quinn v. City of Boston*, 325 F.3d 18, 27 (1st Cir. 2003).

Once the past violations are remedied, the companies are normally entitled to be regulated as to the details of their operations on the same basis as other companies that do or might operate in Maine. If the Maine Board's permit is defective in its detailed prescriptions, the remedy lies with an EPA veto or review in the state courts. Given that the companies have not raised this objection directly, we think the sound course is to leave it to them to seek modification of the injunction if and when they can show that their past harms have been remedied.

The judgment of the district court is affirmed without prejudice to future requests in the district court for modifications of the injunction.

---

4. Penalties

Penalties are an important part of any environmental enforcement scheme, both for their deterrent effect and as a (somewhat rough) form of restitution for the environmental or public health damage caused. In appropriate cases, penalties also represent a form of punishment for wrongdoing. In authorizing the federal courts to assess penalties in suits brought to enforce the Clean Water Act, for example, Congress intended that the courts consider the need for *retribution*, restitution, and deterrence. See *Tull v. United States*, 481 U.S. 412, 422–23 (1987).

As noted earlier, those who have avoided coming into compliance with the law often have enjoyed significant economic benefit through avoided and delayed compliance costs (the latter affording them the opportunity to use the funds for financially profitable purposes during the interim). This has given them a financial advantage over competitors who have complied with the law. Moreover, the prospect of such an economic benefit gives firms a financial incentive to remain out of compliance. For this reason, a common tenet of deterrence theory is that a penalty should be of sufficient size to fully "disgorge" the economic benefit from the violator. Indeed, unless the penalty is somewhat *larger* than the economic benefit, the best that a penalty can do—from a market economics perspective—is to put the violator back in the position it would have been in had it complied with the law in a timely fashion. Most federal statutes specify a number of factors (including economic benefit) that are to be considered by the court in imposing a penalty. See, e.g., 33 U.S.C. §1319(a) (Clean Water Act), 42 U.S.C. §7413(a) (Clean Air Act). In addition, EPA has developed a complex but thorough penalty policy and economic benefit formula. Under the EPA penalty policy, the penalty assessed must address two fundamental components: the economic benefit component, and the "gravity" component (which is designed to reflect the relative seriousness of the harm caused to the environment or public health). See U.S. EPA, *Interim Clean Water Act Settlement Penalty Policy* (March 1, 1995) (available from EPA's website).

Most federal environmental statutes (and their state components) grant the enforcing agency the authority to impose penalties administratively (i.e., without going to court), although they also provide (as they must under the Fifth Amendment's due process clause) the penalized party the right to appeal that assessment to the appropriate court. Often they also afford citizens the right to file an appeal to seek a higher penalty assessment, but this right generally is a circumscribed one. At the federal level, and often at the state level, the administrative penalty procedure is reserved for the relatively smaller penalty assessments. For the imposition of more significant penalties, the agency (or, in the appropriate case, the concerned citizen) will go to court, where the judge sets the amount of the penalty.

Courts have held that where the statute in question requires that penalties be paid to the U.S. Treasury, "penalties" may not be used for other purposes, such as environmental restitution or enhancement. See, e.g., *Public Interest Research Group of New Jersey v. Powell Duffryn Terminals, Inc.*, 913 F.2d 64 (3d Cir. 1990) (construing the Clean Water Act). In general, unless the statute specifically authorizes the use of penalties for environmental projects, as the Clean Air Act does, see 42 U.S.C.

§7604(g)(2) (authorizing payment of penalties to be used for "beneficial mitigation projects"), penalties paid under federal environmental laws may not be earmarked for particular purposes.

■ **NOTES**

1. For a statistical study and analysis indicating that penalties are considerably more effective at encouraging compliance than increased inspections and other nonmonetary "sanctions," see Jay Shimshack and Michael Ward (2005) "Regulator Reputation, Enforcement, and Environmental Compliance," *Journal of Environmental Economics and Management* 50(3): 519–540. The authors studied compliance with water pollution laws within the pulp and paper industry and found that penalties reduced the violations rate within the industry by roughly two thirds, both among firms that had been penalized and among those that had not been penalized themselves but were aware of the imposition of penalties within the industry.

2. An EPA study of Clean Water Act reporting data for 1999–2001 found that approximately 25% of all major industrial facilities were in significant noncompliance with the discharge and/or reporting requirements of their NPDES discharge permits, and noted that this rate had remained steady since 1994. Of those firms in significant noncompliance, just 24% had faced formal or informal enforcement of some kind. See "EPA Report Finds Many Not Penalized for Violating Water Pollution Violations," *Environment Reporter* 18(24): 578 (2003).   ■

5. Settlements

As is true for lawsuits generally, the great bulk of environmental enforcement actions, whether brought administratively or in the courts, are settled by agreement of the parties. In the enforcement context, these settlements usually are effectuated through an administrative or judicial *consent decree*, a contract between the parties that must be reviewed and approved by, and entered as an order of, the appropriate administrative or judicial adjudicatory body. In a federal enforcement lawsuit, then, the consent decree is signed by the federal court in which the suit is filed.

The parties often will prefer a consent decree to a litigated judgment, not only because a settlement can avoid the time and expense of extensive litigation and trial, but also because it provides both greater flexibility and greater certainty. The approval of the court (or, in an administrative action, of the appropriate administrative adjudicator) is necessary to ensure that the settlement proposed by the parties is adequate to serve the public interest (as defined by the environmental statute or statutes at issue in the case). Consent decrees can be a means of providing for (judicially mandated) relief that goes beyond that which would ordinarily be available under the statute in question. As discussed in chapter 8, for example, a citizen suit against EPA for its failure to implement the toxic pollutant provisions of the Clean Water Act led to a consent decree that fundamentally restructured the act's approach to such pollutants. See *Citizens for a Better Env't. v. Gorsuch*, 718 F.2d 1117 (D.C. Cir. 1983).

In enforcement suits against violators of federal environmental laws, the consent decree tends to be the primary mechanism by which all or a portion of a defendant's "penalty" payment is directed toward environmental projects. A variety of creative settlements of this type have been negotiated in citizen enforcement suits, from payments into trust funds to benefit particular resource areas, to payments to establish nonprofit groups to act as advocates and stewards on behalf of particular resource areas, to payments to state or local environmental agencies. The federal courts have sanctioned this approach, even over the objection of the federal government, noting that even where the environmental statute in question requires that penalties be paid to the federal treasury, the parties are free agree to other monetary payments that will serve the purposes of that statute. See, e.g., *Sierra Club v. Electronic Controls Design, Inc.*, 909 F.2d 1350 (9th Cir. 1990). More recently both EPA and the Department of Justice have embraced this approach, both for citizen suits and for suits brought by the federal government. Some years ago, EPA amended its penalty policy to provide a framework through which defendants in a federal government environmental enforcement action can reduce their penalty obligation by making approved payments for supplemental environmental projects (SEPs). See chapter 13 for a discussion of EPA's SEP policy as a means of encouraging pollution prevention.

Certain caveats are appropriate here. The projects being funded, of course, should be worthy and legitimate ones, should not inure to the financial benefit of the defendant (or the plaintiff), and should not be something that the defendant is or will already be obligated to do under the law. Further, unless the statute specifically authorizes the use of penalties for environmental projects, payments to fund environmental projects generally are characterized in a consent decree as "payments for alleged violations" (or some other similarly suitable designation) instead of "penalties." To ensure that such payments have the financial impact of penalties, however, the consent decree should not contain any language—such as a characterization of the payments as "contributions"—that might be read to suggest that the payments are tax deductible. Under federal tax law, civil penalties generally are not deductible, and payments in lieu of penalties should be treated similarly. See *Colt Indus. Inc. v. United States*, 880 F.2d 1311 (Fed. Cir. 1989); *True v. United States*, 894 F.2d 1197 (10th Cir. 1990). Where there is any question, it will be best to specify in the consent decree that the payments are not tax deductible.

6.   Enforcement Actions Against the Government

Enforcement of environmental laws against governmental actors is circumscribed by certain legal principles that flow from the fundamental nature of government. In general, as discussed in the *Weinberger* case excerpted earlier in this chapter, Congress has specified that federal departments and instrumentalities are subject to the same environmental laws and regulations as private industry. That is, Congress has waived the federal government's *sovereign immunity* (the inherent immunity from laws that the federal government, as the "sovereign," is said to enjoy) with regard to these laws. Quite often, as is the case under the Clean Air Act, the Clean Water Act, and RCRA, that waiver extends to state (and sometime local) environmental laws as well. However, the Supreme Court has made it clear that absent an express waiver by Congress, the federal government is immune from the enforcement of environmental laws. See *U.S. Dept. of Energy v.* Ohio, 503 U.S. 607 (1992). Furthermore, as discussed in chapter 5, the Court has held that the state sovereign immunity provisions of the Eleventh Amendment forbid Congress from authorizing suits by private citizens against state governments, which places certain limitations on the reach of federal citizen suits against state departments or instrumentalities.

Finally, the Department of Justice has developed a "unitary theory of the executive," which acts as a restriction on *federal* enforcement of environmental laws against the federal government. Under this theory, all agencies and departments within the executive branch of government are treated—in theory—as the same entity. And because they are the same entity, the theory goes, one may not bring suit against another. Thus, for example, the United States EPA may not bring suit against the United States Army for violations of hazardous waste law because it would essentially be the federal government suing itself. It is for this reason that most environmental enforcement actions brought by EPA and other federal agencies against federal facilities (such as military bases) are done administratively. It is also what makes the federal citizen suit a particularly effective tool in encouraging federal facilities to comply with environmental laws.

E.   THE SPECIAL RULES GOVERNING CITIZEN ENFORCEMENT

1.   Article III Principles: Standing and Mootness

As discussed in chapter 5, any private party seeking to invoke the jurisdiction of the federal courts must satisfy the requirements that the Supreme Court has fashioned from the "case or controversy" language in Article III of the Constitution. These requirements often come to the fore in enforcement suits (private rights of action) brought under federal citizen-suit provisions, and the Supreme Court has developed a rather extensive Article III jurisprudence on the issue of when the citizen plaintiff has the right to bring, and to maintain, such actions.

The three prongs of the Supreme Court's standing requirement—injury in fact, traceability, and redressability—have all been put to the test in citizen-suit litigation. In *Friends of the Earth, Inc. v. Laidlaw Envt'l. Serv. (TOL)*, 528 U.S. 167 (2000), excerpted later in this section, the defendant argued that a citizen-suit plaintiff could not establish injury from the defendant's unlawful discharges of mercury to a river because the district court had found that that there had been "no demonstrated proof of harm to the environment" from those discharges. In rejecting this argument, the Supreme Court noted that, "The relevant showing for purposes of Article III standing . . . is not injury to the environment but injury to the plaintiff" (528 U.S. at 181). As discussed in chapter 5, aesthetic injury (injury to one's "environmental interest" in a particular environmental amenity) is sufficient to establish injury in fact, so long as that interest is personal rather than conceptual. If the claimed injury were the inability to view a mountain vista through the defendant's illegal air emissions, for example, the citizen plaintiff would need to establish that he or she actually visits the area in question, rather than simply reading about it in magazines.

Beyond aesthetic injuries, plaintiffs often establish injury in fact in environmental enforcement cases by establishing actual or threatened harm to their health. In *Laidlaw*, the Supreme Court held that injury in fact is established where plaintiffs decline to utilize an environmental resource because of a "reasonable" fear that they may be harmed as a result of unlawful pollution that they seek to abate through their lawsuit. "[W]e see nothing 'improbable'," noted the Court, "about the proposition that a company's continuous and pervasive illegal discharges of pollutants into a river would cause nearby residents to curtail their recreational use of that waterway and would subject them to other economic and aesthetic harms. The proposition is entirely reasonable, the district court found it was true in this case, and that is enough for injury in fact" (528 U.S. at 184–85).

A common defense argument in citizen enforcement suits is that the plaintiff's injury is not "fairly traceable" to the defendant's pollution because there are numerous sources of pollution affecting the environmental amenity in question. Defendants in Clean Water Act enforcement suits, for example, often argue that because their violations contribute only a small portion of the overall pollutant loading to the body of water in question, they cannot be said to have caused the plaintiff's injury. Similarly, they often argue that for the same reason, the plaintiff's injury cannot possibly be "redressed" by the lawsuit because the waterway will remain polluted regardless of the extent of the relief afforded against the defendant. The courts have uniformly rejected arguments of this nature. To meet the "fairly traceable" requirement in such cases, plaintiffs need show only that the defendant's violations *contributed* to their injury. See, e.g., *PIRG of New Jersey v. Powell Duffryn Terminals*, 913 F.2d 64, 72 (3rd Cir. 1990) (plaintiffs need not show "that defendant's effluent, and defendant's effluent alone, caused the precise harm suffered by the plaintiffs"); *Sierra Club v. Cedar Point Oil*, 73 F.3d 546, 558 (5th Cir. 1996) (same); *Natural Resources Defense Council, Inc. v. Watkins*, 954 F.2d 974, 980 (4th Cir. 1992) ("plaintiffs need not show that a particular defendant is the only cause of their injury, and that, therefore, absent the defendant's activities, the plaintiff would enjoy undisturbed use of a resource"). The Third Circuit's *Powell Duffryn* opinion is the leading case in this area; under the widely adopted *Powell Duffryn* standard, a plaintiff's injury is said to be fairly traceable to a defendant's discharge where the defendant has

1) discharged some pollutant in concentrations greater than allowed by its [NPDES] permit 2) into a waterway in which the plaintiffs have an interest that is or may be adversely affected by the pollutant and 3) that this pollutant causes or contributes to the kinds of injuries alleged by the plaintiffs. (913 F.2d at 72)

Consistent with this approach, the courts also have held that an enforcement suit need not eliminate the pollution of a resource in order to be said to be capable of "redressing" the plaintiff's injury. The partial redress available through the issuance of an injunction against further violation is routinely held to be sufficient (*e.g., PIRG of New Jersey v. Powell Duffryn*, 913 F.2d at 73, *Sierra Club v. Cedar Point Oil*, 73 F.3d at 556), as is the partial redress available through the imposition of civil penalties [*e.g., Sierra Club v. Simkins*, 847 F.2d 1109, 1113 (1988), *PIRG of New Jersey v. Powell Duffryn*, 913 F.2d at 73].

But since penalties, by their nature, are imposed for violations that have already occurred, some questioned whether penalties could ever be said to "redress" the *present* injury-in-fact alleged by the citizen plaintiff in filing suit. As we will see, the Supreme Court has answered this question in the affirmative, for the reason that penalties for past violation can have a deterrent effect on the defendant; that is, they tend to discourage the defendant from committing further violations in the future. That said, however, the Court has determined that Article III does place some limitation on the right of the citizen plaintiff to use the federal courts to seek the imposition of penalties for past violations of a federal environmental law. The first case to address this point was framed as one of statutory, not constitutional, interpretation. The Clean Water Act authorizes the commencement of citizen suits "against any person . . . who is alleged to be in violation" of "an effluent standard or limitation" promulgated under the act [33 U.S.C. §1365(a)(1)]. In the following case, the Supreme Court addressed the meaning of that language and, ultimately, the question of how Article III of the U.S. Constitution is to be applied in the context of the federal citizen suit.

Gwaltney of Smithfield, Ltd. v. Chesapeake Bay Foundation, Inc., et al.
Justice MARSHALL delivered the opinion of the Court.
United States Supreme Court
484 U.S. 49 (1987)

In this case, we must decide whether §505(a) of the Clean Water Act, also known as the Federal Water Pollution Control Act, 33 U.S.C. §1365(a), confers federal jurisdiction over citizen suits for wholly past violations.

I

The Clean Water Act (Act), 33 U.S.C. §1251 et seq., was enacted in 1972 "to restore and maintain the chemical, physical, and biological integrity of the Nation's waters." §1251(a). In order to achieve these goals, §301(a) of the Act makes unlawful the discharge of any pollutant into navigable waters except as authorized by specified sections of the Act. 33 U.S.C. §1311(a).

One of these specified sections is §402, which establishes the National Pollutant Discharge Elimination System (NPDES). 33 U.S.C. §1342. Pursuant to §402(a), the Administrator of the Environmental Protection Agency (EPA) may issue permits authorizing the discharge of pollutants in accordance with specified conditions. §1342(a). Pursuant to §402(b), each State may establish and administer its own permit program if the program conforms to federal guidelines and is approved by the Administrator. §1342(b). The Act calls for the Administrator to suspend the issuance of federal permits as to waters subject to an approved state program. §1342(c)(1).

The holder of a federal NPDES permit is subject to enforcement action by the Administrator for failure to comply with the conditions of the permit. The Administrator's enforcement arsenal includes administrative, civil, and criminal sanctions. §1319. The holder of a state NPDES permit is subject to

both federal and state enforcement action for failure to comply. §§1319, 1342(b)(7). In the absence of federal or state enforcement, private citizens may commence civil actions against any person "alleged to be in violation of" the conditions of either a federal or state NPDES permit. §1365(a)(1). If the citizen prevails in such an action, the court may order injunctive relief and/or impose civil penalties payable to the United States Treasury. §1365(a).

The Commonwealth of Virginia established a federally approved state NPDES program administered by the Virginia State Water Control Board (Board). Va. Code §62.1-44.2 et seq. (1950). In 1974, the Board issued a NPDES permit to ITT-Gwaltney authorizing the discharge of seven pollutants from the company's meatpacking plant on the Pagan River in Smithfield, Virginia. The permit, which was reissued in 1979 and modified in 1980, established effluent limitations, monitoring requirements, and other conditions of discharge. In 1981, petitioner Gwaltney of Smithfield acquired the assets of ITT-Gwaltney and assumed obligations under the permit.

Between 1981 and 1984, petitioner repeatedly violated the conditions of the permit by exceeding effluent limitations on five of the seven pollutants covered. These violations are chronicled in the Discharge Monitoring Reports that the permit required petitioner to maintain. See 9 Record, Exh. 10. The most substantial of the violations concerned the pollutants fecal coliform, chlorine, and total Kjeldahl nitrogen (TKN). Between October 27, 1981, and August 30, 1984, petitioner violated its TKN limitation 87 times, its chlorine limitation 34 times, and its fecal coliform limitation 31 times. Petitioner installed new equipment to improve its chlorination system in March 1982, and its last reported chlorine violation occurred in October 1982. Id., at 7–8. The new chlorination system also helped to control the discharge of fecal coliform, and the last recorded fecal coliform violation occurred in February 1984. 9 Record, Exh. 10-A. Petitioner installed an upgraded wastewater treatment system in October 1983, and its last reported TKN violation occurred on May 15, 1984. 9 Record, Stipulation, p. 10.

Respondents Chesapeake Bay Foundation and Natural Resources Defense Council, two nonprofit corporations dedicated to the protection of natural resources, sent notice in February 1984 to Gwaltney, the Administrator of EPA, and the Virginia State Water Control Board, indicating respondents' intention to commence a citizen suit under the Act based on petitioner's violations of its permit conditions. Respondents proceeded to file this suit in June 1984, alleging that petitioner "has violated . . . [and] will continue to violate its NPDES permit." Respondents requested that the District Court provide declaratory and injunctive relief, impose civil penalties, and award attorney's fees and costs. The District Court granted partial summary judgment for respondents in August 1984, declaring Gwaltney "to have violated and to be in violation" of the Act. No. 84-0366-R (ED

Va. Aug. 30, 1984). The District Court then held a trial to determine the appropriate remedy.

Before the District Court reached a decision, Gwaltney moved in May 1985 for dismissal of the action for want of subject-matter jurisdiction under the Act. Gwaltney argued that the language of §505(a), which permits private citizens to bring suit against any person "alleged to be in violation" of the Act,[1] requires that a defendant be violating the Act at the time of suit. Gwaltney urged the District Court to adopt the analysis of the Fifth Circuit in *Hamker v. Diamond Shamrock Chemical Co.*, 756 F. 2d 392 (1985), which held that "a complaint brought under [§505] must allege a violation occurring at the time the complaint is filed." Id., at 395. Gwaltney contended that because its last recorded violation occurred several weeks before respondents filed their complaint, the District Court lacked subject-matter jurisdiction over respondents' action.

The District Court rejected Gwaltney's argument, concluding that §505 authorizes citizens to bring enforcement actions on the basis of wholly past violations. The District Court found that "[t]he words 'to be in violation' may reasonably be read as comprehending unlawful conduct that occurred solely prior to the filing of the lawsuit as well as unlawful conduct that continues into the present." 611 F. Supp. 1542, 1547 (ED Va.

---

1. In its entirety, §505(a), as codified, 33 U.S.C. §1365(a), provides:

"Except as provided in subsection (b) of this section, any citizen may commence a civil action on his own behalf—

"(1) against any person (including (i) the United States, and (ii) any other governmental instrumentality or agency to the extent permitted by the eleventh amendment to the Constitution) who is alleged to be in violation of (A) an effluent standard or limitation under this chapter or (B) an

order issued by the Administrator or a State with respect to such a standard or limitation, or
"(2) against the Administrator where there is alleged a failure of the Administrator to perform any act or duty under this chapter which is not discretionary with the Administrator.

"The district courts shall have jurisdiction, without regard to the amount in controversy or the citizenship of the parties, to enforce such an effluent standard or limitation, or such an order, or to order the Administrator to perform such act or duty, as the case may be, and to apply any appropriate civil penalties under section 1319(d) of this title."

1985). In the District Court's view, this construction of the statutory language was supported by the legislative history and the underlying policy goals of the Act. Id., at 1550. The District Court held in the alternative that respondents satisfied the jurisdictional requirements of §505 because their complaint alleged in good faith that Gwaltney was continuing to violate its permit at the time the suit was filed. Id., at 1549, n. 8.

The Court of Appeals affirmed, expressly rejecting the Fifth Circuit's approach in *Hamker* and holding that §505 "can be read to comprehend unlawful conduct that occurred only prior to the filing of a lawsuit as well as unlawful conduct that continues into the present." 791 F. 2d 304, 309 (CA4 1986). The Court of Appeals concluded that its reading of §505 was consistent with the Act's structure, legislative history, and purpose. Although it observed that "[a] very sound argument can be made that [respondents'] allegations of continuing violations were made in good faith," the Court of Appeals declined to rule on the District Court's alternative holding, finding it unnecessary to the disposition of the case. Id., at 308, n. 9.

Subsequent to the issuance of the Fourth Circuit's opinion, the First Circuit also had occasion to construe §505. It took a position different from that of either the Fourth or the Fifth Circuit, holding that jurisdiction lies under §505 when "the citizen-plaintiff fairly alleges a continuing likelihood that the defendant, if not enjoined, will again proceed to violate the Act." *Pawtuxet Cove Marina, Inc. v. Ciba-Geigy Corp.*, 807 F. 2d 1089, 1094 (1986). The First Circuit's approach precludes suit based on wholly past violations, but permits suit when there is a pattern of intermittent violations, even if there is no violation at the moment suit is filed. We granted certiorari to resolve this three-way conflict in the Circuits. 479 U.S. 1029 (1987).

We now vacate the Fourth Circuit's opinion and remand the case.

II

A

It is well settled that "the starting point for interpreting a statute is the language of the statute itself." *Consumer Product Safety Comm'n. v. GTE Sylvania, Inc.*, 447 U.S. 102, 108 (1980). The Court of Appeals concluded that the "to be in violation" language of §505 is ambiguous, whereas petitioner asserts that it plainly precludes the construction adopted below. We must agree with the Court of Appeals that §505 is not a provision in which Congress' limpid prose puts an end to all dispute. But to acknowledge ambiguity is not to conclude that all interpretations are equally plausible. The most natural reading of "to be in violation" is a requirement that citizen-plaintiffs allege a state of either continuous or intermittent violation—that is, a reasonable likelihood that a past polluter will continue to pollute in the future. Congress could have phrased its requirement in language that looked to the past ("to have violated"), but it did not choose this readily available option.

Respondents urge that the choice of the phrase "to be in violation," rather than phrasing more clearly directed to the past, is a "careless accident," the result of a "debatable lapse of syntactical precision." But the prospective orientation of that phrase could not have escaped Congress' attention. Congress used identical language in the citizen suit provisions of several other environmental statutes that authorize only prospective relief. See, e.g., Clean Air Act, 42 U.S.C. §7604; Resource Conservation and Recovery Act of 1976, 42 U.S.C. §6972 (1982 ed. and Supp. III); Toxic Substances Control Act, 15 U.S.C. §2619 (1982 ed. and Supp. IV). Moreover, Congress has demonstrated in yet other statutory provisions that it knows how to avoid this prospective implication by using language that explicitly targets wholly past violations.[2]

Respondents seek to counter this reasoning by observing that Congress also used the phrase "is in violation" in §309(a) of the Act, which authorizes the Administrator of EPA to issue compliance orders. 33 U.S.C. §1319(a). That language is incorporated by reference in §309(b), which authorizes the Administrator to bring civil enforcement actions. §1319(b). Because it is little questioned that the Administrator may bring enforcement actions to recover civil penalties for wholly past violations, respondents contend, the parallel language of §309(a) and §505(a) must mean that citizens, too, may maintain such actions.

Although this argument has some initial plausibility, it cannot withstand close scrutiny and comparison of the two statutory provisions. The Administrator's ability to seek civil penalties is not discussed in either §309(a) or §309(b); civil penalties are not mentioned until §309(d), which does not contain the "is in violation" language. 33 U.S.C. §1319(d). This Court recently has recognized that §309(d) constitutes a separate grant of enforcement authority:

"Section 1319 [§309] does not intertwine equitable relief with the imposition of civil penalties. Instead each kind of relief is separably authorized in a separate and distinct statutory provision. Subsection (b), providing injunctive relief, is independent of subsection (d), which provides only for civil penalties." *Tull v. United States*, 481 U.S. 412, 425 (1987).

In contrast, §505 of the Act does not authorize civil penalties separately from injunctive relief; rather, the two forms of relief are referred to in the same subsection, even in the same sentence. 33 U.S.C. §1365(a). The citizen suit provision suggests a connection between injunctive relief and civil penalties that is noticeably absent from the provision authorizing agency enforcement. A comparison of §309 and §505 thus supports rather than refutes our conclusion that citizens, unlike the Administrator, may seek civil penalties only in a suit brought to enjoin or otherwise abate an ongoing violation.

B

Our reading of the "to be in violation" language of §505(a) is bolstered by the language and structure of the rest of the citizen suit provisions in §505 of the Act. These provisions together make plain that the interest of the citizen-plaintiff is primarily forward-looking.

One of the most striking indicia of the prospective orientation of the citizen suit is the pervasive use of the present tense throughout §505. A citizen suit may be brought only for violation of a permit limitation "which is in effect" under the Act. 33 U.S.C. §1365(f). Citizen-plaintiffs must give notice to the alleged violator, the Administrator of EPA, and the State in which the alleged violation "occurs." §1365(b)(1)(A). A Governor of a State may sue as a citizen when the Administrator fails to enforce an effluent limitation "the violation of which is occurring in an-

---

2. For example, the Solid Waste Disposal Act was amended in 1984 to authorize citizen suits against any "past or present" generator, transporter, owner, or operator of a treatment, storage, or disposal facility "who has contributed or who is contributing" to the "past or present" handling, storage, treatment, transportation, or disposal of certain hazardous wastes. 42 U.S.C. §6972(a)(1)(B) (1982 ed., Supp. III). Prior to 1984, the Solid Waste Disposal Act contained language

identical to that of §505(a) of the Clean Water Act, authorizing citizen suits against any person "alleged to be in violation" of waste disposal permits or standards. 42 U.S.C. §6972(a)(1). Even more on point, the most recent Clean Water Act amendments permit EPA to assess administrative penalties without judicial process on any person who "has violated" the provisions of the Act. Water Quality Act of 1987, §314, Pub. L. 100-4, 101 Stat. 46.

other State and is causing an adverse effect on the public health or welfare in his State." §1365(h). The most telling use of the present tense is in the definition of "citizen" as "a person ... having an interest which is or may be adversely affected" by the defendant's violations of the Act. §1365(g). This definition makes plain what the undeviating use of the present tense strongly suggests: the harm sought to be addressed by the citizen suit lies in the present or the future, not in the past.

Any other conclusion would render incomprehensible §505's notice provision, which requires citizens to give 60 days' notice of their intent to sue to the alleged violator as well as to the Administrator and the State. §1365(b)(1)(A). If the Administrator or the State commences enforcement action within that 60-day period, the citizen suit is barred, presumably because governmental action has rendered it unnecessary.[3] §1365(b)(1)(B). It follows logically that the purpose of notice to the alleged violator is to give it an opportunity to bring itself into complete compliance with the Act and thus likewise render unnecessary a citizen suit. If we assume, as respondents urge, that citizen suits may target wholly past violations, the requirement of notice to the alleged violator becomes gratuitous. Indeed, respondents, in propounding their interpretation of the Act, can think of no reason for Congress to require such notice other than that "it seemed right" to inform an alleged violator that it was about to be sued. Brief for Respondents 14.

Adopting respondents' interpretation of §505's jurisdictional grant would create a second and even more disturbing anomaly. The bar on citizen suits when governmental enforcement action is under way suggests that the citizen suit is meant to supplement rather than to supplant governmental action. The

legislative history of the Act reinforces this view of the role of the citizen suit. The Senate Report noted that "[t]he Committee intends the great volume of enforcement actions [to] be brought by the State," and that citizen suits are proper only "if the Federal, State, and local agencies fail to exercise their enforcement responsibility." S. Rep. No. 92-414, p. 64 (1971), reprinted in 2 A Legislative History of the Water Pollution Control Act Amendments of 1972, p. 1482 (1973) (hereinafter Leg. Hist.). Permitting citizen suits for wholly past violations of the Act could undermine the supplementary role envisioned for the citizen suit. This danger is best illustrated by an example. Suppose that the Administrator identified a violator of the Act and issued a compliance order under §309(a). Suppose further that the Administrator agreed not to assess or otherwise seek civil penalties on the condition that the violator take some extreme corrective action, such as to install particularly effective but expensive machinery, that it otherwise would not be obliged to take. If citizens could file suit, months or years later, in order to seek the civil penalties that the Administrator chose to forgo, then the Administrator's discretion to enforce the Act in the public interest would be curtailed considerably. The same might be said of the discretion of state enforcement authorities. Respondents' interpretation of the scope of the citizen suit would change the nature of the citizens' role from interstitial to potentially intrusive. We cannot agree that Congress intended such a result.

C

The legislative history of the Act provides additional support for our reading of §505. Members of Congress frequently characterized the

---

3. The notice provisions specifically provide that citizen suits are barred only if the Administrator or State has commenced an action "to require compliance." 33 U.S.C. §1365(b)(1)(B) (emphasis

added). This language supports our conclusion that the precluded citizen suit is also an action for compliance, rather than an action solely for civil penalties for past, nonrecurring violations.

citizen suit provisions as "abatement" provisions or as injunctive measures. See, e.g., Water Pollution Control Legislation, Hearings before the Subcommittee on Air and Water Pollution of the Senate Committee on Public Works, 92d Cong., 1st Sess., pt. 1, p. 114 (1971) (staff analysis of S. 523) ("Any person may sue a polluter to abate a violation . . ."); id., pt. 2, at 707 (Sen. Eagleton) ("Citizen suits . . . are brought for the purpose of abating pollution"); H. R. Rep. No. 92-911, p. 407 (1972), 1 Leg. Hist. 876 (additional views of Reps. Abzug and Rangel) ("[C]itizens may institute suits against polluters for the purpose of halting that pollution"); 118 Cong. Rec. 33693 (1972), 1 Leg. Hist. 163 (Sen. Muskie) ("Citizen suits can be brought to enforce against both continuous and intermittent violations"); id., at 33717, 1 Leg. Hist. 221 (Sen. Bayh) ("These sorts of citizen suits—in which a citizen can obtain an injunction but cannot obtain money damages for himself—are a very useful additional tool in enforcing environmental protection laws"). . . .

Our conclusion that §505 does not permit citizen suits for wholly past violations does not necessarily dispose of this lawsuit, as both lower courts recognized. The District Court found persuasive the fact that "[respondents'] allegation in the complaint, that Gwaltney was continuing to violate its NPDES permit when plaintiffs filed suit[,] appears to have been made fully in good faith." 611 F. Supp., at 1549, n. 8. On this basis, the District Court explicitly held, albeit in a footnote, that "even if Gwaltney were correct that a district court has no jurisdiction over citizen suits based entirely on unlawful conduct that occurred entirely in the past, the Court would still have jurisdiction here." Ibid. The Court of Appeals acknowledged, also in a footnote, that "[a] very sound argument can be made that [respondents'] allegations of continuing violations were made in good faith," 791 F. 2d, at 308, n. 9, but expressly declined to rule on this alterna-

tive holding. Because we agree that §505 confers jurisdiction over citizen suits when the citizen-plaintiffs make a good-faith allegation of continuous or intermittent violation, we remand the case to the Court of Appeals for further consideration.

Petitioner argues that citizen-plaintiffs must prove their allegations of ongoing noncompliance before jurisdiction attaches under §505. Brief for Petitioner 37–43. We cannot agree. The statute does not require that a defendant "be in violation" of the Act at the commencement of suit; rather, the statute requires that a defendant be "alleged to be in violation." Petitioner's construction of the Act reads the word "alleged" out of §505. As petitioner itself is quick to note in other contexts, there is no reason to believe that Congress' drafting of §505 was sloppy or haphazard. We agree with the Solicitor General that "Congress's use of the phrase 'alleged to be in violation' reflects a conscious sensitivity to the practical difficulties of detecting and proving chronic episodic violations of environmental standards." Brief for United States as Amicus Curiae 18. Our acknowledgment that Congress intended a good-faith allegation to suffice for jurisdictional purpose, however, does not give litigants license to flood the courts with suits premised on baseless allegations. Rule 11 of the Federal Rules of Civil Procedure, which requires pleadings to be based on a good-faith belief, formed after reasonable inquiry, that they are "well grounded in fact," adequately protects defendants from frivolous allegations.

Petitioner contends that failure to require proof of allegations under §505 would permit plaintiffs whose allegations of ongoing violation are reasonable but untrue to maintain suit in federal court even though they lack constitutional standing. Petitioner reasons that if a defendant is in complete compliance with the Act at the time of suit, plaintiffs have suffered no injury remediable by the citizen suit provisions of the Act. Petitioner, however, fails to recognize that our standing cases uniformly recognize that allegations of injury are sufficient to invoke the jurisdiction of a court. In *Warth v. Seldin*, 422 U.S. 490, 501 (1975), for example, we made clear that a suit will not be dismissed for lack of standing if there are sufficient "allegations of fact"—not proof—in the complaint or supporting affidavits.[5] This is not to say, however, that such allegations may not be challenged. In *United States v. SCRAP*, 412 U.S. 669, 689 (1973), we noted that if the plaintiffs' "allegations [of standing] were in fact untrue, then the [defendants] should have moved for summary judgment on the standing issue and demonstrated to the District Court that the allegations were sham and raised no genuine issue of fact." If the defendant fails to make such a showing after the plaintiff offers evidence to support the allegation, the case proceeds to trial on the merits, where the plaintiff must prove the allegations in order to prevail.

But the Constitution does not require that the plaintiff offer this proof as a threshold matter in order to invoke the District Court's jurisdiction.

Petitioner also worries that our construction of §505 would permit citizen-plaintiffs, if their allegations of ongoing noncompliance become false at some later point in the litigation because the defendant begins to comply with the Act, to continue nonetheless to press their suit to conclusion. According to petitioner, such a result would contravene both the prospective purpose of the citizen suit provisions and the "case or controversy" requirement of Article III. Longstanding principles of mootness, however, prevent the maintenance of suit when "'there is no reasonable expectation that the wrong will be repeated'." *United States v. W. T. Grant Co.*, 345 U.S. 629, 633 (1953) (quoting *United States v. Aluminum Co. of America*, 148 F. 2d 416, 448 (CA2 1945)). In seeking to have a case dismissed as moot, however, the defendant's burden "is a heavy one." 345 U.S., at 633. The defendant must demonstrate that it is "absolutely clear that the allegedly wrongful behavior could not reasonably be expected to recur." *United States v. Phosphate Export Assn., Inc.*, 393 U.S. 199, 203 (1968) (emphasis added). Mootness doctrine thus protects defendants from the maintenance of suit under the Clean Water Act based solely on violations wholly unconnected to any present or future wrongdoing, while it also protects plaintiffs from defendants who seek to evade sanction by predictable "protestations of repentance and reform." *United States v. Oregon State Medical Society*, 343 U.S. 326, 333 (1952).[6]

Because the court below erroneously concluded that respondents could maintain an action based on wholly past violations of the

---

5. See also *Warth v. Seldin*, 422 U.S., at 501 ("Art. III's requirement remains: the plaintiff still must allege a distinct and palpable injury to himself....") (emphasis added); *Linda R. S. v. Richard D.*, 410 U.S. 614, 617 (1973) ("[W]e have steadfastly adhered to the requirement that...federal plaintiffs must allege some threatened or actual injury resulting from the putatively illegal action before a federal court may assume jurisdiction") (footnotes omitted; emphasis added); *Baker v. Carr*, 369 U.S. 186, 204 (1962) ("Have the [plaintiffs] alleged such a personal stake in the outcome of the controversy as to assure that concrete adverseness which sharpens the presentation of issues upon which the court so largely depends for illumination of difficult constitutional questions?") (emphasis added).

6. Under the Act, plaintiffs are also protected from the suddenly repentant defendant by the authority of the district courts to award litigation costs "whenever the court determines such award is appropriate." 33 U.S.C. §1365(d). The legislative history of this provision states explicitly that the award of costs "should extend to plaintiffs in actions which result in successful abatement but do not reach a verdict. For instance, if as a result of a citizen proceeding and before a verdict is issued, a defendant abated a violation, the court may award litigation expenses borne by the plaintiffs in prosecuting such actions." S. Rep. No. 92-414, p. 81 (1971), 2 Leg. Hist. 1499.

Act, it declined to decide whether respondents' complaint contained a good-faith allegation of ongoing violation by petitioner. We therefore remand the case for consideration of this question. The judgment of the Court of Appeals is vacated, and the case is remanded for further proceedings consistent with this opinion.

It is so ordered.

CONCUR: JUSTICE SCALIA, WITH WHOM JUSTICE STEVENS AND JUSTICE O'CONNOR JOIN, CONCURRING IN PART AND CONCURRING IN THE JUDGMENT:

I join Parts I and II of the Court's opinion. I cannot join Part III because I believe it misreads the statute to create a peculiar new form of subject-matter jurisdiction.

I

The Court concludes that subject-matter jurisdiction exists under §505 if there is a good-faith allegation that the defendant is "in violation." Thereafter, according to the Court's interpretation, the plaintiff can never be called on to prove that jurisdictional allegation. Ante, at 65. This creates a regime that is not only extraordinary, but to my knowledge unique. I can think of no other context in which, in order to carry a lawsuit to judgment, allegations are necessary but proof of those allegations (if they are contested) is not. The Court thinks it necessary to find that Congress produced this jurisprudential anomaly because any other conclusion, in its view, would read the word "alleged" out of §505. It seems to me that, quite to the contrary, it is the Court's interpretation that ignores the words of the statute.

Section 505(a) states that "any citizen may commence a civil action on his own behalf ... against any person ... who is alleged

to be in violation ..." (emphasis added). There is of course nothing unusual in the proposition that only an allegation is required to commence a lawsuit. Proof is never required, and could not practically be required, at that stage. From this clear and unexceptionable language of the statute, one of two further inferences can be made: (1) The inference the Court chooses, that the requirement for commencing a suit is the same as the requirement for maintaining it, or (2) the inference that, in order to maintain a suit the allegations that are required to commence it must, if contested, be proved. It seems to me that to favor the first inference over the second is to prefer the eccentric to the routine. It is well ingrained in the law that subject-matter jurisdiction can be called into question either by challenging the sufficiency of the allegation or by challenging the accuracy of the jurisdictional facts alleged. See, e.g., *Land v. Dollar*, 330 U.S. 731, 735, n. 4 (1947); *Thomson v. Gaskill*, 315 U.S. 442, 446 (1942); *KVOS, Inc. v. Associated Press*, 299 U.S. 269, 278 (1936); *McNutt v. General Motors Acceptance Corp.*, 298 U.S. 178, 189 (1936). Had Congress intended us to eliminate the second form of challenge, and to create an extraordinary regime in which the jurisdictional fact consists of a good-faith belief, it seems to me it would have delivered those instructions in more clear fashion than merely specifying how a lawsuit can be commenced.

In my view, therefore, the issue to be resolved by the Court of Appeals on remand of this suit is not whether the allegation of a continuing violation on the day suit was brought was made in good faith after reasonable inquiry, but whether petitioner was in fact "in violation" on the date suit was brought. The phrase in §505(a), "to be in violation," unlike the phrase "to be violating" or "to have committed a violation," suggests a state rather than an act—the opposite of a state of compliance. A good or lucky day is not a state of compliance. Nor is the dubious state in which a past effluent problem is not recurring at the moment but the cause of that problem has not been completely and clearly eradicated. When a company has violated an effluent standard or limitation, it remains, for purposes of §505(a), "in violation" of that standard or limitation so long as it has not put in place remedial measures that clearly eliminate the cause of the violation. It does not suffice to defeat subject-matter jurisdiction that the success of the attempted remedies becomes clear months or even weeks after the suit is filed. Subject-matter jurisdiction "depends on the state of things at the time of the action brought"; if it existed when the suit was brought, "subsequent events" cannot "ous[t]" the court of jurisdiction. *Mollan v. Torrance*, 9 Wheat. 537, 539 (1824); see, e.g., *Smith v. Sperling*, 354 U.S. 91, 93, n. 1 (1957); *St. Paul Mercury Indemnity Co. v. Red Cab Co.*, 303 U.S. 283, 289–290 (1938). It is this requirement of clarity of cure for a past violation, contained in the phrase "to be in violation," rather than a novel theory of subject-matter jurisdiction by good faith allegation, that meets the Court's concern for " 'the practical difficulties of detecting and proving chronic episodic violations'," ante, at 65, quoting Brief for United States as Amicus Curiae 18.

Thus, I think the question on remand should be whether petitioner had taken remedial steps that had clearly achieved the effect of curing all past violations by the time suit was brought. I cannot claim that the Court's standard and mine would differ greatly in their practical application. They would, for example, almost certainly produce identical results in this lawsuit. See 611 F. Supp. 1542, 1549, n. 8 (ED Va. 1985) (District Court, in stating that allegation of continuing violation was in good faith, relied entirely on postcomplaint uncertainty as to whether cause of TKN violation was cured). This practical insignificance, however, makes all the more

puzzling the Court's willingness to impute to Congress creation of an unprecedented scheme where that which must be alleged need not be proved.

II

Even if the Court were correct that no evidence of a state of noncompliance has to be produced to survive a motion for dismissal on grounds of subject-matter jurisdiction, such evidence would still be required in order to establish the plaintiff's standing. While Gwaltney did not seek certiorari (or even appeal to the Court of Appeals) on the denial of its motion to dismiss for lack of standing, it did raise the standing issue before us here, see Reply Brief for Petitioner 17–18, and we in any event have an independent obligation to inquire into standing where it is doubtful, see *Bender v. Williamsport Area School Dist.*, 475 U.S. 534, 541 (1986). If it is undisputed that the defendant was in a state of compliance when this suit was filed, the plaintiffs would have been suffering no remediable injury in fact that could support suit. The constitutional requirement for such injury is reflected in the statute itself, which defines "citizen" as one who has "an interest which is or may be adversely affected." 33 U.S.C. §1365(g). See *Middlesex County Sewerage Authority v. National Sea Clammers Assn.*, 453 U.S. 1, 16 (1981).

Accordingly, even on the Court's theory of this case it seems to me that the remand should require the lower court to consider not just good-faith allegation of a state of violation but its actual existence. To be sure, nothing in the Court's opinion precludes such consideration of standing, but under sound practice the remand should require it. See, e.g., *Havens Realty Corp. v. Coleman*, 455 U.S. 363, 378 (1982); *Combs v. United States*, 408 U.S. 224, 227–228 (1972) (per curiam). Of course that disposition would call attention to the fact that we have interpreted

the statute to confer subject-matter jurisdiction over a class of cases in which, by the
terms of the statute itself, there cannot possibly be standing to sue.

Justice Scalia's concurrence proved to be correct: the federal courts did make clear in
subsequent cases that Article III requires that the defendant be in "ongoing violation" of the law when the citizen plaintiff files suit, because this establishes that there
is ongoing harm to the plaintiff that can be redressed by enforcing the law against
this defendant. To prevail in a federal court enforcement suit, the citizen plaintiff
must allege—and ultimately prove—that the defendant was in a state of "ongoing"
violation *at the time the suit was filed.* When the case is filed, this requirement is met
by including good faith factual allegations of ongoing violation in the complaint. At
trial or summary judgment, however, the citizen plaintiff must place sufficient evidence in the record to prove that the defendant's violations were, in fact, ongoing.
On the remand of the *Gwaltney* case, the Fourth Circuit held that citizen plaintiffs
establish ongoing violation either:

by proving violations that continue on or after the date the complaint is filed or by adducing
evidence from which a reasonable trier of fact could find a continued likelihood of a recurrence
in intermittent or sporadic violations. Intermittent or sporadic violations do not cease to be
ongoing until the date when there is no real likelihood of repetition. [*Chesapeake Bay Found.,
Inc. v. Gwaltney of Smithfield, Ltd.*, 844 F.2d 170, 171–72 (4th Cir. 1988)]

This test for determining ongoing violation has been rather universally adopted by
the various federal courts that have addressed the issue, including a majority of the
Circuit Courts of Appeal.

■ **NOTES**

1. In yet another decision in the *Gwaltney* case, the Fourth Circuit held that this test
must be satisfied independently for each discharge parameter for which violations are
alleged unless the violations of one parameter are functionally related to the violations of another parameter (as where, e.g., both violations are caused by the same
treatment system deficiency). See *Chesapeake Bay Found., Inc. v. Gwaltney of Smithfield, Ltd.*, 890 F.2d 690, 698 (4th Cir. 1989); see also *Natural Resources Defense
Council, Inc. v. Texaco Ref. and Mktg., Inc.*, 2 F.3d 493, 499 (3d Cir. 1993).

2. As a practical matter, the first prong of the *Gwaltney* test can be satisfied by intro-
ducting into evidence discharge monitoring reports demonstrating that the defendant
committed at least one postcomplaint violation of the parameter(s) in question. In
the absence of postcomplaint violations, the citizen plaintiff will need to introduce
evidence demonstrating that at the time the complaint was filed, the defendant had

not taken all of the steps necessary to prevent violations from recurring. See, e.g., *Carr v. Alta Verde Indus., Inc.*, 931 F.2d 1055, 1061 (5th Cir. 1991) ("It does not suffice to defeat subject matter jurisdiction that the success of the attempted remedies becomes clear months or even weeks after the suit is filed . . . 'subsequent events' cannot 'oust[ ]' the court of jurisdiction.") [quoting *Chesapeake Bay Found., Inc. v. Gwaltney of Smithfield, Ltd.*, 484 U.S. at 69 (Scalia, J., concurring); *Sierra Club v. Union Oil Co. of California*, 853 F.2d 667, 671 (9th Cir. 1988) (the test is "*whether the risk of defendant's continued violation had been completely eradicated* when citizen-plaintiffs filed suit") (emphasis in original)].   ■

In a subsequent Article III decision, the Supreme Court held that civil penalties payable to the federal treasury could not be said to "redress" injuries inflicted by illegal activity that has wholly ceased before the plaintiff files suit. In *Steel Co. v. Citizens for a Better Environment*, 523 U.S. 83 (1998), the plaintiff filed suit under the citizen suit provision of the Emergency Planning and Community Right-to-Know Act (EPCRA) for the defendant's failure to timely file chemical release information required by the act. As required by the EPCRA citizen suit provision, the plaintiff had provided the defendant 60 days' notice of the alleged violations before filing suit. After receipt of the notice, the defendant filed the delinquent reporting forms within the 60-day notice period. The defendant thus was no longer in violation of the act by the time the plaintiff filed suit, and the plaintiff did not allege that there was a likelihood that the defendant would continue to violate the act in the future. Under these circumstances, reasoned the Court, the only remedy available to the plaintiff in the suit would be the imposition of civil penalties for the defendant's wholly past violations of the act. Since payment of such penalties to the treasury would not provide any personal benefit to the plaintiff, and since the deterrent effect of such penalties could only affect the defendant's future compliance with the act, the Court held that the imposition of penalties would not redress the injury alleged to have been suffered by the plaintiff as a result of the defendant's wholly past violations of the act. As the Court noted, however, "if [the plaintiff] had alleged a continuing violation or the imminence of a future violation," judicial relief designed to deter future violations would "remedy that alleged harm" [*Steel Co. v. Citizens for a Better Env't.*, 523 U.S. at 108].

In *Gwaltney*, the Supreme Court had noted that a citizen plaintiff's case for injunctive relief will become moot when the defendant is able to meet the "heavy burden" of "demonstrat[ing] that it is 'absolutely clear that the allegedly wrongful behavior could not reasonably be expected to recur'" [*Chesapeake Bay Found., Inc. v. Gwaltney of Smithfield, Ltd.*, 484 U.S. at 66 (citation omitted)]. In *Friends of the Earth, Inc. v. Laidlaw Envtl. Servs.*, 149 F.3d 303 (4th Cir. 1998), the Fourth Circuit held that a Clean Water Act citizen suit had become moot after the trial court declined, at a trial held some years after the case had been filed, to issue injunctive relief, even though the trial court also imposed a sizable civil penalty. Citing the Supreme Court's *Steel Co.* decision, the Fourth Circuit held that, as a matter of law, civil penalties payable to the federal treasury do not "redress" a citizen plaintiff's injuries for purposes of an Article III mootness inquiry. This case was appealed to the Supreme Court, which responded with a spirited discussion both of the requirements of Article III and of the nature of deterrence under federal environmental laws.

Friends of the Earth, Inc., et al. v. Laidlaw Environmental Services (TOC), Inc.
Justice GINSBURG delivered the opinion of the Court.
United States Supreme Court
528 U.S. 167 (2000)

This case presents an important question concerning the operation of the citizen-suit provisions of the Clean Water Act. Congress authorized the federal district courts to entertain Clean Water Act suits initiated by "a person or persons having an interest which is or may be adversely affected." 33 U.S.C. §§1365(a), (g). To impel future compliance with the Act, a district court may prescribe injunctive relief in such a suit; additionally or alternatively, the court may impose civil penalties payable to the United States Treasury. §1365(a). In the Clean Water Act citizen suit now before us, the District Court determined that injunctive relief was inappropriate because the defendant, after the institution of the litigation, achieved substantial compliance with the terms of its discharge permit. 956 F. Supp. 588, 611 (D. S.C. 1997). The court did, however, assess a civil penalty of $405,800. 956 F. Supp. at 610. The "total deterrent effect" of the penalty would be adequate to forestall future violations, the court reasoned, taking into account that the defendant "will be required to reimburse plaintiffs for a significant amount of legal fees and has, itself, incurred significant legal expenses." 956 F. Supp. at 610–611.

The Court of Appeals vacated the District Court's order. 149 F.3d 303 (CA4

1998). The case became moot, the appellate court declared, once the defendant fully complied with the terms of its permit and the plaintiff failed to appeal the denial of equitable relief. "Civil penalties payable to the government," the Court of Appeals stated, "would not redress any injury Plaintiffs have suffered." Id. at 307. Nor were attorneys' fees in order, the Court of Appeals noted, because absent relief on the merits, plaintiffs could not qualify as prevailing parties. Id. at 307, n. 5.

We reverse the judgment of the Court of Appeals. The appellate court erred in concluding that a citizen suitor's claim for civil penalties must be dismissed as moot when the defendant, albeit after commencement of the litigation, has come into compliance. In directing dismissal of the suit on grounds of mootness, the Court of Appeals incorrectly conflated our case law on initial standing to bring suit, see, e.g., *Steel Co. v. Citizens for Better Environment*, 523 U.S. 83, 140 L. Ed. 2d 210, 118 S. Ct. 1003 (1998), with our case law on post-commencement mootness, see, e.g., *City of Mesquite v. Aladdin's Castle, Inc.*, 455 U.S. 283, 71 L. Ed. 2d 152, 102 S. Ct. 1070 (1982). A defendant's voluntary cessation of allegedly unlawful conduct ordinarily does not suffice to moot a case. The

Court of Appeals also misperceived the remedial potential of civil penalties. Such penalties may serve, as an alternative to an injunction, to deter future violations and thereby redress the injuries that prompted a citizen suitor to commence litigation.

I

A

In 1972, Congress enacted the Clean Water Act (Act), also known as the Federal Water Pollution Control Act[·] . . .

The Act authorizes district courts in citizen-suit proceedings to enter injunctions and to assess civil penalties, which are payable to the United States Treasury. §1365(a). In determining the amount of any civil penalty, the district court must take into account "the seriousness of the violation or violations, the economic benefit (if any) resulting from the violation, any history of such violations, any good-faith efforts to comply with the applicable requirements, the economic impact of the penalty on the violator, and such other matters as justice may require." §1319(d). In addition, the court "may award costs of litigation (including reasonable attorney and expert witness fees) to any prevailing or substantially prevailing party, whenever the court determines such award is appropriate." §1365(d).

B

In 1986, defendant-respondent Laidlaw Environmental Services (TOC), Inc., bought a hazardous waste incinerator facility in Roebuck, South Carolina, that included a wastewater treatment plant. (The company has since changed its name to Safety-Kleen (Roebuck), Inc., but for simplicity we will refer to it as "Laidlaw" throughout.) Shortly after Laidlaw acquired the facility, the South Carolina Department of Health and Environmental Control (DHEC), acting under 33

U.S.C. §1342(a)(1), granted Laidlaw an NPDES permit authorizing the company to discharge treated water into the North Tyger River. The permit, which became effective on January 1, 1987, placed limits on Laidlaw's discharge of several pollutants into the river, including—of particular relevance to this case—mercury, an extremely toxic pollutant. The permit also regulated the flow, temperature, toxicity, and pH of the effluent from the facility, and imposed monitoring and reporting obligations.

Once it received its permit, Laidlaw began to discharge various pollutants into the waterway; repeatedly, Laidlaw's discharges exceeded the limits set by the permit. In particular, despite experimenting with several technological fixes, Laidlaw consistently failed to meet the permit's stringent 1.3 ppb (parts per billion) daily average limit on mercury discharges. The District Court later found that Laidlaw had violated the mercury limits on 489 occasions between 1987 and 1995. 956 F. Supp. at 613–621.

On April 10, 1992, plaintiff-petitioners Friends of the Earth (FOE) and Citizens Local Environmental Action Network, Inc. (CLEAN) (referred to collectively in this opinion, together with later joined plaintiff-petitioner Sierra Club, as "FOE") took the preliminary step necessary to the institution of litigation. They sent a letter to Laidlaw notifying the company of their intention to file a citizen suit against it under §505(a) of the Act after the expiration of the requisite 60-day notice period, i.e., on or after June 10, 1992. Laidlaw's lawyer then contacted DHEC to ask whether DHEC would consider filing a lawsuit against Laidlaw. The District Court later found that Laidlaw's reason for requesting that DHEC file a lawsuit against it was to bar FOE's proposed citizen suit through the operation of 33 U.S.C. §1365(b)(1)(B). 890 F. Supp. 470, 478 (SC 1995). DHEC agreed to file a lawsuit against Laidlaw; the company's lawyer then drafted the complaint for DHEC and paid the filing fee. On June 9, 1992, the last day before FOE's 60-day notice period expired, DHEC and Laidlaw reached a settlement requiring Laidlaw to pay $100,000 in civil penalties and to make "'every effort'" to comply with its permit obligations. 890 F. Supp. at 479–481.

On June 12, 1992, FOE filed this citizen suit against Laidlaw under §505(a) of the Act, alleging noncompliance with the NPDES permit and seeking declaratory and injunctive relief and an award of civil penalties. Laidlaw moved for summary judgment on the ground that FOE had failed to present evidence demonstrating injury in fact, and therefore lacked Article III standing to bring the lawsuit. Record, Doc. No. 43. In opposition to this motion, FOE submitted affidavits and deposition testimony from members of the plaintiff organizations. Record, Doc. No. 71 (Exhs. 41–51). The record before the District Court also included affidavits from the organizations' members submitted by FOE in support of an earlier motion for preliminary injunctive relief. Record, Doc. No. 21 (Exhs. 5–10). After examining this evidence, the District Court denied Laidlaw's summary judgment motion, finding—albeit "by the very slimmest of margins"—that FOE had standing to bring the suit. App. in No. 97-1246 (CA4), pp. 207–208 (Tr. of Hearing 39-40 (June 30, 1993)).

Laidlaw also moved to dismiss the action on the ground that the citizen suit was barred under 33 U.S.C. §1365(b)(1)(B) by DHEC's prior action against the company. The United States, appearing as amicus curiae, joined FOE in opposing the motion. After an extensive analysis of the Laidlaw-DHEC settlement and the circumstances under which it was reached, the District Court held that DHEC's action against Laidlaw had not been "diligently prosecuted"; consequently, the court allowed FOE's citizen suit to proceed. 890 F. Supp. at 499.[1] The record indicates that after FOE initiated the suit, but before the District Court rendered judgment, Laidlaw violated the mercury discharge limitation in its permit 13 times. 956 F. Supp. at 621. The District Court also found that Laidlaw had committed 13 monitoring and 10 reporting violations during this period. 956 F. Supp. at 601. The last recorded mercury discharge violation occurred in January 1995, long after the complaint was filed but about two years before judgment was rendered. 956 F. Supp. at 621.

On January 22, 1997, the District Court issued its judgment. 956 F. Supp. 588 (SC 1997). It found that Laidlaw had gained a total economic benefit of $1,092,581 as a result of its extended period of noncompliance with the mercury discharge limit in its permit. 956 F. Supp. at 603. The court concluded, however, that a civil penalty of $405,800 was adequate in light of the guiding factors listed in 33 U.S.C. §1319(d). 956 F. Supp. at 610. In particular, the District Court stated that the lesser penalty was appropriate taking into account the judgment's "total deterrent effect." In reaching this determination, the court "considered that Laidlaw will be required to reimburse plaintiffs for a significant amount of legal fees." 956 F. Supp. at 610–611. The court declined to grant FOE's request for injunctive relief, stating that an injunction was inappropriate because "Laidlaw has been in substantial compliance with

---

1. The District Court noted that "Laidlaw drafted the state-court complaint and settlement agreement, filed the lawsuit against itself, and paid the filing fee." 890 F. Supp. at 489. Further, "the settlement agreement between DHEC and Laidlaw was entered into with unusual haste, without giving the Plaintiffs the opportunity to intervene." Ibid.

The court found "most persuasive" the fact that "in imposing the civil penalty of $100,000 against Laidlaw, DHEC failed to recover, or even to calculate, the economic benefit that Laidlaw received by not complying with its permit." 890 F. Supp. at 491.

all parameters in its NPDES permit since at least August 1992." 956 F. Supp. at 611.

FOE appealed the District Court's civil penalty judgment, arguing that the penalty was inadequate, but did not appeal the denial of declaratory or injunctive relief. Laidlaw cross-appealed, arguing, among other things, that FOE lacked standing to bring the suit and that DHEC's action qualified as a diligent prosecution precluding FOE's litigation. The United States continued to participate as amicus curiae in support of FOE.

On July 16, 1998, the Court of Appeals for the Fourth Circuit issued its judgment. 149 F.3d 303. The Court of Appeals assumed without deciding that FOE initially had standing to bring the action, 149 F.3d at 306, n. 3, but went on to hold that the case had become moot. The appellate court stated, first, that the elements of Article III standing—injury, causation, and redressability—must persist at every stage of review, or else the action becomes moot. 149 F.3d at 306. Citing our decision in Steel Co., the Court of Appeals reasoned that the case had become moot because "the only remedy currently available to [FOE]—civil penalties payable to the government—would not redress any injury [FOE has] suffered." 149 F. 3d at 306–307. The court therefore vacated the District Court's order and remanded with instructions to dismiss the action. In a footnote, the Court of Appeals added that FOE's "failure to obtain relief on the merits of [its] claims precludes any recovery of attorneys' fees or other litigation costs because such an award is available only to a 'prevailing or substantially prevailing party'." 149 F.3d at 307, n. 5 (quoting 33 U.S.C. §1365(d)).

According to Laidlaw, after the Court of Appeals issued its decision but before this Court granted certiorari, the entire incinerator facility in Roebuck was permanently closed, dismantled, and put up for sale, and all discharges from the facility permanently ceased. Respondent's Suggestion of Mootness 3.

We granted certiorari, 525 U.S. 1176 (1999), to resolve the inconsistency between the Fourth Circuit's decision in this case and the decisions of several other Courts of Appeals, which have held that a defendant's compliance with its permit after the commencement of litigation does not moot claims for civil penalties under the Act. See, e.g., *Atlantic States Legal Foundation, Inc. v. Stroh Die Casting Co.*, 116 F.3d 814, 820 (CA7), cert. denied, 522 U.S. 981, 139 L. Ed. 2d 379, 118 S. Ct. 442 (1997); *Natural Resources Defense Council, Inc. v. Texaco Rfg. and Mktg., Inc.*, 2 F.3d 493, 503–504 (CA3 1993); *Atlantic States Legal Foundation, Inc. v. Pan American Tanning Corp.*, 993 F.2d 1017, 1020–1021 (CA2 1993); *Atlantic States Legal Foundation, Inc. v. Tyson Foods, Inc.*, 897 F.2d 1128, 1135–1136 (CA11 1990).

II

A

The Constitution's case-or-controversy limitation on federal judicial authority, Art. III, §2, underpins both our standing and our mootness jurisprudence, but the two inquiries differ in respects critical to the proper resolution of this case, so we address them separately. Because the Court of Appeals was persuaded that the case had become moot and so held, it simply assumed without deciding that FOE had initial standing. See *Arizonans for Official English v. Arizona*, 520 U.S. 43, 66–67, 137 L. Ed. 2d 170, 117 S. Ct. 1055 (1997) (court may assume without deciding that standing exists in order to analyze mootness). But because we hold that the Court of Appeals erred in declaring the case moot, we have an obligation to assure ourselves that FOE had Article III standing at the outset of the litigation. We therefore address the question of standing before turning to mootness.

In *Lujan v. Defenders of Wildlife*, 504 U.S. 555, 560–561, 119 L. Ed. 2d 351, 112 S. Ct.

2130 (1992), we held that, to satisfy Article III's standing requirements, a plaintiff must show (1) it has suffered an "injury in fact" that is (a) concrete and particularized and (b) actual or imminent, not conjectural or hypothetical; (2) the injury is fairly traceable to the challenged action of the defendant; and (3) it is likely, as opposed to merely speculative, that the injury will be redressed by a favorable decision. An association has standing to bring suit on behalf of its members when its members would otherwise have standing to sue in their own right, the interests at stake are germane to the organization's purpose, and neither the claim asserted nor the relief requested requires the participation of individual members in the lawsuit. *Hunt v. Washington State Apple Advertising Comm'n.*, 432 U.S. 333, 343, 53 L. Ed. 2d 383, 97 S. Ct. 2434 (1977).

Laidlaw contends first that FOE lacked standing from the outset even to seek injunctive relief, because the plaintiff organizations failed to show that any of their members had sustained or faced the threat of any "injury in fact" from Laidlaw's activities. In support of this contention Laidlaw points to the District Court's finding, made in the course of setting the penalty amount, that there had been "no demonstrated proof of harm to the environment" from Laidlaw's mercury discharge violations. 956 F. Supp. at 602; see also ibid. ("The NPDES permit violations at issue in this citizen suit did not result in any health risk or environmental harm.").

The relevant showing for purposes of Article III standing, however, is not injury to the environment but injury to the plaintiff. To insist upon the former rather than the latter as part of the standing inquiry (as the dissent in essence does) is to raise the standing hurdle higher than the necessary showing for success on the merits in an action alleging noncompliance with an NPDES permit. Focusing properly on injury to the plaintiff, the District Court found that FOE had demonstrated sufficient injury to establish standing. App.

in No. 97-1246 (CA4), pp. 207–208 (Tr. of Hearing 39-40 (June 30, 1993)). For example, FOE member Kenneth Lee Curtis averred in affidavits that he lived a half-mile from Laidlaw's facility; that he occasionally drove over the North Tyger River, and that it looked and smelled polluted; and that he would like to fish, camp, swim, and picnic in and near the river between 3 and 15 miles downstream from the facility, as he did when he was a teenager, but would not do so because he was concerned that the water was polluted by Laidlaw's discharges. Record, Doc. No. 71 (Exhs. 41, 42). Curtis reaffirmed these statements in extensive deposition testimony. For example, he testified that he would like to fish in the river at a specific spot he used as a boy, but that he would not do so now because of his concerns about Laidlaw's discharges. Ibid. (Exh. 43, at 52–53; Exh. 44, at 33).

Other members presented evidence to similar effect. . . .

These sworn statements, as the District Court determined, adequately documented injury in fact. We have held that environmental plaintiffs adequately allege injury in fact when they aver that they use the affected area and are persons "for whom the aesthetic and recreational values of the area will be lessened" by the challenged activity. *Sierra Club v. Morton*, 405 U.S. 727, 735, 31 L. Ed. 2d 636, 92 S. Ct. 1361 (1972). See also *Defenders of Wildlife*, 504 U.S. at 562–563 ("Of course, the desire to use or observe an animal species, even for purely esthetic purposes, is undeniably a cognizable interest for purposes of standing.").

Our decision in *Lujan v. National Wildlife Federation*, 497 U.S. 871, 111 L. Ed. 2d 695, 110 S. Ct. 3177 (1990), is not to the contrary. In that case an environmental organization assailed the Bureau of Land Management's "land withdrawal review program," a program covering millions of acres, alleging that the program illegally opened up public lands to mining activities. The defendants moved for summary judgment, challenging the plaintiff organization's standing to initiate the action under the Administrative Procedure Act, 5 U.S.C. §702. We held that the plaintiff could not survive the summary judgment motion merely by offering "averments which state only that one of [the organization's] members uses unspecified portions of an immense tract of territory, on some portions of which mining activity has occurred or probably will occur by virtue of the governmental action." 497 U.S. at 889.

In contrast, the affidavits and testimony presented by FOE in this case assert that Laidlaw's discharges, and the affiant members' reasonable concerns about the effects of those discharges, directly affected those affiants' recreational, aesthetic, and economic interests. These submissions present dispositively more than the mere "general averments" and "conclusory allegations" found inadequate in National Wildlife Federation. 497 U.S. at 888. Nor can the affiants' conditional statements—that they would use the nearby North Tyger River for recreation if Laidlaw were not discharging pollutants into it—be equated with the speculative "'some day' intentions" to visit endangered species halfway around the world that we held insufficient to show injury in fact in *Defenders of Wildlife*. 504 U.S. at 564.

Los Angeles v. Lyons, 461 U.S. 95, 75 L. Ed. 2d 675, 103 S. Ct. 1660 (1983), relied on by the dissent, does not weigh against standing in this case. In Lyons, we held that a plaintiff lacked standing to seek an injunction against the enforcement of a police chokehold policy because he could not credibly allege that he faced a realistic threat from the policy. 461 U.S. at 107, n. 7. In the footnote from Lyons cited by the dissent, we noted that "the reasonableness of Lyons' fear is dependent upon the likelihood of a recurrence of the allegedly unlawful conduct," and that his "subjective apprehensions" that such a recurrence would even take place were not enough to support standing. 461 U.S. at 108,

n. 8. Here, in contrast, it is undisputed that Laidlaw's unlawful conduct—discharging pollutants in excess of permit limits—was occurring at the time the complaint was filed. Under *Lyons*, then, the only "subjective" issue here is "the reasonableness of [the] fear" that led the affiants to respond to that concededly ongoing conduct by refraining from use of the North Tyger River and surrounding areas. Unlike the dissent, we see nothing "improbable" about the proposition that a company's continuous and pervasive illegal discharges of pollutants into a river would cause nearby residents to curtail their recreational use of that waterway and would subject them to other economic and aesthetic harms. The proposition is entirely reasonable, the District Court found it was true in this case, and that is enough for injury in fact.

Laidlaw argues next that even if FOE had standing to seek injunctive relief, it lacked standing to seek civil penalties. Here the asserted defect is not injury but redressability. Civil penalties offer no redress to private plaintiffs, Laidlaw argues, because they are paid to the government, and therefore a citizen plaintiff can never have standing to seek them.

Laidlaw is right to insist that a plaintiff must demonstrate standing separately for each form of relief sought. See, e.g., *Lyons*, 461 U.S. at 109 (notwithstanding the fact that plaintiff had standing to pursue damages, he lacked standing to pursue injunctive relief); see also *Lewis v. Casey*, 518 U.S. 343, 358, n. 6, 135 L. Ed. 2d 606, 116 S. Ct. 2174 (1996) ("Standing is not dispensed in gross."). But it is wrong to maintain that citizen plaintiffs facing ongoing violations never have standing to seek civil penalties.

We have recognized on numerous occasions that "all civil penalties have some deterrent effect." *Hudson v. United States*, 522 U.S. 93, 102, 139 L. Ed. 2d 450, 118 S. Ct. 488 (1997); see also, e.g., *Department of Revenue of Mont. v. Kurth Ranch*, 511 U.S. 767, 778, 114 S. Ct. 1937, 128 L. Ed. 2d 767

(1994). More specifically, Congress has found that civil penalties in Clean Water Act cases do more than promote immediate compliance by limiting the defendant's economic incentive to delay its attainment of permit limits; they also deter future violations. This congressional determination warrants judicial attention and respect. "The legislative history of the Act reveals that Congress wanted the district court to consider the need for retribution and deterrence, in addition to restitution, when it imposed civil penalties.... [The district court may] seek to deter future violations by basing the penalty on its economic impact." *Tull v. United States*, 481 U.S. 412, 422–423, 95 L. Ed. 2d 365, 107 S. Ct. 1831 (1987).

It can scarcely be doubted that, for a plaintiff who is injured or faces the threat of future injury due to illegal conduct ongoing at the time of suit, a sanction that effectively abates that conduct and prevents its recurrence provides a form of redress. Civil penalties can fit that description. To the extent that they encourage defendants to discontinue current violations and deter them from committing future ones, they afford redress to citizen plaintiffs who are injured or threatened with injury as a consequence of ongoing unlawful conduct.

The dissent argues that it is the availability rather than the imposition of civil penalties that deters any particular polluter from continuing to pollute. This argument misses the mark in two ways. First, it overlooks the interdependence of the availability and the imposition; a threat has no deterrent value unless it is credible that it will be carried out. Second, it is reasonable for Congress to conclude that an actual award of civil penalties does in fact bring with it a significant quantum of deterrence over and above what is achieved by the mere prospect of such penalties. A would-be polluter may or may not be dissuaded by the existence of a remedy on the books, but a defendant once hit in its pocketbook will surely think twice before polluting again.[2]

We recognize that there may be a point at which the deterrent effect of a claim for civil penalties becomes so insubstantial or so remote that it cannot support citizen standing. The fact that this vanishing point is not easy to ascertain does not detract from the deterrent power of such penalties in the ordinary case. Justice Frankfurter's observations for the Court, made in a different context nearly 60 years ago, hold true here as well:

"How to effectuate policy—the adaptation of means to legitimately sought ends—is one of the most intractable of legislative problems. Whether proscribed conduct is to be deterred by qui tam action or triple damages or injunction, or by criminal prosecution, or merely by defense to actions in contract, or by some, or all, of these remedies in combination, is a matter within the legislature's range of choice. Judgment on the deterrent effect of the various weapons in the armory of the law can lay little claim to scientific basis." *Tigner v. Texas*, 310 U.S. 141, 148, 84 L. Ed. 1124, 60 S. Ct. 879 (1940).[3]

In this case we need not explore the outer limits of the principle that civil penalties pro-

---

2. The dissent suggests that there was little deterrent work for civil penalties to do in this case because the lawsuit brought against Laidlaw by DHEC had already pushed the level of deterrence to "near the top of the graph." This suggestion ignores the District Court's specific finding that the penalty agreed to by Laidlaw and DHEC was far too low to remove Laidlaw's economic benefit from noncompliance, and thus was inadequate to deter future violations. 890 F. Supp. 470, 491–494, 497–498 (SC 1995). And it begins to look especially farfetched when one recalls that Laidlaw itself prompted the DHEC lawsuit, paid the filing fee, and drafted the complaint. See supra, at 5, 6, n. 1.

3. In *Tigner* the Court rejected an equal protection challenge to a statutory provision exempting agricultural producers from the reach of the Texas antitrust laws.

vide sufficient deterrence to support redressability. Here, the civil penalties sought by FOE carried with them a deterrent effect that made it likely, as opposed to merely speculative, that the penalties would redress FOE's injuries by abating current violations and preventing future ones—as the District Court reasonably found when it assessed a penalty of $405,800. 956 F. Supp. at 610–611.

Laidlaw contends that the reasoning of our decision in *Steel Co.* directs the conclusion that citizen plaintiffs have no standing to seek civil penalties under the Act. We disagree. *Steel Co.* established that citizen suitors lack standing to seek civil penalties for violations that have abated by the time of suit. 523 U.S. at 106–107. We specifically noted in that case that there was no allegation in the complaint of any continuing or imminent violation, and that no basis for such an allegation appeared to exist. 523 U.S. at 108; see also *Gwaltney*, 484 U.S. at 59 ("the harm sought to be addressed by the citizen suit lies in the present or the future, not in the past"). In short, Steel Co. held that private plaintiffs, unlike the Federal Government, may not sue to assess penalties for wholly past violations, but our decision in that case did not reach the issue of standing to seek penalties for violations that are ongoing at the time of the complaint and that could continue into the future if undeterred.[4]

B

Satisfied that FOE had standing under Article III to bring this action, we turn to the question of mootness.

The only conceivable basis for a finding of mootness in this case is Laidlaw's voluntary conduct—either its achievement by August 1992 of substantial compliance with its NPDES permit or its more recent shutdown of the Roebuck facility. It is well settled that "a defendant's voluntary cessation of a challenged practice does not deprive a federal court of its power to determine the legality of the practice." *City of Mesquite*, 455 U.S. at 289. "If it did, the courts would be compelled to leave 'the defendant . . . free to return to his old ways'." 455 U.S. at 289, n. 10

---

4. In insisting that the redressability requirement is not met, the dissent relies heavily on *Linda R. S. v. Richard D.*, 410 U.S. 614, 35 L. Ed. 2d 536, 93 S. Ct. 1146 (1973). That reliance is sorely misplaced. In Linda R. S., the mother of an out-of-wedlock child filed suit to force a district attorney to bring a criminal prosecution against the absentee father for failure to pay child support. 410 U.S. at 616. In finding that the mother lacked standing to seek this extraordinary remedy, the Court drew attention to "the special status of criminal prosecutions in our system," 410 U.S. at 619, and carefully limited its holding to the "unique context of a challenge to [the nonenforcement of] a criminal statute," 410 U.S. at 617. Furthermore, as to redressability, the relief sought in *Linda R. S.*—a prosecution which, if successful, would automatically land the delinquent father in jail for a fixed term, 410 U.S. at 618, with predictably negative effects on his earning power—would scarcely remedy the plaintiff's lack of child support payments. In this regard, the Court contrasted "the civil contempt model whereby the defendant 'keeps the keys to the jail in his own pocket' and may be released whenever he complies with his legal obligations." Ibid. The dissent's contention, that "precisely the same situation exists here" as in Linda R. S. is, to say the least, extravagant.

Putting aside its mistaken reliance on Linda R. S., the dissent's broader charge that citizen suits for civil penalties under the Act carry "grave implications for democratic governance," seems to us overdrawn. Certainly the federal Executive Branch does not share the dissent's view that such suits dissipate its authority to enforce the law. In fact, the Department of Justice has endorsed this citizen suit from the outset, submitting amicus briefs in support of FOE in the District Court, the Court of Appeals, and this Court. As we have already noted, the Federal Government retains the power to foreclose a citizen suit by undertaking its own action. 33 U.S.C. §1365(b)(1)(B). And if the Executive Branch opposes a particular citizen suit, the statute allows the Administrator of the EPA to "intervene as a matter of right" and bring the Government's views to the attention of the court. §1365(c)(2).

(citing *United States v. W. T. Grant Co.*, 345 U.S. 629, 632, 97 L. Ed. 1303, 73 S. Ct. 894 (1953)). In accordance with this principle, the standard we have announced for determining whether a case has been mooted by the defendant's voluntary conduct is stringent: "A case might become moot if subsequent events made it absolutely clear that the allegedly wrongful behavior could not reasonably be expected to recur." *United States v. Concentrated Phosphate Export Assn., Inc.*, 393 U.S. 199, 203, 21 L. Ed. 2d 344, 89 S. Ct. 361 (1968). The "heavy burden of persuading" the court that the challenged conduct cannot reasonably be expected to start up again lies with the party asserting mootness. Ibid.

The Court of Appeals justified its mootness disposition by reference to *Steel Co.*, which held that citizen plaintiffs lack standing to seek civil penalties for wholly past violations. In relying on *Steel Co.*, the Court of Appeals confused mootness with standing. The confusion is understandable, given this Court's repeated statements that the doctrine of mootness can be described as "the doctrine of standing set in a time frame: The requisite personal interest that must exist at the commencement of the litigation (standing) must continue throughout its existence (mootness)." *Arizonans for Official English*, 520 U.S. at 68, n. 22 (*quoting United States Parole Comm'n. v. Geraghty*, 445 U.S. 388, 397, 63 L. Ed. 2d 479, 100 S. Ct. 1202 (1980), in turn quoting *Monaghan, Constitutional Adjudication: The Who and When*, 82 Yale L. J. 1363, 1384 (1973)) (internal quotation marks omitted).

Careful reflection on the long-recognized exceptions to mootness, however, reveals that the description of mootness as "standing set in a time frame" is not comprehensive. As just noted, a defendant claiming that its voluntary compliance moots a case bears the formidable burden of showing that it is absolutely clear the allegedly wrongful behavior could not reasonably be expected to recur.

Concentrated Phosphate Export Assn., 393 U.S. at 203. By contrast, in a lawsuit brought to force compliance, it is the plaintiff's burden to establish standing by demonstrating that, if unchecked by the litigation, the defendant's allegedly wrongful behavior will likely occur or continue, and that the "threatened injury [is] certainly impending." *Whitmore v. Arkansas*, 495 U.S. 149, 158, 109 L. Ed. 2d 135, 110 S. Ct. 1717 (1990) (citations and internal quotation marks omitted). Thus, in *Lyons*, as already noted, we held that a plaintiff lacked initial standing to seek an injunction against the enforcement of a police chokehold policy because he could not credibly allege that he faced a realistic threat arising from the policy. 461 U.S. at 105–110. Elsewhere in the opinion, however, we noted that a citywide moratorium on police chokeholds—an action that surely diminished the already slim likelihood that any particular individual would be choked by police—would not have mooted an otherwise valid claim for injunctive relief, because the moratorium by its terms was not permanent. 461 U.S. at 101. The plain lesson of these cases is that there are circumstances in which the prospect that a defendant will engage in (or resume) harmful conduct may be too speculative to support standing, but not too speculative to overcome mootness.

Furthermore, if mootness were simply "standing set in a time frame," the exception to mootness that arises when the defendant's allegedly unlawful activity is "capable of repetition, yet evading review" could not exist. When, for example, a mentally disabled patient files a lawsuit challenging her confinement in a segregated institution, her postcomplaint transfer to a community-based program will not moot the action, *Olmstead v. L. C.*, 527 U.S. 581, 594, n. 6, 144 L. Ed. 2d 540, 119 S. Ct. 2176 (1999), despite the fact that she would have lacked initial standing had she filed the complaint after the transfer. Standing admits of no similar exception; if a plaintiff lacks standing at the time the action commences, the fact that the dispute is capable of repetition yet evading review will not entitle the complainant to a federal judicial forum. See *Steel Co.*, 523 U.S. at 109 ("'the mootness exception for disputes capable of repetition yet evading review . . . will not revive a dispute which became moot before the action commenced'") (quoting *Renne v. Geary*, 501 U.S. 312, 320, 115 L. Ed. 2d 288, 111 S. Ct. 2331 (1991)). . . .

Standing doctrine functions to ensure, among other things, that the scarce resources of the federal courts are devoted to those disputes in which the parties have a concrete stake. In contrast, by the time mootness is an issue, the case has been brought and litigated, often (as here) for years. To abandon the case at an advanced stage may prove more wasteful than frugal.[5] . . .

In its brief, Laidlaw appears to argue that, regardless of the effect of Laidlaw's compliance, FOE doomed its own civil penalty claim to mootness by failing to appeal the District Court's denial of injunctive relief. This argument misconceives the statutory scheme. Under §1365(a), the district court has discretion to determine which form of relief is best suited, in the particular case, to abate current violations and deter future ones. "[A] federal judge sitting as chancellor is not mechanically obligated to grant an injunction for every violation of law." *Weinberger v. Romero-Barcelo*, 456 U.S. 305, 313, 72 L. Ed. 2d 91, 102 S. Ct. 1798 (1982). Denial of injunctive relief does not necessarily mean that the district court has concluded there is no prospect of future violations for

civil penalties to deter. Indeed, it meant no such thing in this case. The District Court denied injunctive relief, but expressly based its award of civil penalties on the need for deterrence. See 956 F. Supp. at 610–611. . . .

Laidlaw also asserts, in a supplemental suggestion of mootness, that the closure of its Roebuck facility, which took place after the Court of Appeals issued its decision, mooted the case. The facility closure, like Laidlaw's earlier achievement of substantial compliance with its permit requirements, might moot the case, but—we once more reiterate—only if one or the other of these events made it absolutely clear that Laidlaw's permit violations could not reasonably be expected to recur. *Concentrated Phosphate Export Assn.*, 393 U.S. at 203. The effect of both Laidlaw's compliance and the facility closure on the prospect of future violations is a disputed factual matter. FOE points out, for example—and Laidlaw does not appear to contest—that Laidlaw retains its NPDES permit. These issues have not been aired in the lower courts; they remain open for consideration on remand.[6] . . .

For the reasons stated, the judgment of the United States Court of Appeals for the Fourth Circuit is reversed, and the case is remanded for further proceedings consistent with this opinion.

It is so ordered.

JUSTICE STEVENS, CONCURRING:

Although the Court has identified a sufficient reason for rejecting the Court of Appeals'

---

5. Of course we mean sunk costs to the judicial system, not to the litigants. *Lewis v. Continental Bank Corp.*, 494 U.S. 472, 108 L. Ed. 2d 400, 110 S. Ct. 1249 (1990) (cited by the dissent, post, at 17) dealt with the latter, noting that courts should use caution to avoid carrying forward a moot case solely to vindicate a plaintiff's interest in recovering attorneys' fees.

6. We note that it is far from clear that vacatur of the District Court's judgment would be the appro-

priate response to a finding of mootness on appeal brought about by the voluntary conduct of the party that lost in the District Court. See *U.S. Bancorp Mortgage Co. v. Bonner Mall Partnership*, 513 U.S. 18, 130 L. Ed. 2d 233, 115 S. Ct. 386 (1994) (mootness attributable to a voluntary act of a nonprevailing party ordinarily does not justify vacatur of a judgment under review); see also *Walling v. James V. Reuter, Inc.*, 321 U.S. 671, 88 L. Ed. 1001, 64 S. Ct. 826 (1944).

mootness determination, it is important also to note that the case would not be moot even if it were absolutely clear that respondent had gone out of business and posed no threat of future permit violations. The District Court entered a valid judgment requiring respondent to pay a civil penalty of $405,800 to the United States. No post-judgment conduct of respondent could retroactively invalidate that judgment. A record of voluntary post-judgment compliance that would justify a decision that injunctive relief is unnecessary, or even a decision that any claim for injunctive relief is now moot, would not warrant vacation of the valid money judgment.

Furthermore, petitioners' claim for civil penalties would not be moot even if it were absolutely clear that respondent's violations could not reasonably be expected to recur because respondent achieved substantial compliance with its permit requirements after petitioners filed their complaint but before the District Court entered judgment. As the Courts of Appeals (other than the court below) have uniformly concluded, a polluter's voluntary post-complaint cessation of an alleged violation will not moot a citizen-suit claim for civil penalties even if it is sufficient to moot a related claim for injunctive or declaratory relief.* This conclusion is consistent with the structure of the Clean Water Act, which attaches liability for civil penalties at the time a permit violation occurs. 33 U.S.C. §1319(d) ("Any person who violates [certain provisions of the Act or certain permit conditions and limitations] shall be subject to a civil penalty...."). It is also consistent with

the character of civil penalties, which, for purposes of mootness analysis, should be equated with punitive damages rather than with injunctive or declaratory relief. See *Tull v. United States*, 481 U.S. 412, 422–423, 95 L. Ed. 2d 365, 107 S. Ct. 1831 (1987). No one contends that a defendant's post-complaint conduct could moot a claim for punitive damages; civil penalties should be treated the same way.

The cases cited by the Court in its discussion of the mootness issue all involved requests for injunctive or declaratory relief. In only one, *Los Angeles v. Lyons*, 461 U.S. 95, 75 L. Ed. 2d 675, 103 S. Ct. 1660 (1983), did the plaintiff seek damages, and in that case the opinion makes it clear that the inability to obtain injunctive relief would have no impact on the damages claim. Id. at 105, n. 6, 109. There is no precedent, either in our jurisprudence, or in any other of which I am aware, that provides any support for the suggestion that post-complaint factual developments that might moot a claim for injunctive or declaratory relief could either moot a claim for monetary relief or retroactively invalidate a valid money judgment.

JUSTICE KENNEDY, CONCURRING:

Difficult and fundamental questions are raised when we ask whether exactions of public fines by private litigants, and the delegation of Executive power which might be inferable from the authorization, are permissible in view of the responsibilities committed to the Executive by Article II of the

---

* *Comfort Lake Assn. v. Dresel Contracting, Inc.*, 138 F.3d 351, 356 (CA8 1998); *Atlantic States Legal Foundation, Inc. v. Stroh Die Casting Co.*, 116 F.3d 814, 820 (CA7), cert. denied, 522 U.S. 981, 139 L. Ed. 2d 379, 118 S. Ct. 442 (1997); *Natural Resources Defense Council v. Texaco Refining and Mktg., Inc.*, 2 F.3d 493, 502–503 (CA3 1993); *Atlantic States Legal Foundation, Inc. v. Pan Am. Tanning Corp.*, 993 F.2d 1017, 1020–1021 (CA2 1993); *Atlantic States Legal Foundation, Inc. v.*

Tyson Foods, Inc., 897 F.2d 1128, 1134–1137 (CA11 1990); *Chesapeake Bay Foundation, Inc. v. Gwaltney of Smithfield, Ltd.*, 890 F.2d 690, 696–97 (CA4 1989). Cf. *Powell v. McCormack*, 395 U.S. 486, 496, n. 8, 23 L. Ed. 2d 491, 89 S. Ct. 1944 (1969) ("Where several forms of relief are requested and one of these requests subsequently becomes moot, the Court has still considered the remaining requests").

Constitution of the United States. The questions presented in the petition for certiorari did not identify these issues with particularity; and neither the Court of Appeals in deciding the case nor the parties in their briefing before this Court devoted specific attention to the subject. In my view these matters are best reserved for a later case. With this observation, I join the opinion of the Court.

JUSTICE SCALIA, WITH WHOM JUSTICE THOMAS JOINS, DISSENTING:

The Court begins its analysis by finding injury in fact on the basis of vague affidavits that are undermined by the District Court's express finding that Laidlaw's discharges caused no demonstrable harm to the environment. It then proceeds to marry private wrong with public remedy in a union that violates traditional principles of federal standing—thereby permitting law enforcement to be placed in the hands of private individuals. Finally, the Court suggests that to avoid mootness one needs even less of a stake in the outcome than the Court's watered-down requirements for initial standing. I dissent from all of this.

I

Plaintiffs, as the parties invoking federal jurisdiction, have the burden of proof and persuasion as to the existence of standing. *Lujan v. Defenders of Wildlife*, 504 U.S. 555, 561, 119 L. Ed. 2d 351, 112 S. Ct. 2130 (1992) (hereinafter *Lujan*); *FW/PBS, Inc. v. Dallas*, 493 U.S. 215, 231, 107 L. Ed. 2d 603, 110 S. Ct. 596 (1990). The plaintiffs in this case fell far short of carrying their burden of demonstrating injury in fact. The Court cites affiants' testimony asserting that their enjoyment of the North Tyger River has been diminished due to "concern" that the water was polluted, and that they "believed" that Laidlaw's mercury exceedances had reduced the value of

their homes. These averments alone cannot carry the plaintiffs' burden of demonstrating that they have suffered a "concrete and particularized" injury, Lujan, 504 U.S. at 560. General allegations of injury may suffice at the pleading stage, but at summary judgment plaintiffs must set forth "specific facts" to support their claims. 504 U.S. at 561. And where, as here, the case has proceeded to judgment, those specific facts must be " 'supported adequately by the evidence adduced at trial'," ibid. (quoting *Gladstone, Realtors v. Village of Bellwood*, 441 U.S. 91, 115, n. 31, 60 L. Ed. 2d 66, 99 S. Ct. 1601 (1979)). In this case, the affidavits themselves are woefully short on "specific facts," and the vague allegations of injury they do make are undermined by the evidence adduced at trial.

Typically, an environmental plaintiff claiming injury due to discharges in violation of the Clean Water Act argues that the discharges harm the environment, and that the harm to the environment injures him. This route to injury is barred in the present case, however, since the District Court concluded after considering all the evidence that there had been "no demonstrated proof of harm to the environment," 956 F. Supp. 588, 602 (SC 1997), that the "permit violations at issue in this citizen suit did not result in any health risk or environmental harm," ibid., that "all available data . . . fail to show that Laidlaw's actual discharges have resulted in harm to the North Tyger River," 956 F. Supp. at 602–603, and that "the overall quality of the river exceeds levels necessary to support . . . recreation in and on the water," 956 F. Supp. at 600.

The Court finds these conclusions unproblematic for standing, because "the relevant showing for purposes of Article III standing . . . is not injury to the environment but injury to the plaintiff." This statement is correct, as far as it goes. We have certainly held that a demonstration of harm to the environment is not enough to satisfy the injury-in-fact requirement unless the plaintiff can demonstrate how he personally was harmed. E.g., *Lujan*, supra, at 563. In the normal course, however, a lack of demonstrable harm to the environment will translate, as it plainly does here, into a lack of demonstrable harm to citizen plaintiffs. While it is perhaps possible that a plaintiff could be harmed even though the environment was not, such a plaintiff would have the burden of articulating and demonstrating the nature of that injury. Ongoing "concerns" about the environment are not enough, for "it is the reality of the threat of repeated injury that is relevant to the standing inquiry, not the plaintiff's subjective apprehensions," *Los Angeles v. Lyons*, 461 U.S. 95, 107, n. 8, 75 L. Ed. 2d 675, 103 S. Ct. 1660 (1983). At the very least, in the present case, one would expect to see evidence supporting the affidavits' bald assertions regarding decreasing recreational usage and declining home values, as well as evidence for the improbable proposition that Laidlaw's violations, even though harmless to the environment, are somehow responsible for these effects. Cf. *Gladstone*, supra, at 115 (noting that standing could be established by "convincing evidence" that a decline in real estate values was attributable to the defendant's conduct). Plaintiffs here have made no attempt at such a showing, but rely entirely upon unsupported and unexplained affidavit allegations of "concern."

Indeed, every one of the affiants deposed by Laidlaw cast into doubt the (in any event inadequate) proposition that subjective "concerns" actually affected their conduct. Linda Moore, for example, said in her affidavit that she would use the affected waterways for recreation if it were not for her concern about pollution. Record, Doc. No. 71 (Exhs. 45, 46). Yet she testified in her deposition that she had been to the river only twice, once in 1980 (when she visited someone who lived by the river) and once after this suit was filed. Record, Doc. No. 62 (Moore Deposition 23-24). Similarly, Kenneth Lee Curtis, who claimed he was injured by being deprived of

recreational activity at the river, admitted that he had not been to the river since he was "a kid," (Curtis Deposition, pt. 2, p. 38), and when asked whether the reason he stopped visiting the river was because of pollution, answered "no," id. at 39. As to Curtis's claim that the river "looked and smelled polluted," this condition, if present, was surely not caused by Laidlaw's discharges, which according to the District Court "did not result in any health risk or environmental harm." 956 F. Supp. at 602. The other affiants cited by the Court were not deposed, but their affidavits state either that they would use the river if it were not polluted or harmful (as the court subsequently found it is not), Record, Doc. No. 21 (Exhs. 7, 8, and 9), or said that the river looks polluted (which is also incompatible with the court's findings), ibid. (Exh. 10). These affiants have established nothing but "subjective apprehensions."

The Court is correct that the District Court explicitly found standing—albeit "by the very slimmest of margins," and as "an awfully close call." App. in No. 97-1246 (CA4), p. 207–208 (Tr. of Hearing 39-40 (June 30, 1993)). That cautious finding, however, was made in 1993, long before the court's 1997 conclusion that Laidlaw's discharges did not harm the environment. As we have previously recognized, an initial conclusion that plaintiffs have standing is subject to reexamination, particularly if later evidence proves inconsistent with that conclusion. *Gladstone*, 441 U.S. at 115, and n. 31; *Wyoming v. Oklahoma*, 502 U.S. 437, 446, 117 L. Ed. 2d 1, 112 S. Ct. 789 (1992). Laidlaw challenged the existence of injury in fact on appeal to the Fourth Circuit, but that court did not reach the question. Thus no lower court has reviewed the injury-in-fact issue in light of the extensive studies that led the District Court to conclude that the environment was not harmed by Laidlaw's discharges.

Inexplicably, the Court is untroubled by this, but proceeds to find injury in fact in the most casual fashion, as though it is merely confirming a careful analysis made below. Although we have previously refused to find standing based on the "conclusory allegations of an affidavit" *Lujan v. National Wildlife Federation*, 497 U.S. 871, 888, 111 L. Ed. 2d 695, 110 S. Ct. 3177 (1990), the Court is content to do just that today. By accepting plaintiffs' vague, contradictory, and unsubstantiated allegations of "concern" about the environment as adequate to prove injury in fact, and accepting them even in the face of a finding that the environment was not demonstrably harmed, the Court makes the injury-in-fact requirement a sham. If there are permit violations, and a member of a plaintiff environmental organization lives near the offending plant, it would be difficult not to satisfy today's lenient standard.

II

The Court's treatment of the redressability requirement—which would have been unnecessary if it resolved the injury-in-fact question correctly—is equally cavalier. As discussed above, petitioners allege ongoing injury consisting of diminished enjoyment of the affected waterways and decreased property values. They allege that these injuries are caused by Laidlaw's continuing permit violations. But the remedy petitioners seek is neither recompense for their injuries nor an injunction against future violations. Instead, the remedy is a statutorily specified "penalty" for past violations, payable entirely to the United States Treasury. Only last Term, we held that such penalties do not redress any injury a citizen plaintiff has suffered from past violations. *Steel Co. v. Citizens for Better Environment*, 523 U.S. 83, 106–107, 140 L. Ed. 2d 210, 118 S. Ct. 1003 (1998). The Court nonetheless finds the redressability requirement satisfied here, distinguishing Steel Co. on the ground that in this case the petitioners allege ongoing violations; payment of the penalties, it says, will remedy petitioners' in-

jury by deterring future violations by Laidlaw. It holds that a penalty payable to the public "remedies" a threatened private harm, and suffices to sustain a private suit.

That holding has no precedent in our jurisprudence, and takes this Court beyond the "cases and controversies" that Article III of the Constitution has entrusted to its resolution. Even if it were appropriate, moreover, to allow Article III's remediation requirement to be satisfied by the indirect private consequences of a public penalty, those consequences are entirely too speculative in the present case. The new standing law that the Court makes—like all expansions of standing beyond the traditional constitutional limits—has grave implications for democratic governance. I shall discuss these three points in turn.

A

In *Linda R. S. v. Richard D.*, 410 U.S. 614, 35 L. Ed. 2d 536, 93 S. Ct. 1146 (1973), the plaintiff, mother of an illegitimate child, sought, on behalf of herself, her child, and all others similarly situated, an injunction against discriminatory application of Art. 602 of the Texas Penal Code. Although that provision made it a misdemeanor for "any parent" to refuse to support his or her minor children under 18 years of age, it was enforced only against married parents. That refusal, the plaintiff contended, deprived her and her child of the equal protection of the law by denying them the deterrent effect of the statute upon the father's failure to fulfill his support obligation. The Court held that there was no Article III standing. There was no "'direct' relationship," it said, "between the alleged injury and the claim sought to be adjudicated," since "the prospect that prosecution will, at least in the future, result in payment of support can, at best, be termed only speculative." Id. at 618. "[Our cases] demonstrate that, in American jurisprudence at least, a private citizen lacks a judicially cognizable interest in the prosecution or non-prosecution of another." Id. at 619.

Although the Court in *Linda R. S.* recited the "logical nexus" analysis of *Flast v. Cohen*, 392 U.S. 83, 20 L. Ed. 2d 947, 88 S. Ct. 1942 (1968), which has since fallen into desuetude, "it is clear that standing was denied . . . because of the unlikelihood that the relief requested would redress appellant's claimed injury." *Duke Power Co. v. Carolina Environmental Study Group, Inc.*, 438 U.S. 59, 79, n. 24, 57 L. Ed. 2d 595, 98 S. Ct. 2620 (1978). There was no "logical nexus" between nonenforcement of the statute and Linda R. S.'s failure to receive support payments because "the prospect that prosecution will . . . result in payment of support" was "speculative," *Linda R. S.*, supra, at 618—that is to say, it was uncertain whether the relief would prevent the injury.[1] Of course precisely the same situation exists here. The principle that "in American jurisprudence . . . a private citizen lacks a judicially cognizable interest in the prosecution or nonprosecution of another" applies no less to prosecution for civil penalties payable to the State than to prosecution for criminal penalties owing to the State.

The Court's opinion reads as though the only purpose and effect of the redressability requirement is to assure that the plaintiff receive some of the benefit of the relief that a court orders. That is not so. If it were, a federal tort plaintiff fearing repetition of the injury could ask for tort damages to be paid, not only to himself but to other victims as well, on the theory that those damages would have at least some deterrent effect beneficial to him. Such a suit is preposterous because the "remediation" that is the traditional business of Anglo-American courts is relief specifically tailored to the plaintiff's injury, and not any sort of relief that has some incidental benefit to the plaintiff. Just as a "generalized grievance" that affects the entire citizenry cannot satisfy the injury-in-fact requirement even though it aggrieves the plaintiff along with everyone else, see *Lujan*, 504 U.S. at 573–574, so also a generalized remedy that deters all future unlawful activity against all persons cannot satisfy the remediation requirement, even though it deters (among other things) repetition of this particular unlawful activity against these particular plaintiffs.

Thus, relief against prospective harm is traditionally afforded by way of an injunction, the scope of which is limited by the scope of the threatened injury. *Lewis v. Casey*, 518 U.S. 343, 357–360, 135 L. Ed. 2d 606, 116 S. Ct. 2174 (1996); *Lyons*, 461 U.S. at 105–107, and n. 7. In seeking to overturn that tradition by giving an individual plaintiff the power to invoke a public remedy, Congress has done precisely what we have said it cannot do: convert an "undifferentiated public interest" into an "individual right" vindicable in the courts. *Lujan*, 504 U.S. at 577; *Steel Co.*, 523 U.S. at 106. The sort of scattershot redress approved today makes nonsense of our statement in *Schlesinger v. Reservists Comm. to Stop the War*, 418 U.S. 208, 222, 41 L. Ed. 2d 706, 94 S. Ct. 2925 (1974), that the requirement of injury in fact "insures the framing of relief no broader than required by the precise facts." A claim of particularized future injury has today been made the vehicle for pursuing generalized penalties for past violations, and a threshold showing of injury in fact has become a lever that will move the world.

---

1. The decision in *Linda R. S.* did not turn, as today's opinion imaginatively suggests, on the father's short-term inability to pay support if imprisoned. Ante, at 17, n. 4. The Court's only comment upon the imprisonment was that, unlike imprisonment for civil contempt, it would not condition the father's release upon payment. The Court then continued: "The prospect that prosecution will, at least in the future,"—i.e., upon completion of the imprisonment—"result in payment of support can, at best, be termed only speculative." *Linda R. S.*, 410 U.S. at 618.

B

As I have just discussed, it is my view that a plaintiff's desire to benefit from the deterrent effect of a public penalty for past conduct can never suffice to establish a case or controversy of the sort known to our law. Such deterrent effect is, so to speak, "speculative as a matter of law." Even if that were not so, however, the deterrent effect in the present case would surely be speculative as a matter of fact.

The Court recognizes, of course, that to satisfy Article III, it must be "likely," as opposed to "merely speculative," that a favorable decision will redress plaintiffs' injury, *Lujan*, 504 U.S. at 561. Further, the Court recognizes that not all deterrent effects of all civil penalties will meet this standard—though it declines to "explore the outer limits" of adequate deterrence. It concludes, however, that in the present case "the civil penalties sought by FOE carried with them a deterrent effect" that satisfied the "likely [rather than] speculative" standard. There is little in the Court's opinion to explain why it believes this is so.

The Court cites the District Court's conclusion that the penalties imposed, along with anticipated fee awards, provided "adequate deterrence." 956 F. Supp. at 611. There is absolutely no reason to believe, however, that this meant "deterrence adequate to prevent an injury to these plaintiffs that would otherwise occur." The statute does not even mention deterrence in general (much less deterrence of future harm to the particular plaintiff) as one of the elements that the court should consider in fixing the amount of the penalty. (That element can come in, if at all, under the last, residual category of "such other matters as justice may require." 33 U.S.C. §1319(d).) The statute does require the court to consider "the seriousness of the violation or violations, the economic benefit (if any) resulting from the violation, any history of such violations, any good-faith efforts

to comply with the applicable requirements, [and] the economic impact of the penalty on the violator...." Ibid; see 956 F. Supp. at 601. The District Court meticulously discussed, in subsections (a) through (e) of the portion of its opinion entitled "Civil Penalty," each one of those specified factors, and then—under subsection (f) entitled "Other Matters As Justice May Require," it discussed "1. Laidlaw's Failure to Avail Itself of the Reopener Clause," "2. Recent Compliance History," and "3. The Ever-Changing Mercury Limit." There is no mention whatever—in this portion of the opinion or anywhere else—of the degree of deterrence necessary to prevent future harm to these particular plaintiffs. Indeed, neither the District Court's final opinion (which contains the "adequate deterrence" statement) nor its earlier opinion dealing with the preliminary question whether South Carolina's previous lawsuit against Laidlaw constituted "diligent prosecution" that would bar citizen suit, see 33 U.S.C. §1365(b)(1)(B), displayed any awareness that deterrence of future injury to the plaintiffs was necessary to support standing.

The District Court's earlier opinion did, however, quote with approval the passage from a District Court case which began: "'Civil penalties seek to deter pollution by discouraging future violations. To serve this function, the amount of the civil penalty must be high enough to insure that polluters cannot simply absorb the penalty as a cost of doing business'." App. 122, quoting *PIRG v. Powell Duffryn Terminals, Inc.*, 720 F. Supp. 1158, 1166 (NJ 1989). When the District Court concluded the "Civil Penalty" section of its opinion with the statement that "taken together, this court believes the above penalty, potential fee awards, and Laidlaw's own direct and indirect litigation expenses provide adequate deterrence under the circumstances of this case," 956 F. Supp. at 611, it was obviously harking back to this general statement of what the statutorily prescribed factors (and the "as justice may require" factors, which in this case did not include particularized or even generalized deterrence) were designed to achieve. It meant no more than that the court believed the civil penalty it had prescribed met the statutory standards.

The Court points out that we have previously said "'all civil penalties have some deterrent effect'," (quoting *Hudson v. United States*, 522 U.S. 93, 102, 139 L. Ed. 2d 450, 118 S. Ct. 488 (1997)). That is unquestionably true: As a general matter, polluters as a class are deterred from violating discharge limits by the availability of civil penalties. However, none of the cases the Court cites focused on the deterrent effect of a single imposition of penalties on a particular lawbreaker. Even less did they focus on the question whether that particularized deterrent effect (if any) was enough to redress the injury of a citizen plaintiff in the sense required by Article III. They all involved penalties pursued by the government, not by citizens. See *Hudson*, supra, at 96; *Department of Revenue of Mont. v. Kurth Ranch*, 511 U.S. 767, 773, 114 S. Ct. 1937, 128 L. Ed. 2d 767 (1994); *Tull v. United States*, 481 U.S. 412, 414, 95 L. Ed. 2d 365, 107 S. Ct. 1831 (1987).

If the Court had undertaken the necessary inquiry into whether significant deterrence of the plaintiffs' feared injury was "likely," it would have had to reason something like this: Strictly speaking, no polluter is deterred by a penalty for past pollution; he is deterred by the fear of a penalty for future pollution. That fear will be virtually nonexistent if the prospective polluter knows that all emissions violators are given a free pass; it will be substantial under an emissions program such as the federal scheme here, which is regularly and notoriously enforced; it will be even higher when a prospective polluter subject to such a regularly enforced program has, as here, been the object of public charges of pollution and a suit for injunction; and it will surely be near the top of the graph when, as

here, the prospective polluter has already been subjected to state penalties for the past pollution. The deterrence on which the plaintiffs must rely for standing in the present case is the marginal increase in Laidlaw's fear of future penalties that will be achieved by adding federal penalties for Laidlaw's past conduct.

I cannot say for certain that this marginal increase is zero; but I can say for certain that it is entirely speculative whether it will make the difference between these plaintiffs' suffering injury in the future and these plaintiffs' going unharmed. In fact, the assertion that it will "likely" do so is entirely farfetched. The speculativeness of that result is much greater than the speculativeness we found excessive *in Simon v. Eastern Ky. Welfare Rights Organization*, 426 U.S. 26, 43, 48 L. Ed. 2d 450, 96 S. Ct. 1917 (1976), where we held that denying §501(c)(3) charitable-deduction tax status to hospitals that refused to treat indigents was not sufficiently likely to assure future treatment of the indigent plaintiffs to support standing. And it is much greater than the speculativeness we found excessive in *Linda R. S. v. Richard D.*, discussed supra, where we said that "the prospect that prosecution [for nonsupport] will...result in payment of support can, at best, be termed only speculative," 410 U.S. at 618.

In sum, if this case is, as the Court suggests, within the central core of "deterrence" standing, it is impossible to imagine what the "outer limits" could possibly be. The Court's expressed reluctance to define those "outer limits" serves only to disguise the fact that it has promulgated a revolutionary new doctrine of standing that will permit the entire body of public civil penalties to be handed over to enforcement by private interests.

C

Article II of the Constitution commits it to the President to "take Care that the Laws be faithfully executed," Art. II, §3, and provides specific methods by which all persons exercising significant executive power are to be appointed, Art. II, §2. As JUSTICE KENNEDY's concurrence correctly observes, the question of the conformity of this legislation with Article II has not been argued—and I, like the Court, do not address it. But Article III, no less than Article II, has consequences for the structure of our government, see *Schlesinger*, 418 U.S. at 222, and it is worth noting the changes in that structure which today's decision allows.

By permitting citizens to pursue civil penalties payable to the Federal Treasury, the Act does not provide a mechanism for individual relief in any traditional sense, but turns over to private citizens the function of enforcing the law. A Clean Water Act plaintiff pursuing civil penalties acts as a self-appointed mini-EPA. Where, as is often the case, the plaintiff is a national association, it has significant discretion in choosing enforcement targets. Once the association is aware of a reported violation, it need not look long for an injured member, at least under the theory of injury the Court applies today. And once the target is chosen, the suit goes forward without meaningful public control.[2] The availability of civil penalties vastly disproportionate to the individual injury gives citizen plaintiffs massive bargaining power—which is often used to achieve settlements requiring the defendant to support environmental projects of the plaintiffs' choosing. See Greve, *The Pri-*

vate Enforcement of Environmental Law, 65 Tulane L. Rev. 339, 355–359 (1990). Thus is a public fine diverted to a private interest.

To be sure, the EPA may foreclose the citizen suit by itself bringing suit. 33 U.S.C. §1365(b)(1)(B). This allows public authorities to avoid private enforcement only by accepting private direction as to when enforcement should be undertaken—which is no less constitutionally bizarre. Elected officials are entirely deprived of their discretion to decide that a given violation should not be the object of suit at all, or that the enforcement decision should be postponed.[3] See §1365(b)(1)(A) (providing that citizen plaintiff need only wait 60 days after giving notice of the violation to the government before proceeding with action). This is the predictable and inevitable consequence of the Court's allowing the use of public remedies for private wrongs.

III

Finally, I offer a few comments regarding the Court's discussion of whether FOE's claims became moot by reason of Laidlaw's substantial compliance with the permit limits. I do not disagree with the conclusion that the Court reaches. Assuming that the plaintiffs had standing to pursue civil penalties in the first instance (which they did not), their claim might well not have been mooted by Laidlaw's voluntary compliance with the permit, and leaving this fact-intensive question open

---

2. The Court points out that the government is allowed to intervene in a citizen suit, n. 4; 33 U.S.C. §1365(c)(2), but this power to "bring the Government's views to the attention of the court," is meager substitute for the power to decide whether prosecution will occur. Indeed, according the Chief Executive of the United States the ability to intervene does no more than place him on a par with John Q. Public, who can intervene—whether the government likes it or not—when the United States files suit. §1365(b)(1)(B).

3. The Court observes that "the federal Executive Branch does not share the dissent's view that such suits dissipate its authority to enforce the law," since it has "endorsed this citizen suit from the outset." Of course, in doubtful cases a long and uninterrupted history of presidential acquiescence and approval can shed light upon the constitutional understanding. What we have here—acquiescence and approval by a single Administration—does not deserve passing mention.

for consideration on remand, as the Court does, seems sensible.[4] In reaching this disposition, however, the Court engages in a troubling discussion of the purported distinctions between the doctrines of standing and mootness. I am frankly puzzled as to why this discussion appears at all. Laidlaw's claimed compliance is squarely within the bounds of our "voluntary cessation" doctrine, which is the basis for the remand.[5] There is no reason to engage in an interesting academic excursus upon the differences between mootness and standing in order to invoke this obviously applicable rule.[6]

Because the discussion is not essential—indeed, not even relevant—to the Court's decision, it is of limited significance. Nonetheless, I am troubled by the Court's too-hasty retreat from our characterization of mootness as "the doctrine of standing set in a time frame." *Arizonans for Official English v. Arizona*, 520 U.S. 43, 68, n. 22, 137 L. Ed. 2d 170, 117 S. Ct. 1055 (1997). We have repeatedly recognized that what is required for litigation to continue is essentially identical to what is required for litigation to begin: There must be a justiciable case or controversy as required by Article III. "Simply

---

4. In addition to the compliance and plant-closure issues, there also remains open on remand the question whether the current suit was foreclosed because the earlier suit by the State was "diligently prosecuted." See 33 U.S.C. §1365(b)(1)(B). Nothing in the Court's opinion disposes of the issue. The opinion notes the District Court's finding that Laidlaw itself played a significant role in facilitating the State's action. But there is no incompatibility whatever between a defendant's facilitation of suit and the State's diligent prosecution—as prosecutions of felons who confess their crimes and turn themselves in regularly demonstrate. Laidlaw was entirely within its rights to prefer state suit to this private enforcement action; and if it had such a preference it would have been prudent—given that a State must act within 60 days of receiving notice of a citizen suit, see §1365(b)(1)(A), and given the number of cases State agencies handle—for Laidlaw to make sure its case did not fall through the cracks. South Carolina's interest in the action was not a feigned last minute contrivance. It had worked with Laidlaw in resolving the problem for many years, and had previously undertaken an administrative enforcement action resulting in a consent order. 890 F. Supp. 470, 476 (SC 1995). South Carolina has filed an amicus brief arguing that allowing citizen suits to proceed despite ongoing state enforcement efforts "will provide citizens and federal judges the opportunity to relitigate and second-guess the enforcement and permitting actions of South Carolina and other States." Brief for South Carolina as Amicus Curiae 6.

5. Unlike Justice Stevens' concurrence, the opinion for the Court appears to recognize that a claim for civil penalties is moot when it is clear that no future injury to the plaintiff at the hands of the defendant

can occur. The concurrence suggests that civil penalties, like traditional damages remedies, cannot be mooted by absence of threatened injury. The analogy is inapt. Traditional money damages are payable to compensate for the harm of past conduct, which subsists whether future harm is threatened or not; civil penalties are privately assessable (according to the Court) to deter threatened future harm to the plaintiff. Where there is no threat to the plaintiff, he has no claim to deterrence. The proposition that impossibility of future violation does not moot the case holds true, of course, for civil-penalty suits by the government, which do not rest upon the theory that some particular future harm is being prevented.

6. The Court attempts to frame its exposition as a corrective to the Fourth Circuit, which it claims "confused mootness with standing." The Fourth Circuit's conclusion of nonjusticiability rested upon the belief (entirely correct, in my view) that the only remedy being pursued on appeal, civil penalties, would not redress FOE's claimed injury. 149 F.3d 303, 306 (1998). While this might be characterized as a conclusion that FOE had no standing to pursue civil penalties from the outset, it can also be characterized, as it was by the Fourth Circuit, as a conclusion that, when FOE declined to appeal denial of the declaratory judgment and injunction, and appealed only the inadequacy of the civil penalties (which it had no standing to pursue) the case as a whole became moot. Given the Court's erroneous conclusion that civil penalties can redress private injury, it of course rejects both formulations—but neither of them necessitates the Court's academic discourse comparing the mootness and standing doctrines.

stated, a case is moot when the issues presented are no longer 'live' or the parties lack a legally cognizable interest in the outcome." *Powell v. McCormack*, 395 U.S. 486, 496, 23 L. Ed. 2d 491, 89 S. Ct. 1944 (1969). A Court may proceed to hear an action if, subsequent to its initiation, the dispute loses "its character as a present, live controversy of the kind that must exist if [the Court is] to avoid advisory opinions on abstract propositions of law." *Hall v. Beals*, 396 U.S. 45, 48, 24 L. Ed. 2d 214, 90 S. Ct. 200 (1969) (per curiam). See also *Preiser v. Newkirk*, 422 U.S. 395, 401, 45 L. Ed. 2d 272, 95 S. Ct. 2330 (1975); *Steffel v. Thompson*, 415 U.S. 452, 459, n. 10, 39 L. Ed. 2d 505, 94 S. Ct. 1209 (1974). Because the requirement of a continuing case or controversy derives from the Constitution, *Liner v. Jafco, Inc.*, 375 U.S. 301, 306, n. 3, 11 L. Ed. 2d 347, 84 S. Ct. 391 (1964), it may not be ignored when inconvenient, *United States v. Alaska S. S. Co.*, 253 U.S. 113, 116, 64 L. Ed. 808, 40 S. Ct. 448 (1920) (moot question cannot be decided, "however convenient it might be"), or, as the Court suggests, to save "sunk costs," [see] *Lewis v. Continental Bank Corp.*, 494 U.S. 472, 480, 108 L. Ed. 2d 400, 110 S. Ct. 1249 (1990) ("Reasonable caution is needed to be sure that mooted litigation is not pressed forward . . . solely in order to obtain reimbursement of sunk costs").

It is true that mootness has some added wrinkles that standing lacks. One is the "voluntary cessation" doctrine to which the Court refers. But it is inaccurate to regard this as a reduction of the basic requirement for standing that obtained at the beginning of the suit. A genuine controversy must exist at both stages. And just as the initial suit could be brought (by way of suit for declaratory judgment) before the defendant actually violated the plaintiff's alleged rights, so also the initial suit can be continued even though the defendant has stopped violating the plaintiff's alleged rights. The "voluntary cessation" doctrine is nothing more than an evidentiary presumption that the controversy reflected by the violation of alleged rights continues to exist. *Steel Co.*, 523 U.S. at 109. Similarly, the fact that we do not find cases moot when the challenged conduct is "capable of repetition, yet evading review" does not demonstrate that the requirements for mootness and for standing differ. "Where the conduct has ceased for the time being but there is a demonstrated probability that it will recur, a real-life controversy between parties with a personal stake in the outcome continues to exist." *Honig v. Doe*, 484 U.S. 305, 341, 98 L. Ed. 2d 686, 108 S. Ct. 592 (1988) (SCALIA, J., dissenting) (emphasis omitted).

Part of the confusion in the Court's discussion is engendered by the fact that it compares standing, on the one hand, with mootness based on voluntary cessation, on the other hand. The required showing that it is "absolutely clear" that the conduct "could not reasonably be expected to recur" is not the threshold showing required for mootness, but the heightened showing required in a particular category of cases where we have sensibly concluded that there is reason to be skeptical that cessation of violation means cessation of live controversy. For claims of mootness based on changes in circumstances other than voluntary cessation, the showing we have required is less taxing, and the inquiry is indeed properly characterized as one of "'standing set in a time frame'." See *Arizonans*, supra, at 67, 68, n. 22 (case mooted where plaintiff's change in jobs deprived case of "still vital claim for prospective relief"); *Spencer v. Kemna*, 523 U.S. 1, 7, 140 L. Ed. 2d 43, 118 S. Ct. 978 (1998) (case mooted by petitioner's completion of his sentence, since "throughout the litigation, the plaintiff must have suffered, or be threatened with, an actual injury traceable to the defendant and likely to be redressed by a favorable judicial decision") (internal quotation marks omitted); *Lewis*, 494 U.S. at 478–480 (case against state mooted by change in federal law that eliminated parties' "personal stake" in the outcome).

In sum, while the Court may be correct that the parallel between standing and mootness is imperfect due to realistic evidentiary presumptions that are by their nature applicable only in the mootness context, this does not change the underlying principle that "'the requisite personal interest that must exist at the commencement of the litigation...must continue throughout its existence....'" *Arizonans*, supra, at 68, n. 22 (quoting *United States Parole Comm'n. v.*

Geraghty, 445 U.S. 388, 397, 63 L. Ed. 2d 479, 100 S. Ct. 1202 (1980))....

By uncritically accepting vague claims of injury, the Court has turned the Article III requirement of injury in fact into a "mere pleading requirement," Lujan, 504 U.S. at 561; and by approving the novel theory that public penalties can redress anticipated private wrongs, it has come close to "making the redressability requirement vanish," *Steel Co.*, supra, at 107. The undesirable and unconstitutional consequence of today's decision is to place the immense power of suing to enforce the public laws in private hands. I respectfully dissent.

■ **NOTES**

1. As a comparison between the majority and dissenting opinions in this case illustrates, some members of the Supreme Court are more comfortable with citizen enforcement of federal laws (in the federal courts) than are others. Regardless of one's political, social, or cultural views on the topic, does the concept of a congressionally sanctioned private right of action to enforce delineated public laws actually raise *constitutional* issues? Would the views expressed in Justice Scalia's dissent also apply to the traditional use by Congress of *qui tam* laws—federal statutes that authorize citizens to file suit against violators of a (specified) federal law, to recover a judgment on behalf of the United States, and to receive a percentage of that judgment as compensation for having brought the suit? (See, for example, 31 U.S.C. §3730, which authorizes private citizens to file suit on behalf of the United States against violators of the False Claims Act, and to receive up to 30% of any proceeds recovered, in addition to attorneys' fees and costs.)

2. One way of thinking about citizen enforcement suits is as a bridge between the embodiment of congressional policies in federal statute and the implementation of those policies in practice. In general, the level of federal enforcement of environmental laws (and of regulatory statutes generally) tends to vary with the attitude of the reigning presidential administration toward government regulation of business. For example, an analysis of Syracuse University's Transactional Records Access Clearinghouse (TRAC) database of records compiled by the Executive Office of U.S. Attorneys indicates that civil and criminal enforcement of federal environmental stat-

utes dropped considerably under the administration of President George W. Bush, compared with the administrations of presidents Bill Clinton and George H. W. Bush. When governmental enforcement takes a downturn of this nature, citizen enforcement arguably becomes an especially necessary component of the overall system for implementing environmental law. Yet it is at these times that the conflict noted by Justice Scalia comes most prominently to the fore. That is, the citizen-plaintiff's desire to enforce a particular legal standard clashes with the federal regulator's desire for a more lenient approach. From a constitutional law perspective, however, the real conflict is between Congress (who articulated the policies to be enforced) and the president (who disagrees with those policies). Unless the balance struck in the Constitution is to be reformulated, it would appear that Congress—as the authorized constitutional policymaker—has the upper legal hand in such a debate.

3. As the Court's opinion in the *Laidlaw* case also reflects, the citizen-suit provisions in federal environmental statutes generally provide that citizen plaintiffs may be awarded reasonable attorneys' fees, expert witness fees, and other costs of litigation (to be paid by the defendant). Many of these provisions explicitly limit such fee awards to those cases in which the citizen plaintiff is the "prevailing or substantially prevailing" party, and all limit recovery to those situations in which the citizen lawsuit has affirmatively advanced the federal policies embodied in the environmental statute(s) under which suit is brought.   ∎

2. The Relationship between Citizen Enforcement and Government Oversight

All federal environmental citizen suit provisions draw a balance between encouraging citizen enforcement suits, on the one hand, and protecting the violator from multiple enforcement actions, on the other. In general, Congress has chosen to (1) clearly specify those situations in which a private citizen may file a judicial enforcement action, (2) give EPA or the state the opportunity to preclude such a suit by filing its own enforcement suit, and (3) allow the citizen suit to go forward if the agency declines this opportunity. Under the Clean Water Act, for example, a citizen is precluded from filing a suit "if [the EPA] or State has commenced and is diligently prosecuting a civil or criminal action in a court of the United States, or a State to require compliance with the standard, limitation, or order, but in any such action in a court of the United States any citizen may intervene as a matter of right" [33 U.S.C. §1365 (b)(1)(B)]. Similar language can be found in 42 U.S.C. §300j-8(b)(1)(B) (Safe Drinking Water Act); 42 U.S.C. §9659(d)(2) (CERCLA); 42 U.S.C. §7604(b)(1)(B) (Clean Air Act); 15 U.S.C. §2619(b)(1)(B) (TSCA); and 42 U.S.C. §11046 (Emergency Planning and Community Right-to-Know Act).

■ **NOTES**

1. Such provisions have been held not to be triggered by *municipal* enforcement suits. See, e.g., *Ohio Pub. Interest Research Group v. Laidlaw Envtl. Serv., Inc.*, 963 F.Supp. 635, 638–39 (S.D. Ohio 1996), and cases cited therein.)

2. To facilitate the agency's consideration of the matter prior to the filing of a citizen action, Congress typically has required the citizen to give notice of the alleged violations to the agency and the violater and has specified a prescribed waiting period (typically 60 days) during which the agency may evaluate a potential enforcement suit.

3. The typical 60-day (or, in some cases, 90-day) notice provision in most of the federal environmental legislation is considered jurisdictional in nature and cannot be waived. In *Hallstrom v. Tillamook County*, 493 U.S. 20 (1989), a case under RCRA, the Supreme Court dismissed a case after the plaintiff had prevailed at trial because the plaintiff had not provided presuit notice as required by RCRA. The Court held that the notice requirement is jurisdictional in nature. The Court also held that strict construction of the requirement that notice be given was in furtherance of the clear congressional objectives of providing the EPA and state enforcement agencies with the first opportunity to enforce the law and of promoting voluntary compliance by the alleged violator in a nonadversarial setting (*Hallstrom v. Tillamook County*, 493 U.S. at 28–29).

4. The statutory notice provisions usually provide that the EPA is to promulgate regulations implementing the notice requirement. The EPA has done so, and the resulting regulations specify, inter alia, the required content of the notice and the required manner of service.

5. Is the citizen plaintiff is required to give additional notice of violations that occur, or are discovered, after notice is given? The accepted rule appears to be that no additional notice need be given for postnotice violations that are the same type for which notice has already been given. *See PIRG of New Jersey v. Hercules, Inc.*, 50 F.3d 1239 (3d Cir. 1995). If the postnotice violations are of a different type, however, the issue likely will turn on the question of whether the postnotice violations are sufficiently related to the violations described in the notice that the notice can fairly be said to have included them within its scope (Id.). Where the additional violations actually occurred prior to the original notice but were not discovered until after the notice was served, the courts have tended to apply something of a fairness analysis. If it can be said that the citizen plaintiff reasonably should have discovered the additional violations prior to giving notice (e.g., where the violations were apparent from publicly available records), it is highly likely that additional notice will be required. However, if the citizen plaintiff reasonably could not have been expected to

discover the violations prior to giving notice (e.g., where the defendant took steps to conceal the violations), additional notice may not be required.

6. In *Hallstrom*, the Supreme Court did not address the issue of the requisite *content* of the notice. Consistent with EPA regulation, some courts have held that the notice is sufficient so long as it provides information from which the recipient can determine the nature of the violation alleged, even if the notice is not precisely accurate. See, e.g., *Atlantic States Legal Found. v. Stroh Die Casting Co.*, 116 F.3d 814 (7th Cir. 1997) (Clean Water Act notice was sufficient even though it did not specifically identify the outfall at which the discharge violations allegedly were occurring). ▪

Some federal statutes also provide that some prior federal or state *administrative* enforcement actions bar (in whole or in part) the filing of a citizen suit addressing the same violations. See, e.g., Section 309(g)(6) of the Clean Water Act, 33 U.S.C. §1319(g)(6) (a citizen is barred from filing a "civil penalty action" where the EPA or state begins a "diligently" prosecuted administrative penalty action for the same violations before the citizen gives a 60-day notice of suit); Section 7002(b)(2)(B) of RCRA, 42 U.S.C. §6972(b)(2)(B) (a citizen action for "imminent and substantial endangerment" may not be commenced to the extent that the situation has already been addressed by an administrative order issued by the EPA under Section 106 of CERCLA).

In *North and South Rivers Watershed Association, Inc. v. Scituate*, 949 F.2d 552 (1st Cir. 1991), the First Circuit departed from the language and legislative history of Section 309(g)(6) of the Clean Water Act to hold (1) that a state administrative compliance action bars a Clean Water Act citizen suit regardless of whether the state actually seeks penalties against the violator; and (2) that even though the statute states that only "civil penalty" actions are precluded, citizen actions for injunctive relief are barred as well. On both points, this decision violates a fundamental principle of statutory construction in that the court substituted its own view of appropriate Clean Water Act enforcement policy for the policy articulated by Congress in the plain language of the statute. The Ninth Circuit has twice rejected the *Scituate* court's analysis on the first point, holding that only administrative *penalty* actions have a preclusive effect under the Clean Water Act. See *Washington Pub. Interest Research Group v. Pendleton Woolen Mills*, 11 F.3d 883, 886 (9th Cir. 1993) ("[W]e are not persuaded by the First Circuit's reasoning...The most persuasive evidence of...[congressional] intent is the words selected by Congress, not a court's sense of the general role of citizen suits in the enforcement of the Act.") (citation and internal quotation marks omitted); *Citizens for a Better Env't. v. Union Oil Co.*, 83 F.3d 1111, 1118 (9th Cir. 1996).

The Eighth Circuit, while noting that the plain language of Section 309(g)(6) does not bar citizen suits for injunctive relief, nonetheless agreed with the *Scituate* court on the second point: that a citizen suit for injunctive relief should not be allowed to go forward where the citizen's penalty claim is barred. *See Arkansas Wildlife Fed'n. v. ICI Americas, Inc.*, 29 F.3d 376 (8th Cir. 1994). This conflicts in two important respects with the analysis the Supreme Court applied to the Clean Water Act in the *Gwaltney* decision. In *Gwaltney*, the Court stressed that the role of a court in interpreting the act is to give effect to the plain language of Congress according to its "most natural reading," and that Congress' primary purpose in including a citizen-suit provision in the act was to enable citizens to obtain relief (including injunctive relief) to restrain future violations. Noting these conflicts, the Tenth Circuit declared itself "compelled to disagree with the First and Eighth Circuits," and held that the citizen plaintiff's claim for injunctive relief is not barred in such circumstances. See *Paper, Allied-Industrial, Chemical and Energy Workers Intern. Union v. Continental Carbon Co.*, 428 F.3d 1285, 1299 (10th Cir. 2005).

3. Strategic Lawsuits Against Public Participation (SLAPP Suits)

No contemporary treatment of environmental enforcement would be complete without mention of "SLAPP" (strategic lawsuit against public participation) suits. A SLAPP suit is a complaint or counterclaim filed against an individual or group seeking to challenge a project or activity on environmental or other similar grounds, filed by the proponent of that project or activity. The SLAPP plaintiff is usually a commercial interest, although at least one municipality in Massachusetts has pursued such an action against its own residents. The action often is brought as a tort claim for libel, slander, or interference with business relationship. Relief is sought in the form of monetary damages (regularly and intentionally in the millions of dollars) with accompanying efforts to place liens against residential real estate, and prayers for injunctive relief.

SLAPP suits are rare, and successful ones are rarer still. They have, nevertheless, caught the attention of the public, and potential citizen plaintiffs in environmental enforcement litigation frequently express concern about them. Although these suits rarely succeed on the merits, they are not usually filed for that purpose. To the contrary, their strategic value is as a threat and a deterrent against citizen involvement. By forcing a SLAPP defendant to defend a suit and respond to abusive and costly discovery tactics, plaintiffs in these sorts of actions attempt to bludgeon citizens into forgoing their constitutionally protected First Amendment rights to petition the government and to free speech. Indeed, under the Supreme Court's well-developed *Noerr-Pennington* doctrine, citizens are immunized from liability associated with their having petitioned governmental bodies. See, e.g., *California Motor Transport Co. v. Trucking Unlimited*, 404 U.S. 508 (1972).

Several states, including Massachusetts, New Jersey, New York, California, and Washington, have enacted anti-SLAPP legislation. Other states, like Colorado, have fashioned judicial rules that place a heavy burden on SLAPP plaintiffs. See, e.g., *Protect Our Mountain Env't., Inc. v. District Court*, 677 P.2d 1361 (Colo. 1984). A number of SLAPP defendants have "SLAPPed back" and recovered substantial actual damages and fees as well as punitive damages. See, e.g., *Leonardini v. Shell Oil Co.*, 216 Cal.App.3d 547, 264 Cal.Rptr. 883 (1989) ($5 million awarded in punitive damages).

A useful general resource on the topic is George W. Pring and Penelope Canon (1996) *SLAPPs: Getting Sued for Speaking Out.* Temple University Press, Philadelphia, Pa.

ACKNOWLEDGMENT

Portions of this chapter were drawn from Charles C. Caldart, Stephen H. Burrington, and Peter Shelley, Public Interest Environmental Litigation, chapter 4 of Gregor I. McGregor, ed. (2006). *Massachusetts Environmental Law*. Boston: MCLE.

12 Alternative Forms of Government Intervention to Promote Pollution Reduction

Excess pollution has been defined as an "economic" problem arising from the failure to internalize the social costs of industrial, agricultural, transportation, energy, and other activities. (See, for example, the classic article by Lawrence Ruff excerpted in chapter 1). In chapter 3 we identified some of the imperfections in the operation of private markets that result in excessive levels of pollution and environmental damage relative to what individuals and/or society desire. Here, having now addressed the current regulatory system in some detail in chapters 5 through 11, we take a step back and turn to an examination of various types of government policies that can, at least in theory, be introduced to remedy these market imperfections (and thereby improve economic and environmental performance).

One should keep in mind, however, that there are instances in which policy considerations may justify doing more than simply correcting market imperfections. Society may, for example, choose to transcend markets entirely in limiting exposure to toxic substances and promoting technological change, especially where the effects of pollution fall most heavily on disadvantaged subgroups of the population or are borne by subsequent generations not adequately represented at the political table. Society may also choose to invoke the Precautionary Principle when definitive scientific knowledge is not available and the consequences of not acting could be serious, as in the case of persistent, bioaccumulative substances.

Five major categories of government intervention are considered in this chapter: (1) direct controls (often called command-and-control regulation); (2) indirect controls (often called market-based approaches); (3) other policy instruments, such as information sharing, technical assistance, and government purchasing practices; (4) statutory and common-law liability for harm, and (5) encouragement of so-called voluntary initiatives. Government programs coming within this last category tend to be premised either on industry's presumed interest in meeting social demands for a cleaner environment, or on industry's desire to avoid more stringent regulation. While perhaps not strictly governmental policies, voluntary approaches of this nature often require government acquiescence and encouragement to succeed.

Direct controls are legal commands, imposed by a government agency, requiring firms to take some action (e.g., reduce emissions to meet environmental objectives, or provide specified information to government, the community, or the public). Firms do not have the choice of *not* complying with direct controls if they wish to operate within the confines of legal behavior. Noncompliance would be a violation of the law, and could subject a firm to legal sanctions, including civil (and possibly criminal) penalties. Consequently, noncompliance tends to carry with it a stigma of wrongdoing. This form of government intervention is sometimes called command-and-control regulation because it is characterized by legal compulsion.

Indirect controls provide incentives whose purpose is to induce firms to take some action to improve environmental quality. However, firms are not required by law to take the desired action, and normally no sense of wrongdoing accompanies a failure to do so. An emissions fee or "tax" that is imposed on firms for every unit of pollution they emit is a type of "negative" indirect control, while tax deductions and credits are types of "positive" indirect controls. Because indirect controls generally take the form of an economic charge or subsidy or some other type of financial incentive, they are often referred to as *economic instruments* or *market-based instruments*. We will follow this convention and use the terms "indirect controls," "economic instruments," and "market-based instruments" interchangeably throughout this chapter.

There are *other "positive" policy instruments* that also are designed to indirectly stimulate industry to reduce pollution. Broadly speaking, these programs involve government provision of goods or services that private industry has been unable or unwilling to provide or develop. Examples are the creation of pollution and waste control and prevention information databases and clearinghouses, the establishment of a state office of technical assistance, the sponsoring of technical conferences, the creation of a waste recovery facility to separate out recyclable materials, government projects to demonstrate the feasibility and effectiveness of new pollution-reducing technologies, and the use of government purchasing power to promote cleaner production. Although these programs are conceptually linked to positive market-based incentives such as subsidies and tax credits, they typically involve a greater level of government involvement in the process.

Liability statutes and common-law suits that result in damage awards for health or environmental consequences can, under some circumstances, be incentives to reduce pollution and waste. CERCLA is the most prominent of such liability statutes on the federal level. Also included in this category are financial responsibility requirements that mandate firms, or their agents, to provide collateral (such as financial bonds) to guarantee that there will be funds available to pay for future environmental damage resulting from their operations.

The types of *voluntary initiatives* that can be encouraged by governmental programs include so-called industrial ecology practices involving exchange of wastes and materials among commercial and industrial firms, industry self-enforcement encouraged by industry codes of practice, and voluntary programs or covenants between industry and governments to go beyond compliance.

▪ NOTE

1. The distinction between indirect and direct controls is not always a clear one. Economic incentives, normally associated with indirect controls, may accompany direct controls. The monetary penalties imposed for violations of direct controls, for example, are a type of economic or market-based incentive. Conversely, indirect controls are typically supported by various requirements or prohibitions, noncompliance with which would be a violation of the law (as where, for example, firms are required to pay a specified emissions fee for every unit of pollution they choose to emit, and are prohibited from disconnecting or otherwise tampering with monitoring equipment used to measure the amount of pollution they are emitting). ▪

In evaluating each type of government intervention, we will examine its performance in terms of *static* efficiency or cost-effectiveness, i.e., whether a particular policy instrument can achieve environmental objectives using existing technology at minimum cost. However, we will also examine the performance of these policy instruments from the perspective of *dynamic* efficiency, i.e., the extent to which a particular policy instrument has the potential to induce *technological change* to reduce environmental and human risk.

Other criteria for evaluating alternative instruments are suggested by the following questions:

• What substance or activity is being controlled?
• Who ultimately pays for the pollution or waste reduction?
• Who is likely to comply?
• What is the likelihood that the pollution or waste reduction goal will be achieved?
• What is the likelihood that the public health or environmental goals will be achieved?
• How "tunable" (readily adjustable) is the instrument?
• Is there opportunity for political interference?

Depending on the answers to these questions (and their relative importance to the policymaker), particular policy approaches may be more attractive in one situation than in another, reflecting, for example, differences in equity outcomes, or certainty of result versus flexibility. In our discussions of alternative approaches, we focus on the question of the effectiveness of the approach in fostering innovation and technological change, because it is in that realm that most gains can be made with regard to both achieving extensive risk reduction and conferring economic benefits to the industry. Before proceeding with our investigation of the various forms of government intervention, a brief discussion of three important caveats is in order.

The first caveat relates to the fact that the policy instruments introduced in this chapter are, for the most part, discussed individually. One might therefore conclude, erroneously, that the issue at hand is which single policy instrument to select. In reality, regulators will typically select a mixture of policy instruments that complement each other to achieve environmental objectives. Furthermore, some policy instruments are hybrids that are difficult to pigeonhole in a single category. One example is a combination of direct and indirect controls that places an upper limit on a firm's emissions—or a cap that decreases over time, such as the reduction of emissions of SO_2 and NO_X under the acid rain program—while also imposing an economic charge on every unit of pollution. A related matter is that certain policy instruments, while conceptually distinct, may function equivalently in some cases. For instance, if an economic charge—the epitome of an indirect control—is set so high that no one is willing to pollute, then it is equivalent to a ban, the most extreme type of direct control. Finally, we note that as a general matter there is no single "best" policy instrument. Each type of policy instrument has its place, and the relative efficacies of the various approaches will vary with the nature and source of the pollutant, the geographical setting, the presence or absence of complementary, mutually reinforcing policies, and various technical, political, and administrative considerations (including the issues discussed earlier).

The second caveat is that the focus in this chapter is on the various *types* of policy instruments. Largely absent from this discussion is a consideration of several other factors that can influence the performance of government programs designed to reduce pollution. The *stringency* of an environmental program, for example, often is a key determinant of whether the program induces a significant reduction in emissions. In general, an environmental requirement can be considered stringent because compliance necessitates a significant reduction in exposure to pollutants, because compliance using existing technology is costly, or because compliance requires a significant technological change. It makes little difference which type of policy instrument is selected if the level of stringency is too low to affect the behavior of polluters. This in fact has been a persistent complaint about the use of economic charges, which often have been set at amounts too modest to elicit a response from the regulated community (Organization for Economic Co-operation and Development, 1997). *Monitoring and enforcement* are also critical to the success of most environmental programs because they will determine (1) whether one can identify the type and magnitude of emissions generated by each pollution source, and (2) whether the prescribed response to detected emissions—such as collecting the appropriate emissions charge from pollution sources or imposing penalties for emissions violations—can be implemented. In the absence of credible monitoring and enforcement, polluters will have little incentive to respond to risk-reduction initiatives.

A related third caveat is that in comparing alternative approaches, one must be conscious of comparing them *as they are likely to be applied*, rather than according to theoretical criteria. For example, comparing a (theoretical) perfectly working pollution tax with the existing regulatory system would be as inappropriate as comparing a (theoretical) perfectly functioning regulatory system with market instruments operating in an imperfect market. At best, we have second-best approaches competing for our attention and selection. Ideological preferences are best put aside if one is to fully appreciate the complexity of the variety of possible approaches to reducing pollution. This is not to say, however, that "values" concerns about outcomes or processes are to be ignored. Indeed, the Polluter Pays Principle embodies a quasi-moral concern about pollution, as does erring on the side of caution in applying the Precautionary Principle. (See the discussion of these concepts in chapter 3.) In general, considerations of values and equity, as well as cost-effectiveness, will tend to enter into one's preferences for particular approaches.

A. DIRECT CONTROLS

Pollution reduction standards—the most well known of what we call direct controls—may be classified in a number of ways. A *performance standard* is one that specifies a particular outcome—such as a specified emission level above which it is illegal to emit a specified air pollutant—but does not specify how that outcome is to be achieved. Sometimes the level of performance is determined with reference to the level achieved by a certain technology in use, and this is called a technology-based standard, but this should not be confused with requiring a specific technology. A *design* or *specification standard*, on the other hand, specifies a particular technology, such as a catalytic converter, that must be utilized. In either case, the standard can be based on (1) a desired level of protection for human health or environmental quality, (2) some level of presumed technological feasibility, (3) some level of presumed economic feasibility, or (4) some balancing of social costs and social benefits. Within each of these options, there is a wide spectrum of possible approaches. A human health-based standard, for example, might be designed to protect only the average member of the population, or it might be designed to protect the most sensitive subgroup. A technology-based standard might be based on what is deemed feasible for an entire industry, for the average performing firm within the industry, or for the average of the top performing firms within the industry. Moreover, standards can be based on a combination of these factors. Many standards based on technological feasibility, for example, are also based on some concept of economic feasibility.

Direct controls also include a wide variety of information-based obligations, such as to monitor and report emission levels, to disclose exposure, toxicity, chemical content, and production data, and to conduct testing or screening of chemical products. (See the discussion on right-to-know initiatives in chapter 10.) Adequate access to information is regarded as essential both by advocates of command-and-control approaches and by advocates of more market-based or laissez-faire policies.

The recognized advantages of direct controls, if enforced, are that they carry with them the force of legal compulsion and may be especially desirable when the substance being controlled is extremely hazardous. In addition, direct controls can be tiered for various industrial sectors and can distinguish between new and existing firms. They have the advantage of relative certainty of obligation, which allows industry to set longer-range investment goals.

Depending on their stringency and scheduling, and on the opportunities for revision and experimentation, direct standards can stimulate technological development or, alternatively, can "lock in" inferior or obsolete technologies. The following article describes a technology-focused approach to standard setting that aims to stimulate an innovative response.

Using Regulation to Change the Market for Innovation

Nicholas A. Ashford, Christine Ayers, and Robert F. Stone

Source: 9 *Harvard Environmental Law Review* (No. 2), 419–466 (1985), excerpted with permission.

INTRODUCTION

Technological innovation[1] is both a significant determinant of economic growth and important for reducing health, safety, and environmental hazards. It may be major, involving radical shifts in technology, or incremental, involving adaptation of prior technologies. Technological innovation is different from diffusion, which is the widespread adoption of technology already developed.

Several commentators and researchers have investigated the effects of regulation on technological change.[2] Based on this work and experience gained from the history of industrial responses to regulation over the past fifteen years, designers may now be able to fashion regulatory strategies for eliciting the best possible technological response to achieve specific health, safety, or environmental goals. These technological responses to environmental regulation include adoption of compliance technology, change in process technology, and product substitution. In some cases, regulation need only create a climate in which existing technologies, known to produce the desired environmental results, will be adopted or diffused on a large scale. In others, however, the requisite technology may be lacking altogether, and thus regulation must stimulate research and development. Underlying a regulatory strategy based on an assessment of technological options is a rejection of the premise that regulation must achieve a *balance* between environmental integrity and industrial growth, or between job safety and competition in world markets.[3] Rather, such a strategy builds on the thesis that health, safety, and environmental goals can be *co-optimized* with economic growth through technological innovation.

The concept of technological change is the foundation of a regulatory design strategy

---

1. Technological innovation is the first commercially successful application of a new technical idea. By definition, it occurs in those institutions, primarily private profit-seeking firms, that compete in the marketplace. Innovation should be distinguished from invention, which is the development of a new technical idea, and from diffusion, which is the subsequent widespread adoption of an innovation by those who did not develop it. The distinction between innovation and diffusion is complicated by the fact that innovations can rarely be adopted by new users without modification. When modifications are extensive, the result may be a new innovation. Definitions used in this article draw on a history of several years' work at the Center for Policy Alternatives at the Massachusetts Institute of Technology, beginning with a five-country study: National Support for Science & Technology: An Explanation of the Foreign Experience (Aug. 18, 1975) (CPA No. 75-12). Some definitions appear in that study at pages 1–12.

2. Stewart, *Regulation, Innovation, and Administrative Law: A Conceptual Framework*, 69 CALIF. L. REV. *1259* (1981): Magat, *The Effects of Environmental Regulation on Innovation*, 43 LAW & CONTEMP. PROBS., Winter-Spring 1979, at 4. For a review of prior research at the Center for Policy Alternatives and elsewhere, see Ashford & Heaton. *Regulation and Technological Innovation in the Chemical Industry*. 46 LAW & CONTEMP. PROBS., Summer 1983, at 109.

3. Environmental, health, and safety regulation, as seen by economists, should correct market imperfections by internalizing the social costs of industrial production. Regulation results in a redistribution of the costs and benefits of industrial activity among manufacturers, employers, workers, consumers, and other citizens. Within the traditional economic paradigm, economically efficient solutions reflecting the proper *balance* between costs and benefits of given activities are the major concern.

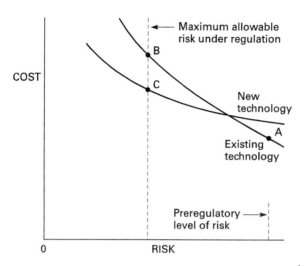

Figure 12.1
An innovative response to regulation. (Source: Nicholas A. Ashford, Christine Ayers, and Robert F. Stone, "Using Regulation to Change the Market for Innovation," 9 *Harvard Environmental Law Review* (No. 2), 419–466 (1985).)

based on the promotion of innovation.[4] While a new technology may be more a costly method of attaining *current* environmental standards, it may achieve stricter standards at less cost than adaptation of existing technology. [Figure 12.1] illustrates the difference.

Suppose it is determined (by either market demand or regulatory fiat) that a reduction in health risk from point "A" to the dotted line is desirable. Use of existing technological capabilities would impose a cost represented by point "B." However, if it were possible to elicit technological innovation, a new "supply curve" would arise, allowing the same degree of health risk reduction at a lower cost represented by point "C." Alternatively, a greater degree of health protection could be afforded if expenditures equal to costs represented by point "B" were applied instead to new

---

4. The work of Burton Klein best describes the kind of industry and economic environment in which innovation flourishes. Burton KLEIN, DYNAMIC ECONOMICS (1977) [Cambridge, Mass.: Harvard University Press] Klein's work concerns the concept of dynamic efficiency, as opposed to the static economic efficiency of the traditional economic theorists. In a state of static efficiency, resources are used most effectively within a fixed set of alternatives. Dynamic efficiency, in contrast, takes into account a constantly shifting set of alternatives, particularly in the technological realm. Thus, a dynamic economy, industry, or firm is flexible and can respond effectively to a constantly changing external environment.

Several conditions are critical to the achievement of dynamic efficiency. A dynamically efficient firm

is open to technological development, has a relatively nonhierarchical structure, possesses a high level of internal and external communication, and shows a willingness to redefine organizational priorities as new opportunities emerge. Dynamically efficient industry groups are open to new entrants with superior technologies and encourage "rivalrous" behavior among industries already in the sector. In particular, dynamic efficiency flourishes in an environment that is conducive to entrepreneurial risk-taking and does not reward those who adhere to the technological status quo. Thus, Klein emphasizes structuring a macroeconomy containing strong incentives for firms to change, adapt, and redefine the alternatives facing them. Regulation is one of several stimuli which can promote such a restructuring of a firm's market strategy.

technological solutions. Note that co-optimization resulting in "having your cake and eating it too" can occur because a new *dynamic* efficiency is achieved.

In creating an atmosphere conducive to innovation, a regulator must assess the innovative capacity of the target industrial sector. The target sector may be the regulated industry, the pollution control industry, or a related industry capable of producing substitute technology. The analysis should focus principally on the process of technological *change* within the possible responding sectors. The regulator should analyze a sector's "innovative dynamic" rather than its existing, static technological capability. An assessment of this innovative dynamic requires a historical examination of the pattern of innovation in the regulated industry, an evaluation of the technological capabilities of related sectors having incentives to develop compliance or substitute technology, and a comparison between the regulated sector and analogous sectors with documented technological responses to regulation. The assessment should include an analysis of the industry's existing technological capabilities as well as a reasoned prediction of its innovative potential under the challenge of regulation. This kind of assessment will assist the design of regulations promoting innovation beneficial both to public health and the environment, and to economic growth within the responding industrial sector.

This article will present a model of the effects of regulation on technological change, provide a brief history of environmental regulation affecting innovation, and review innovation waivers under the Clean Air Act, the Clean Water Act, and the Resource Conservation and Recovery Act ("RCRA"). Finally, it will discuss concerns regarding the design of regulations which do not pit technological innovation against other social concerns.

I. A MODEL OF THE EFFECTS OF REGULATION ON TECHNOLOGICAL CHANGE

Prior work has developed models for explaining the effects of regulation on technological change in the chemical, pharmaceutical, and automobile industries.[9] [Figure 12.2] presents a modified model, structured to assist in designing regulations, rather than simply to trace the effects of regulation on innovation.

A. The Regulatory Stimulus

Environmental, health, and safety regulations affecting the chemical industry include controls on air quality, water quality, solid and hazardous waste, pesticides, food additives, pharmaceuticals, toxic substances, workplace health and safety, and consumer product safety. These regulations control different aspects of development or production, change over time, and are "technology-forcing" to different degrees.[11] Thus, designers of regulations

9. *See* Ashford & Heaton, *supra* note 2. *See also* Ashford, Heaton & Priest, *Environmental.Health, and Safety Regulation and Technological Innovation*, in TECHNOLOGICAL INNOVATION FOR A DYNAMIC ECONOMY 161 (1979); Ashford & Heaton, *The Effects of Health and Environmental Regulation on Technological Change in the Chemical Industry: Theory and Evidence*, in FEDERAL REGULATION AND CHEMICAL INNOVATION 45 (C. Hill ed. 1979) [hereinafter cited as FEDERAL REGULATION AND CHEMICAL INNOVATION].

11. Technology-forcing refers to the tendency of a regulation to force industry to develop new tech-

nology. Regulations may force development of new technology by different types of restrictions. For example, air and water pollution regulation focuses on "end-of-pipe" effluents.... OSHA, in contrast, regulates chemical exposures incident to the production process.... The FDCA, FIFRA, and TSCA impose a pre-market approval process on new chemicals.... The degree of technology-forcing ranges from pure "health-based" mandates, such as those in the ambient air quality standards of the Clean Air Act, to a technology diffusion standard, such as "best available technology" under the Clean Water Act....

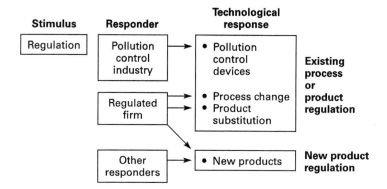

Figure 12.2
A model for regulation-induced technological change. (Source: Nicholas A. Ashford, Christine Ayers, and Robert F. Stone, "Using Regulation to Change the Market for Innovation," 9 *Harvard Environmental Law Review* (No. 2), 419–466 (1985).)

should consider that the effects on technological innovation will differ among regulations which:

a) require demonstration of product safety prior to marketing (pesticides, food additives, pharmaceuticals, and new chemicals);
b) require demonstration of the efficacy of products prior to marketing (pharmaceuticals);
c) require proof of safety or the control of product use after marketing (existing chemicals under the Toxic Substances Control Act, worker protection, and consumer products);
d) control production technology to reduce risks to workplace health and safety; and
e) control emissions, effluents, or wastes (air, water, and hazardous waste regulation).

Furthermore, the internal structure of regulations may alter the general climate for innovation. Elements of that structure include:

a) the form of the regulation (product versus process regulation);
b) the mode (performance versus specification standards);
c) the time for compliance;
d) the uncertainty;
e) the stringency of the requirements; &
f) the existence of other economic incentives which complement the regulatory signal.

The distinction between regulation of products and regulation of processes suggests yet a further division.[17] New products differ from existing products, and production process components differ from unwanted by-products or pollutants.[18] Regulations relying on detailed specification standards may discourage innovation while prompting rapid diffusion of state-of-the-art technology. Similarly, though a phased-in compliance schedule may prompt only incremental improvements

---

17. In practice, product and process regulations may be difficult to distinguish. If a process regulation is stringent enough, it effectively becomes a product ban. Product regulation generally gives rise to product substitution and process regulation generally gives rise to process change. *See* FED-

ERAL REGULATION AND CHEMICAL INNOVATION, *supra* note 10, at 58. *See also generally* Ashford & Heaton, *supra* note 3.
18. Note, however, that component regulations normally specify elements of the production process designed to prevent undesirable by-products....

in technology, it allows a timely industry response.

An industry's perception of the need to alter its technological course often precedes promulgation of a regulation. Most environmental regulations arise only after extended scrutiny of a potential problem by government, citizens, workers, and industry. Prior scrutiny, according to a study done by the Massachusetts Institute of Technology,[19] often has greater effects on industry than formal rulemaking, because anticipation of regulation stimulates innovation. For example, formal regulation of polychlorinated biphenyls ("PCBs") followed years after the government expressed initial concern. Aware of this concern, the original manufacturer and other chemical companies began to search for substitutes prior to regulation. Similarly, most firms in the asbestos products industry substantially complied with the Occupational Safety and Health Administration ("OSHA") asbestos regulation years before it was promulgated. This preregulation period allows industry time to develop compliance technologies, process changes, or product substitutes, while allowing leeway for it to adjust to ensure continued production or future commercial innovation.

The government's initial show of concern is often, however, an unreliable stimulus to technological change. Both technical uncertainties and application of political pressures may cause uncertainty regarding future regulatory requirements. Nevertheless, regulatory uncertainty is frequently beneficial. Although excessive regulatory uncertainty may cause industry inaction, too much certainty will stimulate only minimum compliance technology. Similarly, too frequent change of regulatory requirements may frustrate technological development.

Regulatory stringency is the most important factor influencing technological innovation. A regulation is stringent either (1) because it requires a *significant* reduction in exposure to toxic substances, (2) because compliance using existing technology is costly, or (3) because compliance requires a *significant* technological change. Policy considerations dictate different degrees of stringency as well, since some statutes require that standards be based predominantly on environmental, health, and safety concerns, some on existing technological capability, and others on the technology within reach of a vigorous research and development effort. In the early 1970's, most environmental, health, and safety regulations set standards at a level attainable by existing technology. The regulations reflected both a perceived limit to legislative authority and substantial industry influence over the drafting of standards. More recent regulations have tended toward greater stringency.

The effect of the agency's strategy on innovation is not confined to standard-setting. Innovation waivers, which stimulate innovation by allowing noncompliance with existing regulation while encouraging the development of a new technology, are affected by enforcement strategies as well. The degree to which the requirements of a regulation are strictly enforced may influence the willingness of an industrial sector to attempt to innovate. The implementing agency ultimately may strictly enforce environmental regulations against those firms receiving waivers or, alternatively, it may adopt a "fail-soft" strategy where a firm has made an imperfect effort, but good

19. N. Ashford, D. Hattis, G. Heaton, A. Jaffe, S. Owen & W. Priest, Environmental/Safety Regulation and Technological Change in the U.S. Chemical Industry (Mar. 1979) (report to the National Science Foundation) (CPA No. 79-6) [hereinafter cited as CPA Chemical Industry Study]. Results of this study were published in FEDERAL REGULATION AND CHEMICAL INNOVATION, *supra* note 9.

faith attempt to comply. The latter strategy is an important element of the regulatory stimulus to innovation as it decreases an innovator's risk of severe agency action in the event of failure.

B. Characteristics of the Responding Industrial Sector

The industry responding to regulation may be the regulated industry, the pollution control industry, or a related industry.[29] Regulation of *existing* chemical products or processes might elicit (1) a pollution control device, (2) a manufacturing process change, or (3) a product substitution. The regulated industry will likely supply new processes; the pollution control industry, new devices; and either the regulated industry or new entrants, product substitutions. Regulation of *new* chemicals, however, will simply affect the development of new products.

Recent research on the innovation process has focused on the innovation "dynamic" in diverse industrial segments throughout the economy.[30] The model refers to a "productive segment" in industry,[31] defined by the nature of its technology. Over time the nature and rate of innovation in the segment will change. Initially, the segment creates a market niche by selling a new product, superior in performance to the old technology it replaces. The new technology is typically unrefined, and product change occurs rapidly as technology improves.[32] Because of the rapid product change, the segment neglects process improvements in the early period.

Later, however, as the product becomes better defined, more rapid process change occurs. In this middle period, the high rate of process change reflects the segment's need to compete on the basis of price rather than product performance. In the latter stages, both product and process change decline, and the segment becomes static or rigid. At this point in its cycle, the segment may be vulnerable to invasion by new ideas or disruption by external forces that could cause a reversion to an earlier stage.

C. The Design of Regulatory Strategies

The implications of this model of innovation relate directly to the design of regulation to promote innovation in three ways. First, the model suggests that innovation is predictable in a given industrial context. Second, it asserts that the characteristics of a particular technology determine the probable nature of future innovation within an industrial segment. Third, it describes a general process of industrial maturation which appears relatively uniform across different productive segments. The model does not, however, describe sources of innovation, nor does it elucidate the forces that may transform a mature segment into a more innovative one.

The value of this theory of innovation is that of providing a rationale upon which the designer may fashion a regulation aimed at the industry most likely to achieve his regulatory goal. Consistently, the theory relies on the assumption that the designer may determine the extent of an industry's innovative

---

29. *See supra* [figure 12.2].

30. In particular, the work of Abernathy and Utterback offers an important model of the differences in the nature of innovation across industries and over time. *See* Abernathy & Utterback, *Patterns of Industrial Innovation*, TECH. REV., June–July 1978, at 41. For a fuller discussion of the model in the context of regulation. See generally Ashford & Heaton, *supra* note 2.

31. Automobile engine manufacture would be a productive segment as would vinyl chloride monomer production, but neither the automobile industry nor the vinyl chloride industry would be a productive segment since they both encompass too many diverse technologies.

32. It is typical for the old technology to improve as well, although incrementally, when a new approach challenges its dominance.

rigidity (or flexibility) and its likely response to regulatory stimuli with reference to objective determinable criteria.

Thus the regulatory designer must make the following three determinations:

a) what technological response is desirable (for example, should a regulation force a product or a process change and, further, should it promote diffusion of existing technology, simple adaptation, accelerated development of radical innovation already in progress, or radical innovation);

b) which industrial sector will most likely innovate; and

c) what kind of regulation will most likely elicit the desired response.

The first determination requires a technological assessment, the second a knowledge of a variety of industrial segments, and the third an application of the model considered in this article....

■ **NOTES**

1. For the most part, EPA has not focused deliberately on transforming industry as a primary motivation. Rather, it has tended to set stringent standards when driven by health or environmental concerns, and has been willing to force technology as a result. While EPA may view this approach as being dictated by its various mandates from Congress, the agency actually has the authority in many circumstances to drive technological change much more directly, even with technology-based standards. For example, Section 304 of the Clean Water Act directs EPA to consider process technology as well as control technology when setting BAT standards for industrial dischargers, and clearly authorizes the agency both to assess the technological potential of each industrial subcategory separately and to set the standard according to the technological "cutting edge" within that subcategory (so long as doing so will not drive that subcategory out of business). While this stops short of authorization to require innovation, it does give EPA the authority to set standards that may well be stringent enough to strongly encourage innovation.

2. For a later review of the positive effects regulation can have on technological change, see Strasser (1997), a portion of which is excerpted in chapter 13.

3. For a look at technology forcing from a market economics perspective, see the discussion of static versus dynamic efficiency in chapter 3. For a discussion of how one might design a regulatory system to promote technological change toward pollution prevention and a sustainable economy, see chapter 13.   ■

B. INDIRECT CONTROLS I: "NEGATIVE" INCENTIVES

The chief conceptual difference between direct and indirect controls is that the latter do not command a particular response (such as a particular level of pollution reduction), but rather endeavor to induce the desired response through the creation of an *economic incentive*. As most commonly conceptualized, these market-based approaches involve the creation of an *economic disincentive* to pollute, such as an emission fee. In theory, these "negative" market-based incentives offer several advantages as a mechanism to correct for the market imperfections discussed in chapter 3, although (as discussed here) practical considerations may limit or negate some of these advantages.

• First, emissions fees and other economic disincentives help to internalize the costs of pollution damage. As a result, they satisfy both static efficiency and equity objectives in that the parties who cause the pollution pay for (at least a portion of) the costs their actions impose on society, i.e., they satisfy the Polluter Pays Principle.

• Second, economic disincentives can, in principle, facilitate achievement of environmental objectives at minimum cost. Direct controls, such as emission or effluent standards, sometimes apply pollution control requirements uniformly to all firms, regardless of their cost of compliance. When this is the case, the use of economic instruments may reduce total compliance costs by inducing a shift in emissions reductions from firms with relatively high pollution abatement costs to those with relatively low pollution abatement costs. It should be noted, however, that the "uniformity" characteristic of direct controls has often been significantly overstated by advocates of indirect controls. Emission requirements placed on individual polluters by the states in implementing uniform federal ambient air quality standards under the Clean Air Act, for example, are not themselves uniform. The actual federal standards are media-based concentration standards, rather than firm-based emission requirements. States, through state implementation plans, do in fact place stricter emission requirements on firms more able to sustain the economic burden of pollution reduction. Moreover, where technology-based performance standards distinguish old from new firms, or are industry sector specific, uniformity of response by various firms is neither intended nor achieved. Furthermore, where uniform emission standards do apply, it is often because of the serious nature of particular hazardous pollutants or because of the desire to avoid local hot spots.

• Third, economic disincentives can be fashioned to provide a continuing impetus for firms to further reduce pollution levels under arrangements by which every unit of pollution imposes an economic cost on the firm. In contrast, once a firm complies with a mandated pollution reduction standard, the firm has no incentive—other than that provided by the uncertainty of more stringent environmental regulations in the future—to reduce pollution levels further.

• Fourth, emissions charges and other economic disincentives generate revenue. These revenues may simply be added to the general government revenue fund to finance government activities as a whole, or they can be earmarked to recover, fully or in part, the costs of administering government programs to control environmental pollution. For example, charges and fees for waste are typically revenue generating and are used to offset the costs to government for waste handling and treatment. Economic instruments of this type, introduced to correct for externalities, are the ideal public finance mechanism in that (unlike corporate taxes, income taxes, or most other taxes) they remedy rather than create market distortions and efficiency losses. (See, for instance, Nichols, 1984, pp. 34–35.) In addition, these economic instruments can be made revenue neutral if they are accompanied by an equivalent reduction in corporate taxes, personal income taxes, or other distortionary taxes.

The remainder of this section examines in more detail the two types of economic disincentives most commonly offered as a substitute for command-and-control regulation: emissions charges and tradable emissions permits.

1.   Emissions Charges

The classic example of an economic instrument to achieve environmental objectives is a charge imposed on firms for every unit of pollution they emit.[1] The derivation and effect of emissions charges are demonstrated in figure 12.3. The horizontal axis indicates the amount of pollution generated by all firms. A movement from right to left denotes a reduction in total emissions. Curve A represents the marginal cost of emissions reduction summed over all polluting firms. The shape of the curve reflects the fact that additional reductions in emissions (from a maximum level of pollution E′ to 0) become increasingly more expensive to achieve. Curve B represents the marginal social cost of pollution damage, which increases as the amount of pollution increases (from 0 to E′). In the absence of any requirement to reduce pollution, the emissions damage is not borne by the firms that pollute, and therefore the (marginal) cost of pollution damage to them is zero. The total amount of pollution emitted would be E′. From a classical economics perspective, however, the socially optimal

---

1. The terminology applied to pollution charges is not standardized. For the purposes of this chapter, we use the terms "pollution," "waste," "discharges," "emissions," and "effluents" somewhat interchangeably, most often referring to them collectively as "emissions." Technically, however, emissions refer specifically to air pollution and effluents refer specifically to water pollution. Charges include *user charges* (payments for the costs of collective or public treatment of effluents); *product charges* (fees placed on the price of products that contribute to pollution in their manufacturing, consumption, or disposal; and *administrative charges* (fees paid to support government services related to chemical or product registration or regulatory enforcement). The terms "charge," "fee," and "tax" are often used interchangeably. In fact, the term "Pigouvian tax"—named in recognition of Arthur Pigou, the British economist who first proposed the use of these fees to correct resource misallocations resulting from externalities—specifically refers to economic charges. In this chapter, however, we will reserve the term "tax" for government levies whose primary purpose is to provide revenues to finance government activities.

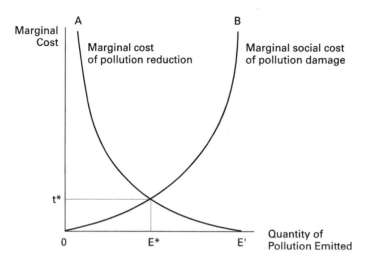

Figure 12.3
Pollution reduction by means of an emission charge.

emissions level is E^*, the point at which the damage caused by an additional unit of pollution is just equal to the marginal cost of avoiding it.[2]

The government can induce firms to reduce total emissions from E' to the socially optimal level, E^*, by imposing an emissions charge of t^* per unit of pollution—equal to the marginal social cost of pollution damage at the point at which this cost equals the marginal cost to firms of reducing emissions. With an emissions charge of t^* per unit of pollution, movement from E' to E^* is profitable to firms because the cost of pollution reduction within that range is less than the emissions charge t^*. Further emissions reductions will not occur below E^* because firms would minimize costs by paying the charge rather than further reducing emissions since with emissions less than E^*, the cost of additional pollution reduction is more than emissions charge t^*.

It is important to realize that the effect of an emissions charge is *not* the same as the effect of a uniform emissions standard, even though both reduce the pollution level to E^*. This can be seen by referring to figure 12.4, in which it is assumed for simplicity that there are only two polluters, firm 1 and firm 2. Their marginal costs of pollution reduction are curves MC_1 and MC_2, respectively. In the absence of government intervention, firm 1 and firm 2 would generate pollution levels of E_1' and E_2',

---

2. Note that this concept of social optimality—"Pareto optimality" in economics jargon—is an economic efficiency criterion. See chapter 3. The acceptable level of pollution from a societal perspective may be quite different.

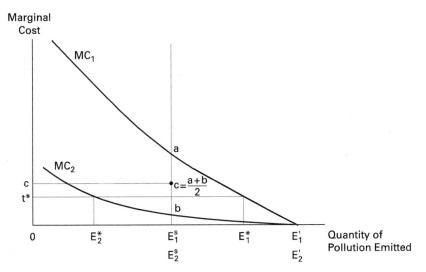

Figure 12.4
Efficiency gains from an emissions charge.

respectively. For convenience, E_1' and E_2' have been set equal to each other in figure 12.4.[3] A uniform emissions standard would typically impose identical pollution restrictions on all firms, thereby limiting each firm's emissions to a maximum of E^S; this is indicated in figure 12.4 as E_1^S for firm 1 and E_2^S for firm 2 (where E_1^S and E_2^S sum to E^*). Firm 1's cost of achieving the emissions standard, evaluated at the last unit of pollution reduction, is equal to "a" in figure 12.4, while firm 2's cost, again evaluated at the margin, is equal to "b" in figure 12.4. Averaging over both firms, the marginal cost of achieving the emissions standard is "c" (equal to $(a + b)/2$) in figure 12.4.

In contrast, an emissions charge of t^* can achieve a pollution reduction to E^* at lower cost. In response to the emissions charge, both firms would reduce emissions until the marginal cost of pollution reduction equaled t^*. As a consequence, more of the pollution reduction is undertaken by firm 2, the firm with the lower marginal cost of reducing pollution, and less is undertaken by firm 1, the firm with the higher marginal cost of reducing pollution. (In figure 12.4, firm 2 expands its pollution reduction efforts to E_2^*, while firm 1 limits its emission reduction to E_1^*, where E_2^* and E_1^* total to E^*.) That is why the marginal cost of reducing emissions to E^* is lower for an emissions charge than for an emissions standard by an amount equal to the

---

3. Note that the horizontal summation of MC_1 and MC_2 in figure 12.4 would yield the marginal cost curve A in figure 12.3, and E_1' and E_2' in figure 12.4 would sum to E' in figure 12.3.

difference between t* and "c" in figure 12.4.[4] These cost savings can be significant. The results of a extensive body of empirical research indicate that the compliance costs under uniform emissions standards have often been several times higher than what they would have been had emissions charges been used instead.[5] This may not be the case, however, when the uniform emissions standard induces the industry to introduce a technological change that lowers the cost of compliance significantly. Here, the resultant change in the compliance cost may be such that complying with the uniform standard is actually cheaper than paying the emission fee.

We emphasize that the effectiveness of economic charges as a mechanism to reduce environmental pollution—as described here—requires that the charges be imposed directly in relation to the amount of pollution being emitted. In particular, it is generally inappropriate to base such charges on a firm's output or on some other measure of a firm's productive activity.[6] Despite this fact, many environmental economics textbooks introduce economic charges on firm output as the standard mechanism to reduce pollution, an approach illustrated in figure 12.5. (Note that figure 12.5 looks deceptively like figure 12.3; the difference is that the horizontal axis measures the level of economic activity rather than the level of pollution being emitted.) It is not a firm's productive activity, however, that is the problem, but rather the firm's emissions resulting from its productive activity, and there is in general no fixed relationship between a firm's productive activity and its emissions. Furthermore, unlike what figure 12.5 suggests, the last method a firm would normally choose to reduce pollution, and typically the most costly, would be to cut back on production. Instead, the firm would usually prefer either to install filters to trap pollutants before they are released to the environment or alter the production process (such as by sub-

---

4. For ease of presentation, the cost savings that are due to emissions charges were described in terms of the marginal cost of the last unit of pollution reduction. A more accurate measure is total cost savings, which involves comparing areas under the marginal cost curves. The total compliance cost of the emissions standard is the sum of the area under MC_1 between E_1' and E_1^S and the area under MC_2 between E_2' and E_2^S. The total compliance cost using an emissions charge is the sum of the area under MC_1 between E_1' and E_1^* and the area under MC_2 between E_2' and E_2^*. The cost savings of the emissions charge are equal to the difference between the area under MC_1 between E_1^* and E_1^S and the area under MC_2 between E_2^* and E_2^S. Under these assumptions, compliance costs could never be lower for an emissions standard, relative to emissions charges that achieve the same pollution reduction, since by construction, the distance from E_2^* to E_2^S must equal the distance from E_1^* to E_1^S, and the maximum marginal cost for MC_2 between E_1^* and E_1^S (that is, t*) is the minimum marginal cost for MC_1 between E_1^* and E_1^S.

5. The estimated cost savings of emissions charges, relative to emissions standards in general, may occasionally have been overstated, particularly in those cases where the actual baseline emissions standard was exceptionally restrictive, specifying not only emissions limits but also the pollution abatement equipment to be adopted. See Tietenberg (1985).

6. There is one broad exception to this principle. When the optimal emissions charge is impossible to calculate because of informational problems (see below in the text) or impractical to administer because of nonpoint or mobile sources of pollution whose emissions are difficult to measure, a reasonable second-best approach may be to impose economic charges on inputs or outputs, such as fuels or pesticides, whose use in production is potentially hazardous to human health or the environment. See Hanley, Shogren, and White (1997, pp. 71–72).

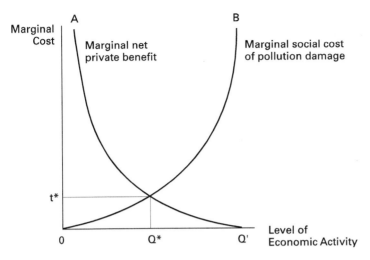

Figure 12.5
Pollution levels and responses based on economic activity.

stituting less hazardous inputs) to reduce the pollutants created per unit of output as a by-product of the firm's productive activities. An emissions charge would elicit this desired technological response, but a charge on a firm's output might not.

Up to this point, we have analyzed the functioning of emissions charges in theoretical terms. In practice, "real world" problems are likely to complicate the use of emissions charges and potentially compromise their effectiveness. As explained later, these problems include the following: (1) spatial effects of pollution on environmental quality; (2) temporal considerations, such as inflation or industry growth; and (3) informational requirements.

In most cases, the specific *location* of a pollution source will influence the effects its emissions have on environmental quality at the various monitoring (or "receptor") points. For instance, consider two pollution sources—one in town and the other upstream from a town—that discharge identical amounts of effluent into a river. The pollution source further upstream would tend to create less environmental damage in town, assuming the upstream part of the river is sufficiently unpolluted to permit natural processes to disperse and degrade the wastes before they reach the town. In principle, such spatial effects require a separate emissions charge for each pollution source, depending on its location in an environmental region or zone[7]—since a

7. The impact of a unit of emissions from a particular pollution source on environmental quality at a particular monitoring point is termed its "transfer coefficient." The economic charge for that pollution source would equal the sum of its economic charges at each monitoring point, which in turn reflect the environmental target (which might vary because of population density, etc.) and the pollution source's transfer coefficient at each monitoring point. See, for example, Hanley, Shogren, and White (1997, pp. 115–117).

uniform emissions charge in such circumstances would forestall attainment of environmental objectives, or at least their attainment at minimum cost. In practice, however, such differentiation of emissions charges among pollution sources is likely to be explicitly illegal or politically infeasible.

A related problem concerns various *temporal considerations* that influence the effectiveness of emissions charges over time. Inflation, for instance, will erode the real value of an emissions charge fixed in nominal terms. Similarly, industrial expansion will tend to increase the amount of pollution for any given emissions charge. Because of these regular disturbances, periodic increases in the emissions charge will be necessary to maintain environmental quality. Frequent adjustment of emissions charges to accommodate these changing conditions, however, may be administratively impractical and therefore unlikely to occur.

Another problem in converting theory into practice concerns the prodigious informational requirements needed to determine the optimal emissions charge.[8] Referring back to figure 12.3, in order to estimate the optimal emissions charge (t*), environmental regulators need to obtain reasonable estimates of both curve A (the marginal cost of pollution reduction as a function of the quantity of pollution emitted) and curve B (the marginal social cost of pollution damage as a function of the quantity of pollution emitted). Just calculating current pollution levels, estimating the resulting pollution damage, and then imputing a monetary value of the pollution damage is a daunting task. (See section E.1 of chapter 3 for a discussion of the difficulties associated with developing monetary estimates of pollution damage.) However, the information required is not the marginal social cost of pollution damage at *current* pollution levels, but what the marginal social cost of pollution damage would be if emissions were adjusted to their *optimal* level (to E* in figure 12.3). Similarly, the information required is not the marginal cost of pollution reduction to achieve the current level of pollution, but what the marginal social cost of pollution reduction would be to achieve the optimal pollution level. These informational requirements are further compounded by the spatial and temporal factors previously mentioned.

Because of the vast amount of information required to identify the optimal emissions charge, environmental regulators might reasonably adopt a second-best approach and attempt to impose a system of emissions charges so as to achieve an acceptable—but not necessarily optimal—standard of environmental quality, in

---

8. It should be emphasized that these informational requirements are not peculiar to an emissions charge. When the goal is *optimal* emissions reduction, full information about the marginal costs and benefits of pollution abatement is required regardless of the type of government intervention employed (i.e., whether the method of emissions control is direct or indirect, or whether the method of indirect control is an emissions charge, a tradable emissions permit, or an emissions subsidy).

terms of strict economic efficiency.[9] (See Baumol and Oates, 1988, pp. 159–176, for a discussion of the merits and limitations of this approach.) A continuing advantage of this second-best type of indirect control, relative to direct controls, is that it will achieve any given level of emissions reduction at minimum cost. One disadvantage of this approach, however, is that given uncertainty about the marginal costs and benefits of emissions reduction, a particular emissions charge may not achieve the target level of environmental quality. This is particularly likely to be a problem when the curve representing the marginal social cost of pollution damage is steep. In that case, failure to control pollution to target levels could have dire environmental consequences. On the other hand, in the presence of steeply increasing costs of pollution abatement, an emissions charge provides a valuable upper limit of the costs to industry of emissions reduction, since when the marginal cost of emissions reduction exceeds the emissions charge, the firm will simply pay the emissions charge rather than reduce emissions further. See Weitzman (1974).

In theory, this problem could be overcome by iterative adjustments to the emissions charge until emissions were reduced to an acceptable level, i.e., the amount of the charge could be "tuned" to achieve the desired result. (Furthermore, if attainment of the environmental targets were to prove to be unexpectedly inexpensive, environmental regulators could entertain the prospect of raising the minimally acceptable level of environmental quality.) In practice, frequent modification of emissions charges, as previously noted, may simply be administratively impractical. Of further concern is the possibility that high or low initial emissions charges could induce firms to make irreversible (sunk) investments in the wrong type of pollution reduction technology. The risk of such technological "lock-in" arises because emissions reduction technologies tend to be "lumpy"; that is, they can't be added in marginal units and usually alternative emissions reduction technologies can't be combined effectively. Hence, firms must typically commit to one type of emissions reduction technology or another. (On the issue of technological lock-in, see, for example, Pearce and Turner, 1990, p. 115.)

The characteristically laudable features of charges—their flexibility and tunability—are also the features that may render them undesirable as a means of encouraging technological innovation. If government wants to stimulate long-term investment in innovative changes in inputs, processes, and final products, there has to be relative certainty of longer-term pollution requirements, or firms will not make those investments. Thus, while some commentators have suggested that flexibility in signals and a continuing incentive to reduce pollution offered by charges

---

9. As discussed in chapters 3 and 5, considerable political pressure from the Office of Management and Budget may be applied to ensure that (according to EPA's own calculations) the estimated costs of major regulations do not exceed their estimated benefits, i.e., to ensure that the total benefits of the regulation equal (or exceed) its total costs, rather than that the *marginal* benefits are equal to the *marginal* costs.

facilitate innovation (e.g., Stewart, 2000, p. 186), we argue that while incremental, easy changes may well flow from flexible signals, significant technological change is less likely. (See chapter 13 for a discussion of this concept; also see Driesen, 2003, 2004.)

- **NOTES**

1. For a more extensive discussion of emission fees, see Stensvaag (1999, pp. 560–574).

2. As discussed in chapter 9, the costs associated with the handling, treatment, and disposal of solid and hazardous waste operate as a de facto tax on the generation of such wastes. These costs have grown dramatically over the past 30 years and often provide a meaningful financial incentive for reducing wastes. And when they were in effect, the levies on chemical production and use imposed under the Hazardous Substance Superfund provided an additional impetus to reduce chemicals throughout the life cycle of production. ∎

2. Tradable Emissions Permits

Another major category of indirect control that provides economic disincentives to pollute is the *tradable (or marketable) emissions permit*: a legal right, created by government, for a firm to emit a specified quantity of pollution.[10] As the name implies, what distinguishes tradable emissions permits from more traditional environmental permits (such as the Clean Water Act's NPDES permit or the Clean Air Act's Title V operating permits) is that they can be bought and sold like regular commodities.

The theoretical functioning of the market for tradable emissions permits can be demonstrated by referring to figure 12.3. Recall that the horizontal axis indicates the amount of pollution generated by all firms, Curve A represents the marginal cost of emissions reduction summed over all firms, and curve B represents the marginal social cost of pollution damage. Suppose that instead of imposing an emissions charge of t^*, the government simply issues E^* emissions permits, where each permit allows the firm that has the permit to emit one "unit" of pollution. Curve A, which reflects the marginal cost of emissions reduction, is in effect the demand curve for emissions permits, since firms would purchase an (additional) emissions permit only if the permit price were lower than their cost of reducing emissions by one unit. For that reason, firms with higher costs of emissions reduction will, other things being equal, tend to purchase a larger share of the tradable emissions permits (and the firms with lower reduction costs will tend to reduce emissions more). This can be seen by referring to figure 12.4, where at an equilibrium emissions permit price of

---

10. Although they are hardly a new concept, tradable emissions permits are a more recent innovation in environmental policy than economic charges. J. H. Dales is credited with introducing the idea. See Dales (1968).

t^*, firm 1—with higher costs of emissions reduction—would purchase E_1^* emissions permits, while firm 2—with lower costs—would purchase only E_2^* emissions permits. As figure 12.3 indicates, when the number of emissions permits is set by the government at E^*, the market-clearing price of a permit will be t^*. (If the price fell below t^*, the demand for emissions permits would exceed E^*; if the price rose above t^*, demand would be insufficient to sell all E^* emissions permits.)

Note that under conditions of perfect information, emissions charges and tradable emissions permits yield equivalent outcomes: emissions reduced to E^* with firms paying t^* per unit of pollution emitted. The only difference is that emissions charges are a price-based approach, while tradable emissions permits are a quantity-based approach. Of course, as was the case with emissions charges, practical considerations complicate the use of tradable emissions permits and raise important issues for the design of an actual system of tradable permits. As discussed in the next section, these issues include the development of a permit system to address the geographical dimensions of polluting activity, the initial allocation of permits, and other factors that affect efficient trading.

■ **NOTE**

1. For a more extensive discussion of "transferable rights" of this nature, see Stensvaag (1999, pp. 574–588).　　　　　　　　　　　　　　　　　　　　　　　　■

a. Types of Permit Systems

Recall that a unit of emissions from a particular pollution source will generally have a nonuniform effect on environmental quality at each of the monitoring points in an environmental region. Three broad types of tradable pollution permit systems have been developed to deal with these *spatial effects* of pollution on environmental quality: an ambient permit system, an emissions permit system, and a pollution-offset system.

In an *ambient permit system*, separate permits are issued for each monitoring point based on the allowed contribution to the pollution concentration at that monitoring point. Such a system would effectively establish a separate permit market for each monitoring point and require a pollution source to obtain a portfolio of permits from the various monitoring points at which its emissions contribute to pollution levels. As a result, an ambient permit system would impose high transaction costs on polluting firms.

An *emissions permit system* offers a simpler solution to the problem of spatial effects of pollution on environmental quality. In such a system, each pollution source is assigned to a particular zone within which permits would be traded one-for-one. This approach greatly reduces transaction costs for industry. The major objection to an emissions permit system is that it ignores differences in the dispersion characteristics of emissions within each zone. This is not a serious problem if pollution sources within a zone generate emissions with similar dispersion characteristics. If the ambient effects of emissions vary significantly with a zone, however, then the efficiency loss—either in achieving the desired level of environmental quality or in achieving it at minimum cost—may be substantial.

A *pollution offset system* is a sort of hybrid alternative that combines attractive features of the emissions permit system and the ambient permit system. Under a pollution offset system, permits are defined in terms of emissions, and trades take place only within a specified zone (as in an emissions permit system). However, trades in permits are subject to the restriction that ambient quality standards not be violated at any monitoring point. When a binding pollution constraint is encountered at any monitoring point, permits are not traded on a one-for-one basis, but rather in proportion to the relative effects of emissions from one pollution source versus another at that monitoring point (as in an ambient permit system). A pollution offset system can avoid the efficiency losses associated with an emissions permit system; and although it is not as simplified as an emissions permit system, a pollution offset system promises to provide substantial savings in transaction costs, relative to an ambient permit system, because polluting firms are not required to trade in a multitude of separate permit markets. Several variations of the trading restriction are possible, including (1) a "nondegradation offset," which imposes an additional requirement that total emissions not increase and (2) a "modified offset," which imposes the requirement that the pretrade or the target level of environmental quality, whichever is the stricter, not be violated. For further discussion of these alternatives, see Atkinson and Tietenberg (1987).

b.   The Initial Allocation of Permits

A major issue in designing a tradable pollution permit system is how to fashion the initial allocation of permits. One method is for the government to auction off the initial stock of permits. Several types of auction designs are possible. Perhaps the simplest is to have firms submit sealed bids for permits, with the permits sold to all the winning bidders at the bid price for the last permit sold (the clearing price) and the proceeds retained by government.[11] The problem with this method is that it might draw considerable political resistance from the preauction polluters, who would be forced to pay possibly large sums of money for rights to pollute that they previously enjoyed for free.

---

11. This type of auction is known to encourage strategic behavior in the sense that bidders will understate their willingness to pay if they believe their bid could be the lowest accepted bid. An alternative auction mechanism that avoids this problem is to award the permits to the highest bidder, but at the price bid by the second-highest bidder. A bidder has no incentive to understate its willingness to pay under this alternative because its own bid never affects the price it pays. See, for example, Hanley, Shogren, and White (1997, pp. 146–147). On the issue whether to auction or give away the permits for free, see Cramton and Kerr (1998). '

An alternative method that would remedy this problem would be to distribute the initial stock of permits free of charge to existing polluters in proportion to their currently allowable level of emissions. In fact, a similar result could be obtained by auctioning off the initial stock of permits as before and distributing the proceeds of the auction to the preauction polluters in proportion to their preauction allowable level of emissions. This auction is termed "the Hahn-Noll zero-revenue auction" and is discussed in Ortolano (1997, pp. 227–229). If this scheme is deemed to be too generous to polluters, then only a portion of the auction revenues need be returned to them.

c.   Other Factors that Affect the Efficiency of Trading

There are several strategies government can adopt to facilitate the efficient functioning of a tradable pollution permit system: limiting the number of permits issued; refraining from making unexpected changes in the number of permits, allowing permits to be usable in future years (time banking), making rights granted to permit holders unambiguous and stable, confiscating permits only under extreme circumstances (and, preferably, rarely), avoiding high transaction costs, and enforcing permit trading rules. See Hahn and Noll (1990). In general, adherence to these strategies can be expected to increase industry's willingness to participate in markets for tradable pollution permits.

Several practical factors may, nevertheless, impede the efficient operation of a tradable pollution permit system. First, where permit markets are characterized by bilateral, sequential trades under conditions of imperfect information—rather than by multilateral, simultaneous trades under conditions of perfect information, as assumed by economic theory—participants often make early suboptimal trades that considerably reduce future cost-saving opportunities. See Hanley, Shogren, and White (1997, pp. 147–150). Second, because of imperfect information, the trading of emissions permits may entail significant search costs as willing buyers and sellers attempt to identify each other. However, where tradable permit markets are well established, as is true for the permit market for the precursors of acid rain, SO_2 and NO_X, these limitations disappear. Third, firms may, in some cases, treat their pollution permits as strategic inputs and therefore hoard them. Firms may, for example, be unwilling to sell pollution permits to business competitors. This may be a particular problem in permit markets that are already thin.

Despite their drawbacks, however, tradable pollution permits offer several advantages over economic charges.[12] First, tradable pollution permits reduce the

---

12. It is possible to develop more complicated economic instruments that combine tradable permits and economic charges. In one ingenious scheme, both an economic charge and an economic subsidy supplement a system of tradable permits. In effect, the economic charge and the economic subsidy serve as safety valves that limit the detrimental effects arising from government issuing too many or too few tradable permits. See Roberts and Spence (1976).

uncertainty as to whether the acceptable level of environmental quality will be attained, since the government can directly set the total emissions allowed by permit so as to achieve that level. (That is, the government can effectively "cap" the pollution.) In comparison, the government cannot be sure how polluting firms will respond to an emissions charge of a particular magnitude. Second, unlike emissions charges, tradable pollution permits do not need periodic adjustment to accommodate the effects of inflation or industrial expansion, since these changes will be directly reflected in a higher market-clearing permit price. Third, as previously noted, a system of tradable pollution permits can capture the spatial effects of pollution on environmental quality in a manner that, relative to a comparable set of emissions charges, is less administratively and politically objectionable. Fourth, as previously discussed, the financial burden on polluters can, if desired, be reduced either by distributing the initial stock of permits to polluting firms free of charge, or by redistributing some or all of the proceeds from the initial auction.

Tradable pollution permit systems have been widely deployed for air pollution in the United States, probably more so than in any other country. A prominent example is EPA's use of emission reduction credits under the Clean Air Act. As discussed in chapter 6, existing stationary sources of air pollution qualify for an emissions reduction credit by reducing their emissions below the maximum allowable by law. Beginning in 1977, EPA established an *offset policy*, which requires proposed new stationary sources desiring to locate in nonattainment areas—regions that violate national ambient air quality standards (for pollutants that the new source would discharge)—to obtain sufficient emission reduction credits (ERCs) from others to (more than) offset the new source's emissions. In 1979, EPA extended its program to single business and corporate organizations with multiple existing sources of pollution at a single site in a nonattainment area. This so-called bubble policy allows an organization to meet an aggregate emissions limit for its facilities (under an imaginary "bubble") rather than having to meet the limits for each pollution source under the bubble. This policy allows a firm to exchange emission reductions at facilities with low abatement costs for increased emissions at its facilities that are expensive to control. Another variant is *netting*, which allows existing sources seeking to expand to avoid stringent new emissions requirements if they reduce discharges elsewhere on site in an amount equal to the increased discharges caused by the expansion. Finally, *banking* allows a firm that earns emission reduction credits in one time period to retain them for its own future use or for future sale to another firm. All of these schemes—offsets, bubbles, netting, and banking—are limited to "trades" for a specific pollutant. No interpollutant trading is allowed, with the exception that for hazardous air pollutants, a single firm may increase its emissions of a relatively less hazardous pollutant, such as toluene, by reducing in equal amounts emissions of a more hazardous pollutant, such as benzene.

■ **NOTES**

1. For a more detailed examination of EPA's emission reduction credit policies, see chapter 6 and Ortolano (1997, pp. 229–232).

2. One criticism of tradable pollution permits that is sometimes raised by environmental groups is that they are objectionable on ethical grounds because they allow firms to purchase a legal right to pollute. Such criticism seems more a matter of semantics than substance, however, given that direct controls allow firms to pollute *for free* until they reach the discharge limit specified by the pollution standard.   ■

d. History, Evidence, and Analysis of Effectiveness of Emissions Trading

One of the initiatives to reduce acid rain put in place by the 1990 amendments to the Clean Air Act is a program of tradable permits for the release of SO_2 and NO_X from stationary sources. This is a classic "cap-and-trade" policy, administered by EPA, under which the total amount of allowable emissions is reduced each year. The goal of this program is to use emissions trading both to stimulate an overall reduction in emissions and to achieve such reduction at a lower overall cost than would be incurred if uniform reduction requirements were imposed on all sources. The following two articles discuss the emissions trading program for SO_2. The first, written when the program was in its infancy, explains historical origins and identifies expected outcomes. The second provides an evaluation some 3 years into the program.

Environmental Effects of SO_2 Trading and Banking
Dallas Burtraw and Erin Mansur

Source: Reprinted in part with permission from *Environmental Science and Technology* 33(20): 3489–3494 (1999). Copyright 1999, American Chemical Society.

INTRODUCTION

The widely acknowledged innovation of Title IV of the 1990 Clean Air Act Amendments (CAAA) is sulfur dioxide (SO_2) allowance trading, which is designed to encourage the electricity industry to minimize the cost of reducing emissions. Title IV sets an annual cap on average aggregate SO_2 emissions by electricity generators. The cap ultimately will fall to about one-half of emissions in 1980. Firms surrender one emission allowance for each ton of sulfur dioxide emitted. Allowances are allocated to individual facilities roughly in proportion to fuel consumption during the 1985–1987 period. Firms may transfer allowances among facilities or to other firms. In addition, the emission cap accommodates an allowance bank, enabling firms to accumulate surplus allowances for use in subsequent years.

The environmental consequences of trading have been the subject of considerable speculation and acrimony, especially in the Northeast, which is widely thought to be the recipient of pollution emitted by power plants in the Midwest....

Similarly, the environmental consequences of banking are ambiguous. To build up a bank, emissions are reduced in the near-term, leading to greater environmental benefits in the early years of the program. "Overcompliance" to date has been trumpeted by the Environmental Protection Agency as a measure of success. However, the depletion of the aggregate allowance bank that is expected to begin in 2000 will enable annual emissions to exceed annual allowance allocations for several years and is likely to ignite unfavorable opinions from environmental advocates.

The SO_2 program now serves as an international model for reducing the costs of pollution reduction. In September 1998, the EPA announced another substantial trading program for NO_x emissions that will affect electric utilities in 22 eastern states and which is explicitly based on the "success" of the SO_2 program. The proposed NO_x program differs from the SO_2 program because states would opt in or out of a regional trading program. Also, banking of emission allowances would be restricted due to concern about NO_x as a precursor to ozone, which is an episodic pollution problem....

We used an integrated assessment computer model to evaluate changes in emissions of SO_2, atmospheric concentrations of sulfates and deposition of sulfur, and public health benefits from reduced exposure to SO_2 and particulate matter. We assessed geographic and temporal changes at the state level that result from trading and banking and compared them with estimated cost savings.

In brief, we find a sizable geographic and temporal shift in emissions, in some states over 20% of emissions, due to trading and banking. However, the geographic consequences are not consistent with the fears of the program's critics. By holding aggregate emissions constant at the expected levels obtained under the program, pollutant concentrations decrease and health benefits actu-

ally increase in the East and Northeast due to trading. The expected result is health related benefits nationally of nearly $125 million in 2005 as compared to a scenario with equal aggregate emissions that did not allow trading. Deposition of sulfur in the eastern regions also decreases by a slight amount as a result of trading, even in New York State. Meanwhile, cost savings from trading totals $531 million, about 37% of compliance cost in 2005.

Banking has a predictable effect on the timing of emissions and the benefits of emission reductions, but the geographic pattern of emission changes is not simple. In 1995, emission reductions due to banking led uniformly to decreased concentrations and deposition. Some states reduce emissions in 2005, but there is an overall increase, uniformly leading to increased concentrations and deposition.

BACKGROUND

Economists urge the use of market-based approaches such as emission permit trading because they are expected to control pollution at a lower cost than traditional command-and-control approaches. Rather than forcing firms to emit SO_2 at a uniform rate or to install specific control technology, the opportunity for trading should provide an incentive for low-cost firms to assume a relatively greater share of emission reductions.

Banking is thought to offer similar opportunities for cost savings by offering firms flexibility in timing their compliance activities. Title IV is implemented in two phases. The first phase began in 1995 and affected the largest coal-fired power plants. The second phase will begin in 2000 and will tighten average emission rates and affect several hundred additional facilities. A firm may overcomply at one facility (a frequent occurrence during the first phase of the program) to create an allowance surplus that can be sold or used to delay further investments at other facilities.

Ultimately, total emissions will be cut about in half; however, the full effect of the emission reductions will not be felt until about 2010, when the allowance bank built up in Phase I is depleted. To date, the program has achieved full compliance, and a substantial bank is accumulating, primarily for use in Phase II....

DISCUSSION

The emission changes we identify only pertain to trading and banking, which are only a small part of the story with respect to the overall impact of the SO_2 program. Overall, the program will result in dramatic emission reductions of nearly 50%.

Furthermore, it is important to note that the overall emission reductions might not otherwise have been achieved without the opportunity to trade and bank. The flexibility offered by these aspects of the program led to significant decreases in cost and made the program economically affordable and politi-

cally acceptable. Finally, this analysis leaves aside entirely an evaluation of the proper level of emission reductions and the question of whether environmental resources and public health are adequately protected.

These findings do not generalize to other potential trading programs, but the questions do. In particular, one cannot be sanguine about the environmental effects of trading of NO_x emissions by electric utilities. Although NO_x emissions contribute to acidification and to the creation of secondary particulates in analogous fashion to SO_2, abatement strategies vary greatly; so the trading of NO_x allowances is unlikely to mirror the trading of SO_2 allowances. Also, NO_x contributes to a different set of problems, including ground-level ozone. What may generalize from the SO_2 experience is the opportunity for cost savings through allowance trading. Nonetheless, public policy should remain sensitive to the environmental consequences of trading, and programs should be designed to take this into account.

Are Cap and Trade Programs More Effective in Meeting Environmental Goals than Command-and-Control Alternatives?

A. Denny Ellerman

Source: http://web.mit.edu/ceepr/www/2003-015.pdf (2003). Also published in *Moving to Markets in Environmental Regulation: Lessons from Twenty Years of Experience*. Charles Kolstad and Jody Freeman (eds.). Oxford University Press, New York, 2006, pp. 48–62, excerpted with permission.

INTRODUCTION

Market-based instruments (MBI's) are advocated because of their presumed lower economic cost in comparison with conventional regulatory instruments. The environmental effectiveness of the MBI is typically assumed to be the same as that of the conventional alternative.... Recent experience with cap-and-trade systems has confirmed the economic advantages of MBI's and failed to find a degradation of environmental perfor-

mance. As a result, MBI's, and especially cap-and-trade systems, have become widely accepted in the policy community. Recognizing this circumstance, opponents of the use of MBIs tend to attack the assumption that the environmental performance is equal.... Their argument is that, while the economic performance may be better, the environmental performance is worse, and that the increased environmental damages outweigh the savings in abatement cost.

This paper makes the contrary argument that the experience with the cap-and-trade programs suggests that at least this form of MBI may be more environmentally effective than the usual command-and-control alternatives in addition to being more economically efficient. The evidence rests mainly on the SO_2 cap-and-trade system created by Title IV of the 1990 Clean Air Act Amendments (also known as the Acid Rain Program), but corroborating evidence emerges from the Northeastern NO_x Budget Program and the RECLAIM programs for trading NO_x and SO_2 emissions in the Los Angeles Basin....

FOUR ENVIRONMENTALLY ADVANTAGEOUS FEATURES

Four features describe the environmental performance of the Acid Rain Program. First, a large reduction of emissions was accomplished rather quickly—in the fifth year following passage of the enabling legislation. Second, the schedule of emission reduction was accelerated significantly as a result of banking. Third, no exemptions, exceptions, or relaxations from the program's requirements were granted. Four, the "hot spots" that were feared to result from emissions trading have not appeared....

The program caused a significant reduction of SO_2 emissions relatively quickly: in the fifth year following enactment and the first year in which the program was effective. Moreover, most of the reduction observed in 1995 was due to banking, which was not mandated, but a form of voluntary, early action on the part of program participants. Banking implies that the early "overcompliance" will be followed by later "under-compliance," as can be observed in the first three years of Phase II; however, if a positive discount rate is attached to the timing of emission reductions, this behavior constitutes a net gain. During the entire five years of Phase I, emissions were reduced by

twice as much as was required to meet the Phase I cap. On a yearly basis, the annual emission reduction has increased steadily from 3.9 million tons in the first year, 1995, to 4.4 million tons in 1999, the last year of Phase I, and to 6.9 million tons in 2002, a 77% increase in abatement by the eighth year.

EPA often notes that Title IV has achieved 100% compliance.... What is meant is that the program was implemented without the granting of the exemptions, exceptions, or relaxations of the regulatory requirement that are typically issued to avoid the undue hardship that can result when a more or less uniform mandate is imposed on sources exhibiting cost heterogeneity. Since the sources incurring less onerous costs never step forward to request more stringent regulation and the regulator does not have the information or will to impose a compensating tightening of the standard on these units, deviations from the presumed performance are all in one direction. The Acid Rain Program avoided this loosening bias through the trading mechanism, which automatically provided compensating reductions and made them cheaper than seeking some form of regulatory exemption.

The term "hot spots" refers to the possibility that the required emission reductions might be made in less critical areas as a result of emissions trading. A well-designed trading program would not allow hot spots, but the practical requirements of program design and implementation will often allow this possibility. In the Acid Rain Program, the fear was that the required emission reductions would not be made in the Midwest, which was the source of the emissions most responsible for acidification in the Northeast, but in other areas such as the Southeast. As it turned out, most of the emission reductions did take place in the Midwest. Sources in the eight main Midwestern states (PA, WV, OH, IN, IL, KY, TN, MO) have provided about 80% of the nationwide emission reduction achieved by Title IV while accounting for about 50% of current emissions and about 60% of what emissions would have been absent Title IV.

It is hard to imagine an alternative command-and-control program that would have had equal environmental performance, even assuming that such a program could have achieved the legislative consensus accorded to Title IV after nearly a decade of stalemated command-and-control proposals. Although there is surprisingly little ex post evaluation of the performance of command-and-control regulations, they are typically not characterized by quick implementation with significant emission reductions relatively soon after enactment, nor by voluntary actions that have the effect of accelerating required emission reductions. More usually, implementation occurs only after a long period of regulatory rulemaking, administrative proceedings, and litigation as participants seek to shape the rules and to gain some form of relaxation and competitive advantage over other firms.

■ NOTES

1. Cap-and-trade programs can be more complicated than they seem. The companion program for NO_X, for example, is complicated by the fact that the same amount of NO_X can lead to different amounts of ozone production, depending on the season, temperature, time of day, sunlight, the presence of VOCs, and other meteorological conditions. This suggests that changing fees (or trading amounts)—in other words placing temporal and geographical restraints on trading depending on the conditions enumerated above—would be required to achieve the health-relevant reductions in ozone concentrations and exposure. See Mauzerall et al. (2005).

2. Not all commentators agree that indirect controls are more economically efficient in practice than direct controls. Cole and Grossman (1999, p. 937) argue that, "where abatement costs are relatively low and monitoring costs are relatively high, command-and-control is likely to be as efficient and effective as effluent taxes or a tradable emissions program." Further, they argue that administrative cost differentials between economic instruments and standards may offset the compliance cost advantages of economic instruments, rendering the latter superior. See Cole and Grossman (2002).

3. For a valuable analysis of environmental policy instruments, see Friedman et al. (2000). See also Stewart (2001).

4. For a thoughtful discussion of the strengths and weakness of indirect controls versus direct controls, see "Comparing Standards, Emission Fees, and Transferable Rights" and "The Limits of Economic Incentives" in Stensvaag (1999, pp. 588–593).

5. In a survey article on the relationship between environmental policy and technological change, Jaffe, Newell, and Stavins (2002) identify the following barriers, among others, to encouraging the diffusion of less-polluting technology: (1)

inadequate information, (2) uncertainty (in the effectiveness or net costs or benefits of adopting environmental technology), (3) constrained capital financing (necessary to fund environmental investments), and (4) inability to appropriate all (i.e., profit from) the positive adoption spillovers (that benefit others) from environmental investments. Encouraging environmental innovation, as distinct from diffusion, is further complicated by the riskiness of innovation in general.

6. Scholars commenting on the merits of different types of environmental policy instruments have tended to fall into one of four categories: (1) those who analyze policy options according to their effects on economic costs, usually implicitly assuming static efficiency with no mention of the effects on technological innovation; (2) those who do mention the effect on innovation as an evaluation criterion, but do not incorporate it into their analysis; (3) those who simply state, without discussion or analysis, that market-based instruments are more likely than command-and-control regulation to favor innovation, both because market-based instruments allow industry greater discretion in how to respond and because they can provide a financial incentive to exceed targeted pollution reduction goals; and (4) those who undertake a serious analysis of the dynamic effects of innovation, recognizing that the stringency of a regulatory strategy—whether it be command and control or market-based—will be a major determinant of whether innovation is preferentially promoted by one approach over another. For a sharp contrast in commentaries about instrument choices and approaches for addressing environmental pollution, compare Jaffe, Newell, and Stavins (2002), Stewart (2000, 2001), Steinzor (1998, 2001), and Driesen (2003, 2004, 2005).

7. Often, the advocates of one approach will criticize another without applying the same critical analysis to their preferred option. Richard Stewart, for example, has criticized command-and-control regulation for preventing the desirable exit of old, inefficient, polluting firms:

[L]egislators and environmental regulators also tend to impose disproportionately more stringent command burdens on new products and processes than on existing ones, thus discouraging the turnover of capital stock necessary for innovation and perpetuating older products and processes that yield greater pollution (Stewart, 2001, p. 6).

Stewart, an advocate of market-based controls, does not discuss the fact that emissions trading does exactly the same thing by allowing older, less efficient firms to opt out of reducing their emissions by purchasing pollution credits. This same tendency to identify problems with direct controls without acknowledging their corollaries among indirect controls can be found in Jaffe, Newell, and Stavins (2002).

8. Hemmelskamp (2000), examining empirical data from Germany, has analyzed the assertion of neoclassical economists that environmental taxes (charges) necessarily

lead to greater innovation than command-and-control standards. He finds little support for this conclusion, which appears to be based on the unsubstantiated assumption, articulated by Jaffe and Palmer (1997), that environmental expenditures divert funds from the research and development necessary to spur technological innovation. In fact, Hemmelskamp observes that the firms participating in his study ascribed little importance to research and development in their implementation of environmentally friendly technology.

One explanation may be the current dominance of end-of-pipe technologies, which are essentially merely incremental improvements to existing technological solutions, so that R&D is only required to a limited extent. This is supported by the significant negative relationship between the innovation risk and the importance of the development of environmental friendly products as an innovation objective (Hemmelskamp, 2000, p. 19).

In other words, without sufficient incentive to channel their research and development toward more fundamental process or product innovation, firms are likely to focus on easily achievable, low-risk, incremental advances. Years previously, Ashford, Heaton, and Priest (1979) questioned the commonplace assumption that funds expended for environmental compliance would have in fact been used for research and development dedicated to new product development or other profit-generating activity.

9. Jaffe, Newell, and Stavins (2002) argue that there is no generalizable statement that can be made about whether command-and-control or market-driven incentives will be more likely to foster innovation or diffusion. Acknowledging that command-and-control approaches can induce innovation, they note that when a firm undertakes such innovation for environmental purposes, it may do so at the opportunity cost of forgoing innovation focused on expanding its business. This certainly can be true, but that does not mean it is (necessarily) undesirable. The decision to favor one type of innovation over another is a social policy choice. If the goal is to encourage less-polluting products and processes, and to discourage their more-polluting counterparts, the nature of business-related innovation will be asked to change accordingly. Moreover, the need to reduce pollution often offers an opportunity to take business technology in new, and perhaps more profitable, directions.

10. David Driesen (1998, 2005) raises the central question of whether, as alleged by many neoclassical environmental economists, emissions trading stimulates the necessary innovation for significant environmental improvements.

If a regulation allows facilities to use trading to meet standards, the low-cost facilities tend to provide more of the total reductions than they would provide under a comparable traditional [i.e., uniform emissions] regulation [because, in practice, traditional regulation would seek a (uniform) compromise among firms incurring different costs for achieving the regulation, while under trading, firms who could reduce emissions more cheaply would do so]. Conversely, the high-cost facilities will provide less of the total required reductions than they would have under a comparable traditional regulation. The low-cost facilities probably have a greater ability to provide reductions without substantial [additional] innovation than high-cost facilities. A high-cost facility may need to innovate to escape the high costs of routine compliance; the low-cost facility does not have this same motivation. Hence, emissions trading, by shifting reductions from high-cost to low cost-facilities, may lessen the incentives for innovation. (Driesen, 1998, p. 335)

Driesen may or may not be correct, depending on how much reduction the cap in the cap-and-trade regulations require. The low-cost firms may be more modern, more inherently innovative, and easily capable of more innovation.

More important, Driesen's analysis should be taken a step further. If technology forcing were a central tenet of regulatory design, the designers of uniform emissions restrictions would not only be willing to have the regulations phase out old, high-cost firms, they would also push the next generation of firms to do even better. Under this scenario, the low-cost firms would not have many pollution credits to spare, but would have a continuous incentive to innovate. Thus, emissions trading encourages the regulations to be *less* technology forcing than they might otherwise be under a more aggressive strategy (See Ashford, Ayers, and Stone, 1985 and the discussion in chapter 13.) This underscores the importance of stringency, not only in regulatory design, but also in the analysis of alternatives. Different alternatives can look better or worse, depending on upon what level of stringency is assumed.

11. Driesen (2005) also points out that the allegation that cap-and-trade provides an incentive for continual innovation is without merit. Even with a declining cap, the incentive for innovation ends when eventually the cap is reached. This is, of course, also true with mandated performance standards.

12. In a study of power plants by Taylor, Rubin, and Hounshell (2005), the authors found that "[i]ncreased diffusion of the technology results in significant and predictable operating cost reductions in existing systems, as well as notable efficiency improvements and capital cost reductions in new systems" (p. 697) lending empirical support to (the weak form of) the Porter Hypothesis. They further concluded that "the case provides little evidence for the claim that cap-and-trade instruments induce innovation more than other instruments" (p. 697) because most of the innovation occurred before the 1990 amendments and was spurred on by stringent regulation.

13. For a comprehensive critique of recommended changes within the existing regulatory framework, see a variety of reports written in the 1980s by the multistakeholder Technology, Innovation and Economics Committee of the National Advisory Council on Environmental Policy and Technology (NACEPT, 1991, 1992, 1993).

14. Confusion about the nature and history of command-and-control regulation pervades the literature. For example, many critiques of technology-based standards

wrongly state or imply that these standards *require* the adoption of specific technology to attain compliance with environmental law (i.e., that they are *design*, or *specification*, standards). See, for example, Hockenstein et al. (1997). In fact, very few technology-based standards are of this nature. Most are *performance* standards. That is, they are established with reference to the (pollution reduction) performance deemed achievable through the application of particular technology or practices, but they leave the regulated entity free to attain that performance level through any means at its disposal. (The national technology-based effluent limitations set by EPA under the Clean Water Act, for example, typically are expressed simply as a numeric discharge limit; it is up to the individual discharger to determine how best to meet that limit.)

15. It is also argued that command-and-control systems are necessarily fragmented and uncoordinated (Stewart, 1999, 2001). This need not be the case. During the Carter administration, the heads of the major environmental and public health regulatory agencies (EPA, OSHA, CPSC, and FDA) worked closely together through the Interagency Regulatory Liaison Group (IRLG), which helped to coordinate regulatory policy and standard setting. The IRLG was disbanded by the Reagan administration precisely because its absence was likely to reduce the level of cooperation and integration among the different regimes and agencies, thus making regulation less effectual. Ample opportunities for agency coordination, such as coordinated permitting, remain. That more has not been made of them is largely indicative of a dearth of political will and not of an inherent structural defect.

16. Aidt, Skousgaard, and Dutta (2004) analyze the differing pathways taken by the United States and western Europe as limitations on air emissions have become more stringent. They argue that both have moved away from uniform emission standards, but in different ways. While the United States is increasingly emphasizing tradable permits, the approach favored by industry, western Europe is increasingly moving toward emissions taxes whose revenues can be used to further improve the environment, an approach favored by environmental nongovernmental organizations (NGOs). For evidence that the United States and Europe have effectively "traded places" when it comes to stringency and enforcement of environmental laws in general (with Europe now taking a more aggressive regulatory approach), see Vogel (2003a, b). ∎

C. INDIRECT CONTROLS II: "POSITIVE" INCENTIVES

One obvious alternative to attaching a financial penalty to the generation of pollution would be to reward firms for reducing the amount (and/or the toxicity) of pollution they generate. Such rewards could, for example, take the form of direct grants-in-aid, tax credits, or tax reductions.

1. Economic Subsidies

In the most general terms, one might consider providing a monetary subsidy to firms based on their pollution reductions. In theory, the consequences of an economic charge and an economic subsidy are equivalent. This can be seen by referring to figure 12.3. An economic charge of t^* per unit of pollution induces firms to reduce emissions from E' to E^*, and no further, since the cost of additional pollution reductions below E^* would exceed the economic charge. Suppose that the economic charge t^* were removed and replaced by a subsidy payment of t^* to firms per unit of pollution reduction.[13] In that case, firms would still reduce total emissions from E' to E^*, since they would profit economically from that reduction. Because the subsidy payment would be less than the cost of reducing emissions below E^*, the firms would have no economic incentive to reduce their emissions below that level.

Although both will operate to correct externalities, an economic subsidy suffers from two serious disadvantages relative to an economic charge. First, while a pollution charge will reduce the profitability of polluting firms and typically induce some of them to exit a competitive industry, a pollution-reduction subsidy will increase firm profitability and stimulate firm entry and industry expansion. [In terms of competitive industry dynamics, the subsidy for pollution reduction will shift the average cost curve downward for firms in the industry and increase their profits, but that will stimulate new entrants into the industry and drive down prices to the firms' minimum level of average cost. At the new equilibrium, firm output and pollution levels will be lower than prior to the subsidy, but because of new entries, industry output will be higher, and it is conceivable that total industry emissions levels could be higher as well (see Baumol and Oates, 1988, pp. 218–228).] Consequently, an economic subsidy will generally result in a greater number of polluting firms and a greater overall amount of pollution than would have resulted had an economic charge of equal magnitude been used instead. Second, an economic subsidy fails to provide the revenue-generating benefits of an economic charge. Indeed, the subsidy must *itself* be financed by an increase in government taxation of some type, with attendant market distortions and efficiency losses.

For these reasons, economic subsidies would be a poor choice as a general-purpose mechanism to promote reductions in pollution. On the other hand, subsidies could be an effective policy instrument if they were specifically targeted toward pollution-

---

13. We ignore here the serious administrative issue of determining the presubsidy level of pollution emitted by the firm and the potential strategic options available to the firm for obtaining larger subsidy payments. On these matters, see, for example, Kamien, Schwartz, and Dolbear (1966) and Wenders (1975).

reducing technologies. Technological and economic risks are major impediments to the successful development and adoption of pollution-reducing innovations. Grants to fund the research and development of promising, but high-risk, pollution-reducing technologies (particularly those R&D investments that private markets are unwilling to underwrite), low-interest loans to allow cash-strapped or marginal firms to adopt pollution-reducing innovations, and tax advantages for firms investing in pollution-reducing activities could all help to overcome these impediments.

Nevertheless, such subsidies, particularly tax allowance subsidies, must be implemented with care. Tax credits and accelerated depreciation allowances for investments in pollution control equipment, for example, arguably have been counterproductive.[14] Because they were designed to reward end-of-pipe methods of pollution control, but not other, typically more efficient means of reducing pollution, such as changing inputs or modifying the production process, these tax allowance subsidies have often induced firms to make suboptimal investment decisions and have actually discouraged investment in pollution prevention. (In France, by comparison, pollution prevention, as opposed to pollution control, is accorded accelerated depreciation.) In addition, a limitation of tax allowance subsidies in general is that the firms often most in need of financial assistance—namely, those firms that operate at a loss—are effectively precluded from taking advantage of tax allowance subsidies since they have no corporate income taxes to reduce.

▪ **NOTE**

1. While emission fees, marketable permits, and other "negative" market-based instruments continue to be advocated as alternatives to command-and-control regulation, the enthusiasm for subsidies has waned greatly. This might be partly explained by the fact that they clearly violate the Polluter Pays Principle. While a Coasean analysis (see chapter 3) could be used to argue against assigning responsibility for pollution abatement to any one party, including the polluter (in the absence of transaction costs)—thus vitiating the need for the Polluter Pays Principle—it has not been used to resurrect the case for subsidies. If products or energy resources are underpriced because pollution externalities are not included, and the consumer and the public thereby benefit economically, could a case be made for taxpayers sharing the burden of reducing pollution through public subsidies of abatement? What are the arguments against this rationale?   ▪

---

14. Tax credits result in a reduction of tax payments, while accelerated depreciation allowances for investment result in a postponement of tax payments (as a result of allowing fast write-offs for investments in pollution control). The economic benefits of accelerated depreciation allowances, then, arise through changes in the timing of tax payments by reducing the discounted net present value of tax liabilities. See Rajah and Smith (1993, pp. 51–53).

2. The Coordination of Tax Policy and Environmental Policy

The tendency of pollution control subsidies to discourage investment in pollution prevention is simply one example of a broader public policy issue: the imperfect coordination between tax policy and environmental policy. Often the two operate at cross-purposes, with the environment being the apparent loser. This can happen, as with the foregoing example, with tax policies that were designed to improve environmental performance (in this case at a time when end-of-pipe approaches were a favored strategy for pollution reduction). More commonly, this disjuncture occurs with policies that were not designed with environmental consequences in mind. One such example is the depletion allowance for natural resources, which permits firms to take a tax deduction for their investment in a natural resource as the resource is depleted.[15] The availability of a depletion allowance serves to make the extraction and use of virgin materials more profitable relative to the use of recycled materials. Moreover, in the case of hard-rock minerals, different minerals qualify for differing depletion rates. The four minerals allowed the highest depletion rate of 22% (compared with the average depletion rate of 12.1%) are among the most hazardous to human health and the environment: asbestos, uranium, lead, and mercury (Westin and Gaines, 1989, p. 765). The favorable depletion allowance for these hazardous materials provides a continuing incentive to utilize them in preference to other, safer materials.

In general, the tax system's treatment of production inputs, outputs, and development costs can have a profound influence on the choice of technology and thus has a potentially significant effect on the environment. For the most part, however, tax policies and strategies are developed without environmental goals in mind. Better coordination of environmental and tax policies would be a logical objective of any system of indirect environmental incentives.

Taxes have three general functions: (1) to raise revenue (which may or may not be used for environmental purposes), (2) to create incentives and disincentives to guide industrial activity, and (3) to address equity considerations (e.g., to implement the Polluter Pays Principle, or to achieve distributional fairness of environmental costs among industries and the general public).

In some industrial economies, investments in pollution control are given the more favorable tax treatment of accelerated depreciation while industrial investment in pollution prevention (input substitution, process redesign, product reformulation,

---

15. A depletion allowance for natural materials parallels the tax deduction granted for other capital assets as their economic value depreciates with use or over time. One difference, however, is that a percentage depletion allowance (unlike a cost depletion allowance) is unrelated to the taxpayer's investment in the resource. See Westin and Gaines (1989, pp. 763–765).

and the like) is depreciated in a straight-line fashion. To the extent that this occurs, there is a bias toward end-of-pipe approaches and a bias toward older firms (since they are the ones that are most likely to retrofit). Moreover, since no extra tax advantage accrues to a firm for devoting a higher percentage of its human resources to environmental matters or worker safety, the tax system biases firms toward a technological or capital investment solution, rather than the more creative use of human capital. Finally, it is widely understood that without carryover provisions, those firms not making profits are not aided by this public subsidy.

Tax deductions that subsidize undesirable activity may also detract from the effort to achieve environmental goals. Two particularly questionable examples are deductions for the cost of cleaning up industrial waste and the deduction of punitive damages imposed for egregious environmental misconduct. (See Westin and Gaines, 1989, pp. 759–762.) Tax deductions of this nature amount to a public subsidy for the polluter and arguably are socially undesirable.

Governments sometimes provide tax-exempt financing to the private sector for the construction and maintenance of waste treatment facilities. This encourages end-of-pipe approaches to pollution and relieves the pressure on industrial firms to engage in pollution prevention or source reduction.

These are just a few examples of tax policies that either encourage continued pollution or miss the opportunity for encouraging prevention of pollution.

■ **NOTE**

1. Richards (2000) argues that the benefits of alternative instruments for reducing pollution should be evaluated according to their impact on three types of costs: (1) the production costs borne by the polluting firm; (2) the implementation costs borne by government, such as information gathering, enforcement etc.; and (3) public finance impacts related to the administrative costs associated with revenue-raising activities from charges, etc. In addition, he argues that the legal and political constraints affecting the practical use of various policy instruments must be factored into the ultimate choice of instruments.   ■

3. Other "Positive" Instruments: Information Sharing, Technical Assistance, and Government Purchasing Practices

There are a variety of other government policies that can assist firms and citizens in achieving greater pollution control and prevention. Much can be accomplished through the creation and sharing of pertinent information. Government can, for example, sponsor research on the health and environmental effects of pollution and/or the development of pollution-reducing technologies. The government can also create and maintain databases on toxicity and/or environmental technology[16] and disseminate that information through the Internet and by means of conferences and workshops.

Providing citizens and workers with information about chemical releases and exposures can be a powerful informational tool, as it helps create political and economic pressure for reducing pollution reduction.[17] Mandating industry disclosure of such information, through what are often called right-to-know laws, is a form of direct control, and is discussed in detail in chapter 10. Some state governments, such as Massachusetts, New Jersey, and Illinois, have created nonregulatory offices of technical assistance that directly advise and help industries with pollution reduction. The resultant technical assistance programs have taken a variety of forms, such as demonstration projects that showcase better pollution reduction activities, or workshops that facilitate the sharing of technical information among firms and industries. In addition, some states provide waste recovery facilities and deposit-refund systems for recyclable materials (see EPA, 2001).

Applying life-cycle principles, state and federal governments can also lead the market in stimulating environmentally sound products and services through their purchasing power. The Environmental Protection Agency has established a program to further these goals.

---

16. See the discussion in chapter 13 on the Pollution Prevention Information Clearinghouse established by the Pollution Prevention Act.

17. This is sometimes called "the third wave in pollution control policy" after regulation and economic incentives. See Tietenberg (1998). Also see Graham (2001) and Graham and Miller (2001). For a somewhat contrarian view, see Bui (2005).

Environmentally Preferable Purchasing Program
Environmental Protection Agency
Source: EPA Report 742-R-99-001, June 1999.

During the past 20 years, U.S. federal agencies have operated under a series of federal statutes and Presidential Executive Orders mandating the purchase of products and services that pose fewer burdens on the environment. As a result, federal agencies are increasihgly selecting products based in part on environmental attributes such as recycled-content percentages, energy- and water-efficiency ratings, lower toxicity, and the use of renewable resources. Many state and local governments are embarking upon similar initiatives. The U.S. Environmental Protection Agency's (EPA's) Environmentally Preferable Purchasing (EPP) Program is assisting these efforts and documenting federal, state, and local government attempts to implement environmentally preferable purchasing strategies.

According to Executive Order 13101, Greening the Government Through Waste Prevention, Recycling, and Federal Acquisition (September 1998), environmentally preferable purchasing means selecting "products or services that have a lesser or reduced effect on human health and the environment when compared with competing products or services that serve the same purpose." An earlier Executive Order, Federal Acquisition, Recycling and Waste Prevention (October 20, 1993), initiated EPA's work on environmental preferability by mandating EPA to develop environmentally preferable purchasing guidance for federal agencies. EPA proposed seven guiding principles and provided further clarification to help federal agencies comply with the Executive Order mandates.

EPA recommends that agencies select products to maximize beneficial environmental attributes and to minimize adverse environmental effects consistent with price and performance considerations. EPA encourages agencies to evaluate the multiple environmental impacts of every product throughout the product's life cycle—raw material acquisition, manufacture, packaging and distribution, use, and disposal. Environmental impacts can include: 1) Energy-efficiency, 2) Recycled content, 3) Water-efficiency, 4) Resource conservation, 5) Waste prevention, 6) Renewable material percentages, 7) Adverse effects to workers, animals, plants, air, water, and soil, 8) Toxic material content, 9) Packaging and 10) Transportation.

When these products are available, Federal Acquisition Regulations require federal agencies to purchase products meeting the United States Environmental Protection Agency's guidelines for Environmentally Preferable Products as follows:

Pollution Prevention. Consideration of environmental preferabiliy should begin early in the process and be rooted in the ethic of pollution prevention that strives to eliminate or reduce, up front, potential risks to human health and the environment.

Life-cycle Perspective. Environmental preferability should reflect life-cycle consideration of products and services to the extent feasible.

Magnitude of Impact. Environmental preferability should consider the scale (global versus local) and temporal aspects (reversibility) of the impacts.

Local Conditions. Environmental preferability should be tailored to local conditions where appropriate.

Competition. Environmental attributes of products or services should be an important factor or "subfactor" in competition among vendors, where appropriate.

Product Attribute Claims. Agencies need to examine product attribute claims.

Multiple Attributes. A product or service's environmental preferability is a function of multiple environmental attributes: energy reduction, source reduction, indoor air quality, waste reduction, recycling program, and recycled content.

■ NOTES

1. For a general description of the opportunities in "green" (or "environmentally preferable") purchasing, see Verschoor and Reijnders (1997). For applications in California, see Swanson et al. (2005).

2. Green purchasing is increasingly being used to promote the development of cleaner technology and is finding its way into international voluntary standards such as ISO 14000 as a way of encouraging greener inputs, final products, and manufacturing and industrial processes, and to influence ISO 14001 regarding environmental management systems. See Chen (2005). ■

D. LIABILITY STANDARDS

Another set of policies that can provide incentives for pollution reduction is the system of laws that impose monetary liability on those who can be shown to have caused health or environmental harm. This system of laws is a disparate one that comprises both statutory and common law standards. Claims for personal injury or property damage alleged to have resulted from environmental pollution are usually brought under state tort law, as are product liability claims against chemical manufacturers (see chapter 4). Claims for injury or disease from *occupational* exposure to toxic chemicals, on the other hand, are generally handled under state (and sometimes federal) workers' compensation statutes. These statutes generally provide compensation without proof of employer negligence, but place limits on the amount of monetary recovery and disallow recovery for pain and suffering. See Ashford (2006). Another important form of liability is that imposed by federal or state statutes for the cost of remediating contamination by hazardous substances. Chief among these statutes, of course, is the Comprehensive Environmental Response, Compensation, and Liability Act, commonly known as the federal Superfund law (see chapter 9). The private insurance industry plays a role in the practical application of all of these liability systems because many firms seek insurance coverage for some or all of these areas of potential liability.

Although all of these liability programs are focused on providing compensation for, or remediation of, injuries caused by chemical exposures, they also play a role in deterring the behavior that may lead to such exposures. Quite simply, the more certain it is that a firm will be held liable for monetary damages or cleanup costs as a result of engaging in some risk-generating activity, the stronger the financial incentive for the firm to take steps to reduce that risk (and thus reduce or eliminate the likelihood of being held liable in the future). The federal Superfund statute, CERCLA, which imposes strict and (presumptively) joint and several liability on those who send waste to a site that later becomes the subject of a Superfund cleanup, sends a relatively strong deterrent signal. Tort or worker compensation liability for health damage caused by exposure to chemicals, however, presents an unclear incentive for reducing pollution or accidents. This is especially the case for *long-term health effects* of exposure to chemicals, such as chronic disease, that are difficult if not impossible to link to specific chemical exposures. Here potential liability often does not present a significant incentive to reduce pollution. It also appears that liability for even relatively near-term damage that is due to sudden and accidental releases does not provide a particularly strong incentive for reducing risk (see the discussion of chemical accidents in chapter 13). Moreover, insurance actually can remove (or reduce) the risk averseness of high-risk operators. And where insurance is not available or is prohibitively expensive, firms are often insufficiently self-insured.

Liability, Innovation, and Safety in the Chemical Industry
Nicholas A. Ashford and Robert F. Stone

Source: Peter W. Huber and Robert E. Litan (eds.), *The Liability Maze*, 1991, Washington, D.C.: Brookings Institution, pp. 392–402, excerpted with permission.

THE DEGREE OF DETERRENCE

...[O]f the several objectives of the liability system, deterrence is the most relevant to concerns about stimulating the adoption or development of safer products and processes. The liability costs stemming from chemical harm provide a signal to the chemical firm and to other private actors to engage in hazard prevention activities.[62]

The deterrence effects of the liability system need to be examined with great care. From an economic perspective, optimal deterrence is achieved by the internalization of all social costs of chemical production and use. In general, overdeterrence may arise if costs that exceed or are unrelated to the social costs are imposed on private actors. However, we argue that the imposition of punitive damages should not be confused with overdeterrence, because those damages serve a moral and symbolic function, satisfying a need for just punishment of wrongdoers. Good-faith and knowledgeable chemical firms have little to fear from punitive damages, because it is highly unlikely that such damages would be imposed on them. Never-

theless, the specter of punitive damages not only encourages good-faith industrial activity but also prods the firm to gain the knowledge required to assess the risks of its technology.

Many factors influence the firm's response to the expected value of economic costs associated with chemical harm, such as the role of insurance, the extent to which the firm produces a diversified mix of products, and the desire of the firm to maintain its reputation as a good corporate citizen.[63] Table [12.1] presents some possible scenarios for the firm under which it feels varying degrees of motivation to engage in hazard-reducing activity, including the search for safer products and processes.

Firms that are fully insured for worker injuries through workers' compensation have little incentive to engage in preventive activities, beyond an interest in reducing the wage premium for risk that workers demand; the only exceptions are those rare cases where compensation premiums are a high percentage of the cost of doing business and the firm is merit-rated. The same is true for injuries to consumers for chemical firms insured by product liability insurance,[65] and for injuries

62. This is one of the essential lessons to be derived from the earlier examination of the innovation process. Acquiring information and engaging in innovative search are costly to the firm. The uncertainty of liability costs attracts the attention of management and redirects its activities to exploit profitable safety opportunities that arise from the avoidance of these tort system costs. Liability awards not only bring to the attention of industry the advantages of minimizing the hazardous effects of technology but also raise the importance of safety in technological planning in general.

63. One important factor, not usually relevant for *acute* chemical injuries (except perhaps in Bhopal-

sized accidents), is the size of the chemical firm's assets in relation to the magnitude of its tort liability burden and the ease with which the firm can evade that burden by seeking bankruptcy protection.

65. However, the fact that product liability insurance has become exceedingly expensive in recent years, and often become unavailable, has forced many firms to self-insure. These consequences of the insurance "crisis" have generally served to stimulate risk-prevention incentives (though they may be accompanied by some efficiency losses as well)....

Table 12.1
Motivation for Developing or Adopting Safer Products and Processes[a]

Item	Economic costs from compensating damage awards			Punitive damages	Reputation	Likely overall incentives
	Expected losses		Reasonably likely upper bound to losses for self-insured firms with few products or hazards (risk averse)			
	All firms	Self-insured firms with many products or hazards				
Under insurance						
Workers' compensation (workers)	—			$(+)^b$	+	—
Product liability (consumers)	$(-)^c$			+	+	+
Enterprise (others)	$(-)^d$			+	+	+
Without insurance						
Workers		+	++	+	+	++
Consumers		+	++	+	+	++
Others		+	++	+	+	++

Notes:
a. — denotes great underdeterrence; – denotes some underdeterrence; + denotes slight deterrence; ++ denotes modest deterrence, but still less than optimal.
b. Available as a surcharge in a minority of jurisdictions.
c. Possibly unavailable or very expensive.
d. Possibly available for injuries; unavailable for chronic disease.

to others for chemical firms insured through enterprise liability insurance. Through its risk-spreading properties, insurance shifts the total social costs of chemical damage away from the firm, causing underdeterrence. As regards worker injuries or enterprise liability, the incentives that do exist for insured firms are probably directed to limiting the effects of an accident once it occurs (such as providing fire extinguishers) rather than to preventing it in the first place.[66] Furthermore, minimal loss prevention advice originates with the insurance carriers, who usually lack the requisite technical and scientific expertise to suggest technological changes in chemical products and processes.[67]

66. However, some, though incomplete, deterrence is provided even if the chemical firm has product liability insurance, since many consumers recognize and value safety features and are willing to pay extra for them. Similarly, chemical firms with workers' compensation and enterprise insurance are still motivated to prevent safety hazards that threaten to damage or destroy their own property (though that is usually insured as well). Finally, the terms of most insurance policies contain some deterrence features of their own, such as coinsurance and deductibles, but these clearly are of secondary importance.
67. "Insurers have little knowledge of the loss-prevention or loss-protection technologies available to the insured chemical handlers. Interviews with underwriters reveal little interest in developing their own knowledge base about either technologies or

Probability of expenditures

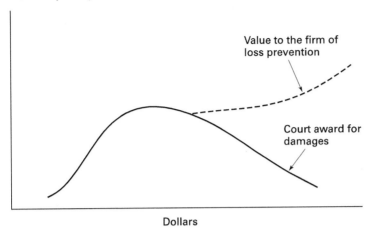

Value to the firm of
loss prevention

Court award for
damages

Dollars

Figure 12.6
Probability of court awards and resources devoted to prevention by a risk-averse firm. (Source: Nicholas A. Ashford and Robert F. Stone, "Liability, Innovation, and Safety in the Chemical Industry," in Peter W. Huber and Robert E. Litan, eds., *The Liability Maze*, 1991. Washington, D.C.: Brookings Institution Press.)

As for chemical firms that manufacture many chemical products, the expected value of economic losses due to chemical harm to workers, consumers, and bystanders provides a degree of deterrence, at least insofar as the firms are not insured and must self-insure. For the uninsured chemical firm that manufactures few products, it is the reasonably likely upper bound of a loss, rather than the expected value of the loss, that drives the firm's preventive activities. This extra incentive reflects the risk averseness of those firms against business disruption and sudden catastrophic economic loss. Such firms will go an extra measure to prevent chemical harm, but

that should not be confused with overdeterrence. Rather, when firms are insured, there is underdeterrence.

In figure [12.6], the smooth curve depicts the *hypothetical* probability of an award as a function of its size. The value to the firm of avoiding damage is identical with this curve for small awards. As awards increase in size, the risk-averse firm will increasingly value risk reduction and will spend increasing amounts to avoid liability, as shown in the dashed curve.[68] The capping of awards (shown as a solid vertical line in figure [12.7] and/or risk spreading through insurance (where premiums are collected, as shown by

losses." (Katzman 1988, 86.) But the recent development of risk retention groups, group captives, and other user-financed insurance mechanisms promises to improve risk management skills and to provide a payoff for the firms that participate. See Ashford, Moran, and Stone 1989, V-5, V-6.

68. One possible functional relationship is: $V = p \times (d + k_1 d^2 + \cdots + k_n d^{n+1})$, where V is the value to the firm of avoiding damage costs; p is the probability of damage; and d is the severity of damage. The firm's risk averseness is reflected in the higher-order terms of this expression.

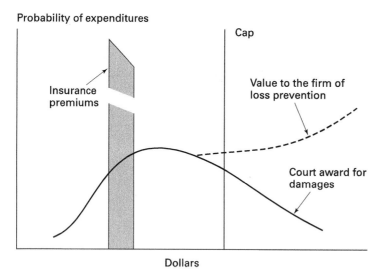

Probability of expenditures

Cap

Insurance premiums

Value to the firm of loss prevention

Court award for damages

Dollars

Figure 12.7
Probability of court awards and resources devoted to prevention by a risk-averse firm (illustrating the effects of insurance and caps on awards). (Source: Nicholas A. Ashford and Robert F. Stone, "Liability, Innovation, and Safety in the Chemical Industry," in Peter W. Huber and Robert E. Litan, eds., *The Liability Maze*, 1991. Washington, D.C.: Brookings Institution Press.)

the hatched area*) decreases the risk averseness of the firm and, hence, expenditures for developing or adopting safer products and processes.

Attempts to avoid liability claims (with or without the possibility of punitive damages) may drive either an uninsured or an insured firm to take special efforts for prevention. If so, the firm is responding not only to its expected economic losses but also to the value *it* places on maintaining a good reputation. Poor corporate images are avoided by good corporate citizens. Expenditures incurred by firms to develop safer products or processes may exceed the expected value of losses for not doing so or even the reasonably likely upper bound of a loss. That too should not be attributed to overdeterrence, since the

* [The area under the smooth curve for court-awarded damages and the hatched area are assumed to be equal.]

firm *values* the avoidance of liability beyond the immediate or monetizable economic costs. Similarly, risk-averse firms that decide not to market or use unsafe products or processes may do so because they value the avoidance of liability risk more than the net profits that might have been enjoyed. If the firms that decide not to market unsafe products or to use unsafe processes do not have the intellectual resources to develop new technology, they may suffer economically. However, other firms—notably new entrants—may develop new technologies and profit from them.

As we determined in the previous analysis, the liability system does not impose on the chemical firm even the expected value of the social costs of acute chemical injuries. Rather, it provides an underdeterrence for the development of safer products and processes. But though there is underdeterrence from an economic perspective, the deterrence that does occur because of prospective liability tends to promote safer technologies for those firms that value "doing the right thing."[69] Ensuring that the economic costs associated with acute chemical hazards are fully internalized would create even greater incentives.

SAFETY AND INNOVATIVE PERFORMANCE RELATED TO TORT LIABILITY

Although, as we have just concluded, tort liability provides inadequate deterrence in the area of acute chemical injuries, the tort system—in many cases, in combination with regulation—has stimulated the development of safer products and processes. For example, consumer products with potentially explosive containers (such as some former drain cleaners) have been removed from the market and replaced by safer alternatives, and almost all chemical products contain detailed warnings and instructions about their safe use so as to inform and protect the consumer.

The evidence of liability-induced chemical innovations is probably greatest in the area of process technology, but most of those innovations are incremental (though valuable) ones, and because of underdeterrence many have not been widely adopted as yet. Examples of incremental process innovations include the removal or reduction of toxic chemicals used in the manufacturing process, improved chemical containment technology, and the development of user-friendly technol-ogy that can tolerate less than ideal human performance without initiating a chemical accident.

Partly in response to the Bhopal disaster—both because of the risk of massive tort liability and because of the regulatory activities that were themselves initiated partly in response to what happened in Bhopal[70]—chemical firms and secondary manufacturers have reduced the amount of hazardous chemicals they store on site and, in some instances, the amounts they use. . . .

TORT LIABILITY AND CHRONIC CHEMICAL ILLNESSES

Our analysis of the effects of tort liability for chronic chemical diseases parallels the tasks performed in the preceding analysis: an estimation of the chemical firm's payout for chronic diseases relative to the social costs of those diseases; an assessment of the amount of deterrence created by these chemical firm liabilities; and an evaluation of the deterrence effects of liability for chronic chemical diseases on chemical safety and innovation. Because much of the groundwork was provided in the evaluation of liability for acute injuries, the following analysis is greatly simplified.

Recall that chronic disease may develop weeks to years after initial exposure to a toxic chemical. Examples of chemical-caused disease are cancer of all organ systems; respiratory diseases including emphysema; reproductive system damage including sterility, impotence, miscarriages, and birth defects;

---

69. For these firms, liability operates much like regulation, in the sense that factors beyond economic considerations stimulate them to engage in a search for better products or processes. For example, an impending ban on a product encourages certain firms to develop substitute products. In the context of tort suits, the possibility of punitive damages or a damage to reputation also stimulates the search for new products and processes, even though the economic factors associated with those damages might not in and of themselves stimulate a search for new products.

70. The most prominent example is title 111 (the Emergency Planning and Community Right to Know Act of 1986) of the Superfund Amendments and Reauthorization Act of 1986 (SARA), which has imposed significant reporting requirements on industry concerning the identity and amounts of hazardous materials stored, used, and released and has created several emergency planning mechanisms as well.

heart disease; and neurotoxicity. Many of these chronic diseases caused by chemical exposures are considered "ordinary diseases of life." Hence, unless there is strong epidemiologic evidence linking exposure with excess incidence of these diseases in the workplace, in a specific geographic area, or associated with a particular consumer use, causation is extremely difficult to establish in either the tort or administrative compensation systems now in operation.

Sometimes chronic diseases constitute so-called signature diseases, which are so rare that, as a practical matter, their incidence can be explained only by exposure to a specific chemical. Examples are angiosarcoma (liver cancer), associated with vinyl chloride exposure, and mesothelioma, associated with asbestos exposure. In some instances the presence of the chemical causing an ordinary disease of life can be ascertained, for example lead in blood and other tissues, or DNA-adduct formation that is chemically specific. In these cases chemical causation may be unequivocally established as a result of biological monitoring. . . .

One way for the government to compensate for the inadequacy of environmental insurance as an incentive for reducing long-term health risks (owing, for example, to the long time it may take for toxic pollutants to migrate through soil into drinking water supplies, or to the long latency period of some environmental diseases) would be to require high-risk operations to post performance bonds or other "up-front money" to serve as a guaranty that damages would be paid and that responsible parties would not escape liability even if they go out of business or file for bankruptcy.

Financial responsibility requirements are imposed by the federal government under RCRA and CERCLA, but can also be imposed by the states. Since insurance activities are regulated at the state level, states may be in a unique position to coordinate efforts from state departments of insurance, environmental protection, and public health. There is a real opportunity for state initiatives to serve as a complement to federal legislation on financial responsibility. Further, imposing financial responsibility requirements on *potential polluters* may be the only effective way to ensure that high-risk operations pay current attention to future low-probability, but possibly catastrophic, risks.

■ NOTES

1. For an extensive discussion of financial responsibility requirements, see Boyd (2002).

2. To prevail in a tort case, the plaintiff generally must prove both that the defendant's behavior violated a (common law or statutory) duty of care and that such violation was the proximate cause of the plaintiff's injuries. When the injury in question is a common disease with many potential causes, such as lung cancer, proof of this second element may well be impossible. See chapter 4 for a more detailed look at

the operation of the tort system, and for an examination of the extent to which it is able to meaningfully engage environmental issues. For a discussion of why tort liability is not likely to match command-and-control regulation in generating incentives for prevention because of crucial differences in procedural, remedial, and substantive characteristics, see Schroeder (2002).

3. Insurance may not cover injuries that are the result of deliberate acts, such as knowingly dumping harmful chemicals into an aquifer, or knowingly exposing workers to harmful chemicals. In this latter situation, as discussed in chapter 4, the injured worker may be able to bypass the state workers' compensation statute, and sue the employer directly in tort.

4. While liability per se may not provide a strong incentive to improve environmental performance, shareholders' reactions to firms violating standards and incurring liability costs could encourage better practices. Johnston (2005a) argues that capital markets do in fact respond adversely to objectionable environmental, health, safety, and labor practices by publicly owned firms, and that better-enforced and expanded Security and Exchange Commission disclosure laws would facilitate an even larger market response. For a contrary view (drawing on the experience with petroleum refineries), see Bui (2005) and Bui and Mayer (2003).   ▪

E. "VOLUNTARY" INITIATIVES AND NEGOTIATION-BASED STRATEGIES

Beginning with the administration of Ronald Reagan in the 1980s, recent presidential administrations have demonstrated a general disillusionment with (and often a strong antagonism toward) command-and-control approaches to environmental protection. This, along with a general (and often industry-sponsored) effort to find "nonconfrontational" solutions to environmental issues, has helped spawn a number of so-called voluntary initiatives in the environmental and energy fields. As discussed in the following materials, these initiatives can be broadly characterized as *public voluntary schemes* (designed by the government, with optional participation by industry), *unilateral commitments* (made by industry), and *negotiated environmental agreements* (between industry and government). The central unifying feature of all of these initiatives is that, at least in theory, industry is improving its environmental performance on its own, without being required by government to do so. Although the same could also be said for some of the indirect control policies discussed earlier in this chapter, voluntary initiatives tend to be discussed separately in policy and academic circles, and we will follow that convention here.

Those who advocate voluntary initiatives of this nature usually cite a list of purported advantages, including (1) environmental effectiveness (encouraging improvements beyond mandated compliance); (2) economic efficiency (encouraging flexibility in achieving "win-win" technological improvements); (3) reductions in administrative, monitoring, and enforcement costs; (4) increased environmental awareness (and concomitant attitudinal changes) within industry; and (5) innovation and other dynamic effects (through learning by doing and by anticipating future environmental demands). See, for example, Brouhle et al. (2005) and OECD (1997, 1999, 2003). As one might expect, however, the performance of voluntary initiatives has been a mixed bag. While there is much to be gained by encouraging industry to take a serious interest in charting its own environmental future, participation in a voluntary environmental program may also be a convenient way to avoid making serious environmental improvements. In fact, many of the voluntary initiatives that have achieved real environmental progress were not strictly "voluntary" per se, but rather were carried out in the face of overriding regulatory imperatives. The following discussion of voluntary initiatives is written from a European perspective, during a time when Europe was intrigued with nonregulatory approaches.

1. Overview of Voluntary Initiatives

The Rationale and Potential of Voluntary Approaches
Carlo Carraro and Francois Leveque

Source: Carlo Carraro and Francois Leveque (eds.), *Voluntary Approaches in Environmental Policy*, Kluwer, Boston, 1999, pp. 1–15, excerpted with permission.

What are voluntary approaches? Are they an effective means to improve the environment? Which context and provisions enhance the performance of these new environmental policy instruments? Why would firms voluntarily commit themselves to pollution abatement? Is self-regulation potentially anticompetitive? . . .

1.1. WHAT ARE VOLUNTARY APPROACHES?

Voluntary approaches are commitments from polluting firms [to improve] their environmental performances. They include three . . . instruments: (1) negotiated environmental agreements between industry and public authorities, (2) unilateral commitments made by polluters, and (3) public volun-

tary schemes developed by environmental agencies. The common element of voluntary approaches, as the name implies, is that a firm's decision to abate pollution is not *de jure* required. As a consequence, in contrast to laws, voluntary approaches do not apply to all polluting firms. . . .

Voluntary approaches cover a large variety of different arrangements. This is reflected by a rich terminology. Self-regulation, voluntary initiatives, voluntary codes, environmental charters, voluntary accords, voluntary agreements, co-regulation, covenants, [and] negotiated environmental agreements are just a few of the names used to refer to voluntary approaches. A key feature which differentiates voluntary approaches is . . . whether the environmental commitments were set by industry, public authorities, or both.

1.1.1. Unilateral Commitments

These consist of environmental improvement programmes set up by firms themselves and communicated to their stakeholders (employees, shareholders, clients, etc.). The definition of the environmental obligations to be achieved, as well as of the provisions governing compliance, are determined by the committed firms. Nevertheless, firms may delegate monitoring and dispute resolution to a third party in order to strengthen the credibility and the environmental effectiveness of their commitments. One example of such [a] self-regulatory arrangement is provided by the Responsible Care [I]nitiative undertaken by the Canadian Chemical Producers Association [that] was devised in response to a decline in public confidence in the chemical industry and to a threat of more stringent regulations. The programme contains principles and rules designed to improve a firm's performances in safety and environmental protection. Each participant must submit its plants to regular compliance verification which is undertaken by an external committee composed [of] industry experts and community representatives. The results of this monitoring are made public.

1.1.2. Public Voluntary Scheme

[In] this type of voluntary approach, participating firms agree on standards (related to their [environmental] performance, their technology or their [internal administration]) which are developed by environmental agencies. The scheme defines the conditions of individual membership, the provisions to be complied with by the firms, the monitoring criteria, and the evaluation of the results. Economic benefits in the form of R&D subsidies, technical assistance, and reputation in using an environmental logo [may] be provided by public authorities. An example of such a non-mandatory regulation is provided by the Eco-Management and Auditing Scheme (EMAS) implemented within the European Union since 1993 [see the excerpt from Gouldson and Murphy in section E.3 of this chapter]. To register under EMAS a firm must establish a company environmental policy, conduct an environmental review of its sites, set and implement an environmental improvement programme and an environmental management system, and have its policy, sites' review, improvement programme, and management system examined [by an independent third party] to verify that they meet the requirements of EMAS. Registered firms are then able to use and display a statement of participation.

1.1.3. Negotiated [Environmental] Agreements

These are contracts between the public (national, federal or regional) authorities and industry. They contain a target (i.e. a pollution abatement objective) and a time within which it is to be achieved. The public authority commitment generally consists of not introducing new [legal requirements] (e.g., a compulsory environmental standard or an environmental tax) unless the voluntary action fails to meet the agreement target. The contracts may be legally binding (as in The Netherlands) or not (as in Germany), depending on whether executive branches of government are empowered by national constitutions to sign such.... Negotiated [environmental] agreements are the key instrument of the National Environmental Policy Plan in The Netherlands, where they are called covenants. Covenants related to reduction of greenhouse gas emissions and other pollutants have been signed with more than fifty industry sectors, including industries dominated by large companies, such as oil and chemical industries, but also including sectors dominated by small and medium-sized enterprises such as textiles, leather, dairy, printing, and packaging printers....

1.3. STRATEGIC INCENTIVES TO VOLUNTARY ENVIRONMENTAL COMMITMENTS

A firm which voluntarily commits to additional abatement efforts must [believe it will] be compensated by additional benefits. Pollution abatement is costly for a firm, for it requires new investments (e.g., adding end-of-pipe technologies [or] organizing an environmental management department). Firms are motivated by profit, and therefore any expenditures cannot be voluntarily made if they are not counter-balanced with some expected gains. The gains may come from three sources:

• Better use of, and access to, inputs (energy and material savings; easier [ability] to recruit employees and to raise money on financial markets, thanks to a greener reputation, etc.);
• A[n increase in] sales... because of [the] consumer's willingness to pay more for green products[,] which enables firms to increase their price (or because at the same price, consumers opt for greener products and therefore the greener firm is rewarded by an increase[d] market share);
• Avoidance of [the] costs of public regulation imposing a new standard or a new [economic] charge.

The sum of these gains sets the cap of the abatement efforts that may be expected from a firm's voluntary action. In the absence of corrective mechanisms, a firm will try to capture the benefits of making a voluntary commitment without bearing the corresponding abatement costs. The best [economic] outcome for a polluting firm is to convince everybody that it has abated pollution without actually incurring abatement costs. Such... strategic behaviour enables a firm to maximize its net gain of pollution "abatement." For instance, when the voluntary approach involves an industry association, an individual company has an interest in [actually] not implementing the environmen-

tal programme (to free ride) because it would benefit from the collective gain in reputation without paying the related cost. To make voluntary approaches [effective], a firm's [strategic behaviour] has to be limited by using various corrective mechanisms, such as:

• Access [of] third parties in the discussion dealing with the setting of environmental targets;
• A monitoring and reporting system checked] by [an] independent [third] party;
• A credible mechanism of sanctions for non-compliance;
• A system to limit free-riding in collective agreements.

Oversight can be provided by peers from other firms, green groups, consumers and citizens associations and public authorities. It is noteworthy that the setting of these barriers to free-riding may be in the interest of the industry itself. If they are not implemented, a firm's commitment cannot be distinguished from just talk and, therefore, consumers and public authorities [may] not reward the concerned company by buying its product or by not regulating [it, respectively]. When a voluntary approach is not [viewed as] credible [by] public opinion and [the] public authorities, a firm [may] not commit [to a] voluntary approach.

1.4. PERFORMANCE AND POTENTIAL OF VOLUNTARY AGREEMENTS

The performance of voluntary agreements can be analysed across several dimensions.

1.4.1. Environmental Effectiveness

There are two reasons why voluntary approaches [might be expected] not to result in significant effects on the environment. One is that firms do not respect their commitments: they do not achieve the environmental objective they publicly declared. The second [reason] concerns the low ambition of the objective itself: firms may have declared an easy target to reach.

It is often argued that voluntary approaches only contain a pollution reduction programme which follows a natural trend, a business-as-usual pattern. As technology evolves and improves, it "automatically" increases the efficiency with which natural resources are used, and therefore reduces the emissions per unit of resource used. As economies develop, and [an] old technology is replaced by a new one, there is a corresponding improvement in environmental performance, which owes nothing to a firm's environmental policy *per se*. It is the automatic consequence of economic development. If the voluntary approach does not advance the target beyond what would have been naturally achieved anyway, then it cannot be said to be environmentally effective. . . .

Because of market and technological uncertainties, the business as usual scenario is difficult to foresee. The assessment whether an environmental target is ambitious raises controversial issues. An example is provided by the voluntary agreement of the Federal Association of German Industry (BDI). This involved the publication in March 1995 of a *Joint Declaration of the German Industry on Climate Protection* stating their objective to reduce their specific energy consumption up to 20% (with reference to 1987 as a base year) in the period up to 2005. This was agreed by 14 industrial associations, including the steel and non-ferrous metals industries. This target has been criticized as being lower than the business as usual trend. From 1970 to 1993, the energy efficiency increased in Germany with an annual rate of 1.8% whereas the declared objective by BDI corresponds with an annual rate of 1.2% for the period 1987–2005. It was argued by industry that this gap does not mean the absence of specific efforts because marginal gains in energy efficiency are more difficult to achieve, especially in the industries involved in the

voluntary initiative. However, another forecasting study which carried out a detailed technological analysis at the sectoral level showed that, except for the tiles and glass industries, the target was inferior to the business as usual pattern.

Eventually, the German industrial associations revised their commitments. 1990 was chosen as the year of reference instead of 1987, the former being characterized by higher energy consumption and the declaration of "up to 20%" was changed to "by 20%" by the year 2005. Moreover, a monitoring system supervised by an independent institution (Rheinisch-Wesfalisches fur Wirtschafts-forschung) was established.

To ensure that the objectives set in voluntary approaches are above the business-as-usual pattern, the target setting process has to be open and transparent. Consultation with, or contractual participation from, nongovernmental representatives and government agencies are a key element in this regard. A regulatory threat is generally another necessary ingredient . . .

1.4.2. Implementation Effectiveness

Once a voluntary approach has been put into place, the initial pressures may dissipate and firms may have the opportunity not to comply with their commitments. The voluntary approach must address all aspects necessary to ensure compliance: clear objectives, unambiguous obligations, monitoring and reporting requirements, a mechanism for dispute resolution, and sanctions for non-compliance.

Which of the hundreds of voluntary approaches recently adopted in OECD countries will contribute significantly to a better environment? No robust answers can be provided yet. Most voluntary approaches have been initiated in association with a regulatory threat. But were they credible? Most do not include monitoring and sanction for non-compliance mechanisms, although this is changing. For instance, neither the Canadian

Responsible Care programme nor the voluntary agreement of the German industry on
climate protection included a monitoring system by an independent party, but they were
amended and now they do so. Similarly,
negotiated agreements with public authorities increasingly contain explicit systems of
sanctions. . .

1.4.3. Cost Effectiveness

With voluntary approaches, the choice of the
abatement strategy is left to firms, which are
most likely to have information about it, and
[which] have the incentive to implement the
least-cost options. In this regard, voluntary
approaches are likely to lead to cost-
effectiveness, that is, the achievement of a
given environmental improvement at least
cost. On the other hand, when voluntary
approaches involve industry associations, the
burden sharing of the environmental objective is more driven by equity considerations
than individual costs. Firms are given equivalent targets rather than the reductions being
allocated to firms with the lower abatement
costs. In such cases, voluntary approaches are
less efficient than charges or tradable permits.

1.4.4. Stimulation of Innovation

Will voluntary approaches stimulate innovation? Experience seems to indicate that if the
target of the voluntary approach is ambitious, thus demanding more than the routine
technology available off the shelf to achieve
it, then it will stimulate innovation. Conversely, if the target can be achieved with a
business as usual approach, then there will
be little incentive to introduce a new technology. There are theoretical arguments and empirical evidence that voluntary approaches
which involve several firms enable individual
companies to share information and experiments on abatement technologies and that
such a collective learning process stimulates
innovation and decreases its costs.

1.4.5. Feasibility

The large number of voluntary approaches
now in place [in Europe] is evidence that
these instruments can be developed and
implemented. It is clear from experience,
however, that the design of an effective voluntary approach is far from simple and takes
time. . . . The biggest threat to [the] political
sustainability [of voluntary approaches] is
likely to arise when voluntary approaches
lack credibility in the eyes of public opinion
and non-governmental organizations. Citizens and environmental groups may perceive
that voluntary approaches are being used by
firms, as well as by governments, as a smoke
screen to avoid substantive environmental
improvements. To avoid this type of perception, voluntary approaches should share
some common features [mentioned earlier]: a
set of verifiable and clearly-stated objectives,
a monitoring system involving independent
parties, and so on. However, this may not be
sufficient whenever public confidence in industry commitments is low because of bad
experiences in the past.

1.4.6. Competition

Are voluntary approaches anti-competitive?
There is a fundamental fear that voluntary
approaches will lessen competition within industry and raise non tariff barriers. Until
now, evidence has been lacking [in] this regard and only a few claims have been submitted to antitrust authorities. The potential
danger of industry collusion is greatest when
the voluntary approach concerns a concentrated sector, where a relatively small number
of firms dominates the market. The potential
danger with regard to barriers to trade within
[the] European Union is greatest when voluntary approaches are nationally designed and
are championed by the national Department
of Industry. However, existing competition
laws seem to contain sufficient provisions to
cope with anticompetitive collusion and the

trade barriers to which voluntary approaches may lead in the future. Furthermore, voluntary approaches may contribute to the equalization of environmental performances across different countries. It is not possible for a national government to require a company in another country to meet its environmental standards, but a company can require its suppliers and units localized elsewhere to meet the standards of its home country. Voluntary approaches can create an environmental policy with extraterritorial effects.

1.5. POLICY CONCLUSIONS AND RECOMMENDATIONS

Evidence shows that voluntary approaches may be encountered anywhere. They are flexible and various enough to adapt to different industrial contexts, environmental concerns, and geographic jurisdictions, constitutional laws, and so forth.... [T]he following features may facilitate an extensive use of voluntary approaches:

• The jurisdiction in question has an administration in place which can interpret the terms of a voluntary approach such that participants and citizens understand that the voluntary approach has standing and is not a trivialization of environmental policy.
• Environmental interests are organized in non-profit organizations and political parties such they can effectively fulfill a role of watchdog vis-à-vis both government and industry.
• Government and non-governmental organizations are sufficiently informed concerning the environmental performance and potential of individual firms and industry sectors to be able to distinguish between commitments which correspond with genuine abatement efforts from those which follow a business-as-usual pattern.
• Government is a multi-tier structure organized with agencies which can understand a firm's concerns and their technological potential. The agencies [are] under the control of an upper administrative branch to limit the collusion between agencies and industry interests.

■ NOTES

1. Farber (2000) divides the various efforts to "reinvent" environmental regulation into the following three categories: (1) self-regulation by individual firms, (2) bilateral negotiation between individual firms and the government, and (3) multilateral governance of environmental problems involving consensus building. Presumably the three categories identified here by Carraro and Leveque would all fit within Farber's first two categories. His third category, on the other hand, might incorporate initiatives such as the negotiation of a "good neighbor agreement" between a firm and the surrounding community. See Lewis and Henkels (1997), Adriatico (1999), and Siegel (2002).

2. Carraro and Leveque assess the performance of voluntary initiatives according to six criteria: (1) environmental effectiveness, (2) implementation effectiveness, (3) cost effectiveness, (4) stimulation of innovation, (5) feasibility, and (6) competition. Brouhle, Griffiths, and Wolverton (2005) use similar criteria. For a more concentrated

focus on the effects of voluntary initiatives on dynamic efficiency and innovation, see Ashford (1999), Caldart and Ashford (1999), and Aggeri and Hatchuel (1999).

3. In contrast, Alberini and Segerson (2002) offer an assessment of voluntary programs based on two criteria: whether a particular scheme is effective in providing environmental protection and whether it offers (economic) efficiency advantages over other approaches. Here, as with other neoclassical economic analyses, *static* efficiency is the focus, rather than dynamic change and innovation. For a similar neoclassical analysis, see Barde (2000).

4. See Brouhle, Griffiths, and Wolverton (2005) for a detailed review of EPA's voluntary programs, and see OECD (1999, 2003) for a detailed review of U.S. and European voluntary initiatives.

5. An examination of a voluntary packaging initiative (Repak) implemented in Ireland concluded that "innovations resulting from the voluntary approach were nothing beyond business as usual" (Cunningham and Clinch, 2005, p. 390). This is in line with the OECD's finding that the environmental impacts of voluntary agreements "are likely to be modest" (OECD, 2003, p. 15).

6. Participation by other interested parties (such as community groups) in voluntary environmental programs (VEPs) may be an important means both of checking the performance of such programs and of enhancing their legitimacy. Carmin, Darnell, and Mil-Homens (2003, p. 9) assessed the degree of stakeholder influence on the design of government, industry, and third-party (independent) VEPs, which they defined as "any program, code, agreement, or commitment that encourage[s] business organizations to voluntarily reduce their environmental [pollution] impacts beyond that required by the environmental regulatory system." They found that government-sponsored VEPs provided for more overall stakeholder involvement than industry-sponsored VEPs, which in turn provided for greater involvement than third-party VEPs. Not surprisingly, industry representatives were found to have had the highest "intensity of involvement" in governmental VEPs, and to have had a disproportionate level of involvement compared with other stakeholders. Nonetheless, this research suggests that stakeholder involvement is becoming an institutionalized aspect of environmental program design, regardless of sponsor or regulatory requirements.   ▪

2. Public Voluntary Programs: The EPA Experience

The majority of U.S. voluntary efforts are public voluntary programs. See OECD (2003) and Brouhle, Griffiths, and Wolverton (2005). Two prominent examples are EPA's 33/50 and WasteWise programs. Under these programs, participating firms enter into agreements with the agency to meet specified environmental goals, but there typically is no penalty for nonattainment (beyond possible revocation of membership in the program). See Darnall and Carmin (2005).

Begun in 1991, the 33/50 program (also known as the Voluntary Industrial Toxics Program) focused on the reduction of toxic air emissions. Firms participating in the program agreed in the first phase to reduce their emissions of seventeen priority toxic chemicals by 33% by 1992, and in the second phase by 50% by 1995, relative to the 1988 baseline. Not coincidentally, these same seventeen chemicals were also the subject of impending MACT standards (emission limitations) under Section 112 of the Clean Air Act. In other words, the participating firms had an independent regulatory incentive to reduce their emissions of these chemicals. Initially, the program was at best considered a moderate success; industry achieved a 28% reduction in the first phase against a target of 33% (Khanna and Damon, 1999). In large part, industry did this by applying readily available measures but did not make significant changes in their processes. Ultimately, the program met its goal and reduced the seventeen chemical emissions by more than 750 million pounds by the end of 1995, but that may be credited more to MACT regulation than to voluntary efforts.

WasteWise involves voluntary commitments to implement certain pollution practices, to improve the collection of recyclable material, and to increase the purchase of recycled material, to the extent desired by the firms themselves. In a detailed analysis, Gamper-Rabindran (2006, p. 391) found that participants in that program "do not reduce their health-indexed emissions of target chemicals in several key industries" and that "[w]here reductions are detected in selected industries, participants' increased off-site transfers to recyclers give reasons to question whether this program truly reduced emissions."

A third EPA voluntary program—this one focused on a single industry—is the Strategic Goals Program (SGP), a cooperative effort between the agency and the metal-finishing industry. Begun in 1998, the SGP encourages companies to go beyond environmental compliance, and endeavors to offer them incentives, resources, and a means for removing regulatory and policy barriers as they work to achieve specific environmental goals. Although the decentralized nature of this industry, which includes a number of smaller companies without substantial resources, would appear to make it an ideal candidate for this approach, Johnston (2005b, p. 391) found that the SGP "did not seem to provide the necessary financial assistance," "did not appear to have extended the regulator's reach to cover the most egregiously noncomplying firms in the industry," and did not create "the firm-specific data-base which is necessary to evaluate why firms did or did not participate and whether the initiative caused changes in the participants' environmental performance."

In these and other programs of this nature, EPA has followed through with neither a commitment of the necessary resources, a serious engagement of the key stakeholders, nor attention to preventing media and problem shifting that might otherwise have resulted in greater success.

■ **NOTES**

1. A 2005 evaluation of EPA voluntary programs by EPA's Inspector General noted the paucity of agency data and analysis suitable for performing such an evaluation, and recommended that the agency engage in more aggressive target-setting and assessment activities with regard to its voluntary programs. See "Ongoing Management Improvements and Further Evaluation Vital to EPA Stewardship and Voluntary Programs" at http://www.epa.gov/oig/reports/2005/20050217-2005-P-00007.pdf.

2. For an investigation of the extent to which there may be environmental justice impacts of the 33/50 program, see Gamper-Rabindran (2006).

3. See chapters 10 and 13 for a discussion of the successes and failures of the Toxics Release Inventory provisions requiring the reporting of (1) voluntary reductions in actual emissions (which reduced emissions to air but increased chemical waste) and (2) voluntary pollution prevention measures (which were few).   ■

3.   Unilateral Commitments

a.   Self-Enforcement, Environmental Management Systems, and Industry Codes
One strain of the voluntary initiative movement emphasizes a form of self-regulation by industry. This approach generally involves an emphasis on the development and implementation of environmental management systems—management structures and planning activities dedicated to hazard management and risk reduction—with few (if any) performance requirements.

Toward a Management-Based Environmental Policy?
Cary Coglianese and Jennifer Nash
Source: C. Coglianese and J. Nash (eds.), *Regulating from the Inside*. Resources for the Future, Washington, D.C., 2001, pp. 222–234, excerpted with permission.

Private firms and public environmental agencies today are devoting increasing amounts of attention to environmental management systems (EMSs). Managers of private organizations are learning about the EMSs that their competitors and customers have adopted and are considering the strategic advantage of implementing similar systems. They are assessing the environmental impacts of their facilities, setting goals to reduce those impacts, documenting procedures, training workers, measuring progress, and engaging third parties to assess their systems. Encouraged by the results of the EMSs they have implemented, some managers are requiring that their suppliers adopt similar systems as a condition of business. Public policy makers, too, are paying close attention to EMSs.

More than a dozen states have begun to create tiered regulatory systems, making entry into the privileged tier dependent on EMS adoption. The U.S. Environmental Protection Agency (EPA) has launched the National Environmental Performance Track, which offers recognition and other incentives to facilities that adopt EMSs with certain characteristics.

What are the benefits of EMS adoption, and how should public policy adapt, if at all, to their widespread use? In this chapter, we revisit the main lessons from the research presented in this book and point out the direction for future research that will be needed to determine how far current policy should shift toward becoming a management-based system of environmental policy.

BENEFITS FOR FIRMS AND SOCIETY

One clear lesson is that companies respond differently to environmental pressures. In many firms, the natural environment is still only a peripheral factor in business decisions. It is rarely discussed except in the context of regulatory compliance. The environmental manager's primary function is [as a] "chief compliance officer" who makes sure permits are up-to-date and control equipment is operated as specified so business managers will not have to concern themselves with the environment at all.

But for other firms, ... the environment has assumed an altogether different importance. Environmental performance is viewed as a business need. Managers are attuned to various external and internal actors who value environmental performance: customers, competitors, shareholders, insurers, environmental advocacy groups, regulators, labor unions, and employees. The managers of these firms may or may not be environmentalists themselves; they are simply good managers. If they want to build their customer base, borrow capital, buy insurance, and attract skilled workers, they must invest in improving environmental performance. For such companies, the definition of *strong environmental performance* is expanding. In the past, compliance was sufficient; now it is only a first step. The managers' job is to find ways to reduce materials inputs and waste by tightening operating processes and bringing environmental concerns into business planning. They engage community residents and other people whose values may be different from their own in an effort to identify new strategies. They work to ensure that foreign facilities that operate under far less stringent regulatory systems meet the same standards as home-country plants.

EMSs are a part of many of such companies' environmental programs. They provide a way for managers to institutionalize corporate environmental goals and the practices that will work toward achieving those goals .... EMSs have the potential not only to improve regulatory compliance but also to create a system of continual improvements toward reducing a facility's most pressing environmental problems. Most of the facilities participating in the National Database on Environmental Management Systems (NDEMS) used the EMS design process as an opportunity to examine all their activities to identify those that would have a potential impact on the environment. EMSs have the potential to engage managers in an investigation of the root causes of environmental problems, allowing them to prevent—not only control—pollution.

... EMSs offer benefits because they operationalize management commitments. Managers may know and understand that business and environmental interests increasingly intersect but fail to act effectively. Compensation systems may not reward environmental performance, for example, and work routines may keep environmental managers organizationally separated form process engineers. ENS design is a deliberate process in which managers assess and prioritize environmental impacts and determine how best to focus organizational attention on reducing those impacts. When designing an EMS, managers have the opportunity to correct mistakes in established practices that have kept business and environmental interests from meshing. The EMS process establishes a cycle in which managers continually seek better outcomes by setting targets, establishing routines, checking progress, and striving to do better next time. People from diverse functions may take part in this process so that environmental managers are no longer lone voices urging attention to environmental needs; they are joined by marketing managers and process engineers who have come to see environmental protection as their job, too. In this way, as Coglianese observes, EMSs may "draw in" managers and employees who otherwise would be left out.

Research...suggests that facilities with EMSs may perform better than the norm in terms of several criteria. EMS adoption appears to correlate with advanced management practices generally....[M]anagers of EMS plants who also have pollution prevention programs are likely to adopt a "broad bundle" of innovative approaches such as total quality management, employee involvement, and performance measurement systems. Managers use EMSs as one of many approaches to make their firms more competitive.

Facilities with EMSs also may pose lower environmental risk than comparable plants without such systems. Although there is little direct research yet that compares the environmental risks posed by EMS plants with those posed by non-EMS plants,...EMS plant managers tend to rate their environmental performance better than managers of non-EMS facilities. Managers of EMS plants are far more likely than their non-EMS peers

to cite recycling, air emissions reduction, and solid waste reduction as sources of environmental problems for surrounding communities.

EMSs may help managers reduce the costs of their environmental programs. [There are] examples of firms that turned waste streams into products, decreased water and energy use, and therefore reduced their utility bills. Numerous organizations appear to reduce compliance costs after EMS adoption. Exactly how these cost savings are achieved is not yet clear. Presumably, as more workers are drawn in to help meet a facility's environmental goals, more ideas are generated about how to do so efficiently. The savings reported in some facilities are substantial. Some firms that report financial savings from EMS adoption had already implemented pollution prevention programs so their ability to identify further cost reductions is even more notable....

POLICY RESPONSES

How should environmental policy respond to the widespread adoption of EMSs? We have argued that EMSs allow managers to operationalize their commitments to strong environmental performance. In some cases, firms can use EMSs to outperform their non-EMS peers, perhaps even posing lower risks to their communities and achieving greater efficiency. Many policymakers in business and government see the movement toward EMS adoption as an opportunity for large-scale changes in the regulatory system. What would a management-based environmental policy look like? Would such a system be desirable?

Conceivably, environmental policy could shift from a system that relies on technology-based [i.e., specification] standards to a system built more explicitly around performance standards. In the EMS design process, managers generate performance targets on the basis of their understanding of their company's most significant impacts. These targets could become the basis of a performance-driven regulatory system, especially if progress toward meeting the targets were regularly monitored and periodically verified by qualified third parties. By setting performance targets instead of technology standards, firms would retain flexibility in selecting the means to achieve these targets, allowing them to choose the lowest-cost method of making environmental improvements. Performance targets could be set for pollutants in any media, allowing firms to "trade" between water and air emissions. Eventually, with additional developments in risk analysis, firms' targets could be set in terms of the overall risk created by the firm. Firms that secured reliable third-party audits of their environmental performance as part of an EMS could pave the way for a potentially dramatic shift toward a much more flexible style of regulation.

With a management-based environmental policy, government agencies could more efficiently allocate their monitoring, permitting, and enforcement resources. With effective EMSs, firms would engage in what essentially amounts to a system of self-regulation, but still one with the threat of regulation or other policy incentives in the background. Government agencies could require new reporting requirements, under which firms and independent auditors would become the principal monitors of environmental performance. They could rely on the information generated by these reports as a basis for assessing compliance or allocating regulatory resources. The mere presence of a verifiable management system that included internal and third-party auditing would provide assurance that a firm's environmental impacts were being well managed. Ultimately, government agencies could shift resources toward managing a system of management systems.

Over time, the widespread use of EMSs might create changes in the relationships among business, environmental groups, and local communities. If the information gener-

ated by EMSs were readily accessible on the Internet, community groups could closely monitor the environmental impacts of local firms. If firms routinely used a transparent, systematic process for their environmental management, outside organizations could more feasibly provide input into that process. With transparent EMSs, these organizations also may be able to participate more effectively in government decisions about setting a firm's performance targets....

Finally, the presence of an EMS, particularly one based on ISO 14001, is not necessarily a good metric for differentiating among firms.... Firms can adopt an EMS without investing in environmental performance improvement. Only through careful observation of a firm's environmental targets and performance over time can agencies assess whether a firm's EMS is intended to build the legitimacy of the organization or designed to motivate and guide action.

Furthermore, meshing performance-based programs with traditional regulatory programs will be difficult, as several authors point out. In theory, at least, agencies could offer incentives powerful enough to change the values of managers. They could offer firms with particularly strong EMSs exemption from regulatory requirements that are particularly costly, or they could decide not to subject these facilities to regular inspections. In practice, however, agencies are constrained when it comes to providing meaningful benefits. Agencies face a trade-off between giving more and asking more. That is, the more government seeks to give managers by way of an incentive, the more it will ask for in terms of proof that those managers' firms are deserving. This is why most performance-based programs, such as EPA's Project XL, have attracted relatively few participants. When the benefits are meaningful, the costs of participation are too high for most organizations. EPA's National Environmental Performance Track so far has attracted a comparatively large number of participants, because the costs of admission are quite low. The benefits to firms, in terms of substantive reforms to the regulatory system, are correspondingly small.

The conclusion we draw ... is that although EMSs may be an effective tool that managers can use to achieve their environmental objectives, the best policy response to their widespread adoption may be no response at all. It is, after all, quite possible for the widespread use of EMSs to coexist with the current system of environmental regulation. Further-more, private mandates may be far stronger than public ones in encouraging EMS adoption. When a customer announces that it will require its suppliers to register to ISO 14001 as a condition of business, firms that rely on this customer for a substantial portion of their sales will face an overwhelming incentive to adopt that management system. Certainly, such an incentive is more likely to get the attention of managers than the package of benefits being offered in agency performance track programs....

■ NOTES

1. Note that the improved environmental performance anticipated here by Coglianese and Nash derives partly from their incorrect characterization of environmental standards as *specification (design)* standards. As discussed previously, most environmental standards are in fact *performance* standards. That is, they do not mandate the use of any particular technology, but rather allow the regulated entity the flexibility to use any available means to meet the designated performance end point (as long as it is otherwise lawful).

2. While these authors are somewhat tentative here in their conclusions about the potential positive impact of EMSs on environmental performance, they have subsequently suggested that governments may want to consider *mandating* the development of environmental management systems. See Coglianese and Nash (2002).

3. Another group of researchers has undertaken an extensive empirical analysis of a sample of Standard and Poor (S&P) 500 firms, and has come to generally positive conclusions regarding the performance of environmental management systems:

Firms are increasingly addressing environmental concerns in a more proactive manner through the adoption of EMSs that integrate environmental considerations in various facets of production. Regulators are seeking to encourage this trend towards self-regulation by providing technical and financial assistance and through regulatory incentives. EMSs can differ considerably among firms in the comprehensiveness of their coverage and the ambitiousness of their goals. Analysis of the count of environmental practices adopted by S&P 500 firms shows that the threat of liabilities and market-based pressures from consumers, investors and other firms are significant motivators for the adoption of a more comprehensive EMS. Further, consumer pressure has a stronger effect on firms that would have otherwise been adopters of a less comprehensive EMS given their (other) characteristics.

We also find that the adoption of a more comprehensive EMS has a significant negative impact on the intensity of toxic releases and that this impact is greater on firms that have inferior past environmental records. In addition, we find a differential impact of these incentives on a firm's choice of pollution control method. Results show that EMSs have a negative effect on the intensity of on-site releases and off-site transfers, though not on HAP [hazardous air pollutants] per unit sales. These findings suggest that adoption of EMSs leads to source reduction of total waste generation or to pollution prevention and reduces end-of-pipe disposal. By and large, none of the market-based or regulatory pressures considered are found to have had a significant direct impact on the pollution intensity of firms. Rather, their effect is indirect and operates through inducing the adoption of a more comprehensive EMS. Our results, taken together, suggest that public policy can play a role in inducing the prevention of toxic pollution by creating regulatory and market-based pressures that induce adoption of EMSs. These pressures include a threat of stringent mandatory regulation and the provision of environmental information about firms to the public. These results also suggest that promoting the adoption of EMSs particularly by firms with large toxic release intensity can be considered as an effective policy tool. (Anton, Deltas, and Khanna, 2004, p. 633)

4. Lori Snyder (2003) examined fourteen state-based regulatory systems that mandated management-based regulation (MBR), and found that MBR had a "measurable positive effect on the environmental performance of manufacturing plants . . . [i.e.,] larger decreases in total pounds of toxic chemicals released and a [greater likelihood] to engage in source reduction activities" (p. 1). She concluded that "[t]he results provide preliminary support for the hypothesis that plants with greater complementarity between planning effort and pollution reduction will have larger effects from [mandated] MBR" (p. 32). She also found that the more positive responses tended to occur in firms that were not members of Responsible Care, the chemical industry's flagship voluntary program, "casting doubt on the effectiveness of Responsible Care as an industry self-regulatory initiative" (p. 32) (id.). Similarly, King and Lenox (2000) report that U.S. chemical companies that have signed onto Responsible Care improve their environmental performance more slowly than non-participating firms. In later work, King, Lenox, and Terlaak (2005) found no evidence that ISO 14001 certification (for having an environmental management system) serves as a signal of superior environmental performance. Consistent with previous results, they found that firms that certified with ISO 14001 tend to have lower environmental performance relative to peers in their industry. See also Karkkainen (2001), excerpted in chapter 10.

5. Dorothy Daley (2002) investigated the factors influencing the formation of state voluntary programs designed to facilitate the remediation of hazardous waste sites outside of federal or state Superfund programs. These sites included, but were not limited to, brownfield sites, and the programs were voluntary initiatives that had arisen in response to inadequate progress under prior federal and state programs. She found that the more successful programs tended to be found in states with larger chemical releases, smaller resources, greater "professional" legislatures, and pressure from both industrial interest groups and environmental groups.

6. Conclusions about the expected improvements in environmental performance from self-regulation deserve careful consideration. See MacDonald (2005). Again, we stress that although these approaches are often discussed as if they were a full-fledged alternative to regulation, it would appear that their success often depends on the threat of stringent mandatory regulation and the mandatory provision of environmental information about firms to the public. (Laws requiring the disclosure of chemical information to the public are discussed in chapter 10.)   ∎

Europe has had considerable experience with voluntary initiatives and audit systems. The following piece discusses the European perspective on self-regulation and describes an important EU initiative, the EU Eco-Management and Audit System (EMAS).

Voluntary Regulation and the European Union's Eco-Management and Audit System

A. Gouldson and J. Murphy

Source: *Regulatory Realities*. London: Earthscan, 1998, pp. 54–69, excerpted with permission.

INTRODUCTION

... The contribution that voluntary regulation might make to environmental protection is an important aspect of the debate about alternative policy instruments. From both government and industry perspectives voluntary regulation can have a number of advantages. For government, effective voluntary action might deliver benefits which reduce the need for mandatory regulation and therefore the requirement for costly regulatory agencies. For industry, reductions in the level of government intervention may allow scarce resources to be channeled toward environmental improvement rather than bureaucratic compliance. However, particularly amongst the public and pressure groups, voluntary regulation commonly generates suspicion that voluntary regulation may in fact mean no regulation. ...

DEFINING VOLUNTARY REGULATION

... Jacobs (1991, p. 134) defines voluntary action as "all those actions unforced by law and unpersuaded by financial incentives, which individuals, groups and firms take to protect the environment." Thus, the defining features of voluntary action are that it is unforced by law and unpersuaded by financial incentives. While it is important to acknowledge that any definition is likely to be found wanting in some respect, these features require further examination.

By its very nature voluntary regulation must be unforced by law. However, this does not necessarily mean that government has no influence over the design, implementation and impact of voluntary regulation. Government and its agencies can facilitate and encourage the use of voluntary regulation in a variety of ways. Government can catalyze voluntary action by establishing frameworks or institutions to develop and administer voluntary initiatives or to verify their quality and integrity. It may encourage companies to take voluntary action by providing various forms of business support or by requesting evidence of voluntary action in their purchasing or contracting criteria. It can provide the impetus for voluntary action by negotiating targets for environmental improvement with industrial groups. Government can also establish a legal context that encourages, but does not require, voluntary action. For example, it may threaten to bring forward legislation unless voluntary action is taken. Similarly, if regulators perceive voluntary action to be effective, they might subject companies that are taking such action to less intensive scrutiny than those that are not. Therefore, although voluntary regulation is unforced by law, it can be encouraged by government in a variety of other ways. At the extreme this encouragement could evolve into a *de facto* requirement for voluntary action.

The extent to which voluntary action is unpersuaded by financial incentives is unclear. As discussed above, government may encourage voluntary action by providing various forms of business support or by requesting evidence of voluntary action in their purchasing or contracting criteria. Government may encourage voluntary action by reforming the fiscal system to present various incentives and disincentives for environmental improvement. The framework of mandatory regulation can be used to encourage companies to apply voluntary initiatives to minimise the costs of compliance and the risk of fines for non-compliance. A framework of civil law can encourage voluntary action to minimise exposure to various financial liabilities. Measures that raise awareness and ensure freedom of access to information and the courts can allow different stakeholders to put pressure on companies to improve their environmental performance and thereby encourage voluntary action to protect market share or to maintain public relations. As a result it is not at all clear that voluntary action is undertaken unpersuaded by financial incentives.

Thus it can be seen that the only distinguishing feature of voluntary action is that it is unforced by law. However, while by its nature voluntary action cannot be secured by legal imperative, it may come about in response to the threat of legal action, it may be linked with the demands of mandatory regulation and it may be persuaded by financial incentives and other inducements....

THE CASE FOR VOLUNTARY REGULATION

Jenkins (1995) outlines a number of arguments that may be used to support calls for a move away from mandatory regulation and toward voluntary regulation. Broadly, these arguments suggest that voluntary regulation may be both more efficient and more effective than mandatory regulation in a number of respects.

In relation to efficiency it is suggested that voluntary regulation might impose lower costs on both government and industry than mandatory regulation. From the government perspective, voluntary action may allow a reduction in the public expenditure that is associated with environmental protection or a diversion of that expenditure toward more productive uses. Primarily this may be the case if a shift from mandatory to voluntary regulation reduces the need for an expensive regulatory agency. However, if the agency implementing mandatory regulation is obliged to recover its costs from the companies that it regulates, the cost savings that might follow a shift from mandatory to voluntary regulation may in effect be passed on to industry. Efficiency gains may also be realized if voluntary regulation allows industry to search for, develop and apply environmental initiatives in a more flexible way. A lack of flexibility in mandatory regulation can result in environmental problems being dealt with in an effective but costly way. The increased flexibility that voluntary action might allow may save money by allowing industry to adopt the least cost responses to environmental problems.

In relation to effectiveness it is suggested that voluntary regulation might secure higher or accelerated levels of environmental improvement than those which typically arise from mandatory regulation. Aside from its flexibility, voluntary regulation may be better able to foster commitment to environmental improvement than mandatory regulation precisely because it is voluntary. The benefits of this commitment are particularly apparent when compared to the defensive position that some companies adopt when faced with the demands of mandatory regulation. In such instances companies may spend time and money resisting or trying to avoid the demands of mandatory regulation rather than improving their environmental performance. Finally, voluntary action can often be enacted over a shorter time frame than mandatory regulation as it does not have to go through the same governmental and legislative procedures. Consequently it is possible to speculate that voluntary regulation may secure higher levels of environmental improvement than mandatory regulation and in a shorter time frame.

However, drawing on an analysis of voluntary regulation in practice, Jenkins (1995) argues that practical experience with the application of voluntary regulation commonly contradicts the arguments put forward above. Far from encouraging innovation and accelerated environmental improvement, Jenkins (1995) suggests that a switch to voluntary regulation alone removes what is commonly a major impetus for innovation, namely the imperative to comply with the demands of mandatory regulation. In essence, in the absence of mandatory regulation companies are free to assign a higher priority to the economic pressures of the short term than to the environmental opportunities of the medium to long term.

More broadly, a shift from mandatory to voluntary regulation can mean that government hands over responsibility for significant areas of public policy to the private sector. This generates concern about the credibility of voluntary regulation and the accountability of voluntary regulators. For example, there is a suspicion that because of their voluntary and sometimes commercial nature, the verification structures that are developed to assure the quality and demonstrate the integrity of voluntary regulation may be more susceptible to regulatory capture than those that seek to ensure compliance with mandatory regulation. Finally, the costs that are saved through a reduction in the administration of mandatory regulation may be offset by an increase in the costs that follow a rise in voluntary regulation. Aside from the distributional issues, in aggregate the cost savings associated with a shift from mandatory to voluntary regulation depend upon the relative efficiencies of each.

It is clear from the discussion above that in principle a range of different agendas favour the wider application of voluntary regulation. The critical issue then is whether voluntary regulation can replace mandatory regulation or whether it can merely supplement it. In some instances voluntary action is clearly motivated by the threat of mandatory regulation. In other instances voluntary initiatives are taken either to ensure compliance with the requirements of mandatory regulation or to respond to the financial incentives and disincentives that are established by mandatory regulation. Given the central role that mandatory regulation plays in stimulating the development and application of voluntary regulation it is likely that voluntary regulation will have a greater influence on industrial behaviour where it is applied as a complement to mandatory regulation rather than as a replacement for it.

THE CASE OF THE EU'S ECO-MANAGEMENT AND AUDIT SCHEME

Having considered the general issues associated with voluntary regulation in some detail, this section will assess the nature of the EU's Eco-Management and Audit Scheme (EMAS) as an example of voluntary regulation. EMAS is also an example of a broader category of environmental management systems (EMS) standards. Although there are differences between EMAS and other EMS standards, the similarities are sufficient to allow them to be considered under the same heading. The following discussion briefly considers the history behind the development of EMS standards in general before assessing the nature of EMAS in particular. The analysis draws on the findings of interviews with representatives of DGXI (Environment) of the European Commission, the body that coordinated the development of EMAS and that is ultimately responsible for its administration.

The development of the various EMS standards can be viewed as the result of two relatively recent trends, namely the success of various quality management systems (QMS) standards in the 1980s and the general rise in environmental awareness in the late 1980s and early 1990s. Although lagging behind quality management by at least a decade, the development of systems based approaches to environmental management has undoubtedly benefited from the experience that has accumulated with QMS standards in industry. Following the success of these QMS standards, and reacting in some way to an upsurge in public concern about the environment, industry began to request the development of an EMS standard toward the end of the 1980s.

In the UK, the British Standards Institute developed the first EMS standard (BS7750) which after an earlier pilot scheme was finally launched in 1994. In order to allow the introduction of a common international EMS standard, the British standard was subsequently withdrawn and replaced in 1997 by the International Standards Organization's (ISO) EMS standard (ISO14001). At the EU level a separate EMS based initiative was developed and launched in 1993 as the EMAS Regulation. Together, EMAS and ISO14001 represent the most important EMS standards currently available. Both EMAS and ISO14001 provide an opportunity for industry to establish an EMS which can be certified or verified against the requirements of an external standard by an independent agency. The following discussion will examine the broader nature of EMS standards by focusing on EMAS.

The EMAS Regulation "allowing voluntary participation by companies in the industrial sector in a Community eco-management and audit scheme" was developed by the European Committee for Standardization (CEN) and became operational in 1995. EMAS is generally regarded as the most demanding EMS standard. The objective of EMAS is to promote "continuous improvement in environmental performance" on a site-specific basis. For registered sites this is to be achieved by ensuring that these sites:

• Adopt a company environmental policy;
• conduct an environmental review;
• introduce an environmental programme and an environmental management system;
• carry out an environmental audit;
• prepare an environmental statement to be released to the public.

EMAS establishes the principles upon which each of these stages must be based. Theoretically the environmental programme must be based on the adoption of objectives and targets which address a range of the site's environmental impacts, including some of its most significant ones. Once developed an accredited environmental verifier must check that the approach taken by the site complies with the requirements of the scheme. Once compliance has been assured, a site is able to register its participation in the scheme.

EMAS was established as an EU Regulation and thus does not require enabling legislation at the national level. Instead it demanded that member states establish structures to promote and administer the scheme by early 1995. Thus, member states were obliged to designate a competent body to administer the scheme and to establish a body and a system to accredit independent environmental verifiers who essentially act as regulators by checking the compliance of those sites that choose to register under the scheme.

Within each member state, the primary role of the competent body is to hold and maintain a register of registered sites. The competent body may be a government department or agency or an independent organization. The accreditation body is charged with the task of accrediting individuals or organizations as environmental verifiers, indicating that they have the necessary skills and capacities to assess a site against the requirements of EMAS. The accreditation body must supervise the performance of verifiers over time to ensure their continuing compliance with the accreditation criteria. Finally, the role of the verifier is to assess the performance of companies wishing to register under the scheme and therefore to ensure that they comply with the requirements of EMAS. This includes the validation of the environmental statement. If this is completed successfully the site can be registered with the competent body....

[A]lthough EMAS is a voluntary scheme, those sites that wish to register for the scheme choose to subject themselves to a considerable degree of external scrutiny from an independent organization. Despite its voluntary nature, EMAS can demand a considerable input from government if it assumes responsibility for establishing and running the institutional structures that are required to administer the scheme. Government can also influence the way that mandatory regulations interact with voluntary schemes such as EMAS. However, despite the involvement and influence of government, EMAS registration is at this point voluntary for all companies.

THE STRENGTHS AND WEAKNESSES OF ENVIRONMENTAL MANAGEMENT SYSTEMS STANDARDS

... The potential strengths that can be associated with the application of an EMS can be outlined as follows:

• *They can provide a framework for a comprehensive approach to the environment:* A management system can help to reduce the uncertainty and complexity associated with the environment as a business issue. In particular it may increase the amount of meaningful data available to managers, thus helping to improve the level of control that they are able to exert over the environmental performance of their business.

• *They create the potential for improved economic performance:* A systematic and periodic assessment of the environmental problems of a business may reveal opportunities for a range of waste minimization and energy efficiency gains which previously had not been recognized or exploited. Where action is taken to exploit these opportunities, economic competitiveness may be enhanced.

• *They can improve public image and reputation:* A well designed management system can aid effective communication by helping to relay information to and from stakeholders both inside and outside the firm. The presence of a management system can also improve a company's image by helping to communicate commitment and responsibility.

• *They can change the relationship between regulators and business:* Management systems can help to ensure compliance with the demands of mandatory regulation. They may also help to improve the relationship between the business and the mandatory regulator, particularly by developing trust and by creating conditions that are conducive to compliance and continual improvement.

• *They can establish a new learning network:* An externally verified management system can help to develop links between the business and other organizations with related experience and expertise. Whilst interacting in this network the opportunity is presented for a company to learn about alternative approaches to environmental management.

Thus, an EMS can offer a number of benefits. These include direct cost savings, enhanced management control and improved relationships with regulators and stakeholders. However, it is important to note that the benefits outlined above do not necessarily follow the application of an EMS as the performance of management systems can vary considerably. It is also apparent that there are a number of potential weaknesses associated with the development and application of an EMS:

• *They do not guarantee any level of environmental performance:* The presence of a management system does not in itself demonstrate any particular standard of environmental performance although registration with an EMS standard normally demands a minimum level of compliance with mandatory regulation. Furthermore, although EMS standards commonly require continuous improvement, the speed of improvement required to retain registration is not specified. Thus, they may lend legitimacy and credibility to environmentally damaging companies that are only improving slowly.

• *They may be costly to develop and apply:* Particularly during their development but also throughout their application, management systems can draw on the managerial capacity and financial capital of a firm. These costs and the associated opportunity costs may not be recouped, particularly in the short term.

• *They may increase the risks associated with legislative non-compliance:* Although management systems can help companies to minimize the risk of noncompliance, the information that a management system collects and presents may enable prosecution or litigation if it is disclosed or discovered. This may also increase the consequences of noncompliance by making it easier to allocate blame and by allowing charges to be pursued on the basis of negligence rather than ignorance.

• *They may encourage short termism:* In cases where companies communicate their performance and publish targets for environ-mental improvement they can be held to account more readily by various stakeholders. If these stakeholders demand improvement in the short term, attention and resources may be diverted from longer term opportunities with the potential to realize more significant benefits.

• *They increase the likelihood that the means are confused with the ends:* Companies may channel their resources toward the development of a management system or registration with an EMS standard. As management systems in themselves do not secure environmental improvement this may reduce or delay the benefits which they are designed to realize.

• *They may engender complacency:* Once a company has installed an EMS, or is registered with an EMS standard, its interest in further initiatives may decline. In such instances the EMS may be passively relied upon to deliver environmental improvement rather than being used as an active mechanism for environmental improvement. Similarly, the management system may limit the emphasis of environmental management initiatives to operational rather than strategic change.

It is clear then that, as with any form of regulation, voluntary regulation in general and EMS standards in particular have a range of potential strengths and weaknesses. Other than in limited instances, the economic and environmental performance of voluntary regulation has yet to be generally established. However, in the case of EMS standards practical experience associated with the application of voluntary regulation is accumulating rapidly. It is clear from this experience that there are potential benefits associated with the application of this form of regulation. Despite this experience it is as yet unclear whether the external verification structures that have been designed to administer and ensure the integrity of EMS standards are sufficiently developed to ensure that the potential weaknesses of voluntary regulation are avoided. . . .

CONCLUSIONS

It is increasingly acknowledged that governments have traditionally relied on a restricted number of policy instruments in their attempts to influence the relationship between economic development and environmental protection. More recently, however, governments have begun to explore the ability of alternative policy instruments to mobilise the problem solving capacities of industry for environmental ends. While various approaches to regulation demonstrate some potential in this respect, as Jaenicke and Weidner (1995, p. 18) have noted, it is apparent that "there is no single ideal instrument or type of instrument, we need the full orchestra."

The review of voluntary regulation provided above has suggested that it has the potential to influence the relationship between economic development and environmental protection. However, it has also been argued that voluntary action is commonly motivated by the direct and indirect impacts of mandatory regulation. Consequently, it is likely that voluntary regulation will have a greater influence on industrial behaviour where it is applied as a complement to mandatory regulation rather than as a replacement for it.

In addition to the nature of its interaction with mandatory regulation, the performance of voluntary regulation depends upon the manner of its application . . . [T]his chapter has suggested that the performance of voluntary regulations such as EMAS can be analysed with reference to the frameworks, structures and styles that characterize their implementation. . . .

REFERENCES

Jacobs, M. (1991). *The Green Economy*, London: Pluto Press, p. 134

Jaenicke, M. and Weidner, H. (1995). *Successful Environmental Policy: A Critical Evaluation of 24 Cases*, Berlin: Sigma, p. 18

Jenkins, T. (1995). *The Superficial Attraction: The Voluntary Approach and Sustainable Development*, London: Friends of the Earth

---

■ **NOTES**

1. In the book from which this reading was taken, the authors examine both the EMAS regulation and the European Union's Integrated Pollution Prevention and Control (IPPC) Directive. They compare the experiences of the United Kingdom (in using a more truly voluntary approach similar to that at present promoted in the United States) and the Netherlands (in using a cooperative, but firmer approach closer to that utilized in the Nordic countries and Germany). They find that greater technological innovation has been fostered in the latter, more stringent regulatory system.

2. For a further discussion of the IPPC directive, see chapter 13.   ■

b.   Industrial Ecology as a Special Example of Unilateral Commitments

One industrial response to the costs of reducing emissions to air and water, and the costs of handling and treating hazardous wastes, has been the emphasis on voluntary waste and material exchange that is popularly known as "industrial ecology." The following reading explains this concept and highlights its differences from pollution prevention.

Overview of the Special Issue on Industrial Ecology

N. A. Ashford

Source: *Journal of Cleaner Production*, 1997, 5(1/2), pp. i–iv, excerpted with permission.

...[In an essay on industrial ecology, John] Ehrenfeld [1997] traces the evolution [of] world views or paradigms from one in which scarcity, limits and sustainability are not viewed as physical problems; to concerns with environmental externalities to the need for resource management; to industrial ecology which acknowledges the limits of resources, energy and the assimilative capacity of natural systems and the need to embark on a sustainable economic and industrial pathway. Through the lens of product design and focusing on supply-side strategies, rather than demand-side policies affecting consumption, Ehrenfeld articulates four specific avenues to product design: (1) improving the metabolic pathways of industrial processes and materials use, (2) creating loop-closing industrial ecosystems, (3) de-materializing industrial output, and (4) systematizing patterns of energy use. Emphasis on dematerialization reflects a change from increasing consumption of material goods, to improved utilization of materials/goods, the satisfaction of needs by longer product life and greater serviceability (including re-manufacturing), and functional substitution. Anastas and Breen (1997) discuss design-for-the-environment (DfE) and green chemistry for both products and processes as the "heart and soul" of the industrial ecology, and the key to achieving sustainability. Both are seen as essential for promoting pollution prevention. Like Ehrenfeld, the authors acknowledge the need to search for functional substitutes for toxic chemicals, but they also emphasize alternative synthetic pathways (green chemis-

try) for the production of materials and goods. Special importance is placed on the design of environmentally sound processes and products, observing that "some 70% of the costs of a product's development, manufacture, and use is determined in the initial design of a product."...

[In a second essay, excerpted in chapter 13, Kristen] Oldenburg and [Kenneth] Geiser [1997] discuss the compatibilities and incompatibilities between industrial ecology and pollution prevention, noting the definitional problems both have had in their evolution. Industrial ecology continues to have those problems. In contrast, "pollution prevention has advanced... from a concept to a proven, practical deed." Citing similarities in their emphasis on promoting the reduction of pollutant discharges to the environment and their utilization of life cycle analysis and materials accounting, they nonetheless identify important differences. While both strive for efficiency in production, pollution prevention may require more of firms in order to sufficiently reduce the use and discharges of toxic substances. The operational boundaries of the two concepts are different, with pollution prevention focused on the individual firm and industrial ecology promoting efficiency in environmental management through the linkages of participating firms at the industrial or regional level. Further, pollution prevention sees government (regulation) as playing a central role, while industrial ecology seems to generally bypass a role for government. Further, strict regulation of RCRA, for example, is regarded as a barrier to recycling schemes essential to industrial ecology. The greatest incompatibilities are viewed in terms of their effects on recycling, materials efficiency, and risk reduction. Arguing that waste recycling has a "spotty history," the authors point out that the aim of pollution prevention is to prevent (especially off-site) recycling. Industrial ecology's focus on closing the loop encourages recycling; eventually, however, toxics enter the waste stream, unlike pollution prevention. The authors observe that improved material efficiencies at the firm level do not automatically mean improved efficiencies at the industry or market level, again reflecting different operational boundaries of the two concepts. Of special concern are the disincentives for technological innovation and pollution prevention that industrial ecology creates by interlocking the activities of firms in static rigidity, with "waste-to-input material" dependencies. Finally, unlike industrial ecology, pollution prevention requires a focus and prioritization on the magnitude and nature of the risks associated with specific pollutants. Industrial ecology is driven much more by a search for optimal material and energy utilization, and other economic efficiencies, rather than a focus on maximizing risk reduction....A potential for convergence is seen where both industrial ecology and pollution prevention...focus beyond industry's waste streams to consider industry's product streams (see Ehrenfeld). The authors observe "[i]ndustrial ecology needs to consider the recycling and so-called 'take back' of products as well as wastes, and pollution prevention needs to more effectively deal with the prevention of pollution from products. If industrial ecology schemes are to be made compatible with pollution preven-

tion programs, industrial ecology should de-emphasize the current concept of firms made interdependent by linking waste streams and input needs" (p. iii).

Providing a contrasting view to that of Oldenburg and Geiser, [Gunter] Pauli [1997] argues that since the goal of cleaner production (what is called pollution prevention in North America) is zero waste, and since individual firms cannot achieve that ideal in a cost-effective manner, then "[c]lusters of industries, where waste of one is input for the other, will emerge as the solution" (p. iii). Pauli directs his remarks to both manufacturing and agricultural systems..., arguing that the zero waste concept must be applied to all minerals and biomass. He advocates that cleaner production can evolve from its linear approach to existing operations to application in systems of industrial and agricultural activities. Implicit in his essay is that linkages between firms can provide complementary solutions to a firm-centered cleaner production approach, augmenting the reduction of pollution achieved by cleaner production to the ultimate desirable goal of zero waste through exchange of materials between different operations. (In other words cleaner production *plus* material/waste exchange.)...

REFERENCES

Ehrenfeld, John (1997) "Industrial Ecology: A Framework for Product and Process Design," *J. Cleaner Prod.*, Volume 5, Number 1-2

Oldenburg, Kristin and Kenneth Geiser (1997) "Pollution Prevention and...or Industrial Ecology?" *J. Cleaner Prod.* Volume 5, Number 1-2

Pauli, Gunter (1997) "Zero Emissions: The Ultimate Goal of Cleaner Production," *J. Cleaner Prod.* Volume 5, Number 1-2

■ **NOTES**

1. In a very real sense, industrial ecology is a paradigm that competes with both pollution prevention *and* pollution control. For a further discussion of the paradigmatic differences, see the Oldenburg and Geiser article excerpted in chapter 13.

2. For a thoughtful article of where industrial ecology is headed, see Ehrenfeld (2004).

3. For an in-depth review of industrial ecology practices, see two special issues of the *Journal of Cleaner Production* dedicated to the subject: volume 12, issues 8–10, October–December 2004 and volume 5, issues 1–2, 1997.   ■

4. Negotiated Outcomes

The following readings survey the use of negotiation in formulating and implementing environmental policy in the United States and assess the potential of negotiation to foster improved environmental outcomes and stimulate technological change.

Negotiated Regulation, Implementation and Compliance in the United States
Nicholas A. Ashford and Charles C. Caldart

Source: E. Croci (ed.), *The Handbook of Voluntary Agreements*. Dordrecht, the Nether lands: Springer; 2005, pp. 135–159, excerpted with permission.

1. INTRODUCTION

Negotiation—as an alternative or an adjunct to the adversarial process—is increasingly touted as the wave of the future. Negotiation, it is argued, is a more efficient use of societal resources, because it is more likely to produce a result that all sides can accept. Moreover, negotiation is said to be more likely to produce creative solutions, because it forces the parties to focus on cooperation rather than confrontation....

2. MODES OF NEGOTIATION

In a broad sense, there are three major instances in which negotiation is used to *make* or *effectuate* policy within the federal administrative system of the United States.

First, there is *negotiated rulemaking*, wherein negotiation is used to help set regulatory standards. Originally an informal process, negotiated rulemaking has now been formalized through legislation. Second, there is *negotiated implementation*, where negotiation is used to determine how a regulatory standard, once set, is to be applied to a particular firm (or other member of the regulated community). Under United States environmental statutes, negotiated implementation often occurs when a permit is being issued or revised, as was the case with EPA's *Project XL* initiative. Such negotiation also occurs when the regulated firm seeks a waiver or variance from the regulatory standard at issue. Of particular interest here are the *innovation waivers* that have been made available by Congress in certain environmental statutes.

When such a waiver is granted by EPA, the firm is given additional time to comply with the standard so that it may perfect a promising innovative compliance technology.

Third, there is *negotiated compliance*, where negotiation is used to determine the terms by which regulatory standards will be enforced against a particular firm (or other regulated entity) that is out of compliance with a particular regulatory standard. By its nature, of course, almost all enforcement involves some amount of negotiation between the enforcing agency (or, in the case of citizen enforcement suits, the enforcing citizen) and the alleged violator. Of interest here are those compliance negotiations that result in (a) compliance through the use of innovative technology, and/or (b) environmental gains *beyond* compliance. Since the early 1990's, EPA has pioneered the use of what it terms "Supplemental Environmental Projects" in an attempt to meet these goals within the compliance context.

In addition, there is what might be classified as a fourth type of policy-relevant negotiation—*regulatory reinvention*—that was begun (at least under that name) in the Clinton administration, and continues today in evolving forms. The most prominent early example was EPA's *Common Sense Initiative* (CSI), wherein the agency assembled groups of interested parties to focus on regulatory issues concerning a particular industry sector (e.g., automobile manufacturing), with an eye toward developing "cleaner, cheaper, smarter" ways of reducing or preventing pollution. In contrast, EPA's "Project XL," mentioned above, focused on negotiations with individual firms. Both programs have now been phased out, and the Bush Administration's National Environmental Performance Track program is now occupying center stage in regulatory reinvention. This program focuses on creating partnerships with individual firms in which the firms agree to exceed regulatory requirements, implement environmental management systems, work closely with their communities, and set three-year goals to continuously improve their environmental performance, in exchange for reduced priority status for inspections, reduced regulatory, administrative, and reporting requirements and positive public recognition.[1]

---

1. Approximately 350 firms have joined the program from a diverse cross-section of the economy. In contrast to Project XL [discussed in the following article], regulatory flexibility seems to relate to discretionary activities of agency inspection and reporting policies, rather than extensive exclusion of individual firms from mandatory regulatory provisions. See http://www.epa.gov/performancetrack.

A detailed discussion of the practice and performance of negotiated rulemaking can be found in chapter 5. A discussion of negotiated implementation, negotiated compliance, and negotiated "regulatory reinvention" follows.

Negotiation as a Means of Developing and Implementing Environmental and Occupational Health and Safety Policy

Charles C. Caldart and Nicholas A. Ashford

Source: 23 *Harvard Environmental Law Review* 141 (1999), excerpted with permission.

IV. NEGOTIATED IMPLEMENTATION

In contrast to its role when it is *enforcing* a regulatory standard (discussed below), an agency's role in *implementing* the standard (that is, when it addresses the question of the timing and the extent of the applicability of the standard to a particular firm) is a circumscribed one. Nonetheless, there are circumstances in which the agency may be able to use negotiation at this stage of the process to encourage innovation and/or incidental health, safety, or environmental gains....

Over its history, EPA has made some use of negotiated implementation both within its explicit statutory mandates (using...waivers made available under certain environmental statutes) and outside of them (using its Project XL program).

1. Innovation Waivers

Various U.S. environmental statutes...have had provisions allowing EPA to issue *innovation waivers* to qualifying firms, thus allowing them additional time to develop innovative approaches to compliance. [The Clean Air Act and Clean Water Act both contain provisions authorizing EPA to grant innovation waivers in certain circumstances.] Under these provisions, EPA is authorized to extend the deadline by which a firm must meet emission or effluent limitations, so long as the agency is persuaded that the firm is actively pursuing an innovative approach to compliance that shows real promise of coming to fruition. Innovation waivers are meant to focus squarely on the innovation of new technology, and are not designed to promote diffusion of an existing technology.

Conceptually, the innovation waiver makes a great deal of sense. Development of an innovative idea into an operational reality—which often requires several periods of trial and error—can take substantial time, during which a firm might otherwise find itself liable for penalties for violations of emission or effluent standards. The innovation waiver exempts the firm from such penalties during a designated trial period, and offers it the prospect of the cost savings that may be derived from the development of a superior technology. [Although it may be unrealistic to expect EPA to use innovation waivers to promote radical process innovation, because of the long time generally needed to develop the innovation, the agency might well use such waivers to encourage both incremental process innovation and the acceleration of radical innovation already underway.]

In practice, however, innovation waivers have been used sparingly by EPA, both because industry has been unsure of their application (and thus has been wary of risking non-compliance), and because the agency has not encouraged their use [Ashford et al. (1985); EPA (1994)]. Success will require EPA to give early, clear, and certain signals to the firm, thus minimising the risk of its technology being found unacceptable. Furthermore, good faith efforts resulting in significant, though not complete, achievement of the pollution reduction goal may need to be rewarded by "fail-soft" enforcement strategies, such as a reduction of otherwise applicable penalties, if industry is to be persuaded to take a technological and legal risk that the innovation waiver often poses. In this context, one can make a case for "risk sharing" between government and industry in the interest of fostering innovative solutions.

2.   Extra-statutory Efforts: Project XL

In an effort to add to those opportunities for flexibility that are specifically authorized by statute, such as innovation waivers, EPA sometimes endeavors to incorporate flexibility into its regulatory implementation by agency fiat. A recent example [now terminated] is the Clinton EPA's Excellence in Leadership Project, popularly known as Project XL. The Clinton White House announced this program, with considerable fanfare, in a 1995 policy statement, and EPA published a set of guidelines for approving Project XL proposals in 1996.

The basic idea of Project XL [was] to allow regulatory flexibility, in return for superior environmental performance, at selected facilities, on a facility-by-facility basis. As conceived, the cornerstone on which Project XL was to rest is negotiation among the regulators, the facility owners, and the affected community, resulting in a Final Project Agreement ("FPA") governing environmental performance at the facility. The underlying rationale for Project XL was the belief that, for appropriately selected (new and existing) facilities, such negotiations could produce a plan for limiting pollutant discharge from the facility that will both cost *less*, and reduce environmental and public health risks *more*, than would have been the case under existing regulations.[219] The program was far from a clear success.... Few FPAs [were] negotiated, and some of those that [were became] the subject of considerable debate and opposition.

A fundamental problem with Project XL [was] that it envisione[d] a kind of regulatory flexibility that has not been authorized by Congress. Because it was not authorized by statute, the regulatory plan set forth in the negotiated FPA did not supersede existing regulations. Thus, to the extent that the regulatory "flexibility" negotiated by the participants involve[d] a failure to comply with certain regulations (even if also involve[d] *outperforming* certain other regulations), the facility [was] operating in violation of the law. And, since relief from existing regulations is precisely what [made] this program attractive to the business community, most FPAs [were] expected to involve violations of applicable environmental regulations. Indeed, one source reported that an expression among EPA staff familiar with Project XL [was] that "if it ain't illegal, it ain't XL." This [made] Project XL an unsafe bet for the participating firm. For, even if EPA and the state give informal assurances that they will not take enforcement action that is inconsistent with the FPA, the agencies cannot guarantee that such enforcement action will not be taken under the "citizen suit" provision of the applicable federal statute.

In theory, the threat of a citizen enforcement suit was to be eradicated (or at least greatly minimized) by the inclusion of the affected community in the negotiation process. Yet this points to a second fundamental problem with XL: the difficulty of defining the relevant "community." Is it limited to those living near the plant, or does it include national and regional environmental groups with an interest in the issue? Does it include labor? Does it include those who speak on behalf of the protection of sensitive popula-

---

219. Negotiation between the agency and the facility owner (sometimes also involving environmental groups and/or local community groups) is commonplace in the permitting process. Project XL negotiations [were] different, however, in that they purported to *replace* current standards with an al-

ternative approach, while traditional permit negotiations generally are over the proper way to *apply* current standards to the facility in question. Thus, XL purport[ed] to be the negotiation of environmental *policy*, albeit on a facility-by-facility basis.

tions, or on behalf of disadvantaged neighborhoods? These are high-stakes issues for two reasons.

First, any interested party who is excluded from the negotiation process is less likely to be satisfied with the result, and thus is more likely to challenge it, through a citizen enforcement suit, a public organizing and publicity campaign, or both. Probably the best-known Project XL agreement[,] for example, pertains to [a new Intel Corporation facility built at the company's] semiconductor production site in Chandler, Arizona. The five-year project agreement, which cover[ed] operations at a 720-acre site, was negotiated among the company, federal and state regulators, and five Chandler residents. Although the participants presumably [were] satisfied with the FPA negotiated through this process, many non-participants [were] not. Two vociferous critics [were] the Silicon Valley Toxics Coalition, a California-based group that addresses pollution problems in the semiconductor industry, and the Natural Resources Defense Council, a national environmental group. These two groups, [who were] concerned about the national and industry-wide implications of this agreement as much as, if not more than, its local environmental impacts, mounted a high-profile campaign against the Intel agreement, and against Project XL itself. This level of opposition clearly indicates that the negotiating committee that devised the regulatory plan for the Intel facility was *not* representative of the "relevant" community.

Second, the composition of the negotiating committee is of obvious *substantive* importance as well. If important constituencies are left underrepresented, the agreement negotiated is much less likely to be the "right" result. The five community representatives who helped negotiate the Intel agreement were also members of a pre-existing Intel Community Advisory Panel, and were generally representative of a community sentiment that values the important role that Intel has

played over the past sixteen years in helping transform Chandler from a small agrarian town into the third fastest-growing city in the United States. While this obviously is a legitimate perspective, it may well not be the one that places environmental and public health protection (much less the health concerns of particularly sensitive populations) at the forefront. Indeed, the tendency of local interests to sacrifice long-term environmental and public health interests in favor of short-term economic gain was one of the factors that drove Congress to begin setting *national* pollution standards in the 1970s.

One of the beliefs underlying Project XL [was] that sufficient public involvement and scrutiny at a site could greatly diminish the need for a national regulatory presence. This is unlikely to be the case, however, unless the "public" is broadly and fairly represented, and unless its "involvement" is truly meaningful. At the Intel site, it is not at all clear that the regulatory flexibility negotiated by Intel—such as relaxed permitting requirements for new product lines—is offset by "superior" environmental performance. While EPA concluded that the Intel plant would outperform certain regulatory requirements, there appears to have been no showing that the facility attained, much less outperformed, the current state of art for the semiconductor industry. For example, based on a comparison of projected toxic emissions from the new Intel facility to reported emissions from similarly-sized semiconductor facilities from 1992 through 1994, EPA was able to conclude only that "Intel is well within, if not exceeding, the standard for the industry . . .".

Had groups such as the Silicon Valley Toxics Coalition and the Natural Resources Defense Council been involved as full-fledged negotiating participants at the Intel site, it is likely that any resultant FPA would have been substantively different from the one actually negotiated. It is questionable, however, whether Intel would have agreed to negotiate a FPA with such groups participating. Indeed, when these and other environmental groups requested that the Intel agreement be augmented with legally-enforceable pollution prevention requirements, Intel was not receptive. [An Intel representative was quoted as asking incredulously, "Citizens are going to make decisions...that are binding on Fortune 500 companies?"]

[Mazurek (1999).] Although this clearly does not represent the sentiments of all companies regarding all situations, the hesitancy that many firms would feel about sitting down as equal participants with environmental groups in site-specific negotiations is another factor that would tend to limit the success of an initiative such as Project XL. In addition, meaningful involvement of the public, even where it is acceptable to the company, likely would considerably extend the time necessary to develop the FPA.

...EPA appears to have recognized that a site-specific negotiated solution is fraught with potential problems, and that, like negotiated rulemaking, it cannot be expected to be done successfully without a substantial commitment of time and resources. A Project XL success story makes the point. In 1997, the agency completed negotiations on what has been characterized as a "small, focused" FPA involving an OSi Specialties organosilicone plant on the Ohio River. According to a company attorney who participated in the process, the negotiations were "enormously burdensome" for the agency. "Unless they can think of a more efficient way to do it," he opined, "I'd be surprised if the program survives." To some degree, of course, the amount of time and resources that the agency [found it necessary to] devote to a Project XL negotiation [was] a function of the relative novelty of the XL concept within EPA, the level of mistrust of the XL process within the environmental community, and the pressure on the agency to "make good" on its promise to deliver increased regulatory flexibility without sacrificing environmental goals. Even if [a program such as] Project XL were to one day become a routinized part of EPA's activities, however, one would expect the resource demand to continue to be

substantial. Real negotiation of environmental policy, even if it is only the policy for a single facility, requires considerable effort....

V. NEGOTIATED COMPLIANCE

Roughly 90% of firms cited with noncriminal violations of federal environmental statutes in the United States resolve the matter through a negotiated settlement (rather than through an administrative hearing or court trial). The settlement of an enforcement action often offers an agency an excellent opportunity to promote pollution prevention, rather than conventional end-of-pipe control technology. The firm's attention has been commanded, and a need for creative (and less costly) approaches to compliance may well have become apparent. Outside of the enforcement process, an agency has little statutory or regulatory authority to require firms to implement pollution prevention; the regulated community can choose the means by which it will comply with federal requirements. But once an enforcement action is initiated, a window of opportunity for pollution prevention opens, because the means of achieving compliance likely will be subject to negotiation between the agency and the violator.

[An agency program that has taken good advantage of this opportunity is EPA's supplemental environmental project (SEP) program, which is discussed in chapter 13.]...

VI. REGULATORY REINVENTION: EPA'S "COMMON SENSE" INITIATIVE

Under the Clinton Administration, EPA [determined] that fundamental changes in approach will be necessary if significant additional progress in protecting the environment is to be made, and if the environmental challenges of the future are to be resolved satisfactorily. The agency refer[red] to this as the need for "regulatory reinvention." In July 1994, EPA began its *Common Sense Initiative* (CSI), which it termed the "centerpiece" of its regulatory reinvention efforts. The primary goals of CSI [were] to find "cleaner, cheaper, smarter" ways of reducing pollution, and to formulate proposed changes in the existing regulatory structure to effectuate them. As with Project XL, negotiation among interested parties [was] the means by which EPA hope[d] to achieve the goals of the program. Unlike XL, however, the focus of the negotiations [was] *industry-wide*. To carry out CSI, the agency [assembled] six advisory committees, one for each of six industrial sectors: automobile manufacturing, computers and electronics, iron and steel, metal finishing, petroleum refining, and printing. Each advisory committee consist[ed] of representatives from EPA, the relevant industry sector, state and local regulatory agencies, national and local environmental groups, labor, and community organizations. The work of these committees [was] overseen by a separate Council, whose membership [was] drawn from the same sources. The Council [was] chaired by the EPA Administrator, and each of the six sector committees [was] chaired by an EPA official. The work of the Council and the committees [was] assisted by EPA staff.

This industry-sector structure [was] based on a fundamentally sound premise: that, for a variety of reasons, different industries often differ in their technological and economic potential for reducing pollution, and also in the way in which they respond to various types of regulatory signals. By bringing together people who are knowledgeable about the opportunities for reducing pollution within a particular industry, and who have a stake in how, when, and under what terms that reduction will occur, EPA hoped to harness the potential of each industry to a fuller extent than it had heretofore been able to do. The agency also hoped that, by creating an atmosphere in which innovation and flexibility were emphasized, the focus of the committees would be on pollution prevention rather than end-of-pipe pollution control. [In December 1998,

arguing that the CSI approach had been proven a success, EPA announced that CSI itself would be phased out, but that the lessons learned from the initiative would be expanded to other industry segments in a future action plan.]

[In fact,] the results of the CSI experiment [were] mixed. On the one hand, as EPA points out, the initiative brought together six groups of people representing a diverse set of interests, and [encouraged] an ongoing dialogue on issues that are important to the future development of environmental policy .... [Indeed,] if CSI succeed[ed] at nothing more than promoting a better understanding of the issues among different stakeholders, and of each other, among those likely to participate in environmental policy-making and implementation affecting these industries, it arguably [had] a positive impact.

On the other hand, however, CSI has been criticized for its lack of substantive results. A series of reviews of CSI have raised this issue, including a 1997 report issued by the U.S. General Accounting Office ("GAO"), a research arm of Congress [GAO (1997), hereafter "GAO Report"]. ... In general, GAO and other reviewers found that the CSI process move[d] considerably more slowly than most of the participants [would have liked]. The reasons for CSI's slow pace, GAO found, [were] multifold: the time necessary to collect and analyze data; the variations in the participants' understanding of the technical issues involved; the time taken by the participants "in reaching consensus on the approaches needed to address large, complex issues or policies;" the time taken by participants "discussing how they would carry out their work and developing their own operating standards;" and the difficulties experienced by some participants in making the necessary time commitment. None of this should be particularly surprising. Indeed, when one adds to this list the overall need to establish a degree of trust among the participants in each sector group sufficient to permit a meaningful discussion on substantive issues, it is not particularly difficult to understand why substantive progress [was] slow in coming. . . .

Nonetheless, there appears to [have been] a growing feeling among participants that a failure to meaningfully step up the pace of substantive progress [would mean] the death-knell of the initiative. The automobile and petroleum refining industries [ ] ended their participation, and other participants [indicated] that they would leave unless EPA [made] changes [in response to the various reviews of the project to make the process more efficient].[284] To address this issue, GAO [had] proposed that EPA

. . . provide an improved operating framework that (1) more clearly defines the Initiative's "cleaner, cheaper, smarter" environmental protection goal—including its expected results—and (2) specifies how the Council and its subcommittees and work-groups will accomplish their work, clarifying issues such as how and when consensus will be achieved, how the Initiative's goal should be interpreted and applied to individual projects, and to what extent representatives of all stakeholder groups should be included in activities at each level of the Initiative, including its projects and workgroups [GAO Report, note 13 at 7].

EPA [indicated at the time that it would] introduce reforms of this nature, but GAO fault[ed] the agency for not having done much of this at the outset. It is not at all clear, however, that this would have been the right approach. It is arguable that, had EPA attempted to dictate terms of this nature to the participants at the beginning of the process, rather than allowing the participants to first address these issues on their own, it would have engendered considerable resentment among some of the participants.

Moreover, the changes envisioned by GAO [were] unlikely to address the more deep-seated issues that [slowed or prevented] substantive results along the lines originally

anticipated by EPA. It is likely that a major factor inhibiting real progress [was] the fact that, in contrast to negotiated rulemaking, the CSI negotiations [did not proceed] within a formal legal context, with a known and meaningful set of potential consequences. In negotiated rulemaking, the participants all know that, regardless of whether they reach agreement on a proposed rule, a rule is likely to be issued. The "stakes" for each partici-pant thus are fairly clear: if they do not nego-tiate, the agency likely will promulgate a regulation without them, and the result may be something they will not like. In the CSI negotiations, however, the consequences of inaction [usually were] both far less clear and far less dramatic. Indeed, in most cases the failure of a negotiating committee to agree on a particular "regulatory reinvention" pro-posal [would have had] no greater practical effect than simply the preservation of the sta-tus quo.

Accordingly, the chief factor likely to be motivating industry's participation in [CSI-type] negotiations is the opportunity to push for regulatory alternatives that are less ex-pensive (to industry) than the status quo. Industry's interest, then, is likely to be in "streamlining" or eliminating current regula-tion, and not in extending the scope of regu-lation into new areas. . . . [And], since the environmental representatives should not be expected to agree to a cheaper alternative if it does not also represent increased environ-mental benefit, progress [in these types of negotiations] may be slow in coming, espe-cially in those industry sectors where few easy and obvious "win/win" (i.e., cheaper *and* cleaner) regulatory improvements present themselves.

Thus, it should not be surprising that the petroleum and automobile industries decided to abandon their participation in the CSI Initiative. Effective participation in nego-tiations of this nature takes a considerable commitment of resources. As noted by the American Petroleum Institute in a letter to

---

284. Eventually, several environmental justice groups, as well as representatives from the State of Michigan, also withdrew from the CSI negotiations.

EPA explaining the withdrawal of its member companies from the CSI negotiations, the companies "believe the refining industry's resources...can be more productively directed toward other approaches."...

Another systemic problem one would expect to encounter in negotiations of this nature stems from the participants' unequal access to relevant data. If effective strategies to encourage pollution prevention are to be crafted by consensus, reliable technical information, especially information relating to the technological potential for pollution prevention, is likely to be important. Much of the relevant data, of course, will be in the hands of industry. Without a clear incentive to make these data available to the other participants, industry is likely to prefer to pick and choose what it will share, thus making meaningful negotiations all the more difficult. This reportedly [was] a major issue, for example, in the computer and electronics work group. Firms reportedly [were] reluctant to divulge information because "they feared that regulators would use data to extract further concessions," and because they believed that environmental groups would "use any information divulged during CSI meetings to mount lawsuits." This, in turn, contributed to a sense of mistrust among the environmental group participants.

This is not to say that [cooperative approaches are] not capable of producing any meaningful results of substance. There are cleaner/cheaper opportunities in a number of industries that may be able to be realized without the "push" of additional regulatory pressure, and [cooperative approaches] could bring some of these to light. The CSI metal finishing work group, for example, began a successful demonstration of a new technology for filtering chromium from air releases that should decrease chromium emissions while reducing costs by about 90%, and [ ] announced agreement on an emission reduction program that is reported to rely, in part, on pollution prevention strategies. In addition, the CSI printing

work group [developed] an education and outreach project designed "to achieve fundamental change" by incorporating the philosophy of pollution prevention into everyday work practices. [In general, however, the bulk of the CSI negotiations reportedly did *not* focus on pollution prevention strategies, let alone innovation, thus falling well below EPA's original expectations.]

In 1999, two years after the GAO report, EPA issued a report by an independent contractor evaluating some 40 CSI projects [Bruninga (1999)]. The report concluded that, although there had been a small number of sector-specific modifications, EPA made little progress in addressing broad regulatory changes through CSI, and CSI successes were not integrated into core EPA programs.

VII. CONCLUSION

Negotiation should hardly be viewed as a panacea for the various difficulties that typically confront the policymaker. Used in the right context, however, negotiation can be a useful tool in the establishment, implementation, and enforcement of environmental and occupational safety and health policy. Negotiation can facilitate a better understanding of issues, concerns, facts, and positions among adversaries. It can also promote the sharing of relevant information, and can provide an opportunity for creative problem-solving. Whether negotiation will be better than other, generally more adversarial mechanisms as a means of fostering improved environmental, health, and safety outcomes, or of stimulating meaningful technological change, will depend on the situation in which it is used. In general, negotiation would appear to work best as a means of securing these goals in situations in which the necessary regulatory signals for improvement and innovation are already in place.

This is one of the reasons that EPA's use of *negotiated compliance*, as embodied in its SEP policy, has been as successful as it has been. To the firm that is the target of the enforcement action, the "stakes" are clear: so long as it believes it faces higher costs (in the form of a larger fine and/or higher transaction costs and/or adverse publicity) if it does not identify and execute a SEP that is acceptable to EPA, the firm has a meaningful incentive to participate in good faith in the SEP process. Additionally, because the agency has structured the program to allow maximum credit for pollution prevention projects, pollution prevention can become the focus, *and the goal*, of the negotiations. The pollution prevention results of the SEP program have been relatively modest—mostly diffusion and, sometimes, incremental innovation—but this is in keeping with the relatively modest nature of the financial incentives typically involved, and with the relatively short time period within which the SEP typically must be identified and completed. Especially because negotiation is the traditional means of resolving enforcement disputes, even outside of the SEP process, negotiation appears to work well here. . . .

One would also expect negotiation to work well in those *negotiated implementation* situations that have a clear, formal focus on technological change, such as the innovation waiver opportunities created by certain environmental statutes. . . . The chief signal to innovate—the new regulatory standard—is already in place (or clearly on the horizon) before negotiation over the waiver or variance begins, and the statutes typically provide an extended period of time for the firm to develop and test the proposed innovation. Thus, so long as the new standard is stringent enough to command the firm's attention, firms should have a meaningful incentive to negotiate time to pursue an innovative compliance alternative.

The fact that EPA's innovation waiver program has thus far not lived up to expectations appears largely due to a failure of [leadership and] administration. This, in turn, may have contributed to what appears to be a reticence by Congress to include innovation waiver provisions in its revisions to existing statutes.

If EPA could develop and promote its innovation waiver program the way it has the SEP program, the innovation waiver might become a much more important means of securing environmentally beneficial technological change. . . .

In contrast to negotiated compliance and negotiated implementation, *negotiated rulemaking* is a situation in which the chief regulatory signal for improvement and innovation is *not* already established, at least not in full. Rather, one of the functions of negotiation in this context is to *establish*, either in part or in full, the stringency of the regulatory standard. If the goal is innovation, this may well be problematic. If the nature of the regulated industry is such that it will require a dramatic impetus, such as the promulgation of an unexpectedly stringent standard (or the fear that such a standard will be promulgated), before it will be motivated to innovate, negotiated rulemaking may well be inadvisable. Since negotiated rulemaking seeks consensus among the participants, and since such an industry is unlikely to agree to a standard that it views as having a "dramatic" impact, negotiated rulemaking is unlikely to produce a standard of this nature. In such situations, negotiated rulemaking's focus on consensus can effectively *remove* the potential to spur innovation [Goulding and Murphy, 1998].

In situations in which the desired technological change is likely to come more easily, negotiated rulemaking should be expected to have a better chance of success. Here, the advantages of negotiation, such as information-sharing and creative problem-solving, may work to encourage productive technological change. The key to the willingness of industry representatives to explore the technological options in good faith is likely to be tied to what they perceive the likely "default" standard to be. If they believe that, in the absence of a negotiated rule, the agency will promulgate a stringent rule on its own, their willingness to focus on creative technological solutions is likely to be higher. The agency can facilitate this process by making clear at the outset that promoting technological change will be a focus of the regulation. If technologically literate stakeholders, such as trade unions or sophisticated non-profit groups, are involved, the dominance of industry's technical expertise may be minimized, and outcomes that advance the state of the technology may emerge.

Another important difference between negotiated rulemaking and negotiations over SEPs and innovation waivers, however, is that the scope of the negotiations in negotiated rulemaking is (at least) industry-wide, rather than firm-specific. Interest in the negotiations thus is much stronger, and the number of participants who must be involved, if the negotiations are to succeed, is an order of magnitude higher. Accordingly, management of the negotiation process becomes a formidable task, and the agency must have the resources to be able to keep pace. There is always the risk that the process itself, and not the ultimate results of the process, will assume centre stage, and that a focus on technological change will give way to a focus on achieving consensus.

Many of these same concerns are germane when negotiation is used in an *extra-statutory* sense [as was the case with EPA's Project XL and Common Sense Initiative], in an attempt to change regulatory policy. If the focus is industry-wide ... the resource demands will be large. Further, where there is no meaningful incentive for industry negotiators to move away from the status quo—that is, where there is no impending "default" standard or requirement that they perceive as onerous— they may well be interested only in those regulatory changes that save them money.

In the last analysis, it must be recognized that negotiation is a process that facilitates *market solutions* to questions regarding the appropriate ends or means of compliance. That is, the relative bargaining power of the stakeholders largely determines the outcome, unless it is checked at the end of the process

by a government agency with a strong sense of trusteeship for the congressional policy it is charged with implementing. Agencies who see themselves as *mediators* of the negotiation, or who otherwise relinquish their statutory role as trustees, help to promote a market-like result through the operation of the consensus process. In this case, negotiation is unlikely to produce impressive environmental gains linked to technological change. When this happens, the relative success of the negotiations likely will depend on whether some *other* factor, such as a court ruling or a scientific study, can produce the kind of incentives that are likely to promote technological change. If a superior result is to be achieved, it likely will require the participation of agencies with both the means and the will to take a firm position in support of health, safety, and the environment, and in support of the development of new technologies.

REFERENCES

Ashford N, Ayers C, Stone R. Using regulation to change the market for innovation. Harvard Env Law Rev 1985; 9(419): 443–62.

Bruninga, Susan "CSI Successes Not Being Integrated Into Core EPA Programs, Stakeholders Say" *Environment Reporter* 29(50) Friday, April 23, 1999.

EPA, Office of Water. Providing waivers from NPDES permit compliance for industrial pollution prevention technology: the industrial pollution prevention project (IP3). Analysis of Sections 301(K) and 307(E) of the Clean Water Act, 1994.

Mazurek, Jan. *Making Microchips: Policy, Globalization, and Economic Restructuring in the Semiconductor Industry* (1999), p. 187.

[GAO] United States General Accounting Office. Regulatory reinvention: EPA's common sense initiative needs an improved operating framework and progress measures, July 1997.

Goulding A, Murphy J. Regulatory realities: the implementation and impact of industrial environmental regulation. London: Earthscan Publications Ltd, 1998. 120

■ NOTES

1. At least one court has held that the federal Pollution Prevention Act requires EPA to give preference to pollution prevention in its administration of all waivers issued under federal environmental statutes, and not only innovation waivers. See the discussion of *Monsanto v. EPA* in chapter 13.

2. For a 2001 EPA report documenting the U.S. experience with economic incentives and voluntary programs, see EPA (2001). See also EPA (2004) for a discussion of the international experience with these regulatory alternatives.   ■

ACKNOWLEDGMENT

The authors are indebted to Robert F. Stone for his contributions to the writing of this chapter.

REFERENCES

Adriatico, Marianne F. 1999. "The Good Neighbor Agreement: Environmental Excellence Without Compromise," *Hastings West-Northwest Journal of Environmental Law and Policy* 5: 285–302.

Aggieri, F., and A. Hatcheul. 1999. "A Dynamic Model of Environmental Policies: The Case of Innovation Oriented Voluntary Agreements," in *Voluntary Approaches in Environmental Policy*, C. Carraro and F. Leveque (eds.) Boston: Kluwer, pp. 151–186.

Aidt, T. S. Toke Skovsgaard, and Jayasri Dutta. 2004. "Transitional Politics: Emerging Incentive-Based Instruments in Environmental Regulation," *Journal of Environmental Economics and Management* 47(3): 458–479, May.

Alberini, Anna, and Kathleen Segerson. 2002. "Assessing Voluntary Programs to Improve Environmental Quality," *Environment and Resource Economics* 22: 157–184.

Anastas, Paul T. and Joseph J. Breen. 1997. "Design for the Environment and Green Chemistry: The Heart and Soul of Industrial Ecology," *Journal of Cleaner Production* 5(1/2): 97–102.

Anton, Wilma Rose Q., George Deltas, and Madhu Khanna. 2004. "Incentives for Environmental Self-Regulation and Implications for Environmental Performance," *Journal of Environmental Economics and Management* 48(1): 632–654, July.

Ashford, Nicholas A. 1999. "The Influence of Information-based Initiatives and Negotiated Environmental Agreements on Technological Change," in *Voluntary Approaches in Environmental Policy*, C. Carraro and F. Leveque (eds.) Boston: Kluwer, pp. 137–150.

Ashford, Nicholas A. 2006. "Workers' Compensation," in *Environmental and Occupational Medicine*, 4th ed. W. N. Rom (ed.) Philadelphia, Pa.: Lippincott-Raven.

Ashford, N. A., C. Ayers, and R. F. Stone. 1985. "Using Regulation to Change the Market for Innovation," *Harvard Environmental Law Review* 9(2): 419–466.

Atkinson, S., and T. Tietenberg. 1987. "Economic Implications of Emissions Trading Rules," *Canadian Journal of Economics* 20: 370–386.

Barde, J.-P. 2000. "Environmental Policy and Policy Instruments," in *Principles of Environmental and Resource Economics: A Guide for Students and Decision-makers*, 2nd ed. Henk Folmer and H. Landis Gabel (eds.) Cheltenham, UK: Edward Elgar.

Baumol, W. J., and W. E. Oates. 1988. *The Theory of Environmental Policy*, 2nd ed. Cambridge: Cambridge University Press.

Bohm, P. 1981. *Deposit-Refund Systems: Theory and Applications to Environmental, Conservation, and Consumer Policy*. Baltimore: Johns Hopkins University Press.

Boyd, James. 2002. "Financial Responsibility for Environmental Obligations: Are Bonding and Assurance Rules Fulfilling their Promise?" *Research in Law and Economics* 20: 417–485.

Brouhle, K., C. Griffiths, and A. Wolverton. 2005. "The Use of Voluntary Approaches for Environmental Protection Policymaking in the U.S.," in *The Handbook of Voluntary Agreements*, E. Croci (ed.) Dordrecht, the Netherlands: Springer, pp. 107–134.

Bui, Linda, and Christopher Mayer. 2003. "Regulation and Capitalization of Environmental Amenities: Evidence from the Toxics Release Inventory," *Review of Economics and Statistics*, 85(3): 693–708.

Bui, Linda. 2005. "Public Disclosure of Private Information As a Tool for Regulating Environmental Emissions: Firm-level Responses by Petroleum Refineries to the Toxics Release Inventory," CES 05-13 October 2005. (47 pages) Available at http://www.ces.census.gov/index.php/ces/1.00/cespapers?detail_key=101723.

Caldart Charles C., and Nicholas A. Ashford. 1999. "Negotiation As a Means of Developing and Implementing Environmental and Occupational Health and Safety Policy," *Harvard Environmental Law Review* 23(1): 141–202.

Carmin, JoAnn, Nicole Darnall, and Joao Mil-Homens. 2003. "Stakeholder Involvement in the Design of U.S. Voluntary Environmental Programs: Does Sponsorship Matter?" *Policy Studies Journal* 31(4): 527–543.

Chen, Chung-Chiang. 2005. "Incorporating Green Purchasing into the Frame of ISO 14000," *Journal of Cleaner Production* 13(9): 927–933.

Coglianese, Cary, and Jennnifer Nash. 2002. "Policy Options for Improving Environmental Management," *Environment* 44(9): 13–22.

Cole, Daniel H., and Grossman, Peter Z. 1999. "When Is Command-and-Control Efficient? Institutions, Technology, and the Comparative Advantage of Alternative Regulatory Regimes for Environmental Protection," *Wisconsin Law Review*, 1999: 887–938.

Cole, Daniel H., and Grossman, Peter Z. 2002. "An Introduction to the Law and Economics of Environmental Policy: Issues in Institutional Design," *Research in Law and Economics* 20: 223–241.

Cramton, Peter and Suzi Kerr. 1998. "Tradable Carbon Permit Auctions: How and Why to Auction Not Grandfather," Discussion Paper 98-34, May 1998, Resources for the Future, Washington, D.C.

Cunningham, James A., and Peter Clinch. 2005. "Innovation and Environmental Voluntary Approaches," *Journal of Environmental Planning and Management* 48(3): 373–392.

Darnall, Nicole, and JoAnn Carmin. 2005. "Greener and Cleaner? The Signaling Accuracy of U.S. Environmental Programs," *Policy Sciences* 38(2–3): 71–90.

Dales, J. H. 1968. *Pollution, Property and Prices*. Toronto: University of Toronto Press.

Daley, Dorothy M. 2002. "Understanding the Rise of Voluntary Programs: Exploring Diffusion of Innovation in State Environmental Policy," paper presented at the 2002 Annual Meeting of the American Political Science Association, August 29–September 1, 2002.

Driesen, David M. 1998. "Is Emissions Trading an Economic Incentive Program?: Replacing the Command and Control/Economic Incentive Dichotomy," 55 *Washington and Lee Law Review* 298.

Driesen, David M. 2003. *The Economic Dynamics of Environmental Law*. Cambridge, Mass.: MIT Press.

Driesen, David M. 2004. "The Economic Dynamics of Environmental Law: Cost-Benefit Analysis, Emissions Trading, and Priority Setting," 31 *British Columbia Environmental Affairs Law Review* 501–528.

Driesen, David M. 2005. "Distributing the Costs of Environmental, Health, and Safety Protection: The Feasibility Principle, Cost-Benefit Analysis, and Regulatory Reform," 32 *British Columbia Environmental Affairs Law Review* 1–95.

Ehrenfeld, John. 2004. "Industrial Ecology: A New Field or Only a Metaphor?" *Journal of Cleaner Production* 12(8–10): 825–831.

EPA (U.S. Environmental Protection Agency). (2001). *The United States Experience with Economic Incentives for Protecting the Environment*. EPA-240-R-01-001, Washington, D.C.

EPA (U.S. Environmental Protection Agency). (2004). *International Incentives Report: International Experiences with Economic Incentives for Protecting the Environment*, EPA National Center for Environmental Economics. Accessible at http://www.epa.gov/economics.

Farber, Daniel. 2000. "Symposium: Innovations in Environmental Policy: Triangulating the Future of Reinvention: Three Emerging Models of Environmental Protection," 2000 *University of Illinois Law Review* 61–80.

Friedman, Robert M., Donna Downing, and Elizabeth M. Gunn. 2000. "Comment: Environmental Policy Instrument Choice: The Challenge of Competing Goals," 10 *Duke Environmental Law and Policy Forum* 327–387. See also *Environmental Policy Tools: A User's Guide*, Office of Technology Assessment, OTA-ENV-634; GPO stock No. 052-003-01441-6, Washington, D.C., September 1995.

Gamper-Rabindran, Shanti. 2006. "Did the EPA's Voluntary Industrial Toxics Program Reduce Emissions? A GIS Analysis of Distributional Impacts and By-media Analysis of Substitution," *Journal of Environmental Economics and Management* 52: 391–410.

Graham, Mary. 2001. "Information as Risk Regulation: Lessons from Experience," Occasional Paper, Institute for Government Innovation, John F. Kennedy School of Government, Harvard University, Cambridge, Mass.

Graham Mary, and Catherine Miller. 2001. "Disclosure of Toxic Releases in the United States," *Environment* October, 8–20.

Hahn, R. W., and R. Noll. 1990. "Environmental Markets in the Year 2000," *Journal of Risk and Uncertainty* 3: 351–367.

Hanley, N., J. F. Shogren, and B. White. 1997. *Environmental Economics: Theory and Practice*. New York: Oxford University Press.

Hemmelskamp, Jens. 2000. "Environmental Taxes and Standards: An Empirical Analysis of the Impact on Innovation," in *Innovation-Oriented Environmental Regulation: Theoretical Approach and Empirical Analysis*, J. Hemmelskamp, K. Rennings, and F. Leone (eds.) ZEW Economic Studies. Heidelberg, New York: Springer Verlag.

Hockenstein, Jeremy B., Robert N. Stavins, and Bradley W. Whitehead. 1997. "Crafting the Next Generation of Market-Based Environmental Tools," *Environment* 39(4): 12–33.

Jaffe, A. B., and K. Palmer. 1997. "Environmental Regulation: A Panel Data Study," *Review of Economics and Statistics* 79(4): 610–619.

Jaffe, Adam B., Richard E. Newell, and Robert Stavins. 2002. "Environmental Policy and Technological Change," *Environmental and Resource Economics* 22: 41–69.

Johnston, Jason Scott. 2005a. "Signaling Social Responsibility: On the Law and Economics of Market Incentives for Corporate Environmental Performance," paper presented May 11, 2005 at the John F. Kennedy School of Government, Harvard University. Paper available at http://www.ksg.harvard.edu/cbg/CSR%20and%20the%20Law.pdf.

Johnston, Jason Scott. 2005b. "The Promise and Limits of Voluntary Management-Based Regulatory Reform: An Analysis of EPA's Strategic Goals Program." University of Pennsylvania Institute for Law and Economics Research Paper 05-17, April 2005. Available at http://papers.ssrn.com/sol3/papers.cfm?abstract_id=712103.

Kamien, M. I., N. L. Schwartz, and F. T. Dolbear. 1966. "Asymmetry between Bribes and Charges," *Water Resources Research* 2(1): 147–157.

Karkkainen, Bradley C. 2001. "Information as Environmental Regulation: TRI and Performance Benchmarking, Precursor to a New Paradigm?" *Georgetown Law Journal* 89: 257–370.

Khanna, Madhu, and Lisa A. Damon. 1999. "EPA's Voluntary 33/50 Program: Impact on Toxic Releases and Economic Performance of Firms," *Journal of Environmental Economics and Management* 37(1): 1–25.

King, Andrew, and Michael Lenox. 2000. "Industry Self-Regulation Without Sanction: The Chemical Industry's Responsible Care Program," *Academy of Management Journal* 43(4): 698–716.

King, Andrew, Michael Lenox, and Ann Terlaak. 2005. "The Strategic Use of Decentralized Institutions: Exploring Certification with the ISO 14001 Management Standard," accepted for publication in the *Academy of Management Journal*.

Koch, Lars, and Nicholas A. Ashford. 2006. "Rethinking the Role of Information in Chemicals Policy: Implications for TSCA and REACH," *Journal of Cleaner Production* 14(1): 31–46.

Lewis, Sanford, and Diane Henkels. 1997. "Good Neighbor Agreements: A Tool for Environmental and Social Justice," *Social Justice* 23(4): 134–151. Available at http://www.cpn.org/topics/environment/ igoodneighbor.html.

MacDonald, Jamie P. 2005. "Strategic Sustainable Development Using the ISO 14001 Standard," *Journal of Cleaner Production* 13(6): 631–643.

Mauzerall, Denise, Babar Sultan, Namsoug Kim, and David F. Bradford. 2005. "NO_x Emissions from Large Point Sources: Variability in Ozone Production, Resulting Health Damages and Economic Costs," *Atmospheric Environment* 39(16): 2851–2866.

NACEPT (National Advisory Council for Environmental Policy and Technology). (1991). *Permitting and Compliance Policy: Barriers to U.S. Environmental Technology Innovation.* Report and Recommendations of the Technology Innovation and Economics Committee of the National Advisory Council for Environmental Policy and Technology. Washington, D.C.: U.S. EPA.

NACEPT (National Advisory Council for Environmental Policy and Technology). (1992). *Improving Technology Diffusion for Environmental Protection.* Report and Recommendations of the Technology Innovation and Economics Committee of the National Advisory Council for Environmental Policy and Technology. Washington, D.C.: U.S. EPA.

NACEPT (National Advisory Council for Environmental Policy and Technology). (1993). *Transforming Environmental Permitting and Compliance Policies to Promote Pollution Prevention.* Report and Recommendations of the Technology Innovation and Economics Committee of the National Advisory Council for Environmental Policy and Technology. Washington, D.C.: U.S. EPA.

Nichols, A. L. 1984. *Targeting Economic Incentives for Environmental Protection.* Cambridge, Mass.: MIT Press.

OECD (Organization for Economic Co-operation and Development). 1997. *Evaluating Economic Instruments for Environmental Policy.* Paris: OECD.

OECD (Organization for Economic Co-operation and Development). 1999. *Voluntary Approaches for Environmental Policy.* Paris: OECD.

OECD (Organization for Economic Co-operation and Development). 2003. *Voluntary Approaches for Environmental Policy: Effectiveness, Efficiency and Usage in Policy Mixes.* Paris: OECD.

Ortolano, Leonard. 1997. *Environmental Regulation and Impact Assessment.* New York: Wiley.

Pearce, D. W., and R. K. Turner. 1990. *Economics of Natural Resources and the Environment.* London: Harvester Wheatsheaf.

Rajah, N., and S. Smith. 1993. "Taxes, Tax Expenditures, and Environmental Regulation," *Oxford Review of Economic Policy* 9(4): 41–65.

Richards, Kenneth R. 2000. "Framing Environmental Policy Instrument Choice," 10 *Duke Environmental Law and Policy Forum* 221–285.

Roberts, M. J., and M. Spence. 1976. "Effluent Charges and Licenses Under Uncertainty," *Journal of Public Economics* 5(3)(4): 193–208.

Schroeder, Christopher H. 2002. "Lost in the Translation: What Environmental Regulation Does that Tort Cannot Duplicate," 41 *Washburn Law Journal* 583.

Siegel, Janet V. 2002. "Negotiating for Environmental Justice: Turning Polluters into 'Good Neighbors' Through Collaborative Bargaining," 10 *New York University Environmental Law Journal* 147–195.

Snyder, Lori D. 2003. "Are Management-Based Regulations Effective?: Evidence from State Pollution Prevention Programs" (manuscript) 51 pages (available as Regulatory Policy Program Working Paper No. RPP-2003-21), Center for Business and Government, John F. Kennedy School of Government, Harvard University, Cambridge, Mass. Accessible at http://www.innovations.harvard.edu/showdoc .html?id=34 or http://www.ksg.harvard.edu/cbg/research/rpp/RPP-2003-21.pdf.

Steinzor, Rena I. 1998. "Reinventing Environmental Regulation: The Dangerous Journey from Command to Self-Control," 22 *Harvard Environmental Law Review* 103–202.

Steinzor, Rena I. 2001. "Essay: Myths of the Reinvented State," 29 *Capital University Law Review* 223–243.

Stensvaag, John-Mark. 1999. *Materials on Environmental Law*. St. Paul, Minn.: West Group.

Stewart, R. B. 2000. "Economic Incentives for Environmental Protection: Opportunities and Obstacles," in *Environmental Law, The Economy and Sustainable Development*, R. L. Revesz, P. Sands, and R. B. Stewart (eds.) Cambridge: Cambridge University Press.

Stewart, Richard B. 2001. "A New Generation of Environmental Regulation," 29 *Capital University Law Review* 21–182.

Strasser, Kurt A. 1997. "Cleaner Technology, Pollution Prevention, and Environmental Regulation," *Fordham Environmental Law Journal* 9(1): 1–106.

Swanson, Mary, Arthur Weissman, Gary Davis, Maria Leet Socolof, and Kim Davis. 2005. "Developing Priorities for Greener State Government Purchasing: A California Case Study," *Journal of Cleaner Production* 13(7): 669–677.

Taylor, Margaret R., Edward S. Rubin, and David A. Hounshell. 2005. "Control of SO_2 Emissions from Power Plants: A Case of Induced Technological Innovation in the U.S.," *Journal of Technological Forecasting and Social Change* 72: 697–718.

Tietenberg, T. 1985. *Emissions Trading: An Exercise in Reforming Pollution Policy*. Washington, D.C.: Resources for the Future.

Tietenberg, Tom. 1998. "Disclosure Strategies for Pollution Control," *Environment and Resource Economics* 11(3–4): 587–602.

Verschoor, A. H., and L. Reijnders. 1997. "How the Purchasing Department Can Contribute to Toxics Reduction," *Journal of Cleaner Production* 5(3): 187–191.

Vogel, David. 2003a. "The Hare and Tortoise Revisited: The New Politics of Consumer and Environmental Regulation in Europe," *British Journal of Political Science* 33, Part 4, October. Reprinted in *Environmental Risk*, vol. II, John Applegate (ed.) Aldershot, UK: Ashgate, 2004.

Vogel, David. 2003b. "Risk Regulation in Europe and the US," in *The Yearbook of European Environmental Law*, vol. 3, H. Somsen (ed.) New York: Oxford University Press.

Weitzman, M. L. 1974. "Prices vs. Quantities," *Review of Economic Studies* 41(4): 477–491.

Wenders, J. T. 1975. "Methods of Pollution Control and the Rate of Change in Pollution Abatement Technology," *Water Resources Research* 11(3): 343–346.

Westin, R. A., and S. E. Gaines. 1989. "The Relationship of Federal Income Taxes to Toxic Wastes: A Selective Study," *Boston College Environmental Affairs Law Review* 16(4): 753–791.

13 Policies to Promote Pollution Prevention and Inherent Safety

A. Background
   1. The Limits of Traditional Pollution Control and the Emergence of Pollution Prevention
   2. The Winds of Change: Dissatisfaction with End-of-Pipe Regulatory Approaches
   3. Industrial Ecology as a Competing Paradigm to Pollution Prevention
B. Chemical Accident Prevention and Its Relationship to Pollution Prevention
   1. The Nature of Chemical Accidents
   2. Chemical Safety and Accident Prevention: Inherent Safety and Inherently Safer Production
   3. The Enhanced Need for Inherent Safety after 9/11
C. Moving from Characterizing Problems and Assessing Risk to Finding Technology-Based Solutions
   1. The Technology Options Analysis
   2. The U.S. Experience
   3. The European Experience: The Cleaner Technology Movement and Ecological Modernization
D. U.S. and European Union Legislation Focusing on Pollution and Accident Prevention
   1. The Pollution Prevention Act
   2. The Chemical Safety Provisions of the Clean Air Act
      a. General Provisions
      b. OSHA's Process Safety Management Standard
      c. EPA's Risk Management Plan Regulation
   3. The Massachusetts Toxics Use Reduction Act
   4. Coordinating Accident Prevention with Pollution Prevention
   5. European Union Legislation
      a. The Integrated Pollution Prevention and Control Directive
      b. The Seveso Directives

E. Using Traditional Environmental Statutes to Encourage Pollution and Accident
   Prevention
   1. Stringent Standards
   2. Innovation Waivers
   3. EPA's Supplemental Environmental Project (SEP) Program
F. Worker and Citizen Involvement in Pollution Prevention and Technology
   Choices
References

A. BACKGROUND

1. The Limits of Traditional Pollution Control and the Emergence of Pollution Prevention

As many of the previous chapters have illustrated, approaches to environmental
pollution have been evolving over the past four decades from (1) the dispersion of
pollution and waste (the "dilution solution"), to (2) end-of-pipe control, to (3) waste
and material exchange and consolidation ("industrial ecology"), to (4) pollution prevention and "inherently cleaner" technology, to (5) systemic changes and the promotion of sustainable development. At present, different industrial sectors, processes,
and countries are at different places along this continuum.

The encouragement of dispersion and dilution tended to spread pollution over
wider areas and populations, sometimes by creating greater environmental and public health damage, depending on the specific hazardous substance and its associated
dose-response relationship (see chapter 2). It also contributed to transboundary pollution, such as when tall stacks were used to disperse SO_2 and NO_X, the precursors
of acid rain.

End-of-pipe control focuses on collecting the harmful emissions, effluents, or waste
from industrial processes (or in the case of workers' exposure, on ventilating the
workplace or providing personal protective equipment), usually without altering
inputs, feedstocks, processes, or final products. Early preoccupation with minimizing
air and water pollution often shifted the problem to the hazardous waste stream and/
or increased workplace exposure, resulting in what is popularly known as a "media
shift." It also often changed the *nature* of the hazard by increasing the potential
for chemical accidents (sudden and unexpected chemical releases, sometimes with
accompanying fires and explosions), thus resulting in what is popularly known as a
"problem shift."

The exchange and consolidation of materials and waste—the core of what has
come to be called industrial ecology—generally saves money through the reuse of

industrial residues, and promotes economies of scale if practiced widely enough. However, this approach does not usually involve fundamental changes to inputs, final products, or production processes, and it sometimes creates increased transportation hazards and handling risks for workers.

Pollution prevention—what the Europeans call "cleaner" production or technology—received its first political push in this country with the mid-1980s pursuit of "waste minimization," an economically driven movement that grew out of a recognition that the best way to avoid the rising costs of treatment and disposal of hazardous wastes often is simply to generate less waste. See Caldart and Ryan (1985), U.S. Congress (1986), Hirschhorn (1988), and Hirschhorn and Oldenburg (1991).

Depending on the context and the time period, pollution prevention has also been known as "elimination of pollution at the source," "source reduction," and "toxics use reduction." This approach (by whatever name it is known) *does* entail fundamental changes to inputs and feedstocks, final products, and/or production processes. These changes often are associated with improvements in ecoefficiency and energy efficiency. See Freeman (1995) and Allen and Shonard (2002). In the context of chemical production, they often involve the exploration of alternative synthetic pathways and green chemistry initiatives. See Anastas and Warner (2000) and Ashford and Tsamis (2000). The search for and identification of alternative production methods may also promote the development and use of inherently safer production technology, although, as we will see, this will not always be the case because the minimization of accident potential may require a somewhat different set of changes. See Bollinger et al. (1996).

The fifth approach, the promotion of systemic changes and sustainable development, involves rethinking how a particular human need can be satisfied by technology in order to change a larger system; e.g., rather than substituting a safer pesticide, making changes in the agricultural system so that pesticides are not needed. In evolutionary terms, this approach lies beyond pollution prevention and it is the focus of the final chapter of this book. The present chapter explores the design and implementation of systems to promote pollution prevention and inherent chemical safety.

Pollution prevention is not a refined version of pollution control. It involves fundamental changes in production technology: substitution of inputs, redesign and reengineering of processes, and/or reformulation of the final product. It may require organizational and institutional changes as well.[1] "Inherent safety"—also known as "primary" accident prevention—is the analogous concept for the prevention of

---

1. See *Government Strategies and Policies for Cleaner Production*. United Nations Environment Program, Paris, 1994, 32 pp. See also N. A. Ashford and G. Zwetsloot (1999) "Encouraging Inherently Safer Production in European Firms: A Report from the Field," *Journal of Hazardous Materials*, Special Issue on Risk Assessment and Environmental Decision Making, A. Amendola and D. Wilkinson (eds.), 78(1–3): 123–144.

sudden and accidental chemical releases. Inherent safety is a concept similar to—and often is a natural extension of—pollution prevention. The common thread linking the two concepts is that they both attempt to prevent the *possibility* of harm, rather than to reduce the *probability* of harm, by eliminating the problem (chemical accidents and chemical pollution) *at its source*.

The Pollution Prevention Act of 1990, discussed later in this chapter, endeavors to encourage both pollution prevention and inherent safety by requiring EPA to give preference to "source reduction" in the implementation of all of its environmental programs. Thus far, however, the agency has not embarked upon the fundamental regulatory revisions that this law envisions, and pollution prevention has lagged accordingly. As discussed in the following reading, an effective policy for promoting the prevention of pollution is likely to require a transformation of the current regulatory approach (although not necessarily a change in the basic laws themselves).

Cleaner Technology, Pollution Prevention and Environmental Regulation
Kurt Strasser
Source: 9 *Fordham Environmental Law Journal* 1 (1997), excerpted with permission.

INTRODUCTION

Preventing pollution, rather than controlling it after it has been produced, seems like such a good policy on its face that one wonders how executing it could be so problematic.[1] . . .

Prevention is important for three main reasons.[2] First, controlling pollution after it has been produced has only limited potential to achieve further environmental protection. While pollution control's emphasis on the end-of-the-pipe has already accomplished substantial environmental protection, further

improvements will be increasingly difficult and expensive. Today, pollution control leads to more and more rules and standards, but with less and less actual environmental improvement to show for them. Second, prevention is a strategy that can support both environmental protection and economic development goals, by harnessing the creative energy of business to serve both. "Encouraging technological changes for production purposes and for environmental compliance purposes must be seen as interrelated rather than separable activities."[3] Pollution preven-

---

1. These advantages are surveyed and the literature discussing them collected in Kurt A. Strasser, *Preventing Pollution*, 8 FORDHAM ENVTL. L.J. 1, 7–15 (1996).
2. The definition of pollution prevention has proved contentious. EPA wishes to limit the term to source reduction of pollutants, with recycling or reuse defined as separate categories. *See* Pollution Prevention Act of 1990, 42 U S C. §13,101 (1994); Environmental Protection Agency Pollution Prevention Strategy, 56 Fed. Reg. 7849, 7854 (1991).

The agency's usage emphasizes a policy preference for prevention over other waste reuse, treatment or disposal methods . . . [EPA includes in-process recycling in the definition, but excludes other recycling methods].
3. N. Ashford *Government Strategies and Policies for Cleaner Production*, United Nations Environmental Program, Paris, 1994, ISBN 92-807-1442-2, 32 pp. Available at http://hdl.handle.net/1721.1/1560.

tion shows most clearly that the choice between economic growth or environmental protection, though oft posed, is false. Third, pollution prevention is more effective environmental protection because it treats the problem—the creation of pollution—rather than simply shifting it around to less strictly regulated media.

To prevent pollution, business must do much more than simply add clean-up gadgets at the end-of-the-pipe or the smokestack. Business organizations and the people in them have a central role in preventing pollution. Successful pollution prevention requires an effort inside the plant, and even earlier when designing products and choosing raw materials. Pollution is the unfortunate byproduct of producing goods and services. The people who do the producing will have a primary role in learning to produce with less pollution; ideally with none. This will require changes in raw materials, production processes and technologies, and in [the final] products themselves. Innovative ideas and organizational support to implement them are both essential. This Article will consider how the traditional environmental regulatory system encourages and discourages business from these new ways of acting and thinking....

[This Article also]...evaluate[s] the traditional regulatory system's positive and negative effects on pollution prevention and environmental technology development. In addition, this Article...suggest[s] that whereas a compliance/enforcement culture may hinder prevention efforts, a multimedia approach, which encourages innovation and dissemination of technology, may yield better results.

I. ENVIRONMENTAL REGULATION AND POLLUTION PREVENTION

Traditional environmental regulation has been primarily aimed at achieving pollution control, rather than pollution prevention. Thus, its primary concern has been to set and enforce standards limiting the discharge of pollutants from the end-of-the-pipe or the smokestack [into the air, water or land], or standards for storage and treatment of wastes.... At first blush, it seems that a regulatory system that successfully controls pollution will inevitably motivate polluters to prevent that pollution at the outset. To a degree, the traditional regulatory system has achieved some substantial success in this regard over the last twenty-five years.[10] The present regulatory system, however, oriented as it is to pollution control rather than pollution prevention, has some inadvertent but quite serious disincentives to pollution prevention.

Four broad themes describe the extent to which traditional environmental regulation motivates—and fails to motivate—business to prevent pollution. The first theme is that, despite Congressional, EPA and White House policy statements, pollution control remains the current policy and prevention is pursued only marginally, if at all. To be sure, there is a long history of pilot projects and other one-time efforts that have experimented with a prevention approach. However, the sheer number of these projects, the extent of this history, as well as the unending and uncoordinated progression of new initiatives, show that pollution prevention has not yet been institutionalized within the regulatory bureaucracies. Accordingly, the current

---

10. For example, from the 1970 enactment of the Clean Air Act to 1994, the combined emissions of the six principal air pollutants decreased 24% while U.S. population increased 27%, vehicle miles traveled increased 111% and gross domestic produce increased 90%. During this period the introduction of unleaded gas decreased lead emissions by 98%.

system fails to support the business efforts and initiatives that prevention demands.

The second theme is that the regulatory system could be a most potent motivator of pollution prevention by business. Clearly, the regulatory system is a critically important motivator of business behavior. Of all environmental policies, the regulatory system sends the sharpest and loudest message to business, although unfortunately not always the clearest or most consistent one. The regulatory system is built around mandates and penalties that business ignores only at its considerable peril. The evidence suggests that, even in pollution prevention programs, business spends most of its environmental protection budget on compliance rather than on prevention. Business responds to the regulatory system; that system will determine whether the business response includes pollution prevention.

Further, the regulatory system determines what new pollution prevention technology will be developed. The standards set in the regulatory system will effectively define at least the minimum market for environmental technology. If regulators do not set and enforce standards that require new technology to be adopted, business has little incentive to develop and deploy it. Conversely, when new technology is developed, if regulators do not approve it in their permitting and enforcement decisions, then that technology will not be profitable and ultimately will not survive in the market. A history of such disapproval will discourage firms from even developing new technology in the first place.

The third theme is that the present regulatory system could support business pollution prevention efforts without fundamental statutory change. Several specific provisions of the statutes authorize flexibility in writing standards and in issuing and enforcing permits. This flexibility affords regulators a measure of discretion that they can exercise to encourage business to prevent pollution. In addition,

regulators could coordinate their efforts to partially accomplish multimedia results, particularly with permitting and compliance. Finally, EPA can support more prevention-friendly regulation by the states: through supervision, guidance and in grants which support pollution prevention.

The last theme is that a truly robust pollution prevention and environmental technology policy would require radical change that embraces fundamentally different approaches to environmental protection regulation. To encourage prevention, environmental regulation should adopt a multimedia approach, looking broadly at all the environmental consequences of a particular business operation across all environmental media. Present regulation tends to focus narrowly on one environmental medium at a time, e.g., air, water or land based waste disposal. This single-medium philosophy leads, in turn, to a focus on the end-of-the-pipe, and the technology available for application there. Effective pollution prevention by business requires new technology within the plant and business decisions that embrace it.

Multimedia regulation should ideally be organized by industrial sectors rather than by the different environmental media. Organization by industrial sectors will encourage the agencies to develop greater expertise and sophistication in assessing the technology and innovation possibilities within each business sector. Fundamental changes in regulatory thinking, as well as a wholesale reorganization of regulatory agency structure will be essential; rewriting of the basic environmental statutes to require multimedia regulation would further this goal.

Regulators must develop a clearer idea of what business must do to prevent pollution and consider the industry and firm specific characteristics that might affect it. Environmental technological innovation is influenced by many factors other than the regulatory system....

F. Policy Approaches to Promote Technological Change in Standard Setting

To promote technological change, environmental standards must promote responsive business decision-making in order to insure that business will embrace technological change needed to prevent pollution rather than just control it at the end-of-the-pipe. Three main arguments will be discussed in this subsection. First, standards that regulate across all environmental media would promote prevention and technological change more effectively than the current single-medium standards. Second, such standards can be set to directly promote and support needed types of change and to target the most likely actors. Third, standards promoting technological change must allow for the uncertainty and delay inherent in the process.

Common themes run throughout these discussions. A technology-oriented policy must consider firm-specific and industry-specific factors if the policy is to be effective. It is at the individual firm and industry levels that innovation and diffusion opportunities are either embraced or discarded. Thus, sophisticated regulators will require a deep familiarity with the specifics of individual industries and firms to anticipate and support technological change in them. Ultimately, this will also require new training and technical support for regulatory personnel. . . .

CONCLUSION

Pollution prevention, using better environmental technology, is crucial for the future of environmental protection. For the last twenty-five years we have been trying to protect the environment by controlling pollution and this effort has had considerable success. However, more environmental protection is needed, and getting it through pollution control is proving harder and harder. The regulatory system keeps adding more and more rules, and increasingly specific controls, yet its progress in protecting the environment seems to be slowing down. To continue to move toward the needed level of environmental protection, we must add pollution prevention to our present pollution control efforts.

In addition, prevention offers the possibility of achieving environmental protection at less cost and in ways that may be supportive of other economic objectives. Preventing the pollution in the first place is often cheaper than treating it after the fact, and this will surely become even more true as the required level of treatment inevitably increases over time. Further, prevention is typically built on technological innovations that can also support other business productivity and competitiveness goals.

Pollution prevention requires that business learn to produce economic goods and services without creating as many harmful wastes. . . . In most situations, better environmental performance turns on using environmentally better technology. Some technology is still to be developed; in other cases, there is simply a need for wider diffusion of existing technology. In either situation, the key is to require or inspire business corporations to develop and use the technology that is best for the environment. This Article is concerned with whether, and how, the traditional environmental regulatory system discourages and encourages business in this effort.

The traditional environmental regulatory system is of such great concern because, for better or worse, it is the prime motivator of business environmental performance. Regulation determines the minimum environmental performance requirements for business. But beyond this, it effectively defines the market for existing and new environmental technology. If a given technology is not approved for companies to meet their environmental requirements, that technology will disappear from the market, if it is even developed in the first place. A technology friendly environmental policy, so essential for pollution prevention, begins with a hospitable and supportive approach from the traditional regulatory system.

However, that system has not shown much concern for its impact on technology. The traditional system—writing regulations, issuing permits to individual sources, and seeking compliance and enforcement—has emphasized controlling pollution at the end-of-the-pipe or smokestack and has given little thought to preventing pollution by using new environmental technology inside the plant. This regulatory system inadvertently creates many incentives related to new technology: some supportive, many discouraging. The process of setting standards is so slow that it cannot itself prescribe the latest technology, and it has not generally done so. However, business reaction to the standards that do get set is varied. Both emissions standards and product standards have sometimes encouraged innovation and diffusion of cleaner technology, although each has often discouraged it. The process of issuing permits, as well as the compliance and enforcement process, show a deep-seated bias in favor of known, established pollution control technologies, although some exceptions can be found and there are some encouraging recent developments that show the beginnings of a change in regulatory thinking. . . .

Technology-friendly regulation must consider a number of aspects of each particular business and industry situation. The most important single factor is the degree of youthful fluidity or mature rigidity in the firm or industry's underlying technology. After this, other important factors include the technological opportunities available, the nature of the firm's processes, the individual firm's culture and values, and the prospects for innovation from outsiders. The key point is that the extent to which a business is likely to develop or embrace new technology in response to regulatory stimuli is a reasonably knowable and predictable process. Regulators can craft environmental policies that will be con-

sciously supportive of environmental technology, although they have not frequently done so.

A technology-friendly environmental policy can be crafted at two levels. There is much that can be done within the framework of existing environmental laws. When specific regulatory standards are set, they can expressly consider who is likely to create and apply new technology and what is likely to motivate those parties' behavior. The permitting process need not manifest its present bias in favor of familiar existing pollution control technology; neither must compliance and enforcement. However, all of these efforts require substantial technical and organizational support for agency personnel as they wrestle with the necessarily more complex questions presented by new technology, particularly new technology inside the plant rather than at the end-of-the-pipe. Further, new technology often takes longer to develop and perfect than installation of known options, and it presents a greater risk of failure; the regulatory system needs to make allowance for this to be truly effective. . . .

Along with such a change in regulatory culture, a truly robust environmental technology policy would make more fundamental changes in the regulatory structure. A multimedia approach is key. This strategy requires multimedia statutes, supporting multimedia regulations, and regulatory agencies structured around specific industry sectors rather than individual environmental media as is now the case. Agencies organized by industry sectors will develop the knowledge of industry operations and technology possibilities. Companies genuinely and deeply committed to environmental technological advancement can be offered the option of alternative regulatory requirements and enforcement, keyed to alternative environmental management systems, in exchange [for] truly superior environmental performance.

Getting to this second level will be difficult and other priorities and policy concerns will have to be considered and accounted for. At best, it must be seen as a long-term objective, but certainly a worthwhile one. Such an environmental regulatory regime would provide much better long-term environmental protection, and it would support long-term goals of economic development and productivity.

■ **NOTE**

1. See Gutowski et al. (2005) for a study of "environmentally benign manufacturing" (inherently cleaner and safer technology) in the automotive and electronics sectors based on interviews in Japan, Europe, and the United States that document its importance as a "significant competitive dimension between companies" (p. 1). Also see Eder (2003) for a similar Delphi study of experts in the chemical industry in the United States and Europe, which concludes that "innovation leading to alternative synthetic pathways" (i.e., green chemistry) has an "especially high potential for both strong positive ecological effects and . . . competitiveness," (p. 347).   ■

2.   The Winds of Change: Dissatisfaction with End-of-Pipe Regulatory Approaches

The fundamental concept of pollution prevention—changing the nature of industrial activities so as to reduce or eliminate the creation of pollutants—is most likely as old as pollution itself. The concept did not gain any real prominence in the United States, however, until the mid-1980s, when a number of factors helped spur a growing dissatisfaction with end-of-pipe approaches to reducing pollution. The focus on end-of-pipe controls had contributed to a fragmented regulatory approach—with air, water, waste, and workplace issues addressed separately—that many viewed as cumbersome and inefficient. Furthermore, as regulations (especially those governing hazardous waste disposal) tightened, the technical limits of media-specific end-of-pipe controls led to increased marginal costs relative to the corresponding marginal reductions in pollution risks. Moreover, there was a growing disillusionment among many in government and industry, and among some environmental groups, with command-and-control regulation generally.

Thus there was a call from various quarters for coupling environmental improvements with the natural tendency of industrial firms to improve their technology for business purposes. (See the discussion in chapter 3 of the Massachusetts Institute of Technology and Porter hypotheses and the potential for "win-win" opportunities and "first mover" advantages.) There was also a call for decoupling pollution and production preferentially through the use of economic incentives rather than command-and-control regulation. Finally, there was a growing recognition, both in government and among some industry actors, that a more integrated and technology-focused approach was needed.

To varying degrees, each of these somewhat disparate movements touted pollution prevention as a preferable alternative to end-of-pipe pollution control. The resulting rhetoric of pollution prevention, however, tended to far outstrip its actual accomplishments.

Pollution Prevention: A New Ethic or New Rhetoric?
N. A. Ashford

Source: "Understanding Technological Responses of Industrial Firms to Environmental Problems: Implications for Government Policy," in K. Fischer and I. Schot (eds.), *Environmental Strategies for Industry: International Perspectives on Research Needs and Policy Implications*. Island Press, Washington, D.C., 1993, pp. 277–307, excerpted with permission.

The current...emphasis on pollution prevention must be understood in a historical context. [R]egulations [which] had their origin in the 1970s, when somewhat aggressive government intervention was in vogue, [did challenge industry]. The environmental progress and technology forcing that occurred resulted from clear and stringent regulatory requirements. Understandably, industry not only did not want to be "forced" to develop new technology, it did not want to be forced to make any technological changes that were costly or that compromised production efficiency. Government regulation was criticized as being too focused on "command and control," but for different reasons. Industry objected originally because regulation was seen to require (i.e., to command) unnecessarily low levels of permissible emissions or effluents—that is, [industry objected to] the *stringency* of the regulations.... On the other hand, some economists objected because they believed that economic measures such as pollution taxes that would affect the prices of inputs and final products were superior to mandated pollution levels for achieving environmental improvement—that is, [they objected to] the method of achieving compliance.... In addition, industry and the economists argued that specification standards (of

which there were precious few) stifled industry's use of more innovative and efficient ways to comply. Industry [they argued] should be left to choose its method of complying. Industry, in fact, was never in favor of the economists' pollution charges, although pollution credits and trading did appeal to those industries that had pollution reduction capability to spare....

Although companies such as 3M had long argued that "pollution prevention pays," that rhetoric became identified with the idea that pollution prevention made good sense because it was grounded in the economic rationality of the industrial firm. It was argued that the firm, faced with its own hidden costs of pollution, and presented with the correct information, would change its operations to reduce environmental pollution.[2] Industry began to embrace pollution prevention (initially without any deep understanding of what it meant), partly because the costs of waste disposal were becoming prohibitive and partly because pollution prevention contributed to a positive corporate image.

---

2. In Europe, this conviction was expressed in the concept of ecological modernization [discussed later in this chapter].

Government, faced with renewed citizen demands for reduction of environmental pollution but still ideologically committed to economic instruments, began to realize that if economic incentives were to reduce environmental pollution, those incentives had to be fashioned as supplements to, rather than as wholesale replacements for, regulations. Regulations continued to adhere to traditional emission and effluent restrictions and actually went even further in entertaining product phase-outs (e.g., for chlorofluorocarbons) and product bans (e.g., for asbestos). Rhetoric continued against command-and control regulation, but now the objection... concerned overspecification of the means of achieving pollution reduction rather than the stringency of levels of pollution control. Government became increasingly committed to stringent (but flexibly implemented) regulation backed up by tough enforcement. How did industry come to accept this return of government to more serious concern with the environment?

The credibility of chemical-using and chemical producing industries suffered greatly in the 1980s, and the fact that industrial product and emissions information was now accessible to citizens and workers through ... right-to-know legislation convinced companies that they must do something. The increasing prohibition on landfilling, cleanup costs at contaminated sites, and citizen action ended the do-nothing period for pollution prevention. But what, in fact, did industry do during the 1980s while waving the pollution prevention banner?

Several studies... throw light on the question. It turns out that, while pollution control technology was *in situ*, most industrial firms were not using [most of] the pollution prevention options open to them. Their first response was to undertake housekeeping changes and equipment modifications that could have been instituted much earlier had they perceived the federal government to be serious about environmental regulation. The firms also discovered that they could save money. Recycling...was financially attractive, partly because it was accompanied by material reclamation and partly because off-site waste treatment was becoming expensive. In other words, firms had been so suboptimal in their industrial operations that almost anything they did yielded an improvement in the efficiency of pollution abatement.... What the record shows, however, is that input substitution, process redesign, and product reformulation were rare events. They were rare events because environmental requirements were not stringent enough on their face and/or because there was inadequate enforcement [of such regulations] to force technological change.

Although a number of specific self-reports of individual accomplishments of "pollution prevention" in industry are found in the available literature, three comprehensive and critical overviews compiled [in the period from 1985 through 1991] discovered little fundamental technological change. [See INFORM (1985) *Cutting Chemical Waste: What 29 Organic Chemical Plants Are Doing to Reduce Hazardous Waste*, Washington, D.C.: INORM; Office of Technology Assessment (1986), *Serious Reduction of Hazardous Waste*, Washington, D.C., OTA; and Environmental Protection Agency (1991) *Pollution Prevention 1990: Progress on Reducing Industrial Pollution*, EPA 21 P-3.3, Washington, D.C.: EPA.]

■ NOTE

1. Ochsner (1998) has argued that addressing the dissatisfaction with fragmented end-of-pipe approaches by moving away from command-and-control regulation

as a means of encouraging pollution prevention is neither necessary nor desirable. As discussed in the next section, regulation could be the driver of fundamental changes through a comprehensive, technology-focused strategy. (See the discussion of regulation-induced technological change in chapter 12.)   ■

3. Industrial Ecology as a Competing Paradigm to Pollution Prevention

While some in industry pursued (or experimented with) pollution prevention, others promoted industrial ecology as an alternative approach. Indeed, the argument that firms would voluntarily gravitate toward industrial ecology, with its emphasis on waste and materials exchange, was increasingly offered as a reason to forgo a more determined regulatory push for pollution prevention. In a very real sense, then, pollution prevention and industrial ecology became, and remain, policy competitors.

Pollution Prevention and . . . or Industrial Ecology?
K. Oldenburg and K. Geiser
Source: *Journal of Cleaner Production* 5(2): 103–108 (1997), excerpted with permission.

INTRODUCTION

The concepts of pollution prevention and industrial ecology both claim similar roots. The two ideas also attempt to solve similar problems. Both concepts begin by assuming that current economic activity is increasingly harmful to the environment and conclude that changes are needed. Both concepts assert that the changes must begin with how people think about the nexus between the environment and economic activity. But, when it comes to how to make the changes, pollution prevention and industrial ecology start to diverge, so much so that incompatibilities emerge. Yet, these differences are not so broad that there is not a reasonable potential for convergence.

Conceptually, pollution prevention has always been simple. Find the source of the environmental problem, and change the source to reduce or eliminate the problem. The objective? To reduce risk to workers, communities, and the environment by preventing pollution where it is first generated

[1]. If the pollutant does not exist, the problem (the risk) does not either.

Operationally, pollution prevention has been defined as the top of an environmental protection hierarchy, and is followed, in order, by recycling, treatment, and disposal [2]. From the pollution prevention perspective, these latter options are ways to deal with pollutants that, despite efforts to prevent them, have nevertheless been generated. This form of definition was codified by the US Congress in the Pollution Prevention Act of 1990 (PPA) in which pollution prevention was equated with source reduction as [3]:

. . . any practice which reduces the amount of any hazardous substance, pollutant, or contaminant entering any waste stream or otherwise released into the environment (including fugitive emissions) prior to recycling, treatment and disposal; and reduces the hazards to public health and environment . . .

Not everyone agrees with this definition. For over a decade there have been sharp debates over the definition of pollution prevention. Some consider pollution prevention to include only those processes, product and material changes that reduce pollution at the source, while others also include various forms of materials and waste recycling. At one extreme are those, such as the Chemical Manufacturers Association [now the American Chemistry Council], who write of "a hierarchy of pollution prevention practices, including source reduction, recycling, recovery for energy, and treatment" [4].

Industrial ecology is in the midst of its own definitional problems. Among industrial ecology proponents the controversy seems to be about the pace and extent of change. Robert Frosch and Nicholas Gallopoulos were early drafters of the concept. For them [5]:

(a)n industrial ecosystem is the transformation of the traditional model of industrial activity, in which individual manufacturing takes in raw materials and generates products to be sold plus wastes to be disposed of, into a more integrated system, in which the consumption of energy and materials is optimized and the effluents of one process serve as the raw material for another process.

Brad Allenby in an early article on industrial ecology drew an even more ambitious agenda when he argued that [6]:

...industrial ecology may be defined as the means by which a state of sustainable development is approached and maintained. It consists of a systems view of human economic activity and its interrelationships with fundamental biological, chemical, and physical systems with the goal of establishing and maintaining the human species at levels that can be sustained indefinitely—given continued economic, cultural, and technological evolution.

Meanwhile, Jelinski and others, writing in a special issue of the *Proceedings of the National Academy of Sciences of the USA* in 1992 took a more narrow approach, focusing centrally on the efficiency of industrial materials flows, where they defined industrial ecology as [7]:

...a new approach to the industrial design of products and processes and the implementation of sustainable manufacturing strategies. It is a concept in which an industrial system is viewed not in isolation from its surrounding systems but in concert with them. Industrial ecology seeks to optimize the total materials cycle from virgin material, to finished material, to component, to product, to waste product, and to ultimate disposal.

In a more recent text, Graedel and Allenby accept this wording, but expand the concept by adding additional commitments so that industrial ecology is seen as [8]:

...the means by which humanity can deliberately and rationally approach and maintain a desirable carrying capacity, given continued economic, cultural, and technological evolution. The concept requires that an industrial system be viewed not in isolation from its surrounding systems, but in concert with them. It is a systems view in which one seeks to optimize the total materials cycle from virgin material, to finished material, to component, to product, to obsolete product, and to ultimate disposal. Factors to be optimized include resources, energy, and capital.

Thus, industrial ecology becomes either "an incremental extension of efficiency improvements underway in industry, or a radical new paradigm that must be embraced if we are to save the planet from industrial development [9]."

By contrast, despite resolution of a universally agreed upon definition, pollution prevention has advanced in 10 years from a concept to a proven, practical deed. In fact, the long struggle over its definition has kept pollution prevention in the forefront among those advocating progressive environmentalism, garnered the interest of others, and helped to clarify priorities in conventional waste management practices.

SIMILAR YET DIFFERENT

Despite their differing rhetoric and state of development, functionally pollution prevention and industrial ecology are similar in several ways. Both promote reduction in the volume of pollutant discharges to the environment. Both require materials flow information to measure performance. And, both use many of the same analytical methods

Table 13.1
Primary Attributes of Pollution Prevention and Industrial Ecology

	Pollution Prevention	Industrial Ecology
Primary goals	Prevent pollution Reduce risk	Optimize resource flows Promote sustainability
Primary focus	Individual firm	Networks of firms
Core concept	Planning process	Integrated system
Primary techniques	Life-cycle assessment Process characterization Materials accounting Waste audits Full-cost accounting	Life-cycle assessment Materials accounting Design for environment
Role of recycling	Only in-process	In-process, off-site and between firms
Role of government	Technical assistance	Barriers removal
Economic domain	Multiple sectors	Industrial sector
Mode of evaluation	Materials tracking	Materials tracking

to determine and choose among options. Among the common tools, for example, are life cycle assessment, design for the environment, materials accounting, total cost accounting, and production process assessments.

For both pollution prevention and industrial ecology, life cycle assessment is a strategic tool. It usually focuses on a single product or product function, collecting and analyzing a comprehensive set of data on the materials and energy consumed and wastes generated over the stages of a product from materials extraction to residual product disposal. The other tools are more operational. Materials accounting gives a materials balance (the inputs and outputs) of a manufacturing process. Production process assessments use materials accounting and other information to identify the source reduction changes necessary for pollution prevention. And, finally, financial tools, such as total cost accounting and activity based accounting, add the necessary economic values to options derived by the technical tools.

Yet, there are essential differences between industrial ecology and pollution prevention. Table [13.1] summarizes some of the similarities and differences between the two con-

cepts. While both pollution prevention and industrial ecology strive for efficiency in production, efficiency appears to be an industrial ecology end-point. For pollution prevention, efficiency is but one way to achieve its goal of risk reduction and efficiency improvements alone may not be sufficient. A very efficient production process or system can be, at the same time, highly toxic. An efficient leather tanning process using hexavalent chromium does not prevent pollution. A chemical process that produces tons of product and parts per million of a pollutant is efficient. But, from an environmental viewpoint, the tiny amounts of pollutant may be unacceptable. In ways similar to efficiency, conservation of materials is an industrial ecology core goal but [it is] simply one method for pollution prevention.

Industrial ecology and pollution prevention system boundaries often differ. Most pollution prevention activity today is focused at the firm level although, as firms start to demand pollution prevention activities by their suppliers and product designers, that boundary expands. Industrial ecology emphasizes the interconnectivity of industrial activity as a system and promotes action at the regional or industrial level. Industrial ecology proponents describe the current industrial system as linear and aim to close the materials loop. Conceptually, there are no limits to how many firms it may take (or to their geographic location) to achieve this loop-closing state [10].

Pollution prevention and industrial ecology both use environmental protection concepts to improve economic activity. Pollution prevention attracts individual firms who, independent of one another and each at their own pace, move towards this improved state. Industrial ecology creates linkages among firms or industrial sectors and moves them forward, together. Both schemes require industry to change the way it conducts itself and measures its progress.

Industrial ecology is based on the model of a system with looping material and information flows. Pollution prevention programs are based on a planning protocol that iteratively guides activities from hazard identification to option analysis to goal setting to implementation and evaluation. Systems approaches are useful in analyzing current conditions and designing new ones, but offer little practical guidance on how to get from a current condition to a more desirable future one. It is in guiding such transitions that planning protocols excel.

Pollution prevention proponents have long acknowledged the role that government has to play to foster and enable such changes, yet little is written about the role of government among those who promote industrial ecology. Initially, pollution prevention was adopted as an adjunct to existing environmental agency and extension service operations. Increasingly, pollution prevention is now being integrated, thereby changing how these agencies operate and interact with industry. In Massachusetts, integration brought about a full reorganization of the state's environmental agency system and the adoption of an over-arching toxics use reduction approach to environmental protection. Meanwhile, industrial ecology proponents tend to concentrate on changing industry and industrial systems irrespective of government, except when government creates barriers to industrial ecology.

Industrial ecology's "natural systems" model has been applied almost exclusively to industrial activities. Pollution prevention started in that limited fashion, but the strategy has spread to other sectors, such as agriculture, transportation, and services. Agriculture's Integrated Pest Management, fuel switching by electric utilities, electronic transfers that avoid paper use in the services sector, and shifts from motor vehicles to public transit in transportation are all forms of prevention.

Symptomatic of pollution prevention's expansion is its proven practicability. While industrial ecology remains mostly theoretical, there is now a decade of operational experience with pollution prevention. There are thousands of examples of how it works (or doesn't), what it costs, and the benefits it produces. The number of state and federal pollution prevention programs continues to grow. Many tangible lessons have been learned.

INCOMPATIBLE DIFFERENCES

Despite the differences enumerated above, it is possible from an industrial ecology perspective to see pollution prevention as but one of many industrial ecology actions within the materials cycle. Yet, there are aspects of industrial ecology that, in fact, make the two concepts incompatible. These involve recycling, materials efficiency, and risk reduction.

Recycling

Given the lofty vision put forward by the more ambitious advocates of industrial ecology, it is surprising how many papers on industrial ecology focus almost solely on material and waste recycling among firms. With

few concrete examples to document industrial
ecology, the inter-firm waste transfer system
at Kalundborg, Denmark, is often used as
the signature icon of the concept [10]. In the
USA, recent efforts to model the Kalundborg
example have appeared in "eco-industrial
parks" in Baltimore and Texas. These projects are primarily centered on inter-firm
waste recycling. While it is a worthy materials conservation approach, waste recycling
has had a spotty environmental history. Pollution prevention may promote in-process
recycling and on-site materials reuse; but, in
keeping with the PPA definition, it does not
include off-site materials recycling. In fact, it
is an aim of pollution prevention as defined
by the PPA to prevent recycling from occurring, just as it attempts to remove the need
for waste treatment or disposal. Industrial
ecology, in closing the materials loop, encourages recycling and the transfer of materials
from one place to another.

When firms or industrial sectors set up the
systematic transfers of wastes under industrial
ecology, they must cope with the accompanying liability issue. Under current laws,
transfers of hazardous wastes are recorded.
Should an environmental problem arise with,
say, a transfer storage point, all those in the
chain of custody could be liable for clean-up
costs. This is not a theoretical problem.
Sham recycling operations rise and fall. A
significant percentage of today's hazardous
waste dump sites were once waste recycling
centers. The Silrisim site in Lowell, Massachusetts, and the Port Elizabeth site in New
Jersey are two notorious examples. Total
cost accounting systems factor in future liability costs...and can make pollution prevention the economic choice. So, while
current liability provisions act as deterrents
to industrial ecology, they promote pollution
prevention.

Other regulations similarly impact pollution prevention and industrial ecology differently. For example, industrial ecology

proponents argue that the way waste materials are defined and the cumbersome permitting procedures required under the US
Resource Conservation and Recovery Act
create a major barrier to the waste trading
that is central to many industrial ecology
schemes. Yet these regulations may be a
valuable tool to control the kind of sham
recycling noted above, and they help to encourage pollution prevention.

Recycling wastes from one firm to another
often involves some "downgrading" of the
quality of the material being recycled. And,
even with good recycling, most industrial
materials will eventually become waste.
Thus, industrial waste recycling may delay,
but it does not prevent, materials from
becoming wastes. To the degree that such
materials eventually enter the waste stream
pollution is not prevented by recycling
wastes. Admittedly, not all materials down-
grade during recycling. Glass and aluminium
are two materials that can be reprocessed
without loss of quality. Yet, many industrial
wastes are difficult to recycle into the same
or comparable uses.

Spent solvent is a useful example. Solvents
used in cleaning metal parts may become
soiled with the greases or oils on those parts
and thus no longer acceptable for parts
cleaning. These solvents are considered waste
when new solvents are substituted and the
spent solvent is drummed up for disposal.
Properly marketed, these spent solvents may
still find productive use as a raw material in
manufacturing some paints and coatings or
as a fuel in some boilers. Yet, these secondary
uses are more crude processes requiring a
lesser quality raw material than the pure solvent that replaced the spent solvent.

Plastic food packaging requires a high
grade of polystyrene. Once the food packaging is used federal regulations will not permit
it to be reused for food packaging. Indeed,
the process of regrinding the plastic, pelletiz-
ing it, and preparing it for reprocessing dete-

riorates the material until it can not meet the same standards of the original material. Thus, recycled plastic food packaging often finds reuse as cheap waste disposal bags or construction product fillers.

Materials Efficiency

Firms are clearly attracted to the economic gains found from using pollution prevention to solve environmental problems. Under industrial ecology, however, many such economic gains may have to be shared.

The materials cycles of industrial ecology promotes materials efficiencies as both an economic and environmental benefit. Extending the life of valuable materials in commercial use maintains efficiencies in the economy as a whole. But it is not clear that such efficiencies immediately accrue to the firm. Finding markets for wastes, preparing wastes to meet the needs of future customers, and complying with the necessary government laws that regulate materials recycling all add expenses that will need to be captured in the pricing of the waste. In many cases virgin materials are cheap enough that reprocessed wastes will have difficulty competing.

It is true that the market could be adjusted to encourage waste recycling. Today, the purchase price of many major raw materials from wood products to organic chemicals is subsidized by government investment or tax expenditure programs. Theoretically, these subsidies could be converted to encourage the use of recycled materials but, politically, the power of special industrial interests makes this unlikely.

On the other hand, pollution prevention programs are typically promoted and adopted on their capacity to lower costs at the firm level. Preventing pollution can result in lower waste handling and treatment costs, less raw material purchases, reduced liability costs and lower compliance costs. Polaroid, 3M, AT&T, Dow, DuPont, and General Motors,

among others, including a growing number of smaller firms, report millions of dollars of savings from implementing pollution prevention programs. The economic efficiencies for the firm are either immediate or, more often, are achieved through a relatively short pay-back period. While some of these cost savings-reduced liability and compliance costs-are transaction savings that do not involve materials efficiencies, others such as reduced raw material purchases or improved yields in production do result in efficiencies of material use.

The boundary issue raised by industrial ecology advocates becomes important here, because improved materials efficiencies at the firm level do not automatically mean improved efficiencies at the industry or market level. For instance, polystyrene cup manufacturers can reduce pollution from their facilities by carefully controlling styrene inputs, by improving the ratio of cups to waste, and by reducing the number of quality rejects. Yet, once the cup enters the market it becomes waste and the disposing of the cup in a landfill is not a highly efficient means of materials use at the level of society. Thus, in the aggregate, pollution prevention programs can and do achieve efficiencies in the larger market, but this is not a given and is seldom the way in which these programs are conceived or promoted.

Industrial ecology schemes do present two potentials for inefficiencies that need to be carefully considered. First, the type of materials dependencies that may be created among firms that are sequentially linked in a "waste-to-input-material" relationship may inhibit and stall technological innovations. If firms must somehow guarantee a fixed amount or condition of waste to their potential customers, they may be reluctant to institute changes in waste handling and treatment that might otherwise make technical, environmental, or even economic sense for themselves alone.

Second, these "waste-to-input-material" dependencies may actually reduce the incentive to institute pollution prevention projects. Investments that might reduce or eliminate certain dangerous materials in a waste stream would likely be resisted internally because this might adversely affect the firm's waste customers. If pollution prevention does actually lead to efficiencies at the firm level then these rigid dependencies among firms might actually distort overall market efficiencies.

Risk Reduction

A fundamental objective of pollution prevention is to promote reduction in risk. Most of the literature on industrial ecology pays little attention to the concept of risk or risk reduction. Graedel and Allenby [8] argue that materials selection is important and that there is a need for an unambiguous, if general, risk prioritization in performing the life cycle assessment necessary for implementing industrial ecology programs. Yet, the Graedel and Allenby definition and the wide-ranging visions of industrial ecology suggest that a world of efficient materials cycles would reduce risk as well. Where the two concepts diverge is over the prioritizing of materials for reduction.

Preventing pollution requires a focus on pollutants. By definition, a pollutant is an undesirable contaminant of an ecosystem or an organism. Pollution prevention programs do not view all material wastes as equal. Some wastes are regarded as more prone to generate risks than others. Some state pollution prevention programs in the USA include a list of pollutants that are considered dangerous wastes. Federal pollution prevention programs often make reference to the Toxics Release Inventory List established under the Emergency Planning and Community Right to Know Act of 1986. This list, which today includes some 630 substances, serves as a target for pollution prevention. Indeed, the

US Environmental Protection Agency's "33-50 Program," which was designed to promote the voluntary reduction in pollution first by 33% and then by 50%, identified 17 high-priority chemicals for special emphasis [11].

Risk reduction is also addressed in another way by many pollution prevention programs. Implementing pollution prevention programs at the firm level often requires changing the materials, technologies or work practices of the production systems. In such cases, good pollution prevention projects seek to reduce pollution without introducing new risks to workers or the environment. Following the US Environmental Protection Agency's successful *Pollution Prevention Opportunities Assessment Manual* [12], many pollution prevention programs often involve some assessment phase where potential options for preventing pollution are compared in term[s] of the overall potential to reduce risks.

The more global approach to materials efficiency central to industrial ecology schemes does not include operations that prioritize materials in terms of risk. Nor does it assess how alternative approaches to improving materials efficiencies may differentially affect environmental quality or occupational safety. The apparent industrial ecology assumption that all material recycling and all materials efficiencies leads equally to environmental or health benefits needs to be more carefully considered.

THE POTENTIAL FOR CONVERGENCE

For all of their differences, there could be benefits to finding the compatibility between pollution prevention and industrial ecology. The possibility is enhanced by the difference in the stage of development of the two schemes. The operational sophistication of pollution prevention and the theoretical vision of industrial ecology invite an effort to "nest" pollution prevention as a practical tool within the broader concept of industrial ecology. Indeed, Graedel and Allenby [8] and O'Rourke, Connelly and Koshland [9] make brief note of this potential, but surprisingly few promoters of industrial ecology even mention pollution prevention.

Advocates of pollution prevention could also find benefit in such "nesting." Pollution prevention might be more effectively promoted if the focus included regional networks of firms in the fashion that is advocated by industrial ecology advocates. The fundamental systems concepts inherent in industrial ecology could assist in prioritizing and guiding pollution prevention investments. But to better integrate these two concepts will require that the direct incompatibilities be resolved. The idea of designing an industrial economy around an ecological metaphor is attractive and rich in possibility. Yet there are many differences between a natural ecological cycle and what we desire out of our industrial economy. For instance, we are not seeking a final "climax" equilibrium in the economy in the way in which ecological systems seek stasis. But we are looking for a production and consumption system that is balanced, efficient and safe.

To do so, both pollution prevention and industrial ecology schemes should look beyond industry's waste streams to consider industry's product streams as well. After all, in the current economy, products all become waste sooner or later and, from a biological perspective, there is little to distinguish products from waste. Industrial ecology needs to consider the recycling and so-called "take-back" of products as well as wastes, and pollution prevention needs to more effectively deal with the prevention of pollution from products. In addition, pollution prevention can be faulted for pushing the balance of the hierarchy (recycling, treatment, and disposal) totally out of its sphere and leaving those actions to traditional waste management. Indeed, industrial ecologists also offer limited consideration of waste treatment and disposal practices.

If industrial ecology schemes are to be made compatible with pollution prevention programs, industrial ecology should de-emphasize the current concept of firms made interdependent by linking waste streams and input needs. This is only one tenet of an ecological system and a narrow one at that. Sound ecological systems also build the health of niche organisms through careful selection and avoidance behaviors.

Instead of a narrow focus on waste recycling, industrial ecology schemes should incorporate risk reduction, target those parts of the economy that are most endangering, and assist in identifying and developing materials and technologies that fit comfortably into ecological cycles and support human and ecological health. Considered from this perspective pollution prevention programs that serve to "correct" and tailor production systems could be seen as a powerful tool in an industrial ecologist's instrument bag and industrial ecology could become a source of vision for the detailed operations of pollution prevention programs at the firm level.

REFERENCES

1. US Congress, Office of Technology Assessment, *Serious Reduction of Hazardous Wastes.* Office of Technology Assessment, Washington, DC, 1986.

2. Hirschhorn, J. and Oldenburg, K., *Prosperity Without Pollution: The Prevention Strategy for Industry and Consumers.* Van Nostrand Reinhold. New York. 1991.

3. US Congress, *Pollution Prevention Act of 1990. 42 U.S.C.* Section 13106.

4. Chemical Manufacturers Association, *Pollution Prevention in the Chemical Industry: A Progress Report, 1988–1993.* Chemical Manufacturers Association, Washington, DC, 1994.

5. Frosch, R. and Gahopoulos, N., *Scientific American, 1989, 260,144.*

6. Allenby, B., *MRS Bulletin, 1992,* March, 47.

7. Jelinski, L., *Proceedings of the National Academy of Sciences,* 1992, 89, 793.

8. Graedel, T. and Allenby, B., *Industrial Ecology.* PrenticeHall, Englewood Cliffs, NJ, 1995.

9. O'Rourke, D., Connelly, L. and Koshland, C., *Industrial Ecology: A Critical Review, International Journal of Environment and Pollution*, 1996, 26(2/ 3), 89–111.

10. Tibbs, H., *Whole Earth Review, 1992,* p. 9.

11. US Environmental Protection Agency, 1992 *Toxics Release Inventory.* US EPA, Washington, DC, 1994.

12. US Environmental Protection Agency, *Pollution Prevention Opportunities Assessment Manual.* US EPA, Washington, DC, 1990.

■ NOTES

1. Although Oldenburg and Geiser explore here some of the ways in which pollution prevention and industrial ecology could be compatible, the respective underlying principles of these two approaches remain fundamentally at odds: while industrial ecology operates by creating a market for industrial wastes, pollution prevention strives to minimize or eliminate the production of such wastes. To the extent that pollution prevention is successful, then, the rationale for industrial ecology disappears.

2. In table 13.1 the authors identify promotion of sustainability and design for the environment as goals of industrial ecology, but not of pollution prevention. This is puzzling. Certainly the design of production processes and products to be free of toxic substances, which is the touchstone of any serious attempt to promote sustainability, is much more clearly the province of pollution prevention than of industrial ecology.

3. For a thoughtful discussion of where industrial ecology may be heading, see Ehrenfeld (2004).   ■

B. CHEMICAL ACCIDENT PREVENTION AND ITS RELATIONSHIP TO POLLUTION PREVENTION

Often, discussions of "clean" technology omit any concomitant discussion of "inherently safer" technology. This omission has real-world consequences. Not only are pollution prevention and primary accident prevention related concepts, as discussed here, but the threat of chemical accidents is (especially in this post 9/11 world) a matter of increasing importance. If strategies to promote pollution prevention are to take full advantage of the opportunities for reducing chemical risks, they must also promote primary prevention of accidents. This requires an integrated strategy, one that flows both from an understanding of the nature of chemical pollution and from an understanding of the nature of chemical accidents.

1. The Nature of Chemical Accidents

The Encouragement of Technological Change for Preventing Chemical Accidents: Moving Firms from Secondary Prevention and Mitigation to Primary Prevention

Nicholas A. Ashford, James Victor Gobbell, Judith Lachman, Mary Matthiesen, Ann Minzner, and Robert Stone

Source: *A Report to the U.S. Environmental Protection Agency*, Center for Technology, Policy and Industrial Development at MIT, Cambridge, Mass., July 1993. Excerpted with permission. Available at http://hdl.handle.net/1721.1/1561

II. A MODEL OF ACUTE CHEMICAL ACCIDENTS[1]

In order to prevent chemical accidents, we first need to understand how and why they arise; that is, we require a conceptual framework or model of chemical accidents. In this chapter, we construct such a model, which is based on earlier models developed by Roger Kasperson and others at Clark University and by Nicholas Ashford. The usefulness of the construct here is to demonstrate that opportunities for primary prevention can be identified and chosen over, or as supplements to, the traditional secondary prevention and mitigation approaches.

A. Development of an Accident Model

Kasperson's framework for analyzing accidents is depicted in figure [13.1], which provides a causal model of hazards and related hazard-control opportunities.[2] The model builds upon the customary division of hazards into events and consequences: the evolution of an accident involves a series of stages that culminate in unintended and undesired consequences. The "upstream" stages of the

model begin with basic human needs (e.g., food) which are converted into human wants (e.g., increased food production through pest control). Satisfying human wants requires the making of technological choices (e.g., pesticide manufacture using highly toxic chemicals in the production process), based on considerations of benefits, costs, and risks. However, the choice of "appropriate technologies" has traditionally been driven more by utility concerns than by concerns for risk. Some initiating event (e.g., a break in a pipe or some other component failure) can trigger a fire or explosion or toxic release. The "downstream" portion of the accident sequence consists of human exposure to the released hazard and the subsequent adverse consequences. Note that each step in the accident sequence presents an opportunity to introduce control measures designed to prevent the unintended and undesired consequences from being realized. These opportunities are represented in figure [13.1] by the bottom row of boxes. Ashford's model, presented in figure [13.2], focuses on intervention points in the accident sequence and develops a three-category taxonomy of accident control measures—primary prevention, secondary

---

1. A more detailed explication of the model developed in this chapter is provided in Minzner (1990) and in Ashford (1991).

2. See Hohenemser and Kasperson (1982); Kates, Hohenemser, and Kasperson (1985); and Kasperson *et al.* (1988).

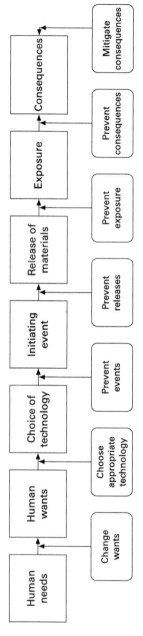

*as developed in Kasperson et al. (1988)

Figure 13.1
Causal structure of hazard. (Source: Kasperson, R. E., J. X. Kasperson, C. Hohenemser, and R. W. Kates. 1988. *Corporate Management of Health and Safety Hazards: A Comparison of Current Practice.* Boulder, CO: Westview Press as reproduced in Nicholas A. Ashford, James Victor Gobbell, Judith Lachman, Mary Matthiesen, Ann Minzner, and Robert Stone, *The Encouragement of Technological Change for Preventing Chemical Accidents: Moving Firms from Secondary Prevention and Mitigation to Primary Prevention: A Report to the U.S. Environmental Protection Agency.* Center for Technology, Policy and Industrial Development, Massachusetts Institute of Technology, Cambridge, Mass., July 1993.)

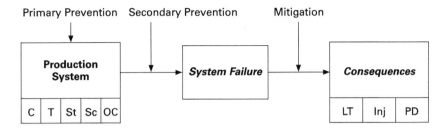

**as developed in Ashford (1991)

Legend:

C: chemicals   OC: operating conditions
T: technology   LT: life threatening
St: storage   Inj: non-life-threatening
Sc: scope   PD: property damage

Figure 13.2
Acute hazardous release model. (Source: Nicholas A. Ashford, James Victor Gobbell, Judith Lachman, Mary Matthiesen, Ann Minzner, and Robert Stone, *The Encouragement of Technological Change for Preventing Chemical Accidents: Moving Firms from Secondary Prevention and Mitigation to Primary Prevention: A Report to the U.S. Environmental Protection Agency*. Center for Technology, Policy and Industrial Development, Massachusetts Institute of Technology, Cambridge, Mass., July 1993.)

prevention, and mitigation—based on the point of intervention.[3]

Mitigation measures are those that [arise] in response to a released hazard, but do not prevent the release of the hazard from occurring. These measures correspond to the stages of accident intervention to the right of the release of materials in Kasperson's model and include exposure prevention, consequence prevention, and consequence mitigation. Mitigation measures generally exist as stand-by systems intended to minimize the amount of personal injury and property damage given the occurrence of a release. [They minimize injury or damage, but do not prevent accidental releases.] Many emergency evacuation procedures, initiated in response to the detection of a hazardous release, fall into this category. Other forms of accident mitigation

include add-on mechanical systems which are designed to decrease the rate or duration of a release, or interfere with the transport of a release or reduce its toxic concentration. Examples include emergency vent-gas scrubbers and water sprays.

Secondary prevention measures intervene between the production system and prerelease hazards. In Kasperson's model, these measures arise after the choice of technology and before the hazardous release; they are to the left of, and perform prior to, mitigation measures. Secondary prevention systems are often applied continuously to prevent an initiating event. Examples include pressure vessels designed to withstand high pressures, refrigeration systems designed to maintain an appropriate temperature, and pressure and temperature monitoring equipment to detect critical deviations. Other secondary prevention measures include seals and check valves designed to contain hazardous substances

---

3. See Ashford (1991).

within process chambers and safety measures to stabilize temperature and pressure after critical deviations have been realized.

Primary prevention measures are those that are an intrinsic part of the production technology. In Kasperson's model, activation of these measures typically coincides with, or precedes, the choice of technology. Examples of primary prevention measures include redesigning the production process, choosing different process technology, selecting more benign inputs, and reformulating the final product in ways that eliminate the possibility of (certain types of) hazard or accident. Another approach to primary prevention is to alter the scope of the production process, such as by expanding the production process to encompass creating and consuming small amounts of the toxic material as an intermediate product in a closed-loop system or by shifting from an inventory system where large quantities of a toxic input are stored on-site to a just-in-time delivery system.[4] Obviously, there may be instances in which it is difficult to draw a sharp line between primary and secondary prevention, but the distinction does serve a valuable purpose in thinking about process re-design and accident prevention options.

Figure [13.3] presents a simplified accident model which integrates Kasperson's and Ashford's models. This hybrid model facilitates a pictorial visualization of the distinctions between primary prevention, secondary prevention, and mitigation. While also distinguishing between various prevention and mitigation measures, this model focuses on the concept of inherent (versus extrinsic) safety. Inherent safety is defined as being able to withstand deviations from normal operating conditions without having to rely on safety systems to prevent accidents.[5] Inherent safety corresponds closely to primary prevention measures in Ashford's model, while extrinsic safety corresponds to secondary prevention and mitigation measures. With reference to our (and Kasperson's) model, a system will be inherently safer the further the employed prevention methods are to the left.

Factors affecting the inherent safety of a production technology include the following: (1) the scale of production; (2) the quantity of hazardous chemicals involved; (3) the hazardousness of the chemicals involved; (4) batch versus continuous processing; (5) the presence of pressure or temperature extremes; (6) storage of intermediates versus closed loop processing; and (7) multistream versus single-stream plants. These factors are discussed briefly below.

The Scale of Production
Chemical production is typically characterized by economies of scale. Based on a generalized formula for the chemical industry, a doubling of plant capacity increases the capital cost by only about 60%.[6] However, larger-scale plants require a larger inventory of chemicals, which tends to increase the hazard potential of the plant. Therefore, from a safety standpoint, the optimal scale of production may involve smaller plants because chemical releases, though sometimes more frequent, would be smaller and easier to control.

The Quantity of Hazardous Chemicals Involved
The amount of hazardous chemicals on-site can be reduced by methods other than altering the scale of production. For example, the

---

4. Of course, if reduced inventory on-site results in greater amounts stored in another facility, or in many more deliveries, not only may this cause a mere shift of the locus of the hazard, it may also create a greater overall risk.

5. See various discussions in Kletz (1989) and Lees (1984), Volume 1.
6. See, for example, Lees (1984), page 4.

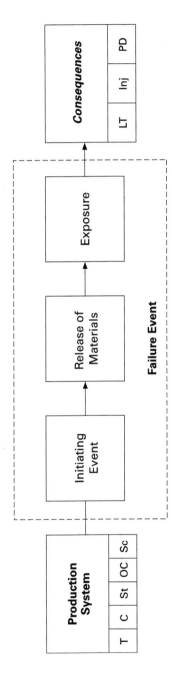

Figure 13.3
Combined model of acute hazardous release. (Source: Nicholas A. Ashford, James Victor Gobbell, Judith Lachman, Mary Matthiesen, Ann Minzner, and Robert Stone, *The Encouragement of Technological Change for Preventing Chemical Accidents: Moving Firms from Secondary Prevention and Mitigation to Primary Prevention: A Report to the U.S. Environmental Protection Agency.* Center for Technology, Policy and Industrial Development, Massachusetts Institute of Technology, Cambridge, Mass., July 1993.)

amount of hazardous material stored on-site can often be significantly reduced, and if not, the hazardous materials can be stored in many small containers in separate facilities rather than in a single container. Thus, if a container fails, the size and catastrophic potential of the release is much reduced.

In addition, the amount of material needed in the production process can be reduced by using specially-designed equipment (such as Higee columns, which replace conventional distillation columns).[7]

The Hazardousness of the Chemicals Involved

An obvious method for increasing the inherent safety of a production process is to substitute safer chemicals for more hazardous ones wherever possible. For example, flammable chemicals might be replaced by non-flammable ones; explosive chemicals might be replaced by less reactive ones; and highly toxic chemicals might be replaced by less toxic ones.[8]

Batch Versus Continuous Processing

Batch processing involves loading feedstock chemicals into a process vessel, closing it, and reacting the vessel's contents to the desired final product.[9] At this point, the vessel is emptied, and the entire process is repeated. Continuous processing, as the name implies, involves feeding raw materials to a reactor continuously and yields a continuous stream of desired reaction product.[10]

Continuous processing is generally inherently safer than batch processing because smaller amounts of hazardous substances are present at any one time and because of the automated nature of the process.[11] However, there may be size considerations that need to be taken into account regarding continuous processing. Connecting and disconnecting continuous processes may be especially hazardous (and this hazard will depend on the size of the processing vessel). On the other hand, utilizing smaller processing volume may lead to smaller hazards per connecting/disconnecting event, but may involve a larger number of events, the sum of which may represent a larger total risk.

A certain scale of production is normally required to make continuous processing feasible. For that reason, continuous production is sometimes considered to be more hazardous than batch processing.[12] However, it is the scale of production which creates the hazard, not the mode of production, *per se.* In many cases, techniques exist to adapt continuous processing to smaller volume production.[13]

---

7. See Kletz (1989), page 20.
8. See, for example, Zanetti (1986); Chowdhury (1987), and Kletz (1989).
9. See Luyben and Wenzel (1988), pages 25–27.
10. See Luyben and Wenzel (1988), page 28.
11. For example, if the explosive chemical nitroglycerin is produced using a batch process, at the end of the reaction the process vessel will be filled with highly unstable and temperature-sensitive nitroglycerin. However, by using a continuous process, only small quantities of nitroglycerin are present at any one time, because the dangerous product is continuously being formed and drawn off. Since the chemical reaction is exothermic, producing more heat than it consumes, cooling is necessary to prevent the temperature from rising above the explosion point of nitroglycerin, regardless of

the processing mode. However, the temperature control in continuous processing involves the much easier and simpler process of directly cooling the coil of tubing that contains the nitroglycerin (rather than attempting to mix the contents of the batch process vessel to avoid any local "hot spots," which could cause the reactor to explode). These characteristics, although specific to the production of nitroglycerin, illustrate the inherent safety of continuous processing.
12. See, for example, Garrison (1989), page 56.
13. There are some instances where concerns with final product restrict the practicality of some primary prevention measures. For example, in the high volume ethoxylation of esters for surfactants, batch processes are needed to produce the required high range of molecular chain lengths.

The Presence of High Pressures or Temperatures

High (or low) pressure and high (or low) temperature storage and processing of hazardous chemicals is much riskier than the storage and processing of hazardous chemicals at ambient pressures and temperatures. High pressures and high temperatures place storage and process equipment closer to the failure point and thus make them more susceptible to an accidental release. In addition, accidental releases from high-pressure vessels have a much higher rate of release than do comparable releases from near-atmospheric pressure units. Low temperatures may make materials brittle, and low pressures may provide significant pressure differentials which would allow the entrance of air into reactant vessels.

The advantages of high pressures and temperatures in reactant vessels or pipes are that smaller volume equipment is required when the chemicals are under pressure and that, for many chemical reactions, the conversion of the reactants into desired products is facilitated, or the rates increased, under high pressure and temperature. However, in some cases, this latter advantage can be overcome by using catalysts under ambient conditions to increase the rate of reaction to a comparable level achieved under high pressure and temperature—while at the same time increasing the inherent safety of the process.[14]

Storage of Intermediates Versus Closed Loop Processing

Closed loop processing involves having intermediate chemical substances formed in the conversion process (from feedstock chemicals to the desired final product) recycled back into the process stream until they react to form more of the final product. Both produc-

tion economics and safety generally favor closed loop processing when such technology is available because the intermediate chemicals are completely transformed into valuable final product instead of remaining as an undesirable and problematic hazardous chemical byproduct. Because the research and development required is expensive, a closed loop processing technology, in many cases, does not exist. However, where the impetus to change has been strong (such as in the production of carbaryl pesticides after the Bhopal tragedy), spectacular advances in inherently-safer closed loop processing have been achieved.[15]

Multistream Versus Single-Stream Plants

In order to enhance production flexibility and to take advantage of different feedstock pricing patterns, chemical plants in some productive segments or product lines are designed to use a variety of alternative process inputs to produce a variety of products. While economically attractive in a narrow production sense, such multistream plants increase the interactive complexity of the production process and thereby enhance the potential for system accidents.[16] It is inherently safer to build simpler, single-stream plants dedicated to producing one product.[17]

B. Illustrations of the Model Applied to Examples of Accidents and Accident Prevention

In the remainder of this chapter, we illustrate the use of our accident model (1) by reviewing several well-publicized, large-scale accidents and (2) by examining a few recent examples of production modifications that

---

14. One example demonstrating the successful use of catalysts under ambient conditions is in the production of polyethylene. See Mark (1986), pages 430–431.

15. See, for instance, Zanetti (1986).
16. See Perrow (1984), page 70.
17. See Kletz (1989).

have been alleged to improve the chemical plant's inherent safety. . . .

Union Carbide
(Figure 13.4) The Union Carbide plant in Bhopal, India was equipped with secondary prevention and mitigation systems specifically designed to prevent a release of methyl isocyanate (MIC), a deadly gas. However, inadequate design, component failures, and lagging maintenance activities resulted in every one of these systems being compromised. Specific elements in the causal structure of the eventual release include:

• the refrigeration unit, designed to maintain an appropriate temperature in the MIC unit and therefore prevent an exotherm, was not in operation,
• the vent gas line, intended for carrying MIC to an emergency scrubber, leaked MIC directly to the atmosphere,
• the gas that did get to the scrubber was not neutralized because of a lack of alkali in the scrubber,
• the vent gas scrubber was designed for a capacity of 5 to 8 tonnes. The MIC tank's capacity was 70 tonnes,
• the temperature indicator on the MIC tank was not functioning,
• the flare tower for burning off the released MIC was not functioning, and
• the water curtain (high pressure water sprayers) for neutralizing MIC could reach a height of only 10 meters whereas MIC leaked from the vent gas line at about 33 meters.

The devastation which resulted from these failures has been documented many times over.[18]

Another Union Carbide accident occurred at its Institute, West Virginia plant in August, 1985.[19] (See figure [13.5].) In the wake of

Bhopal, the plant was the focus of much safety concern, since MIC is also produced there. Safety system upgrades, including a hazardous gas detection system and a water-spray system designed to impede the migration of a release off-site, were installed. Despite these improvements, a noxious cloud of methylene chloride and aldicarb oxide escaped from the plant. The escape went undetected by plant personnel due to the following factors:

• a high temperature alarm was out of service,
• a level indicator in the tank was broken,
• the newly installed gas detection system had not been programmed to test for aldicarb oxide, and
• the water spray curtain intended to impede the migration of the gas offsite was inadequately designed for the given release.

Citizens in four neighboring communities were affected; 135 people were hospitalized. . . .

DuPont
(Figure [13.6]) DuPont, which has been making a crop-protection insecticide at its plant in LaPorte, Texas using MIC purchased from Union Carbide, has found a way to avoid keeping 40,000 to 50,000 pounds of MIC in storage. Though it will now actually produce MIC as an intermediate, the firm will immediately consume it in a closed-loop process. The result is a maximum of two pounds of MIC on-premises at any one time.[31]

The preceding examples illustrate that, for the manufacture of many products, primary prevention opportunities to improve chemical safety are available, and that some firms are taking advantage of these opportunities. Given the proper incentives, both regulatory

---

18. See, in particular, Bowonder, Kasperson, and Kasperson (1985).

19. See, for example, Kasperson *et al.* (1988), page 115.
31. See Windsor (1988).

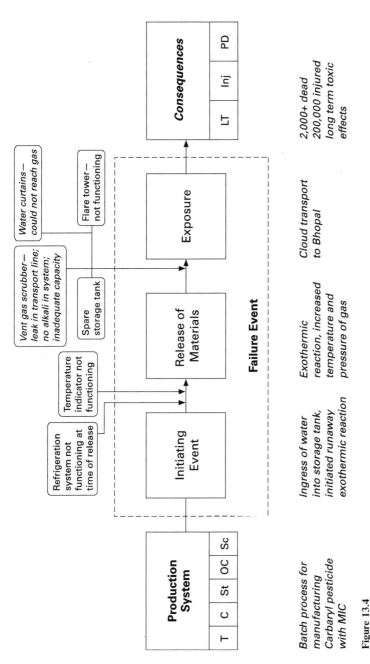

Figure 13.4

Union Carbide at Bhopal. (Source: Nicholas A. Ashford, James Victor Gobbell, Judith Lachman, Mary Matthiesen, Ann Minzner, and Robert Stone, *The Encouragement of Technological Change for Preventing Chemical Accidents: Moving Firms from Secondary Prevention and Mitigation to Primary Prevention: A Report to the U.S. Environmental Protection Agency*. Center for Technology, Policy and Industrial Development, Massachusetts Institute of Technology, Cambridge, Mass., July 1993.)

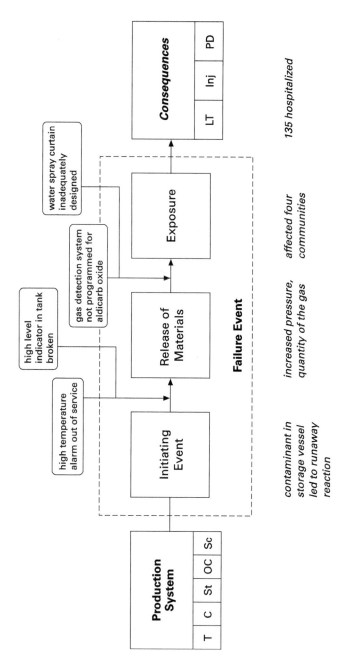

Figure 13.5
Union Carbide at Institute, West Virginia. (Source: Nicholas A. Ashford, James Victor Gobbell, Judith Lachman, Mary Matthiesen, Ann Minzner, and Robert Stone, *The Encouragement of Technological Change for Preventing Chemical Accidents: Moving Firms from Secondary Prevention and Mitigation to Primary Prevention: A Report to the U.S. Environmental Protection Agency*. Center for Technology, Policy and Industrial Development, Massachusetts Institute of Technology, Cambridge, Mass., July 1993.)

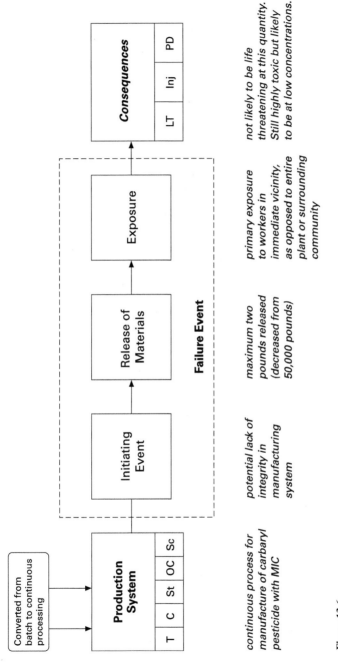

Figure 13.6
DuPont. (Source: Nicholas A. Ashford, James Victor Gobbell, Judith Lachman, Mary Matthiesen, Ann Minzner, and Robert Stone, *The Encouragement of Technological Change for Preventing Chemical Accidents: Moving Firms from Secondary Prevention and Mitigation to Primary Prevention: A Report to the U.S. Environmental Protection Agency.* Center for Technology, Policy and Industrial Development, Massachusetts Institute of Technology, Cambridge, Mass., July 1993.)

and economic, we might expect additional innovations in primary accident prevention to be developed and adopted by industry....

REFERENCES

Ashford, N. A. January 1991. "Policy Considerations for Anticipating and Preventing Accidents." Proceedings of Enprotech '91 International Environmental Conference.

Bowonder, B., J. X. Kasperson, and R. E. Kasperson. September 1985. "Avoiding Future Bhopals." *Environment* 27: 7, pages 6–13, 31–37.

Chowdhury, J. March 16, 1987. "Chemical-Plant Safety: An International Drawing Card," *Chemical Engineering*, pages 14–17.

Garrison, W. G. 1989. *Large Property Damage Losses in the Hydrocarbon-Chemical Industries—A Thirty-Year Review* (12th ed.). Chicago: Marsh & McLennan Protection Consultants.

Hohenemser, C., and J. X. Kasperson (eds.). 1982. *Risk in the Technological Society.* Boulder, Colorado: Westview Press.

Kasperson, R. E., J. X. Kasperson, C. Hohenemser, and R. W. Kates. 1988. *Corporate Management of Health and Safety Hazards: A Comparison of Current Practice.* Boulder, CO: Westview Press.

Kates, R. W., C. Hohenemser, and J. X. Kasperson (eds.). 1985. *Perilous Progress: Managing the Hazards of Technology.* Boulder CO: Westview Press.

Kletz, T. July 1989. "Friendly Plants." *Chemical Engineering Progress*, pages 18–26.

Lees, F. P. 1984. *Loss Prevention in the Process Industries,.* Volumes 1 and 2. London: Butterworths.

Luyben, W. L., and L. A. Wenzel. 1988. *Chemical Process Analysis: Mass and Energy Balances.* Englewood Cliffs, New Jersey: Prentice Hall.

Mark, H. F. 1986. *Encyclopedia of Polymer Science and Engineering*, Volume 6, 2nd Edition. John Wiley and Sons.

Minzner, A. M. 1990. "Chemical Accident Prevention: An Analysis of Current Practices and Policy Recommendations for the Future." Unpublished Master's Thesis, Massachusetts Institute of Technology.

Perrow, C. 1984. *Normal Accidents: Living with High-Risk Technologies.* New York: Basic Books.

Windsor, D. G. November 10, 1988. "The Art of Safety: Working. Job Opportunities for Human Factors and Ergonomics." *Safety and Health*, page 35.

Zanetti, R. November 10, 1986. "CPI Alter Their Ways of Dealing with Toxics." *Chemical Engineering Progress*, 53: 21, pages 27–30.

---

2.   Chemical Safety and Accident Prevention: Inherent Safety and Inherently Safer Production

Although the concept of inherent safety is endorsed by the American Institute of Chemical Engineers, it is not in widespread practical use in U.S. industry. When chemical engineers discuss the "root causes" of chemical accidents, they usually mean faulty equipment, pipes, vessels, and pressure valves. These really are "secondary" causes of accidents, and addressing them (e.g., through the use of stronger vessels and piping able to sustain higher pressures, neutralizing baths, automatic shut-off devices, and the like) constitutes "secondary" prevention. This bias in the chemical engineering profession has been one of the reasons that progress in eliminating chemical accidents has been relatively slow. See Kletz (2003). *Primary* accident prevention, on the other hand, involves a fundamental redesign of the production process, with an emphasis on inherently safer chemicals and technology.

It is generally recognized that a significant reduction in the incidence of even "garden variety" industrial accidents—spills of acids or caustics, falls from high places, electrical shocks, machinery cuts, and the like—could not be obtained without the redesign of production and manufacturing technologies and would require new organizational approaches to work and to production. The same is true for chemical accidents involving sudden and accidental releases of highly toxic, flammable, or explosive chemicals.

Encouraging Inherently Safer Production in European Firms: A Report from the Field

Nicholas A. Ashford and Gerard Zwetsloot

Source: *Journal of Hazardous Materials*, Special Issue on Risk Assessment and Environmental Decision Making, A. Amendola and D. Wilkinson (eds.) 78(1–3): 123–144 (1999), excerpted with permission.

1. THE CONCEPT OF INHERENT SAFETY

...Inherent safety is an approach to chemical accident prevention that differs fundamentally from secondary accident prevention and accident mitigation [1–9]. Sometimes also referred to as "primary prevention" [1, 2], inherent safety relies on the development and deployment of technologies that prevent the possibility of a chemical accident.[2] By comparison, "secondary prevention" reduces the probability of a chemical accident, and "mitigation" and emergency responses seek to reduce the seriousness of injuries, property damage, and environmental damage resulting from chemical accidents. [Most chemical safety efforts to date have concentrated on secondary prevention and accident mitigation. Some reductions in inventory of hazardous materials, while heralded as primary prevention, may simply shift the locus of risk and increase the probability of transport accidents.]

Secondary prevention and mitigation, by themselves, are unable to eliminate the risk of serious or catastrophic chemical accidents, although improved process safety management can reduce their probability and severity. Most chemical production involves "transformation" processes, which are inherently complex and tightly coupled. "Normal accidents" are an unavoidable risk of systems with these characteristics [11]. However, the

---

2. The authors are cognizant of the conventional wisdom that no technology is entirely safe, and that it might be more accurate to describe various technologies as saf*er*. However, some technologies are in fact absolutely safe along certain dimensions. For example, some chemicals are not flammable, or explosive, or toxic. Some reactions carried out under atmospheric pressure simply will not release their byproducts in a violent way. Thus, inherent safety is, in some sense, an idea analogous to pollution prevention. Just as some might argue that pollution prevention can never be 100% achieved, purists may argue that technologies can only be made inherently safer, not safe. Articulating the ideal, however, makes an important point: dramatic, not marginal, changes are required to achieve both. Like pollution prevention, the term "inherently safe" focuses attention on the proper target.

risk of serious, or catastrophic, consequences need not be. Specific industries use many different processes. In many cases, alternative chemical processes exist which completely or almost completely eliminate the use of highly toxic, volatile, or flammable chemicals. [Normal accidents arising in these systems result in significantly less harmful chemical reactions or releases. Replacement of existing production systems with such benign chemical processes, a practice sometimes called "green chemistry," as well as nonchemical approaches, are examples of primary accident prevention.] [12]

Inherent safety is similar in concept to pollution prevention or cleaner production. Both attempt to prevent the possibility of harm—from accidents or pollution—by eliminating the problem at its source. Both typically involve [primary prevention encouraging] fundamental changes in production technology: substitution of inputs, process redesign and re-engineering, and/or final product reformulation. [Examples include changing from a batch process using large amounts of explosive or toxic intermediates to a continuous flow process where the intermediates exist in very small amounts for very short periods of time.]

Secondary prevention and mitigation are similar in concept to pollution control and remediation measures, respectively, in that each involves only minimal change to the core production system. In particular, secondary accident prevention focuses on improving the structural integrity of production vessels and piping, neutralising escaped gases and liquids, and shut-off devices rather than changing the basic production methods. When plants expand beyond the capacity they were initially designed for, secondary prevention capacities may be exceeded. Sometimes, overconfidence in these added-on safety measures may invite an expansion of production capacity. Accidents, of course, may also dis-

able secondary safety technology, leading to runaway chemical reactions.

The superiority of pollution prevention and cleaner production as a tool of environmental policy has been recognised for more than a decade in both Europe and North America [13, 14]. International meetings of the Cleaner Production Roundtables and the Pollution Prevention Roundtables are held annually in Europe and North America, respectively. The United Nations Environment Programme has spearheaded an aggressive cleaner production program [13]. The U.S. EPA has established a hierarchy of policy choices, with pollution prevention given the highest priority over reuse or recycling, treatment, or disposal [15]. In 1990, the U.S. Congress codified, as national environmental policy, a preference for pollution prevention over pollution control, when it passed the Pollution Prevention Act. The EU supports its Directive on Integrated Pollution Prevention and Control (IPPC) by funding research in Seville, Spain for the identification of Best Available Techniques (BAT)....

Finally, a discussion of inherent safety (or cleaner production) would be incomplete without noting the importance of the stage of the production process where inherent safety is implemented. Production systems can be thought of as being comprised of at least four stages, which are found in each product line or productive segment in complex, multi-productline operations:

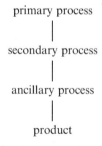

primary process

secondary process

ancillary process

product

The distinction between primary, secondary, and ancillary manufacturing and production processes—and final products as well—is an important one for the identification of inherent safety opportunities. It also helps to explain why the receptivity to the adoption of inherent safety technology might be different for firms that (1) are already in existence and do not contemplate change, (2) firms that are contemplating changes or contraction/expansion of capacity (what we call operations in transition), and (3) new facilities or operations.

An illustrative example is offered in the context of casting and electro-plating metal screws. The primary process is the casting of the screw (both toxic fumes and dangers from workers coming in contact with molten metals are recognised hazards). The secondary process is electroplating (this too presents both toxic and corrosive hazards). The ancillary process is cleaning or degreasing the screw using organic solvents (which can be both toxic and flammable). The screw itself may have sharp edges and present an occupational hazard. If the firm focuses on the ancillary process, it might be relatively easy for it to search for and find an alternative, non-polluting, non-flammable cleaning process. Technological innovation would be not likely be required. If the electroplating is the process that needs to be modified, at least a new process might have to be brought into the firm—usually by the diffusion of alternative plating technology—but the firm would be expected to be uncomfortable about changing a proven method and taking a chance on altering the appearance of its product, even if it is a separate operation. The most resistance could be expected by demands on the primary process. Here innovation might be necessary and the firm is not likely to invest in developing an entirely new casting process.

Even if an alternative casting technology were available, the firm is unlikely to be enthusiastic about changing its core technology.

On the other hand, firms that have already been searching to change even their core technologies because of high energy, water and materials costs, or for safety and environmental reasons, may be willing to plan for change. However, some firms in transition to new or expanded operation may delay implementing approaches to safety that require new investments if the remaining life of the existing facility, or portions of the facility, is limited. New operations would expected to be the most receptive to examining technology options that affect core, secondary and ancillary processes—and even final products.

2. INCENTIVES, BARRIERS, AND OPPORTUNITIES FOR THE ADOPTION OF INHERENTLY SAFER TECHNOLOGY

[Although they are conceptually similar, pollution prevention and accident prevention differ in the response they have thus far received from industry. While many firms are embracing pollution prevention (some enthusiastically, some more tentatively), far fewer are moving to primary accident prevention. In all likelihood, this disparity is due to a difference in incentives.]

The reasons that firms are embracing pollution prevention and cleaner production today are because of (1) the increased costs of continuing the current practices of waste transport/treatment and pollution control, (2) liability for environmental damage due to industrial releases of toxic substances, (3) increasingly available information about pollution and toxic releases to the public,* and (4) the EU IPPC Directive [18] (and possibly

---

* The Emergency Planning and Community Right-to-Know Act (EPCRA) has provided firms *and the public* with plant-specific information

revealing large inventories and emissions of toxic substances.

the EMAS [19] and ISO 14000 [20] requirements), and to a lesser extent the Pollution Prevention Act of 1996 in the United States [21], force increased attention to changing production technology, rather than relying solely on end-of-pipe, add-on technologies. Thus, both economic and informational mechanisms are causing a gradual cultural shift away from pollution control and waste treatment and towards pollution prevention and cleaner production. [Similar factors are not present with regard to primary accident prevention.]

With regard to primary accident prevention, the same economic signals are not really there [2]. Firms do not pay the full social costs of injuries to workers (or to the public) and firms are under-insured. Unlike pollution, which has to be reckoned with as a part of production planning, accidents are rare events and their consequences are not factored into the planning process. [Thus, firms may anticipate accidents, and may be motivated to take some steps to avoid them, but they do not feel a strong financial incentive to invest in primary accident prevention. Further, while some of the information reportable under EPCRA is relevant to chemical accidents, this information alone—without detailed and plant-specific data on production processes—does not allow the firm, or the public, to assess the accident potential of a particular facility.]

Furthermore, an organisation's gradual emissions or wastes can be observed and calculated for any given time period, and this information can be used to measure the effectiveness of the organisation's pollution prevention efforts. Because acute chemical accidents are relatively rare events, an organisation implementing an effective chemical safety program may therefore receive no form of positive feedback whatsoever. Because the safety system is working, accidents do not occur. Of course, a hazardous chemical plant may eventually receive negative

feedback, but only when it is too late to take preventive measures.

In earlier work, one of the authors [2] summarised the barriers to primary prevention:

These include: (1) *inadequate information* about the potential for catastrophic accidents, the significant costs of secondary prevention and mitigation and the costs of chemical accidents, and the existence of inherently-safe[r] alternatives; (2) *insufficient economic incentives*—in the form of workers' compensation, the tort system, regulatory fines, and insurance; (3) *organisational and managerial barriers*—linked to corporate attitudes, objectives, structure, and internal incentives, and the lack of a labour-management dialogue on safety; (4) *a lack of managerial awareness and expertise* about inherently safe[r] technologies; (5) *inadequate worker knowledge* about primary accident prevention; (6) *technological barriers* limiting primary accident prevention; and (7) *regulatory problems*. Primary prevention shares some of these barriers with secondary prevention and mitigation, but these barriers are of different importance.

Although firms sometimes do anticipate accidents and try to avoid them, the expenditures for adequate prevention have not been, and are not likely to be, invested without the right incentives. To the extent that the firm *knows* that the costs of maintenance and the inflexibility of traditional safety approaches are greater than using more reliable inherently safer approaches, the firm may respond by changing its technology.

One way of providing firms with *more visible* economic incentives would be to encourage them to exploit the opportunity to prevent accidents and accidental releases (1) by identifying *where* in the production process changes to inherently safer inputs, processes, and final products could be made and (2) by identifying the *specific inherently safer technologies that could be substituted*. The former we call Inherent Safety Opportunity Audits (ISOAs). The latter we call Technology Options Analysis (TOAs). Unlike a hazard, risk, or technology assessment, these techniques seek to identify *where and what superior technologies could be adopted* to eliminate the possibility, or to dramatically reduce the probability, of accidents and accidental releases.[6] . . .

From a general safety perspective, it is widely recognised that safety performance is determined by three elements:

- management and organisational factors,
- technological factors, and
- behavioural factors (also referred to as the human dimension, i.e., people)

These three factors interact and influence the safety of industrial manufacturing and production processes through their effects on the *willingness, opportunity, and capability* of organisations and people to change.

In some approaches that promote the adoption of inherent safety, the emphasis is on mainly technological factors, i.e., on identifying and disseminating information on superior technologies. In the current approaches to safety management—especially those falling under the rubric of Safety Management Systems—the emphasis is on management and organisational factors, and also on the human dimension, addressing the management of safety; these approaches assume minimal technological change, implicitly leaving the core and secondary production technologies essentially unchanged. Both of these distinct approaches are by themselves insufficient to maximise the adoption of desirable inherently safer technologies and frustrate further progress in safety performance and continual progress in safety management. There is therefore a clear need, both from a technical point of view and from an industrial practice perspective, for a gener-

ally accepted approach that bridges traditional safety management with inherently safer technology.

REFERENCES

[1]. Ashford, N. A. (1991), "Policy Considerations for Anticipating and Preventing Accidents," Proceedings of Enprotech '91 International Environmental Conference, Taiwan, 30–31.

[2]. Ashford, N. A., Gobbel, J. V., Lachman, J., Matthiesen, M., Minzner, A. and R. F. Stone. (1993), *The Encouragement of Technological Change for Preventing Chemical Accidents: Moving Firms from Secondary Prevention and Mitigation to Primary Prevention.* Cambridge, Massachusetts: Center for Technology, Policy and Industrial Development, Massachusetts Institute of Technology, Boston.

[3]. Bollinger R. E., & D. G. Clarck, A. M. Dowel III, R. M. Ewbank, D. C. Henderschot, W. K. Lutz, S. I. Meszaros, D. E. Park, E. D. Wixom (1996), *Inherently Safer Chemical Processes; A life Cycle Approach*, The Center for Chemical Process Safety (CCPS) of The American Institute of Chemical Engineers (AIChE), New York.

[4]. Hendershot, D. C. (1993), "Inherently Safer Plants," Chapter 2 in *Guidelines for Engineering Design for Process Safety*, edited by the Center for Chemical Process Safety, American Institute of Chemical Engineers, NY.

[5]. Kletz, T. A. (1989), "Friendly Plants," *Process Safety Progress*, (85): 18–26.

[6]. Kletz, T. A. (1990), "The need for friendly plants," *Journal of Occupational Accidents*, 13 (1/2) Special issue: Product Life: From Design to Disposal, pp. 3–13.

[7]. Kletz, T. A. (1991), *Plant Design for Safety*, Hemisphere Publishing Corporation, New York.

[8]. Lutz, W. K. (1995), "Take Chemistry and Physics into Consideration in all Phases of Chemical

---

6. A [risk] assessment, in practice, is generally limited to an evaluation of the risks associated with the firm's established production technology and does not include the identification or consideration of alternative production technologies that may be inherently safer than the ones currently being employed. Consequently, [risk] assessments tend to invite secondary accident prevention and mitigation strategies, which impose engineering and administrative controls on an existing production

technology, rather than primary accident prevention strategies, which utilize input substitution and process redesign to modify a production technology. In contrast to a [risk] assessment that suggests "fixing the current production system defects, by end-of-pipe additions," a technology options analysis would expand the evaluation to include alternative production technologies and would facilitate the development of primary accident prevention strategies.

Plant Design," *Process Safety Progress* 14(3): 153–160.

[9]. Zwetsloot, G. I. J. M. (1998), Book review of *Inherently Safer Chemical Processes; A life Cycle Approach*; Published in 1996 by The Center for Chemical Process Safety (CCPS) of The American Institute of Chemical Engineers (AIChE), *Safety Science*, 28(3): 213–214.

[10]. Rasmussen, J. (1997), "Risk Management in a Dynamic Society: A modeling problem", *Safety Science* 27(2/3): 183–213.

[11]. Perrow, C. (1984), *Normal Accidents: Living with High-Risk Technologies*. New York: Basic Books.

[12]. Anastas, P. T. and Williamson, T. C. (eds.) (1998), *Green Chemistry: Frontiers in Benign Chemical Synthesis and Processes*, Oxford University Press, New York. ISBN 0 19 850170 6.

[13]. Ashford, N. A. (1994), *Government Strategies and Policies for Cleaner Production*, United Nations Environment Programme, Paris, 32 pp.

[14]. Caldart, C. C., and C. W. Ryan (1985), "Waste Generation Reduction: A First Step Toward Developing a Regulatory Policy to Encourage Hazardous Substance Management through Production Process Change," *Hazardous Waste & Hazardous Materials*, 2(3): 309–331.

[15]. Hirschhorn, J. S., and K. U. Oldenburg (1990), *Prosperity Without Pollution: The Preven-* *tion Strategy for Industry and Consumers*. Van Nostrand Reinhold, New York.

[16]. Von Moltke, K. (1985), "Bhopal and Seveso: Avoiding a Recurrence," *The Environmental Forum*, June 1985, pp. 21–23.

[17]. Papadakis, G. A. and Amendola, A. (eds.) (1997), *Guidance on the Preparation of the Safety Report to Meet the Requirements of Council Directive 96/82/EC (Seveso II)*, EUR 17690, European Commission, Joint Research Centre, Institute for Systems, Informatics and Safety, Major Accident Hazards Bureau, Ispra (VA)-Italy. For other aspects of guidance, see Mitchison, N. (1999) "The Seveso II Directive: Guidance and Fine-tuning" *Journal of Hazardous Materials* 65(1/2): 23–36.

[18]. EEC (1996) Integrated Pollution Prevention and Control (IPPC) Directive 96/61/EC.

[19]. EEC (1993) Council Regulation (EEC) no. 1836/93: Regulation on the voluntary participation by companies in the industrial sector in a Community eco-management and audit scheme.

[20]. ISO (1996), ISO Standard 14001, "Environmental management systems—Specification with guidance for use," ISO, Geneva.

[21]. USA (1996), Pollution Prevention Act of 1996, 42 USC 13101 et seq.

[22]. Baas, L., H. Hofman, and D. Huisingh (1990), *Protection of the North Sea: Time for Clean Production*, Erasmus University Rotterdam, ESM.

▪ NOTES

1. One way to enhance the incentives for primary accident prevention would be to significantly increase the workers' compensation payments available to workers injured by industrial accidents. This would increase the cost of liability insurance to the firm, and would thus encourage primary accident prevention as a means of obtaining lower insurance premiums. This approach would require widespread changes in workers' compensation law and is unlikely to be effectuated.

2. As discussed above, another approach would be the use of a mandated technology options analysis (TOA), to be conducted by firms within high-risk industries, and to be made available to the agency and the public. In performing such a TOA, firms would be required to systematically identify and prioritize accident prevention technologies. Industry has been less than enthusiastic about this approach, largely because of the fear of tort liability. If a firm identified superior accident prevention technologies but did not implement them, this most likely would increase the firm's

vulnerability to lawsuits in the event a preventable chemical accident occurred. (This concern is not as prevalent with regard to a *pollution prevention* TOA, because the causal link between gradual pollution and environmental disease is much more difficult to establish than the link between chemical accident and chemical injury.)

3. A TOA will be most effective when it is preceded by an inherent safety opportunity audit (ISOA). A firm would perform an ISOA at a particular facility to identify precisely where in its operations inherently unsafe practices, material usage, processes, equipment, or products are present. This would then be followed by a search for, or the development of, inherently safer technology options through a TOA.   ∎

3. The Enhanced Need for Inherent Safety after 9/11

In general, chemical professionals agree that secondary prevention measures—no matter how aggressively they are applied to buttress the structural integrity of chemical plants and to provide control measures for runaway reactions—will not be adequate in the event of a deliberate attack. Deliberate attacks on high-risk chemical plants and oil refineries remain an unappreciated, serious, widespread threat, potentially affecting a significant number of Americans. It has been estimated that there are more than a hundred such facilities where a release could threaten more than a million people, 700 facilities that each put at least 100,000 people at risk; and 3,000 facilities that each put at least 10,000 people at risk (Baumann, 2001), although these figures have been disputed by the Bush administration. Documents possessed and statements made by the 9/11 terrorists reveal that they were well aware of the safety vulnerabilities of high-risk industrial plants. No current security plan eliminates, or can eliminate, the vulnerability of U.S. chemical sites to the sudden, catastrophic release of chemicals by accident or intent. The current technology of chemical production, use, and transportation, which is inherited from decades-old design, is largely *inherently unsafe*. This is a problem that could be productively addressed through a program to promote primary accident prevention.

Safety engineers are not design engineers. They oversee the safety of industrial technology as designed and built by others. For the most part, as discussed here, the predominant focus of both safety and chemical engineers has been on end-of-process, secondary safety technology, leaving many industrial plants vulnerable to chemical explosions and sudden and accidental releases of highly toxic chemicals, such as has occurred in a number of U.S. petroleum refinery accidents in the recent past.

Various bills dealing with chemical security have been introduced in Congress without success. Some emphasize inherently safer production as a means of significantly reducing risks from high-risk chemical facilities, while others emphasize simply "policing" those facilities for would-be terrorists. Industry generally objects to any legislation that would mandate that facilities be made inherently safer, including legislation that would mandate the performance of a technology options analysis. Studies of European plants suggest that inherently safer production is practical and cost-effective, both for existing and new plants. It not only can lead to the reduction of risk from catastrophic accidents, but can also provide an opportunity to modernize older plants, find alternative synthetic pathways for production and use of chemicals, and eliminate unnecessary waste. On the other hand, placing a security guard at the gates of high-risk chemical plants, limiting plane flights over these plants, and other such "band-aid" approaches cannot be done practically on the scale needed and will not provide real security in any event.

Some in government have long recognized the importance of inherent safety, but government has thus far failed to press industry to adopt these measures. There are laws and institutions already in place that could contribute to the enhancement of chemical safety, but they are largely uncoordinated and underfunded. EPA itself has an Office of Pollution Prevention, but its focus is on preventing the gradual and expected releases of chemicals, not sudden, accidental, or deliberate releases leading to catastrophic events. Its activities are carried out independently of the EPA Office of Chemical Preparedness and Emergency Response, and that latter office has yet to press for modern prevention approaches, inherent safety, or technological redesign. Similarly, the Occupational Safety and Health Administration has yet to recognize the importance of preventing pollution *at the source*, let alone the importance of inherent safety. The federal government does have an agency with relevant expertise on the safety of chemical processes: the Chemical Safety and Hazard Investigation Board (CSB), which was created by the 1990 Clean Air Act Amendments as part of a chemical safety initiative discussed later in this chapter. However, the CSB's creation was long delayed and resisted by the chemical industry, and it remains understaffed and underfunded. On the community level, the Local Emergency Planning Committees (LEPCs) created by EPCRA could be important assets, but they have thus far focused on secondary prevention and population evacuation measures, and they are largely unfunded.

In December 2003, the Bush administration assigned chemical security to the new Department of Homeland Security (DHS), but that body has no authority to enforce the chemical safety provisions of the Clean Air Act. Even without any new legislation focusing explicitly on inherent safety, the promotion of inherent safety could be enhanced considerably through a coordinated governmental effort. Consideration might be given, for example, to the creation of a chemical safety coordinating council consisting of EPA, OSHA, DOT, CSB, and DHS, the involvement of all stakeholders—industry, workers, and citizens—in a "chemical safety watch" (perhaps through a federal advisory committee to the council), and to increasing the resources made available to EPA, OSHA, CSB, and LEPCs, to enable them to enhance and expand their expertise and activities in encouraging inherently safer production.

■ **NOTES**

1. In response to chemical safety concerns expressed after the events of 9/11, many agencies removed documents from Internet sites "to keep them away from terrorists." Similarly, EPA dismantled its risk management website containing general information about emergency plans and chemicals used at 15,000 sites nationwide, allowing selective access to sensitive information about "worst case" chemical accidents (contained in offsite consequence analyses) only in special reading rooms. See Guy Gugilotta (2001) "Agencies Scrub Web Sites of Sensitive Chemical Data: Government Debates Safety Versus Security," *Washington Post*, October 4, p. A29.

2. In her book *It's My Party Too* (Penguin, 2005), former EPA Administrator Christie Whitman reveals that industry lobbyists worked with key Republican lawmakers to scuttle new security regulations for chemical plants after the 9/11 attacks.

3. Responding to pre-9/11 chemical safety concerns raised during the 1999 passage of the Chemical Safety Information, Site Security and Fuels Regulatory Relief Act, P.L.106-40, 113 Stat. 207 (1999), the U.S. General Accounting Office surveyed the emergency response community (emergency planners, firefighters, and EPA officials) as to the adequacy of chemical safety information and its delivery for response purposes. The resulting report, released in 2002, concluded that the information was generally adequate, though lacking in sufficient specificity about the chemicals and with too much emphasis on "worst-case scenarios" rather than on "probable-case scenarios." See GAO (2002) *Chemical Safety: Emergency Response Community Views on the Adequacy of Federally Required Chemical Information*, Report to Congressional Committees.

4. Public interest groups have also been active in the policy debate on chemical safety. In 2001, the U.S. Public Interest Research Group (PIRG) published *Protecting Our Hometowns: Preventing Chemical Terrorism in America: A Guide for Policymakers and Advocates* (see Baumann, 2001), and the Safe Hometowns Initiative published *The Safe Hometowns Initiative: How to Do a Community Reassessment of Chemical Site Safety and Security after September 11, 2001* (available at http://www.safehometowns.org; see also Lewis, 2001).

5. In 2004, Public Citizen issued *Homeland Unsecured: The Bush Administration's Hostility to Regulation and Ties to Industry Leave America Vulnerable* (available at

www.HomelandUnsecured.org), which details "how the Bush administration has failed to harden our defenses against terrorism and secure the most vulnerable, high-impact targets." The report is based on an analysis of five key areas—chemical plants, nuclear power plants, hazardous material transport, ports, and water systems. Greenpeace and OMB Watch have also taken up the cudgel in favor of enhanced chemical plant security, arguing that the measures taken by the chemical industry to date represent largely cosmetic approaches to a serious public safety threat.

6. In July 2005 the Congressional Research Service released a state-by-state breakdown of chemical facilities that possess significant amounts of toxic and flammable chemicals, based on the size of the populations that could potentially be affected by disasters. The analysis is based on EPA data from May 2005. The number of plants in each category is the maximum believed to pose a danger, but the report (available at http://www.chron.com/cs/CDA/ssistory.mpl/front/3254502) does not specify the facilities' names or the cities where they are located.

7. In 1996 the European Union identified inherent safety as the preferred approach of the Seveso II Directive on the Prevention of Chemical Accidents, adopted in response to the industrial disasters at Bhopal and Seveso. See Papadakis and Amendola (1997). The Seveso Directives are discussed later in this chapter.

8. Under the leadership of Governor Jon Corzine, a strong proponent of inherent safety while in the U.S. Senate, New Jersey is proposing rules to expand the coverage of New Jersey's Toxic Catastrophic Prevention Act (TPCA). The original rules required TPCA-covered facilities to perform an inherently safer technology review only if they added a new process. The proposed rules would require all TCPA-covered facilities to do such a review within 120 days after the rules are finalized and to repeat the analysis every 5 years thereafter [*Toxics Law Reporter* 22(15): 345 (2007)].

9. In contrast, the U.S. Department of Homeland Security in an interim final rule issued in 2007 continues to follow a risk-based approach advocated by the American Chemistry Council, focusing on risk analysis of existing facilities and on "security standards" that emphasize securing the perimeter of the chemical facility and critical targets, controlling access, deterring the theft of dangerous chemicals, and preventing internal sabotage [*Environmental Reporter* 38(14): 812 (2007)]. These are at best secondary prevention approaches, and are not focused on technology-based controls. While it does not preempt state law, the oversight authority that DHS exercises over state efforts has left many concerned that state efforts aggressively promoting inherent safety could be weakened as a practical matter, and some have called for congressional action to preserve the freedom of the states to take such initiative. ∎

C. MOVING FROM CHARACTERIZING PROBLEMS AND ASSESSING RISK TO FINDING TECHNOLOGY-BASED SOLUTIONS

As we have stressed at various points throughout this text, there are fundamental differences between a risk-based and a technology-based approach to addressing environmental problems and setting environmental priorities. The first approach asks: How do we identify and rank the risks (or opportunities for reducing risks) to human health and the environment? The second approach, on the other hand, begins with the following question: How do we identify and exploit the opportunities for changing the basic technologies of production, extraction, agriculture, and transportation that cause damage to the environment and health? As a corollary to this inquiry, it also asks whether we want to effectuate a transformation of the existing polluting or problem industrial sectors, or stimulate more radical innovation that might result in replacement of a technology.

Considerations of risks, costs, and equity are relevant to all these questions, of course. Historically, the U.S. EPA and most economists, scientists, and risk analysts have dedicated their efforts to exploring rational approaches to answering the first question. In general, they also implicitly assume a static technological world. In contrast, those who focus on the second approach argue for the application of political will and creative energy toward changing the ways we do business in the industrial state. The first effort promotes rationalism within a static world; the second is arational, but not irrational, and promotes transformation of the industrial state as something of an art form. It is interesting that it is the first approach that is criticized as being too technocratic, but it is the second that argues for technological change.

The authors of this text believe that the second approach is much more clearly compatible with the promotion of pollution prevention and primary accident prevention. We believe that a comparison between *risk assessment*—a basic tool of this first approach—and *technology options analysis*—a basic tool of the second—makes the point.

1. The Technology Options Analysis

Suppose a given industrial firm is interested in determining how best to reduce the risk that it will harm the environment or public health through gradual chemical pollution and sudden and accidental chemical releases. It could do a risk assessment in an effort to determine the nature and extent of these risks and then work backward to perform a technology assessment—an assessment of the technologies and methodologies available for reducing the more pressing of these risks. On the surface, this appears to be an eminently logical approach, for no one would argue that a risk reduction strategy should proceed without an appreciation of the degree of the risk. In practice, however, a risk-technology assessment is generally limited to an evaluation of the risks associated with the firm's established production technology, and does not include the identification or consideration of alternative production technologies that could be adopted or developed that may be inherently cleaner or safer than the ones currently employed. Consequently, risk assessments tend to emphasize end-of-pipe pollution control, rather than the type of process, input, and product changes that are consistent with preventing pollution. Furthermore, they tend to emphasize secondary accident prevention and mitigation strategies, which impose engineering and administrative controls on an existing production technology, rather than primary accident prevention strategies, which utilize input substitution and process redesign to modify a production technology.

Instead of simply performing the usual risk and technology assessment, however, the firm could conduct an inherent safety opportunity audit and a technology options analysis. As discussed earlier in this chapter, an ISOA followed by a TOA examines *where* in the production process cleaner and/or safer technologies could be adopted or developed, and *what* those technologies could be. In contrast to a risk and technology assessment, then, a TOA expands the risk reduction evaluation to include alternative production technologies and thus facilitates the implementation of strategies to prevent pollution and primary accidents. Pointedly, the TOA looks not only to the array of technologies already in use within a particular industry, but also to the adaptation of technologies from related industries and the opportunities for reducing risk through technological innovation.

This comparison can be generalized to the current environmental regulatory system as a whole. In general, the conventional approach to regulating chemicals, which is often driven by specific regulation, envisions a three-step sequential process: (1) producing or collecting risk-relevant information, (2) performing a risk assessment and characterization, and (3) adopting risk management practices. We argue that such a sequential process is too static, or linear, and that it channels a disproportionate level of societal resources to the search for, and the generation of information about, present hazards (i.e., toxicity and exposure data). We believe that resources should be redirected to searching for and generating information about safer alternatives (i.e., input substitution, final product reformulation, and process changes). Further, we argue that the generation of the information necessary for risk assessment and the search for cleaner and safer alternative technologies should be approached simultaneously, in two parallel quests. This parallel approach would blur the bright line often asserted to lie between risk assessment and risk management, but would allow the integration of risk and risk-reduction options. See Koch and Ashford (2006).

■ **NOTE**

1. To the extent that a firm adopts, rather than develops, pollution prevention technology, this response would be characterized as *diffusion*-driven pollution prevention. The resulting changes, while beneficial, could very well be suboptimal because the firm would not undertake to innovate and thus may achieve static, rather than dynamic, efficiency. (See the discussion of dynamic efficiency in chapter 3.)   ■

2. The U.S. Experience

Although the U.S. regulatory establishment has flirted with a more technology-focused approach, it has made little sustained movement in this direction. In a 1994 report detailing its "Technology Innovation Strategy," EPA indicated that it was moving from a preoccupation with risk to a concern for fundamental technological change:

Technology innovation is indispensable to achieving our national and international environmental goals. Available technologies are inadequate to solve many present and emerging environmental problems or, in some cases, too costly to bear widespread adoption. Innovative technologies offer the promise that the demand for continuing economic growth can be reconciled with the imperative of strong environmental protection. In launching this Technology Innovation Strategy, the Environmental Protection Agency aims to inaugurate an era of unprecedented technological ingenuity in the service of environmental protection and public health.... This strategy signals EPA's commitment to making needed changes and reinventing the way it does its business so that the United States will have the best technological solutions needed to protect the environment....

We are progressing from an environmental paradigm based on cleanup and control to one including assessment, anticipation and avoidance.... The environmental problems of greatest immediate concern have changed over the past quarter of a century, and the technologies required to address those problems have changed as well. In the 1970's, environmental protection focused on "end-of-pipe" equipment for controlling air and water pollution. In the 1980's, the physical cleanup of waste sites received particular attention. Today, environmental protection is beginning to involve changes in the fundamental ways our energy, food, fiber, shelter and consumer goods are produced. The emphasis has shifted from the control and remediation of pollution to the avoidance ... of many kinds of environmental harm. (U.S. EPA, 1994)

Although this clear, bold statement might have been expected to signal a significantly revised regulatory approach, this proved not to be the case. EPA did initiate several activities or programs in the 1990s that focused on pollution prevention. As required by the Pollution Prevention Act of 1990, the agency created an Office of Pollution Prevention within the Office of Pesticides and Toxic Substances, and charged it with emphasizing source reduction in the manufacturing or use of chemicals and materials. That office subsequently launched a "Design for the Environment" initiative to encourage green chemistry. The agency also created a Technology Innovation Office

in the Office of Solid Waste and Emergency Response, which was charged with promoting alternative remediation technologies. Further, EPA established an advisory
committee, the National Advisory Council for Environmental Policy and Technology (NACEPT), to address policies and incentives for encouraging diffusion and
innovation of environmentally relevant technologies from pollution control to pollution prevention. In the early 1990s, NACEPT operated as a complement to EPA's
science and risk-focused Science Advisory Board (SAB). Unlike the SAB, NACEPT
was conceived as a multistakeholder advisory committee, with participation by
industry, environmentalists, and academics. The core committee of NACEPT, the
Technology, Innovation and Economics (TIE) committee, produced significant
technology-focused studies. See NACEPT (1991, 1992, 1993). TIE has since been disbanded, however, and NACEPT is not currently a vehicle for pollution prevention.

In 2001, the General Accounting Office issued a report evaluating pollution prevention efforts in the United States. The GAO found that pollution prevention was
not yet a major activity among industrial firms, and that the EPA had not yet developed an effective set of programs to track and promote pollution prevention. Among
its findings were the following:

[L]imitations of available data inhibit [EPA's] ability to ascertain the extent to which companies use pollution prevention practices....

For many companies, the opportunity for a financial return [rather than agency pressure or
encouragement] is the primary impetus for pursuing pollution prevention....

Technical challenges associated with new and sometimes unproven techniques are one of the
principal barriers hindering the wider use of pollution prevention.... These technical challenges are sometimes compounded by the preferences among key decisionmakers to use "tried
and tested" methods....

[Although] the Pollution Prevention Act requires that EPA review its regulatory proposals
and determine their effect on source reduction[,] EPA has not systematically tracked its compliance with this provision and therefore does not know the extent to which source reduction
has, in fact, been considered in the promulgation of EPA regulations. (GAO, 2001, pp. 3–4)

In all, the GAO's findings would appear to indicate a disinterested agency that has
only a reluctant commitment to pollution prevention, much less to advancing a comprehensive environmental technology policy.

3. The European Experience: The Cleaner Technology Movement and Ecological Modernization

In Europe, especially in Germany, Scandinavia, and the Netherlands, there is a
burgeoning "clean technology" movement. National governments have played an
important role in encouraging technological transformation and sustainable development. In general, this has been done by setting clear standards and policy goals while
allowing industry the flexibility to choose the means (risk-reduction strategies and

practices) of achieving those goals.[3] The goals are set as much as 50 years ahead, and policies are put in place in the interim to encourage the transformations that are likely to be necessary to meet those goals. See, e.g., Keijzers (2002, 2000) and Vollenbroek (2002).[4]

Negotiated and consensual approaches in Europe are often implemented under the scrutinizing eyes of government, and this process has given rise to a system of "ecological modernization" or "reflexive law" premised on the assumption that industry will benefit from modernizing to reduce or eliminate pollution, especially when the focus is on flexibility to adopt or develop cleaner and inherently safer technology. The Dutch "polder model," for example, boasts of success in stimulating environmentally superior technological solutions by involving industry with other stakeholders in a "covenant" to engage in continuous improvement of environmental performance. See Gouldson and Murphy (1998). These Dutch covenants are often much more than simple agreements between industry and government. There generally is participation by environmentalists as well. Moreover, the covenants generally specify milestones, provide for oversight, and are legally enforceable. Thus far, some success at promoting incremental or modest innovation is apparent.

■ NOTES

1. If an order-of-magnitude (or greater) reduction in pollution, or in materials or energy usage, is what is desired, a policy based on cooperation with existing firms could limit success, especially if the targets, as well as the means and schedule for reaching the targets, are negotiated between government and those firms. (See the discussion of negotiated rulemaking in chapter 5, and the discussion of negotiation generally in chapter 12.)

2. Although the European Community has done more than the United States in the past several years to promote a technology-focused approach to environmental policy, neither the United States nor Europe has embraced the idea of radical technological innovation, especially where it would mean the displacement of dominant technologies or firms. See Koch and Ashford (2006). This tends to exacerbate the risk that dominant technological regimes will "capture" or unduly influence government regulation or negotiation processes. See, generally, Ashford et al. (2001). If

---

3. This is commonly done in the spirit of "backcasting" (as opposed to forecasting), as done in the Netherlands for the Dutch national environmental policy plans (see Vergragt and van Grootveld, 1994). That is, one assumes that the desired future goal will be met, and then identifies the key policies that would have had to have been in place to secure that result.

4. Some argue that these transformations or "transitions" can be managed through "strategic niche management" (see Rotmans, Kemp, and van Asselt, 2001), but others are skeptical about the adequacy of this evolutionary approach (see Ashford et al., 2001).

technological transformation and long-term sustainability are the goals, new entrants and new technologies must be given a chance to evolve to address environmental problems.

3. The design and implementation of regulatory policy is ultimately in the hands of government. If a government simply serves as a referee or arbiter of competing interests, future technologies may not be adequately represented by the existing industrial stakeholders. For this reason we believe that government must act as a trustee for new technology. See Ashford (2005). As discussed in chapter 12, direct support of research and development, tax incentives for investment in sustainable technologies, and other technical assistance initiatives that fall under the rubric of "industrial policy" are other areas where government can make a difference. See Nelson (1996) and Nelson and Rosenberg (1993).

4. See Ashford (2005) for a review of different perspectives on the emerging "ecological modernization" movement in Europe, and for a discussion of the degree to which its success is likely to be linked to concerns for dynamic change.   ∎

D. U.S. AND EUROPEAN UNION LEGISLATIVE INITIATIVES FOCUSING ON POLLUTION AND ACCIDENT PREVENTION

In this section we examine three U.S. laws—two federal, and one state—that focus explicitly on preventing pollution and/or chemical accidents. We also explore how these or similar laws might be used to promote pollution prevention and inherent safety as part of the same coordinated effort. Finally, although a review of European Union environmental law is beyond the scope of this text, we briefly examine two important EU directives promoting cleaner and inherently safer technology.

1. The Pollution Prevention Act

Just as Congress endeavored with the National Environmental Policy Act of 1969 to imbue federal agencies with an environmental consciousness, so did Congress endeavor with the Pollution Prevention Act of 1990 to imbue federal environmental and public health agencies with a preference for preventing pollution. The Pollution Prevention Act (PPA), 42 U.S.C. §13101, *et seq.*, enunciates a clear federal policy preference for achieving environmental goals through pollution prevention.

The PPA does this through the rubric of "source reduction," which it defines as

any practice which (i) reduces the amount of any hazardous substance, pollutant, or contaminant entering any waste stream or otherwise released into the environment (including fugitive emissions) *prior to* recycling, treatment, or disposal; *and* (ii) reduces the hazards to public health and the environment associated with the release of such substances, pollutants, or contaminants. [42 U.S.C. §13102(5)(A), emphasis added]

Explicitly included within the statuatory definition are "equipment or technology modifications, process or procedure modifications, reformulation or redesign of products, substitution of raw materials, and improvements in housekeeping, maintenance, training, or inventory control," while explicitly *excluded* is any practice that "alters the physical, chemical, or biological characteristics or the volume of a hazardous substance, pollutant, or contaminant *through a process or activity which itself is not integral to and necessary for the production of a product or the providing of a service*" [42 U.S.C. §13102(5)(A) and (B), emphasis added]. Thus, pollution prevention and primary accident prevention (as we use the terms in this text) both come within the PPA's definition of "source reduction." On the other hand, recycling or reuse does not meet this definition unless it is done as part of a closed-loop production process (as is often done within the metal-finishing industry, when metals are recovered at the end of the process and immediately returned to the beginning of the process).

The PPA declares, as the "national policy," that pollution is to be addressed in a hierarchical fashion. First, "pollution should be prevented or reduced at the source whenever feasible." Second, "pollution that cannot be prevented should be recycled in an environmentally safe manner, whenever feasible." And, third, "disposal or other release into the environment should be employed only as a last resort" [42 U.S.C. §13101(b)]. As an articulated first step toward achieving these goals, the PPA directs the EPA to establish a separate office to "develop and implement a strategy to promote source reduction" [42 U.S.C. §13103(a)]. The three regulatory cornerstones of this source reduction strategy are to be (1) the evaluation of existing and proposed EPA regulations to ensure that they are consistent with the promotion of source reduction, (2) coordination of source reduction activities in all other EPA offices, and (3) coordination with other agencies to promote source reduction and research into source reduction "techniques and processes," as a comprehensive federal policy. See 42 U.S.C. §13103(b)(2) and (3). EPA's source reduction strategy is also to include the establishment of "standard methods" to measure source reduction; the identification of "measurable goals" for implementing a source reduction policy; measures to "facilitate" the implementation of source reduction techniques by industry (including source reduction training programs and workshops and an awards program for "outstanding or innovative" source reduction activities); identification of institutional barriers to, and opportunities to use federal procurement to promote, source reduction; and development of methods of "coordinating, streamlining, and assuring" public access to data collected under federal environmental statutes. See 42 U.S.C. §13103(b).

EPA did establish an Office of Pollution Prevention to carry out these activities but, as discussed, the agency's overall commitment to implementing the PPA has waned considerably since the early 1990s. Neither the Clinton nor Bush administrations wholeheartedly embraced the potential opportunities for fundamental change that the PPA represents, and the agency's "source reduction strategy" has largely been allowed to languish. This is not particularly surprising, given the general regulatory philosophies of these administrations and given the relatively "soft" mandates of the PPA. With few specific, measurable statutory benchmarks—either for EPA or for industry—to guide its implementation, the PPA is very much a creature of administrative discretion. Not only can its influence and importance be expected to rise and fall according to the level of enthusiasm of those who administer the EPA, but its directives will (even in the most enthusiastic of administrations) find themselves competing for the agency's attention with the much more specific, time-sensitive mandates of the various media-based environmental statutes.

As discussed in chapter 10, one concrete mandate in the PPA is its requirement that firms subject to the Toxic Release Inventory reporting requirements of the Emergency Planning and Community Right-to-Know Act include specific information in their annual Toxic Chemical Release forms regarding the source reduction and recycling activities they have undertaken. This reporting is to include (1) the amount of each listed chemical entering the environment before recycling, treatment, or disposal, the percentage change from the previous year, and the predictions for the next 2 years; (2) the amount of each such chemical recycled, the percentage change from the previous year, and the predictions for the next 2 years; (3) the amount of each such chemical treated and the percentage change from the previous year; (4) the amount of any such chemical released via "catastrophic" or other one-time event; (5) the ratio of this year's production to the previous year's, (6) the "source reduction practices" utilized over the past year (divided according to four categories—equipment, technology, or process modification; product reformulation or redesign; input substitution; and management, training, or other "operational" improvements); and (7) the techniques utilized to identify source reduction opportunities. See 42 U.S.C. §13106. The PPA also directed EPA to establish a source reduction clearinghouse to compile information on "management, technical, and operational approaches to source reduction" [42 U.S.C. §13105(a)], and the agency created the Pollution Prevention Information Clearinghouse (PPIC) to meet this requirement. True to its statutory function, PPIC has developed into an often-valuable repository of information on various aspects of pollution prevention. See http://www.epa.gov/oppt/ppic

■ **NOTES**

1. The language of the PPA is largely directed toward the protection of the environment and there is very little explicit focus on workplace health and safety. However,

included in the list of findings in the law's opening section are both a recognition that prevention of pollution at its source will "reduce risks to worker health and safety" and an expression of a congressional preference for "multimedia management of pollution." See 42 U.S.C. §13102(a)(2) and (3). This, plus the obvious opportunities for cooptimizing environmental and workplace gains through a coordinated pollution and accident reduction strategy, should encourage EPA to manage its pollution prevention program with a firm commitment toward reducing chemical risks in the workplace. See section F of this chapter.

2. Under the PPA, the states are to receive matching federal grants to establish programs that encourage "the use of source reduction techniques by businesses" [42 U.S.C §13104(a)]. The state programs are expected to make technical assistance available to businesses seeking information about source reduction opportunities, assist targeted businesses that lack the information to develop source reduction plans on their own, and provide training in source reduction techniques. See 42 U.S.C. §13104(b). As discussed later, several states have their own omnibus pollution prevention statutes and some of these, such as the Massachusetts Toxics Use Reduction Act, require more from industry than does the PPA.

3. The information contained in the annual toxic chemical release forms, as well as the information in the annual Toxic Chemical Source Reduction and Recycling Report, is available to the general public (including individual workers). The data and information collected by the Pollution Prevention Information Clearinghouse are also available to the general public (http://www.epa.gov/oppt/ppic/). Such information includes source reduction opportunities, available source reduction technologies, and the data collected by state source reduction programs. ∎

2. The Chemical Safety Provisions of the Clean Air Act[5]

Although EPCRA, passed in 1986, was the first congressional response to the country's "Bhopal" concerns, the chemical safety provisions of that law are focused almost solely on mitigation and not on accident prevention. A much greater potential for a direct focus on primary accident prevention can be found in the 1990 amendments to the Clean Air Act, although that potential has yet to be realized.

a. General Provisions
Section 112(r) of the Clean Air Act, added in 1990, directs EPA to develop regulations regarding the prevention and detection of accidental chemical releases, and to

---

5. This section is based on materials found in Ashford and Caldart (1996).

publish a list of at least 100 chemical substances (with associated threshold quantities) to be covered by the regulations. The regulations must include requirements for the development of risk management plans by facilities using any of the regulated substances in amounts above the relevant threshold. These risk management plans must include a hazard assessment, an accident prevention program, and an emergency release program. See 42 U.S.C. §§7412 (r)(3) and 7412(r)(7)(ii). Similarly, Section 304 of the Clean Air Act Amendments of 1990 directed the Occupational Safety and Health Administration to promulgate a chemical process safety standard under the Occupational Safety and Health Act, 29 U.S.C. §651, *et seq.*

Section 112(r) also imposes a "general duty" on *all* "owners and operators of stationary sources [of air pollution]," regardless of the particular identity or quantity of the chemicals used on site. These parties have a duty to:

...*identify hazards* that may result from [accidental chemical] releases using appropriate hazard assessment techniques,

...*design and maintain a safe facility* taking such steps as are necessary to prevent releases, and

...*minimize the consequences* of accidental releases which do occur. [42 U.S.C. §7412(r)(1), emphasis added]

Thus, firms are under a general duty to *anticipate, prevent, and mitigate* accidental releases.

In defining the nature of this duty, Section 112(r) specifies that it is "a general duty in the same manner and to the same extent as" that imposed by 29 U.S.C. §654, a section of the OSHAct, commonly known as the general duty clause, which requires every employer to provide a workplace free from recognized hazards that are likely to cause serious harm. Because Section 112 specifically ties its general duty obligation to the general duty clause of the OSHAct, case law interpreting that provision should be directly relevant. For example, in *U.A.W. v. General Dynamics*, 815 F.2nd 626 (D.C.Cir. 1987), the D.C. Circuit Court of Appeals held that the OSHAct's general duty obligation is separate and distinct from occupational safety and health standards established under the OSHAct, and that compliance with a standard does not discharge an employer's duty to comply with the general duty obligation. Similarly, compliance with other Clean Air Act chemical safety requirements should not relieve a firm's duty to comply with Section 112(r)'s general duty clause.

The 1990 amendments to the Clean Air Act also require each state to establish programs to provide small businesses with technical assistance in addressing chemical safety. These programs could provide information on alternative technologies, process changes, products, and methods of operation that help reduce emissions to air. However, these state mandates are unfunded and may not be uniformly implemented. Where they are established, linkage with state offices of technical assistance, especially those that provide guidance on pollution prevention, could be particularly beneficial.

Finally, Section 112(r) established an independent Chemical Safety and Hazard Investigation Board. As discussed earlier, the board is empowered to investigate the causes of accidents, perform research on prevention, and make recommendations for preventive approaches, much in the way the Air Transportation Safety Board does with regard to airplane safety. Initially, however, President Clinton provided no funding for the CSB in his annual budget. The CSB was ultimately activated in response to pressure from environmental and labor groups, but it has remained chronically underfunded.

▪ NOTES

1. Four states—New Jersey, California, Nevada, and Delaware—have regulations on prevention of accidental releases. More stringent state programs are not preempted by Section 112(r), and some of these state regulations go beyond the requirements of that provision. For example, as discussed earlier, New Jersey mandates a "state-of-art review" which is akin to a technology options analysis for accident prevention technologies. See note 8 in Section B-3.

2. The risk management plans required by the CAA are to be registered with the EPA and submitted to the CSB, as well as to state and local emergency response entities.

3. In 2006, the CSB proposed a rule requiring firms to ensure the preservation of crucial evidence after a significant explosion or spill. See Hess (2006).   ▪

b.   OSHA's Process Safety Management Standard

As required by the 1990 Clean Air Act amendments, OSHA promulgated a standard requiring chemical process safety management (PSM) in the workplace in 1992. See 29 C.F.R. §1910.119. The PSM standard is designed to protect employees working in facilities that use "highly hazardous chemicals," and employees working in facilities with more than 10,000 pounds of flammable liquids or gases present in one location. The list of highly hazardous chemicals in the standard includes acutely toxic, highly flammable, and reactive substances. The PSM standard requires employers to compile safety information (including process flow information) on chemicals and processes used in the workplace, complete a workplace process hazard analysis every 5 years, conduct triennial compliance safety audits, develop and implement written operating procedures to maintain the integrity of process equipment, conduct extensive worker training, perform prestartup reviews for new (and significantly modified) facilities, develop and implement written procedures to manage changes in production methods, establish an emergency action plan, and investigate accidents and near-misses at their facility.

■ **NOTES**

1. In essence, the OSHA PSM standard seeks to improve safety management only in facilities that are likely to experience sudden and accidental releases of highly hazardous chemicals that may injure workers. It imposes no affirmative duty on these facilities to change any element of their production system.

2. Many aspects of chemical safety are not covered by specific workplace standards. Most that do apply to chemical safety have their origin in the consensus standards adopted under Section 6(a) of the OSHAct in 1971 and hence are greatly out of date. The general duty obligation in Section 5 of the Occupational Safety and Health Act requires employers "to furnish...employment and a place of employment free from recognized hazards that are...likely to cause death and serious physical harm to his employees" [28 U.S.C. §654(a)] Does this impose a duty on the employer to seek out technological improvements that would improve safety for workers? If a worker were injured, could an employer be cited under the general duty clause of the OSHAct for failure to look for and implement these improvements? Even if a technology options analysis (TOA) were not otherwise required of the employer, would the failure to perform a TOA that would have identified a clearly safer technology constitute a per se violation of the employer's general duty to provide a safe and healthy workplace? If a TOA were required and did identify affordable superior technologies, would the failure to implement these changes be a violation of the general duty obligation under the OSHAct? Note that the general duty obligation in Section 112(r) of the Clean Air Act requires the firm to "design and maintain a safe facility." Is this a stronger mandate for chemical safety than the OSHAct's obligation to "furnish" a workplace that is "free from recognized hazards" to employees? The Clean Air Act's focus on public health and safety generally clearly is broader than the OSHAct's exclusive focus on employee safety, but protection of employees from chemical hazards may well require measures that are equally extensive as (or more extensive than) those required to protect the public in general. Further, although the Clean Air Act specifically references the obligation to "design" a safe facility, while the OSHAct does not, the obligation to "furnish" such a facility would appear to extend to design as well as maintenance.   ■

c. EPA's Risk Management Plan Regulation
In 1996, EPA promulgated regulations setting forth requirements for the "risk management plans" specified in Section 112(r) of the Clean Air Act. See 61 *Fed. Reg.*

31,668, *et seq.* (June 20, 1996), codified at 40 C.F.R. Part 68. Previously, EPA had issued a draft risk management plan (RMP) rule, which had engendered considerable—and often acrimonious—public comment. Labor and environmental groups criticized the draft rule for its lack of emphasis on primary prevention and inherent safety. Industry, on the other hand, bristled at the suggestion that the rule mandate TOAs requiring identification of inherently safer technologies. In promulgating the final rule, EPA announced that it had "decided not to mandate inherently safer technology analysis" [61 *Fed. Reg.* 31,699].

The final RMP rule was modeled on the OSHA PSM standard. It requires a hazard assessment (involving an off-site consequence analysis—including worst-case risk scenarios—and compilation of a 5-year accident history), a prevention program to address the hazards identified, and an emergency response program. The rule does not emphasize primary accident prevention. Rather than focusing on the need to promote technological change, the rule takes existing production technologies as a given, and thus has largely failed to encourage significant changes in chemical processes, final products, or inputs.

EPA revised its reporting requirements in 2004, and now requires that a reportable accident be entered into a facility's 5-year accident history within 6 months of its occurrence. Previously, the incident was to be included in the next 5-year reporting cycle. The revised requirements also specify that the reports must indicate whether the accident involved an uncontrolled or runaway chemical reaction. In response to industry's argument that chemical accident information could find its way to would-be terrorists, the revised RMP rule also removes the off-site consequence analyses from the executive summary available to the public. See 69 *Fed. Reg.* 18,819 (April 9, 2004).

■ **NOTE**

1. For a discussion of the value of chemical safety information, see Beierle (2003).   ■

3. The Massachusetts Toxics Use Reduction Act

Some states, especially New Jersey, Minnesota, Illinois, and Massachusetts, have made a more concerted effort than the federal government to promote pollution prevention. Of particular interest, both because of its apparent effectiveness and because of its relative longevity, is the Toxics Use Reduction Act (TURA) passed by the Massachusetts legislature in 1989.

Information as Environmental Regulation: TRI and Performance Benchmarking, Precursor to a New Paradigm?

Bradley C. Karkkainen

Source: 89 *Georgetown Law Journal* 257 (2001), excerpted with permission.

D. STRUCTURED SELF-MONITORING AND BENCHMARKING: MASSACHUSETTS TOXICS USE REDUCTION ACT

Building on TRI [the Toxics Release Inventory reporting required by EPCRA], a number of states have adopted toxics use reduction (TUR) programs, explicitly seeking to enlist facilities in "source reduction" planning to reduce both the use and generation of toxic substances. Many of these programs are purely voluntary, consisting largely of free technical assistance, but a few states, including Massachusetts, Oregon, and New Jersey, have established mandatory (or so-called "mandatory-voluntary") programs. Of these, the Massachusetts Toxics Use Reduction Act (TURA) is perhaps the most ambitious variant. It sets a statewide goal of reducing toxic waste generation by fifty percent, focusing on toxics use reduction as the preferred means to achieve this goal. The Act requires "Large Quantity Toxics Users" to develop inventories of chemicals flowing into and through their production processes, establish process-specific toxics use reduction plans, and file their inventories and summaries of their reduction plans, including projected future levels of toxic chemical use and emissions, with state officials. Toxics use reduction plans must be certified by credentialed toxics use reduction planners (TURPs). Each facility is free to select its own reduction goals and means of implementation, but it must have both goals and an implementation plan. Once the plan is properly prepared and filed, however, the program becomes "voluntary." The facility has discretion to decide whether

to actually implement the plan, in whole or in part.

The Massachusetts program also provides free state-funded technical assistance through an Office of Technical Assistance. The Toxics Use Reduction Institute (TURI) at the University of Massachusetts-Lowell, a statutorily created, independent entity, provides training for toxics users, TURPs, and state employees, conducts research and publishes evaluations of toxics use reduction methods, develops demonstration projects, and periodically assesses the overall program. Finally, a cabinet-level Administrative Council, with advice from an Advisory Board consisting of representatives from industry, environmental, and health groups, recommends program budget allocations and may also designate specific industrial sectors as "priority user segments," triggering regulatory authority to set minimum performance standards based on "reasonably proven public domain technologies."

The Massachusetts TUR program can be seen as a logical extension of the TRI approach. It formalizes, deepens, and expands the scope of mandatory self-monitoring, benchmarking, and regulatory monitoring, requiring facilities to engage in careful self-examination and systematic reporting, under structured state supervision, not only of emissions data but also of the inputs and production processes that generate waste, and of the best available alternatives [emphasis added].[5] ... TURA does not leave firm and

---

5. Perhaps the most controversial aspect of TURA is that unlike both TRI and 33/50, it explicitly aims to reduce the use of toxic substances, not merely

facility managers entirely to their own devices to identify improvement opportunities. The TURP certification requirements, TURI research and demonstration projects, and state-provided technical assistance are designed to formalize and deepen industry-wide benchmarking and the rolling advance of best practices. A cadre of private sector, academic, and governmental experts play a central role in this process, identifying and evaluating evolving "state-of-the-art" technologies and production processes, making facility managers cognizant of them, and encouraging their incorporation into facility-specific toxics use reduction plans. To that extent, TURA goes well beyond TRI's emphasis on monitoring and benchmarking of objective indicators of environmental performance, instead focusing on benchmarking and continuous improvement of the means of achieving environmental objectives—that is to say, of production processes themselves.

Massachusetts officials claim the TURA program has achieved dramatic results, pointing to a seventy-three percent reduction in reported TRI releases since 1990, significantly above the national average.[6] EPA survey data indicate that Massachusetts firms engage in more pollution prevention activities and pollution-reducing process changes and input substitutions than their peers in other states.[7] This suggests that supervised mandatory planning leads many to identify opportunities for cost-effective alternatives that otherwise might not have been apparent.

But individualized goal-setting as practiced in Massachusetts also comes at the price of limited opportunities for public participation, transparency, and accountability to parties other than those designated by the state. Toxics use reduction plans are generally highly complex technical documents and, under the Massachusetts statute, are treated as proprietary information and, therefore, are not disclosed to the public. The TUR planning process also does not produce much in the way of publicly reported comparable data by which the public can hold individual facilities or firms accountable, a role that continues to fall primarily to TRI. Indeed, Massachusetts officials themselves rely on TRI data as evidence of TURA's success, suggesting that TRI remains the best available public metric of TURA's effectiveness. Yet while TRI and TURA might be thought to be broadly complementary programs, TRI data on environmental releases is ultimately poorly suited to measure firm- or facility-level progress toward toxics use reduction, the stated purpose of the Massachusetts statute. That remains, under the Massachusetts program, a matter for experts alone.

The Massachusetts TUR program thus represents a professional-technocratic extension of the TRI approach, requiring an intensive form of performance self-monitoring,

---

emissions or other forms of waste. The CMA and some other business groups insist that use reduction is an inappropriate goal, arguing that harm results only from human exposures and environmental releases which may be regulated independently. The merits of the use-versus-emissions question are hotly debated, and beyond the scope of this Article. That issue aside, the critical and interesting elements of the Massachusetts approach are that it requires mandatory, explicit, detailed goal-setting and planning, under a structure designed to incorporate and formalize benchmarking and regulatory supervision while retaining TRI's flexibility and discretion.

6. Notably, however, other states in the New England region and in the northeast more generally have made comparable gains through other means... (showing steep declines in TRI-reported releases in New York and in all New England states).

7. ... ([In an] EPA survey, ninety-five percent of plant managers in Massachusetts and New Jersey reported implementing pollution prevention activities, compared with seventy-nine percent in the rest of the U.S.; seventy-seven percent of Massachusetts and New Jersey respondents reported that they had substituted chemicals or raw materials or modified their products, compared with sixty percent from the rest of the United States).

goal-setting, and implementation planning by managers and certified experts, assisted and disciplined by external expert monitoring and formalized benchmarking. But the TUR process does not expose firms to non-expert monitoring by markets and the citizenry. The political tradeoff for closer scrutiny by experts and regulators has been insulation from further transparency and accountability to the lay public.

The following reading evaluates the efficacy of the Massachusetts law as a form of mandatory environmental management planning and suggests some implications for environmental management systems generally.

Policy Options for Improving Environmental Management
Cary Coglianese and Jennnifer Nash
Source: *Environment* 44(9): 13–22 (2002), excerpted with permission.

Although environmental management systems are currently conceived as alternatives to conventional regulation, they could in principle be incorporated into governmental mandates. In other fields of regulation, such as securities, banking, and food safety, government agencies require operational procedures comparable to management and auditing systems.[4] Even in the environmental arena, governmental requirements to engage in planning and other management activities can be found in several contexts, including in settlements of...government enforcement actions, the regulations requiring chemical firms to engage in risk management planning, and in state pollution prevention laws.[25]

The advantage of a governmental mandate is that it can be imposed on all firms. If the goal is simply to increase the number of firms using EMSs, then a governmental mandate is probably the best option to pursue. However, just as firms may respond to private sector customer mandates only begrudgingly, firms' responses to governmental mandates may also turn out to be only token or ritualistic. The specter of EMS regulations and possible sanctions for noncompliance may also breed resistance from firms, especially from those whose managers do not see the need for such systems. Firms may perceive EMS requirements simply as one more unreasonable regulatory burden imposed by government and may react by complying only minimally with the rules.[26] Mandating environmental management systems might dramatically increase the number of firms using EMSs without necessarily increasing the number of firms using them effectively.[27]

---

4. C. Coglianese and D. Lazer, "Management-Based Regulatory Strategies," in J. Donahue and J. Nye, eds., Market-Based Governance (Washington, D.C.: Brookings Institution Press, 2002).
25. C. Coglianese and D. Lazer, Management-Based Regulation: Using Private Sector Management to Achieve Public Goals, (John F. Kennedy School Faculty Working Paper, 2001).

26. E. Bardach and R. Kagan, Going by the Book: The Problem of Regulatory Unreasonableness (Temple University Press, 1982).
27. Moreover, a sharp increase in the number of firms seeking to implement environmental management systems could potentially overwhelm the current capacity for qualified third-party verification, thereby reducing the effectiveness of one of the critical methods for ensuring EMS credibility and effectiveness.

On the other hand, if environmental management systems tend to take on a "life of their own" once implemented, such that even those firms that begrudgingly undertake them later see how beneficial they can be, then regulation might be a sensible way to get firms to overcome their initial resistance. Requiring firms to engage in systematic planning and management effectively compels them to invest more resources in a search for cost-effective opportunities for environmental improvement. When required to engage in planning, firms may well identify ways to reduce risks that would have otherwise gone overlooked.[28]

To anticipate the impact of governmental EMS requirements, it is instructive to examine the area of toxic use reduction where regulators have imposed management-based requirements on firms. In fact, more than twenty states in the late 1980s passed laws requiring facilities to develop plans to reduce their use or generation of toxic materials.[29] The Commonwealth of Massachusetts adopted one of the most notable of such laws in 1989. The Massachusetts Toxics Use Reduction Act (TURA) aimed to reduce the use of toxic chemicals in the state by 50 percent during the period 1987–1997, but without requiring facilities to implement toxic use reduction projects or meet specific reduction goals. Instead, the Act required managers at approximately 600 facilities in the state to report publicly on their use of toxic materials

and undertake a planning process to identify opportunities for reduction.

While Massachusetts does not characterize its mandated toxic use reduction plans as "environmental management systems," TURA essentially incorporates the main elements of an EMS. Managers of TURA-regulated facilities must submit to the state a policy statement every two years that includes goals for the reduction of toxics use and waste. Plans must describe the industrial processes in which the listed chemicals are used, the costs of the toxic chemicals, and options for reducing their use. Managers are encouraged to establish planning teams that enlist workers in analyzing production processes and identifying opportunities for improvement. Plans must be signed by an officer of the firm as well as by a toxic use reduction planner who has been certified by the state.

An evaluation commissioned by the state's Toxics Use Reduction Institute in 1996 concluded that managers of facilities covered by the Act significantly increased planning to reduce toxics during the period 1990 to 1996. For example, of the 434 facilities surveyed, 48% tracked quantities of chemicals used before 1990, while 90% did so in 1996.[30] Even though the Act does not require facilities to implement their plans (only to create them), 81% of the surveyed facilities had implemented at least a few toxic use reduction projects that they identified through the planning process.[31] In addition, participating

---

28. We make no claims here about how widespread the potential win-win opportunities available might be, a point that has garnered some debate in the literature. *See* M. Porter and C. van der Linde, "Green and Competitive: Ending the Stalemate," Harvard Business Review 73 (1995): 120–134; K. Palmer, W. Oates, and P. Portney, "Tightening Environmental Standards: The Benefit-Cost or No-Cost Paradigm?," Journal of Economic Perspectives 9 (1995): 119–132. Our point here is simply that there will likely be some such opportunities that would have been overlooked because of information costs, but that once an investment in

risk identification and planning is compelled by regulation some of these information costs effectively will become sunk costs to the firm.
29. T. Greiner, "Tiered Approach to EMS," (presentation at the annual meeting of the Multi-State Working Group on Environmental Management Systems, Orlando, FL, 2002).
30. M. Becker and K. Geiser, "Evaluating Progress: A Report on the Findings of the Massachusetts Toxic Use Reduction Program Evaluation," (Lowell, MA: Toxic Use Reduction Institute, 1997).
31. Ibid.

managers perceived the benefits of the program, in terms of facility operating expenses, to exceed the costs of planning, certification, and implementation.[32]

Massachusetts' experience with TURA suggests that a mandatory approach, with appropriate sanctions for noncompliance, can provide substantial incentives for firms to use environmental management systems. Nearly all managers complied with the mandate to develop plans, and most implemented at least part of them. Data compiled by the state's Toxic Use Reduction Institute indicates that facilities covered under the law reduced their toxic chemical use by 41% over the period 1990 to 1999 and generated 57% less waste per unit of production.[33] Because comparable data have not been compiled for similar facilities not governed by the mandate, the degree to which these improvements should be credited to the Act is far from clear. Many of the states in the New England region saw marked declines in toxic emissions during the same period, even in the absence

of toxic use planning requirements.[34] Moreover, in recent years environmental improvements implemented as a result of TURA planning may have begun to taper off and firms may now be routinizing their compliance with TURA's requirements.[35] In addition, government proposals to expand TURA-type requirements to other environmental concerns have so far gone nowhere due to industry resistance.

The TURA experience suggests that mandates [on industry to undertake and report planning] would indeed increase firms' use and implementation of EMSs, and that such use may help some firms make improvements in environmental performance. The overall impact on the environment from such a requirement is much harder to assess, but the experience with TURA seems to suggest that when such planning requirements are imposed at least some firms will respond to achieve meaningful change even though other firms are more likely just to go through the motions.

---

32. R. Currier and C. Van Atten, Benefit-Cost Analysis of The Massachusetts Toxics Use Reduction Act, (Lowell, Massachusetts: The Massachusetts Toxics Use Reduction Institute, 1997).
33. TURA Data—Results to Date, accessed at http://www.turi.org/turadata/Success/Results-ToDate.html. On July 19, 2002.

34. B. Karkkainen, "Information as Environmental Regulation: TRI and Performance Benchmarking, Precursor to a New Paradigm?," Georgetown Law Journal 89 (2001): 257–370.
35. T. Greiner, supra.

■ **NOTE**

1. O'Rourke and Lee (2004) conclude that "TURA has been able to motivate deeper, more systematic changes that support continuous process improvements and that support more extensive production process changes." What lessons could the federal government draw from the TURA experience? Could EPA use the Pollution Prevention Act and Section 112(r) of the Clean Air Act to require firms to evaluate and report on the opportunities for the development and use of cleaner and inherently safer technologies and practices at their facilities? Would the agency's hand be strengthened if Congress amended the Pollution Prevention Act to explicitly require such evaluation and reporting?   ■

4. Coordinating Accident Prevention with Pollution Prevention

By now, the interconnectedness of chemical pollution and chemical accidents, and the joint opportunities for prevention, should be apparent. It should also be clear that if production processes and technology are to be redesigned to reduce environmental and workplace exposures through pollution prevention, it makes sense to redesign them to prevent accidents *at the same time*. This would encourage industries to rethink production processes in a comprehensive, prevention-oriented fashion, and would be more likely to encourage the kinds of innovation that would lead to cleaner and safer production technologies.

Such an approach also would be consistent with the mandate of the Pollution Prevention Act. The scope of the PPA clearly extends to chemical accidents, and not merely to chemical pollution. As discussed, the PPA seeks to promote the use of "source reduction," with a primary emphasis on pollution prevention. The goals of source reduction, in turn, are defined to include "reduc[ing] the hazards to public health...associated with the release of [hazardous chemicals]," and reducing "[t]he amount of any toxic chemical released into the environment...from a catastrophic event" [42 U.S.C §§13102(5)(A)(ii) and 13106(b)(7)]. Coordination of federal pollution prevention and accident prevention efforts thus is required by the PPA, which directs EPA to "coordinate source reduction activities in each Agency Office," and to "coordinate with appropriate offices to promote source reduction practices in other Federal agencies" [42 U.S.C. §13103(b)(3)].

The EPA RMP rule does not integrate the concepts of accident prevention with those of pollution prevention or source reduction and thus fails to take advantage of an important opportunity to cooptimize EPA safety and pollution goals. Furthermore, while there is a memorandum of understanding between EPA and OSHA regarding chemical safety, little interagency coordination on the issue actually takes place.

As suggested earlier, one way in which EPA and OSHA could coordinate pollution prevention and accident prevention would be the requirement of comprehensive technology options analyses. If they are to succeed in promoting primary accident prevention, TOAs should be required well before the prestartup safety review. Further, TOAs should also be filed with the Chemical Safety and Hazard Investigation Board (and with other appropriate federal, state, and local regulatory authorities) *before design of the facility commences*. The advantages of conducting these analyses at the design stage were acknowledged by EPA in its supplemental notice on the draft RMP rule. See 60 *Fed. Reg.* 13535 (March 13, 1995). Furthermore, if they are to help promote technologies to reduce workplace exposures, TOAs should be made available to joint management-labor safety committees.

5.   European Union Legislation

The European Union, once a follower, is now a leader in environmental law and has taken aggressive steps to modernize its approach to preventing pollution and chemical accidents. See, e.g., Vogel (2003). The mid-1990s saw the emergence of two strong EU initiatives, one directed at promoting pollution prevention and one directed at promoting inherent safety.

a.   The Integrated Pollution Prevention and Control Directive

The purpose of the European Union's Integrated Pollution Prevention and Control (IPPC) Directive, adopted in 1996, is to provide a high level of environmental protection by preventing wherever practicable, or otherwise reducing, emissions to air, water, and land from a range of industrial processes, including the energy sector, metals production and processing, the mineral and chemical industries, waste management facilities, and food production and intensive livestock operations. Like the U.S. Pollution Prevention Act, the IPPC Directive clearly favors prevention over end-of-pipe control and recycling as the preferred approach.

Unlike the PPA, however, the IPPC Directive also imposes a set of standards designed to accelerate the implementation of this approach throughout industry. As of the end of 2007, approximately 60,000 installations across the EU were required to have operating permits.[6] The permits are to be coordinated, addressing together all waste and pollution streams, and are to impose performance standards based on the application of "best available techniques" (BAT). In contrast to the BAT (best available technology) requirements typically imposed under the U.S. Clean Air and Clean Water acts, this European version is not limited to existing technology, but can incorporate pollution reduction gains deemed attainable through anticipated innovation. In many cases, then, the European BAT will mean radical improvement within the regulated industry, and it is expected that sometimes it may be costly for companies to adapt their plants to BAT standards. Identification of required performance levels achievable by BAT is undertaken by the EU Center in Seville, Spain.

b.   The Seveso Directives

In 1982, in response to the chemical accident at Bhopal, India, the European Union adopted its Directive on Major Accident Hazards of Certain Industrial Activities, which has come to be known as the "Seveso Directive." This early version of the Seveso Directive required EU member states to ensure that all manufacturers prove to a "competent authority" that major hazards had been identified in their industrial

---

6. http://europa.eu.int/comm/environment/ippc/index.htm (accessed 01/02/08). Actual permit allocation appears to be lagging behind this requirement.

activities; that appropriate safety measures, including emergency plans, had been adopted; and that information, training, and safety equipment had been provided to on-site employees. See von Moltke (1985). A revised version of this directive, known as the Seveso II Directive, went into effect in 1997. Seveso II strengthens the original provisions and extends their coverage to a broader range of facilities. Moreover, the revised directive requires the implementation of safety management approaches, and the accompanying guidance document highlights inherent safety as a preferred approach to preventing chemical accidents, Unlike the IPPC Directive, however, Seveso II does not reinforce its prevention-oriented goals with performance standards.

■ **NOTES**

1. As is the custom in the EU, each directive is "transposed" into the national law of the member states. See Gouldson and Murphy (1998) for a comparison of approaches to the IPPC Directive taken by the United Kingdom and the Netherlands.

2. See Papadakis and Amendola (1997) for a discussion of the potential of the Seveso II Directive for promoting inherent safety. For a more comprehensive overview of EU environmental law in general, see Sands (2003).   ■

E. USING TRADITIONAL ENVIRONMENTAL STATUTES TO ENCOURAGE POLLUTION AND ACCIDENT PREVENTION

As suggested at the outset of this chapter (and throughout this text), media-based statutes such as the Clean Air Act and Clean Water Act, as well as information-based statutes such as EPCRA, can be utilized to encourage pollution and accident prevention. Indeed, the use of "traditional" environmental statutes for this purpose would appear to be required by the Pollution Prevention Act. As discussed earlier, EPA is obligated under the Pollution Prevention Act to examine its regulations for their possible impact on pollution prevention and inherent safety, giving these approaches hierarchical preference over all other methods of meeting environmental goals. There is much that EPA and other agencies could do on this score, and we offer three examples here. (1) Stringent standards can be used to foster both the adoption of existing prevention technology (technology diffusion) and the innovation of cleaner and/or inherently safer technology. (2) Agencies can encourage firms to take advantage of statutory waiver provisions to "buy" the time necessary to develop innovative technology and approaches. (3) Agencies can secure industry commitment to implement pollution and/or accident prevention in settlement agreements when regulations have been violated.

1. Stringent Standards

Regulatory stringency is the most important factor influencing technological innovation. Stringent standards, properly implemented, can stimulate innovation in pollution and/or accident prevention. A regulation is considered stringent where compliance requires a significant reduction in (environmental or workplace) pollution or chemical accident risk, where compliance using existing technology is costly, or where compliance is not possible with existing technology and hence requires a significant technological change. In practice, of course, a variety of legislative policy considerations will dictate the permissible bounds of regulatory stringency. As we have seen, some statutes require that standards be based predominantly on environmental, health, or safety concerns; some on existing technological capability; and others on the technology within reach of a vigorous research and development effort. While much will depend on the particulars of the situation, each type of statute will generally provide considerable opportunity for a stringent regulatory approach.

Beginning in 1979 a number of MIT studies found that regulation can stimulate significant fundamental changes in product and process technology that benefit the industrial innovator, provided the regulations are stringent and focused. This empirical work was conducted 15 years earlier than the emergence in the 1990s of the relatively weaker Porter hypothesis, which holds that firms on the cutting edge of developing and implementing pollution reduction will benefit economically, through cost-saving "innovation offsets," by being "first-movers" (i.e., the first within the industry to comply with regulation). See Nicholas A. Ashford, Christine Ayers, and Robert F. Stone, "Using Regulation to Change the Market for Innovation," 9 *Harvard Environmental Law Review* 419 (1985), portions of which are reproduced in chapter 12. See also Strasser (1997), excerpted at the beginning of this chapter.

2. Innovation Waivers

As discussed in chapter 12, EPA has been reluctant to utilize its authority under several environmental statutes to grant innovation waivers to selected firms. Such waivers, which allow the firms additional time to meet new regulations, could be used by the agency as a means of stimulating innovation. EPA could better publicize and promote the availability of these waivers, and could enhance their attractiveness by creating a regulatory climate that makes their advantages clear. The willingness of a regulated firm to seek an innovation waiver will be influenced by a variety of factors; chief among these are likely to be the stringency of the new regulation and the perceived seriousness of the effort to enforce it. Here again, then, stringency will be a key. At the same time, however, the firm needs to know that it will not be penalized for a good-faith failure to find a workable innovative approach to compliance. Thus the regulatory approach must be both firm and flexible and must be tailored (at least in general) to the technological realities of the industry in question. The following decision of the Seventh Circuit Court of Appeals in Chicago, which arises out of an application for a waiver under the Clean Air Act, illustrates the importance of flexibility in allowing industry to experiment with the development of new technology. Moreover, this case suggests that the Pollution Prevention Act may *require* such flexibility in the implementation of statutory waiver provisions, even where (as here) they are not "innovation waivers" per se.

Monsanto Company v. Environmental Protection Agency
FOREMAN, District Judge
19 F.3d 1201 (7th Cir. 1994)

The Monsanto Company brings this petition for review of an Environmental Protection Agency decision that denied Monsanto's request for additional time to comply with certain hazardous emissions standards under the Clean Air Act. For the reasons given below, we grant the petition and reverse the agency's decision.

At issue in these proceedings is Monsanto's compliance with the EPA's emissions limit for benzene.... This standard was promulgated by the EPA on September 14, 1989, and became effective for new or modified sources on that date.... The Clean Air Act ... gave the EPA Administrator authority to grant a waiver to existing sources for a period of up to two years "if he finds that such period is necessary for the installation of controls and that steps will be taken during the period of the waiver to assure that the health of persons will be protected from imminent endangerment." ...

Monsanto was not prepared to comply with the new benzene standard in December 1989 and, therefore, requested a waiver until August 15, 1990, to allow the company to install water scrubbing equipment designed to satisfy the standard. The EPA granted this request. However, after the equipment was installed, Monsanto discovered that the equipment did not perform as anticipated. In-

stead of achieving the 95 percent emissions reduction that the benzene standard requires, the water scrubber system appeared to be operating at about an 80 percent reduction level. The company, therefore, asked the EPA for an extension of the waiver so that it could install a carbon adsorption system as a secondary means of filtering out the harmful emissions that were not captured by the primary system. The EPA denied this second request, leading to the pending petition for review....

Under §112(c)(1)(B)(ii) of the Clean Air Act, the Administrator of the EPA "may grant a waiver permitting [a stationary source] a period of up to two years after the effective date of a standard to comply with the standard, if he finds that such period is necessary for the installation of controls" and that steps in the interim will "assure that the health of persons will be protected from imminent endangerment." ...

The EPA granted Monsanto's initial request for a waiver. Thus, there appears to be no dispute that as of December 1989, the company needed additional time in which to install the equipment needed to control its benzene emissions....

... The company explained that in designing its original system, it had decided to install a water scrubber system because that system would allow the company to recover and reuse the benzene and other organic chemicals. The company decided against using the alternative control measure of carbon adsorption, which uses carbon filters to reduce benzene emissions, because this "end-of-the-pipe" technology would produce benzene-contaminated carbon. In short, instead of recapturing and reusing the benzene, carbon adsorption would create a hazardous waste that would require special treatment or disposal. . . .

The company similarly decided against incineration because that "end-of-the-pipe" alternative would produce waste gases. . . . [In the words of the company] "In the final analysis and in keeping with the U.S. EPA's 'preferred waste treatment' policy, Monsanto sought to eliminate wastes first, recycle or reuse second, and only if those two options were not available, 'dispose' of the waste." . . .

However, after construction was complete, Monsanto's tests showed for the first time that the equipment was actually removing less than 80 percent of the benzene. The company then promptly contacted the EPA and began the process of requesting an extension of its waiver so that the company could install a secondary system, using carbon absorption to capture the benzene that escaped through the primary water scrubber system. Monsanto, therefore, provided the information that was lacking in its original request.

In upholding its preliminary decision to deny the extension, the EPA maintained its position that additional time was not "necessary" because Monsanto could have installed carbon adsorption in the first place. . . .

The EPA expressly rejected Monsanto's claim that it "proceeded reasonably in terms of developing and implementing controls," and that carbon adsorption was "a choice of last resort because it offered the least opportunity for waste immunization and the greatest concern for safety[.]" [EPA continued:] "The CAA does not authorize the Administrator to grant a waiver of compliance in or-

der to allow a source more time to "proceed reasonably" in experimenting with the various available technologies, saving those technologies the source believes cause "considerable expense" and increase "safety concerns" for last. . . . If a source can install technology that will control the emissions, it must; only if additional time beyond the required compliance date "is necessary for the installation of controls," may the Administrator grant it additional time. In that Monsanto acknowledges that carbon adsorption could [have been] used at its facility in December 1989, and that, when in operation at its facility it did achieve greater than 95% consistent removal, U.S. EPA cannot find that additional time beyond that granted in the original waiver was "necessary for the installation of controls." . . .

The EPA's decision . . . ignores the fact that Monsanto chose the water scrubber system to comply with the EPA's own pollution prevention policy. See Pollution Prevention Policy Statement, 54 Fed.Reg. 3845 (Jan. 26, 1989). . . .

We recognize that the Clean Air Act required companies like Monsanto to comply with the emissions standards, if possible, by December 1989. . . . However, the record shows that Monsanto did not have the controls needed to comply with the benzene standard at that time; it clearly needed additional time to install appropriate controls. The question then becomes whether the EPA should follow its pollution prevention policy by allowing Monsanto to choose the control strategy that was designed to meet the benzene standard in the most environmentally sound manner or whether Monsanto was required to use the carbon adsorption strategy. . . .

EPA seems to be saying that if a "quick fix" is available, sources are required to employ that "quick fix" without regard to its adverse environmental ramifications. This viewpoint is short-sighted and bad environmental policy. Instead of eliminating an environmental problem, the EPA's "quick fix" would merely change the form of the problem—i.e., it would remove the environmental hazard from the air but create a hazardous waste disposal problem....

[W]e are unconvinced that the EPA's construction of the waiver provision is reasonable—especially when it is contrary to the agency's own pollution prevention policy and the Pollution Prevention Act of 1990 and the EPA has not provided any explanation for a departure from that policy. Indeed, the EPA's decision is devoid of any rationale to support its rigid construction of the waiver provision....

[I]f a company like Monsanto has a choice between two control strategies, the EPA has the authority to grant a waiver for a pollution prevention strategy even if that strategy would take slightly longer to implement than the less desirable strategy. This assumes, of course, that the pollution prevention strategy will work and can be installed within the two-year waiver period.

Those requirements were satisfied in this case....Although full compliance was not achieved within the eleven-month time frame that Monsanto first envisioned, it was accomplished within two years after the statutory deadline. Neither Monsanto nor the EPA had any reason to believe that Monsanto's initial system of choice would not perform up to expectations. Thus, it was arbitrary and capricious to deny Monsanto the additional time it needed to perfect its system....

In sum, Monsanto's original choice of the water scrubber system was environmentally and scientifically sound. The system was designed to achieve full compliance within the initial waiver period granted by the EPA. Although the system did not live up to its full expectations, Monsanto promptly asked the EPA for additional time to add a carbon adsorption process that would bring the system into full compliance with the emissions standard within the two years allowed by the statute. The reasons given by the EPA for denying the request have no foundation in the record. Therefore, we find that the EPA was arbitrary and capricious in denying Monsanto's request for an extension of its waiver. Accordingly, we hereby [grant] Monsanto's petition for review and [reverse] the EPA's decision.

[Dissenting opinion of Easterbrook, Circuit Judge, omitted]

---

3.   EPA's Supplemental Environmental Project (SEP) Program

Negotiation as a Means of Developing and Implementing Environmental and Occupational Health and Safety Policy
Charles C. Caldart and Nicholas A. Ashford
Source: 23 *Harvard Environmental Law Review* 141 (1999), excerpted with permission.

Roughly 90% of firms cited with noncriminal violations of federal environmental statutes in the United States resolve the matter through a negotiated settlement, rather than through an administrative hearing or court trial. The settlement of an enforcement action often offers an agency an excellent opportunity to promote pollution prevention, rather than conventional end-of-pipe control technology. The firm's attention has been commanded, and a need for creative (and less costly) approaches to compliance may well have become apparent. Outside of the enforcement process, an agency has little statutory or regulatory authority to require firms to implement pollution prevention; the regulated community can choose the means by which it will comply with federal requirements. But once an enforcement action is initiated, a window of opportunity for pollution prevention opens, because the means of achieving compliance likely will be subject to negotiation between the agency and the violator.

EPA has sought to capitalize on this opportunity by encouraging the use of *Supplemental Environmental Projects* (SEPs) to promote pollution prevention. SEPs are environmentally beneficial activities, which the violator agrees to perform and/or fund as part of its settlement with EPA, and which the violator is not otherwise legally required to perform. In the settlement process, EPA and company attorneys typically agree both on a penalty and on a set of activities designed to achieve and maintain compliance. In 1991, EPA adopted a SEP policy authorizing agency enforcement personnel to reduce the amount of the penalty in exchange for the execution of a SEP. Encouraged by initial results from this approach, the agency has revised and expanded its SEP policy since that time.

The key to the SEP policy is the trade-off between penalties and SEPs. Current EPA penalty policy anticipates that, unless the SEP policy is invoked, the penalty assessed in any enforcement action will be the sum of (a) the amount of the *economic benefit* gained by the violator as a result of non-compliance (typically, the investment earnings from delayed capital expenditures, together with any avoided operation and maintenance costs), and (b) a *gravity* component (calculated according to agency guidelines) that is meant to reflect the relative seriousness of the violations. Under the present SEP policy, SEPs may be used to reduce this amount, so

long as the final penalty paid is at least as large as what EPA characterizes as the *minimum penalty*: the larger of (a) the economic benefit plus 10% of the gravity component or (b) 25% of the gravity component.

Currently, there are seven categories of acceptable SEPs: pollution prevention, public health, pollution reduction, environmental restoration and protection, assessments and audits, environmental compliance promotion, and emergency planning and preparedness. The key feature linking these various categories is the expectation that the project will result in some benefit to the environment or public health. Some SEPs, such as an off-site stream restoration project, offer direct, predictable public benefits while returning no direct benefit to the violator. Others, such as an agreement by the violator to conduct a comprehensive environmental audit of its facility, offer potential (and far less predictable) benefits both to the public and to the violator. In general, *pollution prevention* SEPs—which involve expenditures by the violator to implement technology or practices that reduce its generation of pollution—offer the greatest potential for the development of innovative production technologies and practices with widespread application.

So long as it does not reduce the penalty below the acceptable minimum, EPA will (depending on the assessed merits of the project) credit up to 80% of the after-tax cost of most approved SEPs (net of any savings—such as reduced operations costs—that the SEP may offer to the violator) against the amount of the penalty. In order to encourage certain types of projects, however, the agency revised its policy in 1995 to offer a credit of up to 100% for SEPs judged to be "of outstanding quality" according to a set of specified criteria.[250] Two of the six criteria specified in the most recent version of

---

250. Five criteria were specified in the 1995 policy: benefits to the public or environment at large; pollution prevention; innovativeness; environmen-

tal justice; and multimedia impacts. In 1998, a sixth criterion—community input—was added.

the SEP policy are: (a) the extent to which the project develops or implements *pollution prevention* techniques or practices; and (b) the extent to which the project develops or implements *innovative* technological approaches.

EPA reports that, from Fiscal Year 1992 through Fiscal Year 1994, it negotiated more than 700 SEPs, with an estimated total value (i.e., cost to violators) of over $190 million. Of these, approximately 14% were pollution prevention SEPs, with an estimated total value of approximately $57 million. EPA estimates that these pollution prevention SEPs will reduce the discharge of toxic chemicals and the production of hazardous waste by a total of some 65 million pounds.

A case study analysis of ten pollution prevention SEPs negotiated by EPA through Fiscal Year 1992—selected because they reflect a range of technological responses—found that the technologies utilized included chemical substitution, process change, and closed-loop recycling [Becker and Ashford, 1994]. Representatives from all nine of the firms involved expressed support for the SEP policy. They indicated that they were glad to have had the option to implement a pollution prevention project in exchange for some penalty reduction, and noted their belief that the SEPs took some of the "sting" out of the enforcement process without eliminating the significant economic and psychological impacts of the enforcement action. Several company representatives also stated that the SEP process helped their firm to recognize other opportunities for environmentally beneficial improvements.

The technological changes undertaken by firms through pollution prevention projects can be categorized according to *the locus* of the change and according to the *degree of innovation* of the change. The majority of technological changes made by the SEP case study firms were diffusion-driven. A smaller number can be considered incremental innovations, and only one case can be considered a major innovation. There was a fairly even distribution of technological changes across the spectrum of primary, secondary, and ancillary processes. If a random case-study selection process had been used, the sample would have been more heavily weighted toward diffusion-driven changes to ancillary production processes. The larger universe of EPA settlements containing pollution prevention consisted mainly of the adoption of off-the-shelf technologies. This suggests there are unexploited opportunities in enforcement for stimulating innovative technological change. Realisation of this potential likely would require changes in attitudes and knowledge levels, both within industry and within EPA. One move in this direction has been the agency's more recent willingness to allow up to two years for the completion of selected pollution prevention SEPs, as a longer-term time window is essential if more significant innovation is to take place.

REFERENCE

Becker, Monica and Nicholas Ashford. 1995. "Exploiting Opportunities for Pollution Prevention in EPA Enforcement Agreements," *Environmental Science & Technology* 29(5): 220A–226A.

F. WORKER AND CITIZEN INVOLVEMENT IN POLLUTION PREVENTION AND TECHNOLOGY CHOICES

As logic would suggest, there often is much to be gained from involving workers and the community in the pollution and accident prevention process. A word or two of caution is appropriate here, however. At times community or worker involvement will be offered as a substitute for actual regulation and meaningful technological change; see, for example, the discussion of negotiation and "voluntary" approaches in chapter 12. Moreover, community members and workers are sometimes brought into the regulatory process for the precise purpose of avoiding or delaying stringent implementation and enforcement, usually as part of an effort to reframe the policy debate so that it appears to be an issue of jobs and economic security versus environmental protection. Conversely, as the discussion of hazardous waste activism in chapter 9 illustrates, communities and workers can be a strong political force for preventing pollution. Moreover, they can bring important practical and technical insights to the table.

Worker participation is likely to be particularly important. Involving workers in planning pollution reduction is one way to help ensure that chemical releases in the workplace are given proper consideration. The minimization of such releases is important, not only to occupational health and safety, but also to pollution prevention and chemical accident prevention generally. Often, however, pollution prevention analyses and activities proceed with little or no consideration of the workplace component.

Industrial Safety: The Neglected Issue in Industrial Ecology
N. A. Ashford

Source: *Journal of Cleaner Production*, Special Issue on Industrial Ecology, N. A. Ashford and R. P. Côté, (eds.), 5(1/2): i–iv, March–June 1997, excerpted with permission.

There is a great deal of effort being devoted in both North America and in Europe to the identification of pollution prevention/cleaner technology opportunities. In the United States, the Environmental Protection Agency has created the Pollution Prevention Information Clearinghouse which contains electronic information on promising technologies. The United Nations Environment Programme (UNEP) has created a similar system, the International Cleaner Production Information Clearinghouse (ICPIC) drawing upon U.S., European and other sources.

In a project conducted for the European Commission, Directorate for Health, Safety, and Public Health (DG-V), the author and his colleagues (Ashford et al. 1996) examined a representative selection of cases in the ICPIC system. Summary observations and criticisms of the content of the ICPIC cases are:

The most striking feature of the case studies is their complete lack of information regarding the interactions of human beings with the production processes, materials, or products. Process engineers generally do not consider workers or jobs as part of the production process. Manufacturing engineers often can not answer the question "Where do workers fit into your new framework of process design for the environment and for product safety?" From a worker health perspective, this is a serious problem that must be solved if risk shifting from the environment to people is to be limited.

No information is given regarding the physical or economic context for the processes. It is very difficult to know what the processes in the UNEP database [ICPIC] actually looked like with respect to the physical space in which they were located, the degree of automation, the quality and maintenance status of the equipment, engineering controls, or administrative practices used to run the processes

Table 13.2
Characteristics of Selected Cleaner Production Technologies

Technology	Type	External Pollution or Waste Status	Worker Health Status	Accident Potential Status	Raw Material Use	Water Use	Energy Efficiency
Rapeseed oil extraction by enzymes	Adverse for workers	++	−−	+	++	−	−−
Flame spray zinc	Adverse for workers	+	−	(0, −)	n/a	++	(0, +)
Recovery of sulfated mother liquor	Adverse for workers	+	−	−−	++	++	(0, +)
Recycling of cyanide water	Adverse for workers	++	−−	−−	++	0	(0, +)
Solvent substitution in paint	Missed opportunity	+	0	0	+	0	n/a
Production of casting molds	Missed opportunity	++	+	+	+	0	0
Hydrocarbon-based dry cleaning	Missed opportunity and adverse for workers	++	0	(0, −)	n/a	−	−
Wood and furniture surface treatment	Missed opportunity	+	0	0	+	0	0

Legend: ++ = significant   improvement,   + = improvement,   0 = no change,   − = deterioration, −− = significant deterioration, and n/a = information not available.

including shift work. From an industrial hygiene perspective, it is well-known that the actual conduct of the processes described in these case studies can vary considerably depending on the economic context and physical surroundings of the workplace. Many of these processes are used in the U.S., Italy, and China and, in each of these countries, chemical manufacturing is performed using practices that range from manual reactor vessel charging, mixing, packaging, and maintenance to process steps that are almost completely enclosed and automatic. The same process under these different conditions could have very different implications for worker health.

Limited information is given regarding the physical form of the substances at certain stages in the process so that should a worker be exposed, the physiologic route of entry can not be adequately anticipated. The physical form of substances can

occasionally be determined by knowing process specifications such as temperature and pressure but these process specifications are not given consistently. Information is lacking about the manner in which materials are added to a process, maintained, stored and disposed.

The authors undertook an in-depth analysis of eight technologies in the ICPIC system that represented a process or product line that has significance for the EU from an economic or industrial policy perspective. The features for the eight technologies are represented in table [13.2]. The first four technologies actually worsen the health and safety of workers. Cases 5, 6 and 8 describe technologies that do not trade off environmental benefits for worsened worker health and safety but, on the other hand, are sub-optimal from a worker protection perspective. That is, in cases 5, 6 and 8, missed opportunities for even better environmental and worker protection performance were identified. Case 7 represents an example of a technology with both characteristics: the substitution of fluorocarbons by hydrocarbons introduces a risk of explosion (creating an adverse effect for workers) and the use of multi-process wet cleaning would eliminate both the use of fluorocarbons and hydrocarbons (a missed opportunity). Other examples from the literature include the substitution of HCFCs for CFCs, leading to lessened damage to the ozone layer, but creating a carcinogenic risk for workers, and the use of water-based paints, eliminating volatile organic solvents, but introducing a biocide hazard for workers.

REFERENCES

Ashford, N., I. Banoutsos, K. Christiansen, B. Hummelmose, and D. Stratikopoulos. 1996. *Evaluation of the Relevance for Worker Health and Safety of Existing Environmental Technology Databases for Cleaner and Inherently Safer Technologies: A Report to the European Commission*, April 1996.

As this discussion suggests, an exclusive focus on environmental concerns and/or on gradual pollution may overlook real problems and miss real opportunities for change, with regard both to worker health and safety and to sudden and accidental chemical releases. (As discussed earlier, an exchange of wastes and materials creates similar but different issues.) Involvement of workers in the evaluative process—while no ultimate guarantee of a broader focus—can generally be expected to bring issues of workplace exposure and chemical accident potential more to the fore. The Pollution Prevention Act does contemplate that firms required to report their source reduction activities (with their TRI data) will consult their workers for input on such activities; indeed, it arguably requires them to do so. See 42 U.S.C. §13106(b)(6), which requires the listing of "techniques which were used to identify source reduction activities," and specifies that the techniques listed "should include" both "employee recommendations" and "participative team management." Moreover as discussed earlier, the PPA contemplates that pollution prevention ("source reduction") will both improve worker health and safety and reduce the risk of chemical accidents. The Massachusetts Toxics Use Reduction Act also places an emphasis on workplace protection; it defines toxics use reduction as "in-plant changes in production processes or raw materials or hazardous substances that reduce, avoid, or eliminate the use of toxic or hazardous substances or generation of hazardous by-product per unit of product...*without shifting risks between workers, consumers, or parts of the environment.*" An evaluation of TURA some 10 years into that law's implementation (Roelofs, Moure-Eraso, and Ellenbecker, 2000) found that "toxics use reduction activities have resulted in improvements to the work environment" in almost half of thirty-five published case studies, but that such improvements were "rarely a direct concern of these efforts, thus creating the potential for new negative worker health and safety impacts and missed opportunities to coordinate environmental and worker health and safety improvements" (p. 843). The authors recommended that technical assistance agencies and companies better integrate worker health and safety issues with pollution prevention activities.

■ **NOTES**

1. Based on an analysis of the 1991–1992 TRI database, and using the definition of source reduction in the Pollution Prevention Act, Bunge, Cohen-Rosenthal, and Ruiz-Quintanilla (1996) found statistically relevant evidence that manufacturers using a combination of three formal employee participation practices tripled the reduction of emissions over those manufacturers using none of those practices. (See chapter 10, section D, note 5 for an expanded discussion of this study.)

2. Over the past decade there has been an increased recognition of the importance of improving indoor air quality in nonindustrial workplaces, such as offices, and in non-occupational environments, such as public facilities, housing, and schools. This in turn has further opened the way for the types of risk reduction approaches that benefit both the workplace *and* the environment.

3. For an examination of some of the occupational health and safety benefits of involving workers in decisions regarding the choice and design of workplace technology, see Ashford and Ayers (1987).

4. Note that the data in table 13.2 provide empirical support for the Porter hypothesis. The adoption of measures to improve the environment (column 3) is often accompanied by improvements ("innovation offsets" in Porter's language) in raw material use, water use, and energy efficiency (columns 6, 7, and 8). ■

Community involvement in pollution prevention activities at a particular plant or industry can take many forms, ranging from the cooperative to the confrontational. One variant that draws from both forms is the "good neighbor agreement" between industry and the community. These agreements tend to be the result of activism by citizen and environmental groups concerned with implementing pollution prevention activities to address chemical releases (both gradual and sudden and accidental) in their immediate neighborhoods. See Lewis (1990, 1993) and Lewis and Henkels (1997). For an evaluation of how these agreements have developed and what they have accomplished in Minnesota, see Murdock and Sexton (2002). In the right circumstances (and with the right participants), good neighbor agreements can be a meaningful way of involving the community, the workers in the plant, and plant management in informal consensus building that benefits the economy, the workplace, and the environment.

REFERENCES

Allen, David T., and Shonnard, David R. 2002. *Green Engineering: Environmentally Conscious Design of Chemical Processes.* Upper Saddle River, N.J.: Prentice Hall.

Anastas, Paul, and John Warner. 2000. *Green Chemistry Theory and Practice.* Oxford: Oxford University Press.

Ashford, Nicholas. 2005. "Government and Environmental Innovation in Europe and North America," in *Towards Environmental Innovation Systems,* Matthias K. Weber and Jens Hemmelskamp (eds.) Heidelberg: Springer, pp. 159–174.

Ashford, Nicholas A., and Christine Ayers. 1987. "Changes and Opportunities in the Environment for Technology Bargaining," 62 *Notre Dame Law Review* 5: 810–858. Available at http://hdl.handle.net/1721.1/1546.

Ashford, Nicholas A., and Charles C. Caldart. 1996. *Technology, Law, and the Working Environment,* Revised ed. Washington, D.C.: Island Press.

Ashford, Nicholas, and Achilleas Tsamis. 2000. "Green Chemistry, Pollution Prevention, and Worker Health and Safety." Report to the Green Chemistry Institute, American Chemical Society, Washington, D.C.

Ashford, Nicholas, Wim Hafkamp, Frits Prakke, and Philip Vergragt. 2001. *Pathways to Sustainable Industrial Transformations: Cooptimising Competitiveness, Employment, and Environment.* Final Report to the Ministry of Environment and Spatial Planning, Government of the Netherlands, Ashford Associates, Boston.

Baumann, Jeremiah. 2001. *Protecting Our Hometowns: Preventing Chemical Terrorism in America.* A Guide for Policymakers and Advocates, U.S. Public Interest Research Group Education Fund, Washington, D.C.

Beierle, Thomas C. 2003. *The Benefits and Costs of Environmental Information Disclosure: What Do We Know About Right-to-Know?* RFF Discussion Paper 03-05. Washington, D.C.: Resources for the Future.

Bollinger, Robert E., David G. Clark, Roger M. Dowell, and Roger M. Ewbank. 1996. "Inherently Safer Chemical Processes: A Life Cycle Approach." Center for Chemical Process Safety of the American Institute of Chemical Engineers: New York.

Bunge, John, Edward Cohen-Rosenthal, and Antonio Ruiz-Quintanilla. 1996. "Employee Participation in Pollution Reduction: Preliminary Analysis of the TRI," *Journal of Cleaner Production* 4(1): 9–16.

Caldart, Charles C., and C. William Ryan. 1985. "Waste Generation Reduction: A First Step Toward Developing a Regulatory Policy to Encourage Hazardous Substance Management Through Production Process Change," *Hazardous Waste and Hazardous Materials* 2: 309–351.

Eder, P. 2003. "Expert Inquiry on Innovation Options for Cleaner Production in the Chemical Industry," *Journal of Cleaner Production* 11(4): 347–364.

Ehrenfeld, John. 2004. "Industrial Ecology: A New Field or Only a Metaphor?" *Journal of Cleaner Production* 12(8–10): 825–831.

Freeman, Harry M. 1995. *Industrial Pollution Prevention Handbook.* New York: McGraw-Hill.

GAO (General Accounting Office) 2001. *Environmental Protection: EPA Should Strengthen Its Efforts to Measure and Encourage Pollution Prevention.* GAO-01-283. Washington, D.C.: GAO.

Gouldson, A., and Murphy, J. 1998. *Regulatory Realities: The Implementation and Impact of Industrial Environmental Regulation.* London: Earthscan.

Gutowski, Timothy, Cynthia Murphy, David Allen, Diana Bauer, Bert Bras, Thomas Piwonka, Paul Sheng, John Sutherland, Deborah Thurston and Egon Wolff. 2005. "Environmentally Benign Manufacturing: Observations from Japan, Europe and the United States," *Journal of Cleaner Production* 13: 1–17.

Hess, Glenn. 2006. "Evidence Rule Stirs Up Debate," *Chemical & Engineering News* 84(15): 49–52.

Hirschhorn, Joel S. 1988. "Cutting Production of Hazardous Wastes," *Technology Review* 91: 52.

Hirschhorn, J., and Oldenburg, K. 1991. *Prosperity Without Pollution: The Prevention Strategy for Industry and Consumers.* New York: Van Nostrand Reinhold.

Keijzers, Gerard. 2000. "The Evolution of Dutch Environmental Policy: The Changing Ecological Arena from 1970–2000 and Beyond," *Journal of Cleaner Production* 8(3): 179–200.

Keijzers, Gerard. 2002. "The Transition to the Sustainable Enterprise," *Journal of Cleaner Production* 10(4): 349–359.

Kletz, Trevor A. 2003. "Inherently Safer Design: Its Scope and Future," *Transactions of the Institution of Chemical Engineering* 81(PartB): 401–405.

Koch, L., and N. A. Ashford. 2006. "Rethinking the Role of Information in Chemicals Policy: Implications for TSCA and REACH," *Journal of Cleaner Production* 14(1): 31–46.

Lewis, Sanford. 1990. "Citizens as Regulators of Local Polluters and Toxic Users," *New Solutions* 1(1): 20–21.

Lewis, Sanford. 1993. *The Good Neighbor Handbook: A Community-Based Strategy for Sustainable Industry*, 2nd ed. Center for the Study of Public Policy, Waverley, Mass., Available from Apex Press, New York.

Lewis, Sanford. 2001. "The Safe Hometowns Initiative: How to Do a Community Reassessment of Chemical Site Safety and Security after September 11, 2001." Available at available at http://www.safehometowns.org or from the publications tab at http://home.earthlink.net/~gnproject.

Lewis, Sanford, and Diane Henkels. 1997. "Good Neighbor Agreements: A Tool for Environmental and Social Justice," *Social Justice* 23(4): 134–151. Available at http://www.cpn.org/topics/environment/goodneighbor.html.

Murdock, Barbara Scott, and Ken Sexton. 2002. "Promoting Pollution Prevention through Community-Industry Dialogues: The Good Neighbor Model In Minnesota," *Environmental Science Technology* 36: 2130–2137.

NACEPT (National Advisory Council for Environmental Policy and Technology). 1991. *Permitting and Compliance Policy: Barriers to U.S. Environmental Technology Innovation.* Report and Recommendations of the Technology Innovation and Economics Committee of the National Advisory Council for Environmental Policy and Technology. Washington, D.C.: U.S. EPA.

NACEPT (National Advisory Council for Environmental Policy and Technology). 1992. *Improving Technology Diffusion for Environmental Protection.* Report and Recommendations of the Technology Innovation and Economics Committee of the National Advisory Council for Environmental Policy and Technology. Washington, D.C.: U.S. EPA.

NACEPT (National Advisory Council for Environmental Policy and Technology). 1993. *Transforming Environmental Permitting and Compliance Policies to Promote Pollution Prevention.* Report and Recommendations of the Technology Innovation and Economics Committee of the National Advisory Council for Environmental Policy and Technology. Washington, D.C.: U.S. EPA.

Nelson, Richard R. 1996. "National Innovation Systems: A Retrospective on a Study," in *The Sources of Economic Growth*, Richard R. Nelson (ed.) Cambridge, Mass.: Harvard University Press, pp. 274–302.

Nelson, Richard R., and Nathan Rosenberg. 1993. *National Innovation Systems: A Comparative Analysis.* New York: Oxford University Press.

Ochsner, Michele. 1998. "Pollution Prevention: An Overview of Regulatory Incentives and Barriers," 6 *New York University Environmental Law Journal* 586–617.

O'Rourke, Dara, and Eungkyoon Lee. 2004. "Mandatory Planning for Environmental Innovation: Evaluating Regulatory Mechanisms for Toxic Use Reduction," *Journal of Environmental Planning and Management* 47(2): 181–200.

Papadakis, G. A., and A. Amendola (eds.) 1997. *Guidance on the Preparation of the Safety Report to Meet the Requirements of Council Directive 96/82/EC (Seveso II), EUR 17690*, European Commission, Joint Research Centre, Institute for Systems, Informatics and Safety, Major Accident Hazards Bureau, Ispra (VA)-Italy. For other aspects of guidance, see N. Mitchison. 1999. "The Seveso II Directive: Guidance and Fine-tuning," *Journal of Hazardous Materials* 65(1/2): 23–36.

Roelofs, Cora R., Rafael Moure-Eraso, and Michael J. Ellenbecker. 2000. "Pollution Prevention and the Massachusetts Experience," *Applied Occupational and Environmental Hygiene* 15(11): 843–850.

Rotmans, Jan, René Kemp, and Marjolein van Asselt. 2001. "More Evolution than Revolution: Transition Management in Public Policy," *Foresight* 3(1): 015–031.

Sands, Phillipe. 2003. *Principles of International Environmental Law*, 2nd ed. Cambridge, UK: Cambridge University Press.

Strasser, Kurt A. 1997. "Cleaner Technology, Pollution Prevention, and Environmental Regulation," *Fordham Environmental Law Journal* 9(1): 1–106.

U.S. Congress, Office of Technology Assessment. 1986. *Serious Reduction of Hazardous Wastes*. Washington, D.C.: Office of Technology Assessment.

U.S. EPA (Environmental Protection Agency). 1994. *Technology Innovation Strategy*. EPA 543-K-93 002. Washington, D.C.: U.S. EPA.

Vergragt, Philip J., and Geert van Grootveld. 1994. "Sustainable Technology Development in the Netherlands: The First Phase of the Dutch STD Program," *Journal of Cleaner Production* 2(3–4): 133–139.

Vogel, David. 2003. "The Hare and the Tortoise Revisited: The New Politics of Consumer and Environmental Regulation in Europe," *British Journal of Political Science* 33: 557–580.

Vollenbroek, Frans A. 2002. "Sustainable Development and the Challenge of Innovation," *Journal of Cleaner Production* 10(3): 215–223.

Von Moltke, K. 1985. "Bhopal and Seveso: Avoiding a Recurrence," *Environmental Forum* June 1985, pp. 21–23.

14 Epilogue—Beyond Pollution Control and Prevention: Sustainable Development

A. The Unsustainable Industrial State
B. Conceptualizations of Sustainable Development
C. Incremental Change by Incumbent Firms Is Inadequate for Achieving Sustainability
D. The Role of Government

Currently several environmental problems face both industrialized and developing nations. These include (1) chemical pollution, (2) climate change, (3) resource and energy depletion, and (4) the loss of biodiversity and ecosystem integrity. While often addressed separately, all four of these environmental problems are related to advancing industrialization, population growth, and the globalization of production and commerce. Societies that produce and consume more also tend to deplete more natural resources, create more pollution, produce more greenhouse gases, and have a relatively greater adverse impact on the ecosystem. In addition, the interconnectedness of nations through globalization has produced "lock-in" of, and dependence on, a particular development model. We believe that this model needs thoughtful reexamination.

Environmental burdens are often felt unequally within nations, between nations, and between generations, giving rise to intranational, international, and intergenerational equity concerns that are often expressed as a concern for environmental justice. Not only do environmental problems affect different people differently, but they are also addressed differently within and between nations and between generations. At present, global climate change, with its intergenerational consequences and with different implications for industrialized and developing nations, has captured center stage, but all environmental problems raise a variety of equity concerns.

This text on environmental pollution has focused largely on the first of the environmental problems identified above and has examined a variety of policies designed to reduce gradual releases of chemicals into the environment and/or the sudden and accidental releases associated with chemical mishaps. Historically, the approach to reducing pollution was framed independently of the approaches to the other three kinds of environmental problems. As we have seen, national approaches in the United States and Europe for reducing pollution have been evolving in the past four decades, first emphasizing the dispersion of pollution and waste (the "dilution solution"), then end-of-pipe control, then waste and material exchange and consolidation (industrial ecology), and now (at least to a certain extent) pollution prevention and cleaner and inherently safer technology. Only recently has attention turned to system changes and the promotion of sustainable development. In evolutionary terms, these newer approaches lie beyond changing a single industrial process, transportation vehicle, energy source, or agricultural practice, and involve a larger set of fundamental changes than either pollution control or pollution prevention are likely to bring.

Incremental or even moderate improvements in energy efficiency, ecoefficiency, and dematerialization may not be sufficient to offset trends of increased pollution and increased energy and resource consumption tied to industrial and commercial development. Significant transformations may be needed in manufacturing, housing, agriculture, transportation, energy systems, services, and consumption patterns to reduce the impacts caused by pollution. For some, sustainable development implicitly focuses on environmental sustainability. For others, sustainability includes more far-reaching changes in (1) the nature and level of goods and services produced and used by a society, (2) employment, and (3) environmental sustainability. In other words, environmental concerns are "nested" within, and are connected to, wider concerns of competitiveness and employment.

A.   THE UNSUSTAINABLE INDUSTRIAL STATE

Those who argue that the industrialized state, whether developed or developing, is currently unsustainable emphasize several problems. These are depicted schematically in figure 14.1. In the "economic" realm, there may be a failure of a society to provide adequate goods and services to all of its members. This of course places enormous pressure on an economy to produce more, but this in turn may increase the ecological footprint of that society. Environmental problems stem from the activities involved with agriculture, manufacturing, extraction, transportation, housing, energy, services, and information and communication technology (ICT)—all driven by the demand of consumers, commercial entities, and government. In addition, these activities have significant effects on the amount, security, and skill of employment, on the nature and conditions of work, and on the purchasing power associated

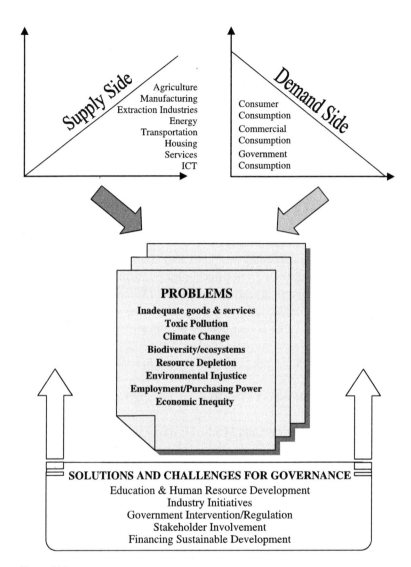

Figure 14.1
The sources and drivers of unsustainability, resulting problems, and solutions.

with wages. An increasing concern is economic inequity stemming from inadequate and unequal purchasing power within and between nations and for the workers and citizens of the future. Policies to increase employment are often fashioned in terms of producing (and consuming) more, again with adverse environmental consequences. On the other hand, reducing production to accommodate environmental pressures may create undesirable consequences for growth and employment. Is there a way out of this seeming dilemma in which one social goal must be compromised to satisfy another? Is it a question of achieving the proper balance among competing social goals? This may be the case only if a society remains technologically static.

Whether education, industrial initiatives, government intervention, stakeholder involvement, and financing will be able to solve these problems will depend on whether a number of fundamental characteristics of the modern industrial state can be corrected or overcome: (1) the fragmentation of the knowledge base, which leads to a myopic understanding of fundamental problems and the fashioning of single-purpose or narrowly fashioned solutions by technical and political decision makers, (2) the inequality of access to economic and political power, (3) the tendency toward "gerontocracy"—governance of industrial systems by old ideas, (4) the failure of markets to correctly price the adverse consequences of industrial activity, and (5) the inherent failure of even "perfect" markets to deal adequately with effects that span long time horizons (for which correct pricing is not likely to be the answer).

B.   CONCEPTUALIZATIONS OF SUSTAINABLE DEVELOPMENT

Whether one views sustainable development as just an environmental issue or as a multidimensional challenge in the three dimensions—economic, environmental, and social—makes quite a difference. We argue that competitiveness, environment, and employment are the operationally important dimensions of sustainability. Together these three dimensions drive sustainable development along different pathways and lead to different places than does a singular concern for environmental sustainability. The latter will almost invariably lead to tradeoffs, e.g., between environmental improvements and jobs or economic growth, that will ultimately be counterproductive. The interrelatedness of competitiveness, environment, and employment is depicted in figure 14.2.

A *sustainable development* agenda is, almost by definition, an agenda of *system* change. This is not to be confused with an *environmental policy* agenda, which is, or should be, explicitly effects-based: a program of policies and legislation directed toward environmental improvements and relying on specific goals and conditions. The sustainable development policy agenda focuses on products and processes (e.g., related to manufacturing, transport, energy, or construction), but extends to changes in technological and social systems that cut across many dimensions.

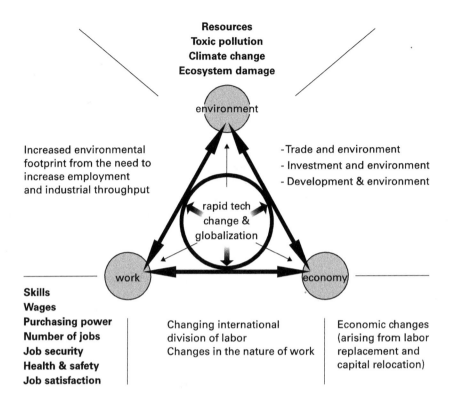

Resources
Toxic pollution
Climate change
Ecosystem damage

environment

Increased environmental
footprint from the need to
increase employment
and industrial throughput

- Trade and environment
- Investment and environment
- Development & environment

rapid tech
change &
globalization

work

economy

Skills
Wages
Purchasing power
Number of jobs
Job security
Health & safety
Job satisfaction

Changing international
division of labor
Changes in the nature of work

Economic changes
(arising from labor
replacement and
capital relocation)

Figure 14.2
The dimensions of sustainability.

Note that *current strategy agendas*, even those that go beyond environmental goals, are focused on policies that (1) improve profit and market share by enhancing the performance of current technologies or by cutting costs, and by finding new sources of energy, (2) control pollution and/or make simple substitutions and changes and conserve energy and resources, or (3) ensure an adequate supply of appropriately skilled labor, and safe and healthy workplaces. See table 14.1. In the context of technological change, we would describe these strategies as reactive rather than proactive. Each usually is the responsibility of a different unit of government or a different department in the industrial firm, and each usually is pursued separately by different private sector stakeholders. At best, current policies affecting competitiveness, environment, and employment are *coordinated* but not integrated.

In contrast, *sustainable agendas* are those policies that are focused on (1) technological changes that alter the ways goods and services are provided, (2) the prevention

Table 14.1
The Interrelationship of Competitiveness, Environment, and Employment

Agenda	Competitiveness	Environment	Employment
Current	Improve performance/cut costs Find new sources of energy	Control pollution and make simple substitutions or changes to products and processes Conserve energy and resources	Ensure supply of adequately trained people; dialogue with workers Provide safe workplaces
Sustainable	Change nature of meeting market needs through radical or disrupting innovation (a systems change)	Prevent pollution through system changes Design safe and environmentally sound products and processes Change resource and energy dependence	Radical improvement in human–technology interfaces (a systems change)

of pollution and the reduction of energy and resource use through more far-reaching system changes, and (3) the encouragement of the development of novel sociotechnical systems—involving both technological and organizational elements—that enhance the many dimensions of meaningful employment through the integration, rather than the coordination, of policy design and implementation. Sustainable agendas address all important social goals simultaneously rather than in a piecemeal fashion.

C. INCREMENTAL CHANGE BY INCUMBENT FIRMS IS INADEQUATE FOR ACHIEVING SUSTAINABILITY

The kind of innovation likely to be managed successfully by industrial corporations is relevant to the differences between current and sustainable technology agendas. We argue that the needed transformations in products, processes, and systems may exceed the capacity of the dominant industries and firms to change easily, at least by themselves. Furthermore, industry and other sectors may not have the intellectual capacity and trained human resources to do what is necessary.

This argument is centered on the idea of "the winds of creative destruction" developed by Joseph Schumpeter[1] in explaining technological advance. The distinction between incremental and radical innovations—be they technological, organizational, institutional, or social—is not simply line-drawing along points on a continuum. Incremental innovation generally involves a series of continuous improvements, while

---

1. Joseph Schumpeter (1939) *Business Cycles: A Theoretical, Historical and Statistical Analysis of the Capitalist Process.* McGraw-Hill, New York, as discussed in Jurg Niehans (1990) "Joseph Schumpeter," in *A History of Economic Theory: Classic Contributions 1720–1980.* Johns Hopkins University Press, Baltimore, p. 448.

radical innovations are discontinuous,[2] rather than evolutionary transformations, possibly involving *displacement* of dominant firms, institutions, *and ideas*. In semantic contrast, Clayton Christensen[3] distinguishes continuous improvements as "sustaining innovation" and uses the term "disrupting innovation" instead of radical innovation, arguing that both sustaining and disrupting innovations can be either incremental or radical, where the term "radical" is reserved for rapid or significant performance changes within a particular technological trajectory.

Thus in Christensen's terminology, a radical sustaining innovation is a major change in a technology *along the lines that the technology has been changing historically* (for example, a much more efficient air pollution scrubber) and is often pioneered by incumbent firms. A major innovation that represents an entirely new approach, even if it synthesizes previously invented artifacts, is termed "disrupting," and in product markets it almost always is developed by firms that are not in the prior markets or business. This is consistent with the important role of outsiders—both for existing firms and as new competitors—in bringing forth new concepts and ideas.[4]

Counting only or mainly on existing industries or on traditionally trained technical expertise for a sustainable transformation ignores increasing evidence that it is not simply willingness, opportunity, and motivation that are required for change. Another factor—the ability or capacity of firms and people to change—also is essential.[5] In some situations they may change because society or market demand sends a strong signal, but this is not true in all or even in most cases.

An essential concept in fostering innovative technical responses is that of "design space." As originally introduced by Tom Allen and his colleagues at MIT, design space is a cognitive concept that refers to the dimensions along which the designers of technical systems concern themselves.[6] Especially in industrial organizations that limit themselves to current or traditional strategies or agendas, there is a one-sided utilization of the available design space. Solutions to design problems are only sought along traditional engineering lines. In many cases unconventional

2. Chris Freeman (1992) *The Economics of Hope*. Pinter, London.

3. Clayton Christensen (2000) *The Innovator's Dilemma: When New Technologies Cause Great Firms to Fail*, 2nd ed. Harvard Business School Press, Cambridge, Mass.

4. Ibo de Poel (2000) "On the Role of Outsiders in Technical Development," *Technology Analysis and Strategic Management* 12(3): 383–397.

5. Nicholas Ashford (2000) "An Innovation-Based Strategy for a Sustainable Environment," in *Innovation-Oriented Environmental Regulation: Theoretical Approach and Empirical Analysis*, J. Hemmelskamp, K. Rennings, and F. Leone (eds.) ZEW Economic Studies. Springer Verlag, Heidelberg, New York, pp. 67–107.

6. Thomas J. Allen, James M. Utterback, Marvin A. Sirbu, Nicholas A. Ashford, and J. Herbert Hollomon (1978) "Government Influence on the Process of Innovation in Europe and Japan," *Research Policy* 7(2): 124–149.

solutions that may or may not be hi-tech are ignored. For that reason, radical, disrupting innovations are often produced by industry mavericks or as a result of some disruptive outside influence (such as significantly new or more stringent environmental regulation, foreign competition, or the input of an outsider to the organization).

Given that a sustainable future requires technological, organizational, institutional, and social change, it is likely that an evolutionary pathway is not sufficient for achieving improvements of a factor of ten or greater in eco- and energy efficiency and reductions in the production and use of, and exposure to, toxic substances. Such improvements require more systemic, multidimensional, and disruptive changes. The capacity to change can be the limiting factor, and this is often a crucial missing factor in optimistic scenarios. Such significant industrial transformations occur less often within dominant technology firms than in new firms that displace existing products, processes, and technologies. This can be seen in examples of significant technological innovations over the past 50 years, including transistors, computers, and substitutes for PCBs.

D. THE ROLE OF GOVERNMENT

An intelligent government policy is likely to play an essential role both in encouraging the appropriate systemic responses and in assisting in the necessary educational transformations. As noted, successful management of disruptive product and process innovations often requires initiatives from outsiders to help expand the design space that limits the paths likely to be pursued by dominant technology firms. Rigid industries whose processes have remained stagnant will face considerable difficulties in any efforts to become significantly more sustainable. Shifts from products to product services will rely on transformations in the use, location, and ownership of products. Mature product manufacturers may participate in such transformations, but this will require them to make significant changes and will involve both managerial and social (customer) innovations. Changes in sociotechnical systems, such as transportation or agriculture, are likely to be even more difficult to achieve. This collection of formidable challenges, each involving one or a series of entrenched interests, suggests that the creative use of government intervention is likely to be a more promising strategic approach for achieving sustainable industrial transformations than reliance on policies that tend to emphasize firms' short-term economic self-interest.

This is not to say that enhancement of an industry's analytical and technical capabilities, and of its communication and cooperation with suppliers, customers, workers, and other industries (as well as environmental, consumer, and community groups), are not valuable adjuncts in the transformation process. In most cases, however, these means and strategies are unlikely to be sufficient by themselves to bring about significant transformations. Further, they will not work without clear, mandated targets to enhance the triple goals of competitiveness, environmental quality, and employment.

Government has a significant role to play, but it cannot simply serve as a referee or arbiter of existing competing interests because neither future generations nor future technologies are adequately represented by the existing stakeholders. The government should work with stakeholders to define targets far into the future without allowing the agenda to be captured by the incumbents, and then use its position as trustee to represent future generations *and* future technologies. Through this process government should attempt to "backcast" the specific policies that will be necessary to produce the desired technical, organizational, and social transformations. To do this, government will need to go beyond its historical focus on coordinating public and private sector policies. Approaches for achieving sustainability must be multidimensional and must directly address the present fragmentation of governmental functions, not only at the national level but also among national, regional, and local governmental entities.

It may be unreasonable to expect that government can (or should) play too definitive a role in creating a future. Accordingly, rather than attempting tight management of the pathways necessary for the type of transformations that are sustainable in the broad sense in which we define the term here, the government role might be better conceived as one of enabling or facilitating change while at the same time *lending visionary leadership for cooptimizing competitiveness, environment, and employment.* This means that the various policies must be mutually reinforcing. This newly conceptualized leadership role—focused on opening up the problem space of the engineer and designer—will require the creative participation of more than one government department or organization. Without a collective approach, sustainable development is likely to remain an elusive goal.

About the Authors

Nicholas A. Ashford is Professor of Technology and Policy and Director of the Technology and Law Program at MIT. He is also an adjunct faculty member at the Harvard University and Boston University schools of public health. He is the author of *Crisis in the Workplace: Occupational Disease and Injury* (MIT Press, 1976) and the coauthor (with Claudia S. Miller) of *Chemical Exposures: Low Levels and High Stakes*. He holds a Ph.D. in chemistry and a law degree and has graduate training in economics. He and Charles C. Caldart are the authors of *Technology, Law, and the Working Environment* and (with Christine J. Spadafor and Dale B. Hattis) of *Monitoring the Worker for Exposure and Disease: Scientific, Legal, and Ethical Considerations in the Use of Biomarkers* (1990, Johns Hopkins University Press).

Charles C. Caldart is Director of Litigation for the nonprofit National Environmental Law Center (offices in Boston, Seattle, and San Francisco) and a Lecturer in the Department of Civil and Environmental Engineering in the Engineering Systems Division at MIT. He holds a law degree, a master's degree in public health, and a degree in economics.

Index of Cases

Subject Index